BARRON'S

GRE®

22ND EDITION

Sharon Weiner Green, M.A.
Former Instructor of English

Ira K. Wolf, Ph.D.
Former Professor of Mathematics
Former Director of University Teacher Preparation Program

Acknowledgement

In 1967, Barron's Educational Series published *How to Prepare for the GRE* by Samuel Brownstein and Mitchel Weiner. Today, fifty years later, with the publication of this 22nd Edition of *Barron's GRE*, we are pleased to announce that Lexy Green, granddaughter of original co-author Mitchel Weiner, has joined the Barron's team as contributing author. In this new edition, Ms. Green, Director of Forensics at The College Preparatory School in Oakland, California, and a nationally-known debate coach, brings her insights to the section on Analytical Writing.

All inquiries should be addressed to:
Barron's Educational Series, Inc.
250 Wireless Boulevard
Hauppauge, New York 11788
www.barronseduc.com

Library of Congress Control Number: 2016959852

ISBN: 978-1-4380-0915-5

PRINTED IN THE UNITED STATES OF AMERICA

9 8 7 6 5 4 3 2

10%
POST-CONSUMER
WASTE
Paper contains a minimum of 10% post-consumer waste (PCW). Paper used in this book was derived from certified, sustainable forestlands.

Contents

PART 3: ANALYTICAL WRITING: TACTICS, STRATEGIES, AND PRACTICE

PART 4: QUANTITATIVE ABILITY: TACTICS, STRATEGIES, PRACTICE, AND REVIEW

PART 5: MODEL TESTS

Acknowledgments

The authors gratefully acknowledge the following for permission to reprint reading passages in the book or online.

BOOK PASSAGES

Page 32: From *Classic Authors of the Gilded Age* by Darrel Abel. Copyright © 1963 by Barron's Educational Series.

Page 36: From the National Biological Information Infrastructure.

Page 128: From "So Many Female Rivals" by Christine Froula, *The New York Times Book Review*, February 7, 1988.

Page 129: Ladislas Segy, "African Sculpture Speaks," Dover Publications, New York, 1958. By permission of Helena Segy.

Page 582: From *Black Leaders of the Twentieth Century*. Copyright 1982 by the Board of Trustees of the University of Illinois. Used with permission of the University of Illinois Press.

Page 625: From Vol. 15 of *Americas*, Copyright © 1963 by the Organization of American States.

Page 635: From *Eyes on the Prize: Civil Rights Years*, edited by Clayborne Carson et al. Copyright © 1987 by Penguin Books. Blackside, Inc. 1991, with permission.

ONLINE EXAM PASSAGES

From *Black History and the Historical Profession, 1915–1980*. Copyright 1986, by the Board of Trustees of the University of Illinois. Used with permission of the author and the University of Illinois Press.

From *India and Democracy* by Sir George Schuster and Guy Wint, p. 10. Copyright © 1941 by Macmillan and Co.

From "James Lind and the Cure of Scurvy" by R. E. Hughes, courtesy of the National Center for Biotechnology Information.

From "What Are Greenhouse Gases?" by the U.S. Energy Information Administration.

Preface

As a prospective graduate student concerned with professional advancement, you know the importance of using good tools and drawing on solid research. In this Twenty-second Edition of *Barron's GRE,* we offer you both.

This revision contains the fruits of our close study of the 2011 changes to the GRE General Test. We have scrutinized hundreds of actual GRE questions, traced dozens of GRE reading passages to their sources and analyzed subsets of questions by order of difficulty and question type. We have gone through all the topics in the analytical writing section, categorizing the actual issues you will encounter on your test and analyzing the argument passages, pinpointing their logical flaws. In the process, we have come up with the following features, which should make this Twenty-second Edition particularly helpful to you:

Visit *barronsbooks.com/TP/GRE/* to take two free online practice tests.

TYPICAL GRE QUESTIONS ANALYZED

We will take you step by step through more than 1,000 practice verbal and mathematical questions that simulate actual GRE questions, showing you how to solve them and how to avoid going wrong.

TESTING TACTICS

We provide you with dozens of proven testing tactics that will help you attack the different types of questions on the GRE.

HIGH-FREQUENCY WORD LIST

This edition contains the revised 320-word High-Frequency Word List—320 critical words from *abate* to *zealot* that have occurred and recurred on actual published GREs—plus Barron's GRE Master Word List, your guide to the level of vocabulary expected of graduate school students.

COMPREHENSIVE MATHEMATICS REVIEW

We present you with extensive mathematical review of all the topics that you need to know. This is especially valuable for college students and adults who haven't taken math since high school.

GRE-MODELED TESTS

We have created for you a compact Diagnostic Test that will enable you to pinpoint your areas of weakness right away and concentrate your review on subjects in which you need the most work, plus two Model Tests, all with answers completely explained, that in format, difficulty, and content echo today's GRE. Two additional tests are available online at *barronsbooks.com/TP/GRE/*.

COMPUTER GRE UPDATE

In this edition we will introduce you to the latest version of the computer-delivered GRE and explain everything you need to know about how to take the computerized GRE.

ANALYTICAL WRITING UPDATE

We provide you with an introduction to the GRE analytical writing section, familiarizing you with the range of topics covered and giving you helpful hints on how to write clear, cogent essays in no time at all.

This Twenty-second Edition once more upgrades what has long been a standard text. It reflects the contributions of numerous teachers, editors, and coaches, and the dedication of the staff at Barron's. It also reflects the forensic and rhetorical skills of Lexy Green, Director of Debate at the College Preparatory School, who is joining our authorial team. We, the authors, are indebted to all these individuals for their ongoing efforts to make this book America's outstanding GRE study guide.

Timetable for a Typical Computer-Delivered Graduate Record Examination

TOTAL TIME: 4 HOURS

Section	Time Allowed	Description
1*	60 minutes	*Analytical Writing* Essay 1: Giving one's perspective on an issue Essay 2: Analyzing an argument (30 minutes each)
1-minute break		
2	30 minutes	*Verbal Ability* 6 text completion questions 5 sentence equivalence questions 9 reading comprehension questions
1-minute break		
3	35 minutes	*Quantitative Ability* 8 quantitative comparison questions 9 discrete quantitative questions 3 data interpretation questions
10-minute break		
4	30 minutes	*Verbal Ability* 6 text completion questions 5 sentence equivalence questions 9 reading comprehension questions
1-minute break		
5	35 minutes	*Quantitative Ability* 7 quantitative comparison questions 10 discrete quantitative questions 3 data interpretation questions
1-minute break		
6	30 or 35 minutes	*Experimental Section* a third verbal or quantitative section

*The paper-delivered GRE splits the Analytical Writing Test into two sections, as shown below:

1	30 minutes	*Analytical Writing* Issue Essay: Giving one's perspective on an issue
2	30 minutes	*Analytical Writing* Argument Essay: Analyzing an argument

NOTE: Sections 2 through 6 can come in any order—for example, Section 2 could be a Quantitative Ability section and the Experimental Section could be any section except Section 1. Although the Experimental Section will not count in your score, it will look identical to one of the other sections—you won't know which section it is, so you must do your best on every section of the test.

PART 1
Introduction/ Diagnostic Test

1 What You Need to Know About the GRE

AN OVERVIEW OF THE COMPUTER-DELIVERED GRE GENERAL TEST

Visit *barronsbooks.com/TP/GRE/* for access to two complete online practice tests, conveniently accessible on your computer, smartphone, or tablet.

The GRE General Test is an examination designed by the Educational Testing Service (ETS) to measure the verbal, quantitative, and analytical writing skills you have developed in the course of your academic career. High GRE scores strongly correlate with the probability of success in graduate school: the higher you score, the more likely you are to complete your graduate degree. For this reason, many graduate and professional schools require applicants to take the GRE General Test, a test now given only on computer. (They may also require you to take a GRE Subject Test in your particular field. Subject Tests currently are available in 14 fields.)

The computer-delivered GRE General Test you take will have five or six sections. There will always be

- one Analytical Writing section composed of two 30-minute tasks (60 minutes)*
- two 20-question Verbal Ability sections (30 minutes each)
- two 20-question Quantitative Ability sections (35 minutes each)

In addition, there *may* be

- an unidentified Experimental Section, which would be a third verbal or quantitative section

Occasionally, there *may* be

- an identified optional research section (but *not* if there is an Experimental Section)

*Unlike the computer-delivered GRE, the paper-delivered GRE will include not one but two Analytical Writing sections. There will be a 30-minute section for the Issue task and a separate 30-minute section for the Argument task.

The verbal section measures your ability to use words as tools in reasoning; you are tested not only on the extent of your vocabulary but on your ability to discern the relationships that exist both within written passages and among individual groups of words. The quantitative section measures your ability to use and reason with numbers and mathematical concepts; you are tested not on advanced mathematical theory but on general concepts expected to be part of everyone's academic background. The mathematics covered should be familiar to most students who took at least two years of math in a high school in the United States. The writing section measures your ability to make rational assessments about unfamiliar, fictitious relationships and to logically present your perspective on an issue.

COMMONLY ASKED QUESTIONS ABOUT THE COMPUTER-DELIVERED GRE

How Does the GRE Differ from Other Tests?

Most tests college students take are straightforward achievement tests. They attempt to find out how much you have learned, usually in a specific subject, and how well you can apply that information. Without emphasizing memorized data, the GRE General Test attempts to measure verbal, quantitative, and analytical writing skills that you have acquired over the years both in and out of school.

Although the ETS claims that the GRE General Test measures skills that you have developed over a long period, even a brief period of intensive study can make a great difference in your eventual GRE scores. By thoroughly familiarizing yourself with the process of computer-delivered testing, the GRE test format, and the various question types, you can enhance your chances of doing well on the test and of being accepted by the graduate school of your choice.

What Is It Like to Take a Computer-Delivered GRE?

For practice using the actual GRE testing platform, you can go to the ETS's official GRE website—*www.ets.org/GRE/*—and download their free *PowerPrep® II* software, which includes a test preview tool and a practice test. You can also take the two online tests available at *barronsbooks.com/TP/GRE/*.

When you actually take the GRE, you sit in a carrel in a computer lab or testing center, facing a computer screen. You may be alone in the room, or other test-takers may be taking tests in nearby carrels. With your mouse, you click on an icon to start your test. The first section of the test is the Analytical Writing section, and you will have 60 minutes in which to complete the two writing tasks. When you have finished the writing section, you will have a one-minute break to take a few deep breaths and get ready for the next four or five sections, each of which will consist of 20 multiple-choice verbal or quantitative questions. When the break is over, the first question in Section 2 appears on the screen. You answer it, clicking on the oval next to your answer choice, and then, ready to move on, you click on the box marked Next. A new question appears on screen, and you go through the process again. Be sure to answer every question. Because there is no penalty for an incorrect answer on the GRE General Test, when you don't know an answer, try to make an educated guess by eliminating clearly incorrect choices; if you can't eliminate any choices, make a wild guess, and move on.

At the end of the second section, you are given another one-minute break. After finishing the third section, you have a ten-minute break. There will be two more one-minute breaks—after the fourth and fifth sections.

Why Do Some People Call the Computer-Delivered General Test a CAT?

CAT stands for Computer-Adaptive Test. What does this mean? It means that the test adapts to your skill level: it is customized.

What happens is that after you complete the first quantitative or verbal section, the computer program assesses your performance and adjusts the difficulty level of the questions you will have to answer in the second quantitative or verbal section. The more questions you answer correctly in the first section, the harder will be the questions that you will be given in the second section. However, the harder the questions are, the more they are worth. So your raw score depends on both the number of questions you answer correctly and the difficulty level of those questions.

Actually, the GRE is much less computer-adaptive than it used to be. It used to adapt the level of questions you received continuously; after every question the program would assess your performance and determine the level of difficulty of the next question. Now, it doesn't make that determination until you have completed an entire section.

BE PREPARED

1. Make sure to bring your photo ID to the test center.
2. Do not bring food, drinks, or tobacco products to the test center.
3. No cell phones, smartphones, PDAs, or other electronic devices are allowed in the testing center.
4. All personal items brought with you to the test center are subject to inspection.

Can I Tell How Well I'm Doing on the Test from the Questions the Computer Assigns Me?

Don't even try; it never pays to try to second-guess the computer. There's no point in wasting time and energy wondering whether it's feeding you harder questions or easier ones. Let the computer keep track of how well you're doing—you concentrate on answering correctly as many questions as you can and on pacing yourself.

Should I Guess?

Yes, you must! You are not going to know the correct answer to every question on the GRE. That's a given. But you should *never* skip a question. Remember, there is no penalty for an incorrect answer. So if a question has you stumped, eliminate any obviously incorrect answer choices, and then guess and don't worry whether you've guessed right or wrong. Your job is to get to the next question you *can* answer. Just remember to use the process of elimination to improve your guessing odds.

How Can I Determine the Unidentified Experimental Section?

You can't. Do not waste even one second in the exam room trying to identify the Experimental Section. Simply do your best on every section. Some people claim that most often the last section is the Experimental Section. Others claim that the section with unusual questions is the one that does not count. Ignore the claims: you have no sure way to tell. If you encounter a series of questions that seem strange to you, do your best. Either these are experimental and will not count, in which case you have no reason to worry about them, or they will count, in which case they probably will seem just as strange and troublesome to your fellow examinees.

How Are GRE Scores Calculated and When Are They Reported?

On both the verbal and quantitative sections of the GRE, your *raw score* is the number of questions you answered correctly, adjusted for the difficulty level of those questions. Each raw score is then adjusted to a *scaled score*, which lies between 130 and 170. The written score report that you will receive in the mail will include both your scaled scores and your percentile rank indicating the percent of examinees scoring below your scaled scores on the General Test.

Your analytical writing score will be the average of the scores assigned to your essays by two trained readers. These scores are rounded up to the nearest half-point. Your combined analytical writing score can vary from 0 to 6, with 6 the highest score possible.

As soon as you have finished taking the test, the computer will calculate your *unofficial* scaled scores for the verbal and quantitative sections and display them to you on the screen. Because your essays are sent to trained readers for holistic scoring, you will not receive a score for the analytical writing section on the day of the test. You should receive in the mail an *official* report containing all three scores approximately three weeks after the test date.

After you take one of the Model Tests in the back of this book and/or online, you cannot calculate your exact scores, because there is no way to factor in the difficulty level of the questions. To give yourself a rough idea of how you did, on both the verbal and quantitative sections, assume that your raw score is equal to the number of correct answers, and that your scaled score is equal to 130 plus your raw score. For example, if you answered correctly 30 of the 40 quantitative questions, assume that your raw score would be 30 and that your scaled score would be 160.

GRE TEST FORMAT

Verbal Reasoning

The two verbal sections consist of a total of 40 questions. These questions fall into two basic types: discrete short-answer questions and critical reading questions.

Here is how a 20-question verbal section generally breaks down:

- 10 discrete short-answer questions
- 10 critical reading questions (including logical reasoning questions)

NOTE

For all of the multiple-choice questions in the verbal and quantitative sections of the tests and practice exercises in this book, the answer choices are labeled A, B, C, D, and E, and these letters are used in the Answer Keys and the answer explanations. On an actual GRE exam, these letters never appear on the screen. Rather, each choice is preceded by a blank oval or square, and you will answer a question by clicking with the mouse on the oval or square in front of your choice.

Although the amount of time spent on each type of question varies from person to person, in general, discrete short-answer questions take less time to answer than critical reading questions.

DISCRETE SHORT-ANSWER QUESTIONS

In these fill-in-the-blank questions, you are asked to choose the best way to complete a sentence or short passage from which one, two, or three words have been omitted. These questions test a combination of reading comprehension and vocabulary skills. You must be able to recognize the logic, style, and tone of the sentence so that you will be able to choose the answer that makes sense in context. You must also be able to recognize differences in usage. The sentences cover a wide variety of topics from a number of academic fields. They do not, however, test specific academic knowledge. You may feel more comfortable if you are familiar with the topic the sentence is discussing, but you should be able to handle any of the sentences using your knowledge of the English language.

Here is a typical fill-in-the-blank question, using one of the new question formats. In this question, you are asked to find ***not one but two*** correct answers; both answers must produce completed sentences that are like each other in meaning. This is what the test-makers call a **sentence equivalence** question.

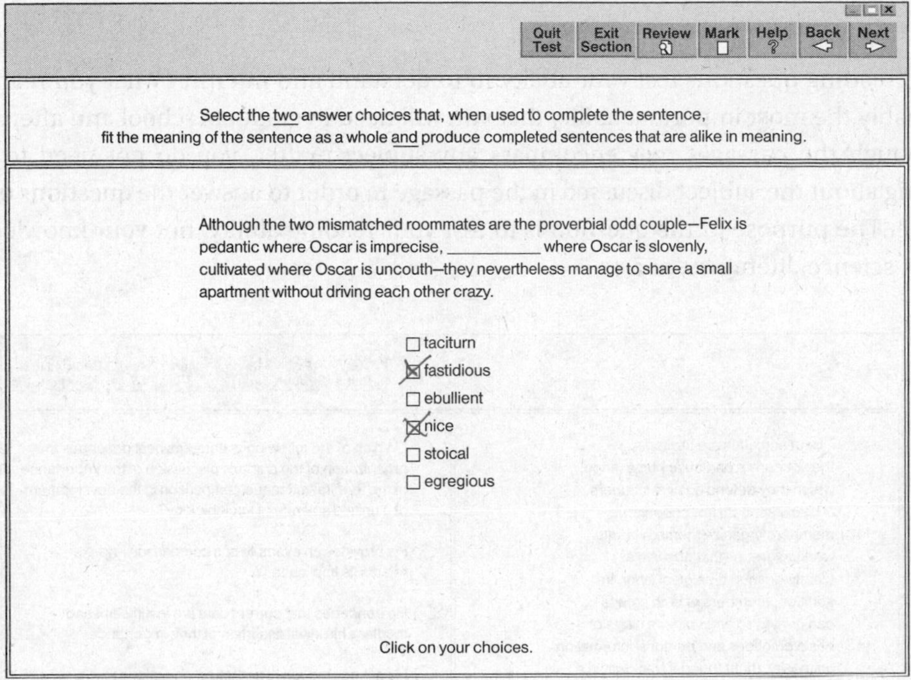

Unlike Oscar, Felix is *not* slovenly (messy and untidy); instead, he is a compulsive neatnik. Felix is *fastidious* or *nice* in his habits, excessively sensitive in matters of taste. (Note the use of *nice* in a secondary sense.)

Look at the same question, restructured into what the test-makers call a **text completion** question. In this type of question, you are asked to find only one correct answer per blank. However, you must have a correct answer for each and every blank.

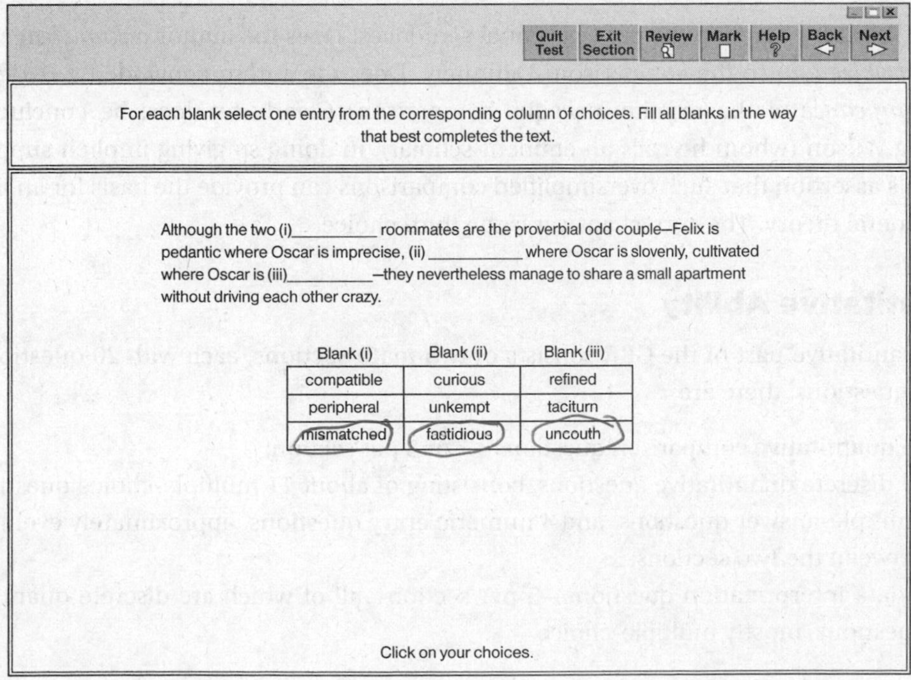

See page 72 for fill-in-the-blank question tactics and practice exercises that will help you handle both of the new question types.

CRITICAL READING QUESTIONS

Critical reading questions test your ability to understand and interpret what you read. This is probably the most important ability that you will need in graduate school and afterward.

Although the passages may encompass any subject matter, you do not need to know anything about the subject discussed in the passage in order to answer the questions on that passage. The purpose of the question is to test your reading ability, not your knowledge of history, science, literature, or art.

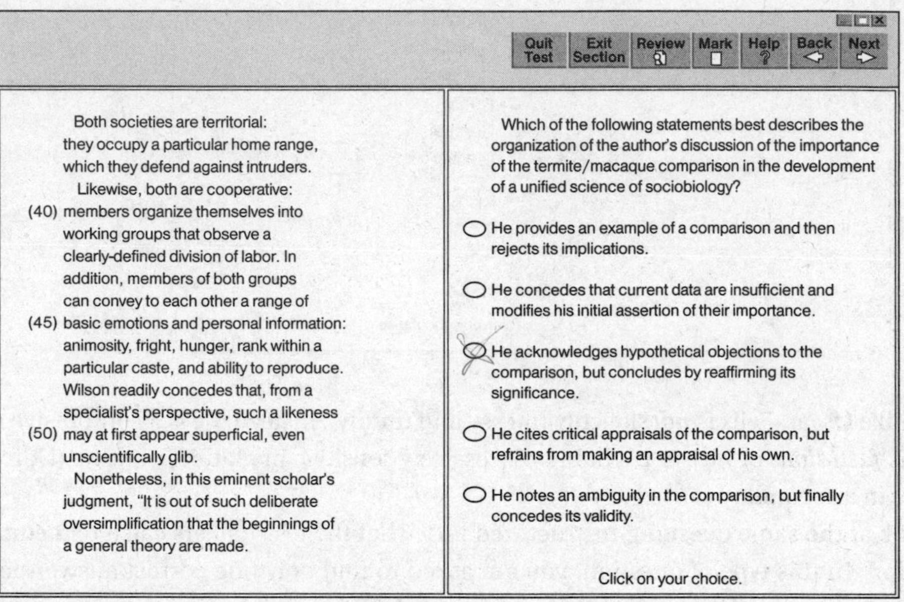

The key lines here are the passage's final sentences. Does the author *acknowledge hypothetical objections* to the comparison? Definitely. Does the author conclude by *reaffirming the significance* of the termite/macaque comparison? Clearly he does: he concludes by quoting Wilson (whom he calls an eminent scholar), in doing so giving implicit support to Wilson's assertion that such oversimplified comparisons can provide the basis for an important general theory. The correct answer is the third choice.

Quantitative Ability

The quantitative part of the GRE consists of two math sections, each with 20 questions. Of the 40 questions, there are

- 15 quantitative comparison questions—7 or 8 per section;
- 19 discrete quantitative questions, consisting of about 11 multiple-choice questions, 4 multiple-answer questions, and 4 numeric entry questions, approximately evenly split between the two sections;
- 6 data interpretation questions—3 per section—all of which are discrete quantitative questions, mostly multiple-choice.

In order to answer these questions, you need to know arithmetic, some very elementary algebra, and a little geometry. Much of this material you learned in elementary and middle school; the rest you learned during the first two years of high school. You do not need to know *any* advanced mathematics. The questions are intended to determine if you have a basic knowledge of elementary mathematics, and if you have the ability to reason clearly.

If you haven't done any mathematics in a while, go through the math review in this book before attempting the Model Tests, and certainly before registering to take the GRE. If you feel that your math skills are still pretty good, you can try the Diagnostic Test first, and then read only those sections of the math review relating to those topics that gave you trouble.

QUANTITATIVE COMPARISON QUESTIONS

Of the 40 mathematics questions on the GRE, 15 are what is known as quantitative comparisons. Unless you prepared for the SAT before 2005, it is very possible that you have never even seen such a question. Even if you have had some contact with this type of question, you need to review the basic idea and learn the essential tactics for answering them. Therefore, read these instructions *very* carefully.

TIP

You will be provided with scratch paper to help you work out problems and take notes.

In these questions there are two quantities—Quantity A and Quantity B—and it is your job to compare them. For these problems there are *only four possible answers*:

Quantity A is greater;
Quantity B is greater;
The two quantities are equal; and
It is impossible to determine which quantity is greater.

In this book, these four answer choices will be referred to as A, B, C, and D, respectively. In some of the questions, information about the quantities being compared is centered above them. This information *must* be taken into consideration when comparing the two quantities.

In Chapter 10, you will learn several important strategies for handling quantitative comparisons. For now, let's look at three examples to make sure that you understand the concepts involved.

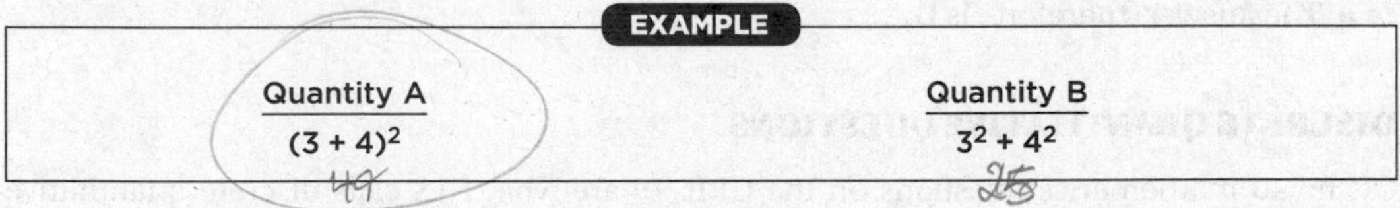

Quantity A	Quantity B
$(3 + 4)^2$	$3^2 + 4^2$

- Evaluate each quantity: $(3 + 4)^2 = 7^2 = \mathbf{49}$, whereas $3^2 + 4^2 = 9 + 16 = \mathbf{25}$.
- Since $49 > 25$, Quantity A is greater. The answer is A.

EXAMPLE

$a + b = 16$

Quantity A	Quantity B
The average (arithmetic mean) of a and b	8

Quantity A is the average of a and b: $\frac{a+b}{2}$. Since we are told that $a + b = 16$, Quantity A is $\frac{a+b}{2} = \frac{16}{2} = \mathbf{8}$.

So, Quantity A and Quantity B are equal. The answer is **C**.

NOTE: We cannot determine the value of either a or b; all we know is that their sum is 16. Perhaps $a = 10$ and $b = 6$, or $a = 0$ and $b = 16$, or $a = -4$ and $b = 20$. *It doesn't matter.* The average of 10 and 6 is 8; the average of 0 and 16 is 8; and the average of -4 and 20 is 8. Since $a + b$ is 16, the average of a and b is 8, *all the time, no matter what.* The answer, therefore, is **C**.

EXAMPLE

Quantity A	Quantity B
a^3	a^2

- If $a = 1$, $a^3 = 1$, and $a^2 = 1$. *In this case,* the quantities in the two columns are equal.
- This means that the answer to this problem *cannot* be A or B. Why?
- The answer can be A (or B) only if Quantity A (or B) is greater *all the time.* But it isn't — not when $a = 1$.
- So, is the answer C? *Maybe.* But for the answer to be C, the quantities would have to be equal *all the time.* Are they?
- No. If $a = 2$, $a^3 = 8$, and $a^2 = 4$, and *in this case* the two quantities are *not equal.*
- The answer, therefore, is **D**.

DISCRETE QUANTITATIVE QUESTIONS

Of the 40 mathematics questions on the GRE, 19 are what ETS calls discrete quantitative questions. More than half of those questions are standard ***multiple-choice questions***, for which there are five answer choices, exactly one of which is correct. The way to answer such a question is to do the necessary work, get the solution, and then look at the five choices to find your answer. In Chapter 9, we will discuss other techniques for answering these questions, but for now let's look at one example.

EXAMPLE

Edison High School has 840 students, and the ratio of the number of students taking Spanish to the number not taking Spanish is 4:3.
How many of the students take Spanish?

Ⓐ 280 Ⓑ 360 Ⓒ 480 Ⓓ 560 Ⓔ 630

To solve this problem requires only that you understand what a ratio is. Ignore the fact that this is a multiple-choice question. *Don't even look at the choices.*

- Let $4x$ and $3x$ be the number of students taking and not taking Spanish, respectively.
- Then $4x + 3x = 840 \Rightarrow 7x = 840 \Rightarrow x = 120$.
- The number of students taking Spanish is $4 \times 120 = 480$.
- Having found the answer to be 480, *now look at the five choices.* The answer is C.

A second type of discrete quantitative question that appears on the GRE is what ETS calls a "multiple-choice question—more than one answer possible," and what for simplicity we call a ***multiple-answer question***. In this type of question, there could be as many as 12 choices, although usually there are no more than 7 or 8. Any number of the answer choices, from just one to all of them, could be correct. To get credit for such a question, you must select *all* of the correct answer choices and *none* of the incorrect ones. Here is a typical example.

EXAMPLE

If x is negative, which of the following statements *must* be true?

Indicate *all* such statements.

[A] $x^2 < x^4$

[B] $x^3 < x^2$

[C] $x + \frac{1}{x} < 0$

[D] $x = \sqrt{x^2}$

To solve this problem, examine each statement independently, and think of it as a true-false question.

A. For many negative values of x, x^2 is less than x^4, but if $x = -1$, then x^2 and x^4 are each 1, so it is *not* true that x^2 *must* be less than x^4. A is false.

B. If x is negative, x^3 is negative, and so *must* be less than x^2, which is positive. Statement B is true.

C. If x is negative, so is $\frac{1}{x}$, and the sum of two negative numbers is negative. Statement C is true.

D. The square root of a number is *never* negative, and so could *not possibly* equal x. Statement D is false.

You must choose B and C and neither A nor D.

The third type of discrete quantitative question is called a ***numeric entry question.*** The numeric entry questions are the only questions on the GRE for which no answer choices are given. For these questions, you have to determine the correct numerical answer and then use the number keys on the keyboard to enter the answer. If the answer is negative, type a hyphen for the negative sign. There are two possibilities: if the answer is an integer or a number that contains a decimal point, there will be a single box for your answer; if the answer is to be entered as a fraction, there will be two boxes—one for the numerator and one for the denominator.

Here is a typical numeric entry question.

EXAMPLE

Directions: The answer to the following question is a fraction. Enter the numerator in the upper box and the denominator in the lower box.

On Monday, $\frac{1}{5}$ of the students at Central High went on a field trip to a museum. On Tuesday, $\frac{5}{8}$ of the students who hadn't gone to the museum on Monday had the opportunity to go. What fraction of the students in the school did not go to the museum either day?

In Section H of Chapter 12, we will discuss the algebraic way to solve a problem such as this one, but on the GRE the best approach is just to assume that the school has 40 students, 40 being the least common multiple of 5 and 8, the two denominators in the problem. Then, 8 students ($\frac{1}{5}$ of 40) went to the museum on Monday, and of the remaining 32 students, 20 of them ($\frac{5}{8}$ of 32) went on Tuesday. So, 28 students went to the museum and 12 did not. So the fraction of the students in the school who did not go to the museum either day is $\frac{12}{40}$.

Enter 12 in the upper box for the numerator and 40 in the lower box for the denominator. Note that $\frac{12}{40}$ can be reduced to $\frac{6}{20}$ and $\frac{3}{10}$ and you would get full credit for either of those answers, but on the GRE it is *not* necessary to reduce fractions.

DATA INTERPRETATION QUESTIONS

In each of the two quantitative sections there are three consecutive questions that are based on the same set of data. Most data interpretation questions are multiple-choice questions, but you may have a multiple-answer and/or a numeric entry question. No data interpretation questions are quantitative comparisons. As you might guess from their name, all of these questions are based on information provided in graphs, tables, or charts. The questions test your ability to interpret the data that have been provided. You will either have to do a calculation or make an inference from the given data. The various types of questions that could arise will be explored in Chapter 11. Here is a typical data interpretation question.

EXAMPLE

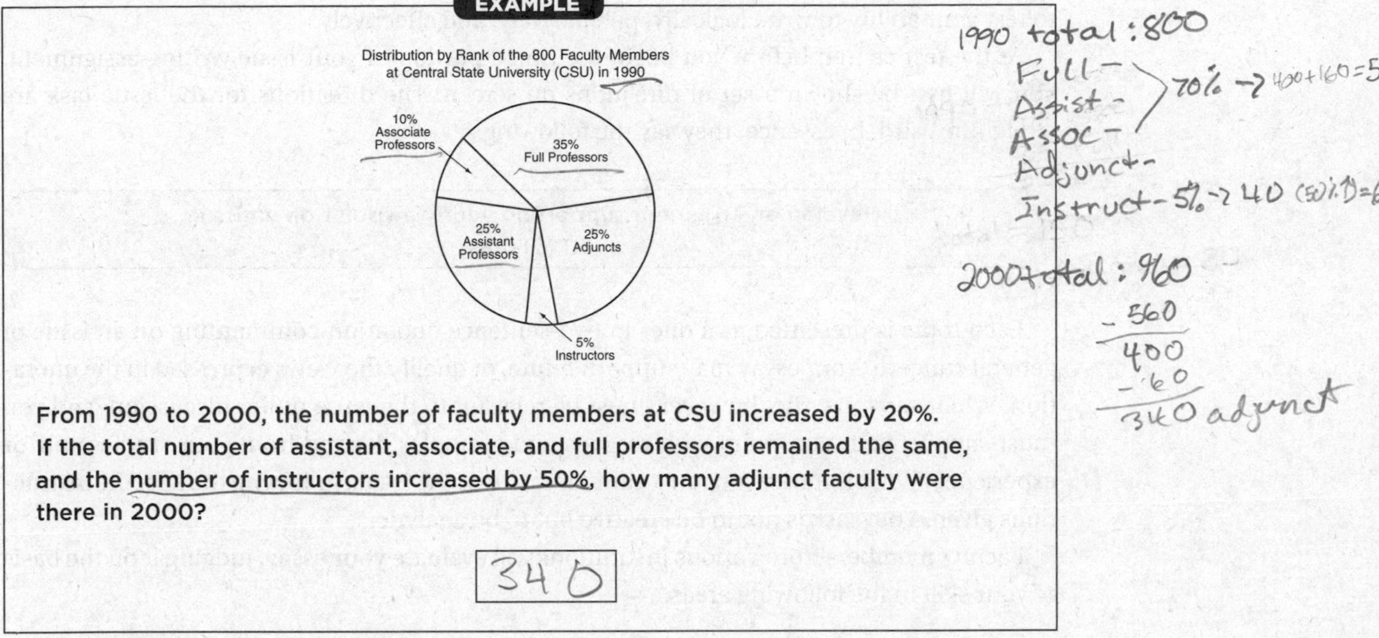

From 1990 to 2000, the number of faculty members at CSU increased by 20%. If the total number of assistant, associate, and full professors remained the same, and the number of instructors increased by 50%, how many adjunct faculty were there in 2000?

This question is not difficult, but it requires several calculations.

- Since the number of faculty members increased by 20%, in 2000 there were 960 people on the faculty (20% of 800 = 160, and 800 + 160 = 960).
- In 1990, 70% (35% + 10% + 25%) of the faculty were professors, and 70% of 800 = 560.

So in 1990 and also in 2000, there were 560 professors.

- In 1990, there were 40 instructors (5% of 800 = 40); since that number increased by 50%, and 50% of 40 is 20, there were 60 instructors in 2000.
- Of the 960 faculty members in 2000, 560 were professors and 60 were instructors. The remaining **340** were adjuncts (960 – 560 – 60 = 340).

Enter 340 in the box.

Analytical Writing

The analytical writing portion of the GRE consists of two tasks:

- Writing an essay presenting your point of view on an issue of general intellectual concern.
- Writing an essay analyzing the line of reasoning in an argument.

You are allotted 30 minutes to complete the issue task, and 30 minutes to complete the argument analysis task. You must finish one task before you begin the other. You will find suggestions for tackling both writing tasks in Chapter 7.

THE ISSUE TASK

In this task, you are asked to respond to a particular issue, clearly presenting your viewpoint on that issue and supporting your position with reasons and examples. This task is intended to test your ability to write logically, persuasively, and effectively.

At the test center, before you begin the timed portion of your issue writing assignment, you will first be shown a set of directions on screen. The directions for the issue task are straightforward. In essence, they say the following:

> **Develop an argument supporting your viewpoint on an issue.**
> **30 Minutes**

Each topic is presented as a one- to two-sentence quotation commenting on an issue of general concern. Your essay may support, refute, or qualify the views expressed in the quotation. Whatever you write, however, must be relevant to the issue under discussion, and you must support your viewpoint with reasons and examples derived from your studies and/or experience. What is more, you must carefully analyze the issue, following the specific instructions given. Your task is not to be creative but to be analytic.

Faculty members from various institutions will evaluate your essay, judging it on the basis of your skill in the following areas:

- ☑ Coverage of each of the elements in the topic instructions
- ☑ Analysis of the question's implications
- ☑ Organization and articulation of your ideas
- ☑ Use of relevant examples and arguments to support your case
- ☑ Handling of the mechanics of standard written English

To begin the timed portion of this task, click on the box labeled CONTINUE. Once you click on CONTINUE, a second screen will appear. This screen contains some general words of advice about how to write an issue essay:

- Think before you write. Plan what you are going to say.
- Work out your ideas in detail.
- Be coherent.
- Leave yourself enough time to revise.

None of this is rocket science. You already know what you are supposed to do. Don't waste your time reading pro forma advice, just click on the CONTINUE box and get to work.

Here are two issue topics modeled on the issue tasks on the GRE. Please note that these are not official GRE issue topics, although they do resemble official topics closely in subject matter and form.

SAMPLE ISSUE TASK 1

Claim: If we are serious about solving the problem of income inequality, our primary focus should be on improving funding for public colleges and universities.

Reason: Higher education is the key to career advancement.

Compose an essay that identifies how greatly you concur (or differ) with the claim provided and its rationale.

SAMPLE ISSUE TASK 2

The key to success is found not in following your passion, but rather in bringing passion to the work you do.

Compose an essay that identifies how greatly you concur (or differ) with the statement provided, describing in detail the rationale for your argument. As you build and provide evidence for your argument, include examples that demonstrate circumstances in which the statement could (or could not) be valid. Be sure to explain the impact these examples have on your argument.

THE ARGUMENT TASK

In this task, you are asked to critique the line of reasoning of an argument given in a brief passage, clearly pointing out that argument's strengths and weaknesses and supporting your position with reasons and examples. This task is intended to test both your ability to evaluate the soundness of a position and your ability to get your point across to an academic audience.

Again, before you begin the timed portion of your argument analysis task, you will first be shown a set of directions on screen. The directions for the argument task are straightforward. In essence, they say the following:

Evaluate an argument.
30 Minutes

In 30 minutes, prepare a critical analysis of the argument expressed in a short paragraph. You may not offer an analysis of any other argument.

As you critique the argument, think about the author's underlying assumptions. Ask yourself whether any of them are questionable. Also, evaluate any evidence that the author brings up. Ask yourself whether it actually supports the author's conclusions.

In your analysis, you may suggest additional kinds of evidence to reinforce the author's argument. You may also suggest methods to refute the argument or additional data that might be useful to you as you assess the soundness of the argument. You may not, however, present your personal views on the topic. Your job is to analyze the elements of an argument, not to support or contradict that argument.

Faculty members from various institutions will judge your essay, assessing it on the basis of your skills in the following areas:

- ☑ Coverage of each of the elements in the topic instructions
- ☑ Identification and assessment of the argument's main elements
- ☑ Organization and articulation of your thoughts
- ☑ Use of relevant examples and arguments to support your case
- ☑ Handling of the mechanics of standard written English

Here is an argument analysis topic modeled on the argument analysis task of the GRE. Please note that this is not an official GRE argument analysis topic, although it does resemble the official topics closely in subject matter and form.

> **SAMPLE ARGUMENT TASK**
>
> **The following appeared in an editorial in the *Springfield Morning Leader*.**
>
> **"The time is now for Springfield to step up to the plate and demonstrate that it is a city on the move. By building a new stadium that meets the standards of Major League Baseball, we can strengthen the local economy and inspire civic pride. Building the stadium will create construction jobs for local workers. Additionally, the new stadium will help woo a Major League team to the area, which will create jobs and make Springfield more attractive to businesses that are considering relocating. Building a new stadium is an investment of public funds that will pay off for Springfield today and for generations to come."**
>
> ***Compose an essay that identifies and considers the evidence required to assess the validity of the argument provided. In writing your essay be sure to clarify whether this evidence would bolster or undermine the argument.***

Editorial claims that building a new stadium alone will strengthen the econ & ↑ civic pride. And while the claim that the project will create jobs is almost certainly true, it is not certain the stadium will "woo" a team or that, if that occurs, that will lead to an ↑ in jobs and businesses.

Many areas that have stadiums an MLB teams do not have burgeoning economies or a large job market.

A stadium would be an investment that could pay off in creating jobs, but the pay off for Springfield is not necessarily as large as the editorial claims.

Test-Taking Tactics for the Computer-Delivered GRE

2

In this chapter, we will take you step-by-step through a discussion of all the screens you will see as you take the computer-delivered GRE. But first let's look at a few sample questions to show you what the screens actually look like, to familiarize you with the various icons, and to demonstrate how to use the mouse to navigate through the exam.

Here is a simple ***multiple-choice*** math question as it would appear on a computer screen. Right now the arrow is off to one side.

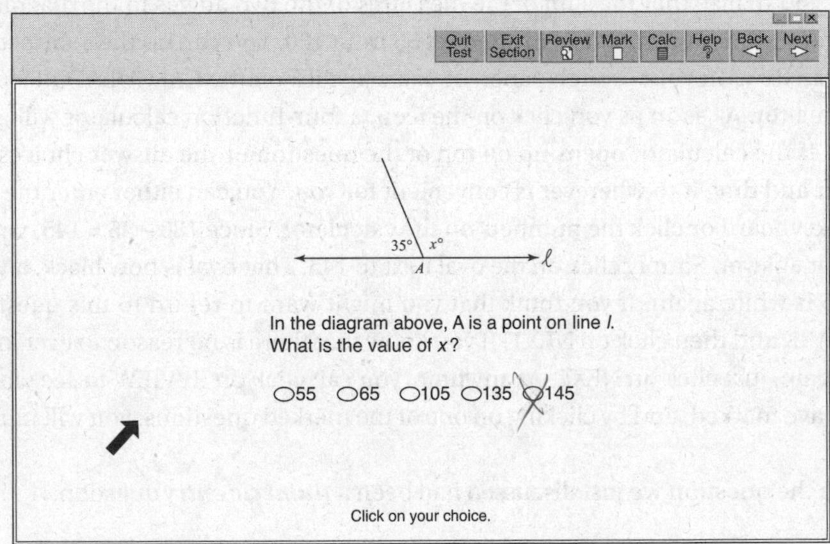

Quit Test
Exit Section
Review
Mark
Calc
Help
Back
Next
35°
x°
A
ℓ
In the diagram above, A is a point on line l.
What is the value of x?
55
65
105
135
145
Click on your choice.

Suppose that in looking at the diagram, you see that the angle is a little greater than 90° and so decide that the answer must be 105. Move the mouse until the arrow is on the oval next to 105 and click. Note that the oval on which you clicked is now black.

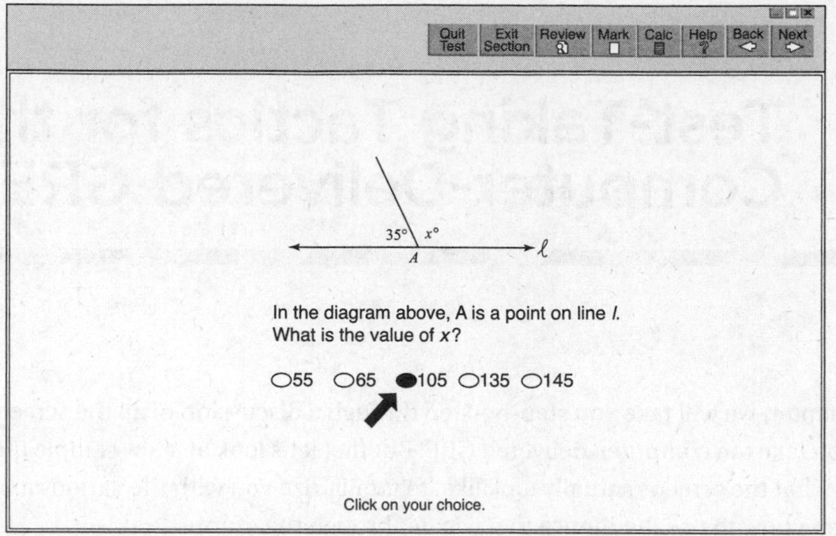

Suppose that just as you are about to click on NEXT to go to the next question, you remember that diagrams on the GRE are not drawn to scale, and so the answer may not be 105. Hopefully, you realize that the sum of the measures of the two angles in the diagram is 180°, and so to get the answer, you have to subtract 35 from 180. You can do the subtraction mentally, you can do it on your scratch paper, or you can click on the CALCULATOR icon and do it on a calculator. As soon as you click on the icon, a four-function calculator will appear on the screen. If the calculator opens up on top of the question or the answer choices, click on the top of it and drag it to wherever is convenient for you. You can either enter the numbers from your keyboard or click the numbers on the calculator. Since 180 – 35 = 145, you want to change your answer. Simply click on the oval next to 145. That oval is now black, and the one next to 105 is white again. If you think that you might want to return to this question later, click on MARK and then click on NEXT. If you know that there is no reason to ever look at this question again, just click on NEXT. At any time, you can click on REVIEW to see which questions you have marked, and by clicking on one of the marked questions, you will immediately return to it.

Suppose the question we just discussed had been a ***numeric entry*** question.

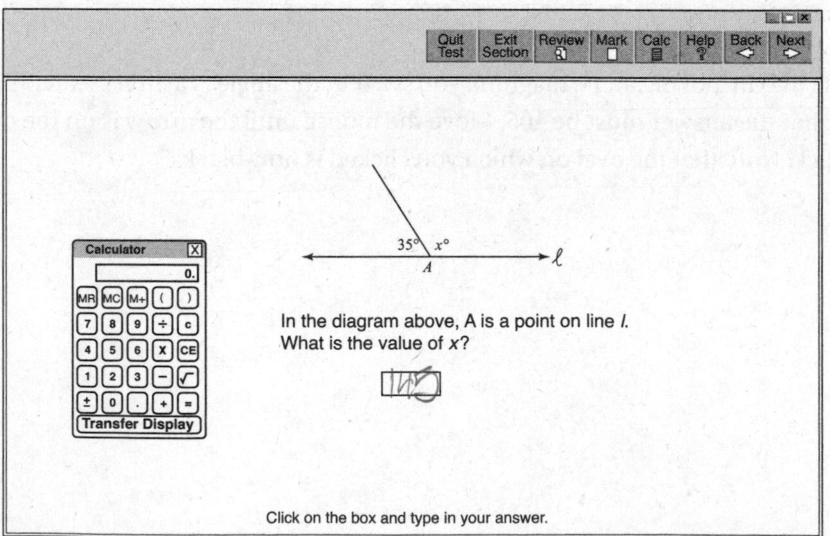

If you subtracted 35 from 180 in your head, and you knew that the answer was 145, you could click in the box and type 145. If you used your calculator to subtract, you could still type 145 in the box, but if you prefer, instead of typing 145, you could click on the bar labeled TRANSFER DISPLAY at the bottom of the calculator, and the 145 that is in the calculator's digital readout will automatically appear in the box. Note that the only time you can click on the TRANSFER DISPLAY bar is when the question on the screen is a numeric entry question; at all other times that bar is grayed out.

> **If you use the calculator to answer a question and then click on NEXT to go to the next question, the calculator will remain on the screen (with whatever your previous answer was still in the digital readout). You may leave it there, but it is better to close it by clicking on the X in the upper-right-hand corner, and then just clicking on the calculator icon the next time you need it.**

Finally, let's look at a ***multiple-answer*** question. Notice that on multiple-answer questions there are squares, instead of ovals, in front of each answer choice.

On multiple-answer questions, when you click on a square in front of an answer choice, an X appears in the square. In the question below, suppose you clicked on 17, 37, and 57, the screen would then look like this.

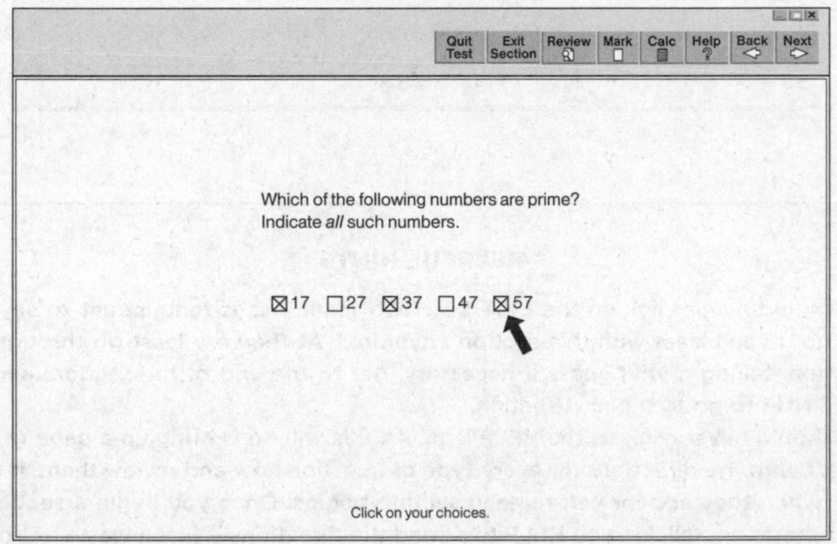

If you then realize that 47 is also a prime, just click on it; an X will appear in its square.

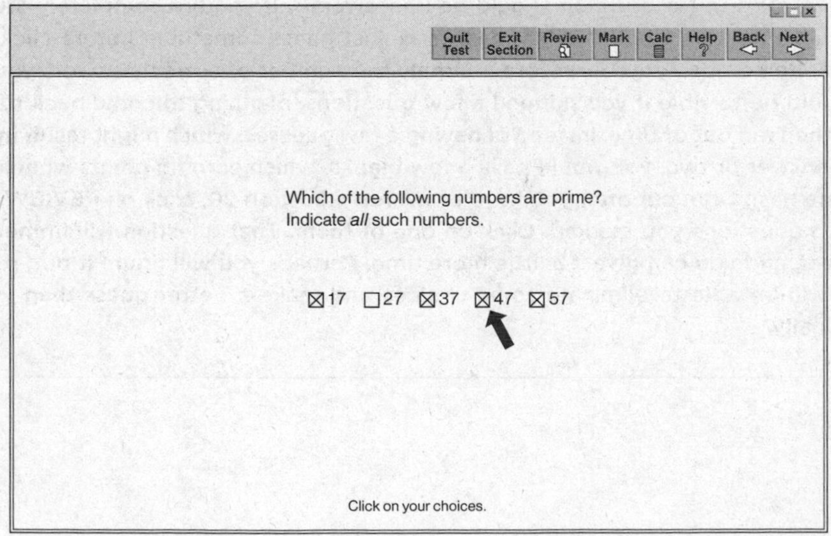

Finally, if you realize that you made another mistake, by including 57 ($57 = 3 \times 19$), just click on the square in front of 57 and the X will go away.

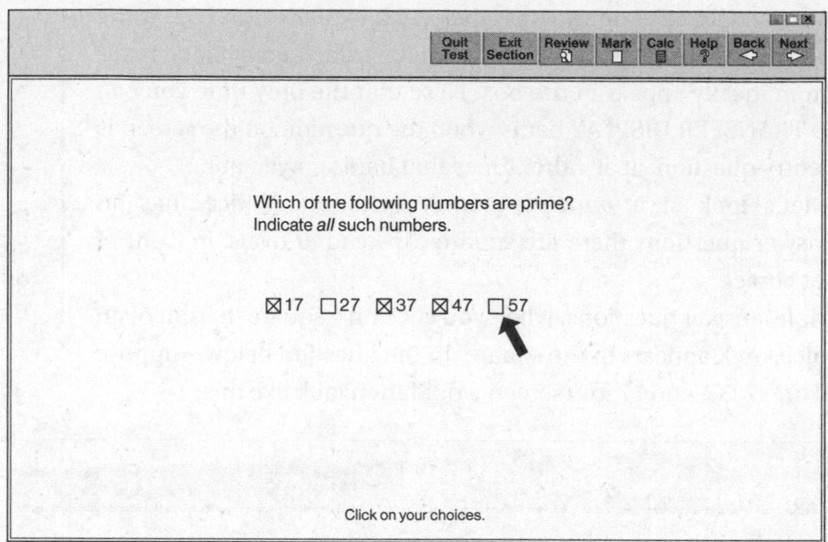

HELPFUL HINTS

1. You should *never* click on the EXIT SECTION icon. This is tantamount to saying, "I give up. I can't deal with this section anymore." At the very least go through each question, taking a wild guess if necessary, get to the end of the section, and click CONTINUE to go to the next section.
2. You should never click on the HELP icon. All this will do is bring up a page of directions. Learn the directions for every type of question now and review them, if necessary, when they appear before each section begins. Once you begin a section, the clock starts and clicking on HELP to reread the directions is just a waste of time.
3. Don't click on REVIEW until you have gotten to the end of the section. When you click on REVIEW, all you will see is a list numbered from 1–20, indicating for each question whether it has been ANSWERED or UNANSWERED and whether or not it has been MARKED. No question should be unanswered. If you are completely stumped and have no idea what the right answer is, just guess something before clicking on NEXT. Remember, your raw score is simply the number of correct answers you have. It would be terrible if you skipped a few questions, planning to come back to them, and then ran out of time. Instead of having a few guesses, which might result in a correct answer or two, you would have a few blanks, which earn no points whatsoever.
4. If time hasn't run out after you have answered Question 20, click on REVIEW to see which questions you marked. Click on one of them. That question will immediately appear, and you can give it a little more time. Perhaps you will figure it out; perhaps you will be able to eliminate some choices and make a better guess than you did originally.

A GUIDED TOUR OF THE COMPUTER-DELIVERED GRE

The following outline tells you exactly what you will see, screen by screen, when you take the computerized GRE. To some extent you can alter the flow of screens. For example, after answering the fourteenth math question, we assume that you would click on NEXT to bring up the screen for question 15. However, at that point, if you chose to, you could click on MARK to put a check mark next to question 14 in the list of questions you have looked at; you could click on BACK to return to question 13 or click on BACK repeatedly to return to any previous question in the section; you could click on REVIEW to see exactly which questions you had already answered, which ones you had skipped, and which ones you had marked; or you could click on HELP to reread the directions for the math questions. As you will see shortly, most of those would be poor choices, but you could do any of them.

SCREEN 1

When you are ready to begin the test, the first screen you will see is a page of TEST CENTER REGULATIONS. You may take as much time as you like to read over this list of rules—no eating, no drinking, no smoking, no creating disturbances, no tampering with the computer—but you shouldn't need to because you should have already read it when you looked at *POWERPREP II* on the GRE website. When you are through looking at this screen, click on CONTINUE.

SCREEN 2

The second screen is a CONFIDENTIALITY AGREEMENT. This is where you promise not to cheat or to take any test materials or scrap paper out of the room. The way you say "I agree" is to click on CONTINUE.

SCREEN 3

The third screen contains GENERAL TEST INFORMATION. Much of this information—when you can take breaks; how long the breaks are; when you can leave the room—is included in this book, but feel free to take as much time as you like to read it over. When you are ready to proceed, click on CONTINUE.

SCREEN 4

This screen gives you the DIRECTIONS FOR THE ANALYTICAL WRITING section of the GRE. Again, once you read this book, you should know all of these directions. When you are ready to move on, click on CONTINUE.

SCREEN 5

This screen has the DIRECTIONS FOR TASK 1 (ANALYZE AN ISSUE). The most important point to remember is that although you have 60 minutes for Section 1, you have a maximum of 30 minutes for each of the two tasks. If, for example, you finish Task 1 in 23 minutes, you may move on to Task 2, but once you do, you can never return to Task 1 to write for 7 more minutes. Nor can you tack those 7 minutes on to the time you have for Task 2. Once you leave Task 1, you will have exactly 30 minutes for Task 2. Once you are ready to leave this screen, TAKE A DEEP BREATH: as soon as you click on CONTINUE, the test officially begins.

SCREEN 6

This screen has Task 1. On the left of the screen will be the issue you are to analyze; on the right of the screen will be a blank page on which you are to type your analysis. In the upper-right-hand corner of the screen, below the row of icons, you will see a digital readout of the amount of time remaining. If you find that distracting, you may click on HIDE TIME to make it go away, but it will reappear when there are only five minutes left. During every section, the countdown clock will be visible unless you choose to hide it. Even if you do, in every section, the clock will reappear during the last five minutes. If you finish your essay in less than 30 minutes, read it over and make any changes you like. If you still have time left, and don't want to look at the essay any more, you *can* hit NEXT, but you don't have to. You can relax. When the 30 minutes are up, the computer will automatically close that screen and take you to the next one. If you do click on NEXT, the computer will give you one last chance to change your mind.

SCREEN 7

If your full 30 minutes for Task 1 has not expired, this screen will remind you that you still have time left and give you the option of returning to Task 1 (RETURN) or moving on (CONTINUE).

SCREEN 8

Once you have left Task 1, the next screen has the DIRECTIONS FOR TASK 2 (ANALYZE AN ARGUMENT). Note: the clock is *not* running while you read these directions. So if you want an extra minute or so before starting your second essay, wait before clicking on CONTINUE.

SCREEN 9

This screen has Task 2. The argument you are to analyze will be on the left, and just as in Task 1, on the right there will be a blank page on which you are to type your analysis. And as in Task 1, the moment this screen appears, the clock will start counting down from 30:00. When you have finished your essay, you may look it over, rest a while, or click on NEXT.

SCREEN 10

If your full 30 minutes for Task 2 has not expired, this screen will remind you that you still have time left and give you the option of returning to Task 2 (RETURN) or moving on (CONTINUE).

SCREEN 11

Once you have left Task 2, the next screen will tell you that you have finished Section 1 and are about to begin Section 2. When you are ready, click on CONTINUE.

SCREEN 12

This screen will tell you that the next section will begin in 60 seconds. This is your first official break. You *should* take this short break to relax before beginning Section 2, but you don't have to. At any time before your 60 seconds are up, you can click on CONTINUE to move on.

NOTE

Section 2 will either be a 30-minute verbal section or a 35-minute quantitative section. In the practice tests in this book, Sections 2 and 4 are verbal and Sections 3 and 5 are quantitative. On an actual GRE, however, the sections can come in any order, and it is very likely that there will be an Experimental Section—either a third verbal section or a third quantitative section—which can come at any point in the test. The Experimental Section will not affect your score, but there is no way to know which section it is, so you must do your very best on each section.

SCREEN 13

This screen gives you the DIRECTIONS FOR THE VERBAL ABILITY sections of the GRE. Reading this screen, slowly, if you like, gives you a little longer break before resuming the test. When you are ready to begin Section 2, click on CONTINUE.

SCREENS 14–33

Screens 14–33 will be the 20 verbal questions in Section 2, one question per screen. Go through the section, answering *every* question, guessing whenever necessary. If, when you click on CONTINUE after question 20, your 30 minutes for Section 2 aren't up, the next screen you see will give you the option of returning to Section 2, by clicking on RETURN, or going on to Section 3, by again clicking on CONTINUE.

SCREEN 34

This screen will tell you that the next section will begin in 60 seconds. This is your second official break. You *should* take this short break to relax before beginning Section 3, but you don't have to. At any time before your 60 seconds are up, you may click on CONTINUE to move on.

SCREEN 35

This screen gives you the DIRECTIONS FOR THE QUANTITATIVE ABILITY sections of the GRE. Reading this screen, slowly, if you like, gives you a little longer break before resuming the test. When you are ready to start Section 3, click on CONTINUE.

SCREENS 36–55

Screens 36–55 will be the 20 quantitative questions in Section 3, one question per screen. Go through the section, answering *every* question, guessing whenever necessary. If there is a question that has you stumped, you can MARK it, but still answer it (even if your answer is a wild guess) before clicking on NEXT. Just as in Section 2, after answering question 20, you may click on CONTINUE, but if you still have time left, a screen will appear that will give you the chance to change your mind: you can click on RETURN to go back to the questions in Section 3 or you can really end the section by once again clicking on CONTINUE.

SCREEN 56

This screen will tell you that the next section will begin in 10 minutes. This is your third official break, and the only one that lasts more than 60 seconds. TAKE THIS BREAK! Whether you need to or not, go to the restroom now. If you have to go later during the test, the clock will be running. Outside the room, you can have a drink and/or a snack. And, of course, you can use this break to take some deep breaths and to relax before beginning the rest of the test. Having said this, you should know that you don't have to take the full 10-minute break. At any time before the 10 minutes are up, you may click on CONTINUE to move on.

At this point, the screens essentially repeat. There will be at least two more sections (one verbal and one quantitative), and probably three (the third section being yet another verbal or another quantitative one). Remember that if there are six sections, any section other than the writing section can be the experimental one, even Section 2 or 3. Each verbal section will have 20 questions and be 30 minutes long, just like Section 2, and each quantitative section will have 20 questions and be 35 minutes long, just like Section 3.

FINAL SCREEN

After you have answered question 20 in Section 6 and clicked on CONTINUE, the test is over. At this point you will see the following screen.

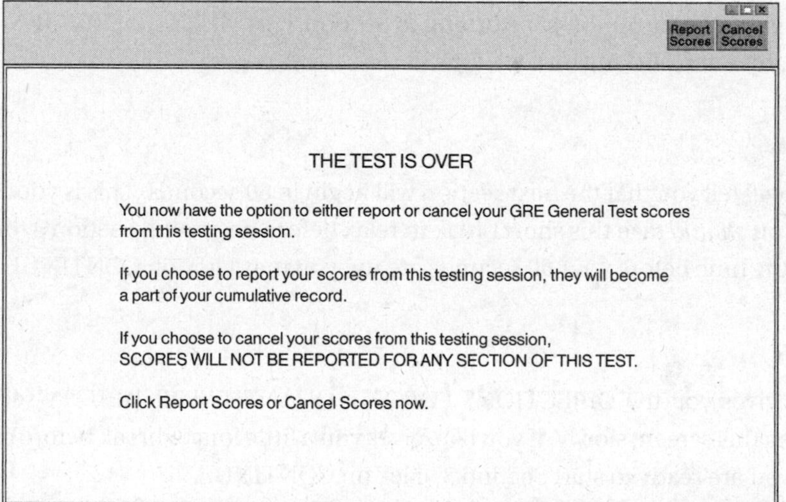

NOTE

If you click on CANCEL, the next screen will give you a chance to avoid a disaster, in case you clicked CANCEL accidentally. Once again, you will be asked to REPORT or CANCEL your scores, and this time your decision is irreversible.

If you choose to REPORT your scores, the next screen will give you your unofficial scores for the verbal and quantitative sections. Your official scores will arrive in the mail about three weeks after you take the test and, of course, will include your writing score, as well.

3 A Diagnostic Test

The Diagnostic Test in this chapter consists of three complete sections: one each of analytical writing, verbal ability, and quantitative ability. The format of each section is identical to that of the corresponding section of an actual GRE. The main difference between this Diagnostic Test and the Model Tests at the back of the book, the model tests online, and the real GRE is that the Diagnostic Test is shorter—one verbal section and one quantitative section instead of two of each. Of course, unlike a real GRE, this Diagnostic Test isn't computerized. Later in your preparation, to get a feel for what it is like to take a computerized GRE, do one or two model tests online at *barronsbooks.com/TP/GRE/*.

After taking the Diagnostic Test, score your answers and evaluate your results, using the self-rating guides provided. (Be sure also to read the answer explanations for questions you answered incorrectly and questions you answered correctly but found difficult.)

You should now be in a position to approach your review program realistically and allot your time for study. For example, you should know which topics in mathematics require review and drill. You should also know which of your verbal and analytical writing skills require concentrated study.

SIMULATE TEST CONDITIONS

To best simulate actual test conditions, find a quiet place to work. Have a stop watch or a clock handy so that you can keep perfect track of the time. Go through each section by answering the questions in the order in which they appear. If you don't know the answer to a question, guess (making an educated guess, if possible) and move on. Knowing how much time you have for each section and how many questions there are, try to pace yourself so that you have time to finish each section in the time allowed. Do not spend too much time on any one question. Again, if you get stuck, just guess and go on to the next question. If any time remains, you may return to a question that you were unsure of or check your work.

ANSWER SHEET
Diagnostic Test

Section 2

1. Ⓐ Ⓑ Ⓒ Ⓓ Ⓔ Ⓕ
2. Ⓐ Ⓑ Ⓒ Ⓓ Ⓔ Ⓕ
3. Ⓐ Ⓑ Ⓒ Ⓓ Ⓔ Ⓕ
4. Ⓐ Ⓑ Ⓒ Ⓓ Ⓔ Ⓕ
5. Ⓐ Ⓑ Ⓒ Ⓓ Ⓔ Ⓕ
6. Ⓐ Ⓑ Ⓒ Ⓓ Ⓔ Ⓕ
7. Ⓐ Ⓑ Ⓒ Ⓓ Ⓔ
8. Ⓐ Ⓑ Ⓒ Ⓓ Ⓔ
9. Ⓐ Ⓑ Ⓒ Ⓓ Ⓔ
10. Ⓐ Ⓑ Ⓒ Ⓓ Ⓔ
11. Ⓐ Ⓑ Ⓒ Ⓓ Ⓔ
12. Ⓐ Ⓑ Ⓒ Ⓓ Ⓔ
13. Ⓐ Ⓑ Ⓒ Ⓓ Ⓔ Ⓕ
14. Ⓐ Ⓑ Ⓒ Ⓓ Ⓔ Ⓕ
15. Ⓐ Ⓑ Ⓒ Ⓓ Ⓔ Ⓕ
16. Ⓐ Ⓑ Ⓒ Ⓓ Ⓔ Ⓕ
17. Ⓐ Ⓑ Ⓒ Ⓓ Ⓔ
18. Ⓐ Ⓑ Ⓒ Ⓓ Ⓔ
19. Ⓐ Ⓑ Ⓒ
20. Ⓐ Ⓑ Ⓒ Ⓓ Ⓔ

Section 3

1. Ⓐ Ⓑ Ⓒ Ⓓ
2. Ⓐ Ⓑ Ⓒ Ⓓ
3. Ⓐ Ⓑ Ⓒ Ⓓ
4. Ⓐ Ⓑ Ⓒ Ⓓ
5. Ⓐ Ⓑ Ⓒ Ⓓ
6. Ⓐ Ⓑ Ⓒ Ⓓ
7. Ⓐ Ⓑ Ⓒ Ⓓ
8. Ⓐ Ⓑ Ⓒ Ⓓ
9. Ⓐ Ⓑ Ⓒ Ⓓ Ⓔ
10. Ⓐ Ⓑ Ⓒ Ⓓ Ⓔ
11. Ⓐ Ⓑ Ⓒ Ⓓ Ⓔ
12. [ ]
13. Ⓐ Ⓑ Ⓒ Ⓓ Ⓔ Ⓕ Ⓖ Ⓗ Ⓘ
14. Ⓐ Ⓑ Ⓒ Ⓓ Ⓔ
15. Ⓐ Ⓑ Ⓒ Ⓓ Ⓔ
16. [ ]
17. Ⓐ Ⓑ Ⓒ Ⓓ Ⓔ
18. Ⓐ Ⓑ Ⓒ Ⓓ Ⓔ
19. Ⓐ Ⓑ Ⓒ Ⓓ Ⓔ
20. Ⓐ Ⓑ Ⓒ Ⓓ Ⓔ

SECTION 1 ANALYTICAL WRITING

TIME: 60 MINUTES—2 WRITING TASKS

Task 1: Analyze an Issue

30 MINUTES

Directions: In 30 minutes, compose an essay on the topic below. You may not write on any other topic.

The topic is presented in a one- to two-sentence quotation commenting on an issue of general concern. Your essay may support, refute, or qualify the views expressed in the quotation. Whatever you write, however, must be relevant to the issue under discussion, and you must support your viewpoint with reasons and examples derived from your studies and/or experience.

If you will be taking the computer-delivered test, write your essay using a word-processing program with its spelling and grammar checker turned off. If you will be taking the paper-delivered test, write your essay on lined paper using a #2 pencil.

Faculty members from various institutions will evaluate your essay, judging it on the basis of your skill in the following areas:

- ☑ Coverage of each of the elements in the task instructions
- ☑ Analysis of the statement's implications
- ☑ Organization and articulation of your ideas
- ☑ Use of relevant examples and arguments to support your case
- ☑ Handling of the mechanics, grammar, and usage of standard written English

ISSUE TOPIC

"Question authority. Only by questioning accepted wisdom can we advance our understanding of the world."

Compose an essay that identifies how greatly you concur (or differ) with the recommendation provided and describe the rationale for your argument. As you build and provide evidence for your argument, include examples that demonstrate circumstances in which implementing the recommendation might (or might not) be beneficial. Be sure to explain the impact these examples have on your argument.

Task 2: Analyze an Argument

30 MINUTES

Directions: In 30 minutes, prepare a critical analysis of an argument expressed in a short paragraph, following the specific task instructions provided. You may not offer an analysis of any other argument.

Be sure to support your analysis with evidence (reasons and/or examples) but **do not present your personal views on the topic.** Your job is to analyze the elements of an argument, not to support or contradict that argument.

If you will be taking the computer-delivered test, write your essay using a word-processing program with its spelling and grammar checker turned off. If you will be taking the paper-delivered test, write your essay on lined paper using a #2 pencil.

Faculty members from various institutions will evaluate your essay, judging it on the basis of your skill in the following areas:

- ☑ Coverage of each of the elements in the task instructions
- ☑ Identification and assessment of the argument's main elements
- ☑ Organization and articulation of your thoughts
- ☑ Use of relevant examples and arguments to support your case
- ☑ Handling of the mechanics, grammar, and usage of standard written English

ARGUMENT TOPIC

The following appeared in an editorial in the *Bayside Sentinel.*

"Bayside citizens need to consider raising local taxes if they want to see improvements in the Bayside School District. Test scores, graduation and college admission rates, and a number of other indicators have long made it clear that the Bayside School District is doing a poor job educating our youth. Our schools look run down. Windows are broken, bathrooms unusable, and classrooms hopelessly out of date. Yet just across the Bay, in New Harbor, school facilities are up-to-date and in good condition. The difference is money. New Harbor spends twenty-seven percent more per student than Bayside does, and test scores and other indicators of student performance are stronger in New Harbor as well."

Compose an essay that identifies and considers the assumptions (implicit and/or explicit) on which the argument is based. The essay must clarify the importance of these assumptions to the argument and explain the impact on the argument's validity should the assumptions be faulty.

SECTION 2 VERBAL REASONING

TIME: 30 MINUTES—20 QUESTIONS

> **Directions:** For each of the following sentences, select the two answers of the six choices given that, when substituted in the sentence, both logically complete the sentence as a whole and create sentences that are equivalent to one another in meaning.

QUESTIONS 1–6 (SENTENCE EQUIVALENCE)

1. Many of us attempt to rewrite our personal stories to present ourselves in the best light; indeed, we are almost universally _______ to do so.

   [A] reluctant
   [B] illuminated
   [C] apt
   [D] prone
   [E] intimidated
   [F] comprehensive

2. Far from condemning Warhol for his apparent superficiality and commercialism, critics today _______ him for these very qualities, contending that in these superficial, commercial artworks he had captured the essence of American culture in the 1970s.

   [A] belittle
   [B] chastise
   [C] tolerate
   [D] extol
   [E] flaunt
   [F] hail

3. A born trickster, he was as inclined to _______ as an embezzler is inclined to fraud.

   [A] bravado
   [B] chicanery
   [C] cowardice
   [D] candor
   [E] ingenuousness
   [F] artifice

4. Paradoxically, the very admonitions intended to reform the prodigal served only to _______ his wicked ways.

   [A] turn him from
   [B] confirm him in
   [C] distress him about
   [D] absolve him of
   [E] reinforce
   [F] transform

5. Although no two siblings could have disagreed more in nature—where she was gregarious, he was introverted; where she was outspoken, he was _______—the twins nevertheless got on amazingly well.

   [A] reserved
   [B] discreet
   [C] garrulous
   [D] insensitive
   [E] imprudent
   [F] fluent

6. Amusingly enough, lawyers sometimes drive their sport cars in the same fashion that they construct their cases: a lawyer noted for the _______ of his arguments, for example, may also be known for the circuitousness of his routes.

   [A] brevity
   [B] pertinacity
   [C] judiciousness
   [D] deviousness
   [E] conciseness
   [F] indirectness

Directions: Questions 7 through 11 are based on the content of the following passages. Read the passage and then determine the best answer choice for each question. Base your choice on what the passage *states directly* or *implies*, not on any information you may have gained elsewhere.

For questions 7–11, select *one* answer choice unless otherwise instructed.

QUESTIONS 7–9 ARE BASED ON THE FOLLOWING PASSAGE.

James's first novels used conventional narrative techniques: explicit characterization, action that related events in distinctly phased sequences, settings firmly outlined and specifically described. But this method gradually gave way to a subtler, more deliberate, more diffuse style of accumulation of minutely discriminated details whose total significance the reader can grasp only by constant attention and sensitive inference. His later novels play down scenes of abrupt and prominent action, and do not so much offer a succession of sharp shocks as slow piecemeal additions of perception. The curtain is not suddenly drawn back from shrouded things, but is slowly moved away. Such a technique is suited to James's essential subject, which is not human action itself but the states of mind that produce and are produced by human actions and interactions. James was less interested in what characters do, than in the moral and psychological antecedents, realizations, and consequences which attend their doings. This is why he more often speaks of "cases" than of actions. His stories, therefore, grow more and more lengthy while the actions they relate grow simpler and less visible; not because they are crammed with adventitious and secondary events, digressive relief, or supernumerary characters, as overstuffed novels of action are; but because he presents in such exhaustive detail every nuance of his situation. Commonly the interest of a novel is in the variety and excitement of visible actions building up to a climactic event which will settle the outward destinies of characters with storybook promise of permanence. A James novel, however, possesses its characteristic interest in carrying the reader through a rich analysis of the mental adjustments of characters to the realities of their personal situations as they are slowly revealed to them through exploration and chance discovery.

7. The passage supplies information for answering which of the following questions?
   - Ⓐ Did James originate the so-called psychological novel?
   - Ⓑ Is conventional narrative technique strictly chronological in recounting action?
   - Ⓒ Can novels lacking overtly dramatic incident sustain the reader's interest?
   - Ⓓ Were James's later novels more acceptable to the general public than his earlier ones?
   - Ⓔ Is James unique in his predilection for exploring psychological nuances of character?

8. In which sentence of the passage does the author use figurative language to clarify James's technique in his later novels?

Note: *In the computer-delivered GRE, the directions for this question would be:* ***Click on the sentence in the passage.***

Ⓐ The first sentence ("James's first novels ... described.")
Ⓑ The second sentence ("But this method ... inference.")
Ⓒ The fourth sentence ("The curtain ... moved away.")
Ⓓ The fifth sentence ("Such a technique ... interactions.")
Ⓔ The sixth sentence ("James was ... doings.")

9. In the context in which it appears, "attend" (line 24) most nearly means

Ⓐ take care of
Ⓑ watch over
Ⓒ pay attention to
Ⓓ accompany
Ⓔ celebrate

QUESTIONS 10–11 ARE BASED ON THE FOLLOWING PASSAGE.

According to the theory of plate tectonics, the lithosphere (Earth's relatively hard and solid outer layer consisting of the crust and part of the underlying mantle) is divided into a few dozen plates that vary in size and shape; in general, these plates move in relation to one another. They move away from one another at a mid-ocean ridge, a long chain of sub-oceanic mountains that forms a boundary between plates. At a mid-ocean ridge, new lithospheric material in the form of hot magma pushes up from the Earth's interior. The injection of this new lithospheric material from below causes the phenomenon known as sea-floor spreading.

Given that the earth is not expanding in size to any appreciable degree, how can "new" lithosphere be created at a mid-ocean ridge? For new lithosphere to come into being in one region, an equal amount of lithospheric material must be destroyed somewhere else. This destruction takes place at a boundary between plates called a subduction zone. At a subduction zone, one plate is pushed down under another into the red-hot mantle, where over a span of millions of years it is absorbed into the mantle.

10. According to the passage, a mid-ocean ridge differs from a subduction zone in that

Ⓐ it marks the boundary line between neighboring plates
Ⓑ only the former is located on the ocean floor
Ⓒ it is a site for the emergence of new lithospheric material
Ⓓ the former periodically disrupts the earth's geomagnetic field
Ⓔ it is involved with lithospheric destruction rather than lithospheric creation

11. It can be inferred from the passage that as new lithospheric material is injected from below

Ⓐ the plates become immobilized in a kind of gridlock
Ⓑ it is incorporated into an underwater mountain ridge
Ⓒ the earth's total mass is altered
Ⓓ it reverses its magnetic polarity
Ⓔ the immediately adjacent plates sink

DIAGNOSTIC TEST

Directions: Each of the following sentences or groups of sentences contains one, two, or three blanks. These blanks signify that a word or set of words has been left out. Below each sentence are columns of words or sets of words. For each blank, pick the *one* word or set of words from the corresponding column that *best* completes the text.

12. By ________ strict rules of hygiene in maternity wards, Ignaz Semmelweis saved many women from dying of childbed fever, a fate that many expectant mothers feared.

Ⓐ challenging
Ⓑ instituting
Ⓒ intimating
Ⓓ invalidating
Ⓔ sanitizing

13. The earth is a planet bathed in light; it is therefore (i) ________ that many of the living organisms that have evolved on the earth have (ii) ________ the biologically advantageous capacity to trap light energy.

Blank (i)
Ⓐ anomalous
Ⓑ unsurprising
Ⓒ problematic

Blank (ii)
Ⓓ encapsulated
Ⓔ divested
Ⓕ developed

14. To contrast the demeanor of Austen's clergyman brothers James and Henry with that of Mr. Collins, the much-abused figure of fun in *Pride and Prejudice*, is instructive, for where the Austen brothers were properly (i) ________ to their social superiors and benevolent to their dependents, the odious Mr. Collins was invariably (ii) ________ to his betters, fawning in particular on his patron, Lady Catherine de Burgh.

Blank (i)
Ⓐ deferential
Ⓑ disingenuous
Ⓒ demonstrative

Blank (ii)
Ⓓ responsible
Ⓔ sycophantic
Ⓕ sardonic

15. The reclassification of the solar system that demoted Pluto to a "dwarf planet" did not go (i) _______, for several hundred indignant astronomers petitioned the International Astronomical Union to (ii) _______ its decision.

Blank (i)
Ⓐ astray
Ⓑ uncontested
Ⓒ unrewarded

Blank (ii)
Ⓓ reconsider
Ⓔ initiate
Ⓕ promulgate

16. Relatively few politicians willingly (i) _______ center stage, although a touch of (ii) _______ on their parts now and again might well increase their popularity with the voting public.

Blank (i)
Ⓐ forsake
Ⓑ embrace
Ⓒ endure

Blank (ii)
Ⓓ garrulity
Ⓔ misanthropy
Ⓕ self-effacement

Directions: Questions 17 through 20 are based on the content of the following passages. Read the passage and then determine the best answer choice for each question. Base your choice on what the passage *states directly* or implies, not on any information you may have gained elsewhere.

For questions 17–20, select *one* answer choice unless otherwise instructed.

QUESTIONS 17–18 ARE BASED ON THE FOLLOWING PASSAGE.

The stability that had marked the Iroquois Confederacy's generally pro-British position was shattered with the overthrow of James II in 1688, the colonial uprisings that followed in Massachusetts, New York, and Maryland, and the commencement of King William's War against Louis XIV of France. The increasing French threat to English hegemony in the interior of North America was signalized by French-led or French-inspired attacks on the Iroquois and on outlying colonial settlements in New York and New England. The high point of the Iroquois response was the spectacular raid of August 5, 1689, in which the Iroquois virtually wiped out the French village of Lachine, just outside Montreal. A counter-raid by the French on the English village of Schenectady in March 1690 instilled an appropriate measure of fear among the English and their Iroquois allies.

The Iroquois position at the end of the war, which was formalized by treaties made during the summer of 1701 with the British and the French, and which was maintained throughout most of the eighteenth century, was one of "aggressive neutrality" between the two competing European powers. Under the new system the Iroquois initiated a peace policy toward the "far Indians," tightened their control over the nearby tribes, and induced both English and French to support their neutrality toward the European powers by appropriate gifts and concessions.

17. The author's primary purpose in this passage is to
    - Ⓐ denounce the imperialistic policies of the French
    - Ⓑ disprove the charges of barbarism made against the Indian nations
    - Ⓒ expose the French government's exploitation of the Iroquois balance of power
    - Ⓓ describe and assess the effect of European military power on the policy of an Indian nation
    - Ⓔ show the inability of the Iroquois to engage in European-style diplomacy

18. With which of the following statements would the author be LEAST likely to agree?
    - Ⓐ The Iroquois were able to respond effectively to French acts of aggression.
    - Ⓑ James II's removal from the throne preceded the outbreak of dissension among the colonies.
    - Ⓒ The French sought to undermine the generally positive relations between the Iroquois and the British.
    - Ⓓ Iroquois negotiations involved playing one side against the other.
    - Ⓔ The Iroquois ceased to receive trade concessions from the European powers early in the eighteenth century.

QUESTIONS 19–20 ARE BASED ON THE FOLLOWING PASSAGE.

A recent assessment of the status of global amphibian populations identified habitat loss as the single greatest identifiable factor contributing to amphibian declines. Habitat loss primarily results from the residential, agricultural, arboricultural, or recreational development of an area.

Anthropogenic conversion of land has caused significant reductions in the wetland, forest, and grassland habitat that amphibians require for their survival. Outright habitat loss probably has the greatest effect on amphibians, but habitat degradation, or the general decline in the health of a habitat, often results from environmental contamination, the introduction of exotic invasive species, or a reduction in required resources within a habitat, and similarly affects amphibians. Likewise, habitat fragmentation (the disruption or fragmentation of habitat into discontinuous or isolated remnants of viable habitat) emerges from isolated patches of habitat loss and can often have delayed effects on animal populations.

19. Which of the following statements about habitat loss is supported by the passage?

    Select *all* that apply.

    - [A] The role of habitat loss in the decline of global amphibian populations is the subject of current evaluation.
    - [B] Outright habitat loss causes less damage to amphibian populations than either habitat degradation or habitat fragmentation.
    - [C] Introducing non-native species to an area may prove detrimental to the native animal populations.

20. Throughout the passage, the author never takes the opportunity to
    - Ⓐ define a term
    - Ⓑ cite an authority
    - Ⓒ state a probability
    - Ⓓ qualify a statement
    - Ⓔ make an assertion

SECTION 3 QUANTITATIVE ABILITY

TIME: 35 MINUTES—20 QUESTIONS

Directions: In each of questions 1-8, there are two quantities—Quantity A and Quantity B. You are to compare those quantities, taking into consideration any additional information given. The correct answer to such a question is

Ⓐ if Quantity A is greater;
Ⓑ if Quantity B is greater;
Ⓒ if the two quantities are equal;
Ⓓ if it is impossible to determine which quantity is greater.

Note: The given information, if any, is always centered above the two quantities. In any question, if a symbol or letter appears more than once, it represents the same thing each time.

1.

$a > 0$

Quantity A	Quantity B
a^4a^5	$(a^3)^2$

2.

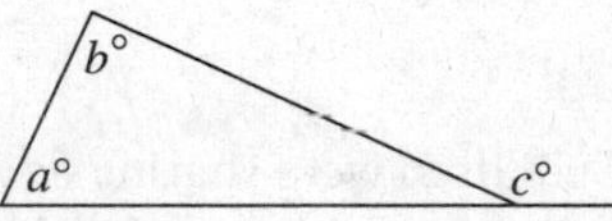

Quantity A	Quantity B
$a + b - c$	0

3.

$0 < a < b < 1$

Quantity A	Quantity B
$\sqrt{a+b}$	$\sqrt{a} + \sqrt{b}$

4.

There are 250 people lined up outside a theater. Jack is the 25th person from the front, and Jill is the 125th person from the front.

Quantity A	Quantity B
The number of people between Jack and Jill	100

5.

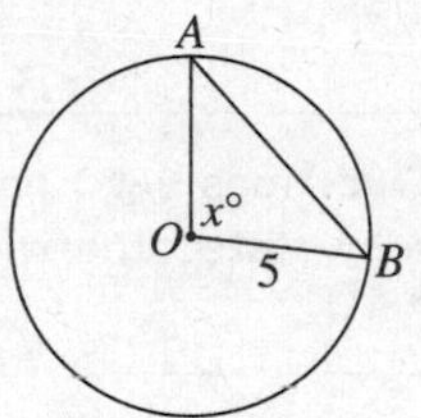

$90 < x < 180$

Quantity A	Quantity B
The perimeter of $\triangle AOB$	17

6.

Set 1 = {10, 20, 30, 40}
Set 2 = {30, 60, 90, 120}
Set 3 = {60, 70, 80, 90}

Quantity A	Quantity B
The standard deviation of the numbers in Set 2	The standard deviation of the numbers in Set 3

DIAGNOSTIC TEST

7.

Quantity A	Quantity B
The average (arithmetic mean) of the measures of the three angles of a triangle whose largest angle measures 75°	The average (arithmetic mean) of the measures of the three angles of a triangle whose largest angle measures 105°

8.

The three circles have the same center. The radii of the circles are 3, 4, and 5.

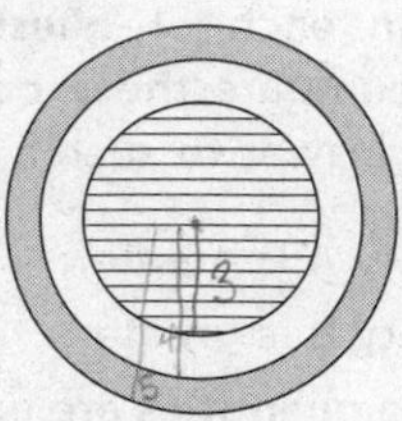

Quantity A	Quantity B
The area of the shaded region	The area of the striped region

Directions: Questions 9–20 have three different formats. Unless a question has its own directions that specifically state otherwise, each question has five answer choices, exactly one of which is correct.

9. In the figure below, what is the value of $a + b + c$?

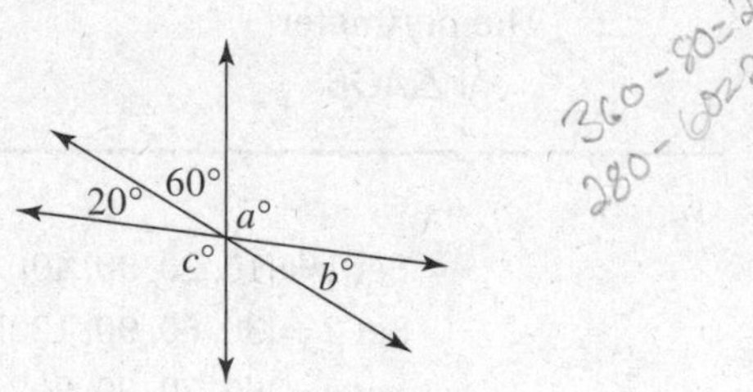

Ⓐ 210
Ⓑ 220
Ⓒ 240
Ⓓ 270
Ⓔ 280

10. What is the value of n if $4^{10} \times 64^2 = 16^2 \times 4^n$?

Ⓐ 6
Ⓑ 10
Ⓒ 12
Ⓓ 15
Ⓔ 30

11. Twenty children were sharing equally the cost of a present for their teacher. When 4 of the children decided not to contribute, each of the other children had to pay \$1.50 more. How much did the present cost, in dollars?

Ⓐ 50
Ⓑ 80
Ⓒ 100
Ⓓ 120
Ⓔ 150

Directions: For the following question, enter your answer in the box.

12. Of the 200 seniors at Monroe High School, exactly 40 are in the band, 60 are in the orchestra, and 10 are in both. How many seniors are in neither the band nor the orchestra?

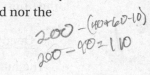

[ ]

Directions: For the following question, consider each of the choices separately and select *all* that apply.

13. Benjamin's average (arithmetic mean) on the six biology tests he took last semester was 89. On each of his first five tests, his grade was between 90 and 100, inclusive. Which of the following could have been his grade on his sixth test?

    Indicate *all* such grades.

[A]	15	[D]	45	[G]	75
[B]	25	[E]	55	[H]	85
[C]	35	[F]	65	[I]	95

QUESTIONS 14–16 REFER TO THE FOLLOWING GRAPHS.

1993
Total Exports to Eastern Europe = $98 Billion

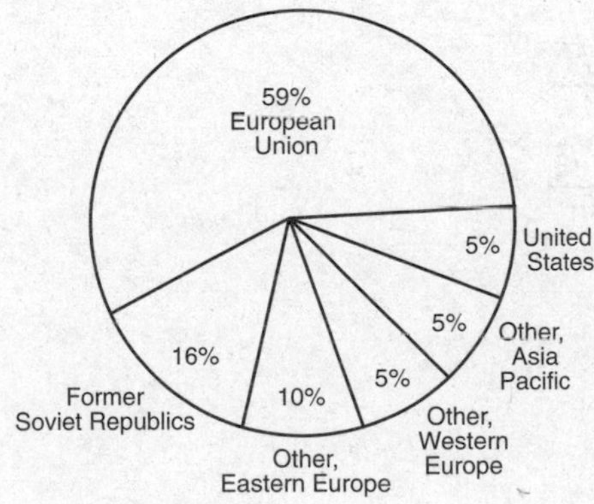

1996
Total Exports to Eastern Europe = $174 Billion

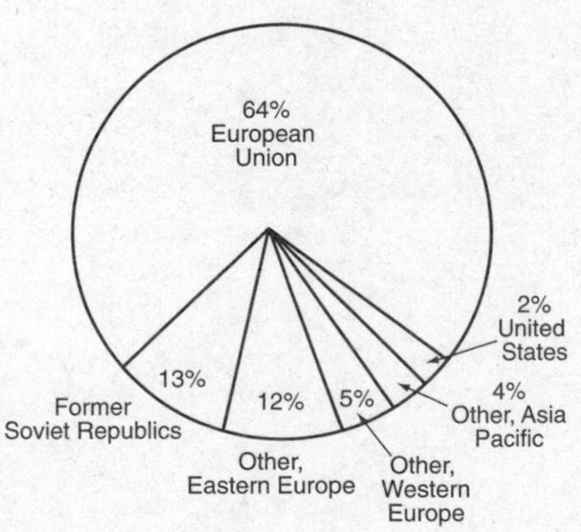

14. Which of the following statements concerning the value of exports to Eastern Europe from other Eastern European countries from 1993 to 1996 is the most accurate?

    Ⓐ They increased by 2%.
    Ⓑ They increased by 12%.
    Ⓒ They increased by 20%.
    Ⓓ They increased by 50%.
    Ⓔ They increased by 100%.

15. France is one of the countries in the European Union. If in 1996 France's exports to Eastern Europe were four times those of the United States, then what percent of the European Union's exports to Eastern Europe came from France that year?

    Ⓐ 5%
    Ⓑ 8%
    Ⓒ 12.5%
    Ⓓ 20%
    Ⓔ 25%

Directions: For the following question, enter your answer in the box.

16. If from 1996 to 2000 the percent increase in total exports to Eastern Europe was the same as the percent increase from 1993 to 1996, and the percent of exports from the European Union remained the same as in 1996, to the nearest billion, what was the value, in dollars, of exports from the European Union to Eastern Europe in 2000?

    [ ] dollars

17. Let the lengths of the sides of a triangle be represented by $x + 3$, $2x - 3$, and $3x - 5$. If the perimeter of the triangle is 25, what is the length of the shortest side?

Ⓐ 5
Ⓑ 6
Ⓒ 7
Ⓓ 8
Ⓔ 10

18. In 1990, twice as many boys as girls at Adams High School earned varsity letters. From 1990 to 2000 the number of girls earning varsity letters increased by 25% while the number of boys earning varsity letters decreased by 25%. What was the ratio in 2000 of the number of girls to the number of boys who earned varsity letters?

Ⓐ $\frac{5}{3}$
Ⓑ $\frac{6}{5}$
Ⓒ $\frac{1}{1}$
Ⓓ $\frac{5}{6}$
Ⓔ $\frac{3}{5}$

19. If $x + 2y = a$ and $x - 2y = b$, which of the following expressions is equal to xy?

Ⓐ ab
Ⓑ $\frac{a+b}{2}$
Ⓒ $\frac{a-b}{2}$
Ⓓ $\frac{a^2-b^2}{4}$
Ⓔ $\frac{a^2-b^2}{8}$

20. Square and an equilateral triangle each have sides of length 5. What is the ratio of the area of the square to the area of the triangle?

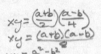

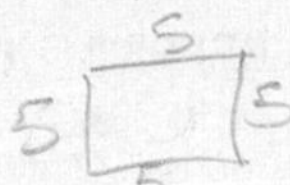
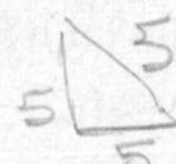

Ⓐ $\frac{4}{3}$
Ⓑ $\frac{16}{9}$
Ⓒ $\frac{\sqrt{3}}{4}$
Ⓓ $\frac{4\sqrt{3}}{3}$
Ⓔ $\frac{16\sqrt{3}}{9}$

SELF-APPRAISAL

Now that you have completed the Diagnostic Test, evaluate your performance. Identify your strengths and weaknesses, and then plan a practical study program based on what you have discovered.

Use the Answer Key on the next page to check your answers. Your raw score for each section is equal to the number of questions you answered correctly. Once you have determined your raw score for each ability area, use the conversion chart that follows to get your scaled score. Note that this conversion chart is provided to give you a very rough estimate of the GRE score you would achieve if you took the test now without any further preparation. When you take the computer-based GRE, your scaled score will be determined not only by the number of questions you answer correctly, but also by the difficulty level of those questions. The unofficial conversion chart presented here gives you only an approximate idea of how raw scores convert into scaled scores.

Use this Diagnostic Test to identify areas you may be weak in. You may find that you had trouble with a particular question type (for example, you didn't do well on the reading comprehension questions in the verbal section), or with particular subject matter (for example, you didn't do well on the geometry questions, whether they were quantitative comparisons or discrete quantitative). Determining what you need to concentrate on will help you plan an effective study program.

Remember, in addition to evaluating your scores and identifying weak areas, you should read all the answer explanations for questions you answered incorrectly, questions you guessed on, and questions you answered correctly but found difficult. Reviewing the answer explanations will help you understand concepts and strategies, and may point out shortcuts.

Score Conversion Chart for the Verbal and Quantitative Sections

Raw Score	Scaled Score	Raw Score	Scaled Score
20	170	9	148
19	168	8	146
18	166	7	144
17	164	6	142
16	162	5	140
15	160	4	138
14	158	3	136
13	156	2	134
12	154	1	132
11	152	0	130
10	150		

ANSWER KEY

Section 1—Analytical Writing

The Analytic Writing sections are scored holistically in accordance with the following guidelines.

First, estimate your score on the Issue Essay by using the following rubric.

	Argument	Support	Structure	Fluency	Conventions
6	Presents a clear and perceptive argument that responds to the specific task instructions	Provides strong reasoning and/or examples to fully support its thesis	Is focused and very well organized and has logical and skillful transitions between ideas	Expresses ideas clearly and fluently, with sophisticated word choice and varied sentence structure	Displays impressive command of the grammar, usage, and mechanics of standard written English
5	Presents a clear and thoughtful argument that responds to the specific task instructions	Provides logical reasoning and/or appropriate examples to support its thesis	Is focused and well organized and has logical transitions between ideas	Expresses ideas effectively, with appropriate word choice and varied sentence structure	Displays solid command of the grammar, usage, and mechanics of standard written English
4	Presents a clear argument that adequately responds to the specific task instructions	Provides adequate reasoning and/or examples to support its thesis	Is reasonably well focused and organized	Expresses ideas effectively, with appropriate word choice	Displays command of the grammar, usage, and mechanics of standard written English
3	Presents an argument that is somewhat unclear or that does not clearly respond to the specific task instructions	Makes unsupported claims or has limited relevant examples to support its thesis	Is minimally focused and/or organized	Is somewhat unclear due to incorrect word choice or sentence structure	Includes infrequent major or frequent minor errors in grammar, usage, and/or mechanics
2	Presents an argument that is unclear or fails to address the specific task instructions	Provides nearly no relevant examples or reasons to support its thesis	Is unfocused and/or disorganized	Is unclear due to frequent incorrect word choice or sentence structure	Includes significant errors in grammar, usage, and/or mechanics that render its meaning unclear
1	Presents an argument that demonstrates severely limited understanding of the topic	Provides little to no examples or reasoning that are related to the assigned topic	Is extremely disorganized or excessively short	Is very unclear due to pervasive incorrect word choice or sentence structure	Includes pervasive errors in grammar, usage, and/or mechanics that render it indecipherable
0	Addresses a topic other than the one assigned, is written in a language other than English, is nothing more than the words in the topic and/or task instructions, is nothing more than random characters, is not legible.				

As you examine the rubric you will notice that all of the scores below four are shaded gray. The reason for this is that ETS, the maker of the GRE, states that essays scoring below four display **one or more** of the characteristics listed in the shaded area. In other words, if your essay displays even one characteristic listed in the shaded area, that low score will determine your overall score. If all of your essay's characteristics are found in the boxes above the shaded area, your score should be the average of the five scores (for argument, support, structure, fluency, and writing conventions).

SCORING THE ISSUE ESSAY

Using the Issue Essay Rubric, check the box in each column that best describes your work. If each of the boxes you have checked is above the shaded area, add those five scores together and calculate their average.

Example:

Argument	4
Support	4
Structure	5
Fluency	4
Conventions	4
Total	21

The average is 4.2, rounded down to a likely score of 4.

If, however, **any** of your scores fall into the shaded area of the rubric, the lowest score marked will be your final score.

Next, estimate your score on the Argument Essay by using the following rubric.

	Argument	Support	Structure	Fluency	Conventions
6	Pinpoints the elements of the argument at issue and evaluates them with great insight	Provides detailed and persuasive support for its main points	Expresses ideas clearly and is very well organized, with logical and clear transitions between ideas	Expresses ideas clearly and fluently, with sophisticated word choice and varied sentence structure	Displays impressive command of the grammar, usage, and mechanics of standard written English
5	Pinpoints the elements of the argument at issue and evaluates them thoughtfully	Provides thoughtful and persuasive support for its main points	Expresses ideas clearly and is well organized, with suitable transitions between ideas	Expresses ideas effectively, with appropriate word choice and varied sentence structure	Displays solid command of the grammar, usage, and mechanics of standard written English
4	Identifies the elements of the argument at issue and evaluates them, but may include less relevant points	Provides sufficient, though possibly uneven, support for its main points	Expresses ideas reasonably clearly and is organized, but transitions between ideas are inadequate or absent	Expresses ideas effectively, with appropriate word choice	Displays command of the grammar, usage, and mechanics of standard written English
3	Fails to distinguish or evaluate the most relevant elements of the argument, though some relevant aspects may be discussed	Provides support that is sometimes irrelevant to its main points	Expresses ideas with little depth and/or organizes them illogically	Is somewhat unclear due to incorrect word choice or sentence structure	Includes infrequent major or frequent minor errors in grammar, usage, and/or mechanics
2	Fails to evaluate the argument using logic, but may provide the writer's personal views on the topic	Provides support that is generally irrelevant to its main points	Expresses ideas inadequately and organizes them illogically	Is unclear due to frequent incorrect word choice or sentence structure	Includes significant errors in grammar, usage, and/or mechanics that render its meaning unclear
1	Fails to demonstrate any grasp of the argument at issue	Provides no support for its main points	Is extremely disorganized or excessively short	Is very unclear due to pervasive incorrect word choice or sentence structure	Includes pervasive errors in grammar, usage, and/or mechanics that render it indecipherable
0	Addresses a topic other than the one assigned, is written in a language other than English, is nothing more than the words in the topic and/or task instructions, is nothing more than random characters, is not legible.				

SCORING THE ARGUMENT ESSAY

Using the Argument Essay Rubric, check the box in each column that best describes your work. If each of the boxes you have checked is above the shaded area, add those five scores together and calculate their average.

CALCULATING YOUR OVERALL SCORE

To determine your overall Analytical Writing score, add the scores for both essays (Issue and Argument) together and divide by 2. The overall score is given in half-point increments, so you should round up to the nearest half point when calculating this score. As an example, if you earn a score of 5 on the Issue Essay and a score of 4.5 on the Argument Essay, your overall Analytical Writing score will be 4.75, rounded up to 5.

Section 2—Verbal Reasoning

1. **C, D**	6. **D, F**	11. **B**	16. **A, F**
2. **D, F**	7. **C**	12. **B**	17. **D**
3. **B, F**	8. **C**	13. **B, F**	18. **E**
4. **B, E**	9. **D**	14. **A, E**	19. **A, C**
5. **A, B**	10. **C**	15. **B, D**	20. **B**

Section 3—Quantitative Ability

Note: The letters in brackets following the Quantitative Ability answers refer to the sections of Chapter 12 in which you can find the information you need to answer the questions. For example, 1. **C** [E] means that the answer to question 1 is C, and that the solution requires information found in Section 12-E: Averages. Also, 14. **E** [11] means that the answer to question 14 is based on information in Chapter 11: Data Interpretation Questions.

1. **D** [A]	6. **A** [E]	11. **D** [G]	16. **198** [11]
2. **C** [J]	7. **C** [E, J]	12. **110** [O]	17. **C** [G]
3. **B** [A, B]	8. **C** [L]	13. **C, D, E, F, G** [E]	18. **D** [C, D]
4. **B** [O]	9. **B** [I]	14. **E** [11]	19. **E** [G]
5. **A** [J, L]	10. **C** [A]	15. **C** [11]	20. **D** [J, K]

DIAGNOSTIC TEST

ANSWER EXPLANATIONS

Section 1—Analytical Writing: Issue Essay

Though there are no right or wrong answers to the essay questions, you can get an idea of the level of writing required to achieve a particular score by reviewing the sample essays that follow. We have included a sample essay for each score from 6 (the best) through 1 (the poorest). Each sample essay also includes a short explanation of how the score was derived by using the rubric. In evaluating your own essays you should apply the rubric in a similar fashion.

PROMPT #1

"Question authority. Only by questioning accepted wisdom can we advance our understanding of the world."

Compose an essay that identifies how greatly you concur (or differ) with the recommendation provided and describe the rationale for your argument. As you build and provide evidence for your argument, include examples that demonstrate circumstances in which implementing the recommendation might (or might not) be beneficial. Be sure to explain the impact these examples have on your argument.

SCORE 6 ISSUE ESSAY

In their infamous 1984 ad campaign for Macintosh computers, Apple, Inc. showed a mass of gray, unblinking faces entranced by a droning voice emanating from a massive screen—suddenly, a beautiful blonde woman in a brightly-colored jumpsuit appears and smashes the screen with a hammer. The video was followed by an imprint of Apple's fluorescent logo and a command: "Think Differently." The call to "question authority" is certainly a convenient catch-phrase for corporations; however, the circumstances of an individual's relationship to authority are often much more complex than walking to an Apple Store and buying a smartphone. "Question authority" is a blunt command that fails to account for the potentially grave consequences of defiance.

It is undeniable that challenging conventional wisdom is necessary to advance our understanding of the mysterious universe in which we find ourselves. A classic example is the case of Galileo Galilei, the Italian astronomer. In the 17th century, Galileo used a telescope to map the celestial bodies, using methods of logical inference that today most children are taught as "the scientific method." His profound insight led him to the conclusion that the Earth revolved around the Sun—this was not an entirely "new" idea, but it was a highly controversial one at the time. During the Roman Inquisition, the Catholic Church attempted to root out those who promulgated views contradicting the religious doctrine; this, of course, included Galileo's writings on the "heliocentric" theory, and he was eventually imprisoned, and his works censored.

Galileo's case illustrates that questioning authority is a rare privilege, with often serious consequences. We can find more humble examples in our own society: for example, a single mother in a major metropolitan area who works several jobs to support her children—one week into a new job as cashier at a fast food restaurant, she asks for overtime in order to make an upcoming rent payment. Her employer not only refuses, but berates her for having the audacity to ask for overtime, the right to which belongs to more established employees. Of course, she may have the instinct to challenge this arbitrary rule; but, more likely, she would lose her job for lack of obedience. After all, there is no shortage of people who could fill her position.

In both examples—a philosopher in a theocratic society, or a laborer in a situation of exploitation—the desire to openly challenge authority comes up against a pragmatic need to keep quiet in the interest of one's welfare. Although there is something quite powerful about adopting an ethos of "Thinking Differently" (and perhaps this explains its success as a marketing slogan), the circumstances in which we have opportunities to challenge authority figures are contingent and complex. Rather than an inflexible command, perhaps we should understand the call to "question authority" as an ethical guide—encouraging us to have the courage to say what we feel is true, when the cost of failing to speak outweighs the reprisals we may invite. This way, "Think Differently" might become, more than a corporate platitude, a meaningful motto for a progressive society.

APPLYING THE RUBRIC

Argument	5
Support	6
Structure	6
Fluency	6
Conventions	6
Total	29

The average is 5.8, rounded up to a likely score of 6.

ARGUMENT The essay presents a clear and perceptive argument that the command to question authority is too simplistic and that the cost of complying with it may be too high for some to pay. The writer does an especially good job responding to the task instruction to describe situations in which adopting the recommendation could be disadvantageous. One shortcoming is that the author accepts without examination the second half of the quotation, which asserts that questioning authority is the *only* way to advance knowledge.

SUPPORT The essay includes two strong examples of situations in which questioning authority was dangerous to the questioner. It also provides an example in the introductory paragraph that demonstrates how the command to question authority is an oversimplified catch-phrase, much like those used in advertising.

STRUCTURE The essay is well focused and does not stray from the task of proving its thesis. The transitions, especially those from the second to third paragraph and from the third to fourth paragraph, are graceful and clearly link one topic to the next.

FLUENCY The essay displays sophisticated vocabulary and varied sentence structure throughout.

CONVENTIONS Outstanding. The essay includes no noticeable errors in grammar, usage, or mechanics.

SCORE 5 ISSUE ESSAY

Recently, a friend of mine posted the following status on Facebook: "Those who are obedient will be blessed." Although it sounds like perhaps it is scripture, it may just have been a simple moment of alleged wisdom in her own words. Whatever the case, I reflected on this post for quite some time. Am I obedient? Do I aspire to follow in the footsteps of other obedient people? And I am blessed?

The post brought to mind another favorite quote, one I am sure can be attributed to an actual person, although the original speaker escapes me: "Well behaved women rarely make history." This is true of women, and it is true of the people of all oppressed groups in the history of the United States. An overview of American history shows us pretty clearly that the questioning of authority has shaped the entire destiny of this country and its inhabitants. Obedience has guaranteed rights to no one. Women following the rules and expectations for them were not simply granted the right to vote out of the kindness of men's hearts. They suffered for suffrage, toiling, protesting, marching, and lobbying the public and the political leaders in order to gain this right. If the women of the Seneca Falls convention accepted the wisdom of the day—that politics was the work of men—millions of Americans would still be disenfranchised.

Similarly, the Voting Rights Act created a pathway to civic participation that had been blocked to African-Americans simply because of race. While Black men were granted the right to vote in theory long before women of any race were, prohibitive laws and customs prevented African-American voting from reconstruction until the middle of the 20th century. (Indeed, there is good reason to believe that the suppression of Black voting is still active and accepted de facto law in some parts of the country despite the Voting Rights Act). While constitutionally originally 3/5 of a person, Black people have been a backbone of this country, but accepting authority never ensured political representation or even political consideration. African-Americans living under Jim Crow laws during reconstruction and beyond were not rewarded for good behavior with equal rights socially, politically, or economically. Those rights had to be demanded. Our present political landscape, including the Black Lives Matter movement, shows us that Black people questioning authority is an ongoing need. Without vocal and strategic demands that authority be interrogated, we see that authority does what it does best—uphold its own interest at the risk of the well-being of those being governed by its power.

Voting rights, of course, are not the only rights that have been prevented by maintaining the status quo. Japanese-Americans needed only be Japanese (and, in fact, often needed only be any Asian group) to be interned as possible traitors whether they had obeyed all US laws or not. Their heritage made them suspect, and obeying authority did not protect them from internment. Until recently, LGBTQ people law-abidingly living without marriage rights were able to vote but missed out on minor perks and major life-changing powers that heterosexual couples enjoyed via custom and via the law. In today's headlines, we see abuse or neglect of authority everywhere from the Flint, Michigan, water scandal to the current standoff at Standing Rock in protest of the Dakota Pipeline.

APPLYING THE RUBRIC

Argument	5
Support	6
Structure	5
Fluency	5
Conventions	5
Total	26

The average is 5.2, rounded down to a likely score of 5.

ARGUMENT The essay presents a clear argument that authority must be questioned in order for social progress to be made. While the thesis is clear, it does not consider the possibility that there may be instances in which questioning authority may be disadvantageous. A more perceptive and complex argument would take potential disadvantages into account (while still concluding that those disadvantages are outweighed).

SUPPORT The essay includes compelling and detailed examples that provide strong support for its thesis that progress cannot be made without questioning authority.

STRUCTURE The essay is generally well focused, though the introduction is a bit of a diversion. Transitions between paragraphs are logical. The conclusion is abrupt, and reads as if the writer was unable to finish their thought.

FLUENCY The ideas in the essay are clear, and its vocabulary use is appropriate and effective, if a bit colloquial at times. Sentence structure is varied.

CONVENTIONS The essay demonstrates solid command of the grammar, usage, and mechanics of standard written English. There are few, if any, obvious errors.

SCORE 4 ISSUE ESSAY

There is a great thrill from questioning authority. Young children question the authority of their parents by testing boundaries and pushing them. Students question the authority of their teachers with disrespect or refusing to submit their assignments. When confronted with progress, knowledge itself is challenged. In this essay, I will argue that questioning authority is a critical part of changing human knowledge. This can be observed in both historical and modern times.

Questioning authority does create greater understanding of the world, as we can see from the historical example of Galileo. This historical era scientist questioned common knowledge of astronomy and the earth's place in the universe. His research made him think that the sun was the center, and that planets like Earth revolve around it. This is why Galileo is a founding father of modern science. His questioning of the common knowledge of his time was a challenge to authority that changed many things we know about the universe today.

Questioning authority is not just part of history, but is also a modern day occurrence. LGBT marriage is an example of this, which ended in several court cases and laws being changed. Until recently, the common knowledge of most Americans was that marriage is between a man and a woman, but now the United States Supreme Court has ruled that same-sex marriage is legal in all 50 states. But someone had to question that common knowledge before the law could be changed.

As you can see, this quotation can be proven true with historical examples and current events. But there is still one flaw. The "Only by" in the quotation says that there is a single way to change understanding of the world, and that is to question authority. This is too simple a solution to resolve all of the questions about progress and advancement of knowledge. Galileo's work was destroyed when he questioned the authority that said earth was the center of the universe. He was punished and placed under house arrest for the rest of his life. Today the movement for LGBT marriage has caused some backlash. This has magnified homophobia and increased violence against LGBT people. Questioning authority may be a good way to challenge conventional wisdom, but it cannot be considered the only option.

APPLYING THE RUBRIC	
Argument	4
Support	4
Structure	4
Fluency	4
Conventions	4
Total	20

The average is 4, for a score of 4.

ARGUMENT The essay presents a reasonably clear argument on the statement, agreeing that questioning authority is needed for progress in human understanding. The argument grows muddled, however, at the end of the essay, when the writer, in describing possible risks to questioning authority, posits that there are other options for promoting change.

SUPPORT The essay includes relevant examples to support its thesis, though with less detail than is provided in higher scoring essays.

STRUCTURE The essay is adequately focused and organized to support its thesis, though the final paragraph appears to undermine, or at least moderate, its primary argument.

FLUENCY The essay demonstrates adequate control of the conventions of standard written English, though it is at times repetitive or awkward.

CONVENTIONS There are minor errors in grammar and mechanics, but they do not undermine the meaning.

SCORE 3 ISSUE ESSAY

I think it is imperative that authority be questioned. In fact, I would go as far to say that it is immoral for anything to not be questioned. Only when statements and authority are protected against criticism is when our freedom is truly encroached.

In the United States, the first amendment of the Bill of Rights protects the right to free speech. Under this, theoretically Americans have the ability to speak out against not only the authority of the government, but against other forms of authority as well. For example, without protected free speech in the political realm, the authority of the government upholding racist laws in the Jim Crow era of America might not have been questioned as people might have been too scared to stand up to the abhorrent laws.

Furthermore, authority should be questioned not just on the governmental level, but on all levels of academia and media as well. A common misconception that permeates today (whether in newspapers or television shows) is the danger difference, or lack thereof, between powder cocaine and crack cocaine. In truth, pharmacologically, the two are very similar—the main difference is that crack cocaine has a methylated branch while the powder does not. This structural difference has no pharmacological difference in the biochemical effects the drug has, but the media and the majority of academia reject to see this. Only a few researcher, Dr. Carl Hart, for example, are advocates against the majority. These advocates have no fear in standing up and questioning the larger authority, and I think that this is greatly beneficial for society. Without their work, it still could be a reality that crack offenders would be punished more harshly by a ratio of 100:1 than powder offenders. Because of their work, crack possessors are punished instead 18:1 more harshly. Even though there is an improvement made, things still have a ways to go.

I do see that the constant barrage of questioning of authority can prove problematic. In fact, it can be likened to herding cats sometimes when authority is always being questioned. When there is no faith in a system, then it is near impossible to enact any meaningful change. However, only by questioning a government can it be ensured that its power is kept in check and that the people's rights are protected.

APPLYING THE RUBRIC

Argument	3
Support	4
Structure	4
Fluency	4
Conventions	3
Total	18

The average is 3.6. Because one or more of the individual scores is a 3, the final score for this essay is likely a 3.

ARGUMENT The essay presents a reasonably clear argument, but it does not respond to the topic. Instead of addressing the topic, that questioning authority is necessary in order to advance understanding of the world, the essay focuses on questioning authority as a necessary check on government power.

SUPPORT The essay includes two examples in which questioning authority has been beneficial. The second example provides greater detail than needed, so much detail that it obscures the point the example is attempting to demonstrate.

STRUCTURE The essay is reasonably well focused and organized, though its transitions are awkward or minimal. Additionally, the length and level of detail in the third paragraph is out of proportion with the rest of the essay.

FLUENCY The essay is reasonably effective in expressing its ideas, and its word choice is generally appropriate.

CONVENTIONS The essay includes frequent minor errors in grammar and usage, some of which obscure meaning.

SCORE 2 ISSUE ESSAY

"Question authority" is a famous saying in the United States. It is popular but it is the wrong thing to do.

Example 1 is American children are very disrespectful to there parents. They do not listen to advise from them, sometimes they even call them a disrespectful name. Children in other cultures show much more respect, that is the proper way.

Example 2 is students. In the United States they do not respect teachers. If they talk when the teacher is talking you visit school to see it. Sometimes they attack even the teacher and vandalize the class room. Teacher in the United States also is receive poor pay checks. Why would any one be teacher when the student "question authority"?

Example 3 is police. They do the very dangerous job to keep safe from preventing crime. Today people do not follow there order when they tell them stop. They make a high speed chase that is very dangerous for the community. Inoccent peoples are killed in high speed chase.

In conclusion, the United States saying "Question authority" is a bad idea.

APPLYING THE RUBRIC

Argument	2
Support	3
Structure	4
Fluency	3
Conventions	2
Total	14

The average is 2.8, but because one or more of the individual scores is a 2, the final score for this essay is likely a 2.

ARGUMENT The essay presents an argument that is clear, but fails to address the full topic or the specific task instructions. No mention is made of advancing understanding of the world, though this is the topic's justification for questioning authority.

SUPPORT The essay includes three examples to support its thesis, but they are rather limited in this role.

STRUCTURE The essay appears to be organized, as a result of its explicit numerical structure. At the same time, transitions are abrupt, signaled by nothing more than numbering.

FLUENCY The essay is somewhat unclear due to incorrect word choice or sentence structure.

CONVENTIONS The essay includes major errors in grammar and mechanics, some of which obscure meaning.

SCORE 1 ISSUE ESSAY

People should question authority because authority might be wrong and not understanding the real issue very well.

APPLYING THE RUBRIC

Argument	2
Support	1
Structure	1
Fluency	4
Conventions	3
Total	11

The average is 2.2, but because one or more of the individual scores is a 1, the final score for this essay is likely a 1.

ARGUMENT The essay presents an argument that is on topic, but fails to address the specific requirement in the task instructions.

SUPPORT The essay includes no examples and very limited reasoning to support its thesis.

STRUCTURE The essay is excessively short.

FLUENCY The essay is reasonably clear in making its argument.

CONVENTIONS The essay includes an error in grammar. A single error would not be significant in a longer piece, but it is glaring in an essay this brief.

Section 1—Analytical Writing: Argument Essay

Though there are no right or wrong answers to the essay questions, you can get an idea of the level of writing required to achieve a particular score by reviewing the sample essays that follow. We have included a sample essay for each score from 6 (the best) through 1 (the poorest). Each sample essay also includes a short explanation of how the score was derived by using the rubric. In evaluating your own essays you should apply the rubric in a similar fashion.

PROMPT #2:

The following appeared in an editorial in the *Bayside Sentinel.*

"Bayside citizens need to consider raising local taxes if they want to see improvements in the Bayside School District. Test scores, graduation and college admission rates, and a number of other indicators have long made it clear that the Bayside School District is doing a poor job educating our youth. Our schools look run down. Windows are broken, bathrooms unusable, and classroom equipment hopelessly out of date. Yet just across the Bay, in New Harbor, school facilities are up-to-date and in good condition. The difference is money; New Harbor spends twenty-seven percent more per student than Bayside does, and test scores and other indicators of student performance are stronger in New Harbor as well."

Compose an essay that identifies and considers the assumptions (implicit and/or explicit) on which the argument is based. The essay must clarify the importance of these assumptions to the argument and explain the impact on the argument's validity should the assumptions be faulty.

SCORE 6 ARGUMENT ESSAY

Though conservative pundits have long claimed that there is no link between education spending and student outcomes, the editors of the *Bayside Sentinel* disagree, arguing that higher taxes and education spending are needed to improve the academic performance of Bayside students. While I am a staunch advocate of increased funding for public education, the argument presented by the *Bayside Sentinel* is disappointingly weak because it makes fundamental errors in causation, assuming the existence of a causal link without adequate evidence. Though poor funding may, in fact, lead to poor educational outcomes, this editorial has not demonstrated this to be the case. As a result, it has failed to make a strong argument for Bayside voters to increase their taxes.

The first error in causation made by the *Bayside Sentinel's* editors involves their focus on the condition of Bayside school facilities when compared to those in New Harbor. Though it is possible that poor facilities cause poor student outcomes, the editorial only implies this by observing that Bayside schools have both poor facilities and poor results, while New Harbor schools have both new facilities and better student performance. The editorial makes no direct claim of causation, simply assuming that a causal relationship exists and providing no evidence that there is more afoot in this case than a simple correlation.

Due to this lack of evidence, it is entirely possible that the editors have even gotten the causal relationship between Bayside students' academic performance and the condition of their school facilities reversed. One alternate explanation for the relationship might be that students who are alienated from and perform poorly in school are more likely to vandalize school facilities. It is also possible that the academic challenges faced by Bayside students, unlike those faced by their counterparts in New Harbor, are so great that the Bayside district is forced to spend so much on remediation that it cannot adequately fund facilities maintenance. In other words, the academic challenges Bayside students face may be the cause of the poor condition of their school facilities, rather than their result.

The editorial commits an additional error in causation by failing to consider alternate causes for the poor performance of Bayside schools. It is quite possible that the real cause of the disparity in performance between the schools in Bayside and New Harbor is not their per pupil spending, but the wealth of members of the respective communities. If high test scores, graduation rates, and college admission rates are, as many studies suggest, products of high socio-economic status, it is possible that disparities in wealth between the two communities are the real cause of Bayside's poor results. Ironically, this disparity may also explain the difference in per pupil spending between the two districts, as the residents of Bayside may be less able to spend on education than are their neighbors in New Harbor.

If the editors of the *Bayside Sentinel* want to provide a strong justification to Baysiders for increasing their taxes, they need to provide evidence that poor funding is causing poor student outcomes in Bayside schools. They also need to identify how new funds would be spent and demonstrate that those changes are likely to improve student performance. Without this information, Baysiders can be forgiven for their reluctance to spend more on their schools.

APPLYING THE RUBRIC

Argument	6
Support	6
Structure	6
Fluency	6
Conventions	6
Total	30

The average is 6.

ARGUMENT The essay displays significant insight in pinpointing two ways in which the argument presented fails to prove its thesis. It does this first by observing that the argument assumes causation, while only demonstrating correlation, and second by proposing several alternate theories that might explain both why Bayside schools are in poor condition and why Bayside students do not perform as well as New Harbor students.

SUPPORT The essay offers detailed and persuasive support by means of multiple examples of factors that might also (or even better) explain the relationship between school funding and student results in Bayside and New Harbor.

STRUCTURE The essay expresses its ideas in a well-organized and clear manner. Transitions between ideas are clear and logical.

FLUENCY The essay expresses its ideas clearly and utilizes sophisticated vocabulary and varied sentence structure throughout.

CONVENTIONS Impressive. The essay includes no noticeable errors in grammar, usage, or mechanics.

SCORE 5 ARGUMENT ESSAY

The opinion piece in the *Bayside Sentinel* regarding raising taxes to improve our schools makes several arguments. There are three pieces of evidence the author considers valuable for comparison: metrics like standardized test scores, equipment and facilities, and revenue stream. In this piece he compares these three metrics between two different school districts. These comparisons are designed to convince the reader that an increase in revenue stream will create an increase in standardized test scores and equipment and facilities. However, there are several hidden assumptions within this opinion piece that undercut the strength of the argument as presented.

The most glaring of these assumptions is the author's claim that raising local taxes will mean an increase in funding for the school district. While the author lays out a careful argument about what an increase in revenue stream could provide for the community, they do not provide a piece of evidence that an increase in local taxes would benefit the school district. They argue that New Harbor is spending more money per student, but do not indicate from where New Harbor received that funding. There is a logical leap that more taxes would mean more funding for Bayside schools, without a warrant to prove that is true.

An additional problem with this opinion piece is that it wholly omits a discussion of teachers and the differences between the two school districts in terms of teachers. It is possible that New Harbor has twice as many teachers as Bayside, or that the teachers in New Harbor have more current training than the teachers in Bayside. The author here argues that by improving facilities and equipment with increased tax revenue, test scores would increase. However, teachers are a crucial component to educational success. No one writes a thank you letter to their favorite computer station upon graduating from high school. Without a discussion of teachers, it is impossible to know if increased revenue stream will actually improve performance.

The final problem I will highlight here is that there is no causal relationship between increased revenue and increases in other metrics such as test scores. The proposed revenue stream may not be allocated to the school, or may be allocated in such a way that it does not resolve the problems laid out in the original letter. It is easy to assume that an increase in taxes would return to the community, but unless specially earmarked for improving facilities or increasing test scores, it is questionable whether or not the funding would reach its intended target. There is no interrogation of why New Harbor spends more per student; it is possible that other problems in Bayside are affecting students, such as political corruption or mismanagement of existing tax dollars.

While this opinion piece attempts to locate a problem and suggest a solution for that problem, it falls short of making a complete argument. Too many questions are unanswered about the comparison between Bayside and New Harbor in terms of existing socio-economic status, the current revenue streams and expenses, and teachers. Absent these and other comparisons, this argument is severely weakened. While increases in measurable success such as standardized test scores and college admission ratings is an admirable community goal, the steps to get there are much more complicated than simply raising local taxes.

APPLYING THE RUBRIC

Argument	6
Support	5
Structure	4
Fluency	5
Conventions	5
Total	25

The average is 5.

ARGUMENT The essay pinpoints the elements of the argument at issue and evaluates them with great insight, focusing primarily on the questions of whether funds from a tax increase will be allocated to the schools and whether funds allocated to the schools will be spent in a manner that will improve test scores. It also, though less clearly, questions whether the differences in academic performance between Bayside and New Harbor may result from differences in the number or quality of teachers in the two districts.

SUPPORT The essay provides thoughtful and persuasive support for its main points by pointing out that the proposed increase in tax revenue may not be spent on the schools, or that it may be misspent. It also includes teacher quality as another variable that is unexamined in the original argument.

STRUCTURE The essay expresses ideas clearly and is generally well organized, with suitable transitions between ideas. Two exceptions are the abrupt and incomplete ending of the third paragraph (almost certainly accidental) and the odd placement of that paragraph. It seems out of place between two paragraphs on funding, and would have been more logically placed before or after them.

FLUENCY The essay expresses ideas effectively, with appropriate word choice and varied sentence structure, though the abrupt ending of the third paragraph is a bit confusing.

CONVENTIONS The essay displays solid command of the grammar, usage, and mechanics of standard written English, though it includes a few careless errors.

SCORE 4 ARGUMENT ESSAY

Although I am generally for increased school spending, I want to examine the argument that additional funding would automatically improve the state of Bayside schools. This is an unproven assumption. While spending in New Harbor is higher per student than in Bayside, this does not mean that higher spending is the only factor in higher test scores for New Harbor students.

First, let us note that standardized testing can be a flawed way of measuring student learning. There are numerous critiques of this system, and many of those critiques are based on examining whether standardized testing actually measures knowledge or simply measures testing ability. That said, standardized testing, while it is flawed, is the system we use. It would be useful to know which scores are differnet and how different they are.

If cultural factors such as parent education or language (especially ESL) play a factor in standardized test scores, this may be as much an influence on those scores as much as spending. Thus raising per student spending in Bayside might not have as much impact as one would hope on helping those students match New Harbor scores.

Still, I lean toward agreeing with the argument that more spending per student would help. When schools are in disarray, not only is it distracting for students, its demoralizing. A student who has seen New Harbor schools in comparison with their own is likely to see the community's acceptance of subpar schools as an issue of pride and faith—if my community believed in me as much as New Harbor believes in their kids, they would invest in me the same way, but they must not, so I must not be worth it.

However, an increase in spending doesn't automatically equal improved facilities. The editorial would be stronger if it said how taxes would be used. How much would go into facilities and how much would go into things like professional development for teachers, after school programs, tutoring, and so on? And is there evidence that this spending will turn things around for students in Bayside?

In other words, I'm all for spending more on schools. Of all the things my tax dollars could be going towards, schools are actually my favorite. However, the editorial arguing for more school fudning leaves me with questions because it does not say what the money will be spent on. I'm willing to spend the money, but I'd be more convinced by an editorial that laid out more of a plan. The premise—more money will fix it—is probably true, but I want to know how more money will fix it.

APPLYING THE RUBRIC

Argument	4
Support	4
Structure	4
Fluency	4
Conventions	4
Total	20

The average is 4.

ARGUMENT The essay identifies the elements of the argument at issue and evaluates them, but may include less relevant points.

SUPPORT The essay provides sufficient, though possibly uneven, support for its main points.

STRUCTURE The essay expresses ideas reasonably clearly and is organized, but transitions between ideas are inadequate or absent.

FLUENCY The essay expresses ideas effectively, with appropriate word choice.

CONVENTIONS Despite some obvious typographical errors, the essay displays command of the grammar, usage, and mechanics of standard written English.

SCORE 3 ARGUMENT ESSAY

The *Bayside Sentinel* editorial places the blame for Bayside School District's low levels of academic achievement squarely on lack of funds. Certainly, there is hardly a public school system in the world that could not use more money—however, the editorial's proposal of increased local taxation, specifically toward funding infrastructural improvement (e.g., repairing and remodeling old buildings and purchasing new equipment), is wasteful when those funds could be better spent. While I might support increasing taxes to improve education in Bayside, I do not agree that this new revenue should be spent on infrastructure.

The most important factor in student academic success is the relationship between teachers and students, the *social* environment in which students are learning. If teachers are not well-prepared and well-trained, and not well-attuned to the particular needs of students in that specific cohort, they will not be able to make their students engaged or interested in their schoolwork. Because teachers play such an important role in student academic success, the proposed new tax revenue should be spent on teacher training rather than improved facilities.

Even if Bayside can afford to take on the burden of additional taxation, improved infrastructure is not the best use of those funds. Given the importance of culture and academic climate to student achievement, it might be better to increase funding for programs that more directly influence those factors. For example, an after school program offering one-on-one tutoring is more likely to improve student performance than is a new coat of paint, and an academic activity like a debate or mock trial team is more likely to drive student engagement than is a new globe in the History classroom. Additionally, providing greater opportunity for students to work closely with college counselors is a proven method of increasing student engagement and improving academic outcomes. If Bayside taxes are to be raised, it should be done to support programs like these, rather than for updating infrastructure.

The editorial's author clearly has good intentions, but their investment proposal leaves much to be desired. If the Bayside community can afford to spend more on its schools, those monies should be utilized in the areas that will have the greatest impacts on student academic performance.

APPLYING THE RUBRIC

Argument	3
Support	4
Structure	4
Fluency	5
Conventions	5
Total	21

The average is 4.2. Because one or more of the individual scores is a 3, the final score for this essay is likely a 3.

ARGUMENT While the essay presents a clear response to the argument presented in the prompt, it fails to meet the demands of the specific task instructions. The task instructions require the writer to examine the stated and unstated assumptions in the argument. The essay's focus on its author's disagreement with the argument, rather than on the assumptions made in the argument, is not relevant to the task instructions. This essay is a classic example of an otherwise satisfactory effort's being brought down by its failure to meet the requirements stated in the task instructions.

SUPPORT The essay provides sufficient but uneven support for its main argument, sometimes making assertions without evidence. Examples of this tendency are the claims that after school tutoring and increased college counseling are likely to have a greater impact on student performance than are facilities improvements.

STRUCTURE The essay expresses its ideas in a reasonably organized and clear manner, but the transitions between ideas are somewhat jarring.

FLUENCY The essay expresses its ideas clearly and utilizes appropriate vocabulary and varied sentence structure throughout.

CONVENTIONS The essay displays solid command of the grammar, usage, and mechanics of standard written English.

SCORE 2 ARGUMENT ESSAY

First and foremost, in this statement that appeared in the editorial, the writer clearly by mistake believes that external and internal have a direct relationship. This is false. The vast majority of the editorial is the physical appearances and differences between the two schools. There is only one sentence regarding the good of the school—test scores, graduation, and college admissions.

In my opinion, the purpose of school is to prepare someone for life, and this involves learning life skills. These skills can be proper socialization according to society, communication skills, accountability, honesty, and many other positive personality traits can be fostered by mentors like teachers at a young age. The test score does not make the kind of person a child is.

Different socio economic status can have a extremely massive impact on education that is completely separate from schooling but can effect education. For example, a child from a lower socio economic class might have a partime job to add income while those in a more rich neighborhood would be ignorant of struggles like these.

A different solution instead of raising local taxes in which might already be a less affluent area would to look into a different allocation of resources.

APPLYING THE RUBRIC

Argument	3
Support	3
Structure	2
Fluency	2
Conventions	2
Total	12

The average is 2.4. Because one or more of the individual scores is a 2, the final score for this essay is likely a 2.

ARGUMENT The essay fails to distinguish or evaluate the most relevant elements of the argument, though it does lightly examine the relationship of money to educational outcomes. It does not, however, explicitly examine the assumptions made in the argument, which was the charge in the specific task instructions.

SUPPORT The essay provides support that is sometimes irrelevant to its point, when that point can be identified. For example, the discussion of students of lower socioeconomic status does not appear to be offered in support of any particular idea.

STRUCTURE The essay's purpose is unclear because it expresses its ideas inadequately. Additionally, although the author uses language to signal the beginning of the essay, there is no logic to its organization.

FLUENCY The essay's point is unclear due to its frequent use of faulty sentence structure.

CONVENTIONS The essay includes frequent errors in grammar that render its meaning unclear.

SCORE 1 ARGUMENT ESSAY

Bayside citizens should increase taxes for the education of better test scores and colleges rates. Money is difference of broken windows and out of date bathrooms. Good conditions is the difference for New Harbor. 27% more student gets test scores and indicators stronger in New Harbor. Bayside needs 27% more indicators of student performance to. Bayside increase taxes fixes the hopelessly of the students. Then there indicators of student performance is in good condition.

APPLYING THE RUBRIC

Argument	2
Support	1
Structure	1
Fluency	2
Conventions	2
Total	8

The average is 1.6. Because one or more of the individual scores is a 1, the final score for this essay is likely a 1.

ARGUMENT The essay fails to evaluate the argument using logic, though it is on topic. Generally, the essay parrots back terms from the essay prompt in a manner that demonstrates some limited grasp of the argument.

SUPPORT The essay provides no support for its main point.

STRUCTURE The essay's organization is unclear and it is excessively short.

FLUENCY The essay is unclear due to frequent incorrect word choice and poor sentence structure.

CONVENTIONS The essay includes significant errors in grammar, usage, and mechanics that render its meaning unclear.

Section 2—Verbal Reasoning

1. **(C, D)** Both *apt* and *prone* have several meanings. *Apt*, for example, can mean appropriate, as in an apt remark, or it can mean unusually quick and intelligent, as in an apt pupil. *Prone* can mean prostrate; it can also mean having a downward slope. Here both *apt* and *prone* are used in the sense of inclined or liable.

   Note the use of *indeed* to both confirm and emphasize the preceding statement. Not only do many of us try to rewrite our lives, but we are almost universally inclined to do so.

2. **(D, F)** *Far from* is a contrast signal. It indicates that you are looking for an antonym for *condemn*. The critics do not condemn Warhol for what seems to be superficiality and commercialism. Instead, they *extol* or *hail* him for having captured the superficial, commercial nature of American culture during the 1970s.

   Note that *hail* in this context is synonymous with acclaim or approve enthusiastically (secondary meaning).

3. **(B, F)** By definition, embezzlers are inclined to fraud. By definition, tricksters are inclined to trickery, that is, to *chicanery* or *artifice*. Here *artifice* means subtle but base deception, not skill or ingenuity.

4. **(B, E)** *Paradoxically* inherently signals a contrast. It indicates that something unexpected and unwanted has occurred. An admonition or warning intended to reform a spendthrift failed to have the desired result. Instead, it *reinforced* his profligate behavior, *confirming* or strengthening *him in* his wasteful habits.

5. **(A, B)** You are looking for an antonym for *outspoken* (frank and unreserved in speech). To be *reserved* is to be restrained or reticent in manner. To be *discreet* is to be judicious in conduct or speech.

6. **(D, F)** The key word here is *circuitousness.* The writer here is developing an analogy between the way lawyers drive their cars and the way they build or construct their legal arguments. Thus, someone known for choosing circuitous (roundabout; twisty) routes might also be known for coming up with *devious* (tricky; oblique) or *indirect* (roundabout; not direct) arguments.

7. **(C)** The author states that the later novels of James play down prominent action. Thus, they lack *overtly dramatic incident.* However, the author goes on to state that James's novels *do* possess interest; they carry the reader through "a rich analysis of the mental adjustments of the characters to the realities of their personal situations." It is this implicitly dramatic psychological revelation that sustains the reader's interest.

   Question A is unanswerable on the basis of the passage. It is evident that James wrote psychological novels; it is nowhere stated that he originated the genre.

   Question B is unanswerable on the basis of the passage. Although conventional narrative technique relates "events in distinctly phased sequences," clearly separating them, it does not necessarily recount action in *strictly* chronological order.

   Question D is unanswerable on the basis of the passage. The passage does not deal with the general public's reaction to James.

   Question E is unanswerable on the basis of the passage. The passage talks of qualities in James as a novelist in terms of their being *characteristic,* not in terms of their making him *unique.*

8. **(C)** In the third sentence the author describes James's later novel as offering "slow piecemeal additions of perception." To clarify the process, he goes on in sentence four to paint a picture in words, using figurative language. No literal curtain is drawn away here; however, the image of a curtain being slowly drawn away helps the reader develop a feeling for James's method of psychological revelation.

9. **(D)** The word "attend" here is used in the sense of "to accompany or go with as a concurrent circumstance or result." People's actions inevitably involve moral and psychological realizations and consequences; they go with the territory, so to speak.

10. **(C)** The subduction zone is the site of the destruction or consumption of existing lithospheric material. In contrast, the mid-ocean ridge is the site of the creation or emergence of new lithospheric material.

    Choice A is incorrect. Both mid-ocean ridges and subduction zones are boundaries between plates.

    Choice B is incorrect. Both are located on the ocean floor.

    Choice D is incorrect. It is unsupported by the passage.

    Choice E is incorrect. The reverse is true.

11. **(B)** Choice B is correct. You are told that the new lithospheric material is injected into a mid-ocean ridge, a suboceanic mountain range. This new material does not disappear; it is added to the material already there. Thus, it is *incorporated into* the existing mid-ocean ridge.

Choice A is incorrect. "In general the plates are in motion with respect to one another." Nothing suggests that they become immobilized; indeed, they are said to diverge from the ridge, sliding as they diverge.

Choice C is incorrect. The passage specifically denies it. ("The size of the earth is essentially constant.")

Choice D is incorrect. It is the earth itself whose magnetic field reverses. Nothing in the passage suggests the new lithospheric material has any such potential.

Choice E is incorrect. At a mid-ocean ridge, the site at which new lithospheric material is injected from below, the plates diverge; they do not sink. (They sink, one plate diving under another, at a subduction zone.)

12. **(B)** How did Semmelweis save women from dying of childbed fever? He did so by establishing or *instituting* strict rules of hygiene.

13. **(B, F)** Given the ubiquity of light, it is *unsurprising* that creatures have *developed* the biologically helpful ability to make use of light energy.

    Note the use of *therefore* indicating that the omitted portion of the sentence supports or continues a thought developed elsewhere in the sentence.

14. **(A, E)** Here the author is contrasting appropriate clerical behavior with inappropriate clerical behavior. The Austen brothers behave appropriately: they are properly *deferential* to their social superiors, paying them proper respect. The fictional Mr. Collins, however, behaves inappropriately: he is *sycophantic* (obsequious, fawning) to his social superiors.

15. **(B, D)** To *contest* an action is to dispute it or call it in question. The reclassification of Pluto did not go *uncontested,* for a large number of astronomers asked the International Astronomical Union to *reconsider* or rethink its decision, calling the union's action in question.

    Note the use of *for,* indicating a relationship of cause and effect.

16. **(A, F)** The politicians are unwilling to *forsake* or abandon center stage. However, if they did leave center stage once in a while, the public might like them better for their *self-effacement* (withdrawal from attention).

17. **(D)** The opening sentence describes the shattering of the Iroquois leadership's pro-British policy. The remainder of the passage describes how Iroquois policy changed to reflect changes in European military goals.

    Choice A is incorrect. The passage is expository, not accusatory.

    Choice B is incorrect. Nothing in the passage suggests that such charges were made against the Iroquois.

    Choice C is incorrect. It is unsupported by the passage.

    Choice E is incorrect. The passage demonstrates the Iroquois were able to play European power politics.

    Remember, when asked to find the main idea, be sure to check the opening and summary sentences of each paragraph.

18. **(E)** Lines 22–34 indicate that in the early 1700s and through most of the eighteenth century the Iroquois *did* receive concessions from the European powers. Therefore, Choice E is the correct answer.

Choice A is incorrect. The raid on Lachine was an effective response to French aggression, as was the Iroquois-enforced policy of aggressive neutrality.

Choice B is incorrect. James II's overthrow was followed by colonial uprisings.

Choice C is incorrect. In response to the Iroquois leaders' supposed favoring of the British, the French initiated attacks on the Iroquois (lines 7–13).

Choice D is incorrect. This sums up the policy of aggressive neutrality.

19. **(A, C)** Choice A is supported by the passage: the opening sentence of the passage discusses a "recent assessment" of the status of global amphibian populations. Likewise, Choice C is supported by the passage: habit degradation, which negatively affects amphibians, can be caused by "the introduction of exotic invasive species," that is, *non-native species.* Note that to receive credit for this question you must have chosen *both* correct answers, not just one.

20. **(B)** The author never *cites* or quotes *an authority.*

    Choice A is incorrect. The author *defines* the term habit fragmentation.

    Choice C is incorrect. The author *states a probability.* He asserts, "Outright habitat loss *probably* has the greatest effect on amphibians."

    Choice D is incorrect. The author *qualifies a statement.* He first states, "Outright habitat loss probably has the greatest effect on amphibians." He then qualifies what he has said by stating that habitat degradation similarly affects amphibians.

    Choice E is incorrect. The author *makes* several *assertions.*

Section 3—Quantitative Ability

1. **(D)** Use the laws of exponents. (See KEY FACT A17 on page 337.)

    Quantity A is $a^4a^5 = a^{4+5} = a^9$.

    Quantity B is $(a^3)^2 = a^{3\times2} = a^6$.

    If $a = 1$, the quantities are equal; but if $a = 2$, Quantity A is much greater. Neither quantity is always greater, and the two quantities are not always equal (D).

2. **(C)** Since the measure of an exterior angle of a triangle is equal to the sum of the measures of the two opposite interior angles. (See KEY FACT J2 on page 457.)

$$c = a + b \Rightarrow a + b - c = 0$$

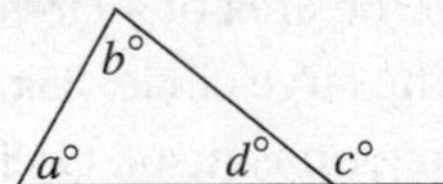

The quantities are equal (C).

Alternative Solution. Plug in easy-to-use numbers. If $a = 60$ and $b = 70$, then $d = 50 \Rightarrow c = 130$, and $60 + 70 - 130 = 0$.

3. **(B)**

	Quantity A	Quantity B
	$\sqrt{a+b}$	$\sqrt{a}+\sqrt{b}$
Since both quantities are positive, we can square them.	$a+b$	$a+2\sqrt{ab}+b$
Subtract $a+b$ from each quantity	0	$2\sqrt{ab}$

Since a and b are positive, $2\sqrt{ab}$ is positive. Quantity B is greater.

4. **(B)** From the 124 people in front of Jill, remove Jack plus the 24 people in front of Jack: $124 - 25 = 99$. Quantity B is greater.

5. **(A)** Since *OA* and *OB* are radii, they are each equal to 5. With no restrictions on x, chord *AB* could be any positive number less than 10 (the length of a diameter). If x were 90, by the Pythagorean theorem (page 459), $AB^2 = 5^2 + 5^2 = 50$. So, *AB* would be $\sqrt{50}$; since $x > 90$, $AB > \sqrt{50} > 7$. Therefore, the perimeter of $\triangle AOB$ is greater than $5 + 5 + 7 = 17$. Quantity A is greater.

6. **(A)** Do not waste time calculating any standard deviations.

- Quantity A: Every number in Set 2 is three times the corresponding number in Set 1, so the standard deviation of the numbers in Set 2 is three times greater than the standard deviation of the numbers in Set 1.
- Quantity B: Every number in Set 3 is 50 more than the corresponding number in Set 1, so the standard deviation of the numbers in Set 3 is equal to the standard deviation of the numbers in Set 1.
- Quantity A is greater.

7. **(C)** Since the sum of the measures of the three angles of *any* triangle is 180°, the average of the three measures is $180° \div 3 = 60°$. The quantities are equal (C).

8. **(C)** By KEY FACT L8 (page 491), the area of a circle whose radius, r, is πr^2. The area of the shaded region is the area of the large circle, 25π, minus the area of the middle circle, 16π: $25\pi - 16\pi = 9\pi$. The striped region is just a circle of radius 3. Its area is also 9π. The quantities are equal (C).

9. **(B)** By KEY FACT I4 (page 447), the unmarked angle opposite the 60° angle also measures 60°, and by KEY FACT I3 (page 447), the sum of the measures of all six angles in the diagram is 360°. So,

$$\begin{aligned} 360 &= a + b + c + 20 + 60 + 60 \\ &= a + b + c + 140 \end{aligned}$$

Subtracting 140 from each side, we get that $a + b + c = 220$.

10. **(C)** $4^{10} \times 64^2 = 4^{10} \times (4^3)^2 = 4^{10} \times 4^6 = 4^{16}$.
Also, $16^2 \times 4^n = (4^2)^2 \times 4^n = 4^4 \times 4^n = 4^{4+n}$.
So, $4^{16} = 4^{4+n}$ and $16 = 4 + n$. Then $n = 12$.

11. **(D)** Let x be the amount in dollars that each of the 20 children were going to contribute; then $20x$ represents the cost of the present. When 4 children dropped out, the remaining 16 each had to pay $(x + 1.50)$ dollars. So, $16(x + 1.5) = 20x \Rightarrow 16x + 24 = 20x \Rightarrow 24 = 4x \Rightarrow x = 6$, and so the cost of the present was $20 \times 6 = 120$ dollars.
Alternative Solution. Since each of the 16 remaining children had to pay an extra \$1.50, the extra payments totaled $16 \times \$1.50 = \$24$. This is the amount that would have been paid by the 4 children who dropped out, so each of the 4 would have paid \$6. The cost of the gift was $20 \times \$6 = \$120$.

12. **110** Draw a Venn diagram (see page 530). Since 10 seniors are in *both* band and orchestra, 30 are in band only and 50 are in orchestra only.

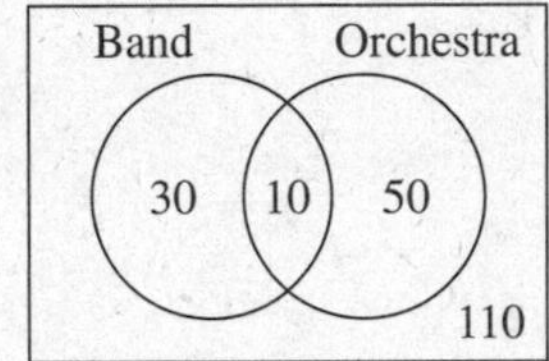

Therefore, $10 + 30 + 50 = 90$ seniors are in at least one group, and the remaining 110 are in neither.

13. **(C, D, E, F, G)** On the six tests, Benjamin earned a total of $6 \times 89 = 534$ points. On his first five tests, he earned at least $5 \times 90 = 450$ points, but no more than $5 \times 100 = 500$ points. So his grade on the sixth test was at least $534 - 500 = 34$ and at most $534 - 450 = 84$.
Only answer Choices C, D, E, F, and G are between 34 and 84.

14. **(E)** Exports to Eastern Europe from other Eastern European countries increased from \$9.8 billion (10% of \$98 billion) to \$20.88 billion (12% of \$174 billion)—an increase of slightly more than 100%.

15. **(C)** If France's exports to Eastern Europe were four times those of the United States, then France accounted for 8% of the total exports. Since 8% is $\frac{1}{8}$ of 64%, France accounted for $\frac{1}{8}$ or 12.5% of the exports from the European Union.

16. **198** The percent increase in total exports to Eastern Europe from 1993 to 1996 was

$$\frac{\text{the actual increase}}{\text{original amount}} \times 100\% = \frac{174-98}{98} \times 100\% = \frac{76}{98} \times 100\% = 77.55\%$$

So, in billions of dollars, the increase in total exports to Eastern Europe from 1996 to 2000 was $0.7755 \times 174 = 134.94$, making total exports $174 + 135 = 309$ billion dollars. The value of exports from the European Union was 64% of $309 = 197.76$ billion dollars. To the nearest billion, the figure was 198.

17. **(C)** Set up the equation:

$$(x + 3) + (2x - 3) + (3x - 5) = 25$$

Collect like terms: $6x - 5 = 25$
Add 5 to each side: $6x = 30$
Divide each side by 6: $x = 5$
Plugging in 5 for x, we get that the lengths of the sides are 8, 7, and 10.
The length of the shortest side is 7.

18. **(D)** A nice way to answer this question is to pick easy-to-use numbers. Assume that in 1990 there were 200 boys and 100 girls who earned varsity letters. Then in 2000, there were 150 boys and 125 girls. So, the ratio of girls to boys was 125:150 = 5:6 or $\frac{5}{6}$.

19. **(E)** The easiest way to solve this is to plug in numbers. Let $x = 2$ and $y = 1$. Then $xy = 2$, $a = 4$, and $b = 0$. Now, plug in 4 for a and 0 for b and see which of the five choices is equal to 2. Only Choices C and E work:

(C) $\frac{a-b}{2} = \frac{4-0}{2} = 2$

(E) $\frac{a^2-b^2}{8} = \frac{4^2-0^2}{8} = \frac{16}{8} = 2.$

To determine whether Choice C or E is the correct answer, plug in different numbers. If $x = 3$ and $y = 1$, then $xy = 3$, $a = 5$, and $b = 1$. Now Choice C doesn't work:
$\frac{a-b}{2} = \frac{5-1}{2} = \frac{4}{2} = 2 \neq 3.$

Choice E does work: $\frac{a^2-b^2}{8} = \frac{25-1}{8} = \frac{24}{8} = 3.$

Here is the correct algebraic solution.

Add the two equations:

$$\begin{aligned} x + 2y &= a \\ + \; x - 2y &= b \\ \hline 2x &= a + b \end{aligned}$$

Divide by 2: $x = \frac{a+b}{2}$

Multiply the second equation by −1 and add it to the first:

$$\begin{aligned} x + 2y &= a \\ + \; -x + 2y &= -b \\ \hline 4y &= a - b \end{aligned}$$

Divide by 4: $y = \frac{a-b}{4}$

Then $xy = \frac{a+b}{2} \cdot \frac{a-b}{4} = \frac{a^2-b^2}{8}.$

This is the type of algebra you want to avoid.

20. **(D)** Since you need a ratio, the length of the side is irrelevant. The area of a square whose sides are s is s^2 (KEY FACT K9, page 479), and the area of an equilateral triangle whose sides are s is $\frac{s^2\sqrt{3}}{4}$ (KEY FACT J15, page 466).

Then the ratio is $s^2 \div \frac{s^2\sqrt{3}}{4} = s^2 \times \frac{4}{s^2\sqrt{3}} = \frac{4}{\sqrt{3}} = \frac{4\sqrt{3}}{3}$.

Of course, you could have used 5 (or any number) instead of s, and if you forgot (or didn't know) the formula for the area of an equilateral triangle, you could have used the formula $A = \frac{1}{2}bh$ (KEY FACT J14, page 465).

PART 2
Verbal Ability: Tactics, Review, and Practice

Sentence Equivalence and Text Completion Questions 4

Sentence equivalence and text completion questions are those old favorites, fill-in-the-blank questions. The GRE presents some variations on this familiar form. The packaging is different, but the task remains the same.

We sometimes refer to the first question type, the **sentence equivalence question**, as the **double or nothing question**. To get credit for answering a sentence equivalence question correctly, you must come up with not one correct answer choice, but ***two*** correct answer choices that work equally well.

Sentence equivalence questions look like this:

The medical researchers replied to the charge that their proposed new treatment was ________ by demonstrating that it in fact observed standard medical practices.

- [A] deleterious
- [B] untested
- [C] unorthodox
- [D] expensive
- [E] intricate
- [F] unconventional

YOUR CLUE

The answer choices to sentence equivalence questions are marked with square boxes, not with ovals. Square boxes are your clue that you must select two answer choices to get the question right.

The medical researchers defend their new treatment by saying that it follows accepted, standard practices. What, therefore, must have been the critic's charge or accusation about the treatment? They must have alleged it was nonstandard, violating acceptable medical practices. The two words that best complete this sentence are *unorthodox* and *unconventional.*

We refer to the second question type, the **text completion question**, as the **mix and match question.** In a text completion question, you will be presented with a sentence or group of sentences containing one to three blanks. Instead of seeing a single list of answer choices, you will see one, two, or three independent columns of choices; for each blank in the sentence, you must select one correct answer choice from the appropriate column, mixing and matching your choices until you come up with a combination that makes sense.

Text completion questions look like this:

> Her novel published to universal (i)_______, her literary gifts acknowledged by the chief figures of the Harlem Renaissance, her reputation as yet (ii)_______ by envious slights, Hurston clearly was at the (iii)_______ of her career.

Blank (i)	Blank (ii)	Blank (iii)
indifference	belittled	zenith
derision	resented	extremity
acclaim	untarnished	ebb

Think about the structure of the sentence. It begins with three parallel absolute phrases, each telling about some aspect of Hurston's literary position at a particular time in her career. All three phrases are positive in tone. The concluding independent clause ("Hurston clearly was at the _______ of her career") should be positive as well.

Now examine the first blank. What reaction did people have to Hurston's novel? Look at the part of the sentence without any blanks: "her literary gifts (were) acknowledged by the chief figures of the Harlem Renaissance." In acknowledging Hurston's gifts, these literary luminaries were praising her novel. Her novel clearly had been published to great *acclaim* (approval).

Next, study the second blank. You know that, at the time this writer is discussing, Hurston's standing in the literary world was high. Her novel was acclaimed; her gifts were acknowledged (recognized). This third absolute phrase also must state something positive about Hurston. Recast it as a sentence: Her reputation (was) as yet _______ by envious slights. Envious slights (insults or slurs, prompted by jealousy) would have had a negative effect on Hurston's reputation. However, as yet, at the time under discussion, no negative comments had besmirched Hurston's reputation, which was *untarnished* (spotless; unblemished).

Finally, consider the third blank. How would you describe Hurston's career at the time under discussion? It was at its highest point: in years to come envious slights would tarnish her reputation and her novels would be forgotten, but for the moment Hurston was riding high: she was at the *zenith* (peak) of her career.

TESTING TACTICS

The Sentence Equivalence Question

To answer this type of short answer question correctly, you must come up with a pair of words, both equally fit to complete the meaning of the sentence as a whole. ***If you fail to get both answers correct, you get no credit for the question.***

These are the GRE website's directions for these double or nothing sentence equivalence questions:

> **Directions:** For the following questions, select the **two** answer choices that, when used to complete the sentence, fit the meaning of the sentence as a whole **and** produce completed sentences that are alike in meaning.

TACTIC

Before You Look at the Sentence, Look Over the Answer Choices to Locate Any Obvious Synonyms

Your task is to find **two** words that can complete the sentence in thought and style, and that can function interchangeably in the context. In other words, you may be looking for synonyms; you definitely are looking for words that complete the sentence in the same fashion.

Before you look at the sentence itself, examine the answer choices. See if you can spot a pair of synonyms. Then substitute these two words in the sentence. If both make logical sense in the context, you may well have found your answer pair. To check yourself, look over the other four choices. Try each of them in the sentence. Satisfy yourself that the synonyms you spotted work better than any of these other words.

Here are six answer choices to a sentence equivalence question.

[A] extravagant
[B] tawdry
[C] parsimonious
[D] optimistic
[E] profligate
[F] pedestrian

Extravagant and *profligate* are synonyms; both mean spendthrift or wasteful.

Now here is the sentence. Do the synonyms that you spotted work in this context?

> Although the young duke's trustees had tried to teach him fiscal prudence, they feared he would never learn to curb his ________ ways.

Clearly, they do. If the young duke has not learned to be careful about his finances, it is understandable that his trustees might worry about his inability to curb or restrain his *profligate* and *extravagant* ways.

NOTE: ***Be very careful when you apply this tactic.*** The test-makers are very aware that some examinees simply scan the answer choices looking for synonyms. Therefore, often they will deliberately plant obvious synonym pairs among the answer choices. These eye-catchers or distractors are there to trick the unwary. Because you will recognize these words as synonyms, you may want to select them without reading the sentence closely. However, the test-makers are not testing your knowledge of vocabulary *per se.* They are testing your reading comprehension. The words you choose do not have to be synonyms. However, they must both make sense in the sentence in an equivalent way.

TIP

Every sentence equivalence question has *two* correct answer choices. To get credit for the question, *you must get both answers right.*

TACTIC

If You Fail to Detect a Pair of Synonyms Right Away, Read the Sentence and Think of a Word That Makes Sense

This tactic is helpful because it enables you to get a sense of the sentence as a whole without being distracted by any misleading answers among the answer choices. You are free to concentrate on spotting key words or phrases in the body of the sentence and to call on your own "writer's intuition" in arriving at a stylistically apt choice of word.

See how the process works in a typical model question.

Because experience had convinced her that Hector was both self-seeking and avaricious, she rejected the possibility that the motivation behind his donation had been wholly ________.

A redundant
B frivolous
C egotistical
D ephemeral
E altruistic
F benevolent

This sentence presents a simple case of cause and effect. The key phrase here is *self-seeking* and *avaricious.* The woman has found the man to be selfish and greedy. *Therefore,* she refuses to believe his motivation for donating money can be ________. She expects selfishness (*self-seeking*) and greed (*avaricious*), not their opposite.

You are looking for words that are antonyms for *selfish.* What words immediately come to mind? *Selfless, generous, charitable*? The missing words are, of course, *altruistic* and *benevolent.* They are the correct answer pair.

Practice Tactic 2 extensively to develop your intuitive sense of the *mot juste*—the exactly right word.

TACTIC 3

Consider Secondary Meanings of the Answer Choices As Well as Their Primary Meanings

Frequently, the test-makers attempt to mislead you by using familiar words in an unfamiliar way. Suppose you have found one answer choice that perfectly fits the meaning of the sentence as a whole but cannot find a second answer choice that seems exactly right.

Reread the sentence, substituting that perfect answer choice for the blank. Then take a fresh look at the other answer choices. Remember that these words or phrases may have multiple meanings. Think of contexts in which you have heard these words or phrases used. That may help you come up with additional meanings for them.

See how this tactic helps you answer the following sentence equivalence question.

Snakes are the most stationary of all vertebrates; as long as a locality ________ them a sufficiency of food and some shelter to which they can readily retreat, they have no inducement to change it.

A provides
B constitutes
C affords
D denies
E disallows
F withholds

Snakes tend to be stationary creatures. Why? They stay put because a particular locality meets their needs: it *provides* or offers them food and shelter.

Look at the other answer choices. Can you rule out any of them? *Denies, disallows,* and *withholds* are all negative terms; none of them seem appropriate in this context. After all, if a locality *denied* or *disallowed* the snakes food and shelter or *withheld* food and shelter from them, that would not be an inducement or incentive for the snakes to stay put. Likewise, *constitutes* (composes; establishes) does not seem appropriate in the context. It feels awkward, even ungrammatical (the verb does not normally take an indirect object).

Only *affords* is left. Here it clearly is *not* used with its primary meaning, "to be able to meet the expense of," as in affording to buy a new car.

Try to think of other contexts for *afford*. "It affords me great pleasure to be here." "Gustavo's Facebook entries afford us a glimpse into the daily life of a musician on tour." These sentences use *afford* with a secondary meaning: to give, offer, or provide. The correct answers to this sentence equivalence question are *affords* and *provides.*

TACTIC 4 Look at All the Possible Choices Before You Choose an Answer Pair

Never decide on your answer before you have read all the choices. You are looking for *two* words that *both* make sense in the sentence. What is more, not only do both these words have to make sense in the sentence, but they have to make the same kind of sense. You have to be able to substitute one for the other in the sentence without changing the meaning of the sentence as a whole.

In order to be sure you have not been hasty in making your decision, substitute all the answer choices for the missing word. Do not spend a lot of time doing so, but do try them all. Then decide which two of these words function in the same way. That way you can satisfy yourself that you have come up with the *best* possible pair.

See how this tactic helps you deal with another question patterned on examples from the GRE.

> The evil of class and race hatred must be eliminated while it is still in ________ state; otherwise, it may grow to dangerous proportions.
>
> A an amorphous
> B an overt
> C a rudimentary
> D a threatening
> E an independent
> F an embryonic

On the basis of a loose sense of this sentence's meaning, you might be tempted to select the first choice, *amorphous*. After all, this sentence basically tells you that you should wipe out hatred before it gets too dangerous. Clearly, if hatred is vague or *amorphous,* it is less formidable than if it is well-defined. However, this reading of the sentence is inadequate: it fails to take into account the sentence's key phrase.

The key phrase here is "may grow to dangerous proportions." The writer fears that class and race hatred may grow large enough to endanger society. He wants us to wipe out this hatred before it is fully grown. Examine each answer choice, eliminating those answers that carry no suggestion that something lacks its full growth or development. Does *overt* suggest that something isn't fully grown? No, it suggests that something is obvious or evident. Does *rudimentary* suggest that something isn't fully grown? Yes, it suggests that something is unfinished or immature. This may well be one of your two correct answer choices.

Look for a second word that suggests a lack of full growth. Does *independent* suggest that something isn't fully grown? No, it suggests that something is free and unconstrained. Does *threatening* suggest that something isn't fully grown? No, it suggests that something is a source of danger or cause for alarm. Only one word is left: *embryonic* (at an early, incomplete stage of development). If you substitute *embryonic* for *rudimentary* in the sentence, you will not change the sentence's essential meaning. The correct answer choices are *rudimentary* and *embryonic.*

TACTIC

Watch for Signal Words That Link One Part of the Sentence to Another

Writers use transitions to link their ideas logically. These transitions or signal words are clues that can help you figure out what the sentence actually means.

GRE sentence equivalence and text completion questions often contain several signal words, combining them in complex ways.

CAUSE AND EFFECT SIGNALS

Look for words or phrases explicitly indicating that one thing **causes** another or **logically determines** another.

Cause and Effect Signal Words	
accordingly	in order to
because	so . . . that
consequently	therefore
given	thus
hence	when . . . then
if . . . then	

SUPPORT SIGNALS

Look for words or phrases explicitly indicating that the omitted part of the sentence **supports** or **continues a thought** developed elsewhere in the sentence. In such cases, a synonym or near-synonym for another word in the sentence may provide the correct answer.

Support Signal Words	
additionally	furthermore
also	indeed
and	likewise
as well	moreover
besides	too

EXPLICIT CONTRAST SIGNALS

Look for function words or phrases (conjunctions, sentence adverbs, etc.) that explicitly **indicate a contrast** between one idea and another, setting up a reversal of a thought. In such cases, an antonym or near-antonym for another word in the sentence may provide the correct answer.

Explicit Contrast Signal Words	
albeit	nevertheless
although	nonetheless
but	notwithstanding
despite	on the contrary
even though	on the other hand
however	rather than
in contrast	still
in spite of	while
instead of	yet

IMPLICIT CONTRAST SIGNALS

Look for content words whose meaning inherently indicates a contrast. These words can turn a situation on its head. They indicate that something unexpected, possibly even unwanted, has occurred.

Implicit Contrast Signal Words		
anomaly	anomalous	anomalously
illogic	illogical	illogically
incongruity	incongruous	incongruously
irony	ironic	ironically
paradox	paradoxical	paradoxically
surprise	surprising	surprisingly
	unexpected	unexpectedly

Note the function of such a contrast signal word in the following question.

Paradoxically, the more ________ the details this artist chooses, the better able she is to depict her fantastic, other-worldly landscapes.

- A ethereal
- B realistic
- C fanciful
- D mundane
- E extravagant
- F sublime

The artist creates imaginary landscapes that do not seem to belong to this world. We normally would expect the details comprising these landscapes to be as fantastic and other-worldly as the landscapes themselves. The truth of the matter, however, is *paradoxical*: it contradicts what we expect. The details she chooses may be *realistic* (true to life) or *mundane* (ordinary, everyday), yet the more lifelike and unremarkable they are, the more fantastic the paintings seem. The correct answers are *realistic* and *mundane*.

TACTIC 6 Use Your Knowledge of Word Parts and Parts of Speech to Get at the Meanings of Unfamiliar Words

If a word used by the author is unfamiliar, or if an answer choice is unknown to you, two approaches are helpful.

1. Break down the word into its component parts—prefixes, suffixes, roots—to see whether they provide any clues to its meaning. For example, in the preceding list of Implicit Contrast Signal Words, the word *incongruous* contains three key word parts. *In-* here means not; *con-* means together; *gru-* means to move or come. *Incongruous* behavior, therefore, is behavior that does not go together or agree with someone's usual behavior; it is unexpected.

2. Change the unfamiliar word from one part of speech to another. If the adjective *embryonic* is unfamiliar to you, cut off its adjective suffix *–nic* and recognize the familiar word *embryo*. If the noun *precocity* is unfamiliar to you, cut off its noun suffix *–ity* and visualize it with different endings. You may come up with the adjective *precocious* (maturing early). If the verb *appropriate* is unfamiliar to you, by adding a word part or two you may come up with the common noun *appropriation* or the still more common noun *misappropriation* (as in the misappropriation of funds).

Note the application of this tactic in the following example.

TIP

Remember, if you can eliminate two or more answer choices, it pays to guess.

This island is a colony; however, in most matters it is ________ and receives no orders from the mother country.

[A] synoptic
[B] independent
[C] methodical
[D] autonomous
[E] heretical
[F] disinterested

First, locate any answer choices that are obviously correct. If a colony receives no orders from its mother country, it is *independent* to act according to its own wishes: it is essentially self-governing. It is not necessarily *methodical* (systematic), nor is it by definition *heretical* (unorthodox) or *disinterested* (impartial). Thus, you may rule out Choices C, E, and F.

The two answer choices remaining may be unfamiliar to you. Analyze them, using what you know of related words. *Synoptic* is related to the noun *synopsis*, a summary or abridgement. Does this term have anything to do with how a colony might govern itself? Definitely not. *Autonomous*, however, comes from the prefix *auto-* (self) and the root *nom-* (law). An autonomous nation is independent; it rules itself. Thus, the correct answers are *independent* and *autonomous*.

The Testing Tactics for Text Completion Questions

To answer this type of short answer question correctly, you must come up with the right word for each and every blank in the sentence or group of sentences. As in a Cloze procedure, you have to insert words in a text, monitoring for meaning as you read. Your goal is closure: the completion of a partly finished semantic pattern.

These are the GRE website's directions for text completion questions:

STRATEGY FOR ANALYZING QUESTION TYPES

There is no partial credit for text completion questions: to get any credit, you must fill in *every blank in the text correctly*.

Directions: For the following questions, select one entry for each blank from the corresponding column of choices. Fill all blanks in the way that best completes the text.

TACTIC

In Double- and Triple-Blank Texts, Go Through One Column at a Time, Eliminating the Answer Choices That Don't Fit

In a text completion question with two or three blanks, read through the entire text to get a sense of it as a whole. Pay special attention to the parts of the text (subordinate clauses, participial phrases, etc.) *without* any blanks. See whether you can predict what the first missing word may be. Then go through the first column, inserting each word in the sentence's first blank. Ask yourself whether a given word would make sense in this blank. If it makes no sense, eliminate it. If it makes possible sense, keep it in mind as you work on filling in the next blank.

Critics of the movie version of *The Color Purple* (i)________ its saccharine, overoptimistic tone as out of keeping with the novel's more (ii)________ quality.

Blank (i)	Blank (ii)
acclaimed	acerbic
decried	cloying
echoed	sanguine

For a quick, general sense of the opening clause, break it down. What does it say? *Critics ______ the movie's sugary sweet tone.*

How would critics react to something sugary sweet and overly hopeful? Most likely they would *not* acclaim (praise) it. You are probably safe to cross out the word *acclaimed.* However, they might well *decry* or disparage it. They might even *echo* or copy it, although that answer choice seems unlikely.

You have two possibilities for the first blank, *decried* and *echoed,* with the former more likely than the latter. Now consider the second blank. The movie's sugary, overly hopeful tone is out of keeping with the novel's quality: the two tones disagree. Therefore, the novel's tone is not *sanguine* (hopeful) or *cloying* (sickly sweet). It is instead on the bitter or sour side; in a word, *acerbic.*

TIP

Do *not* assume that you have to work your way through the blanks sequentially. It may be easier to fill in the second blank first!

Now that you are sure of your second answer choice, go back to the first blank. Reread the sentence:

> Critics of the movie ________ its saccharine, overoptimistic tone as out of keeping with the novel's more acerbic quality. Clearly, the critics would not echo the movie's tone. Instead, they decried or disparaged it. By rereading the text you have confirmed your answer choices.

TACTIC 

Break Down Complex Passages into Simple Components

In analyzing long, complex text completion items, you may find it useful to simplify the texts by breaking them down. Rephrase dependent clauses and long participial phrases, turning them into simple sentences.

See how this tactic helps you to analyze the following complex sentence.

> Museum director Hoving (i)________ refers to the smuggled Greek urn as the "hot pot," not because there are doubts about its authenticity or even great reservations as to its price, but because the (ii)________ of its acquisition is open to question.

Blank (i)	Blank (ii)
characteristically	timeliness
colloquially	manner
repeatedly	expense

What do we know?

1. The urn has been smuggled.
2. Hoving calls it a "hot pot."
3. It is genuine. (There are no doubts about its authenticity.)
4. It did not cost too much. (There are no great reservations as to its price.)

In calling the smuggled urn a "hot pot," Hoving is not necessarily speaking *characteristically*: we have no information about his typical mode of speech. Similarly, we have no evidence that Hoving has *repeatedly* called it a hot pot: we know only that he called it a hot pot at least once. Hoving is speaking *colloquially*, that is, informally. (*Hot* here is a slang term meaning stolen or illegally obtained.) You have your first correct answer choice, *colloquially*.

Now consider the second blank. The urn's expense is not being questioned, nor is the *timeliness* (well-timed occurrence) of its acquisition. However, because the urn has been smuggled into the country, there clearly are unresolved questions about how it got here, in other words, about its mode or *manner* of acquisition. The second correct answer choice is *manner*.

TACTIC 9 If a Sentence Contains a Metaphor, Check to See Whether That Metaphor Controls the Writer's Choice of Words (and Your Answer Choice)

Writers sometimes indulge in extended metaphors, complex analogies that imaginatively identify one object with another.

In the following example, the mind of a prejudiced person is compared to the pupil of an eye in its response to light or illumination.

> The mind of a bigot is like the pupil of the eye: the more light you pour upon it, the more it will ______.

blink
veer
stare
reflect
contract

The image of light unifies this sentence. In choosing an answer, you must complete the sentence in such a way as to develop that metaphor fully and accurately. Exactly what takes place when you shine a light into someone's eye? The person may stare back or blink; you may see the light reflected in the person's eye. But what happens to the pupil of the eye? It neither blinks nor reflects. Instead it shrinks in size: it *contracts.* Likewise, exposed to the light of tolerance, the bigot's mind resists illumination, shrinking from light. *Contract* completes the metaphor; it is the correct answer choice.

TACTIC

Once You Have Filled In All the Blanks to Your Satisfaction, Reread the Completed Passage to Make Sure It Makes Sense

No matter how confident you are that you have filled in an individual blank correctly, you cannot be sure you have successfully completed the passage until you have confirmed your word choice(s) by rereading the entire text. This is what you did in working out the answers to the sample question in Tactic 4. Remember: you are aiming for closure. Do not omit this stage in the procedure.

PRACTICE EXERCISES

Exercise A (Sentence Equivalence)

Directions: For the following questions, select the **two** answer choices that, when used to complete the sentence, fit the meaning of the sentence as a whole **and** produce completed sentences that are alike in meaning.

1. Normally an individual thunderstorm lasts about 45 minutes, but under certain conditions the storm may ________, becoming ever more severe, for as long as four hours.

   A wane
   B moderate
   C persist
   D endure
   E vacillate
   F disperse

2. Perhaps because something in us instinctively distrusts such displays of natural fluency, some readers approach John Updike's fiction with ________.

   A wariness
   B indifference
   C suspicion
   D veneration
   E bewilderment
   F remorse

3. We lost confidence in him because he never ________ the grandiose promises he had made.

   A forgot about
   B reneged on
   C carried out
   D tired of
   E delivered on
   F retreated from

4. We were amazed that a man who had been heretofore the most ________ of public speakers could, in a single speech, electrify an audience and bring them cheering to their feet.

   A prosaic
   B enthralling
   C accomplished
   D pedestrian
   E auspicious
   F iconoclastic

5. Despite the mixture's ________ nature, we found that by lowering the temperature in the laboratory we could dramatically reduce its tendency to vaporize.

   A resilient
   B homogeneous
   C volatile
   D insipid
   E acerbic
   F unstable

6. In a revolutionary development in technology, some manufacturers now make biodegradable forms of plastic; some plastic trash bags, for example, gradually ________ when exposed to sunlight.

   A harden
   B stagnate
   C inflate
   D propagate
   E decompose
   F disintegrate

7. Aimed at curbing European attempts to seize territory in the Americas, the Monroe Doctrine was a warning to ________ foreign powers.

A pertinacious
B cautionary
C credulous
D rapacious
E predatory
F remote

8. Few other plants can grow beneath the canopy of the sycamore tree, whose leaves and pods produce a natural herbicide that leaches into the surrounding soil, ________ other plants that might compete for water and nutrients.

A inhibiting
B distinguishing
C nourishing
D suppressing
E harvesting
F fertilizing

9. The child was so spoiled by her indulgent parents that she pouted and became ______ when she did not receive all of their attention.

A discreet
B suspicious
C elated
D sullen
E tranquil
F grumpy

10. The reasoning in this editorial is so ________ that we cannot see how anyone can be deceived by it.

A unsound
B coherent
C astute
D dispassionate
E scrupulous
F specious

11. Because Inspector Morse could not contain his scorn for the police commissioner, he was imprudent enough to make ______ remarks about his superior officer.

A ambiguous
B impartial
C unfathomable
D contemptuous
E scathing
F pertinent

12. Though he was theoretically a friend of labor, his voting record in Congress ______ that impression.

A implied
B confirmed
C created
D belied
E tallied
F contradicted

13. Modern architecture has discarded ________ trimming on buildings and has concentrated on an almost Greek simplicity of line.

A flamboyant
B ornate
C austere
D inconspicuous
E aesthetic
F derivative

14. The young clerk was quickly promoted when his employers saw how ________ he was.

A indigent
B assiduous
C autocratic
D industrious
E intractable
F self-serving

15. After medical school, the three friends followed ________ paths, as Jan went on to become a neurologist, Dana an emergency room physician, and Morgan a consultant to a major pharmaceutical company.

A lucrative
B implausible
C divergent
D dissimilar
E traditional
F quixotic

Exercise B (Sentence Equivalence)

Directions: For the following questions, select the **two** answer choices that, when used to complete the sentence, fit the meaning of the sentence as a whole **and** produce completed sentences that are alike in meaning.

1. Truculent in defending their individual rights of sovereignty under the Articles of Confederation, the newly formed states ________ constantly.

A digressed
B conferred
C bickered
D dismembered
E rebuffed
F squabbled

2. In Anglo Saxon times, the monastic scribes made ________ distinction between Latin texts and texts in the vernacular by assigning the former an Anglo-Caroline script and reserving the pointed insular script for texts in Old English.

A a nice
B a subtle
C a pointless
D an obvious
E an unconventional
F a judgmental

3. Written in an amiable style, the book provides a comprehensive overview of European wines that should prove ________ to both the virtual novice and the experienced connoisseur.

A inviting
B tedious
C engaging
D inspirational
E perplexing
F opaque

4. Shy and hypochondriacal, Madison was uncomfortable at public gatherings; his character made him a most ________ orator and practicing politician.

A conscientious
B unlikely
C fervent
D gregarious
E improbable
F effective

5. Alec Guinness has few equals among English-speaking actors, and in his autobiography he reveals himself to possess an uncommonly ________ prose style as well.

   A ambivalent
   B infamous
   C felicitous
   D happy
   E redundant
   F ephemeral

6. Because Pauling stubbornly continued to believe in the power of vitamin C to cure cancer despite much evidence to the contrary, his colleagues felt he had lost his scientific ________.

   A tenacity
   B inventiveness
   C contrariness
   D impartiality
   E hypothesis
   F objectivity

7. The distinctive qualities of African music were not appreciated or even ________ by Westerners until fairly recently.

   A deprecated
   B discerned
   C ignored
   D revered
   E remarked on
   F neglected

8. Bored by the verbose and rambling prose of the typical Victorian novelist, the student welcomed the change to the ________ prose of Ernest Hemingway.

   A consistent
   B terse
   C florid
   D equivocal
   E pithy
   F discursive

9. She is a pragmatist, as ________ to base her future on impractical dreams as she would be to build a castle on shifting sand.

   A determined
   B disinclined
   C loath
   D quick
   E diligent
   F foolhardy

10. Although eighteenth-century English society as a whole did not encourage learning for its own sake in women, it illogically ________ women's sad lack of education.

    A decried
    B postulated
    C criticized
    D tolerated
    E vaunted
    F legitimized

11. Unlike the gregarious Capote, who was never happier than when he was in the center of a crowd of celebrities, Faulkner, in later years, grew somewhat ________ and shunned company.

    A dispassionate
    B infamous
    C reclusive
    D ambivalent
    E withdrawn
    F notorious

12. Studded starfish are well protected from most predators and parasites by ________ surface whose studs are actually modified spines.

    A a vulnerable
    B an armored
    C an obtuse
    D a brittle
    E a concave
    F a rugged

13. Traffic speed limits are set at a level that achieves some balance between the desire of most people to travel as quickly as possible and the danger of ________ speed.

- [A] inordinate
- [B] marginal
- [C] inadvertent
- [D] inadequate
- [E] regulated
- [F] excessive

14. Baldwin's brilliant *The Fire Next Time* is both so eloquent in its passion and so penetrating in its candor that it is bound to ________ any reader.

- [A] embarrass
- [B] disgust
- [C] disquiet
- [D] unsettle
- [E] disappoint
- [F] bore

15. Glendon provides a dark underside to Frederick Jackson Turner's frontier thesis that saw rugged individualism as the essence of American society—an individualism that Glendon sees as ________ atomism.

- [A] antithetical toward
- [B] skeptical of
- [C] degenerating into
- [D] aspiring to
- [E] regressing to
- [F] revitalized by

Exercise C (Text Completion)

Directions: For the following questions, select one entry for each blank from the corresponding column of choices. Fill all blanks in the way that best completes the text.

1. Unlike other examples of ________ verse, Milton's *Lycidas* does more than merely mourn the death of Edward King; it also denounces corruption in the church in which King was ordained.

Ⓐ satiric
Ⓑ elegiac
Ⓒ free
Ⓓ didactic
Ⓔ pedestrian

2. Just as disloyalty is the mark of the renegade, (i)________ is the mark of the (ii)________.

Blank (i)	Blank (ii)
Ⓐ avarice	Ⓓ craven
Ⓑ cowardice	Ⓔ laggard
Ⓒ vanity	Ⓕ misanthrope

3. Because she had a reputation for (i)________, we were surprised and pleased when she greeted us so (ii)________.

Blank (i)	Blank (ii)
Ⓐ graciousness	Ⓓ affably
Ⓑ credulity	Ⓔ disdainfully
Ⓒ petulance	Ⓕ irascibly

4. Despite an affected (i)________ that convinced casual observers that he was (ii)________ about his painting and cared only for frivolity, Warhol cared deeply about his art and labored at it (iii)________.

Blank (i)	Blank (ii)	Blank (iii)
Ⓐ fervor	Ⓓ indifferent	Ⓖ ambivalently
Ⓑ gloom	Ⓔ passionate	Ⓗ diligently
Ⓒ nonchalance	Ⓕ systematic	Ⓘ intermittently

5. Although a few years ago the fundamental facts about the Milky Way seemed fairly well (i)________, now even its mass and its radius have come into (ii)________.

Blank (i)	Blank (ii)
Ⓐ diminished	Ⓓ disrepute
Ⓑ established	Ⓔ prominence
Ⓒ disparaged	Ⓕ question

6. One of the most (i)________ educators in New York, Dr. Shalala (ii)________ a controversy in 1984 by calling the city public schools a "rotten barrel" in need of (iii)________ reform.

Blank (i)	Blank (ii)	Blank (iii)
Ⓐ indifferent	Ⓓ diverted	Ⓖ partial
Ⓑ outspoken	Ⓔ ignited	Ⓗ superficial
Ⓒ eclectic	Ⓕ defused	Ⓘ systemic

7. The newest fiber-optic cables that carry telephone calls cross-country are made of glass so ________ that a piece 100 miles thick is clearer than a standard windowpane.

Ⓐ fragile
Ⓑ immaculate
Ⓒ iridescent
Ⓓ tangible
Ⓔ transparent

8. The texts as we have them were written down and edited carefully by Christians proud of their ancestors but unable to bear the thought of their indulging in heathen practices; thus, all references to the ancient religion of the Celts were (i)________, if not (ii)________.

Blank (i)	Blank (ii)
Ⓐ aggrieved	Ⓓ ironic
Ⓑ detailed	Ⓔ overawed
Ⓒ muddied	Ⓕ suppressed

9. To alleviate the problem of contaminated chicken, the study panel recommends that the federal government shift its inspection emphasis from cursory bird-by-bird check to a more ________ random sampling for bacterial and chemical contamination.

Ⓐ discreet
Ⓑ perfunctory
Ⓒ rigorous
Ⓓ solicitous
Ⓔ symbolic

10. The orator was so (i)________ that the audience soon became (ii)________.

Blank (i)	Blank (ii)
Ⓐ bombastic	Ⓓ drowsy
Ⓑ inaudible	Ⓔ irresolute
Ⓒ soporific	Ⓕ moribund

11. Her true feelings (i)________ themselves in her sarcastic asides; only then was her (ii)________ revealed.

Blank (i)	Blank (ii)
Ⓐ anticipated	Ⓓ anxiety
Ⓑ concealed	Ⓔ bitterness
Ⓒ manifested	Ⓕ charm

12. The sugar dissolved in water (i)________; finally all that remained was an almost (ii)________ residue on the bottom of the glass.

Blank (i)	Blank (ii)
Ⓐ gradually	Ⓓ fragrant
Ⓑ quickly	Ⓔ imperceptible
Ⓒ subsequently	Ⓕ problematic

13. After the Japanese attack on Pearl Harbor on December 7, 1941, Japanese-Americans were (i)________ of being spies for Japan, although there was no evidence to (ii)________ this accusation.

Blank (i)	Blank (ii)
Ⓐ acquitted	Ⓓ back up
Ⓑ reminded	Ⓔ carry out
Ⓒ suspected	Ⓕ shrug off

14. Mencken's readers enjoyed his (i)________ wit, but his victims often (ii)________ at the broad, yet pointed satire.

Blank (i)	Blank (ii)
Ⓐ cutting	Ⓓ connived
Ⓑ kindly	Ⓔ smiled
Ⓒ subtle	Ⓕ winced

15. Given the current anti-regulatory mood in government circles, critics of for-profit colleges questioned whether regulators and law enforcement agencies would ever (i) _______ those predatory schools that enriched themselves and their shareholders by (ii) _______ their programs in order to entice underqualified students to apply despite the school's low rates of graduation and the high cost of student loans.

Blank (i)	Blank (ii)
Ⓐ bear with	Ⓓ misrepresenting
Ⓑ rein in	Ⓔ retrofitting
Ⓒ profit from	Ⓕ disseminating

Exercise D (Text Completion)

Directions: For the following questions, select **one** entry for each blank from the corresponding column of choices. Fill all blanks in the way that best completes the text.

1. Chaotic in conception but not in _______, Kelly's canvases are as neat as the proverbial pin.

Ⓐ conceit
Ⓑ execution
Ⓒ intent
Ⓓ origin
Ⓔ theory

2. During the middle of the eighteenth century, the (i)_______ style in furniture and architecture, marked by elaborate scrollwork and (ii)_______ decoration, flourished.

Blank (i)	Blank (ii)
Ⓐ abstract	Ⓓ austere
Ⓑ medieval	Ⓔ excessive
Ⓒ rococo	Ⓕ functional

3. Tocqueville decided to swear the oath of loyalty to the new Orleanist king in part (i)_______ (he wanted to keep his position as magistrate), and in part (ii)_______ (he was convinced that the democratization of politics represented by the new regime was inevitable).

Blank (i)	Blank (ii)
Ⓐ opportunistically	Ⓓ altruistically
Ⓑ selflessly	Ⓔ irresolutely
Ⓒ theoretically	Ⓕ pragmatically

4. In seeking to rediscover Zora Neale Hurston, it is intriguing to look at the figure she cut in the minds of her contemporaries, the high regard she (i)________ before shifting aesthetic values (ii)________ her to curio status.

Blank (i)
Ⓐ deplored
Ⓑ enjoyed
Ⓒ offered

Blank (ii)
Ⓓ elevated
Ⓔ relegated
Ⓕ suspended

5. The tapeworm is an example of (i)________ organism, one that lives within or on another creature, (ii)________ some or all of its nutrients from its host.

Blank (i)
Ⓐ an autonomous
Ⓑ a hospitable
Ⓒ a parasitic

Blank (ii)
Ⓓ converting
Ⓔ deriving
Ⓕ sublimating

6. Ms. Sutcliffe's helpful notes on her latest wine discoveries and her no-nonsense warnings to consumers about (i)________ wines provide (ii)________ guide to the numbing array of wines of Burgundy.

Blank (i)
Ⓐ overpriced
Ⓑ superior
Ⓒ vintage

Blank (ii)
Ⓓ an inadequate
Ⓔ a spotty
Ⓕ a trusty

7. Measurement is, like any other human endeavor, a complex activity, subject to (i)________, not always used properly, and frequently misinterpreted and (ii)________.

Blank (i)
Ⓐ correlation
Ⓑ error
Ⓒ legislation

Blank (ii)
Ⓓ analyzed
Ⓔ incorporated
Ⓕ misunderstood

8. Just as insincerity is the mark of the (i)________, boastfulness is the mark of the (ii)________.

Blank (i)
Ⓐ zealot
Ⓑ skeptic
Ⓒ hypocrite

Blank (ii)
Ⓓ glutton
Ⓔ autocrat
Ⓕ braggart

9. For Miró, art became (i)________ ritual; paper and pencils were holy objects to him, and he worked as though he were (ii)________ a religious rite.

Blank (i)	Blank (ii)
Ⓐ a cryptic	Ⓓ absolving
Ⓑ an eclectic	Ⓔ performing
Ⓒ a sacred	Ⓕ protracting

10. If the *Titanic* had hit the iceberg head on, its watertight compartments might have saved it from (i)________, but the great liner swerved to (ii)________ the iceberg, and in the collision so many compartments were opened to the sea that disaster was (iii)________.

Blank (i)	Blank (ii)	Blank (iii)
Ⓐ adversity	Ⓓ avoid	Ⓖ averted
Ⓑ denouement	Ⓔ contract	Ⓗ inevitable
Ⓒ foundering	Ⓕ mollify	Ⓘ limited

11. We have become so democratic in our habits of thought that we are convinced that truth is (i)________ through a (ii)________ of facts.

Blank (i)	Blank (ii)
Ⓐ assimilated	Ⓓ hierarchy
Ⓑ determined	Ⓔ plebiscite
Ⓒ exculpated	Ⓕ transcendence

12. The writer's (i)________ use of language renders a usually uninspiring topic, economics, known as "the dismal science," uncommonly (ii)________.

Blank (i)	Blank (ii)
Ⓐ pedestrian	Ⓓ engaging
Ⓑ felicitous	Ⓔ abstruse
Ⓒ grandiloquent	Ⓕ contentious

13. The leader of the group is the passionately committed Crimond, whose (i)________ politics is (ii)________ proportional to his disciples' lapsed political faith.

Blank (i)	Blank (ii)
Ⓐ engagement in	Ⓓ critically
Ⓑ indifference to	Ⓔ inversely
Ⓒ retreat from	Ⓕ marginally

14. Although the economy suffers (i)_______, it also has strong (ii)_______ and self-correcting tendencies.

Blank (i)	Blank (ii)
Ⓐ contradictions	Ⓓ recidivist
Ⓑ digressions	Ⓔ recuperative
Ⓒ downturns	Ⓕ unstable

15. Faced with these massive changes, the government keeps its own counsel; although generally benevolent, it has always been _______ regime.

Ⓐ an altruistic
Ⓑ an indifferent
Ⓒ a reticent
Ⓓ a sanguine
Ⓔ an unpredictable

ANSWER KEY

Exercise A

1. **C**, **D**
2. **A**, **C**
3. **C**, **E**
4. **A**, **D**
5. **C**, **F**
6. **E**, **F**
7. **D**, **E**
8. **A**, **D**
9. **D**, **F**
10. **A**, **F**
11. **D**, **E**
12. **D**, **F**
13. **A**, **B**
14. **B**, **D**
15. **C**, **D**

Exercise B

1. **C**, **F**
2. **A**, **B**
3. **A**, **C**
4. **B**, **E**
5. **C**, **D**
6. **D**, **F**
7. **B**, **E**
8. **B**, **E**
9. **B**, **C**
10. **A**, **C**
11. **C**, **E**
12. **B**, **F**
13. **A**, **F**
14. **C**, **D**
15. **C**, **E**

Exercise C

1. **B**
2. (i) **B**; (ii) **D**
3. (i) **C**; (ii) **D**
4. (i) **C**; (ii) **D**; (iii) **H**
5. (i) **B**; (ii) **F**
6. (i) **B**; (ii) **E**; (iii) **I**
7. **E**
8. (i) **C**; (ii) **F**
9. **C**
10. (i) **C**; (ii) **D**
11. (i) **C**; (ii) **E**
12. (i) **A**; (ii) **E**
13. (i) **C**; (ii) **D**
14. (i) **A**; (ii) **F**
15. (i) **A**; (ii) **D**

Exercise D

1. **B**
2. (i) **C**; (ii) **E**
3. (i) **A**; (ii) **F**
4. (i) **B**; (ii) **E**
5. (i) **C**; (ii) **E**
6. (i) **A**; (ii) **F**
7. (i) **B**; (ii) **F**
8. (i) **C**; (ii) **F**
9. (i) **C**; (ii) **E**
10. (i) **C**; (ii) **D**; (iii) **H**
11. (i) **B**; (ii) **E**
12. (i) **B**; (ii) **D**
13. (i) **A**; (ii) **E**
14. (i) **C**; (ii) **E**
15. **C**

ANSWER EXPLANATIONS

Exercise A

1. **(C, D)** If, rather than ending in 45 minutes, a storm lasts for four hours, then clearly it *persists* or *endures.*

2. **(A, C)** A reader who distrusts fluency (eloquence, articulateness) in authors might well regard the fluent author John Updike with *wariness* or *suspicion.*

3. **(C, E)** What made people lose confidence in this person? He made promises, but failed to *carry* them *out* or *deliver on* them.

4. **(A, D)** What amazed people? The speaker had made an electrifying, exciting speech. Why were they amazed? They were amazed because he was known to be a *prosaic, pedestrian* (unimaginative, dull) public speaker.

5. **(C, F)** The mixture had a tendency to vaporize or evaporate. Therefore, its nature was *volatile* (easily evaporated) or *unstable.*

6. **(E, F)** By definition, *biodegradable* means capable of being decomposed by bacteria or other living organisms. The plastic trash bags *decompose* or *disintegrate* in the sunlight.

7. **(D, E)** The European nations are attempting to seize territory in the Americas. For this reason, the Americans regard them as *rapacious* (aggressively greedy) and *predatory* (seeking to exploit others).

8. **(A, D)** If few plants can grow under the canopy of the sycamore tree, the sycamore must be doing something to *inhibit* or *suppress* the growth of other plants. In fact, sycamore leaves and pods produce a natural herbicide, a substance that is toxic to plants.

9. **(D, F)** To pout is to push one's lips forward to express annoyance. The spoiled child is annoyed because she is not getting all her parents' attention. For this reason, she is *sullen* (bad-tempered and sulky) and *grumpy.*

10. **(A, F)** The speaker is being critical of the reasoning in the editorial, which is flawed: it can't fool anyone. The missing words must be negative. Check the answer choices for their positive and negative connotations. Only two answers, *unsound* (not based on reliable reasoning or evidence) and *specious* (plausible on the surface, but actually wrong), are negative. They are the correct answers.

11. **(D, E)** Someone who cannot contain his scorn for his boss is likely to make negative comments about his superior. Again, check the answers for their positive and negative connotations. Only two answers, *contemptuous* (scornful) and *scathing* (severely critical) are negative. They are the correct answers.

12. **(D, F)** "Though" signals a contrast, in this case a contrast between the Congressman's supposed position (a "friend of labor" would in theory have a voting record that was favorable to labor unions) and his actual position (his voting record is anti-labor). His voting record thus *belies* or *contradicts* the impression that he is pro-labor.

13. **(A, B)** The simple lines of modern buildings are neither *flamboyant* (elaborate) nor *ornate* (highly decorated).

14. **(B, D)** Employers would most likely promote someone for his positive qualities, not his negative ones. The missing words must be positive. Check the answer choices for their positive and negative connotations. Only two answers, *assiduous* (careful and diligent) and *industrious* (hard-working) are positive. They are the correct answers.

15. **(C, D)** What is most significant about the career paths chosen by the three young doctors? Although they are all possible careers for graduates of medical schools, they are very different in nature. In other words, these paths are *divergent* (developing in different directions) or *dissimilar*. While *lucrative* (financially rewarding) and *traditional* may describe a career in medicine, these terms do not emphasize how greatly these three careers vary in nature. Likewise, while *unrealistic* and *quixotic* are alike in meaning, they do not work in the context, for all three career paths are quite practical.

Exercise B

1. **(C, F)** The key word here is *truculent,* quick to argue or fight. The states are quick to take action to defend their rights from outside interference. Thus, they *bicker* and *squabble* (quarrel, often about trivial things).

2. **(A, B)** Watch out for words that have uncommon secondary meanings. At first glance none of the answer choices appear to be alike in meaning. However, *nice,* which commonly means *enjoyable* or *good,* as in having a nice time, has the secondary meaning of *very slight* or *subtle.* In using one script for Latin texts and a different script for Old English texts, the scribes subtly distinguished the texts from one another.

3. **(A, C)** The book is described in positive terms: it is "(w)ritten in an amiable (agreeable; pleasing) style;" it "provides a comprehensive (broad, wide-ranging) overview." Therefore, it should be *engaging* or *inviting* to anyone with an interest in wine. However, it would not necessarily be *inspirational* (soul-stirring; emotionally moving) to such a person.

4. **(B, E)** Would you expect someone shy and uncomfortable at public gatherings to be a natural politician? No, he would be an *unlikely, improbable* politician.

5. **(C, D)** As an actor, Guinness is described in highly positive terms: he "has few equals among ... actors." His writing is described in similarly positive terms: it is "uncommonly *felicitous* (well expressed) or *happy* (apt, as in "a happy turn of phrase"). Again, check words for possible secondary meanings. *Happy,* commonly means *joyful* or *merry,* as in "Have a happy birthday!," which has the secondary meaning of *fitting* or *apt.*

6. **(D, F)** An *objective, impartial* scientist would trust solid evidence, even when that evidence contradicted his cherished beliefs. Pauling stuck to his beliefs despite the evidence. Therefore, his colleagues feared he had lost his scientific *objectivity* or *impartiality.*

7. **(B, E)** The adverb *even* is used here to emphasize something surprising. Not only didn't these dumb Westerners fail to appreciate what made African music distinctive (special and noteworthy), they didn't even *discern* (recognize, spot) it or *remark* (show they noticed by commenting) *on* it. While *ignored* and *neglected* are alike in meaning, they do not work in the context.

8. **(B, E)** The student welcomes a change from a verbose (wordy) and rambling (aimlessly wandering) prose style. This suggests that the student wants prose that is the opposite of wordy. In other words, she would like prose that is *terse* (effectively concise) and *pithy* (brief).

9. **(B, C)** A pragmatist is a practical person, one who is concerned whether a particular course of action will work. Such a person would be unwilling to try to build a castle (which needs a solid foundation) on sands that moved or shifted. Likewise, the woman described here is *disinclined* or *loath* (reluctant, averse) to base her future on impractical dreams. Watch out for words that look alike. The verb *loathe* means hate. Sue *loathes* beets. The adjective *loath* means unwilling. Because her boyfriend loved beets, Sue was *loath* to tell him that she *loathed* his favorite vegetable.

10. **(A, C)** The key word here is *illogically.* If eighteenth-century English society did not encourage women to get an education, then it was clearly illogical for society to *decry* (denounce, condemn) or *criticize* women's lack of education.

11. **(C, E)** Someone who shuns or avoids society may well be described as *reclusive* (avoiding other people's company) and *withdrawn* (unsociable; remote). While *infamous* and *notorious* are alike in meaning, they do not work in the context.

12. **(B, F)** If the studded surface is able to protect the starfish from external threats, then it is unlikely to be *brittle* (easily broken) or *vulnerable* (an easy target for attack). The surface is far more likely to be described as *armored* (protected by armor) or *rugged* (tough).

13. **(A, F)** What sort of speed is dangerous? *Inordinate* (extreme, unreasonable), *excessive* speed.

14. **(C, D)** What sort of response would a brilliant, passionate, eloquent book most likely inspire? Probably some sort of positive response. However, Baldwin's book is described as "penetrating (piercing or sharp) in its candor (directness, outspokenness)." It is also likely that the book's frankness may be more than its readers can comfortably handle. Thus, the conclusion that the book is bound to *disquiet* (agitate, alarm) or *unsettle* (disturb) any reader. None of the other choices are likely responses to a brilliant, eloquent book.

15. **(C, E)** The key phrase here is "a dark underside." According to Glendon, there is something fundamentally wrong with the American adherence to rugged individualism (the belief that individuals should be independent and self-reliant). If you take this adherence too far, it can *degenerate* (go bad and fall) into or *regress* (deteriorate) to atomism. (Social atomism looks on all individuals as interchangeable units; it ignores the idea that each individual is unique, formed by individual circumstances and having individual needs.)

Exercise C

1. **(B)** The key word here is "mourn." By definition, examples of *elegiac* verse (verse expressing grief or lamentation) mourn. Milton's *Lycidas* differs from other examples of elegiac verse because in addition to mourning King's death, the poem condemns wickedness and depravity in the church.

2. **(B, D)** By definition, *cowardice* is the mark of the *craven* (person lacking in courage).

3. **(C, D)** The key word here is "surprised." We would expect someone with a reputation for *petulance* (sulkiness, bad temper) to greet people in an irritable, grumpy way. It would be surprising for someone petulant to greet people *affably* (in a good-natured, friendly way).

4. **(C, D, H)** The key phrase here is "cared deeply." Someone who cared deeply about his art would be unlikely to work at it ambivalently (with mixed feelings about what he was doing). Likewise, someone who cared deeply about his art would be unlikely to work at it only intermittently (sporadically; at odd moments). No. We would expect someone with such deep feelings to work at his art *diligently* (carefully, conscientiously). "Despite" signals a contrast. The contrast is between Warhol's deep feelings for his art and the appearance he affected or shammed. He tries to appear *nonchalant* (unconcerned), and his affected *nonchalance* makes people who don't look closely think he is *indifferent* (uncaring) about his paintings.

5. **(B, F)** "Although" signals a contrast. The contrast here is between how the basic facts about the Milky Way were regarded a few years ago and how they are regarded now. Back then, folks thought they understood the Milky Way; they regarded the basic facts about it as *established* (generally accepted). Now, even its dimensions and mass are no longer generally accepted; they have come into *question.*

6. **(B, E, I)** What sort of educator would call the New York City's public school system a "rotten barrel"? Dr. Shalala was clearly an *outspoken* educator, one who frankly stated her opinions, especially if they were shocking or controversial, and the opinion she stated was shocking enough to *ignite* (trigger, spark) controversy. Finally, if the school system was rotten through and through, what kind of reform was needed to mend it? The answer is *systemic* reform, reform that would affect the entire organization, not just one particular classroom or school.

7. **(E)** If a piece of glass cable 100 miles thick is clearer than an ordinary windowpane, then the glass that makes up the cable must be extraordinarily *transparent.*

8. **(C, F)** The Christians considered the ancient religion of the Celts to be heathen (pagan; non-Christian, and therefore heretical). They were proud of their Celtic ancestors, but had a hard time thinking of these ancestors as wicked pagans. So Christian texts either *muddied* (obscured or made unclear) any references to the Celts' ancient religion or completely *suppressed* (concealed; hid) such references.

9. **(C)** The key words here are "alleviate" and "cursory." A problem exists: "contaminated chicken" is making people sick. A study panel hopes to alleviate this problem, making it less severe. They recommend changing inspections from cursory (hasty, and therefore *not* thorough) checks to *rigorous* (extremely thorough and careful) random sampling.

10. **(C, D)** The structure "so . . . that" signals cause and effect. The orator's voice was *soporific* (sleep-inducing). By definition, it caused people to become *drowsy* (sleepy). That was its effect.

11. **(C, E)** The key words here are "sarcastic" and "revealed." What trait would be revealed in sarcastic (scornful, contemptuous) asides (sidecomments; remarks not meant to be heard by everyone)? Certainly not *charm* or *anxiety* (unease, worry). Clearly, the

sarcastic asides reveal the woman's *bitterness*. Because she is bitter and resentful, her true feelings *manifest* (show) themselves in her snarky comments.

12. **(A, E)** By definition, "finally" means after a long time, typically when there has been some delay. In this case, it has taken a long time for the sugar to dissolve; it dissolved only *gradually* (slowly, by degrees). What was left? An almost *imperceptible* (unnoticeable, impossible to detect) leftover small amount on the bottom of the glass.

13. **(C, D)** The Japanese-Americans were neither *acquitted* (found innocent) of spying nor *reminded* of (caused to remember) spying for Japan. Instead they were *suspected* (believed guilty) of spying even though no proof existed to *back up* (support) that belief.

14. **(A, F)** How would victims of pointed (unambiguously critical; biting) satire most likely react to being the targets of such sharp criticism? Most likely they would *wince* (flinch or make a face indicating their distress). However, Mencken's readers who were *not* the targets of his satire might well have enjoyed his *cutting* wit.

15. **(B, D)** "Given" here means considering something or taking it into account. If you take into account that the current mood in government circles is anti-regulatory (against controlling something, especially a business activity, by means of rules and regulations), what would you expect regulators and law enforcement agencies to do about the activities of predatory (greedy, exploitative) for-profit schools? Sadly, not much. That's what critics of for-profit colleges think: they question whether the regulators and law enforcement agencies would ever *rein in* (check, control) the greedy schools that fool underqualified students into wasting their money signing up for worthless or inappropriate classes. How do the colleges fool these students into signing up? The for-profit colleges *misrepresent* their programs, giving a false impression of their nature.

Exercise D

1. **(B)** The key word here is "conception," which here means the forming or devising of an idea. Kelly is a painter. The ideas behind his paintings may be chaotic (messy, disorganized), but the paintings themselves are neat as a pin. So, the paintings are messy in conception, but neat in *execution* (the way a plan or course of action is carried out). Note that the writer is using a secondary meaning of the noun *execution* here.

2. **(C, E)** By definition, the *rococo* style in furniture was characterized by elaborate scrollwork and *excessive* ornamentation. It was over the top.

3. **(A, F)** The missing words are explained by the parentheses following each blank.

   Go through the answer choices, testing each one to see whether it makes sense. Eliminate any choices that you can. If you don't know the meaning of an answer choice, go on to the next one to see whether you can eliminate that. If you can eliminate two answer choices, the third choice must be the correct answer. If you swear an oath of loyalty in order to keep your job, are you being *opportunistic*? The word is unfamiliar; go on to the next answer choice.

   If you swear an oath of loyalty in order to keep your job, are you being *selfless* (unselfish, altruistic)? No, you are thinking of yourself. You can eliminate choice B. If you swear an oath of loyalty in order to keep your job, are you being *theoretical* (conceptual, not practical)? No, you are being practical. You can eliminate Choice C. The correct answer must be Choice A, *opportunistically.* To be opportunistic is to be ready to exploit immediate opportunities, regardless of principle. Toqueville decided to swear an oath that he was loyal because that was his chance to keep his job.

Now, go through the answer choices for the second blank. If you swear an oath of loyalty because you believe that the new government's policies inevitably will win, are you being *altruistic* (unselfish)? No, you are simply accepting the inevitable. You can eliminate Choice D. Are you being *irresolute* (indecisive or uncertain)? No, you are certain that the democratization of politics will inevitably occur. You can eliminate Choice E. Are you being *pragmatic* (practical)? Yes, it was practical for Toqueville to go along with the regime whose success he believed was inevitable. Choice F is correct.

4. **(B, E)** The key words here are "rediscover" and "curio status." Someone who needs to be rediscovered is someone who has been forgotten. Once, Hurston was respected as a writer: she *enjoyed* or possessed the "high regard" of literary society. Then, aesthetic values shifted. Her writing was no longer valued. The change in aesthetic values *relegated* (downgraded or consigned) her to curio status, the status of a no longer fashionable literary curiosity.

5. **(C, E)** Use the process of elimination to fill in the first blank. A tapeworm is an organism that lives within or on another creature. By definition it is not *autonomous* (independent, self-sufficient). You can eliminate Choice A. A tapeworm is an organism that depends on a host (an animal or plant that provides nutrition for an organism living within or on it). It is not *hospitable* in any sense of the word. You can eliminate Choice B. A tapeworm, however, by definition is *parasitic, deriving* (obtaining) some or all of its nutrients from its host.

6. **(A, F)** The key words here are "helpful" and "warnings." "Warnings" is your clue to the correct answer choice for the first blank. Why would consumers need to be warned about certain wines? Not because those wines were *superior* (higher in quality) or *vintage* (of high quality), but because they were *overpriced* (too highly priced). Likewise, the fact that her wine notes are helpful is your clue that these notes provide *a trusty* (reliable) guide to the wines of Burgundy.

7. **(B, F)** To be subject to something is to be likely to be affected by it, especially if it is unwelcome or unpleasant. In this case, measurement is a complex activity that is subject to *error.* What is more, even when no actual errors of measurement occur, measurement can be misinterpreted and *misunderstood.*

8. **(C, F)** Use the process of elimination to fill in the first blank. A *zealot* is a fanatic who refuses to make any compromises about his or her religious, political, or other ideals. Zealots are marked by fanaticism, not by insincerity. You can eliminate Choice A. A *skeptic* is a person inclined to question or doubt that something is true. Skeptics are marked by a lack of belief, not by a lack of sincerity. You can eliminate Choice B. Insincerity, however, is the mark of a *hypocrite*: "a person who feigns some desirable or publicly approved attitude, especially one whose private life, opinions, or statements belie his or her public statements." Such a person by definition is insincere. Tackle the second blank the same way. Is boastfulness the mark of the *glutton* (overly greedy eater)? No, greed marks the glutton. You can eliminate Choice D. Is boastfulness the mark of the *autocrat* (person who insists on absolute obedience from others)? No,

domineering arrogance marks the autocrat. You can eliminate Choice E. Only Choice F is left. Boastfulness is the mark of the *braggart.*

9. **(C, E)** The key words here are "ritual," "holy," and "rite ." They reinforce the idea that, in Miro's view, to create art is to *perform a sacred* (holy) ritual or religious ceremony.

10. **(C, D, H)** More than a century after the supposedly "unsinkable" *R.M.S. Titanic* went down in the North Atlantic, the sinking of the *Titanic* still fascinates people. Look at the "If . . . then" structure of the opening portion of the sentence. *If* the ship had hit the iceberg head on, *then* the ship might have been saved from ________. What words come to mind? *Sinking, disaster, destruction.* Clearly, the first missing word must be negative. *Adversity* (misfortune, ill luck, hardship) is a negative term; however, it may not be a negative enough term to describe the *Titanic*'s fate. Check the other answer choices before settling on Choice A. A *denouement* is the outcome of a situation, the time when things are made clear. The word makes no sense in this context; you can eliminate Choice B. To *founder* is to fill with water and sink. Clearly, Choice C, *foundering,* is the best choice for the first missing word.

    Now, examine the context for the second missing word. The key word here is "swerved" (changed direction abruptly). Why would the *Titanic* swerve? To *avoid* the iceberg. Neither *contract* (decrease in size) nor *mollify* (pacify, soften) makes sense in the context. Finally, what effect would opening the watertight compartments to the sea have on the vessel's fate? It would neither *avert* (prevent) nor *limit* the disaster. Instead, it would make the disaster *inevitable* (unavoidable).

11. **(B, E)** The key word here is "democratic." To be democratic in one's habits of thought is to believe that whether something is true or not can be settled by voting. In other words, that truth can be *determined* (established) by a *plebiscite* (the direct vote of all the members of an electorate on an important public question) of facts.

12. **(B, D)** The phrase "usually uninspiring" signals a contrast between the way economics is usually presented and the way the so-called dismal science is presented by this writer. "Uninspiring" and "dismal" are negative terms. The missing words must be positive. Neither choice A, *pedestrian* (dull; unexciting), nor Choice C, *grandiloquent* (pompous, overdone), is positive. Choice B, *felicitous* (apt, well-chosen), however, is decidedly positive. Similarly, Choice D, *engaging* (appealing) is positive as well.

13. **(A, E)** What do we know about Crimond and his group? Crimond is the leader; he is passionately committed to a political cause. He is neither *indifferent* to (uninterested in) politics nor in *retreat* from politics. Instead, he is deeply *engaged* (involved) in politics.

    Crimond's disciples or followers, however, are far less committed than their leader; their political faith has lapsed. Thus, it is fair to say that Crimond's passionate engagement in politics is *inversely* proportional to his followers' lack of engagement. Their reactions are opposite.

14. **(C, E)** To suffer something is to experience or be subjected to (something bad or unpleasant). Therefore, the first missing word must be negative. Also, it must be something negative that can happen to the economy. *Contradictions* (refutations, denials) may be bad or unpleasant. However, "contradictions" is not a term used in economic circles: it has no specific application to economics. You can eliminate choice

A. *Digressions* (departures from the topic, ramblings) may be positive or negative; in addition, the term has no specific economic definition. You can eliminate Choice B. A *downturn*, however, by definition, is a decline in economic, business, or other activity. The economy frequently suffers downturns.

Although signals a contrast. Despite the downturns, the economy can recover: it has strong *recuperative* and self-correcting tendencies.

15. **(C)** To keep one's own counsel is to say nothing about what one thinks or plans. Thus, a government that keeps its own counsel can be described figuratively as a *reticent* (tight-lipped, uncommunicative) regime.

Reading Comprehension Questions

5

GRE reading comprehension questions test your ability to understand what you read—both content and technique. Each verbal section on the GRE includes two to five relatively short passages, each passage followed by one to four questions. A passage may deal with the **sciences** (including medicine, botany, zoology, chemistry, physics, geology, astronomy); the **humanities** (including art, literature, music, philosophy, folklore); or the **social sciences** (including history, economics, sociology, government). Some passages are strictly objective, explaining or describing a phenomenon or process neutrally. Others reflect a particular bias or point of view: the author is trying to convince the reader to share his or her opinion about the subject being discussed.

The GRE tends to take its reading passages from *The New York Review of Books*, from prestigious university presses (Harvard, Princeton, Oxford), from government publications, and from scholarly journals. Often the test-makers hit academically "hot" topics—biodiesel fuels, plate tectonics, damage to the ozone layer, Arthurian romance, the status of women's literature—that have aroused controversy over the past several decades. Frequently they edit these passages to make them more demanding both in vocabulary level and in grammatical complexity.

Some of the reading comprehension questions on the GRE are factual, asking you about specific details in the passages. Others ask you to interpret the passages, to make judgments about them. Still others ask you to recognize various techniques used by the authors or possible applications of their ideas to other circumstances. Some questions include lengthy and complex statements, as lengthy and complex as any sentences in the passage. Read the questions closely, as closely as you read the text. Be sure, in answering reading comprehension questions, that you read *all* the answer choices before deciding which is correct.

The reading comprehension portions of the GRE contain a few different question types. Some require you to click on a sentence within the passage that fits a particular description; others require you to select one or more answer choices to get a question right. In addition, logical reasoning questions appear in the reading comprehension portions of the test. Logical reasoning questions resemble questions found on the Logical Reasoning sections of the LSAT, the verbal sections of the GMAT, and so on. These questions ask you to determine the logical conclusion of an argument, to analyze the function and relationship of individual statements within an argument, to isolate the assumptions underlying an argument, and to distinguish what strengthens an argument from what weakens it.

Read the question *first*! Know what info you're seeking before you start your search.

The reading comprehension questions following each passage are not arranged in order of difficulty. They are arranged to reflect the way the passage's content is organized. A question based on information found at the beginning of the passage generally will come before a question based on information at the passage's end.

TESTING TACTICS

First Read the Question, Then Read the Passage

In responding to reading comprehension passages on the GRE, you often will have to consider more material than can fit conveniently on a single screen. You will confront a split screen similar to the one below. On one-half of the screen you will see the question you must answer; on the other you will see a segment of the passage under consideration. You will have to scroll through the passage in order to read the text in its entirety.

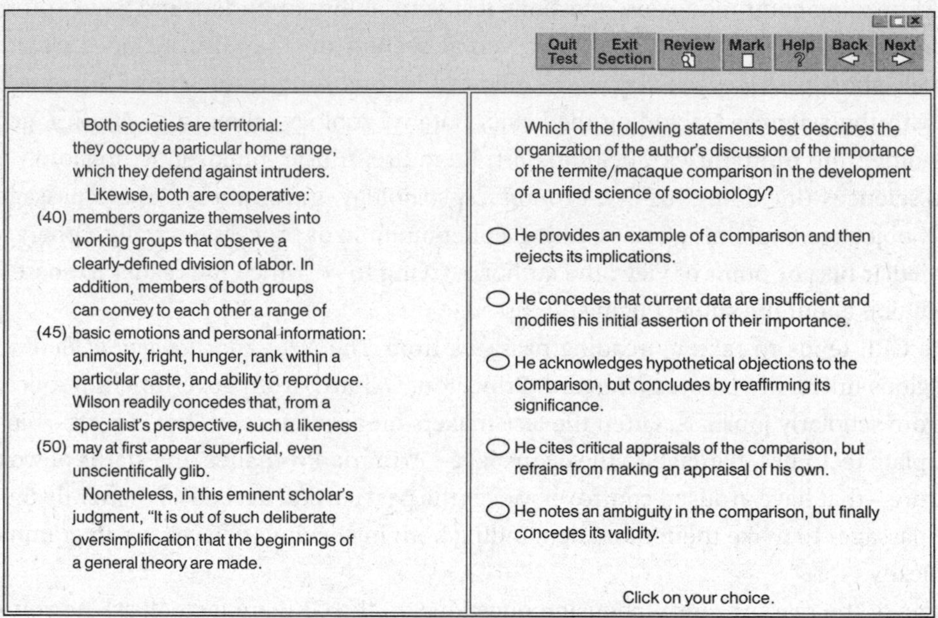

Under these conditions, clearly only one tactic works: first read the question, then read the passage.

It is particularly important to follow this tactic when you are dealing with the logical reasoning questions on the GRE. You must look at the question before you look at the argument.

Rather than jumping in blindly and analyzing each and every aspect of the argument—assumptions, central point, evidence, further application, logical flaws—do no more work than necessary. Look at the question stem. Then examine the argument. Know what aspect of the argument you are to concentrate on, and focus on it. You will save time and effort.

The logical reasoning reading question in the example below consists of a short passage followed by the question, "Which of the following best serves as an assumption that would make the argument above logically correct?" If you read the question before you read the passage, you will know that, as presented, the argument is faulty. As a result, you will be looking for the flaw as you read the passage and may already realize what's wrong before reading through the five answer choices. If you read the passage first, you may not catch the subtle flaw, and you may find the conclusion perfectly reasonable. Then when you read the question, and learn that the argument was not logically correct, you will be forced to go back and reread the passage, wasting valuable time.

CAUTION

Read only the question itself—do not read the answer choices before reading the passage. Doing so will confuse you and waste time.

EXAMPLE

In order to save $500,000 in this year's budget, the city council voted to freeze the salaries of its school building inspectors. This shortsighted decision is yet another example of the council's being penny wise and pound foolish. The cursory inspections that will result from this action will cause many structural defects to go undetected, resulting in millions more dollars being spent on repairs in the future.

In order for his argument to be logically correct, the author of the above argument used which of the following statements as an unstated underlying assumption?

- Ⓐ **City inspectors are already overpaid and so the wage freeze is warranted.**
- Ⓑ **The city council cares less about the safety of the school children than it does about saving money.**
- Ⓒ **If they do not receive an increase in their wages, school inspectors will become lax in performing their jobs.**
- Ⓓ **The council does not feel that cursory inspections will necessarily result in defects going undetected.**
- Ⓔ **The council will not authorize repairs in the future, so it will never have to incur the extra costs.**

The passage attempts to justify the conclusion that the city will eventually have to pay much more than it is now saving. Having first read the question, you were on the lookout for a flaw in the passage's logic (the passage's failure to state an underlying assumption). Therefore, you probably picked up the subtle shift from "freeze the salaries" in the first sentence to perform "cursory inspections" in the third sentence. If you did, you might have said to yourself, "The fact that the wages of the inspectors are not being raised does not necessarily mean that they will retaliate by rendering poorer service." This then is the gap in the passage's logic. To justify the conclusion presented, you need to assume that freezing salaries will result in cursory or slipshod inspections; and this is precisely what Choice C says.

In the preceding example, none of the other choices is an assumption upon which the argument depends. You can read and analyze each of the other choices before eliminating it, but that takes time. It is always better if you can anticipate the correct choice.

READING COMPREHENSION STRATEGIES

1. Read the question carefully, so that you are sure you understand what it is asking. Decide whether it is asking about a specific, readily identifiable detail within the passage, or whether it is asking about the passage as a whole. Note any key words in the question that may help you spot where the answer may be found.
2. Next, turn to the passage. Read as rapidly as you can with understanding, but do not force yourself. Do not worry about the time element. If you worry about not finishing the test, you will begin to take shortcuts and miss the correct answer in your haste.
3. As you read the opening sentences, try to anticipate what the passage will be about. Whom or what is the author talking about? What, in other words, is the *topic* of this passage?
4. As you scroll through the passage, think about what kind of writing this is. What is the author trying to do?

   Is the author trying to *explain* some aspect of the topic?
   Is the author trying to *describe* some aspect of the topic?
   Is the author trying to *argue* or debate some aspect of the topic?

   What does the author feel about this topic? What audience is the author addressing here? Answering these questions will give you a sense of the passage as a whole.
5. Use your scratch paper intelligently. Take brief notes of important words or phrases in different paragraphs so that you can scroll back to them quickly when you want to verify an answer choice. You may also want to note key words in question stems (words like EXCEPT and LEAST, which the test-makers capitalize for emphasis, and that restrict your answer choice).
6. Your first scrolling through the passage should give you a general impression of the scope of the passage and of the location of its major subdivisions. In order to answer the question properly, **you must go back to the passage to verify your answer choice.** Do not rely on your memory. Above all, do not rely on anything you may have learned from your reading or courses about the topic of this passage. Base your answer on what this passage says, not on what you know from other sources.

TACTIC

Learn to Spot the Major Reading Question Types

It helps to familiarize yourself with the major types of reading questions on the test. If you can recognize just what a given question is asking for, you will be better able to tell which reading tactic to apply.

Here are seven categories of reading questions you are likely to face:

1. **MAIN IDEA** Questions that test your ability to find the central thought of a passage or to judge its significance often take one of the following forms:

   The main point of the passage is to . . .
   The passage is primarily concerned with . . .
   The author's primary purpose in this passage is to . . .
   The chief theme of the passage can best be described as . . .
   Which of the following titles best states the central idea of the passage?
   Which of the following statements best expresses the main idea of the passage?

2. **FINDING SPECIFIC DETAILS** Questions that test your ability to understand what the author states *explicitly* are often worded:

   According to the author, . . .
   The author states all of the following EXCEPT . . .
   According to the passage, which of the following is true of the . . .
   The passage supplies information that would answer which of the following questions?
   Which of the following statements is (are) best supported by the passage?
   Which of the following is NOT cited in the passage as evidence of . . .?

3. **DRAWING INFERENCES** Questions that test your ability to go beyond the author's explicit statements and see what these statements imply may be worded:

   It can be inferred from the passage that . . .
   The author implies that . . .
   The passage suggests that . . .
   Which of the following statements about . . . can be inferred from the passage?

4. **APPLICATION TO OTHER SITUATIONS** (These are logical reasoning questions.) Questions that test your ability to recognize how the author's ideas might apply to other situations often are worded:

   With which of the following statements would the author of the passage be most likely to agree?
   With which of the following aphorisms would the author be in strongest agreement?
   The author's argument would be most weakened by the discovery of which of the following?
   The author's contention would be most clearly strengthened if which of the following were found to be true?
   Which of the following examples could best be substituted for the author's example of . . .?
   Which of the following statements would be most likely to begin the paragraph immediately following the passage?
   The author is most probably addressing which of the following audiences?

5. **TONE/ATTITUDE** Questions that test your ability to sense an author's emotional state often take the form:

   The author's attitude toward the problem can best be described as . . .
   The author regards the idea that . . . with . . .
   The author's tone in the passage is that of a person attempting to . . .
   Which of the following best describes the author's tone in the passage?

6. **TECHNIQUE** Questions that test your ability to recognize a passage's method of organization or technique often are worded:

   Which of the following best describes the development of this passage?
   In presenting the argument, the author does all of the following EXCEPT . . .
   The relationship between the second paragraph and the first paragraph can best be described as . . .
   In the passage, the author makes the central point primarily by . . .
   The organization of the passage can best be described as . . .

7. **DETERMINING THE MEANING OF WORDS FROM THEIR CONTEXT** Questions that test your ability to work out the meaning of unfamiliar words from their context often are worded:

    As it is used in the passage, the term . . . can best be described as . . .
    The phrase . . . is used in the passage to mean that . . .
    As used by the author, the term . . . refers to . . .
    The author uses the phrase . . . to describe . . .

TACTIC

3 When Asked to Find the Main Idea, Be Sure to Check the Opening and Summary Sentences of Each Paragraph

The opening and closing sentences of a paragraph are key sentences for you to read. They can serve as guideposts, pointing out the author's main idea.

When you are asked to determine a passage's main idea, *always* check the opening and summary sentences of each paragraph. Authors typically provide readers with a sentence that expresses a paragraph's main idea succinctly. Although such *topic sentences* may appear anywhere in the paragraph, readers customarily look for them in the opening or closing sentences.

Note that in GRE reading passages topic sentences are sometimes implied rather than stated directly. If you cannot find a topic sentence, ask yourself these questions:

1. Who or what is this passage about?
   (The subject of the passage can be a *person*, *place*, or *thing*. It can be something abstract, such as an *idea*. It can even be a *process*, or something in motion, for which no single-word synonym exists.)

2. What aspect of this subject is the author talking about?

3. What is the author trying to get across about this aspect of the subject?
   (Decide the most important thing that is being said about the subject. Either the subject must be *doing* something, or something is *being done* to it.)

Read the following natural science passage and apply this tactic.

According to Wilson,[1] only when we are able to apply the same parameters and mathematical principles to weighing both troops of rhesus macaques and termite colonies will a unified science of sociobiology finally exist. While recognizing that many of his colleagues question such an outcome, Wilson, one of sociobiology's leading proponents, finds himself simultaneously more and more struck by the functional similarities that characterize both insect and vertebrate societies and less concerned with the structural differences that divide them to such an apparently irreconcilable degree. Thus, he freely compares termites and macaques, pointing out numerous likenesses between them. Both societies are territorial: they occupy a particular home range, which they defend against intruders. Likewise, both are cooperative: members organize themselves into working groups that observe a clearly defined division of labor. In addition, members of both groups can convey to each other a range of basic emotions and personal information: animosity, fright, hunger, rank within a particular caste, and ability

[1]Edwin O. Wilson, Harvard professor and author of *Sociobiology*.

to reproduce. Wilson readily concedes that, from a specialist's perspective, such a likeness may at first appear superficial, even unscientifically glib. Nonetheless, in this eminent scholar's judgment, "it is out of such deliberate oversimplification that the beginnings of a general theory are made."

Now look at a typical main idea question on this passage.

EXAMPLE

Which of the following best summarizes the author's main point?

- **Ⓐ Facile and simplistic comparisons of animal societies could damage the prospects for the establishment of a unified science of sociobiology.**
- **Ⓑ It is necessary to study both biology and sociology in order to appreciate how animals as different as termites and rhesus macaques can be said to resemble each other.**
- **Ⓒ The majority of animal species arrange themselves in societies whose patterns of group behavior resemble those of human societies.**
- **Ⓓ It is worthwhile noting that animals as dissimilar as termites and rhesus monkeys observe certain analogous and predictable behavior patterns.**
- **Ⓔ An analysis of the ways in which insect and vertebrate societies resemble one another could supply the foundation for a unified science of sociobiology.**

Look at the opening and summary sentences of the passage: "only when we are able to apply the same parameters and mathematical principles to weighing both troops of rhesus macaques and termite colonies will a unified science of sociobiology finally exist . . . it is out of such deliberate oversimplification that the beginnings of a general theory are made." First, is there a person, place, thing, idea, or process that is common to both sentences? Are there any words in the last sentence that repeat something in the first? *A general theory* repeats the idea of *a unified science* of sociobiology. The paragraph's subject seems to be the unified science of sociobiology. Note as well the words pointing to expectations for the future—*will . . . finally exist, beginnings.* The tone of both sentences appears positive: when certain conditions are met, then, in Wilson's view, a specific result will follow—we will have a unified science or general theory of sociobiology. This result, however, is not guaranteed; it can come about only if the conditions are met.

Now turn to the answer choices. What does Choice A say about a unified science of sociobiology? It states some things could make it less likely, not more likely, to come about. Choice A is incorrect; it contradicts the passage's sense that a unified science of sociobiology is a *likely* outcome. Choices B, C, and D also may be incorrect: not one of them mentions a unified science of sociobiology. On closer inspection, Choice B proves incorrect: it makes an unsupported statement that one needs biological and sociological education to understand the resemblances between insects and vertebrates. Choice C also proves incorrect: it goes far beyond what the passage actually states. Where the passage speaks in terms of termites and rhesus macaques, Choice C speaks in terms of the *majority* of animal species and extends the comparison to include humans as well. Choice D, while factually correct according to the passage, is incorrect because it is too narrow in scope. It ignores the author's main point; it fails to include Wilson's interest in the possibility that a study of such similar patterns of behavior might lead to a general theory of sociobiology. The correct answer is Choice E. It is the only statement that speaks of a unified science of sociobiology as a likely possibility.

TACTIC

When Asked to Choose a Title, Watch Out for Choices That Are Too Specific or Too Broad

A paragraph has been defined as a group of sentences revolving around a central theme. An appropriate title for a paragraph, therefore, must express this central theme that each of the sentences in the paragraph develops. It should be neither too broad nor too narrow in scope; it should be specific and yet comprehensive enough to include all the essential ideas presented by the sentences. A good title for a passage of two or more paragraphs should express the thoughts of ALL the paragraphs.

When you are trying to select the best title for a passage, watch out for words that come straight out of the passage. They may not always be your best choice.

This second question on the sociobiology passage is a title question. Note how it resembles questions on the passage's purpose or main idea.

EXAMPLE

Which of the following is the best title for the passage?

Ⓐ Deceptive Comparisons: Oversimplification in Biological Research

Ⓑ An Uncanny Likeness: Termites and Rhesus Macaques

Ⓒ Structural Dissimilarities Between Insects and Vertebrates

Ⓓ Arguments Against a Science of Sociobiology

Ⓔ Sociobiology: Intimations of a General Theory

Choice A is incorrect: it is at once too narrow and too broad. It is too narrow in that the passage refers to *oversimplification* only in passing; it does not have oversimplification as its subject. It is too broad in that the passage emphasizes sociobiology, not the whole realm of biological research. It is also misleading; the passage never asserts that the deliberate oversimplification of the comparison between termites and macaques is intended to deceive.

Choice B is incorrect: it is too narrow. True, the author discusses the resemblance between termite and macaque societies; however, this likeness is not his subject. He discusses it to provide an example of the sort of comparison that may lay the groundwork for a potential science of sociobiology.

Choice C is also incorrect because it is not inclusive enough. It fails to mention the potential science of sociobiology. In addition, while the passage refers to *structural differences* between insect and vertebrate societies, it stresses structural similarities, not structural dissimilarities.

Choices D and E both mention the theory of sociobiology. Which is the better title for the piece? Clearly, Choice E: the author is not arguing against the potential science of sociobiology; he is reporting Wilson's opinions concerning the likelihood of sociobiology's emergence as a unified science. Thus, he finds in the termite-macaque comparison *intimations* or hints of an incipient general theory.

When Asked to Determine Questions of Attitude, Mood, or Tone, Look for Words That Convey Emotion, Express Values, or Paint Pictures

In determining the attitude, mood, or tone of an author, examine the specific diction used. Is the author using adjectives to describe the subject? If so, are they words like *fragrant, tranquil, magnanimous*—words with positive connotations? Or are they words like *fetid, ruffled, stingy*—words with negative connotations?

When we speak, our tone of voice conveys our mood—frustrated, cheerful, critical, gloomy, angry. When we write, our images and descriptive phrases get our feelings across.

The next model question on the Wilson passage is an attitude question. Note the range of feelings in the answer choices.

EXAMPLE

According to the author, Wilson's attitude toward the prospect of a unified theory in sociobiology can best be characterized as which of the following?

- **Ⓐ Unconditional enthusiasm**
- **Ⓑ Cautious optimism**
- **Ⓒ Unbiased objectivity**
- **Ⓓ Resigned acquiescence**
- **Ⓔ Strong displeasure**

How does Wilson feel about the possibility of a unified theory of sociobiology? The answer choices range from actively negative (*strong displeasure*) to actively positive (*unconditional enthusiasm*), with passively negative (*resigned acquiescence*), neutral (*unbiased objectivity*), and guardedly positive (*cautious optimism*) in between.

Wilson's attitude toward the possibility of a unified theory of sociobiology is implicit in the author's choice of words. It is clear that Wilson views this possibility positively; the whole thrust of his argument is that the current studies of the similarities between insect and vertebrate societies could mark the beginnings of such a unified theory and that the specialist should not dismiss these studies as glib or simpleminded. Note in the second sentence how the author describes Wilson as a leading proponent or champion of sociobiology, someone whose feelings about the field are by definition positive.

Wilson is certainly not unhappy or *strongly displeased* with this potential unified theory, nor is he merely long-suffering or *resigned* to it. Similarly, he is not *unbiased* and *objective* about it; he actively involves himself in arguing the case for sociobiology. Thus, you can eliminate Choices C, D, and E. But how do you decide between the two positive terms, *enthusiasm* and *optimism*, Choice A and Choice B? To decide between them, you must look carefully at the adjectives modifying them. Is Wilson's enthusiasm unqualified or *unconditional?* You may think so, but look again. The opening sentence states a basic condition that must be met before there can be a unified science of sociobiology: the same parameters and mathematical principles must be used to analyze insect and vertebrate societies. Though a proponent of sociobiology, Wilson is first and foremost a scientist, one who tests hypotheses and comes to logical conclusions about them. *Unconditional enthusiasm* seems to overstate his attitude.

Choice A appears incorrect. What about Choice B? Is Wilson's optimism *cautious* or guarded? Yes. According to the passage, Wilson is aware that specialists may well find fault with the sociobiologist's conclusions; the passage uses terms that convey values, first the negative "superficial, even unscientifically glib" to suggest the specialist's negative attitude toward sociobiology, then the positive "deliberate" to convey Wilson's own more positive response. The correct answer is Choice B.

TACTIC 6 When Asked About Specific Details in the Passage, Spot Key Words in the Question and Scan the Passage to Find Them (or Their Synonyms)

In developing the main idea of a passage, a writer will make statements to support his or her point. To answer questions about such supporting details, you *must* find a word or group of words in the passage supporting your choice of answer. The words "according to the passage" or "according to the author" should focus your attention on what the passage explicitly states. Do not be misled into choosing an answer (even one that makes good sense) if you cannot find it supported by the text.

Detail questions often ask about a particular phrase or line. In such cases, use the following technique:

1. Look for key words (nouns or verbs) in the answer choices.
2. Scroll through the passage, looking for those key words or their synonyms. (This is *scanning*. It is what you do when you look up someone's number in the phone directory.)
3. When you find a key word or its synonym in a sentence, reread that sentence to make sure the test-makers haven't used the original wording to mislead you.

Read the following brief passage and apply this tactic.

What is involved in the process of visual recognition? First, like computer data, visual memories of an object must be stored; then, a mechanism must exist for them to be retrieved. But how does this process work? The eye triggers the nerves into action. This neural activity constructs a picture in the brain's memory system, an internal image of the object observed. When the eye once again confronts that object, the object is compared with its internal image; if the two images match, recognition takes place.

Among psychologists, the question as to whether visual recognition is a parallel, single-step operation or a sequential, step-by-step one is the subject of much debate. Gestalt psychologists contend that objects are perceived as wholes in a parallel operation: the internal image is matched with the retinal impression in one single step. Psychologists of other schools, however, suggest the opposite, maintaining that the individual features of an object are matched serially with the features of its internal image. Some experiments have demonstrated that the more well-known an object is, the more holistic its internal image becomes, and the more parallel the process of recognition tends to be. Nonetheless, the bulk of the evidence appears to uphold the serial hypothesis, at least for simple objects that are relatively unfamiliar to the viewer.

Now look at the following question on a specific detail in the passage.

EXAMPLE

According to the passage, psychologists of the Gestalt school assume which of the following about the process of visual recognition?

Select *all* that apply.

A The image an object makes on the retina is exactly the same as its internal image.

B The mind recognizes a given object as a whole; it has no need to analyze the object's constituent parts individually.

C The process of matching an object with its internal image takes place in a single step.

You can arrive at the correct answer to this question by elimination.

First, quickly scan the passage looking for the key word *Gestalt.* The sentence mentioning Gestalt psychologists states they maintain that objects are recognized as wholes in a parallel procedure. The sentence immediately preceding defines a parallel procedure as one that takes only one step.

Now examine the statements. Do Gestalt psychologists maintain that an object's retinal image is exactly the same as its internal image? Statement A is unsupported by the passage.

Statement B is supported by the passage: lines 10–11 indicate that Gestalt psychologists believe objects are recognized as wholes.

Statement C is supported by the passage: lines 11–12 indicate that Gestalt psychologists believe matching is a parallel process that occurs in one step.

Choices B and C are both correct.

Note how necessary it is to point to specific lines in the passage when you answer questions on specific details.

TACTIC

When Asked to Make Inferences, Base Your Answers on What the Passage Implies, Not What It States Directly

In *Language in Thought and Action,* S. I. Hayakawa defines an inference as "a statement about the unknown made on the basis of the known."

Inference questions require you to use your own judgment. You must not take anything directly stated by the author as an inference. Instead, you must look for clues in the passage that you can use in deriving your own conclusion. You should choose as your answer a statement that is a logical development of the information the author has provided.

Try this relatively easy inference question, based on the previous passage about visual recognition.

EXAMPLE

One can infer from the passage that, in visual recognition, the process of matching

(A) requires neural inactivity

(B) cannot take place if an attribute of a familiar object has been altered in some way

(C) cannot occur when the observer looks at an object for the very first time

(D) has now been proven to necessitate both serial and parallel processes

(E) can only occur when the brain receives a retinal image as a single unit

Go through the answer choices, eliminating any choices that obviously contradict what the passage states or implies. Remember that in answering inference questions you must go beyond the obvious, beyond what the authors explicitly state, to look for logical implications of what they say.

Choice A is incorrect. Nothing in the passage suggests that the matching process requires or demands neural inactivity. Rather, the entire process of visual recognition, including the matching of images, requires neural *activity.*

Choice D is incorrect. It is clear from the passage that the matching process is not fully understood; nothing yet has been absolutely *proven.* The weight of the evidence *seems to* support the serial hypothesis, but controversy still surrounds the entire question.

Choice E is incorrect. It can be eliminated because it directly contradicts information in the passage stating that recognition most likely is a serial or step-by-step process rather than a parallel one receiving an image as a single unit.

Choices B and C are left. Which is a possible inference? Choice C seems a possible inference. Although the author never says so, it seems logical that you could not match an object if you had never seen it before. After all, if you had never seen the object before, you would have no prior internal image of it and would have nothing with which to match it. What about Choice B? Nothing in the passage mentions altering any attributes or features of a familiar object. Therefore, *on the basis of the passage* you have no way to deduce whether matching would or would not be possible if such a change took place. There is not enough information in the passage to justify Choice B as an inference. The correct answer is Choice C.

Another, more difficult inference question is based on the previous excerpt reviewing Wilson's *Sociobiology.* Review the passage briefly and see how you do with a question that very few of the examinees would have answered correctly.

EXAMPLE

According to Wilson, only when we are able to apply the same parameters and mathematical principles to weighing both troops of rhesus macaques and termite colonies will a unified science of sociobiology finally exist. While recognizing that many of his colleagues question such an outcome, Wilson, one of sociobiology's leading proponents, finds himself simultaneously more and more struck by the functional similarities that characterize both insect and vertebrate societies and less concerned with the structural differences that divide them to such an apparently irreconcilable degree. Thus, he freely compares termites and macaques, pointing out numerous likenesses between them. Both societies are territorial: they occupy a particular home range, which they defend against intruders. Likewise, both are cooperative: members organize themselves into working groups that observe a clearly-defined division of labor. In addition, members of both groups can convey to each other a range of basic emotions and personal information: animosity, fright, hunger, rank within a particular caste, and ability to reproduce. Wilson readily concedes that, from a specialist's perspective, such a likeness may at first appear superficial, even unscientifically glib. Nonetheless, in this eminent scholar's judgment, "it is out of such deliberate oversimplification that the beginnings of a general theory are made."

In analyzing insect and vertebrate societies, the passage suggests which of the following?

Ⓐ A clearly-defined division of labor is a distinguishing feature of most insect and vertebrate societies.

Ⓑ The caste structures of insect and vertebrate societies share certain likenesses.

Ⓒ Most insect and vertebrate societies utilize cooperative groups to hold and defend their home range.

Ⓓ The system of communication employed by members of insect societies resembles the system that members of vertebrate societies follow.

Ⓔ Major structural differences exist between insect and vertebrate societies.

Why would most examinees answer this question incorrectly? The reason is simple: it is easy to confuse statements made about specific insect and vertebrate societies with statements made about insect and vertebrate societies in general. In this passage, in the fourth sentence, the author switches from talking about Wilson's views of insect and vertebrate societies in general and refers to his comments on termites and macaques in specific.

Go through the answer choices one by one. Does the passage suggest that a clearly-defined division of labor distinguishes *most* insect and vertebrate societies? No. It merely states that, according to Wilson, a clearcut division of labor is a characteristic of termite and rhesus macaque societies. Choice A is incorrect: you cannot justify leaping from a single type of insect (*termites*) and a single type of vertebrate (*rhesus macaques*) to most insects and most vertebrates.

Does the passage suggest that the caste structure of insect societies shares certain likenesses with that of their counterparts in vertebrate societies? No. It merely states that, according to Wilson, termites and macaques both can communicate rank within a particular caste. Choice B is incorrect. You cannot assume that the caste structure of insect societies is similar to the caste structure of vertebrate societies just because termites and rhesus macaques both have some way to communicate caste status or rank.

Does the passage suggest that *most* insect and vertebrate societies form cooperative groups in order to hold and defend their home range or territory? No. It merely states that termites and macaques organize themselves into cooperative groups, and that both species occupy and defend territories. Choice C is incorrect: again, you cannot justify leaping from termites and rhesus macaques to *most* insects and *most* vertebrates.

Does the passage suggest that the system of communication employed by members of insect societies resembles that employed by members of vertebrate societies? No. It merely states that communication among termites and macaques serves similar ends; it says nothing about the specific systems of communication they use, nor about those systems of communication used by other insects and vertebrates. Choice D is incorrect.

The correct answer is Choice E. In the passage, the author states that Wilson has grown less impressed "with the structural differences that divide them (i.e., insect and vertebrate societies) to such an apparently irreconcilable degree." This suggests that, even though Wilson may be unimpressed with them, these differences exist and are *major.*

TACTIC

When Asked to Apply Ideas from the Passage to a New Situation, Put Yourself in the Author's Place

GRE application questions require you to do three things:

1. **REASON—**If X is true, then Y must also be true.
2. **PERCEIVE FEELINGS—**If the author feels this way about subject A, he probably feels a certain way about subject B.
3. **SENSE A LARGER STRUCTURE—**This passage is part of an argument for a proposal, or part of a description of a process, or part of a critique of a hypothesis.

Like inference questions, application questions require you to go beyond what the author explicitly states. Application questions, however, ask you to go well beyond a simple inference, using clues in the passage to interpret possible reasons for actions and possible outcomes of events. Your concern is to comprehend how the author's ideas might apply to other situations, or be affected by them. To do so, you have to put yourself in the author's place.

Imagine you are the author. What are you arguing for? Given what you have just stated in the passage, what would you want to say next? What might hurt your argument? What might make it stronger? What kind of audience would appreciate what you have to say? Whom are you trying to convince? If you involve yourself personally with the passage, you will be better able to grasp it in its entirety and see its significance.

Answer the following application question based on the previous passage discussing Wilson's *Sociobiology.*

EXAMPLE

Which of the following statements would be most likely to begin the paragraph immediately following the passage?

- **(A) Wilson has raised a problem in ethical philosophy in order to characterize the essence of the discipline of sociobiology.**
- **(B) It may not be too much to say that sociology and the other social sciences are the last branches of biology waiting to be integrated into neo-Darwinist evolutionary theory.**
- **(C) Although behavioral biology is traditionally spoken of as if it were a unified subject, it is now emerging as two distinct disciplines centered on neurophysiology and sociobiology, respectively.**
- **(D) The formulation of a theory of sociobiology constitutes, in Wilson's opinion, one of the great manageable problems of biology for the next twenty or thirty years.**
- **(E) In the past, the development of sociobiology has been slowed by too close an identification with ethology and behavioral psychology.**

As you know from answering the previous main idea and attitude questions, Wilson's point is that students of insect and vertebrate societies may be on the verge of devising a general theory of sociobiology. Like Wilson, the author of the passage appears optimistic about the likelihood of developing this unified science. At the same time, again like Wilson, he is cautious; he too does not wish to overstate the case.

Put yourself in the author's place. What would you be likely to say next? The author has just been describing Wilson's hopeful view of the prospects for putting together a general theory of sociobiology. What would be more natural than for him next to discuss Wilson's opinion of a time frame for formulating this general theory? Choice D, with its confident yet judicious view of the formulation of a theory of sociobiology as "one of the great *manageable* problems of biology for the next twenty or thirty years," seems a logical extension of what the passage has just been saying. While Choices A, B, C, and E all touch on sociobiology in some way, none of them follows as naturally from the passage's immediate argument.

TACTIC

When Asked to Give the Meaning of an Unfamiliar Word, Look for Nearby Context Clues

When a question in the reading comprehension part of an examination asks for the meaning of a word, that meaning can usually be deduced from the word's context. The purpose of this kind of question is to determine how well you can extract meaning from the text, not how extensive your general vocabulary is.

Sometimes the unknown word is a common word used in one of its special or technical meanings. For example:

> **He *threw* the pot in an hour. The wheel turned busily and the shape grew quickly as his fingers worked the wet, spinning clay. (*Throw* here means to shape on a potter's wheel.)**

At other times, the unknown word may bear a deceptive resemblance to a known word.

> **He fell *senseless* to the ground. (He was unconscious. He did not fall foolishly or nonsensically to the ground.)**

Just because you know *one* meaning of a word, do not assume that you know its meaning as it is used in a particular passage. You must look within the passage for clues. Often authors will use an unfamiliar word and then immediately define it within the same sentence. The two words or groups of words are juxtaposed—set beside one another—to make their relationship clear. Commas, hyphens, and parentheses may signal this relationship.

1. The *rebec*, a medieval stringed instrument played with a bow, has only three strings.
2. *Paleontologists*—students of fossil remains—explore the earth's history.
3. Most mammals are *quadrupeds* (four-footed animals).

Often an unfamiliar word in one clause of a sentence will be defined or clarified in the sentence's other clause.

1. The early morning dew had frozen, and everything was covered with a thin coat of *rime*.
2. Cowards, we use *euphemisms* when we cannot bear the truth, calling our dead "the dear departed," as if they have just left the room.

Refer once more to the passage on visual recognition to answer the following question.

EXAMPLE

What is involved in the process of visual recognition? First, like computer data, visual memories of an object must be stored; then, a mechanism must exist for them to be retrieved. But how does this process work? The eye triggers the nerves into action. This neural activity constructs a picture in the brain's memory system, an internal image of the object observed. When the eye once again confronts that object, the object is compared with its internal image; if the two images match, recognition takes place.

Among psychologists, the question as to whether visual recognition is a parallel, single-step operation or a sequential, step-by-step one is the subject of much debate. Gestalt psychologists contend that objects are perceived as wholes in a parallel operation: the internal image is matched with the retinal impression in one single step. Psychologists of other schools, however, suggest the opposite, maintaining that the individual features of an object are matched serially with the features of its internal image. Some experiments have demonstrated that the more well-known an object is, the more holistic its internal image becomes, and the more parallel the process of recognition tends to be. Nonetheless, the bulk of the evidence appears to uphold the serial hypothesis, at least for simple objects that are relatively unfamiliar to the viewer.

Which of the following phrases could best replace "the more holistic its internal image becomes" (lines 15–16) without significantly changing the sentence's meaning?

Ⓐ the more its internal image increases in detail
Ⓑ the more integrated its internal image grows
Ⓒ the more its internal image decreases in size
Ⓓ the more it reflects its internal image
Ⓔ the more indistinct its internal image appears

What words or phrases in the vicinity of "the more holistic its internal image becomes" give you a clue to the phrase's meaning? The phrase immediately following, "becomes more parallel." If the recognition process becomes more parallel as an object becomes more familiar, then matching takes place in one step in which all the object's features are simultaneously transformed into a single internal representation. Thus, to say that an object's internal image becomes more holistic is to say that it becomes more *integrated* or whole. The correct answer is Choice B.

TACTIC 10 Familiarize Yourself with the Technical Terms Used to Describe a Passage's Organization

Another aspect of understanding the author's point is understanding how the author organizes what he has to say. You have to understand how the author makes his point, figure out whether he begins with his thesis or main idea or works up to it gradually. Often this means observing how the opening sentence or paragraph relates to the passage as a whole.

Here is a technique question based on the last two sentences of the passage about sociobiology. Those lines are repeated so that you can easily refer to them.

EXAMPLE

". . . Wilson readily concedes that, from a specialist's perspective, such a likeness may at first appear superficial, even unscientifically glib. Nonetheless, in this eminent scholar's judgment, "it is out of such deliberate oversimplification that the beginnings of a general theory are made."

Which of the following statements best describes the organization of the author's discussion of the importance of the termite/macaque comparison in the development of a unified science of sociobiology (lines 15–18)?

Ⓐ He provides an example of a comparison and then rejects its implications.
Ⓑ He concedes that current data are insufficient and modifies his initial assertion of their importance.
Ⓒ He acknowledges hypothetical objections to the comparison, but concludes by reaffirming its significance.
Ⓓ He cites critical appraisals of the comparison, but refrains from making an appraisal of his own.
Ⓔ He notes an ambiguity in the comparison, but finally concedes its validity.

Consider the first clause of each answer choice.

In his comment on how things may seem from the specialist's point of view, does the author *provide an example* of a comparison? No. He refers to a comparison made earlier. Therefore, you can eliminate Choice A.

Does he *concede the insufficiency* of current data? Not quite. He states that some people may quarrel with the comparison because it seems glib to them; he does not grant that they are right or that the data are inadequate. Therefore, you can eliminate Choice B.

Does he *acknowledge hypothetical objections* to the comparison? Definitely. Make a note to come back later to Choice C.

Does he cite *critical appraisals* of the comparison? Possibly. Again, make a note of Choice D.

Does he *note an ambiguity* in the comparison? No. He notes an objection to the comparison; he mentions no ambiguities within it. Therefore, you can eliminate Choice E.

Now consider the second clause of Choices C and D. Does the author *refrain from making an appraisal* of the comparison? No. He calls it a deliberate oversimplification that may bear fruit. Choice D is incorrect. Does the author conclude by *reaffirming the significance* of the termite/macaque comparison? Clearly he does; he quotes Wilson's conclusion that such oversimplified comparisons can provide the basis for an important general theory. The correct answer is Choice C.

TACTIC 11 In Answering Logical Reasoning Questions, Read Each Argument Very Carefully

Some students, who find that they can answer many reading comprehension questions correctly by skimming the passage without reading every word, attack logical reasoning questions in the same way. This is a very poor strategy.

First of all, the temptation to skim logical argument passages should be less, since these passages are much shorter than the usual run of reading comprehension passages, and skimming them will save less time. More important, in logical reasoning passages, it is not enough to have a general idea about the argument; you must be able to analyze the argument very closely.

A cursory reading is not sufficient to pick up a subtle flaw in logic or to ascertain what unstated premise the author is assuming to be true.

TACTIC 12 In Tackling Logical Reasoning Questions, Always Identify the Conclusion of the Argument

It is imperative that you are absolutely clear about what conclusion the author of the argument claims to have reached. The three most common situations are as follows:

- The conclusion is the last sentence of the passage, often introduced by a word such as *therefore, so, thus, hence,* or *consequently.* Here is a simple example of this type of argument:

  Joan Smith has those qualities that we seek in our congressional leaders. She is honest, hardworking, intelligent, and dedicated. Having served for ten years in the House of Representatives, she has the requisite experience to be an effective United States Senator. Therefore, you should enthusiastically vote for Ms. Smith in this year's election.

- The conclusion is the first sentence of the passage, followed by the supporting evidence. In such a case, there is no word such as therefore signaling the conclusion, but it is still very easy to spot. For example, the preceding argument could have been presented as follows:

Joan Smith deserves your vote for United States Senator. She has those qualities that we seek in our congressional leaders. She is honest, hardworking, intelligent, and dedicated. In addition, having served for ten years in the House of Representatives, she has the requisite congressional experience to be an effective United States Senator.

- The conclusion is not in the passage. In such cases, the question usually asks you to identify the conclusion that is implicit in the argument. For example, if in the two preceding arguments the last or first sentence, respectively, had been omitted, you would have had no difficulty determining that the author of the passage wanted you to vote for Joan Smith. The question might have asked, "Which of the following five statements can most reasonably be inferred from the statements in the given passage?"

TACTIC 13 In Tackling Logical Reasoning Questions, Pay Particular Attention to Signal Words in the Question (and in the Argument As Well)

In answering logical reasoning questions, you must read closely both the argument and the question or questions based on it. When you do so, be on the lookout for certain signal words that can clarify the situation. In particular, be alert for:

CAUSE AND EFFECT SIGNAL WORDS

The following words often signal the conclusion of an argument:

accordingly	so
consequently	therefore
for this reason	thus
hence	

CONTRAST SIGNAL WORDS

The following words often suggest a reversal of thought within an argument or question stem:

although	instead
but	nevertheless
despite	not
even though	on the contrary
except	on the other hand
however	rather than
in contrast	unlike

Notice that in the following logical reasoning problem several of these words are present: the argument contains the words *despite, not,* and *consequently,* and the question stem has the word *except.* Each of these words plays a role in your reasoning.

EXAMPLE

Despite the fact that River City increased the average class size by more than 15% in all grades two years ago, this year's average SAT scores for the junior class were the highest ever. This shows that class size is not a good determinant of student performance. Consequently, other school districts should follow River City's lead and save money by increasing the size of their classes.

Each of the following statements, if true, is a valid objection to this argument EXCEPT:

Ⓐ The advantages of smaller classes are more pronounced in elementary school than in high school.

Ⓑ The number of classroom discipline problems reported by teachers is directly proportional to the number of students in the classroom.

Ⓒ Japanese schools have a lower teacher-to-student ratio than American schools do and have generally better results on international standardized tests.

Ⓓ Three years ago, the eighth graders in River City Middle School had very high scores on their standardized tests.

Ⓔ The effects on students of learning in larger classes take at least three or four years to manifest themselves completely.

It is implicit in the question stem that the argument is not very persuasive, and that there are several possible objections to it that could be raised. In fact, the question stem tells you that four of the five statements listed raise valid objections to the argument presented. Your job is to determine the only one that does not.

The conclusion that larger class sizes are not detrimental to student learning is based on a single piece of data concerning high school juniors.

Choice A raises the objection that looking at the results of high school students on the SAT does not tell the whole story and that elementary school students will suffer from the larger classes.

Choice E raises an even stronger objection. It suggests that all students may suffer the consequences of increased class sizes; it will just take more time until the results are clearly discernible.

Choice B raises a completely different objection. Even if student academic performance is not adversely affected by larger class sizes, there are behavioral disadvantages to having large classes.

Choice D raises still another objection to the argument, the support for which is based on the performance of this year's junior class. Because three years ago, as eighth graders, the members of this class had very high test scores, it is possible that this group of students is brighter than the average. If so, it is likely that they would excel regardless of class size, whereas other students might suffer more.

Choice C is slightly harder to analyze. If the word *lower* makes you think *smaller,* Choice C seems to say that smaller classes, at least in Japan, result in higher test scores, and are thus beneficial. This then would be yet another valid objection to the given argument. If, however, you are confident in your analysis to this point and are sure that Choices A, B, D, and E are incorrect, by the process of elimination, Choice C *must* be the correct answer. So look at Choice C again. In fact, Choice C refers to a lower teacher-to-student ratio. A lower teacher-to-student ratio means more students per teacher, not fewer students. If there are more students per teacher, that means there will be larger class sizes, not smaller. Choice

C then is not an objection to the argument; it supports the argument by showing that good results can occur in larger classes.

As this example shows, logical reasoning reading questions must be read very carefully. Do not attempt to analyze them too quickly.

TACTIC

Always Use the Process of Elimination to Reject Incorrect Choices

From Tactic 1, you know that in logical reasoning reading questions, as in all computer-based reading questions, you should always read the question first. This, of course, does not guarantee that you will know the correct answer before you read the answer choices; in fact, more often than not, you won't. What do you do then? Use the process of elimination. In the best-case scenario, using the process of elimination will allow you to zoom in on the correct answer; at worst, it will eliminate some obvious wrong choices and allow you to make an educated guess and move on.

See how the process of elimination works on the next logical reasoning reading question.

EXAMPLE

In the United States between 1993 and 1998, the number of people on death row continued to increase, but at a rate lower than that of the general prison population.

Which of the following statements directly contradicts this claim?

- **Ⓐ The number of death row inmates increased slightly from 1993 to 1998.**
- **Ⓑ Among people convicted of murder, the proportion of those who were sentenced to death decreased from 1993 to 1998.**
- **Ⓒ Each year from 1993 to 1998, more death row inmates were executed than in the previous year.**
- **Ⓓ Each year from 1993 to 1998, fewer people were sentenced to death than in the previous year.**
- **Ⓔ The proportion of death row inmates among the general prison population rose from 0.6% in 1993 to 0.8% in 1998.**

Even though the passage is only one sentence long, you should have read the question "Which of the following statements directly contradicts this claim?" first. Unfortunately, there are many ways to contradict the claim made in that sentence. So there is no point in trying to think of one, and then looking to see if it is one of the five choices. You simply must read each choice, and then, by process of elimination, find the correct one.

- The passage states that the death row population increased. Choice A confirms this (and says nothing about the general prison population). Choice A is incorrect.
- Choice B compares the proportion of new death row inmates to the number of people convicted of murder, not to the general prison population. Choice B is incorrect.
- Choice C states that the number of people executed each year went up. If the number of people executed each year went up, the death row population might have decreased (thereby contradicting the first part of the claim), but not necessarily (not if they were replaced by many more people being sentenced to death). Choice C is incorrect.

CAUTION

Do not spend even one second deciding whether you think the claim in the passage or any of the choices is true. This is completely irrelevant. Examine only the logic of the argument. Look for a statement that, if true, would mean that the claim is false.

- Choice D doesn't guarantee that the claim is true, but it comes closer to confirming it than to contradicting it. Even if fewer people were sentenced to death each year, some still were, so the number of people on death row might have increased. Again, this answer choice makes no reference to the general prison population. Choice D is incorrect.
- Choice E is a little harder to analyze. Because it refers to an increase, many students would not choose it, thinking it confirms rather than refutes the claim. However, you must analyze it. Having definitively rejected Choices A, B, C, and D, you know, by the process of elimination, that Choice E must be the correct answer. Let's examine why, in fact, it is.
- The passage claims the death row population increased at a slower rate than the prison population did. This means that the proportion of death row inmates in the prison population actually decreased. Choice E, which states that the proportion increased, is a direct contradiction of that claim.

NOTE

1. **Although any of the Choices A, B, C, and D could be true without the claim's being true, none of them is inconsistent with the truth of the claim.**
2. **Choices B, C, and D each introduce an extraneous issue. None of the following—the number of murder convictions, the number of executions, the number of people sentenced to death—is directly relevant to the claim.**

TACTIC 15 In Questions About Weakening or Strengthening an Argument, Examine the Argument for Any Unstated Assumptions It Makes

An argument is based upon certain assumptions made by its author. If an argument's basic premises are sound, the argument is strengthened. If the argument's basic premises are flawed, the argument is weakened.

Pinpoint what the argument assumes. Then compare that assumption with the answer choices. If the question asks you to choose an answer that most strengthens the argument, look for the answer choice that is most in keeping with the argument's basic assumption. If the question asks you to choose an answer that most weakens the argument, look for the answer choice that casts the most doubt on that assumption.

Apply this tactic to the following question.

EXAMPLE

In a recent speech, the president of a major college said, "It is extremely valuable for college-educated adults entering the workplace to be able to speak at least one foreign language fluently. I am, therefore, proposing that all of our students be encouraged to spend their junior year abroad."

Which of the following, if true, most weakens the president's argument?

Ⓐ Most students who study abroad for a full year return home with a good working knowledge of the language spoken in the country.
Ⓑ Only students who already know a language well will choose to study in a country where that language is spoken.
Ⓒ Some colleges do a much better job than others in teaching foreign languages.
Ⓓ Some students learn to speak foreign languages fluently by taking intensive immersion courses in the United States.
Ⓔ Many students who spend their junior year abroad learn to speak the language fluently, but cannot read and write with ease.

The argument claims that, in order for students to learn to speak foreign languages well, they should study abroad. It clearly assumes a high correlation between studying in a foreign country and learning to speak the language well. It assumes, at the least, that students who have studied abroad can speak a foreign language well, and, possibly, that students who have not studied abroad cannot.

Choice A is in keeping with the assumption inherent in the president's argument. If true, it would strengthen the argument, not weaken it. Choice E, by stating that many students who study abroad do not learn to read and write the language well, seems to cast doubt on the value of the junior year abroad program. However, since the president talked only about the value of being able to speak a foreign language well, Choice E also strengthens his argument.

Choices B and C are also incorrect. They neither strengthen nor weaken the president's argument. At worst, Choice B suggests that it may be difficult to convince some students to study abroad; however, it does not state that they should not be encouraged to do so. In order to weaken the president's argument, Choice C would have to go much further than it does; it would have to state explicitly that some colleges do such a good job that their students actually learn to speak foreign languages fluently.

The correct answer is Choice D. It states that it is possible for American students to learn to speak foreign languages fluently without studying abroad. Choice D weakens the president's argument. It does so by suggesting an alternative method by which college students could achieve the president's goal of speaking a foreign language fluently.

PRACTICE EXERCISES

Note: Although the reading passages on the computer-based GRE range from 50 to 400 words in length, the paper-based GRE taken by students in foreign countries includes reading passages of up to 800 words in length. Therefore, the following practice exercises present a selection of long and short passages to help students to prepare for either the computer-based or the paper-based test.

> **Directions:** Each of the following reading comprehension questions is based on the content of a passage. Read the passage and then determine the best answer choice for each question. Base your choice on what this passage *states directly* or *implies*, not on any information you may have gained elsewhere.

QUESTIONS 1–3 ARE BASED ON THE FOLLOWING PASSAGE.

One phase of the business cycle is the expansion phase. This phase is a twofold one, including recovery and prosperity. During the recovery period there is ever-growing expansion of existing facilities, and new facilities for production are created. More businesses are created and older ones expanded. Improvements of various kinds are made. **There is an ever-increasing optimism about the future of economic growth.** Much capital is invested in machinery or "heavy" industry. More labor is employed. More materials are required. As one part of the economy develops, other parts are affected. For example, a great expansion in automobiles results in an expansion of the steel, glass, and rubber industries. Roads are required; thus the cement and machinery industries are stimulated. Demand for labor and materials results in greater prosperity for workers and suppliers of raw materials, including farmers. This increases purchasing power and the volume of goods bought and sold. Thus, prosperity is diffused among the various segments of the population. This prosperity period may continue to rise and rise without an apparent end. However, a time comes when this phase reaches a peak and stops spiraling upwards. This is the end of the expansion phase.

1. Which of the following statements best exemplifies the optimism mentioned in the boldfaced sentence of the passage as being part of the expansion phase?

   Ⓐ Public funds are designated for the construction of new highways designed to stimulate tourism.
   Ⓑ Industrial firms allocate monies for the purchase of machine tools.
   Ⓒ The prices of agricultural commodities are increased at the producer level.
   Ⓓ Full employment is achieved at all levels of the economy.
   Ⓔ As technology advances, innovative businesses replace antiquated firms.

2. It can be inferred from the passage that the author believes that

   Ⓐ when consumers lose their confidence in the market, a recession follows
   Ⓑ cyclical ends to business expansion are normal
   Ⓒ luxury goods such as jewelry are unaffected by industrial expansion
   Ⓓ with sound economic policies, prosperity can become a fixed pattern
   Ⓔ the creation of new products is essential for prosperity

3. Which of the following statements would be most likely to begin the paragraph immediately following the passage?
   - Ⓐ Union demands may also have an effect on business cycles.
   - Ⓑ Some industries are, by their very nature, cyclical, having regular phases of expansion and recession.
   - Ⓒ Information is a factor that must be taken into consideration in any discussion of the expansion phase.
   - Ⓓ The farmer's role during the expansion phase is of vital importance.
   - Ⓔ The other phase of the business cycle is called the recession phase.

QUESTIONS 4 AND 5 ARE BASED ON THE FOLLOWING PASSAGE.

Both plants and animals of many sorts show remarkable changes in form, structure, growth habits, and even mode of reproduction in becoming adapted to a different climatic environment, type of food supply, or mode of living. This divergence in response to evolution is commonly expressed by altering the form and function of some part or parts of the organism, the original identity of which is clearly discernible. For example, the creeping foot of the snail is seen in related marine pteropods to be modified into a flapping organ useful for swimming, and is changed into prehensile arms that bear suctorial disks in the squids and other cephalopods. The limbs of various mammals are modified according to several different modes of life—for swift running (cursorial) as in the horse and antelope; for swinging in trees (arboreal) as in the monkeys; for digging (fossorial) as in the moles and gophers; for flying (volant) as in the bats; for swimming (aquatic) as in the seals, whales, and dolphins; and for other adaptations. The structures or organs that show main change in connection with this adaptive divergence are commonly identified readily as **homologous**, in spite of great alterations. Thus, the finger and wrist bones of a bat and whale, for instance, have virtually nothing in common except that they are definitely equivalent elements of the mammalian limb.

4. The author provides information that would answer which of the following questions? Select *all* that apply.
   - [A] What factors can cause change in organisms?
   - [B] What is the theory of evolution?
   - [C] How are horses' legs related to seals' flippers?

5. Which of the following words could best be substituted for the boldfaced word **homologous** without substantially changing the author's meaning?
   - Ⓐ altered
   - Ⓑ mammalian
   - Ⓒ corresponding
   - Ⓓ divergent
   - Ⓔ tactile

QUESTION 6 IS BASED ON THE FOLLOWING PASSAGE.

Although there are no physical differences between the visual organs of the two groups, the inhabitants of the Bilge Islands, when shown a card displaying a spectrum of colors, perceived fewer colors than do most persons in the United States.

6. Which of the following conclusions can most reliably be drawn from the information above?
   - Ⓐ Human color perception is at least partly determined by factors other than the physical structure of the visual organs.
   - Ⓑ The Bilge Islanders are probably taught in childhood to recognize fewer colors than are persons in the United States.
   - Ⓒ Differences in social structure probably affect color perception.
   - Ⓓ Color perception in humans is influenced by differences in physical environment.
   - Ⓔ Bilge Islanders may have fewer terms denoting colors in their language than do English-speaking persons.

QUESTIONS 7–9 ARE BASED ON THE FOLLOWING PASSAGE.

The layer of air next to the earth, which extends upward for about 10 miles, is known as the troposphere. On the whole, the troposphere makes up about 75% of all the weight of the atmosphere. It is the warmest part of the atmosphere because most of the solar radiation is absorbed by the earth's surface, which warms the air immediately surrounding it. A steady decrease of temperature with increasing elevation is a most striking characteristic of this region, whose upper layers are colder because of their greater distance from the earth's surface and because of the rapid radiation of heat into space. (Temperatures within the troposphere decrease about 3.5° per 1,000-foot increase in altitude.) Within the troposphere, winds and air currents distribute heat and moisture. Strong winds, called jet streams, are located at the upper levels of the troposphere. These jet streams are both complex and widespread in occurrence. They normally show a wave-shaped pattern and move from west to east at velocities of 150 mph, but velocities as high as 400 mph have been noted. The influences of changing locations and strengths of jet streams upon weather conditions and patterns are no doubt considerable. Current intensive research may eventually reveal their true significance.

7. It can be inferred from the passage that a jet plane will usually have its best average rate of speed on its run from

Ⓐ New York to San Francisco
Ⓑ Los Angeles to New York
Ⓒ Boston to Miami
Ⓓ Bermuda to New York
Ⓔ London to Washington, DC

8. It can be inferred from the passage that at the top of Jungfrau, which is 12,000 feet above the town of Interlaken in Switzerland, the temperature is usually

Ⓐ below freezing
Ⓑ about 42° colder than on the ground
Ⓒ warmer than in Interlaken
Ⓓ affected by the ionosphere
Ⓔ about 75° colder than in Interlaken

9. The passage states that the troposphere is the warmest part of the atmosphere because it

Ⓐ is closest to the sun
Ⓑ contains electrically charged particles
Ⓒ radiates heat into space
Ⓓ has winds and air currents that distribute the heat
Ⓔ is warmed by the earth's heat

QUESTIONS 10 AND 11 ARE BASED ON THE FOLLOWING PASSAGE.

"The emancipation of women," James Joyce told one of his friends, "has caused the greatest revolution in our time in the most important relationship there is—that between men and women." Other modernists agreed: Virginia Woolf, claiming that in about 1910, "human character changed," and, illustrating the new balance between the sexes, urged "Read the 'Agamemnon,' and see whether your sympathies are not almost entirely with Clytemnestra." D. H. Lawrence wrote, "perhaps the deepest fight for 2,000 years and more, has been the fight for women's independence."

But if modernist writers considered women's revolt against men's domination one of their "greatest" and "deepest" themes, only recently—in perhaps the past 15 years—has literary criticism begun to catch up with it. Not that the images of sexual antagonism that abound in modern literature have gone unremarked; far from it. But what we are able to see in literary works depends on the perspectives we bring to them, and now that women—enough to make a difference—are reforming canons and interpreting literature, the landscapes of literary history and the features of individual books have begun to change.

10. Acording to the passage, women are changing literary criticism by
    - Ⓐ noting instances of hostility between men and women
    - Ⓑ seeing the literature from fresh points of view
    - Ⓒ studying the works of early 20th-century writers
    - Ⓓ reviewing books written by feminists
    - Ⓔ resisting masculine influence

11. The author quotes James Joyce, Virginia Woolf, and D. H. Lawrence primarily in order to show that
    - Ⓐ these were feminist writers
    - Ⓑ although well-intentioned, they were ineffectual
    - Ⓒ before the 20th century there was little interest in women's literature
    - Ⓓ modern literature is dependent on the women's movement
    - Ⓔ the interest in feminist issues is not new

QUESTION 12 IS BASED ON THE FOLLOWING PASSAGE.

When you first saw a piece of African art, it impressed you as a unit; you did not see it as a collection of shapes or forms. This, of course, means that the shapes and volumes within the sculpture itself were coordinated so successfully that the viewer was affected emotionally.

It is entirely valid to ask how, from a purely artistic point of view, this unity was achieved. And we must also inquire whether there is a recurrent pattern or rules or a plastic language and vocabulary that is responsible for the powerful communication of emotion which the best African sculpture achieves. If there is such a pattern of rules, are these rules applied consciously or instinctively to obtain so many works of such high artistic quality?

It is obvious from the study of art history that an intense and unified emotional experience, such as the Christian credo of the Byzantine or 12th or 13th century Europe, when espoused in art forms, gave great unity, coherence, and power to art. But such an integrated feeling was only the inspirational element for the artist, only the starting point of the creative act. The expression of this emotion and its realization in the work could be done only with discipline and thorough knowledge of the craft. And the African sculptor was a highly trained workman. He started his apprenticeship with a master when a child, and he learned the tribal styles and the use of tools and the nature of woods so thoroughly that his carving became what Boas calls "motor action." He carved automatically and instinctively.

12. The information in the passage suggests that a mature African carver might best be compared to a
    - Ⓐ chef following a recipe
    - Ⓑ fluent speaker of English just now beginning to study French
    - Ⓒ batter who hits a home run the first time at bat
    - Ⓓ veteran fiddler expertly varying a traditional tune
    - Ⓔ senior editor correcting the prose of an unidiomatic author

QUESTION 13 IS BASED ON THE FOLLOWING PASSAGE.

The likelihood of America's exhausting her natural resources is growing less. All kinds of waste are being recycled, and new uses are constantly being found for almost everything. We are getting more use out of what we produce, and are manufacturing many new byproducts out of what we formerly threw away. It is, therefore, unnecessary for us to continue to ban logging in national parks, nature reserves, or areas inhabited by endangered species of animals.

13. Which one of the following most seriously undermines the conclusion of this argument?

Ⓐ The increasing amount of recycled material made available each year is equal to one-tenth of the increasing amount of natural material consumed annually.

Ⓑ Recent studies have shown that the number of endangered animals throughout the world fluctuates sharply and is chiefly determined by changes in meteorological conditions.

Ⓒ The logging industry contributes huge sums of money to political campaigns in states where it has a financial interest.

Ⓓ The techniques that make recycling possible are constantly improved so that more is reclaimed for lower costs each year.

Ⓔ Political contributions by the recycling industry are now greater than those of either the logging or animal protection interests.

ANSWER KEY

1. **B**
2. **B**
3. **E**
4. **A, C**
5. **C**
6. **A**
7. **B**
8. **B**
9. **E**
10. **B**
11. **E**
12. **D**
13. **A**

ANSWER EXPLANATIONS

1. **(B)** Take a close look at the sentences that immediately precede and follow the boldfaced sentence. What do they discuss? They talk about changes in business, in the facilities for production, in investments in "machinery or 'heavy' industry." These changes reflect business owners' optimism about the future of economic growth. If the owners of industrial firms were not optimistic that their businesses were going to grow, they would be unwilling to invest money in purchasing new equipment. The correct answer is Choice B.

2. **(B)** To the author, it is no big deal that an end comes to the business cycle's expansion phase. He describes the end of the prosperity cycle in a matter-of-fact manner: "a time comes when this phase reaches a peak and stops spiraling upwards." To him, *cyclical ends to business expansion are normal.*

   Use the process of elimination to make sure you have come up with the correct answer. Does the author believe that *when consumers lose their confidence in the market, a recession follows*? There is no evidence to support this statement: the passage never even mentions recessions or consumer loss of confidence. You can eliminate Choice A. Does the author believe that *luxury goods such as jewelry are unaffected by industrial expansion*? While the author discusses industrial expansion, he never mentions luxury goods. You can eliminate Choice C. Does the author believe that *with sound economic policies, prosperity can become a fixed pattern*? Definitely not. He states that a time comes when the prosperity period stops spiraling upwards; rather than becoming a fixed pattern, prosperity comes to an end. You can eliminate Choice D. Does the author believe that *the creation of new products is essential for prosperity*? Most likely not. He doesn't talk about new products; he certainly never asserts that their creation is essential for prosperity. You can eliminate Choice E. Only Choice B is left. It is the correct answer.

3. **(E)** What is the topic of this passage? It is the business cycle's expansion phase. From the passage's opening sentence ("One phase of the business cycle is the expansion phase.") to its concluding sentence ("This is the end of the expansion phase."), the author has been describing this one phase. By definition, a phase is one stage in a process of change or development. The business cycle therefore must consist of more than one phase. Thus, it is likely that the paragraph immediately following a description of the business cycle's expansion phase would describe a different phase of the business cycle. Choice E, *The other phase of the business cycle is called the recession phase,* is a likely introductory sentence for such a paragraph.

4. **(A, C)** The passage's opening sentence lists factors that may cause plants and animals to change or adapt. These factors include changes in the climate or in the sort of food

supply available. Thus, the author provides information to answer the question "What factors can cause change in organisms?" Choice A is correct.

Although the passage mentions the word *evolution*, it fails to provide information that would serve to answer the question "What is the theory of evolution?" Choice B is incorrect.

The passage also answers the question of how horses' legs are related to seals' flippers. Although adaptive divergence has caused them to look very different and to serve very different functions, they are definitely related as "equivalent elements of the mammalian limb." Choice C also is correct.

Pay particular attention to the instruction "Select *all* that apply." One, two, or three answers may be correct.

5. **(C)** The term *homologous*, as used in biology, means similar in position, structure, and evolutionary origin but not necessarily in function. In spite of great alterations, the structures or organs are equivalent elements; they *correspond* to one another.

6. **(A)** We are not told *why* the Bilge Islanders perceive fewer colors than most persons in the United States do. We are told only that the Bilge Islanders do perceive fewer colors than most Americans do, and that there are no physical differences between the islanders' visual organs and the visual organs of most Americans. From this information we can conclude only that *(h)uman color perception is at least partly determined by factors other than the physical structure of the visual organs.*

7. **(B)** If the jet streams move from west to east at high velocities, then this suggests that jet planes flying from the west (Los Angeles) to the east (New York) will enjoy a better rate of speed than jet planes flying from the east to the west.

8. **(B)** Lines 14–16 state that "[t]emperatures within the troposphere decrease about 3.5° per 1,000-foot increase in altitude." The question specifies that the top of Jungfrau is 12,000 feet above the town of Interlaken. If you multiply 3.5° by 12, your answer is 42°. This suggests that the temperature on the mountaintop should be *about 42° colder than on the ground.*

9. **(E)** Scan the passage looking for the key phrase "warmest part." You will find the phrase, and the answer to this question, in lines 5–9: "It is the warmest part of the atmosphere because most of the solar radiation is absorbed by the earth's surface, which warms the air immediately surrounding it." The warmth or heat of the earth's surface makes the troposphere the warmest part of the atmosphere.

10. **(B)** Scan the passage looking for the key phrase "literary criticism." You will find the phrase, and the answer to this question in lines 18–20, and the sentences immediately following. Women are interpreting literature from their own perspective; thus, they are changing literary criticism by *seeing literature from* their own *fresh points of view.*

11. **(E)** The passage's opening paragraph uses quotes from Joyce, Woolf, and Lawrence to establish the point that *the interest in feminist issues is not new.* Indeed, the passage states that Woolf claimed the shift took place early in the 20th century.

12. **(D)** We are told that the African sculptor was highly trained and followed the rules without thinking about them. Analogously, a *veteran fiddler* can expertly improvise variations on *a traditional tune* without giving the process much thought. Both creative

artists have over the course of time developed a mastery of their chosen medium. They need neither to follow recipes nor to impose rules on others.

13. **(A)** The passage argues that, because America's recycling efforts are so successful, we no longer need "to ban logging in national parks" and other environmentally sensitive areas. Choice A, however, points out that our recycling efforts have been far less successful than the passage attempts to show. Thus, Choice A seriously undermines the argument's conclusion.

Reviewing Vocabulary 6

The best way to develop a powerful vocabulary is to read extensively and well. However, it is possible to fine-tune your vocabulary by exploring unabridged dictionaries, in which usage notes make clear the fine distinctions between related words, by visiting dictionary websites, and by studying high-level vocabulary lists, such as our GRE Master Word List.

This chapter presents the GRE Master Word List and the GRE High-Frequency Word List, 320 words that have occurred and reoccurred on previously published GREs.

THE GRE HIGH-FREQUENCY WORD LIST

How many of the following words do you think you know? Half? Even more? First, check off those words that you recognize. Then, look up all 320 words and their definitions in our Master Word List. Pay particular attention to the following:

1. Words you recognize but cannot use in a sentence or define. You have a feel for these words—you are on the brink of knowing them. Effort you put into mastering these "borderline" words will pay off soon.
2. Words you thought you knew—but didn't. See whether any of them are defined in an unexpected way. If they are, make a special note of them. As you know from the preceding chapters, the GRE often stumps students with questions based on unfamiliar meanings of familiar-looking words.

In the course of your undergraduate career, you have undoubtedly developed your own techniques for building your vocabulary. One familiar technique—flash cards—often is used less than effectively. Students either try to cram too much information onto a flash card or try to cram too many flash cards into a practice session. If you wish to work with flash cards, try following these suggestions.

Writing the Flash Card

Be brief—but include all the information you need. On one side write the word. On the other side write a concise definition—two or three words at most—for each major meaning of the word you want to learn. Include an antonym, too: the synonym-antonym associations can help you remember both words. To fix the word in your mind, use it in a short phrase. Then write that phrase down.

Memorizing the Flash Card

Carry a few of your flash cards with you every day. Look them over whenever you have a spare moment or two. Work in short bursts. Try going through five flash cards at a time, shuffling through them quickly so that you can build up your rapid sight recognition of the words for the test. You want these words and their antonyms to spring to your mind instantaneously.

Test Your Memory

Don't look at the back of the card unless you must. Go through your five cards several times a day. Then, when you have mastered two or three of the cards and have them down pat, set those cards aside and add a couple of new ones to your working pile. That way you will always be working with a limited group, but you won't be wasting time reviewing words you already recognize on sight.

Never try to master a whole stack of flash cards in one long cram session. It won't work.

GRE HIGH-FREQUENCY WORDS

abate
aberrant
abeyance
abscond
abstemious
admonish
adulterate
aesthetic
aggregate
alacrity
alleviate
amalgamate
ambiguous
ambivalence
ameliorate
anachronism
analogous
anarchy
anomalous
antipathy
apathy
appease
apprise
approbation
appropriate [v.]
arduous
artless
ascetic
assiduous
assuage
attenuate
audacious
austere
autonomous
aver
banal
belie
beneficent
bolster
bombastic
boorish
burgeoning
burnish
buttress
cacophonous
capricious
castigation
catalyst
caustic
chicanery
cogent
commensurate
compendium
complaisant
compliant
conciliatory
condone
confound
connoisseur
contention
contentious
contrite
conundrum
converge
convoluted
craven
daunt
decorum
default
deference
delineate
denigrate
deride
derivative
desiccate
desultory
deterrent
diatribe
dichotomy
diffidence
diffuse
digression
disabuse
discerning
discordant
discredit
discrepancy
discrete
disingenuous
disinterested
disjointed
dismiss
disparage
disparate
dissemble
disseminate
dissolution
dissonance
distend
distill
diverge
divest
document [v.]
dogmatic
dormant
dupe
ebullient
eclectic
efficacy
effrontery
elegy
elicit
embellish
empirical
emulate
endemic
enervate
engender
enhance
ephemeral
equanimity
equivocate
erudite
esoteric
eulogy
euphemism
exacerbate
exculpate
exigency
extrapolation
facetious
facilitate
fallacious
fatuous
fawning
felicitous
fervor
flag [v.]
fledgling
flout
foment
forestall
frugality
futile
gainsay
garrulous
goad
grandiloquent
gregarious
guileless
gullible
harangue
homogeneous
hyperbole
iconoclastic
idolatry
immutable
impair
impassive
impede
impermeable
imperturbable
impervious
implacable
implicit
implode
inadvertently
inchoate
incongruity
inconsequential
incorporate
indeterminate
indigence
indolent
inert
ingenuous
inherent
innocuous
insensible
insinuate

insipid
insularity
intractable
intransigence
inundate
inured
irascible
irresolute
itinerary
laconic
lassitude
latent
laud
lethargic
levity
log
loquacious
lucid
luminous
magnanimity
malingerer
malleable
maverick
mendacious
metamorphosis
meticulous
misanthrope
mitigate
mollify
morose
mundane
negate
neophyte
obdurate
obsequious
obviate
officious
onerous
opprobrium
oscillate
ostentatious
paragon
partisan
pathological
paucity
pedantic
penchant
penury
perennial
perfidious
perfunctory
permeable
pervasive
phlegmatic
piety
placate
plasticity
platitude
plethora
porous
pragmatic
precarious
precipitate (ADJ.)
precursor
presumptuous
prevaricate
pristine
probity
problematic
prodigal
profound
prohibitive
proliferate
propensity
propitiate
propriety
proscribe
qualified
quibble
quiescent
rarefied
recalcitrant
recant
recondite
refractory
refute
relegate
reproach
reprobate
repudiate
rescind
resolution
resolve
reticent
reverent
sage [N.]
salubrious
sanction
satiate
saturate
savor
secrete
shard
skeptic
solicitous
soporific
specious
spectrum
sporadic
stigma
stint [V.]
stipulate
stolid
subpoena
subside
substantiate
supersede
supposition
tacit
tangential
tenuous
tirade
torpor
tortuous
tractable
transgression
truculence
vacillate
venerate
veracious
verbose
viable
viscous
vituperative
volatile
warranted
wary
welter
whimsical
zealot

THE GRE MASTER WORD LIST

The GRE Master Word List begins on the following page. As a graduate student you should be familiar with the majority of these words. You do not, however, need to memorize every word.

For those of you who wish to work your way through the word list and feel the need for a plan, we recommend that you follow the procedure described below in order to use the lists and the exercises most profitably:

1. Allot a definite time each day for the study of a list.
2. Devote at least one hour to each list.
3. First go through the list looking at the short, simple-looking words (seven letters at most). Mark those you don't know. In studying, pay particular attention to them.
4. Go through the list again looking at the longer words. Pay particular attention to words with more than one meaning and familiar-looking words with unusual definitions that come as a surprise to you. Many tests make use of these secondary definitions.
5. List unusual words on index cards, which you can shuffle and review from time to time. (Use the flash card technique described earlier in this chapter.)
6. Using the illustrative sentences in the list as models, make up new sentences on your own.

For each word, the following is provided:

- The word (printed in heavy type).
- Its part of speech (abbreviated).
- A brief definition.
- A sentence or sentences illustrating the word's use.
- Whenever appropriate, related words together with their parts of speech.

The word lists are arranged in strict alphabetical order. In each list, words that appear also on the High-Frequency GRE Word List are marked with a square bullet (■).

Word List 1 abase–adverse

abase V. lower; degrade; humiliate. Anna expected to have to curtsy to the King of Siam; when told to cast herself down on the ground before him, however, she refused to *abase* herself. abasement, N.

abash V. embarrass. He was not at all *abashed* by her open admiration.

■ **abate** V. subside or moderate. Rather than leaving immediately, they waited for the storm to *abate*.

abbreviate V. shorten. Because we were running out of time, the lecturer had to *abbreviate* her speech.

abdicate V. renounce; give up. When Edward VIII *abdicated* the British throne, he surprised the entire world.

■ **aberrant** ADJ. abnormal or deviant. Given the *aberrant* nature of the data, we came to doubt the validity of the entire experiment.

aberration N. abnormality; departure from the norm; mental irregularity or disorder. It remains the consensus among investors on Wall Street that current high oil prices are a temporary *aberration* and that we shall soon see a return to cheap oil.

abet V. assist, usually in doing something wrong; encourage. She was unwilling to *abet* him in the swindle he had planned.

■ **abeyance** N. suspended action. Hostilities between the two rival ethnic groups have been in *abeyance* since the arrival of the United Nations peacekeeping force last month.

abhor V. detest; hate. She *abhorred* all forms of bigotry. abhorrence, N.

abjure V. renounce upon oath; disavow. Pressure from university authorities caused the young scholar to *abjure* his heretical opinions. abjuration, N.

abolish V. cancel; put an end to. The president of the college refused to *abolish* the physical education requirement. abolition, N.

abominable ADJ. detestable; extremely unpleasant; very bad. Mary liked John until she learned he was also dating Susan; then she called him an *abominable* young man, with *abominable* taste in women.

abortive ADJ. unsuccessful; fruitless. Attacked by armed troops, the Chinese students had to abandon their *abortive* attempt to democratize Beijing peacefully. abort, V.

abrasive ADJ. rubbing away; tending to grind down. Just as *abrasive* cleaning powders can wear away a shiny finish, *abrasive* remarks can wear away a listener's patience. abrade, V.

abridge V. condense or shorten. Because the publishers felt the public wanted a shorter version of *War and Peace*, they proceeded to *abridge* the novel.

abrogate V. abolish. Responding to conservative attacks against an outspoken radical professor, the dean pledged to resist such attempts to *abrogate* academic freedom.

■ **abscond** V. depart secretly and hide. The teller who *absconded* with the bonds went uncaptured until someone recognized him from his photograph on *America's Most Wanted*.

absolute ADJ. complete; totally unlimited; certain. Although the King of Siam was an *absolute* monarch, he did not want to behead his unfaithful wife without *absolute* evidence of her infidelity.

absolve V. pardon (an offense). The father confessor *absolved* him of his sins. absolution, N.

abstain V. refrain; withhold from participation. After considering the effect of alcohol on his athletic performance, he decided to *abstain* from drinking while he trained for the race.

■ **abstemious** ADJ. sparing in eating and drinking; temperate. Concerned whether her vegetarian son's *abstemious* diet provided him with sufficient protein, the worried mother pressed food on him.

abstinence N. restraint from eating or drinking. The doctor recommended total *abstinence* from salted foods. abstain, V.

abstract ADJ. theoretical; not concrete; nonrepresentational. To him, hunger was an *abstract* concept; he had never missed a meal.

abstruse ADJ. obscure; profound; difficult to understand. Baffled by the *abstruse* philosophical texts assigned in class, Dave asked Lexy to explain Kant's *Critique of Pure Reason*.

abysmal ADJ. bottomless. His arrogance is exceeded only by his *abysmal* ignorance.

academic ADJ. related to a school; not practical or directly useful. The dean's talk about reforming *academic* policies was only an *academic* discussion: we knew little, if anything, would change.

accede V. agree. If I *accede* to this demand for blackmail, I am afraid that I will be the victim of future demands.

acclaim V. applaud; announce with great approval. The sportscasters *acclaimed* every American victory in the Olympics and decried every American defeat. acclamation, N.

accolade N. award of merit. In Hollywood, an "Oscar" is the highest *accolade*.

accommodate V. oblige or help someone; adjust or bring into harmony; adapt. Mitch always did everything possible to *accommodate* his elderly relatives, from driving them to medical appointments to helping them with paperwork. (secondary meaning)

accomplice N. partner in crime. Because he had provided the criminal with the lethal weapon, he was arrested as an *accomplice* in the murder.

accord N. agreement. She was in complete *accord* with the verdict.

accretion N. growth; increase. Over the years Bob put on weight; because of this *accretion* of flesh, he went from size M to size XL. accrete, V.

acerbic ADJ. bitter or sour in nature; sharp and cutting. Noted for her *acerbic* wit and gossiping, Alice Roosevelt Longworth had a pillow in her home embroidered with the legend "If you can't say something good about someone, sit right here by me."

acerbity N. bitterness of speech and temper. The meeting of the United Nations Assembly was marked with such *acerbity* that observers held little hope of reaching any useful settlement of the problem.

acknowledge V. recognize; admit. Although I *acknowledge* that the Beatles' tunes sound pretty dated nowadays, I still prefer them to the gangsta rap songs my brothers play.

acme N. peak; pinnacle; highest point. Welles's success in *Citizen Kane* marked the *acme* of his career as an actor; never again did he achieve such popular acclaim.

acquiesce V. assent; agree passively. Although she appeared to *acquiesce* to her employer's suggestions, I could tell she had reservations about the changes he wanted made. acquiescence, N.; acquiescent, ADJ.

acquittal N. deliverance from a charge. His *acquittal* by the jury surprised those who had thought him guilty. acquit, V.

acrid ADJ. sharp; bitterly pungent. The *acrid* odor of burnt gunpowder filled the room after the pistol had been fired.

acrimonious ADJ. bitter in words or manner. The candidate attacked his opponent in highly *acrimonious* terms. acrimony, N.

acuity N. sharpness. In time his youthful *acuity* of vision failed him, and he needed glasses.

acumen N. mental keenness. Her business *acumen* helped her to succeed where others had failed.

acute ADJ. quickly perceptive; keen; brief and severe. The *acute* young doctor realized immediately that the gradual deterioration of her patient's once-*acute* hearing was due to a chronic illness, not an *acute* one.

adamant ADJ. hard; inflexible. In this movie Bronson played the part of a revenge-driven man, *adamant* in his determination to punish the criminals who destroyed his family. adamancy, N.

adapt V. alter; modify. Some species of animals have become extinct because they could not *adapt* to a changing environment.

address V. direct a speech to; deal with or discuss. Due to *address* the convention in July, Brown planned to *address* the issue of low-income housing in his speech.

adept ADJ. expert at. She was *adept* at the fine art of irritating people. also N.

adhere V. stick fast. I will *adhere* to this opinion until proof that I am wrong is presented. adhesion, N.; adherence, N.

adherent N. supporter; follower. In the wake of the scandal, the senator's one-time *adherents* quietly deserted him.

adjacent ADJ. adjoining; neighboring; close by. Philip's best friend Jason lived only four houses down the block, near but not immediately *adjacent*.

■ **admonish** V. warn; reprove. When her courtiers questioned her religious beliefs, Mary Stuart *admonished* them, declaring that she would worship as she pleased.

adorn V. decorate. Wall paintings and carved statues *adorned* the temple. adornment, N.

adroit ADJ. skillful. Her *adroit* handling of the delicate situation pleased her employers.

adulation N. flattery; admiration. The rock star thrived on the *adulation* of his groupies and yes-men. adulate, V.

■ **adulterate** V. make impure by adding inferior or tainted substances. It is a crime to *adulterate* foods without informing the buyer; when consumers learned that Beechnut had *adulterated* its apple juice by mixing the juice with water, they protested vigorously. adulteration, N.

advent N. arrival. Most Americans were unaware of the *advent* of the Nuclear Age until the news of Hiroshima reached them.

adversary N. opponent; enemy. Batman struggled to save Gotham City from the machinations of his wicked *adversary*, the Joker.

adverse ADJ. unfavorable; hostile. The recession had a highly *adverse* effect on Father's investment portfolio: he lost so much money that he could no longer afford the butler and the upstairs maid.

Word List 2 adversity–anarchy

adversity N. poverty; misfortune. We must learn to meet *adversity* gracefully.

advocacy N. support; active pleading on behalf of someone or something. No threats could dissuade Bishop Desmond Tutu from his *advocacy* of the human rights of black South Africans.

■ **aesthetic** ADJ. artistic; dealing with or capable of appreciating the beautiful. The beauty of Tiffany's stained glass appealed to Alice's *aesthetic* sense. aesthete, N.

affable ADJ. easily approachable; warmly friendly. Accustomed to cold, aloof supervisors, Nicholas was amazed at how *affable* his new employer was. affability, N.

affected ADJ. artificial; pretended; assumed in order to impress. His *affected* mannerisms—his "Harvard" accent, his air of boredom, his use of obscure foreign words—bugged us: he acted as if he thought he was too good for his old high school friends. affectation, N.

affiliation N. joining; associating with. Our hospital's *affiliation* with top medical facilities, such as Boston Children's Hospital and Beth Israel Medical Center, has enabled us to expand the expert care we provide to residents of the North Shore.

affinity N. kinship. She felt an *affinity* with all who suffered; their pains were her pains.

affirmation N. positive assertion; confirmation; solemn pledge by one who refuses to take an oath. Despite Tom's *affirmations* of innocence, Aunt Polly still suspected he had eaten the pie.

affliction N. state of distress; cause of suffering. Even in the midst of her *affliction*, Elizabeth tried to keep up the spirits of those around her.

affluence N. abundance; wealth. Foreigners are amazed by the *affluence* and luxury of the American way of life.

affront N. insult; offense; intentional act of disrespect. When Mrs. Proudie was not seated beside the Archdeacon at the head table, she took it as a personal *affront* and refused to speak to her hosts for a week. also V.

agenda N. items of business at a meeting. We had so much difficulty agreeing upon an *agenda* that there was very little time for the meeting.

agglomeration N. collection; heap. It took weeks to assort the *agglomeration* of miscellaneous items she had collected on her trip.

aggrandize V. increase or intensify; raise in power, wealth, rank or honor. The history of the past quarter century illustrates how a President may *aggrandize* his power to act aggressively in international affairs without considering the wishes of Congress.

■ **aggregate** V. gather; accumulate. Before the Wall Street scandals, dealers in so-called junk bonds managed to *aggregate* great wealth in short periods of time. also ADJ. aggregation, N.

aggressor N. attacker. Before you punish both boys for fighting, see whether you can determine which one was the *aggressor*.

aghast ADJ. horrified; dumbfounded. Miss Manners was *aghast* at the crude behavior of the fraternity brothers at the annual toga party.

agility N. nimbleness. The *agility* of the acrobat amazed and thrilled the audience.

agitate V. stir up; disturb. Her fiery remarks *agitated* the already angry mob.

agnostic N. one who is skeptical of the existence of a god or any ultimate reality. *Agnostics* say we can neither prove nor disprove the existence of God; we simply have no way to know. also ADJ.

■ **alacrity** N. cheerful promptness; eagerness. Phil and Dave were raring to get off to the mountains; they packed up their ski gear and climbed into the van with *alacrity*.

alienate V. make hostile; separate. Her attempts to *alienate* the two friends failed because they had complete faith in each other.

allay V. calm; pacify. The crew tried to *allay* the fears of the passengers by announcing that the fire had been controlled.

allege V. state without proof. Although it is *alleged* that she has worked for the enemy, she denies the *allegation* and, legally, we can take no action against her without proof. allegation, N.

allegiance N. loyalty. Not even a term in prison could shake Lech Walesa's *allegiance* to Solidarity, the Polish trade union he had helped to found.

■ **alleviate** V. relieve. This should *alleviate* the pain; if it does not, we shall have to use stronger drugs.

allocate V. assign. Even though the Red Cross had *allocated* a large sum for the relief of the sufferers of the disaster, many people perished.

alloy N. a mixture as of metals. *Alloys* of gold are used more frequently than the pure metal.

alloy V. mix; make less pure; lessen or moderate. Our delight at the baseball team's victory was *alloyed* by our concern for our nephew Tim, who injured his pitching arm in the game.

allude V. refer indirectly. Try not to mention divorce in Jack's presence because he will think you are *alluding* to his marital problems with Jill.

allure V. entice; attract. *Allured* by the song of the sirens, the helmsman steered the ship toward the reef. also N.

allusion N. indirect reference. When Amanda said to the ticket scalper, "One hundred bucks? What do you want, a pound of flesh?" she was making an *allusion* to Shakespeare's *Merchant of Venice.*

aloof ADJ. apart; reserved. Shy by nature, she remained *aloof* while all the rest conversed.

altercation N. noisy quarrel; heated dispute. In that hot-tempered household, no meal ever came to a peaceful conclusion; the inevitable *altercation* sometimes even ended in blows.

altruistic ADJ. unselfishly generous; concerned for others. In providing tutorial assistance and college scholarships for hundreds of economically disadvantaged youths, Eugene Lang performed a truly *altruistic* deed. altruism, N.

■ **amalgamate** V. combine; unite in one body. The unions will attempt to *amalgamate* their groups into one national body.

amass V. collect. The miser's aim is to *amass* and hoard as much gold as possible.

ambience N. environment; atmosphere. She went to the restaurant not for the food but for the *ambience.*

■ **ambiguous** ADJ. unclear or doubtful in meaning. His *ambiguous* instructions misled us; we did not know which road to take. ambiguity, N.

■ **ambivalence** N. the state of having contradictory or conflicting emotional attitudes. Torn between loving her parents one minute and hating them the next, she was confused by the *ambivalence* of her feelings. ambivalent, ADJ.

ambulatory ADJ. able to walk; not bedridden. Calvin was a highly *ambulatory* patient; not only did he refuse to be confined to bed, but also he insisted on riding his skateboard up and down the halls.

■ **ameliorate** V. improve. Many social workers have attempted to *ameliorate* the conditions of people living in the slums.

amenable ADJ. readily managed or willing to be led; answerable or accountable legally. Although the ambassador was usually *amenable* to friendly suggestions, he balked when we hinted he should pay his parking tickets. As a foreign diplomat, he claimed he was not *amenable* to minor local laws.

amend V. correct; change, generally for the better. Hoping to *amend* his condition, he left Vietnam for the United States.

amenities N. convenient features; courtesies. In addition to the customary *amenities* for the business traveler—fax machines, modems, a health club—the hotel offers the services of a butler versed in the social *amenities.*

amiable ADJ. agreeable; lovable; warmly friendly. In *Little Women,* Beth is the *amiable* daughter whose loving disposition endears her to all who know her.

amicable ADJ. politely friendly; not quarrelsome. Beth's sister Jo is the hot-tempered tomboy who has a hard time maintaining *amicable* relationships with those around her. Jo's quarrel with her friend Laurie finally reaches an *amicable* settlement, but not because Jo turns amiable overnight.

amiss ADJ. wrong; faulty. Seeing her frown, he wondered if anything were *amiss.* also ADV.

amity N. friendship. Student exchange programs such as the Experiment in International Living were established to promote international *amity.*

amnesty N. pardon. When his first child was born, the king granted *amnesty* to all in prison.

amoral ADJ. nonmoral. The *amoral* individual lacks a code of ethics; he cannot tell right from wrong. The immoral person can tell right from wrong; he chooses to do something he knows is wrong.

amorous ADJ. moved by sexual love; loving. "Love them and leave them" was the motto of the *amorous* Don Juan.

amorphous ADJ. formless; lacking shape or definition. As soon as we have decided on our itinerary, we shall send you a copy; right now, our plans are still *amorphous.*

ample ADJ. abundant. Bond had *ample* opportunity to escape. Why, then, did he let us capture him?

amplify V. broaden or clarify by expanding; intensify; make stronger. Charlie Brown tried to *amplify* his remarks, but he was drowned out by jeers from the audience. Lucy was smarter: she used a loudspeaker to *amplify* her voice.

amputate V. cut off part of body; prune. When the doctors had to *amputate* Ted Kennedy, Jr.'s leg to prevent the spread of cancer, he did not let the loss of his leg keep him from participating in sports.

■ **anachronism** N. something or someone misplaced in time. Shakespeare's reference to clocks in *Julius Caesar* is an *anachronism;* no clocks existed in Caesar's time. anachronistic, ADJ.

■ **analogous** ADJ. comparable. Actors exploring a classic text often improvise, working through an *analogous* situation closer to their own experience: for example, to explore the balcony scene in *Romeo and Juliet,* they may improvise a doorstep "goodnight" scene between a newly met boy and girl.

analogy N. similarity; parallelism. A well-known *analogy* compares the body's immune system with an army whose defending troops are the lymphocytes or white blood cells.

■ **anarchy** N. absence of governing body; state of disorder. The assassination of the leaders led to a period of *anarchy.*

Word List 3 anathema-arduous

anathema N. solemn curse; someone or something regarded as a curse. The Ayatolla Khomeini heaped *anathema* upon "the Great Satan," that is, the United States. To the Ayatolla, America and the West were *anathema;* he loathed the democratic nations, cursing them in his dying words. anathematize, V.

ancestry N. family descent. David can trace his *ancestry* as far back as the seventeenth century, when one of his *ancestors* was a court trumpeter somewhere in Germany. ancestral, ADJ.

anchor V. secure or fasten firmly; be fixed in place. We set the post in concrete to *anchor* it in place. anchorage, N.

ancillary ADJ. serving as an aid or accessory; auxiliary. In an *ancillary* capacity Doctor Watson was helpful; however, Holmes could not trust the good doctor to solve a perplexing case on his own. also N.

anecdote N. short account of an amusing or interesting event. Rather than make concrete proposals for welfare reform, President Reagan told *anecdotes* about poor people who became wealthy despite their impoverished backgrounds.

anguish N. acute pain; extreme suffering. Visiting the site of the explosion, the president wept to see the *anguish* of the victims and their families.

animated ADJ. lively; spirited. Jim Carrey's facial expressions are highly *animated*: when he played Ace Ventura, he was practically rubber-faced.

animosity N. active enmity. He incurred the *animosity* of the ruling class because he advocated limitations of their power.

animus N. hostile feeling or intent. The *animus* of the speaker became obvious to all when he began to indulge in sarcastic and insulting remarks.

annex V. attach; take possession of. Mexico objected to the United States' attempts to *annex* the territory that later became the state of Texas.

annihilate V. destroy. Archaeologists have found proof of the first ever use on British soil of a terrifying new weapon at the Battle of Killiecrankie, at which 2,500 Jacobites *annihilated* a force of 4,000 redcoats.

annotate V. comment; make explanatory notes. In the appendix to the novel, the critic sought to *annotate* many of the more esoteric references.

annul V. make void. The parents of the eloped couple tried to *annul* the marriage.

■ **anomalous** ADJ. abnormal; irregular. She was placed in the *anomalous* position of seeming to approve procedures that she despised.

anomaly N. irregularity. A bird that cannot fly is an *anomaly.*

anonymity N. state of being nameless; anonymousness. The donor of the gift asked the college not to mention her by name; the dean readily agreed to respect her *anonymity.* anonymous, ADJ.

antagonism N. hostility; active resistance. Barry showed his *antagonism* toward his new stepmother by ignoring her whenever she tried talking to him. antagonistic, ADJ.

antecede V. precede. The invention of the radiotelegraph *anteceded* the development of television by a quarter of a century.

antecedents N. preceding events or circumstances that influence what comes later; ancestors or early background. Susi Bechhofer's ignorance of her Jewish background had its *antecedents* in the chaos of World War II. Smuggled out of Germany and adopted by a Christian family, she knew nothing of her birth and *antecedents* until she was reunited with her Jewish family in 1989.

anthology N. book of literary selections by various authors. This *anthology* of science fiction was compiled by the late Isaac Asimov. anthologize, V.

anticlimax N. letdown in thought or emotion. After the fine performance in the first act, the rest of the play was an *anticlimax.* anticlimactic, ADJ.

antidote N. remedy to counteract a poison or disease. When Marge's child accidentally swallowed some cleaning fluid, the local poison control hotline instructed Marge how to administer the *antidote.*

■ **antipathy** N. aversion; dislike. Tom's extreme *antipathy* for disputes keeps him from getting into arguments with his temperamental wife. Noise in any form is *antipathetic* to him. Among his other *antipathies* are honking cars, boom boxes, and heavy metal rock.

antiquated ADJ. obsolete; outdated. Accustomed to editing his papers on word processors, Philip thought typewriters were too *antiquated* for him to use.

antithesis N. contrast; direct opposite of or to. This tyranny was the *antithesis* of all that he had hoped for, and he fought it with all his strength. antithetical or antithetic, ADJ.

■ **apathy** N. lack of caring; indifference. A firm believer in democratic government, she could not understand the *apathy* of people who never bothered to vote. apathetic, ADJ.

apex N. tip; summit; climax. At the *apex* of his career, the star received offers of leading roles daily; two years later, he was reduced to taking bit parts in B-movies.

aplomb N. poise; assurance. Gwen's *aplomb* in handling potentially embarrassing moments was legendary around the office; when one of her clients broke a piece of her best crystal, she coolly picked up her own goblet and hurled it into the fireplace.

apocalyptic ADJ. prophetic; pertaining to revelations. The crowd jeered at the street preacher's *apocalyptic* predictions of doom. The *Apocalypse* or *Book of Revelations* of Saint John prophesies the end of the world as we know it and foretells marvels and prodigies that signal the coming doom. apocalypse, N.

apocryphal ADJ. spurious; not authentic; invented rather than true. Although many versions exist of the famous story of Emerson's visit to Thoreau in jail, in his writings Thoreau never mentions any such visit by Emerson, and so the tale is most likely *apocryphal.*

apolitical ADJ. having an aversion or lack of concern for political affairs. It was hard to remain *apolitical* during the Vietnam War; even people who generally ignored public issues felt they had to take political stands.

apologist N. one who writes in defense of a cause or institution. Rather than act as an *apologist* for the regime in Beijing and defend its brutal actions, the young diplomat decided to defect to the West.

apostate N. one who abandons his religious faith or political beliefs. Because he switched from one party to another, his former friends shunned him as an *apostate.* An apostle passionately adheres to a belief or cause; an *apostate* passionately renounces or abandons one. apostasy, N.

appall V. dismay; shock. We were *appalled* by the horrifying conditions in the city's jails.

apparition N. ghost; phantom. On the castle battlements, an *apparition* materialized and spoke to Hamlet, warning him of his uncle's treachery. In *Ghostbusters,* hordes of *apparitions* materialized, only to be dematerialized by the specialized apparatus wielded by Bill Murray.

■ **appease** V. pacify or soothe; relieve. Tom and Jody tried to *appease* the crying baby by offering him one toy after another. However, he would not calm down until they *appeased* his hunger by giving him a bottle. appeasement, N.

append V. attach. When you *append* a bibliography to a text, you have created an *appendix.*

application N. diligent attention. Pleased with how well Tom had whitewashed the fence, Aunt Polly praised him for his *application.* (Tom had *applied* himself to *applying* the paint.) (secondary meaning) apply, V.

apposite ADJ. appropriate; fitting. She was always able to find the *apposite* phrase, the correct expression for every occasion.

appraise V. estimate value of. It is difficult to *appraise* old paintings; it is easier to call them priceless. appraisal, N.

appreciate V. be thankful for; increase in worth; be thoroughly conscious of. Little Orphan Annie truly *appreciated* the stocks Daddy Warbucks gave her, whose value *appreciated* considerably over the years.

apprehend V. arrest (a criminal); dread; perceive. The police will *apprehend* the culprit and convict him before long.

apprehensive ADJ. fearful; discerning. His *apprehensive* glances at the people who were walking in the street revealed his nervousness.

■ **apprise** V. inform. When NASA was *apprised* of the dangerous weather conditions, the head of the space agency decided to postpone the shuttle launch.

■ **approbation** N. approval. Wanting her parents' regard, she looked for some sign of their *approbation.* Benjamin Franklin, that shrewd observer of mankind, once wrote, "We must not in the course of public life expect immediate *approbation* and immediate grateful acknowledgment of our services."

■ **appropriate** V. acquire; take possession of for one's own use. The ranch owners *appropriated* the lands that had originally been set aside for the Indians' use.

apropos ADJ. to the point and timely. When Bob spoke out against drunk driving, some of our crowd called him a spoilsport, but the rest of us found his comments extremely *apropos.*

apropos PREP. with reference to; regarding. *Apropos* the waltz, the dance has its faults.

aptitude N. fitness; talent. The American aviator Bessie Coleman grew up in Waxahatchie, Texas, where her mathematical *aptitude* freed her from working in the cotton fields with her twelve brothers and sisters.

arable ADJ. fit for growing crops. The first settlers wrote home glowing reports of the New World, praising its vast acres of *arable* land ready for the plow.

arbiter N. person with power to decide a matter in dispute; judge. As an *arbiter* in labor disputes, she has won the confidence of the workers and the employers.

arbitrary ADJ. unreasonable or capricious; tyrannical. The coach claimed the team lost because the umpire made some *arbitrary* calls.

arbitrate V. act as judge. She was called upon to *arbitrate* the dispute between the union and the management.

arcane ADJ. secret; mysterious; known only to the initiated. Secret brotherhoods surround themselves with *arcane* rituals and trappings to mystify outsiders. So do doctors. Consider the *arcane* terminology they use and the impression they try to give that what is *arcane* to us is obvious to them.

archaeology N. study of artifacts and relics of early mankind. The professor of *archaeology* headed an expedition to the Gobi Desert in search of ancient ruins.

archaic ADJ. antiquated. "Methinks," "thee," and "thou" are *archaic* words that are no longer part of our normal vocabulary.

archetype N. prototype; primitive pattern. The Brooklyn Bridge was the *archetype* of the spans that now connect Manhattan with Long Island and New Jersey.

archives N. public records; place where public records are kept. These documents should be part of the *archives* so that historians may be able to evaluate them in the future.

ardor N. heat; passion; zeal. Katya's *ardor* was contagious; soon all her fellow demonstrators were busily making posters and handing out flyers, inspired by her *ardent* enthusiasm for the cause. ardent, ADJ.

■ **arduous** ADJ. hard; strenuous. Her *arduous* efforts had sapped her energy.

Word List 4 arid–autonomous

arid ADJ. dry; barren. The cactus has adapted to survive in an *arid* environment.

aristocracy N. hereditary nobility; privileged class. Americans have mixed feelings about hereditary *aristocracy*: we say all men are created equal, but we describe particularly outstanding people as natural *aristocrats*.

aromatic ADJ. fragrant. Medieval sailing vessels brought *aromatic* herbs from China to Europe.

arraign V. charge in court; indict. After his indictment by the Grand Jury, the accused man was *arraigned* in the County Criminal Court.

array V. marshal; draw up in order. His actions were bound to *array* public sentiment against him. also N.

array V. clothe; adorn. She liked to watch her mother *array* herself in her finest clothes before going out for the evening. also N.

arrears N. being in debt. Because he was in *arrears* with his car payments, the repo men repossessed his Porsche.

arrest V. stop or check; seize or capture (the attention). According to Connolly's "Theory of Permanent Adolescence," the triumphs and disappointments that boys experience at the great British public schools are so intense as to dominate their lives and to *arrest* their development.

arrhythmic ADJ. lacking rhythm or regularity. The doctors feared his *arrhythmic* heartbeat might be the first symptom of an imminent heart attack. arrhythmia, N.

arrogance N. pride; haughtiness. Convinced that Emma thought she was better than anyone else in the class, Ed rebuked her for her *arrogance*.

artful ADJ. cunning; crafty; sly. By using accurate details to suggest a misleading picture of the whole, the *artful* propagandist turns partial truths into more effective instruments of deception than lies.

articulate ADJ. effective; distinct. Her *articulate* presentation of the advertising campaign impressed her employers. also V.

artifact N. object made by human beings, either handmade or mass-produced. Archaeologists debated the significance of the *artifacts* discovered in the ruins of Asia Minor but came to no conclusion about the culture they represented.

artifice N. deception; trickery. The Trojan War proved to the Greeks that cunning and *artifice* were often more effective than military might.

artisan N. manually skilled worker; craftsman, as opposed to artist. Elderly *artisans* from Italy trained Harlem teenagers to carve the stone figures that would decorate the new wing of the cathedral.

■ **artless** ADJ. without guile; open and honest. Red Riding Hood's *artless* comment, "Grandma, what big eyes you have!" indicates the child's innocent surprise at her "grandmother's" changed appearance.

ascendancy N. controlling influence. President Marcos failed to maintain his *ascendancy* over the Philippines.

ascertain V. find out for certain. Please *ascertain* her present address.

■ **ascetic** ADJ. practicing self-denial; austere. The wealthy, self-indulgent young man felt oddly drawn to the strict, *ascetic* life led by members of some monastic orders. also N. asceticism, N.

ascribe V. refer; attribute; assign. Although some friends *ascribe* Bob's depression to the disintegration of his marriage, I believe the depression came first and contributed to the eventual marital breakup.

asperity N. sharpness (of temper). Lady Bracknell reacted sharply to Jack's admission that as a baby he had been found in the cloakroom of Victoria Station's Brighton Line, saying, with marked *asperity*, "The line is immaterial."

aspersion N. slanderous remark. Rather than attacking President Cleveland's arguments with logic, his opponent resorted to casting *aspersions* on the president's moral character.

aspire V. seek to attain; long for. Because he *aspired* to a career in professional sports, Philip enrolled in a graduate program in sports management. aspiration, N.

assail V. assault. He was *assailed* with questions after his lecture.

assay V. analyze; evaluate. When they *assayed* the ore, they found that they had discovered a very rich vein. also N.

assent V. agree; accept. It gives me great pleasure to *assent* to your request. also N.

assert V. state strongly or positively; insist on or demand recognition of (rights, claims, etc.). When Jill *asserted* that nobody else in the junior class had such an early curfew, her parents *asserted* themselves, telling her that if she didn't get home by nine o'clock she would be grounded for the week. assertion, N.

assessment N. estimation; appraisal. I would like to have your *assessment* of the situation in South Africa.

■ **assiduous** ADJ. diligent. It took Rembrandt weeks of *assiduous* labor before he was satisfied with his portrait of his son.

assimilate V. absorb; cause to become homogenous. The manner in which the United States was able to *assimilate* the hordes of immigrants during the nineteenth and early part of the twentieth centuries will always be a source of pride.

■ **assuage** V. ease or lessen (pain); satisfy (hunger); soothe (anger). Jilted by Jane, Dick tried to *assuage* his heartache by indulging in ice cream. One gallon later, he had *assuaged* his appetite but not his grief. assuagement, N.

assumption N. something taken for granted; the taking over or taking possession of. The young princess made the foolish *assumption* that the regent would not object to her *assumption* of power. assume, V.

assurance N. promise or pledge; certainty; self-confidence. When Guthrie gave Guinness his *assurance* that rehearsals were going well, he spoke with such *assurance* that Guinness was convinced. assure, V. assured, ADJ.

astringent ADJ. binding; causing contraction; harsh or severe. The *astringent* quality of the unsweetened lemon juice made swallowing difficult. also N.

astronomical ADJ. enormously large or extensive. The government seemed willing to spend *astronomical* sums on weapons development.

astute ADJ. wise; shrewd; keen. The painter was an *astute* observer, noticing every tiny detail of her model's appearance and knowing exactly how important each one was.

asylum N. place of refuge or shelter; protection. The refugees sought *asylum* from religious persecution in a new land.

asymmetric ADJ. not identical on both sides of a dividing central line. Because one eyebrow was set markedly higher than the other, William's face had a particularly *asymmetric* appearance. asymmetry, N.

atheist N. one who denies the existence of God. "An *atheist* is a man who has no invisible means of support."

atone V. make amends for; pay for. He knew no way in which he could *atone* for his brutal crime.

atrocity N. brutal deed. In time of war, many *atrocities* are committed by invading armies.

atrophy N. wasting away. Polio victims need physiotherapy to prevent the *atrophy* of affected limbs. also V.

attentive ADJ. alert and watchful; considerate; thoughtful. Spellbound, the *attentive* audience watched the final game of the tennis match, never taking their eyes from the ball. A cold wind sprang up; Stan's *attentive* daughter slipped a sweater over his shoulders without distracting his attention from the game.

■ **attenuate** V. make thinner; weaken or lessen (in density, force, degree). The long, dry spell *attenuated* the creek to the merest trickle. When a meteor strikes the ground, the initially intense shock *attenuates* or lessens as it diverges outward.

attest V. testify; bear witness. Having served as a member of a grand jury, I can *attest* that our system of indicting individuals is in need of improvement.

attribute N. essential quality. His outstanding *attribute* was his kindness.

attribute V. ascribe; explain. I *attribute* her success in science to the encouragement she received from her parents.

attrition N. gradual decrease in numbers; reduction in the work force without firing employees; wearing away of opposition by means of harassment. In the 1960s urban churches suffered from *attrition* as members moved from the cities to the suburbs. Rather than fire staff members, church leaders followed a policy of *attrition*, allowing elderly workers to retire without replacing them.

atypical ADJ. not normal. The child psychiatrist reassured Mrs. Keaton that playing doctor was not *atypical* behavior for a child of young Alex's age. "Perhaps not," she replied, "but charging for house calls is!"

■ **audacious** ADJ. daring; bold. Audiences cheered as Luke Skywalker and Princess Leia made their *audacious*, death-defying leap to freedom and escaped Darth Vader's troops. audacity, N.

audit N. examination of accounts. When the bank examiners arrived to hold their annual *audit*, they discovered the embezzlements of the chief cashier. also V.

augment V. increase; add to. Armies *augment* their forces by calling up reinforcements; teachers *augment* their salaries by taking odd jobs.

august ADJ. impressive; majestic. Visiting the palace at Versailles, she was impressed by the *august* surroundings in which she found herself.

auspicious ADJ. favoring success. With favorable weather conditions, it was an *auspicious* moment to set sail. Thomas, however, had doubts about sailing: a paranoid, he became suspicious whenever conditions seemed *auspicious*.

■ **austere** ADJ. forbiddingly stern; severely simple and unornamented. The headmaster's *austere* demeanor tended to scare off the more timid students, who never visited his study willingly. The room reflected the man, *austere* and bare, like a monk's cell, with no touches of luxury to moderate its *austerity*.

authenticate V. prove genuine. An expert was needed to *authenticate* the original Van Gogh painting, distinguishing it from its imitation.

authoritarian ADJ. subordinating the individual to the state; completely dominating another's will. The leaders of the *authoritarian* regime ordered the suppression of the democratic protest movement. After years of submitting to the will of her *authoritarian* father, Elizabeth Barrett ran away from home with the poet Robert Browning.

authoritative ADJ. having the weight of authority; peremptory and dictatorial. Impressed by the young researcher's well-documented presentation, we accepted her analysis of the experiment as *authoritative*.

autocratic ADJ. having absolute, unchecked power; dictatorial. A person accustomed to exercising authority may become *autocratic* if his or her power is unchecked. Dictators by definition are *autocrats*. Bosses who dictate behavior as well as letters can be *autocrats* too. autocracy, N.

■ **autonomous** ADJ. self-governing. Although the University of California at Berkeley is just one part of the state university system, in many ways Cal Berkeley is *autonomous*, for it runs several programs that are not subject to outside control. autonomy, N.

Word List 5 auxiliary–bent

auxiliary ADJ. offering or providing help; additional or subsidiary. To prepare for the emergency, they built an *auxiliary* power station. also N.

avarice N. greediness for wealth. Montaigne is correct in maintaining that it is not poverty, but rather abundance, that breeds *avarice*: the more shoes Imelda Marcos had, the more she craved.

avenge V. take vengeance for something (or on behalf of someone). Hamlet vowed he would *avenge* his father's murder and punish Claudius for his horrible crime.

■ **aver** V. assert confidently or declare; as used in law, state formally as a fact. The self-proclaimed psychic *averred* that, because he had extrasensory perception on which to base his predictions, he needed no seismographs or other gadgets in order to foretell earthquakes.

averse ADJ. reluctant; disinclined. The reporter was *averse* to revealing the sources of his information.

aversion N. firm dislike. Bert had an *aversion* to yuppies; Alex had an *aversion* to punks. Their mutal *aversion* was so great that they refused to speak to one another.

avert V. prevent; turn away. She *averted* her eyes from the dead cat on the highway.

avid ADJ. greedy; eager for. He was *avid* for learning and read everything he could get. avidity, N.

avocation N. secondary or minor occupation. His hobby proved to be so fascinating and profitable that gradually he abandoned his regular occupation and concentrated on his *avocation*.

avow V. declare openly. Lana *avowed* that she never meant to steal Debbie's boyfriend, but no one believed her *avowal* of innocence.

avuncular ADJ. like an uncle. *Avuncular* pride did not prevent him from noticing his nephew's shortcomings.

awe N. solemn wonder. The tourists gazed with *awe* at the tremendous expanse of the Grand Canyon.

awry ADV. distorted; crooked. He held his head *awry*, giving the impression that he had caught cold in his neck during the night. also ADJ.

axiom N. self-evident truth requiring no proof. The Declaration of Independence records certain self-evident truths or *axioms*, the first of which is "All men are created equal." To Sherlock Holmes, it was *axiomatic* that the little things were infinitely the most important; he based his theory of detection on this obvious truth.

badger V. pester; annoy. She was forced to change her telephone number because she was *badgered* by obscene phone calls.

baffle V. frustrate; perplex. The new code *baffled* the enemy agents.

bait V. harass; tease. The school bully *baited* the smaller children, terrorizing them.

baleful ADJ. threatening; menacing; sinister; foreshadowing evil. The bully's *baleful* glare across the classroom warned Tim to expect trouble after school. Blood-red in color, the planet Mars has long been associated with warfare and slaughter because of its ominous, *baleful* appearance.

balk V. stop short, as if faced with an obstacle, and refuse to continue. The chief of police *balked* at sending his officers into the riot-torn area.

balk V. foil. When the warden learned that several inmates were planning to escape, he took steps to *balk* their attempt.

balm N. something that relieves pain. Friendship is the finest *balm* for the pangs of disappointed love.

balmy ADJ. mild; fragrant. A *balmy* breeze refreshed us after the sultry blast.

■ **banal** ADJ. hackneyed; commonplace; trite; lacking originality. The hack writer's worn-out clichés made his comic sketch seem *banal.* He even resorted to the *banality* of having someone slip on a banana peel!

bandy V. discuss lightly or glibly; exchange (words) heatedly. While the president was happy to *bandy* patriotic generalizations with anyone who would listen to him, he refused to *bandy* words with unfriendly reporters at the press conference.

bane N. curse; cause of ruin. Lucy's little brother was the *bane* of her existence, scribbling on walls with her lipstick and pouring her shampoo down the drain. While some factions praised technology as the mainspring of social progress, others criticized it as the *bane* of modern man, responsible for the tyranny of the machine and the squalor of urban life.

baneful ADJ. destructive; causing ruin or death. Anointment seems intended to apply the power of natural and supernatural forces to the sick and thus to ward off the *baneful* influences of diseases and of demons.

bantering ADJ. good-naturedly ridiculing. They resented his *bantering* remarks because they misinterpreted his teasing as sarcasm.

barb N. sharp projection from fishhook or other object; openly cutting remark. If you were a politician, which would you prefer, being caught on the *barb* of a fishhook or being subjected to malicious verbal *barbs*? Who can blame the president if he's happier fishing than he is listening to his critics' *barbed* remarks?

barefaced ADJ. shameless; bold; unconcealed. Shocked by Huck Finn's *barefaced* lies, Miss Watson prayed the good Lord would give him a sense of his unregenerate wickedness.

baroque ADJ. highly ornate. Accustomed to the severe, angular lines of modern skyscrapers, they found the flamboyance of *baroque* architecture amusing.

barterer N. trader. The *barterer* exchanged trinkets for the natives' furs.

bask V. luxuriate; take pleasure in warmth. *Basking* on the beach, she relaxed so completely that she fell asleep.

bastion N. stronghold; something seen as a source of protection. The villagers fortified the town hall, hoping this improvised *bastion* could protect them from the guerrilla raids.

bawdy ADJ. indecent; obscene. Jack took offense at Jill's *bawdy* remarks. What kind of young man did she think he was?

beatific ADJ. showing or producing joy; blissful. When Johnny first saw the new puppy, a *beatific* smile spread across his face. In his novel, Waugh praises Limbo, not Heaven: "Limbo is the place. In Limbo one has natural happiness without the *beatific* vision; no harps; no communal order; but wine and conversation and imperfect, various, humanity."

beatify V. bless or sanctify; proclaim someone dead to be one of the blessed. In 1996 Pope John Paul II traveled to Belgium to *beatify* Joseph De Veuster, better known as Father Damien, who died in 1889 after caring for lepers in Hawaii. How can you tell the pope from a cosmetologist? A cosmetologist beautifies someone living; the Pope *beatifies* someone dead.

bedraggle V. wet thoroughly. We were so *bedraggled* by the severe storm that we had to change into dry clothing. bedraggled, ADJ.

beeline N. direct, quick route. As soon as the movie was over, Jim made a *beeline* for the exit.

befuddle V. confuse thoroughly. His attempts to clarify the situation succeeded only in *befuddling* her further.

beget V. father; produce; give rise to. One good turn may deserve another; it does not necessarily *beget* another.

begrudge V. resent. I *begrudge* every minute I have to spend attending meetings.

beguile V. mislead or delude; cheat; pass time. With flattery and big talk of easy money, the con men *beguiled* Kyle into betting his allowance on the shell game. The men quickly *beguiled* poor Kyle of his money. Broke, he *beguiled* himself during the long hours by playing solitaire.

beholden ADJ. obligated; indebted. Since I do not wish to be *beholden* to anyone, I cannot accept this favor.

behoove V. be necessary or proper for; be incumbent upon. Because the interest of the ruler and the ruled are incompatible, it *behooves* the ruler to trust no one; to be suspicious of sycophants; to permit no one to gain undue power or influence; and, above all, to use guile to unearth plots against the throne.

belabor V. explain or go over excessively or to a ridiculous degree; assail verbally. The debate coach warned her student not to bore the audience by *belaboring* his point.

belated ADJ. delayed. He apologized for his *belated* note of condolence to the widow of his friend and explained that he had just learned of her husband's untimely death.

beleaguer V. besiege or attack; harass. The babysitter was surrounded by a crowd of unmanageable brats who relentlessly *beleaguered* her.

■ **belie** V. contradict; give a false impression. His coarse, hard-bitten exterior *belied* his innate sensitivity.

belittle V. disparage; deprecate. Parents should not *belittle* their children's early attempts at drawing, but should encourage their efforts.

bellicose ADJ. warlike; pugnacious; naturally inclined to fight. Someone who is spoiling for a fight is by definition *bellicose.*

belligerent ADJ. quarrelsome. Whenever he had too much to drink, he became *belligerent* and tried to pick fights with strangers. belligerence, N.

bemoan V. lament; express disapproval of. The widow *bemoaned* the death of her beloved husband. Although critics *bemoaned* the serious flaws in the author's novels, each year his latest book topped the best-seller list.

bemused ADJ. confused; lost in thought; preoccupied. Jill studied the garbled instructions with a *bemused* look on her face.

benediction N. blessing. The appearance of the sun after the many rainy days was like a *benediction.*

benefactor N. gift giver; patron. Scrooge later became Tiny Tim's *benefactor* and gave him gifts.

■ **beneficent** ADJ. kindly; doing good. The overgenerous philanthropist had to curb his *beneficent* impulses before he gave away all his money and left himself with nothing.

beneficial ADJ. helpful; useful. Tiny Tim's cheerful good nature had a *beneficial* influence on Scrooge's once-uncharitable disposition.

benevolent ADJ. generous; charitable. Mr. Fezziwig was a *benevolent* employer who wished to make Christmas merrier for young Scrooge and his other employees. benevolence, N.

benign ADJ. kindly; favorable; not malignant. Though her *benign* smile and gentle bearing made Miss Marple seem a sweet little old lady, in reality she was a tough-minded, shrewd observer of human nature. benignity, N.

bent ADJ.; N. determined; natural talent or inclination. *Bent* on advancing in the business world, the secretary-heroine of *Working Girl* had a true *bent* for high finance.

Word List 6 bequeath–burgeoning

bequeath V. leave to someone by means of a will; hand down. In his will, Father *bequeathed* his watch to Philip; the *bequest* meant a great deal to the boy. bequest, N.

berate V. scold strongly. He feared she would *berate* him for his forgetfulness.

beseech V. beg; plead with. The workaholic executive's wife *beseeched* him to spend more time with their son.

beset V. harass or trouble; hem in. Many vexing problems *beset* the American public school system. Sleeping Beauty's castle was *beset* on all sides by dense thickets that hid it from view.

besiege V. surround with armed forces; harass (with requests). When the bandits *besieged* the village, the villagers holed up in the town hall and prepared to withstand a long siege. Members of the new administration were *besieged* with job applications from people who had worked on the campaign.

besmirch V. soil, defile. The chancellor declared, "Our campus police officers would never do anything that might *besmirch* the reputation of the university."

bestow V. confer. "Freedom is not a gift *bestowed* upon us by other men, but a right that belongs to us by the laws of God and nature." (Benjamin Franklin)

betoken V. signify; indicate. The well-equipped docks, tall piles of cargo containers, and numerous vessels being loaded all *betoken* Oakland's importance as a port.

betray V. be unfaithful; reveal (unconsciously or unwillingly). The spy *betrayed* his country by selling military secrets to the enemy. When he was taken in for questioning, the tightness of his lips *betrayed* his fear of incriminating himself. betrayal, N.

bicker V. quarrel. The children *bickered* morning, noon, and night, exasperating their parents.

biennial ADJ. every two years. Seeing no need to meet more frequently, the group held *biennial* meetings instead of annual ones. Plants that bear flowers *biennially* are known as *biennials.*

bigotry N. stubborn intolerance. Brought up in a democratic atmosphere, the student was shocked by the *bigotry* and narrowness expressed by several of his classmates.

bizarre ADJ. fantastic; violently contrasting. The plot of the novel was too *bizarre* to be believed.

bland ADJ. soothing or mild; agreeable. Jill tried a *bland* ointment for her sunburn. However, when Jack absentmindedly patted her on the sunburned shoulder, she couldn't maintain her *bland* persona. blandness, N.

blare N. loud, harsh roar or screech; dazzling blaze of light. I don't know which is worse: the steady *blare* of a boom box deafening your ears or a sudden *blare* of flashbulbs dazzling your eyes. also V.

blasé ADJ. bored with pleasure or dissipation. Although Beth was as thrilled with the idea of a trip to Paris as her classmates were, she tried to act supercool and *blasé,* as if she'd been abroad hundreds of times.

blasphemy N. irreverence; sacrilege; cursing. In my father's house, the Dodgers were the holiest of holies; to cheer for another team was to utter words of *blasphemy.* blasphemous, ADJ.

blatant ADJ. extremely obvious; loudly offensive. Caught in a *blatant* lie, the scoundrel had only one regret: he wished that he had lied more subtly. blatancy, N.

bleak ADJ. cold or cheerless; unlikely to be favorable. The frigid, inhospitable Aleutian Islands are *bleak* military outposts. It's no wonder that soldiers assigned there have a *bleak* attitude toward their posting.

blighted ADJ. suffering from a disease; destroyed. The extent of the *blighted* areas could be seen only when viewed from the air.

blithe ADJ. carefree and unconcerned (perhaps foolishly so); cheerful and gay. Micawber's *blithe* optimism that something would turn up proved unfounded, and he wound up in debtors' prison. Marie Antoinette's famous remark, "Let them eat cake!" epitomizes her *blithe* ignorance of the harsh realities endured by the common people.

bluff ADJ. rough but good-natured. Jack had a *bluff* and hearty manner that belied his actual sensitivity; he never let people know how thin-skinned he really was.

bluff N. pretense (of strength); deception; high cliff. Claire thought Lord Byron's boast that he would swim the Hellespont was just a *bluff;* she was astounded when he dove from the high *bluff* into the waters below.

blunder N. error. The criminal's fatal *blunder* led to his capture. also V.

blurt V. utter impulsively. Before she could stop him, he *blurted* out the news.

bluster V. blow in heavy gusts; threaten emptily; bully. "Let the stormy winds *bluster,*" cried Jack, "we'll set sail tonight." Jill let Jack *bluster:* she wasn't going anywhere, no matter what he said. also N.

bode V. foreshadow; portend. The gloomy skies and the sulfurous odors from the mineral springs seemed to *bode* evil to those who settled in the area.

bogus ADJ. counterfeit; not authentic. The police quickly found the distributors of the *bogus* twenty-dollar bills.

bohemian ADJ. unconventional (in an artistic way). Gertrude Stein ran off to Paris to live an eccentric, *bohemian* life with her writer friends. Oakland was not *bohemian:* it was too bourgeois, too middle-class.

boisterous ADJ. violent; rough; noisy. The unruly crowd became even more *boisterous* when he tried to quiet them.

■ **bolster** V. support; reinforce. The debaters amassed file boxes full of evidence to *bolster* their arguments.

bolt N. door bar; fastening pin or screw; length of fabric. The carpenter shut the workshop door, sliding the heavy metal *bolt* into place. He sorted through his toolbox for the nuts and *bolts* and nails required for the job. Before he cut into the *bolt* of canvas, he measured how much fabric he would need.

bolt V. dash or dart off; fasten (a door); gobble down. Jack was set to *bolt* out the front door, but Jill *bolted* the door. "Eat your breakfast," she said, "don't *bolt* your food."

bombardment N. attack (as with missiles). The enemy *bombardment* demolished the town. Members of the opposition party *bombarded* the prime minister with questions about the enemy attack.

■ **bombastic** ADJ. pompous; using inflated language. Puffed up with conceit, the orator spoke in such a *bombastic* manner that we longed to deflate him. bombast, N.

boon N. blessing; benefit. The recent rains that filled our empty reservoirs were a *boon* to the whole community.

■ **boorish** ADJ. rude; insensitive. Though Mr. Potts constantly interrupted his wife, she ignored his *boorish* behavior, for she had lost hope of teaching him courtesy.

bountiful ADJ. abundant; graciously generous. Thanks to the good harvest, we had a *bountiful* supply of food and we could be as *bountiful* as we liked in distributing food to the needy.

bourgeois ADJ. middle class; selfishly materialistic; dully conventional. Technically, anyone who belongs to the middle class is *bourgeois,* but, given the word's connotations, most people resent it if you call them that.

boycott V. refrain from buying or using. To put pressure on grape growers to stop using pesticides that harmed the farm workers' health, Cesar Chavez called for consumers to *boycott* grapes. also N.

braggadocio N. boasting. Hip hop is a culture built on *braggadocio,* arrogance, and confidence in one's own abilities and appearance.

braggart N. boaster. Modest by nature, she was no *braggart,* preferring to let her accomplishments speak for themselves.

bravado N. swagger; assumed air of defiance. The *bravado* of the young criminal disappeared when he was confronted by the victims of his brutal attack.

brawn N. muscular strength; sturdiness. It takes *brawn* to become a champion weight-lifter. brawny, ADJ.

brazen ADJ. insolent. Her *brazen* contempt for authority angered the officials.

breach N. breaking of contract or duty; fissure or gap. Jill sued Jack for *breach* of promise, claiming he had broken their engagement. The attackers found a *breach* in the enemy's fortifications and penetrated their lines. also V.

breadth N. width; extent. We were impressed by the *breadth* of her knowledge.

brevity N. conciseness. *Brevity* is essential when you send a telegram or cablegram; you are charged for every word.

brittle ADJ. easily broken; difficult. My employer's *brittle* personality made it difficult for me to get along with her.

broach V. introduce; open up. Jack did not even try to *broach* the subject of religion with his in-laws. If you *broach* a touchy subject, the result may be a *breach*.

brook V. tolerate; endure. The dean would *brook* no interference with his disciplinary actions. (secondary meaning)

browbeat V. bully; intimidate. Billy resisted Ted's attempts to *browbeat* him into handing over his lunch money.

browse V. graze; skim or glance at casually. "How now, brown cow, *browsing* in the green, green grass." I remember lines of verse that I came across while *browsing* through the poetry section of the local bookstore.

brunt N. main impact or shock. Tom Sawyer claimed credit for painting the fence, but the *brunt* of the work fell on others. However, Tom bore the *brunt* of Aunt Polly's complaints when the paint began to peel.

brusque ADJ. blunt; abrupt. She was offended by his *brusque* reply.

bulwark N. earthwork or other strong defense; person who defends. The navy is our principal *bulwark* against invasion.

bungle V. mismanage; blunder. Don't botch this assignment, Bumstead; if you *bungle* the job, you're fired!

buoyant ADJ. able to float; cheerful and optimistic. When the boat capsized, her *buoyant* life jacket kept Jody afloat. Scrambling back on board, she was still in a *buoyant* mood, certain that despite the delay she'd win the race. buoyancy, N.

bureaucracy N. overregulated administrative system marked by red tape. The Internal Revenue Service is the ultimate *bureaucracy*: taxpayers wasted so much paper filling out IRS forms that the IRS *bureaucrats* printed up a new set of rules requiring taxpayers to comply with the Paperwork Reduction Act. bureaucratic, ADJ.

■ **burgeoning** ADJ. flourishing; growing quickly; putting out buds. Phil and Adam could scarcely keep up with the *burgeoning* demand for the services of their production company.

Word List 7 burlesque-celibate

burlesque V. give an imitation that ridicules. In *Galaxy Quest*, Alan Rickman *burlesques* Mr. Spock of *Star Trek*, outrageously parodying Spock's unemotional manner and stiff bearing. also N.

■ **burnish** V. make shiny by rubbing; polish. The maid *burnished* the brass fixtures until they reflected the lamplight.

■ **buttress** V. support; prop up. Just as architects *buttress* the walls of cathedrals with flying *buttresses*, debaters *buttress* their arguments with facts. also N.

buxom ADJ. full-bosomed; plump; jolly. High-fashion models usually are slender rather than *buxom*.

cabal N. small group of persons secretly united to promote their own interests. Some conspiracy theorists contend that a shadowy *cabal* of powerful tycoons secretly rules the world.

cache N. hiding place. The detectives followed the suspect until he led them to the *cache* where he had stored his loot. also V.

■ **cacophonous** ADJ. discordant; inharmonious. Do the students in the orchestra enjoy the *cacophonous* sounds they make when they're tuning up? I don't know how they can stand the racket. cacophony, N.

cadge V. beg; mooch; panhandle. While his car was in the shop, Bob had to *cadge* a ride to work each day. Unwilling to be a complete moocher, however, he offered to pay for the gas.

cajole V. coax; wheedle. Cher tried to *cajole* her father into letting her drive the family car. cajolery, N.

calamity N. disaster; misery. As news of the *calamity* spread, offers of relief poured in to the stricken community.

calculated ADJ. deliberately planned; likely. Lexy's choice of clothes to wear to the debate tournament was carefully *calculated*. Her conventional suit was *calculated* to appeal to the conservative judges.

caliber N. ability; quality. Einstein's cleaning the blackboards again? Albert, quit it! A man of your *caliber* shouldn't have to do such menial tasks.

calligraphy N. beautiful writing; excellent penmanship. As we examine ancient manuscripts, we become impressed with the *calligraphy* of the scribes.

callous ADJ. hardened; unfeeling. He had worked in the hospital for so many years that he was *callous* to the suffering in the wards. callus, N.

callow ADJ. youthful; immature; inexperienced. As a freshman, Jack was sure he was a man of the world; as a sophomore, he made fun of freshmen as *callow* youths. In both cases, his judgment showed just how *callow* he was.

calumny N. malicious misrepresentation; slander. He could endure his financial failure, but he could not bear the *calumny* that his foes heaped upon him. According to Herodotus, someone *calumniated* is doubly injured, first by the person who utters the *calumny*, and then by the person who believes the slander.

camaraderie N. good-fellowship. What he loved best about his job was the sense of *camaraderie* he and his coworkers shared.

camouflage V. disguise; conceal. In order to rescue Han Solo, Princess Leia *camouflaged* herself in the helmet and cloak of a space bandit. also N.

candor N. frankness; open honesty. Jack can carry *candor* too far: when he told Jill his honest opinion of her, she nearly slapped his face. candid, ADJ.

canny ADJ. shrewd; thrifty. The *canny* Scotsman was more than a match for the swindlers.

canon N. collection or authoritative list of books (e.g., by an author, or accepted as scripture). Scholars hotly debated whether the newly discovered sonnet should be accepted as part of the Shakespearean *canon*.

canon N. rule or principle, frequently religious. "One catastrophe, one locality, one day"—these are Aristotle's rules for tragedy, and classic French plays strictly follow them; Shakespeare, however, disregards all these *canons*. A born rebel, Katya was constitutionally incapable of abiding by the *canons* of polite society.

cant N. insincere expressions of piety; jargon of thieves. Shocked by news of the minister's extramarital love affairs, the worshippers dismissed his talk about the sacredness of marriage as mere *cant*. *Cant* is a form of hypocrisy: those who can, pray; those who *cant*, pretend.

cantankerous ADJ. ill-humored; irritable. Constantly complaining about his treatment and refusing to cooperate with the hospital staff, he was a *cantankerous* patient.

canvass V. determine or seek opinions, votes, etc. After *canvassing* the sentiments of his constituents, the congressman was confident that he represented the majority opinion of his district. also N.

capacious ADJ. spacious. In the *capacious* areas of the railroad terminal, thousands of travelers lingered while waiting for their trains.

capacity N. mental or physical ability; role; ability to accommodate. Mike had the *capacity* to handle several jobs at once. In his *capacity* as president of SelecTronics he marketed an electronic dictionary with a *capacity* of 200,000 words.

capitulate V. surrender. Once the allied forces converged on Berlin in April 1945, the end was near; the Berlin garrison commander *capitulated* on the second of May.

■ **capricious** ADJ. unpredictable; fickle. The storm was *capricious*: it changed course constantly. Jill was *capricious*, too: she changed boyfriends almost as often as she changed clothes.

caption N. title; chapter heading; text under illustration. The *captions* that accompany *The Far Side* cartoons are almost as funny as the pictures. also V.

captious ADJ. faultfinding. His criticisms were always *captious* and frivolous, never offering constructive suggestions.

carcinogenic ADJ. causing cancer. Many supposedly harmless substances have been revealed to be *carcinogenic*.

cardinal ADJ. chief. If you want to increase your word power, the *cardinal* rule of vocabulary-building is to read.

caricature N. distortion; burlesque. The *caricatures* he drew always emphasized personal weaknesses of the people he burlesqued. also V.

carnage N. destruction of life. The film *The Killing Fields* vividly depicts the *carnage* wreaked by Pol Pot's followers in Cambodia.

carnal ADJ. fleshly. Is the public more interested in *carnal* pleasures than in spiritual matters? Compare the number of people who read *Playboy* daily to the number of those who read the Bible every day.

carnivorous ADJ. meat-eating. The lion's a *carnivorous* beast; a hunk of meat makes up his feast. A cow is not a *carnivore*; she likes the taste of grain, not gore.

carping N. petty criticism; fault-finding. Welcoming constructive criticism, Lexy appreciated her editor's comments, finding them free of *carping*. also ADJ.

caste N. one of the hereditary classes in Hindu society, social stratification; prestige. The differences created by *caste* in India must be wiped out if true democracy is to prevail in that country.

■ **castigation** N. punishment; severe criticism. Sensitive even to mild criticism, Woolf could not bear the *castigation* that she found in certain reviews. Ben Jonson was a highly moral playwright: in his plays, his purpose was to *castigate* vice and hypocrisy by exposing them publicly.

casualty N. serious or fatal accident. The number of automotive *casualties* on this holiday weekend was high.

cataclysm N. deluge; upheaval. A *cataclysm* such as the French Revolution affects all countries. cataclysmic, ADJ.

■ **catalyst** N. agent that influences the pace of a chemical reaction while it remains unaffected and unchanged; person or thing that causes action. After a banana is harvested, certain enzymes within its cells continue to act as a *catalyst* for the biochemical processes of ripening, thereby causing the banana eventually to rot. In 1969 the IRA split into two factions: the "officials," who advocated a united socialist Ireland but disavowed terrorist activities, and the "provisionals," who argued that terrorism was a necessary *catalyst* for unification.

catastrophe N. calamity; disaster. The 1906 San Francisco earthquake was a *catastrophe* that destroyed most of the city. A similar earthquake striking today could have even more *catastrophic* results.

catechism N. book for religious instruction; instruction by question and answer. He taught by engaging his pupils in a *catechism* until they gave him the correct answer.

categorical ADJ. without exceptions; unqualified; absolute. Though the captain claimed he was never, never sick at sea, he finally qualified his *categorical* denial: he was "hardly ever" sick at sea.

catharsis N. purging or cleansing of any passage of the body. Aristotle maintained that tragedy created a *catharsis* by purging the soul of base concepts.

cathartic N. purgative. Some drugs act as laxatives when taken in small doses but act as *cathartics* when taken in much larger doses. also ADJ.

catholic ADJ. universal; wide-ranging; liberal. He was extremely *catholic* in his taste and read everything he could find in the library.

caucus N. private meeting of members of a party to select officers or determine policy. At the opening of Congress the members of the Democratic Party held a *caucus* to elect the majority leader of the House and the party whip.

causal ADJ. implying a cause-and-effect relationship. The psychologist maintained there was a *causal* relationship between the nature of one's early childhood experiences and one's adult personality. causality, N.

■ **caustic** ADJ. burning; sarcastically biting. The critic's *caustic* remarks angered the hapless actors who were the subjects of his sarcasm.

cauterize V. burn with hot iron or caustic. In order to prevent infection, the doctor *cauterized* the wound.

cavalcade N. procession; parade. As described by Chaucer, the *cavalcade* of Canterbury pilgrims was a motley group.

cavalier ADJ. casual and offhand; arrogant. Sensitive about having her ideas taken lightly, Marcia felt insulted by Mark's *cavalier* dismissal of her suggestion.

cavil V. make frivolous objections. I respect your sensible criticisms, but I dislike the way you *cavil* about unimportant details. also N.

cede V. yield (title, territory) to; surrender formally. Eventually the descendants of England's Henry II were forced to *cede* their French territories to the King of France. cession, N.

celerity N. speed; rapidity. Hamlet resented his mother's *celerity* in remarrying within a month after his father's death.

celestial ADJ. heavenly. She spoke of the *celestial* joys that awaited virtuous souls in the hereafter.

celibate ADJ. abstaining from sexual intercourse; unmarried. Though the late Havelock Ellis wrote extensively about sexual customs and was considered an expert in such matters, recent studies maintain he was *celibate* throughout his life. celibacy, N.

Word List 8 censor–coalesce

censor N. overseer of morals; person who eliminates inappropriate matter. Soldiers dislike having their mail read by a *censor* but understand the need for this precaution. also V.

censorious ADJ. critical. *Censorious* people delight in casting blame.

censure V. blame; criticize. The senator was *censured* for behavior inappropriate to a member of Congress. also N.

cerebral ADJ. pertaining to the brain or intellect. Cumberbatch portrayed Holmes as a *cerebral*, almost affectless figure, someone whose passions were intellectual rather than emotional.

cerebration N. thought. "The mystic leans towards celebration; the mathematician to *cerebration*." (John D. Barrow)

ceremonious ADJ. marked by formality. Ordinary dress would be inappropriate at so *ceremonious* an affair.

certitude N. certainty. Though there was no *certitude* of his getting the job, Lou thought he had a good chance of being hired.

cessation N. stoppage. The airline's employees threatened a *cessation* of all work if management failed to meet their demands. cease, V.

cession N. yielding (something) to another; ceding. The Battle of Lake Erie, a major U.S. naval victory in the War of 1812, ensured U.S. control over Lake Erie and ruled out any territorial *cession* in the Northwest to Great Britain in the peace settlement.

chagrin N. vexation (caused by humiliation or injured pride); disappointment. Embarrassed by his parents' shabby, working-class appearance, Doug felt their visit to his school would bring him nothing but *chagrin*. A person filled with *chagrin* doesn't grin: he's too mortified.

chameleon N. lizard that changes color in different situations. Like the *chameleon*, he assumed the political coloration of every group he met.

champion V. support militantly. Martin Luther King, Jr., won the Nobel Peace Prize because he *championed* the oppressed in their struggle for equality. also N.

chaotic ADJ. in utter disorder. He tried to bring order into the *chaotic* state of affairs. chaos, N.

charisma N. divine gift; great popular charm or appeal. Political commentators have deplored the importance of a candidate's *charisma* in these days of television campaigning.

charlatan N. quack; pretender to knowledge. When they realized that the Wizard didn't know how to get them back to Kansas, Dorothy and her friends were sure they'd been duped by a *charlatan*.

chary ADJ. cautious; sparing or restrained about giving. A prudent, thrifty New Englander, DeWitt was as *chary* of investing money in junk bonds as he was *chary* of paying people unnecessary compliments.

chasm N. abyss. They could not see the bottom of the *chasm*.

chaste ADJ. pure; virginal; modest. To ensure that his bride would stay *chaste* while he was off to the wars, the crusader had her fitted out with a *chastity* belt. chastity, N.

chasten V. correct by punishment or scolding; restrain; rebuke. No matter how much a child deserves to be *chastened* for doing wrong, the maxim "Spare the rod and spoil the child" never justifies physical abuse. Someone sadder but wiser has been *chastened* or subdued by experience.

chastise V. punish or scold; reprimand. Miss Watson liked nothing better than to *chastise* Huck for his alleged offenses.

chauvinist N. blindly devoted patriot; zealous adherent of a group or cause. A *chauvinist* cannot recognize any faults in his country, no matter how flagrant they may be. Likewise, a male *chauvinist* cannot recognize how biased he is in favor of his own sex, no matter how flagrant that bias may be. chauvinistic, ADJ.

check V. stop motion; curb or restrain. Thrusting out her arm, Grandma *checked* Bobby's lunge at his sister. "Young man," she said, "you'd better *check* your temper." (secondary meaning)

checkered ADJ. marked by changes in fortune. During his *checkered* career he had lived in palatial mansions and in dreary boardinghouses.

cherubic ADJ. angelic; innocent-looking. With her cheerful smile and rosy cheeks, she was a particularly *cherubic* child.

■ **chicanery** N. trickery; deception. Those sneaky lawyers misrepresented what occurred, made up all sorts of implausible alternative scenarios to confuse the jurors, and in general depended on *chicanery* to win the case.

chide V. scold. Grandma began to *chide* Steven for his lying.

chimerical ADJ. fantastically improbable; highly unrealistic; imaginative. As everyone expected, Ted's *chimerical* scheme to make a fortune by raising ermines in his backyard proved a dismal failure. chimera, N.

chivalrous ADJ. courteous; faithful; brave. *Chivalrous* behavior involves noble words and good deeds.

choleric ADJ. hot-tempered. His flushed, angry face indicated a *choleric* nature.

choreography N. art of representing dances in written symbols; arrangement of dances. Merce Cunningham used a computer in designing *choreography*: a software program allowed him to compose arrangements of possible moves and immediately view them onscreen.

chortle V. chuckle with delight. When she heard that her rival had just been jailed for embezzlement, she *chortled* with joy. She was *not* a nice lady.

chronic ADJ. long established, as a disease. The doctors were finally able to attribute his *chronic* headaches and nausea to traces of formaldehyde gas in his apartment.

chronicle V. report; record (in chronological order). The gossip columnist was paid to *chronicle* the latest escapades of the socially prominent celebrities. also N.

churlish ADJ. boorish; rude. Dismayed by his *churlish* manners at the party, the girls vowed never to invite him again.

cipher N. nonentity; worthless person or thing. She claimed her ex-husband was a total *cipher* and wondered why she had ever married him.

cipher N. secret code. Lacking his code book, the spy was unable to decode the message sent to him in *cipher*.

circuitous ADJ. roundabout. Because of the traffic congestion on the main highways, she took a *circuitous* route. circuit, N.

circumlocution N. unnecessarily wordy and indirect speech; evasive language. Don't beat about the bush, but just say what you want to say: I'm fed up with listening to your *circumlocutions*.

circumscribe V. limit narrowly; confine or restrict; define. The great lords of state tried to *circumscribe* the queen's power by having her accept a set of conditions that left the decisive voice in all important matters to the privy council.

circumspect ADJ. prudent; cautious. Investigating before acting, she tried always to be *circumspect*.

circumvent V. outwit; baffle. In order to *circumvent* the enemy, we will make two preliminary attacks in other sections before starting our major campaign.

citadel N. fortress. The *citadel* overlooked the city like a protecting angel.

cite V. quote; commend. She could *cite* passages in the Bible from memory. citation, N.

civil ADJ. having to do with citizens or the state; courteous and polite. Although Internal Revenue Service agents are *civil* servants, they are not always *civil* to suspected tax evaders.

clairvoyant ADJ., N. having foresight; fortuneteller. Cassandra's *clairvoyant* warning was not heeded by the Trojans. clairvoyance, N.

clamber V. climb by crawling. She *clambered* over the wall.

clamor N. noise. The *clamor* of the children at play outside made it impossible for her to take a nap. also V.

clandestine ADJ. secret. After avoiding their chaperon, the lovers had a *clandestine* meeting.

clangor N. loud, resounding noise. The blacksmith was accustomed to the *clangor* of hammers on steel.

cleave V. split or sever; cling to; remain faithful to. With her heavy *cleaver*, Julia Child could *cleave* a whole roast duck in two. Soaked through, the soldier tugged at the uniform that *cleaved* annoyingly to his body. He would *cleave* to his post, come rain or shine. cleavage, N. cloven, ADJ.

clemency N. disposition to be lenient; mildness, as of the weather. Why did the defense lawyer look pleased when his case was sent to Judge Bland's chambers? Bland was noted for her *clemency* to first offenders.

cliché N. phrase dulled in meaning by repetition. High school compositions are often marred by such *clichés* as "strong as an ox."

clientele N. body of customers. The rock club attracted a young, stylish *clientele*.

climactic ADJ. relating to the highest point. When he reached the *climactic* portions of the book, he could not stop reading. climax, N.

clime N. region; climate. His doctor advised him to move to a milder *clime*.

clique N. small, exclusive group. Fitzgerald wished that he belonged to the *clique* of popular athletes and big men on campus who seemed to run Princeton's social life.

clout N. great influence (especially political or social). Gatsby wondered whether he had enough *clout* to be admitted to the exclusive club.

cloying ADJ. distasteful (because excessive); excessively sweet or sentimental. Disliking the *cloying* sweetness of standard wedding cakes, Jody and Tom chose a homemade carrot cake for their reception. cloy, V.

coagulate V. thicken; congeal; clot. Even after you remove the pudding from the burner, it will continue to *coagulate* as it stands. coagulant, N.

coalesce V. combine; fuse. The brooks *coalesce* into one large river. When minor political parties *coalesce*, their *coalescence* may create a major coalition.

Word List 9 coalition–concentric

coalition N. partnership; league; union. The Rainbow *Coalition* united people of all races in a common cause.

coda N. concluding section of a musical or literary composition; something that rounds out, summarizes, or concludes. The piece concluded with a distinctive *coda* that strikingly brought together various motifs. Several months after Charlie Chaplin's death, his body was briefly kidnapped from a Swiss cemetery by a pair of bungling thieves—a macabre *coda* that Chaplin might have concocted for one of his own two-reelers.

coddle V. treat gently; pamper. Don't *coddle* the children so much; they need a taste of discipline.

codify V. arrange (laws, rules) as a code; classify. We need to take the varying rules and regulations of the different health agencies and *codify* them into a national health code.

coercion N. use of force to get someone to obey. The inquisitors used both physical and psychological *coercion* to force Joan of Arc to recant her assertions that her visions were sent by God. coerce, V.

■ **cogent** ADJ. convincing. It was inevitable that David chose to go to Harvard: he had several *cogent* reasons for doing so, including a full-tuition scholarship. Katya argued her case with such *cogency* that the jury had to decide in favor of her client.

cogitate V. think over. *Cogitate* on this problem; the solution will come.

cognate ADJ. related linguistically; allied by blood; similar or akin in nature. The English word "mother" is *cognate* to the Latin word "mater," whose influence is visible in the words "maternal" and "maternity." also N.

cognitive ADJ. having to do with knowing or perceiving related to the mental processes. Though Jack was emotionally immature, his *cognitive* development was admirable; he was very advanced intellectually.

cognizance N. knowledge. During the election campaign, the two candidates were kept in full *cognizance* of the international situation.

cohabit V. live together. Many unwed couples who *cohabit* peacefully for years wind up fighting night and day once they marry.

cohere V. stick together. Solids have a greater tendency to *cohere* than liquids.

cohesion N. tendency to keep together. A firm believer in the maxim "Divide and conquer," the emperor, by lies and trickery, sought to disrupt the *cohesion* of the free nations.

coincidence N. the chance occurrence, at the same time, of two or more seemingly connected events. Was it just a *coincidence* that John and she had met at the market for three days running, or was he deliberately trying to seek her out? coincidental, ADJ.

colander N. utensil with perforated bottom used for straining. Before serving the spaghetti, place it in a *colander* to drain it.

collaborate V. work together. Two writers *collaborated* in preparing this book.

collate V. arrange in order; examine in order to verify authenticity. Ashby Village in Berkeley is *collating* details of organizations that provide services to senior citizens, with the expectation of eventually publishing a list.

collateral N. security given for loan. The sum you wish to borrow is so large that it must be secured by *collateral*.

colloquial ADJ. pertaining to conversational or common speech; informal. Some of the new *colloquial* reading passages on standardized tests have a conversational tone intended to make them more appealing to test-takers.

collusion N. secret cooperation to cheat; conspiring in a fraudulent scheme. One method of *collusion* between test takers on multiple-choice tests involves signaling the correct answers by silently tapping one's fingers in a prearranged code.

colossal ADJ. huge. Radio City Music Hall has a *colossal* stage.

colossus N. gigantic statue. The legendary *Colossus* of Rhodes, a bronze statue of the sun god that dominated the harbor of the Greek seaport, was one of the Seven Wonders of the World.

comatose ADJ. in a coma; extremely sleepy. The long-winded orator soon had his audience in a *comatose* state.

combustible ADJ. easily burned. After the recent outbreak of fires in private homes, the fire commissioner ordered that all *combustible* materials be kept in safe containers. also N.

comeuppance N. rebuke; deserts. After his earlier rudeness, we were delighted to see him get his *comeuppance*.

comity N. courtesy; civility. A spirit of *comity* should exist among nations.

commandeer V. to draft for military purposes; to take for public use. The policeman *commandeered* the first car that approached and ordered the driver to go to the nearest hospital.

commemorative ADJ. remembering; honoring. The new *commemorative* stamp honors the late Martin Luther King, Jr.

■ **commensurate** ADJ. corresponding in extent, degree, amount, etc.; proportionate. By the close of World War II much progress had been made in assigning nurses rank and responsibilities *commensurate* with their training and abilities. Critics in the industry charged that imposing new meat inspection regulations without dismantling the traditional system would raise costs without bringing about a *commensurate* improvement in safety.

commiserate V. feel or express pity or sympathy for. Her friends *commiserated* with the widow.

commodious ADJ. spacious and comfortable. After sleeping in small roadside cabins, they found their hotel suite *commodious*.

communal ADJ. held in common; a group of people. When they were divorced, they had trouble dividing their *communal* property.

compact N. agreement; contract. The signers of the Mayflower *Compact* were establishing a form of government.

compact ADJ. tightly packed; firm; brief. His short, *compact* body was better suited to wrestling than to basketball.

compatible ADJ. harmonious; in harmony with. They were *compatible* neighbors, never quarreling over unimportant matters. compatibility, N.

compelling ADJ. overpowering; irresistible in effect. The prosecutor presented a well-reasoned case, but the defense attorney's *compelling* arguments for leniency won over the jury.

■ **compendium** N. brief, comprehensive summary. This text can serve as a *compendium* of the tremendous amount of new material being developed in this field.

compensatory ADJ. making up for; repaying. Can a *compensatory* education program make up for the inadequate schooling he received in earlier years?

compilation N. listing of statistical information in tabular or book form. The *compilation* of available scholarships serves a very valuable purpose.

compile V. assemble; gather; accumulate. We planned to *compile* a list of the words most frequently used on the GRE.

complacency N. self-satisfaction; smugness. Full of *complacency* about his latest victories, he looked smugly at the row of trophies on his mantelpiece. complacent, ADJ.

■ **complaisant** ADJ. trying to please; overly polite; obliging. Fearing that the king might become enraged if his will were thwarted, the *complaisant* Parliament recognized Henry VIII as king of Ireland. Someone *complaisant* is not smug or complacent; he yields to others because he has an excessive need to please.

complement V. complete; consummate; make perfect. The waiter recommended a glass of port to *complement* the cheese. also N.

complementary ADJ. serving to complete something. John's and Lexy's skills are *complementary*: he's good at following a daily routine, while she's great at improvising and handling emergencies. Together they make a great team.

compliance N. readiness to yield; conformity in fulfilling requirements. Bullheaded Bill was not noted for his easy *compliance* to the demands of others. As an architect, however, Bill recognized that his design for the new school had to be in *compliance* with the local building code.

■ **compliant** ADJ. yielding; conforming to requirements. Because Joel usually gave in and went along with whatever his friends desired, his mother worried that he might be too *compliant*.

complicity N. involvement in a crime; participation. Queen Mary's marriage to Lord Darnley, her suspected *complicity* in his murder, and her hasty marriage to the earl of Bothwell stirred the Protestant lords to revolt. Although Spanish *complicity* in the sinking of the battleship *Maine* was not proved, U.S. public opinion was aroused and war sentiment rose.

component N. element; ingredient. I wish all the *components* of my stereo system were working at the same time.

comport V. bear one's self; behave. He *comported* himself with great dignity.

composure N. mental calmness. Even the latest work crisis failed to shake her *composure*.

compound V. combine; constitute; pay interest; increase. The makers of the popular cold remedy *compounded* a nasal decongestant with an antihistamine. also N.

comprehensive ADJ. thorough; inclusive. This book provides a *comprehensive* review of verbal and math skills for the GRE.

compress V. squeeze or press together; make more compact. Miss Watson *compressed* her lips in disapproval as she noted the bedraggled state of Huck's clothes. On farms, roller-packers are used in dry seasons to *compress* and pack down the soil after plowing.

comprise V. include; consist of. If the District of Columbia were to be granted statehood, the United States of America would *comprise* fifty-one states, not just fifty.

compromise V. adjust or settle by making mutual concessions; endanger the interests or reputation of. Sometimes the presence of a neutral third party can help adversaries *compromise* their differences. Unfortunately, you're not neutral. Therefore, your presence here *compromises* our chances of reaching an agreement. also N.

compunction N. remorse. The judge was especially severe in his sentencing because he felt that the criminal had shown no *compunction* for his heinous crime.

compute V. reckon; calculate. He failed to *compute* the interest, so his bank balance was not accurate.

concede V. admit; yield. Despite all the evidence Monica had assembled, Mark refused to *concede* that she was right.

conceit N. vanity or self-love; whimsical idea; extravagant metaphor. Although Jack was smug and puffed up with *conceit*, he was an entertaining companion, always expressing himself in amusing *conceits* and witty turns of phrase.

concentric ADJ. having a common center. The target was made of *concentric* circles.

Word List 10 conception–contiguous

conception N. notion or idea; act of beginning something, especially of *conceiving* a child. Back in the nineteenth century, scientists had no *conception* that a child's *conception* could take place outside a mother's body through the process of *in vitro* fertilization. conceive, V.

concerted ADJ. mutually agreed on; done together. All the Girl Scouts made a *concerted* effort to raise funds for their annual outing. When the movie star appeared, his fans let out a *concerted* sigh.

concession N. an act of yielding. Before they could reach an agreement, both sides had to make certain *concessions*.

■ **conciliatory** ADJ. reconciling; soothing. She was still angry despite his *conciliatory* words. conciliate, V.

concise ADJ. brief and compact. When you define a new word, be *concise*: the shorter the definition, the easier it is to remember.

conclusive ADJ. decisive; ending all debate. When the stolen books turned up in John's locker, we finally had *conclusive* evidence of the identity of the mysterious thief.

concoct V. prepare by combining; make up in concert. How did the inventive chef ever *concoct* such a strange dish? concoction, N.

concomitant N. that which accompanies. A decrease of gastric juice secretion may be a congenital abnormality or a *concomitant* of advanced age. The word *hubbub* emphasizes turbulent activity and *concomitant* din: the hubbub of Wall Street traders shouting out buy orders, for example.

concord N. harmony. Watching Tweedledum and Tweedledee battle, Alice wondered why the two brothers could not manage to live in *concord*.

concur V. agree. Did you *concur* with the decision of the court or did you find it unfair?

concurrent ADJ. happening at the same time. In America, the colonists were resisting the demands of the mother country; at the *concurrent* moment in France, the middle class was sowing the seeds of rebellion.

condescend V. bestow courtesies with a superior air. The king *condescended* to grant an audience to the friends of the condemned man. condescension, N.

condole V. express sympathetic sorrow. His friends gathered to *condole* with him over his loss. condolence, N.

■ **condone** V. overlook; forgive; give tacit approval; excuse. Unlike Widow Douglass, who *condoned* Huck's minor offenses, Miss Watson did nothing but scold.

conducive ADJ. helpful; contributive. Rest and proper diet are *conducive* to good health.

confidant N. trusted friend. He had no *confidants* with whom he could discuss his problems at home.

confine V. shut in; restrict. The terrorists had *confined* their prisoner in a small room. However, they had not chained him to the wall or done anything else to *confine* his movements. confinement, N.

confiscate V. seize; commandeer. The army *confiscated* all available supplies of uranium.

conflagration N. great fire. In the *conflagration* that followed the 1906 earthquake, much of San Francisco was destroyed.

conflate V. meld or fuse; confuse; combine into one. In his painting *White Crucifixion*, which depicts German Jews terrorized by a Nazi mob, Chagall *conflates* Jewish and Christian symbols, portraying the crucified Christ wrapped in a *tallith*, a Jewish prayer shawl. The anthropologist Mahmood Mamdani maintains that terrorism is a unique product of the modern world and should not be *conflated* with Islam.

confluence N. flowing together; crowd. They built the city at the *confluence* of two rivers.

conformity N. harmony; agreement. In *conformity* with our rules and regulations, I am calling a meeting of our organization.

■ **confound** v. confuse; puzzle. No mystery could *confound* Sherlock Holmes for long.

congeal v. freeze; coagulate. His blood *congealed* in his veins as he saw the dread monster rush toward him.

congenial ADJ. pleasant; friendly. My father loved to go out for a meal with *congenial* companions.

congenital ADJ. existing at birth. Doctors are able to cure some *congenital* deformities such as cleft palates by performing operations on infants.

conglomeration N. mass of material sticking together. In such a *conglomeration* of miscellaneous statistics, it was impossible to find a single area of analysis.

congruence N. correspondence of parts; harmonious relationship. The student demonstrated the *congruence* of the two triangles by using the hypotenuse-leg theorem.

congruent ADJ. in agreement; corresponding. In formulating a hypothesis, we must keep it *congruent* with what we know of the real world; it cannot disagree with our experience.

conjecture v. infer on the basis of insufficient data; surmise; guess. In the absence of any eyewitness reports, we can only *conjecture* what happened in the locked room on the night of the 13th. Would it be a reasonable *conjecture* to decide that the previous sentence is an excerpt from a mystery novel?

conjure v. summon a devil; practice magic; imagine or invent. Sorcerers *conjure* devils to appear. Magicians *conjure* white rabbits out of hats. Political candidates *conjure* up images of reformed cities and a world at peace.

connivance N. pretense of ignorance of something wrong; assistance; permission to offend. With the *connivance* of his friends, he plotted to embarrass the teacher. connive, v.

■ **connoisseur** N. person competent to act as a judge of art, etc.; a lover of an art. Bernard Berenson, the American art critic and *connoisseur* of Italian art, was hired by wealthy art lovers to select paintings for their collections.

connotation N. suggested or implied meaning of an expression. Foreigners frequently are unaware of the *connotations* of the words they use.

conscientious ADJ. scrupulous; careful. A *conscientious* editor, she checked every definition for its accuracy.

consecrate v. dedicate; sanctify. In 1804, Napoleon forced Pope Pius VII to come to Paris to *consecrate* him as emperor, only to humiliate Pius at the last minute by taking the crown from the pope's hands and crowning himself.

consensus N. general agreement; opinion reached by a group as a whole. Letty Cottin Pogrebin argues that, although the ultra-right would like us to believe that families disintegrate because of secular education and sexual liberation, the *consensus* of Americans is that what tears families apart is unemployment, inflation, and financial worries.

consequential ADJ. pompous; self-important. Convinced of his own importance, the actor strutted about the dressing room with a *consequential* air.

consign v. deliver officially; entrust; set apart. The court *consigned* the child to her paternal grandmother's care. consignment, N.

consistency N. absence of contradictions; dependability; uniformity; degree of thickness. Holmes judged puddings and explanations on their *consistency*: he liked his puddings without lumps and his explanations without improbabilities.

console v. lessen sadness or disappointment; give comfort. When her father died, Marius did his best to *console* Cosette. consolation, N.

consolidation N. unification; process of becoming firmer or stronger. The recent *consolidation* of several small airlines into one major company has left observers of the industry wondering whether room still exists for the "little guy" in aviation. consolidate, v.

consonance N. harmony; agreement. Her agitation seemed out of *consonance* with her usual calm. The 1815 so-called "Holy Alliance" of the emperors of Russia and Austria and the king of Prussia accomplished nothing, since it was merely a vague agreement that the sovereigns would conduct themselves in *consonance* with Christian principles.

consort v. associate with. We frequently judge people by the company with whom they *consort*.

consort N. husband or wife. The search for a *consort* for the young Queen Victoria ended happily.

conspiracy N. treacherous plot. Brutus and Cassius joined in the *conspiracy* to kill Julius Caesar.

consternation N. dismay; sudden alarm. To her *consternation*, when she arrived at the airport, she discovered that she had left her passport at home.

constituent N. supporter. The congressman received hundreds of letters from angry *constituents* after the Equal Rights Amendment failed to pass.

constraint N. compulsion; repression of feelings. There was a feeling of *constraint* in the room because no one dared to criticize the speaker. constrain, v.

construe v. explain; interpret. If I *construe* your remarks correctly, you disagree with the theory that the previous speaker advanced.

consummate ADJ. wholly without flaw; supremely skilled; complete and utter. Free of her father's autocratic rule, safely married to the man she loved, Elizabeth Barrett Browning felt *consummate* happiness. Da Vinci depicted in his drawings, with scientific precision and *consummate* artistry, subjects ranging from flying machines to intricate anatomical studies of people, animals, and plants. There is no one as boring as Boris; he is a *consummate* bore.

contagion N. infection. Fearing *contagion*, they took drastic steps to prevent the spread of the disease.

contaminate v. pollute. The sewage system of the city so *contaminated* the water that swimming was forbidden.

contempt N. scorn; disdain. The heavyweight boxer looked on ordinary people with *contempt*, scorning them as weaklings who couldn't hurt a fly. We thought it was *contemptible* of him to be *contemptuous* of people for being weak.

contend v. struggle; compete; assert earnestly. In *Revolt of the Black Athlete*, sociologist Harry Edwards *contends* that young black athletes have been exploited by some college recruiters. contention, N.

■ **contention** N. claim; thesis. It is our *contention* that, if you follow our tactics, you will boost your score on the GRE. contend, v.

■ **contentious** ADJ. quarrelsome. Disagreeing violently with the referees' ruling, the coach became so *contentious* that the referees threw him out of the game.

contest v. dispute. The defeated candidate attempted to *contest* the election results.

context N. writings preceding and following the passage quoted. Because these lines are taken out of *context*, they do not convey the message the author intended.

contiguous ADJ. adjacent to; touching upon. The two countries are *contiguous* for a few miles; then they are separated by the gulf.

Word List 11 contingent–cumbersome

contingent ADJ. dependent on; conditional. Cher's father informed her that any increase in her allowance was *contingent* on the quality of her final grades. contingency, N.

contingent N. group that makes up part of a gathering. The New York *contingent* of delegates at the Democratic National Convention was a boisterous, sometimes rowdy lot.

contortions N. twistings; distortions. As the effects of the opiate wore away, the *contortions* of the patient became more violent and demonstrated how much pain she was enduring.

contraband N. illegal trade; smuggling; smuggled goods. The Coast Guard tries to prevent *contraband* in U.S. waters. also ADJ.

contravene V. contradict; oppose: infringe on or transgress. Mr. Barrett did not expect his frail daughter Elizabeth to *contravene* his will by eloping with Robert Browning.

■ **contrite** ADJ. penitent. Her *contrite* tears did not influence the judge when he imposed sentence. contrition, N.

contrived ADJ. forced; artificial; not spontaneous. Feeling ill at ease with his new in-laws, James made a few *contrived* attempts at conversation and then retreated into silence.

controvert V. oppose with arguments; attempt to refute; contradict. The witness's testimony was so clear and her reputation for honesty so well established that the defense attorney decided it was wiser to make no attempt to *controvert* what she said.

contumacious ADJ. disobedient; resisting authority. The *contumacious* mob shouted defiantly at the police. contumacy, N.

conundrum N. riddle; difficult problem. During the long car ride, she invented *conundrums* to entertain the children.

convene V. assemble. Because much needed legislation had to be enacted, the governor ordered the legislature to *convene* in special session by January 15.

convention N. social or moral custom; established practice. Flying in the face of *convention,* George Sand (Amandine Dudevant) shocked her contemporaries by taking lovers and wearing men's clothes.

conventional ADJ. ordinary; typical. His *conventional* upbringing left him wholly unprepared for his wife's eccentric family.

■ **converge** V. approach; tend to meet; come together. African-American men from all over the United States *converged* on Washington to take part in the historic Million Man March. convergence, N.

conversant ADJ. familiar with. In this age of specialization, someone reasonably *conversant* with modern French literature may be wholly unacquainted with the novels of Latin America and Spain.

converse N. opposite. The inevitable *converse* of peace is not war but annihilation.

convert N. one who has adopted a different religion or opinion. On his trip to Japan, though the president spoke at length about the merits of American automobiles, he made few *converts* to his beliefs. also V.

conviction N. judgment that someone is guilty of a crime; strongly held belief. Even her *conviction* for murder did not shake Lord Peter's *conviction* that Harriet was innocent of the crime.

convivial ADJ. festive; gay; characterized by joviality. The *convivial* celebrators of the victory sang their college songs.

convoke V. call together. To the surprise of Vatican observers, the new Pope John XXIII announced his intention to *convoke* an ecumenical council. convocation, N.

■ **convoluted** ADJ. coiled around; involved; intricate. His argument was so *convoluted* that few of us could follow it intelligently.

copious ADJ. plentiful. Unlike Sharon, who took *copious* notes during lectures, David did not take notes in class but waited until back in the dorm to write a brief summary of what he had learned.

cordial ADJ. gracious; heartfelt. Our hosts greeted us at the airport with a *cordial* welcome and a hearty hug.

corollary N. consequence; accompaniment. Brotherly love is a complex emotion, with sibling rivalry its natural *corollary.*

corporeal ADJ. bodily; material. The doctor had no patience with spiritual matters: his job was to attend to his patients' *corporeal* problems, not to minister to their souls.

correlation N. mutual relationship. He sought to determine the *correlation* that existed between ability in algebra and ability to interpret reading exercises. correlate, V., N.

corroborate V. confirm; support. Though Huck was quite willing to *corroborate* Tom's story, Aunt Polly knew better than to believe either of them.

corrode V. destroy by chemical action. The girders supporting the bridge *corroded* so gradually that no one suspected any danger until the bridge suddenly collapsed. corrosion, N.

corrosive ADJ. eating away by chemicals or disease. Stainless steel is able to withstand the effects of *corrosive* chemicals.

cosmic ADJ. pertaining to the universe; vast. *Cosmic* rays derive their name from the fact that they bombard the earth's atmosphere from outer space. cosmos, N.

countenance V. approve; tolerate. Miss Manners refused to *countenance* such rude behavior on their part.

countenance N. face. When José saw his newborn daughter, a proud smile spread across his *countenance.*

countermand V. cancel; revoke. The general *countermanded* the orders issued in his absence.

counterpart N. person or thing that functions in the same way as another; equivalent. Among the many differences that set folk musicians apart from their pop music *counterparts* is longevity.

coup N. highly successful action or sudden attack. As the news of his *coup* spread throughout Wall Street, his fellow brokers dropped by to congratulate him.

couple V. join; unite. The Flying Karamazovs *couple* expert juggling and amateur joking in their nightclub act.

courier N. messenger. The publisher sent a special *courier* to pick up the manuscript.

covenant N. agreement. We must comply with the terms of the *covenant.*

covert ADJ. secret; hidden; implied. Investigations of the Central Intelligence Agency and other secret service networks reveal that such *covert* operations can get out of control.

covetous ADJ. avaricious; eagerly desirous of. The poor man wants many things; the *covetous* man, all. During the Civil War, the Confederates cast *covetous* eyes on California, hoping to seize ports for privateers, as well as gold and silver to replenish the South's sagging treasury. covet, V.

cow V. terrorize; intimidate. The little boy was so *cowed* by the hulking bully that he gave up his lunch money without a word of protest.

cower V. shrink quivering, as from fear. The frightened child *cowered* in the corner of the room.

coy ADJ. shy; modest; coquettish. Reluctant to commit herself so early in the game, Kay was *coy* in her answers to Ken's offer.

crass ADJ. very unrefined; grossly insensible. The film critic deplored the *crass* commercialism of movie-makers who abandon artistic standards in order to make a quick buck.

■ **craven** ADJ. cowardly. Lillian's *craven* refusal to join the protest was criticized by her comrades, who had expected her to be brave enough to stand up for her beliefs.

credence N. belief. It is unlikely that Richard III killed his queen, but his evident alarm at the thought that such a story might gain *credence* even among his faithful followers clearly shows how fragile he felt his reputation to be.

credo N. creed. Just two months before his death, as he talked about life with some friends, the writer Jack London proclaimed his *credo*: "The proper function of man is to live, not to exist. I shall not waste my days in trying to prolong them. I shall use my time."

credulity N. belief on slight evidence; gullibility; naiveté. Con artists take advantage of the *credulity* of inexperienced investors to swindle them out of their savings. credulous, ADJ.

creed N. system of religious or ethical belief. I have a dream that one day this nation will rise up and live out the true meaning of its *creed*: "We hold these truths to be self-evident that all men are created equal."(Martin Luther King, Jr.)

crescendo N. increase in the volume or intensity, as in a musical passage; climax. The overture suddenly changed from a quiet pastoral theme to a *crescendo* featuring blaring trumpets and clashing cymbals.

crestfallen ADJ. dejected; dispirited. We were surprised at his reaction to the failure of his project; instead of being *crestfallen*, he was busily engaged in planning new activities.

cringe V. shrink back, as if in fear. The dog *cringed*, expecting a blow.

criteria N. PL. standards used in judging. What *criteria* did you use when you selected this essay as the prize winner? criterion, SING.

crux N. essential or main point. Will the Turkish people as a whole embrace Islamism, or will they adopt European values and standards? This is the *crux* of the matter; the answer will determine Europe's future for decades to come. crucial, ADJ.

crypt N. secret recess or vault usually used for burial. Until recently only bodies of rulers and leading statesmen were interred in this *crypt*.

cryptic ADJ. mysterious; hidden; secret. Thoroughly baffled by Holmes's *cryptic* remarks, Watson wondered whether Holmes was intentionally concealing his thoughts about the crime.

cull V. pick out; reject. Every month the farmer *culls* the nonlaying hens from his flock and sells them to the local butcher. also N.

culmination N. attainment of highest point. His inauguration as President of the United States marked the *culmination* of his political career.

culpable ADJ. deserving blame. Corrupt politicians who condone the activities of the gamblers are equally *culpable*.

cumbersome ADJ. heavy; hard to manage. She was burdened with *cumbersome* parcels.

Word List 12 cumulative–delusion

cumulative ADJ. growing by addition. Vocabulary-building is a *cumulative* process: as you go through your flash cards, you will add new words to your vocabulary, one by one.

cupidity N. greed. The defeated people could not satisfy the *cupidity* of the conquerors, who demanded excessive tribute.

curator N. superintendent; manager. The members of the board of trustees of the museum expected the new *curator* to plan events and exhibits that would make the museum more popular.

cursory ADJ. casual; hastily done. Because a *cursory* examination of the ruins indicates the possibility of arson, we believe the insurance agency should undertake a more extensive investigation of the fire's cause.

curtail V. shorten; reduce. When Elton asked Cher for a date, she said she was really sorry she couldn't go out with him, but her dad had ordered her to *curtail* her social life.

cynical ADJ. skeptical or distrustful of human motives. *Cynical* from birth, Sidney was suspicious whenever anyone gave him a gift "with no strings attached." cynic, N. cynicism, N.

dabble V. work at in a nonserious fashion; splash around. The amateur painter *dabbled* at art, but seldom produced a finished piece. The children *dabbled* their hands in the bird bath, splashing one another gleefully.

damp V. lessen in intensity; diminish; mute. Not even the taunts of his brother, who considered ballet no proper pursuit for a lad, could *damp* Billy Elliot's enthusiasm for dancing.

dank ADJ. damp. The walls of the dungeon were *dank* and slimy.

daub V. smear (as with paint). From the way he *daubed* his paint on the canvas, I could tell he knew nothing of oils. also N.

■ **daunt** V. intimidate; frighten. "Boast all you like of your prowess. Mere words cannot *daunt* me," the hero answered the villain.

dauntless ADJ. bold. Despite the dangerous nature of the undertaking, the *dauntless* soldier volunteered for the assignment.

dawdle V. loiter; waste time. We have to meet a deadline. Don't *dawdle*; just get down to work.

deadlock N. standstill; stalemate. Because negotiations had reached a *deadlock*, some of the delegates had begun to mutter about breaking off the talks. also V.

deadpan ADJ. wooden; impassive. Silent film comedian Buster Keaton earned the nickname "The Great Stone Face" for the invariably stoic, *deadpan* expression he maintained throughout his slapstick escapades.

dearth N. scarcity. The *dearth* of skilled labor compelled the employers to open trade schools.

debacle N. sudden downfall; complete disaster. In the *Airplane* movies, every flight turns into a *debacle*, with passengers and crew members collapsing, engines falling apart, and carry-on baggage popping out of the overhead bins.

debase V. reduce the quality or value; lower in esteem; degrade. In *The King and I*, Anna refuses to kneel down and prostrate herself before the king; she feels that to do so would *debase* her position, and she will not submit to such *debasement*.

debauch V. corrupt; seduce from virtue. Did Socrates' teachings lead the young men of Athens to be virtuous citizens, or did they *debauch* the young men, causing them to question the customs of their fathers? Clearly, Socrates' philosophical talks were nothing like the wild *debauchery* of the toga parties in *Animal House*.

debilitate V. weaken; enfeeble. Michael's severe bout of the flu *debilitated* him so much that he was too tired to go to work for a week.

debonair ADJ. urbane and suave; amiable; cheerful and carefree. Reporters frequently describe polished and charming leading men—Cary Grant or Pierce Brosnan, for example—as *debonair*.

debris N. rubble. A full year after the earthquake in Mexico City, workers were still carting away the *debris*.

debunk V. expose as false, exaggerated, worthless, etc.; ridicule. Pointing out that he consistently had voted against strengthening antipollution legislation, reporters *debunked* the candidate's claim that he was a fervent environmentalist.

decadence N. decay. The moral *decadence* of the people was reflected in the lewd literature of the period.

decelerate V. slow down. Seeing the emergency blinkers in the road ahead, he *decelerated* quickly.

decimate V. kill, usually one out of ten. We do more to *decimate* our population in automobile accidents than we do in war.

decipher V. decode. I could not *decipher* the doctor's handwriting.

■ **decorum** N. propriety; orderliness and good taste in manners. Even the best-mannered students have trouble behaving with *decorum* on the last day of school. decorous, ADJ.

decoy N. lure or bait. The wild ducks were not fooled by the *decoy*. also V.

decrepitude N. state of collapse caused by illness or old age. I was unprepared for the state of *decrepitude* in which I had found my old friend; he seemed to have aged twenty years in six months.

decry V. express strong disapproval of; disparage. The founder of the Children's Defense Fund, Marian Wright Edelman, strongly *decries* the lack of financial and moral support for children in America today.

deducible ADJ. derived by reasoning. If we accept your premise, your conclusions are easily *deducible*.

deface V. mar; disfigure. If you *deface* a library book you will have to pay a hefty fine.

defame V. harm someone's reputation; malign; slander. If you try to *defame* my good name, my lawyers will see you in court. If rival candidates persist in *defaming* one another, the voters may conclude that all politicians are crooks. defamation, N.

■ **default** N. failure to act. When the visiting team failed to show up for the big game, they lost the game by *default*. When Jack failed to make the payments on his Jaguar, the dealership took back the car because he had *defaulted* on his debt.

defeatist ADJ. resigned to defeat; accepting defeat as a natural outcome. If you maintain your *defeatist* attitude, you will never succeed. also N.

defection N. desertion. The children, who had made him an idol, were hurt most by his *defection* from our cause.

defer V. delay till later; exempt temporarily. In wartime, some young men immediately volunteer to serve; others *defer* making plans until they hear from their draft boards. During the Vietnam War, many young men, hoping to be *deferred*, requested student *deferments*.

defer V. give in respectfully; submit. When it comes to making decisions about purchasing software, we must *defer* to Michael, our computer guru; he has the final word. Michael, however, can *defer* these questions to no one; only he can decide.

■ **deference** N. courteous regard for another's wish. In *deference* to the minister's request, please do not take photographs during the wedding service.

defiance N. refusal to yield; resistance. When John reached the "terrible two's," he responded to every parental request with howls of *defiance*. defy, V. defiant, ADJ.

defile V. pollute; profane. The hoodlums *defiled* the church with their scurrilous writing.

definitive ADJ. most reliable or complete. Carl Sandburg's *Abraham Lincoln* may be regarded as the *definitive* work on the life of the Great Emancipator.

deflect V. turn aside. His life was saved when his cigarette case *deflected* the bullet.

defray V. provide for the payment of. Her employer offered to *defray* the costs of her postgraduate education.

deft ADJ. neat; skillful. The *deft* waiter uncorked the champagne without spilling a drop.

defunct ADJ. dead; no longer in use or existence. The lawyers sought to examine the books of the *defunct* corporation.

degenerate V. become worse; deteriorate. As the fight dragged on, the champion's style *degenerated* until he could barely keep on his feet.

degradation N. humiliation; debasement; degeneration. Some secretaries object to fetching the boss a cup of coffee because they resent the *degradation* of being made to perform such lowly tasks. degrade, V.

dehydrate V. remove water from; dry out. Running under a hot sun quickly *dehydrates* the body; joggers avoid *dehydration* by carrying water bottles and drinking from them frequently.

deify V. turn into a god; idolize. Admire the rock star all you want; just don't *deify* him.

deign V. condescend; stoop. The celebrated fashion designer would not *deign* to speak to a mere seamstress; his overburdened assistant had to convey the master's wishes to the lowly workers assembling his great designs.

delete V. erase; strike out. If you *delete* this paragraph, the composition will have more appeal.

deleterious ADJ. harmful. If you believe that smoking is *deleterious* to your health (and the Surgeon General surely does), then quit!

deliberate V. consider; ponder. Offered the new job, she asked for time to *deliberate* before she made her decision.

■ **delineate** V. portray; depict; sketch. Using only a few descriptive phrases, Austen *delineates* the character of Mr. Collins so well that we can predict his every move. delineation, N.

delirium N. mental disorder marked by confusion. In his *delirium*, the drunkard saw pink panthers and talking pigs. Perhaps he wasn't *delirious*: he might just have wandered into a movie house.

delude V. deceive. The mistress *deludes* herself into believing that her lover will leave his wife and marry her.

deluge N. flood; rush. When we advertised the position we received a *deluge* of applications. also V.

delusion N. false belief; hallucination. Don suffers from *delusions* of grandeur: he thinks he's a world-famous author when he's published just one paperback book.

Word List 13 delusive–diatribe

delusive ADJ. deceptive; raising vain hopes. Do not raise your hopes on the basis of his *delusive* promises.

delve V. dig; investigate. *Delving* into old books and manuscripts is part of a researcher's job.

demagogue N. person who appeals to people's prejudice; false leader. He was accused of being a *demagogue* because he made promises that aroused futile hopes in his listeners.

demean V. degrade; humiliate. Standing on his dignity, he refused to *demean* himself by replying to the offensive letter. If you truly believed in the dignity of labor, you would not think it would *demean* you to work as a janitor.

demeanor N. behavior; bearing. His sober *demeanor* quieted the noisy revelers.

demented ADJ. insane. Doctor Demento was a radio personality who liked to act as if he were truly *demented*. If you're *demented*, your mental state is out of whack; in other words, you're wacky.

demise N. death. Upon the *demise* of the dictator, a bitter dispute about succession to power developed.

demographic ADJ. related to population balance. In conducting a survey, one should take into account *demographic* trends in the region. demography, N.

demolition N. destruction. One of the major aims of the air force was the complete *demolition* of all means of transportation by the bombing of rail lines and terminals. demolish, V.

demoniac ADJ. fiendish. Gleeful at the success of his fiendish plot, the Joker howled with *demoniac* laughter. demon, N.

demur N. objection; protest. Michelangelo regularly denied that Leonardo Da Vinci had influenced him, and critics have usually accepted his statements without *demur*.

demur V. object (because of doubts, scruples); hesitate. When offered a post on the board of directors, David *demurred*: he had scruples about taking on the job because he was unsure he could handle it in addition to his other responsibilities.

demure ADJ. grave; serious; coy. She was *demure* and reserved, a nice modest girl whom any young man would be proud to take home to his mother.

■ **denigrate** V. blacken. All attempts to *denigrate* the character of our late president have failed; the people still love him and cherish his memory.

denizen N. inhabitant or resident; regular visitor. In *The Untouchables*, Eliot Ness fights Al Capone and the other *denizens* of Chicago's underworld. Ness's fight against corruption was the talk of all the *denizens* of the local bars.

denotation N. meaning; distinguishing by name. A dictionary will always give us the *denotation* of a word; frequently, it will also give us its connotation.

denouement N. outcome; final development of the plot of a play or other literary work. The play was childishly written; the *denouement* was obvious to sophisticated theatergoers as early as the middle of the first act.

denounce V. condemn; criticize. The reform candidate *denounced* the corrupt city officers for having betrayed the public's trust. denunciation, N.

depict V. portray. In this sensational exposé, the author *depicts* Beatle John Lennon as a drug-crazed neurotic. Do you question the accuracy of this *depiction* of Lennon?

deplete v. reduce; exhaust. We must wait until we *deplete* our present inventory before we order replacements.

deplore v. regret. Although I *deplore* the vulgarity of your language, I defend your right to express yourself freely.

deploy v. spread out [troops] in an extended though shallow battle line. The general ordered the battalion to *deploy* in order to meet the enemy offensive.

depose v. dethrone; remove from office. The army attempted to *depose* the king and set up a military government.

depravity N. extreme corruption; wickedness. The *depravity* of Caligula's behavior eventually sickened even those who had willingly participated in his earlier, comparatively innocent orgies. deprave, v.

deprecate v. express disapproval of; protest against; belittle. A firm believer in old-fashioned courtesy, Miss Post *deprecated* the modern tendency to address new acquaintances by their first names. deprecatory, ADJ.

depreciate v. lessen in value. If you neglect this property, it will *depreciate.*

depredation N. plundering. After the *depredations* of the invaders, the people were penniless.

derange v. make insane; disarrange. Hamlet's cruel rejection *deranged* poor Ophelia; in her madness, she drowned herself.

derelict ADJ. abandoned; negligent. The *derelict* craft was a menace to navigation. Whoever abandoned it in the middle of the harbor was *derelict* in living up to his responsibilities as a boat owner. also N.

■ **deride** v. ridicule; make fun of. The critics *derided* his pretentious dialogue and refused to consider his play seriously. Despite the critics' *derision*, however, audiences were moved by the play, cheering its unabashedly sentimental conclusion. derisive, ADJ.

■ **derivative** ADJ. unoriginal; obtained from another source. Although her early poetry was clearly *derivative* in nature, the critics thought she had promise and eventually would find her own voice.

derogatory ADJ. expressing a low opinion. Because the word *Eskimo* has come under strong attack in recent years for its supposedly *derogatory* connotations, many Americans today either avoid the term or feel uneasy using it.

descry v. catch sight of. In the distance, we could barely *descry* the enemy vessels.

desecrate v. profane; violate the sanctity of. Shattering the altar and trampling the holy objects underfoot, the invaders *desecrated* the sanctuary.

■ **desiccate** v. dry up. A tour of this smokehouse will give you an idea of how the pioneers used to *desiccate* food in order to preserve it.

desolate ADJ. unpopulated; joyless. After six months in the crowded, bustling metropolis, David was so sick of people that he was ready to head for the most *desolate* patch of wilderness he could find.

desolate v. rob of joy; lay waste to; forsake. The bandits *desolated* the countryside, burning farms and carrying off the harvest.

despise v. look on with scorn; regard as worthless or distasteful. Mr. Bond, I *despise* spies; I look down on them as mean, *despicable*, honorless men, whom I would wipe from the face of the earth with as little concern as I would scrape dog droppings from the bottom of my shoe.

despoil v. strip of valuables; rob. Seeking plunder, the raiders *despoiled* the village, carrying off any valuables they found.

despondent ADJ. depressed; gloomy. To the distress of his parents, William became seriously *despondent* after he broke up with Jan. despondency, N.

despot N. tyrant; harsh, authoritarian ruler. How could a benevolent king turn overnight into a *despot*? despotism, N.

destitute ADJ. extremely poor. Because they had no health insurance, the father's costly illness left the family *destitute.* destitution, N.

desuetude N. state of disuse. Overshadowed by the newly popular waltzes and cotillions, the English country dances of Jane Austen's time fell into *desuetude* until they were rediscovered during the folk dance revival of the early twentieth century.

■ **desultory** ADJ. aimless; haphazard; digressing at random. In prison Malcolm X set himself the task of reading straight through the dictionary; to him, reading was purposeful, not *desultory.*

detached ADJ. emotionally removed; calm and objective; physically separate. A psychoanalyst must maintain a *detached* point of view and stay uninvolved with her patients' personal lives. To a child growing up in an apartment or a row house, to live in a *detached* house was an unattainable dream. (secondary meaning) detachment, N.

determination N. resolve; measurement or calculation; decision. Nothing could shake his *determination* that his children would get the best education that money could buy. Thanks to my pocket calculator, my *determination* of the answer to the problem took only seconds of my time.

■ **deterrent** N. something that discourages; hindrance. Does the threat of capital punishment serve as a *deterrent* to potential killers? also ADJ.

detraction N. slandering; aspersion. Because Susan B. Anthony and Elizabeth Cady Stanton dared to fight for women's rights, their motives, manners, dress, personal appearance, and character were held up to ridicule and *detraction.*

detrimental ADJ. harmful; damaging. The candidate's acceptance of major financial contributions from a well-known racist ultimately proved *detrimental* to his campaign, for he lost the backing of many of his early grassroots supporters. detriment, N.

deviate v. turn away from (a principle, norm); depart; diverge. Richard never *deviated* from his daily routine: every day he set off for work at eight o'clock, had his sack lunch at noon, and headed home at the stroke of five.

devious ADJ. roundabout; erratic; not straightforward. The Joker's plan was so *devious* that it was only with great difficulty we could follow its shifts and dodges.

devise v. think up; invent; plan. How clever he must be to have *devised* such a devious plan! What ingenious inventions might he have *devised* if he had turned his mind to science rather than crime.

devoid ADJ. lacking. You may think Cher's mind is a total void, but she's actually not *devoid* of intelligence. She just sounds like an airhead.

devolve v. be transferred to another; delegate to another; gradually worsen. Because Humpty Dumpty was too shattered by his fall to clean up his own mess, all the work of picking up the pieces *devolved* upon poor Alice.

devotee N. enthusiastic follower. A *devotee* of the opera, she bought season tickets every year.

devout ADJ. pious. The *devout* man prayed daily.

dexterous ADJ. skillful. The magician was so *dexterous* that we could not follow his movements as he performed his tricks.

diabolical ADJ. devilish. "What a fiend I am, to devise such a *diabolical* scheme to destroy Gotham City," chortled the Joker.

dialectical ADJ. relating to the art of debate; mutual or reciprocal. The debate coach's students grew to develop great forensic and *dialectical* skill. Teaching, however, is inherently a *dialectical* situation: the coach learned at least as much from her students as they learned from her. dialectics, N.

■ **diatribe** N. bitter scolding; invective. "Luther's vitriolic *diatribes* against the Jews are part of the history that leads to Kristallnacht." (John Stendahl)

Word List 14 dichotomy–disparity

■ **dichotomy** N. split; branching into two parts (especially contradictory ones). Willie didn't know how to resolve the *dichotomy* between his ambition to go to college and his childhood longing to run away and join the circus. Then he heard about Ringling Brothers Circus College, and he knew he'd found his school.

dictum N. authoritative and weighty statement; saying; maxim. University administrations still follow the old *dictum* "Publish or perish." They don't care how good a teacher you are; if you don't publish enough papers, you're out of a job.

didactic ADJ. teaching; instructional. Pope's lengthy poem *An Essay on Man* is too *didactic* for my taste: I dislike it when poets turn preachy and moralize. didacticism, N.

■ **diffidence** N. shyness. You must overcome your *diffidence* if you intend to become a salesperson.

■ **diffuse** ADJ. wordy; rambling; spread out (like a gas). If you pay authors by the word, you tempt them to produce *diffuse* manuscripts rather than brief ones. also V. diffusion, N.

■ **digression** N. wandering away from the subject. Nobody minded when Professor Renoir's lectures wandered away from their official theme; his *digressions* were always more fascinating than the topic of the day. digress, V.

dilapidated ADJ. ruined because of neglect. The *dilapidated* old building needed far more work than just a new coat of paint. dilapidation, N.

dilate V. expand. In the dark, the pupils of your eyes *dilate*.

dilatory ADJ. tending to delay; intentionally delaying. If you are *dilatory* in paying your bills, your credit rating may suffer.

dilemma N. problem; choice of two unsatisfactory alternatives. Elizabeth Barrett faced a terrible *dilemma*: if she eloped with Robert Browning, she would be disinherited by her father; if she waited for her father's permission to wed, she would never marry the man she loved.

dilettante N. aimless follower of the arts; amateur; dabbler. According to Turgenev, without painstaking work, any writer or artist remains a *dilettante*. In an age of increasing professionalism, the terms *amateur* and *dilettante* have taken on negative connotations they did not originally possess.

diligence N. steadiness of effort; persistent hard work. Her employers were greatly impressed by her *diligence* and offered her a partnership in the firm.

dilute V. make less concentrated; reduce in strength. She preferred her coffee *diluted* with milk.

diminution N. lessening; reduction in size. Old Jack was as sharp at eighty as he had been at fifty; increasing age led to no *diminution* of his mental acuity.

din N. continued loud noise. The *din* of the jackhammers outside the classroom window drowned out the lecturer's voice. also V.

dint N. means; effort. By *dint* of much hard work, the volunteers were able to control the raging forest fire.

dire ADJ. disastrous. People ignored her *dire* predictions of an approaching depression.

dirge N. lament with music. The funeral *dirge* stirred us to tears.

■ **disabuse** V. correct a false impression; undeceive. Once Sharon started teaching junior high on the Lower East Side, she was quickly *disabused* of any romantic notions she had about her role.

disaffected ADJ. disloyal. Once the most loyal of Bradley's supporters, Senator Moynihan found himself becoming increasingly *disaffected*.

disapprobation N. disapproval; condemnation. The conservative father viewed his daughter's radical boyfriend with *disapprobation*.

disarray N. a disorderly or untidy state. After the New Year's party, the once orderly house was in total *disarray*.

disavowal N. denial; disclaiming. The novelist André Gide was controversial both for his early support of communism and for his subsequent *disavowal* of it after a visit to the Soviet Union. disavow, V.

disband V. dissolve; disperse. The chess club *disbanded* after its disastrous initial season.

disburse V. pay out. When you *disburse* money on the company's behalf, be sure to get a receipt.

discernible ADJ. distinguishable; perceivable. The ships in the harbor were not *discernible* in the fog.

■ **discerning** ADJ. mentally quick and observant; having insight. Though no genius, the star was sufficiently *discerning* to distinguish her true friends from the countless phonies who flattered her. discern, V. discernment, N.

disclaim V. disown; renounce claim to. Maintaining the injury had occurred during an afterschool program run by outside contractors, the school *disclaimed* any responsibility for Santiago's injured wrist.

disclose V. reveal. Although competitors offered him bribes, he refused to *disclose* any information about his company's forthcoming product. disclosure, N.

discombobulated ADJ. confused; discomposed. The novice square dancer became so *discombobulated* that he wandered into the wrong set.

discomfit V. make someone feel uneasy; disconcert; thwart. In Coppola's film *The Conversation*, as mime Robert Shields follows people around while mimicking their gestures and gait, he *discomfits* a dour-looking man, who looks distinctly uncomfortable when Shields starts trailing him. discomfiture, N. discomfited, ADJ.

disconcert V. upset; unsettle; confuse. Noise, crowds, and sudden changes from routine are likely to *disconcert* autistic children and cause a possible meltdown.

disconsolate ADJ. sad. The death of his wife left him *disconsolate*.

discord N. conflict; lack of harmony. Watching Tweedledum battle Tweedledee, Alice wondered what had caused this pointless *discord*.

■ **discordant** ADJ. not harmonious; conflicting. Nothing is quite so *discordant* as the sound of a junior high school orchestra tuning up.

discount V. disregard. Be prepared to *discount* what he has to say about his ex-wife.

discourse N. formal discussion; conversation. The young Plato was drawn to the Agora to hear the philosophical *discourse* of Socrates and his followers. also V.

■ **discredit** V. defame; destroy confidence in; disbelieve. The campaign was highly negative in tone; each candidate tried to *discredit* the other.

■ **discrepancy** N. lack of consistency; difference. The police noticed some *discrepancies* in his description of the crime and did not believe him.

■ **discrete** ADJ. separate; unconnected; consisting of distinct parts. In programmed instruction, the information to be learned is presented in *discrete* units; you must respond correctly to each unit before you may advance to the next. Because human populations have been migrating and intermingling for hundreds of centuries, it is hard to classify humans into *discrete* racial groups. Do not confuse *discrete* (separate) with *discreet* (prudent in speech and actions).

discretion N. prudence in speech, actions; ability to decide responsibly; freedom to act on one's own. Charlotte was the soul of *discretion*: she never would repeat anything told to her in confidence. Because we trusted our architect's judgment, we left many decisions about the house renovation to his *discretion*.

discriminating ADJ. able to see differences; prejudiced. A superb interpreter of Picasso, she was sufficiently *discriminating* to judge the most complex works of modern art. discrimination, N.

discursive ADJ. digressing; rambling. As the lecturer wandered from topic to topic, we wondered what if any point there was to his *discursive* remarks.

disdain V. view with scorn or contempt. In the film *Funny Face*, the bookish heroine *disdained* fashion models for their lack of intellectual interests. also N.

disenfranchise V. deprive of a civil right. The imposition of the poll tax effectively *disenfranchised* poor Southern blacks, who lost their right to vote.

disengage V. uncouple; separate; disconnect. A standard movie routine involves the hero's desperate attempt to *disengage* a railroad car from a moving train.

disfigure V. mar the appearance of; spoil. An ugly frown *disfigured* her normally pleasant face.

disgruntle V. make discontented. The passengers were *disgruntled* by the numerous delays.

dishearten V. discourage. His failure to pass the bar exam *disheartened* him.

disheveled ADJ. untidy; disordered. Every time Felipe tried to untangle his son's long, *disheveled* locks, Santiago would run his fingers through his hair, undoing his father's work.

disinclination N. unwillingness. Some mornings I feel a great *disinclination* to get out of bed.

■ **disingenuous** ADJ. lacking genuine candor; insincere. Now that we know that the mayor and his wife are engaged in a bitter divorce fight, we find their earlier remarks regretting their lack of time together remarkably *disingenuous.*

■ **disinterested** ADJ. unprejudiced. Given the judge's political ambitions and the lawyers' financial interest in the case, the only *disinterested* person in the courtroom may have been the court reporter.

■ **disjointed** ADJ. lacking coherence; separated at the joints. Unable to think of anything to say about the assigned topic, the unprepared student scribbled a few *disjointed* sentences on his answer sheet.

dislodge V. remove (forcibly). Thrusting her fist up under the choking man's lower ribs, Margaret used the Heimlich maneuver to *dislodge* the food caught in his throat.

dismantle V. take apart. When the show closed, they *dismantled* the scenery before storing it.

■ **dismiss** V. eliminate from consideration; reject. Believing in John's love for her, she *dismissed* the notion that he might be unfaithful. (secondary meaning)

■ **disparage** V. belittle. A doting mother, Emma was more likely to praise her son's crude attempts at art than to *disparage* them.

■ **disparate** ADJ. basically different; unrelated. Unfortunately Tony and Tina have *disparate* notions of marriage: Tony sees it as a carefree extended love affair, while Tina sees it as a solemn commitment to build a family and a home.

disparity N. difference; condition of inequality. Their *disparity* in rank made no difference at all to the prince and Cinderella.

Word List 15 dispassionate–ductile

dispassionate ADJ. calm; impartial. Known in the company for his cool judgment, Bill could impartially examine the causes of a problem, giving a *dispassionate* analysis of what had gone wrong, and go on to suggest how to correct the mess.

dispatch N. speediness; prompt execution; message sent with all due speed. Young Napoleon defeated the enemy with all possible *dispatch*; he then sent a *dispatch* to headquarters, informing his commander of the great victory. also V.

dispel V. scatter; drive away; cause to vanish. The bright sunlight eventually *dispelled* the morning mist.

disperse V. scatter. The police fired tear gas into the crowd to *disperse* the protesters. dispersion, N.

dispirited ADJ. lacking in spirit. The coach used all the tricks at his command to buoy up the enthusiasm of his team, which had become *dispirited* at the loss of the star player.

disputatious ADJ. argumentative; fond of arguing. Convinced he knew more than his lawyers, Tony was a *disputatious* client, ready to argue about the best way to conduct the case.

disquietude N. uneasiness; anxiety. When Holmes had been gone for a day, Watson felt only a slight sense of *disquietude*, but after a week with no word, Watson's uneasiness about his missing friend had grown into a deep fear for Holmes's safety. disquiet, V., N.

disquisition N. a formal systematic inquiry; an explanation of the results of a formal inquiry. In his *disquisition,* he outlined the steps he had taken in reaching his conclusions.

dissection N. analysis; cutting apart in order to examine. The *dissection* of frogs in the laboratory is particularly unpleasant to some students.

■ **dissemble** V. disguise; pretend. Even though John tried to *dissemble* his motive for taking modern dance, we all knew he was there not to dance but to meet girls.

■ **disseminate** V. distribute; spread; scatter (like seeds). By their use of the Internet, propagandists have been able to *disseminate* their pet doctrines to new audiences around the globe.

dissent V. disagree. In the recent Supreme Court decision, Justice Sotomayor *dissented* from the majority opinion. also N.

dissertation N. formal essay. In order to earn a graduate degree from many of our universities, a candidate is frequently required to prepare a *dissertation* on some scholarly subject.

dissident ADJ. dissenting; rebellious. In the purge that followed the student demonstrations at Tiananmen Square, the government hunted down the *dissident* students and their supporters. also N.

dissimulate V. pretend; conceal by feigning. Although the governor tried to *dissimulate* his feelings about the opposing candidate, we all knew he despised his rival.

dissipate V. squander; waste; scatter. Young Robert is a promising violinist, but I fear he may *dissipate* his gifts if he keeps wasting his time playing video games.

■ **dissolution** N. disintegration; looseness in morals. The profligacy and *dissolution* of life in Caligula's Rome appall some historians. dissolute, ADJ.

■ **dissonance** N. discord; opposite of harmony. Composer Charles Ives often used *dissonance*—clashing or unresolved chords—for special effects in his musical works. dissonant, ADJ.

dissuade V. persuade not to do; discourage. Since Tom could not *dissuade* Huck from running away from home, he decided to run away with his friend. dissuasion, N.

distant ADJ. reserved or aloof; cold in manner. Her *distant* greeting made me feel unwelcome from the start. (secondary meaning)

■ **distend** V. expand; swell out. I can tell when he is under stress by the way the veins on his forehead *distend.*

■ **distill** V. purify; refine; concentrate. A moonshiner *distills* mash into whiskey; an epigrammatist *distills* thoughts into quips.

distinction N. honor; contrast; discrimination. A holder of the Medal of Honor, George served with great *distinction* in World War II. He made a *distinction,* however, between World War II and Vietnam, which he considered an immoral conflict.

distort V. twist out of shape. It is difficult to believe the newspaper accounts of the riots because of the way some reporters *distort* and exaggerate the actual events. distortion, N.

distraught ADJ. upset; distracted by anxiety. The *distraught* parents frantically searched the ravine for their lost child.

diurnal ADJ. daily. A farmer cannot neglect his *diurnal* tasks at any time; cows, for example, must be milked regularly.

■ **diverge** V. vary; go in different directions from the same point. The spokes of the wheel *diverge* from the hub.

divergent ADJ. differing; deviating. Since graduating from medical school, the two doctors have followed *divergent* paths, the one going on to become a nationally prominent surgeon, the other dedicating himself to a small family practice in his hometown. divergence, N.

diverse ADJ. differing in some characteristics; various. A steady influx of immigrants during the 20th century, together with thousands of African-American war-industry workers who relocated from the Deep South during the 1940s, has made Oakland one of the most ethnically *diverse* major cities in the country.

diversion N. act of turning aside; pastime. After studying for several hours, he needed a *diversion* from work. divert, V.

diversity N. variety; dissimilitude. When power narrows the area of man's concern, poetry reminds him of the richness and *diversity* of existence. (John Fitzgerald Kennedy)

■ **divest** V. strip; deprive. Before Eisenhower appointed Charlie Wilson as the Secretary of Defense, he required Wilson to *divest* himself of his holdings in General Motors (Wilson sold his stock at a considerable financial loss). divestiture, N.

divine V. perceive intuitively; foresee the future. Nothing infuriated Tom more than Aunt Polly's ability to *divine* when he was not telling the truth.

divulge V. reveal. No lover of gossip, Charlotte would never *divulge* anything that a friend told her in confidence.

docile ADJ. obedient; easily managed. As *docile* as he seems today, that old lion was once a ferocious, snarling beast. docility, N.

doctrinaire ADJ. unable to compromise about points of doctrine; dogmatic; unyielding. Weng had hoped that the student-led democracy movement might bring about change in China, but the repressive response of the *doctrinaire* hard-liners crushed his dreams of democracy.

doctrine N. teachings in general; particular principle (religious, legal, etc.) taught. He was so committed to the *doctrines* of his faith that he was unable to evaluate them impartially.

■ **document** V. provide written evidence. She kept all the receipts from her business trip in order to *document* her expenses for the firm. also N.

dogged ADJ. determined; stubborn. *Les Miserables* tells of Inspector Javert's long, *dogged* pursuit of the criminal Jean Valjean.

■ **dogmatic** ADJ. opinionated; arbitrary; doctrinal. We tried to discourage Doug from being so *dogmatic*, but never could convince him that his opinions might be wrong.

doleful ADJ. mournful; causing sadness. Eeyore, the lugubrious donkey immortalized by A. A. Milne, looked at his cheerful friend Tigger and sighed a *doleful* sigh.

domicile N. home. Although his legal *domicile* was in New York City, his work kept him away from home for many years. also V.

domineer V. rule over tyrannically. Students prefer teachers who guide, not ones who *domineer*.

■ **dormant** ADJ. sleeping; lethargic; latent. At fifty her long-*dormant* ambition to write flared up once more; within a year she had completed the first of her great historical novels. dormancy, N.

dossier N. file of documents on a subject. Ordered by J. Edgar Hoover to investigate the senator, the FBI compiled a complete *dossier* on him.

dotage N. senility. In his *dotage*, the old man bored us with long tales of events in his childhood.

dote V. be excessively fond of; show signs of mental decline. Not only grandmothers bore you with stories about their brilliant grandchildren; grandfathers *dote* on the little rascals, too.

dour ADJ. sullen; severe; gloomy. The Protestant missionaries who settled on Tahiti in the early nineteenth century were followers of a *dour* and cheerless creed, who routinely dressed in black and never let themselves forget for a moment the awful burden of the sins of the world.

dowdy ADJ. slovenly; untidy. She tried to change her *dowdy* image by buying a fashionable new wardrobe.

downcast ADJ. disheartened; sad. Cheerful and optimistic by nature, Beth was never *downcast* despite the difficulties she faced.

drab ADJ. dull; lacking color; cheerless. The Dutch woman's *drab* winter coat contrasted with the distinctive, colorful native costume she wore beneath it.

draconian ADJ. extremely severe. When the principal canceled the senior prom because some seniors had been late to school that week, we thought the *draconian* punishment was far too harsh for such a minor violation of the rules.

dregs N. sediment; worthless residue. David poured the wine carefully to avoid stirring up the *dregs*.

drivel N. nonsense; foolishness. Why do I have to spend my days listening to such idiotic *drivel? Drivel* is related to dribble: think of a dribbling, *driveling* idiot.

droll ADJ. queer and amusing. He was a popular guest because his *droll* anecdotes were always entertaining.

drone N. idle person; male bee. Content to let his wife support him, the would-be writer was in reality nothing but a *drone*.

drone V. talk dully; buzz or murmur like a bee. On a gorgeous day, who wants to be stuck in a classroom listening to the teacher *drone?*

drudgery N. menial work. Cinderella's fairy godmother rescued her from a life of *drudgery*.

dubious ADJ. questionable; filled with doubt. Some critics of the GRE contend the test is of *dubious* worth. Tony claimed he could get a perfect score on the test, but Tina was *dubious:* she knew he hadn't cracked a book in three years. dubiety, N.

ductile ADJ. malleable; flexible; pliable. Copper is an extremely *ductile* material: you can stretch it into the thinnest of wires, bend it, even wind it into loops. ductility, N.

Word List 16 dumbfound–emulate

dumbfound V. astonish. Egbert's perfect score on the GRE *dumbfounded* his classmates, who had always found him to be utterly dumb.

■ **dupe** N. someone easily fooled. While the gullible Watson often was made a *dupe* by unscrupulous parties, Sherlock Holmes was far more difficult to fool.

duplicity N. double-dealing; hypocrisy. When Tanya learned that Mark had been two-timing her, she was furious at his *duplicity*. duplicitous, ADJ.

duration N. length of time something lasts. Because she wanted the children to make a good impression on the dinner guests, Mother promised them a treat if they'd behave well for the *duration* of the meal.

duress N. forcible restraint, especially unlawful. The hostages were held under *duress* until the prisoners' demands were met.

dutiful ADJ. respectful; obedient. When Mother told Billy to kiss Great-Aunt Hattie, the boy obediently gave the old woman a *dutiful* peck on her cheek.

dwindle V. shrink; reduce. The food in the lifeboat gradually *dwindled* away to nothing; in the end, they ate the ship's cook.

dynamic ADJ. energetic; vigorously active. The *dynamic* aerobics instructor kept her students on the run; she was a little *dynamo*.

earthy ADJ. unrefined; coarse. His *earthy* remarks often embarrassed the women in his audience.

ebb V. recede; lessen. Sitting on the beach, Mrs. Dalloway watched the tide *ebb:* the waters receded, drawing away from her as she sat there all alone. also N.

■ **ebullient** ADJ. showing excitement; overflowing with enthusiasm. Amy's *ebullient* nature could not be repressed; she was always bubbling over with excitement. ebullience, N.

eccentric ADJ. irregular; odd; whimsical; bizarre. The comet veered dangerously close to the earth in its *eccentric* orbit. People came up with some *eccentric* ideas for dealing with the emergency: one kook suggested tying a knot in the comet's tail!

ecclesiastic ADJ. pertaining to the church. The minister donned his *ecclesiastic* garb and walked to the pulpit. also N.

■ **eclectic** ADJ. selective; composed of elements drawn from disparate sources. His style of interior decoration was *eclectic:* bits and pieces of furnishings from widely divergent periods, strikingly juxtaposed to create a unique decor. eclecticism, N.

eclipse V. darken; extinguish; surpass. The new stock market high *eclipsed* the previous record set in 1985.

ecologist N. person concerned with the interrelationship between living organisms and their environment. The *ecologist* was concerned that the new dam would upset the natural balance of the creatures living in Glen Canyon.

economy N. efficiency or conciseness in using something. Reading the epigrams of Pope, I admire the *economy* of his verse: in few words he conveys worlds of meaning. (secondary meaning)

ecstasy N. rapture; joy; any overpowering emotion. When Allison received her long-hoped-for letter of acceptance from Harvard, she was in *ecstasy.* ecstatic, ADJ.

edict N. decree (especially one issued by a sovereign); official command. The emperor issued an *edict* decreeing that everyone should come see him model his magnificent new clothes.

edify V. instruct; correct morally. Although his purpose was to *edify* and not to entertain his audience, many of his listeners were amused and not enlightened.

eerie ADJ. weird. In that *eerie* setting, it was easy to believe in ghosts and other supernatural beings.

effectual ADJ. able to produce a desired effect; valid. Medical researchers are concerned because of the development of drug-resistant strains of bacteria; many once-useful antibiotics are no longer *effectual* in curing bacterial infections.

effeminate ADJ. having womanly traits. "*Effeminate* men intrigue me more than anything in the world. I see them as my alter egos. I feel very drawn to them. I think like a guy, but I'm feminine. So I relate to feminine men." (Madonna)

effervescence N. inner excitement or exuberance; bubbling from fermentation or carbonation. Nothing depressed Sue for long; her natural *effervescence* soon reasserted itself. Soda that loses its *effervescence* goes flat. effervescent, ADJ. effervesce, V.

effete ADJ. lacking vigor; worn out; sterile. Is the Democratic Party still a vital political force, or is it an *effete*, powerless faction, wedded to outmoded liberal policies?

■ **efficacy** N. power to produce desired effect. The *efficacy* of this drug depends on the regularity of the dosage. efficacious, ADJ.

■ **effrontery** N. impudence; shameless boldness; sheer nerve; presumptuousness. When the boss told Frank she was firing him for laziness and insubordination, he had the *effrontery* to ask her for a letter of recommendation.

effusive ADJ. pouring forth; gushing. Unmoved by Martha's many compliments on his performance, George dismissed her *effusive* words of praise as the sentimental outpourings of an emotional fool.

egoism N. excessive interest in one's self; belief that one should be interested in one's self rather than in others. His *egoism* prevented him from seeing the needs of his colleagues.

egotistical ADJ. excessively self-centered; self-important; conceited. Typical *egotistical* remark: "But enough of this chitchat about you and your little problems. Let's talk about what's really important: me!" egotistic, ADJ. egotism, N.

egregious ADJ. notorious; conspicuously bad or shocking. She was an *egregious* liar; we all knew better than to believe a word she said. Ed's housekeeping was *egregious:* he let his dirty dishes pile up so long that they were stuck together with last week's food.

ejaculation N. exclamation. He could not repress an *ejaculation* of surprise when he heard the news.

elaboration N. addition of details; intricacy. Tell what happened simply, without any *elaboration.* elaborate, V.

elated ADJ. overjoyed; in high spirits. Grinning from ear to ear, Bonnie Blair was clearly *elated* by her fifth Olympic gold medal. elation, N.

■ **elegy** N. poem or song expressing lamentation. On the death of Edward King, Milton composed the *elegy* "Lycidas." elegiacal, ADJ.

■ **elicit** V. draw out by discussion. The detectives tried to *elicit* where he had hidden his loot.

elixir N. cure-all; something invigorating. The news of her chance to go abroad acted on her like an *elixir.*

ellipsis N. omission of words from a text. Sometimes an *ellipsis* can lead to a dangling modifier, as in the sentence "Once dressed, . . . you should refrigerate the potato salad."

elliptical ADJ. oval; ambiguous, either purposely or because key words have been left out. An *elliptical* billiard ball wobbles because it is not perfectly round; an *elliptical* remark baffles because it is not perfectly clear.

eloquence N. expressiveness; persuasive speech. The crowds were stirred by Martin Luther King's *eloquence.*

elucidate V. explain; enlighten. He was called upon to *elucidate* the disputed points in his article.

elusive ADJ. evasive; baffling; hard to grasp. No matter how hard Tom tried to lure the trout into taking the bait, the fish was too *elusive* for him to catch. elude, V.

emaciated ADJ. thin and wasted. A severe illness left him acutely *emaciated,* and he did not recover fully until he had regained most of his lost weight.

emanate V. issue forth. A strong odor of sulfur *emanated* from the spring.

emancipate V. set free. At first, the attempts of the Abolitionists to *emancipate* the slaves were unpopular in New England as well as in the South.

embargo N. ban on commerce or other activity. As a result of the *embargo,* trade with the colonies was at a standstill.

embark V. commence; go on board a boat; begin a journey. In devoting herself to the study of gorillas, Dian Fossey *embarked* on a course of action that was to cost her her life.

■ **embellish** V. adorn; ornament; enhance, as a story. The costume designer *embellished* the leading lady's ball gown with yards and yards of ribbon and lace.

embezzlement N. stealing. The bank teller confessed his *embezzlement* of the funds.

embrace V. hug; adopt or espouse; accept readily; encircle; include. Clasping Maid Marian in his arms, Robin Hood *embraced* her lovingly. In joining the outlaws in Sherwood Forest, she had openly *embraced* their cause. also N.

embroider V. decorate with needlework; ornament with fancy or fictitious details. For her mother's birthday, Beth *embroidered* a lovely design on a handkerchief. When asked what made her late getting home, Jo *embroidered* her account with tales of runaway horses and rescuing people from a ditch. embroidery, N.

embroil V. throw into confusion; involve in strife; entangle. He became *embroiled* in the heated discussion when he tried to arbitrate the dispute.

embryonic ADJ. undeveloped; rudimentary. The CEO reminisced about the good old days when the computer industry was still in its *embryonic* stage and start-up companies were being founded in the family garage.

emend V. correct, usually a text. In editing *Beowulf* for his new scholarly edition, Professor Oliver freely *emended* the manuscript's text whenever it seemed to make no sense.

emendation N. correction of errors; improvement. Please initial all the *emendations* you have made in this contract.

eminent ADJ. high; lofty. After her appointment to this *eminent* position, she seldom had time for her former friends.

emissary N. agent; messenger. The Secretary of State was sent as the president's special *emissary* to the conference on disarmament.

empathy N. ability to identify with another's feelings, ideas, etc. What made Ann such a fine counselor was her *empathy,* her ability to put herself in her client's place and feel his emotions as if they were her own. empathize, V.

■ **empirical** ADJ. based on experience. He distrusted hunches and intuitive flashes; he placed his reliance entirely on *empirical* data.

■ **emulate** V. imitate; rival. In a brief essay, describe a person you admire, someone whose virtues you would like to *emulate.*

Word List 17 enamored–escapade

enamored ADJ. in love. Narcissus became *enamored* of his own beauty.

encipher V. encode; convert a message into code. In one of Bond's first lessons he learned how to *encipher* the messages he sent to Miss Moneypenny so that none of his other lady friends could read them.

enclave N. territory enclosed within an alien land. The Vatican is an independent *enclave* in Italy.

encomium N. high praise; eulogy. Uneasy with the *encomiums* expressed by his supporters, Tolkien felt unworthy of such high praise.

encompass V. surround or encircle; enclose; include. A moat, or deep water-filled trench, *encompassed* the castle, protecting it from attack. The term *alternative medicine* can *encompass* a wide range of therapies, including chiropractic, homeopathy, acupuncture, herbal medicine, meditation, biofeedback, massage therapy, and various "new age" therapies such as guided imagery and naturopathy.

encroachment N. gradual intrusion. The *encroachment* of the factories upon the neighborhood lowered the value of the real estate.

encumber V. burden. Some people *encumber* themselves with too much luggage when they take short trips.

endearment N. fond word or act. Your gifts and *endearments* cannot make me forget your earlier insolence.

■ **endemic** ADJ. prevailing among a specific group of people or in a specific area or country. This disease is *endemic* in this part of the world; more than 80 percent of the population are at one time or another affected by it.

endorse V. approve; support. Everyone waited to see which one of the rival candidates for the city council the mayor would *endorse.* (secondary meaning) endorsement, N.

enduring ADJ. lasting; surviving. Keats believed in the *enduring* power of great art, which would outlast its creators' brief lives.

energize V. invigorate; make forceful and active. Rather than exhausting Maggie, dancing *energized* her.

■ **enervate** V. weaken. She was slow to recover from her illness; even a short walk to the window *enervated* her. enervation, N.

enfranchise V. admit to the rights of citizenship (especially the right to vote). Although blacks were *enfranchised* shortly after the Civil War, women did not receive the right to vote until 1920.

engage V. attract; hire; pledge oneself; confront. "Your case has *engaged* my interest, my lord," said Holmes. "You may *engage* my services."

engaging ADJ. charming; attractive. Everyone liked Nancy's pleasant manners and *engaging* personality.

■ **engender** V. cause; produce. To receive praise for real accomplishments *engenders* self-confidence in a child.

engross V. occupy fully. John was so *engrossed* in his studies that he did not hear his mother call.

■ **enhance** V. increase; improve. You can *enhance* your chances of being admitted to the college of your choice by learning to write well; an excellent essay will *enhance* any application.

enigma N. puzzle; mystery. "What do women want?" asked Dr. Sigmund Freud. Their behavior was an *enigma* to him.

enigmatic ADJ. obscure; puzzling. Many have sought to fathom the *enigmatic* smile of the *Mona Lisa.*

enjoin V. command; order; forbid. The owners of the company asked the court to *enjoin* the union from picketing the plant.

enmity N. ill will; hatred. At Camp David President Carter labored to bring an end to the *enmity* that prevented Egypt and Israel from living in peace.

ennui N. boredom. The monotonous routine of hospital life induced a feeling of *ennui* that made her moody and irritable. "This vacation is boring!" complained Heather, tired of being stuck riding in the car with no way to relieve her growing *ennui.*

enormity N. hugeness (in a bad sense). He did not realize the *enormity* of his crime until he saw what suffering he had caused.

enrapture V. please intensely. The audience was *enraptured* by the freshness of the voices and the excellent orchestration.

ensue V. follow as a consequence; result. What a holler would *ensue* if people had to pay the minister as much to marry them as they have to pay a lawyer to get them a divorce. (Claire Trevor)

entail V. require; necessitate; involve. Building a college-level vocabulary will *entail* some work on your part.

enterprising ADJ. full of initiative. By coming up with fresh ways to market the company's products, Mike proved himself to be an *enterprising* businessman.

enthrall V. capture; enslave. From the moment he saw her picture, he was *enthralled* by her beauty.

entice V. lure; attract; tempt. Will the mayor's attempts to *entice* the members of the International Olympic Committee to select Los Angeles as the site of the 2024 Olympic Games succeed? Only time will tell.

entity N. real being. As soon as the charter was adopted, the United Nations became an *entity* and had to be considered as a factor in world diplomacy.

entrance V. put under a spell; carry away with emotion. Shafts of sunlight on a wall could *entrance* her and leave her spellbound.

entreat V. plead; ask earnestly. She *entreated* her father to let her stay out till midnight.

entree N. entrance; a way in. Because of his wealth and social position, he had *entree* into the most exclusive circles.

entrepreneur N. businessperson; contractor. Opponents of our present tax program argue that it discourages *entrepreneurs* from trying new fields of business activity.

enumerate V. list; mention one by one. Huck hung his head in shame as Miss Watson *enumerated* his many flaws.

enunciate V. utter or speak, especially distinctly. Stop mumbling! How will people understand you if you do not *enunciate* clearly?

eon N. long period of time; an age. It has taken *eons* for our civilization to develop.

■ **ephemeral** ADJ. short-lived; fleeting. The mayfly is an *ephemeral* creature: its adult life lasts little more than a day.

epic N. long heroic poem, novel, or similar work of art. Kurosawa's film *Seven Samurai* is an *epic* portraying the struggle of seven warriors to destroy a band of robbers. also ADJ.

epigram N. witty thought or saying, usually short. Poor Richard's *epigrams* made Benjamin Franklin famous.

epilogue N. short speech at conclusion of dramatic work. The audience was so disappointed in the play that many did not remain to hear the *epilogue.*

episodic ADJ. loosely connected. Though he tried to follow the plot of *Gravity's Rainbow,* John found the novel too *episodic.*

epithet N. word or phrase characteristically used to describe a person or thing. So many kings of France were named Charles that modern students need *epithets* to tell them apart: Charles the Wise, for example, was someone far different from Charles the Fat.

epitome N. perfect example or embodiment. Singing "I am the very model of a modern Major-General" in *The Pirates of Penzance,* Major-General Stanley proclaimed himself the *epitome* of an officer and a gentleman. epitomize, V.

epoch N. period of time. The glacial *epoch* lasted for thousands of years.

equable ADJ. tranquil; steady; uniform. After the hot summers and cold winters of New England, she found the climate of the West Indies *equable* and pleasant.

■ **equanimity** N. calmness of temperament; composure. Even the inevitable strains of caring for an ailing mother did not disturb Bea's *equanimity.*

equilibrium N. balance. After the divorce, he needed some time to regain his *equilibrium.*

equitable ADJ. fair; impartial. I am seeking an *equitable* solution to this dispute, one that will be fair and acceptable to both sides.

equity N. fairness; justice. Our courts guarantee *equity* to all.

equivocal ADJ. ambiguous; intentionally misleading. Rejecting the candidate's *equivocal* comments on tax reform, the reporters pressed him to state clearly where he stood on the issue. equivocate, V. equivocation, N.

■ **equivocate** V. lie; mislead; attempt to conceal the truth. No matter how bad the news is, give it to us straight. Above all, don't *equivocate.*

erode V. eat away. The limestone was *eroded* by the dripping water until only a thin shell remained. erosion, N.

erotic ADJ. Films with significant *erotic* content are rated R; pornographic films are rated X.

erratic ADJ. odd; unpredictable. Investors become anxious when the stock market appears *erratic.*

erroneous ADJ. mistaken; wrong. I thought my answer was correct, but it was *erroneous.*

■ **erudite** ADJ. learned; scholarly. Unlike much scholarly writing, Huizinga's prose was entertaining as well as *erudite,* lively as well as learned. erudition, N.

escapade N. prank; flighty conduct. The headmaster could not regard this latest *escapade* as a boyish joke and expelled the young man.

Word List 18 eschew–explicate

eschew V. avoid. Hoping to present himself to his girlfriend as a totally reformed character, he tried to *eschew* all the vices, especially chewing tobacco and drinking bathtub gin.

■ **esoteric** ADJ. hard to understand; known only to the chosen few. *New Yorker* short stories often include *esoteric* allusions to obscure people and events. The implication is, if you are in the in-crowd, you'll get the reference; if you come from Cleveland, you won't. esoterica, N.

espionage N. spying. In order to maintain its power, the government developed a system of *espionage* that penetrated every household.

espouse V. adopt; support. She was always ready to *espouse* a worthy cause.

essay V. make an attempt at; test. In an effort to enrich the contemporary operatic repertoire, the Santa Fe Opera commissioned three new operas by American composers who had not previously *essayed* the form. Although Lydgate *essayed* courtly verse in Chaucer's manner, his imitations of the master's style rarely succeeded. In 1961 the actor Paul Newman *essayed* the role that perhaps best defined his screen persona, that of pool shark "Fast" Eddie Felson in *The Hustler.*

esteem V. respect; value. Jill *esteemed* Jack's taste in music, but she deplored his taste in clothes. also N.

estimable ADJ. worthy of esteem; admirable. Tennis star Andre Agassi survived a near loss in the semifinals to win the seventh Grand Slam tournament title of his uneven yet *estimable* career.

estranged ADJ. separated; alienated. The *estranged* wife sought a divorce. estrangement, N.

ethereal ADJ. light; heavenly; unusually refined. In Shakespeare's *The Tempest,* the spirit Ariel is an *ethereal* creature, too airy and unearthly for our mortal world.

ethical ADJ. moral; in line with standards of right and wrong. During a national drug shortage, the decision as to which of two deserving patients should receive a scarce antibiotic can create an *ethical* dilemma for the physician.

ethnic ADJ. relating to races. Wikipedia defines an *ethnic* group as "a social group of people who identify with each other based on common ancestral, social, cultural, or national experience." Such an excessively broad definition would include ballroom dancers and bird watchers as *ethnic* groups!

ethos N. underlying character of a culture, group, etc. Seeing how tenderly Spaniards treated her small daughter made author Barbara Kingsolver aware of how greatly children were valued in the Spanish *ethos.*

etymology N. study of word parts. A knowledge of *etymology* can help you on many English tests: if you know what the roots and prefixes mean, you can determine the meanings of unfamiliar words.

■ **eulogy** N. expression of praise, often on the occasion of someone's death. Instead of delivering a spoken *eulogy* at Genny's memorial service, Jeff sang a song he had written in her honor. eulogize, V.

■ **euphemism** N. mild expression in place of an unpleasant one. The expression "he passed away" is a *euphemism* for "he died."

euphony N. sweet sound. Noted for its *euphony* even when it is spoken, the Italian language is particularly pleasing to the ear when sung. euphonious, ADJ.

euphoria N. feeling of exaggerated (or unfounded) well-being. "Jill's been on cloud nine ever since Jack asked her out," said Betty, dismissing her friend's *euphoria.*

euthanasia N. mercy killing. Many people support *euthanasia* for terminally ill patients who wish to die.

evanescent ADJ. fleeting; vanishing. For a brief moment, the entire skyline was bathed in an orange-red hue in the *evanescent* rays of the sunset.

evasive ADJ. not frank; eluding. Your *evasive* answers convinced the judge that you were withholding important evidence. evade, V.

evince V. show clearly. When he tried to answer the questions, he *evinced* his ignorance of the subject matter.

evenhanded ADJ. impartial; fair. Do men and women receive *evenhanded* treatment from their teachers, or, as recent studies suggest, do teachers pay more attention to male students than to females?

evocative ADJ. tending to call up (emotions, memories). Scent can be remarkably *evocative.* The aroma of pipe tobacco *evokes* the memory of my father; a whiff of talcum powder calls up images of my daughter as a child.

evoke V. call forth. call up; elicit. Music has the power to *evoke* strong emotions and memories: Whenever I hear the rousing strains of "Do You Hear the People Sing," I remember the thrill of attending the opening night of *Les Miserables* in New York. evocation, N.

■ **exacerbate** V. worsen; embitter. The latest bombing *exacerbated* England's already existing bitterness against the IRA, causing the Prime Minister to break off the peace talks abruptly. exacerbation, N.

exact V. require or demand, often forcibly; take. In feudal times, landowners *exacted* heavy payments from their peasants in both goods and labor. Asa Philip Randolph proclaimed, "Freedom is never granted; it is won. Justice is never given; it is *exacted.*" The war in Algeria *exacted* a heavy toll in casualties.

exacting ADJ. extremely demanding. Cleaning the ceiling of the Sistine Chapel was an *exacting* task, one that demanded extremely meticulous care on the part of the restorers. exaction, N.

exalt V. raise in rank or dignity; praise. The actor Sean Connery was *exalted* to the rank of knighthood by the Queen; he now is known as Sir Sean Connery.

exasperate V. vex. Johnny often *exasperates* his mother with his pranks.

excerpt N. selected passage (written or musical). The cinematic equivalent of an *excerpt* from a novel is a clip from a film. also V.

excise V. cut away; cut out. When you *excise* the dead and dying limbs of a tree, you not only improve its appearance but also enhance its chances of bearing fruit. excision, N.

exclaim V. cry out suddenly. "Watson! Behind you!" Holmes *exclaimed*, seeing the assassin hurl himself on his friend. exclamation, N. exclamatory, ADJ.

excoriate V. scold with biting harshness; strip the skin off. Seeing the rips in Bill's new pants, his mother furiously *excoriated* him for ruining his good clothes. The tight, starched collar chafed and *excoriated* his neck, rubbing it raw.

■ **exculpate** V. clear from blame. Fearful of being implicated as a conspirator in the plot to kill Hitler, General Fromm equivocated, prevaricated, and lied outright in an attempt to *exculpate* himself.

execrable ADJ. very bad. The anecdote was in such *execrable* taste that the audience hissed and booed.

execrate V. curse; express abhorrence for. The world *execrated* the memory of Hitler and hoped that genocide would never again be the policy of any nation.

execute V. put into effect; carry out. The choreographer wanted to see how well she could *execute* a pirouette. (secondary meaning) execution, N.

exegesis N. explanation, especially of biblical passages. The minister based her sermon on her *exegesis* of a difficult passage from the book of Job.

exemplary ADJ. serving as a model; outstanding. At commencement the dean praised Ellen for her *exemplary* behavior as class president.

exemplify V. show by example; furnish an example. Three-time winner of the Super Bowl, Joe Montana *exemplifies* the ideal quarterback.

exempt ADJ. not subject to a duty or obligation. Because of his flat feet, Foster was *exempt* from serving in the armed forces. also V.

exertion N. effort; expenditure of much physical work. The *exertion* involved in unscrewing the rusty bolt left her exhausted.

exhilarating ADJ. invigorating and refreshing; cheering. Though some of the hikers found tramping through the snow tiring, Jeffrey found the walk on the cold, crisp day *exhilarating*. His *exhilaration* was so great that, at the hike's end, he wanted to walk another five miles.

exhort V. urge. The evangelist *exhorted* all the sinners in the audience to repent. exhortation, N.

■ **exigency** N. urgent situation; pressing needs or demands; state of requiring immediate attention. The *exigencies* of war gave impetus and funding to computer research in general and in particular to the development of code-breaking machines. Denmark's Gustav I proved to be a harsh master and an *exigent* lord, known for his heavy taxes and capricious demands.

exodus N. departure. The *exodus* from the hot and stuffy city was particularly noticeable on Friday evenings.

exonerate V. acquit; exculpate. The defense team feverishly sought fresh evidence that might *exonerate* their client.

exorbitant ADJ. excessive. While most motels and budget hotels offer free Internet service, luxury hotels generally charge *exorbitant* rates for a wifi connection.

exorcise V. drive out evil spirits. By incantation and prayer, the medicine man sought to *exorcise* the evil spirits that had taken possession of the young warrior.

exotic ADJ. not native; strange. Because of his *exotic* headdress, he was followed in the streets by small children who laughed at his strange appearance.

expansive ADJ. outgoing and sociable; broad and extensive; able to increase in size. Mr. Fezziwig was in an *expansive* humor, cheerfully urging his guests to join in the Christmas feast. Looking down on his *expansive* paunch, he sighed: if his belly expanded any further, he'd need an *expansive* waistline for his pants.

expatiate V. talk at length. Robert Marlock, the University Orator, welcomed the Queen with a Latin oration in which he (at some length) *expatiated* on the wonders of Elizabeth's scholarship and on the indebtedness of the University to her.

expatriate N. exile; someone who has withdrawn from his native land. Henry James was an American *expatriate* who settled in England.

expedient ADJ. suitable; practical; politic. A pragmatic politician, she was guided by what was *expedient* rather than by what was ethical. expediency, N.

expedite V. hasten. Because we are on a tight schedule, we hope you will be able to *expedite* the delivery of our order. The more *expeditious* your response is, the happier we'll be.

expenditure N. payment or expense; output. When you are operating on an expense account, you must keep receipts for all your *expenditures*. If you don't save your receipts, you won't get repaid without the *expenditure* of a lot of energy arguing with the firm's accountants.

expertise N. specialized knowledge; expert skill. Although she was knowledgeable in a number of fields, she was hired for her particular *expertise* in computer programming.

expiate V. make amends for (a sin). Jean Valjean tried to *expiate* his crimes by performing acts of charity.

expletive N. interjection; profane oath. Fred was so foul-mouthed that, if you deleted all the *expletives* from his comments, very little would have been left.

explicate V. explain; interpret; clarify. Harry Levin *explicated* James Joyce's novels with such clarity that even *Finnegan's Wake* seemed comprehensible to his students.

Word List 19 explicit-fervor

explicit ADJ. totally clear; definite; outspoken. Don't just hint around that you're dissatisfied: be *explicit* about what's bugging you.

exploit N. deed or action, particularly a brave deed. Raoul Wallenberg was noted for his *exploits* in rescuing Jews from Hitler's forces.

exploit V. make use of, sometimes unjustly. Cesar Chavez fought attempts to *exploit* migrant farmworkers in California. exploitation, N.

expository ADJ. explanatory; serving to explain. The manual that came with my blueray player was no masterpiece of *expository* prose: its explanations were so garbled that I couldn't even figure out how to play the disc.

expostulation N. protest; remonstrance. Despite the teacher's scoldings and *expostulations*, the class remained unruly.

exposure N. risk, particularly of being exposed to disease or to the elements; unmasking; act of laying something open. *Exposure* to sun and wind had dried out her hair and weathered her face. She looked so changed that she no longer feared *exposure* as the notorious Irene Adler, one-time antagonist of Sherlock Holmes.

expropriate V. take possession of. He questioned the government's right to *expropriate* his land to create a wildlife preserve.

expunge V. cancel; remove. To bowdlerize a text is to censor it, *expunging* objectionable material and replacing it with less offensive matter.

expurgate V. clean; remove offensive parts of a book. The editors felt that certain passages in the book had to be *expurgated* before it could be used in the classroom.

extant ADJ. still in existence. Although the book is out of print, some copies are still *extant.* Unfortunately, all of them are in libraries or private collections; none is for sale.

extemporaneous ADJ. not planned; impromptu. Because her *extemporaneous* remarks were misinterpreted, she decided to write all her speeches in advance.

extenuating ADJ. representing (a crime or effense) as less serious than it seems; mitigating. Unless extraordinarily strong *extenuating* circumstances exist, someone convicted of murder can expect to be condemned to serve a lengthy sentence.

extirpate V. root up. The Salem witch trials were a misguided attempt to *extirpate* superstition and heresy.

extol V. praise; glorify. The president *extolled* the astronauts, calling them the pioneers of the Space Age.

extort V. wring from; get money by threats, etc. The blackmailer *extorted* money from his victim.

extradition N. surrender of prisoner by one state to another. The lawyers opposed the *extradition* of their client on the grounds that for more than five years he had been a model citizen.

extraneous ADJ. not essential; superfluous. No wonder Ted can't think straight! His mind is so cluttered up with *extraneous* trivia, he can't concentrate on the essentials.

■ **extrapolation** N. projection; conjecture. Based on their *extrapolation* from the results of the primaries on Super Tuesday, the networks predicted that George W. Bush would be the Republican candidate for the presidency. extrapolate, V.

extricate V. free; disentangle. Icebreakers were needed to *extricate* the trapped whales from the icy floes that closed them in.

extrinsic ADJ. external; not essential; extraneous. A critically acclaimed *extrinsic* feature of the Chrysler Building is its ornate spire. The judge would not admit the testimony, ruling that it was *extrinsic* to the matter at hand.

extrovert N. person interested mostly in external objects and actions. A good salesperson is usually an *extrovert* who likes to mingle with people.

exuberance N. overflowing abundance; joyful enthusiasm; flamboyance; lavishness. I was bowled over by the *exuberance* of Amy's welcome. Cheeks glowing, she was the picture of *exuberant* good health.

exult V. rejoice. We *exulted* when our team won the victory.

fabricate V. build; lie. If we *fabricate* the buildings in this project out of standardized sections, we can reduce construction costs considerably. Because of Jack's tendency to *fabricate,* Jill had trouble believing a word he said.

facade N. front (of building); superficial or false appearance. The ornate *facade* of the church was often photographed by tourists, who never bothered to walk around the building to view its other sides. Cher's outward show of confidence was just a *facade* she assumed to hide her insecurity.

facet N. aspect; feature; side. With so many different *facets* to the job, a proposal writer must often be a Jack of all trades, able to manage the project, motivate the proposal team, perform needed research, and, of course, write.

■ **facetious** ADJ. joking (often inappropriately); humorous. I'm serious about this project; I don't need any *facetious,* smart-alecky cracks about do-good little rich girls.

facile ADJ. easily accomplished; ready or fluent; superficial. Words came easily to Jonathan: he was a *facile* speaker and prided himself on being ready to make a speech at a moment's notice. facility, N.

■ **facilitate** V. help bring about; make less difficult. Rest and proper nourishment should *facilitate* the patient's recovery.

facsimile N. copy. Many museums sell *facsimiles* of the works of art on display.

faction N. party; clique; dissension. The quarrels and bickering of the two small *factions* within the club disturbed the majority of the members.

factious ADJ. inclined to form factions; causing dissension. The pollsters' practice of dividing up the map of America into Red and Blue states reinforces *factious* feelings among Americans, who increasingly define themselves as members of one of the two major political parties. Do not confuse *factious* with *fractious* (unruly; unmanageable) or with *factitious* (not natural; not genuine; bogus).

factitious ADJ. artificial; sham. Hollywood actresses often create *factitious* tears by using glycerine.

faculty N. mental or bodily powers; teaching staff. As he grew old, Professor Twiggly feared he might lose his *faculties* and become unfit to teach. However, while he was in full possession of his *faculties,* the school couldn't kick him off the *faculty.*

■ **fallacious** ADJ. false; misleading. Paradoxically, *fallacious* reasoning does not always yield erroneous results: even though your logic may be faulty, the answer you get may be correct.

fallacy N. mistaken idea based on flawed reasoning; invalid argument. The challenge that today's social scientists face is to use computers in ways that are most suited to them without falling into the *fallacy* that, by themselves, computers can guide and organize the study of human society.

fallible ADJ. liable to err. Although I am *fallible,* I feel confident that I am right this time.

falter V. hesitate. When told to dive off the high board, she did not *falter,* but climbed up the ladder at once.

familial ADJ. pertaining to the family. Even though the younger generation had moved away from Michigan, they still maintained close *familial* ties, chatting regularly on Facebook and holding yearly family reunions.

fanaticism N. excessive zeal; extreme devotion to a belief or cause. When Islamic fundamentalists demanded the death of Salman Rushdie because his novel questioned their faith, world opinion condemned them for their *fanaticism.* fanatic, ADJ., N.

farce N. broad comedy; mockery. Nothing went right; the entire interview degenerated into a *farce.* farcical, ADJ.

fastidious ADJ. difficult to please; squeamish. Bobby was such a *fastidious* eater that he would eat a sandwich only if his mother first cut off every scrap of crust.

fatalism N. belief that events are determined by forces beyond one's control. With *fatalism,* he accepted the hardships that beset him. fatalistic, ADJ.

fathom V. comprehend; investigate. I find his motives impossible to *fathom;* in fact, I'm totally clueless about what goes on in his mind.

■ **fatuous** ADJ. brainless; inane; foolish, yet smug. Attacking the notion that women should defer to men's supposedly superior intelligence, Germaine Greer wrote that she was sick of pretending that some *fatuous* male's self-important pronouncements were the objects of her undivided attention. Fatheads are by definition *fatuous.*

■ **fawning** ADJ. trying to please by behaving obsequiously, flattering, or cringing. In *Pride and Prejudice,* Mr. Collins is the archetypal *fawning* clergyman, wholly dependent for his living on the goodwill of his patron, Lady Catherine, whom he flatters shamelessly. Courtiers *fawn* upon princes; groupies *fawn* upon rock stars.

faze V. disconcert; dismay. No crisis could *faze* the resourceful hotel manager.

feasible ADJ. practical. Is it *feasible* to build a new stadium for the Yankees on New York's West Side? Without additional funding, the project is clearly unrealistic.

feckless ADJ. feeble and ineffective; careless and irresponsible. Richard II proved such a *feckless* ruler that Bolingbroke easily convinced Parliament to elect him king in Richard's place. The film *The Perfect Circle* tells the tale of a *feckless* poet who, unwillingly saddled with two war orphans, discovers a sense of responsibility and community that had eluded him in his own previous family life.

fecundity N. fertility; fruitfulness. The *fecundity* of her mind is illustrated by the many vivid images in her poems. Rabbits are noted for their *fecundity*: in the absence of natural predators, they multiply, well, like rabbits, as the Australians learned to their dismay.

feign V. pretend. Although she claimed that the car accident had left her with a bad case of whiplash, when we saw her gyrating at her jazzercise class, we realized she was only *feigning* injury.

feint N. trick; shift; sham blow. Fooled by his opponent's *feint*, the boxer dropped his guard. also V.

■ **felicitous** ADJ. apt; suitably expressed; well chosen. He was famous for his *felicitous* remarks and was called upon to serve as master-of-ceremonies at many a banquet.

felicity N. happiness; appropriateness (of a remark, choice, etc.). She wrote a note to the newlyweds wishing them great *felicity* in their wedded life.

felon N. person convicted of a grave crime. A convicted *felon* loses the right to vote.

feral ADJ. not domestic; wild. Abandoned by their owners, dogs may revert to their *feral* state, roaming the woods in packs.

ferment N. agitation; commotion. With the breakup of the Soviet Union, much of Eastern Europe was in a state of *ferment*. also V.

ferret V. drive or hunt out of hiding. She *ferreted* out their secret.

fervent ADJ. ardent; hot. Modest by nature, Susan felt that the *fervent* praise was excessive and somewhat undeserved.

■ **fervor** N. glowing ardor; intensity of feeling. At the protest rally, the students cheered the strikers and booed the dean with equal *fervor*.

Word List 20 fester–foster

fester V. rankle; produce irritation or resentment. Joe's insult *festered* in Anne's mind for days, and made her too angry to speak to him.

festive ADJ. joyous; celebratory. Their wedding in the park was a *festive* occasion.

fiasco N. total failure. Despite the wedding planner's careful arrangements, the event turned into a total *fiasco* when the drunken best man toppled over into the four-tier wedding cake.

fiat N. command; authorization. Although the bill abolishing the allowances and privileges of the former princes was rejected by the upper house, it was put into effect by presidential *fiat*.

fickle ADJ. changeable; faithless. As soon as Romeo saw Juliet, he forgot all about his crush on Rosaline. Was Romeo *fickle*?

fictitious ADJ. imaginary. Although this book purports to be a biography of George Washington, many of the incidents are *fictitious*.

fidelity N. loyalty. Iago wickedly manipulates Othello, arousing his jealousy and causing him to question his wife's *fidelity*.

figment N. invention; imaginary thing. Was he hearing real voices in the night, or were they just a *figment* of his imagination?

figurative ADJ. not literal, but metaphorical; using a figure of speech. "To lose one's marbles" is a *figurative* expression; if you're told Jack has lost his marbles, no one expects you to rush out to buy him a replacement set.

filibuster V. block legislation by making long speeches. Even though we disapproved of Senator Foghorn's political goals, we were impressed by his ability to *filibuster* endlessly to keep an issue from coming to a vote.

finale N. conclusion. Mexico's Bicentennial celebration culminated with an extraordinary fireworks *finale* that lit up the night sky above Mexico City.

finesse N. delicate skill. The *finesse* and adroitness with which the surgeon wielded her scalpel impressed the observers in the operating theater.

finicky ADJ. too particular; fussy. The little girl was *finicky* about her food, leaving anything that wasn't to her taste.

finite ADJ. limited. It is difficult for humanity with its *finite* existence to grasp the infinite.

firebrand N. hothead; troublemaker. The police tried to keep track of all the local *firebrands* when the president came to town.

fitful ADJ. spasmodic; intermittent. On the airplane, Sharon finally managed to doze off, but it was a *fitful*, restless sleep, interrupted by announcements from the pilot and wails from the baby in the next row.

flaccid ADJ. flabby. His sedentary life had left him with *flaccid* muscles.

■ **flag** V. droop; grow feeble. When the opposing hockey team scored its third goal only minutes into the first period, the home team's spirits *flagged*. flagging, ADJ.

flagrant ADJ. conspicuously wicked; blatant; outrageous. The governor's appointment of his brother-in-law to the state Supreme Court was a *flagrant* violation of the state laws against nepotism (favoritism based on kinship).

flair N. talent. She has an uncanny *flair* for discovering new artists before the public has become aware of their existence.

flamboyant ADJ. ornate. Modern architecture has discarded the *flamboyant* trimming on buildings and emphasizes simplicity of line.

flaunt V. display ostentatiously. Mae West saw nothing wrong with showing off her considerable physical charms, saying, "Honey, if you've got it, *flaunt* it!"

■ **fledgling** ADJ. inexperienced. The folk dance club set up an apprentice program to allow *fledgling* dance callers a chance to polish their skills. also N.

flinch V. hesitate; shrink. She did not *flinch* in the face of danger but fought back bravely.

flippant ADJ. lacking proper seriousness. When Mark told Mona he loved her, she dismissed his earnest declaration with a *flippant* "Oh, you say that to all the girls!" flippancy, N.

florid ADJ. ruddy; reddish; flowery. If you go to Florida and get a sunburn, your complexion will look *florid*. If your postcards about your trip praise it in flowery words, your prose will be *florid*, too.

flounder V. struggle and thrash about; proceed clumsily or falter. Up to his knees in the bog, Floyd *floundered* about, trying to regain his footing. Bewildered by the new software, Flo *floundered* until Jan showed her how to get started.

flourish V. grow well; prosper; make sweeping gestures. The orange trees *flourished* in the sun.

■ **flout** V. reject; mock; show contempt for. The painter Julian Schnabel is known for works that *flout* the conventions of high art, such as paintings on velvet or linoleum. Do not confuse *flout* with *flaunt*: to flaunt something is to show it off; to flout something is to show your scorn for it. Perhaps by *flouting* the conventions of high art, Schnabel was *flaunting* his ability to get away with breaking the rules.

fluctuate V. waver; shift. The water pressure in our shower *fluctuates* wildly; you start rinsing yourself off with a trickle, and two minutes later a blast of water nearly knocks you off your feet. I'll never get used to these *fluctuations*.

fluency N. smoothness of speech. She spoke French with *fluency* and ease.

fluke N. unlikely occurrence; stroke of fortune. When Douglas defeated Tyson for the heavyweight championship, some sportscasters dismissed his victory as a *fluke*.

fluster V. confuse. The teacher's sudden question *flustered* him and he stammered his reply.

flux N. flowing; series of changes. While conditions are in such a state of *flux*, I do not wish to commit myself too deeply to any one position.

foible N. minor eccentricity; slight weakness or flaw. Eating oysters for dessert is just one of David's little *foibles.*

foil N. contrast. In *Star Wars,* dark, evil Darth Vader is a perfect *foil* for fair-haired, naive Luke Skywalker.

foil V. defeat; frustrate. In the end, Skywalker is able to *foil* Vader's diabolical schemes.

foist V. insert improperly; palm off. Susan had no desire to have her late aunt's ancient Boston terrier *foisted* on her, but someone had to look after the poor beast.

■ **foment** V. stir up; instigate. Cher's archenemy Heather spread some nasty rumors that *fomented* trouble in the club. Do you think Cher's foe meant to *foment* such discord?

foolhardy ADJ. rash. Don't be *foolhardy.* Get the advice of experienced people before undertaking this venture.

foray N. raid. The company staged a midnight *foray* against the enemy outpost.

forbearance N. patience. Be patient with John. Treat him with *forbearance:* he is still weak from his illness.

forebears N. ancestors. Reverence for one's *forebears* (sometimes referred to as ancestor worship) plays an important part in many Oriental cultures.

foreboding N. premonition of evil. Suspecting no conspiracies against him, Caesar gently ridiculed his wife's *forebodings* about the Ides of March.

forensic ADJ. suitable to debate or courts of law. In her best *forensic* manner, the lawyer addressed the jury.

foreshadow V. give an indication beforehand; portend; prefigure. In retrospect, political analysts realized that Yeltsin's defiance of the attempted coup *foreshadowed* his emergence as the dominant figure of the new Russian republic.

foresight N. ability to foresee future happenings; prudence. A wise investor, she had the *foresight* to buy land just before the current real estate boom.

■ **forestall** V. prevent by taking action in advance. By setting up a prenuptial agreement, the prospective bride and groom hoped to *forestall* any potential arguments about money in the event of a divorce.

forgo V. give up; do without. Determined to lose weight for the summer, Ida decided to *forgo* dessert until she could fit into a size eight again.

forlorn ADJ. sad and lonely; wretched. Deserted by her big sisters and her friends, the *forlorn* child sat sadly on the steps awaiting their return.

formality N. ceremonious quality; something done just for form's sake. The president received the visiting heads of state with due *formality:* flags waving, honor guards standing at attention, bands playing anthems at full blast. The audition for the starring role was a mere *formality,* for the producer's girlfriend was sure to get the part.

formidable ADJ. inspiring fear or apprehension; difficult; awe-inspiring. In the film *Meet the Parents,* the hero is understandably nervous around his fiancée's father, a *formidable* CIA agent.

forsake V. desert; abandon; renounce. No one expected Foster to *forsake* his wife and children and run off with another woman.

forswear V. renounce; abandon. The captured knight could escape death only if he agreed to *forswear* Christianity and embrace Islam as the one true faith.

forte N. strong point or special talent. I am not eager to play this rather serious role, for my *forte* is comedy.

forthright ADJ. straightforward; direct; frank. I prefer Jill's *forthright* approach to Jack's tendency to beat around the bush. Never afraid to call a spade a spade, she was perhaps too *forthright* to be a successful party politician.

fortitude N. bravery; courage. After her father's death, Cinderella was forced to toil as a servant in her own home; she endured many hardships with true patience and *fortitude.*

fortuitous ADJ. accidental; by chance. Though he pretended their encounter was *fortuitous,* he'd actually been hanging around her usual haunts for the past two weeks, hoping she'd turn up.

foster V. rear; encourage. According to the legend, Romulus and Remus were *fostered* by a she-wolf that raised the abandoned infants as her own. also ADJ.

Word List 21 founder–gibberish

founder V. fail completely; sink. After hitting the submerged iceberg, the *Titanic* started taking in water rapidly and soon *foundered.*

founder N. person who establishes (an organization, business). Among those drowned when the *Titanic* sank was the *founder* of the Abraham & Straus department store chain.

fracas N. brawl, melee. The military police stopped the *fracas* in the bar and arrested the belligerents.

fractious ADJ. unruly; disobedient; irritable. Bucking and kicking, the *fractious* horse unseated its rider.

frail ADJ. weak. The delicate child seemed too *frail* to lift the heavy carton. frailty, N.

franchise N. right granted by authority; right to vote; license to sell a product in a particular territory. The city issued a *franchise* to the company to operate surface transit lines on the streets for 99 years. For most of American history women lacked the right to vote: not until the early twentieth century was the *franchise* granted to women. Stan owns a Carvel's ice cream *franchise* in Chinatown.

frantic ADJ. wild. At the time of the collision, many people became *frantic* with fear.

fraudulent ADJ. cheating; deceitful. The government seeks to prevent *fraudulent* and misleading advertising.

fraught ADJ. filled or charged with; causing emotional distress. "Parenting, like brain surgery, is now all-consuming, *fraught* with anxiety, worry, and self-doubt. We have allowed what used to be simple and natural to become bewildering and intimidating." (Fred Gosman)

frenetic ADJ. frenzied; frantic. The novels of the beat generation reflect a *frenetic,* restless pursuit of new sensation and experience, and a disdain for the conventional measures of economic and social success.

frenzied ADJ. madly excited. As soon as they smelled smoke, the *frenzied* animals milled about in their cages.

fret V. be annoyed or vexed. To *fret* over your poor grades is foolish; instead, decide to work harder in the future.

friction N. clash in opinion; rubbing against. The activist Saul Alinsky wrote, "Change means movement. Movement means *friction.* Only in the *frictionless* vacuum of a nonexistent abstract world can movement or change occur without that abrasive *friction* of conflict."

frigid ADJ. intensely cold. Alaska is in the *frigid* zone.

frivolous ADJ. lacking in seriousness; self-indulgently carefree; relatively unimportant. Though Nancy enjoyed Bill's *frivolous,* lighthearted companionship, she sometimes wondered whether he could ever be serious. frivolity, N.

frolicsome ADJ. playful; full of liveliness. The *frolicsome* puppy tried to lick the face of its master.

■ **frugality** N. thrift; economy. In economically hard times, anyone who doesn't learn to practice *frugality* risks bankruptcy. frugal, ADJ.

fruition N. bearing of fruit; fulfillment; realization. After years of scrimping and saving, her dream of owning her own home finally came to *fruition.*

frustrate V. thwart; defeat. Constant partisan bickering *frustrated* the governor's efforts to persuade the legislature to approve his proposed budget.

fugitive ADJ. fleeting or transitory; roving. The film brought a few *fugitive* images to her mind, but on the whole it made no lasting impression upon her.

fulminate v. denounce thunderously; explode. Known for his "fire and brimstone" sermons, the preacher *fulminated* against sinners and backsliders, consigning them to the flames of hell.

fulsome ADJ. disgustingly excessive. Disgusted by her fans' *fulsome* admiration, the movie star retreated from the public, crying, "I want to be alone!"

functionary N. official. As his case was transferred from one *functionary* to another, he began to despair of ever reaching a settlement.

fundamental V. basic; primary; essential. The committee discussed all sorts of side issues without ever getting down to addressing the *fundamental* problem.

funereal ADJ. sad; solemn. Sympathetic with Queen Victoria's loss, the British people shared her grief, enduring without protest the *funereal* atmosphere that shadowed her court.

furor N. frenzy; great excitement. The story of her embezzlement of the funds created a *furor* on the stock exchange.

furtive ADJ. stealthy; sneaky. Noticing the *furtive* glance the customer gave the diamond bracelet on the counter, the jeweler wondered whether he had a potential shoplifter on his hands.

fusion N. union; blending; synthesis. So-called rockabilly music represents a *fusion* of country music and blues that became rock and roll.

■ **futile** ADJ. useless; hopeless; ineffectual. It is *futile* for me to try to get any work done around here while the telephone is ringing every 30 seconds. futility, N.

gadfly N. animal-biting fly; an irritating person. Like a *gadfly,* he irritated all the guests at the hotel; within forty-eight hours, everyone regarded him as an annoying busybody.

gaffe N. social blunder. According to Miss Manners, to call your husband by your lover's name is worse than a mere *gaffe;* it is a tactical mistake.

■ **gainsay** V. deny. She was too honest to *gainsay* the truth of the report.

galaxy N. large, isolated system of stars, such as the Milky Way; a collection of brilliant personalities. Science fiction speculates about the possible existence of life in other *galaxies.* The deaths of such famous actors as Peter O'Toole and Paul Newman tells us that the *galaxy* of Hollywood superstars is rapidly disappearing.

gall V. annoy; chafe. Their taunts *galled* him.

galvanize V. stimulate by shock; stir up; revitalize. News that the prince was almost at their door *galvanized* the ugly stepsisters into a frenzy of combing and primping.

gambit N. opening in chess in which a piece is sacrificed. The player was afraid to accept his opponent's *gambit* because he feared a trap that as yet he could not see.

gamely ADV. in a spirited manner; with courage. Because he had fought *gamely* against a much superior boxer, the crowd gave him a standing ovation when he left the arena.

gamut N. entire range. In a classic put-down of actress Katharine Hepburn, the critic Dorothy Parker wrote that the actress ran the *gamut* of emotions from A to B.

gape V. open widely. The huge pit *gaped* before him; if he stumbled, he would fall in. Slack-jawed in wonder, Huck *gaped* at the huge stalactites hanging from the ceiling of the limestone cavern.

garbled ADJ. mixed up; jumbled; distorted. A favorite party game involves passing a whispered message from one person to another; by the time it reaches the last player, the message has become totally *garbled.* garble, V.

gargantuan ADJ. huge; enormous. The *gargantuan* wrestler was terrified of mice.

garish ADJ. overbright in color; gaudy. She wore a rhinestone necklace with a *garish* red and gold dress trimmed with sequins.

garner V. gather; store up. In her long career as an actress, Katharine Hepburn *garnered* many awards, including the coveted Oscar.

■ **garrulous** ADJ. loquacious; wordy; talkative. My Uncle Henry can out-talk any other three people I know. He is the most *garrulous* person in Cayuga County. garrulity, N.

gauche ADJ. clumsy; coarse and uncouth. Compared to the sophisticated young ladies in their elegant gowns, tomboyish Jo felt *gauche* and out of place.

gaudy ADJ. flashy; showy. The newest Trump skyscraper is typically *gaudy,* covered in gilded panels that gleam in the sun.

gawk V. stare foolishly; look in open-mouthed awe. The country boy *gawked* at the skyscrapers and neon lights of the big city.

gazette N. official periodical publication. He read the *gazettes* regularly for the announcement of his promotion.

genealogy N. record of descent; lineage. He was proud of his *genealogy* and constantly referred to the achievements of his ancestors.

generality N. vague statement. This report is filled with *generalities;* you must be more specific in your statements.

generate V. cause; produce; create. In his first days in office, President Clinton managed to *generate* a new mood of optimism; we hoped he could also *generate* a few new jobs.

generic ADJ. characteristic of an entire class or species. Sue knew so many computer programmers who spent their spare time playing fantasy games that she began to think that playing Dungeons & Dragons was a *generic* trait.

genesis N. beginning; origin. Tracing the *genesis* of a family is the theme of "Roots."

geniality N. cheerfulness; kindliness; sympathy. This restaurant is famous and popular because of the *geniality* of the proprietor, who tries to make everyone happy. genial, ADJ.

genre N. particular variety of art or literature. Both a short story writer and a poet, Langston Hughes proved himself equally skilled in either *genre.*

genteel ADJ. well-bred; elegant. We are looking for a man with a *genteel* appearance who can inspire confidence by his cultivated manner.

germane ADJ. pertinent; bearing upon the case at hand. The lawyer objected that the testimony being offered was not *germane* to the case at hand.

germinal ADJ. pertaining to a germ; creative. Such an idea is *germinal;* I am certain that it will influence thinkers and philosophers for many generations.

germinate V. cause to sprout; sprout. After the seeds *germinate* and develop their permanent leaves, the plants may be removed from the cold frames and transplanted to the garden.

gesticulation N. motion; gesture. Operatic performers are trained to make exaggerated *gesticulations* because of the large auditoriums in which they appear.

ghastly ADJ. horrible. The murdered man was a *ghastly* sight.

gibberish N. nonsense; babbling. Did you hear that foolish boy spouting *gibberish* about monsters from outer space?

Word List 22 gibe–hazy

gibe V. mock. As you *gibe* at their superstitious beliefs, do you realize that you, too, are guilty of similarly foolish thoughts?

gingerly ADV. very carefully. To separate egg whites, first crack the egg *gingerly.* also ADJ.

gist N. essence. She was asked to give the *gist* of the essay in two sentences.

glacial ADJ. like a glacier; extremely cold. Never a warm person, when offended Hugo could seem positively *glacial.*

glaring ADJ. highly conspicuous; harshly bright. *Glaring* spelling or grammatical errors in your résumé will unfavorably impress potential employers.

glean v. gather leavings. After the crops had been harvested by the machines, the peasants were permitted to *glean* the wheat left in the fields.

glib ADJ. fluent; facile; slick. Keeping up a steady patter to entertain his customers, the kitchen gadget salesman was a *glib* speaker, never at a loss for a word.

glimmer v. shine erratically; twinkle. In the darkness of the cavern, the glowworms hanging from the cavern roof *glimmered* like distant stars.

gloat v. express evil satisfaction; view malevolently. As you *gloat* over your ill-gotten wealth, do you think of the many victims you have defrauded?

gloss over v. explain away. No matter how hard he tried to talk around the issue, President Bush could not *gloss over* the fact that he had raised taxes after all.

glossary N. brief explanation of words used in the text. I have found the *glossary* in this book very useful; it has eliminated many trips to the dictionary.

glut v. overstock; fill to excess. The many manufacturers *glutted* the market and could not find purchasers for the many articles they had produced. also N.

■ **goad** v. urge on; prod; incite. Laura was furious with herself for having lost her temper, and even more furious with Jo for having *goaded* her into losing it. also N.

gouge v. tear out. In that fight, all the rules were forgotten; the adversaries bit, kicked, and tried to *gouge* each other's eyes out.

gouge v. overcharge. During the World Series, ticket scalpers tried to *gouge* the public, asking astronomical prices even for bleacher seats.

graduated ADJ. arranged by degrees (of height, difficulty, etc.). Margaret loved her *graduated* set of Russian hollow wooden dolls; she spent hours happily putting the smaller dolls into their larger counterparts.

grandeur N. impressiveness; stateliness; majesty. No matter how often he hiked through the mountains, David never failed to be struck by the *grandeur* of the Sierra Nevada range.

■ **grandiloquent** ADJ. pompous; bombastic; using high-sounding language. The politician could never speak simply; she was always *grandiloquent.*

grandiose ADJ. pretentious; high-flown; ridiculously exaggerated; impressive. The aged matinee idol still had *grandiose* notions of his supposed importance in the theatrical world.

graphic ADJ. pertaining to the art of delineating; vividly described. I was particularly impressed by the *graphic* presentation of the storm.

grapple v. wrestle; come to grips with. He *grappled* with the burglar and overpowered him.

grate v. make a harsh noise; have an unpleasant effect; shred. The screams of the quarreling children *grated* on her nerves.

gratify v. please. Lori's parents were *gratified* by her successful performance on the GRE.

gratis ADV. free. The company offered to give one package *gratis* to every purchaser of one of their products. also ADJ.

gratuitous ADJ. given freely; unwarranted; uncalled for. Quit making *gratuitous* comments about my driving; no one asked you for your opinion.

gratuity N. tip. Many service employees rely more on *gratuities* than on salaries for their livelihood.

gravity N. seriousness. We could tell we were in serious trouble from the *gravity* of her expression. grave, ADJ.

■ **gregarious** ADJ. sociable. Typically, party-throwers are *gregarious;* hermits are not.

grievance N. cause of complaint. When her supervisor ignored her complaint, she took her *grievance* to the union.

grievous ADJ. causing sorrow or pain; very severe. A pedestrian who suffered *grievous* injuries after being struck by a city bus last year will receive a $575,000 settlement from the transit agency.

grotesque ADJ. fantastic; comically hideous. On Halloween people enjoy wearing *grotesque* costumes.

grouse v. complain; fuss. Students traditionally *grouse* about the abysmal quality of "mystery meat" and similar dormitory food.

grovel v. crawl or creep on ground; remain prostrate. Even though we have been defeated, we do not have to *grovel* before our conquerors.

grudging ADJ. unwilling; reluctant; stingy. We received only *grudging* support from the mayor despite his earlier promises of aid.

grueling ADJ. exhausting. The marathon is a *grueling* race.

gruesome ADJ. grisly; horrible. His face was the stuff of nightmares: all the children in the audience screamed when Freddy Kruger's *gruesome* countenance was flashed on the screen.

gruff ADJ. rough-mannered. Although he was blunt and *gruff* with most people, he was always gentle with children.

guile N. deceit; duplicity; wiliness; cunning. Iago uses considerable *guile* to trick Othello into believing that Desdemona has been unfaithful.

■ **guileless** ADJ. without deceit. He is naive, simple, and *guileless;* he cannot be guilty of fraud.

guise N. appearance; costume. In the *guise* of a plumber, the detective investigated the murder case.

■ **gullible** ADJ. easily deceived. *Gullible* people have only themselves to blame if they fall for con artists repeatedly. As the saying goes, "Fool me once, shame on you. Fool me twice, shame on me."

habituate v. accustom or familiarize; addict. Macbeth gradually *habituated* himself to murder, shedding his scruples as he grew accustomed to his bloody deeds.

hackneyed ADJ. commonplace; trite. When the reviewer criticized the movie for its *hackneyed* plot, we agreed; we had seen similar stories hundreds of times before.

haggle v. argue about prices. I prefer to shop in a store that has a one-price policy because, whenever I *haggle* with a shopkeeper, I am never certain that I paid a fair price for the articles I purchased.

hallowed ADJ. blessed; consecrated. Although the dead girl's parents had never been active churchgoers, they insisted that their daughter be buried in *hallowed* ground.

hallucination N. delusion. I think you were frightened by a *hallucination* that you created in your own mind.

halting ADJ. hesitant; faltering. Novice extemporaneous speakers often talk in a *halting* fashion as they grope for the right words.

hamper v. obstruct. The new mother hadn't realized how much the effort of caring for an infant would *hamper* her ability to keep an immaculate house.

haphazard ADJ. random; by chance. His *haphazard* reading left him unacquainted with many classic books.

hapless ADJ. unfortunate. This *hapless* creature had never known a moment's pleasure.

■ **harangue** N. long, passionate, and vehement speech. In her lengthy *harangue,* the principal berated the offenders. also v.

harass v. annoy by repeated attacks. When he could not pay his bills as quickly as he had promised, he was *harassed* by his creditors.

harbor v. provide a refuge for; hide. The church *harbored* illegal aliens who were political refugees. also N.

hardy ADJ. sturdy; robust; able to stand inclement weather. We asked the gardening expert to recommend particularly *hardy* plants that could withstand our harsh New England winters.

harping N. tiresome dwelling on a subject. After he had reminded me several times about what he had done for me I told him to stop his *harping* on my indebtedness to him. harp, v.

harrowing ADJ. agonizing; distressing; traumatic. At first Terry Anderson did not wish to discuss his *harrowing* months of captivity as a political hostage. harrow, V.

harry V. harass, annoy, torment; raid. The guerrilla band *harried* the enemy nightly.

haughtiness N. pride; arrogance. When she realized that Darcy believed himself too good to dance with his inferiors, Elizabeth took great offense at his *haughtiness.*

haven N. place of safety; refuge. For Ricardo, the school library became his *haven,* a place to which he could retreat during chaotic times.

hazardous ADJ. dangerous. The frayed electrical wiring in their house was so *hazardous* that the contractor recommended they completely rewire the building.

hazy ADJ. slightly obscure. In *hazy* weather, you cannot see the top of this mountain.

Word List 23 headlong–illusory

headlong ADJ. hasty; rash. The slave seized the unexpected chance to make a *headlong* dash across the border to freedom.

headstrong ADJ. stubborn; willful; unyielding. Because she refused to marry the man her parents had chosen for her, everyone scolded Minna and called her a foolish, *headstrong* girl.

heckler N. person who verbally harasses others. The *heckler* kept interrupting the speaker with rude remarks. heckle, V.

hedonist N. one who believes that pleasure is the sole aim in life. A thoroughgoing *hedonist,* he considered only his own pleasure and ignored any claims others had on his money or time. hedonism, N.

heedless ADJ. not noticing; disregarding. She drove on, *heedless* of the warnings that the road was dangerous. heed, V.

hegemony N. dominance, especially of one nation over others. As one Eastern European nation after another declared its independence, commentators marveled at the sudden breakdown of the once monolithic Soviet *hegemony.*

heinous ADJ. atrocious; hatefully bad. Hitler's *heinous* crimes will never be forgotten.

heresy N. opinion contrary to popular belief; opinion contrary to accepted religion. Galileo's assertion that the earth moved around the sun directly contradicted the religious teachings of his day; as a result, he was tried for *heresy.* heretic, N. heretical, ADJ.

hermetic ADJ. sealed by fusion so as to be airtight. After you sterilize the bandages, place them in a container and seal it with a *hermetic* seal to protect them from contamination by airborne bacteria.

hermetic ADJ. obscure and mysterious; occult. It is strange to consider that modern chemistry originated in the *hermetic* teachings of the ancient alchemists. (secondary meaning)

heterodox ADJ. unorthodox; unconventional. To those who upheld the belief that the earth did not move, Galileo's theory that the earth circled the sun was disturbingly *heterodox.*

heterogeneous ADJ. dissimilar; mixed. This year's entering class is a remarkably *heterogeneous* body: it includes students from 40 different states and 26 foreign countries, some the children of billionaires, others the offspring of welfare families. heterogeneity, N.

heyday N. time of greatest success; prime. In their *heyday,* the San Francisco Forty-Niners won the Super Bowl two years running.

hiatus N. gap; pause. Except for a brief two-year *hiatus,* during which she enrolled in the Peace Corps, Ms. Clements has devoted herself to her medical career.

hierarchy N. arrangement by rank or standing; authoritarian body divided into ranks. To be low man on the totem pole is to have an inferior place in the *hierarchy.* hierarchical, ADJ.

hilarity N. boisterous mirth. With superb timing they did a knockabout comedy act that provoked *hilarity* from the audience. hilarious, ADJ.

hindmost ADJ. furthest behind. The coward could always be found in the *hindmost* lines whenever a battle was being waged.

hindrance N. block; obstacle. Stalled cars along the highway are a *hindrance* to traffic that tow trucks should remove without delay. hinder, V.

histrionic ADJ. theatrical. Proud of his *histrionic* ability, Lawrence wanted to play the role of Hamlet. histrionics, N.

hoard V. stockpile; accumulate for future use. Whenever there are rumors of a food shortage, people are tempted to *hoard* food. also N.

hoax N. trick; practical joke. Virginia Woolf's brother Adrian Stephen and a friend enacted an elaborate *hoax* on the British Navy, dressing up as the Emperor of Abyssinia and his entourage, and touring the newest warship of His Majesty's Fleet. also V.

holocaust N. destruction by fire. Citizens of San Francisco remember that the destruction of the city was caused not by the earthquake but by the *holocaust* that followed.

homage N. honor; tribute. In her speech she tried to pay *homage* to a great man.

■ **homogeneous** ADJ. of the same kind. Because the student body at Elite Prep was so *homogeneous,* Sara and James decided to send their daughter to a school that offered greater cultural diversity. homogeneity, N.

hone V. sharpen. To make shaving easier, he *honed* his razor with great care.

hoodwink V. deceive; delude. Having been *hoodwinked* once by the fast-talking salesman, he was extremely cautious when he went to purchase a used car.

horde N. crowd. Just before Christmas the stores are filled with *hordes* of shoppers.

hortatory ADJ. earnestly advising; didactic; preachy. "Film acting schooled Reagan in the *hortatory* oratory of movie dialogue—speeches crafted to sell an ideal or an emotion, and still sound like plain-spoken common sense—techniques he used so dynamically in politics." (Richard Corliss)

hostility N. unfriendliness; hatred. A child who has been the sole object of his parents' affection often feels *hostility* toward a new baby in the family, resenting the newcomer who has taken his place. hostile, ADJ.

hover V. hang about; wait nearby. The police helicopter *hovered* above the accident.

hubbub N. confused uproar. The marketplace was a scene of *hubbub* and excitement; in all the noise, we could not distinguish particular voices.

hubris N. arrogance; excessive self-conceit. Filled with *hubris,* Lear refused to heed his friends' warnings.

hue N. color; aspect. The aviary contained birds of every possible *hue.*

hue and cry N. outcry. When her purse was snatched, she raised such a *hue and cry* that the thief was captured.

humane ADJ. marked by kindness or consideration. It is ironic that the *Humane* Society sometimes must show its compassion toward mistreated animals by killing them to end their misery.

humdrum ADJ. dull; monotonous. After her years of adventure, she could not settle down to a *humdrum* existence.

humid ADJ. damp. Normally, on hot days, sweat evaporates swiftly and cools our bodies, but on *humid* days, the sweat evaporates more slowly, and we feel hotter.

humility N. humbleness of spirit. He spoke with a *humility* and lack of pride that impressed his listeners.

husband V. use sparingly; conserve; save. Marathon runners must *husband* their energy so that they can keep going for the entire distance.

husbandry N. frugality; thrift; agriculture. He accumulated his small fortune by diligence and *husbandry.* husband, V.

hybrid N. mongrel; mixed breed. Mendel's formula explains the appearance of *hybrids* and pure species in breeding. also ADJ.

■ **hyperbole** N. exaggeration; overstatement. As far as I'm concerned, Apple's claims about the new computer are pure *hyperbole:* no machine is that good! hyperbolic, ADJ.

hypercritical ADJ. excessively exacting. You are *hypercritical* in your demands for perfection; we all make mistakes.

hypochondriac N. person unduly worried about his health; worrier without cause about illness. The doctor prescribed chocolate pills for her patient who was a *hypochondriac.*

hypocritical ADJ. pretending to be virtuous; deceiving. Because he believed Eddie to be interested only in his own advancement, Greg resented Eddie's *hypocritical* protestations of friendship. hypocrisy, N.

hypothetical ADJ. based on assumptions or hypotheses; supposed. Suppose you are accepted by Harvard, Stanford, and Yale. Which graduate school will you choose to attend? Remember, this is only a *hypothetical* situation. hypothesis, N.

■ **iconoclastic** ADJ. attacking cherished traditions. Deeply *iconoclastic,* Jean Genet deliberately set out to shock conventional theatergoers with his radical plays. iconoclasm, N.

ideology N. system of ideas characteristic of a group or culture. For people who had grown up believing in the Communist *ideology,* it was hard to adjust to capitalism.

idiom N. expression whose meaning as a whole differs from the meanings of its individual words; distinctive style. The phrase "to lose one's marbles" is an *idiom:* if I say that Joe has lost his marbles, I'm not asking you to find them for him. I'm telling you *idiomatically* that he's crazy.

idiosyncrasy N. individual trait, usually odd in nature; eccentricity. One of Richard Nixon's little *idiosyncrasies* was his liking for ketchup on cottage cheese. One of Hannibal Lecter's little *idiosyncrasies* was his liking for human flesh. idiosyncratic, ADJ.

■ **idolatry** N. worship of idols; excessive admiration. "(P)ublic display of the ruler's countenance, whether on the coinage, the postage stamp, or the wall, is very recent, and in the more conservative countries is still regarded as a blasphemy verging on *idolatry.*" (Bernard Lewis)

idyllic ADJ. charmingly carefree; simple. Far from the city, she led an *idyllic* existence in her rural retreat.

ignoble ADJ. unworthy; not noble. A true knight, Sir Galahad never stooped to perform an *ignoble* deed.

ignominy N. deep disgrace; shame or dishonor. To lose the Ping-Pong match to a trained chimpanzee! How could Rollo endure the *ignominy* of his defeat? ignominious, ADJ.

illicit ADJ. illegal. The defense attorney claimed that the police had entrapped his client; that is, they had elicited the *illicit* action of which they now accused him.

illimitable ADJ. infinite. The notion of *illimitable* or limitless power is alien to our Constitution, for it was designed to guard against abuses of such unlimited power.

illuminate V. brighten; clear up or make understandable; enlighten. Just as a lamp can *illuminate* a dark room, a perceptive comment can *illuminate* a knotty problem.

illusion N. misleading vision. It is easy to create an optical *illusion* in which lines of equal length appear different.

illusive ADJ. deceiving. During the Second World War, Hannah Arendt attempted to rescue endangered Jewish children by sending them to safety in Jerusalem—an *illusive* safety, for some would die in Arab attacks.

illusory ADJ. deceptive; not real. Unfortunately, the costs of running the lemonade stand were so high that Tom's profits proved *illusory.*

Word List 24 imbalance–impunity

imbalance N. lack of balance or symmetry; disproportion. To correct racial *imbalance* in the schools, school boards have bused black children into white neighborhoods and white children into black ones.

imbroglio N. complicated situation; painful or complex misunderstanding; entanglement; confused mass (as of papers). The humor of Shakespearean comedies often depends on cases of mistaken identity that involve the perplexed protagonists in one comic *imbroglio* after another. embroil, V.

immaculate ADJ. spotless; flawless; absolutely clean. Ken and Jessica were wonderful tenants who left the apartment in *immaculate* condition when they moved out.

imminent ADJ. near at hand; impending. Rosa was such a last-minute worker that she could never start writing a paper till the deadline was *imminent.*

immobility N. state of being immovable. Prolonged *immobility,* especially when seated, can lead to pooling of blood in the legs, which in turn may cause swelling, stiffness, and discomfort.

immune ADJ. resistant to; free or exempt from. Fortunately, Florence had contracted chicken pox as a child and was *immune* to it when her baby came down with spots. immunity, N.

■ **immutable** ADJ. unchangeable. All things change over time; nothing is *immutable.*

■ **impair** V. injure; hurt. Drinking alcohol can *impair* your ability to drive safely; if you're going to drink, don't drive.

impalpable ADJ. imperceptible; intangible. The ash is so fine that it is *impalpable* to the touch but it can be seen as a fine layer covering the window ledge.

impartial ADJ. not biased; fair. Knowing she could not be *impartial* about her own child, Jo refused to judge any match in which Billy was competing. impartiality, N.

impassable ADJ. not able to be traveled or crossed. A giant redwood had fallen across the highway, blocking all four lanes: the road was *impassable.*

impasse N. predicament from which there is no escape. In this *impasse,* all turned to prayer as their last hope.

■ **impassive** ADJ. without feeling; imperturbable; stoical. Refusing to let the enemy see how deeply shaken he was by his capture, the prisoner kept his face *impassive.*

impeach V. charge with crime in office; indict. The angry congressman wanted to *impeach* the president for his misdeeds.

impeccable ADJ. faultless. The uncrowned queen of the fashion industry, Diana was acclaimed for her *impeccable* taste.

impecunious ADJ. without money. Though Scrooge claimed he was too *impecunious* to give alms, he easily could have afforded to be charitable.

■ **impede** V. hinder; block. The special prosecutor determined that the Attorney General, though inept, had not intentionally set out to *impede* the progress of the investigation.

impediment N. hindrance; stumbling-block. She had a speech *impediment* that prevented her from speaking clearly.

impel V. drive or force onward. A strong feeling of urgency *impelled* her; if she failed to finish the project right then, she knew that she would never get it done.

impending ADJ. nearing; approaching. The entire country was saddened by the news of his *impending* death.

impenetrable ADJ. not able to be pierced or entered; beyond understanding. How could the murderer have gotten into the locked room? To Watson, the mystery, like the room, was *impenetrable.*

impenitent ADJ. not repentant. Because King John remained obstinate and *impenitent,* the Pope placed England under an interdict prohibiting the performance of church services in the kingdom until John would repent.

imperative ADJ. absolutely necessary; critically important. It is *imperative* that you be extremely agreeable to Great-Aunt Maud when she comes to tea: otherwise she may not leave you that million dollars in her will. also N.

imperceptible ADJ. unnoticeable; undetectable. Fortunately, the stain on the blouse was *imperceptible* after the garment had gone through the wash.

imperial ADJ. like an emperor; related to an empire. When hotel owner Leona Helmsley appeared in ads as Queen Leona standing guard over the Palace Hotel, her critics mocked her *imperial* fancies.

imperious ADJ. domineering; haughty. Jane rather liked a man to be masterful, but Mr. Rochester seemed so bent on getting his own way that he was actually *imperious!* imperiousness, N.

■ **impermeable** ADJ. impervious; not permitting passage through its substance. This new material is *impermeable* to liquids.

impertinent ADJ. insolent; rude. His neighbors' *impertinent* curiosity about his lack of dates angered Ted. It was downright rude of them to ask him such personal questions. impertinence, N.

■ **imperturbable** ADJ. calm; placid. Wellington remained *imperturbable* and in full command of the situation in spite of the hysteria and panic all around him. imperturbability, N.

■ **impervious** ADJ. impenetrable; incapable of being damaged or distressed. The carpet salesman told Simone that his most expensive brand of floor covering was warranted to be *impervious* to ordinary wear and tear. Having read so many negative reviews of his acting, the movie star had learned to ignore them, and was now *impervious* to criticism.

impetuous ADJ. violent; hasty; rash. "Leap before you look" was the motto suggested by one particularly *impetuous* young man.

impetus N. moving force; incentive; stimulus. A new federal highway program would create jobs and give added *impetus* to our economic recovery.

impiety N. irreverence; lack of respect for God. When members of the youth group draped the church in toilet paper one Halloween, the minister reprimanded them for their *impiety.* impious, ADJ.

impinge V. infringe; touch; collide with. How could they be married without *impinging* on one another's freedom?

impious ADJ. irreverent. The congregation was offended by her *impious* remarks.

■ **implacable** ADJ. incapable of being pacified. Madame Defarge was the *implacable* enemy of the Evremonde family.

implausible ADJ. unlikely; unbelievable. Though her alibi seemed *implausible,* it in fact turned out to be true.

implement V. put into effect; supply with tools. The mayor was unwilling to *implement* the plan until she was sure it had the governor's backing. also N.

implicate V. incriminate; show to be involved. Here's the deal: if you agree to take the witness stand and *implicate* your partners in crime, the prosecution will recommend that the judge go easy in sentencing you.

implication N. something hinted at or suggested. When Miss Watson said she hadn't seen her purse since the last time Jim was in the house, the *implication* was that she suspected Jim had taken it.

■ **implicit** ADJ. understood but not stated. Jack never told Jill he adored her; he believed his love was *implicit* in his deeds.

■ **implode** V. burst inward. If you break a vacuum tube, the glass tube *implodes.* implosion, N.

implore V. beg. He *implored* her to give him a second chance.

imply V. suggest a meaning not expressed; signify. When Aunt Millie said, "My! That's a big piece of pie, young man!" was she *implying* that Bobby was being a glutton in helping himself to such a huge piece?

impolitic ADJ. not wise. I think it is *impolitic* to raise this issue at the present time because the public is too angry.

imponderable ADJ. difficult or impossible to measure or assess. Fears of a possible Gulf war have driven down airline bookings for February and March; the effects of an actual war on the airline industry would be *imponderable.*

import N. significance. *Scientific American* has covered Einstein's theories—and the refinements and reactions to them—ever since scientists began to grasp the *import* of his landmark 1905 papers.

importunate ADJ. urging; demanding. He tried to hide from his *importunate* creditors until his allowance arrived.

importune V. beg persistently. Democratic and Republican phone solicitors *importuned* her for contributions so frequently that she decided to give nothing to either party.

imposture N. assuming a false identity; masquerade. Maintaining he was Richard of Shrewsbury, younger son of England's late King Edward IV, Perkin Warbeck laid claim to the throne; captured by Henry VII's army, Warbeck eventually confessed his *imposture.*

impotent ADJ. weak; ineffective. Although he wished to break the nicotine habit, he found himself *impotent* in resisting the craving for a cigarette.

impregnable ADJ. invulnerable. Until the development of the airplane as a military weapon, the fort was considered *impregnable.*

impromptu ADJ. without previous preparation; off the cuff; on the spur of the moment. The judges were amazed that she could make such a thorough, well-supported presentation in an *impromptu* speech.

impropriety N. improperness; unsuitableness. Because of the *impropriety* of the punk rocker's slashed T-shirt and jeans, the management refused to admit him to the hotel's very formal dining room.

improvident ADJ. thriftless. He was constantly being warned to mend his *improvident* ways and begin to "save for a rainy day." improvidence, N.

improvise V. compose on the spur of the moment. She would sit at the piano and *improvise* for hours on themes from Bach and Handel.

imprudent ADJ. lacking caution; injudicious. It is *imprudent* to exercise vigorously and become overheated when you are unwell.

impudence N. impertinence; insolence. Kissed on the cheek by a perfect stranger, Lady Catherine exclaimed, "Of all the nerve! Young man, I should have you horse-whipped for your *impudence.*"

impugn V. dispute or contradict (often in an insulting way); challenge; gainsay. Our treasurer was furious when the finance committee's report *impugned* the accuracy of his financial records and recommended that he take bonehead math.

impunity N. freedom from punishment or harm. A 98-pound weakling can't attack a beachfront bully with *impunity:* the poor, puny guy is sure to get mashed.

Word List 25 impute–indubitable

impute V. attribute; ascribe. If I wished to *impute* blame to the officers in charge of this program, I would say so definitely and immediately.

■ **inadvertently** ADV. unintentionally; by oversight; carelessly. Judy's great fear was that she might *inadvertently* omit a question on the exam and mismark her whole answer sheet.

inalienable ADJ. not to be taken away; nontransferable. The Declaration of Independence mentions the *inalienable* rights that all of us possess.

inane ADJ. silly; senseless. There's no point in what you're saying. Why are you bothering to make such *inane* remarks? inanity, N.

inanimate ADJ. lifeless. Fashioning a huge, manlike figure out of *inanimate* body parts, Victor Frankenstein harnessed the galvanic power of lightning to bring his creation to life.

inarticulate ADJ. speechless; producing indistinct speech. She became *inarticulate* with rage and uttered sounds without meaning.

inaugurate V. begin formally; install in office. The candidate promised that he would *inaugurate* a new nationwide health care plan as soon as he was *inaugurated* as president. inauguration, N.

incapacitate V. disable. During the winter, respiratory ailments *incapacitated* many people.

incarcerate V. imprison. The civil rights workers were willing to be arrested and even *incarcerated* if by their imprisonment they could serve the cause.

incense V. enrage; infuriate. Cruelty to defenseless animals *incensed* Kit: the very idea brought tears of anger to her eyes.

incentive N. spur; motive. Mike's strong desire to outshine his big sister was all the *incentive* he needed to do well in school.

inception N. start; beginning. She was involved with the project from its *inception.*

incessant ADJ. uninterrupted; unceasing. In a famous TV commercial, the frogs' *incessant* croaking goes on and on until eventually it turns into a single word: "Bud-weis-er."

■ **inchoate** ADJ. recently begun; rudimentary; elementary. Before the Creation, the world was an *inchoate* mass.

incidence N. rate of occurrence; particular occurrence. Health professionals expressed great concern over the high *incidence* of infant mortality in major urban areas.

incidental ADJ. not essential; minor. The scholarship covered his major expenses at college and some of his *incidental* expenses as well.

incipient ADJ. beginning; in an early stage. I will go to sleep early for I want to break an *incipient* cold.

incisive ADJ. cutting; sharp. Her *incisive* remarks made us see the fallacy in our plans. incision, N.

incite V. arouse to action; goad; motivate; induce to exist. In a fiery speech, Mario *incited* his fellow students to go out on strike to protest the university's anti-affirmative-action stand.

inclement ADJ. stormy; unkind. In *inclement* weather, I like to curl up on the sofa with a good book and listen to the storm blowing outside.

inclined ADJ. tending or leaning toward; bent. Though I am *inclined* to be skeptical, the witness's manner *inclines* me to believe his story. incline, V.

inclusive ADJ. tending to include all. The comedian turned down the invitation to join the Players' Club, saying any club that would let him in was too *inclusive* for him.

incognito ADV. with identity concealed; using an assumed name. The monarch enjoyed traveling through the town *incognito* and mingling with the populace. also ADJ.

incoherent ADJ. unintelligible; muddled; illogical. The excited fan blushed and stammered, her words becoming almost *incoherent* in the thrill of meeting her favorite rock star face to face. incoherence, N.

incompatible ADJ. inharmonious. The married couple argued incessantly and finally decided to separate because they were *incompatible.* incompatibility, N.

■ **incongruity** N. lack of harmony; absurdity. The *incongruity* of his wearing sneakers with formal attire amused the observers. incongruous, ADJ.

■ **inconsequential** ADJ. insignificant; unimportant. Brushing off Ali's apologies for having broken the wine glass, Tamara said, "Don't worry about it; it's *inconsequential.*"

inconsistency N. state of being self-contradictory; lack of uniformity or steadiness. How are lawyers different from agricultural inspectors? Where lawyers check *inconsistencies* in witnesses' statements, agricultural inspectors check *inconsistencies* in Grade A eggs. inconsistent, ADJ.

incontinent ADJ. lacking self-restraint; licentious. His *incontinent* behavior off stage so shocked many people that they refused to attend the plays and movies in which he appeared.

incontrovertible ADJ. indisputable; not open to question. Unless you find the evidence against my client absolutely *incontrovertible,* you must declare her not guilty of this charge.

■ **incorporate** V. introduce something into a larger whole; combine; unite. Breaking with precedent, President Truman ordered the military to *incorporate* blacks into every branch of the armed services. also ADJ.

incorporeal ADJ. lacking a material body; insubstantial. Although Casper the friendly ghost is an *incorporeal* being, he and his fellow ghosts make quite an impact on the physical world.

incorrigible ADJ. uncorrectable. Though Widow Douglass hoped to reform Huck, Miss Watson pronounced him *incorrigible* and said he would come to no good end.

incredulous ADJ. withholding belief; skeptical. When Jack claimed he hadn't eaten the jelly doughnut, Jill took an *incredulous* look at his smeared face and laughed.

increment N. increase. The new contract calls for a ten percent *increment* in salary for each employee for the next two years.

incriminate V. accuse; serve as evidence against. The witness's testimony against the racketeers *incriminates* some high public officials as well.

incubate V. hatch. Because our supply of electricity has been cut off, we shall have to rely on the hens to *incubate* these eggs.

inculcate V. teach. In an effort to *inculcate* religious devotion, the officials ordered that the school day begin with the singing of a hymn.

incumbent ADJ. obligatory; currently holding an office. It is *incumbent* upon all *incumbent* elected officials to keep accurate records of expenses incurred in office. also N.

incur V. bring upon oneself. His parents refused to pay any future debts he might *incur.*

incursion N. temporary invasion. The nightly *incursions* and hit-and-run raids of our neighbors across the border tried the patience of the country to the point where we decided to retaliate in force.

indefatigable ADJ. tireless. Although the effort of taking out the garbage exhausted Wayne for the entire morning, when it came to partying, he was *indefatigable.*

indelible ADJ. not able to be erased. The *indelible* ink left a permanent mark on my shirt. Young Bill Clinton's meeting with President Kennedy made an *indelible* impression on the youth.

indemnify V. make secure against loss; compensate for loss. The city will *indemnify* all home owners whose property is spoiled by this project.

■ **indeterminate** ADJ. uncertain; not clearly fixed; indefinite. That interest rates shall rise appears certain; when they will do so, however, remains *indeterminate.*

indicative ADJ. suggestive; implying. A lack of appetite may be *indicative* of a major mental or physical disorder.

indices N. PL. signs; indications. Many college admissions officers believe that SAT scores and high school grades are the best *indices* of a student's potential to succeed in college. index, N. SING.

indict V. charge. The district attorney didn't want to *indict* the suspect until she was sure she had a strong enough case to convince a jury. indictment, N.

indifferent ADJ. unmoved or unconcerned by; mediocre. Because Ann felt no desire to marry, she was *indifferent* to Carl's constant proposals. Not only was she *indifferent* to him personally, but she felt that, given his general inanity, he would make an *indifferent* husband.

■ **indigence** N. poverty. Neither the economists nor the political scientists have found a way to wipe out the inequities of wealth and eliminate *indigence* from our society. indigent, ADJ., N.

indigenous ADJ. native. Cigarettes are made of tobacco, a plant *indigenous* to the New World.

indigent ADJ. poor; destitute. Someone who is truly *indigent* can't even afford to buy a pack of cigarettes. [Don't mix up *indigent* and *indigenous.* See preceding entry.] also N.

indignation N. anger at an injustice. She felt *indignation* at the ill-treatment of the helpless animals.

indignity N. offensive or insulting treatment. Although he seemed to accept cheerfully the *indignities* heaped upon him, he was inwardly very angry.

indiscriminate ADJ. choosing at random; confused. She disapproved of her son's *indiscriminate* television viewing and decided to restrict him to educational programs.

indisputable ADJ. too certain for anyone to dispute. In the face of these *indisputable* statements, I withdraw my complaint.

indissoluble ADJ. permanent. The *indissoluble* bonds of marriage are all too often being dissolved.

■ **indolent** ADJ. lazy. Couch potatoes lead an *indolent* life lying back in their Lazyboy recliners watching TV. indolence, N.

indomitable ADJ. unconquerable; unyielding. Focusing on her game despite all her personal problems, tennis champion Steffi Graf displayed an *indomitable* will to win.

indubitable ADJ. unable to be doubted; unquestionable. Auditioning for the chorus line, Molly was an *indubitable* hit: the director fired the leading lady and hired Molly in her place!

Word List 26 induce–insuperable

induce V. persuade; bring about. After the quarrel, Tina said nothing could *induce* her to talk to Tony again. inducement, N.

inductive ADJ. pertaining to induction or proceeding from the specific to the general. The discovery of Pluto is an excellent example of the results that can be obtained from *inductive* reasoning.

indulgent ADJ. humoring; yielding; lenient. Jay's mom was excessively *indulgent:* she bought him every computer game on the market. In fact, she *indulged* Jay so much, she spoiled him rotten.

industrious ADJ. diligent; hard-working. Look busy when the boss walks by your desk; it never hurts to appear *industrious.* industry, N.

inebriated ADJ. habitually intoxicated; drunk. Abe was *inebriated* more often than he was sober. Because of his *inebriety,* he was discharged from his job as a bus driver.

ineffable ADJ. unutterable; cannot be expressed in speech. Such *ineffable* joy must be experienced; it cannot be described.

ineffectual ADJ. not effective; weak. Because the candidate failed to get across her message to the public, her campaign was *ineffectual.*

inept ADJ. lacking skill; unsuited; incompetent. The *inept* glovemaker was all thumbs. ineptness, N.

inequity N. unfairness. In demanding equal pay for equal work, women protest the basic *inequity* of a system that allots greater financial rewards to men. inequitable, ADJ.

■ **inert** ADJ. inactive; lacking power to move. "Get up, you lazybones," Tina cried to Tony, who lay in bed *inert.* inertia, N.

inevitable ADJ. unavoidable. Though death and taxes are both supposedly *inevitable,* some people avoid paying taxes for years.

inexorable ADJ. relentless; unyielding; implacable. After listening to the pleas for clemency, the judge was *inexorable* and gave the convicted man the maximum punishment allowed by law.

infallible ADJ. unerring. We must remember that none of us is *infallible;* we all make mistakes.

infamous ADJ. notoriously bad. Charles Manson and Jeffrey Dahmer are two examples of *infamous* killers.

infer V. deduce; conclude. From the students' glazed looks, it was easy for me to *infer* that they were bored out of their minds. inference, N.

infernal ADJ. pertaining to hell; devilish. Batman was baffled: he could think of no way to hinder the Joker's *infernal* scheme to destroy the city.

infidel N. unbeliever. The Saracens made war against the *infidels.*

infiltrate V. pass into or through; penetrate (an organization) sneakily. In order to *infiltrate* enemy lines at night without being seen, the scouts darkened their faces and wore black coveralls. infiltrator, N.

infinitesimal ADJ. very small. In the twentieth century, physicists made great discoveries about the characteristics of *infinitesimal* objects like the atom and its parts.

infirmity N. weakness. Her greatest *infirmity* was lack of willpower.

inflated ADJ. exaggerated; pompous; enlarged (with air or gas). His claims about the new product were *inflated;* it did not work as well as he had promised.

influx N. flowing into. The *influx* of refugees into the country has taxed the relief agencies severely.

infraction N. violation (of a rule or regulation); breach. When basketball star Dennis Rodman butted heads with the referee, he committed a clear *infraction* of NBA rules.

infringe V. violate; encroach. When copyrighted material is used without authorization, the owner's first step is to send a letter informing the user of the material that he has *infringed* upon the owner's rights.

ingenious ADJ. clever; resourceful. Kit admired the *ingenious* way that her computer keyboard opened up to reveal the built-in CD-ROM below. ingenuity, N.

■ **ingenuous** ADJ. naive and trusting; young; unsophisticated. The woodsman did not realize how *ingenuous* Little Red Riding Hood was until he heard that she had gone off for a walk in the woods with the Big Bad Wolf. ingenue, N.

ingrained ADJ. deeply established; firmly rooted. Try as they would, the missionaries were unable to uproot the *ingrained* superstitions of the natives.

ingrate N. ungrateful person. That *ingrate* Bob sneered at the tie I gave him.

ingratiate V. become popular with. He tried to *ingratiate* himself into her parents' good graces.

■ **inherent** ADJ. firmly established by nature or habit. Katya's *inherent* love of justice caused her to champion anyone she considered to be treated unfairly by society.

inhibit V. restrain; retard or prevent. Only two things *inhibited* him from taking a punch at Mike Tyson: Tyson's left hook, and Tyson's right jab. The protective undercoating on my car *inhibits* the formation of rust. inhibition, N.

inimical ADJ. unfriendly; hostile; harmful; detrimental. I've always been friendly to Martha. Why is she so *inimical* to me?

inimitable ADJ. matchless; not able to be imitated. We admire Auden for his *inimitable* use of language; he is one of a kind.

iniquitous ADJ. wicked; immoral; unrighteous. Whether or not King Richard III was responsible for the murder of the two young princes in the Tower, it was an *iniquitous* deed. iniquity, N.

initiate V. begin; originate; receive into a group. The college is about to *initiate* a program for reducing math anxiety among students.

injurious ADJ. harmful. Smoking cigarettes can be *injurious* to your health.

inkling N. hint. This came as a complete surprise to me as I did not have the slightest *inkling* of your plans.

innate ADJ. inborn. Mozart's parents soon recognized young Wolfgang's *innate* talent for music.

■ **innocuous** ADJ. harmless. An occasional glass of wine with dinner is relatively *innocuous* and should have no ill effect on most people.

innovation N. change; introduction of something new. Although Richard liked to keep up with all the latest technological *innovations,* he didn't always abandon tried and true techniques in favor of something new. innovate, V. innovative, ADJ.

innuendo N. hint; insinuation. I can defend myself against direct accusations; *innuendos* and oblique attacks on my character are what trouble me.

inopportune ADJ. untimely; poorly chosen. A rock concert is an *inopportune* setting for a quiet conversation.

inordinate ADJ. unrestrained; excessive. She had an *inordinate* fondness for candy, eating two or three boxes in a single day.

inquisitor N. questioner (especially harsh); investigator. Fearing being grilled ruthlessly by the secret police, Marsha faced her *inquisitors* with trepidation.

insalubrious ADJ. unwholesome; not healthful. The mosquito-ridden swamp was an *insalubrious* place, a breeding ground for malarial contagion.

insatiable ADJ. not easily satisfied; unquenchable; greedy. The young writer's thirst for knowledge was *insatiable;* she was always in the library.

inscrutable ADJ. impenetrable; not readily understood; mysterious. Experienced poker players try to keep their expressions *inscrutable,* hiding their reactions to the cards behind a so-called poker face.

insensate ADJ. without feeling. She lay there as *insensate* as a log.

■ **insensible** ADJ. unconscious; unresponsive. Sherry and I are very different; at times when I would be covered with embarrassment, she seems *insensible* to shame.

insidious ADJ. treacherous; stealthy; sly. The fifth column is *insidious* because it works secretly within our territory for our defeat.

insightful ADJ. discerning; perceptive. Sol thought he was very *insightful* about human behavior, but actually he was clueless as to why people acted the way they did.

■ **insinuate** V. hint; imply; creep in. When you said I looked robust, did you mean to *insinuate* that I'm getting fat?

■ **insipid** ADJ. lacking in flavor; dull. Flat prose and flat ginger ale are equally *insipid:* both lack sparkle.

insolence N. impudent disrespect; haughtiness. How dare you treat me so rudely! The manager will hear of your *insolence.* insolent, ADJ.

insolvent ADJ. bankrupt; lacking money to pay. When rumors that he was *insolvent* reached his creditors, they began to press him for payment of the money due them. insolvency, N.

instigate V. urge; start; provoke. Delighting in making mischief, Sir Toby sets out to *instigate* a quarrel between Sir Andrew and Cesario.

insubordination N. disobedience; rebelliousness. At the slightest hint of *insubordination* from the sailors on the *Bounty,* Captain Bligh had them flogged; finally, they mutinied. insubordinate, ADJ.

insubstantial ADJ. lacking substance; insignificant; frail. His hopes for a career in acting proved *insubstantial;* no one would cast him, even in an *insubstantial* role.

■ **insularity** N. narrow-mindedness; isolation. The *insularity* of the islanders manifested itself in their suspicion of anything foreign. insular, ADJ.

insuperable ADJ. insurmountable; unbeatable. Though the odds against their survival seemed *insuperable,* the Apollo 13 astronauts reached earth safely.

Word List 27 insurgent–irreverence

insurgent ADJ. rebellious. Because the *insurgent* forces had occupied the capital and had gained control of the railway lines, several of the war correspondents covering the uprising predicted a rebel victory. also N. insurgency, N.

insurmountable ADJ. overwhelming; unbeatable; insuperable. Facing almost *insurmountable* obstacles, the members of the underground maintained their courage and will to resist.

insurrection N. rebellion; uprising. In retrospect, given how badly the British treated the American colonists, the eventual *insurrection* seems inevitable.

intangible ADJ. not able to be perceived by touch; vague. Though the financial benefits of his Oxford post were meager, Lewis was drawn to it by its *intangible* rewards: prestige, intellectual freedom, the fellowship of his peers.

integral ADJ. complete; necessary for completeness. Physical education is an *integral* part of our curriculum; a sound mind and a sound body are complementary.

integrate V. make whole; combine; make into one unit. She tried to *integrate* all their activities into one program.

integrity N. uprightness; wholeness. Lincoln, whose personal *integrity* has inspired millions, fought a civil war to maintain the *integrity* of the republic, that these United States might remain undivided for all time.

intellect N. higher mental powers. He thought college would develop his *intellect.*

intelligentsia N. intellectuals; members of the educated elite [often used derogatorily]. She preferred discussions about sports and politics to the literary conversations of the *intelligentsia.*

intercede V. mediate; plead or petition on someone's behalf. The university's athletics director often *interceded* with the admissions committee on behalf of applicants who were promising athletes but who had low high school G.P.A.s.

interdict V. prohibit; forbid. Civilized nations must *interdict* the use of nuclear weapons if we expect our society to live.

interim N. meantime. The company will not consider our proposal until next week; in the *interim,* let us proceed as we have in the past.

interminable ADJ. endless. Although his speech lasted for only twenty minutes, it seemed *interminable* to his bored audience.

intermittent ADJ. periodic; on and off. The outdoor wedding reception had to be moved indoors to avoid the *intermittent* showers that fell on and off all afternoon.

internecine ADJ. mutually destructive. The rising death toll on both sides indicates the *internecine* nature of this conflict.

interpolate V. insert between. She talked so much that I could not *interpolate* a single remark.

interrogate V. question closely; cross-examine. Knowing that the Nazis would *interrogate* him about his background, the secret agent invented a cover story that would help him meet their questions.

intervene V. come between. When two close friends get into a fight, be careful if you try to *intervene;* they may join forces and gang up on you. intervention, N.

intimate V. hint. She *intimated* rather than stated her preferences.

intimidate V. frighten. I'll learn karate and then those big bullies won't be able to *intimidate* me anymore. intimidation, N.

■ **intractable** ADJ. unruly; stubborn; unyielding. Charlie Brown's friend Pigpen was *intractable:* he absolutely refused to take a bath.

■ **intransigence** N. refusal of any compromise; stubbornness. The negotiating team had not expected such *intransigence* from the striking workers, who rejected any hint of a compromise. intransigent, ADJ.

intrepid ADJ. fearless. For her *intrepid* conduct nursing the wounded during the war, Florence Nightingale was honored by Queen Victoria.

intrinsic ADJ. essential; inherent; built-in. Although my grandmother's china has little *intrinsic* value, I shall always cherish it for the memories it evokes.

introspective ADJ. looking within oneself. Though young Francis of Assisi led a wild and worldly life, even he had *introspective* moments during which he examined his soul. introspection, N.

introvert N. one who is introspective; inclined to think more about oneself. In his poetry, he reveals that he is an *introvert* by his intense interest in his own problems.

intrude V. trespass; enter as an uninvited person. She hesitated to *intrude* on their conversation.

intuition N. immediate insight; power of knowing without reasoning. Even though Tony denied that anything was wrong, Tina trusted her *intuition* that something was bothering him. intuitive, ADJ. intuit, V.

■ **inundate** V. overwhelm; flood; submerge. This semester I am *inundated* with work: you should see the piles of paperwork flooding my desk. Until the great dam was built, the waters of the Nile used to *inundate* the river valley every year.

■ **inured** ADJ. accustomed; hardened. She became *inured* to the Alaskan cold.

invalidate V. weaken; destroy. The relatives who received little or nothing sought to *invalidate* the will by claiming that the deceased had not been in his right mind when he signed the document.

invariable ADJ. constant; unchanging. In the early twentieth century, it was the *invariable* custom for the Japanese to remove their shoes before entering the house, and failure to observe this custom, even by a stranger, would have been considered a great breach of etiquettte.

invective N. abuse. He had expected criticism but not the *invective* that greeted his proposal.

inveigh V. denounce; utter censure or invective. He *inveighed* against the demagoguery of the previous speaker and urged that the audience reject his philosophy as dangerous.

inveigle V. persuade; wheedle; coax. Using her popularity and ability to speak convincingly, she *inveigled* several of her friends into volunteering to work at the soup kitchen.

inverse ADJ. opposite. There is an *inverse* ratio between the strength of light and its distance.

invert V. turn upside down or inside out. When he *inverted* his body in a hand stand, he felt the blood rush to his head.

inveterate ADJ. deep-rooted; habitual. She is an *inveterate* smoker and cannot break the habit.

invidious ADJ. designed to create ill will or envy. The Israelis' continuing success after the hour of the cease-fire placed Kissinger in an *invidious* position, for he had promised the Soviet Union that the Israelis would honor the cease-fire, and they had not.

invincible ADJ. unconquerable. Superman is *invincible.*

inviolable ADJ. secure from corruption, attack, or violation; unassailable. Batman considered his oath to keep the people of Gotham City safe *inviolable:* nothing on earth could make him break this promise. inviolability, N.

invocation N. prayer for help; calling upon as a reference or support. The service of Morning Prayer opens with an *invocation* during which we ask God to hear our prayers.

invoke V. cite as authority; call upon; ask for earnestly. At one appearance, President Carter *invoked* the history and accomplishments of Democratic presidents who preceded him in office.

invulnerable ADJ. incapable of injury. Achilles was *invulnerable* except in his heel.

iota N. very small quantity. She hadn't an *iota* of common sense.

■ **irascible** ADJ. irritable; easily angered. Miss Minchin's *irascible* temper intimidated the younger schoolgirls, who feared she'd burst into a rage at any moment.

irate ADJ. angry. When John's mother found out that he had overdrawn his checking account for the third month in a row, she was so *irate* that she could scarcely speak to him.

irksome ADJ. annoying; tedious. He found working on the assembly line *irksome* because of the monotony of the operation he had to perform. irk, V.

ironic ADJ. occurring in an unexpected and contrary manner. It is *ironic* that his success came when he least wanted it.

irony N. hidden sarcasm or satire; use of words that seem to mean the opposite of what they actually mean. Gradually his listeners began to realize that the excessive praise he was lavishing on his opponent was actually *irony;* he was, in fact, ridiculing the poor fool.

irreconcilable ADJ. incompatible; not able to be resolved. Because the separated couple were *irreconcilable,* the marriage counselor recommended a divorce.

irrefutable ADJ. indisputable; incontrovertible; undeniable. No matter how hard I tried to find a good comeback for her argument, I couldn't think of one: her logic was *irrefutable.*

irrelevant ADJ. not applicable; unrelated. No matter how *irrelevant* the patient's mumblings may seem, they give us some indications of what is on his mind. irrelevancy, N.

irremediable ADJ. incurable; uncorrectable. The error she made was *irremediable;* she could see no way to rectify it.

irreparable ADJ. not able to be corrected or repaired. Your apology cannot atone for the *irreparable* damage you have done to her reputation.

irrepressible ADJ. unable to be restrained or held back. My friend Kitty's curiosity was *irrepressible:* she poked her nose into everybody's business and just laughed when I warned her that curiosity killed the cat.

irreproachable ADJ. blameless; impeccable. Homer's conduct at the office party was *irreproachable;* even Marge had nothing bad to say about how he behaved.

■ **irresolute** ADJ. uncertain how to act; weak. Once you have made your decision, don't waver; a leader should never appear *irresolute.*

irretrievable ADJ. impossible to recover or regain; irreparable. The left fielder tried to retrieve the ball, but it flew over the fence, bounced off a wall, and fell into the sewer: it was *irretrievable.*

irreverence N. lack of proper respect. Some people in the audience were amused by the *irreverence* of the comedian's jokes about the pope; others felt offended by his lack of respect for their faith. irreverent, ADJ.

Word List 28 irrevocable–lionize

irrevocable ADJ. unalterable; irreversible. As Sue dropped the "Dear John" letter into the mailbox, she suddenly had second thoughts and wanted to take it back, but she could not: her action was *irrevocable.*

■ **itinerary** N. plan of a trip. Disliking sudden changes in plans when she traveled abroad, Ethel refused to make any alterations in her *itinerary.*

jaded ADJ. fatigued; surfeited. He looked for exotic foods to stimulate his *jaded* appetite.

jargon N. language used by a special group; technical terminology; gibberish. The computer salesmen at the store used a *jargon* of their own that we simply couldn't follow; we had no idea what they were jabbering about.

jaundiced ADJ. prejudiced (envious, hostile, or resentful); yellowed. Because Sue disliked Carolyn, she looked at Carolyn's paintings with a *jaundiced* eye, calling them formless smears. Newborn infants afflicted with *jaundice* look slightly yellow: they have *jaundiced* skin.

jeopardize V. endanger; imperil; put at risk. You can't give me a D in chemistry: you'll *jeopardize* my chances of being admitted to M.I.T. jeopardy, N.

jettison V. throw overboard. In order to enable the ship to ride safely through the storm, the captain had to *jettison* much of his cargo.

jocular ADJ. said or done in jest. Although Bill knew the boss hated jokes, he couldn't resist making one *jocular* remark; his *jocularity* cost him the job.

jovial ADJ. good-natured; merry. A frown seemed out of place on his invariably *jovial* face.

jubilation N. rejoicing. There was great *jubilation* when the armistice was announced.

judicious ADJ. sound in judgment; wise. At a key moment in his life, he made a *judicious* investment that was the foundation of his later wealth.

juncture N. crisis; joining point. At this critical *juncture,* let us think carefully before determining the course we shall follow.

justification N. good or just reason; defense; excuse. The jury found him guilty of the more serious charge because they could see no possible *justification* for his actions.

juxtapose V. place side by side. If you *juxtapose* the two objects, it will make it easier to compare them.

kaleidoscope N. tube in which patterns made by the reflection in mirrors of colored pieces of glass, etc., produce interesting symmetrical effects. People found a new source of entertainment while peering through the *kaleidoscope;* they found the ever-changing patterns fascinating.

ken N. range of knowledge. I cannot answer your question since this matter is beyond my *ken.*

kernel N. central or vital part; whole seed (as of corn). "Watson, buried within this tissue of lies there is a *kernel* of truth; when I find it, the mystery will be solved."

killjoy N. grouch; spoilsport. At breakfast we had all been enjoying our bacon and eggs until that *killjoy* John started talking about how bad animal fats and cholesterol were for our health.

kindle V. start a fire; inspire. One of the first things Ben learned in the Boy Scouts was how to *kindle* a fire by rubbing two dry sticks together. Her teacher's praise for her poetry *kindled* a spark of hope inside Maya.

kindred ADJ. related; similar in nature or character. Tom Sawyer and Huck Finn were two *kindred* spirits. also N.

kinetic ADJ. producing motion. Designers of the electric automobile find that their greatest obstacle lies in the development of light and efficient storage batteries, the source of the *kinetic* energy needed to propel the vehicle.

knave N. untrustworthy person; rogue; scoundrel. Any politician nicknamed Tricky Dick clearly has the reputation of a *knave.*

knotty ADJ. intricate; difficult; tangled. What to Watson had been a *knotty* problem to Sherlock Holmes was simplicity itself.

kudos N. honor; glory; praise. The singer complacently received *kudos* on his performance from his entourage.

laborious ADJ. demanding much work or care; tedious. In putting together his dictionary of the English language, Doctor Johnson undertook a *laborious* task.

labyrinth N. maze. Hiding from Indian Joe, Tom and Becky soon lost themselves in the *labyrinth* of secret underground caves.

lachrymose ADJ. producing tears. His voice has a *lachrymose* quality that is more appropriate at a funeral than a class reunion.

lackadaisical ADJ. lacking purpose or zest; halfhearted; languid. Because Gatsby had his mind more on his love life than on his finances, he did a very *lackadaisical* job of managing his money.

lackluster ADJ. dull. We were disappointed by the *lackluster* performance.

■ **laconic** ADJ. brief and to the point. Many of the characters portrayed by Clint Eastwood are *laconic* types: strong men of few words.

laggard ADJ. slow; sluggish. The sailor had been taught not to be *laggard* in carrying out orders. lag, N., V.

lambaste V. beat; thrash verbally or physically. It was painful to watch the champion *lambaste* his opponent, tearing into him mercilessly.

lament V. grieve; express sorrow. Even advocates of the war *lamented* the loss of so many lives in combat. lamentation, N.

lampoon V. ridicule. This article *lampoons* the pretensions of some movie moguls. also N.

languid ADJ. weary; sluggish; listless. Her siege of illness left her *languid* and pallid.

languish V. lose animation or strength. Left at Miss Minchin's school for girls while her father went off to war, Sarah Crewe refused to *languish;* instead, she hid her grief and actively befriended her less fortunate classmates.

languor N. lassitude; depression. His friends tried to overcome the *languor* into which he had fallen by taking him to parties and to the theater.

larceny N. theft. Because of the prisoner's record, the district attorney refused to reduce the charge from grand *larceny* to petty *larceny.*

largess N. generous gift. Lady Bountiful distributed *largess* to the poor.

■ **lassitude** N. languor; weariness. After a massage and a long soak in the hot tub, I surrendered to my growing *lassitude* and lay down for a nap.

■ **latent** ADJ. potential but undeveloped; dormant; hidden. Polaroid pictures were popular at parties because you could see the *latent* photographic image gradually appear before your eyes. latency, N.

lateral ADJ. coming from the side. In order to get good plant growth, the gardener must pinch off all *lateral* shoots.

latitude N. freedom from narrow limitations. I think you have permitted your son too much *latitude* in this matter.

■ **laud** V. praise. The NFL *lauded* Boomer Esiason's efforts to raise money to combat cystic fibrosis. also N. laudable, laudatory, ADJ.

lavish ADJ. liberal; wasteful. The actor's *lavish* gifts pleased her. also V.

lax ADJ. careless. We dislike restaurants where the service is *lax* and inattentive.

legacy N. a gift made by a will. Part of my *legacy* from my parents is an album of family photographs.

leniency N. mildness; permissiveness. Considering the gravity of the offense, we were surprised by the *leniency* of the sentence. lenient, ADJ.

lethal ADJ. deadly. It is unwise to leave *lethal* weapons where children may find them.

■ **lethargic** ADJ. drowsy; dull. In class, she tried to stay alert and listen to the professor, but the stuffy room made her *lethargic;* she felt as if she was about to nod off. lethargy, N.

■ **levity** N. lack of seriousness or steadiness; frivolity. Stop giggling and wriggling around in the pew: such *levity* is improper in church.

levy V. impose (a fine); collect (a payment). Crying "No taxation without representation!" the colonists demonstrated against England's power to *levy* taxes. also N.

lexicon N. dictionary. I cannot find this word in any *lexicon* in the library.

liability N. drawback; debts. Her lack of an extensive vocabulary was a *liability* that she was able to overcome.

liaison N. contact that keeps parties in communication; go-between; secret love affair. As the *liaison* between the American and British forces during World War II, the colonel had to ease tensions between the leaders of the two armies. Romeo's romantic *liaison* with Juliet ended in tragedy. also ADJ.

libel N. defamatory statement; act of writing something that smears a person's character. If Batman wrote that the Joker was a dirty, rotten, mass-murdering criminal, could the Joker sue Batman for *libel?* libelous, ADJ.

limn V. draw; outline; describe. Paradoxically, the more realistic the details this artist chooses, the better able she is to *limn* her fantastic, other-worldly landscapes.

linger V. loiter or dawdle; continue or persist. Hoping to see Juliet pass by, Romeo *lingered* outside the Capulet house for hours. Though Mother made stuffed cabbage on Monday, the smell *lingered* around the house for days.

linguistic ADJ. pertaining to language. The modern tourist will encounter very little *linguistic* difficulty as English has become an almost universal language.

lionize V. treat as a celebrity. She enjoyed being *lionized* and adored by the public.

Word List 29 liquidate–marital

liquidate V. settle accounts; clear up. He was able to *liquidate* all his debts in a short period of time.

list V. tilt; lean over. That flagpole should be absolutely vertical; instead, it *lists* to one side. (secondary meaning) also N.

listless ADJ. lacking in spirit or energy. We had expected her to be full of enthusiasm and were surprised by her *listless* attitude.

litigation N. lawsuit. Try to settle this amicably; I do not want to start *litigation*. litigant, N.

livid ADJ. lead-colored; black and blue; ashen; enraged. His face was so *livid* with rage that we were afraid that he might have an attack of apoplexy.

loath ADJ. reluctant; disinclined. Romeo and Juliet were both *loath* for him to go.

loathe V. detest. Booing and hissing, the audience showed how much they *loathed* the villain. loathsome, ADJ.

lofty ADJ. very high. Though Barbara Jordan's fellow students used to tease her about her *lofty* ambitions, she rose to hold one of the highest positions in the land.

■ **log** N. record of a voyage or flight; record of day-to-day activities. "Flogged two seamen today for insubordination," wrote Captain Bligh in the *Bounty's log*. To see how much work I've accomplished recently, just take a look at the number of new files listed on my computer *log*. also V.

loiter V. hang around; linger. The policeman told him not to *loiter* in the alley.

loll V. lounge about. They *lolled* around in their chairs watching television.

loom V. appear or take shape (usually in an enlarged or distorted form). The shadow of the gallows *loomed* threateningly above the small boy.

lope V. gallop slowly. As the horses *loped* along, we had an opportunity to admire the ever-changing scenery.

■ **loquacious** ADJ. talkative. Though our daughter barely says a word to us these days, put a phone in her hand and see how *loquacious* she can be: our phone bills are out of sight! loquacity, N.

■ **lucid** ADJ. easily understood; clear; intelligible. Lexy makes an excellent teacher: her explanations of technical points are *lucid* enough for a child to grasp. lucidity, N.

lucrative ADJ. profitable. He turned his hobby into a *lucrative* sideline.

lucre N. money. Preferring *lucre* to undying fame, he wrote stories of popular appeal.

ludicrous ADJ. laughably foolish or unreasonable. Batman may be a serious crime fighter, but why does he wear such a *ludicrous* costume?

lugubrious ADJ. mournful. The *lugubrious* howling of the dogs added to our sadness.

lull N. moment of calm. Not wanting to get wet, they waited under the awning for a *lull* in the rain.

luminary N. celebrity; dignitary. A leading light of the American stage, Ethel Barrymore was a theatrical *luminary* whose name lives on.

■ **luminous** ADJ. shining; issuing light. The sun is a *luminous* body.

lunar ADJ. pertaining to the moon. *Lunar* craters can be plainly seen with the aid of a small telescope.

lurk V. stealthily lie in waiting; slink; exist unperceived. "Who knows what evils *lurk* in the hearts of men? The Shadow knows."

luscious ADJ. pleasing to taste or smell. The ripe peach was *luscious*.

luster N. shine; gloss. The soft *luster* of the silk in the dim light was pleasing.

lustrous ADJ. shining. Her large and *lustrous* eyes gave a touch of beauty to an otherwise drab face.

luxuriant ADJ. abundant; rich and splendid; fertile. Lady Godiva was completely covered by her *luxuriant* hair.

macabre ADJ. gruesome; grisly. The city morgue is a *macabre* spot for the uninitiated.

Machiavellian ADJ. crafty; double-dealing. I do not think he will be a good ambassador because he is not accustomed to the *Machiavellian* maneuverings of foreign diplomats.

machinations N. evil schemes or plots. Fortunately, Batman saw through the wily *machinations* of the Riddler and saved Gotham City from destruction by the forces of evil.

magisterial ADJ. authoritative; imperious. The learned doctor laid down the law to his patient in a *magisterial* tone of voice.

■ **magnanimity** N. generosity. Noted for his *magnanimity*, philanthropist Eugene Lang donated millions to charity. magnanimous, ADJ.

magnate N. person of prominence or influence. Growing up in Pittsburgh, Annie Dillard was surrounded by the mansions of the great steel and coal *magnates* who set their mark on that city.

magniloquent ADJ. boastful, pompous. In their stories of the trial, the reporters ridiculed the *magniloquent* speeches of the defense attorney.

magnitude N. greatness; extent. It is difficult to comprehend the *magnitude* of his crime.

maim V. mutilate; injure. The hospital could not take care of all who had been mangled or *maimed* in the railroad accident.

maladroit ADJ. clumsy; bungling. "Oh! My stupid tongue!" exclaimed Jane, embarrassed at having said anything so *maladroit*.

malady N. illness. A mysterious *malady* swept the country, filling doctors' offices with feverish, purple-spotted patients.

malaise N. uneasiness; vague feeling of ill health. Feeling slightly queasy before going onstage, Carol realized that this touch of *malaise* was merely stage fright.

malcontent N. person dissatisfied with existing state of affairs. He was one of the few *malcontents* in Congress; he constantly voiced his objections to the presidential program. also ADJ.

malefactor N. evildoer; criminal. Mighty Mouse will save the day, hunting down *malefactors* and rescuing innocent mice from peril.

malevolent ADJ. wishing evil. Iago is a *malevolent* villain who takes pleasure in ruining Othello. malevolence, N.

malfeasance N. wrongdoing. The authorities did not discover the campaign manager's *malfeasance* until after he had spent most of the money he had embezzled.

malicious ADJ. hateful; spiteful. Jealous of Cinderella's beauty, her *malicious* stepsisters expressed their spite by forcing her to do menial tasks. malice, N.

malign V. speak evil of; bad-mouth; defame. Putting her hands over her ears, Rose refused to listen to Betty *malign* her friend Susan.

malignant ADJ. injurious; tending to cause death; aggressively malevolent. Though many tumors are benign, some are *malignant*, growing out of control and endangering the life of the patient. malignancy, N.

■ **malingerer** N. one who feigns illness to escape duty. The captain ordered the sergeant to punish all *malingerers* and force them to work. malinger, V.

■ **malleable** ADJ. capable of being shaped by pounding; impressionable. Gold is a *malleable* metal, easily shaped into bracelets and rings. Fagin hoped Oliver was a *malleable* lad, easily shaped into a thief.

mammoth ADJ. gigantic; enormous. To try to memorize every word on this vocabulary list would be a *mammoth* undertaking; take on projects that are more manageable in size.

mandate N. order; charge. In his inaugural address, the president stated that he had a *mandate* from the people to seek an end to social evils such as poverty and poor housing. also V.

mandatory ADJ. obligatory. These instructions are *mandatory;* any violation will be severely punished.

maniacal ADJ. raging mad; insane. Though Mr. Rochester had locked his mad wife in the attic, he could still hear her *maniacal* laughter echoing throughout the house. maniac, N.

manifest ADJ. evident; visible; obvious. Digby's embarrassment when he met Madonna was *manifest:* his ears turned bright pink, he kept scuffing one shoe in the dirt, and he couldn't look her in the eye.

manifestation N. outward demonstration; indication. Mozart's early attraction to the harpsichord was the first *manifestation* of his pronounced musical bent.

manifesto N. declaration; statement of policy. The *Communist Manifesto* by Marx and Engels proclaimed the principles of modern communism.

manifold ADJ. numerous; varied. I cannot begin to tell you how much I appreciate your *manifold* kindnesses.

manipulate V. operate with one's hands; control or play upon (people, forces, etc.) artfully. Jim Henson understood how to *manipulate* the Muppets. Miley Cyrus understands how to *manipulate* publicity (and men).

mannered ADJ. affected; not natural. Attempting to copy the style of his wealthy neighbors, Gatsby adopted a *mannered,* artificial way of speech.

marital ADJ. pertaining to marriage. After the publication of his book on *marital* affairs, he was often consulted by married people on the verge of divorce.

Word List 30 marked–mirage

marked ADJ. noticeable; targeted for vengeance. He walked with a *marked* limp, a souvenir of an old IRA attack. As British ambassador, he knew he was a *marked* man.

marred ADJ. damaged; disfigured. She had to refinish the *marred* surface of the table. mar, V.

marshal V. put in order. At a debate tournament, extemporaneous speakers have only a minute or two to *marshal* their thoughts before addressing their audience.

martial ADJ. warlike. The sound of *martial* music inspired the young cadet with dreams of military glory.

martinet N. No talking at meals! No mingling with the servants! Miss Minchin was a *martinet* who insisted that the schoolgirls in her charge observe each regulation to the letter.

martyr N. one who voluntarily suffers death for his or her religion or cause; great sufferer. By burning her at the stake, the English made Joan of Arc a *martyr* for her faith. Mother played the *martyr* by staying home to clean the house while the rest of the family went off to the beach.

masochist N. person who enjoys his own pain. The *masochist* begs, "Hit me." The sadist smiles and says, "I won't."

materialism N. preoccupation with physical comforts and things. By its nature, *materialism* is opposed to idealism, for where the *materialist* emphasizes the needs of the body, the idealist emphasizes the needs of the soul.

maternal ADJ. motherly. Many animals display *maternal* instincts only while their offspring are young and helpless. maternity, N.

matriarch N. woman who rules a family or larger social group. The *matriarch* ruled her gypsy tribe with a firm hand.

matrix N. point of origin; array of numbers or algebraic symbols; mold or die. Some historians claim the Nile Valley was the *matrix* of Western civilization.

maudlin ADJ. effusively sentimental. Whenever a particularly *maudlin* tearjerker was playing at the movies, Marvin would embarrass himself by weeping copiously.

maul V. handle roughly. The rock star was *mauled* by his overexcited fans.

■ **maverick** N. rebel; nonconformist. To the masculine literary establishment, George Sand with her insistence on wearing trousers and smoking cigars was clearly a *maverick* who fought her proper womanly role.

maxim N. proverb; a truth pithily stated. Aesop's fables illustrate moral *maxims.*

mayhem N. injury to body. The riot was marked not only by *mayhem,* with its attendant loss of life and limb, but also by arson and pillage.

meager ADJ. scanty; inadequate. Still hungry after his *meager* serving of porridge, Oliver Twist asked for a second helping.

mealymouthed ADJ. indirect in speech; hypocritical; evasive. Rather than tell Jill directly what he disliked, Jack made a few *mealymouthed* comments and tried to change the subject.

meander V. wind or turn in its course. Needing to stay close to a source of water, he followed every twist and turn of the stream as it *meandered* through the countryside.

meddlesome ADJ. interfering. He felt his marriage was suffering because of his *meddlesome* mother-in-law.

mediate V. settle a dispute through the services of an outsider. King Solomon was asked to *mediate* a dispute between two women, each of whom claimed to be the mother of the same child.

mediocre ADJ. ordinary; commonplace. We were disappointed because he gave a rather *mediocre* performance in this role.

meditation N. reflection; thought. She reached her decision only after much *meditation.*

medium N. element that is a creature's natural environment; nutrient setting in which microorganisms are cultivated. We watched the dolphins sporting in the sea and marveled at their grace in their proper *medium.* The bacteriologist carefully observed the microorganisms' rapid growth in the culture *medium.*

medium N. appropriate occupation or means of expression; channel of communication; compromise. Film was Anna's *medium:* she expressed herself through her cinematography. However, she never watched television, claiming she despised the *medium.* For Anna, it was all or nothing: she could never strike a happy *medium.*

medley N. mixture. To avoid boring dancers by playing any one tune for too long, bands may combine three or four tunes into a *medley.*

meek ADJ. submissive; patient and long-suffering. Mr. Barrett never expected his *meek* daughter would dare to defy him by eloping with her suitor.

megalomania N. mania for doing grandiose things. Developers who spend millions trying to build the world's tallest skyscraper suffer from *megalomania.*

melancholy ADJ. gloomy; morose; blue. To Eugene, stuck in his small town, a train whistle was a *melancholy* sound, for it made him think of all the places he would never get to see.

melodramatic ADJ. excessively emotional and exaggerated; overdramatic. Completely over the top and *melodramatic,* every moment of the heroine's life is a life or death disaster waiting to happen.

memorialize V. commemorate. Let us *memorialize* his great contribution by dedicating this library in his honor.

■ **mendacious** ADJ. lying; habitually dishonest. Distrusting Huck from the start, Miss Watson assumed he was *mendacious* and refused to believe a word he said. mendacity, N.

menial ADJ. suitable for servants; lowly; mean. Her wicked stepmother forced Cinderella to do *menial* tasks around the house while her ugly stepsisters lolled around painting their toenails. also N.

mentor N. counselor; teacher. During this very trying period, she could not have had a better *mentor,* for the teacher was sympathetic and understanding.

mercantile ADJ. concerning trade. The knowledge that sea traders like Marco Polo brought to Venice increased commercial activity there, transforming the city into one of the great *mercantile* powers of Europe.

mercenary ADJ. motivated solely by money or gain. "I'm not in this war because I get my kicks waving flags," said the *mercenary* soldier. "I'm in it for the dough." also N.

mercurial ADJ. capricious; changing; fickle. Quick as quicksilver to change, he was *mercurial* in nature and therefore unreliable.

merger N. combination (of two business corporations). When the firm's president married the director of financial planning, the office joke was that it wasn't a marriage, it was a *merger.*

mesmerize V. hypnotize. The incessant drone seemed to *mesmerize* him and place him in a trance.

■ **metamorphosis** N. change of form. The *metamorphosis* of caterpillar to butterfly is typical of many such changes in animal life. metamorphose, V.

metaphor N. implied comparison. "He soared like an eagle" is an example of a simile; "He is an eagle in flight," a *metaphor.*

metaphysical ADJ. pertaining to speculative philosophy. The modern poets have gone back to the fanciful poems of the *metaphysical* poets of the seventeenth century for many of their images. metaphysics, N.

mete V. measure; distribute. He tried to be impartial in his efforts to *mete* out justice.

meteoric ADJ. swift; momentarily brilliant. We all wondered at his *meteoric* rise to fame.

methodical ADJ. systematic. An accountant must be *methodical* and maintain order among his financial records.

■ **meticulous** ADJ. excessively careful; painstaking; scrupulous. Martha Stewart was a *meticulous* housekeeper, fussing about each and every detail that went into making up her perfect home.

metropolis N. large city. Every evening this terminal is filled with the thousands of commuters who are going from this *metropolis* to their homes in the suburbs.

microcosm N. small world; the world in miniature. The village community that Jane Austen depicts serves as a *microcosm* of English society in her time, for in this small world we see all the social classes meeting and mingling.

migrant ADJ. changing its habitat; wandering. These *migrant* birds return every spring. also N.

migratory ADJ. wandering. The return of the *migratory* birds to the northern sections of this country is a harbinger of spring.

milieu N. environment; means of expression. Surrounded by smooth preppies and arty bohemians, the country boy from Smalltown, USA, felt out of his *milieu.* Although he has produced excellent oil paintings and lithographs, his proper *milieu* is watercolor.

militant ADJ. combative; bellicose. Although at this time he was advocating a policy of neutrality, one could usually find him adopting a more *militant* attitude. also N.

militate V. work against. Your record of lateness and absence will *militate* against your chances of promotion.

millennium N. thousand-year period; period of happiness and prosperity. I do not expect the *millennium* to come during my lifetime.

mimicry N. imitation. Her gift for *mimicry* was so great that her friends said that she should be in the theater.

minatory ADJ. menacing; threatening. Jabbing a *minatory* forefinger at Dorothy, the Wicked Witch cried, "I'll get you, and your little dog, too!"

minuscule ADJ. extremely small. Why should I involve myself with a project with so *minuscule* a chance for success?

minute ADJ. extremely small. The twins resembled one another closely; only *minute* differences set them apart.

minutiae N. petty details. She would have liked to ignore the *minutiae* of daily living.

mirage N. unreal reflection; optical illusion. The lost prospector was fooled by a *mirage* in the desert.

Word List 31 mire–myopic

mire V. entangle; stick in swampy ground. Their rear wheels became *mired* in mud. also N.

mirth N. merriment; laughter. Sober Malvolio found Sir Toby's *mirth* improper.

misadventure N. mischance; ill luck. The young explorer met death by *misadventure.*

■ **misanthrope** N. one who hates mankind. In *Gulliver's Travels,* Swift portrays human beings as vile, degraded beasts; for this reason, various critics consider him a *misanthrope.* misanthropic, ADJ.

misapprehension N. error; misunderstanding. To avoid *misapprehension,* I am going to ask all of you to repeat the instructions I have given.

miscellany N. mixture of writings on various subjects. This is an interesting *miscellany* of nineteenth-century prose and poetry.

mischance N. ill luck. By *mischance,* he lost his week's salary.

misconstrue V. interpret incorrectly; misjudge. She took the passage seriously rather than humorously because she *misconstrued* the author's ironic tone.

miscreant N. wretch; villain. In Colonial America, an offender would be put into the stocks so that the villagers could jeer and toss offal at the *miscreant.*

misdemeanor N. minor crime. The culprit pleaded guilty to a *misdemeanor* rather than face trial for a felony.

miserly ADJ. stingy; mean. Transformed by his vision on Christmas Eve, mean old Scrooge ceased being *miserly* and became a generous, kind old man. miser, N.

misgivings N. doubts. Hamlet described his *misgivings* to Horatio but decided to fence with Laertes despite his foreboding of evil.

mishap N. accident. With a little care you could have avoided this *mishap.*

misnomer N. wrong name; incorrect designation. His tyrannical conduct proved to all that his nickname, King Eric the Just, was a *misnomer.*

misogynist N. hater of women. The typical *misogynist* treats women as objects to be used and dismissed at will, never as equals to be loved or admired.

mite N. very small object or creature; small coin. Gnats are annoying *mites* that sting.

■ **mitigate** V. lessen in intensity; moderate; appease. Because solar energy has the power to reduce greenhouse gases and provide increased energy efficiency, conversion to the use of solar energy may help *mitigate* global warming.

mnemonic ADJ. pertaining to memory. She used *mnemonic* tricks to master new words.

mobile ADJ. movable; not fixed. The *mobile* blood bank operated by the Red Cross visited our neighborhood today. mobility, N.

mock V. ridicule; imitate, often in derision. It is unkind to *mock* anyone; it is stupid to *mock* anyone significantly bigger than you. mockery, N.

mode N. prevailing style; manner; way of doing something. The rock star had to have her hair done in the latest *mode:* frizzed, with occasional moussed spikes for variety. Henry plans to adopt a simpler *mode* of life: he is going to become a mushroom hunter and live off the land.

modicum N. limited quantity. Although his story is based on a *modicum* of truth, most of the events he describes are fictitious.

modish ADJ. fashionable. She always discarded all garments that were no longer *modish.*

modulate V. tone down in intensity; regulate; change from one key to another. Always singing at the top of her lungs, the budding Brunhilde never learned to *modulate* her voice. modulation, N.

mogul N. powerful person. The oil *moguls* made great profits when the price of gasoline rose.

■ **mollify** V. soothe. The airline customer service representative tried to *mollify* the angry passenger by offering her a seat in first class.

momentous ADJ. very important. When Marie and Pierre Curie discovered radium, they had no idea of the *momentous* impact their discovery would have upon society.

momentum N. quantity of motion of a moving body; impetus. The car lost *momentum* as it tried to ascend the steep hill.

monarchy N. government under a single ruler. Though England today is a *monarchy,* there is some question whether it will be one in 20 years, given the present discontent at the prospect of Prince Charles as king.

monastic ADJ. related to monks or monasteries; removed from worldly concerns. Withdrawing from the world, Thomas Merton joined a contemplative religious order and adopted the *monastic* life.

monetary ADJ. pertaining to money. Jane held the family purse strings: she made all *monetary* decisions affecting the household.

monolithic ADJ. solidly uniform; unyielding. Knowing the importance of appearing resolute, the patriots sought to present a *monolithic* front.

monotony N. sameness leading to boredom. What could be more deadly dull than the *monotony* of punching numbers into a computer hour after hour? monotonous, ADJ.

monumental ADJ. massive. Writing a dictionary is a *monumental* task.

moodiness N. fits of depression or gloom. We could not discover the cause of her recurrent *moodiness.*

moratorium N. legal delay of payment. If we declare a *moratorium* and delay collection of debts for six months, I am sure the farmers will be able to meet their bills.

morbid ADJ. given to unwholesome thought; moody; characteristic of disease. People who come to disaster sites just to peer at the grisly wreckage are indulging their *morbid* curiosity. morbidity, N.

mores N. conventions; moral standards; customs. In America, Benazir Bhutto dressed as Western women did; in Pakistan, however, she followed the *mores* of her people, dressing in traditional veil and robes.

moribund ADJ. dying. Hearst took a *moribund,* failing weekly newspaper and transformed it into one of the liveliest, most profitable daily papers around.

■ **morose** ADJ. ill-humored; sullen; melancholy. Forced to take early retirement, Bill acted *morose* for months; then, all of a sudden, he shook off his gloom and was his usual cheerful self.

mortify V. humiliate; punish the flesh. She was so *mortified* by her blunder that she ran to her room in tears.

mosaic N. picture made of small, colorful inlaid tiles. The mayor compared the city to a beautiful *mosaic* made up of people of every race and religion on earth. also ADJ.

mote N. small speck. The tiniest *mote* in the eye is very painful.

motif N. theme. This simple *motif* runs throughout the score.

motley ADJ. multicolored; mixed. The jester wore a *motley* tunic, red and green and blue and gold all patched together haphazardly. Captain Ahab had gathered a *motley* crew to sail the vessel: old sea dogs and runaway boys, pillars of the church and drunkards, even a tattooed islander who terrified the rest of the crew.

muddle V. confuse; mix up. Her thoughts were *muddled* and chaotic. also N.

mulct V. defraud a person of something. The lawyer was accused of trying to *mulct* the boy of his legacy.

multifarious ADJ. varied; greatly diversified. A career woman and mother, she was constantly busy with the *multifarious* activities of her daily life.

multiform ADJ. having many forms. Snowflakes are *multiform* but always hexagonal.

multilingual ADJ. having many languages. Because they are bordered by so many countries, the Swiss people are *multilingual.*

multiplicity N. state of being numerous. People from the Eastern bloc express dismay at the appalling *multiplicity* of choices in Western supermarkets. What rational person needs twenty-two brands of toothpaste?

■ **mundane** ADJ. worldly as opposed to spiritual; everyday. Uninterested in philosophical or spiritual discussions, Tom talked only of *mundane* matters such as the daily weather forecast or the latest basketball results.

munificent ADJ. very generous. Shamelessly fawning over a particularly generous donor, the dean kept referring to her as "our *munificent* benefactor." munificence, N.

muse V. ponder. For a moment he *mused* about the beauty of the scene, but his thoughts soon changed as he recalled his own personal problems. also N.

muster V. gather; assemble. Washington *mustered* his forces at Trenton.

mutability N. ability to change in form; fickleness. Going from rags to riches, and then back to rags again, the bankrupt financier was a victim of the *mutability* of fortune. mutable, ADJ.

muted ADJ. silent; muffled; toned down. Thanks to the thick, sound-absorbing walls of the cathedral, only *muted* traffic noise reached the worshippers within. mute, V., N.

mutilate V. maim. The torturer threatened to *mutilate* his victim.

mutinous ADJ. unruly; rebellious. The captain had to use force to quiet his *mutinous* crew. mutiny, N.

myopic ADJ. nearsighted; lacking foresight. Stumbling into doors despite the coke-bottle lenses on his glasses, the nearsighted Mr. Magoo is markedly *myopic.* In playing all summer long and failing to store up food for winter, the grasshopper in Aesop's fable was *myopic* as well. myopia, N.

Word List 32 myriad–obtrude

myriad N. very large number. *Myriads* of mosquitoes from the swamps invaded our village every twilight. also ADJ.

nadir N. lowest point. Although few people realized it, the Dow-Jones averages had reached their *nadir* and would soon begin an upward surge.

naiveté N. quality of being unsophisticated; simplicity; artlessness; gullibility. Touched by the *naiveté* of sweet, convent-trained Cosette, Marius pledges himself to protect her innocence. naive, ADJ.

narcissist N. conceited person. A *narcissist* is his own best friend.

narrative ADJ. related to telling a story. A born teller of tales, Olsen used her impressive *narrative* skills to advantage in her story "I Stand Here Ironing." also N. narration, N.

nascent ADJ. incipient; coming into being. If we could identify these revolutionary movements in their *nascent* state, we would be able to eliminate serious trouble in later years.

nauseate V. cause to become sick; fill with disgust. The foul smells began to *nauseate* her.

nautical ADJ. pertaining to ships or navigation. The Maritime Museum contains models of clipper ships, logbooks, anchors, and many other items of a *nautical* nature.

navigable ADJ. wide and deep enough to allow ships to pass through; able to be steered. So much sand had built up at the bottom of the canal that the waterway was barely *navigable.*

nebulous ADJ. vague; hazy; cloudy. Phil and Dave tried to come up with a clear, intelligible business plan, not some hazy, *nebulous* proposal.

nefarious ADJ. very wicked. The villain's crimes, though various, were one and all *nefarious.*

■ **negate** V. cancel out; nullify; deny. A sudden surge of adrenalin can *negate* the effects of fatigue: there's nothing like a good shock to wake you up. negation, N.

negligence N. neglect; failure to take reasonable care. Tommy failed to put back the cover on the well after he fetched his pail of water; because of his *negligence,* Kitty fell in. negligent, ADJ.

negligible ADJ. so small, trifling, or unimportant as to be easily disregarded. Because the damage to his car had been *negligible,* Michael decided he wouldn't bother to report the matter to his insurance company.

nemesis N. someone seeking revenge. Abandoned at sea in a small boat, the vengeful Captain Bligh vowed to be the *nemesis* of Fletcher Christian and his fellow mutineers.

neologism N. new or newly coined word or phrase. As we invent new techniques and professions, we must also invent *neologisms* such as "microcomputer" and "astronaut" to describe them.

■ **neophyte** N. recent convert; beginner. This mountain slope contains slides that will challenge experts as well as *neophytes.*

nepotism N. favoritism (to a relative). John left his position with the company because he felt that advancement was based on *nepotism* rather than ability.

nettle V. annoy; vex. Do not let her *nettle* you with her sarcastic remarks.

nihilist N. one who considers traditional beliefs to be groundless and existence meaningless; absolute skeptic; revolutionary terrorist. In his final days, Hitler revealed himself a power-mad *nihilist,* ready to annihilate all of Western Europe, even to destroy Germany itself, in order that his will might prevail. The root of the word *nihilist* is *nihil,* Latin for "nothing." nihilism, N.

nip V. stop something's growth or development; snip off; bite; make numb with cold. The twins were plotting mischief, but Mother intervened and *nipped* their plan in the bud. The gardener *nipped* off a lovely rose and gave it to me. Last week a guard dog *nipped* the postman in the leg; this week the extreme chill *nipped* his fingers till he could barely hold the mail.

nocturnal ADJ. done at night. Mr. Jones obtained a watchdog to prevent the *nocturnal* raids on his chicken coops.

noisome ADJ. foul-smelling; unwholesome. The *noisome* atmosphere downwind of the oil refinery not only stank but also damaged the lungs of everyone living in the area.

nomadic ADJ. wandering. Several *nomadic* tribes of Indians would hunt in this area each year. nomad, N.

nomenclature N. terminology; system of names. Sharon found Latin word parts useful in translating medical *nomenclature:* when her son had to have a bilateral myringotomy, she figured out that he needed a hole in each of his eardrums to end his earaches.

nominal ADJ. in name only; trifling. He offered to drive her to the airport for only a *nominal* fee.

nonchalance N. indifference; lack of concern; composure. Cool, calm, and collected under fire, James Bond shows remarkable *nonchalance* in the face of danger. nonchalant, ADJ.

noncommittal ADJ. neutral; unpledged; undecided. We were annoyed by his *noncommittal* reply for we had been led to expect definite assurances of his approval.

nondescript ADJ. undistinctive; ordinary. The private detective was a short, *nondescript* fellow with no outstanding features, the sort of person one would never notice in a crowd.

nonentity N. person of no importance; nonexistence. Because the two older princes dismissed their youngest brother as a *nonentity,* they did not realize that he was quietly plotting to seize the throne.

nonplus V. bring to a halt by confusion; perplex. Jack's uncharacteristic rudeness *nonplussed* Jill, leaving her uncertain how to react.

nostalgia N. homesickness; longing for the past. My grandfather seldom spoke of life in the old country; he had little patience with *nostalgia.* nostalgic, ADJ.

notable ADJ. conspicuous; important; distinguished. Normally *notable* for his calm in the kitchen, today the head cook was shaking, for the *notable* chef Alice Waters was coming to dinner. also N.

notoriety N. disrepute; ill fame. To the starlet, any publicity was good publicity: if she couldn't have a good reputation, she'd settle for *notoriety.* notorious, ADJ.

novelty N. something new; newness. Backup cameras are no longer a *novelty* in automobiles. novel, ADJ.

novice N. beginner. Even a *novice* at working with computers can install *Barron's Computer Study Program for the GRE* by following the easy steps outlined in the user's manual.

noxious ADJ. harmful. We must trace the source of these *noxious* gases before they asphyxiate us.

nuance N. shade of difference in meaning or color; subtle distinction. Jody gazed at the Monet landscape for an hour, appreciating every subtle *nuance* of color in the painting.

nullify V. to make invalid. Thai protesters have vowed to stage large rallies in Bangkok and push on with their efforts to *nullify* the results of Sunday's elections.

nuptial ADJ. related to marriage. Reluctant to be married in a traditional setting, they decided to hold their *nuptial* ceremony at the carousel in Golden Gate Park. nuptials, N. PL.

nurture V. nourish; educate; foster. The Head Start program attempts to *nurture* prekindergarten children so that they will do well when they enter public school. also N.

nutrient N. nourishing substance. As a budding nutritionist, Kim has learned to design diets that contain foods rich in important basic *nutrients.* also ADJ.

■ **obdurate** ADJ. stubborn. In this retelling of Barrie's *Peter Pan,* Fiona Button as Wendy is heartbreaking in her stoical disappointment at Peter's *obdurate* refusal to grow up.

obfuscate V. confuse; muddle; cause confusion; make needlessly complex. Was the president's spokesman trying to clarify the Whitewater mystery, or was he trying to *obfuscate* the issue so the voters would never figure out what went on?

objective ADJ. not influenced by emotions; fair. Even though he was her son, she tried to be *objective* about his behavior.

objective N. goal; aim. A degree in medicine was her ultimate *objective.*

obligatory ADJ. binding; required. It is *obligatory* that books borrowed from the library be returned within two weeks.

oblique ADJ. indirect; slanting (deviating from the perpendicular or from a straight line). Casting a quick, *oblique* glance at the reviewing stand, the sergeant ordered the company to march "*Oblique* Right."

obliterate V. destroy completely. The tidal wave *obliterated* several island villages.

oblivion N. obscurity; forgetfulness. After a decade of popularity, Hurston's works had fallen into *oblivion;* no one bothered to read them any more.

oblivious ADJ. inattentive or unmindful; wholly absorbed. Deep in her book, Nancy was *oblivious* to the noisy squabbles of her brother and his friends.

obnoxious ADJ. offensive. The tourists' *obnoxious* behavior included speaking loudly in public, ingnoring traffic laws, spitting, littering, and scribbling graffiti.

obscure ADJ. dark; vague; unclear. Even after I read the poem a fourth time, its meaning was still *obscure.* obscurity, N.

obscure V. darken; make unclear. At times he seemed purposely to *obscure* his meaning, preferring mystery to clarity.

■ **obsequious** ADJ. slavishly attentive; servile; sycophantic. Helen valued people who behaved as if they respected themselves; nothing irritated her more than an excessively *obsequious* waiter or a fawning salesclerk.

obsessive ADJ. related to thinking about something constantly; preoccupying. Ballet, which had been a hobby, began to dominate his life: his love of dancing became *obsessive.* obsession, N.

obsolete ADJ. outmoded. "Hip" is an *obsolete* expression; it went out with love beads and tie-dye shirts.

obstinate ADJ. stubborn; hard to control or treat. We tried to persuade him to give up smoking, but he was *obstinate* and refused to change. Blackberry stickers are the most *obstinate* weeds I know: once established in a yard, they're extremely hard to root out. obstinacy, N.

obstreperous ADJ. boisterous; noisy. What do you do when an *obstreperous* horde of drunken policemen carouses through your hotel, crashing into potted plants and singing vulgar songs?

obtrude V. push (oneself or one's ideas) forward or intrude; butt in; stick out or extrude. Because Fanny was reluctant to *obtrude* her opinions about child-raising upon her daughter-in-law, she kept a close watch on her tongue. obtrusive, ADJ. obtrusion, N.

Word List 33 obtuse–palliate

obtuse ADJ. blunt; stupid. What can you do with somebody who's so *obtuse* that he can't even tell that you're insulting him?

■ **obviate** V. make unnecessary; get rid of. I hope this contribution will *obviate* any need for further collections of funds.

occlude V. shut; close. A blood clot *occluded* an artery to the heart. occlusion, N.

occult ADJ. mysterious; secret; supernatural. The *occult* rites of the organization were revealed only to members. also N.

odious ADJ. hateful; vile. Cinderella's ugly stepsisters had the *odious* habit of popping their zits in public.

odium N. detestation; hatefulness; disrepute. Prince Charming could not express the *odium* he felt toward Cinderella's stepsisters because of their mistreatment of poor Cinderella.

odyssey N. long, eventful journey. The refugee's journey from Cambodia was a terrifying *odyssey.*

offensive ADJ. attacking; insulting; distasteful. Getting into street brawls is no minor offense for professional boxers, who are required by law to restrict their *offensive* impulses to the ring.

offhand ADJ. casual; done without prior thought. Expecting to be treated with due propriety by her hosts, Great-Aunt Maud was offended by their *offhand* manner.

■ **officious** ADJ. meddlesome; excessively pushy in offering one's services. After her long flight, Jill just wanted to nap, but the *officious* bellboy was intent on showing her all the special features of the deluxe suite.

oligarchy N. government by a privileged few. One small clique ran the student council: what had been intended as a democratic governing body had turned into an *oligarchy.*

ominous ADJ. threatening. Those clouds are *ominous;* they suggest that a severe storm is on the way.

omnipotent ADJ. all-powerful. The monarch regarded himself as *omnipotent* and responsible to no one for his acts.

omnipresent ADJ. universally present; ubiquitous. On Christmas Eve, Santa Claus is *omnipresent.*

omniscient ADJ. all-knowing. I do not pretend to be *omniscient,* but I am positive about this fact.

omnivorous ADJ. eating both plant and animal food; devouring everything. Some animals, including humans, are *omnivorous* and eat both meat and vegetables; others are either carnivorous or herbivorous.

■ **onerous** ADJ. burdensome. She asked for an assistant because her work load was too *onerous.*

onslaught N. vicious assault. We suffered many casualties during the unexpected *onslaught* of the enemy troops.

onus N. burden; responsibility. The emperor was spared the *onus* of signing the surrender papers; instead, he relegated the assignment to his generals.

opaque ADJ. dark; not transparent. The *opaque* window shade kept the sunlight out of the room. opacity, N.

opportune ADJ. timely; well-chosen. Cher looked at her father struggling to balance his checkbook; clearly this would not be an *opportune* moment to ask him for an increase in her allowance.

opportunist N. individual who sacrifices principles for expediency by taking advantage of circumstances. Forget about ethics! He's such an *opportunist* that he'll vote in favor of any deal that will give him a break.

■ **opprobrium** N. infamy; vilification. He refused to defend himself against the slander and *opprobrium* hurled against him by the newspapers; he preferred to rely on his record.

optimist N. person who looks on the bright side. The pessimist says the glass is half-empty; the *optimist* says it is half-full.

optimum ADJ. most favorable. If you wait for the *optimum* moment to act, you may never begin your project. also N.

optional ADJ. not compulsory; left to one's choice. I was impressed by the range of *optional* accessories available for my iPad. option, N.

opulence N. extreme wealth; luxuriousness; abundance. The glitter and *opulence* of the ballroom took Cinderella's breath away. opulent, ADJ.

opus N. work. Although many critics hailed his Fifth Symphony, he did not regard it as his major *opus.*

oracular ADJ. prophetic; uttered as if with divine authority; mysterious or ambiguous. Like many others who sought divine guidance from the *oracle* at Delphi, Oedipus could not understand the enigmatic *oracular* warning he received. oracle, N.

orator N. public speaker. The abolitionist Frederick Douglass was a brilliant *orator* whose speeches brought home to his audience the evils of slavery.

ordain V. decree or command; grant holy orders; predestine. The king *ordained* that no foreigner should be allowed to enter the city. The Bishop of Michigan *ordained* David a deacon in the Episcopal Church. The young lovers felt that fate had *ordained* their meeting.

ordeal N. severe trial or affliction. June was so painfully shy that it was an *ordeal* for her to speak up when the teacher called on her in class.

ordinance N. decree. Passing a red light is a violation of a city *ordinance.*

orgy N. wild, drunken revelry; unrestrained indulgence. The Roman emperor's *orgies* were far wilder than the toga party in the movie *Animal House.* When her income tax refund check finally arrived, Sally indulged in an *orgy* of shopping.

orient V. get one's bearings; adjust. Philip spent his first day in Denver *orienting* himself to the city.

orientation N. act of finding oneself in society. Freshman *orientation* provides the incoming students with an opportunity to learn about their new environment and their place in it.

ornate ADJ. excessively or elaborately decorated. With its elaborately carved, convoluted lines, furniture of the Baroque period was highly *ornate.*

orthodox ADJ. traditional; conservative in belief. Faced with a problem, she preferred to take an *orthodox* approach rather than shock anyone. orthodoxy, N.

■ **oscillate** V. vibrate pendulumlike; waver. It is interesting to note how public opinion *oscillates* between the extremes of optimism and pessimism.

ostensible ADJ. apparent; professed; pretended. Although the *ostensible* purpose of this expedition is to discover new lands, we are really interested in finding new markets for our products.

■ **ostentatious** ADJ. showy; pretentious; trying to attract attention. Trump's latest casino in Atlantic City is the most *ostentatious* gambling palace in the East: it easily out-glitters its competitors. ostentation, N.

ostracize V. exclude from public favor; ban. As soon as the newspapers carried the story of his connection with the criminals, his friends began to *ostracize* him. ostracism, N.

oust V. expel; drive out. The world wondered if Aquino would be able to *oust* Marcos from office.

outlandish ADJ. bizarre; peculiar; unconventional. The eccentric professor who engages in markedly *outlandish* behavior is a stock figure in novels with an academic setting.

outmoded ADJ. no longer stylish; old-fashioned. Unconcerned about keeping in style, Lenore was perfectly happy to wear *outmoded* clothes as long as they were clean and unfrayed.

outspoken ADJ. candid; blunt. The candidate was too *outspoken* to be a successful politician; he had not yet learned to weigh his words carefully.

outstrip V. surpass; outdo. Jesse Owens easily *outstripped* his competitors to win the gold medal at the Olympic Games.

outwit V. outsmart; trick. By disguising himself as an old woman, Holmes was able to *outwit* his pursuers and escape capture.

ovation N. enthusiastic applause. When Placido Domingo came on stage in the first act of *La Bohème*, he was greeted by a tremendous *ovation*.

overbearing ADJ. bossy; arrogant; decisively important. Certain of her own importance and of the unimportance of everyone else, Lady Bracknell was intolerably *overbearing* in manner. "In choosing a husband," she said, "good birth is of *overbearing* importance; compared to that, neither wealth nor talent signifies."

overt ADJ. open to view; done openly; not hidden. "Vietnamese culture considers 'face,' an individual's public image, extremely important. Any *overt* public criticism or disparaging remarks can result in a loss of face and cause extreme embarrassment." (Esmond D. Smith, Jr. & Cuong Pham).

overweening ADJ. presumptuous; arrogant. "We are using our children as symbols of leisure-class standing without building in safeguards against an *overweening* sense of entitlement—a sense of entitlement that may incline some young people more toward the good life than toward the hard work that, for most of us, makes the good life possible." (David Elkind)

overwrought ADJ. extremely agitated; hysterical. When Kate heard the news of the sudden tragedy, she became too *overwrought* to work and had to leave the office early.

pacifist N. one opposed to force; antimilitarist. During the war, *pacifists*, though they refused to bear arms, served in the front lines as ambulance drivers and medical corpsmen. also ADJ. pacifism, N.

pacify V. soothe; make calm or quiet; subdue. Dentists criticize the practice of giving fussy children sweets to *pacify* them.

painstaking ADJ. showing hard work; taking great care. The new high-frequency word list is the result of *painstaking* efforts on the part of our research staff.

palatable ADJ. agreeable; pleasing to the taste. Neither Jack's underbaked opinions nor his overcooked casseroles were *palatable* to me.

palatial ADJ. magnificent. He proudly showed us through his *palatial* home.

pall V. grow tiresome. The study of word lists can eventually *pall* and put one to sleep.

palliate V. ease pain; make less severe or offensive. If we cannot cure this disease at present, we can, at least, try to *palliate* the symptoms. palliation, N.

Word List 34 palpable–pensive

palpable ADJ. tangible; easily perceptible. After knee surgery, David noticed a *palpable* bump or swelling below his knee. Reassured that it was a normal development, he felt a *palpable* sense of relief.

palpitate V. throb; flutter. As she became excited, her heart began to *palpitate* more and more erratically.

paltry ADJ. insignificant; petty; trifling. "One hundred dollars for a genuine imitation Rolex watch! Lady, this is a *paltry* sum to pay for such a high-class piece of jewelry."

pan V. criticize harshly. Hoping for a rave review of his new show, the playwright was miserable when the critics *panned* it unanimously.

panacea N. cure-all; remedy for all diseases. There is no easy *panacea* that will solve our complicated international situation.

panache N. flair; flamboyance. Many performers imitated Noel Coward, but few had his *panache* and sense of style.

pandemic ADJ. widespread; affecting the majority of people. They feared the AIDS epidemic would soon reach *pandemic* proportions.

pandemonium N. wild tumult. When the ships collided in the harbor, *pandemonium* broke out among the passengers.

pander V. cater to the low desires of others. The reviewer accused the makers of *Lethal Weapon* of *pandering* to the masses' taste for violence.

panegyric N. formal praise. Blushing at all the praise heaped upon him by the speakers, the modest hero said, "I don't deserve such *panegyrics*."

panoramic ADJ. denoting an unobstructed and comprehensive view. On a clear day, from the top of the Empire State Building you can get a *panoramic* view of New York City and neighboring stretches of New Jersey and Long Island. panorama, N.

pantomime N. acting without dialogue. Because he worked in *pantomime*, the clown could be understood wherever he appeared. also V.

parable N. short, simple story teaching a moral. Let us apply to our own conduct the lesson that this *parable* teaches.

paradigm N. model; example; pattern. Pavlov's experiment in which he trains a dog to salivate on hearing a bell is a *paradigm* of the conditioned-response experiment in behavioral psychology. paradigmatic, ADJ.

paradox N. something apparently contradictory in nature; statement that looks false but is actually correct. Richard presents a bit of a *paradox*, for he is a card-carrying member of both the National Rifle Association and the relatively pacifist American Civil Liberties Union. paradoxical, ADJ.

■ **paragon** N. model of perfection. Her fellow students disliked Lavinia because Miss Minchin always pointed her out as a *paragon* of virtue.

parallelism N. state of being parallel; similarity. Although the twins were separated at birth and grew up in different adoptive families, a striking *parallelism* exists between their lives.

parameter N. limit; independent variable. We need to define the *parameters* of the problem.

paramount ADJ. foremost in importance; supreme. Proper nutrition and hygiene are of *paramount* importance in adolescent development and growth.

paranoia N. psychosis marked by delusions of grandeur or persecution. Suffering from *paranoia*, he claimed everyone was out to get him. Ironically, his claim was accurate; even *paranoids* have enemies. paranoid, paranoiac, N. and ADJ.

paraphernalia N. equipment; odds and ends. Her desk was cluttered with paper, pen, ink, dictionary and other *paraphernalia* of the writing craft.

paraphrase V. restate a passage in one's own words while retaining thought of author. In 250 words or less, *paraphrase* this article. also N.

parasite N. animal or plant living on another; toady; sycophant. The tapeworm is an example of the kind of *parasite* that may infest the human body.

pariah N. social outcast. If everyone ostracized singer Mariah Carey, would she then be Mariah the *pariah*?

parity N. equality; close resemblance. The striking Greyhound bus drivers are demanding pay *parity* with their counterparts in the public transportation system.

parochial ADJ. narrow in outlook; provincial; related to parishes. Although Jane Austen writes novels set in small rural communities, her concerns are universal, not *parochial*.

parody N. humorous imitation; spoof; takeoff; travesty. The show *Forbidden Broadway* presents *parodies* spoofing the year's new productions playing on Broadway. also V.

paroxysm N. fit or attack of pain, laughter, rage. When he heard of his son's misdeeds, he was seized by a *paroxysm* of rage.

parry V. ward off a blow; deflect. Unwilling to injure his opponent in such a pointless clash, Dartagnan simply tried to *parry* his rival's thrusts. What fun it was to watch Katherine Hepburn and Spencer Tracy *parry* each other's verbal thrusts in their classic screwball comedies! also N.

parsimony N. stinginess; excessive frugality. Silas Marner's *parsimony* did not allow him to indulge in any luxuries. parsimonious, ADJ.

partial ADJ. incomplete; having a liking for something. In this issue we have published only a *partial* list of contributors because we lack space to acknowledge everyone. I am extremely *partial* to chocolate eclairs. partiality, N.

partiality N. inclination; bias. As a judge, not only must I be unbiased, but I must also avoid any evidence of *partiality* when I award the prize.

■ **partisan** ADJ. one-sided; prejudiced; committed to a party. Rather than joining forces to solve our nation's problems, the Democrats and Republicans spend their time on *partisan* struggles. also N.

partition V. divide into parts. Before their second daughter was born, Jason and Lizzie decided each child needed a room of her own, and so they *partitioned* a large bedroom into two small but separate rooms. also N.

passé ADJ. old-fashioned; past the prime. Her style is *passé* and reminiscent of the Victorian era.

passive ADJ. not active; acted upon. Mahatma Gandhi urged his followers to pursue a program of *passive* resistance as he felt that it was more effective than violence and acts of terrorism.

pastiche N. imitation of another's style in musical composition or in writing. We cannot even say that her music is a *pastiche* of this or that composer; it is, rather, reminiscent of many musicians.

pastoral ADJ. rural; related to the country. Although there are drawbacks to living in the country, some of us prefer a simple, *pastoral* life to a harried, hectic existence in the big city.

patent ADJ. open for the public to read; obvious. It was *patent* to everyone that the witness spoke the truth.

pathetic ADJ. causing sadness, compassion, pity; touching. Everyone in the auditorium was weeping by the time she finished her *pathetic* tale about the orphaned boy.

■ **pathological** ADJ. pertaining to disease. As we study the *pathological* aspects of this disease, we must not overlook the psychological elements.

pathos N. tender sorrow; pity; quality in art or literature that produces these feelings. The quiet tone of *pathos* that ran through the novel never degenerated into the maudlin or the overly sentimental.

patriarch N. father and ruler of a family or tribe. In many primitive tribes, the leader and lawmaker was the *patriarch*.

patrician ADJ. noble; aristocratic. We greatly admired her well-bred, *patrician* elegance. also N.

patronize V. support; act superior toward; be a customer of. Penniless artists hope to find some wealthy art lover who will *patronize* them. If some condescending wine steward *patronized* me because he saw I knew nothing about fine wine, I'd refuse to *patronize* his restaurant.

■ **paucity** N. scarcity. They closed the restaurant because the *paucity* of customers made it uneconomical to operate.

pauper N. very poor person. Though Widow Brown was living on a reduced income, she was by no means a *pauper*.

peccadillo N. slight offense. Whenever Huck swiped a cookie from the jar, Miss Watson reacted as if he were guilty of armed robbery, not of some mere *peccadillo*.

pecuniary ADJ. pertaining to money. Seldom earning enough to cover their expenses, folk-dance teachers work because they love dancing, not because they expect any *pecuniary* reward.

pedagogue N. teacher. He could never be a stuffy *pedagogue;* his classes were always lively and filled with humor.

pedagogy N. teaching; art of education. Though Maria Montessori gained fame for her innovations in *pedagogy*, it took years before her teaching techniques became common practice in American schools.

pedant N. scholar who overemphasizes book learning or technicalities. I believe that language is a living thing, so I generally laugh at the grammar *pedants* who have fits about every intrusive comma or use of slang.

■ **pedantic** ADJ. showing off learning; bookish. Leavening her decisions with humorous, down-to-earth anecdotes, Judge Judy was not at all the *pedantic* legal scholar. pedantry, N.

pedestrian ADJ. ordinary; unimaginative. Unintentionally boring, he wrote page after page of *pedestrian* prose.

peerless ADJ. having no equal; incomparable. The reigning operatic tenor of his generation, to his admirers Luciano Pavarotti was *peerless*: no one could compare with him.

pejorative ADJ. negative in connotation; having a belittling effect. Instead of criticizing Clinton's policies, the Republicans made *pejorative* remarks about his character.

penance N. self-imposed punishment for sin. The Ancient Mariner said, "I have *penance* done and *penance* more will do," to atone for the sin of killing the albatross.

■ **penchant** N. strong inclination; liking. Dave has a *penchant* for taking risks: one semester he went steady with three girls, two of whom were stars on the school karate team.

penitent ADJ. repentant. When he realized the enormity of his crime, he became remorseful and *penitent*. also N.

pensive ADJ. dreamily thoughtful; thoughtful with a hint of sadness; contemplative. The *pensive* lover gazed at the portrait of his beloved and sighed deeply.

Word List 35 penury–plaintive

■ **penury** N. severe poverty; stinginess. When his pension fund failed, George feared he would end his days in *penury*. He became such a penny-pincher that he turned into a closefisted, *penurious* miser.

peon N. landless agricultural worker; bond servant. The land reformers sought to liberate the *peons* and establish them as independent farmers. peonage, N.

perceptive ADJ. insightful; aware; wise. Although Maud was a generally *perceptive* critic, she had her blind spots: she could never see flaws in the work of her friends.

perdition N. damnation; complete ruin. Praying for salvation, young Daedalus feared he was damned to eternal *perdition.*

peregrination N. journey. Auntie Mame was a world traveler whose *peregrinations* took her from Tijuana to Timbuktu.

peremptory ADJ. demanding and leaving no choice. From Jack's *peremptory* knock on the door, Jill could tell he would not give up until she let him in.

■ **perennial** N. something long-lasting. These plants are hardy *perennials* and will bloom for many years. also ADJ.

■ **perfidious** ADJ. treacherous; disloyal. When Caesar realized that Brutus had betrayed him, he reproached his *perfidious* friend. perfidy, N.

■ **perfunctory** ADJ. superficial; not thorough; lacking interest, care, or enthusiasm. The auditor's *perfunctory* inspection of the books overlooked many errors.

peripatetic ADJ. traveling about; moving from place to place. To scrape together a living, many musicians lead a *peripatetic* life style, always on the road, traveling from one one-night stand to the next.

peripheral ADJ. marginal; outer. We lived, not in central London, but in one of those *peripheral* suburbs that spring up on the outskirts of a great city.

periphery N. edge, especially of a round surface. He sensed that there was something just beyond the *periphery* of his vision.

perjury N. false testimony while under oath. Rather than lie under oath and perhaps be indicted for *perjury,* the witness chose to take the Fifth Amendment, refusing to answer any questions on the grounds that he might incriminate himself.

■ **permeable** ADJ. penetrable; porous; allowing liquids or gas to pass through. If your jogging clothes weren't made out of *permeable* fabric, you'd drown in your own sweat (figuratively speaking). permeate, V.

pernicious ADJ. very destructive. The Athenians argued that Socrates's teachings had a *pernicious* effect on young and susceptible minds; therefore, they condemned him to death.

perpetrate V. commit an offense. Only an insane person could *perpetrate* such a horrible crime.

perpetual ADJ. everlasting. Ponce de Leon hoped to find the legendary fountain of *perpetual* youth.

perpetuate V. make something last; preserve from extinction. Some critics attack *The Adventures of Huckleberry Finn* because they believe Twain's book *perpetuates* a false image of blacks in this country. perpetuity, N.

perquisite N. any gain above stipulated salary. The *perquisites* attached to this job make it even more attractive than the salary indicates.

personable ADJ. attractive. The individual I am seeking to fill this position must be *personable* since he or she will be representing us before the public.

perspicacious ADJ. having insight; penetrating; astute. The brilliant lawyer was known for his *perspicacious* deductions.

perspicuity N. clearness of expression; freedom from ambiguity. One of the outstanding features of this book is the *perspicuity* of its author; her meaning is always clear.

perspicuous ADJ. plainly expressed. Her *perspicuous* comments eliminated all possibility of misinterpretation.

pert ADJ. impertinent; forward. I think your *pert* and impudent remarks call for an apology.

pertinacious ADJ. stubborn; persistent. She is bound to succeed because her *pertinacious* nature will not permit her to quit.

pertinent ADJ. suitable; to the point. "That is the essence of science: ask an impertinent question, and you are on the way to a *pertinent* answer." (Jacob Bronowski)

perturb V. disturb greatly. The thought that electricity might be leaking out of the empty light-bulb sockets *perturbed* my aunt so much that at night she crept about the house screwing fresh bulbs in the vacant spots. perturbation, N.

peruse V. read with care. After the conflagration that burned down her house, Joan closely *perused* her home insurance policy to discover exactly what benefits her coverage provided. perusal, N.

■ **pervasive** ADJ. spread throughout. Despite airing them for several hours, she could not rid her clothes of the *pervasive* odor of mothballs that clung to them. pervade, V.

perverse ADJ. stubbornly wrongheaded; wicked and unacceptable. When Jack was in a *perverse* mood, he would do the opposite of whatever Jill asked him. When Hannibal Lecter was in a *perverse* mood, he ate the flesh of his victims. perversity, N.

pessimism N. belief that life is basically bad or evil; gloominess. Considering how well you have done in the course so far, you have no real reason for such *pessimism* about your final grade. pessimistic, ADJ.

pestilential ADJ. causing plague; baneful. People were afraid to explore the *pestilential* swamp. pestilence, N.

petrify V. turn to stone. (literally or metaphorically). The attack of stage fright *petrified* McKellen so completely that he was unable to say his lines, or even walk offstage.

petty ADJ. trivial; unimportant; very small. She had no major complaints to make about his work, only a few *petty* quibbles that were almost too minor to state.

petulant ADJ. touchy; peevish. If you'd had hardly any sleep for three nights and people kept on phoning and waking you up, you'd sound *petulant,* too. petulance, N.

pharisaical ADJ. pertaining to the Pharisees, who paid scrupulous attention to tradition; self-righteous; hypocritical. Walter Lippmann has pointed out that moralists who do not attempt to explain the moral code they advocate are often regarded as *pharisaical* and ignored.

phenomena N, PL. observable facts; subjects of scientific investigation. We kept careful records of the *phenomena* we noted in the course of these experiments. phenomenon, SING.

philanthropist N. lover of mankind; doer of good. In his role as *philanthropist* and public benefactor, John D. Rockefeller, Sr., donated millions to charity; as an individual, however, he was a tight-fisted old man.

philistine N. narrow-minded person, uncultured and possibily only interested in material gain. "Call me a *philistine,* but I have small patience for Samuel Beckett, can tolerate only small doses of serial atonality, and am bored numb by recitative." (Douglas Hicton)

■ **phlegmatic** ADJ. calm; not easily disturbed. The nurse was a cheerful but *phlegmatic* person, unexcited in the face of sudden emergencies.

phobia N. morbid fear. Her fear of flying was more than mere nervousness; it was a real *phobia.*

phoenix N. symbol of immortality or rebirth. Like the legendary *phoenix* rising from its ashes, the city of San Francisco rose again after its destruction during the 1906 earthquake.

physiological ADJ. pertaining to the science of the function of living organisms. To understand this disease fully, we must examine not only its *physiological* aspects but also its psychological elements.

piecemeal ADV. one part at a time; gradually. Tolstoy's *War and Peace* is too huge to finish in one sitting; I'll have to read it *piecemeal.*

■ **piety** N. devoutness; reverence for God. Living her life in prayer and good works, Mother Teresa exemplified the true spirit of *piety.* pious, ADJ.

pine V. languish, decline; long for; yearn. Though she tried to be happy living with Clara in the city, Heidi *pined* for the mountains and for her gruff but loving grandfather.

pinnacle N. peak. We could see the morning sunlight illuminate the *pinnacle* while the rest of the mountain lay in shadow.

pious ADJ. devout; religious. The challenge for church people today is how to be *pious* in the best sense, that is, to be devout without becoming hypocritical or sanctimonious. piety, N.

piquant ADJ. pleasantly tart-tasting; stimulating. The *piquant* sauce added to our enjoyment of the meal. piquancy, N.

pique N. irritation; resentment. She showed her *pique* at her loss by refusing to appear with the other contestants at the end of the competition.

pique V. provoke or arouse; annoy. "I know something *you* don't know," said Lucy, trying to *pique* Ethel's interest.

pitfall N. hidden danger; concealed trap. The preacher warned his flock to beware the *pitfall* of excessive pride, for pride brought on the angels' fall.

pith N. core or marrow; essence; substance. In preparing a pineapple for the table, first slice it in half and remove the woody central *pith*. Saying the debate team's closing argument lacked *pith*, the judges awarded the trophy to their opponents.

pithy ADJ. concise; meaningful; substantial; meaty. While other girls might have gone on and on about how uncool Elton was, Cher summed it up in one *pithy* remark: "He's bogus!"

pivotal ADJ. central; critical. De Klerk's decision to set Nelson Mandela free was *pivotal;* without Mandela's release, there was no possibility that the African National Congress would entertain talks with the South African government.

■ **placate** V. pacify; conciliate. The store manager tried to *placate* the angry customer, offering to replace the damaged merchandise or to give back her money.

placebo N. harmless substance prescribed as a dummy pill. In a controlled experiment, fifty volunteers were given erythromycin tablets; the control group received only *placebos.*

placid ADJ. peaceful; calm. Avoid getting between a cow and her calf: The maternal instinct can make an otherwise *placid* animal aggressive.

plagiarize V. steal another's ideas and pass them off as one's own. The teacher could tell that the student had *plagiarized* parts of his essay; she recognized whole paragraphs straight from *Barron's Book Notes.* plagiarism, N.

plaintive ADJ. mournful. The dove has a *plaintive* and melancholy call.

Word List 36 plasticity–prefatory

■ **plasticity** N. ability to be molded. When clay dries out, it loses its *plasticity* and becomes less malleable.

■ **platitude** N. trite remark; commonplace statement. In giving advice to his son, old Polonius expressed himself only in *platitudes*; every word out of his mouth was a truism.

platonic ADJ. purely spiritual; theoretical; without sensual desire. Accused of impropriety in his dealings with female students, the professor maintained he had only a *platonic* interest in the women involved.

plaudit N. enthusiastic approval; round of applause. The theatrical company reprinted the *plaudits* of the critics in its advertisements. plauditory, ADJ.

plausible ADJ. having a show of truth but open to doubt; specious. Your mother made you stay home from school because she needed you to program her computer? I'm sorry, you'll have to come up with a more *plausible* excuse than that.

plebeian ADJ. common; unrefined; pertaining to the common people. *New Yorker* articles are entirely too highbrow for my plebeian taste.

plenary ADJ. complete; full. The union leader was given *plenary* power to negotiate a new contract with the employers.

plenitude N. abundance; completeness. Looking in the pantry, we admired the *plenitude* of fruits and pickles we had preserved during the summer.

■ **plethora** N. excess; overabundance. She offered a *plethora* of excuses for her shortcomings.

pliable ADJ. flexible; yielding; adaptable. In remodeling the bathroom, we replaced all the old, rigid lead pipes with new, *pliable* copper tubing.

pliant ADJ. flexible; easily influenced. Pinocchio's disposition was *pliant*; he was like putty in his tempters' hands.

plight N. condition, state (especially a bad state or condition); predicament. Loggers, unmoved by the *plight* of the spotted owl, plan to keep on felling trees whether or not they ruin the bird's habitat.

plumb V. examine critically in order to understand; measure depth (by sounding). Try as he would, Watson could never fully *plumb* the depths of Holmes's thought processes.

plumb ADJ. vertical. Before hanging wallpaper it is advisable to drop a *plumb* line from the ceiling as a guide. also N.

plummet V. fall sharply. Stock prices *plummeted* as Wall Street reacted to the rise in interest rates.

plutocracy N. society ruled by the wealthy. From the way the government caters to the rich, you might think our society is a *plutocracy* rather than a democracy.

poignancy N. quality of being deeply moving; keenness of emotion. Watching the tearful reunion of the long-separated mother and child, the social worker was touched by the *poignancy* of the scene. poignant, ADJ.

polarize V. split into opposite extremes or camps. The abortion issue has *polarized* the country into pro-choice and anti-abortion camps.

polemic N. written or verbal attack. Kunzru maintains that his novel *The Impressionist* is a better book for not being a *polemic* against the excesses of the British in India.

polemical ADJ. aggressive in verbal attack; disputatious. Lexy was a master of *polemical* rhetoric; she should have worn a T-shirt with the slogan "Born to Debate."

politic ADJ. expedient; prudent; well devised. Even though he was disappointed, he did not think it *politic* to refuse this offer.

polity N. state as a political entity; form of government of nation or state. In spite of the facade of the modern state, power in most African *polities* progresses informally between patron and client along lines of reciprocity.

pomposity N. self-important behavior; acting like a stuffed shirt. Although the commencement speaker had some good things to say, we had to laugh at his *pomposity* and general air of parading his own dignity. pompous, ADJ.

ponderous ADJ. weighty; unwieldy. His humor lacked the light touch; his jokes were always *ponderous.*

pontifical ADJ. pertaining to a bishop or pope; pompous or pretentious. From the very beginning of his ministry it was clear from his *pontifical* pronouncements that John was destined for a high *pontifical* office.

pore V. study industriously; ponder; scrutinize. Determined to become a physician, Beth spends hours *poring* over her anatomy text.

■ **porous** ADJ. full of pores; like a sieve. Dancers like to wear *porous* clothing because it allows the ready passage of water and air.

portend V. foretell; presage. The king did not know what these omens might *portend* and asked his soothsayers to interpret them.

portent N. sign; omen; forewarning. He regarded the black cloud as a *portent* of evil.

posterity N. descendants; future generations. We hope to leave a better world to *posterity.*

posthumous ADJ. after death (as of child born after father's death or book published after author's death). The critics ignored his works during his lifetime; it was only after the *posthumous* publication of his last novel that they recognized his great talent.

postulate V. assume something's existence or truth as a basis for further reasoning or discussion. Attachment theory *postulates* that bonds with parents have a significant influence on later adult relationships. also N.

posture V. assume an affected pose; act artificially. No matter how much Arnold boasted or *postured*, I could not believe he was as important as he pretended to be.

potent ADJ. powerful; persuasive; greatly influential. Looking at the expiration date on the cough syrup bottle, we wondered whether the medication would still be *potent*. potency, N.

potentate N. monarch; sovereign. The *potentate* spent more time at Monte Carlo than he did at home on his throne.

potential ADJ. having the capacity to become something. The Bay Area Country Dance Society launched a publicity campaign in hopes of attracting a new crop of *potential* dancers. also N.

practicable ADJ. feasible. The board of directors decided that the plan was *practicable* and agreed to undertake the project.

practical ADJ. based on experience; useful; feasible. While the School of Education offers morning classes on educational theory, its afternoon program consists of student-teaching assignments that provide participants with *practical*, hands-on experience in the classroom.

■ **pragmatic** ADJ. practical (as opposed to idealistic); concerned with the practical worth or impact of something. This coming trip to France should provide me with a *pragmatic* test of the value of my conversational French class.

pragmatist N. practical person. No *pragmatist* enjoys becoming involved in a game that he can never win.

■ **precarious** ADJ. uncertain; risky. Saying the stock was currently overpriced and would be a *precarious* investment, the broker advised her client against purchasing it.

precedent N. something preceding in time that may be used as an authority or guide for future action; an earlier occurrence. The law professor asked Jill to state which famous case served as a *precedent* for the court's decision in *Brown II*. precede, V.

precept N. practical rule guiding conduct. "Love thy neighbor as thyself" is a worthwhile *precept*.

■ **precipitate** ADJ. rash; premature; hasty; sudden. Though I was angry enough to resign on the spot, I had enough sense to keep myself from quitting a job in such a *precipitate* fashion.

precipitate V. throw headlong; hasten. The removal of American political support appeared to have *precipitated* the downfall of the Marcos regime.

precipitous ADJ. steep; overhasty. This hill is difficult to climb because it is so *precipitous;* one slip, and our descent will be *precipitous* as well.

précis N. concise summing up of main points. Before making her presentation at the conference, Ellen wrote a neat *précis* of the major elements she would cover.

precise ADJ. exact. If you don't give me *precise* directions and a map, I'll never find your place.

preclude V. make impossible; eliminate. The fact that the band was already booked to play in Hollywood on New Year's Eve *precluded* their accepting the offer of a New Year's Eve gig in London.

precocious ADJ. advanced in development. Listening to the grown-up way the child discussed serious topics, we couldn't help remarking how *precocious* she was. precocity, N.

■ **precursor** N. forerunner. Though Gray and Burns share many traits with the Romantic poets who followed them, most critics consider them *precursors* of the Romantic Movement, not true Romantics.

predator N. creature that seizes and devours another animal; person who robs or exploits others. Not just cats, but a wide variety of *predators*—owls, hawks, weasels, foxes—catch mice for dinner. A carnivore is by definition *predatory*, for he *preys* on weaker creatures. predation, N.

predecessor N. former occupant of a post. I hope I can live up to the fine example set by my late *predecessor* in this office.

predetermine V. predestine; settle or decide beforehand; influence markedly. Romeo and Juliet believed that Fate had *predetermined* their meeting. Bea gathered estimates from caterers, florists, and stationers so that she could *predetermine* the costs of holding a catered buffet. Philip's love of athletics *predetermined* his choice of a career in sports marketing.

predicament N. tricky or dangerous situation; dilemma. Tied to the railroad tracks by the villain, Pauline strained against her bonds. How would she escape from this terrible *predicament*?

predilection N. partiality; preference. Although the artist used various media from time to time, she had a *predilection* for watercolors.

predispose V. give an inclination toward; make susceptible to. Oleg's love of dressing up his big sister's Barbie doll may have *predisposed* him to become a fashion designer. Genetic influences apparently *predispose* people to certain forms of cancer. predisposition, N.

preeminent ADJ. outstanding; superior. The king traveled to Boston because he wanted the *preeminent* surgeon in the field to perform the operation.

preempt V. head off; forestall by acting first; appropriate for oneself; supplant. Hoping to *preempt* any attempts by the opposition to make educational reform a hot political issue, the candidate set out her own plan to revitalize the public schools. preemptive, ADJ.

prefatory ADJ. introductory. The chairman made a few *prefatory* remarks before he called on the first speaker.

Word List 37 prelude–propitiate

prelude N. introduction; forerunner. In its violent confrontations of pro-slavery and anti-slavery factions, the border war known as "Bleeding Kansas" was a *prelude* to the American Civil War.

premeditate V. plan in advance. She had *premeditated* the murder for months, reading about common poisons and buying weed killer that contained arsenic.

premise N. assumption; postulate. On the *premise* that there's no fool like an old fool, P. T. Barnum hired a 90-year-old clown for his circus.

premonition N. forewarning. We ignored these *premonitions* of disaster because they appeared to be based on childish fears.

premonitory ADJ. serving to warn. You should have visited a doctor as soon as you felt these *premonitory* chest pains.

preponderance N. superiority of power, quantity, etc. The rebels sought to overcome the *preponderance* of strength of the government forces by engaging in guerrilla tactics. preponderate, V. preponderant, ADJ.

preposterous ADJ. absurd; ridiculous. When the candidate tried to downplay his youthful experiments with marijuana by saying he hadn't inhaled, we all thought, "What a *preposterous* excuse!"

prerogative N. privilege; unquestionable right. The President cannot levy taxes; that is the *prerogative* of the legislative branch of government.

presage V. foretell. The vultures flying overhead *presaged* the presence of something dead.

prescience N. ability to foretell the future. Given the current wave of Japan-bashing, it does not take *prescience* for me to foresee problems in our future trade relations with Japan.

presentiment N. feeling something will happen; anticipatory fear; premonition. Saying goodbye at the airport, Jack had a sudden *presentiment* that this was the last time he would see Jill.

prestige N. impression produced by achievements or reputation. Many students want to go to Harvard University, not for the education offered, but for the *prestige* of Harvard's name. prestigious, ADJ.

presume V. take for granted; assume to be true without proof. Just because you are my nephew, don't *presume* there's a job waiting for you in the family firm.

■ **presumptuous** ADJ. arrogant; taking liberties. It seems *presumptuous* for one so relatively new to the field to challenge the conclusions of its leading experts. presumption, N.

pretentious ADJ. ostentatious; pompous; making unjustified claims; overambitious. The other prize winner isn't wearing her medal; isn't it a bit *pretentious* of you to wear yours?

preternatural ADJ. beyond that which is normal in nature. John's mother's total ability to tell when he was lying struck him as almost *preternatural.*

pretext N. excuse. She looked for a good *pretext* to get out of paying a visit to her aunt.

prevail V. induce; triumph over. He tried to *prevail* on her to proofread his essay for him.

prevalent ADJ. widespread; generally accepted. A radical committed to social change, Reed had no patience with the conservative views *prevalent* in the America of his day.

■ **prevaricate** V. lie. Some people believe that to *prevaricate* in a good cause is justifiable and regard the statement as a "white lie."

prey N. target of a hunt; victim. In *Stalking the Wild Asparagus,* Euell Gibbons has as his *prey* not wild beasts but wild plants. also V.

primordial ADJ. existing at the beginning (of time); rudimentary. The Neanderthal Man is one of our *primordial* ancestors.

■ **pristine** ADJ. characteristic of earlier times; primitive, unspoiled. This area has been preserved in all its *pristine* wildness.

privation N. hardship; want. In his youth, he knew hunger and *privation.*

probe V. explore with tools. The surgeon *probed* the wound for foreign matter before suturing it. also N.

■ **probity** N. uprightness; incorruptibility. Everyone took his *probity* for granted; his indictment for embezzlement, therefore, shocked us all.

■ **problematic** ADJ. doubtful; unsettled; questionable; perplexing. Given the way building costs have exceeded estimates for the job, whether the arena will ever be completed is *problematic.*

proclivity N. inclination; natural tendency. Watching the two-year-old voluntarily put away his toys, I was amazed by his *proclivity* for neatness.

procrastinate V. postpone; delay or put off. Looking at four years of receipts and checks he still had to sort through, Bob was truly sorry he had *procrastinated* for so long and had not finished filing his taxes long ago.

procurement N. obtaining. The company has a large budget for the *procurement* of office supplies.

prod V. poke; stir up; urge. If you *prod* him hard enough, he'll eventually clean his room.

■ **prodigal** ADJ. wasteful; reckless with money. Don't be so *prodigal* spending my money; when you've earned some money, you can waste as much of it as you want! also N.

prodigious ADJ. marvelous; enormous. Watching the champion weight lifter heave the weighty barbell to shoulder height and then boost it overhead, we marveled at his *prodigious* strength.

prodigy N. highly gifted child; marvel. Menuhin was a *prodigy,* performing wonders on his violin when he was barely eight years old.

profane V. violate; desecrate; treat unworthily. The members of the mysterious Far Eastern cult sought to kill the British explorer because he had *profaned* the sanctity of their holy goblet by using it as an ashtray. also ADJ.

profligate ADJ. dissipated; wasteful; wildly immoral. Although surrounded by wild and *profligate* companions, she managed to retain some sense of decency. also N. profligacy, N.

■ **profound** ADJ. deep; not superficial; complete. Freud's remarkable insights into human behavior caused his fellow scientists to honor him as a *profound* thinker. profundity, N.

profusion N. overabundance; lavish expenditure; excess. Freddy was so overwhelmed by the *profusion* of choices on the menu that he knocked over his wine glass and soaked his host. He made *profuse* apologies to his host, the waiter, the busboy, the people at the next table, and the man in the men's room giving out paper towels.

progenitor N. ancestor. The Roth family, whose *progenitors* emigrated from Germany early in the nineteenth century, settled in Peru, Illinois.

progeny N. children; offspring. He was proud of his *progeny* in general, but regarded George as the most promising of all his children.

prognosis N. forecasted course of a disease; prediction. If the doctor's *prognosis* is correct, the patient will be in a coma for at least twenty-four hours.

prognosticate V. predict. Although some economists *prognosticated* the imminent failure of the Social Security system, Senator Sanders maintained the system was nowhere near going broke.

■ **prohibitive** ADJ. tending to prevent the purchase or use of something; inclined to prevent or forbid. Susie wanted to buy a new Volvo but had to settle for a used Dodge because the new car's price was *prohibitive.* prohibition, N.

projectile N. missile. Man has always hurled *projectiles* at his enemy whether in the form of stones or of highly explosive shells.

proletarian N. member of the working class; blue collar guy. "Workers of the world, unite! You have nothing to lose but your chains" is addressed to *proletarians,* not preppies. also ADJ. proletariat, N.

■ **proliferate** V. grow rapidly; spread; multiply. Times of economic hardship inevitably encourage countless get-rich-quick schemes to *proliferate.* proliferation, N.

prolific ADJ. abundantly fruitful. She was a *prolific* writer who produced as many as three books a year.

prolixity N. tedious wordiness; verbosity. A writer who suffers from *prolixity* tells his readers everything they *never* wanted to know about his subject (or were too bored to ask). prolix, ADJ.

prologue N. introduction (to a poem or play). In the *prologue* to *Romeo and Juliet,* Shakespeare introduces the audience to the feud between the Montagues and the Capulets.

prolong V. extend; draw out; lengthen. In their determination to discover ways to *prolong* human life, doctors fail to take into account that longer lives are not always happier ones.

prominent ADJ. conspicuous; notable; protruding. Have you ever noticed that Prince Charles's *prominent* ears make him resemble the big-eared character in *Mad* comics?

promiscuous ADJ. mixed indiscriminately; haphazard; irregular, particularly sexually. In the opera *La Bohème,* we get a picture of the *promiscuous* life led by the young artists of Paris. promiscuity, N.

promote V. help to flourish; advance in rank; publicize. Founder of the Children's Defense Fund, Marian Wright Edelman ceaselessly *promotes* the welfare of young people everywhere.

prompt V. cause; provoke; provide a cue for an actor. Whatever *prompted* you to ask for such a big piece of cake when you're on a diet?

promulgate V. proclaim a doctrine or law; make known by official publication. When Moses came down from the mountaintop prepared to *promulgate* God's commandments, he was appalled to discover his followers worshipping a golden calf.

prone ADJ. inclined to; prostrate. She was *prone* to sudden fits of anger during which she would lie *prone* on the floor, screaming and kicking her heels.

propagate V. multiply; spread. Since bacteria *propagate* more quickly in unsanitary environments, it is important to keep hospital rooms clean.

■ **propensity** N. natural inclination. Convinced of his own talent, Sol has an unfortunate *propensity* to belittle the talents of others.

prophetic ADJ. having to do with predicting the future. In interpreting Pharaoh's *prophetic* dream, Joseph said that the seven fat cows eaten by the seven lean cows represented seven years of plenty followed by seven years of famine. prophecy, N.

prophylactic ADJ. used to prevent disease. Despite all *prophylactic* measures introduced by the authorities, the epidemic raged until cool weather set in. prophylaxis, N.

■ **propitiate** V. appease. The natives offered sacrifices to *propitiate* the gods.

Word List 38 propitious–query

propitious ADJ. favorable; fortunate; advantageous. Chloe consulted her horoscope to see whether Tuesday would be a *propitious* day to dump her boyfriend.

proponent N. supporter; backer; opposite of *opponent*. In the Senate, *proponents* of the universal health care measure lobbied to gain additional support for the controversial legislation.

propound V. put forth for analysis. In the early twentieth century, Albert Einstein *propounded* the general theory of relativity, one of the two pillars of modern physics.

■ **propriety** N. fitness; correct conduct. Miss Manners counsels her readers so that they may behave with *propriety* in any social situation and not embarrass themselves.

prosaic ADJ. dull and unimaginative; matter-of-fact; factual. Though the ad writers had come up with a highly creative campaign to publicize the company's newest product, the head office rejected it for a more *prosaic*, down-to-earth approach.

■ **proscribe** V. ostracize; banish; outlaw. Antony, Octavius, and Lepidus *proscribed* all those who had conspired against Julius Caesar.

proselytize V. induce someone to convert to a religion or belief. In these interfaith meetings, there must be no attempt to *proselytize;* we must respect all points of view.

prosperity N. good fortune; financial success; physical well-being. Promising to stay together "for richer, for poorer," the newlyweds vowed to be true to one another in *prosperity* and hardship alike.

prostrate V. stretch out full on ground. He *prostrated* himself before the idol. also ADJ.

protean ADJ. versatile; able to take on many forms. A remarkably *protean* actor, Alec Guinness could take on any role.

protégé N. person receiving protection and support from a patron. Born with an independent spirit, Cyrano de Bergerac refused to be a *protégé* of Cardinal Richelieu.

protocol N. diplomatic etiquette. We must run this state dinner according to *protocol* if we are to avoid offending any of our guests.

prototype N. original work used as a model by others. The crude bulky computer on display in this museum is the *prototype* of the sleek, miniature models in use today.

protract V. prolong. Seeking to delay the union members' vote, the management team tried to *protract* the negotiations endlessly, but the union representatives saw through their strategy.

protrude V. stick out. His fingers *protruded* from the holes in his gloves.

provenance N. origin or source of something. Feliciano's book, *Lost Museum*: The *Nazi Conspiracy to Steal the World's Greatest Works of Art*, traced the *provenance* of stolen, post-war art and led to thousands of works of art being restored to museum collections.

provident ADJ. displaying foresight; thrifty; preparing for emergencies. In his usual *provident* manner, he had insured himself against this type of loss.

provincial ADJ. pertaining to a province; limited in outlook; unsophisticated. As *provincial* governor, Sir Henry administered the Queen's law in his remote corner of Canada. Caught up in local problems, out of touch with London news, he became sadly *provincial*.

provisional ADJ. tentative. Kim's acceptance as an American Express cardholder was *provisional*: before issuing her a card, American Express wanted to check her employment record and credit history.

proviso N. stipulation. I am ready to accept your proposal with the *proviso* that you meet your obligations within the next two weeks.

provocative ADJ. arousing anger or interest; annoying. In a typically *provocative* act, the bully kicked sand into the weaker man's face. provoke, V. provocation, N.

prowess N. extraordinary ability; military bravery. Performing triple axels and double lutzes at the age of six, the young figure skater was world famous for her *prowess* on the ice.

proximity N. nearness. Blind people sometimes develop a compensatory ability to sense the *proximity* of objects around them.

proxy N. authorized agent. Please act as my *proxy* and vote for this slate of candidates in my absence.

prude N. excessively modest or proper person. The X-rated film was definitely not for *prudes*.

prudent ADJ. cautious; careful. A miser hoards money not because he is *prudent* but because he is greedy. prudence, N.

prune V. cut away; trim. With the help of her editor, she was able to *prune* her manuscript into publishable form.

pry V. inquire impertinently; use leverage to raise or open something. Though Nora claimed she didn't mean to *pry*, everyone knew she was just plain nosy. With a crowbar Long John Silver *pried* up the lid of the treasure chest.

pseudonym N. pen name. Samuel Clemens' *pseudonym* was Mark Twain.

psyche N. soul; mind. It is difficult to delve into the *psyche* of a human being.

puerile ADJ. childish. His *puerile* pranks sometimes offended his more mature friends.

pugnacity N. combativeness; disposition to fight. "Put up your dukes!" he cried, making a fist to show his *pugnacity*. pugnacious, ADJ.

pulchritude N. beauty; comeliness. I do not envy the judges who have to select this year's Miss America from this collection of female *pulchritude*.

pulverize V. crush or grind into very small particles. Before sprinkling the dried herbs into the stew, Michael first *pulverized* them into a fine powder.

pummel V. beat or pound with fists. Swinging wildly, Pammy *pummeled* her brother around the head and shoulders.

punctilious ADJ. stressing niceties of conduct or form; minutely attentive (perhaps too much so) to fine points. Percy is *punctilious* about observing the rules of etiquette whenever Miss Manners invites him to stay. punctiliousness, N.

pundit N. authority on a subject; learned person; expert. Some authors who write about the GRE as if they are *pundits* actually know very little about the test.

pungent ADJ. stinging; sharp in taste or smell; caustic. The *pungent* odor of ripe Limburger cheese appealed to Simone but made Stanley gag. pungency, N.

punitive ADJ. punishing. He asked for *punitive* measures against the offender.

purge V. remove or get rid of something unwanted; free from blame or guilt; cleanse or purify. The Communist government *purged* the party to get rid of members suspected of capitalist sympathies, sending those believed to be disloyal to labor camps in Siberia. also N.

purport N. intention; meaning. If the *purport* of your speech was to arouse the rabble, you succeeded admirably. also V.

purported ADJ. alleged; claimed; reputed or rumored. The *purported* Satanists sacrificing live roosters in the park turned out to be a party of Shriners holding a chicken barbecue.

purveyor N. furnisher of foodstuffs; caterer. As *purveyor* of rare wines and viands, he traveled through France and Italy every year in search of new products to sell.

pusillanimous ADJ. cowardly; fainthearted. In *The Wizard of Oz*, Dorothy's friend the Cowardly Lion wishes he were brave and not *pusillanimous*. pusillanimity, N.

putative ADJ. supposed; reputed. Although there are some doubts, the *putative* author of this work is Massinger.

quack N. charlatan; impostor. Do not be misled by the exaggerated claims of this *quack;* he cannot cure you.

quail V. cower; lose heart. He was afraid that he would *quail* in the face of danger.

quaint ADJ. odd; old-fashioned; picturesque. Her *quaint* clothes and old-fashioned language marked her as an eccentric.

■ **qualified** ADJ. limited; restricted. Unable to give the candidate full support, the mayor gave him only a *qualified* endorsement. (secondary meaning)

qualms N. misgivings; uneasy fears, especially about matters of conscience. I have no *qualms* about giving this assignment to Helen; I know she will handle it admirably.

quandary N. dilemma. When both Harvard and Stanford accepted Laura, she was in a *quandary* as to which school she should attend.

quarantine N. isolation of a person, place, or ship to prevent spread of infection. We will have to place this house under *quarantine* until we determine the exact nature of the disease. also V.

quarry N. victim; object of a hunt. The police closed in on their *quarry*.

quarry V. dig into. They *quarried* blocks of marble out of the hillside.

quash V. subdue; crush; squash. The authorities acted quickly to *quash* the student rebellion, sending in tanks to cow the demonstrators.

queasy ADJ. easily nauseated; squeamish. Remember that great chase movie, the one with the carsick passenger? That's right: *Queasy Rider*!

quell V. extinguish; put down; quiet. Miss Minchin's demeanor was so stern and forbidding that she could *quell* any unrest among her students with one intimidating glance.

quench V. douse or extinguish; assuage or satisfy. What's the favorite song of the Fire Department? "Baby, *Quench* My Fire!" After Bob ate the heavily salted popcorn, he had to drink a pitcherful of water to *quench* his thirst.

querulous ADJ. fretful; whining. Even the most agreeable toddlers can begin to act *querulous* if they miss their nap.

query N. inquiry; question. In her column "Ask Beth," the columnist invites young readers to send her their *queries* about life and love. also V.

Word List 39 quibble–redress

■ **quibble** N. minor objection or complaint. Aside from a few hundred teensy-weensy *quibbles* about the set, the script, the actors, the director, the costumes, the lighting, and the props, the hypercritical critic loved the play. also V.

■ **quiescent** ADJ. at rest; dormant; temporarily inactive. After the devastating eruption, fear of Mount Etna was great; people did not return to cultivate its rich hillside lands until the volcano had been *quiescent* for a full two years. quiescence, N.

quietude N. tranquillity. An oasis of *quietude*, the Dr. Sun Yat-Sen Classical Chinese Garden sits serenely in the midst of the tumult of downtown Vancouver.

quintessence N. purest and highest embodiment. Showcasing historical masterpieces that were once part of the decor of the Imperial palace, the exhibition *Treasures of the Imperial Collections* embodies the *quintessence* of modern Japanese art.

quip N. taunt. You are unpopular because you are too free with your *quips* and sarcastic comments. also V.

quirk N. startling twist; caprice, By a *quirk* of fate, he found himself working for the man whom he had discharged years before.

quixotic ADJ. idealistic but impractical. Constantly coming up with *quixotic*, unworkable schemes to save the world, Simon has his heart in the right place, but his head is somewhere off in the clouds.

quizzical ADJ. teasing; bantering; mocking; curious. When the skinny teenager tripped over his own feet stepping into the bullpen, Coach raised one *quizzical* eyebrow, shook his head, and said, "Okay, kid. You're here; let's see what you've got."

quorum N. number of members necessary to conduct a meeting. The senator asked for a roll call to determine whether a *quorum* was present.

quotidian ADJ. daily; commonplace; customary. To Philip, each new day of his internship was filled with excitement; he could not dismiss his rounds as merely *quotidian* routine.

rail V. scold; rant. You may *rail* at him all you want; you will never change him.

rally V. call up or summon (forces, vital powers, etc.); revive or recuperate. Washington quickly *rallied* his troops to fight off the British attack. The patient had been sinking throughout the night, but at dawn she *rallied* and made a complete recovery. also N.

ramble V. wander aimlessly (physically or mentally). Listening to the teacher *ramble*, Judy wondered whether he'd ever get to his point. also N.

ramification N. branching out; subdivision. We must examine all the *ramifications* of this problem.

ramify V. divide into branches or subdivisions. When the plant begins to *ramify*, it is advisable to nip off most of the new branches.

rampant ADJ. growing in profusion; unrestrained. The *rampant* weeds in the garden choked the asters and marigolds until the flowers died. rampancy, N.

rancor N. bitterness; hatred. Thirty years after the war, she could not let go of the past but was still consumed with *rancor* against the foe. rancorous, ADJ.

random ADJ. without definite purpose, plan, or aim; haphazard. Although the sponsor of the raffle claimed all winners were chosen at *random*, people had their suspicions when the grand prize went to the sponsor's brother-in-law.

rankle V. irritate; fester. The memory of having been jilted *rankled* him for years.

rant V. rave; talk excitedly; scold; make a grandiloquent speech. When he heard that I'd totaled the family car, Dad began to *rant* at me like a complete madman.

rapacious ADJ. excessively grasping; plundering. Hawks and other *rapacious* birds prey on a variety of small animals.

rapport N. emotional closeness; harmony. In team teaching, it is important that all teachers in the group have good *rapport* with one another.

rapt ADJ. absorbed; enchanted. Caught up in the wonder of the storyteller's tale, the *rapt* listeners sat motionless, hanging on his every word.

■ **rarefied** ADJ. made less dense [of a gas]. The mountain climbers had difficulty breathing in the *rarefied* atmosphere. rarefy, V. rarefaction, N.

ratify V. approve formally; confirm; verify. Party leaders doubted that they had enough votes in both houses of Congress to *ratify* the constitutional amendment.

ratiocination N. reasoning; act of drawing conclusions from premises. While Watson was a man of average intelligence, Holmes was a genius, whose gift for *ratiocination* made him a superb detective.

rationale N. fundamental reason or justification; grounds for an action. Her need for a vehicle large enough to accommodate five children and a Saint Bernard was Judy's *rationale* for buying a minivan.

rationalize V. give a plausible reason for an action in place of a true, less admirable one; offer an excuse. When David refused gabby Gabrielle a ride to the dance because, he said, he had no room in the car, he was *rationalizing*; actually, he couldn't stand being cooped up in a car with anyone who talked as much as she did. rationalization, N.

raucous ADJ. harsh and shrill; disorderly and boisterous. The *raucous* crowd of New Year's Eve revelers grew progressively noisier as midnight drew near.

ravenous ADJ. extremely hungry. The *ravenous* dog upset several garbage pails in its search for food.

raze V. destroy completely. Spelling matters: to raise a building is to put it up; to *raze* a building is to tear it down.

reactionary ADJ. opposing progress; politically ultraconservative. Opposing the use of English in worship services, *reactionary* forces in the church fought to reinstate the mass in Latin. also N.

realm N. kingdom; field or sphere. In the animal *realm*, the lion is the king of beasts.

rebuff V. snub; beat back. She *rebuffed* his invitation so smoothly that he did not realize he had been snubbed. also N.

rebuke V. scold harshly; criticize severely. No matter how sharply Miss Watson *rebuked* Huck for his misconduct, he never talked back but just stood there like a stump. also N.

rebuttal N. refutation; response with contrary evidence. The defense lawyer confidently listened to the prosecutor sum up his case, sure that she could answer his arguments in her *rebuttal*.

■ **recalcitrant** ADJ. obstinately stubborn; determined to resist authority; unruly. Which animal do you think is more *recalcitrant*, a pig or a mule?

■ **recant** V. disclaim or disavow; retract a previous statement; openly confess error. Hoping to make Joan of Arc *recant* her sworn testimony, her English captors tried to convince her that her visions had been sent to her by the Devil.

recapitulate V. summarize. Let us *recapitulate* what has been said thus far before going ahead.

recast V. reconstruct (a sentence, story, etc.); fashion again. Let me *recast* this sentence in terms your feeble brain can grasp: in words of one syllable, you are a fool.

receptive ADJ. quick or willing to receive ideas, suggestions, etc. Adventure-loving Huck Finn proved a *receptive* audience for Tom's tales of buried treasure and piracy.

recession N. withdrawal; retreat; time of low economic activity. The slow *recession* of the flood waters created problems for the crews working to restore power to the area.

recidivism N. habitual return to crime. Prison reformers in the United States are disturbed by the high rate of *recidivism;* the number of persons serving second and third terms indicates the failure of the prisons to rehabilitate the inmates.

recipient N. receiver. Although he had been the *recipient* of many favors, he was not grateful to his benefactor.

reciprocal ADJ. mutual; exchangeable; interacting. The two nations signed a *reciprocal* trade agreement.

reciprocate V. repay in kind. When people do something for us, we feel indebted to them and feel a great desire to *reciprocate* the gesture in some way. reciprocity, N.

recluse N. hermit; loner. Disappointed in love, Miss Emily became a *recluse*; she shut herself away in her empty mansion and refused to see another living soul. reclusive, ADJ.

recompense V. repay or reward; N. repayment, compensation. There is no way in which our community can adequately *recompense* the members of the volunteer fire department for the hours of dedicated service they provide..

reconcile V. correct inconsistencies; become friendly after a quarrel. Every time we try to *reconcile* our checkbook with the bank statement, we quarrel. However, despite these monthly lovers' quarrels, we always manage to *reconcile*.

■ **recondite** ADJ. abstruse; profound; secret. He read many *recondite* books in order to obtain the material for his scholarly thesis.

reconnaissance N. survey of enemy by soldiers; reconnoitering. If you encounter any enemy soldiers during your *reconnaissance*, capture them for questioning.

recount V. narrate or tell; count over again. About to *recount* the latest adventure of Sherlock Holmes, Watson lost track of exactly how many cases Holmes had solved and refused to begin his tale until he'd *recounted* them one by one.

recourse N. resorting to help when in trouble. The boy's only *recourse* was to appeal to his father for aid.

recrimination N. countercharges. Loud and angry *recriminations* were her answer to his accusations.

rectify V. set right; correct. You had better send a check to *rectify* your account before American Express cancels your credit card.

rectitude N. uprightness; moral virtue; correctness of judgment. The Eagle Scout was a model of *rectitude*; smugness was the only flaw he needed to correct.

recuperate V. recover. The doctors were worried because the patient did not *recuperate* as rapidly as they had expected.

recurrent ADJ. occurring again and again. As a child I had *recurrent* nightmares about being pursued by wolves.

redoubtable ADJ. formidable; causing fear. During the Cold War period, neighboring countries tried not to offend the Russians because they could be *redoubtable* foes.

redress N. remedy; compensation. Do you mean to tell me that I can get no *redress* for my injuries? also V.

Word List 40 redundant–reputable

redundant ADJ. superfluous; repetitious; excessively wordy. The bottle of wine I brought to Bob's party was certainly *redundant*: how was I to know Bob owned a winery? In your essay, you repeat several points unnecessarily; try to avoid *redundancy* in the future.

■ **refractory** ADJ. stubborn; unmanageable. The *refractory* horse was eliminated from the race when he refused to obey the jockey.

refrain V. abstain from; resist. N. chorus. Whenever he heard a song with a lively chorus, Sol could never *refrain* from joining in on the *refrain*.

refurbish V. renovate; make bright by polishing. The flood left a deposit of mud on everything; it was necessary to *refurbish* our belongings.

■ **refute** V. disprove. The defense called several respectable witnesses who were able to *refute* the lying testimony of the prosecution's sole witness. refutation, N.

regeneration N. spiritual rebirth. Rather than leading to the destruction of the North Oakland neighborhood, the construction of Rockridge's new rapid transit station kick-started the *regeneration* of the area.

regime N. method or system of government. When a Frenchman mentions the Old *Regime*, he refers to the government existing before the revolution.

regimen N. prescribed diet and habits. I doubt whether the results warrant our living under such a strict *regimen*.

rehabilitate V. restore to proper condition. The mission of the physical therapy clinic is to *rehabilitate* patients who have been seriously injured or have undergone reconstructive surgery.

reimburse V. repay. Let me know what you have spent and I will *reimburse* you.

reiterate V. repeat. She *reiterated* the warning to make sure everyone understood it.

rejoinder N. retort; comeback; reply. When someone has been rude to me, I find it particularly satisfying to come up with a quick *rejoinder*.

rejuvenate V. make young again. The charlatan claimed that his elixir would *rejuvenate* the aged and weary.

■ **relegate** V. banish to an inferior position; delegate; assign. After Ralph dropped his second tray of drinks that week, the manager swiftly *relegated* him to a minor post cleaning up behind the bar.

relent V. give in. When her stern father would not *relent* and allow her to marry Robert Browning, Elizabeth Barrett eloped with her suitor. relentless, ADJ.

relevant ADJ. pertinent; referring to the case in hand. Teri was impressed by how *relevant* Virginia Woolf's remarks were to her as a woman writer; it was as if Woolf had been writing with Teri's situation in mind. relevance, N. relevancy, N.

relic N. surviving remnant; memento. Egypt's Department of Antiquities prohibits tourists from taking mummies and other ancient *relics* out of the country. Mike keeps his photos of his trip to Egypt in a box with other *relics* of his travels.

relinquish V. give up something with reluctance; yield. Once you get used to fringe benefits like expense-account meals and a company car, it's very hard to *relinquish* them.

relish V. savor; enjoy. Watching Peter enthusiastically chow down, I thought, "Now there's a man who *relishes* a good dinner!" also N.

remediable ADJ. reparable. Let us be grateful that the damage is *remediable.*

reminiscence N. recollection. Her *reminiscences* of her experiences are so fascinating that she ought to write a book.

remiss ADJ. negligent. When the prisoner escaped, the guard was accused of being *remiss* in his duty.

remission N. temporary moderation of disease symptoms; cancellation of a debt; forgiveness or pardon. Though Senator Tsongas had been treated for cancer, his symptoms were in *remission,* and he was considered fit to handle the strains of a presidential race.

remnant N. remainder. I suggest that you wait until the store places the *remnants* of these goods on sale.

remonstrance N. protest; objection. The authorities were deaf to the pastor's *remonstrances* about the lack of police protection in the area. remonstrate, V.

remorse N. guilt; self-reproach. The murderer felt no *remorse* for his crime.

remunerative ADJ. compensating; rewarding. I find my new job so *remunerative* that I may not return to my previous position. remuneration, N.

render V. deliver; provide; represent. He *rendered* aid to the needy and indigent.

rendezvous N. meeting place. The two fleets met at the *rendezvous* at the appointed time. also V.

rendition N. translation; artistic interpretation of a song, etc. The audience cheered enthusiastically as she concluded her *rendition* of the aria.

renegade N. deserter; traitor. Because he had abandoned his post and joined forces with the Indians, his fellow officers considered the hero of *Dances with Wolves* a *renegade.* also ADJ.

renege V. deny; go back on. He *reneged* on paying off his debt.

renounce V. abandon; disown; repudiate. Even though she knew she would be burned at the stake as a witch, Joan of Arc refused to *renounce* her belief that her voices came from God. renunciation, N.

renovate V. restore to good condition; renew. They claim that they can *renovate* worn shoes so that they look like new ones.

renown N. fame. For many years an unheralded researcher, Barbara McClintock gained international *renown* when she won the Nobel Prize in Physiology and Medicine. renowned, ADJ.

reparable ADJ. capable of being repaired. Fortunately, the damage we suffered in the accident was *reparable* and our car looks brand new.

reparation N. amends; compensation. At the peace conference, the defeated country promised to pay *reparations* to the victors.

repartee N. clever reply. He was famous for his witty *repartee* and his sarcasm.

repeal V. revoke; annul. What would the effect on our society be if we decriminalized drug use by *repealing* the laws against the possession and sale of narcotics?

repel V. drive away; disgust. At first, the Beast's ferocious appearance *repelled* Beauty, but she came to love the tender heart hidden behind that beastly exterior.

repercussion N. rebound; reverberation; reaction. The governor's critics charged that his new tax on gasoline would drive up the cost of commuting, and that serious political and economic *repercussions* would result.

repertoire N. list of works of music, drama, etc., a performer is prepared to present. The opera company decided to include *Madame Butterfly* in its *repertoire* for the following season.

replenish V. fill up again. Before she could take another backpacking trip, Carla had to *replenish* her stock of freeze-dried foods.

replete ADJ. filled to the brim or to the point of being stuffed; abundantly supplied. The movie star's memoir was *replete* with juicy details about the love life of half of Hollywood.

replica N. copy. Are you going to hang this *replica* of the Declaration of Independence in the classroom or in the auditorium?

replicate V. reproduce; duplicate. Because he had always wanted a palace, Donald decided to *replicate* the Taj Mahal in miniature on his estate.

repository N. storehouse. Libraries are *repositories* of the world's best thoughts.

reprehensible ADJ. deserving blame. Shocked by the viciousness of the bombing, politicians of every party uniformly condemned the terrorists' *reprehensible* deed.

repress V. restrain; crush; oppress. Anne's parents tried to curb her impetuosity without *repressing* her boundless high spirits.

reprieve N. temporary stay. During the twenty-four-hour *reprieve,* the lawyers sought to make the stay of execution permanent. also V.

reprimand N. strong rebuke; formal reproof; scolding. Every time Ermengarde made a mistake in class, she was terrified that she would receive a harsh *reprimand* from Miss Minchin. also V.

reprisal N. retaliation. In occupied France, despite the increasingly savage Nazi *reprisals* against the civilian population, the Resistance movement continued to gain in strength.

reprise N. musical repetition; repeat performance; recurrent action. We enjoyed the soprano's solo in Act I so much that we were delighted by its *reprise* in the finale. At Waterloo, it was not the effect of any one skirmish that exhausted Colonel Audley; rather, it was the cumulative effect of the constant *reprises* that left him spent.

■ **reproach** V. express disapproval or disappointment. He never could do anything wrong without imagining how the look on his mother's face would *reproach* him afterwards. also N. reproachful, ADJ.

■ **reprobate** N. person hardened in sin, devoid of a sense of decency. "After all, as a conservative of fairly recent vintage, I've seen how easy it is for liberals, assisted by a compliant press, to cast ideological foes as moral *reprobates* and thus avoid engaging their ideas." (Harry Stein)

reprove V. censure; rebuke. Though Aunt Bea at times would *reprove* Opie for inattention in church, she believed he was at heart a God-fearing lad. reproof, N.

■ **repudiate** V. disown; disavow. On separating from Tony, Tina announced that she would *repudiate* all debts incurred by her soon-to-be ex-husband.

repugnance N. loathing. She looked at the snake with *repugnance.*

repulsion N. distaste; act of driving back. Hating bloodshed, she viewed war with *repulsion.* Even defensive battles distressed her, for the *repulsion* of enemy forces is never accomplished bloodlessly. repulse, V.

reputable ADJ. respectable. If you want to buy antiques, look for a *reputable* dealer; far too many dealers today pass off fakes as genuine antiques.

Word List 41 reputed–saccharine

reputed ADJ. supposed. Isaac Newton is *reputed* to have said, "I can calculate the motions of heavenly bodies but not the madness of people." repute, V. repute, N.

requisite N. necessary requirement. Many colleges state that a student must offer three years of a language as a *requisite* for admission.

requite V. repay; revenge. The wretch *requited* his benefactors by betraying them.

■ **rescind** V. cancel. Because of the public outcry against the new taxes, the senator proposed a bill to *rescind* the unpopular financial measure.

resentment N. indignation; bitterness; displeasure. Not wanting to appear a sore loser, Bill tried to hide his *resentment* of Barry's success.

reserve N. self-control; formal but distant manner. Although some girls were attracted by Mark's *reserve,* Judy was put off by it, for she felt his aloofness indicated a lack of openness. reserved, ADJ.

residue N. remainder; balance. In his will, he requested that after payment of debts, taxes, and funeral expenses, the *residue* be given to his wife.

resignation N. patient submissiveness; statement that one is quitting a job. If Bob Cratchit had not accepted Scrooge's bullying with timid *resignation,* he might have gotten up the nerve to hand in his *resignation.* resigned, ADJ.

resilient ADJ. elastic; having the power of springing back. Highly *resilient,* steel makes excellent bedsprings. resilience, N.

■ **resolution** N. determination. Nothing could shake his *resolution* to succeed despite all difficulties. resolute, ADJ.

■ **resolve** N. determination; firmness of purpose. How dare you question my *resolve* to take up sky-diving! Of course I haven't changed my mind! also V.

resolve V. decide; settle; solve. Holmes *resolved* to travel to Bohemia to *resolve* the dispute between Irene Adler and the King.

resonant ADJ. echoing; resounding; deep and full in sound. The deep, *resonant* voice of the actor James Earl Jones makes him particularly effective when he appears on stage.

respite N. interval of relief; time for rest; delay in punishment. For David, the two weeks vacationing in New Zealand were a delightful *respite* from the pressures of his job.

resplendent ADJ. dazzling; glorious; brilliant. While all the adults were commenting how glorious the emperor looked in his *resplendent* new clothes, one little boy was heard to say, "But he's naked!"

responsiveness N. state of reacting readily to appeals, orders, etc. The audience cheered and applauded, delighting the performers by its *responsiveness.*

restitution N. reparation; indemnification. If you make full *restitution* for the damage you have caused, we are willing to let bygones be bygones.

restive ADJ. restlessly impatient; obstinately resisting control. Waiting impatiently in line to see Santa Claus, even the best-behaved children grow *restive* and start to fidget.

restraint N. moderation or self-control; controlling force; restriction. Show some *restraint,* young lady! Three desserts is quite enough!

resumption N. taking up again; recommencement. During the summer break, Don had not realized how much he missed university life: at the *resumption* of classes, however, he felt marked excitement and pleasure. resume, V.

resurge V. rise again; flow to and fro. It was startling to see the spirit of nationalism *resurge* as the Soviet Union disintegrated into a loose federation of ethnic and national groups. resurgence, N. resurgent, ADJ.

retain V. keep; employ. Fighting to *retain* his seat in Congress, Senator Foghorn *retained* a new manager to head his reelection campaign.

retaliation V. repayment in kind (usually for bad treatment). Because everyone knew the Princeton band had stolen Brown's mascot, the whole Princeton student body expected some sort of *retaliation* from Brown. retaliate, V.

retentive ADJ. holding; having a good memory. The pupil did not need to spend much time memorizing texts thanks to his *retentive* mind.

■ **reticent** ADJ. reserved; uncommunicative; inclined to silence. Fearing his competitors might get advance word about his plans from talkative staff members, Hughes preferred *reticent* employees to loquacious ones. reticence, N.

retiring ADJ. modest; shy. Given Susan's *retiring* personality, no one expected her to take up public speaking; surprisingly enough, she became a star of the school debate team.

retort N. quick, sharp reply. Even when it was advisable for her to keep her mouth shut, she was always ready with a *retort.* also V.

retract V. withdraw; take back. When I saw how Fred and his fraternity brothers had trashed the frat house, I decided to *retract* my offer to let them use our summer cottage for the weekend. retraction, N.

retrench V. cut down; economize. If they were to be able to send their children to college, they would have to *retrench.*

retribution N. vengeance; compensation; punishment for offenses. The evangelist maintained that an angry deity would exact *retribution* from the sinners.

retrieve V. recover; find and bring in. The dog was intelligent and quickly learned to *retrieve* the game killed by the hunter. retrieval, N.

retroactive ADJ. taking effect before its enactment (as a law) or imposition (as a tax). Because the new pension law was *retroactive* to the first of the year, even though Martha had retired in February she was eligible for the pension.

retrograde ADJ. reverting to a prior, inferior state. The education writer denounced the decision to eliminate Head Start programs from the public schools as a *retrograde* step. also V.

retrospective ADJ. looking back on the past. The Museum of Graphic Arts is holding a *retrospective* showing of the paintings of Michael Whelan over the past two decades. also N. retrospection, N.

■ **reverent** ADJ. respectful; worshipful. Though I bow my head in church and recite the prayers, sometimes I don't feel properly *reverent.* revere, V. reverence, N.

revert V. relapse; backslide; turn back to. Most of the time Andy seemed sensitive and mature, but occasionally he would *revert* to his smart-alecky, macho, adolescent self. reversion, N.

revile V. attack with abusive language; vilify. Though most of his contemporaries *reviled* Captain Kidd as a notorious, bloody-handed pirate, some of his fellow merchant-captains believed him innocent of his alleged crimes.

revoke V. cancel; retract. Repeat offenders who continue to drive under the influence of alcohol face having their driver's licenses permanently *revoked.* revocation, N.

revulsion N. sudden violent change of feeling; negative reaction. Many people in this country who admired dictatorships underwent a *revulsion* when they realized what Hitler and Mussolini were trying to do.

rhapsodize V. to speak or write in an exaggeratedly enthusiastic manner. She greatly enjoyed her Hawaiian vacation and *rhapsodized* about it for weeks.

rhetoric N. art of effective communication; insincere or grandiloquent language. All writers, by necessity, must be skilled in *rhetoric*. rhetorical, ADJ.

rife ADJ. abundant; current. In the face of the many scandalous rumors *rife* at the moment, it is best to remain silent.

rift N. opening; break. The plane was lost in the stormy sky until the pilot saw the city through a *rift* in the clouds.

rig V. fix or manipulate. The ward boss was able to *rig* the election by bribing people to stuff the ballot boxes with ballots marked in his candidate's favor.

rigid ADJ. stiff and unyielding; strict; hard and unbending. By living with a man to whom she was not married, George Eliot broke Victorian society's most *rigid* rule of respectable behavior.

rigor N. severity. Many settlers could not stand the *rigors* of the New England winters.

rile V. vex; irritate; muddy. Red had a hair-trigger temper: he was an easy man to *rile*.

riveting ADJ. absorbing; engrossing. The reviewer described Byatt's novel *Possession* as a *riveting* tale: absorbed in the story, she had finished it in a single evening.

robust ADJ. vigorous; strong. After pumping iron and taking karate for six months, the little old lady was far more *robust* in health and could break a plank with her fist.

rote N. repetition. He recited the passage by *rote* and gave no indication he understood what he was saying. also ADJ.

rousing ADJ. lively; stirring. "And now, let's have a *rousing* welcome for TV's own Rosie O'Donnell, who'll lead us in a *rousing* rendition of 'The Star-Spangled Banner.'"

rout V. stampede; drive out. The reinforcements were able to *rout* the enemy. also N.

rudimentary ADJ. not developed; elementary; crude. Although my grandmother's English vocabulary was limited to a few *rudimentary* phrases, she always could make herself understood.

rue V. regret; lament; mourn. Tina *rued* the night she met Tony and wondered how she ever fell for such a jerk. also N. rueful, ADJ.

ruminate V. chew over and over (mentally or, like cows, physically); mull over; ponder. Unable to digest quickly the baffling events of the day, Reuben *ruminated* about them till four in the morning.

ruse N. trick; stratagem. You will not be able to fool your friends with such an obvious *ruse*.

rustic ADJ. pertaining to country people; uncouth. The backwoodsman looked out of place in his *rustic* attire.

ruthless ADJ. pitiless; cruel. Captain Hook was a dangerous, *ruthless* villain who would stop at nothing to destroy Peter Pan.

saboteur N. one who commits sabotage; destroyer of property. Members of the Resistance acted as *saboteurs*, blowing up train lines to prevent supplies from reaching the Nazi army.

saccharine ADJ. cloyingly sweet. She tried to ingratiate herself, speaking sweetly and smiling a *saccharine* smile.

Word List 42 sacrilegious–sensuous

sacrilegious ADJ. desecrating; profane. His stealing of the altar cloth was a very *sacrilegious* act.

sacrosanct ADJ. most sacred; inviolable. The brash insurance salesman invaded the *sacrosanct* privacy of the office of the president of the company.

sadistic ADJ. inclined to cruelty. If we are to improve conditions in this prison, we must first get rid of the *sadistic* warden. sadism, N.

saga N. Scandinavian myth; any legend. This is a *saga* of the sea and the men who risk their lives on it.

sagacious ADJ. perceptive; shrewd; having insight. My father was a *sagacious* judge of character: he could spot a phony a mile away. sagacity, N.

■ **sage** N. person celebrated for wisdom. Hearing tales of a mysterious Master of All Knowledge who lived in the hills of Tibet, Sandy was possessed with a burning desire to consult the legendary *sage*. also ADJ.

salient ADJ. prominent. One of the *salient* features of that newspaper is its excellent editorial page.

■ **salubrious** ADJ. healthful. Many people with hay fever move to more *salubrious* sections of the country during the months of August and September.

salutary ADJ. tending to improve; beneficial; wholesome. The punishment had a *salutary* effect on the boy, who became a model student.

salvage V. rescue from loss. All attempts to *salvage* the wrecked ship failed. also N.

sanctimonious ADJ. displaying ostentatious or hypocritical devoutness. You do not have to be so *sanctimonious* to prove that you are devout.

■ **sanction** V. approve; ratify. Nothing will convince me to *sanction* the engagement of my daughter to such a worthless young man.

sanctuary N. refuge; shelter; shrine; holy place. The tiny attic was Helen's *sanctuary* to which she fled when she had to get away from her bickering parents and brothers.

sanguinary ADJ. bloody. The battle of Iwo Jima was unexpectedly *sanguinary*, with many casualties.

sanguine ADJ. cheerful; hopeful. Let us not be too *sanguine* about the outcome; something could go wrong.

sap V. diminish; undermine. The element kryptonite had an unhealthy effect on Superman: it *sapped* his strength.

sarcasm N. scornful remark; stinging rebuke. Though Ralph pretended to ignore the mocking comments of his supposed friends, their *sarcasm* wounded him deeply. sarcastic, ADJ.

sardonic ADJ. disdainful; sarcastic; cynical. The *sardonic* humor of nightclub comedians who satirize or ridicule patrons in the audience strikes some people as amusing and others as rude.

satellite N. small body revolving around a larger one. During the first few years of the Space Age, hundreds of *satellites* were launched by Russia and the United States.

■ **satiate** V. satisfy fully. Having stuffed themselves with goodies until they were *satiated*, the guests were so full they were ready for a nap. satiety, N.

satire N. form of literature in which irony, sarcasm, and ridicule are employed to attack vice and folly. *Gulliver's Travels*, which is regarded by many as a tale for children, is actually a bitter *satire* attacking human folly.

■ **saturate** V. soak thoroughly. Thorough watering is the key to lawn care: you must *saturate* your new lawn well to encourage its growth.

savant N. scholar. Harvard professor George Whitesides is a *savant* with a wide range of scientific interests, whose influence on the more than 500 graduate students he has mentored is considerable.

■ **savor** V. enjoy; have a distinctive flavor, smell, or quality. Relishing his triumph, Costner especially *savored* the chagrin of the critics who had predicted his failure.

savory ADJ. tasty; pleasing, attractive, or agreeable. Julia Child's recipes enable amateur chefs to create *savory* delicacies for their guests.

scanty ADJ. meager; insufficient. Thinking his helping of food was *scanty*, Oliver Twist asked for more.

scapegoat N. someone who bears the blame for others. After the Challenger disaster, NASA searched for *scapegoats* on whom they could cast the blame.

scavenge V. hunt through discarded materials for usable items; search, especially for food. If you need car parts that the dealers no longer stock, try *scavenging* for odd bits and pieces at the auto wreckers' yards. scavenger, N.

scenario N. plot outline; screenplay; opera libretto. Scaramouche startled the other actors in the commedia troupe when he suddenly departed from their customary *scenario* and began to improvise.

schematic ADJ. relating to an outline or diagram; using a system of symbols. In working out the solution to an analytical logic question, you may find it helpful to construct a simple *schematic* diagram illustrating the relationships between the items of information given in the question. schema, N.

schism N. division; split. The movement to ordain women threatened to create a *schism* in the Church, pitting modernizers against traditionalists.

scintilla N. shred; least bit. You have not produced a *scintilla* of evidence to support your argument.

scintillate V. sparkle; flash. I enjoy her dinner parties because the food is excellent and the conversation *scintillates.*

scoff V. mock; ridicule. He *scoffed* at dentists until he had his first toothache.

scotch V. stamp out; thwart; hinder. Heather tried to *scotch* the rumor that she had stolen her best friend's fiancé.

scruple V. fret about; hesitate, for ethical reasons. Fearing that her husband had become involved in an affair, she did not *scruple* to read his diary. also N.

scrupulous ADJ. conscientious; extremely thorough. Though Alfred is *scrupulous* in fulfilling his duties at work, he is less conscientious about his obligations to his family and friends.

scrutinize V. examine closely and critically. Searching for flaws, the sergeant *scrutinized* every detail of the private's uniform.

scurrilous ADJ. insultingly offensive; obscene; indecent. The candidate maintained that there was no trace of evidence to support the irresponsible, *scurrilous* accusations his opponents had made.

scurry V. move briskly. The White Rabbit had to *scurry* to get to his appointment on time.

seasoned ADJ. experienced. Though pleased with her new batch of rookies, the basketball coach wished she had a few more *seasoned* players on the team.

secession N. withdrawal. The *secession* of the Southern states provided Lincoln with his first major problem after his inauguration. secede, V.

seclusion N. isolation; solitude. One moment she loved crowds; the next, she sought *seclusion.*

■ **secrete** V. hide away or cache; produce and release a substance into an organism. The pack rat *secretes* odds and ends in its nest; the pancreas *secretes* insulin in the islets of Langerhans.

sect N. separate religious body; faction. As university chaplain, she sought to address universal religious issues and not limit herself to the concerns of any one *sect.* sectarian, ADJ.

secular ADJ. worldly; not pertaining to church matters; temporal. The church leaders decided not to interfere in *secular* matters.

sedate ADJ. composed; grave. John's parents were worried because they felt their son was too quiet and *sedate.*

sedentary ADJ. requiring sitting. Sitting all day at the computer, Sharon grew to resent the *sedentary* nature of her job.

sedition N. resistance to authority; insubordination. Her words, though not treasonous in themselves, were calculated to arouse thoughts of *sedition.*

sedulous ADJ. diligent. Students who have not been particularly *sedulous* and diligent in keeping up with their coursework may find themselves in difficulties at midterm time. sedulity, N.

seemly ADJ. proper; appropriate. Lady Bracknell did not think it was *seemly* for Ernest to lack a proper family: no baby abandoned on a doorstep could grow up to marry *her* daughter.

seethe V. be disturbed; boil. The nation was *seething* with discontent as the noblemen continued their arrogant ways.

seismic ADJ. pertaining to earthquakes. The Richter scale is a measurement of *seismic* disturbances.

semblance N. outward appearance; guise. Although this book has a *semblance* of wisdom and scholarship, a careful examination will reveal many errors and omissions.

seminal ADJ. germinal; influencing future developments; related to seed or semen. Although Freud has generally been regarded as a *seminal* thinker who shaped the course of psychology, his psychoanalytic methods have come under attack recently.

seminary N. school for training future ministers; secondary school, especially for young women. Sure of his priestly vocation, Terrence planned to pursue his theological training at the local Roman Catholic *seminary.*

senility N. old age; feeblemindedness of old age. Most of the decisions are being made by the junior members of the company because of the *senility* of the president. senile, ADJ.

sensitization N. process of being made sensitive or acutely responsive to an external agent or substance. The paint fumes triggered a bad allergic response in Vicky; even now, her extreme *sensitization* to these chemicals causes her to faint whenever she is around wet paint.

sensual ADJ. devoted to the pleasures of the senses; carnal; voluptuous. I cannot understand what caused him to abandon his *sensual* way of life and become so ascetic.

sensuous ADJ. pertaining to the physical senses; operating through the senses. Stimulated by the sights, sounds, and smells about her, she enjoyed her *sensuous* experience.

Word List 43 sententious–somber

sententious ADJ. preachy and moralizing; pithy. Constantly quoting maxims ("Neither a borrower nor a lender be"), Polonius is depicted as a *sententious,* garrulous old man.

sentient ADJ. capable of sensation; aware; sensitive. In the science fiction story, the hero had to discover a way to prove that the rocklike extraterrestrial creature was actually a *sentient,* intelligent creature. sentience, N.

sentinel N. sentry; lookout. Though camped in enemy territory, Bledsoe ignored the elementary precaution of posting *sentinels* around the encampment.

septic ADJ. putrid; producing putrefaction. The hospital was in such a filthy state that we were afraid that many of the patients would suffer from *septic* poisoning. sepsis, N.

sequester V. isolate; retire from public life; segregate; seclude. To prevent the jurors from hearing news broadcasts about the case, the judge decided to *sequester* the jury.

serendipity N. gift for finding valuable or desirable things by accident; accidental good fortune or luck. Many scientific discoveries are a matter of *serendipity:* Newton was not sitting there thinking about gravity when the apple dropped on his head.

serenity N. calmness, placidity. The *serenity* of the sleepy town was shattered by a tremendous explosion.

servile ADJ. slavish; cringing. Constantly fawning on his employer, humble Uriah Heep was a *servile* creature. servility, N.

servitude N. slavery; compulsory labor. Born a slave, Douglass resented his life of *servitude* and plotted to escape to the North.

sever V. cut; separate. Dr. Guillotin invented a machine that could neatly *sever* an aristocratic head from its equally aristocratic body. Unfortunately, he couldn't collect any *severance* pay.

severity N. harshness; intensity; sternness; austerity. The *severity* of Jane's migraine attack was so great that she took to her bed for a week. severe, ADJ.

sham V. pretend. She *shammed* sickness to get out of going to school. also N.

shambles N. wreck; mess. After the hurricane, the Carolina coast was a *shambles.* After the New Year's Eve party, the host's apartment was a *shambles.*

■ **shard** N. fragment, generally of pottery. The archaeologist assigned several students the task of reassembling earthenware vessels from the *shards* he had brought back from the expedition.

shirk V. avoid (responsibility, work, etc.); malinger. Brian has a strong sense of duty; he would never *shirk* any responsibility.

shoddy ADJ. sham; not genuine; inferior. You will never get the public to buy such *shoddy* material.

shrew N. scolding woman. No one wanted to marry Shakespeare's Kate because she was a *shrew.*

shrewd ADJ. clever; astute. A *shrewd* investor, she took clever advantage of the fluctuations of the stock market.

shun V. keep away from. Cherishing his solitude, the recluse *shunned* the company of other human beings.

shunt V. turn aside; divert; sidetrack. If the switchman failed to *shunt* the Silver Streak onto a side track, the train would plow right into Union Station.

sibling N. brother or sister. We may not enjoy being *siblings,* but we cannot forget that we still belong to the same family.

simile N. comparison of one thing with another, using the word *like* or *as.* "My love is like a red, red rose" is a *simile.*

simplistic ADJ. oversimplified. Though Jack's solution dealt adequately with one aspect of the problem, it was *simplistic* in failing to consider various complicating factors that might arise.

simulate V. feign. She *simulated* insanity in order to avoid punishment for her crime.

sinecure N. well-paid position with little responsibility. My job is no *sinecure;* I work long hours and have much responsibility.

singular ADJ. unique; extraordinary; odd. Though the young man tried to understand Father William's *singular* behavior, he still found it odd that the old man incessantly stood on his head.

sinister ADJ. evil. Several conspiracy websites allege *sinister* motivations behind the mayor's actions; all too ready to see wickedness everywhere, these sites are constantly on the lookout for evil plots to expose.

■ **skeptic** N. doubter; person who suspends judgment until having examined the evidence supporting a point of view. I am a *skeptic* about the new health plan; I want some proof that it can work. skeptical, ADJ. skepticism, N.

skimp V. provide scantily; live very economically. "Never neglect the little things. Never *skimp* on that extra effort, that additional few minutes, that soft word of praise or thanks, that delivery of the very best that you can do." (Og Mandino)

skinflint N. stingy person; miser. Scrooge was an ungenerous old *skinflint* until he reformed his ways and became a notable philanthropist.

skirmish N. minor fight. Custer's troops expected they might run into a *skirmish* or two on maneuvers; they did not expect to face a major battle. also V.

skittish ADJ. lively; frisky. She is as *skittish* as a kitten playing with a piece of string.

skulduggery N. dishonest behavior. The investigation into municipal corruption turned up new instances of *skulduggery* daily.

skulk V. move furtively and secretly. He *skulked* through the less fashionable sections of the city in order to avoid meeting any of his former friends.

slacken V. slow up; loosen. As they passed the finish line, the runners *slackened* their pace.

slake V. quench; sate. When we reached the oasis, we were able to *slake* our thirst.

slander N. defamation; utterance of false and malicious statements. Considering the negative comments politicians make about each other, it's a wonder that more of them aren't sued for *slander.* also V. slanderous, ADJ.

slapdash ADJ. haphazard; careless; sloppy. From the number of typos and misspellings I've found in it, it's clear that Mario proofread the report in a remarkably *slapdash* fashion.

sleight N. dexterity. The magician amazed the audience with his *sleight* of hand.

slight N. insult to one's dignity; snub. Hypersensitive and ready to take offense at any discourtesy, Bertha was always on the lookout for real or imaginary *slights.* also V.

slipshod ADJ. untidy or slovenly; shabby. As a master craftsman, the carpenter prided himself on never doing *slipshod* work.

slothful ADJ. lazy. The British word "layabout" is a splendid descriptive term for someone *slothful*: What did the lazy bum do? He lay about the house all day. sloth, N.

slovenly ADJ. untidy; careless in work habits. Unshaven, sitting around in his bathrobe all afternoon, Gus didn't care about the *slovenly* appearance he presented. sloven, N.

sluggish ADJ. slow; lazy; lethargic. After two nights without sleep, she felt *sluggish* and incapable of exertion.

slur N. insult to one's character or reputation; slander. Polls revealed that the front-runner's standing had been damaged by the *slurs* and innuendoes circulated by his opponent's staff. (secondary meaning) also V.

slur V. speak indistinctly; mumble. When Sol has too much to drink, he starts to *slur* his words: "Washamatter? Cansh you undershtand what I shay?"

smattering N. slight knowledge. I don't know whether it is better to be ignorant of a subject or to have a mere *smattering* of information about it.

smirk N. conceited smile. Wipe that *smirk* off your face! also V.

smolder V. burn without flame; be liable to break out at any moment. The rags *smoldered* for hours before they burst into flame.

sobriety N. moderation (especially regarding indulgence in alcohol); seriousness. Neither falling-down drunks nor stand-up comics are noted for *sobriety.* sober, ADJ.

solace N. comfort in trouble. I hope you will find *solace* in the thought that all of us share your loss.

solemnity N. seriousness; gravity. The minister was concerned that nothing should disturb the *solemnity* of the marriage service.

solicit V. request earnestly; seek. Knowing she needed to have a solid majority for the budget to pass, the mayor telephoned all the members of the city council to *solicit* their votes.

■ **solicitous** ADJ. worried, concerned. The employer was very *solicitous* about the health of her employees because replacements were difficult to get. solicitude, N.

soliloquy N. talking to oneself. The *soliloquy* is a device used by the dramatist to reveal a character's innermost thoughts and emotions.

solitude N. state of being alone; seclusion. Much depends on how much you like your own company. What to one person seems fearful isolation to another is blessed *solitude.* solitary, ADJ.

soluble ADJ. able to be dissolved; able to be worked out. Sugar is *soluble* in water; put a sugar cube in water and it will quickly dissolve. Because the test-maker had left out some necessary data, the problem was not *soluble.*

solvent ADJ. able to pay all debts. By dint of very frugal living, he was finally able to become *solvent* and avoid bankruptcy proceedings. solvency, N.

solvent N. substance that dissolves another. Dip a cube of sugar into a cup of water; note how the water acts as a *solvent,* causing the cube to break down.

somber ADJ. gloomy; depressing. From the doctor's grim expression, I could tell he had *somber* news.

Word List 44 somnolent–studied

somnolent ADJ. half asleep. The heavy meal and the overheated room made us all *somnolent* and indifferent to the speaker. somnolence, N.

sophist N. teacher of philosophy; quibbler; employer of fallacious reasoning. You are using all the devices of a *sophist* in trying to prove your case; your argument is specious.

sophisticated ADJ. worldly wise and urbane; complex. When Sophy makes wisecracks, she thinks she sounds *sophisticated*, but instead she sounds sophomoric. The IBM laptop with the butterfly keyboard and the built-in FAX modem was a pretty *sophisticated* machine for its time. sophistication, N.

sophistry N. seemingly plausible but fallacious reasoning. Instead of advancing valid arguments, he tried to overwhelm his audience with a flood of *sophistries.*

sophomoric ADJ. immature; half-baked, like a sophomore. Even if you're only a freshman, it's no compliment to be told your humor is *sophomoric.* The humor in *Dumb and Dumber* is *sophomoric* at best.

■ **soporific** ADJ. sleep-causing; marked by sleepiness. Professor Pringle's lectures were so *soporific* that even he fell asleep in class. also N.

sordid ADJ. filthy; base; vile. The social worker was angered by the *sordid* housing provided for the homeless.

sparse ADJ. not thick; thinly scattered; scanty. No matter how carefully Albert combed his hair to make it appear as full as possible, it still looked *sparse.*

spartan ADJ. lacking luxury and comfort; sternly disciplined. Looking over the bare, unheated room with its hard cot, he wondered what he was doing in such *spartan* quarters. Only his *spartan* sense of duty kept him at his post.

spasmodic ADJ. fitful; periodic. The *spasmodic* coughing in the auditorium annoyed the performers.

spatial ADJ. relating to space. Certain exercises test your sense of *spatial* relations by asking you to identify two views of an object seen from different points in space.

spawn V. lay eggs. Fish ladders had to be built in the dams to assist the salmon returning to *spawn* in their native streams. also N.

■ **specious** ADJ. seemingly reasonable but incorrect; misleading (often intentionally). To claim that, because houses and birds both have wings, both can fly is extremely *specious* reasoning.

spectral ADJ. ghostly. We were frightened by the *spectral* glow that filled the room.

■ **spectrum** N. colored band produced when a beam of light passes through a prism. The visible portion of the *spectrum* includes red at one end and violet at the other.

spendthrift N. someone who wastes money. Easy access to credit encourages people to turn into *spendthrifts* who shop till they drop.

sphinx-like ADJ. enigmatic; mysterious. The Mona Lisa's *sphinx-like* expression has puzzled art lovers for centuries.

spontaneity N. lack of premeditation; naturalness; freedom from constraint. The cast overrehearsed the play so much that the eventual performance lacked any *spontaneity.* spontaneous, ADJ.

■ **sporadic** ADJ. occurring irregularly. Although you can still hear *sporadic* outbursts of laughter and singing outside, the big Halloween parade has passed; the party's over till next year.

sportive ADJ. playful. Such a *sportive* attitude is surprising in a person as serious as you usually are.

spry ADJ. vigorously active; nimble. She was eighty years old, yet still *spry* and alert.

spurious ADJ. false; counterfeit; forged; illogical. The hero of Jonathan Gash's mystery novels is an antique dealer who gives the reader advice on how to tell *spurious* antiques from the real thing.

spurn V. reject; scorn. The heroine *spurned* the villain's advances.

squabble N. minor quarrel; bickering. Children invariably get involved in petty *squabbles;* wise parents know when to interfere and when to let the children work things out on their own.

squalor N. filth; degradation; dirty, neglected state. Rusted, broken-down cars in the yard, trash piled on the porch, tar paper peeling from the roof—the shack was the picture of *squalor.* squalid, ADJ.

squander V. waste. If you *squander* your allowance on candy and comic books, you won't have any money left to buy the new video game you want.

stagnant ADJ. motionless; stale; dull. Mosquitoes commonly breed in ponds of *stagnant* water. Mike's career was *stagnant;* it wasn't going anywhere, and neither was he! stagnate, V.

staid ADJ. sober; sedate. Junior partners in the traditionally *staid* and respectable law firm were startled to learn that the senior partner had taken on a gangsta rapper as a client.

stalemate N. deadlock. Negotiations between the union and the employers have reached a *stalemate;* neither side is willing to budge from previously stated positions.

stalwart ADJ. strong, brawny; steadfast. His consistent support of the party has proved that he is a *stalwart* and loyal member. also N.

stamina N. strength; staying power. I doubt that she has the *stamina* to run the full distance of the marathon race.

static ADJ. unchanging; lacking development. Why do you watch chess on TV? I like watching a game with action, not something *static* where nothing seems to be going on. stasis, N.

statute N. law enacted by the legislature. The *statute* of limitations sets limits on how much time you have during which you can take legal action in specific cases.

statutory ADJ. created by statute or legislative action. Unlike acupuncturists and homeopaths, practitioners of conventional medicine are subject to *statutory* regulation: special laws ensure that they are properly qualified and adhere to certain codes of practice.

steadfast ADJ. loyal; unswerving. Penelope was *steadfast* in her affections, faithfully waiting for Ulysses to return from his wanderings.

stealth N. slyness; sneakiness; secretiveness. Fearing detection by the sentries on duty, the scout inched his way toward the enemy camp with great *stealth.*

stellar ADJ. pertaining to the stars; outstanding. Most theories of *stellar* evolution portray stars as lone entities or perhaps in a pair with one other star. Unfortunately, the restaurant reviewers gave the new bistro less than *stellar* ratings.

stem V. check the flow. The paramedic used a tourniquet to *stem* the bleeding from the slashed artery.

stem from V. arise from. Milton's problems in school *stemmed from* his poor study habits.

stereotype N. fixed and unvarying representation; standardized mental picture, often reflecting prejudice. Critics object to the character of Jim in *The Adventures of Huckleberry Finn* because he seems to reflect the *stereotype* of the happy, ignorant slave. also V.

stickler N. perfectionist; person who insists things be exactly right. The Internal Revenue Service agent was a *stickler* for accuracy; no approximations or rough estimates would satisfy him.

stifle V. suppress; extinguish; inhibit. Halfway through the boring lecture, Laura gave up trying to *stifle* her yawns.

■ **stigma** N. token of disgrace; brand. I do not attach any *stigma* to the fact that you were accused of this crime; the fact that you were acquitted clears you completely. stigmatize, N.

stilted ADJ. stiff and unnatural. Feeling awkward at the unexpected meeting, Dave made *stilted* conversation with his ex-girlfriend and her parents.

■ **stint** V. be thrifty; set limits. "Spare no expense," the bride's father said, refusing to *stint* on the wedding arrangements.

stint N. supply; allotted amount; assigned portion of work. She performed her daily *stint* cheerfully and willingly.

stipend N. pay for services. There is a nominal *stipend* for this position.

■ **stipulate** V. make express conditions, specify. Before agreeing to reduce American military forces in Europe, the president *stipulated* that NATO teams be allowed to inspect Russian bases.

stock ADJ. typical; standard; kept regularly in supply. Victorian melodramas portrayed *stock* characters—the rich but wicked villain, the sweet young ingenue, the poor but honest young man—in exaggerated situations. Although the stationery store kept only *stock* sizes of paper on hand, the staff would special-order any items not regularly in *stock*.

stodgy ADJ. stuffy; boringly conservative. For a young person, Winston seems remarkably *stodgy:* you'd expect someone his age to have a little more life.

stoic ADJ. impassive; unmoved by joy or grief. I wasn't particularly *stoic* when I had my flu shot; I squealed like a stuck pig. also N. stoicism, N.

stoke V. stir up a fire; feed plentifully. As a Scout, Marisa learned how to light a fire, how to *stoke* it if it started to die down, and how to extinguish it completely.

■ **stolid** ADJ. dull; impassive. The earthquake shattered Stuart's usual *stolid* demeanor; trembling, he crouched on the no longer stable ground. stolidity, N.

stratagem N. clever trick; deceptive scheme. What a gem of a *stratagem*! Watson, I have the perfect plan to trick Moriarty into revealing himself.

stratified ADJ. divided into classes; arranged into strata. As the economic gap between the rich and the poor increased, Roman society grew increasingly *stratified*. stratify, V.

stratum N. layer of earth's surface; layer of society. It is the job of the university to see that its teaching benefits the entire community and not just those elite students drawn from a narrow *stratum* within the community. strata, PL.

stricture N. critical comments; severe and adverse criticism. His *strictures* on the author's style are prejudiced and unwarranted.

strident ADJ. loud and harsh; insistent. We could barely hear the speaker over the *strident* cries of the hecklers. stridency, N.

stringent ADJ. binding; rigid. I think these regulations are too *stringent*.

studied ADJ. unspontaneous; deliberate; thoughtful. Given Jill's previous slights, Jack felt that the omission of his name from the guest list was a *studied* insult.

Word List 45 stultify–sycophant

stultify V. cause to appear or become stupid or inconsistent; frustrate or hinder. His long hours in the blacking factory left young Dickens numb and incurious, as if the menial labor had *stultified* his mind.

stupefy V. make numb; stun; amaze. Disapproving of drugs in general, Laura refused to take sleeping pills or any other medicine that might *stupefy* her.

stupor N. state of apathy; daze; lack of awareness. In his *stupor*, the addict was unaware of the events taking place around him.

stymie V. present an obstacle; stump. The detective was *stymied* by the contradictory evidence in the robbery investigation.

suavity N. urbanity; polish. He is particularly good in roles that require *suavity* and sophistication. suave, ADJ.

subdued ADJ. less intense; quieter. Bob liked the *subdued* lighting at the restaurant because he thought it was romantic. I just thought the place was dimly lit.

subjective ADJ. occurring or taking place within the mind; unreal. Your analysis is highly *subjective;* you have permitted your emotions and your opinions to color your thinking.

subjugate V. conquer; bring under control. As soon as the pasha had *subjugated* one tribe, another tribe immediately rebelled against him.

sublimate V. refine; purify; divert an impulse into something more socially acceptable. Exiled to his estates, the former Roman senator *sublimated* his desire for political glory into the writing of history.

sublime ADJ. exalted; noble and uplifting; utter. Lucy was in awe of Desi's *sublime* musicianship, while he was in awe of her *sublime* naiveté.

subliminal ADJ. below the threshold. We may not be aware of the *subliminal* influences that affect our thinking.

submissive ADJ. yielding; timid. When he refused to permit Elizabeth to marry her poet, Mr. Barrett expected her to be properly *submissive*; instead, she eloped with the guy!

subordinate ADJ. occupying a lower rank; inferior; submissive. Bishop Proudie's wife expected the *subordinate* clergy to behave with great deference to the wife of their superior. also N.

suborn V. persuade to act unlawfully (especially to commit perjury). In *The Godfather*, the mobsters used bribery and threats to *suborn* the witnesses against Don Michael Corleone.

■ **subpoena** N. writ summoning a witness to appear. The prosecutor's office was ready to serve a *subpoena* on the reluctant witness. also V.

subsequent ADJ. following; later. In *subsequent* lessons, we shall take up more difficult problems.

subservient ADJ. behaving like a slave; servile; obsequious. She was proud and dignified; she refused to be *subservient* to anyone. subservience, N.

■ **subside** V. settle down; descend; grow quiet. The doctor assured us that the fever would eventually *subside*.

subsidiary ADJ. subordinate; secondary. This information may be used as *subsidiary* evidence but is not sufficient by itself to prove your argument. also N.

subsidy N. direct financial aid by government, etc. Without this *subsidy*, American ship operators would not be able to compete in world markets.

subsistence N. existence; means of support; livelihood. As unemployment continues to grow, more people will find themselves impoverished and without available means of *subsistence*.

substantial ADJ. ample; solid; essential or fundamental. The generous scholarship represented a *substantial* sum of money. If you don't eat a more *substantial* dinner, you'll be hungry later on.

■ **substantiate** V. establish by evidence; verify; support. These endorsements from satisfied customers *substantiate* our claim that Barron's *GRE* is the best GRE prep book on the market.

substantive ADJ. essential; pertaining to the substance. Although the delegates were aware of the importance of the problem, they could not agree on the *substantive* issues.

subsume V. include; encompass. Does the general theory of relativity contradict Newtonian physics, or is Newton's law of gravity *subsumed* into Einstein's larger scheme?

subterfuge N. pretense; evasion. As soon as we realized that you had won our support by a *subterfuge*, we withdrew our endorsement of your candidacy.

subtlety N. perceptiveness; ingenuity; delicacy. Never obvious, she expressed herself with such *subtlety* that her remarks went right over the heads of most of her audience. subtle, ADJ.

subversive ADJ. tending to overthrow; destructive. At first glance, the notion that Styrofoam cups may actually be more ecologically sound than paper cups strikes most environmentalists as *subversive*.

succinct ADJ. brief; terse; compact. Don't bore your audience with excess verbiage: be *succinct*.

succor V. aid; assist; comfort. If you believe that con man has come here to *succor* you in your hour of need, you're even a bigger sucker than I thought. also N.

succumb v. yield; give in; die. I *succumb* to temptation whenever it comes my way.

suffragist N. advocate of voting rights (for women). In recognition of her efforts to win the vote for women, Congress authorized coining a silver dollar honoring the *suffragist* Susan B. Anthony.

summation N. act of finding the total; summary. In his *summation,* the lawyer emphasized the testimony given by the two witnesses.

sumptuous ADJ. lavish; rich. I cannot recall when I have had such a *sumptuous* Thanksgiving feast.

sundry ADJ. various; several. The economist took dry facts, occasional anecdotes, and a wealth of data from *sundry* sources, and wove them together into a narrative at once both interesting and informative.

supercilious ADJ. arrogant; condescending; patronizing. The *supercilious* headwaiter sneered at customers who he thought did not fit the image of a restaurant catering to an ultrafashionable crowd.

supererogatory ADJ. superfluous; more than needed or demanded. We have more than enough witnesses to corroborate your statement; to present any more would be *supererogatory.*

superficial ADJ. trivial; shallow. Since your report gave only a *superficial* analysis of the problem, I cannot give you more than a passing grade.

superfluous ADJ. excessive; overabundant, unnecessary. Please try not to include so many *superfluous* details in your report; just give me the bare facts. superfluity, N.

superimpose v. place over something else. I used Photoshop to *superimpose* a quote from Martha Graham onto one of my favorite photographs of her dancing.

■ **supersede** v. cause to be set aside; replace; make obsolete. Bulk mailing postal regulation 326D *supersedes* bulk mailing postal regulation 326C. If, in bundling your bulk mailing, you follow regulation 326C, your bulk mailing will be returned. supersession, N.

supplant v. replace; usurp. Did the other woman actually *supplant* Princess Diana in Prince Charles's affections, or did Charles never love Diana at all? Bolingbroke, later to be known as King Henry IV, fought to *supplant* his cousin, Richard III, as King of England.

supplicate v. petition humbly; pray to grant a favor. We *supplicate* Your Majesty to grant him amnesty.

■ **supposition** N. hypothesis; surmise. I based my decision to confide in him on the *supposition* that he would be discreet. suppose, v.

supposititious ADJ. assumed; counterfeit; hypothetical. Perkin Warbeck, the *supposititious* heir to the British throne, eventually confessed that he was a pretender.

suppress v. stifle; overwhelm; subdue; inhibit. Too polite to laugh in anyone's face, Roy did his best to *suppress* his amusement at Ed's inane remark.

surfeit v. satiate; stuff; indulge to excess in anything. Every Thanksgiving we are *surfeited* with an overabundance of holiday treats. also N.

surmise v. guess without actual evidence. I *surmise* that he will be late for this meeting. also N.

surmount v. overcome. I know you can *surmount* any difficulties that may stand in the way of your getting an education.

surpass v. exceed. Her SAT scores *surpassed* our expectations.

surreptitious ADJ. secret; furtive; sneaky; hidden. Hoping to discover where his mom had hidden the Christmas presents, Timmy took a *surreptitious* peek into the master bedroom closet.

surrogate N. substitute. For a fatherless child, a male teacher may become a father *surrogate.*

surveillance N. watching; guarding. The FBI kept the house under constant *surveillance* in the hope of capturing all the criminals at one time.

susceptible ADJ. impressionable; easily influenced; having little resistance, as to a disease; receptive to. Said the patent medicine man to his very *susceptible* customer: "Buy this new miracle drug, and you will no longer be *susceptible* to the common cold." susceptibility, N.

sustain v. experience; support; nourish. He *sustained* such a severe injury that the doctors feared he would be unable to work to *sustain* his growing family.

sustenance N. means of support, food, nourishment. In the tropics, the natives find *sustenance* easy to obtain because of all the fruit trees.

swelter v. be oppressed by heat. I am going to buy an air conditioning unit for my apartment as I do not intend to *swelter* through another hot and humid summer.

swerve v. deviate; turn aside sharply. The car *swerved* wildly as the driver struggled to regain control of the wheel.

swindler N. cheat. She was gullible and trusting, an easy victim for the first *swindler* who came along.

sycophant N. servile flatterer; bootlicker; yes man. Fed up with the toadies and brownnosers who made up his entourage, the star cried, "Get out, all of you! I'm sick of *sycophants*!" sycophantic, ADJ.

Word List 46 symbiosis–topography

symbiosis N. interdependent relationship (between groups, species), often mutually beneficial. Both the crocodile bird and the crocodile derive benefit from their *symbiosis;* pecking away at food particles embedded in the crocodile's teeth, the bird derives nourishment; the crocodile, meanwhile, derives proper dental hygiene. symbiotic, ADJ.

symmetry N. arrangement of parts so that balance is obtained; congruity. By definition, something lopsided lacks *symmetry.* symmetrical, ADJ.

synchronous ADJ. similarly timed; simultaneous with. We have many examples of scientists in different parts of the world who independently have made *synchronous* discoveries.

synoptic ADJ. providing a general overview; summary. The professor turned to the latest issue of *Dissertation Abstracts* for a *synoptic* account of what was new in the field. synopsis, N.

synthesis N. combining parts into a whole. Now that we have succeeded in isolating this drug, our next problem is to plan its *synthesis* in the laboratory. syntheses, PL., synthesize, v.

synthetic ADJ. artificial; resulting from synthesis. During the twentieth century, many *synthetic* products have replaced their natural counterparts. also N.

■ **tacit** ADJ. understood; not put into words. We have a *tacit* agreement based on only a handshake.

taciturn ADJ. habitually silent; talking little. The stereotypical cowboy is a *taciturn* soul, answering lengthy questions with a "Yep" or "Nope."

tactile ADJ. pertaining to the organs or sense of touch. His callused hands had lost their *tactile* sensitivity.

taint v. contaminate; cause to lose purity; modify with a trace of something bad. One speck of dirt on your utensils may contain enough germs to *taint* an entire batch of preserves. also N.

■ **tangential** ADJ. peripheral; only slightly connected; digressing. Despite Clark's attempts to distract her with *tangential* remarks, Lois kept on coming back to her main question: Why couldn't he come out to dinner with Superman and her?

tangible ADJ. able to be touched; real; palpable. Although Tom did not own a house, he had several *tangible* assets—a car, a television, a PC—that he could sell if he needed cash.

tantalize v. tease; torture with disappointment. Tom loved to *tantalize* his younger brother with candy; he knew the boy was forbidden to have it.

tantamount ADJ. equivalent in effect or value. Because so few Southern blacks could afford to pay the poll tax, the imposition of this tax on prospective voters was *tantamount* to disenfranchisement for black voters.

tantrum N. fit of petulance; caprice. The child learned that he could have almost anything if he went into *tantrums.*

tarry V. delay; dawdle. We can't *tarry* if we want to get to the airport on time.

taut ADJ. tight; ready. The captain maintained that he ran a *taut* ship.

tautological ADJ. needlessly repetitious. In the sentence "It was visible to the eye," the phrase "to the eye" is *tautological.* tautology, N.

tawdry ADJ. cheap and gaudy. He won a few *tawdry* trinkets at Coney Island.

tedium N. boredom; weariness. We hope this new Game Boy will help you overcome the *tedium* of your stay in the hospital. tedious, ADJ.

temerity N. boldness; rashness. Do you have the *temerity* to argue with me?

temper V. moderate; tone down or restrain; toughen (steel). Not even her supervisor's grumpiness could *temper* Nancy's enthusiasm for her new job.

temperament N. characteristic frame of mind; disposition; emotional excess. Although the twins look alike, they differ markedly in *temperament:* Tod is calm, but Rod is excitable.

temperate ADJ. restrained; self-controlled; moderate in respect to temperature. Try to be *temperate* in your eating this holiday season; if you control your appetite, you won't gain too much weight. Goldilocks found San Francisco's *temperate* climate neither too hot nor too cold but just right.

tempestuous ADJ. stormy; impassioned; violent. Racket-throwing tennis star John McEnroe was famed for his displays of *tempestuous* temperament.

tempo N. speed of music. I find the band's *tempo* too slow for such a lively dance.

temporal ADJ. secular; not lasting forever; limited by time. An uneasy relationship exists between the city's *temporal* and spiritual leaders.

temporize V. act evasively to gain time; avoid committing oneself. Ordered by King John to drive Robin Hood out of Sherwood Forest, the sheriff *temporized,* hoping to put off any confrontation with the outlaw band.

tenacious ADJ. holding fast. I had to struggle to break his *tenacious* hold on my arm.

tenacity N. firmness; persistence. Jean Valjean could not believe the *tenacity* of Inspector Javert. Here all Valjean had done was to steal a loaf of bread, and the inspector had pursued him doggedly for 20 years!

tendentious ADJ. having an aim; biased; designed to further a cause. This intensive and *tendentious* coverage makes it clear that some news channels are pursuing agendas of their own.

tender V. offer; extend. Although no formal charges had been made against him, in the wake of the recent scandal the mayor felt he should *tender* his resignation.

tenet N. doctrine; dogma. The agnostic did not accept the *tenets* of their faith.

tentative ADJ. hesitant; not fully worked out or developed; experimental; not definite or positive. Unsure of his welcome at the Christmas party, Scrooge took a *tentative* step into his nephew's drawing room.

■ **tenuous** ADJ. thin; rare; slim. The allegiance of our allies is held by such *tenuous* ties that we have little hope they will remain loyal.

tenure N. holding of an office; time during which such an office is held. A special recall election put an end to Gray Davis's *tenure* in office as governor of California.

tepid ADJ. lukewarm. To avoid scalding the baby, make sure the bath water is *tepid,* not hot.

termination N. end. Though the time for *termination* of the project was near, we still had a lot of work to finish before we shut up shop. terminate, V.

terminology N. terms used in a science or art. The special *terminology* developed by some authorities in the field has done more to confuse laypersons than to enlighten them.

terse ADJ. concise; abrupt; pithy. There is a fine line between speech that is *terse* and to the point and speech that is too abrupt.

thematic ADJ. relating to a unifying motif or idea. Those who think of *Moby Dick* as a simple adventure story about whaling miss its underlying *thematic* import.

theocracy N. government run by religious leaders. Though some Pilgrims aboard the Mayflower favored the establishment of a *theocracy* in New England, many of their fellow voyagers preferred a nonreligious form of government.

theoretical ADJ. not practical or applied; hypothetical. Bob was better at applied engineering and computer programming than he was at *theoretical* physics and math. While I can still think of some *theoretical* objections to your plan, you've convinced me of its basic soundness.

therapeutic ADJ. curative. Now better known for its racetrack, Saratoga Springs first gained attention for the *therapeutic* qualities of its famous "healing waters."

thespian ADJ. pertaining to drama. Her success in the school play convinced her she was destined for a *thespian* career. also N.

threadbare ADJ. worn through till the threads show; shabby and poor. The poorly paid adjunct professor hid the *threadbare* spots on his jacket by sewing leather patches on his sleeves.

thrifty ADJ. careful about money; economical. A *thrifty* shopper compares prices before making major purchases.

thrive V. prosper; flourish. Despite the impact of the recession on the restaurant trade, Philip's cafe *thrived.*

throes N. violent anguish. The *throes* of despair can be as devastating as the spasms accompanying physical pain.

throng N. crowd. *Throngs* of shoppers jammed the aisles. also V.

thwart V. baffle; frustrate. He felt that everyone was trying to *thwart* his plans and prevent his success.

tightwad N. excessively frugal person; miser. Jill called Jack a *tightwad* because he never picked up the check.

timidity N. lack of self-confidence or courage. If you are to succeed as a salesperson, you must first lose your *timidity* and fear of failure.

timorous ADJ. fearful; demonstrating fear. Shy when encountering strangers, she was too *timorous* to meet anyone's gaze.

■ **tirade** N. extended scolding; denunciation; harangue. Every time the boss holds a meeting, he goes into a lengthy *tirade,* scolding us for everything from tardiness to padding our expenses.

titanic ADJ. gigantic. *Titanic* waves beat against the majestic S.S. *Titanic,* driving it against the concealed iceberg. titan, N.

title N. right or claim to possession; mark of rank; name (of a book, film, etc.). Though the penniless Duke of Ragwort no longer held *title* to the family estate, he still retained his *title* as head of one of England's oldest families.

titular ADJ. having the title of an office without the obligations. Although he was the *titular* head of the company, the real decisions were made by his general manager.

tome N. large volume. She spent much time in the archives poring over ancient *tomes.*

topography N. physical features of a region. Before the generals gave the order to attack, they ordered a complete study of the *topography* of the region.

Word List 47 torpor–unaccountable

■ **torpor** N. lethargy; sluggishness; dormancy. Throughout the winter, nothing aroused the bear from his *torpor:* he would not emerge from hibernation until spring. torpid, ADJ.

torrid ADJ. passionate; hot or scorching. The novels published by Harlequin Romances feature *torrid* love affairs, some set in *torrid* climates.

■ **tortuous** ADJ. winding; full of curves. Because this road is so *tortuous,* it is unwise to go faster than twenty miles an hour on it.

touchstone N. stone used to test the fineness of gold alloys; criterion. What *touchstone* can we use to measure the character of a person?

touchy ADJ. sensitive; irascible. Do not discuss his acne with Archy; he is very *touchy* about it.

tout V. publicize; praise excessively. I lost confidence in my broker after he *touted* some junk bonds that turned out to be a bad investment.

toxic ADJ. poisonous. We must seek an antidote for whatever *toxic* substance he has eaten. toxicity, N.

tract N. a region of indefinite size; pamphlet. The King granted William Penn a *tract* of land in the New World.

■ **tractable** ADJ. docile; easily managed. Although Susan seemed a *tractable* young woman, she had a stubborn streak of independence that occasionally led her to defy the powers-that-be when she felt they were in the wrong. tractability, N.

traduce V. expose to slander. His opponents tried to *traduce* the candidate's reputation by spreading rumors about his past.

trajectory N. path taken by a projectile. The police tried to locate the spot from which the assassin had fired the fatal shot by tracing the *trajectory* of the bullet.

tranquillity N. calmness; peace. After the commotion and excitement of the city, I appreciate the *tranquillity* of these fields and forests.

transcendent ADJ. surpassing; exceeding ordinary limits; superior. Standing on the hillside watching the sunset through the Golden Gate was a *transcendent* experience for Lise: the sight was so beautiful it surpassed her wildest dreams. transcend, V. transcendency, N.

transcribe V. copy. When you *transcribe* your notes, please send a copy to Mr. Smith and keep the original for our files. transcription, N.

transfigure V. transform outwardly, usually for the better; change in form or aspect. Elizabeth Barrett's love for Robert Browning *transfigured* her poetry as well as transforming her life. Bely's poetic novel, *Peterburg,* is a travel fantasy set within a city that is both real and *transfigured* into a myth.

■ **transgression** N. violation of a law; sin. Although Widow Douglass was willing to overlook Huck's minor *transgressions,* Miss Watson refused to forgive and forget.

transient ADJ. momentary; temporary; staying for a short time. Lexy's joy at finding the perfect Christmas gift for Phil was *transient;* she still had to find presents for the cousins and Uncle Bob. Located near the airport, this hotel caters to the largely *transient* trade. also N.

transition N. going from one state of action to another. During the period of *transition* from oil heat to gas heat, the furnace will have to be shut off.

transitory ADJ. impermanent; fleeting. Fame is *transitory:* today's rising star is all too soon tomorrow's washed-up has-been. transitoriness, N.

transmute V. change; convert to something different. He was unable to *transmute* his dreams into actualities.

transparent ADJ. easily detected; permitting light to pass through freely. John's pride in his son is *transparent;* no one who sees the two of them together can miss it. transparency, N.

transpire V. be revealed; happen. When Austen writes the sentence "It had just *transpired* that he had left gaming debts behind him," her meaning is not that the debts had just been incurred, but that the shocking news had just leaked out.

transport N. strong emotion. Margo was a creature of extremes, at one moment in *transports* of joy over a vivid sunset, at another moment in *transports* of grief over a dying bird. also V.

transpose V. interchange; invert; rearrange in order. Because I have a mild case of dyslexia, I frequently *transpose* numbers and mistake q's for g's and b's for d's when I read too fast.

trappings N. outward decorations; ornaments. He loved the *trappings* of success: the limousines, the stock options, the company jet.

traumatic ADJ. pertaining to an injury caused by violence. In his nightmares, he kept on recalling the *traumatic* experience of being wounded in battle. trauma, N.

travail N. painful physical or mental labor; drudgery; torment. Like every other recent law school graduate she knew, Shelby hated the seemingly endless *travail* of cramming for the bar exam.

traverse V. go through or across. When you *traverse* this field, be careful of the bull.

travesty N. harshly distorted imitation; parody; debased likeness. Phillips's translation of *Don Quixote* is so inadequate and clumsy that it seems a *travesty* of the original.

treatise N. scholarly work treating a subject systematically and thoroughly. The Ed School professors study pedagogical theories and write *treatises* and argue, as scholars will, but none of them can teach a class of middle schoolers to save his life.

trek N. travel; journey. The tribe made their *trek* further north that summer in search of game. also V.

tremor N. trembling; slight quiver. She had a nervous *tremor* in her right hand.

trenchant ADJ. forceful and vigorous; cutting. With his *trenchant* wit, reviewer Frank Rich cut straight to the heart of the matter, panning a truly dreadful play.

trepidation N. fear; nervous apprehension. As she entered the office of the dean of admissions, Sharon felt some *trepidation* about how she would do in her interview.

tribulation N. distress; suffering. After all the trials and *tribulations* we have gone through, we need this rest.

tribute N. tax levied by a ruler; mark of respect. The colonists refused to pay *tribute* to a foreign despot.

trifling ADJ. trivial; unimportant. Why bother going to see a doctor for such a *trifling,* everyday cold? trifle, N.

trigger V. set off. John is touchy today; say one word wrong and you'll *trigger* an explosion.

trilogy N. group of three works. Having read the first two volumes of Philip Pullman's *trilogy,* Alison could hardly wait to read volume three.

trite ADJ. hackneyed; commonplace. The *trite* and predictable situations in many television programs turn off many viewers, who, in turn, turn off their sets.

trivia N. trifles; unimportant matters. Too many magazines ignore newsworthy subjects and feature *trivia.*

■ **truculence** N. aggressiveness; ferocity. Tynan's reviews were noted for their caustic attacks and general tone of *truculence.* truculent, ADJ.

truism N. self-evident truth. Many a *truism* is summed up in a proverb; for example, "Marry in haste, repent at leisure."

truncate V. cut the top off. The top of the cone that has been *truncated* in a plane parallel to its base is a circle.

tumult N. commotion; riot; noise. She could not make herself heard over the *tumult* of the mob.

turbulence N. state of violent agitation. Warned of approaching *turbulence* in the atmosphere, the pilot told the passengers to fasten their seat belts.

turmoil N. great commotion and confusion. Lydia running off with a soldier! Mother fainting at the news! The Bennet household was in *turmoil.*

turncoat N. traitor. The British considered Benedict Arnold a loyalist; the Americans considered him a *turncoat.*

turpitude N. depravity. A visitor may be denied admittance to this country if she has been guilty of moral *turpitude.*

tutelage N. guardianship; training. Under the *tutelage* of such masters of the instrument, she made rapid progress in playing the violin.

tutelary ADJ. protective; pertaining to a guardianship. Each village, no matter how small, boasts dozens of shrines to the local *tutelary* or guardian spirits.

tycoon N. wealthy leader. John D. Rockefeller was a prominent *tycoon.*

tyranny N. oppression; cruel government. Frederick Douglass fought against the *tyranny* of slavery throughout his entire life.

tyro N. beginner; novice. The young lawyer, a *tyro* less than a year out of law school, had never tried a capital case; he was not incompetent, merely too inexperienced to represent his client successfully.

ubiquitous ADJ. being everywhere; omnipresent. That Christmas "The Little Drummer Boy" seemed *ubiquitous:* Justin heard the tune everywhere he went. ubiquity, N.

ulterior ADJ. situated beyond; unstated and often questionable. You must have an *ulterior* motive for your behavior, since there is no obvious reason for it.

ultimate ADJ. final; not susceptible to further analysis. Even though Jill and her husband discuss major purchases together, as the primary wage earner she has control over finances and makes the *ultimate* decision.

ultimatum N. last demand; warning. Since they have ignored our *ultimatum,* our only recourse is to declare war.

umbrage N. resentment; anger; sense of injury or insult. She took *umbrage* at his remarks and stormed away in a huff.

unaccountable ADJ. inexplicable; unreasonable or mysterious. I have taken an *unaccountable* dislike to my doctor: "I do not love thee, Doctor Fell. The reason why, I cannot tell."

Word List 48 unalloyed–vainglorious

unalloyed ADJ. pure; unmixed. Raising children, although rewarding, is not an *unalloyed* delight; it definitely has its ups and downs.

unanimity N. complete agreement. We were surprised by the *unanimity* with which our proposals were accepted by the different factions. unanimous, ADJ.

unassailable ADJ. not subject to question; not open to attack. Penelope's virtue was *unassailable;* while she waited for her husband to come back from the war, no other guy had a chance.

unassuaged ADJ. unsatisfied; not soothed. Tensions grew as the protesters, *unassuaged* by the dean's promise to investigate campus police mistreatment of minority students, surrounded the administration building.

unassuming ADJ. modest. He is so *unassuming* that some people fail to realize how great a man he really is.

unbridled ADJ. violent. She had a sudden fit of *unbridled* rage.

uncanny ADJ. strange; mysterious. You have the *uncanny* knack of reading my innermost thoughts.

unconscionable ADJ. unscrupulous; excessive. She found the loan shark's demands *unconscionable* and impossible to meet.

uncouth ADJ. outlandish; clumsy; boorish. Most biographers portray Lincoln as an *uncouth* and ungainly young man.

underlying ADJ. fundamental; lying below. The *underlying* cause of the student riot was not the strict curfew rule but the moldy cafeteria food. Miss Marple seems a sweet little old lady at first, but an iron will *underlies* that soft and fluffy facade.

undermine V. weaken; sap. The recent corruption scandals have *undermined* many people's faith in the city government.

underscore V. emphasize. Addressing the jogging class, Kim *underscored* the importance to runners of good nutrition.

unearth V. dig up. When they *unearthed* the city, the archeologists found many relics of an ancient civilization.

unearthly ADJ. not earthly; unnatural; weird. The director's brooding presence imposed an *unearthly* silence on the cast. No one dared speak.

unequivocal ADJ. plain; obvious. My answer to your proposal is an *unequivocal* and absolute "No."

unerringly ADV. infallibly. My teacher *unerringly* pounced on the one typographical error in my essay.

unexceptionable ADJ. not offering any basis for criticism; entirely acceptable. Objecting to Jack's lack of a respectable family background, Lady Bracknell declared that Cecily could marry only a man of *unexceptionable* lineage and character.

unfaltering ADJ. steady; resolute. Her voice *unfaltering,* her gaze clear, 12-year-old Kumari read out a list of demands that children of the community had drawn up for implementation.

unfeigned ADJ. genuine; real. She turned so pale that I am sure her surprise was *unfeigned.*

unfettered ADJ. liberated; freed from chains. What can a weakened university system do to preserve the spirit of open and *unfettered* academic inquiry? This is the problem confronting academia today. unfetter, V.

ungainly ADJ. awkward; clumsy; unwieldy. "If you want to know whether Nick's an *ungainly* dancer, check out my bruised feet," said Nora. Anyone who has ever tried to carry a bass fiddle knows it's an *ungainly* instrument.

uniformity N. sameness; monotony. At *Persons* magazine, we strive for *uniformity* of style; as a result, all our writers wind up sounding exactly alike. uniform, ADJ.

unilateral ADJ. one-sided. Relations between the United States and Israel suffered as a result of Israel's *unilateral* decision to invade Lebanon in 1982.

unimpeachable ADJ. blameless and exemplary. "Caesar had always admired men of *unimpeachable* honesty, such as Cicero and Cato, and liked to work with them. Unfortunately men of *unimpeachable* honesty tended to look askance at some of Caesar's methods." (Rose Williams)

uninhibited ADJ. unrepressed. The congregation was shocked by her *uninhibited* laughter during the sermon.

unintimidating ADJ. unfrightening. Though Phil had expected to feel overawed when he met Joe Montana, he found the world-famous quarterback friendly and *unintimidating.*

unique ADJ. without an equal; single in kind. You have the *unique* distinction of being the first student whom I have had to fail in this course.

unison N. unity of pitch; complete accord. The choir sang in *unison.*

universal ADJ. characterizing or affecting all; present everywhere. At first, no one shared Christopher's opinions; his theory that the world was round was met with *universal* disdain.

unkempt ADJ. disheveled; uncared for in appearance. Jeremy hated his neighbor's *unkempt* lawn: he thought its neglected appearance had a detrimental effect on neighborhood property values.

unmitigated ADJ. unrelieved or immoderate; absolute. After four days of *unmitigated* heat, I was ready to collapse from heat prostration. The congresswoman's husband was an *unmitigated* jerk: not only did he abandon her, but also he took her campaign funds!

unobtrusive ADJ. inconspicuous; not blatant. Reluctant to attract notice, the governess took a chair in a far corner of the room and tried to be as *unobtrusive* as possible.

unpalatable ADJ. distasteful; disagreeable. "I refuse to swallow your conclusion," she said, finding his logic *unpalatable.*

unprecedented ADJ. novel; unparalleled. For a first novel, Margaret Mitchell's book *Gone with the Wind* was an *unprecedented* success.

unprepossessing ADJ. unattractive. During adolescence many attractive young people somehow acquire the false notion that their appearance is *unprepossessing.*

unravel V. disentangle; solve. With equal ease Miss Marple *unraveled* tangled balls of yarn and baffling murder mysteries.

unrequited ADJ. not reciprocated. Suffering the pangs of *unrequited* love, Olivia rebukes Cesario for his hardheartedness.

unruly ADJ. disobedient; lawless. The only way to curb this *unruly* mob is to use tear gas.

unsavory ADJ. distasteful; morally offensive. His work as a private detective brings Spenser into contact with some pretty *unsavory* characters with shady pasts.

unscathed ADJ. unharmed. They prayed he would come back from the war *unscathed.*

unseemly ADJ. unbecoming; indecent; in poor taste. When Seymour put whoopee cushions on all the seats in the funeral parlor, his conduct was most *unseemly.*

unsightly ADJ. ugly. Although James was an experienced emergency room nurse, he occasionally became queasy when faced with a particularly *unsightly* injury.

unstinting ADJ. generous; openhanded; liberal. The philanthropist was noted for his *unstinting* support of the arts.

untenable ADJ. indefensible; not able to be maintained. Wayne is so contrary that, the more *untenable* a position is, the harder he'll try to defend it.

unwarranted ADJ. unjustified; groundless; undeserved. Your assumption that I would accept your proposal is *unwarranted,* sir; I do not want to marry you at all. We could not understand Martin's *unwarranted* rudeness to his mother's guests.

unwieldy ADJ. awkward; cumbersome; unmanageable. The large carton was so *unwieldy* that the movers had trouble getting it up the stairs.

unwitting ADJ. unintentional; not knowing. She was the *unwitting* tool of the swindlers.

unwonted ADJ. unaccustomed. He hesitated to assume the *unwonted* role of master of ceremonies at the dinner.

upbraid V. severely scold; reprimand. Not only did Miss Minchin *upbraid* Ermengarde for her disobedience, but also she hung her up by her braids from a coatrack in the classroom.

uproarious ADJ. marked by commotion; extremely funny; very noisy. The *uproarious* comedy hit *Ace Ventura: Pet Detective* starred Jim Carrey, whose comic mugging provoked gales of *uproarious* laughter from audiences coast to coast.

upshot N. outcome. The *upshot* of the rematch was that the former champion proved that he still possessed all the skills of his youth.

urbane ADJ. suave; refined; elegant. The courtier was *urbane* and sophisticated. urbanity, N.

usurp V. seize another's power or rank. The revolution ended when the victorious rebel general succeeded in his attempt to *usurp* the throne. usurpation, N.

utopia N. ideal place, state, or society. Fed up with this imperfect universe, Don would have liked to run off to Shangri-la or some other imaginary *utopia.* utopian, ADJ.

■ **vacillate** V. waver; fluctuate. Uncertain which suitor she ought to marry, the princess *vacillated,* saying now one, now the other. vacillation, N.

vacuous ADJ. empty; lacking in ideas; stupid. The candidate's *vacuous* remarks annoyed the audience, who had hoped to hear more than empty platitudes. vacuity, N.

vagary N. caprice; whim. Without income from Social Security to depend on, senior citizens will be even more vulnerable to the *vagaries* of the stock market than they are today.

vagrant ADJ. stray; random. He tried to study, but could not collect his *vagrant* thoughts.

vagrant N. homeless wanderer. Because he was a stranger in town with no visible means of support, Martin feared he would be jailed as a *vagrant.* vagrancy, N.

vainglorious ADJ. boastful; excessively conceited. Louis XIV consumed the revenues of the state in warlike enterprises, and a million men were sacrificed to his *vainglorious* ambition.

Word List 49 valedictory–vituperative

valedictory ADJ. pertaining to farewell. I found the *valedictory* address too long; leave-taking should be brief. also N.

valid ADJ. logically convincing; sound; legally acceptable. You're going to have to come up with a better argument if you want to convince me that your reasoning is *valid.*

validate V. confirm; ratify. It is important that researchers both describe their methodology accurately and *validate* it using independent data.

valor N. bravery. He received the Medal of Honor for his *valor* in battle.

vapid ADJ. dull and unimaginative; insipid and flavorless. "*Bor*-ing!" said Cher, as she suffered through yet another *vapid* lecture about Dead White Male Poets.

vaunted ADJ. boasted; bragged; highly publicized. This much *vaunted* project proved a disappointment when it collapsed.

veer V. change in direction. After what seemed an eternity, the wind *veered* to the east and the storm abated.

vegetate V. live in a monotonous way. I do not understand how you can *vegetate* in this quiet village after the adventurous life you have led.

vehement ADJ. forceful; intensely emotional; with marked vigor. Alfred became so *vehement* in describing what was wrong with the Internal Revenue Service that he began jumping up and down and gesticulating wildly. vehemence, N.

velocity N. speed. The train went by at considerable *velocity.*

venal ADJ. capable of being bribed. The *venal* policeman accepted the bribe offered him by the motorist whom he had stopped for speeding.

vendetta N. blood feud. The rival mobs engaged in a bitter *vendetta.*

vendor N. seller. The fruit *vendor* sold her wares from a stall on the sidewalk.

veneer N. thin layer; cover. Casual acquaintances were deceived by his *veneer* of sophistication and failed to recognize his fundamental shallowness.

venerable ADJ. deserving high respect. We do not mean to be disrespectful when we refuse to follow the advice of our *venerable* leader.

■ **venerate** V. revere. In Tibet today, the common people still *venerate* their traditional spiritual leader, the Dalai Lama.

venial ADJ. forgivable; trivial. When Jean Valjean stole a loaf of bread to feed his starving sister, he committed a *venial* offense.

venom N. poison; hatred. Bitten on his ankle by a *venomous* snake, the cowboy contortionist curled up like a pretzel and sucked the *venom* out of the wound.

vent N. small opening; outlet. The wine did not flow because the air *vent* in the barrel was clogged.

vent V. express; utter. He *vented* his wrath on his class.

venture V. risk; dare; undertake a risk. Fearing to distress the actors, the timorous reviewer never *ventured* to criticize a performance in harsh terms. also N.

venturesome ADJ. bold. A group of *venturesome* women were the first to scale Mt. Annapurna.

venue N. location. The attorney asked for a change of *venue;* he thought his client would do better if the trial were held in a less conservative county.

■ **veracious** ADJ. truthful. I can recommend him for this position because I have always found him *veracious* and reliable. veracity, N.

veracity N. truthfulness. Trying to prove Hill a liar, Senator Spector repeatedly questioned her *veracity*. veracious, ADJ.

verbalize V. put into words. I know you don't like to talk about these things, but please try to *verbalize* your feelings.

verbatim ADV. word for word. He repeated the message *verbatim*. also ADJ.

verbiage N. pompous array of words. After we had waded through all the *verbiage*, we discovered that the writer had said very little.

■ **verbose** ADJ. wordy. We had to make some major cuts in Senator Foghorn's speech because it was far too *verbose*. verbosity, N.

verge N. border; edge. Madame Curie knew she was on the *verge* of discovering the secrets of radioactive elements. also V.

verisimilar ADJ. probable or likely; having the appearance of truth. Something *verisimilar* is very similar to the truth, or at least seems to be.

verisimilitude N. appearance of truth; likelihood. Critics praised her for the *verisimilitude* of her performance as Lady Macbeth. She was completely believable.

veritable ADJ. actual; being truly so; not false or imaginary. At his computer, Pavel is a *veritable* wizard, creating graphic effects that seem magical to programmers less skilled than he.

verity N. quality of being true; lasting truth or principle. Do you question the *verity* of Kato Kaelin's testimony about what he heard the night Nicole Brown Simpson was slain? To the skeptic, everything was relative: there were no eternal *verities* in which one could believe.

vernacular N. living language; natural style. Cut out those old-fashioned "thee's" and "thou's" and write in the *vernacular*. also ADJ.

versatile ADJ. having many talents; capable of working in many fields. She was a *versatile* athlete, earning varsity letters in basketball, hockey, and track. versatility, N.

verve N. enthusiasm; liveliness. Hamilton maintains that the comic characters of Aristophanes and Shakespeare share a fundamental resemblance, for they possess "the same tremendous energy and *verve* and vitality; the same swinging, swashbuckling spirit; the same exuberant, effervescing flow of language; the same rollicking, uproarious fun."

vestige N. trace; remains. We discovered *vestiges* of early Indian life in the cave.

vex N. annoy; distress. Please try not to *vex* your mother; she is doing the best she can.

■ **viable** ADJ. practical or workable; capable of maintaining life. The plan to build a new baseball stadium, though missing a few details, is *viable* and stands a good chance of winning popular support.

vicarious ADJ. acting as a substitute; done by a deputy. Many people get a *vicarious* thrill at the movies by imagining they are the characters on the screen.

vicissitude N. change of fortune. Humbled by life's *vicissitudes*, the last emperor of China worked as a lowly gardener in the palace over which he had once ruled.

vie V. contend; compete. Politicians *vie* with one another, competing for donations and votes.

vigilant ADJ. watchfully awake; alert to spot danger. From the battlement, the *vigilant* sentry kept his eyes open for any sign of enemy troops approaching. vigilance, N.

vigor N. active strength. Although he was over seventy years old, Jack had the *vigor* of a man in his prime. vigorous, ADJ.

vignette N. picture; short literary sketch. The *New Yorker* published her latest *vignette*.

vilify V. slander. Waging a highly negative campaign, the candidate attempted to *vilify* his opponent's reputation. vilification, N.

vindicate V. clear from blame; exonerate; justify or support. The lawyer's goal was to *vindicate* her client and prove him innocent on all charges. The critics' extremely favorable reviews *vindicate* my opinion that *The Madness of King George* is a brilliant movie.

vindictive ADJ. out for revenge; malicious. Divorce sometimes brings out a *vindictive* streak in people; when Tony told Tina he was getting a divorce, she poured green Jell-O into his aquarium and turned his tropical fish into dessert.

virtual ADJ. effectively so, though not strictly or completely so. The lack of any management policy preventing Atlantic halibut from being overharvested resulted in the *virtual* commercial extinction of the fish.

virtue N. goodness; moral excellence; good quality. A *virtue* carried to extremes can turn into something resembling vice; humility, for example, can degenerate into servility and spinelessness.

virtuoso N. highly skilled artist. The child prodigy Yehudi Menuhin grew into a *virtuoso* whose *virtuosity* on the violin thrilled millions. virtuosity, N.

virulent ADJ. extremely poisonous; hostile; bitter. Laid up with a *virulent* case of measles, Vera blamed her doctors because her recovery took so long. In fact, she became quite *virulent* on the subject of the quality of modern medical care. virulence, N.

visceral ADJ. felt in one's inner organs. She disliked the *visceral* sensations she had whenever she rode the roller coaster.

■ **viscous** ADJ. sticky, gluey. Melted tar is a *viscous* substance. viscosity, N.

visionary ADJ. produced by imagination; fanciful; mystical. She was given to *visionary* schemes that never materialized. also N.

vital ADJ. vibrant and lively; critical; living; breathing. The *vital*, highly energetic first aid instructor stressed that it was *vital* in examining accident victims to note their *vital* signs.

vitiate V. spoil the effect of; make inoperative. The state's interest in effective crime-fighting should never *vitiate* the citizens' Bill of Rights.

vitriolic ADJ. corrosive; sarcastic. Such *vitriolic* criticism is uncalled for.

■ **vituperative** ADJ. abusive; scolding. He became more *vituperative* as he realized that we were not going to grant him his wish.

Word List 50 vivacious–zenith

vivacious ADJ. lively or animated; sprightly. A very bubbly and *vivacious* woman, with a radiant smile, Julie never had any difficulty making new friends.

vociferous ADJ. clamorous; noisy. The crowd grew *vociferous* in its anger and threatened to take the law into its own hands.

vogue N. popular fashion. Jeans became the *vogue* on many college campuses.

■ **volatile** ADJ. changeable; explosive; evaporating rapidly. The political climate today is extremely *volatile*: no one can predict what the electorate will do next. Maria Callas's temper was extremely *volatile*: the only thing you could predict was that she would blow up. Acetone is an extremely *volatile* liquid: it evaporates instantly. volatility, N.

volition N. act of making a conscious choice. According to Henry James, the things that the children thought to do spontaneously, of their own *volition*, were the most important ingredients of their education.

voluble ADJ. fluent; glib; talkative. An excessively *voluble* speaker suffers from logorrhea: he continually runs off at the mouth! volubility, N.

voluminous ADJ. bulky; large. A caftan is a *voluminous* garment; the average person wearing one looks as if he or she is draped in a small tent.

voracious ADJ. ravenous. The wolf is a *voracious* animal, its hunger never satisfied.

vouchsafe V. grant condescendingly; guarantee. Maintaining that power was only *vouchsafed* to the man who dared to stoop and pick it up, Raskolnikov attempted to justify his murder of the pawnbroker.

vulnerable ADJ. susceptible to wounds. His opponents could not harm Achilles, who was *vulnerable* only in his heel. vulnerability, N.

waffle V. speak equivocally about an issue. When asked directly about the governor's involvement in the savings and loan scandal, the press secretary *waffled*, talking all around the issue.

waive V. give up temporarily; yield. Sparing Shylock's life, the Duke offers to *waive* the republic's claim to half of the moneylender's fortune.

wanderlust N. strong longing to travel. Don't set your heart on a traveling man. He's got too much *wanderlust* to settle down.

wane V. decrease in size or strength; draw gradually to an end. To *wane* is the opposite of to wax or increase in size. When lit, does a wax candle *wane*?

wangle V. wiggle out; fake. She tried to *wangle* an invitation to the party.

wanton ADJ. unrestrained; willfully malicious; unchaste. Pointing to the stack of bills, Sheldon criticized Sarah for her *wanton* expenditures. In response, Sara accused Sheldon of making an unfounded, *wanton* attack.

■ **warranted** ADJ. justified; authorized. Before the judge issues the injunction, you must convince her this action is *warranted*.

warranty N. guarantee; assurance by seller. The purchaser of this automobile is protected by the manufacturer's *warranty* that he will replace any defective part for five years or 50,000 miles.

■ **wary** ADJ. very cautious. The spies grew *wary* as they approached the sentry.

wax V. increase; grow. With proper handling, her fortunes *waxed* and she became rich.

waylay V. ambush; lie in wait. They agreed to *waylay* their victim as he passed through the dark alley going home.

wean V. accustom a baby not to nurse; give up a cherished activity. He decided he would *wean* himself away from eating junk food and stick to fruits and vegetables.

weather V. endure the effects of weather or other forces. He *weathered* the changes in his personal life with difficulty, as he had no one in whom to confide.

■ **welter** N. turmoil; bewildering jumble. The existing *welter* of overlapping federal and state claims cries out for immediate reform.

welter V. wallow. At the height of the battle, the casualties were so numerous that the victims *weltered* in their blood while waiting for medical attention.

wheedle V. cajole; coax; deceive by flattery. She knows she can *wheedle* almost anything she wants from her father.

whet V. sharpen; stimulate. The odors from the kitchen are *whetting* my appetite; I will be ravenous by the time the meal is served.

whiff N. puff or gust (of air, scent, etc.); hint. The slightest *whiff* of Old Spice cologne brought memories of George to her mind.

■ **whimsical** N. capricious; fanciful. In *Mrs. Doubtfire*, the hero is a playful, *whimsical* man who takes a notion to dress up as a woman so that he can look after his children, who are in the custody of his ex-wife. whimsy, N.

willful ADJ. intentional; headstrong. Donald had planned to kill his wife for months; clearly, her death was a case of deliberate, *willful* murder, not a crime of passion committed by a hasty, *willful* youth unable to foresee the consequences of his deeds.

wily ADJ. cunning; artful. She is as *wily* as a fox in avoiding trouble.

wince V. shrink back; flinch. The screech of the chalk on the blackboard made her *wince*.

windfall N. fallen fruit; unexpected lucky event. This huge tax refund is quite a *windfall*.

wistful ADJ. vaguely longing; sadly pensive. With a last *wistful* glance at the happy couples dancing in the hall, Sue headed back to her room to study for her exam.

withdrawn ADJ. introverted; remote. Rebuffed by his colleagues, the initially outgoing young researcher became increasingly *withdrawn*.

wither V. shrivel; decay. Cut flowers are beautiful for a day, but all too soon they *wither*.

withhold V. refuse to give; hold back. The tenants decided to *withhold* a portion of the rent until the landlord kept his promise to renovate the building.

withstand V. stand up against; successfully resist. If you can *withstand* all the peer pressure in high school to cut classes and goof off, you should survive college in fine shape.

witless ADJ. foolish; idiotic. If Beavis is a half-wit, then Butthead is totally *witless*.

witticism N. witty saying; wisecrack. I don't mean any criticism, but your last supposed *witticism* really hurt my feelings.

wizardry N. sorcery; magic. Merlin amazed the knights with his *wizardry*.

woe N. deep, inconsolable grief; affliction; suffering. Pale and wan with grief, Wanda was bowed down beneath the burden of her *woes*.

worldly ADJ. engrossed in matters of this earth; not spiritual. You must leave your *worldly* goods behind you when you go to meet your Maker.

wrangle V. quarrel; obtain through arguing; herd cattle. They *wrangled* over their inheritance.

wrath N. anger; fury. She turned to him, full of *wrath*, and said, "What makes you think I'll accept lower pay for this job than you get?"

wreak V. inflict. "The Category 5 storm *wreaked* havoc, doing more than $20 billion in damage and making it by far the costliest hurricane ever in United States history." (*BoatUS*)

wrench V. pull; strain; twist. She *wrenched* free of her attacker and landed a powerful kick to his kneecap.

wrest V. pull away; take by violence. With only ten seconds left to play, our team *wrested* victory from their grasp.

writ N. written command issued by a court. The hero of Leonard's novel is a process server who invents unorthodox ways of serving *writs* on reluctant parties.

writhe V. twist in coils; contort in pain. In *Dances with Snakes*, the snake dancer wriggled sinuously as her boa constrictor *writhed* around her torso.

wry ADJ. twisted; with a humorous twist. We enjoy Dorothy Parker's verse for its *wry* wit.

xenophobia N. fear or hatred of foreigners. When the refugee arrived in America, he was unprepared for the *xenophobia* he found there.

yen N. longing; urge. She had a *yen* to get away and live on her own for a while.

yield N. amount produced; crop; income on investment. An experienced farmer can estimate the annual *yield* of his acres with surprising accuracy. also V.

yield V. give in; surrender. The wounded knight refused to *yield to* his foe.

yoke V. join together, unite. I don't wish to be *yoked* to him in marriage, as if we were cattle pulling a plow. also N.

zany ADJ. crazy; comic. I can watch the Marx brothers' *zany* antics for hours.

zeal N. eager enthusiasm. Wang's *zeal* was contagious; soon all his fellow students were busily making posters, inspired by his ardent enthusiasm for the cause. zealous, ADJ.

■ **zealot** N. fanatic; person who shows excessive zeal. Though Glenn was devout, he was no *zealot;* he never tried to force his religious beliefs on his friends.

zenith N. point directly overhead in the sky; summit. When the sun was at its *zenith*, the glare was not as strong as at sunrise and sunset.

PART 3

Analytical Writing: Tactics, Strategies, and Practice

INTRODUCTION TO PART 3

What sort of test is the analytical writing test? First and foremost, it is not a multiple-choice test. It is a performance test—you have to write two analytical essays in one hour.

The analytical writing section of the GRE is the most substantive of the three sections on the tests. This section is organized in two parts. In Part 1, "Present Your Perspective on an Issue," you have 30 minutes to write an essay expressing your point of view on a particular issue. You will be given a quotation that states an opinion about an issue; you will probably write a better essay if the quotation "grabs" you, but you can write a strong paper even if the topic seems unappealing at first.

Your job is to take a stand and to support it, drawing on your own experiences and on your readings to come up with examples that reinforce your argument. It does not matter what stand you take; there is no "correct" position, no one true answer. Many different approaches can work. You can agree completely with the quotation's point of view or you can dispute it absolutely. You can disagree with some aspects of the quote, but agree with others. What matters is how you present your case.

Part 2 of the analytical writing section asks you to perform a different but complementary task. In Part 2, "Analyze an Argument," you have 30 minutes to write an essay critiquing the logical soundness of an argument. You will be given one short passage in which an author makes a claim and backs it up, giving reasons that may well be flawed. You get no choice of passages to analyze; you must work with whatever passage comes up on your screen.

This time your job is not to advocate a particular point of view. This is not the moment for you to agree or disagree with the author; it is the moment for you to weigh the validity of the author's reasoning. Your approach is analytical and expository, not argumentative or persuasive. It is your task to examine carefully what the author offers as evidence. You will find it helpful to note what the author claims explicitly, and also to note what she or he assumes (not necessarily justifiably!).

If you study the tactics and work through the practice exercises in the following chapter, and take full advantage of the study materials on the GRE's website, *www.gre.org*, you will be well prepared for the analytical writing section of the GRE and should feel confident in your ability to write high-scoring essays.

7 Analytical Writing

THE GOAL

What do the GRE readers want? In essence, a well-reasoned and supported argument that responds to the specific task instructions with clear organization (structure), fluency, and command of the conventions of standard written English. This chapter covers both what you need to do on the day of the test and what you can do now to prepare.

TEST DAY

The Game Plan

The Analytical Writing portion of the GRE requires you to write two essays. The first is your analysis of an issue of universal concern, and the second is your evaluation of an argument. You have 30 minutes to complete each analytical-writing task. To earn a top score, you need to produce a smooth 400–700 word essay with solid content, coherent organization, and few, if any, mechanical errors. You can do it. Just follow Barron's 6-Step Approach.

The Issue Essays and Argument Essays follow slightly different game plans. Study both plans.

6 STEPS TO A POLISHED ISSUE ESSAY

Each issue topic is presented in a 1–2 sentence statement commenting on a subject of general concern. This statement makes a claim (or claims). Your essay may support, refute, or qualify the views expressed in the statement. Whatever you write, however, must be relevant to the issue under discussion, and you must support your viewpoint with data—reasons and examples derived from your studies, experience, and reading.

GRE readers score your essay, evaluating it based on its effectiveness in the following areas:

- Presenting an **argument** that responds to the specific task instructions
- Providing reasoning and/or examples that **support** its thesis
- Having **structure** that is focused and well organized
- Expressing ideas with clarity and **fluency**
- Displaying command of the **conventions** of standard written English

Here is the 6-step plan you should use in writing your Issue Essay. Suggested times are approximate.

1 Minutes	Break It Down
2 Minutes	Brainstorm
3 Minutes	Outline
15 Minutes	Speed-write
5 Minutes	Open and Close
4 Minutes	Review and Refine

Step One: Break Down the Task Instructions (no more than 1 minute)

Each of the Issue Task prompts includes two parts:

1. the topic itself
2. specific task instructions

There are 200 possible topics, but only 6 different sets of task instructions. You can review them all on the ETS website at *https://www.ets.org/gre/revised_general/prepare/analytical_writing/issue/*. Let's look at a version of one.

> Compose an essay that presents your opinion on the policy presented, explicating your rationale for this opinion. As you build and provide evidence for your argument, you must take into account the likely effects of applying the policy and describe the impact these potential effects have on your argument.

When you first read the prompt, pay special attention to the specific elements of the task instructions. If you are taking the test on paper, you may find it helpful to circle or underline each of the required elements of the task.

> Compose an essay that presents your opinion on the policy presented, explicating your rationale for this opinion. As you build and provide evidence for your argument, you must take into account the likely effects of applying the policy and describe the impact these potential effects have on your argument.

If you are taking the test online, list the required elements on scrap paper, as shown below:

- give opinions/views on the policy and explain rationale/reasoning
- consider effects of applying/implementing policy
- describe potential effects that shape the argument

Once you are clear on the task, you can begin to analyze the topic itself. In the case of the preceding task instructions, as you begin to think about the topic, you know that you need to be thinking about what would happen if the policy in the topic were implemented. Later, when writing and reviewing your essay, you should check off each element to ensure that you address it.

It is critical that you address each of the elements of the task instructions, rather than simply giving your opinion on the issue. **Essays that are on topic but fail to clearly address *each* of the elements of the task instructions will receive scores of 3 or lower, regardless of how well they are written.**

Step Two: Begin to Brainstorm (2 minutes)

Let the issue statement and task instructions trigger your brainstorming. Grab your pencil and sum up the claim the author is making on your scrap paper.

ISSUE TASK PROMPT

> **"Public schools should increase graduation requirements in Science, Technology, Engineering, and Math and decrease requirements for classes in the Arts."**
>
> ***Compose an essay that presents your opinion on the policy presented, explicating your rationale for this opinion. As you build and provide evidence for your argument, you must take into account the likely effects of applying the policy and describe the impact these potential effects have on your argument.***

Quick Summation

"Increase STEM, decrease Art."

Now that you're clear about the author's point, start scribbling. Write down as many reasons that support or weaken the author's claim as you possibly can. Be sure to write both reasons for and reasons against. Don't worry right now if any of these reasons strike you as flimsy or implausible; you can always cut them later or find ways to strengthen them if you need to. Just note them down on your scrap paper, together with examples supporting both sides of the issue. For examples, try to focus on what would happen, good or bad, if the policy were adopted, because the prompt specifically asks for this. Other than that, try to stay loose; this is your time for free association, not self-censorship.

Step Three: Organize Your Outline (3 minutes)

The first step in writing your outline is deciding where you stand on the issue. Each of the 6 specific sets of Issue Task instructions asks for your opinion on a statement, recommendation, claim, view, or policy. Your essay must clearly express the extent to which you agree or disagree with that statement, recommendation, claim, view, or policy. Look over the ideas you jotted down while brainstorming and make a quick decision as to which way you want to go based on the strength of the reasons and examples you have listed. You may agree or disagree, and you may do so strongly or with caveats. Do not over-think. Make a decision and move on.

Once you have decided upon a position, stick with it. Don't second-guess yourself or worry about making the best possible argument. There is no "right" answer.

Now that you know what you are setting out to prove, use the best reasons and examples from your brainstorming in creating your outline. As you do this, refer to the elements of the specific task instructions. Be sure to address them all. In the preceding example, the task instructions require that you do **three** things: (1) discuss your views on the policy and explain your reasoning; (2) consider the consequences of implementing the policy; **and** (3) explain how these consequences shape your position.

Your goal should be to write a quick, thumbnail outline that will keep you focused and ensure that you cover everything required by the Issue Task. You can write your outline in the GRE word processing program or on scratch paper, whichever works best for you. You may want to use symbols in order to save time. Avoid giving too much detail in the outline. Save it for your essay.

Here is a sample thumbnail outline for the Issue Task above.

> Th: ↓ Arts ed. → ↓ competitiveness b/c
>
> 1. ↓ designers (Nike, Apple, Ford)
> 2. ↓ content (films, music)
> 3. ↓ HS grads (less skilled)

The thumbnail outline above is spare both because time is short and because you do not require much detail to remind yourself of the arguments and examples that are in your head. Below, you will find an expanded version of the thumbnail outline to help you decipher it. On test day, write a thumbnail outline. ***Always keep your outline as short as possible without sacrificing function.***

Thesis: Policy is counterproductive because it will make American industry less competitive.

I. Decreasing Arts education will harm industry because industry needs designers.

   Examples—Shoes (Nike), cars (Ford), tech (Apple)

II. Decreasing Arts education will harm industry because industry needs content.

   Examples—cell phones/computers, streaming media need music, movies, etc.

III. Decreasing Arts education may harm industry because having fewer arts classes may cause some students to drop out, more workers less skilled.

   Reasoning—students who don't enjoy academic classes may stay in school for drama, band, etc.

Step Four: Write the Body of Your Essay (15 minutes)

You already know your general line of reasoning, the direction you want your essay to take. You need to spend the bulk of your time writing the body of your essay.

- As rapidly as you can, type up your points, writing two to three sentences to flesh out each reason or example in your outline.
- Do not worry if time pressure doesn't allow you to deal with every point you dreamed up.
- Start with a reason or example that you can easily put into words, preferably your best, most compelling reason or example.

Given the 30-minute time limit you're working under, you want to be sure to cover your best points right away, before you run out of time. During the revision period, you can always rearrange your paragraphs, putting the strongest paragraph immediately before the conclusion, so that your essay builds to a solid climax (if you are taking the computer-delivered test).

Step Five: Now Write Your Opening and Summary Paragraphs (5 minutes)

It may seem strange to write your introductory paragraph after you have written the body of your essay, but it is a useful technique. Many writers launch into writing the introduction only to find, once they have finished the essay, that their conclusion is unrelated to, or even contradicts, what they had written in the introduction. By writing the introduction after you have composed the bulk of the essay, you will avoid having to rewrite the introduction to support the conclusion that you *actually* reached, rather than the conclusion that you *expected* to reach.

This is one area in which the technology of the online GRE will greatly assist you. If you are taking the GRE as a hard-copy (paper) exam, you will need to save space on your page to insert your introduction, guessing roughly how much room you will need. If, however, you are taking the computer-delivered GRE, you can simply go back to the top of the page and begin writing the introduction.

While this technique is helpful to many, not everyone finds it comfortable. Experiment with it when writing practice essays and use it if it works for you.

What, then, should your introduction include? Your introductory paragraph should both introduce the topic on which you are writing and clearly indicate your thesis or point. While in some situations it is strategic (or simply more graceful) to reveal your thesis fully only in the conclusion, the GRE is probably not one of those situations. Clarity is key; you do not want to risk leaving your readers uncertain of your line of reasoning or under the impression that you have strayed from the point.

For a top score, your introductory paragraph should also provide some context for the argument. The GRE readers appear to favor introductions that place the topic in a historical or social context, rather than those that simply discuss it in a contextual vacuum. The two introductory paragraphs that follow demonstrate the difference between these two types of introduction.

Introduction with Context
Western society tends to glorify the individual over the group. Our social and political philosophy, based on John Stuart Mill's faith that progress is fostered by competition within the marketplace of ideas, encourages people, as the Apple computer commercial says, to "think different." This cult of the individual overemphasizes the importance of being different and fails to recognize that a healthy person will be both a conformist and an individualist. Ironically, self-conscious dedication to nonconformity will ultimately result in extreme slavishness to custom.

Introduction without Context
A healthy individual is neither a conformist nor an individualist; he is both a conformist and an individualist. Balancing conformity and individualism allows people to follow their interests and passions without wasting time on issues that do not interest them, while a self-conscious dedication to nonconformity ultimately results in an extreme slavishness to custom.

One last note on introductions: While you may have been taught in school that a paragraph must comprise at least three sentences, the GRE readers are not concerned about the length of your introductory paragraph. In fact, they appear willing to grant the highest score to essays whose introduction is only one sentence long. This does not mean that they favor essays with single-sentence introductions, only that they do not discriminate against them. If your introduction makes your thesis clear, it has done its job.

Your conclusion should, however, be longer than one sentence. It should restate your thesis and summarize the arguments that you make in its support. You should mention your supporting arguments in the same order in which they appear in the body of the essay. This technique underscores the organization of your essay, giving it a predictable and orderly appearance.

Step Six: Review and Refine (5 minutes)

The first step in wrapping up your essay is ensuring that it addresses all of the elements in the specific task instructions. Review the items that you circled/underlined or listed and check your essay to be sure that you have addressed them. Check off the elements as you go.

Once you have confirmed that you have met the requirements of the task instructions, you can concentrate on style.

Expert writers often test their work by reading it aloud. In the exam room, you cannot read out loud. However, when you read your essay silently, take your time and listen with your inner ear to how it sounds. Read to get a sense of your essay's logic and rhythm. Does one sentence flow smoothly into the next? Would they flow more smoothly if you were to add a transition word or phrase (*therefore, however, nevertheless, in contrast, similarly*)? Do the sentences follow a logical order? Is any key idea or example missing? Does any sentence seem out of place? How would things sound if you cut out that awkward sentence or inserted that transition word?

Take a minute to act on your response to hearing your essay. If it sounded to you as if a transition word was needed, insert it. If it sounded as if a sentence should be cut, delete it. If it sounded as if a sentence was out of place, move it. Trust your inner ear, but do not attempt to do too much. Have faith in your basic outline for the essay. You have neither the need nor the time to revise everything.

Now, think of yourself as an editor, not an auditor. Just as you need to have an ear for problems of logic and language, you also need to have an eye for errors that damage the text. Take a minute to look over your essay for problems in spelling and grammar. From your English classes you should know which words and grammatical constructions have given you trouble in the past. See whether you can spot any of these words or constructions in your essay. Correct any glaring errors that you find. Do not worry if you fail to catch every mechanical error or awkward phrase. The readers understand that 30 minutes doesn't give you enough time to produce polished, gemlike prose. They won't penalize you for an occasional mechanical glitch.

Here is an example of a solid essay responding to the sample Issue Task prompt.

> Open any newspaper and you are likely to find a report of a politician decrying the failure of American industry and education. According to them, we are "falling behind" our foreign competitors, and our schools are not training the skilled workers that American industry needs in order to compete. Almost invariably, the solution proposed by the politician in question is to require our schools to increase their focus on job readiness and jettison "wasteful and unnecessary" programs, especially in the Arts. The recommendation that our schools decrease graduation requirements in the Arts in favor of increasing them in Science,

Technology, Engineering, and Math (STEM) is, however, a poor one, because following it is likely to cause the reverse of its intended effect.

Those who would sacrifice Arts education in the name of American competitiveness fail to recognize that the Arts are, for a number of reasons, critical to the success of American industry in the global market. First, all products require designers, from those who design the look and feel of the product itself to those who design its packaging and marketing materials. An artist stands behind every new car or shoe design and behind every user interface. America's most successful companies, from Nike to Ford to Apple, all rely on artists to make their products attractive, usable, and popular. If we were to sacrifice Arts education to increase the time spent studying STEM, American businesses would be less competitive because there would be a shortage of those all-important designers.

An additional reason that decreasing the focus on Arts education will hurt American competitiveness is that the Arts are necessary to provide content. Much of the new technology that is driving our economy, from computers to cell phones to streaming media, is dedicated to providing content in new ways. The delivery mechanism may be new, but the need for literature, music, and movies remains the same. Without artists producing quality material, there is no need for the technology used to view or listen to it. The iPhone, for example, would be a far less attractive product if there were not exciting new music to listen to on it.

Finally, even if the Arts had no direct application to industry, their presence in the school curriculum helps connect many students to their schools. Not all students love Mathematics, Science, History, and other academic subjects. For many of these students, Arts classes are the bright spot in an otherwise dull and trying day. They are their motivation for getting out of bed in the morning, the thing that bonds them to their school, and the reason that they are able to make it through to graduation. Decreasing our commitment to the Arts would surely cause some students to leave school prematurely, leaving them less prepared to be productive members of the workforce.

The policy of sacrificing Arts education in order to focus resources on more "practical" subjects is a terrible mistake that will ultimately cause the very problem that it is trying to address. The Arts are practical, and they play a key role in the success of American industry. The importance of the Arts to industry is the reason that the call for STEM education is being replaced by a focus on STEAM—Science, Technology, Engineering, Arts, and Math. If anything, our emphasis on the Arts should be increased, rather than decreased.

6 STEPS TO A POWERFUL ARGUMENT ESSAY

You have 30 minutes to complete the argument-analysis task. To earn a top score, you need to produce a smooth critique with solid content, coherent organization, and few, if any, mechanical errors.

In this task, you are asked to critique the line of reasoning of an argument given in a brief passage, clearly pointing out that argument's strengths and weaknesses and supporting your position with reasons and examples. This task is intended to test both your ability to evaluate the soundness of a position and your ability to get your point across to an academic audience.

*You should **not**, however, present your personal views on the topic.* Your job is to analyze the elements of an argument, not to support or contradict that argument.

GRE readers score your essay, evaluating it based on its effectiveness in the following areas:

- Pinpointing and evaluating the elements of the **argument** at issue
- Providing **support** for the essay's main points
- Expressing ideas in a clear and **organized** manner
- Expressing ideas with clarity and **fluency**
- Displaying command of the **conventions** of standard written English

As with the Issue Essay, follow a 6-step approach in dealing with the Argument Essay.

Here is the 6-step plan you should use in writing your Argument Essay. Suggested times are approximate.

1 Minutes	Break It Down
2 Minutes	Spot the Claims
2 Minutes	Question the Claims
18 Minutes	Speed-write
5 Minutes	Open and Close
5 Minutes	Review and Refine

Step One: Break Down the Task Instructions (no more than 1 minute)

Each of the Argument Essay prompts includes two parts:

1. the topic itself
2. specific task instructions.

There are 200 possible topics, but only eight different sets of task instructions. You can review them all on the ETS website at *https://www.ets.org/gre/revised_general/prepare/analytical_writing/argument/*. Let's look at one:

> Compose an essay that identifies and considers the assumptions (implicit and/or explicit) on which the argument is based. The essay must clarify the importance of these assumptions to the argument and explain the impact on the argument's validity should the assumptions be faulty.

When you first read the prompt, pay special attention to the specific elements of the task instructions. If you are taking the test on paper, you may find it helpful to circle or underline each of the required elements of the task. For example:

> Compose an essay that identifies and considers the assumptions (implicit and/or explicit) on which the argument is based. The essay must clarify the importance of these assumptions to the argument and explain the impact on the argument's validity should the assumptions be faulty.

If you are taking the test online, list the required elements on scrap paper or the GRE word processor, as shown here:

- Identify and consider implicit/explict assumptions
- Clarify importance of assumptions to argument
- Explain impact on argument if assumptions faulty

It is critical that you address each of the elements of the task instructions rather than simply giving your opinion of the argument. **Essays that are on topic but fail to clearly address each of the elements of the task instructions will receive scores of 3 or lower, regardless of how well they are written.**

Step Two: Identify the Claims (2 minutes)

Before you can identify the flaws in an Argument Essay prompt, you must have a clear understanding of the claims it makes. After reading the prompt once for general understanding, examine it more carefully, one sentence at a time. As you do this, use your scrap paper to write a list of the claims made in the prompt. List the claims in the order in which they are made. GRE argument prompts typically contain at least three flaws in the author's reasoning or use of evidence.

Here is an example of the notes you might take if you were writing on the following topic.

ARGUMENT TASK PROMPT

> The following appeared in an article in the Real Estate section of the *Springfield Bugle*.
>
> Springfield is a great place to live. Every year, hundreds of former city dwellers move to Springfield, spurning the sophisticated cultural offerings of the urban setting for Springfield's more relaxed atmosphere. Despite the attractions of big city life, Springfield's new citizens choose their home for its rural setting and small-town atmosphere. If Springfield wants to continue to attract these newcomers, it must adopt aggressive planning regulations to keep out chain stores, fast food establishments, bars, and other businesses more appropriate to an urban setting.
>
> *Compose an essay that identifies and considers the assumptions (implicit and/or explicit) on which the argument is based. The essay must clarify the importance of these assumptions to the argument and explain the impact on the argument's validity should the assumptions be faulty.*

OVERALL POINT: Springfield must control the growth of certain types of businesses in order for it to remain attractive to newcomers.

CLAIM ONE: People come to Springfield to get away from sophisticated city culture and to have a relaxed atmosphere.

CLAIM TWO: People come to Springfield for its rural, small-town atmosphere.

CLAIM THREE: Keeping chain stores, bars, and fast food restaurants out of Springfield will maintain its attractiveness to newcomers.

Step Three: Question the Claims (2 minutes)

Once you have identified the claims made in the prompt, you need to assess the strength of those claims. In this case, you would be wise to focus on the assumptions on which the argument is based, because that is an explicit requirement of the task instructions. In most cases, their shortcomings will be apparent to you. If, however, you are having trouble figuring out the flaws in a given claim, try applying a few handy questions to it.

1. **GROUNDS.** Is there any **evidence** to support the claim?

   The first two claims in the prompt on page 217 are assertions. Though the author might have survey data to support her claim that newcomers move to Springfield to escape urban culture and enjoy a more relaxed, rural, small-town atmosphere, she presents no such data in her argument.

2. **WARRANT.** Does the evidence provided **support** the claim?

   Could other factors cause the effect about which the author is writing? In the situation described in the prompt above, there are many possible reasons to choose to move to Springfield. The author gives no reason for readers to believe that she has correctly identified the cause of Springfield's popularity.

   Does the author assert a general rule based on an overly small sample? For example, if the author of the Springfield argument based her claims about why newcomers generally move to Springfield on the comments of a single new neighbor, her claims would lack adequate support. They would be unwarranted.

   Does the author compare comparable groups? If, for example, the author of the Springfield argument attempted to support her claims about why newcomers move to Springfield with surveys of residents who moved to Springfield twenty years ago, she would have no basis to make claims about people who have moved to Springfield more recently.

Step Four: Write the Body of Your Critique, Following the Order of the Claims Made in the Prompt (18 minutes)

Organization is an important part of writing a clear and coherent essay. The simplest and best approach is to discuss the claims made in the prompt in the order in which they are presented. There is no reason to try anything tricky or fancy. The test-makers have given you an order. Use it. Using the structure of the prompt will save you time. It will also discourage you from writing a discursive essay that wanders unpredictably from one idea to another. High scores go to test-takers who write clear and well-reasoned essays. Creativity in this context is more likely to confuse your readers than to earn you extra points.

As we recommended in the previous section on the Issue Essay, spend the bulk of your time writing the body of your critique. Get those ideas onto the screen or paper, allotting two to three sentences to each claim to flesh it out.

Step Five: Then Add Your Introductory and Summary Paragraphs (5 minutes)

While following the structure of the prompt is a handy way to organize the body of your critique, you still need to write an introduction and conclusion to your essay. Your introductory paragraph should provide a general overview of the criticisms you have made in the body of your essay. Do not give too much detail in the introduction; it is where you introduce, rather than explain, your analysis. *Present your points in the introduction in the same order in which they appear in the body of the essay.* By doing so, you will give your reader a clear idea of where you are going and what you intend to demonstrate.

As with the Issue Essay, the GRE readers are not concerned about the length of your introductory paragraph. They appear willing to grant the highest score to some essays whose introduction is only one sentence long. This does not mean that they favor essays with single-sentence introductions, only that they do not discriminate against them. If your introduction makes your thesis clear, it has done its job.

Your conclusion should, however, be longer than one sentence. *In your conclusion, you should briefly restate the main points you have made in the body of your critique and suggest one or two ways the author could have made his or her argument more persuasive.* Follow the same order that you used in the body of your essay. This technique underscores the organization of your essay, giving it a predictable and orderly appearance.

Step Six: Review and Refine (5 minutes)

Once again, our recommendation is to first listen, then look. Begin by reading your essay silently, listening with your inner ear to how it sounds. Ask yourself whether one sentence flows smoothly into the next and whether any transition words might help the flow. Consider whether any key idea or example might be missing or any sentence seems out of place. Do not make any major changes. Just tweak things slightly to improve your essay's sound and sense.

Now, cast an eye over your essay, looking for mechanical errors. You know the sorts of grammatical constructions and spelling words that create problems for you. See whether you can spot any of them in your essay. Correct any errors that jump out at you.

Here is an example of an argument critique that follows the organization of the prompt:

> Springfield may well be a great place to live, but the author of this article makes a number of unsubstantiated assumptions about the attributes that make Springfield an attractive home. Based on these assumptions, the author makes a bold proposal regarding zoning and city planning. Though this proposal is intended to maintain the positive attributes that bring new residents to Springfield, it may fail to achieve this goal or even have the reverse effect of worsening the quality of life in the town.
>
> The author's first mistake is to assume that she knows why hundreds of former city dwellers move to Springfield each year. She claims that in moving to Springfield, people are rejecting the culture of the city in favor of Springfield's more relaxed suburban lifestyle. This is a classic case of confusing correlation with causation. While Springfield may, in fact, be more relaxed than the city, and while the city may have a more sophisticated culture than Springfield, it does not follow that those who move from the city to Springfield are choosing relaxation over sophistication. Perhaps they are moving to Springfield for entirely different reasons. High urban property values, with their concomitant high urban property taxes, may be driving potential homeowners to less expensive suburban areas. People may also be moving to Springfield for better schools or a lower crime rate.
>
> The claim that people move to Springfield for its small-town atmosphere and rural setting is similarly unsubstantiated. Yes, Springfield is a small, rural suburb.

It does not follow, however, that this is why new residents move to Springfield. They could be moving to Springfield for any of the reasons mentioned above, or for any number of other reasons.

The conclusion that Springfield must keep out businesses that are common in urban areas if it is to remain an attractive community is unsupported. If new residents are really being drawn to Springfield by something other than the ways in which it is different from a big city, there is no reason to believe that keeping Springfield from growing city-like will make it more attractive. In fact, if people move to Springfield in spite of its lack of big-city amenities and because of its lower cost (or some other factor), the addition of big-city businesses may make Springfield more attractive to newcomers.

Ironically, if the author is correct that Springfield's relaxed, small-town feel is what attracts new residents, making Springfield attractive to former city dwellers may, in the long run, destroy Springfield's positive attributes. After all, for how long can Springfield maintain this small-town atmosphere, if hundreds of newcomers are encouraged to move there each year? Ultimately, the author of this article appears to seek the impossible—a quiet, small town with sustained, robust population growth.

Despite the flaws in this author's argument, she may be correct in her assessment of why newcomers move to Springfield. She could strengthen her argument by documenting its most important premise with data. If, for example, she provided survey results from newcomers indicating that they did indeed come to Springfield to escape urban culture and to enjoy a more relaxed, rural, small-town atmosphere, her argument would be far more persuasive. Were this the case, her call for more restrictive zoning might be justified.

PRIOR TO TEST DAY

There is much that you can do in the weeks and months leading up to the test to prepare yourself to perform well on the Analytical Writing portion of the GRE. This work is presented in four sections:

1. General Analytical Writing Testing Tactics
2. Issue Essay Testing Tactics
3. Argument Essay Testing Tactics
4. Practice Exercises

TESTING TACTICS

Preparing for the Analytical Writing Test

Understand How the Essays Are Scored

In order to earn the highest possible score for your essays, it helps to understand how they will be scored.

Two readers will judge your GRE analytical essays, awarding each essay a grade ranging from 0 to 6, with 6 being the highest possible score. The powers-that-be then calculate your analytical writing score by taking the average of your four grades and rounding up the result to the nearest half-point. If one reader awarded your Issue Essay a 5 and your Argument Essay a 4, while the other reader gave both your essays 4s, you'd come out with a score of 4.25, rounded up to 4.5.

You probably have a sense of what score you need in order to be accepted by the graduate school of your choice. If you're seeking admission to Harvard's Ph.D. program in history, you're clearly aiming for a 5.5 or 6. If you're aiming for a graduate program in a field that favors number-crunching over essay-writing—mathematics or electrical engineering, for instance—you may not need to aim so high. But, however high a score you're seeking, you want to come out of the essay-writing section looking good. And to do that, you have to know what the GRE readers are looking for.

Readers will score your essays based on how strong they are in the following areas: Argument, Support, Structure, Fluency, and Conventions.

ARGUMENT

Each analytical writing task has two parts:

1. a topic
2. specific task instructions

The first requirement is that you must make an argument about the topic.

- For the ISSUE task you should agree or disagree with the topic statement. You may also take a middle position, arguing that the statement is true in some, but not all, cases.
- For the ARGUMENT task you should make a claim about the strength or weakness of the argument presented. The question in this case is ***not*** whether you agree with the argument, but rather how strong it is and what additional information would be needed in order to assess it.

The task instructions tell you HOW to respond to the topic. ETS uses 14 different sets of task instructions in the Analytical Writing section of the GRE. Each topic is paired with one of the 14 sets. Pay careful attention to those instructions. You ***must*** follow them.

It is not enough to agree or disagree with the argument you are analyzing, or to take a position on the issue assigned. You ***must*** do so in the manner outlined in the task instructions.

- If the task instructions request that you identify the evidence you would need in order to assess the argument, you must identify that evidence.
- If the task instructions ask you to examine the assumptions on which the argument is based, you must identify and assess those assumptions.
- If the task instructions require you to address the strongest examples that could be used against your analysis, you must identify and respond to those examples.

SUPPORT

Every argument requires support of some kind. An effective essay will provide strong reasoning and compelling examples in making its case. Avoid confusing claims and evidence (examples). "Taking practice exams increases students' test scores" is a claim. "After I started taking practice tests prior to the final exam, my average score increased from 78 percent to 85 percent" is an example that supports that claim.

You do not need any special expertise on the topic in order to support your argument. Examples from history, current events, and even from personal experience are just fine. Remember that this part of the GRE is about assessing your analytical writing ability, not your knowledge of the essay's subject matter.

STRUCTURE

Structure is coherent arrangement. In this case, it is your ability to arrange your thoughts in order, following a clear game plan. The paragraph is the basic unit of composition; the beginning of each new paragraph serves to alert readers that they are coming to a new step in the development of the subject. One paragraph leads to the next, drawing readers on to the essay's conclusion.

State your thesis clearly. You can introduce it in your first paragraph, or you can build up to it, stating it in your conclusion. ETS accepts either approach.

Outlines help. If you jump from subject to subject within a single paragraph, if you leave out critical elements, if you mis-order your points or never manage to state exactly what you mean, then you need to practice outlining your position briefly before you express it in essay form.

FLUENCY

Fluency is smoothness and ease in communicating. In this case, it is your ability to set down a given number of words within a limited period of time. If you freeze on essay examinations, writing only a sentence or two when whole paragraphs are called for, then you need to practice letting your words and ideas flow.

Literary fluency, however, involves more than just the number of words you type. The readers tend to award their highest grades to test-takers who use language well, employing a variety of sentence types and demonstrating a command of vocabulary. If you invariably use short, simple sentences, you need to practice constructing more complex ones. If you have a limited vocabulary, you need to expand it, working with Barron's GRE Flash Cards and other tools to learn the precise meaning of each new word you employ.

LET IT FLOW!

GRE essay readers look for quantity as well as quality. Work on building up your typing speed.

CONVENTIONS OF ENGLISH

The conventions of English are the part of English that most students hate—grammar, spelling, punctuation, and word usage. In this case, it is your ability to produce grammatically correct sentences in standard written English. If your English compositions used to come back to you with the abbreviations "frag" or "agr" or "sp" scribbled all over the margins, then you need to practice reading through your papers to catch any technical mistakes.

There are literally hundreds of handbooks available that will help you handle the mechanics of writing essays. Strunk and White's manual, *The Elements of Style*, provides clear, concise advice, as does William Zinsser's *On Writing Well.* Other good reference tools are *The Harbrace College Handbook*, Edward Johnson's *Handbook of Good English*, and, for the complete grammarphobe, Patricia O'Conner's aptly named *Woe Is I.*

NOTE: Unless you are someone who can't type two words in a row without making a spelling error, do not worry about spelling and punctuation mistakes. The GRE readers generally ignore them. However, if you make so many errors that it becomes difficult for the readers to make sense of what you have written, they will lower your score accordingly.

The rubrics provided on pages 42–44, and again after of each of the Model Tests, will allow you to see what you are aiming for in each of the five areas just described. There are also scored sample essays that demonstrate how the rubrics can function.

TACTIC 2

Take Advantage of the GRE's Free Study Aids

TIP

Download *PowerPrep II*—It's *Free*!

PowerPrep II is software that allows you to practice taking the computer-delivered GRE. The software includes two full practice tests from the authors of the GRE. You can download it immediately from the GRE website, *www.gre.org*.

PowerPrep II is especially helpful because it uses the same GRE word processing software that you will have to use to write your essays when you take your computer-delivered test. It is a very basic word processor that lets you perform very basic tasks. You can insert text, delete text, and move text around using a cut-and-paste function. You can also undo an action you've just performed.

NOTE: The GRE word processing software has a quirk—it has no copy function. You cannot simply copy and paste.

- To move text: cut text & paste elsewhere
- To copy and paste: cut text and paste twice—once in its original location, and a second time in its new location.

The cut text remains on your "clipboard" after pasting, so you can paste it multiple times.

Familiarize yourself with this word processing software so that, on the test date, you'll be comfortable using it. This software simulates actual testing conditions and presents actual essay topics. Practice writing your essays while you keep one eye on the clock. You need to develop a sense of how much time to allow for thinking over your essay and how much time to set aside for the actual writing.

TACTIC

Practice Taking Shortcuts to Maximize Your Typing Efficiency

Slow and steady is not the way to go, at least not when you're taking the analytical writing test on the GRE. Fast typists have a decided advantage here. Unfortunately, you cannot turn yourself into a typing whiz overnight. However, you can use your time right now to practice some shortcuts to help you on the day of the test.

First, using the GRE's own word processing program (which comes when you download *PowerPrep II*), you can **practice using the cut-and-paste function** (described in Tactic 2) **to copy** phrases that you want to repeat in your essay. In an Argument Essay, for example, you might want to reuse such phrases as "the author makes the following assumption" or "another flaw in the author's argument is that . . . ." In an Issues Essay, if you are running out of time and still haven't written your opening and summary paragraphs (which we advise you to compose after you've written the body of your text), you can write just your concluding paragraph, cutting and pasting it to both the beginning and end of the essay. Then, in a few seconds, you can change the wording of that initial paragraph so that it works as an introduction, not as a conclusion. How does that cliché about essay-writing go? "Tell them what you're going to tell them, tell them it, then tell them what you've told them." It's easy to do so, using cut-and-paste.

Remember that to copy a chunk of text, you must first cut it and then paste it back in its original spot and then re-paste it where you want it reproduced. The process may feel cumbersome at first, but by practicing with the word processor you will quickly build up speed copying using cut-and-paste.

Second, you can also **practice abbreviating** multiword names or titles. Consider the following argument topic or prompt:

The parent of a Collegiate High student included these remarks in a letter to the education page of the *Oakville Bugle*.

If you look closely at Oakville's two leading private high schools—Collegiate Preparatory High School and Exover Academy—you must conclude that Collegiate is unmistakably superior to the Academy. Collegiate has a staff of 35 teachers, many of them with doctorates. In contrast, Exover has a staff of 22, several holding only a bachelor's degree. Moreover, Collegiate's average class size is 12, compared to Exover's average class size of 20; Collegiate's students receive much more individual attention than their peers do at the Academy. Students graduating from Collegiate High also are accepted by better universities than Exover graduates are: 40% of last year's Collegiate senior class went on to Ivy League colleges, compared to only 15% of Exover's senior class. Thus, if you want your children to get individual attention from their high school teachers and would like them to get into good colleges, you should send them to Collegiate Prep.

Compose an essay that identifies the questions that must be answered before reaching a conclusion about whether the advice and the argument supporting it make sense. In writing your essay you should describe the impact that the answers to these questions would have on your assessment of the advice.

In critiquing this argument, you can follow the letter writer's example and refer to Exover Academy and Collegiate Preparatory High School simply as Exover and Collegiate. You can also refer to Collegiate by its initials. Be sure, however, to identify the institution fully when you first mention it, inserting its initials in parentheses: Collegiate Preparatory High School (CPHS). Then, your readers will know what you mean by future references to CPHS. Similarly, instead of typing out "for example," you can substitute the abbreviation "e.g."

TACTIC

Acquaint Yourself with the Actual Essay Topics You Will Face

The GRE has posted its entire selection of potential essay topics on its website. The pool of issue topics can be found at *www.ets.org/gre/revised_general/prepare/analytical_writing/issue/pool.* The pool of argument topics can be found at *www.ets.org/gre/revised_general/prepare/analytical_writing/argument/pool.*

There is no point in trying to memorize these topics or in trying to write an essay for each one. There are well over 200 items in the pool of issue topics alone. There is, however, a real point to exploring these potential topics and to noting their common themes.

We suggest that you print out both topic pools so that you can review their contents at leisure. When you do so, you will see that the issue topics fall naturally into groups with common themes. Some of these themes involve contrasts:

- Tradition versus innovation and modernization
- Competition versus cooperation
- Present social needs versus future social needs
- Conformity versus individualism
- Imagination versus knowledge
- Pragmatism versus idealism

Many of the issue topics pose a simple question:

- What makes an effective leader?
- What are education's proper goals?
- How does technology affect our society?
- Why should we study history (or art, literature, etc.)?
- What is government's proper role (in education, art, wilderness preservation, and so on)?
- How do we define progress?

Others ask you to question conventional wisdom:

- Is loyalty always a virtue?
- Is "moderation in all things" truly good advice?
- Does conformity always have a negative impact?

Go over these recurrent questions and themes. They relate to all the areas of the college curriculum: political science, sociology, anthropology, economics, history, law, philosophy, psychology, the physical sciences, the fine arts, literature, even media studies. Whether or not you have any special knowledge of a suggested topic's subject area, you most likely have opinions about it. You probably have class notes on it as well.

If you find yourself stymied by these topics, you may want to review old notebooks from your general education courses. Skim through them to refresh your memory of classroom discussions of typical GRE issues. In the course of flipping through these old notes, you're very likely to come across examples that you might want to note for possible use in writing the Issue Essay.

TACTIC

Make Use of Transitions or Signal Words to Point the Way

Assume that typical GRE readers must read hundreds of Issue Essays in a day. You want to make the readers' job as easy as possible, so that when they come to your essay they breathe a sigh of relief, saying, "Ah! Someone who knows how to write!"

One way to make the readers' job easy is to lead them by the hand from one idea to the next, using signal words to point the way. The GRE readers like it when test-takers use signal words (transitions); in their analyses of sample essays scoring a 5 or 6, they particularly mention the writers' use of transitions as a good thing.

Here are a few helpful transitions. Practice using them precisely: you earn no points for sticking them in at random!

SUPPORT SIGNAL WORDS

Use the following words or abbreviations to signal to the reader that you are going to support your claim with an illustration or example:

e.g., (short for Latin *exemplia gratia*, for the sake of an example)

for example
for instance
let me illustrate
such as

Use these words to signal to the reader that you are about to add an additional reason or example to support your claim:

additionally	furthermore	likewise
also	in addition	moreover

CONTRAST SIGNAL WORDS

Use the following words to signal a switch of direction in your argument:

although	in contrast	on the other hand
but	in spite of	rather than
despite	instead of	still
even though	nevertheless	unlike
except	not	yet
however	on the contrary	

CAUSE AND EFFECT SIGNAL WORDS

Use the following words to signal the next step in your line of reasoning or the conclusion of your argument:

accordingly	in conclusion	therefore
consequently	in short	thus
for this reason	in summary	when ... then
hence	so ... that	

See Tactic 15 for a discussion of how signal words can be helpful to you in the second of your two writing tasks, the argument critique.

Preparing for the Issue Essay

TACTIC

7 Familiarize Yourself with the Issue Essay Task Instructions

Though there are 200 possible topics in the Issue Essay topic pool, there are only six sets of specific task instructions for those topics. GRE essay readers require that you not only adhere to the *subject* of the assigned essay topic, but that you also *meet each of the requirements found in the task instructions.* Making a strong argument on the assigned topic is not enough to receive a high score; you must do so in the manner described in the task instructions.

The list below includes versions of all six of the possible GRE Issue Essay task instructions, followed by a short explanation of each task and how you should approach it. The *exact* wording of the instructions can be found on the ETS website, located at *https://www.ets.org/gre/revised_general/prepare/analytical_writing/issue/*.

1. *Compose an essay that identifies how greatly you concur (or differ) with the statement provided, describing in detail the rationale for your argument. As you build and provide evidence for your argument, include examples that demonstrate circumstances in which the statement could (or could not) be valid. Be sure to explain the impact these examples have on your argument.*

   These task instructions have three elements. (1) Your essay must identify how strongly you agree or disagree with the topic statement. Are you in full agreement or disagreement? Do you agree or disagree, but grudgingly, or with exceptions? An essay that is unclear about the *extent* of your agreement or disagreement cannot receive the highest score. (2) Your essay must include examples that demonstrate *how* the statement might or might not hold true. Taking a position on the topic statement without demonstrating how it might or might not hold true in practice will not fully meet the requirement of the task instructions. (3) Your essay must explain how these examples affect your position on the topic statement. Do they support or moderate your position? You need to be clear about the *purpose* that the example plays in your argument.

2. *Compose an essay that identifies how greatly you concur (or differ) with the recommendation provided and describe the rationale for your argument. As you build and provide evidence for your argument, include examples that demonstrate circumstances in which implementing the recommendation might (or might not) be beneficial. Be sure to explain the impact these examples have on your argument.*

   These task instructions have three elements. (1) Your essay must identify how strongly you agree or disagree with the recommendation made in the topic statement. Are you in full agreement or disagreement? Do you agree or disagree, but grudgingly, or with exceptions? An essay that is unclear about the *extent* of your agreement or disagreement cannot receive the highest score. (2) Your essay must explain the reasoning for the position you take. Do you disagree because the consequences of following the recommendation would be harmful or costly? Do you agree because following the recommendation would be efficient or promote fairness? Your essay must not only specify that you agree or disagree, but *why* you do so. (3) Your essay must include *examples* of circumstances in which following the recommendation would be advantageous or disadvantageous. Without concrete examples to prove your point, your essay cannot receive a high score.

3. *Compose an essay that identifies how greatly you concur (or differ) with the claim provided. As you build and provide evidence for your argument, you must respond to the strongest counterarguments (or examples) that might undermine your argument.*

   These task instructions have three elements. (1) Your essay must identify how strongly you agree or disagree with the claim made in the topic statement. Are you in full agreement or disagreement? Do you agree or disagree, but grudgingly, or with exceptions? An essay that is unclear about the *extent* of your agreement or disagreement cannot receive the highest score. (2) Your essay must include the strongest reasons or examples that could be used *against* your position. This is an unusual requirement, and if you only provide examples that *support* your position, you cannot receive a high score. (3) Your essay must *address* the counterexamples it describes. In other words, it must explain why the examples that challenge your position do not fully undermine your argument. If your essay fails to do this, you will not have sufficiently proven your argument, and your essay cannot receive the highest score.

4. *Compose an essay that identifies which of the two views provided is closest to your own, explaining why you have reached this conclusion. As you build and clarify your argument, be sure to examine both of the views provided.*

These task instructions have three elements. (1) These task instructions are used when the topic includes two conflicting views. Your essay must indicate which of the two views you most agree with. The task instructions do not leave you room to agree or disagree equally with both views. (2) Your essay must explain the reasoning for the position you take. Do you favor one view over the other because it is more fair or practical? Is one of the views more familiar to you? Your essay must not only specify the view you most agree with, but *why* you agree with it. (3) Your essay must discuss *both* of the views presented in the prompt. An essay that focuses solely on the view with which you most agree cannot receive a high score.

5. *Compose an essay that identifies how greatly you concur (or differ) with the claim provided and its rationale.*

These task instructions have two elements. (1) Your essay must identify how strongly you agree or disagree with the claim made in the topic statement. Are you in full agreement or disagreement? Do you agree or disagree, but grudgingly, or with exceptions? An essay that is unclear about the *extent* of your agreement or disagreement cannot receive the highest score. (2) Your essay must discuss and take a position on the reason on which the claim is based. Whether that reason is explicitly stated or merely implied, your essay must identify the reason behind the claim and agree or disagree with it. An essay that does not address the reason supporting the claim cannot receive a high score.

6. *Compose an essay that presents your opinion on the policy presented, explicating your rationale for this opinion. As you build and provide evidence for your argument, you must take into account the likely effects of applying the policy and describe the impact these potential effects have on your argument.*

These task instructions have three elements. (1) Your essay must state your views on the policy presented in the topic statement. It is not enough to describe the policy or explain its purpose or execution; you must take a position on the policy. (2) Your essay must explain your reasoning. *Why* do you take this position on the policy? Is it beneficial or harmful? Is it too costly or impractical? Is it a good compromise? (3) Your essay must describe the *consequences* of implementing the policy. An essay that does not discuss the potential consequences of implementing the policy cannot receive a high score.

TACTIC

8 Break Down the Topic Statement Into Separate Areas to Consider

Here is an example of an issue topic, modeled on actual topics found in the GRE pool.

"The end does justify the means,
if the end is truly meritorious."

Break down the statement into its component elements. Look for key words and phrases. First, consider ***ends*** or goals. These can be divided into personal goals—taking a trip to a foreign country, for example, or providing for one's family—and societal goals—preserving an endangered species, for example, or protecting the health of the elderly.

Next, consider what ***means*** you might use to reach these goals. If you have to spend your savings and take a leave of absence from college to travel abroad, thereby postponing or potentially jeopardizing your eventual graduation, then perhaps your goal is insufficiently meritorious to justify the means. If, however, your goal is not simply to take a pleasure trip but to use the time abroad working in a refugee camp, the worthiness of the cause you are serving might well outweigh the expense and the risk of your not graduating. Similarly, while most people would agree that preserving an endangered species is a worthwhile societal goal, the cost to society of doing so can occasionally outweigh the benefits: think about the societal cost in ruined crops and lost income to Klamath Basin farmers when the government cut off water to their farms in an effort to preserve endangered coho salmon and sucker fish, an action later criticized as unnecessary by the National Academy of Sciences.

Finally, consider the phrase ***truly meritorious***. The author is begging the question, qualifying his assertion to make it appear incontrovertible. But what makes an action meritorious? Even more, what makes an action truly meritorious? How do you measure merit? Whose standards do you use?

Breaking down the topic statement into its components helps start you thinking analytically about the subject. It's a good way to begin composing your Issue Essay.

TACTIC

9 Familiarize Yourself with the Elements of a Sound Argument

According to British rhetorical theorist and philosopher Stephen Toulmin, a sound argument requires three elements: CLAIM, GROUNDS (or data), and WARRANT. Your claim is your thesis; it is an overall statement of the argument you hope to prove. The grounds for your argument are your evidence. Grounds for an argument can include statistics, examples, and even anecdotes. The warrant is the connection between the claim and the grounds. It is an explanation of how the grounds justify the claim.

CLAIM (THESIS): Historians and other social scientists are as useful to society as are biochemists and engineers because society's ills cannot be cured by technological progress alone.

Once you have settled on your claim, look to your brainstorming for the arguments that support it. Each of these arguments requires its own claim, grounds, and warrant.

1. **CLAIM:** War is not prevented by technological progress.
   GROUNDS: Invention of gunpowder, nuclear weapons
   WARRANT: Technological progress is driven by war; in fact, technology tends to make war more destructive.

2. **CLAIM:** Historians and social scientists can prevent, or at least discourage, war through their understanding of why wars have occurred in the past.
   GROUNDS: Treaty of Versailles, Marshall Plan
   WARRANT: An understanding of history can allow us to design policies that encourage peace.

3. **CLAIM:** Technological progress does not prevent poverty.
   GROUNDS: Industrial Revolution, sweatshops
   WARRANT: Technology changes the distribution of wealth, increasing extreme poverty as it increases wealth for some.

4. **CLAIM:** Historians and social scientists can prevent poverty through economic policy.
   GROUNDS: New Deal, Social Security
   WARRANT: Social programs can prevent poverty.

Though not a necessary component of the argument, RESERVATIONS can strengthen a claim. A reservation is a rebuttal to the claim that is introduced and granted by the writer. Reservations strengthen arguments in several ways: First, they moderate the writer's claim, thereby decreasing the level of proof required. Second, reservations make the writer appear more reliable by demonstrating that she is open-minded and that her position is not extreme. Third, reservations allow the writer to defuse criticism before it is made. When you include a reservation in your argument, be sure to take the opportunity to weigh it against your other claims.

5. **RESERVATION:** Biochemists and engineers do contribute to society.
   WEIGHING: Though technological progress can increase the food supply and cure disease, we will always need historians and social scientists to show us how to use technology without causing more harm than good.

TACTIC

Adopt a Balanced Approach

Consider your readers. Who are they? They are academics, junior members of college faculties. What are they looking for? They are looking for articulate and persuasive arguments expressed in scholarly, well-reasoned prose. In other words, they are looking for the sort of essay they might write themselves.

How do you go about writing for an academic audience? First, avoid extremes. You want to come across as a mature, evenhanded writer, someone who can take a strong stand on an issue, but who can see others' positions as well. Restrain yourself: don't get so carried away by the "rightness" of your argument that you wind up sounding fanatical or shrill. Second, be sure to acknowledge that other viewpoints exist. Cite them; you'll win points for scholarly objectivity.

Draw examples to support your position from "the great world" and from the academic realm. In writing about teaching methods, for example, you'll win more points citing current newspaper articles about magnet schools or relevant passages from John Dewey and Maria Montessori than telling anecdotes about your favorite gym teacher in junior high school. While it is certainly acceptable for you to offer an occasional example from personal experience, for the most part your object is to show the readers the *breadth* of your knowledge (without showing off by quoting the most obscure sources you can find!).

One additional point: Do not try to second-guess your readers. Yes, they want you to come up with a scholarly, convincing essay. But there is no "one true answer" that they are looking for. You can argue for the position. You can argue against the position. You can strike a middle ground, arguing both for and against the position, hedging your bet. The readers don't care what position you adopt. Don't waste your time trying to psych them out.

Preparing for the Argument Essay

TACTIC

Familiarize Yourself with the Argument Essay Task Instructions

Though there are 200 possible topics in the Argument Essay topic pool, there are only eight sets of specific task instructions for those topics. GRE essay readers require that you not only adhere to the *subject* of the assigned essay topic, but that you also *meet each of the requirements found in the task instructions.* Writing a well-reasoned critique of the argument provided is not enough to receive a high score; you must do so in the manner described in the task instructions.

The list below includes versions of all eight of the possible GRE Argument Essay task instructions, followed by a short explanation of each task and how you should approach it. Several of the sets of task instructions are slight variations of the others, so they are grouped together at the end of the list. The *exact* wording of the instructions can be found on the ETS website, located at *https://www.ets.org/gre/revised_general/prepare/analytical_writing/argument.*

1. *Compose an essay that identifies and considers the evidence required to assess the validity of the argument provided. In writing your essay be sure to clarify whether this evidence would bolster or undermine the argument.*

   These task instructions have two elements. (1) The argument presented will make claims that are not supported by evidence. Your essay must identify what evidence is *missing* from the argument presented. You may offer examples of possible evidence that would either support or undermine the argument. An essay that does not identify evidence that is missing from the argument cannot receive a high score. (2) Your essay must explain *how* the evidence you identify would weaken or strengthen the argument. Would the evidence demonstrate a possible alternate cause of the situation described in the argument? Would it demonstrate that the argument has proven true in other similar circumstances?

2. *Compose an essay that identifies and considers the assumptions (implicit and/or explicit) on which the argument is based. The essay must clarify the importance of these assumptions to the argument and explain the impact on the argument's validity should the assumptions be faulty.*

   These task instructions have three elements. (1) Your essay must identify and assess the stated and/or unstated assumptions underlying the argument presented. An essay that fails to discuss these assumptions cannot receive a high score. (2) Your essay must explain how these assumptions are crucial to proving the truth of the argument—how the strength of the argument *depends* on these assumptions. (3) Your essay must explain what it would mean for the reliability of the argument if the assumptions it is based on are false. Would the argument be entirely without merit? Could it still be true in some circumstances, or to a limited extent?

3. *Compose an essay that proposes one or more competing theories that might prove more accurate than the explanation provided. Make clear how your theory (or theories) offers a satisfactory explanation of the information provided.*

These task instructions have two elements. (1) The argument presented provides an explanation for a phenomenon. Your essay must propose one or more rival explanations that could account for the same phenomenon. An essay that does not propose at least one alternative explanation for the phenomenon cannot receive a high score. (2) Your essay must explain *how* the alternative explanation(s) *rival(s)* the explanation in the argument provided. In other words, you must discuss the relative plausibility of the competing explanations. Why is your explanation equal to, or more likely than, the explanation given in the topic?

. . .

The following task instructions are very similar. In each of these questions, there are two elements to the task instructions. (1) The first element is to identify and discuss the questions that would need to be answered in order to evaluate the argument that is presented. An essay that does not identify and discuss these questions cannot receive a high score. The second element in each task's instructions is unique and is described below.

4. *Compose an essay identifying the questions that must be answered before reaching a conclusion about whether the recommendation and the argument supporting it make sense. In writing your essay you should describe the impact that the answers to these questions would have on your assessment of the recommendation.*

(2) Your essay must explain *how* the answers to these questions would weaken or strengthen the argument and assist in evaluating the soundness of the recommendation. Your essay will be especially effective if it examines the potential impact of conflicting answers. If the answer to the question is X, how does that support or undermine the recommendation? If, instead, the answer is Y, how does that support or undermine the recommendation?

5. *Compose an essay that identifies the questions that must be answered before reaching a conclusion about whether the advice and the argument supporting it make sense. In writing your essay you should describe the impact that the answers to these questions would have on your assessment of the advice.*

(2) Your essay must explain *how* the answers to these questions would weaken or strengthen the argument and assist in evaluating the soundness of the advice. Your essay will be especially effective if it examines the potential impact of conflicting answers. If the answer to the question is X, how does that support or undermine the advice? If, instead, the answer is Y, how does that support or undermine the advice?

6. *Compose an essay that identifies the questions that must be answered in order to accurately predict whether following the recommendation will achieve the expected consequence. In writing your essay you should describe the impact that the answers to these questions would have on your assessment of the recommendation.*

(2) Your essay must explain *how* the answers to these questions affect the likelihood of the recommendation's achieving its attended result, helping to evaluate the soundness of the recommendation. Your essay will be especially effective if it examines the potential impact of conflicting answers. If the answer to the question is X, how does that affect the odds of the recommendation's achieving its intended result? If, instead, the answer is Y, how does that change the odds?

7. *Compose an essay that identifies the questions that must be answered before reaching a conclusion about whether the prediction and the argument supporting it make sense. In writing your essay you should describe the impact that the answers to these questions would have on your assessment of the prediction.*

(2) Your essay must explain *how* the answers to these questions affect the likelihood that the prediction will prove accurate. Your essay will be especially effective if it examines the potential impact of conflicting answers. If the answer to the question is X, how does that affect the odds that the prediction will prove true? If, instead, the answer is Y, how does that change the odds?

8. *Compose an essay that identifies the questions that must be answered before deciding whether the conclusion and the argument supporting it make sense. In writing your essay you should describe the impact that the answers to these questions would have on your assessment of the conclusion.*

(2) Your essay must explain *how* the answers to these questions affect your evaluation of the reasonableness of the conclusion. Your essay will be especially effective if it examines the potential impact of conflicting answers. If the answer to the question is X, how reasonable is the conclusion? If, instead, the answer is Y, is the conclusion more or less reasonable?

TACTIC 12 Learn to Spot Common Logical Fallacies

You may remember studying a list of logical fallacies during your undergraduate education. It probably included Latin terms such as "post hoc ergo propter hoc" and "argumentum ad hominem.' Fortunately, you do not need to memorize these terms to perform well on the GRE Argument Essay. The GRE's essay readers are not concerned with whether you know the name of a given logical fallacy; they are more concerned with whether you can recognize and explain fallacies as they occur in simulated real-world situations. Labeling a claim a "post hoc" fallacy will not win you a 6 (the top score) unless you can *explain* the flaw in the argument. And a straightforward logical explanation of the argument's flaw can get you a 6, whether or not you use the fancy Latin terminology.

This does not mean, however, that brushing up on the common logical fallacies is a waste of your time. A decent understanding of the ways in which arguments can be wrong will help you write a better essay by enabling you to identify more flaws in the assigned argument (GRE argument statements generally include more than one logical error) and by giving you a clearer understanding of the nature of those flaws. Our advice is, therefore, to review the common logical fallacies without spending too much time trying to memorize their names.

Here are two examples of arguments, or prompts, similar to those in the GRE pool. Read them. The discussion following will point out what common logical fallacies they embody.

ARGUMENT 1

The school board of the Shadow Valley Unified School District included these remarks in a letter sent to the families of all students attending school in the district.

Over the past few years, an increase in disciplinary problems and a high dropout rate have plagued District schools. The Ash Lake School District to our north adopted a mandatory uniform policy three years ago. Since that time, suspensions and expulsions in Ash Lake have fallen by 40 percent, while the mean grade point average of Ash Lake students has risen from 2.3 (C+) to 2.7 (B–). In order to improve the discipline and academic performance of Shadow Valley students, we have adopted a mandatory uniform policy effective on the first day of the new school year.

Compose an essay that identifies and considers the assumptions (implicit and/or explicit) on which the argument is based. The essay must clarify the importance of these assumptions to the argument and explain the impact on the argument's validity should the assumptions be faulty.

ARGUMENT 2

The following is excerpted from a letter to the editor in the *Chillington Gazette.*

The recent residential property tax increase to improve park maintenance in Chillington is a waste of money. There is no need to improve Chillington's parks because the people of Chillington do not enjoy outdoor recreation. I live across the street from Green Park in South Chillington, and I've noticed that there is never anyone in the park. Park use did not increase in Warm Springs last year when they implemented a similar tax. There is no reason to improve parks that will not be used.

Compose an essay that identifies the questions that must be answered before reaching a conclusion about whether the prediction and the argument supporting it make sense. In writing your essay you should describe the impact that the answers to these questions would have on your assessment of the prediction.

CAUSAL FALLACIES

The classic fallacy of causation is often known by a Latin phrase, "post hoc ergo propter hoc," or its nickname, "the post hoc fallacy." The Latin phrase translates to, "after this, therefore because of this." The post hoc fallacy confuses correlation with causation, assuming that when one event follows another, the second event must have been caused by the first. It is as if you were to say that because your birthday precedes your husband's by one month, your birth must have caused him to be born.

The Shadow Valley School District argument presents an excellent example of a post hoc fallacy. The author of this argument assumes that because "suspensions and expulsions in Ash Lake have fallen by 40 percent, while the mean grade point average of Ash Lake students has risen from 2.3 (C+) to 2.7 (B–)" since Ash Lake's adoption of a mandatory uniform policy, the uniform policy has caused the improved student performance. Despite this correlation, it is possible that other factors are responsible for Ash Lake's progress. Perhaps the school uniform policy coincided with a significant decrease in average class size or the arrival of a new superintendent of schools. Or perhaps the recent improvements were brought about by an increase in federal aid for at-risk students. School uniforms may have been a partial cause of Ash Lake's improvements, or they may have played no role at all. Without further information, no reliable conclusion can be reached.

INDUCTIVE FALLACIES

Fallacies of induction involve the drawing of general rules from specific examples. They are among the most common fallacies found in the GRE Argument Essay topics. To induce a general rule correctly from specific examples, it is crucial that the specific examples be representative of the larger group. All too often, this is not the case.

The **hasty generalization** (too small sample) is the most common inductive fallacy. A hasty generalization is a general conclusion that is based on too small a sample set. If, for example, you wanted to learn the most popular flavor of ice cream in Italy, you would need to interview a substantial number of Italians. Drawing a conclusion based on the taste of the three Italian tourists you met last week would not be justified.

The *Chillington Gazette* argument provides another good example of the hasty generalization. The author of this argument concludes that "the people of Chillington do not enjoy outdoor recreation," but he draws this general conclusion from the lack of visitors to the park across the street from his home. Readers are never told just how many parks there are in Chillington. There could be dozens of parks, all possibly overflowing with happy visitors, despite the unpopularity of the one park viewed by the author.

Small sample size is a problem because it increases the risk of drawing a general conclusion from an **unrepresentative sample**. If, for example, you wanted to learn who was most likely to be elected president of the United States, you could not draw a reliable conclusion based on the preferences of the citizens of a single city, or even a single state. The views of the citizens of Salt Lake City are not necessarily the views of the citizens of the nation as a whole, nor are the views of Californians representative of those of the entire nation. This is why pollsters go to such great lengths to ensure that they interview a representative sample of the entire population.

Unrepresentative samples do not, however, always result from too small a sample. The *Chillington Gazette* argument concludes that the citizens of Chillington will not use improved parks because "[p]ark use did not increase in Warm Springs last year when they implemented a similar tax." The author gives no reason to believe, however, that the two towns' situations are similar. Perhaps park use did not increase in Warm Springs because its parks were already extremely popular, unlike those of Chillington. Or perhaps Warm Springs is an industrial city with little housing, while Chillington is a bedroom community with a large number of school-aged children. Should we conclude that the experiences of one city will be mirrored by the experiences of the other?

To learn more about common logical fallacies, consult standard works on rhetoric and critical reasoning. Two currently popular texts are James Herrick's *Argumentation* and T. Edward Darner's *Attacking Faulty Reasoning*.

TACTIC 13

Remember That Your Purpose Is to Analyze, Not to Persuade

You are not asked to agree or disagree with the argument in the prompt. Do not be distracted by your feelings on the subject of the prompt, and do not give in to the temptation to write your own argument. Be especially vigilant against this temptation if the topic is on a subject that you know very well. If, for example, the prompt argues that class size reduction is a poor idea because it did not improve test scores in one city, do not answer this argument with data you happen to know about another city in which test scores improved after class sizes were reduced. Instead, point out that one city is not a large enough sample on which to base a general conclusion. Go on to identify other factors that could have caused test scores to remain the same, despite lower class size. (Perhaps test scores in the sample city were already nearly as high as they could go, or the student population in that city was changing at the time class sizes were reduced.) Remember, the readers are not interested in how much you *know* about the subject of the prompt; they want to know how well you *think*.

TACTIC

Examine the Argument for Unstated Assumptions and Missing Information

An argument is based upon certain assumptions made by its author. If an argument's basic premises are sound, the argument is strengthened. If the argument's basic premises are flawed, the argument is weakened.

Pinpoint what the argument assumes but never states. Then, consider the validity of these unstated assumptions. For example, the Shadow Valley argument assumes that the populations of Shadow Valley and Ash Lake are analogous. Is this unstated assumption warranted? Not necessarily. The two towns might well have distinctly dissimilar populations—one might be a working-class suburb with high unemployment, while the other might be a suburb populated by wealthy professionals. If that were so, there would be no reason to believe that the same factors would cause poor student performance in both towns.

Ask yourself what additional evidence would strengthen or weaken the claim. Generally, GRE argument prompts are flawed but could be true under some circumstances. Only rarely will you find an argument that is absolutely untrue. Instead, you will find plausible arguments for which support (grounds and warrant) is lacking.

Put yourself in the place of the argument's author. If you were trying to prove this argument, what evidence would you need? What missing data should you assemble to support your claim? Use your concluding paragraph to list this evidence and explain how its presence would solve the shortcomings that you identified earlier in your essay.

TACTIC

Pay Particular Attention to Signal Words in the Argument

In analyzing arguments, be on the lookout for transitions or signal words that can clarify the structure of the argument. These words are like road signs, pointing out the direction the author wants you to take, showing you the connection between one logical step and the next. When you spot such a word linking elements in the author's argument, ask yourself whether this connection is logically watertight. Does A unquestionably lead to B? These signal words can indicate vulnerable areas in the argument—points you can attack.

In particular, be alert for:

CAUSE AND EFFECT SIGNAL WORDS

The following words often signal the conclusion of an argument:

accordingly	hence	in summary	therefore
consequently	in conclusion	so	thus
for this reason	in short		

CONTRAST SIGNAL WORDS

The following words often signal a reversal of thought within an argument:

although	except	nevertheless	rather than
but	however	not	still
despite	in contrast	on the contrary	unlike
even though	instead	on the other hand	yet

Notice that in the following argument several of these words are present: *despite, not,* and *consequently.* Each of these words plays an important role in the argument.

ARGUMENT 3

The following is from a letter to the state Department of Education.

Despite the fact that the River City School District increased the average class size by more than 15% in all grades two years ago, this year's average SAT scores for the junior class were the highest ever. This shows that class size is not a good determinant of student performance. Consequently, other school districts should follow River City's lead and save money by increasing the size of their classes.

Compose an essay identifying the questions that must be answered before reaching a conclusion about whether the recommendation and the argument supporting it make sense. In writing your essay you should describe the impact that the answers to these questions would have on your assessment of the recommendation.

Think about each link in the chain of reasoning signaled by the three transition words. These words should act like a red flag, alerting you that danger (flawed logic) may lie ahead. Did the average SAT score for the junior class increase *despite* the increase in class size? Maybe. Then again, maybe not; the average score for that year's junior class may have increased because that year's juniors were unusually bright. Do this year's extra-high SAT scores show that class size is *not* a good determinant of student performance? Not necessarily. Many factors could have contributed to the junior class's high scores. Finally, consider the implications of *consequently.* Even if class size were not a good determinant of student performance, does it necessarily follow *as a consequence* that school districts should increase the size of their classes? In the words of the old song, "It ain't necessarily so."

PRACTICE EXERCISES

Practice for the Issue Task

1. Brainstorm for 5 minutes, jotting down any words and phrases that are triggered by one of the following questions:

   - What should the goals of higher education be?
   - Why should we study history?
   - How does technology affect our society?
   - What is the proper role of art?
   - Which poses the greater threat to society, individualism or conformity?
   - Which is more socially valuable, preserving tradition or promoting innovation?
   - Is it better to be a specialist or a generalist?
   - Can a politician be both honest and effective?

2. In a brief paragraph, define one of the following words:

   - Freedom
   - Originality
   - Honesty
   - Progress

3. To improve your ear for language, read aloud short selections of good prose: editorials from *The New York Times* or *The Christian Science Monitor,* as well as columns or brief essays by prose stylists like Annie Dillard, M. F. K. Fisher, or E. B. White. Listen for the ways in which these authors vary their sentence structure. Note the precision with which they choose their words. The more good prose you hear, the better able you'll be to improve your writing style.

4. Selecting three or four issue topics from the GRE's online pool of topics for the revised test (currently at *http://www.ets.org/gre/revised_general/prepare/analytical_writing/issue/pool),* break down the topic statements in terms of Toulmin's three elements: claim, grounds, and warrant. Ask yourself the following questions. What claims are made in each topic statement? What grounds or data are given to support each of these claims? Is the claim warranted or unwarranted? Why? In what way do the grounds logically justify the claim?

5. Choosing another issue topic from the GRE's published pool of topics, write an essay giving your viewpoint concerning the particular issue raised. Set no time limit; take as long as you want to complete this task, then choose a second issue topic from the pool. *In only 30 minutes,* write an essay presenting your perspective on this second issue.

   Compare your two essays. Ask yourself how working under time pressure affected your second essay. Did its major problems stem from a lack of fluency? A lack of organization? A lack of familiarity with the subject matter under discussion? A lack of knowledge of the mechanics of formal written English? Depending on what problems you spot, review the appropriate sections of this chapter, as well as any style manuals or other texts we suggest.

Practice for the Argument Task

1. Choosing a sample of argument topics from GRE's online pool of topics for the revised test (currently at *http://www.ets.org/gre/revised_general/prepare/analytical_writing/argument/pool*), practice applying the list of logical fallacies to the published prompts. See how many fallacies you can find for each argument. If you have time, write practice essays for some of these arguments. If you are short of time, or would simply like to move more quickly, get together with a friend and explain the fallacies you have found in the argument essay prompts. This will be especially rewarding if you can work with a friend who is also preparing to take the GRE.

2. Write an "original" argument topic, modeling it on one of the argument prompts in the GRE's published pool. Your job is to change the details of the situation (names, figures, and so on) without changing the types of logical fallacies involved. By doing this, you will learn to spot the same old fallacies whenever they crop up in a new guise.

3. Choosing an argument prompt from GRE's online pool of topics for the revised test (currently at *http://www.ets.org/gre/revised_general/prepare/analytical_writing/argument/pool*), write an essay critiquing the particular argument expressed. Set no time limit; take as long as you want to complete this task, then choose a second argument prompt from the pool. *In only 30 minutes*, write an essay critiquing this second argument.

   Compare your two critiques. Ask yourself how working under time pressure affected your second critique. Would more familiarity with the common logical fallacies have helped you? Depending on what problems you spot, review the appropriate sections of this chapter, as well as any other materials we suggest.

PART 4

Quantitative Ability: Tactics, Strategies, Practice, and Review

INTRODUCTION TO PART 4

Part 4 consists of five chapters. Chapter 8 presents several important strategies that can be used on any mathematics questions that appear on the GRE. In Chapters 9, 10, and 11 you will find tactics that are specific to one of the three different types of questions: discrete quantitative questions, quantitative comparison questions, and data interpretation questions, respectively. Chapter 12 contains a complete review of all the mathematics you need to know in order to do well on the GRE, as well as hundreds of sample problems patterned on actual test questions.

Five Types of Tactics

Five different types of tactics are discussed in this book.

1. In Chapters 1 and 2, you learned many basic tactics used by all good test-takers, such as read each question carefully, pace yourself, don't get bogged down on any one question, and never waste time reading the directions. You also learned the specific tactics required to excel on a computerized test. These tactics apply to both the verbal and quantitative sections of the GRE.
2. In Chapters 4 and 5 you learned the important tactics needed for handling each type of verbal question.
3. In Chapter 7 you learned the strategies for planning and writing the two essays that constitute the analytical writing section of the GRE.
4. In Chapters 8–11 you will find all of the tactics that apply to the quantitative sections of the GRE. Chapter 8 contains those techniques that can be applied to all types of mathematics questions; Chapters 9, 10, and 11 present specific strategies to deal with each of the three kinds of quantitative questions found on the GRE: discrete quantitative questions, quantitative comparison questions, and data interpretation questions.
5. In Chapter 12 you will learn or review all of the mathematics that is needed for the GRE, and you will master the specific tactics and key facts that apply to each of the different mathematical topics.

Using these tactics will enable you to answer more quickly many questions that you already know how to do. But the greatest value of these tactics is that they will allow you to correctly answer or make educated guesses on problems that *you do not know how to do.*

When to Study Chapter 12

How much time you initially devote to Chapter 12 should depend on how good your math reasoning skills are, how long it has been since you studied math, and how much of the math you learned in middle school and the first two years of high school you remember. If you think that your math skills are quite good, you can initially skip the instructional parts of Chapter 12. If, however, after doing the Model Tests in Part 5 of this book, you find that you made more than one or two mistakes on questions involving the same topic (averages, percents, geometry, etc.) or you spent too much time on them, you should then study the appropriate sections of Chapter 12. Even if your math skills are excellent, you should do the exercises in Chapter 12; they are a good source of additional GRE questions. If your math skills were never very good or if you feel they are rusty, it is advisable to review the material in Chapter 12, including working out the problems, *before* tackling the Model Tests.

An Important Symbol

Throughout the rest of this book, the symbol "$\Rightarrow$" is used to indicate that one step in the solution of a problem follows *immediately* from the preceding one, and no explanation is necessary. You should read

$3x = 12 \Rightarrow x = 4$

as $3x = 12$ *implies that* $x = 4$

or $3x = 12$, *which implies that* $x = 4$

or *since* $3x = 12$, *then* $x = 4$.

Here is a sample solution to the following problem using $\Rightarrow$:

What is the value of $2x^2 - 5$ when $x = -4$?

$$x = -4 \Rightarrow x^2 = (-4)^2 = 16 \Rightarrow 2x^2 = 2(16) = 32 \Rightarrow 2x^2 - 5 = 32 - 5 = \mathbf{27}$$

When the reason for a step is not obvious, $\Rightarrow$ is not used: rather, an explanation is given, often including a reference to a KEY FACT from Chapter 12. In many solutions, some steps are explained, while others are linked by the $\Rightarrow$ symbol, as in the following example.

In the diagram below, if $w = 10$, what is the value of z?

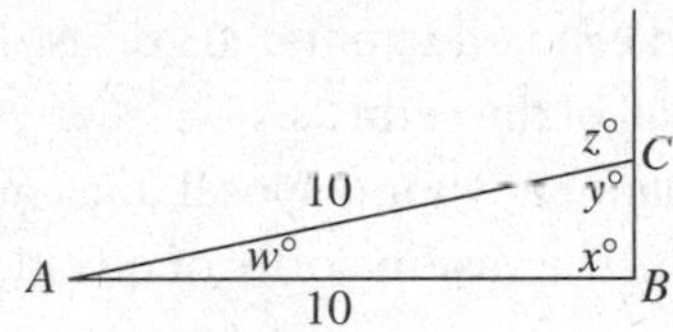

- By KEY FACT J1 (page 456), $w + x + y = 180$.
- Since $\triangle ABC$ is isosceles, $x = y$ (KEY FACT J5, page 459).
- Therefore, $w + 2y = 180 \Rightarrow 10 + 2y = 180 \Rightarrow 2y = 170 \Rightarrow y = 85$.
- Finally, since $y + z = 180$ (KEY FACT I3, page 447), $85 + z = 180 \Rightarrow z = \mathbf{95}$.

Calculators on the GRE

You may *not* bring your own calculator to use when you take the GRE. However, you will have access to an onscreen calculator. While you are working on the math sections, one of the icons at the top of the screen will be a calculator icon. During the verbal and writing sections of the test, either that icon will be greyed out (meaning that you can't click on it) or it will simply not be there at all. During the math sections, however, you will be able to click on that icon at anytime; when you do, a calculator will instantly appear on the screen. Clicking the X in the upper-right-hand corner of the calculator will hide it.

REMEMBER

Use your calculator only when you need to.

Note that when the calculator appears on the screen, it may cover part of the question or the answer choices. If this occurs, just click on the top of the calculator and drag it to a convenient location. If you use the calculator to answer a question and then click NEXT to go to the next question, the calculator remains on the screen, exactly where it was, with the same numerical readout. This is actually a distraction. So, if you do use the calculator to answer a question, as soon as you have answered that question, click on the X to remove the calculator from the screen. Later, it takes only one click to get it back.

The onscreen calculator is a simple four-function calculator, with a square root key. It is not a graphing calculator; it is not a scientific calculator. The only operations you can per-

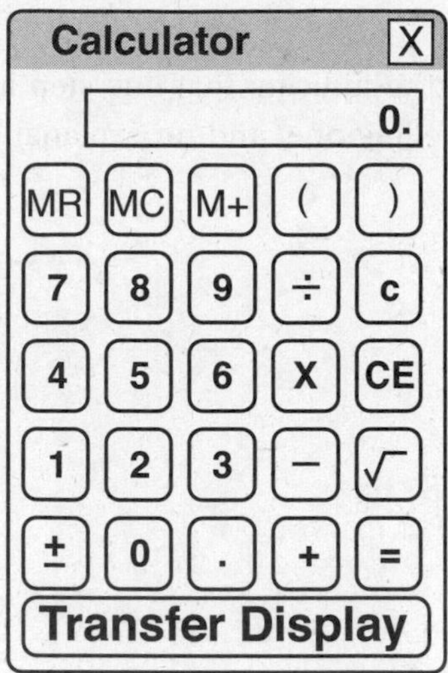

form with the onscreen calculator are adding, subtracting, multiplying, dividing, and taking square roots. Fortunately, these are the only operations you will ever need to answer any GRE question.

At the bottom of the onscreen calculator is a bar labeled TRANSFER DISPLAY. If you are using the calculator on a numeric entry question, and the result of your final calculation is the answer that you want to enter in the box, click on TRANSFER DISPLAY—the number currently displayed in the calculator's readout will instantly appear in the box under the question. This saves the few seconds that it would otherwise take to enter your answer; more important, it guarantees that you won't make an error typing in your answer.

Note: you cannot use TRANSFER DISPLAY to enter either the numerator or denominator of a fraction—you must use the keyboard to enter a number in each box. Also, you must be attentive to what the question is asking. Suppose the question asks for a value rounded to the nearest hundredth, and the last calculation results in a calculator display of 0.8333333. You have two choices: either use the keyboard to enter .83 or use TRANSFER DISPLAY, and then use the delete button to remove all of the extra 3s.

Just because you have a calculator at your disposal does not mean that you should use it very much. In fact, you shouldn't. The vast majority of questions that appear on the GRE do not require any calculations.

8 General Math Strategies

In Chapters 9 and 10, you will learn tactics that are specifically applicable to discrete quantitative questions and quantitative comparison questions, respectively. In this chapter you will learn several important general math strategies that can be used on both of these types of questions.

The directions that appear on the screen at the beginning of the quantitative sections include the following cautionary information:

> **Figures that accompany questions are intended to provide information useful in answering the questions.**
>
> **However, unless a note states that a figure is drawn to scale, you should solve these problems NOT by estimating sizes by sight or measurement, but by using your knowledge of mathematics.**

Despite the fact that they are telling you that you cannot totally rely on *their* diagrams, if you learn how to draw diagrams accurately, *you can trust the ones you draw.* Knowing the best ways of handling diagrams on the GRE is critically important. Consequently, the first five tactics all deal with diagrams.

TACTIC 1.	Draw a diagram.
TACTIC 2.	Trust a diagram that has been drawn to scale.
TACTIC 3.	Exaggerate or change a diagram.
TACTIC 4.	Add a line to a diagram.
TACTIC 5.	Subtract to find shaded regions.

To implement these tactics, you need to be able to draw line segments and angles accurately, and you need to be able to look at segments and angles and accurately estimate their measures. Let's look at three variations of the same problem.

1. If the diagonal of a rectangle is twice as long as the shorter side, what is the degree measure of the angle it makes with the longer side?
2. In the rectangle below, what is the value of x?

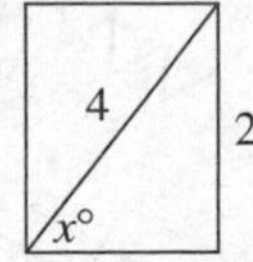

3. In the rectangle below, what is the value of x?

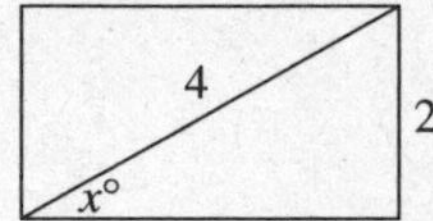

For the moment, let's ignore the correct mathematical way of solving this problem. In the diagram in (3), the side labeled 2 appears to be half as long as the diagonal, which is labeled 4; consequently, you should assume that the diagram has been drawn to scale, and you should see that x is about 30, *certainly* between 25 and 35. In (1) you aren't given a diagram, and in (2) the diagram is useless because you can see that it has not been drawn to scale (the side labeled 2 is nearly as long as the diagonal, which is labeled 4). However, if while taking the GRE, you see a question such as (1) or (2), you should be able to quickly draw on your scrap paper a diagram that looks just like the one in (3), and then look at *your* diagram and see that the measure of x is just about 30. If the answer choices for these questions were

Ⓐ 15 Ⓑ 30 Ⓒ 45 Ⓓ 60 Ⓔ 75

you would, of course, choose **30**, **B**. If the choices were

Ⓐ 20 Ⓑ 25 Ⓒ 30 Ⓓ 35 Ⓔ 40

you might not be quite as confident, but you should still choose **30**, here **C**.

When you take the GRE, even though you are not allowed to have rulers or protractors, you should be able to draw your diagrams very accurately. For example, in (1) on page 245, you should draw a horizontal line, and then, either freehand or by tracing the corner of a piece of scrap paper, draw a right angle on the line. The vertical line segment will be the width of the rectangle; label it 2.

Mark off that distance twice on a piece of scrap paper and use that to draw the diagonal.

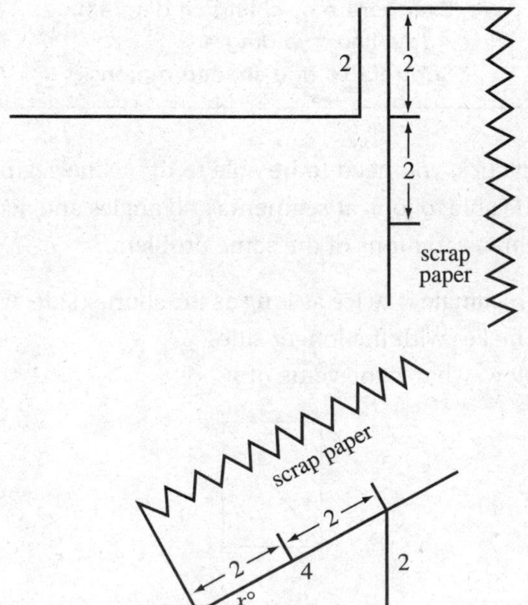

You should now have a diagram that is similar to that in (3), and you should be able to see that x is about 30.

By the way, x is *exactly* 30. A right triangle in which one leg is half the hypotenuse must be a 30-60-90 triangle, and that leg is opposite the 30° angle [see KEY FACT J11, page 462].

Having drawn an accurate diagram, are you still unsure as to how you should know that the value of x is 30 just by looking at the diagram? You will now learn not only how to look at *any* angle and know its measure within 5 or 10 degrees, but how to draw any angle that accurately.

You should easily recognize a 90° angle and can probably draw one freehand; but you can always just trace the corner of a piece of scrap paper. To draw a 45° angle, just bisect a 90° angle. Again, you can probably do this freehand. If not, or to be even more accurate, draw a right angle, mark off the same distance on each side, draw a square, and then draw in the diagonal.

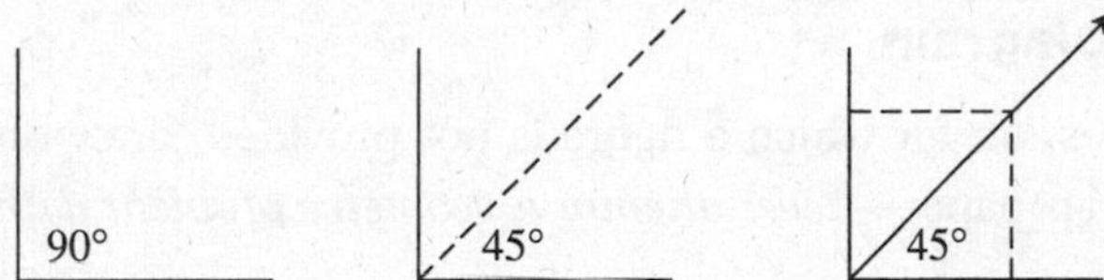

To draw other acute angles, just divide the two 45° angles in the above diagram with as many lines as necessary.

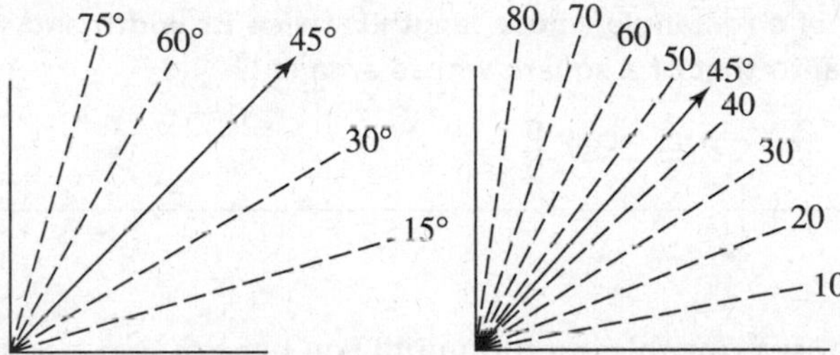

Finally, to draw an obtuse angle, add an acute angle to a right angle.

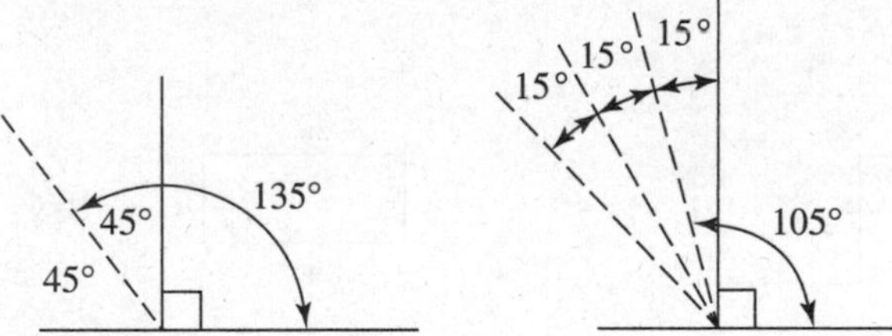

Now, to estimate the measure of a given angle, just draw in some lines.

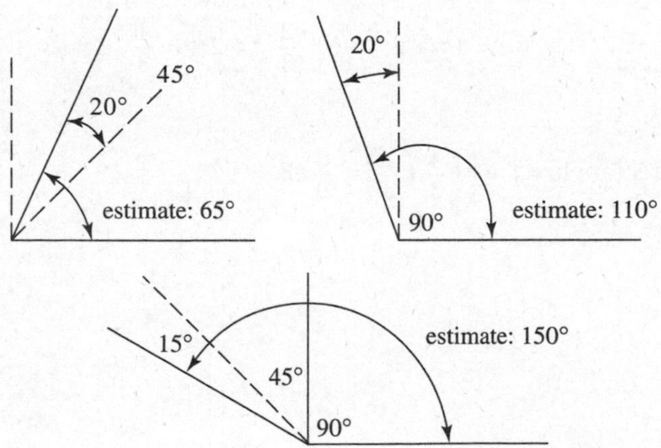

To test yourself, find the measure of each angle shown. The answers are found at the bottom of the page.

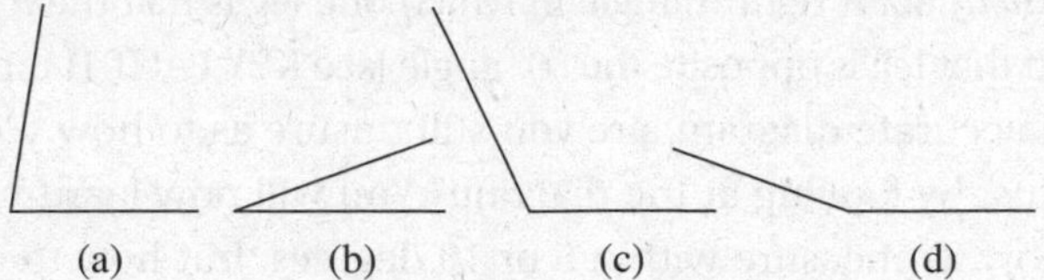

TESTING TACTICS

Draw a Diagram

On *any* geometry question for which a figure is not provided, draw one (as accurately as possible) on your scrap paper—*never attempt a geometry problem without first drawing a diagram.*

EXAMPLE 1

What is the area of a rectangle whose length is twice its width and whose perimeter is equal to that of a square whose area is 1?

Ⓐ 1 Ⓑ 6 Ⓒ $\frac{2}{3}$ Ⓓ $\frac{4}{3}$ Ⓔ $\frac{8}{9}$

SOLUTION.

Don't even think of answering this question until you have drawn a square and a rectangle and labeled each of them: each side of the square is 1, and if the width of the rectangle is w, its length (ℓ) is $2w$.

1, 1, 1, 1 $P = 4$ $2w$, w, w, $2w$ $P = 6w$

Now, write the required equation and solve it:

$$6w = 4 \Rightarrow w = \frac{4}{6} = \frac{2}{3} \Rightarrow 2w = \frac{4}{3}$$

The area of the rectangle $= \ell w = \left(\frac{4}{3}\right)\left(\frac{2}{3}\right) = \mathbf{\frac{8}{9}}$, **E.**

Answers (a) 80° (b) 20° (c) 115° (d) 160°. Did you come within 10° on each one?

EXAMPLE 2

Betty drove 8 miles west, 6 miles north, 3 miles east, and 6 more miles north. How many miles was Betty from her starting place?

[   ] **miles**

SOLUTION.
Draw a diagram showing Betty's route from A to B to C to D to E.

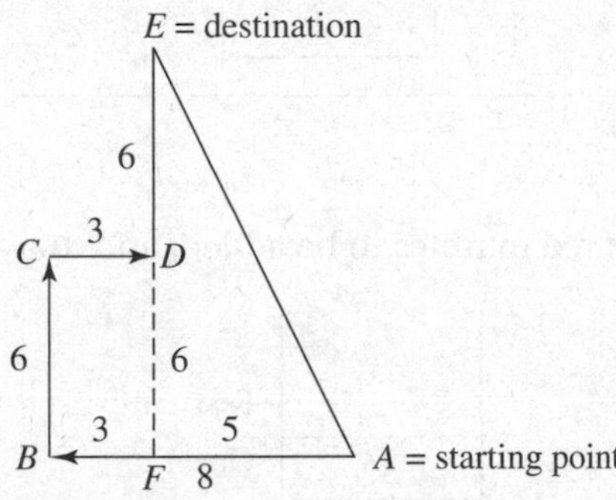

Now, extend line segment ED until it intersects AB at F. Then, AFE is a right triangle, whose legs are 5 and 12. The length of hypotenuse AE represents the distance from her starting point to her destination. Either recognize that $\triangle AFE$ is a 5-12-13 right triangle or use the Pythagorean theorem:

$$5^2 + 12^2 = (AE)^2 \Rightarrow (AE)^2 = 25 + 144 = 169 \Rightarrow AE = \mathbf{13}$$

EXAMPLE 3

What is the difference in the degree measures of the angles formed by the hour hand and the minute hand of a clock at 12:35 and 12:36?

Ⓐ 1° Ⓑ 5° Ⓒ 5.5° Ⓓ 6° Ⓔ 30°

SOLUTION.
Draw a simple picture of a clock. The hour hand makes a complete revolution, 360°, once every 12 hours. So, in 1 hour it goes through 360° ÷ 12 = 30°, and in one minute it advances through 30° ÷ 60 = 0.5°. The minute hand moves through 30° every 5 minutes or 6° per minute. So, in the minute from 12:35 to 12:36 (or any other minute), the *difference* between the hands increased by 6° – 0.5° = **5.5°**, **C**.

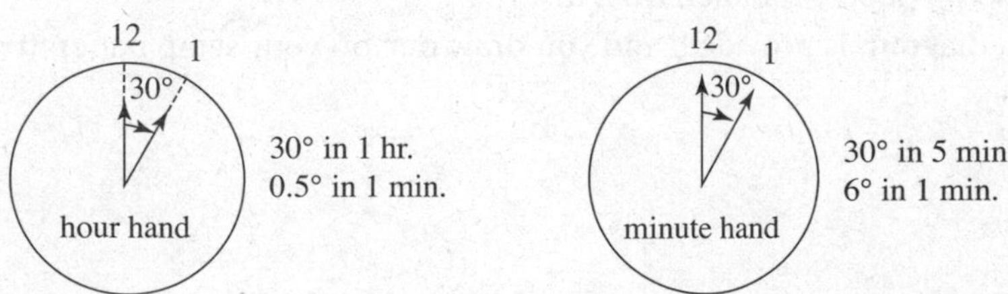

NOTE: It was not necessary, and would have been more time-consuming, to determine the angle between the hands at either 12:35 or 12:36. (See TACTIC 6, page 257: Don't do more than you have to.)

Drawings should not be limited to geometry questions; there are many other questions on which drawings will help.

EXAMPLE 4

A jar contains 10 red marbles and 30 green ones. How many red marbles must be added to the jar so that 60% of the marbles will be red?

SOLUTION.

Let x represent the number of red marbles to be added, and draw a diagram and label it.

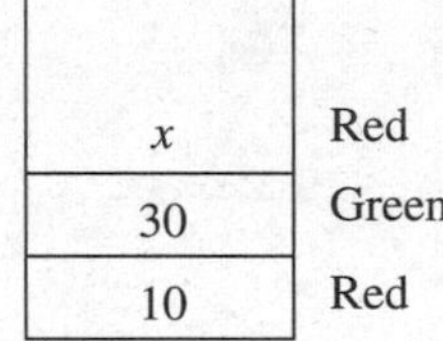

From the diagram it is clear that there are now $40 + x$ marbles in the jar, of which $10 + x$ are red. Since we want the fraction of red marbles to be 60%, we have $\frac{10+x}{40+x} = 60\% = \frac{60}{100} = \frac{3}{5}$.

Cross-multiplying, we get:

$$5(10 + x) = 3(40 + x) \Rightarrow 50 + 5x = 120 + 3x \Rightarrow 2x = 70 \Rightarrow x = \mathbf{35}$$

Of course, you could have set up the equation and solved it without the diagram, but the diagram makes the solution easier and you are less likely to make a careless mistake.

Trust Diagrams That Are Drawn to Scale Redraw Diagrams That Are Not Drawn to Scale

Whenever diagrams have been drawn to scale, they can be trusted. This means that you can look at the diagram and use your eyes to accurately estimate the sizes of angles and line segments.

To take advantage of this situation:

- If a diagram is given that you know has been drawn to scale, trust it.
- If a diagram is given that you can see has not been drawn to scale, try to draw it to scale on your scrap paper, and then trust it.
- When no diagram is provided, and you draw one on your scrap paper, try to draw it to scale.

In Example 5 below, we are told that *ABCD* is a square and that diagonal *BD* is 3. In the diagram provided, quadrilateral *ABCD* does indeed look like a square, and $BD = 3$ does not contradict any other information. We can, therefore, assume that the diagram has been drawn to scale.

EXAMPLE 5

In the figure at the right, diagonal *BD* of square *ABCD* is 3. What is the perimeter of the square?

Ⓐ 4.5 Ⓑ 12 Ⓒ $3\sqrt{2}$ Ⓓ $6\sqrt{2}$ Ⓔ $12\sqrt{2}$

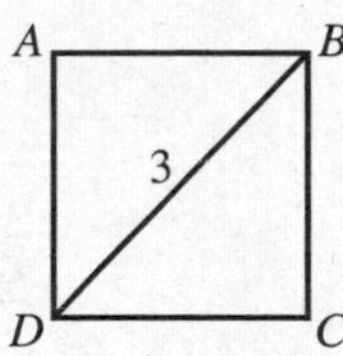

SOLUTION.

Since this diagram has been drawn to scale, you can trust it. The sides of the square appear to be about two thirds as long as the diagonal, so assume that each side is about 2. Then the perimeter is about 8. Which of the choices is approximately 8? Certainly not A or B. Since $\sqrt{2} \approx 1.4$, Choices C, D, and E are approximately 4.2, 8.4, and 12.6, respectively. Clearly, the answer must be **D**.

Direct mathematical solution. Let *s* be a side of the square. Then since $\triangle BCD$ is a 45-45-90 right triangle, $s = \frac{3}{\sqrt{2}} = \frac{3\sqrt{2}}{2}$, and the perimeter of the square is $4s = 4\left(\frac{3\sqrt{2}}{2}\right) = 6\sqrt{2}$.

Remember the goal of this book is to help you get credit for *all* the problems you know how to do, and, by using the TACTICS, to get credit for *many* that you don't know how to do. Example 5 is typical. Many students would miss this question. *You*, however, can be sure that you will answer it correctly, even if you don't remember how to solve it directly.

EXAMPLE 6

In $\triangle ABC$, what is the value of *x*?

Ⓐ 75 Ⓑ 60 Ⓒ 45 Ⓓ 30 Ⓔ 15

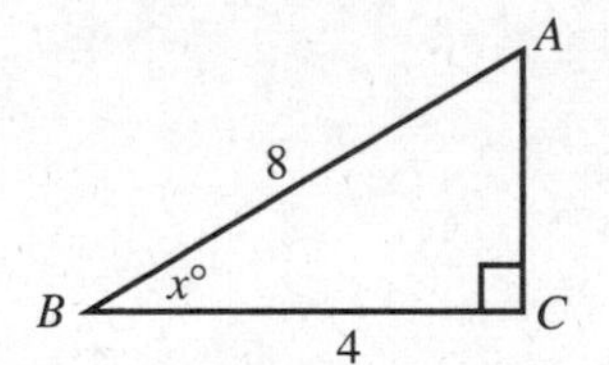

SOLUTION.

If you don't see the correct mathematical solution, you should use TACTIC 2. Clearly, the diagram is not drawn to scale. We are told that $AB = 8$ and $BC = 4$, but in the figure, *AB* and *BC* are almost the same length. So, when you copy the diagram onto your scrap paper, be sure to *fix it*. Redraw it so that *AB is twice as long as BC* (see diagram at right). Now, just look: *x* is about **60, B**.

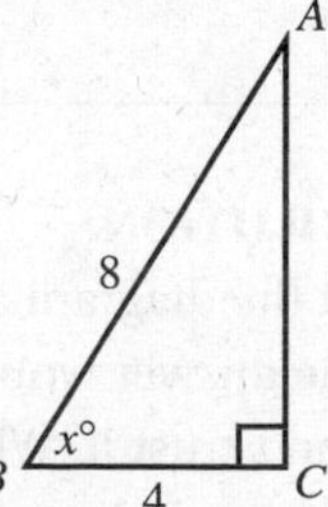

In fact, *x* is exactly 60. If the hypotenuse of a right triangle is twice the length of one of the legs, then it's a 30-60-90 triangle, and the angle formed by the hypotenuse and that leg is 60° (see Section 12-J, page 456).

TACTIC 2 is equally effective on quantitative comparison questions that have diagrams. See pages 9–10 for directions on how to solve quantitative comparison questions.

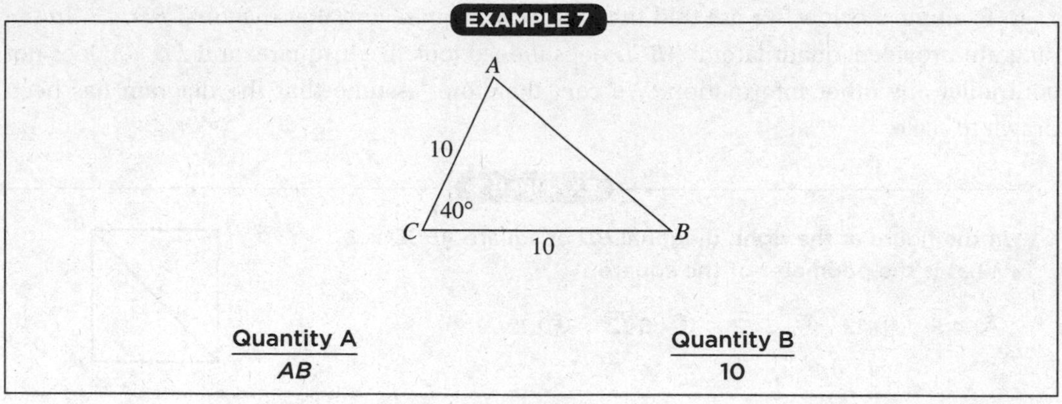

SOLUTION.

There are two things wrong with the given diagram: $\angle C$ is labeled 40°, but looks much more like 60° or 70°, and AC and BC are each labeled 10, but BC is drawn much longer. Therefore, you can't trust the diagram until you fix it. When you copy the diagram onto your scrap paper, be sure to correct these two mistakes: draw a triangle that has a 40° angle and two sides of the same length.

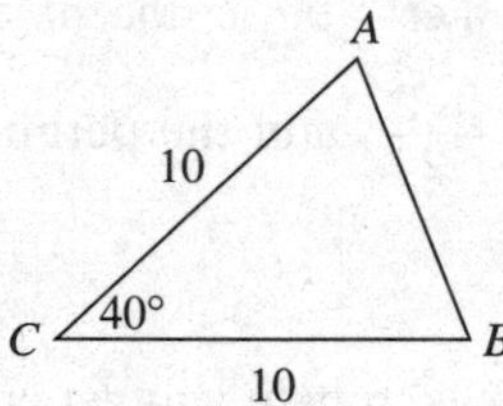

Now, it's clear: $AB < 10$. The answer is **B**.

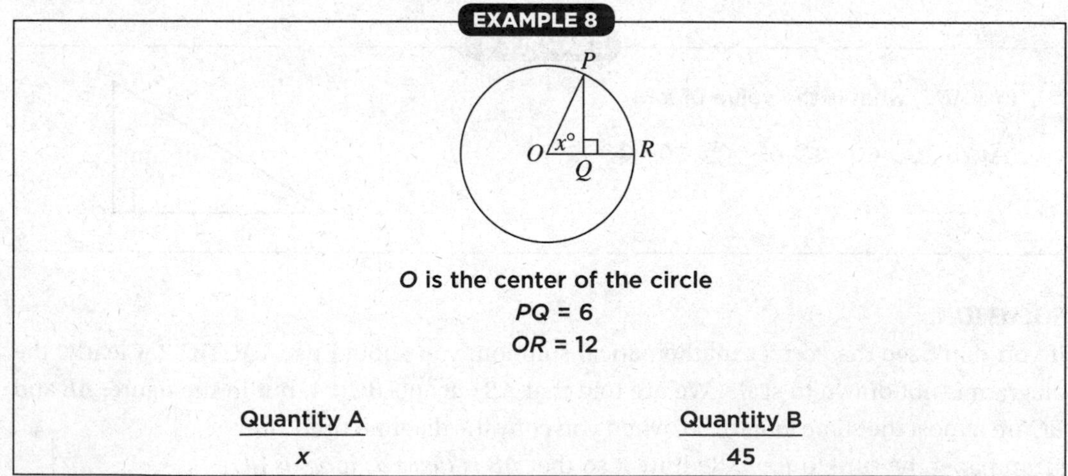

EXAMPLE 8
P
O
x°
R
Q
O is the center of the circle
PQ = 6
OR = 12
Quantity A
x
Quantity B
45

SOLUTION.

In the diagram above, the value of x is at least 60, so if the diagram has been drawn to scale, the answer would be **A**. If, on the other hand, the diagram has not been drawn to scale, we can't trust it. Which is it? The diagram is *not* drawn to scale—PQ is drawn almost as long as OR, even though OR is twice as long. Fix the diagram: do your best to draw it so that OR is twice as long as PQ.

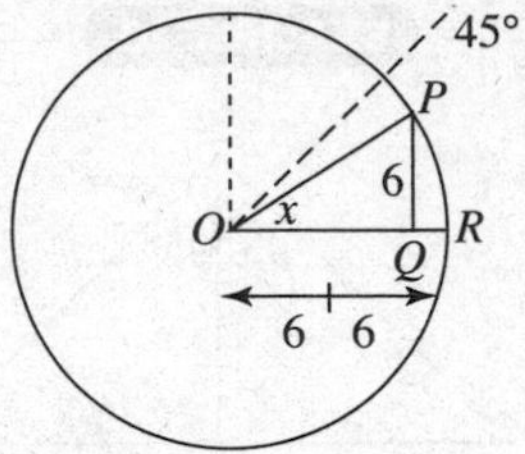

Now you can see that x is less than 45. The answer is **B**.

TACTIC 3 Exaggerate or Otherwise Change a Diagram

Sometimes it is appropriate to take a diagram that appears to be drawn to scale and intentionally exaggerate it. Why would we do this? Consider the following example.

EXAMPLE 9

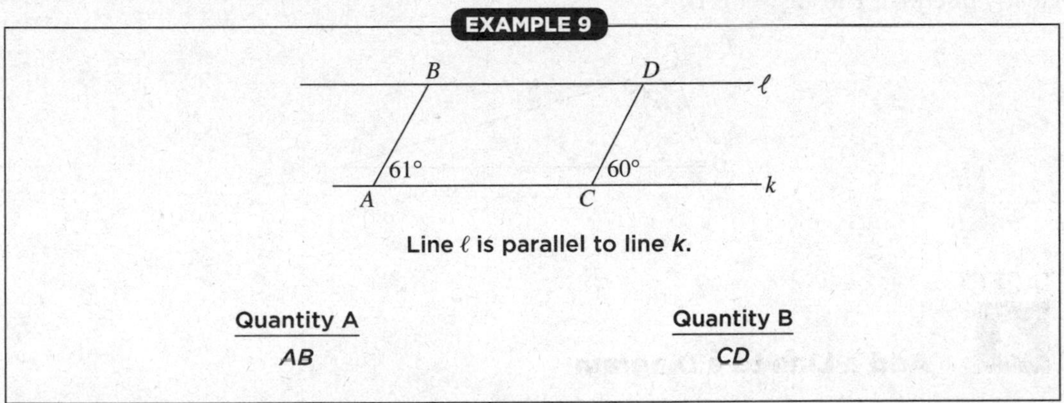

Line ℓ is parallel to line k.

Quantity A	Quantity B
AB	CD

SOLUTION.

In the diagram, which appears to be drawn correctly, AB and CD look as though they are the same length. However, there *might* be an imperceptible difference due to the fact that angle C is slightly smaller than angle A. So exaggerate the diagram: redraw it, making angle C *much* smaller than angle A. Now, it's clear: CD is longer. The answer is **B**.

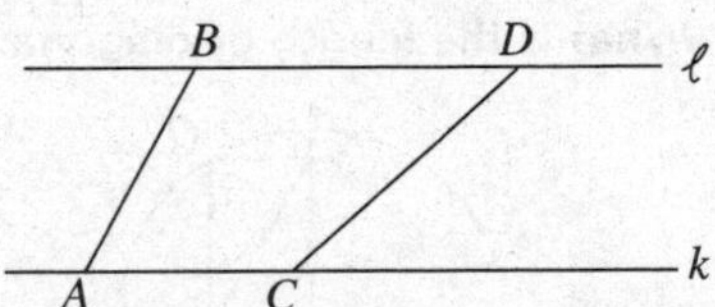

When you copy a diagram onto your scrap paper, you can change anything you like as long as your diagram is consistent with all the given data.

EXAMPLE 10

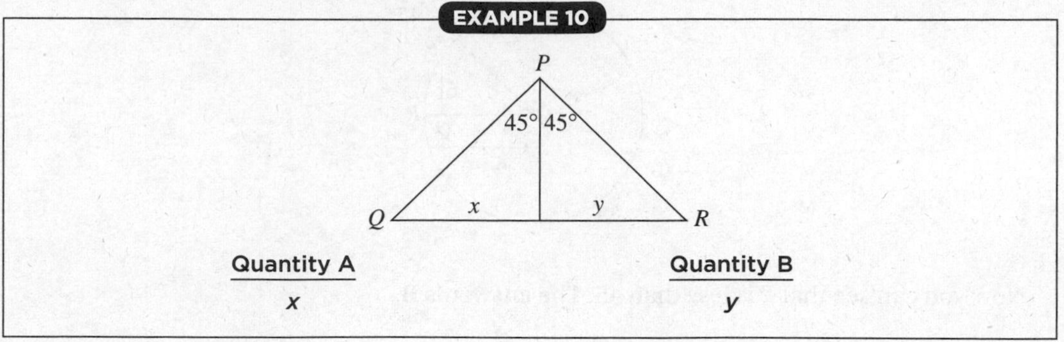

SOLUTION.

You may redraw this diagram any way you like, as long as the two angles that are marked 45° remain 45°. If PQ and PR are equal, as they appear to be in the given diagram, then x would equal y. Since the given information doesn't state that $PQ = PR$, draw a diagram in which PQ and PR are clearly unequal. In the diagram below, PR is much longer than PQ, and x and y are clearly unequal. The answer is **D**.

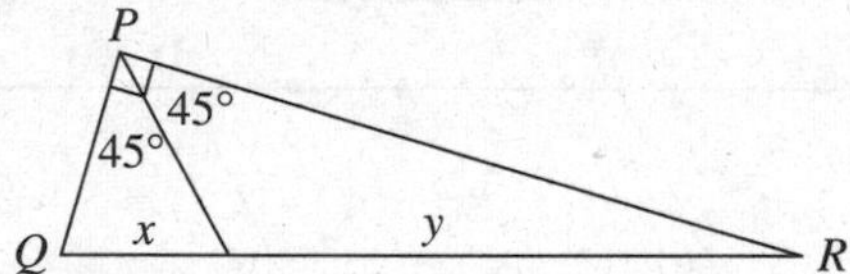

TACTIC

4 Add a Line to a Diagram

Occasionally, after staring at a diagram, you still have no idea how to solve the problem to which it applies. It looks as though not enough information has been given. When this happens, it often helps to draw another line in the diagram.

EXAMPLE 11

In the figure below, *Q* is a point on the circle whose center is *O* and whose radius is *r*, and *OPQR* is a rectangle. What is the length of diagonal *PR*?

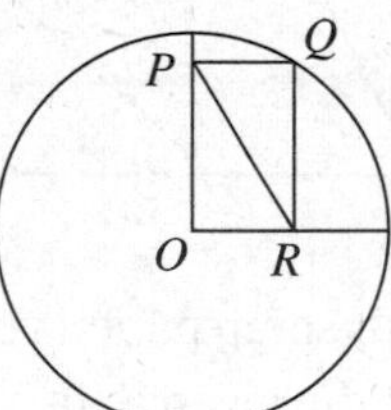

Ⓐ r Ⓑ r^2 Ⓒ $\frac{r^2}{\pi}$ Ⓓ $\frac{r\sqrt{2}}{\pi}$

Ⓔ **It cannot be determined from the information given.**

SOLUTION.
If after staring at the diagram and thinking about rectangles, circles, and the Pythagorean theorem, you're still lost, don't give up. Ask yourself, "Can I add another line to this diagram?" As soon as you think to draw in *OQ*, the other diagonal, the problem becomes easy: the two diagonals of a rectangle have the same length and, since *OQ* is a radius, it is equal to ***r*, A**.

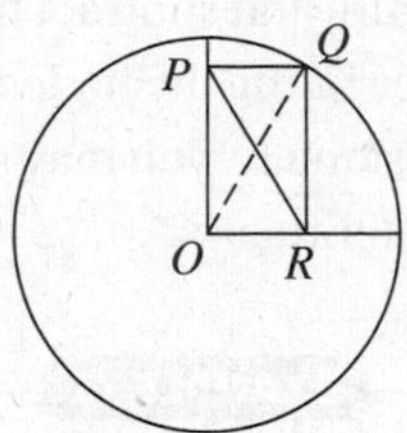

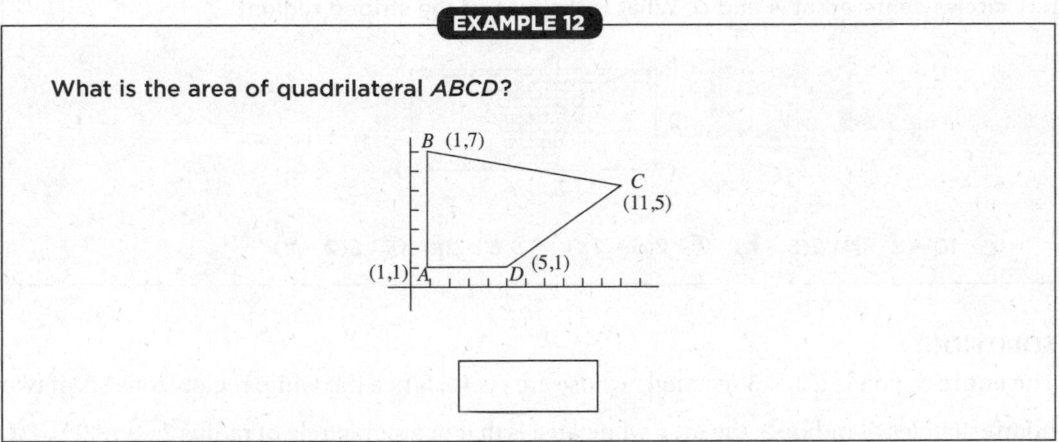

SOLUTION.
Since the quadrilateral is irregular, there isn't a formula to find the area. However, if you draw in *AC*, you will divide *ABCD* into two triangles, each of whose areas can be determined.

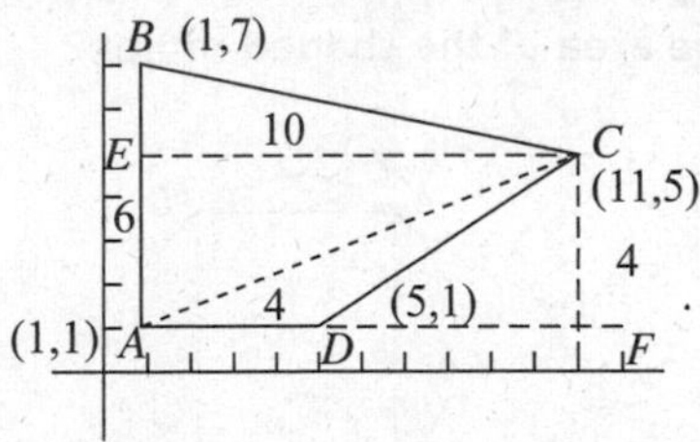

If you then draw in the height of each triangle, you see that the area of $\triangle ACD$ is $\frac{1}{2}(4)(4) = 8$, and the area of $\triangle BAC$ is $\frac{1}{2}(6)(10) = 30$, so the area of *ABCD* is 30 + 8 = **38**.

Note that this problem could also have been solved by drawing in lines to create rectangle *ABEF*, and subtracting the areas of $\triangle BEC$ and $\triangle CFD$ from the area of the rectangle.

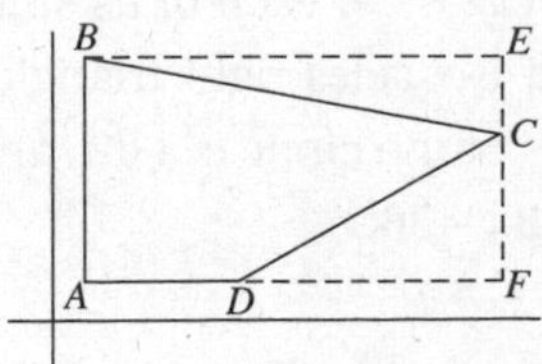

TACTIC

5 Subtract to Find Shaded Regions

Whenever part of a figure is shaded, the straightforward way to find the area of the shaded portion is to find the area of the entire figure and subtract from it the area of the unshaded region. Of course, if you are asked for the area of the unshaded region, you can, instead, subtract the shaded area from the total area. Occasionally, you may see an easy way to calculate the shaded area directly, but usually you should subtract.

EXAMPLE 13

In the figure below, *ABCD* is a rectangle, and *BE* and *CF* are arcs of circles centered at *A* and *D*. What is the area of the striped region?

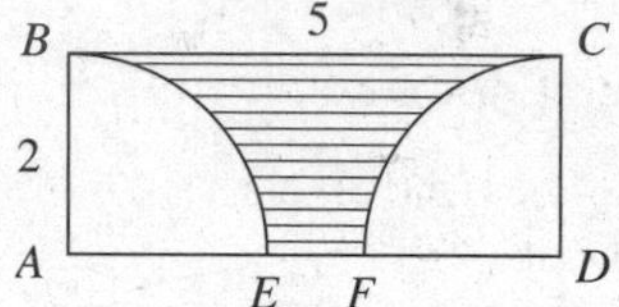

Ⓐ $10 - \pi$ Ⓑ $2(5 - \pi)$ Ⓒ $2(5 - 2\pi)$ Ⓓ $6 + 2\pi$ Ⓔ $5(2 - \pi)$

SOLUTION.

The entire region is a 2×5 rectangle whose area is 10. Since the white region consists of two quarter-circles of radius 2, the total white area is that of a semicircle of radius 2: $\frac{1}{2}\pi(2)^2 = 2\pi$. Therefore, the area of the striped region is $10 - 2\pi =$ $\mathbf{2(5 - \pi)}$, **B**.

EXAMPLE 14

In the figure below, square *ABCD* is inscribed in circle *O*. If the perimeter of *ABCD* is 24, what is the area of the shaded region?

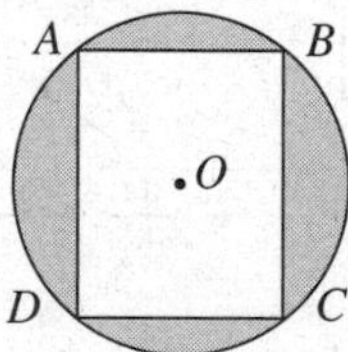

Ⓐ $18\pi - 36$ Ⓑ $18\pi - 24$ Ⓒ $12\pi - 36$ Ⓓ $9\pi - 36$ Ⓔ $9\pi - 24$

SOLUTION.

Since the perimeter of square *ABCD* is 24, each of its sides is 6, and its area is $6^2 = 36$. Since diagonal *AC* is the hypotenuse of isosceles right triangle *ABC*, $AC = 6\sqrt{2}$. But *AC* is also a diameter of circle *O*, so the radius of the circle is $3\sqrt{2}$, and its area is $\pi(3\sqrt{2})^2 = 18\pi$. Finally, the area of the shaded region is $\mathbf{18\pi - 36}$, **A**.

TACTIC

Don't Do More Than You Have To

Very often a problem can be solved in more than one way. You should always try to do it in the easiest way possible. Consider the following examples.

EXAMPLE 15

If $5(3x - 7) = 20$, what is $3x - 8$?

Ⓐ $\frac{11}{3}$ Ⓑ 0 Ⓒ 3 Ⓓ 14 Ⓔ 19

It is not difficult to solve for x:

$$5(3x-7)=20 \Rightarrow 15x-35=20 \Rightarrow 15x=55 \Rightarrow x=\frac{55}{15}=\frac{11}{3}$$

But it's too much work. Besides, once you find that $x=\frac{11}{3}$, you still have to multiply to get $3x$: $3\left(\frac{11}{3}\right)=11$, and then subtract to get $3x-8$: $11-8=\mathbf{3}$.

SOLUTION.

The key is to recognize that you don't need to find x. Finding $3x - 7$ is easy (just divide the original equation by 5), and $3x - 8$ is just 1 less:

$$5(3x-7)=20 \Rightarrow 3x-7=4 \Rightarrow 3x-8=\mathbf{3},\ \mathbf{C}$$

EXAMPLE 16

If $7x + 3y = 17$ and $3x + 7y = 19$, what is the average (arithmetic mean) of x and y?

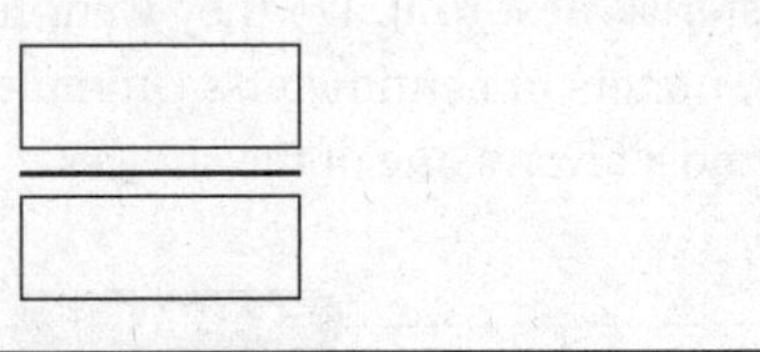

The obvious way to do this is to first find x and y by solving the two equations simultaneously and then to take their average. If you know how to do this, try it now, before reading further. If you worked carefully, you should have found that $x=\frac{31}{20}$ and $y=\frac{41}{20}$, and their average is $\frac{\frac{31}{20}+\frac{41}{20}}{2}=\frac{9}{5}$. Enter 9 as the numerator and 5 as the denominator.

This is not too difficult, but it is quite time-consuming, and questions on the GRE never require you to do that much work. Look for a shortcut. Is there a way to find the average without first finding x and y? Absolutely! Here's the best way to do this.

SOLUTION.

Add the two equations:

$$\begin{array}{r} 7x + 3y = 17 \\ \underline{+\ 3x + 7y = 19} \\ 10x + 10y = 36 \end{array}$$

Divide each side by 10: $x + y = 3.6$

Calculate the average: $\dfrac{x+y}{2} = \dfrac{3.6}{2} = \mathbf{1.8}$

Since this numeric entry question requires a fraction for the answer, note that $1.8 = 1\frac{8}{10} = \frac{18}{10}$. So enter 18 for the numerator and 10 for the denominator. Remember that you don't have to reduce fractions to lowest terms.

EXAMPLE 17

> **Benjamin worked from 9:47 A.M. until 12:11 P.M.**
> **Jeremy worked from 9:11 A.M. until 12:47 P.M.**
>
> | Quantity A | Quantity B |
> |---|---|
> | The number of minutes Benjamin worked | The number of minutes Jeremy worked |

Do not spend any time calculating how many minutes either of them worked. You only need to know which column is greater, and since Jeremy started earlier and finished later, he clearly worked longer. The answer is **B**.

TACTIC

Pay Attention to Units

Often the answer to a question must be in units different from the data given in the question. As you read the question, write on your scratch paper exactly what you are being asked and circle it or put an asterisk next to it. Do they want hours or minutes or seconds, dollars or cents, feet or inches, meters or centimeters? On multiple-choice questions, an answer using the wrong units is almost always one of the choices.

EXAMPLE 18

> **Driving at 48 miles per hour, how many minutes will it take to drive 32 miles?**
>
> Ⓐ $\frac{2}{3}$ Ⓑ $\frac{3}{2}$ Ⓒ 40 Ⓓ 45 Ⓔ 2,400

SOLUTION.

This is a relatively easy question. Just be attentive. Divide the distance, 32, by the rate, 48: $\frac{32}{48} = \frac{2}{3}$, so it will take $\frac{2}{3}$ of an *hour* to drive 32 miles. Choice A is $\frac{2}{3}$, but that is not the correct answer, because you are asked how many *minutes* it will take. To convert hours to minutes, multiply by 60: it will take $\frac{2}{3}(60) = \mathbf{40}$ minutes, **C.**

Note that you could have been asked how many *seconds* it would take, in which case the answer would be 40(60) = 2,400, Choice E.

EXAMPLE 19

At Nat's Nuts a $2\frac{1}{4}$-pound bag of pistachio nuts costs $6.00. At this rate, what is the cost in cents of a bag weighing 9 ounces?

Ⓐ 1.5 Ⓑ 24 Ⓒ 150 Ⓓ 1,350 Ⓔ 2,400

SOLUTION.
This is a relatively simple ratio, but make sure you get the units right. To do this you need to know that there are 100 cents in a dollar and 16 ounces in a pound.

$$\frac{\text{price}}{\text{weight}} : \frac{6 \text{ dollars}}{2.25 \text{ pounds}} = \frac{600 \text{ cents}}{36 \text{ ounces}} = \frac{x \text{ cents}}{9 \text{ ounces}}$$

Now cross-multiply and solve: $36x = 5{,}400 \Rightarrow x =$ **150, C.**

TACTIC

8

Systematically Make Lists

When a question asks "how many," often the best strategy is to make a list of all the possibilities. If you do this it is important that you make the list in a *systematic* fashion so that you don't inadvertently leave something out. Usually, this means listing the possibilities in numerical or alphabetical order. Often, shortly after starting the list, you can see a pattern developing and you can figure out how many more entries there will be without writing them all down. Even if the question does not specifically ask "how many," you may need to count something to answer it; in this case, as well, the best plan may be to write out a list.

EXAMPLE 20

A palindrome is a number, such as 93539, that reads the same forward and backward. How many palindromes are there between 100 and 1,000?

SOLUTION.
First, write down the numbers that begin and end in 1:

101, 111, 121, 131, 141, 151, 161, 171, 181, 191

Next write the numbers that begin and end in a 2:

202, 212, 222, 232, 242, 252, 262, 272, 282, 292

By now you should see the pattern: there are 10 numbers beginning with 1, 10 beginning with 2, and there will be 10 beginning with 3, 4, . . . , 9 for a total of $9 \times 10 =$ **90** palindromes.

EXAMPLE 21

The product of three positive integers is 300. If one of them is 5, what is the least possible value of the sum of the other two?

Ⓐ 16 Ⓑ 17 Ⓒ 19 Ⓓ 23 Ⓔ 32

SOLUTION.

Since one of the integers is 5, the product of the other two is 60. Systematically, list all possible pairs, (a, b), of positive integers whose product is 60 and check their sums. First let $a = 1$, then 2, and so on.

a	b	$a + b$
1	60	61
2	30	32
3	20	23
4	15	19
5	12	17
6	10	16

The least possible sum is **16, A.**

PRACTICE EXERCISES

General Math Strategies

1. At Leo's Lumberyard, an 8-foot long wooden pole costs \$3.00. At this rate, what is the cost, in cents, of a pole that is 16 inches long?

Ⓐ 0.5
Ⓑ 48
Ⓒ 50
Ⓓ 64
Ⓔ 96

2. In the figure below, vertex *Q* of square *OPQR* is on a circle with center *O*. If the area of the square is 8, what is the area of the circle?

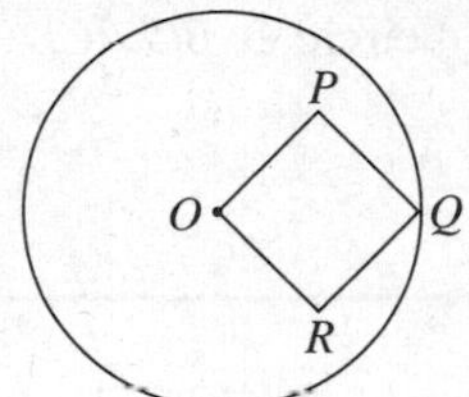

Ⓐ 8π
Ⓑ $8\pi\sqrt{2}$
Ⓒ 16π
Ⓓ 32π
Ⓔ 64π

3. In 1999, Diana read 10 English books and 7 French books. In 2000, she read twice as many French books as English books. If 60% of the books that she read during the two years were French, how many books did she read in 2000?

Ⓐ 16
Ⓑ 26
Ⓒ 32
Ⓓ 39
Ⓔ 48

4. In writing all of the integers from 1 to 300, how many times is the digit 1 used?

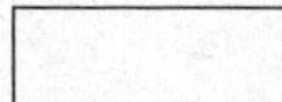

5. In the figure below, if the radius of circle *O* is 10, what is the length of diagonal *AC* of rectangle *OABC*?

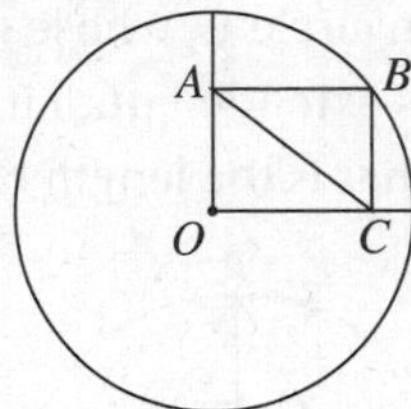

Ⓐ $\sqrt{2}$
Ⓑ $\sqrt{10}$
Ⓒ $5\sqrt{2}$
Ⓓ 10
Ⓔ $10\sqrt{2}$

6. In the figure below, *ABCD* is a square and *AED* is an equilateral triangle. If $AB = 2$, what is the area of the shaded region?

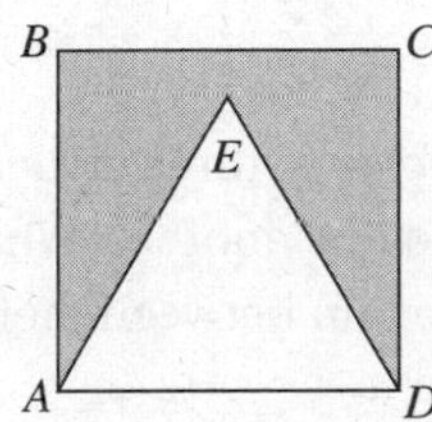

Ⓐ $\sqrt{3}$
Ⓑ 2
Ⓒ 3
Ⓓ $4 - 2\sqrt{3}$
Ⓔ $4 - \sqrt{3}$

7. If $5x + 13 = 31$, what is the value of $\sqrt{5x+31}$?

Ⓐ $\sqrt{13}$
Ⓑ $\sqrt{\frac{173}{5}}$
Ⓒ 7
Ⓓ 13
Ⓔ 169

8. If $a + 2b = 14$ and $5a + 4b = 16$, what is the average (arithmetic mean) of a and b?

9. In the figure below, equilateral triangle ABC is inscribed in circle O, whose radius is 4. Altitude BD is extended until it intersects the circle at E. What is the length of DE?

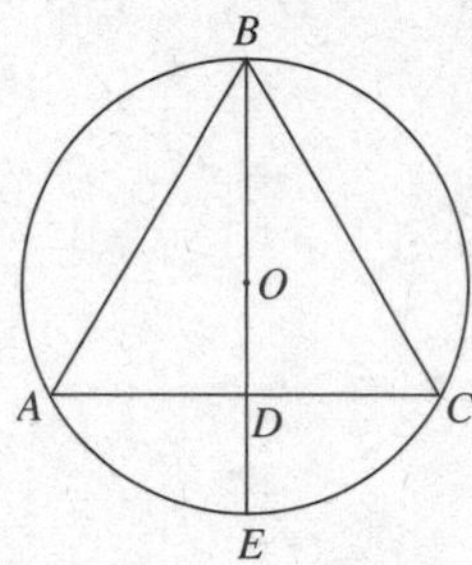

Ⓐ 1

Ⓑ $\sqrt{3}$

Ⓒ 2

Ⓓ $2\sqrt{3}$

Ⓔ $4\sqrt{3}$

10. In the figure below, three circles of radius 1 are tangent to one another. What is the area of the shaded region between them?

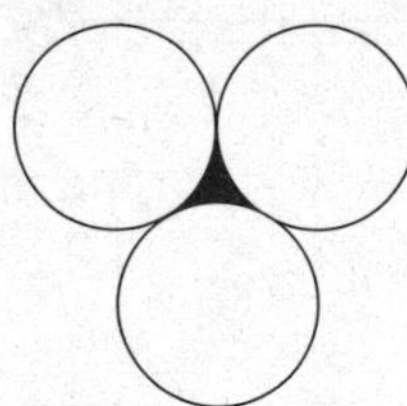

Ⓐ $\frac{\pi}{2} - \sqrt{3}$

Ⓑ 1.5

Ⓒ $\pi - \sqrt{3}$

Ⓓ $\sqrt{3} - \frac{\pi}{2}$

Ⓔ $2 - \frac{\pi}{2}$

11.

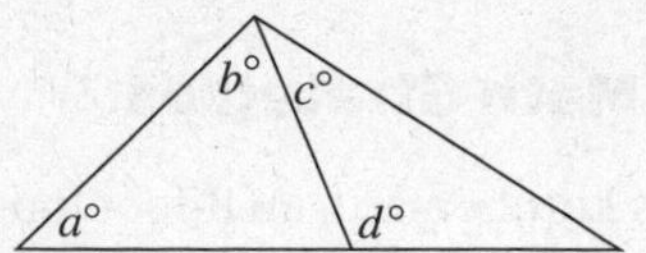

Quantity A	Quantity B
$a + b$	$c + d$

12.

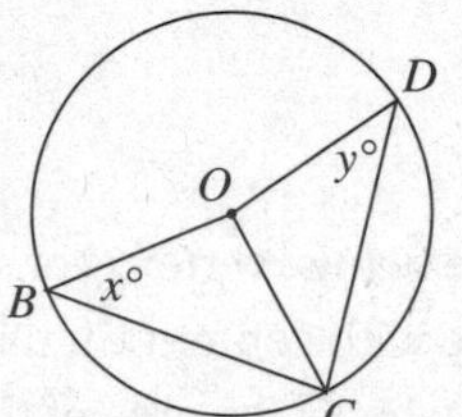

In circle O, $BC > CD$

Quantity A	Quantity B
x	y

13.

Quantity A	Quantity B
The number of odd positive factors of 30	The number of even positive factors of 30

QUESTIONS 14–15 REFER TO THE FOLLOWING DEFINITION.

14.

$\{a, b\}$ represents the remainder when a is divided by b.

Quantity A	Quantity B
$\{10^3, 3\}$	$\{10^5, 5\}$

15.

c and d are positive integers with $c < d$.

Quantity A	Quantity B
$\{c, d\}$	$\{d, c\}$

ANSWER KEY

1. **C**	6. **E**	11. **B**
2. **C**	7. **C**	12. **B**
3. **E**	8. **2.5**	13. **C**
4. **160**	9. **C**	14. **A**
5. **D**	10. **D**	15. **A**

ANSWER EXPLANATIONS

Two asterisks (**) indicate an alternative method of solving.

1. **(C)** This is a relatively simple ratio problem, but use TACTIC 7 (page 258) and make sure you get the units right. To do this you need to know that there are 100 cents in a dollar and 12 inches in a foot.

$$\frac{\text{price}}{\text{weight}} : \frac{3 \text{ dollars}}{8 \text{ feet}} = \frac{300 \text{ cents}}{96 \text{ inches}} = \frac{x \text{ cents}}{16 \text{ inches}}$$

Now cross-multiply and solve:

$$96x = 4,800 \Rightarrow x = 50$$

2. **(C)** Use TACTICS 2 (page 250) and 4 (page 254). On your scrap paper, extend line segments OP and OR.

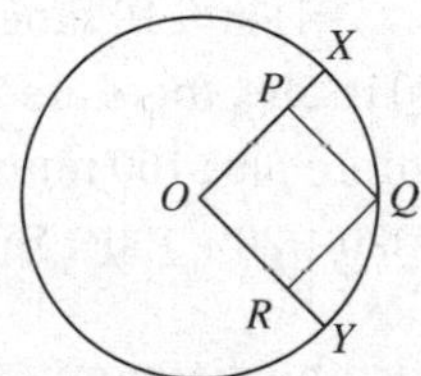

Square $OPQR$, whose area is 8, takes up most of quarter-circle OXY. So the area of the quarter-circle is certainly between 11 and 13. The area of the whole circle is 4 times as great: between 44 and 52. Check the five choices: they are approximately 25, 36, 50, 100, 200. The answer is clearly C.

**Another way to use TACTIC 4 (page 254) is to draw in line segment OQ.

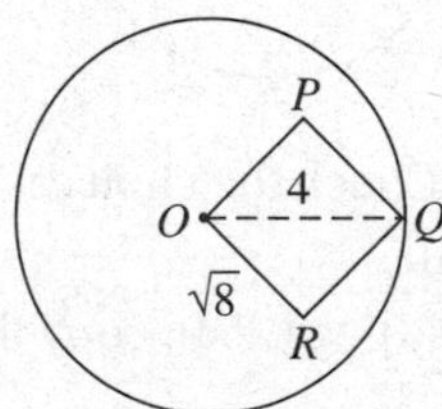

Since the area of the square is 8, each side is $\sqrt{8}$, and diagonal OQ is $\sqrt{8} \times \sqrt{2} = \sqrt{16} = 4$.

But OQ is also a radius, so the area of the circle is $\pi(4)^2 = 16\pi$.

3. **(E)** Use TACTIC 1 (page 248): draw a picture representing a pile of books or a bookshelf.

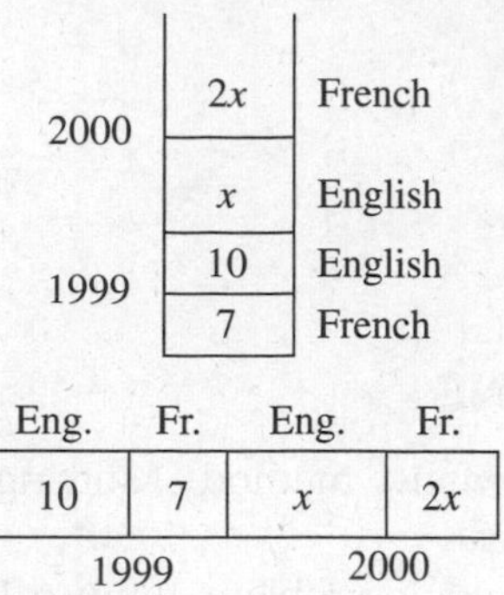

In the two years the number of French books Diana read was $7 + 2x$ and the total number of books was $17 + 3x$. Then 60% or $\frac{3}{5} = \frac{7+2x}{17+3x}$. To solve, cross-multiply:

$$5(7 + 2x) = 3(17 + 3x) \Rightarrow 35 + 10x = 51 + 9x \Rightarrow x = 16$$

In 2000, Diana read 16 English books and 32 French books, a total of 48 books.

4. **160** Use TACTIC 8 (page 259). Systematically list the numbers that contain the digit 1, writing as many as you need to see the pattern. Between 1 and 99 the digit 1 is used 10 times as the units digit (1, 11, 21, . . . , 91) and 10 times as the tens digit (10, 11, 12, . . . , 19) for a total of 20 times. From 200 to 299, there are 20 more (the same 20 preceded by a 2). From 100 to 199 there are 20 more plus 100 numbers where the digit 1 is used in the hundreds place. So the total is 20 + 20 + 20 + 100 = 160.

5. **(D)** Use TACTIC 2 (page 250). Trust the diagram: *AC*, which is clearly longer than *OC*, is approximately as long as radius *OE*.

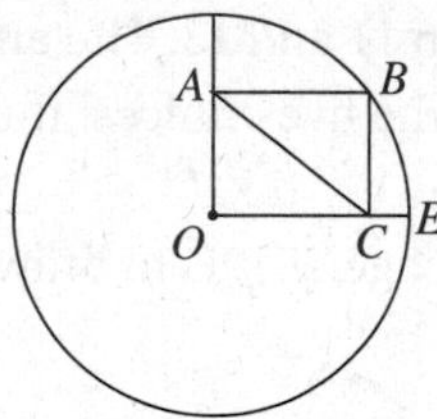

Therefore, *AC* must be about 10. Check the choices. They are approximately 1.4, 3.1, 7, 10, and 14. The answer must be 10.
**The answer *is* 10. Use TACTIC 4 (page 254): copy the diagram on your scrap paper and draw in diagonal *OB*.

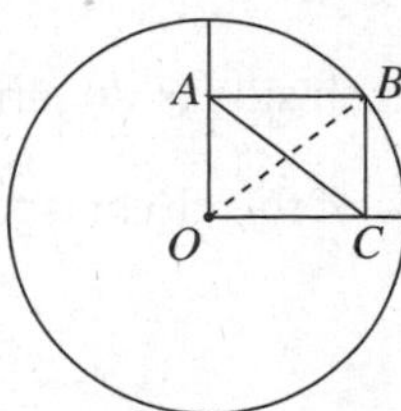

Since the two diagonals of a rectangle are equal, and diagonal *OB* is a radius, $AC = OB = 10$.

6. **(E)** Use TACTIC 5 (page 256): subtract to find the shaded area. The area of the square is 4. The area of the equilateral triangle (see Section 12-J, page 456) is $\frac{2^2\sqrt{3}}{4} = \frac{4\sqrt{3}}{4} = \sqrt{3}$. So the area of the shaded region is $4 - \sqrt{3}$.

7. **(C)** Use TACTIC 6 (page 257): don't do more than you have to. In particular, don't solve for x.

$$5x + 13 = 31 \Rightarrow 5x = 18 \Rightarrow 5x + 31 = 18 + 31 = 49 \Rightarrow \sqrt{5x+31} = \sqrt{49} = 7$$

8. **2.5** Use TACTIC 6 (page 257): don't do more than is necessary. We don't need to know the values of a and b, only their average. Adding the two equations, we get

$$6a + 6b = 30 \Rightarrow a + b = 5 \Rightarrow \frac{a+b}{2} = \frac{5}{2} = 2.5$$

9. **(C)** Use TACTIC 5 (page 256): to get DE, subtract OD from radius OE, which is 4. Draw AO (TACTIC 4, page 254).

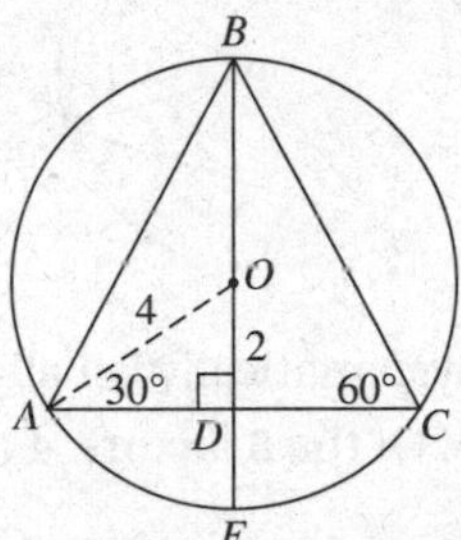

Since $\triangle AOD$ is a 30-60-90 right triangle, OD is 2 (one half of OA). So, $DE = 4 - 2 = 2$.

10. **(D)** Use TACTIC 4 (page 254) and add some lines: connect the centers of the three circles to form an equilateral triangle whose sides are 2.

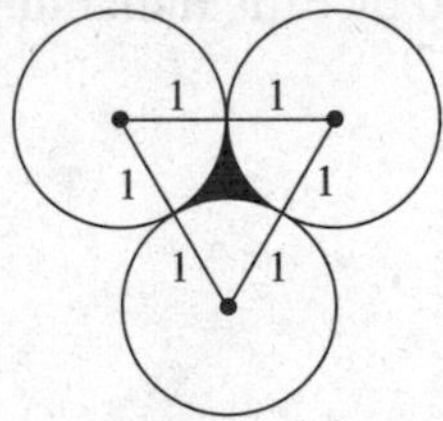

Now use TACTIC 5 (page 256) and find the shaded area by subtracting the area of the three sectors from the area of the triangle. The area of the triangle is $\frac{2^2\sqrt{3}}{4} = \sqrt{3}$ (see Section 12-J, page 456).

Each sector is one sixth of a circle of radius 1. Together they form one half of such a circle, so their total area is $\frac{1}{2}\pi(1)^2 = \frac{\pi}{2}$. Finally, subtract: the shaded area is $\sqrt{3} - \frac{\pi}{2}$.

11. **(B)** If you don't see how to answer this, use TACTIC 2 (page 250): trust the diagram. Estimate the measure of each angle: for example, $a = 45$, $b = 70$, $c = 30$, and $d = 120$. So $c + d$ (150) is considerably greater than $a + b$ (115). Choose B.

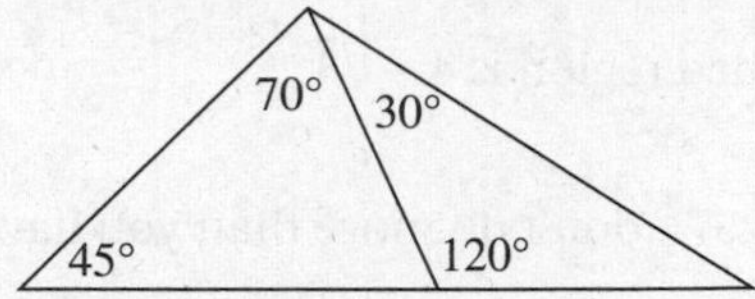

**In fact, d by itself is equal to $a + b$ (an exterior angle of a triangle is equal to the sum of the opposite two interior angles). So $c + d > a + b$.

12. **(B)** From the figure, it appears that x and y are equal, or nearly so. However, the given information states that $BC > CD$, but this is not clear from the diagram. Use TACTIC 3 (page 253): when you draw the figure on your scrap paper, exaggerate it. Draw it with BC much greater than CD. Now it is clear that y is greater.

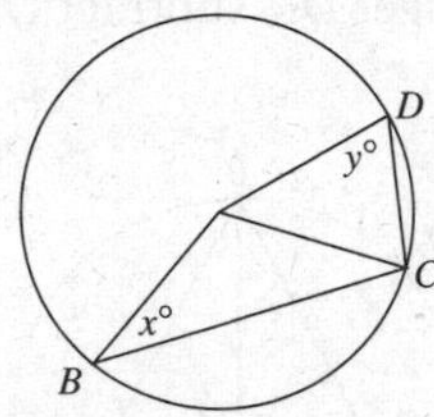

13. **(C)** Use TACTIC 8 (page 259). Systematically list all the factors of 30, either individually or in pairs: 1, 30; 2, 15; 3, 10; 5, 6. Of the 8 factors, 4 are even and 4 are odd.

14. **(A)** Quantity A: When 10^3 (1,000) is divided by 3, the quotient is 333 and the remainder is 1. Quantity B: 10^5 is divisible by 5, so the remainder is 0.
    Quantity A is greater.

15. **(A)** Quantity A: since $c < d$, the quotient when c is divided by d is 0, and the remainder is c. Quantity B: when d is divided by c the remainder must be less than c.
    So Quantity A is greater.

Discrete Quantitative Questions

9

About 20 of the 40 questions in the two math sections are what the ETS calls discrete quantitative questions. These questions are of three types:

- Multiple-choice questions
- Multiple-answer questions
- Numeric entry questions

TIP

When you take the GRE, dismiss the instructions for these questions instantly—do not spend even one second reading them—and certainly never accept their offer of clicking on "HELP" to return to them during the test.

Multiple-choice questions are just the standard multiple-choice questions that you are familiar with. Each one has five answer choices, exactly one of which is the correct answer. To get credit for a multiple-choice question you simply click on the oval in front of the one correct answer choice.

Multiple-answer questions are multiple-choice questions with a twist. These questions could have anywhere from 3 to 12 answer choices, any number of which could be correct, from just one to all of them. To alert you to the fact that there may be, and usually is, more than one correct answer, instead of an oval, a square appears in front of each answer choice. To get credit for a multiple-answer question, you must click on the square in front of each correct answer and leave blank the squares in front of each of the incorrect answers.

Numeric entry questions are the only questions on the test for which no answer choices are given. The answer to such a question may be positive or negative and may be an integer, decimal, or fraction. If the answer is negative, use a hyphen for the negative sign. To get credit for a numeric entry question you must use the keyboard to enter your answer into the box on the screen directly below the question. If in answering a question, you use the onscreen calculator and the digital readout is exactly the answer that you want to enter in the box, you can click on the calculator's TRANSFER DISPLAY bar and the readout will automatically appear in the box. Always enter the exact answer unless the question tells you to round your answer, in which case you must round it to the degree of accuracy asked for.

TIP

On pages 11–12 you can see a worked out example of each of these three types of questions.

If the answer is to be entered as a fraction, there will be two boxes, and you are to enter the numerator in the upper box and the denominator in the lower box. Any answer equivalent to a correct answer earns full credit. If the correct answer to a question is 2.5, then 2.50 is equally acceptable, unless you were told to give the answer to the nearest tenth. Also, fractions do not have to be reduced: if the correct answer is $\frac{1}{2}$, then you would receive full credit for $\frac{3}{6}$ or $\frac{13}{26}$, or any other fraction equivalent to $\frac{1}{2}$.

The majority of discrete quantitative questions are of the multiple-choice variety, and all of the tactics discussed in this chapter apply to them. Some of the tactics also apply to multiple-answer questions and numeric entry questions.

The important strategies you will learn in this chapter help you answer many questions on the GRE. However, as invaluable as these tactics are, use them only when you need them. *If you know how to do a problem and are confident that you can do it accurately and reasonably quickly, JUST DO IT!*

As we have done throughout this book, on multiple-choice questions we will continue to label the five answer Choices A, B, C, D, and E and to refer to them as such. On multiple-answer questions, the choices will be consecutively labeled A, B, C, etc., using as many letters as there are answer choices. Of course, when you take the GRE, these letters will not appear—there will simply be a blank oval in front of each of the answer choices. When we refer to Choice C—as we do, for example, in TACTIC 1 (below)—we are simply referring to the third answer choice among the five presented.

TESTING TACTICS

TACTIC

Test the Choices, Starting with C

TACTIC 1, often called ***backsolving***, is useful when you are asked to solve for an unknown and you understand what needs to be done to answer the question, but you want to avoid doing the algebra. The idea is simple: test the various choices to see which one is correct.

NOTE: On the GRE the answers to virtually all numerical multiple-choice questions are listed in either increasing or decreasing order. Consequently, C is the middle value, and *in applying TACTIC 1, you should always start with C.* For example, assume that Choices A, B, C, D, and E are given in increasing order. Try C. If it works, you've found the answer. If C doesn't work, you should know whether you need to test a larger number or a smaller one, and that permits you to eliminate two more choices. If C is too small, you need a larger number, so A and B are out; if C is too large, eliminate D and E, which are even larger.

Examples 1 and 2 illustrate the proper use of TACTIC 1.

EXAMPLE 1

If the average (arithmetic mean) of 5, 6, 7, and w is 10, what is the value of w?

Ⓐ 8 Ⓑ 13 Ⓒ 18 Ⓓ 22 Ⓔ 28

SOLUTION.

Use TACTIC 1. Test Choice C: $w = 18$.

- Is the average of 5, 6, 7, and 18 equal to 10?
- No: $\frac{5+6+7+18}{4} = \frac{36}{4} = 9$, which is *too small.*
- Eliminate C, and, since for the average to be 10, w must be *greater* than 18, eliminate A and B, as well.
- Try D: $w = 22$. Is the average of 5, 6, 7, and 22 equal to 10?
- Yes: $\frac{5+6+7+22}{4} = \frac{40}{4} = 10$. The answer is **D**.

Every problem that can be solved using TACTIC 1 can be solved directly, often in less time. So we stress: *if you are confident that you can solve a problem quickly and accurately, just do so.*

Here are two direct methods for solving Example 1, each of which is faster than backsolving. (See Section 12-E, page 397, on averages.) If you know either method you should use it, and save TACTIC 1 for those problems that you can't easily solve directly.

DIRECT SOLUTION 1. If the average of four numbers is 10, their sum is 40. So, $5 + 6 + 7 + w = 40 \Rightarrow 18 + w = 40 \Rightarrow w = \mathbf{22}$.

DIRECT SOLUTION 2. Since 5 is *5 less than* 10, 6 is *4 less than* 10, and 7 is *3 less than* 10, to compensate, w must be $5 + 4 + 3 = 12$ more than 10.

So, $w = 10 + 12 = \mathbf{22}$.

EXAMPLE 2

Judy is now twice as old as Adam, but 6 years ago, she was 5 times as old as he was. How old is Judy now?

Ⓐ 10 Ⓑ 16 Ⓒ 20 Ⓓ 24 Ⓔ 32

SOLUTION.

Use TACTIC 1: backsolve starting with C. If Judy is now 20, Adam is 10, and 6 years ago, they would have been 14 and 4. Since Judy would have been less than 5 times as old as Adam, eliminate C, D, and E, and try a smaller value. If Judy is now 16, Adam is 8; 6 years ago, they would have been 10 and 2. That's it; 10 *is* 5 times 2. The answer is **B**.

(See Section 12-H, page 435, on word problems for the correct algebraic solution.)

TIP

Don't start with C if some of the other choices are much easier to work with. If you start with B and it is too small, you may only get to eliminate two choices (A and B), instead of three, but it will save time if plugging in Choice C would be messy.

Some tactics allow you to eliminate a few choices so you can make an educated guess. On those problems where it can be used, TACTIC 1 *always* gets you the right answer. The only reason not to use it on a particular problem is that you can *easily* solve the problem directly.

EXAMPLE 3

If $3x = 2(5 - 2x)$, then $x =$

Ⓐ $-\frac{10}{7}$ Ⓑ 0 Ⓒ $\frac{3}{7}$ Ⓓ 1 Ⓔ $\frac{10}{7}$

SOLUTION.

Since plugging in 0 is so much easier than plugging in $\frac{3}{7}$, start with B: then the left-hand side of the equation is 0 and the right-hand side is 10. The left-hand side is much too small. Eliminate A and B and try something bigger—D, of course; it will be much easier to deal with 1 than with $\frac{3}{7}$ or $\frac{10}{7}$. Now the left-hand side is 3 and the right-hand side is 6. We're closer, but not there. The answer must be **E**. Notice that we got the right answer without ever plugging in one of those unpleasant fractions. Are you uncomfortable choosing E without checking it? Don't be. If you *know* that the answer is greater than 1, and only one choice is greater than 1, that choice has to be right.

Again, we emphasize that, no matter what the choices are, you backsolve *only* if you can't easily do the algebra. Most students would probably do this problem directly:

$$3x = 2(5 - 2x) \Rightarrow 3x = 10 - 4x \Rightarrow 7x = 10 \Rightarrow x = \frac{10}{7}$$

and save backsolving for a harder problem. You have to determine which method is best for you.

TACTIC 2 Replace Variables with Numbers

Mastery of TACTIC 2 is critical for anyone developing good test-taking skills. This tactic can be used whenever the five choices involve the variables in the question. There are three steps:

STEP 1 Replace each letter with an easy-to-use number.
STEP 2 Solve the problem using those numbers.
STEP 3 Evaluate each of the five choices with the numbers you picked to see which choice is equal to the answer you obtained.

Examples 4 and 5 illustrate the proper use of TACTIC 2.

EXAMPLE 4

If *a* is equal to the sum of *b* and *c*, which of the following is equal to the difference of *b* and *c*?

Ⓐ $a - b - c$ Ⓑ $a - b + c$ Ⓒ $a - c$ Ⓓ $a - 2c$ Ⓔ $a - b - 2c$

SOLUTION.

STEP 1 Pick three easy-to-use numbers that satisfy $a = b + c$: for example, $a = 5$, $b = 3$, $c = 2$.

STEP 2 Then, solve the problem with these numbers: the difference of b and c is $3 - 2 = 1$.

STEP 3 Finally, check each of the five choices to see which one is equal to 1:

Ⓐ Does $a - b - c = 1$? NO. $5 - 3 - 2 = 0$
Ⓑ Does $a - b + c = 1$? NO. $5 - 3 + 2 = 4$
Ⓒ Does $a - c = 1$? NO. $5 - 2 = 3$
Ⓓ Does $a - 2c = 1$? YES! $5 - 2(2) = 5 - 4 = 1$
Ⓔ Does $a - b - 2c = 1$? NO. $5 - 3 - 2(2) = 2 - 4 = -2$

The answer is **D**.

EXAMPLE 5

If the sum of five consecutive even integers is *t*, then, in terms of *t*, what is the greatest of these integers?

Ⓐ $\frac{t-20}{5}$ Ⓑ $\frac{t-10}{5}$ Ⓒ $\frac{t}{5}$ Ⓓ $\frac{t+10}{5}$ Ⓔ $\frac{t+20}{5}$

SOLUTION.

STEP 1 Pick five easy-to-use consecutive even integers: say, 2, 4, 6, 8, 10. Then t, their sum, is 30.

STEP 2 Solve the problem with these numbers: the greatest of these integers is 10.

When $t = 30$, the five choices are $\frac{10}{5}, \frac{20}{5}, \frac{30}{5}, \frac{40}{5}, \frac{50}{5}$.

STEP 3 Only $\frac{50}{5}$, Choice **E**, is equal to 10.

Of course, Examples 4 and 5 can be solved without using TACTIC 2 *if your algebra skills are good.* Here are the solutions.

SOLUTION 4. $a = b + c \Rightarrow b = a - c \Rightarrow b - c = (a - c) - c = a - 2c.$

SOLUTION 5. Let n, $n + 2$, $n + 4$, $n + 6$, and $n + 8$ be five consecutive even integers, and let t be their sum. Then,

$$t = n + (n + 2) + (n + 4) + (n + 6) + (n + 8) = 5n + 20$$

So, $n = \frac{t-20}{5} \Rightarrow n + 8 = \frac{t-20}{5} + 8 = \frac{t-20}{5} + \frac{40}{5} = \frac{t+20}{5}$.

The important point is that if you can't do the algebra, you can still use TACTIC 2 and *always* get the right answer. Of course, you should use TACTIC 2 even if you can do the algebra, if you think that by using this tactic you will solve the problem faster or will be less likely to make a mistake. This is a good example of what we mean when we say that with the proper use of these tactics, you can correctly answer many questions for which you may not know the correct mathematical solution.

Examples 6 and 7 are somewhat different. You are asked to reason through word problems involving only variables. Most students find problems like these mind-boggling. Here, the use of TACTIC 2 is essential. Without it, Example 6 is difficult and Example 7 is nearly impossible. This is not an easy tactic to master, but with practice you will catch on.

TIP

Replace the letters with numbers that are easy to use, not necessarily ones that make sense. *It is perfectly OK to ignore reality.* A school can have 5 students, apples can cost 10 dollars each, trains can go 5 miles per hour or 1,000 miles per hour—it doesn't matter.

EXAMPLE 6

If a school cafeteria needs *c* cans of soup each week for each student, and if there are *s* students in the school, for how many weeks will *x* cans of soup last?

Ⓐ csx Ⓑ $\frac{xs}{c}$ Ⓒ $\frac{s}{cx}$ Ⓓ $\frac{x}{cs}$ Ⓔ $\frac{cx}{s}$

SOLUTION.

- Replace *c, s,* and *x* with three easy-to-use numbers. If a school cafeteria needs 2 cans of soup each week for each student, and if there are 5 students in the school, how many weeks will 20 cans of soup last?
- Since the cafeteria needs $2 \times 5 = 10$ cans of soup per week, 20 cans will last 2 weeks.
- Which of the choices equals 2 when $c = 2$, $s = 5$, and $x = 20$?
- $csx = 200$; $\frac{xs}{c} = 50$; $\frac{s}{cx} = \frac{1}{8}$; $\frac{x}{cs} = 2$; and $\frac{cx}{s} = 8$.

  The answer is $\frac{x}{cs}$, **D.**

NOTE: You do not need to get the exact value of each choice. As soon as you see that a choice does not equal the value you are looking for, stop—eliminate that choice and move on. For example, in the preceding problem, it is clear that *csx* is much greater than 2, so eliminate it immediately; you do not need to multiply it out to determine that the value is 200.

CAUTION

In this type of problem it is *not* a good idea to replace any of the variables by 1. Since multiplying and dividing by 1 give the same result, you would not be able to distinguish between $\frac{cx}{s}$ and $\frac{x}{cs}$, both of which are equal to 4 when $c = 1$, $s = 5$, and $x = 20$. It is also not a good idea to use the same number for different variables: $\frac{cx}{s}$ and $\frac{xs}{c}$ are each equal to *x* when *c* and *s* are equal.

EXAMPLE 7

A vendor sells *h* hot dogs and *s* sodas. If a hot dog costs twice as much as a soda, and if the vendor takes in a total of *d* dollars, how many cents does a soda cost?

Ⓐ $\frac{100d}{s+2h}$ Ⓑ $\frac{s+2h}{100d}$ Ⓒ $\frac{d(s+2h)}{100}$ Ⓓ $100d(s+2h)$ Ⓔ $\frac{d}{100(s+2h)}$

SOLUTION.

- Replace *h, s,* and *d* with three easy-to-use numbers. Suppose a soda costs 50¢ and a hot dog \$1.00. Then, if he sold 2 sodas and 3 hot dogs, he took in 4 dollars.
- Which of the choices equals 50 when $s = 2$, $h = 3$, and $d = 4$?
- Only $\frac{100d}{s+2h}$ **(A)**: $\frac{100(4)}{2+2(3)} = \frac{400}{8} = 50$.

Now, practice TACTIC 2 on the following problems.

EXAMPLE 8

Yann will be x years old y years from now. How old was he z years ago?

Ⓐ $x+y+z$ Ⓑ $x+y-z$ Ⓒ $x-y-z$ Ⓓ $y-x-z$ Ⓔ $z-y-x$

SOLUTION.
Assume that Yann will be 10 in 2 years. How old was he 3 years ago? If he will be 10 in 2 years, he is 8 now and 3 years ago he was 5. Which of the choices equals 5 when $x = 10$, $y = 2$, and $z = 3$? Only $x - y - z$, **C.**

EXAMPLE 9

Stan drove for h hours at a constant rate of r miles per hour. How many miles did he go during the final 20 minutes of his drive?

Ⓐ $20r$ Ⓑ $\frac{hr}{3}$ Ⓒ $3rh$ Ⓓ $\frac{hr}{20}$ Ⓔ $\frac{r}{3}$

SOLUTION.
If Stan drove at 60 miles per hour for 2 hours, how far did he go in the last 20 minutes? Since 20 minutes is $\frac{1}{3}$ of an hour, he went 20 $\left(\frac{1}{3}\text{ of } 60\right)$ miles. Only Choice E, $\frac{r}{3}$, is 20 when $r = 60$ and $h = 2$. Notice that h is irrelevant. Whether he had been driving for 2 hours or 20 hours, the distance he covered in the last 20 minutes would be the same.

TACTIC

Choose Appropriate Numbers

TACTIC 3 is similar to TACTIC 2, in that we pick convenient numbers. However, here no variable is given in the problem. TACTIC 3 is especially useful in problems involving fractions, ratios, and percents.

TIP

In problems involving fractions, the best number to use is the least common denominator of all the fractions. In problems involving percents, the easiest number to use is 100. (See Sections 12-B and 12-C, pages 350–380.)

EXAMPLE 10

At Madison High School each student studies exactly one foreign language. Three-fifths of the students take Spanish, and one-fourth of the remaining students take German. If all of the others take French, what <u>percent</u> of the students take French?

Ⓐ 10 Ⓑ 15 Ⓒ 20 Ⓓ 25 Ⓔ 30

SOLUTION.
The least common denominator of $\frac{3}{5}$ and $\frac{1}{4}$ is 20, so assume that there are 20 students at Madison High. (Remember the numbers don't have to be realistic.) The number of students taking Spanish is 12 $\left(\frac{3}{5}\text{ of } 20\right)$. Of the remaining 8 students, 2 of them $\left(\frac{1}{4}\text{ of } 8\right)$ take German. The other 6 take French. Finally, 6 is **30%** of 20. The answer is **E.**

EXAMPLE 11

From 1994 to 1995 the sales of a book decreased by 80%. If the sales in 1996 were the same as in 1994, by what percent did they increase from 1995 to 1996?

Ⓐ 80% Ⓑ 100% Ⓒ 120% Ⓓ 400% Ⓔ 500%

SOLUTION.

Since this problem involves percents, assume that 100 copies of the book were sold in 1994 (and 1996). Sales dropped by 80 (80% of 100) to 20 in 1995 and then increased by 80, from 20 back to 100, in 1996. The percent increase was

$$\frac{\text{the actual increase}}{\text{the original amount}} \times 100\% = \frac{80}{20} \times 100\% = \mathbf{400\%, D}$$

TACTIC 4

Eliminate Absurd Choices and Guess

When you have no idea how to solve a multiple-choice question, you can always make an educated guess—simply eliminate all the absurd choices and then guess from among the remaining ones.

During the course of a GRE, you will probably find at least a few multiple-choice questions that you don't know how to solve. Since you are not penalized for wrong answers, you are surely going to enter answers for them. But before taking a wild guess, take a moment to look at the answer choices. Often two or three of them are absurd. Eliminate those and then guess one of the others. Occasionally, four of the choices are absurd. When this occurs, your answer is no longer a guess.

What makes a choice absurd? Lots of things. Here are a few. Even if you don't know how to solve a problem you may realize that

- the answer must be positive, but some of the choices are negative;
- the answer must be even, but some of the choices are odd;
- the answer must be less than 100, but some choices exceed 100;
- a ratio must be less than 1, but some choices are greater than 1.

Let's look at several examples. In a few of them, the information given is intentionally insufficient to solve the problem; but you will still be able to determine that some of the answers are absurd. In each case, the "solution" will indicate which choices you should have eliminated. At that point you would simply guess. Remember, on the GRE when you guess, don't agonize. Just guess and move on.

EXAMPLE 12

A region inside a semicircle of radius r is shaded and you are asked for its area.

Ⓐ $\frac{1}{4}\pi r^2$ Ⓑ $\frac{1}{3}\pi r^2$ Ⓒ $\frac{1}{2}\pi r^2$ Ⓓ $\frac{2}{3}\pi r^2$ Ⓔ πr^2

SOLUTION.
You may have no idea how to find the area of the shaded region, but you should know that since the area of a circle is πr^2, the area of a semicircle is $\frac{1}{2}\pi r^2$. Therefore, the area of the shaded region must be *less* than $\frac{1}{2}\pi r^2$, so eliminate C, D, and E. On an actual GRE problem, you may be able to make an educated guess between A and B. If so, terrific; if not, just choose one or the other.

EXAMPLE 13

The average (arithmetic mean) of 5, 10, 15, and z is 20. What is z?

Ⓐ 0 Ⓑ 20 Ⓒ 25 Ⓓ 45 Ⓔ 50

SOLUTION.
If the average of four numbers is 20, and three of them are less than 20, the other one must be greater than 20. Eliminate A and B and guess. If you further realize that since 5 and 10 are a *lot less* than 20, z will probably be a *lot more* than 20; eliminate C, as well.

EXAMPLE 14

If 25% of 260 equals 6.5% of a, what is a?

Ⓐ 10 Ⓑ 65 Ⓒ 100 Ⓓ 130 Ⓔ 1,000

SOLUTION.
Since 6.5% of a equals 25% of 260, which is surely greater than 6.5% of 260, a must be greater than 260. Eliminate A, B, C, and D. The answer *must* be **E**!

Example 14 illustrates an important point. *Even if you know how to solve a problem,* if you immediately see that four of the five choices are absurd, just pick the fifth choice and move on.

EXAMPLE 15

A jackpot of \$39,000 is to be divided in some ratio among three people. What is the value of the largest share?

Ⓐ \$23,400 Ⓑ \$19,500 Ⓒ \$11,700 Ⓓ \$7,800 Ⓔ \$3,900

SOLUTION.
If the prize were divided equally, each of the three shares would be worth \$13,000. If it is divided unequally, the largest share is surely worth *more than* \$13,000. Eliminate C, D, and E. In an actual question, you would be told what the ratio is, and that might enable you to eliminate A or B. If not, you just guess.

EXAMPLE 16

In a certain club, the ratio of the number of boys to girls is 5:3. What percent of the members of the club are girls?

Ⓐ 37.5% Ⓑ 50% Ⓒ 60% Ⓓ 62.5% Ⓔ 80%

SOLUTION.

Since there are 5 boys for every 3 girls, there are fewer girls than boys. Therefore, *fewer than half* (50%) of the members are girls. Eliminate B, C, D, and E. The answer is **A**.

EXAMPLE 17

In the figure below, four semicircles are drawn, each one centered at the midpoint of one of the sides of square *ABCD*. Each of the four shaded "petals" is the intersection of two of the semicircles. If *AB* = 4, what is the total area of the shaded region?

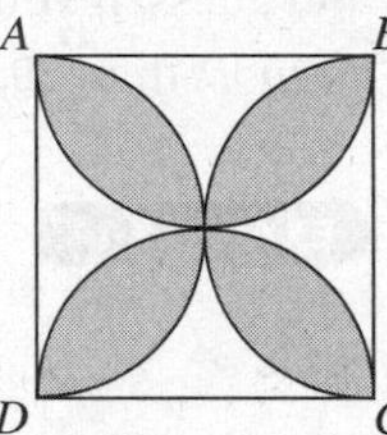

Ⓐ 8π Ⓑ $32 - 8\pi$ Ⓒ $16 - 8\pi$ Ⓓ $8\pi - 32$ Ⓔ $8\pi - 16$

SOLUTION.

- Since $AB = 4$, the area of the square is 16, and so, obviously, the area of the shaded region must be much less.
- Check each choice. Since π is slightly more than 3 ($\pi \approx 3.14$), 8π is somewhat greater than 24, approximately 25.
- (A) $8\pi \approx 25$. More than the area of the whole square: way too big.
- (B) $32 - 8\pi \approx 32 - 25 = 7$.
- (C) $16 - 8\pi$ is negative.
- (D) $8\pi - 32$ is also negative.
- (E) $8\pi - 16 \approx 25 - 16 = 9$.

NOTE: Three of the choices are absurd: A is more than the area of the entire square and C and D are negative; they can be eliminated immediately. The answer must be B or E. If you think the shaded area takes up less than half of the square, guess B; if you think it takes up more than half of the square, guess E. (The answer is **E**.)

Now use TACTIC 4 on each of the following problems. Even if you know how to solve them, don't. Practice this technique and see how many choices you can eliminate *without* actually solving.

EXAMPLE 18

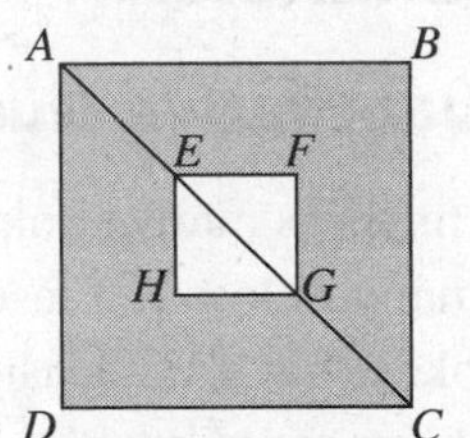

In the figure at the right, diagonal *EG* of square *EFGH* is $\frac{1}{2}$ of diagonal *AC* of the square *ABCD*. What is the ratio of the area of the shaded region to the area of *ABCD*?

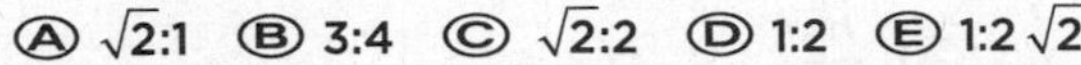

SOLUTION.

Obviously, the shaded region is smaller than square *ABCD*, so the ratio must be less than 1. Eliminate A. Also, from the diagram, it is clear that the shaded region is more than half of square *ABCD*, so the ratio is greater than 0.5. Eliminate D and E. Since 3:4 = .75 and $\sqrt{2}:2 \approx .71$, B and C are too close to tell which is correct just by looking; so guess. The answer is **B**.

EXAMPLE 19

Shari receives a commission of 25¢ for every $20.00 worth of merchandise she sells. What percent is her commission?

Ⓐ $1\frac{1}{4}$% Ⓑ $2\frac{1}{2}$% Ⓒ 5% Ⓓ 25% Ⓔ 125%

SOLUTION.

Clearly, a commission of 25¢ on $20 is quite small. Eliminate D and E and guess one of the small percents. If you realize that 1% of $20 is 20¢, then you know the answer is a little more than 1%, and you should guess A (maybe B, but definitely not C). The answer is **A**.

EXAMPLE 20

From 1980 to 1990, Lior's weight increased by 25%. If his weight was *k* kilograms in 1990, what was it in 1980?

Ⓐ 1.75*k* Ⓑ 1.25*k* Ⓒ 1.20*k* Ⓓ .80*k* Ⓔ .75*k*

SOLUTION.

Since Lior's weight increased, his weight in 1980 was *less than k*. Eliminate A, B, and C and guess. The answer is **D**.

EXAMPLE 21

The average of 10 numbers is −10. If the sum of 6 of them is 100, what is the average of the other 4?

Ⓐ −100 Ⓑ −50 Ⓒ 0 Ⓓ 50 Ⓔ 100

SOLUTION.

Since the average of all 10 numbers is negative, so is their sum. But the sum of the first 6 is positive, so the sum (and the average) of the others must be negative. Eliminate C, D, and E. **B** is correct.

PRACTICE EXERCISES

Discrete Quantitative Questions

1. Evan has 4 times as many books as David and 5 times as many as Jason. If Jason has more than 40 books, what is the least number of books that Evan could have?

Ⓐ 200
Ⓑ 205
Ⓒ 210
Ⓓ 220
Ⓔ 240

2. Judy plans to visit the National Gallery once each month in 2012 except in July and August when she plans to go three times each. A single admission costs $3.50, a pass valid for unlimited visits in any 3-month period can be purchased for $18, and an annual pass costs $60.00. What is the least amount, in dollars, that Judy can spend for her intended number of visits?

[ ] dollars

3. Alison is now three times as old as Jeremy, but 5 years ago, she was 5 times as old as he was. How old is Alison now?

Ⓐ 10
Ⓑ 12
Ⓒ 24
Ⓓ 30
Ⓔ 36

4. What is the largest prime factor of 255?

Ⓐ 5
Ⓑ 15
Ⓒ 17
Ⓓ 51
Ⓔ 255

5. If c is the product of a and b, which of the following is the quotient of a and b?

Ⓐ $\frac{b^2}{c}$
Ⓑ $\frac{c}{b^2}$
Ⓒ $\frac{b}{c^2}$
Ⓓ bc^2
Ⓔ b^2c

6. If w widgets cost c cents, how many widgets can you get for d dollars?

Ⓐ $\frac{100dw}{c}$
Ⓑ $\frac{dw}{100c}$
Ⓒ $100cdw$
Ⓓ $\frac{dw}{c}$
Ⓔ cdw

7. If 120% of a is equal to 80% of b, which of the following is equal to $a + b$?

Ⓐ $1.5a$
Ⓑ $2a$
Ⓒ $2.5a$
Ⓓ $3a$
Ⓔ $5a$

8. In the figure below, *WXYZ* is a square whose sides are 12. *AB*, *CD*, *EF*, and *GH* are each 8, and are the diameters of the four semicircles. What is the area of the shaded region?

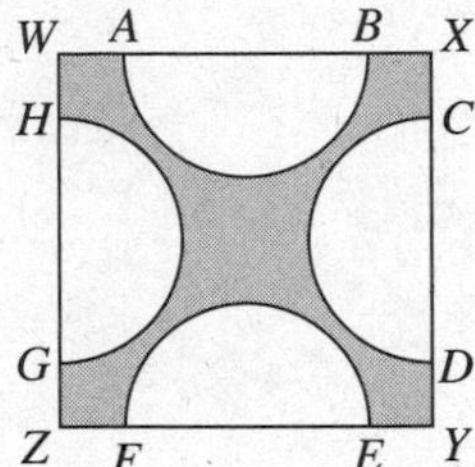

Ⓐ $144 - 128\pi$
Ⓑ $144 - 64\pi$
Ⓒ $144 - 32\pi$
Ⓓ $144 - 16\pi$
Ⓔ 16π

9. If *x* and *y* are integers such that $x^3 = y^2$, which of the following could not be the value of *y*?

Indicate *all* such values.

A −1
B 1
C 8
D 12
E 16
F 27

10. What is *a* divided by *a*% of *a*?

Ⓐ $\frac{a}{100}$
Ⓑ $\frac{100}{a}$
Ⓒ $\frac{a^2}{100}$
Ⓓ $\frac{100}{a^2}$
Ⓔ $100a$

11. If an object is moving at a speed of 36 kilometers per hour, how many meters does it travel in one second?

[ ] meters

12. In a certain French-American committee, $\frac{2}{3}$ of the members are men, and $\frac{3}{8}$ of the men are Americans. If $\frac{3}{5}$ of the committee members are French, what fraction of the members are American women?

$\frac{[\ ]}{[\ ]}$

13. For what value of *x* is $8^{2x-4} = 16^x$?

Ⓐ 2
Ⓑ 3
Ⓒ 4
Ⓓ 6
Ⓔ 8

14. If $12a + 3b = 1$ and $7b - 2a = 9$, what is the average (arithmetic mean) of *a* and *b*?

Ⓐ 0.1
Ⓑ 0.5
Ⓒ 1
Ⓓ 2.5
Ⓔ 5

15. If *x*% of *y* is 10, what is *y*?

Ⓐ $\frac{10}{x}$
Ⓑ $\frac{100}{x}$
Ⓒ $\frac{1,000}{x}$
Ⓓ $\frac{x}{100}$
Ⓔ $\frac{x}{10}$

ANSWER KEY

1. **D**	6. **A**	11. **10**	14. **B**
2. **49.50**	7. **C**	12. $\frac{3}{20}$	15. **C**
3. **D**	8. **C**	13. **D**	
4. **C**	9. **D, E**		
5. **B**	10. **B**		

ANSWER EXPLANATIONS

Two asterisks (**) indicate an alternative method of solving.

1. **(D)** Test the answer choices starting with the smallest value. If Evan had 200 books, Jason would have 40. But Jason has more than 40, so 200 is too small. Trying 205 and 210, we see that neither is a multiple of 4, so David wouldn't have a whole number of books. Finally, 220 works. (So does 240, but we shouldn't even test it since we want the least value.)

   **Since Jason has at least 41 books, Evan has at least 41 × 5 = 205. But Evan's total must be a multiple of 4 and 5, hence of 20. The smallest multiple of 20 greater than 205 is 220.

2. **49.50** Judy intends to go to the Gallery 16 times during the year. Buying a single admission each time would cost 16 × \$3.50 = \$56, which is less than the annual pass. If she bought a 3-month pass for June, July, and August, she would pay \$18 plus \$31.50 for 9 single admissions (9 × \$3.50), for a total expense of \$49.50, which is the least expensive option.

3. **(D)** Use TACTIC 1 (page 268): backsolve starting with C. If Alison is now 24, Jeremy is 8, and 5 years ago, they would have been 19 and 3, which is more than 5 times as much. Eliminate A, B, and C, and try a bigger value. If Alison is now 30, Jeremy is 10, and 5 years ago, they would have been 25 and 5. That's it; 25 is 5 times 5.

   **If Jeremy is now x, Alison is $3x$, and 5 years ago they were $x-5$ and $3x-5$, respectively. Now, solve:

   $$3x - 5 = 5(x - 5) \Rightarrow 3x - 5 = 5x - 25 \Rightarrow 2x = 20 \Rightarrow x = 10 \Rightarrow 3x = 30$$

4. **(C)** Test the choices starting with C: 255 *is* divisible by 17 (255 = 17 × 15), so this is a possible answer. Does 255 have a larger prime factor? Neither Choice D nor E is prime, so the answer must be Choice C.

5. **(B)** Use TACTIC 2 (page 270). Pick simple values for a, b, and c. Let $a = 3$, $b = 2$, and $c = 6$. Then $a \div b = \frac{3}{2}$. Without these values of a, b, and c, only B is equal to $\frac{3}{2}$.

   $$^{**}c = ab \Rightarrow a = \frac{c}{b} \Rightarrow a \div b = \frac{c}{b} \div b = \frac{c}{b} \cdot \frac{1}{b} = \frac{c}{b^2}$$

6. **(A)** Use TACTIC 2 (page 270). If 2 widgets cost 10 cents, then widgets cost 5 cents each, and for 3 dollars, you can get 60. Which of the choices equals 60 when $w = 2$, $c = 10$, and $d = 3$? Only A.

   $$^{**}\frac{\text{widgets}}{\text{cents}} = \frac{w}{c} = \frac{x}{100d} \Rightarrow x = \frac{100dw}{c}$$

7. **(C)** Since 120% of 80 = 80% of 120, let $a = 80$ and $b = 120$. Then $a + b = 200$, and $200 \div 80 = 2.5$.

8. **(C)** If you don't know how to solve this, you must use TACTIC 4 (page 274) and guess after eliminating the absurd choices. Which choices are absurd? Certainly, A and B, both of which are negative. Also, since Choice D is about 94, which is much more than half the area of the square, it is much too big. Guess between Choice C (about 43) and Choice E (about 50). If you remember that the way to find shaded areas is to subtract, guess C.

   **The area of the square is $12^2 = 144$. The area of each semicircle is 8π, one-half the area of a circle of radius 4. So together the areas of the semicircles is 32π.

9. **(D, E)** Test each choice until you find all the correct answers.

   (A) Could $y = -1$? Is there an integer x such that $x^3 = (-1)^2 = 1$? Yes, $x = 1$.
   (B) Similarly, if $y = 1$, $x = 1$.
   (C) Could $y = 8$? Is there an integer x such that $x^3 = (8)^2 = 64$? Yes, $x = 4$.
   (D) Could $y = 12$? Is there an integer such that $x^3 = 12^2 = 144$? No, $5^3 = 125$, which is too small; and $6^3 = 216$, which is too big.
   (E) Could $y = 16$? Is there an integer x such that $x^3 = 16^2 = 256$? No, $6^3 = 216$, which is too small, and $7^3 = 343$, which is too big.
   (F) Could $y = 27$? Is there an integer x such that $x^3 = 27^2 = 729$? Yes, $9^3 = 729$.

   The answer is D and E.

10. **(B)** $a \div (a\% \text{ of } a) = a \div \left(\frac{a}{100} \times a\right) = a \div \left(\frac{a^2}{100}\right) = a \times \frac{100}{a^2} = \frac{100}{a}$.

    **Use TACTICS 2 (page 270) and 3 (page 273): replace a by a number, and use 100 since the problem involves percents. $100 \div (100\% \text{ of } 100) = 100 \div 100 = 1$.

    Test each choice; which ones equal 1 when $a = 100$. Both A and B: $\frac{100}{100} = 1$.

    Eliminate Choices C, D, and E, and test A and B with another value for a.

    $$50 \div (50\% \text{ of } 50) = 50 \div (25) = 2$$

    Now, only B works $\left(\frac{100}{50} = 2, \text{ whereas } \frac{50}{100} = \frac{1}{2}\right)$.

11. **10** Set up a ratio:

    $$\frac{\text{distance}}{\text{time}} = \frac{36 \text{ kilometers}}{1 \text{ hour}} = \frac{36{,}000 \text{ meters}}{60 \text{ minutes}} = \frac{36{,}000 \text{ meters}}{3{,}600 \text{ seconds}} = 10 \text{ meters/second}$$

    **Use TACTIC 1 (page 268): Test choices starting with C:

    100 meters/second = 6,000 meters/minute = 360,000 meters/hour = 360 kilometers/hour

    Not only is that too big, it is too big by a factor of 10. The answer is 10.

12. $\frac{\mathbf{3}}{\mathbf{20}}$ Use TACTIC 3 (page 273). The LCM of all the denominators is 120, so assume that the committee has 120 members. Then there are $\frac{2}{3} \times 120 = 80$ men and 40 women. Of the 80 men 30 $\left(\frac{3}{8}\times 80\right)$ are American. Since there are 72 $\left(\frac{3}{5}\times 120\right)$ French members, there are $120 - 72 = 48$ Americans, of whom 30 are men, so the other 18 are women. Finally, the fraction of American women is $\frac{18}{120} = \frac{3}{20}$.

This is illustrated in the Venn diagram below.

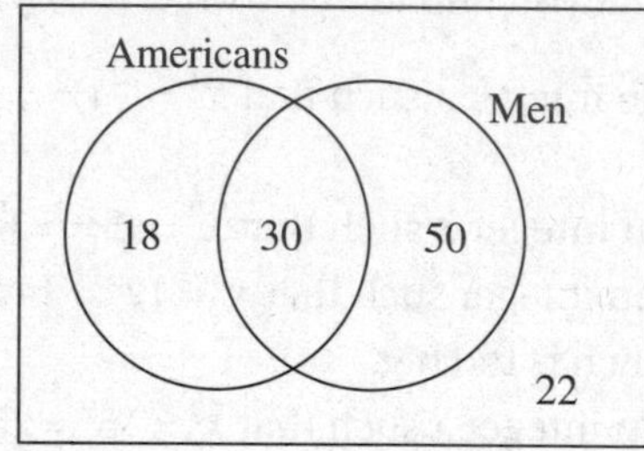

13. **(D)** Use the laws of exponents to simplify the equation, and then solve it:

$$8^{2x-4} = 16^x \Rightarrow (2^3)^{2x-4} = (2^4)^x \Rightarrow 3(2x-4) = 4x \Rightarrow 6x - 12 = 4x \Rightarrow 2x = 12 \Rightarrow x = 6$$

14. **(B)** Add the two equations:

$$10a + 10b = 10 \Rightarrow a + b = 1 \Rightarrow \frac{a+b}{2} = \frac{1}{2}$$

Do not waste time solving for a and b.

15. **(C)** Pick easy-to-use numbers. Since 100% of 10 is 10, let $x = 100$ and $y = 10$. When $x = 100$, Choices C and E are each 10. Eliminate Choices A, B, and D, and try some other numbers: 50% of 20 is 10. Of Choices C and E, only C = 20 when $x = 50$.

10 Quantitative Comparison Questions

About 15 of the 40 questions on the two quantitative sections of the GRE are quantitative comparisons. Unless you took the SAT before 2005, it is very likely that you have never seen questions of this type and certainly never learned the correct strategies for answering them. Don't worry. In this chapter, you will learn all of the necessary tactics. If you master them, you will quickly realize that quantitative comparisons are the easiest mathematics questions on the GRE and will wish that there were more than 15 of them.

Before the first quantitative comparison question appears on the screen, you will see these instructions.

Directions: In each of Questions 1–8, there are two quantities—Quantity A and Quantity B. You are to compare those quantities, taking into consideration any additional information given. The correct answer to such a question is

Ⓐ if Quantity A is greater;
Ⓑ if Quantity B is greater;
Ⓒ if the two quantities are equal;
Ⓓ if it is impossible to determine which quantity is greater.

Note: The given information, if any, is always centered above the two quantities. In any question, if a symbol or letter appears more than once, it represents the same thing each time.

Before learning the different strategies for solving this type of question, let's clarify these instructions. In quantitative comparison questions there are two quantities, and it is your job to compare them. The correct answer to a quantitative comparison question is one of the four statements listed in the directions above. Of course, on the computer screen those choices will not be listed as A, B, C, and D. Rather, you will see an oval in front of each statement, and you will click on the oval in front of the statement you believe is true.

You should click on the oval in front of	if
Quantity A is greater.	Quantity A is greater *all the time, no matter what.*
Quantity B is greater.	Quantity B is greater *all the time, no matter what.*
The two quantities are equal.	The two quantities are equal *all the time, no matter what.*
It is impossible to determine which quantity is greater.	*The answer is not one of the first three choices.*

This means, for example, that *if you can find a single instance* when Quantity A is greater than Quantity B, then you can immediately eliminate two choices: the answer cannot be "Quantity B is greater," and the answer cannot be "The two quantities are equal." In order for the answer to be "Quantity B is greater," Quantity B would have to be greater *all the time*; but you know of one instance when it isn't. Similarly, since the quantities are not equal *all the time*, the answer can't be "The two quantities are equal." The correct answer, therefore, is either "Quantity A is greater" or "It is impossible to determine which quantity is greater." If it turns out that Quantity A *is* greater all the time, then that is the answer; if, however, you can find a single instance where Quantity A is not greater, the answer is "It is impossible to determine which quantity is greater."

By applying the tactics that you will learn in this chapter, you will probably be able to determine which of the choices is correct; if, however, after eliminating two of the choices, you still cannot determine which answer is correct, quickly guess between the two remaining choices and move on.

Before learning the most important tactics for handling quantitative comparison questions, let's look at two examples to illustrate the preceding instructions.

TIP

Right now, memorize the instructions for answering quantitative comparison questions. *When you take the GRE, dismiss the instructions for these questions immediately—do not spend even one second reading the directions (or looking at a sample problem).*

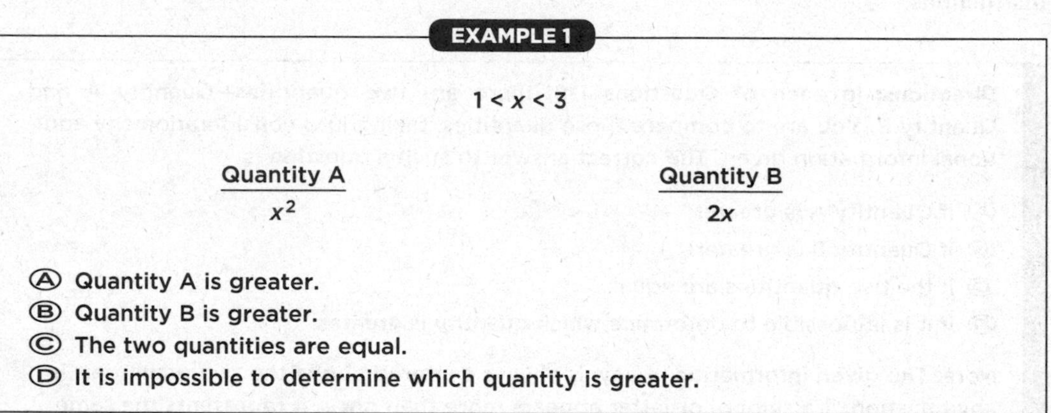
EXAMPLE 1
1 < x < 3
Quantity A
x^2
Quantity B
2x
Ⓐ Quantity A is greater.
Ⓑ Quantity B is greater.
Ⓒ The two quantities are equal.
Ⓓ It is impossible to determine which quantity is greater.

SOLUTION.

Throughout, x represents the same thing—a number between 1 and 3. If x is 2, then x^2 and $2x$ are each 4, and *in this case* the two quantities are equal. We can, therefore, eliminate the first two choices: neither Quantity A nor Quantity B is greater *all the time*. However, in order for the correct answer to be "The two quantities are equal," the quantities would have to be equal *all the time*. Are they? Note that although 2 is the only *integer* between 1 and 3, it is not the only *number* between 2 and 3: x could be 1.1 or 2.5 or any of infinitely many other numbers. And in those cases the quantities are not equal (for example, $2.5^2 = 6.25$, whereas $2(2.5) = 5$). The quantities are *not* always equal, and so the correct answer is the fourth choice: It is impossible to determine which quantity is greater.

EXAMPLE 2

p and q are primes
$p + q = 12$

Quantity A	Quantity B
p	8

Ⓐ Quantity A is greater.
Ⓑ Quantity B is greater.
Ⓒ The two quantities are equal.
Ⓓ It is impossible to determine which quantity is greater.

SOLUTION.
Since 5 and 7 are the only primes whose sum is 12, p could be 5 or 7. In either case, p is less than 8, and so Quantity B is greater, *all the time.* Note that although $1 + 11 = 12$, p cannot be 11, because 1 is not a prime (see Section 12-A, page 328).

NOTE: To simplify the discussion, throughout the rest of this chapter, in the explanations of the answers to all sample questions and in the Model Tests, the four answer choices will be referred to as A, B, C, and D, respectively. For example, we will write

The correct answer is **B**.

rather than

The correct answer is: Quantity B is greater.

TESTING TACTICS

TACTIC

Replace Variables with Numbers

Many problems that are hard to analyze because they contain variables become easy to solve when the variables are replaced by simple numbers.

TACTIC 1 is the most important tactic in this chapter. Using it properly will earn you more points on the quantitative comparison questions of the GRE than you can gain by applying any of the others. *Be sure to master it!*

Most quantitative comparison questions contain variables. When those variables are replaced by simple numbers such as 0 or 1, the quantities become much easier to compare.

The reason that TACTIC 1 is so important is that it *guarantees* that on any quantitative comparison question that involves variables, you will be able to immediately eliminate two of the four choices, and very often a third choice as well, leaving you with at least a 50 percent chance of guessing correctly, and often a certainty. Try the following example, and then read the explanation very carefully.

EXAMPLE 3

$a < b < c < d$

Quantity A	Quantity B
ab	cd

SOLUTION.

- Replace a, b, c, and d with easy-to-use numbers that satisfy the condition $a < b < c < d$: for example, $a = 1$, $b = 3$, $c = 6$, $d = 10$. (See the guidelines on page 287 to learn why 1, 2, 3, 4 is not a good choice.)
- Evaluate the two quantities: $ab = (1)(3) = 3$, and $cd = (6)(10) = 60$.
- So *in this case,* Quantity B is greater.
- Does that mean that B is the correct answer? Not necessarily. Quantity B *is* greater this time, but will it be greater ***every single time, no matter what***?
- What it does mean is that neither A nor C could possibly be the correct answer: Quantity A can't be greater ***every single time, no matter what*** because it isn't greater *this* time; and the quantities aren't equal ***every single time, no matter what*** because they aren't equal *this* time.

So in the few seconds that it took you to plug in 1, 3, 6, and 10 for *a, b, c,* and *d,* you were able to eliminate two of the four choices. You now know that the correct answer is either B or D, and if you could do nothing else, you would now guess with a 50 percent chance of being correct.

But, of course, *you will do something else.* You will try some other numbers. But *which* numbers? Since the first numbers you chose were positive, try some negative numbers this time.

- Let $a = -5$, $b = -3$, $c = -2$, and $d = -1$.
- Evaluate: $ab = (-5)(-3) = 15$ and $cd = (-2)(-1) = 2$.
- So *in this case,* Quantity A is greater.
- Quantity B is *not* greater all the time. B is *not* the correct answer.
- The correct answer is **D**: It is impossible to determine which quantity is greater.

NOTES:

1. If for your second substitution you had chosen 3, 7, 8, 10 or 2, 10, 20, 35 or *any* four positive numbers, Quantity B would have been bigger. No matter how many substitutions you made, Quantity B would have been bigger each time, and you would have incorrectly concluded that B was the answer. In fact, if the given condition had been $0 < a < b < c < d$, then B *would have been* the correct answer.
2. Therefore, knowing which numbers to plug in when you use TACTIC 1 is critical. As long as you comply with the conditions given in the question, you have complete freedom in choosing the numbers. Some choices, however, are much better than others.

Here are some guidelines for deciding which numbers to use when applying TACTIC 1.

1. The very best numbers to use first are: 1, 0, and −1.
2. Often, fractions between 0 and 1 are useful.
3. Occasionally, "large" numbers such as 10 or 100 can be used.
4. If there is more than one letter, it is permissible to replace each with the same number.
5. Do not impose any conditions not specifically stated.

In particular, do not assume that variables must be integers. For example, 3 is not the only number that satisfies $2 < x < 4$ (2.1, 3.95, and π all work). The expression $a < b < c < d$ does not mean that a, b, c, d are *integers*, let alone *consecutive* integers (which is why we didn't choose 1, 2, 3, and 4 in Example 3), nor does it mean that any or all of them are *positive*.

When you replace the variables in a quantitative comparison question with numbers, remember:

If the value of Quantity A is ever greater:	eliminate B and C: the answer must be A or D.
If the value of Quantity B is ever greater:	eliminate A and C: the answer must be B or D.
If the two quantities are ever equal:	eliminate A and B: the answer must be C or D.

You have learned that, no matter how hard a quantitative comparison is, as soon as you replace the variables, two choices can *immediately* be eliminated; and if you can't decide between the other two, just guess. This guarantees that in addition to correctly answering all the questions that you know how to solve, you will be able to answer correctly at least half, and probably many more, of the questions that you don't know how to do.

Practice applying TACTIC 1 on these examples.

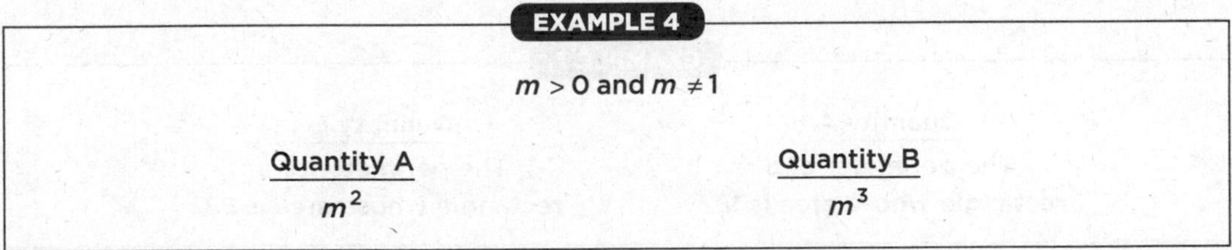

EXAMPLE 4

$m > 0$ and $m \neq 1$

Quantity A	Quantity B
m^2	m^3

SOLUTION.

Use TACTIC 1. Replace m with numbers satisfying $m > 0$ and $m \neq 1$.

	Quantity A	Quantity B	Compare	Eliminate
Let $m = 2$	$2^2 = 4$	$2^3 = 8$	B is greater	A and C
Let $m = \frac{1}{2}$	$\left(\frac{1}{2}\right)^2 = \frac{1}{4}$	$\left(\frac{1}{2}\right)^3 = \frac{1}{8}$	A is greater	B

The answer is **D**.

EXAMPLE 5

Quantity A	Quantity B
$13y$	$15y$

SOLUTION.
Use TACTIC 1. There are no restrictions on *y*, so use the best numbers: 1, 0, –1.

	Quantity A	Quantity B	Compare	Eliminate
Let $y = 1$	13(1) = 13	15(1) =15	B is greater	A and C
Let $y = 0$	13(0) = 0	15(0) = 0	They're equal	B

The answer is **D**.

EXAMPLE 6

Quantity A	Quantity B
$w + 11$	$w - 11$

SOLUTION.
Use TACTIC 1. There are no restrictions on *w*, so use the best numbers: 1, 0, –1.

	Quantity A	Quantity B	Compare	Eliminate
Let $w = 1$	1 + 11 = 12	1 - 11 = -10	A is greater	B and C
Let $w = 0$	0 + 11 = 11	0 - 11 = -11	A is greater	
Let $w = -1$	-1 + 11 = 10	-1 - 11 = -12	A is greater	

Guess **A**. We let *w* be a positive number, a negative number, and 0. Each time, Quantity A was greater. That's not proof, but it justifies an educated guess. (The answer *is* A. Clearly, $11 > -11$, and if we add *w* to each side, we get: $w + 11 > w - 11$.)

EXAMPLE 7

Quantity A	Quantity B
The perimeter of a rectangle whose area is 18	The perimeter of a rectangle whose area is 28

SOLUTION.
What's this question doing here? How can we use TACTIC 1? Where are the variables that we're supposed to replace? Well, each quantity is the perimeter of a rectangle, and the variables are the lengths and widths of these rectangles.

Quantity A	Quantity B	Compare	Eliminate
Choose a rectangle whose area is 18: 9 × 2 rectangle The perimeter here is 9 + 2 + 9 + 2 = 22	Choose a rectangle whose area is 28: 7 × 4 rectangle The perimeter here is 7 + 4 + 7 + 4 = 22	Quantities A and B are equal	A and B
Keep Quantity B, but take a different rectangle of area 18 when evaluating Quantity A:			
6 × 3 rectangle Perimeter = 3 + 6 + 3 + 6 = 18	7 × 4 rectangle Perimeter = 22	B is greater	C

The answer is **D**.

EXAMPLE 8

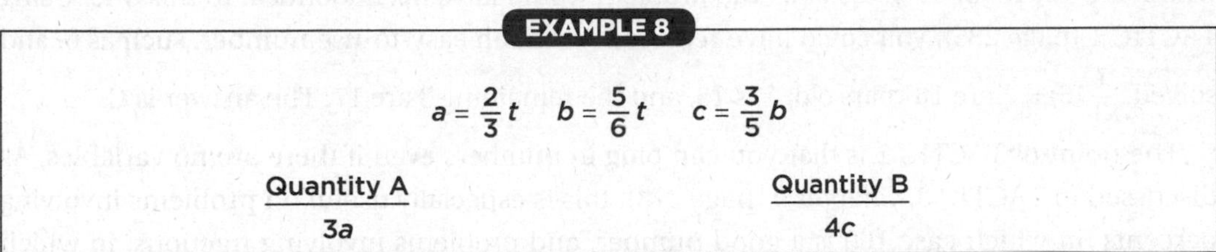

$$a = \frac{2}{3}t \quad b = \frac{5}{6}t \quad c = \frac{3}{5}b$$

Quantity A	Quantity B
$3a$	$4c$

SOLUTION.

Use TACTIC 1. First, try the easiest number: let $t = 0$. Then a, b, and c are each 0, and *in this case*, the quantities are equal—they're both 0. Eliminate A and B. Now, try another number for t. The obvious choice is 1, but then a, b, and c will all be fractions. To avoid this, let $t = 6$. Then, $a = \frac{2}{3}(6) = 4$, $b = \frac{5}{6}(6) = 5$, and $c = \frac{3}{5}(5) = 3$. This time, $3a = 3(4) =$ **12** and $4b = 4(3) =$ **12**. *Again, the two quantities are equal.* Choose **C.**

NOTE: You should consider answering this question directly (i.e., without plugging in numbers), *only if you are very comfortable with both fractions and elementary algebra.* Here's the solution:

$$c = \frac{3}{5}b = \frac{3}{5}\left(\frac{5}{6}t\right) = \frac{1}{2}t$$

Therefore, $2c = t$, and $4c = 2t$. Since $a = \frac{2}{3}t$, $3a = 2t$. So, $4c = 3a$. The answer is **C.**

TACTIC

2 Choose Appropriate Numbers

This is just like TACTIC 1 (page 285). We are replacing a variable with a number, but the variable isn't mentioned in the problem.

EXAMPLE 9

Every band member is either 15, 16, or 17 years old. One third of the band members are 16, and twice as many band members are 16 as 15.

Quantity A	Quantity B
The number of 17-year-old band members	The total number of 15- and 16-year-old band members

If the first sentence of Example 9 had been "There are *n* students in the school band, all of whom are 15, 16, or 17 years old," the problem would have been identical to this one. Using TACTIC 1 (page 285), you could have replaced *n* with an easy-to-use number, such as 6, and solved: $\frac{1}{3}(6) = 2$ are 16 years old; 1 is 15, and the remaining 3 are 17. The answer is **C**.

The point of TACTIC 2 is that you can plug in numbers even if there are no variables. As discussed in TACTIC 3, Chapter 9 (page 273), this is especially useful on problems involving percents, in which case 100 is a good number, and problems involving fractions, in which case the LCD of the fractions is a good choice. However, the use of TACTIC 2 is not limited to these situations. Try using TACTIC 2 on the following three problems.

EXAMPLE 10

The perimeter of a square and the circumference of a circle are equal.

Quantity A	Quantity B
The area of the circle	The area of the square

SOLUTION.

First use TACTIC 1, Chapter 8 (page 248): draw a diagram.

$C = 2\pi(1) = 2\pi$

$A = \pi(1)^2 = \pi \approx 3.14$

Then use TACTIC 2: choose an easy-to-use number. Let the radius of the circle be 1. Then its area is π. Let s be the side of the square:

s $P = 4s$ $A = s^2$

$$4s = 2\pi \approx 6 \Rightarrow s \approx 1.5 \Rightarrow$$
$$\text{area of the square} \approx (1.5)^2 = 2.25$$

The answer is **A**.

EXAMPLE 11

Jen, Ken, and Len divided a cash prize.

Jen took 50% of the money and spent $\frac{3}{5}$ of what she took.

Ken took 40% of the money and spent $\frac{3}{4}$ of what he took.

Quantity A	Quantity B
The amount that Jen spent	The amount that Ken spent

SOLUTION.
Use TACTIC 2. Assume the prize was \$100. Then Jen took \$50 and spent $\frac{3}{5}$(\$50) = \$30. Ken took \$40 and spent $\frac{3}{4}$(\$40) = \$30. The answer is **C**.

EXAMPLE 12

Eliane types twice as fast as Delphine.
Delphine charges 50% more per page than Eliane.

Quantity A	Quantity B
Amount Eliane earns in 9 hours	Amount Delphine earns in 12 hours

SOLUTION.
Use TACTIC 2. Choose appropriate numbers. Assume Delphine can type 1 page per hour and Eliane can type 2. Assume Eliane charges \$1.00 per page and Delphine charges \$1.50. Then in 9 hours, Eliane types 18 pages, earning **\$18.00.** In 12 hours, Delphine types 12 pages, earning $12 \times \$1.50$ = **\$18.00.** The answer is **C**.

TACTIC

3 Make the Problem Easier: Do the Same Thing to Each Quantity

A quantitative comparison question can be treated as an equation or an inequality. Either:

Quantity A < Quantity B, or
Quantity A = Quantity B, or
Quantity A > Quantity B

In solving an equation or an inequality, you can always add the same thing to each side or subtract the same thing from each side. Similarly, in solving a quantitative comparison, you can always add the same thing to Quantities A and B or subtract the same thing from Quantities A and B. You can also multiply or divide each side of an equation or inequality by the same number, *but in the case of inequalities you can do this only if the number is positive.* Since you don't know whether the quantities are equal or unequal, you cannot multiply or divide by a variable *unless you know that it is positive.* If Quantities A and B are both positive you may square them or take their square roots.

To illustrate the proper use of TACTIC 3, we will give alternative solutions to Examples 4, 5, and 6, which we already solved using TACTIC 1 (page 285).

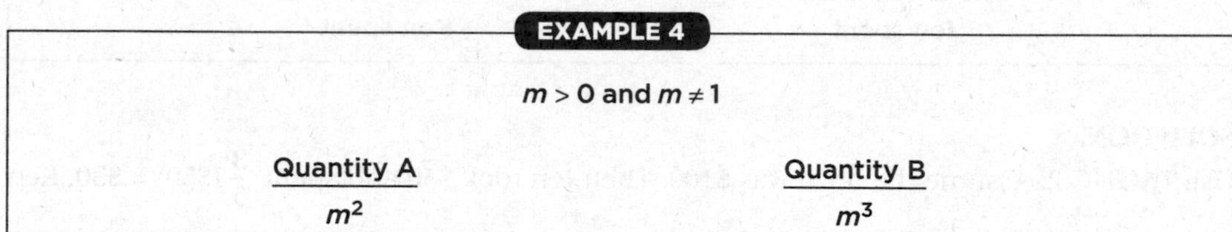

EXAMPLE 4

$m > 0$ and $m \neq 1$

Quantity A	Quantity B
m^2	m^3

SOLUTION.

	Quantity A	Quantity B
Divide each quantity by m^2 (that's OK—m^2 is positive):	$\frac{m^2}{m^2} = 1$	$\frac{m^3}{m^2} = m$

This is a much easier comparison. Which is greater, m or 1? We don't know. We know $m > 0$ and $m \neq 1$, but it could be greater than 1 or less than 1. The answer is **D**.

EXAMPLE 5

Quantity A	Quantity B
$13y$	$15y$

SOLUTION.

	Quantity A	Quantity B
Subtract $13y$ from each quantity:	$13y - 13y = 0$	$15y - 13y = 2y$

Since there are no restrictions on y, $2y$ could be greater than, less than, or equal to 0. The answer is **D**.

EXAMPLE 6

Quantity A	Quantity B
$w + 11$	$w - 11$

SOLUTION.

	Quantity A	Quantity B
Subtract w from each quantity:	$(w + 11) - w = 11$	$(w - 11) - w = -11$

Clearly, 11 is greater than –11. Quantity **A** is greater.

Here are five more examples on which to practice TACTIC 3.

EXAMPLE 13

Quantity A	Quantity B
$\frac{1}{3}+\frac{1}{4}+\frac{1}{9}$	$\frac{1}{9}+\frac{1}{3}+\frac{1}{5}$

SOLUTION.

	Quantity A	Quantity B
Subtract $\frac{1}{3}$ and $\frac{1}{9}$ from each quantity:	$\cancel{\frac{1}{3}} + \frac{1}{4} + \cancel{\frac{1}{9}}$	$\cancel{\frac{1}{9}} + \cancel{\frac{1}{3}} + \frac{1}{5}$

Since $\frac{1}{4} > \frac{1}{5}$, the answer is **A.**

EXAMPLE 14

Quantity A	Quantity B
$(43 + 59)(17 - 6)$	$(43 + 59)(17 + 6)$

SOLUTION.

	Quantity A	Quantity B
Divide each quantity by (43 + 59):	$\cancel{(43 + 59)}(17 - 6)$	$\cancel{(43 + 59)}(17 + 6)$

Clearly, (17 + 6) > (17 – 6). The answer is **B.**

EXAMPLE 15

Quantity A	Quantity B
$(43 - 59)(43 - 49)$	$(43 - 59)(43 + 49)$

SOLUTION.

> **CAUTION**
>
> (43 − 59) is negative, and you may not divide the two quantities by a negative number.

The easiest alternative is to note that Quantity A, being the product of 2 negative numbers, is positive, whereas Quantity B, being the product of a negative number and a positive number, is negative, and so Quantity A is greater.

EXAMPLE 16

a is a negative number

Quantity A	Quantity B
a^2	$-a^2$

SOLUTION.

	Quantity A	Quantity B
Add a^2 to each quantity:	$a^2 + a^2 = 2a^2$	$-a^2 + a^2 = 0$

Since a is negative, $2a^2$ is positive. The answer is **A**.

EXAMPLE 17

Quantity A	Quantity B
$\frac{\sqrt{20}}{2}$	$\frac{5}{\sqrt{5}}$

SOLUTION.

	Quantity A	Quantity B
Square each quantity:	$\left(\frac{\sqrt{20}}{2}\right)^2 = \frac{20}{4} = 5$	$\left(\frac{5}{\sqrt{5}}\right)^2 = \frac{25}{5} = 5$

The answer is **C**.

TACTIC 4 Ask "Could They Be Equal?" and "Must They Be Equal?"

TACTIC 4 has many applications, but is most useful when one of the quantities contains a variable and the other contains a number. In this situation ask yourself, "Could they be equal?" If the answer is "yes," eliminate A and B, and then ask, "Must they be equal?" If the second answer is "yes," then C is correct; if the second answer is "no," then choose D. When the answer to "Could they be equal?" is "no," we usually know right away what the correct answer is. In both questions, "Could they be equal" and "Must they be equal," the word *they* refers, of course, to Quantities A and B.

Let's look at a few examples.

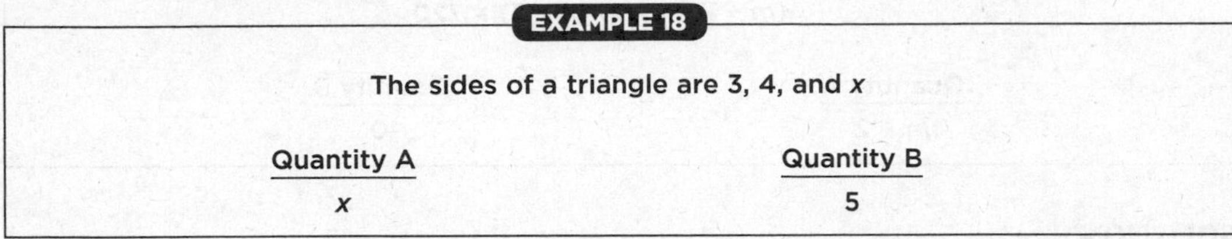

EXAMPLE 18

The sides of a triangle are 3, 4, and x

Quantity A	Quantity B
x	5

SOLUTION.
Could they be equal? Could $x = 5$? Of course. That's the all-important 3-4-5 right triangle. Eliminate A and B. Must they be equal? Must $x = 5$? If you're not sure, try drawing an acute or an obtuse triangle. The answer is No. Actually, x can be any number satisfying: $1 < x < 7$. (See KEY FACT J12, page 463, the triangle inequality, and the figure below.) The answer is **D**.

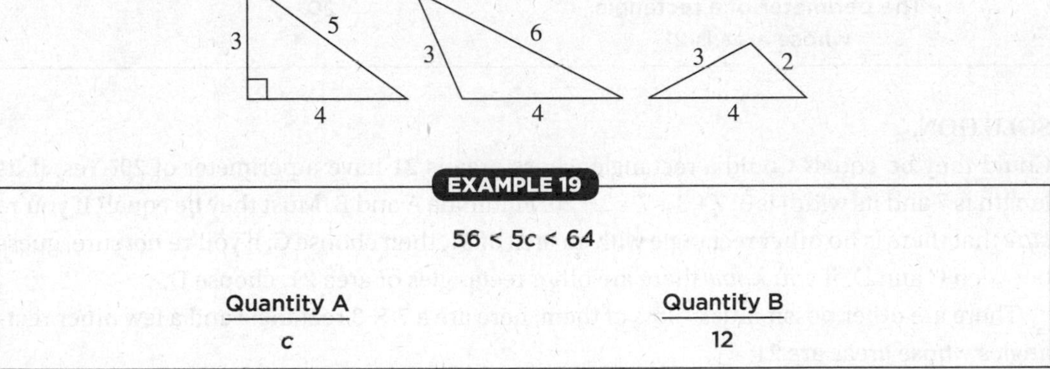

EXAMPLE 19

$56 < 5c < 64$

Quantity A	Quantity B
c	12

SOLUTION.
Could they be equal? Could $c = 12$? If $c = 12$, then $5c = 60$, so, yes, they could be equal. Eliminate A and B. Must they be equal? Must $c = 12$? Could c be more or less than 12? BE CAREFUL: $5 \times 11 = 55$, which is too small; and $5 \times 13 = 65$, which is too big. Therefore, the only *integer* that c could be is 12; but *c doesn't have to be an integer*. The *only* restriction is that $56 < 5c < 64$. If $5c$ were 58 or 61.6 or 63, then c would not be 12. The answer is **D**.

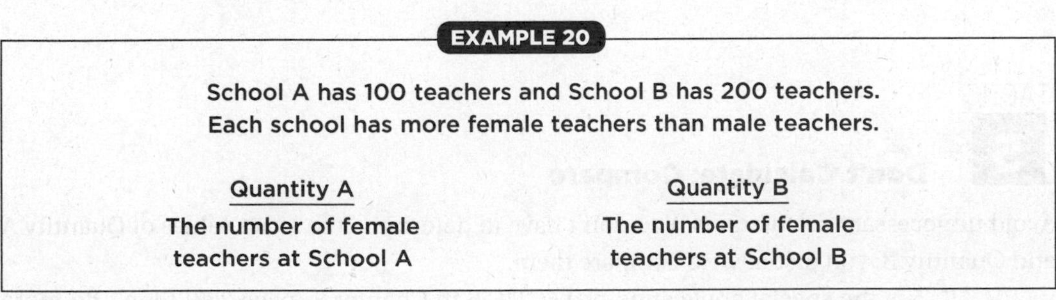

EXAMPLE 20

School A has 100 teachers and School B has 200 teachers.
Each school has more female teachers than male teachers.

Quantity A	Quantity B
The number of female teachers at School A	The number of female teachers at School B

SOLUTION.
Could they be equal? Could the number of female teachers be the same in both schools? No. More than half (i.e., more than 100) of School B's 200 teachers are female, but School A has only 100 teachers in all. The answer is **B**.

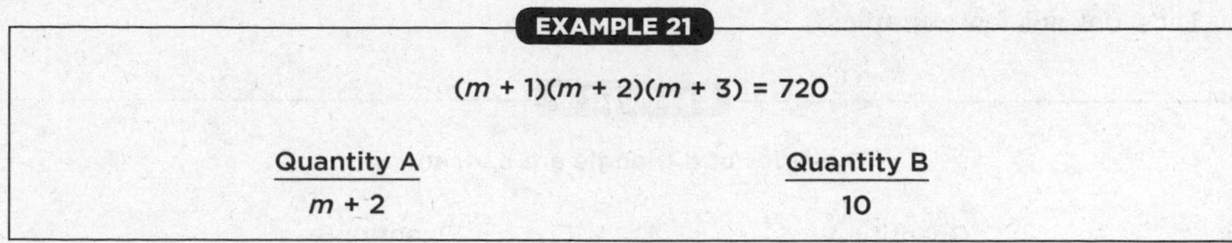

EXAMPLE 21

$(m + 1)(m + 2)(m + 3) = 720$

Quantity A	Quantity B
$m + 2$	10

SOLUTION.

Could they be equal? Could $m + 2 = 10$? No, if $m + 2 = 10$, then $m + 1 = 9$ and $m + 3 = 11$, and $9 \times 10 \times 11 = 990$, which is too big. The answer is *not* C, and since $m + 2$ clearly has to be smaller than 10, the answer is **B**.

EXAMPLE 22

Quantity A	Quantity B
The perimeter of a rectangle whose area is 21	20

SOLUTION.

Could they be equal? Could a rectangle whose area is 21 have a perimeter of 20? Yes, if its length is 7 and its width is 3: $7 + 3 + 7 + 3 = 20$. Eliminate A and B. Must they be equal? If you're *sure* that there is no other rectangle with an area of 21, then choose C; if you're *not* sure, guess between C and D; if you *know* there are other rectangles of area 21, choose D.

There are other possibilities—lots of them; here are a 7×3 rectangle and a few other rectangles whose areas are 21:

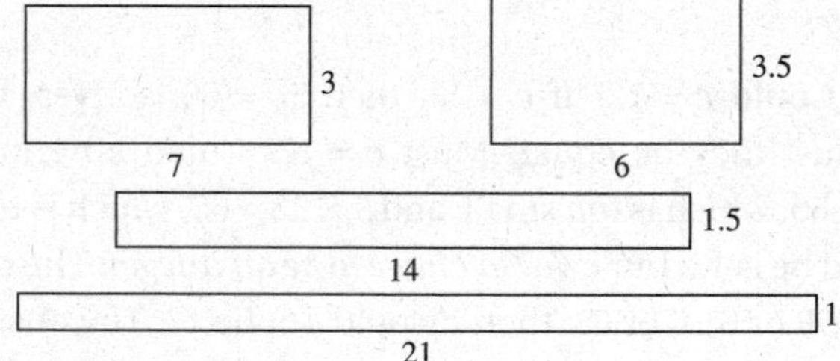

Don't Calculate: Compare

Avoid unnecessary calculations. You don't have to determine the exact values of Quantity A and Quantity B; you just have to compare them.

TACTIC 5 is the special application of TACTIC 6 in Chapter 8 (page 257) (don't do more than you have to) to quantitative comparison questions. Using TACTIC 5 allows you to solve many quantitative comparisons without doing tedious calculations, thereby saving you valuable test time that you can use on other questions. *Before you start calculating*, stop, look at the quantities, and ask yourself, "Can I easily and quickly determine which quantity is greater without doing *any* arithmetic?" Consider Examples 23 and 24, which look very similar, but really aren't.

EXAMPLE 23

Quantity A	Quantity B
37 × 43	30 × 53

EXAMPLE 24

Quantity A	Quantity B
37 × 43	39 × 47

Example 23 is very easy. Just multiply: 37 × 43 = 1,591 and 30 × 53 = 1,590. The answer is **A**.

Example 24 is even easier. *Don't* multiply. In less time than it takes to do the multiplications, even with the calculator, you can see that 37 < 39 and 43 < 47, so clearly 37 × 43 < 39 × 47. The answer is **B**. *You don't get any extra credit for taking the time to determine the value of each product!*

Remember: do not start calculating immediately. Always take a second or two to glance at each quantity. In Example 23 it's not at all clear which product is larger, so you have to multiply. In Example 24, however, no calculations are necessary.

These are problems on which poor test-takers do a lot of arithmetic and good test-takers think! Practicing TACTIC 5 will help you become a good test-taker.

Now, test your understanding of TACTIC 5 by solving these problems.

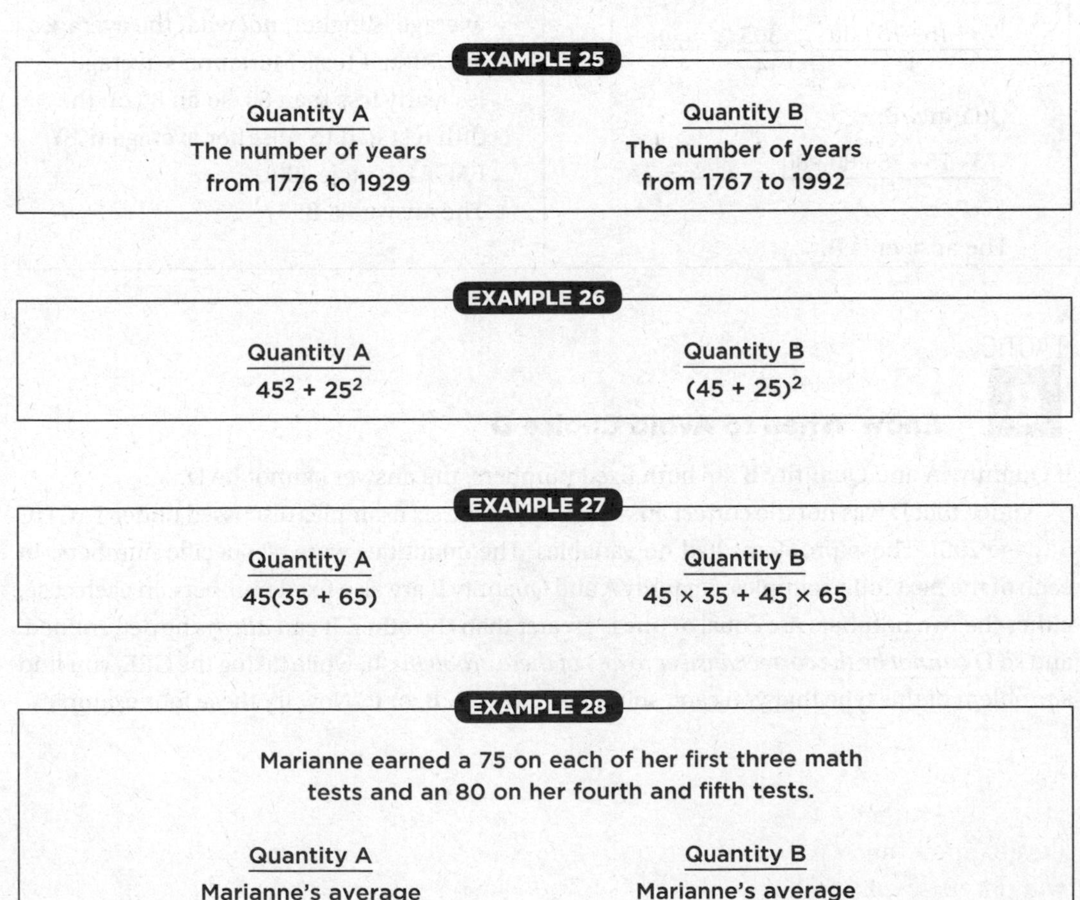

EXAMPLE 25

Quantity A	Quantity B
The number of years from 1776 to 1929	The number of years from 1767 to 1992

EXAMPLE 26

Quantity A	Quantity B
$45^2 + 25^2$	$(45 + 25)^2$

EXAMPLE 27

Quantity A	Quantity B
45(35 + 65)	45 × 35 + 45 × 65

EXAMPLE 28

Marianne earned a 75 on each of her first three math tests and an 80 on her fourth and fifth tests.

Quantity A	Quantity B
Marianne's average after 4 tests	Marianne's average after 5 tests

CAUTION

TACTIC 5 is important, but *don't spend a lot of time looking for ways to avoid a simple calculation.*

SOLUTIONS 25–28.

Performing the Indicated Calculations	Using TACTIC 5 to Avoid Doing the Calculations
25. Quantity A: 1,929 – 1,776 = 153 Quantity B: 1,992 – 1,767 = 225 The answer is **B**.	25. The subtraction is easy enough, but why do it? The dates in Quantity **B** start earlier and end later. Clearly, they span more years. You don't need to know how many years. The answer is **B**.
26. Quantity A: $45^2 + 25^2 =$ $2{,}025 + 625 = 2{,}650$ Quantity B: $(45 + 25)^2 =$ $70^2 = 4{,}900$ The answer is **B**.	26. For *any positive numbers a* and *b*: $(a + b)^2 > a^2 + b^2$. You should do the calculations only if you don't know this fact. The answer is **B**.
27. Quantity A: 45(35 + 65) = 45(100) = 4,500 Quantity B: $45 \times 35 + 45 \times 65 =$ 1,575 + 2,925 = 4,500 The answer is **C**.	27. This is just the distributive property (KEY FACT A20, page 339), which states that, for *any* numbers *a, b, c*: $a(b + c) = ab + ac$. The answer is **C**.
28. Quantity A: $\frac{75+75+75+80}{4} = \frac{305}{4} = 76.25$ Quantity B: $\frac{75+75+75+80+80}{5} = \frac{385}{5} = 77$ The answer is **B**.	28. Remember, you want to know which average is higher, *not* what the averages are. After 4 tests Marianne's average is clearly less than 80, so an 80 on the fifth test had to *raise* her average (KEY FACT E4, page 400). The answer is **B**.

TACTIC 6 Know When to Avoid Choice D

If Quantity A and Quantity B are both fixed numbers, the answer cannot be D.

Notice that D was not the correct answer to any of the six examples discussed under TACTIC 5 (page 296). Those problems had no variables. The quantities were all specific numbers. In each of the next four examples, Quantity A and Quantity B are also fixed numbers. In each case, either the two numbers are equal or one is greater than the other. It can *always* be determined, and so D *cannot be the correct answer to any of these problems.* If, while taking the GRE, you find a problem of this type that you can't solve, just guess: A, B, or C. Now try these four examples.

EXAMPLE 29

Quantity A	Quantity B
The number of seconds in one day	The number of days in one century

EXAMPLE 30

Quantity A	Quantity B
The area of a square whose sides are 4	Twice the area of an equilateral triangle whose sides are 4

EXAMPLE 31

Three fair coins are flipped.

Quantity A	Quantity B
The probability of getting one head	The probability of getting two heads

EXAMPLE 32

Quantity A	Quantity B
The time it takes to drive 40 miles at 35 mph	The time it takes to drive 35 miles at 40 mph

Here's the important point to remember: don't choose D because *you* can't determine which quantity is bigger; choose D only if *nobody* could determine it. *You* may or may not know how to compute the number of seconds in a day, the area of an equilateral triangle, or a certain probability, but *these calculations can be made.*

SOLUTIONS 29–32.

Direct Calculations	Solution Using Various TACTICS
29. Recall the facts you need and calculate. 60 seconds = 1 minute, 60 minutes = 1 hour, 24 hours = 1 day, 365 days = 1 year, and 100 years = 1 century. Quantity A: $60 \times 60 \times 24 = 86{,}400$ Quantity B: $365 \times 100 = 36{,}500$ Even if we throw in some days for leap years, the answer is clearly **A**.	29. The point of TACTIC 6 is that even if you have no idea how to calculate the number of seconds in a day, you can eliminate two choices. The answer *cannot* be D, and it would be an incredible coincidence if these two quantities were actually equal, so don't choose C. *Guess* between A and B.

Direct Calculations	Solution Using Various TACTICS 
30. Calculate both areas. (See KEY FACT J15, page 466 for the easy way to find the area of an equilateral triangle.) Quantity A: $A = s^2 = 4^2 = 16$ Quantity B: $A = \frac{s^2\sqrt{3}}{4} = \frac{4^2\sqrt{3}}{4} = 4\sqrt{3}$; and *twice* A is $8\sqrt{3}$. Since $\sqrt{3} \approx 1.7$, $8\sqrt{3} \approx 13.6$. The answer is **A**.	30. Use TACTIC 5 (page 296): don't calculate—draw a diagram and then compare. 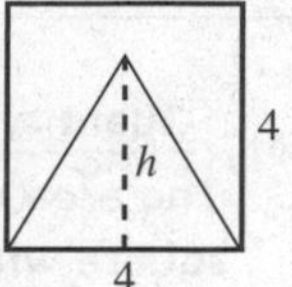 Since the height of the triangle is less than 4, its area is less than $\frac{1}{2}(4)(4) = 8$, and twice its area is less than 16, the area of the square. The answer is **A**. (If you don't see that, and just have to guess in order to move on, be sure not to guess D.)
31. When a coin is flipped 3 times, there are 8 possible outcomes: HHH, HHT, HTH, HTT, THH, THT, TTH, and TTT. Of these, 3 have one head and 3 have two heads. Each probability is $\frac{3}{8}$. The answer is **C**.	31. Don't forget TACTIC 5 (page 296). Even if you know how, you don't *have to* calculate the probabilities. When 3 coins are flipped, getting two heads means getting one tail. Therefore, the probability of two heads equals the probability of one tail, which by symmetry equals the probability of one head. The answer is **C**. (If you don't remember anything about probability, TACTIC 5 at least allows you to eliminate D before you guess.)
32. Since $d = rt$, $t = \frac{d}{r}$ (see Section 12-H, page 435). Quantity A: $\frac{40}{35}$ hours—more than 1 hour. Quantity B: $\frac{35}{40}$ hours—less than 1 hour. The answer is **A**.	32. You *do* need to know these formulas, but *not* for this problem. At 35 mph it takes *more than an hour* to drive 40 miles. At 40 mph it takes *less than an hour* to drive 35 miles. Choose **A**.

PRACTICE EXERCISES

Quantitative Comparison Questions

Ⓐ Quantity A is greater.
Ⓑ Quantity B is greater.
Ⓒ The two quantities are equal.
Ⓓ It is impossible to determine which quantity is greater.

1.

Quantity A	Quantity B
197 + 398 + 586	203 + 405 + 607

2.

$x > 0$

Quantity A	Quantity B
$10x$	$\frac{10}{x}$

3.

Quantity A	Quantity B
The time that it takes to type 7 pages at a rate of 6 pages per hour	The time that it takes to type 6 pages at a rate of 7 pages per hour

4.

$cd < 0$

Quantity A	Quantity B
$(c + d)^2$	$c^2 + d^2$

5.

a, *b*, and *c* are the measures of the angles of isosceles triangle *ABC*.
x, *y*, and *z* are the measures of the angles of right triangle *XYZ*.

Quantity A	Quantity B
The average of *a*, *b*, and *c*	The average of *x*, *y*, and *z*

6.

$b < 0$

Quantity A	Quantity B
$6b$	b^6

7.

Quantity A	Quantity B
The area of a circle whose radius is 17	The area of a circle whose diameter is 35

8.

Line *k* goes through (1,1) and (5,2).
Line *m* is perpendicular to *k*.

Quantity A	Quantity B
The slope of line *k*	The slope of line *m*

9.

x is a positive integer

Quantity A	Quantity B
The number of multiples of 6 between 100 and $x + 100$	The number of multiples of 9 between 100 and $x + 100$

10.

$x + y = 5$
$y - x = -5$

Quantity A	Quantity B
y	0

11.

Quantity A	Quantity B
$\frac{7}{8}$	$\left(\frac{7}{8}\right)^5$

12.

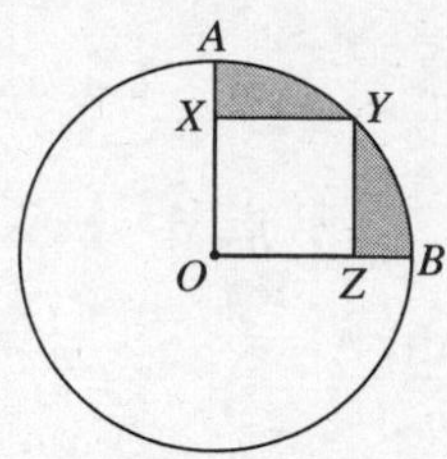

O is the center of the circle of radius 6. *OXYZ* is a square.

Quantity A	Quantity B
The area of the shaded region	12

13.

The number of square inches in the surface area of a cube is equal to the number of cubic inches in its volume.

Quantity A	Quantity B
The length of an edge of the cube	6 inches

14.

$1 < x < 4$

Quantity A	Quantity B
πx	x^2

15.

$AB = AC$

Quantity A	Quantity B
The area of $\triangle ABC$	3

ANSWER KEY

1. **B**	4. **B**	7. **B**	10. **C**	13. **C**
2. **D**	5. **C**	8. **A**	11. **A**	14. **D**
3. **A**	6. **B**	9. **D**	12. **B**	15. **D**

ANSWER EXPLANATIONS

The direct mathematical solution to a problem is almost always the preferable one, so it is given first. It is often followed by one or more alternative solutions, indicated by a double asterisk (**), based on the various tactics discussed in this chapter. Occasionally, a solution based on one of the tactics is much easier than the straightforward one. In that case, it is given first.

1. **(B)** Using the onscreen calculator, this can easily be solved in 20 or 30 seconds by adding, but in only 5 seconds by thinking! Use TACTIC 5 (page 296): don't calculate; compare. Each of the three numbers in Quantity B is greater than the corresponding numbers in Quantity A.

2. **(D)** Use TACTIC 1 (page 285). When $x = 1$, the quantities are equal; when $x = 2$, they aren't.

   **Use TACTIC 3 (page 292)

	Quantity A	Quantity B
	$10x$	$\frac{10}{x}$
Multiply each quantity by x (this is OK since $x > 0$):	$10x^2$	10
Divide each quantity by 10:	x^2	1

   This is a much easier comparison. x^2 *could* equal 1, but doesn't have to. The answer is Choice D.

3. **(A)** You can easily calculate each of the times—divide 7 by 6 to evaluate Quantity A, and 6 by 7 in Quantity B. However, it is easier to just observe that Quantity A is more than one hour, whereas Quantity B is less than one hour.

4. **(B)** Use TACTIC 3 (page 292)

	Quantity A	Quantity B
Expand Quantity A:	$(c + d)^2 =$ $c^2 + 2cd + d^2$	$c^2 + d^2$
Subtract $c^2 + d^2$ from each quantity:	$2cd$	0

   Since it is given that $cd < 0$, so is $2cd$.

   **If you can't expand $(c + d)^2$, then use TACTIC 1 (page 285). Replace c and d with numbers satisfying $cd < 0$.

	Quantity A	Quantity B	Compare	Eliminate
Let $c = 1$ and $d = -1$	$(1 + -1)^2 = 0$	$1^2 + (-1)^2 =$ $1 + 1 = 2$	B is greater	A and C
Let $c = 3$ and $d = -5$	$(3 + -5)^2 =$ $(-2)^2 = 4$	$3^2 + (-5)^2 =$ $9 + 25 = 34$	B is greater	

Both times Quantity B was greater: choose B.

5. **(C)** The average of 3 numbers is their sum divided by 3. Since in *any* triangle the sum of the measures of the 3 angles is 180°, the average in each quantity is equal to $180 \div 3 = 60$.

   **Use TACTIC 1 (page 285). Pick values for the measures of the angles. For example, in isosceles $\triangle ABC$ choose 70, 70, 40; in right $\triangle XYZ$, choose 30, 60, 90. Each average is 60. Choose C.

6. **(B)** Since $b < 0$, $6b$ is negative, whereas b^6 is positive.

   **Use TACTIC 1 (page 285). Replace b with numbers satisfying $b < 0$.

	Quantity A	Quantity B	Compare	Eliminate
Let $b = -1$	$6(-1) = -6$	$(-1)^6 = 1$	B is greater	A and C
Let $b = -2$	$6(-2) = -12$	$(-2)^6 = 64$	B is greater	

Both times Quantity B was greater: choose B.

7. **(B)** Use TACTIC 5 (page 296): don't calculate the two areas; compare them. The circle in Quantity A is the area of a circle whose radius is 17 and whose diameter is 34. Quantity B is the area of a circle whose diameter is 35, and so is clearly greater.

8. **(A)** Use TACTIC 5 (page 296): don't calculate either slope. Quickly, make a rough sketch of line k, going through (1,1) and (5,2), and draw line m perpendicular to it.

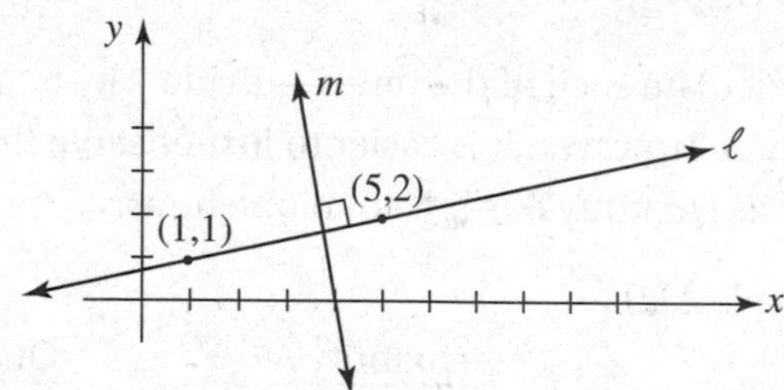

Line k has a positive slope (it slopes upward), whereas line m has a negative slope (it slopes downward). Quantity A is greater.

[Note: The slope of k is $\frac{1}{4}$ and the slope of m is -4, but you don't need to calculate either one. See Section 12-N (page 510) for all the facts you need to know about slopes.]

**If you don't know this fact about slopes, use TACTIC 6 (page 298). The answer cannot be Choice D, and if two lines intersect, their slopes cannot be equal, so eliminate Choice C. Guess Choice A or B.

9. **(D)** Every sixth integer is a multiple of 6 and every ninth integer is a multiple of 9, so in a large interval there will be many more multiples of 6. But in a very small interval, there might be none or possibly just one of each.

**Use TACTIC 1 (page 285). Let $x = 1$. Between 100 and 101 there are *no* multiples of 6 and *no* multiples of 9. Eliminate Choices A and B. Choose a large number for x: 100, for example. Between 100 and 200 there are many more multiples of 6 than there are multiples of 9. Eliminate Choice C.

10. **(C)** Add the equations.

$$\begin{array}{r} x + y = 5 \\ +\ y - x = -5 \\ \hline 2y = 0 \end{array}$$

Since $2y = 0$, $y = 0$.

**Use TACTIC 4 (page 294). Could $y = 0$? In each equation, if $y = 0$, then $x = -5$. So, y can equal 0. Eliminate Choices A and B, and either guess between Choices C and D or continue. Must $y = 0$? Yes, when you have two linear equations in two variables, there is only one solution, so nothing else is possible.

11. **(A)** With a calculator, you can multiply $\frac{7}{8} \times \frac{7}{8} \times \frac{7}{8} \times \frac{7}{8} \times \frac{7}{8}$, but it is annoying and time-consuming. However, you can avoid the arithmetic, if you know KEY FACT A24 (page 342):

If $0 < x < 1$ and $n > 1$, then $x^n < x$.

Since $\frac{7}{8} < 1$, then $\left(\frac{7}{8}\right)^5 < \frac{7}{8}$.

12. **(B)** The area of the shaded region is the area of quarter-circle *AOB* minus the area of the square. Since $r = OA = 6$, the area of the quarter-circle is $\frac{1}{4}\pi r^2 = \frac{1}{4}36\pi = 9\pi$. *OY*, the diagonal of the square, is 6 (since it is a radius of the circle), so *OZ*, the side of the square, is $\frac{6}{\sqrt{2}}$ (see KEY FACT J8, page 461). So the area of the square is $\left(\frac{6}{\sqrt{2}}\right)^2 = \frac{36}{2} = 18$.

Finally, the area of the shaded region is $9\pi - 18$, which is approximately 10.

**The solution above requires several steps. (See Sections 12-J, K, L, pages 456–499 to review any of the facts used.) If you can't reason through this, you still should be able to answer this question correctly. Use TACTIC 6 (page 298). The shaded region has a definite area, which is either 12, more than 12, or less than 12. Eliminate D. Also, the area of a curved region almost always involves π, so assume the area isn't exactly 12. Eliminate Choice C. You can now *guess* between Choices A and B, but if you trust the diagram and know a little bit you can improve your guess. If you know that the area of the circle is 36π, so that the area of the quarter-circle is 9π or about 28, you can estimate the shaded region. It's well less than half of the quarter-circle, so less than 14 and probably less than 12. Guess Choice B.

13. **(C)** Use TACTIC 4 (page 294). Could the edge be 6? Test it. If each edge is 6, the area of each face is $6 \times 6 = 36$, and since a cube has 6 faces, the total surface area is $6 \times 36 = 216$. The volume is $6^3 = 216$. So the quantities could be equal. Eliminate Choices A and B. If you have a sense that this is the only cube with this property,

choose C. In fact, if you had no idea how to do this, you might use TACTIC 6 (page 298), assume that there is only one way, eliminate Choice D, and then guess C. The direct solution is simple enough if you know the formulas. If e is the length of an edge of the cube, then the area is $6e^2$ and the volume is e^3: $6e^2 = e^3 \Rightarrow 6 = e$.

14. **(D)** There are several ways to answer this question. Use TACTIC 1 (page 285): plug in a number for x. If $x = 2$, Quantity A is 2π, which is slightly more than 6, and Quantity B is $2^2 = 4$. Quantity A is greater: eliminate Choices B and C. Must Quantity A be greater? If the only other number you try is $x = 3$, you'll think so, because $3^2 = 9$, but $3\pi > 9$. But remember, x does not have to be an integer: $3.9^2 > 15$, whereas $3.9\pi < 4\pi$, which is a little over 12.

    **Use TACTIC 4 (page 294). Could $\pi x = x^2$? Yes, if $x = \pi$. Must $x = \pi$? No.

    **Use TACTIC 3 (page 292). Divide each quantity by x: Now Quantity A is π and Quantity B is x. Which is bigger, π or x? We cannot tell.

15. **(D)** Use TACTIC 4 (page 294). Could the area of $\triangle ABC = 3$? Since the height is 6, the area would be 3 only if the base were 1: $\frac{1}{2}(1)(6) = 3$. Could $BC = 1$? Sure (see the figure). Must the base be 1? Of course not.

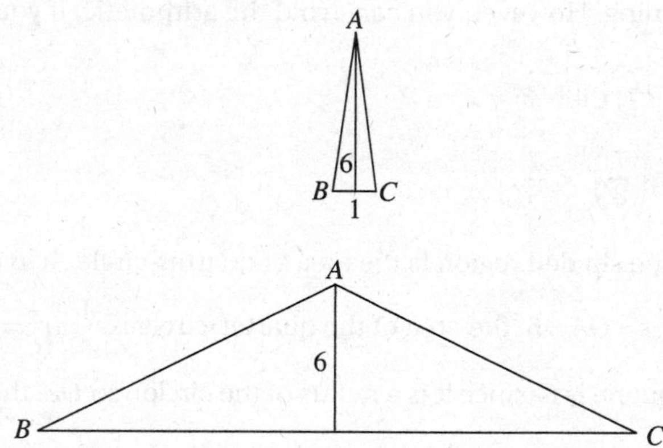

11 Data Interpretation Questions

Three of the 20 questions in each quantitative section of the GRE are data interpretation questions. As their name suggests, these questions are always based on the information that is presented in some form of a graph or a chart. Occasionally, the data are presented in a chart or table, but much more often, they are presented graphically. The three most common types of graphs are ***line graphs***, ***bar graphs***, and ***circle graphs***. It is also possible, but much less likely, that the data are presented in a ***scatter plot***.

In each section, the data interpretation questions are three consecutive questions, say Questions 14, 15, and 16, all of which refer to the same set of graphs or charts.

TIP

Before even reading a question based on a graph or table, take 10 or 15 seconds to look it over. Make sure you understand the information that is being displayed and the units of quantities involved.

When the first data interpretation question appears, either the graphs will be on the left-hand side of the screen, and the question will be on the right-hand side, or the graphs will be at the top of the screen and the question will be below them. It is possible, but unlikely, that you will have to scroll down in order to see all of the data. After you answer the first question, a second question will replace it on the right-hand side (or the bottom) of the screen; the graphs, of course, will still be on the screen for you to refer to.

The tactics discussed in this chapter can be applied to any type of data, no matter how they are displayed. In the practice exercises at the end of the chapter, there are data interpretation questions based on the types of graphs that normally appear on the GRE. Carefully, read through the answer explanations for each exercise, so that you learn the best way to handle each type of graph.

Infrequently, an easy data interpretation question will require only that you read the graph and find a numerical fact that is displayed. Usually, however, you will have to do some calculation on the data that you are analyzing. In harder questions, you may be given hypothetical situations and asked to make inferences based on the information provided in the given graphs.

Most data interpretation questions are multiple-choice questions, but some could be multiple-answer or numeric entry questions. They are never quantitative comparisons.

Line Graphs

A ***line graph*** indicates how one or more quantities change over time. The horizontal axis is usually marked off in units of time; the units on the vertical axis can represent almost any type of numerical data: dollars, weights, exam grades, number of people, and so on.

Here is a typical line graph:

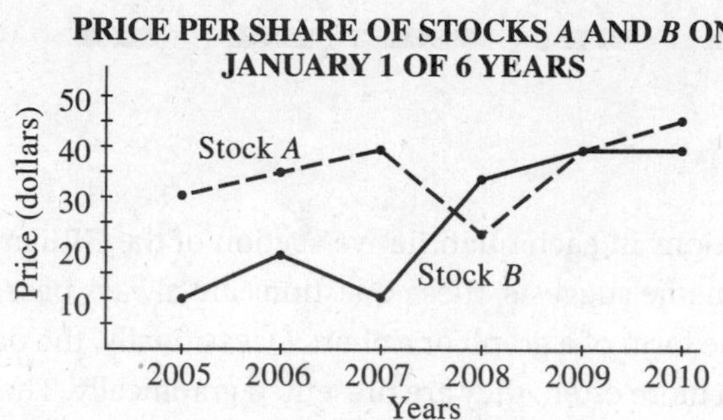

Before reading even one of the questions based on the above graph, you should have acquired *at least* the following information:

(i) The graph gives the values of two different stocks.
(ii) The graph covers the period from January 1, 2005, to January 1, 2010.
(iii) During that time, both stocks rose in value.

There are literally dozens of questions that could be asked about the data in this graph. The next seven examples are typical of the types of questions that could appear on the GRE.

EXAMPLE 1

What is the difference, in dollars, between the highest and lowest values of a share of Stock *A*?

SOLUTION.
The lowest value of Stock *A* was \$25 (in 2005); the highest value was \$40 (in 2010). The difference is **\$15**.

EXAMPLE 2

On January 1 of what year was the difference in the values of a share of Stock *A* and a share of Stock *B* the greatest?

SOLUTION.
Just look at the graph. The difference was clearly the greatest in **2007**. (Note that you don't have to calculate what the difference was.)

EXAMPLE 3

On January 1 of what year was the ratio of the value of a share of Stock *A* to the value of a share of Stock *B* the greatest?

SOLUTION.

From 2008 to 2010 the values of the two stocks were fairly close, so those years are not candidates. In 2007 the ratio was 40:10 or 4:1 or 4. In 2006 the ratio was 35:20 or 7:4 or 1.75. In 2005 the ratio was 30:10 or 3:1 or 3. The ratio was greatest in **2007**.

EXAMPLE 4

In what year was the percent increase in the value of a share of Stock *B* the greatest?

SOLUTION.

Just look at the graph. Since the slope of the graph is steepest in **2007** (between January 1, 2007 and January 1, 2008), the rate of growth was greatest then.

EXAMPLE 5

During how many years did the value of Stock *B* grow at a faster rate than that of Stock *A*?

SOLUTION.

Again, look at the slopes.

- In 2005, *B* rose more sharply than *A*. (✔)
- In 2006, *B* fell while *A* rose.
- In 2007, *B* rose while *A* fell. (✔)
- In 2008, *A* rose more sharply than *B*.
- In 2009, *A* rose; *B* stayed the same.

B grew at a faster rate during **2** years.

EXAMPLE 6

What was the average yearly increase in the value of a share of Stock *A* from 2005 to 2010?

SOLUTION.

Over the 5-year period from January 1, 2005, to January 1, 2010, the value of a share of Stock *A* rose from \$30 to \$45, an increase of \$15. The average yearly increase was \$15 ÷ 5 years or **\$3** per year.

EXAMPLE 7

If from 2005 to 2015 the value of each stock increases at the same rate as it did from 2005 to 2010, what will then be the ratio of the value of a share of Stock *B* to the value of a share of Stock *A*?

SOLUTION.
From 2005 to 2010, the value of Stock *A* increased by 50% (from \$30 to \$45) and the value of Stock *B* quadrupled (from \$10 to \$40). At the same rates, Stock *A* will grow from \$45 to \$67.50 in the years 2010–2015, while Stock *B* will grow from \$40 to \$160. The ratio of the value of a share of Stock *B* to the value of a share of Stock *A* will be 160 to 67.5, or approximately **2.37**.

HELPFUL HINT

On data interpretation questions, ignore the extraneous information you are given. Zero in on exactly what you need.

To answer these seven questions, most (but not all) of the data contained in the graph was used. On the GRE, if you had two questions based on that line graph, you can see that there would be many items of information you would not use.

Bar Graphs

The same information that was given in the preceding line graph, could have been presented in a ***table*** or in a ***bar graph.***

PRICE PER SHARE OF STOCKS *A* AND *B*
ON JANUARY 1 OF 6 YEARS

	Prices (dollars)					
Stock	2005	2006	2007	2008	2009	2010
Stock *A*	30	35	40	25	40	45
Stock *B*	10	20	15	35	40	40

PRICE PER SHARE OF STOCKS *A* AND *B*
ON JANUARY 1 OF 6 YEARS

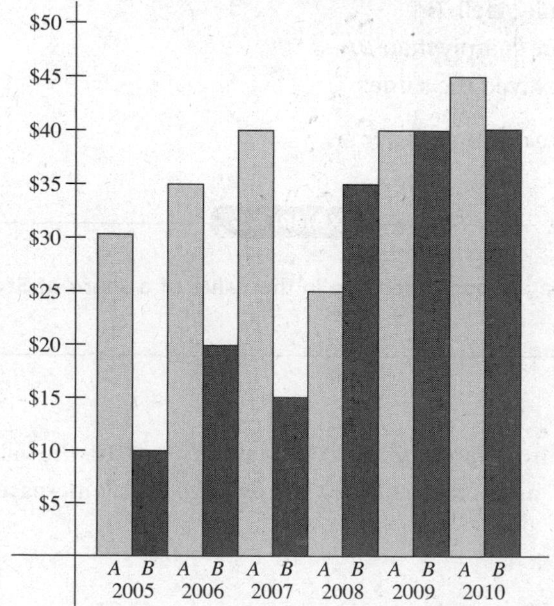

In a bar graph, the taller the bar, the greater is the value of the quantity. Bar graphs can also be drawn horizontally; in that case the longer the bar, the greater is the quantity. You will see examples of each type in the exercises at the end of this section, in the model tests, and, of course, on the GRE.

The following bar graph shows the numbers of students taking courses in the various foreign languages offered at a state college.

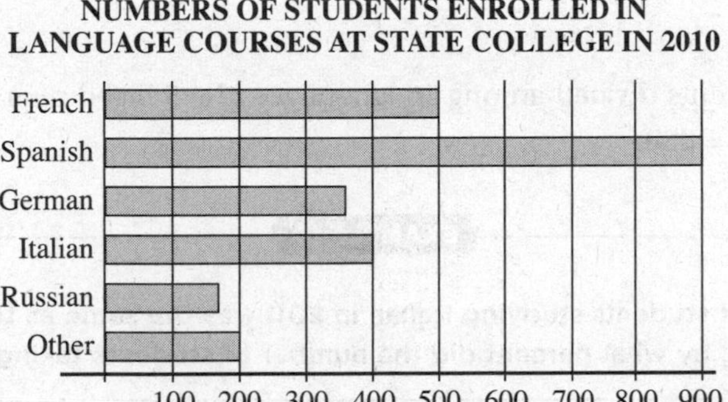

In a slight variation of the horizontal bar graph, the bars are replaced by a string of icons, or symbols. For example, the graph below, in which each picture of a person represents 100 students, conveys the same information as does the preceding bar graph.

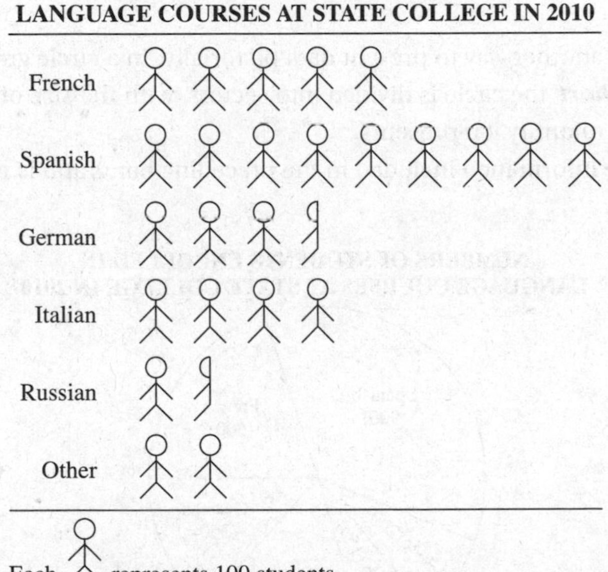

From either of the two preceding graphs, many questions could be asked. Examples 8–10 illustrate a few types.

EXAMPLE 8

What is the total number of students enrolled in language classes in 2010?

SOLUTION.

Just read the graph and add: **2500.**

EXAMPLE 9

> **If the "Other" category includes five languages, what is the average (arithmetic mean) number of students studying each language offered at the college?**

SOLUTION.

There are 2500 students divided among 10 languages (the 5 listed plus the 5 in the "Other" category): $2500 \div 10 =$ **250.**

EXAMPLE 10

> **If the number of students studying Italian in 2011 was the same as the number taking Spanish in 2010, by what percent did the number of students taking Italian increase?**

SOLUTION.

The number of students taking Italian increased by 500 from 400 to 900. This represents a $\frac{500}{400} \times 100\% =$ **125%** increase.

Circle Graphs

A ***circle graph*** is another way to present data pictorially. In a circle graph, which is sometimes called a ***pie chart***, the circle is divided into sectors, with the size of each sector exactly proportional to the quantity it represents.

For example, the information included in the preceding bar graph is presented in the following circle graph.

NUMBERS OF STUDENTS ENROLLED IN LANGUAGE COURSES AT STATE COLLEGE IN 2010

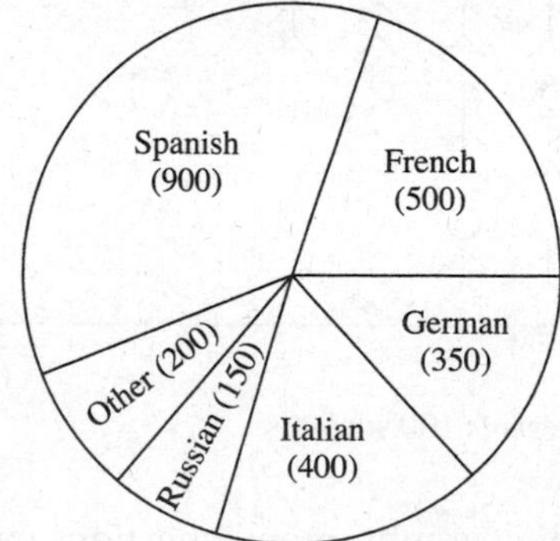

Usually on the GRE, in each sector of the circle is noted the number of degrees of its central angle or the percent of the total data it contains. For example, in the circle graph above, since in 2010, 500 of the 2500 language students at State College were studying French, the sector representing French is exactly $\frac{1}{5}$ of the circle. On the GRE this sector would also be marked either $72° \left(\frac{1}{5} \text{ of } 360°\right)$ or $20\% \left(\frac{1}{5} \text{ of } 100\%\right)$. The GRE graph would look like one of the graphs on the next page.

DISTRIBUTION OF THE 2500 STUDENTS ENROLLED IN LANGUAGE COURSES

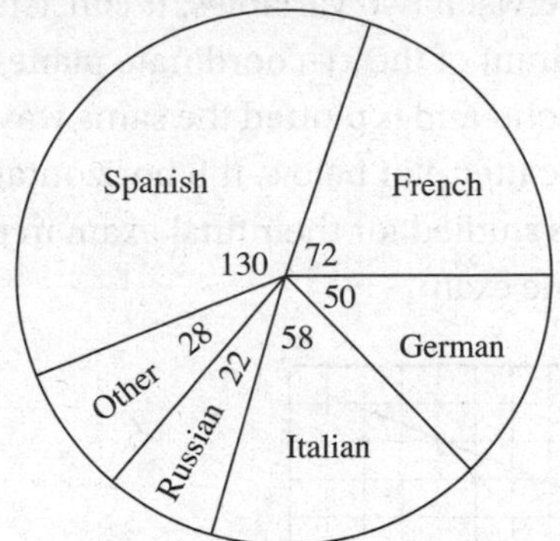

DISTRIBUTION OF THE 2500 STUDENTS ENROLLED IN LANGUAGE COURSES

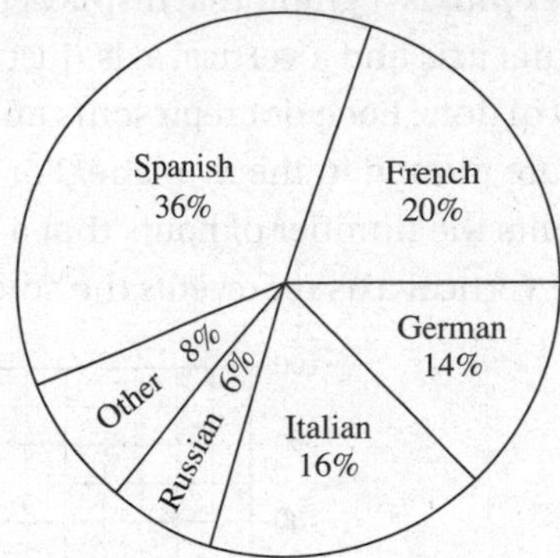

Very often on the GRE, some data are omitted from a circle graph, and it is your job to determine the missing item. Examples 11 and 12 are based on the following circle graph, which shows the distribution of marbles by color in a large jar.

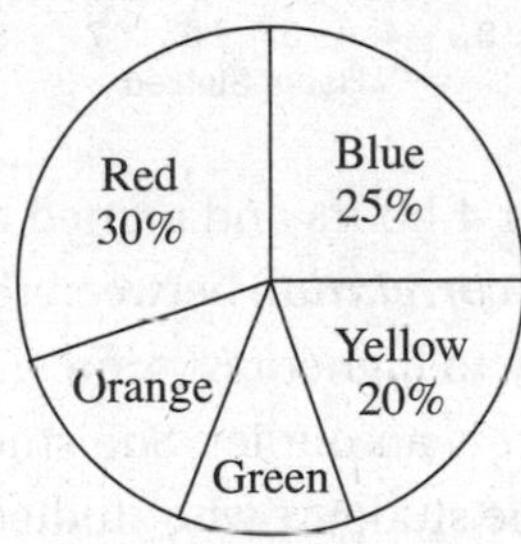

EXAMPLE 11

If the jar contains 1200 marbles and there are twice as many orange marbles as there are green, how many green marbles are there?

SOLUTION.

Since the red, blue, and yellow marbles constitute 75% of the total (30% + 25% + 20%), the orange and green ones combined account for 25% of the total: 25% of 1200 = 300. Then, since the ratio of orange marbles to green ones is 2:1, there are 200 orange marbles and **100** green ones.

EXAMPLE 12

Assume that the jar contains 1200 marbles, and that all of the red ones are removed and replaced by an equal number of marbles, all of which are blue or yellow. If the ratio of blue to yellow marbles remains the same, how many additional yellow marbles are there?

SOLUTION.

Since 30% of 1200 is 360, the 360 red marbles were replaced by 360 blue and yellow ones. To maintain the current blue to yellow ratio of 25 to 20, or 5 to 4, $\frac{5}{9}$ of the new marbles would be blue and $\frac{4}{9}$ would be yellow: $\frac{4}{9}$ of 360 = **160**.

Scatter Plot

A ***scatter plot*** is a graph that displays the relationship between two variables. It consists of a horizontal axis and a vertical axis (just like the first quadrant of the *xy*-coordinate plane) and a series of dots. Each dot represents an individual data point and is plotted the same way that points are plotted in the *xy*-plane. For example, in the scatter plot below, the horizontal axis represents the number of hours that a group of students studied for their final exam in math and the vertical axis represents the students' scores on the exam.

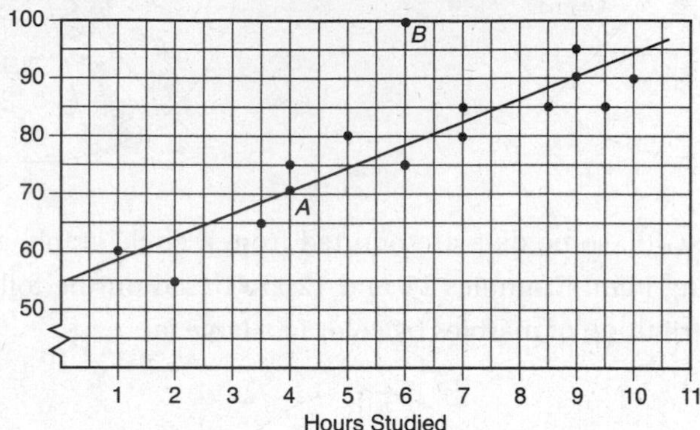

Look at Student *A*. He studied for 4 hours and earned a 70 on the final. Note that in this case, there is a fairly strong ***positive correlation*** between the two variables. The *general trend* is that more hours of study correlate to higher test scores. However, the correlation is clearly not perfect. Student *B*, for example, is an outlier. She studied for only 6 hours but had the highest score—higher than any of the students who studied 9 or 10 hours.

The line that is drawn on the scatter plot is called the ***line of best fit*** and can be used to predict the most likely value of one variable given the other. For example, from the line of best fit we see that a student who studies 8 hours would probably have a test score very close to 87. We also see that a student who earned a 60 on the final probably studied for about $1\frac{1}{2}$ hours.

Some scatter plots have a ***negative correlation***, and some have no correlation at all. An example of two variables whose scatter plot would likely have a negative correlation is one where the variable along the horizontal axis is a person's weight and the variable on the vertical axis is the speed at which that person can run a 100-meters dash. The general trend would likely show that the heavier the person is, the slower he or she can run. An example of variables whose scatter plot would likely show no correlation is people's height and the number of times per month the people go to the movies.

Be very careful. A strong correlation *does not mean* that there is ***causation***. Even if one variable increases whenever a second variable increases, there may be no cause and effect. For example in 2015 in the town of Brest, there was a very high correlation between the number of gallons of ice cream consumed in a week and the number of people who drowned that week. Clearly eating ice cream didn't cause the drownings. Something else was going on. In fact, during the weeks that it was very hot, people ate lots of ice cream. During those same weeks, more people went to the pools and beaches. Hence, there were more drownings. The causative variable was the temperature.

On the GRE, you will not be given a set of data and asked to create a scatter plot, nor will you have to calculate the line of best fit for a given scatter plot. However, you may have to recognize what type of correlation is exhibited and/or make a prediction based on a line of best fit that has been drawn in a scatter plot graph.

TESTING TACTICS

The four questions that follow will be used to illustrate the tactics that you should use in answering data interpretation questions. Remember, however, that on the GRE there will always be three questions that refer to a particular graph or set of graphs.

QUESTIONS 1–4 REFER TO THE FOLLOWING GRAPHS.

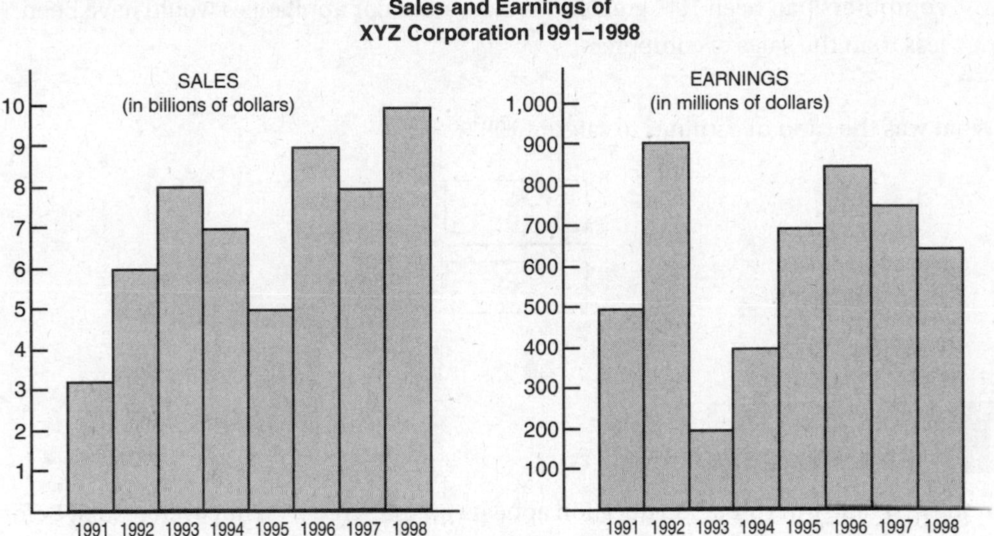

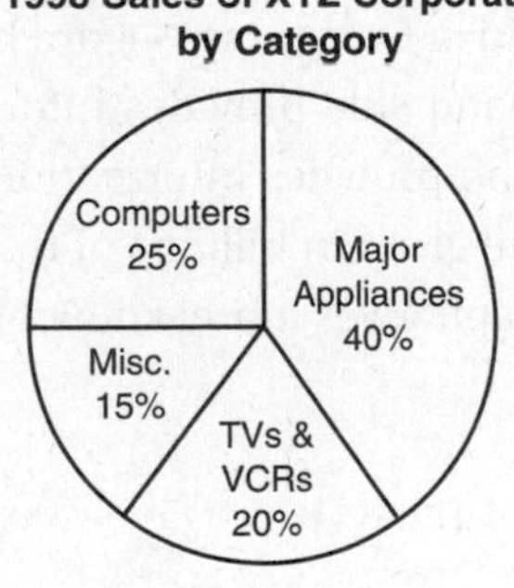

1. What is the average (arithmetic mean) in billions of dollars of the sales of XYZ Corporation for the period 1991–1998?

   Ⓐ 5.5 Ⓑ 6.0 Ⓒ 7.0 Ⓓ 8.0 Ⓔ 8.5

2. For which year was the percentage increase in earnings from the previous year the greatest?

   Ⓐ 1992 Ⓑ 1993 Ⓒ 1994 Ⓓ 1995 Ⓔ 1996

3. Which of the following statements can be deduced from the data in the given charts and circle graph?

   Indicate *all* such statements.

   [A] Sales of major appliances in 1998 exceeded total sales in 1991.

   [B] Earnings for the year in which earnings were greatest were more than sales for the year in which sales were lowest.

   [C] If in 1998, the sales of major appliances had been 10% less, and the sales of computers had been 10% greater, the sales of major appliances would have been less than the sales of computers.

4. What was the ratio of earnings to sales in 1993?

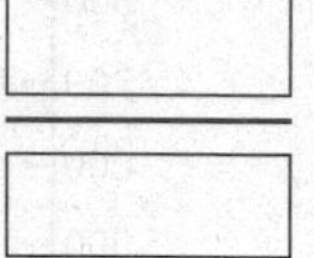

TACTIC

First Read the Titles

When the first data interpretation question appears on the screen, do not even read it! Before you attempt to answer a data interpretation question, take 15 to 30 seconds to study the graphs. Try to get a general idea about the information that is being displayed.

Observe that the bar graphs on which Questions 1–4 are based present two different sets of data. The bar graph on the left-hand side provides information about the sales of XYZ Corporation, and the right-hand graph provides information about the corporation's earnings. Also, note that whereas sales are given in billions of dollars, earnings are given in millions of dollars. Finally, the circle graph gives a breakdown by category of the sales of XYZ Corporation for one particular year.

TACTIC

2

Don't Confuse Percents and Numbers

Many students make mistakes on data interpretation questions because they don't distinguish between absolute numbers and percents. Although few students would look at the circle graph shown and think that XYZ Corporation sold 25 computers in 1998, many would mistakenly think that it sold 15 percent more major appliances than computers.

The problem is particularly serious when the questions involve percent increases or percent decreases. In Question 2 you are not asked for the year in which the increase in earnings from the previous year was the greatest. You are asked for the year in which the percent increase in earnings was the greatest. A quick glance at the right-hand graph reveals that the greatest increase occurred from 1991 to 1992 when earnings jumped by $400 million. However, when we solve this problem in the discussion of TACTIC 3 (page 317), you will see that Choice A is not the correct answer.

NOTE: Since many data interpretation questions involve percents, you should carefully study Section 12-C, page 368, and be sure that you know all of the tactics for solving percent problems. In particular, always try to use the number 100 or 1000, since it is so easy to mentally calculate percents of powers of 10.

TACTIC

3

Whenever Possible, Estimate

Although you have access to the onscreen calculator, when you take the GRE, you will not be expected to do complicated or lengthy calculations. Often, thinking and using some common sense can save you considerable time. For example, it may seem that in order to get the correct answer to Question 2, you have to calculate five different percents. In fact, you only need to do one calculation, and that one you can do in your head!

Just looking at the Earnings bar graph, it is clear that the only possible answers are 1992, 1994, and 1995, the three years in which there was a significant increase in earnings from the year before. From 1993 to 1994 expenditures doubled, from \$200 million to \$400 million—an increase of 100%. From 1991 to 1992 expenditures increased by \$400 million (from \$500 million to \$900 million), but that is less than a 100% increase (we don't care how much less). From 1994 to 1995 expenditures increased by \$300 million (from \$400 million to \$700 million); but again, this is less than a 100% increase. The answer is **C**.

TACTIC

Do Each Calculation Separately

As in all multiple-answer questions, Question 3 requires you to determine which of the statements are true. The key is to work with the statements individually.

To determine whether or not statement A is true, look at both the Sales bar graph and the circle graph. In 1998, total sales were \$10 billion, and sales of major appliances accounted for 40% of the total: 40% of \$10 billion = \$4 billion. This exceeds the \$3 billion total sales figure for 1991, so statement A is true.

In 1992, the year in which earnings were greatest, earnings were \$900 million. In 1991, the year in which sales were lowest, sales were \$3 billion, which is much greater than \$900 million. Statement B is false.

In 1998, sales of major appliances were \$4 billion. If they had been 10% less, they would have been \$3.6 billion. That year, sales of computers were \$2.5 billion (25% of \$10 billion). If computer sales had increased by 10%, sales would have increased by \$0.25 billion to \$2.75 billion. Statement C is false.

The answer is **A**.

TACTIC

Use Only the Information Given

You must base your answer to each question only on the information in the given charts and graphs. It is unlikely that you have any preconceived notion as to the sales of XYZ Corporation, but you might think that you know the population of the United States for a particular year or the percent of women currently in the workplace. If your knowledge contradicts any of the data presented in the graphs, ignore what you know. First of all, you may be mistaken; but more important, the data may refer to a different, unspecified location or year. In any event, *always* base your answers on the given data.

TACTIC

6

Always Use the Proper Units

In answering Question 4, observe that earnings are given in millions, while sales are in billions. If you answer too quickly, you might say that in 1993 earnings were 200 and sales were 8, and conclude that the desired ratio is $\frac{200}{8} = \frac{25}{1}$. You will avoid this mistake if you keep track of units: earnings were 200 *million* dollars, whereas sales were 8 *billion* dollars. The correct ratio is

$$\frac{200,\!\cancel{000,000}}{8,\!\cancel{000,000},000} = \frac{2}{80} = \frac{1}{40}$$

Enter 1 in the box for the numerator and 40 in the box for the denominator.

TACTIC

7

Be Sure That Your Answer Is Reasonable

Before clicking on your answer, take a second to be sure that it is reasonable. For example, in Question 4, from the logic of the situation, you should realize that earnings can't exceed sales. The desired ratio, therefore, must be less than 1. If you use the wrong units (see TACTIC 6, above), your initial thought might be to enter $\frac{25}{1}$. By testing your answer for reasonableness, you will realize that you made a mistake.

Remember that if you don't know how to solve a problem, you should always guess. Before guessing, however, check to see if one or more of the choices are unreasonable. If so, eliminate them. For example, if you forget how to calculate a percent increase, you would have to guess at Question 2. But before guessing wildly, you should at least eliminate Choice B, since from 1992 to 1993 earnings decreased.

TACTIC

8

Try to Visualize the Answer

Because graphs and tables present data in a form that enables you to readily see relationships and to make quick comparisons, you can often avoid doing any calculations. Whenever possible, use your eye instead of your computational skills.

For example, to answer Question 1, rather than reading the sales figures in the bar graph on the left for each of the eight years, adding them, and then dividing by 8, visualize the situation. Where could you draw a horizontal line across the graph so that there would be the same amount of gray area above the line as white area below it? Imagine a horizontal line drawn through the 7 on the vertical axis. The portions of the bars above the line for 1993 and 1996–1998 are just about exactly the same size as the white areas below the line for 1991, 1992, and 1994. The answer is **C**.

PRACTICE EXERCISES

Data Interpretation Questions

On the GRE there will typically be three or four questions based on any set of graphs. Accordingly, in each section of the model tests in this book, there are three data interpretation questions, each referring to the same set of graphs. In this exercise set, however, for each graph or pair of graphs there are only two questions.

QUESTIONS 1–2 REFER TO THE FOLLOWING GRAPHS.

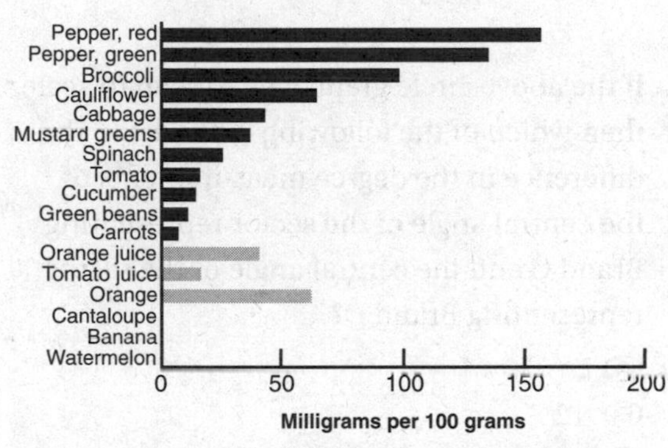

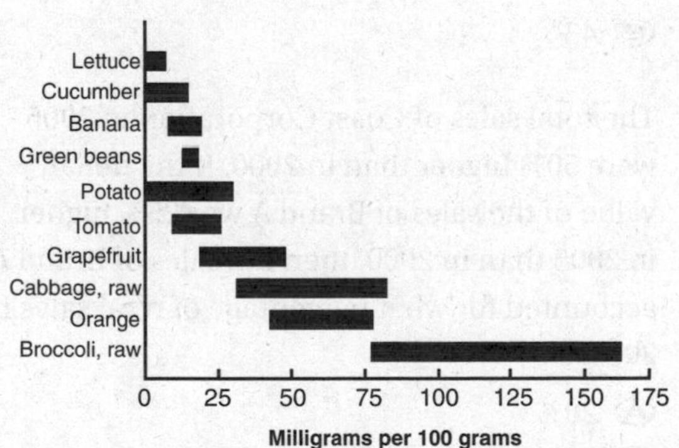

1. Based on the upper graph, what is the ratio of the amount of vitamin C in 500 grams of orange to the amount of vitamin C in 500 grams of orange juice?

Ⓐ 4:7
Ⓑ 1:1
Ⓒ 7:4
Ⓓ 2:1
Ⓔ 4:1

2. Based on the lower graph, how many grams of tomato would you have to eat to be certain of getting more vitamin C than you would get by eating 100 grams of raw broccoli?

Ⓐ 300
Ⓑ 500
Ⓒ 750
Ⓓ 1,200
Ⓔ 1,650

QUESTIONS 3–4 REFER TO THE FOLLOWING GRAPHS.

Percentage of students who reported spending time on homework and watching television

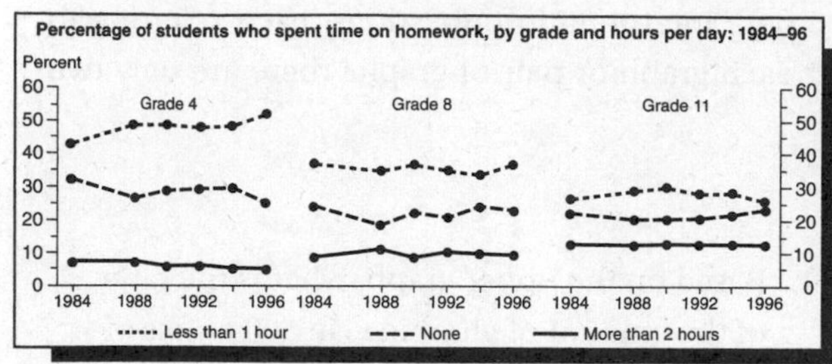

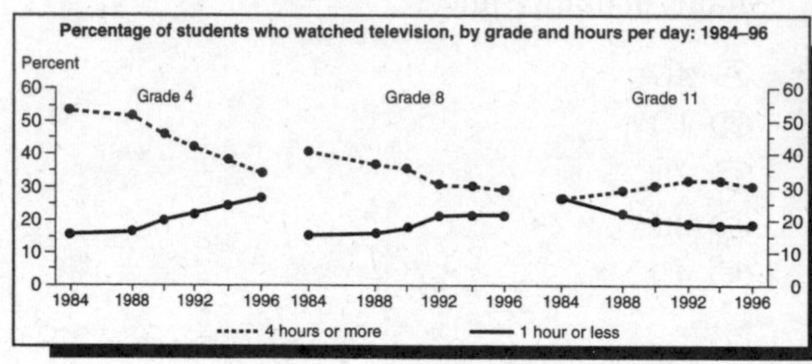

SOURCE: U.S. Department of Education.

3. In 1996, what percent of fourth-graders did between 1 and 2 hours of homework per day?

Ⓐ 5%
Ⓑ 15%
Ⓒ 25%
Ⓓ 40%
Ⓔ 55%

4. If in 1984 there were 2,000,000 eleventh-graders, and if between 1984 and 1996 the number of eleventh-graders increased by 10%, then approximately how many fewer eleventh-graders watched 1 hour or less of television in 1996 than in 1984?

Ⓐ 25,000
Ⓑ 50,000
Ⓒ 75,000
Ⓓ 100,000
Ⓔ 150,000

QUESTIONS 5–6 REFER TO THE FOLLOWING GRAPH.

Total Sales of Coast Corporation in 2000: $1,000,000

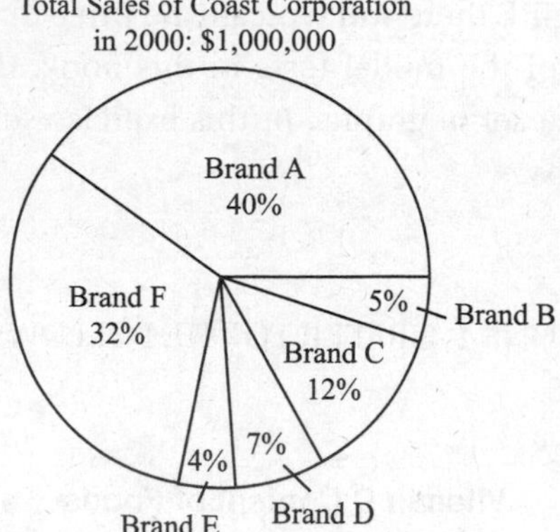

5. If the above circle graph were drawn to scale, then which of the following is closest to the difference in the degree measurements of the central angle of the sector representing Brand C and the central angle of the sector representing Brand D?

Ⓐ 5°
Ⓑ 12°
Ⓒ 18°
Ⓓ 25°
Ⓔ 43°

6. The total sales of Coast Corporation in 2005 were 50% higher than in 2000. If the dollar value of the sales of Brand A was 25% higher in 2005 than in 2000, then the sales of Brand A accounted for what percentage of total sales in 2005?

Ⓐ 20%
Ⓑ 25%
Ⓒ $33\frac{1}{3}$%
Ⓓ 40%
Ⓔ 50%

QUESTIONS 7–8 REFER TO THE FOLLOWING GRAPHS.

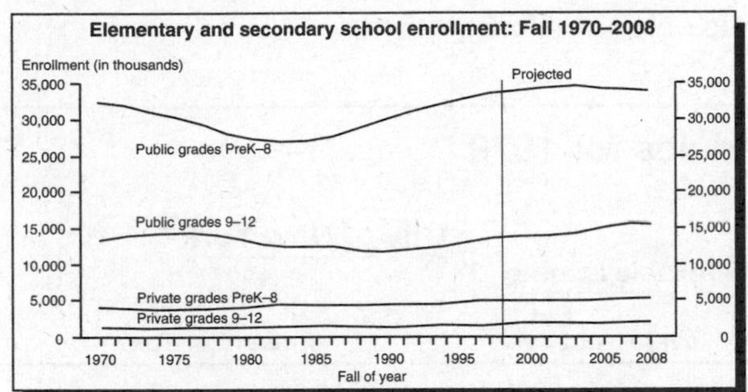

Projected percentage change in public elementary and secondary school enrollment, by region: Fall 1988 to 2008

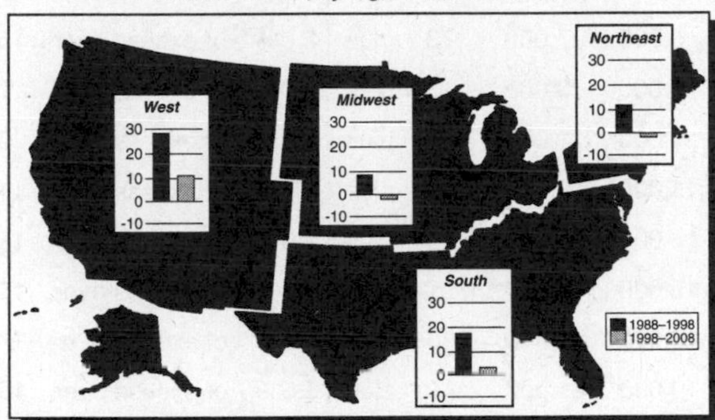

SOURCE: U.S. Department of Education, National Center for Education Statistics.

7. To the nearest million, how many more students were enrolled in school—both public and private, preK–12—in 1970 than in 1988?
   - Ⓐ 3,000,000
   - Ⓑ 6,000,000
   - Ⓒ 10,000,000
   - Ⓓ 44,000,000
   - Ⓔ 51,000,000

8. In 1988 there were 40,000,000 public school students in the United States, of whom 22% lived in the West. Approximately, how many public school students are projected to be living in the West in 2008?
   - Ⓐ 9,000,000
   - Ⓑ 12,000,000
   - Ⓒ 15,000,000
   - Ⓓ 24,000,000
   - Ⓔ 66,000,000

QUESTIONS 9–10 REFER TO THE FOLLOWING GRAPH.

Perceptions of Body Weight Status

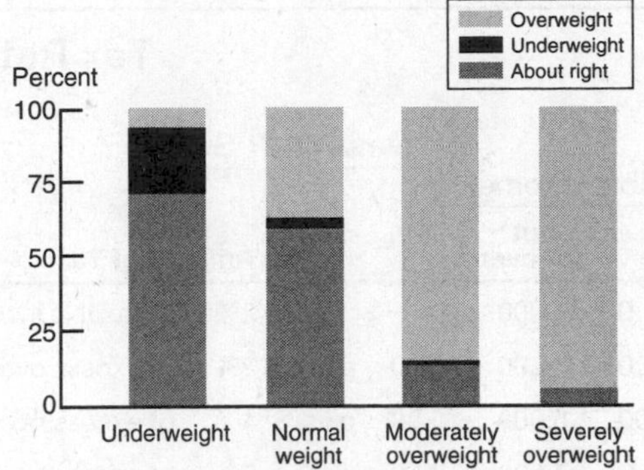

Actual weight status

Perceived compared with actual weight status of adult females.

Source: U.S. Department of Agriculture.

9. To the nearest 5%, what percent of underweight adult females perceive themselves to be underweight?

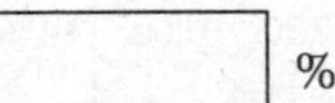 %

10. The members of which of the four groups had the least accurate perception of their body weight?
    - Ⓐ Underweight
    - Ⓑ Normal weight
    - Ⓒ Moderately overweight
    - Ⓓ Severely overweight
    - Ⓔ It cannot be determined from the information given in the graph.

QUESTIONS 11–12 REFER TO THE FOLLOWING TABLE.

In 1979, residents of New York City paid both New York State and New York City tax. Residents of New York State who lived and worked outside of New York City paid only New York State tax.

Tax Rate Schedules for 1979

New York State

Taxable Income over	but not over	Amount of Tax				
$ 0	$1,000			2%	of taxable income	
1,000	3,000	$20	plus	3%	of excess over	$1,000
3,000	5,000	80	plus	4%	of excess over	3,000
5,000	7,000	160	plus	5%	of excess over	5,000
7,000	9,000	260	plus	6%	of excess over	7,000
9,000	11,000	380	plus	7%	of excess over	9,000
11,000	13,000	520	plus	8%	of excess over	11,000
13,000	15,000	680	plus	9%	of excess over	13,000
15,000	17,000	860	plus	10%	of excess over	15,000
17,000	19,000	1,060	plus	11%	of excess over	17,000
19,000	21,000	1,280	plus	12%	of excess over	19,000
21,000	23,000	1,520	plus	13%	of excess over	21,000
23,000		1,780	plus	14%	of excess over	23,000

City of New York

Taxable Income over	but not over	Amount of Tax				
$ 0	$1,000			0.9%	of taxable income	
1,000	3,000	$ 9	plus	1.4%	of excess over	$1,000
3,000	5,000	37	plus	1.8%	of excess over	3,000
5,000	7,000	73	plus	2.0%	of excess over	5,000
7,000	9,000	113	plus	2.3%	of excess over	7,000
9,000	11,000	159	plus	2.5%	of excess over	9,000
11,000	13,000	209	plus	2.7%	of excess over	11,000
13,000	15,000	263	plus	2.9%	of excess over	13,000
15,000	17,000	321	plus	3.1%	of excess over	15,000
17,000	19,000	383	plus	3.3%	of excess over	17,000
19,000	21,000	449	plus	3.5%	of excess over	19,000
21,000	23,000	519	plus	3.8%	of excess over	21,000
23,000	25,000	595	plus	4.0%	of excess over	23,000
25,000		675	plus	4.3%	of excess over	25,000

11. In 1979 how much tax, in dollars, would a resident of New York State who lived and worked outside New York City have paid on a taxable income of $16,100?

[ ] dollars

12. In 1979, how much more total tax would a resident of New York City who had a taxable income of $36,500 pay, compared to a resident of New York City who had a taxable income of $36,000?

Ⓐ $21.50
Ⓑ $43
Ⓒ $70
Ⓓ $91.50
Ⓔ $183

QUESTIONS 13–14 REFER TO THE FOLLOWING TABLES.

Years of Life Expectancy at Birth
(Life expectancy in years)

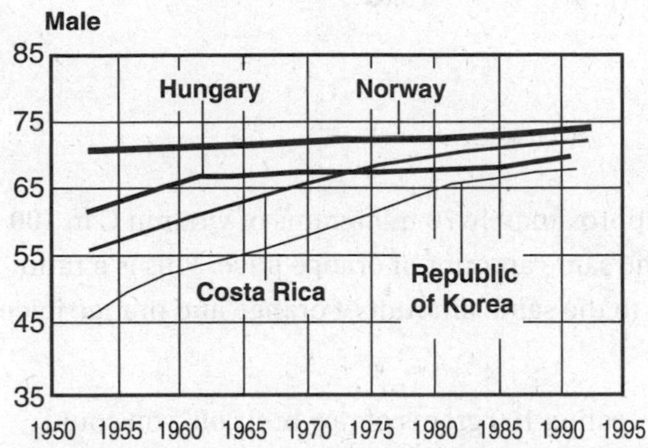

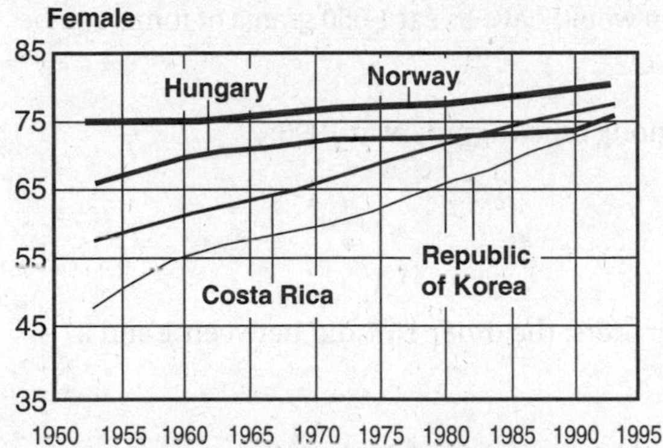

Source: U.S. Bureau of the Census, Center for International Research.

13. For how many of the countries listed in the graphs is it true that the life expectancy of a female born in 1955 was higher than the life expectancy of a male born in 1990?

Ⓐ None
Ⓑ 1
Ⓒ 2
Ⓓ 3
Ⓔ 4

14. By sex and nationality, who had the greatest increase in life expectancy between 1955 and 1990?

Ⓐ A Korean female
Ⓑ A Korean male
Ⓒ A Costa Rican female
Ⓓ A Costa Rican male
Ⓔ A Norwegian female

QUESTIONS 15–16 REFER TO THE FOLLOWING GRAPH.

Bias-Motivated Offenses 1998
Percent Distribution

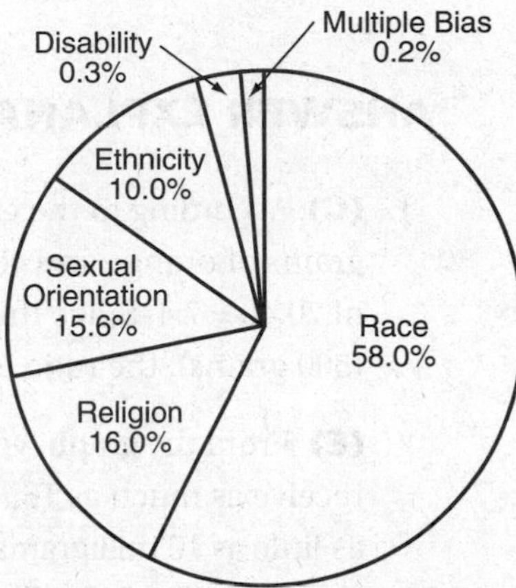

Source: U.S. Department of Justice, Federal Bureau of Investigation.

15. If in 1998 there were 10,000 bias-motivated offenses based on ethnicity, how many more offenses were based on religion than on sexual orientation?

Ⓐ 4
Ⓑ 40
Ⓒ 400
Ⓓ 4,000
Ⓔ 40,000

16. If after further analysis it was determined that between 25% and 50% of the offenses included under Religion were, in fact, not bias-motivated, and those offenses were removed from the study, which of the following could be the percentage of bias-motivated offenses based on race?

Indicate *all* such percentages.

[A] 59%
[B] 60%
[C] 61%
[D] 62%
[E] 63%
[F] 64%
[G] 65%

ANSWER KEY

1. **C**	4. **E**	7. **B**	10. **A**	13. **B**	16. **C, D, E**
2. **E**	5. **C**	8. **B**	11. **970**	14. **A**	
3. **B**	6. **C**	9. **25**	12. **D**	15. **C**	

ANSWER EXPLANATIONS

1. **(C)** According to the graph, there are approximately 70 milligrams of vitamin C in 100 grams of orange and 40 milligrams in the same amount of orange juice. This is a ratio of 70:40 = 7:4. Since the question refers to the same amount of orange and orange juice (500 grams), the ratio is unchanged.

2. **(E)** From the graph, you can see that by eating 100 grams of raw broccoli, you could receive as much as 165 milligrams of vitamin C. Since 100 grams of tomato could have as little as 10 milligrams of vitamin C, you would have to eat 1,650 grams of tomato to be sure of getting 165 milligrams of vitamin C.

3. **(B)** From the top graph, we see that among fourth-graders in 1996:

   25% did no homework;
   55% did less than 1 hour;
   5% did more than 2 hours.

   This accounts for 85% of the fourth-graders; the other 15% did between 1 and 2 hours of homework per day.

4. **(E)** In 1984, approximately 540,000 eleventh-graders watched television 1 hour or less per day (27% of 2,000,000). By 1996, the number of eleventh-graders had increased by 10% to 2,200,000, but the percent of them who watched television 1 hour or less per day decreased to about 18%: 18% of 2,200,000 is 396,000. This is a decrease of 144,000, or approximately 150,000.

5. **(C)** The central angle of the sector representing Brand C is 12% of 360°:

   $$(0.12) \times 360° = 43.2°$$

   The central angle of the sector representing Brand D is 7% of 360°:

   $$(0.7) \times 360° = 25.2°$$

   Finally, $43.2° - 25.2° = 18°$

   **Note this can be done in one step by noticing that the percentage difference between Brands C and D is 5% and 5% of 360 is $(0.05) \times 360 = 18$.

6. **(C)** Since total sales in 2000 were $1,000,000, in 2005 sales were $1,500,000 (a 50% increase).

   In 2000, sales of Brand A were $400,000 (40% of $1,000,000).

   In 2005 sales of Brand A were $500,000 (25% or $\frac{1}{4}$ more than in 2000).

   Finally, $500,000 is $\frac{1}{3}$ or $33\frac{1}{3}$% of $1,500,000.

7. **(B)** Reading from the top graph, we get the following enrollment figures:

	1970	1988
Public PreK–8	33,000,000	28,000,000
Public 9–12	13,000,000	12,000,000
Private PreK–8	4,000,000	4,000,000
Private 9–12	1,000,000	1,000,000
Total	51,000,000	45,000,000

51,000,000 – 45,000,000 = 6,000,000.

8. **(B)** In 1988, 8,800,000 (22% of 40,000,000) students lived in the West. From 1988–1998 this figure increased by 27%—for simplicity use 25%: an additional 2,200,000 students; so the total was then 11,000,000. The projected increase from 1998–2008 is about 10%, so the number will grow by 1,100,000 to 12,100,000.

9. **25** The bar representing underweight adult females who perceive themselves to be underweight extends from about 70% to about 95%, a range of approximately 25%.

10. **(A)** Almost all overweight females correctly considered themselves to be overweight; and more than half of all females of normal weight correctly considered themselves "about right." But nearly 70% of underweight adult females inaccurately considered themselves "about right."

11. **970** Referring only to the New York State table, we see that the amount of tax on a taxable income between $15,000 and $17,000 was $860 plus 10% of the excess over $15,000. Therefore, the tax on $16,100 is $860 plus 10% of $1,100 = $860 + $110 = $970.

12. **(D)** According to the tables, each additional dollar of taxable income over $25,000 was subject to a New York State tax of 14% and a New York City tax of 4.3%, for a total tax of 18.3%. Therefore, an additional $500 in taxable income would have incurred an additional tax of $0.183 \times 500 = \$91.50$.

13. **(B)** In Norway, the life expectancy of a female born in 1955 was 75 years, which is greater than the life expectancy of a male born in 1990. In Hungary, the life expectancy of a female born in 1955 was 66 years, whereas the life expectancy of a male born in 1990 was greater than 67. In the other two countries, the life expectancy of a female born in 1955 was less than 65 years, and the life expectancy of a male born in 1990 was greater than 65.

14. **(A)** The life expectancy of a Korean female born in 1955 was about 51 and in 1990 it was about 74, an increase of 23 years. This is greater than any other nationality and sex.

15. **(C)** Since there were 10,000 bias-motivated offenses based on ethnicity, and that represents 10% of the total, there were 100,000 bias-motivated offenses in total. Of these, 16,000 (16% of 100,000) were based on religion, and 15,600 (15.6% of 100,000) were based on sexual orientation. The difference is 400.

16. **(C, D, E)** Since this is a question about percentages, assume that the total number of bias-motivated offenses in 1998 was 100, of which 16 were based on religion and 58 were based on race.

- If 8 of the religion-based offenses (50% of 16) were deleted, then there would have been 92 offenses in all, of which 58 were based on race.

$$\frac{58}{92} = 0.6304 = 63.04\%$$

- If 4 of the religion-based offenses (25% of 16) were deleted, then there would have been 96 offenses in all, of which 58 were based on race.

$$\frac{58}{96} = 0.6041 = 60.41\%$$

Only Choices C, D, and E lie between 60.41% and 63.04%.

Mathematics Review 12

The mathematics questions on the GRE General Test require a working knowledge of mathematical principles, including an understanding of the fundamentals of algebra, plane geometry, and arithmetic, as well as the ability to translate problems into formulas and to interpret graphs. Very few questions require any math beyond what is typically taught in the first two years of high school, and even much of that is not tested. The following review covers those areas that you definitely need to know.

This chapter is divided into 16 sections, labeled 12-A through 12-P. For each question on the Diagnostic Test and the two Model Tests, the Answer Key indicates which section of Chapter 12 you should consult if you need help on a particular topic.

How much time you initially devote to reviewing mathematics should depend on your math skills. If you have always been a good math student and you have taken some math in college and remember most of your high school math, you can skip the instructional parts of this chapter for now. If while doing the Model Tests in Part 5 or on the accompanying CD-ROM, you find that you keep making mistakes on certain types of problems (averages, percents, circles, solid geometry, word problems, for example), or they take you too long, you should then study the appropriate sections here. Even if your math skills are excellent, and you don't need the review, you should complete the sample questions in those sections; they are an excellent source of additional GRE questions. If you know that your math skills are not very good and you have not done much math since high school, then it is advisable to review all of this material, including working out the problems, *before* tackling the model tests.

No matter how good you are in math, *you should carefully read and do the problems* in Chapters 8, 9, 10, and 11. For many of these problems, two solutions are given: the most direct mathematical solution and a second solution using one or more of the special tactics taught in these chapters.

ARITHMETIC

To do well on the GRE, you need to feel comfortable with most topics of basic arithmetic. In the first five sections of this chapter, we will review the basic arithmetic operations, signed numbers, fractions, decimals, ratios, percents, and averages. Since the GRE uses these concepts to test your reasoning skills, not your ability to perform tedious calculations, we will concentrate on the concepts and not on arithmetic drill. The solutions to more than one-third of the mathematics questions on the GRE depend on your knowing the key facts in these sections. Be sure to review them all.

12-A. BASIC ARITHMETIC CONCEPTS

- The Number Line
- Absolute Value
- Addition, Subtraction, Multiplication, Division
- Integers
- Exponents and Roots
- Squares and Square Roots
- PEMDAS
- Inequalities
- Practice Exercises
- Answer Explanations

Number Line

Let's start by reviewing the most important sets of numbers and their properties. On the GRE the word *number* always means *real number*, a number that can be represented by a point on the number line.

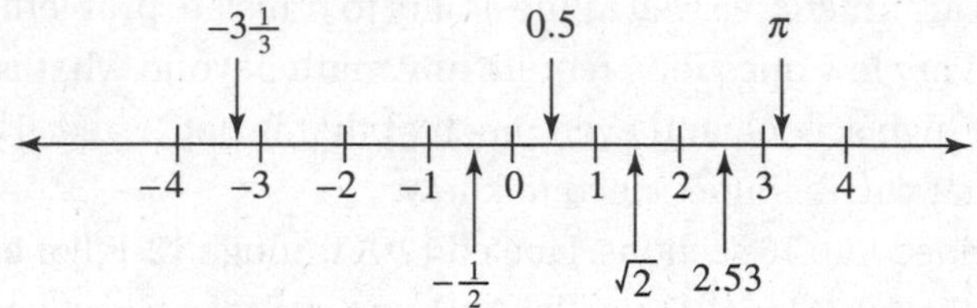

Signed Numbers

The numbers to the right of 0 on the number line are called ***positive*** and those to the left of 0 are called ***negative***. Negative numbers must be written with a *negative sign* (–2); positive numbers can be written with a *plus sign* (+2) but are usually written without a sign (2). All numbers can be called ***signed numbers***.

KEY FACT A1

For any number *a*, exactly one of the following is true:

- ***a* is negative**
- $\boldsymbol{a = 0}$
- ***a* is positive**

TIP

The absolute value of a number is *never* negative.

The ***absolute value*** of a number a, denoted $|a|$, is the distance between a and 0 on the number line. Since 3 is 3 units to the right of 0 on the number line and –3 is 3 units to the left of 0, both have an absolute value of 3:

- $|3| = 3$
- $|-3| = 3$

Two unequal numbers that have the same absolute value are called ***opposites***. So, 3 is the opposite of –3 and –3 is the opposite of 3.

KEY FACT A2

The only number that is equal to its opposite is 0.

EXAMPLE 1

$$a - b = -(a - b)$$

Quantity A	Quantity B
a	b

SOLUTION.
Since $-(a - b)$ is the opposite of $a - b$, $a - b = 0$, and so $a = b$. The answer is **C**.

Addition, Subtraction, Multiplication, Division

In arithmetic we are basically concerned with the addition, subtraction, multiplication, and division of numbers. The third column of the following table gives the terms for the results of these operations.

Operation	Symbol	Result	Example
Addition	+	***Sum***	16 is the sum of 12 and 4 $16 = 12 + 4$
Subtraction	–	***Difference***	8 is the difference of 12 and 4 $8 = 12 - 4$
Multiplication*	×	***Product***	48 is the product of 12 and 4 $48 = 12 \times 4$
Division	÷	***Quotient***	3 is the quotient of 12 and 4 $3 = 12 \div 4$

*Multiplication can be indicated also by a dot, parentheses, or the juxtaposition of symbols without any sign: $2^2 \cdot 2^4$, $3(4)$, $3(x + 2)$, $3a$, $4abc$.

Given any two numbers a and b, we can *always* find their sum, difference, product, and quotient, except that we may *never divide by zero.*

- $0 \div 7 = 0$
- $7 \div 0$ is meaningless

EXAMPLE 2

What is the sum of the product and quotient of 8 and 8?

Ⓐ 16 Ⓑ 17 Ⓒ 63 Ⓓ 64 Ⓔ 65

SOLUTION.
Product: $8 \times 8 = 64$. Quotient: $8 \div 8 = 1$. Sum: $64 + 1 =$ **65** (E).

KEY FACT A3

- **The product of 0 and any number is 0. For any number *a*: $a \times 0 = 0$.**
- **Conversely, if the product of two numbers is 0, *at least one* of them must be 0:**

$$ab = 0 \Rightarrow a = 0 \text{ or } b = 0$$

EXAMPLE 3

Quantity A	Quantity B
The product of the integers from –7 to 2	The product of the integers from –2 to 7

SOLUTION.
Do not multiply. Each quantity is the product of 10 numbers, one of which is 0. So, by KEY FACT A3, each product is 0. The quantities are equal (**C**).

KEY FACT A4

The product and quotient of two positive numbers or two negative numbers are positive; the product and quotient of a positive number and a negative number are negative.

×	+	–
+	+	–
–	–	+

÷	+	–
+	+	–
–	–	+

$6 \times 3 = 18$ $\quad 6 \times (-3) = -18 \quad (-6) \times 3 = -18 \quad (-6) \times (-3) = 18$

$6 \div 3 = 2 \quad 6 \div (-3) = -2 \quad (-6) \div 3 = -2 \quad (-6) \div (-3) = 2$

To determine whether a product of more than two numbers is positive or negative, count the number of negative factors.

KEY FACT A5

- **The product of an *even* number of negative factors is positive.**
- **The product of an *odd* number of negative factors is negative.**

EXAMPLE 4

Quantity A	Quantity B
(–1)(2)(–3)(4)(–5)	(1)(–2)(3)(–4)(5)

SOLUTION.
Don't waste time multiplying. Quantity A is negative since it has 3 negative factors, whereas Quantity B is positive since it has 2 negative factors. The answer is **B**.

KEY FACT A6

- **The *reciprocal* of any nonzero number a is $\frac{1}{a}$.**
- **The product of any number and its reciprocal is 1:**

$$a \times \left(\frac{1}{a}\right) = 1$$

KEY FACT A7

- **The sum of two positive numbers is positive.**
- **The sum of two negative numbers is negative.**
- **To find the sum of a positive and a negative number, find the difference of their absolute values and use the sign of the number with the larger absolute value.**

$$6 + 2 = 8 \qquad (-6) + (-2) = -8$$

To calculate either 6 + (–2) or (–6) + 2, take the *difference*, 6 – 2 = 4, and use the sign of the number whose absolute value is 6. So,

$$6 + (-2) = 4 \qquad (-6) + 2 = -4$$

KEY FACT A8

The sum of any number and its opposite is 0:

$$\boldsymbol{a + (-a) = 0}$$

Many of the properties of arithmetic depend on the relationship between subtraction and addition and between division and multiplication.

KEY FACT A9

- **Subtracting a number is the same as adding its opposite.**
- **Dividing by a number is the same as multiplying by its reciprocal.**

$$\boldsymbol{a - b = a + (-b) \qquad a \div b = a \times \left(\frac{1}{b}\right)}$$

Many problems involving subtraction and division can be simplified by changing them to addition and multiplication problems, respectively.

KEY FACT A10

To subtract signed numbers, change the problem to an addition problem, by changing the sign of what is being subtracted, and use KEY FACT A7.

$$2 - 6 = 2 + (-6) = -4 \qquad 2 - (-6) = 2 + (6) = 8$$

$$(-2) - (-6) = (-2) + (6) = 4 \qquad (-2) - 6 = (-2) + (-6) = -8$$

In each case, the minus sign was changed to a plus sign, and either the 6 was changed to –6 or the –6 was changed to 6.

Integers

The ***integers*** are {..., –4, –3, –2, –1, 0, 1, 2, 3, 4, ...}.
The ***positive integers*** are {1, 2, 3, 4, 5, ...}.
The ***negative integers*** are {..., –5, –4, –3, –2, –1}.

TIP

0 is neither positive nor negative, but it *is* an integer.

There are five integers whose absolute value is less than 3—two negative integers (–2 and –1), two positive integers (1 and 2), and 0.

Consecutive integers are two or more integers written in sequence in which each integer is 1 more than the preceding integer. For example:

$$22, 23 \quad 6, 7, 8, 9 \quad -2, -1, 0, 1 \quad n, n+1, n+2, n+3$$

EXAMPLE 5

If the sum of three consecutive integers is less than 75, what is the greatest possible value of the smallest one?

Ⓐ 23 Ⓑ 24 Ⓒ 25 Ⓓ 26 Ⓔ 27

SOLUTION.
Let the numbers be n, $n + 1$, and $n + 2$. Then,

$$n + (n + 1) + (n + 2) = 3n + 3 \Rightarrow 3n + 3 < 75 \Rightarrow 3n < 72 \Rightarrow n < 24$$

So, the most n can be is **23** (**A**).

CAUTION

Never assume that *number* means *integer*: 3 is not the only number between 2 and 4; there are infinitely many, including 2.5, 3.99, $\frac{10}{3}$, π, and $\sqrt{10}$.

EXAMPLE 6

If $2 < x < 4$ and $3 < y < 7$, what is the largest integer value of $x + y$?

SOLUTION.
If x and y are integers, the largest value is $3 + 6 = 9$. However, although $x + y$ is to be an integer, neither x nor y must be. If $x = 3.8$ and $y = 6.2$, then $x + y =$ **10**.

The sum, difference, and product of two integers are *always* integers; the quotient of two integers may be an integer, but it is not necessarily one. The quotient $23 \div 10$ can be expressed as $\frac{23}{10}$ or $2\frac{3}{10}$ or 2.3. If the quotient is to be an integer, we can say that the quotient is 2 and there is a ***remainder*** of 3. It depends upon our point of view. For example, if 23 dollars is to be divided among 10 people, each one will get \$2.30 (2.3 dollars); but if 23 books are to be divided among 10 people, each one will get 2 books and there will be 3 books left over (the remainder).

KEY FACT A11

If *m* and *n* are positive integers and if *r* is the remainder when *n* is divided by *m*, then *n* is *r* more than a multiple of *m*. That is, $n = mq + r$ where *q* is an integer and $0 \le r < m$.

EXAMPLE 7

How many positive integers less than 100 have a remainder of 3 when divided by 7?

SOLUTION.
To leave a remainder of 3 when divided by 7, an integer must be 3 more than a multiple of 7. For example, when 73 is divided by 7, the quotient is 10 and the remainder is 3: $73 = 10 \times 7 + 3$. So, just take the multiples of 7 and add 3. (*Don't forget that 0 is a multiple of 7.*)

$0 \times 7 + 3 = \underline{3}$; $\quad 1 \times 7 + 3 = \underline{10}$;
$2 \times 7 + 3 = \underline{17}$; $\quad \ldots$;
$13 \times 7 + 3 = \underline{94}$

A total of **14** numbers.

CALCULATOR SHORTCUT

The standard way to find quotients and remainders is to use long division; but on the GRE you *never* do long division: you use the onscreen calculator. To find the remainder when 100 is divided by 7, divide on your calculator: $100 \div 7 = 14.285714\ldots$ This tells you that the quotient is 14. (Ignore everything to the right of the decimal point.) To find the remainder, multiply $14 \times 7 = 98$, and then subtract: $100 - 98 = 2$.

EXAMPLE 8

If today is Saturday, what day will it be in 500 days?

Ⓐ Friday Ⓑ Saturday Ⓒ Sunday Ⓓ Monday Ⓔ Tuesday

SOLUTION.
The days of the week form a repeating sequence. Seven days (1 week), 70 days (10 weeks), 700 days (100 weeks) from Saturday it is again Saturday. If 500 were a multiple of 7, then the answer would be Choice B, Saturday. Is it? With your calculator divide 500 by 7: $500 \div 7 = 71.428\ldots$ So, 500 is not a multiple of 7; since $71 \times 7 = 497$. The quotient when 500 is divided by 7 is 71, and the remainder is 3. Therefore, 500 days is 3 days more than 71 complete weeks. 497 days from Saturday it will again be Saturday; three days later it will be **Tuesday, (E)**.

If a and b are integers, the following four terms are synonymous:

a is a ***divisor*** of b	a is a ***factor*** of b
b is ***divisible*** by a	b is a ***multiple*** of a

They all mean that when b is divided by a there is no remainder (or, more precisely, the remainder is 0). For example:

3 is a divisor of 12	3 is a factor of 12
12 is divisible by 3	12 is a multiple of 3

KEY FACT A12

Every integer has a finite set of factors (or divisors) and an infinite set of multiples.

The factors of 12:	–12, –6, –4, –3, –2, –1, 1, 2, 3, 4, 6, 12
The multiples of 12:	... , –48, –36, –24, –12, 0, 12, 24, 36, 48, ...

The only positive divisor of 1 is 1. All other positive integers have at least 2 positive divisors: 1 and itself, and possibly many more. For example, 6 is divisible by 1 and 6, as well as 2 and 3, whereas 7 is divisible only by 1 and 7. Positive integers, such as 7, that have exactly 2 positive divisors are called ***prime numbers*** or ***primes***. The first ten primes are

2, 3, 5, 7, 11, 13, 17, 19, 23, 29

TIP

1 is *not* a prime.

Memorize this list—it will come in handy.

Positive integers greater than 1 that are not prime are called ***composite numbers***. It follows from the definition that every composite number has at least three distinct positive divisors. The first ten composite numbers are

4, 6, 8, 9, 10, 12, 14, 15, 16, 18

KEY FACT A13

Every integer greater than 1 that is not a prime (i.e., every composite number) can be written as a product of primes.

To find the prime factorization of any integer, find any two factors; if they're both primes, you are done; if not, factor them. Continue until each factor has been written in terms of primes. A useful method is to make a *factor tree*.

For example, here are the prime factorizations of 108 and 240:

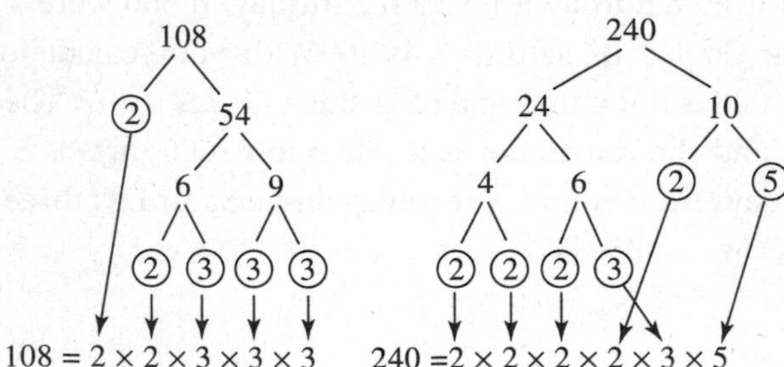

EXAMPLE 9

For any positive integer *a*, let $\lceil a \rfloor$ denote the smallest prime factor of *a*. Which of the following is equal to $\lceil 35 \rfloor$?

Ⓐ $\lceil 10 \rfloor$ Ⓑ $\lceil 15 \rfloor$ Ⓒ $\lceil 45 \rfloor$ Ⓓ $\lceil 55 \rfloor$ Ⓔ $\lceil 75 \rfloor$

SOLUTION.

Check the first few primes; 35 is not divisible by 2 or 3, but is divisible by 5, so 5 is the *smallest* prime factor of 35: $\lceil 35 \rfloor = 5$. Now check the five choices: $\lceil 10 \rfloor = 2$, and $\lceil 15 \rfloor$, $\lceil 45 \rfloor$, and $\lceil 75 \rfloor$ are all equal to 3. Only $\lceil \mathbf{55} \rfloor = 5$. The answer is **D.**

The ***least common multiple*** (**LCM**) of two or more integers is the smallest positive integer that is a multiple of each of them. For example, the LCM of 6 and 10 is 30. Infinitely many positive integers are multiples of both 6 and 10, including 60, 90, 180, 600, 6000, and 66,000,000, but 30 is the smallest one. The ***greatest common factor*** (**GCF**) or ***greatest common divisor*** (**GCD**) of two or more integers is the largest integer that is a factor of each of them. For example, the only positive integers that are factors of both 6 and 10 are 1 and 2, so the GCF of 6 and 10 is 2. For small numbers, you can often find their GCF and LCM by inspection. For larger numbers, KEY FACT A14 is very useful.

KEY FACT A14

The product of the GCF and LCM of two numbers is equal to the product of the two numbers.

TIP

It is usually easier to find the GCF than the LCM. For example, you might see immediately that the GCF of 36 and 48 is 12. You could then use KEY FACT A14 to find the LCM: since GCF × LCM = 36 × 48, then

$$\text{LCM} = \frac{{}^{3}\cancel{36} \times 48}{\cancel{12}_{1}} = 3 \times 48 = 144.$$

An easy way to find the GCF or LCM of two or more integers is to first get their prime factorizations.

- The GCF is the product of all the primes that appear in each factorization, using each prime the smallest number of times it appears in any of the factorizations.
- The LCM is the product of all the primes that appear in any of the factorizations, using each prime the largest number of times it appears in any of the factorizations.

For example, let's find the GCF and LCM of 108 and 240. As we saw:

$$108 = 2 \times 2 \times 3 \times 3 \times 3 \text{ and } 240 = 2 \times 2 \times 2 \times 2 \times 3 \times 5$$

- **GCF.** The primes that appear in both factorizations are 2 and 3: 2 appears twice in the factorization of 108 and 4 times in the factorization of 240, so we take it twice; 3 appears 3 times in the factorization of 108, but only once in the factorization of 240, so we take it just once. The GCF = 2 × 2 × 3 = **12.**
- **LCM.** Take one of the factorizations and add to it any primes from the other that are not yet listed. So, start with 2 × 2 × 3 × 3 × 3 (108) and look at the primes from 240: there are four 2s; we already wrote two 2s, so we need two more; there is a 3 but we already have that; there is a 5, which we need. So, the LCM = (2 × 2 × 3 × 3 × 3) × (2 × 2 × 5) = 108 × 20 = **2,160.**

EXAMPLE 10

What is the smallest number that is divisible by both 34 and 35?

[ ]

SOLUTION.

We are being asked for the LCM of 34 and 35. By KEY FACT A14, LCM = $\frac{34 \times 35}{\text{GCF}}$. But the GCF is 1 since no number greater than 1 divides evenly into both 34 and 35. So, the LCM is $34 \times 35 =$ **1,190.**

The ***even numbers*** are all the multiples of 2:

$$\{\ldots, -4, -2, 0, 2, 4, 6, \ldots\}$$

The ***odd numbers*** are the integers not divisible by 2:

$$\{\ldots, -5, -3, -1, 1, 3, 5, \ldots\}$$

TIP

The terms odd and even apply *only* to integers.

NOTE:

- Every integer (positive, negative, or 0) is either odd or even.
- 0 is an even integer; it is a multiple of 2. ($0 = 0 \times 2$)
- 0 is a multiple of *every* integer. ($0 = 0 \times n$)
- 2 is the only even prime number.

KEY FACT A15

The tables below summarize three important facts:

1. **If two integers are both even or both odd, their sum and difference are even.**
2. **If one integer is even and the other odd, their sum and difference are odd.**
3. **The product of two integers is even unless both of them are odd.**

+ and –	even	odd
even	even	odd
odd	odd	even

×	even	odd
even	even	even
odd	even	odd

Exponents and Roots

Repeated addition of the same number is indicated by multiplication:

$$17 + 17 + 17 + 17 + 17 + 17 + 17 = 7 \times 17$$

Repeated multiplication of the same number is indicated by an exponent:

$$17 \times 17 \times 17 \times 17 \times 17 \times 17 \times 17 = 17^7$$

In the expression 17^7, 17 is called the ***base*** and 7 is the ***exponent.***

At some time, you may have seen expressions such as 2^{-4}, $2^{\frac{1}{2}}$, or even $2^{\sqrt{2}}$. On the GRE, although the base, *b*, can be any number, the exponents you will see will almost always be positive integers.

KEY FACT A16

For any number b: $b^1 = b$, and $b^n = b \times b \times \cdots \times b$, where b is used as a factor n times.

(i) $2^5 \times 2^3 = (2 \times 2 \times 2 \times 2 \times 2) \times (2 \times 2 \times 2) = 2^8 = \mathbf{2^{5+3}}$

(ii) $\frac{2^5}{2^3} = \frac{2\times2\times2\times2\times2}{2\times2\times2} = 2 \times 2 = 2^2 = \mathbf{2^{5-3}}$

(iii) $(2^2)^3 = (2 \times 2)^3 = (2 \times 2) \times (2 \times 2) \times (2 \times 2) = 2^6 = \mathbf{2^{2\times3}}$

(iv) $2^3 \times 7^3 = (2 \times 2 \times 2) \times (7 \times 7 \times 7) = (2 \times 7)(2 \times 7)(2 \times 7) = \mathbf{(2 \times 7)^3}$

These four examples illustrate the following important ***laws of exponents*** given in KEY FACT A17.

KEY FACT A17

For any numbers b and c and positive integers m and n:

(i) $b^m b^n = b^{m+n}$ (ii) $\frac{b^m}{b^n} = b^{m-n}$ (iii) $(b^m)^n = b^{mn}$ (iv) $b^m c^m = (bc)^m$

TIP

Memorize the laws of exponents. They come up often on the GRE.

CAUTION

In (i) and (ii) the bases are the same and in (iv) the exponents are the same. None of these rules applies to expressions such as $7^5 \times 5^7$, in which both the bases and the exponents are different.

EXAMPLE 11

If $2^x = 32$, what is x^2?

Ⓐ 5 Ⓑ 10 Ⓒ 25 Ⓓ 100 Ⓔ 1,024

SOLUTION.

To solve $2^x = 32$, just count (and keep track of) how many 2s you need to multiply to get 32: $2 \times 2 \times 2 \times 2 \times 2 = 32$, so $x = 5$ and $x^2 = \mathbf{25}$ **(C)**.

EXAMPLE 12

If $3^a \times 3^b = 3^{100}$, what is the average (arithmetic mean) of a and b?

[ ]

SOLUTION.

Since $3^a \times 3^b = 3^{a+b}$, we see that $a + b = 100 \Rightarrow \frac{a+b}{2} = \mathbf{50}$.

The next KEY FACT is an immediate consequence of KEY FACTS A4 and A5.

KEY FACT A18

For any positive integer n:

- $0^n = 0$
- **if a is positive, then a^n is positive**
- **if a is negative and n is even, then a^n is positive**
- **if a is negative and n is odd, then a^n is negative**

EXAMPLE 13

Quantity A	Quantity B
$(-13)^{10}$	$(-13)^{25}$

SOLUTION.

Quantity A is positive and Quantity B is negative. So Quantity A is greater.

Squares and Square Roots

The exponent that appears most often on the GRE is 2. It is used to form the square of a number, as in πr^2 (the area of a circle), $a^2 + b^2 = c^2$ (the Pythagorean theorem), or $x^2 - y^2$ (the difference of two squares). Therefore, it is helpful to recognize the ***perfect squares,*** numbers that are the squares of integers. The squares of the integers from 0 to 15 are as follows:

x	0	1	2	3	4	5	6	7
x^2	0	1	4	9	16	25	36	49

x	8	9	10	11	12	13	14	15
x^2	64	81	100	121	144	169	196	225

There are two numbers that satisfy the equation $x^2 = 9$: $x = 3$ and $x = -3$. The positive one, 3, is called the (***principal***) ***square root*** of 9 and is denoted by the symbol $\sqrt{9}$. Clearly, each perfect square has a square root: $\sqrt{0} = 0$, $\sqrt{36} = 6$, $\sqrt{81} = 9$, and $\sqrt{144} = 12$. But, it is an important fact that *every* positive number has a square root.

KEY FACT A19

For any positive number a, there is a positive number b that satisfies the equation $b^2 = a$. That number is called the square root of a and we write $b = \sqrt{a}$.

So, for any positive number a: $(\sqrt{a})^2 = \sqrt{a} \times \sqrt{a} = a$.

The only difference between $\sqrt{9}$ and $\sqrt{10}$ is that the first square root is an integer, while the second one isn't. Since 10 is a little more than 9, we should expect that $\sqrt{10}$ is a little more than $\sqrt{9} = 3$. In fact, $(3.1)^2 = 9.61$, which is close to 10, and $(3.16)^2 = 9.9856$, which is very close to 10. So, $\sqrt{10} \approx 3.16$. On the GRE you will *never* have to evaluate such a square root; if the solution to a problem involves a square root, that square root will be among the answer choices.

EXAMPLE 14

What is the circumference of a circle whose area is 10π?

Ⓐ 5π Ⓑ 10π Ⓒ $\pi\sqrt{10}$ Ⓓ $2\pi\sqrt{10}$ Ⓔ $\pi\sqrt{20}$

SOLUTION.
Since the area of a circle is given by the formula $A = \pi r^2$, we have

$$\pi r^2 = 10\pi \Rightarrow r^2 = 10 \Rightarrow r = \sqrt{10}$$

The circumference is given by the formula $C = 2\pi r$, so $C = 2\pi\sqrt{10}$ **(D)**.

KEY FACT A20

For any positive numbers *a* and *b*:

- $\sqrt{ab} = \sqrt{a} \times \sqrt{b}$
- $\sqrt{\frac{a}{b}} = \frac{\sqrt{a}}{\sqrt{b}}$

CAUTION

$\sqrt{a+b} \neq \sqrt{a} + \sqrt{b}$. For example:

$$\sqrt{9+16} = \sqrt{25} = 5$$

$$\sqrt{9} + \sqrt{16} = 3 + 4 = 7$$

CAUTION

Although it is always true that $(\sqrt{a})^2 = a$, $\sqrt{a^2} = a$ is true *only if a* is positive:

$$\sqrt{(-5)^2} = \sqrt{25} = 5, \textit{ not } -5$$

EXAMPLE 15

Quantity A	Quantity B
$\sqrt{x^{20}}$	$(x^5)^2$

SOLUTION.
Quantity A: Since $x^{10}x^{10} = x^{20}$, $\sqrt{x^{20}} = x^{10}$. Quantity B: $(x^5)^2 = x^{10}$. The quantities are equal **(C)**.

PEMDAS

When a calculation requires performing more than one operation, it is important to carry them out in the correct order. For decades students have memorized the sentence "Please Excuse My Dear Aunt Sally," or just the first letters, PEMDAS, to remember the proper order of operations. The letters stand for:

- Parentheses: first do whatever appears in parentheses, following PEMDAS within the parentheses if necessary.
- Exponents: next evaluate all terms with exponents.
- Multiplication and Division: then do all multiplications and divisions *in order from left to right—do not* multiply first and then divide.
- Addition and Subtraction: finally, do all additions and subtractions *in order from left to right*—do not add first and then subtract.

Here are some worked-out examples.

1. $12 + 3 \times 2 = 12 + 6 = 18$ **[Multiply before you add.]**
   $(12 + 3) \times 2 = 15 \times 2 = 30$ **[First add in the parentheses.]**
2. $12 \div 3 \times 2 = 4 \times 2 = 8$ **[Just go from left to right.]**
   $12 \div (3 \times 2) = 12 \div 6 = 2$ **[First multiply inside the parentheses.]**
3. $5 \times 2^3 = 5 \times 8 = 40$ **[Do exponents first.]**
   $(5 \times 2)^3 = 10^3 = 1000$ **[First multiply inside the parentheses.]**
4. $4 + 4 \div (2 + 6) = 4 + 4 \div 8 = 4 + .5 = 4.5$
   [First add in the parentheses, then divide, and finally add.]
5. $100 - 2^2(3 + 4 \times 5) = 100 - 2^2(23) = 100 - 4(23) = 100 - 92 = 8$
   [First evaluate what's inside the parentheses (using PEMDAS); then take the exponent; then multiply; and finally subtract.]

There is an important situation when you shouldn't start with what's in the parentheses. Consider the following two examples.

(i) What is the value of $7(100 - 1)$?

Using PEMDAS, you would write $7(100 - 1) = 7(99)$, and then multiply: $7 \times 99 = 693$. But you can do this even quicker in your head if you think of it this way: $7(100 - 1) = 700 - 7 = 693$.

(ii) What is the value of $(77 + 49) \div 7$?

If you followed the rules of PEMDAS, you would first add, $77 + 49 = 126$, and then divide, $126 \div 7 = 18$. This is definitely more difficult and time-consuming than mentally doing $\frac{77}{7} + \frac{49}{7} = 11 + 7 = 18$.

Both of these examples illustrate the very important distributive law.

KEY FACT A21

The distributive law

For any real numbers *a*, *b*, and *c*:

- $a(b + c) = ab + ac$
- $a(b - c) = ab - ac$

and if $a \neq 0$

- $\frac{b+c}{a} = \frac{b}{a} + \frac{c}{a}$
- $\frac{b-c}{a} = \frac{b}{a} - \frac{c}{a}$

TIP

Many students who use the distributive law with multiplication forget about it with division. Don't you do that.

EXAMPLE 16

Quantity A	Quantity B
$5(a - 7)$	$5a - 7$

SOLUTION.
By the distributive law, Quantity A = $5a - 35$. The result of subtracting 35 from a number is *always less* than the result of subtracting 7 from that number. Quantity **B** is greater.

EXAMPLE 17

Quantity A	Quantity B
$\frac{50 + x}{5}$	$10 + x$

SOLUTION.

	Quantity A	Quantity B
By the distributive law:	$10 + \frac{x}{5}$	$10 + x$
Subtract 10 from each quantity:	$\frac{x}{5}$	x

The quantities are equal if $x = 0$, but not if $x = 1$.
The answer is **D**.

Inequalities

The number *a* is ***greater than*** the number *b*, denoted $a > b$, if *a* is to the right of *b* on the number line. Similarly, *a* is ***less than*** *b*, denoted $a < b$, if *a* is to the left of *b* on the number line. Therefore, if *a* is positive, $a > 0$, and if *a* is negative, $a < 0$. Clearly, if $a > b$, then $b < a$.

The following KEY FACT gives an important alternate way to describe greater than and less than.

KEY FACT A22

- **For any numbers a and b:**

$$a > b \text{ means that } a - b \text{ is positive.}$$

- **For any numbers a and b:**

$$a < b \text{ means that } a - b \text{ is negative.}$$

KEY FACT A23

- **For any numbers a and b, exactly one of the following is true:**

$$a > b \quad \text{or} \quad a = b \quad \text{or} \quad a < b$$

The symbol ≥ means ***greater than or equal to*** and the symbol ≤ means ***less than or equal to***. The statement "$x \geq 5$" means that x can be 5 or any number greater than 5; the statement "$x \leq 5$" means that x can be 5 or any number less than 5. The statement "$2 < x < 5$" is an abbreviation for the statement "$2 < x$ and $x < 5$." It means that x is a number between 2 and 5 (greater than 2 and less than 5).

Inequalities are very important on the GRE, especially on the quantitative comparison questions where you have to determine which of two quantities is the greater one. KEY FACTS A24 and A25 give some important facts about inequalities.

If the result of performing an arithmetic operation on an inequality is a new inequality in the same direction, we say that the inequality has been ***preserved***. If the result of performing an arithmetic operation on an inequality is a new inequality in the opposite direction, we say that the inequality has been ***reversed***.

KEY FACT A24

- **Adding a number to an inequality or subtracting a number from an inequality preserves it.**

  If $a < b$, then $a + c < b + c$ and $a - c < b - c$.

  $3 < 7 \Rightarrow 3 + 100 < 7 + 100 \quad (103 < 107)$
  $3 < 7 \Rightarrow 3 - 100 < 7 - 100 \quad (-97 < -93)$

- **Adding inequalities in the same direction preserves them.**

  If $a < b$ and $c < d$, then $a + c < b + d$.

  $3 < 7 \text{ and } 5 < 10 \Rightarrow 3 + 5 < 7 + 10 \quad (8 < 17)$

- **Multiplying or dividing an inequality by a positive number preserves it.**

  If $a < b$, and c is positive, then $ac < bc$ and $\frac{a}{c} < \frac{b}{c}$.

  $3 < 7 \Rightarrow 3 \times 100 < 7 \times 100 \quad (300 < 700)$
  $3 < 7 \Rightarrow 3 \div 100 < 7 \div 100 \quad \left(\frac{3}{100} < \frac{7}{100}\right)$

- **Multiplying or dividing an inequality by a negative number reverses it.**

If $a < b$, and c is negative, then $ac > bc$ and $\frac{a}{c} > \frac{b}{c}$.

$$3 < 7 \Rightarrow 3 \times (-100) > 7 \times (-100) \quad (-300 > -700)$$

$$3 < 7 \Rightarrow 3 \div (-100) > 7 \div (-100) \quad \left(-\frac{3}{100} > -\frac{7}{100}\right)$$

- **Taking negatives reverses an inequality.**

If $a < b$, then $-a > -b$ and if $a > b$, then $-a < -b$.

$$3 < 7 \Rightarrow -3 > -7 \text{ and } 7 > 3 \Rightarrow -7 < -3$$

- **If two numbers are each positive or negative, then taking reciprocals reverses an inequality.**

If a and b are both positive or both negative and $a < b$, then $\frac{1}{a} > \frac{1}{b}$.

$$3 < 7 \Rightarrow \frac{1}{3} > \frac{1}{7} \qquad -7 < -3 \Rightarrow -\frac{1}{7} > -\frac{1}{3}$$

KEY FACT A25

Important inequalities for numbers between 0 and 1.

- **If $0 < x < 1$, and a is positive, then $xa < a$. For example: $.85 \times 19 < 19$.**
- **If $0 < x < 1$, and m and n are positive integers with $m > n$, then**

  $x^m < x^n < x$. For example, $\left(\frac{1}{2}\right)^5 < \left(\frac{1}{2}\right)^2 < \frac{1}{2}$.

- **If $0 < x < 1$, then $\sqrt{x} > x$. For example, $\sqrt{\frac{3}{4}} > \frac{3}{4}$.**

- **If $0 < x < 1$, then $\frac{1}{x} > x$. In fact, $\frac{1}{x} > 1$. For example, $\frac{1}{0.2} > 1 > 0.2$.**

TIP

Be sure you understand KEY FACT A24; it is very useful. Also, review the important properties listed in KEY FACTS A25 and A26. These properties come up often on the GRE.

KEY FACT A26

Properties of Zero

- **0 is the only number that is neither positive nor negative.**
- **0 is smaller than every positive number and greater than every negative number.**
- **0 is an even integer.**
- **0 is a multiple of every integer.**
- **For every number a: $a + 0 = a$ and $a - 0 = a$.**
- **For every number a: $a \times 0 = 0$.**

- **For every positive integer n: $0^n = 0$.**
- **For every number a (including 0): $a \div 0$ and $\frac{a}{0}$ are *meaningless symbols.* (They are *undefined.*)**
- **For every number a other than 0: $0 \div a = \frac{0}{a} = 0$.**
- **0 is the only number that is equal to its opposite: $0 = -0$.**
- **If the product of two or more numbers is 0, at least one of them is 0.**

KEY FACT A27

Properties of 1

- **For any number a: $1 \times a = a$ and $\frac{a}{1} = a$.**
- **For any integer n: $1^n = 1$.**
- **1 is a divisor of every integer.**
- **1 is the smallest positive integer.**
- **1 is an odd integer.**
- **1 is *not* a prime.**

PRACTICE EXERCISES—BASIC ARITHMETIC

Discrete Quantitative Questions

1. For how many positive integers, a, is it true that $a^2 \leq 2a$?

   Ⓐ None
   Ⓑ 1
   Ⓒ 2
   Ⓓ 4
   Ⓔ More than 4

2. If $0 < a < b < 1$, which of the following statements are true?

   Indicate *all* such statements.

   [A] $a - b$ is negative
   [B] $\frac{1}{ab}$ is positive
   [C] $\frac{1}{b} - \frac{1}{a}$ is positive

3. If the product of 4 consecutive integers is equal to one of them, what is the largest possible value of one of the integers?

   [ ]

4. At 3:00 A.M. the temperature was 13° below zero. By noon it had risen to 32°. What was the average hourly increase in temperature?

   Ⓐ $\left(\frac{19}{9}\right)^\circ$
   Ⓑ $\left(\frac{19}{6}\right)^\circ$
   Ⓒ 5°
   Ⓓ 7.5°
   Ⓔ 45°

5. If a and b are negative, and c is positive, which of the following statements are true?

   Indicate *all* such statements.

   [A] $a - b < a - c$
   [B] If $a < b$, then $\frac{a}{c} < \frac{b}{c}$
   [C] $\frac{1}{b} < \frac{1}{c}$

6. If $-7 \leq x \leq 7$ and $0 \leq y \leq 12$, what is the greatest possible value of $y - x$?

   Ⓐ −19
   Ⓑ 5
   Ⓒ 7
   Ⓓ 17
   Ⓔ 19

7. If $(7^a)(7^b) = \frac{7^c}{7^d}$, what is d in terms of a, b, and c?

   Ⓐ $\frac{c}{ab}$
   Ⓑ $c - a - b$
   Ⓒ $a + b - c$
   Ⓓ $c - ab$
   Ⓔ $\frac{c}{a+b}$

8. If each of ★ and ❖ can be replaced by +, −, or ×, how many different values are there for the expression 2 ★ 2 ❖ 2?

   [ ]

9. A number is "terrific" if it is a multiple of 2 or 3. How many terrific numbers are there between –11 and 11?

Ⓐ 6
Ⓑ 7
Ⓒ 11
Ⓓ 15
Ⓔ 17

10. If x ✪ y represents the number of integers greater than x and less than y, what is the value of $-\pi$ ✪ $\sqrt{2}$?

Ⓐ 2
Ⓑ 3
Ⓒ 4
Ⓓ 5
Ⓔ 6

QUESTIONS 11 AND 12 REFER TO THE FOLLOWING DEFINITION.

For any positive integer n, $\tau(n)$ represents the number of positive divisors of n.

11. Which of the following statements are true?

Indicate *all* such statements.

[A] $\tau(5) = \tau(7)$
[B] $\tau(5) \cdot \tau(7) = \tau(35)$
[C] $\tau(5) + \tau(7) = \tau(12)$

12. What is the value of $\tau(\tau(\tau(12)))$?

Ⓐ 1
Ⓑ 2
Ⓒ 3
Ⓓ 4
Ⓔ 6

---

13. If p and q are primes greater than 2, which of the following statements must be true?

Indicate *all* such statements.

[A] $p + q$ is even
[B] pq is odd
[C] $p^2 - q^2$ is even

14. If $0 < x < 1$, which of the following lists the numbers in increasing order?

Ⓐ $\sqrt{x}, x, x^2$
Ⓑ $x^2, x, \sqrt{x}$
Ⓒ $x^2, \sqrt{x}, x$
Ⓓ $x, x^2, \sqrt{x}$
Ⓔ $x, \sqrt{x}, x^2$

15. Which of the following is equal to $(7^8 \times 7^9)^{10}$?

Ⓐ 7^{27}
Ⓑ 7^{82}
Ⓒ 7^{170}
Ⓓ 49^{170}
Ⓔ 49^{720}

Quantitative Comparison Questions

Ⓐ Quantity A is greater.
Ⓑ Quantity B is greater.
Ⓒ The two quantities are equal.
Ⓓ It is impossible to determine which quantity is greater.

16.

Quantity A	Quantity B
The product of the odd integers between –8 and 8	The product of the even integers between –9 and 9

17.

a and b are nonzero integers

Quantity A	Quantity B
$a + b$	ab

18.

Quantity A	Quantity B
The remainder when a positive integer is divided by 7	7

19.

Quantity A	Quantity B
$24 \div 6 \times 4$	12

20.

Quantity A	Quantity B
$\frac{2x-17}{2}$	$x - 17$

21.

n is an integer greater than 1 that leaves a remainder of 1 when it is divided by 2, 3, 4, 5, and 6

Quantity A	Quantity B
n	60

22.

Quantity A	Quantity B
The number of primes that are divisible by 2	The number of primes that are divisible by 3

23.

n is a positive integer

Quantity A	Quantity B
The number of different prime factors of n	The number of different prime factors of n^2

24.

Quantity A	Quantity B
The number of even positive factors of 30	The number of odd positive factors of 30

25.

n is a positive integer

Quantity A	Quantity B
$(-10)^n$	$(-10)^{n+1}$

ANSWER KEY

1. **C**	6. **E**	11. **A, B**	16. **A**	21. **A**
2. **A, B**	7. **B**	12. **C**	17. **D**	22. **C**
3. **3**	8. **4**	13. **A, B, C**	18. **B**	23. **C**
4. **C**	9. **D**	14. **B**	19. **A**	24. **C**
5. **B, C**	10. **D**	15. **C**	20. **A**	25. **D**

ANSWER EXPLANATIONS

1. **(C)** Since a is positive, we can divide both sides of the given inequality by a: $a^2 \leq 2a \Rightarrow a \leq 2 \Rightarrow a = 1$ or 2.

2. **(A, B)** Since $a < b$, $a - b$ is negative (A is true). Since a and b are positive, so is their product, ab; and the reciprocal of a positive number is positive (B is true). $\frac{1}{b} - \frac{1}{a} = \frac{a-b}{ab}$, and we have just seen that the numerator is negative and the denominator positive; so the value of the fraction is negative (C is false).

3. **3** If all four integers were negative, their product would be positive, and so could not equal one of them. If all of the integers were positive, their product would be much greater than any of them (even $1 \times 2 \times 3 \times 4 = 24$). So, the integers must include 0, in which case their product *is* 0. The largest set of four consecutive integers that includes 0 is 0, 1, 2, 3.

4. **(C)** In the 9 hours from 3:00 to 12:00, the temperature rose $32 - (-13) = 32 + 13 = 45$ degrees. So, the average hourly increase was $45° \div 9 = 5°$.

5. **(B, C)** Since b is negative and c is positive, $b < c \Rightarrow -b > -c \Rightarrow a - b > a - c$ (A is false). Since c is positive, dividing by c preserves the inequality. (B is true.) Since b is negative, $\frac{1}{b}$ is negative, and so is less than $\frac{1}{c}$, which is positive (C is true).

6. **(E)** To make $y - x$ as large as possible, let y be as big as possible (12), and subtract the smallest amount possible ($x = -7$): $12 - (-7) = 19$.

7. **(B)** $(7^a)(7^b) = 7^{a+b}$, and $\frac{7^c}{7^d} = 7^{c-d}$. Therefore,

$$a + b = c - d \Rightarrow a + b + d = c \Rightarrow d = c - a - b$$

8. **4** Just list the 9 possible outcomes of replacing ★ and ❖ by +, –, and ×, and see that there are 4 different values: –2, 2, 6, 8.

$2 + 2 + 2 = 6$	$2 - 2 - 2 = -2$	$2 \times 2 \times 2 = 8$
$2 + 2 - 2 = 2$	$2 - 2 \times 2 = -2$	$2 \times 2 + 2 = 6$
$2 + 2 \times 2 = 6$	$2 - 2 + 2 = 2$	$2 \times 2 - 2 = 2$

9. **(D)** There are 15 "terrific" numbers: 2, 3, 4, 6, 8, 9, 10, their opposites, and 0.

10. **(D)** There are 5 integers (1, 0, –1, –2, –3) that are greater than –3.14 ($-\pi$) and less than 1.41 $(\sqrt{2})$.

11. **(A, B)** Since 5 and 7 have two positive factors each, $\tau(5) = \tau(7)$. (A is true.) Since 35 has 4 divisors (1, 5, 7, and 35) and $\tau(5) \cdot \tau(7) = 2 \times 2 = 4$. (B is true.) Since the positive divisors of 12 are 1, 2, 3, 4, 6, and 12, $\tau(12)$ is 6, which is *not* equal to 2 + 2. (C is false.)

12. **(C)** $\tau(\tau(\tau(12))) = \tau(\tau(6)) = \tau(4) = 3$

13. **(A, B, C)** All primes greater than 2 are odd, so p and q are odd, and $p + q$, the sum of two odd numbers, is even (A is true). The product of two odd numbers is odd (B is true). Since p and q are odd, so are their squares, and so the difference of their squares is even (C is true).

14. **(B)** For any number, x, between 0 and 1: $x^2 < x$ and $x < \sqrt{x}$.

15. **(C)** First, multiply inside the parentheses: $7^8 \times 7^9 = 7^{17}$; then, raise to the 10th power: $(7^{17})^{10} = 7^{170}$.

16. **(A)** Quantity B is the product of nine factors (–8, –6, –4, –2, 0 2, 4, 6, 8). Since one of the factors is 0, Quantity B is equal to 0. Quantity A is the product of eight factors (–7, –5, –3, –1, 1, 3, 5, 7). The product of the four negative factors is positive, as is the product of the four positive factors. So Quantity A is positive, and, therefore, greater than Quantity B.

17. **(D)** If a and b are each 1, then $a + b = 2$, and $ab = 1$; so, Quantity A is greater. But, if a and b are each 3, $a + b = 6$, and $ab = 9$, then Quantity B is greater.

18. **(B)** The remainder is *always* less than the divisor.

19. **(A)** According to PEMDAS, you divide and multiply from left to right (do *not* do the multiplication first): $24 \div 6 \times 4 = 4 \times 4 = 16$.

20. **(A)** By the distributive law, $\frac{2x-17}{2} = \frac{2x}{2} - \frac{17}{2} = x - 8.5$, which is greater than $x - 17$ (the larger the number you subtract, the smaller the difference).

21. **(A)** The LCM of 2, 3, 4, 5, 6 is 60; and all multiples of 60 are divisible by each of them. So, n could be 61 or 1 more than any multiple of 60.

22. **(C)** The only prime divisible by 2 is 2, and the only prime divisible by 3 is 3. Quantity A and Quantity B are each 1.

23. **(C)** If you make a factor tree for n^2, the first branches could be n and n. Now, when you factor each n, you get exactly the same prime factors. (See the example below.)

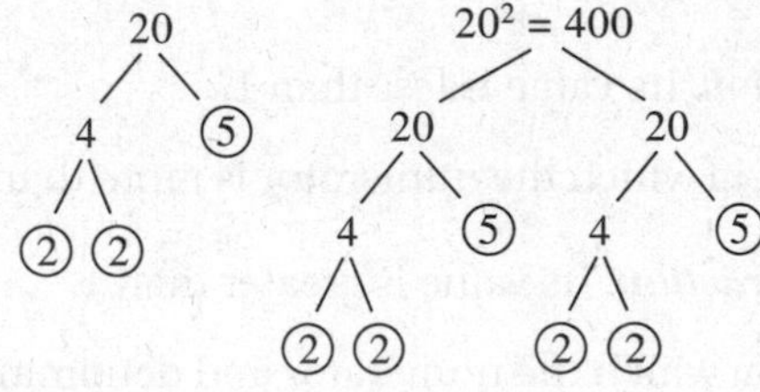

24. **(C)** Just list the factors of 30: 1, 2, 3, 5, 6, 10, 15, 30. Four of them are odd and four are even.

25. **(D)** If n is even, then $n + 1$ is odd, and consequently $(-10)^n$ is positive, whereas $(-10)^{n+1}$ is negative. If n is odd, exactly the opposite is true.

12-B. FRACTIONS AND DECIMALS

Several questions on the GRE involve fractions or decimals. The KEY FACTS in this section cover all of the important facts you need to know for the GRE.

Fractions and Decimals

When a whole is *divided* into n equal parts, each part is called *one-nth* of the whole, written $\frac{1}{n}$. For example, if a pizza is cut (*divided*) into 8 equal slices, each slice is one-eighth $\left(\frac{1}{8}\right)$ of the pizza; a day is *divided* into 24 equal hours, so an hour is one-twenty-fourth $\left(\frac{1}{24}\right)$ of a day; and an inch is one-twelfth $\left(\frac{1}{12}\right)$ of a foot.

- If Donna slept for 5 hours, she slept for five-twenty-fourths $\left(\frac{5}{24}\right)$ of a day.
- If Taryn bought 8 slices of pizza, she bought eight-eighths $\left(\frac{8}{8}\right)$ of a pie.
- If Aviva's shelf is 30 inches long, it measures thirty-twelfths $\left(\frac{30}{12}\right)$ of a foot.

Numbers such as $\frac{5}{24}$, $\frac{8}{8}$, and $\frac{30}{12}$, in which one integer is written over a second integer, are called ***fractions***. The center line is called the fraction bar. The number above the bar is called the ***numerator***, and the number below the bar is called the ***denominator***.

CAUTION

The denominator of a fraction can *never* be 0.

- A fraction, such as $\frac{5}{24}$, in which the numerator is less than the denominator, is called a ***proper fraction***. Its value is less than 1.
- A fraction, such as $\frac{30}{12}$, in which the numerator is more than the denominator, is called an ***improper fraction***. Its value is greater than 1.
- A fraction, such as $\frac{8}{8}$, in which the numerator and denominator are the same, is also ***improper***, but it is equal to 1.

It is useful to think of the fraction bar as a symbol for division. If three pizzas are divided equally among eight people, each person gets $\frac{3}{8}$ of the pizza. If you actually divide 3 by 8, you get that $\frac{3}{8} = 0.375$.

KEY FACT B1

Every fraction, proper or improper, can be expressed in decimal form (or as a whole number) by dividing the numerator by the denominator.

$$\frac{3}{10} = 0.3 \qquad \frac{3}{4} = 0.75 \qquad \frac{5}{8} = 0.625 \qquad \frac{3}{16} = 0.1875$$

$$\frac{8}{8} = 1 \qquad \frac{11}{8} = 1.375 \qquad \frac{48}{16} = 3 \qquad \frac{100}{8} = 12.5$$

Note that any number beginning with a decimal point can be written with a 0 to the left of the decimal point. In fact, some calculators will express 3 ÷ 8 as .375, whereas others will print 0.375.

Unlike the examples above, when most fractions are converted to decimals, the division does not terminate after 2 or 3 or 4 decimal places; rather it goes on forever with some set of digits repeating itself.

$$\frac{2}{3} = 0.666666... \quad \frac{3}{11} = 0.272727... \quad \frac{5}{12} = 0.416666... \quad -\frac{17}{15} = -1.133333...$$

A convenient way to represent repeating decimals is to place a bar over the digits that repeat. For example, the decimal equivalent of the four fractions, above, could be written as follows:

$$\frac{2}{3} = 0.\overline{6} \quad \frac{3}{11} = 0.\overline{27} \quad \frac{5}{12} = 0.41\overline{6} \quad -\frac{17}{15} = -1.1\overline{3}$$

A ***rational number*** is any number that can be expressed as a fraction, $\frac{a}{b}$, where a and b are integers. For example, 2, –2.2, and $2\frac{1}{2}$ are all rational since they can be expressed as $\frac{2}{1}$, $\frac{-22}{10}$, and $\frac{5}{2}$, respectively. When written as decimals, all rational numbers either terminate or repeat. Numbers such as $\sqrt{2}$ and π that cannot be expressed as fractions whose numerators and denominators are integers are called ***irrational numbers***. The decimal expansions of irrational numbers neither terminate nor repeat. For example, $\sqrt{2} = 1.414213562...$ and $\pi = 3.141592654...$

Comparing Fractions and Decimals

KEY FACT B2

To compare two positive decimals, follow these rules.

- **Whichever number has the greater number to the left of the decimal point is greater: since 11 > 9, 11.001 > 9.896; since 1 > 0, 1.234 > 0.8; and since 3 > –3, 3.01 > –3.95. (Recall that if a decimal is written without a number to the left of the decimal point, you may assume that a 0 is there. So, 1.234 > 0.8.)**
- **If the numbers to the left of the decimal point are equal (or if there are no numbers to the left of the decimal point), proceed as follows:**
  1. **If the numbers do not have the same number of digits to the right of the decimal point, add zeros to the end of the shorter one.**
  2. **Now, compare the numbers *ignoring* the decimal point.**

For example, to compare 1.83 and 1.823, add a 0 to the end of 1.83, forming 1.830. Now compare them, *thinking of them as whole numbers*: since, 1,830 > 1,823, then 1.830 > 1.823.

EXAMPLE 1

Quantity A	Quantity B
.2139	.239

SOLUTION.

Do not think that Quantity A is greater because 2,139 > 239. Be sure to add a 0 to the end of 0.239 (forming 0.2390) before comparing. Now, since 2,390 > 2,139, Quantity **B** is greater.

KEY FACT B3

There are two methods of comparing positive fractions:

1. **Convert them to decimals (by dividing), and use KEY FACT B2.**
2. **Cross-multiply.**

For example, to compare $\frac{1}{3}$ and $\frac{3}{8}$, we have two choices.

1. Write $\frac{1}{3}$ = .3333... and $\frac{3}{8}$ = .375. Since .375 > .333, then $\frac{3}{8} > \frac{1}{3}$.

2. Cross-multiply: $\frac{1}{3} \times \frac{3}{8}$. Since $3 \times 3 > 8 \times 1$, then $\frac{3}{8} > \frac{1}{3}$.

KEY FACT B4

When comparing positive fractions, there are three situations in which it is easier just to look at the fractions, and not use either method in KEY FACT B3.

1. **If the fractions have the same denominator, the fraction with the larger numerator is greater. Just as \$9 is more than \$7, and 9 books are more than 7 books, 9 fortieths are more than 7 fortieths: $\frac{9}{40} > \frac{7}{40}$.**
2. **If the fractions have the same numerator, the fraction with the smaller denominator is greater.**
   If you divide a cake into 5 equal pieces, each piece is larger than the pieces you would get if you had divided the cake into 10 equal pieces: $\frac{1}{5} > \frac{1}{10}$, and similarly $\frac{3}{5} > \frac{3}{10}$.
3. **Sometimes the fractions are so familiar or easy to work with, you just know the answer. For example, $\frac{3}{4} > \frac{1}{5}$ and $\frac{11}{20} > \frac{1}{2}$ $\left(\text{since } \frac{10}{20} = \frac{1}{2}\right)$.**

KEY FACTS B2, B3, and B4 apply to *positive* decimals and fractions.

KEY FACT B5

- **Clearly, any positive number is greater than any negative number:**

$$\frac{1}{2} > -\frac{1}{5} \quad \text{and} \quad 0.123 > -2.56$$

- **For negative decimals and fractions, use KEY FACT A24 (page 342), which states that if $a > b$, then $-a < -b$:**

$$\frac{1}{2} > \frac{1}{5} \Rightarrow -\frac{1}{2} < -\frac{1}{5} \quad \text{and} \quad 0.83 > 0.829 \Rightarrow -0.83 < -0.829$$

EXAMPLE 2

Which of the following lists the fractions $\frac{2}{3}$, $\frac{5}{8}$, and $\frac{13}{20}$ in order from least to greatest?

Ⓐ $\frac{2}{3}, \frac{5}{8}, \frac{13}{20}$ Ⓑ $\frac{5}{8}, \frac{2}{3}, \frac{13}{20}$ Ⓒ $\frac{5}{8}, \frac{13}{20}, \frac{2}{3}$ Ⓓ $\frac{13}{20}, \frac{5}{8}, \frac{2}{3}$ Ⓔ $\frac{13}{20}, \frac{2}{3}, \frac{5}{8}$

SOLUTION.
Use your calculator to quickly convert each to a decimal, writing down the first few decimal places: $\frac{2}{3} = 0.666$, $\frac{5}{8} = 0.625$, and $\frac{13}{20} = 0.65$. It is now easy to order the decimals: $0.625 < 0.650 < 0.666$. The answer is **C**.

ALTERNATIVE SOLUTION.
Cross-multiply.

- $\frac{2}{3} > \frac{5}{8}$ since $8 \times 2 > 3 \times 5$.
- $\frac{13}{20} > \frac{5}{8}$ since $8 \times 13 > 20 \times 5$.
- $\frac{2}{3} > \frac{13}{20}$ since $20 \times 2 > 3 \times 13$.

EXAMPLE 3

$0 < x < y$

Quantity A	Quantity B
$\frac{1}{x} - \frac{1}{y}$	0

SOLUTION.
By KEY FACT B4, $x < y \Rightarrow \frac{1}{x} > \frac{1}{y}$, and so by KEY FACT A22 (page 342), $\frac{1}{x} - \frac{1}{y}$ is positive. Quantity **A** is greater.

Equivalent Fractions

If Bill and Al shared a pizza, and Bill ate $\frac{1}{2}$ the pizza and Al ate $\frac{4}{8}$ of it, they had exactly the same amount.

We express this idea by saying that $\frac{1}{2}$ and $\frac{4}{8}$ are ***equivalent fractions***: they have the exact same value.

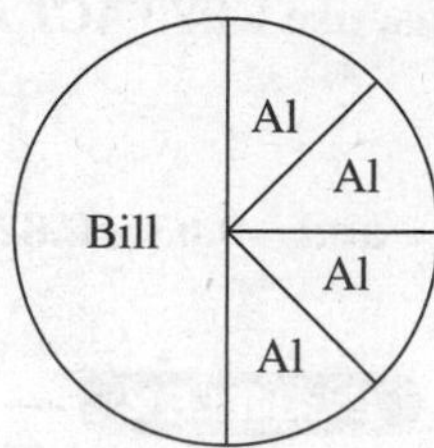

NOTE: If you multiply both the numerator and denominator of $\frac{1}{2}$ by 4 you get $\frac{4}{8}$; and if you divide both the numerator and denominator of $\frac{4}{8}$ by 4 you get $\frac{1}{2}$. This illustrates the next KEY FACT.

KEY FACT B6

Two fractions are equivalent if multiplying or dividing both the numerator and denominator of the first one *by the same number* gives the second one.

Consider the following two cases.

1. When the numerator and denominator of $\frac{3}{8}$ are each multiplied by 15, the products are $3 \times 15 = 45$ and $8 \times 15 = 120$. Therefore, $\frac{3}{8}$ and $\frac{45}{120}$ are equivalent fractions.
2. $\frac{2}{3}$ and $\frac{28}{45}$ are not equivalent fractions because 2 must be multiplied by 14 to get 28, but 3 must be multiplied by 15 to get 45.

KEY FACT B7

To determine if two fractions are equivalent, cross-multiply. The fractions are equivalent if and only if the two products are equal.

For example, since $120 \times 3 = 8 \times 45$, then $\frac{3}{8}$ and $\frac{45}{120}$ are equivalent.

Since $45 \times 2 \neq 3 \times 28$, then $\frac{2}{3}$ and $\frac{28}{45}$ are not equivalent fractions.

A fraction is in ***lowest terms*** if no positive integer greater than 1 is a factor of both the numerator and denominator. For example, $\frac{9}{20}$ is in lowest terms, since no integer greater than 1 is a factor of both 9 and 20; but $\frac{9}{24}$ is not in lowest terms, since 3 is a factor of both 9 and 24.

KEY FACT B8

Every fraction can be *reduced* to lowest terms by dividing the numerator and the denominator by their greatest common factor (GCF). If the GCF is 1, the fraction is already in lowest terms.

For any positive integer *n*: *n*!, read *n factorial,* is the product of all the integers from 1 to *n*, inclusive.

EXAMPLE 4

What is the value of $\frac{6!}{8!}$?

Ⓐ $\frac{1}{56}$ Ⓑ $\frac{1}{48}$ Ⓒ $\frac{1}{8}$ Ⓓ $\frac{1}{4}$ Ⓔ $\frac{3}{4}$

SOLUTION.
Even with a calculator, you do not want to calculate 6! $(1\cdot2\cdot3\cdot4\cdot5\cdot6 = 720)$ and 8! $(1\cdot2\cdot3\cdot4\cdot5\cdot6\cdot7\cdot8 = 40{,}320)$ and then take the time to reduce $\frac{720}{40{,}320}$. Here's the easy solution:

$$\frac{6!}{8!} = \frac{\overset{1}{\cancel{6\times5\times4\times3\times2\times1}}}{8\times7\times\underset{1}{\cancel{6\times5\times4\times3\times2\times1}}} = \frac{1}{8\times7} = \frac{1}{56}$$

Arithmetic Operations with Decimals

Arithmetic operations with decimals should be done on your calculator, unless they are so easy that you can do them in your head.

Multiplying and dividing by powers of 10 is particularly easy and does not require a calculator: they can be accomplished just by moving the decimal point.

KEY FACT B9

To multiply any decimal or whole number by a power of 10, move the decimal point as many places to the *right* as there are 0s in the power of 10, filling in with 0s, if necessary.

$$1.35 \times 10 = 13.5 \ (1) \qquad 1.35 \times 100 = 135 \ (2)$$

$$1.35 \times 1{,}000 = 1{,}350 \ (3)$$

$$23 \times 10 = 230 \ (1) \qquad 23 \times 100 = 2{,}300 \ (2)$$

$$23 \times 1{,}000{,}000 = 23{,}000{,}000 \ (6)$$

KEY FACT B10

To divide any decimal or whole number by a power of 10, move the decimal point as many places to the *left* as there are 0s in the power of 10, filling in with 0s, if necessary.

$$67.8 \div 10 = 6.78 \quad (1) \qquad 67.8 \div 100 = 0.678 \quad (2)$$

$$67.8 \div 1{,}000 = 0.0678 \quad (3)$$

$$14 \div 10 = 1.4 \quad (1) \qquad 14 \div 100 = 0.14 \quad (2)$$

$$14 \div 1{,}000{,}000 = 0.000014 \quad (6)$$

EXAMPLE 5

Quantity A	Quantity B
3.75×10^4	$37{,}500{,}000 \div 10^3$

SOLUTION.
To evaluate Quantity A, move the decimal point 4 places to the right: **37,500**. To evaluate Quantity B, move the decimal point 3 places to the left: **37,500**. The answer is **C**.

Arithmetic Operations with Fractions

KEY FACT B11

To multiply two fractions, multiply their numerators and multiply their denominators:

$$\frac{3}{5} \times \frac{4}{7} = \frac{3\times4}{5\times7} = \frac{12}{35} \qquad \frac{3}{5} \times \frac{\pi}{2} = \frac{3\times\pi}{5\times2} = \frac{3\pi}{10}$$

KEY FACT B12

To multiply a fraction by any other number, write that number as a fraction whose denominator is 1:

$$\frac{3}{5} \times 7 = \frac{3}{5} \times \frac{7}{1} = \frac{21}{5} \qquad \frac{3}{5} \times \pi = \frac{3}{5} \times \frac{\pi}{1} = \frac{3\pi}{5}$$

TACTIC B1

Before multiplying fractions, reduce. You may reduce by dividing any numerator and any denominator by a common factor.

EXAMPLE 6

Express the product, $\frac{3}{4} \times \frac{8}{9} \times \frac{15}{16}$, in lowest terms.

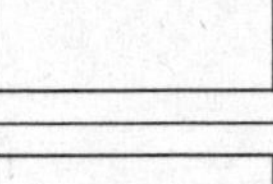

SOLUTION.

You could use your calculator to multiply the numerators and denominators: $\frac{360}{576}$. It is better, however, to use TACTIC B1 and reduce first:

$$\frac{\overset{1}{\cancel{3}}}{4} \times \frac{\overset{1}{\cancel{8}}}{\underset{\underset{1}{\cancel{3}}}{\cancel{9}}} \times \frac{\overset{5}{\cancel{15}}}{\underset{2}{\cancel{16}}} = \frac{1 \times 1 \times 5}{4 \times 1 \times 2} = \mathbf{\frac{5}{8}}$$

TACTIC B2

When a problem requires you to find a fraction of a number, multiply.

EXAMPLE 7

If $\frac{4}{7}$ of the 350 sophomores at Monroe High School are girls, and $\frac{7}{8}$ of them play on a team, how many sophomore girls do <u>not</u> play on a team?

SOLUTION.

There are $\frac{4}{7} \times 350 = 200$ sophomore girls.

Of these, $\frac{7}{8} \times 200 = 175$ play on a team. So, $200 - 175 =$ **25** do not play on a team.

The ***reciprocal*** of any nonzero number x is that number y such that $xy = 1$. Since $x\left(\frac{1}{x}\right) = 1$, then $\frac{1}{x}$ is the reciprocal of x. Similarly, the reciprocal of the fraction $\frac{a}{b}$ is the fraction $\frac{b}{a}$, since $\frac{a}{b} \cdot \frac{b}{a} = 1$.

KEY FACT B13

To divide any number by a fraction, multiply that number by the reciprocal of the fraction.

$$20 \div \frac{2}{3} = \frac{20}{1} \times \frac{3}{2} = 30 \qquad \frac{3}{5} \div \frac{2}{3} = \frac{3}{5} \times \frac{3}{2} = \frac{9}{10}$$

$$\sqrt{2} \div \frac{2}{3} = \frac{\sqrt{2}}{1} \times \frac{3}{2} = \frac{3\sqrt{2}}{2} \qquad \frac{\pi}{5} \div \frac{2}{3} = \frac{\pi}{5} \times \frac{3}{2} = \frac{3\pi}{10}$$

EXAMPLE 8

In the meat department of a supermarket, 100 pounds of chopped meat was divided into packages, each of which weighed $\frac{4}{7}$ of a pound.

How many packages were there?

SOLUTION.

$$100 \div \frac{4}{7} = \frac{100}{1} \times \frac{7}{4} = \mathbf{175}$$

KEY FACT B14

- **To add or subtract fractions with the same denominator, add or subtract the numerators and keep the denominator:**

$$\frac{4}{9} + \frac{1}{9} = \frac{5}{9} \quad \text{and} \quad \frac{4}{9} - \frac{1}{9} = \frac{3}{9} = \frac{1}{3}$$

- **To add or subtract fractions with different denominators, first rewrite the fractions as equivalent fractions with the same denominators:**

$$\frac{1}{6} + \frac{3}{4} = \frac{2}{12} + \frac{9}{12} = \frac{11}{12}$$

NOTE: The *easiest* common denominator to find is the product of the denominators ($6 \times 4 = 24$, in this example), but the best denominator to use is the ***least common denominator,*** which is the least common multiple (LCM) of the denominators (12, in this case). Using the least common denominator minimizes the amount of reducing that is necessary to express the answer in lowest terms.

KEY FACT B15

If $\frac{a}{b}$ is the fraction of a whole that satisfies some property, then $1 - \frac{a}{b}$ is the fraction of that whole that does not satisfy it.

EXAMPLE 9

In a jar, $\frac{1}{2}$ of the marbles are red, $\frac{1}{4}$ are white, and $\frac{1}{5}$ are blue.

What fraction of the marbles are neither red, white, nor blue?

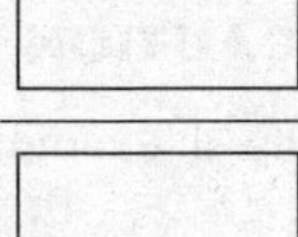

SOLUTION.
The red, white, and blue marbles constitute

$$\frac{1}{2} + \frac{1}{4} + \frac{1}{5} = \frac{10}{20} + \frac{5}{20} + \frac{4}{20} = \frac{19}{20}$$

of the total, so $1 - \frac{19}{20} = \frac{20}{20} - \frac{19}{20} = \mathbf{\frac{1}{20}}$ of the marbles are neither red, white, nor blue.

Alternatively, you could convert the fractions to decimals and use your calculator.

$$0.5 + 0.25 + 0.2 = 0.95$$

$$1 - 0.95 = 0.05 = \frac{5}{100}$$

Remember, on the GRE you do not have to reduce fractions, so $\frac{5}{100}$ is an acceptable answer.

EXAMPLE 10

Lindsay ate $\frac{1}{3}$ of a cake and Emily ate $\frac{1}{4}$ of it. What fraction of the cake was still uneaten?

SOLUTION.

$\frac{1}{3} + \frac{1}{4} = \frac{4}{12} + \frac{3}{12} = \frac{7}{12}$ of the cake was eaten, and $1 - \frac{7}{12} = \mathbf{\frac{5}{12}}$ was uneaten.

EXAMPLE 11

Lindsay ate $\frac{1}{3}$ of a cake and Emily ate $\frac{1}{4}$ of what was left. What fraction of the cake was still uneaten?

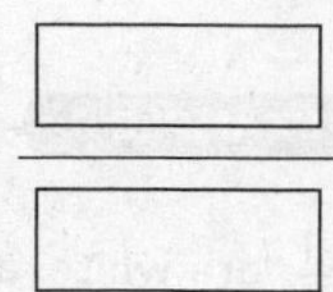

CAUTION

Be sure to read questions carefully. In Example 10, Emily ate $\frac{1}{4}$ of the cake. In Example 11, however, she only ate $\frac{1}{4}$ of the $\frac{2}{3}$ that was left after Lindsay had her piece: she ate $\frac{1}{4} \times \frac{2}{3} = \frac{1}{6}$ of the cake.

SOLUTION.

$\frac{1}{3} + \frac{1}{6} = \frac{2}{6} + \frac{1}{6} = \frac{1}{2}$ of the cake was eaten, and the other $\frac{1}{2}$ was uneaten.

Arithmetic Operations with Mixed Numbers

A ***mixed number*** is a number such as $3\frac{1}{2}$, which consists of an integer followed by a fraction. It is an abbreviation for the *sum* of the number and the fraction; so, $3\frac{1}{2}$ is an abbreviation for $3 + \frac{1}{2}$. Every mixed number can be written as an improper fraction, and every improper fraction can be written as a mixed number:

$$3\frac{1}{2} = 3 + \frac{1}{2} = \frac{3}{1} + \frac{1}{2} = \frac{6}{2} + \frac{1}{2} = \frac{7}{2} \quad \text{and} \quad \frac{7}{2} = \frac{6}{2} + \frac{1}{2} = 3 + \frac{1}{2} = 3\frac{1}{2}$$

On the GRE you should perform all arithmetic operations on mixed numbers in one of the following two ways:

- Change the mixed numbers to improper fractions and use the rules you already know for performing arithmetic operations on fractions.
- Change the mixed numbers to decimals and perform the arithmetic on your calculator.

CAUTION

A common mistake for many students is to think that

$3 \times 5\frac{1}{2}$ is $15\frac{1}{2}$—it isn't!

If you need to multiply $3 \times 5\frac{1}{2}$, use one of the two methods mentioned above.

- $3 \times 5\frac{1}{2} = 3\left(5+\frac{1}{2}\right) = 15 + \frac{3}{2} = 15 + 1\frac{1}{2} = 16\frac{1}{2}$
- $3 \times 5\frac{1}{2} = 3 \times 5.5 = 16.5 = 16\frac{1}{2}$

Complex Fractions

A ***complex fraction*** is a fraction, such as $\frac{1+\frac{1}{6}}{2-\frac{3}{4}}$, which has one or more fractions in its numerator or denominator or both.

KEY FACT B16

There are two ways to simplify a complex fraction:

- **Multiply *every* term in the numerator and denominator by the least common multiple of all the denominators that appear in the fraction.**
- **Simplify the numerator and the denominator, and then divide.**

To simplify $\frac{1+\frac{1}{6}}{2-\frac{3}{4}}$

- either multiply each term by 12, the LCM of 6 and 4:

$$\frac{12(1)+12\left(\frac{1}{6}\right)}{12(2)-12\left(\frac{3}{4}\right)} = \frac{12+2}{24-9} = \frac{14}{15}\text{, or}$$

- simplify the numerator and denominator:

$$\frac{1+\frac{1}{6}}{2-\frac{3}{4}} = \frac{\frac{7}{6}}{\frac{5}{4}} = \frac{7}{6} \times \frac{4}{5} = \frac{14}{15}$$

PRACTICE EXERCISES—FRACTIONS AND DECIMALS

Discrete Quantitative Questions

1. A biology class has 12 boys and 18 girls. What fraction of the class are boys?

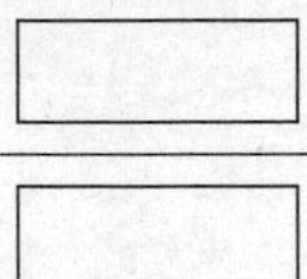

2. For how many integers, a, between 30 and 40 is it true that $\frac{5}{a}$, $\frac{8}{a}$, and $\frac{13}{a}$ are all in lowest terms?

Ⓐ 1
Ⓑ 2
Ⓒ 3
Ⓓ 4
Ⓔ 5

3. What fractional part of a week is 98 hours?

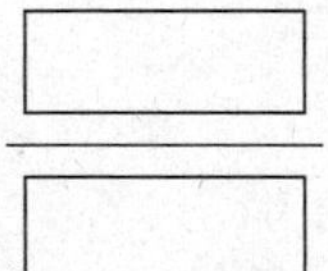

4. What is the value of the product $\frac{5}{5}\times\frac{5}{10}\times\frac{5}{15}\times\frac{5}{20}\times\frac{5}{25}$?

Ⓐ $\frac{1}{120}$
Ⓑ $\frac{1}{60}$
Ⓒ $\frac{1}{30}$
Ⓓ $\frac{5}{30}$
Ⓔ $\frac{1}{2}$

5. If $\frac{3}{11}$ of a number is 22, what is $\frac{6}{11}$ of that number?

Ⓐ 6
Ⓑ 11
Ⓒ 12
Ⓓ 33
Ⓔ 44

6. Jason won some goldfish at the state fair. During the first week, $\frac{1}{5}$ of them died, and during the second week, $\frac{3}{8}$ of those still alive at the end of the first week died. What fraction of the original goldfish were still alive after two weeks?

Ⓐ $\frac{3}{10}$
Ⓑ $\frac{17}{40}$
Ⓒ $\frac{1}{2}$
Ⓓ $\frac{23}{40}$
Ⓔ $\frac{7}{10}$

7. $\frac{5}{8}$ of 24 is equal to $\frac{15}{7}$ of what number?

Ⓐ 7
Ⓑ 8
Ⓒ 15
Ⓓ $\frac{7}{225}$
Ⓔ $\frac{225}{7}$

8. If $7a = 3$ and $3b = 7$, what is the value of $\frac{a}{b}$?

Ⓐ $\frac{9}{49}$

Ⓑ $\frac{3}{7}$

Ⓒ 1

Ⓓ $\frac{7}{3}$

Ⓔ $\frac{49}{9}$

9. What is the value of $\dfrac{\frac{7}{9} \times \frac{7}{9}}{\frac{7}{9} + \frac{7}{9} + \frac{7}{9}}$?

Ⓐ $\frac{7}{27}$

Ⓑ $\frac{2}{3}$

Ⓒ $\frac{7}{9}$

Ⓓ $\frac{9}{7}$

Ⓔ $\frac{3}{2}$

10. Which of the following expressions are greater than x when $x = \frac{9}{11}$?

Indicate *all* such expressions.

[A] $\frac{1}{x}$

[B] $\frac{x+1}{x}$

[C] $\frac{x+1}{x-1}$

11. One day at Lincoln High School, $\frac{1}{12}$ of the students were absent, and $\frac{1}{5}$ of those present went on a field trip. If the number of students staying in school that day was 704, how many students are enrolled at Lincoln High?

[ ]

12. If $a = 0.87$, which of the following expressions are less than a?

Indicate *all* such expressions.

[A] $\sqrt{a}$

[B] a^2

[C] $\frac{1}{a}$

13. For what value of x is

$$\frac{(34.56)(7.89)}{x} = (.3456)(78.9)?$$

Ⓐ .001

Ⓑ .01

Ⓒ .1

Ⓓ 10

Ⓔ 100

14. If $A = \{1, 2, 3\}$, $B = \{2, 3, 4\}$, and C is the set consisting of all the fractions whose numerators are in A and whose denominators are in B, what is the product of all of the numbers in C?

Ⓐ $\frac{1}{64}$

Ⓑ $\frac{1}{48}$

Ⓒ $\frac{1}{24}$

Ⓓ $\frac{1}{12}$

Ⓔ $\frac{1}{2}$

15. For the final step in a calculation, Ezra accidentally divided by 1,000 instead of multiplying by 1,000. What should he do to his incorrect answer to correct it?
    Ⓐ Multiply it by 1,000.
    Ⓑ Multiply it by 100,000.
    Ⓒ Multiply it by 1,000,000.
    Ⓓ Square it.
    Ⓔ Double it.

Quantitative Comparison Questions

Ⓐ Quantity A is greater.
Ⓑ Quantity B is greater.
Ⓒ The two quantities are equal.
Ⓓ It is impossible to determine which quantity is greater.

16.

Quantity A	Quantity B
$\frac{5}{13}$ of 47	$\frac{47}{13}$ of 5

17.

$$x = -\frac{2}{3} \text{ and } y = \frac{3}{5}$$

Quantity A	Quantity B
xy	$\frac{x}{y}$

18.

Quantity A	Quantity B
$\frac{15}{\frac{1}{15}}$	1

19.

Judy needed 8 pounds of chicken. At the supermarket, the only packages available weighed $\frac{3}{4}$ of a pound each.

Quantity A	Quantity B
The number of packages Judy needed to buy	11

20.

Quantity A	Quantity B
$\frac{11}{12}$ of $\frac{13}{14}$	$\frac{14}{15}$

21.

$$a\nabla b = \frac{a}{b} + \frac{b}{a}$$

Quantity A	Quantity B
$3\nabla 4$	$\frac{1}{2}\nabla\frac{2}{3}$

22.

Quantity A	Quantity B
$\frac{100}{2^{100}}$	$\frac{100}{3^{100}}$

23.

Quantity A	Quantity B
$\left(-\frac{1}{2}\right)\left(-\frac{3}{4}\right)\left(-\frac{5}{6}\right)\left(-\frac{7}{8}\right)$	$\left(-\frac{3}{7}\right)\left(-\frac{5}{9}\right)\left(-\frac{7}{11}\right)$

24.

$$a = \frac{1}{2} \text{ and } b = \frac{1}{3}$$

Quantity A	Quantity B
$\frac{a}{b}$	$\frac{b}{a}$

25.

Quantity A	Quantity B
$\left(\frac{3}{11}\right)^2$	$\sqrt{\frac{3}{11}}$

ANSWER KEY

1. $\frac{2}{5}$	4. **A**	9. **A**	14. **A**	19. **C**	24. **A**
	5. **E**	10. **A, B**	15. **C**	20. **B**	25. **B**
2. **C**	6. **C**	11. **960**	16. **C**	21. **C**	
	7. **A**	12. **B**	17. **A**	22. **A**	
3. $\frac{7}{12}$	8. **A**	13. **D**	18. **A**	23. **A**	

ANSWER EXPLANATIONS

1. $\frac{2}{5}$ The class has 30 students, of whom 12 are boys. So, the boys make up $\frac{12}{30} = \frac{2}{5}$ of the class.

2. **(C)** If a is even, then $\frac{8}{a}$ is *not* in lowest terms, since both a and 8 are divisible by 2.

   Therefore, the only possibilities are 31, 33, 35, 37, and 39; but $\frac{5}{35} = \frac{1}{7}$ and $\frac{13}{39} = \frac{1}{3}$, so only 3 integers—31, 33, and 37—satisfy the given condition.

3. $\frac{7}{12}$ There are 24 hours in a day and 7 days in a week, so there are $24 \times 7 = 168$ hours in a week: $\frac{98}{168} = \frac{7}{12}$.

4. **(A)** Reduce each fraction and multiply:

$$1\times\frac{1}{2}\times\frac{1}{3}\times\frac{1}{4}\times\frac{1}{5} = \frac{1}{120}$$

5. **(E)** Don't bother writing an equation for this one; just think. We know that $\frac{3}{11}$ of the number is 22, and $\frac{6}{11}$ of a number is twice as much as $\frac{3}{11}$ of it: $2 \times 22 = 44$.

6. **(C)** The *algebra* way is to let x = the number of goldfish Jason won. During the first week $\frac{1}{5}x$ died, so $\frac{4}{5}x$ were still alive. During week two, $\frac{3}{8}$ of them died and $\frac{5}{8}$ of them survived:

$$\left(\frac{\cancel{5}^{1}}{\cancel{8}_{2}}\right)\left(\frac{\cancel{4}^{1}}{\cancel{5}_{1}}x\right) = \frac{1}{2}x$$

   On the GRE, the best way is to assume that the original number of goldfish was 40, the LCM of the denominators (see TACTIC 3, Chapter 9, page 273).

   Then, 8 died the first week $\left(\frac{1}{5} \text{ of } 40\right)$, and 12 of the 32 survivors $\left(\frac{3}{8} \text{ of } 32\right)$ died the second week. In all, $8 + 12 = 20$ died; the other 20 $\left(\frac{1}{2} \text{ the original number}\right)$ were still alive.

7. **(A)** If x is the number, then $\frac{15}{7}x = \frac{5}{\cancel{8}_1} \times \overset{3}{\cancel{24}} = 15$. So, $\frac{15}{7}x = 15$, which means (dividing by 15) that $\frac{1}{7}x = 1$, and so $x = 7$.

8. **(A)** $7a = 3$ and $3b = 7 \Rightarrow a = \frac{3}{7}$ and $b = \frac{7}{3} \Rightarrow \frac{a}{b} = \frac{3}{7} \div \frac{7}{3} = \frac{3}{7} \times \frac{3}{7} = \frac{9}{49}$.

9. **(A)** Don't start by doing the arithmetic. This is just $\frac{(a)(a)}{a+a+a} = \frac{(a)(\cancel{a})}{3\cancel{a}} = \frac{a}{3}$.

Now, replacing a with $\frac{7}{9}$ gives $\frac{7}{9} \div 3 = \frac{7}{9} \times \frac{1}{3} = \frac{7}{27}$.

10. **(A, B)** The reciprocal of a positive number less than 1 is greater than 1 (A is true). $\frac{x+1}{x} = 1 + \frac{1}{x}$, which is greater than 1 (B is true). Since $\frac{9}{11} + 1$ is positive and $\frac{9}{11} - 1$ is negative, when $x = \frac{9}{11}$, $\frac{x+1}{x-1} < 0$ and, therefore, less than x (C is false).

11. **960** If s is the number of students enrolled, $\frac{1}{12}s$ is the number who were absent, and $\frac{11}{12}s$ is the number who were present. Since $\frac{1}{5}$ of them went on a field trip, $\frac{4}{5}$ of them stayed in school. Therefore,

$$704 = \frac{\overset{1}{\cancel{4}}}{5} \times \frac{11}{\cancel{12}_3}s = \frac{11}{15}s \Rightarrow$$

$$s = 704 \div \frac{11}{15} = 704 \times \frac{15}{11} = 960$$

12. **(B)** Since $a < 1$, $\sqrt{a} > a$ (A is false). Since $a < 1$, $a^2 < a$ (B is true). The reciprocal of a positive number less than 1 is greater than 1 (C is false).

13. **(D)** There are two easy ways to do this. The first is to see that (34.56)(7.89) has 4 decimal places, whereas (.3456)(78.9) has 5, so the numerator has to be divided by 10. The second is to round off and calculate mentally: since $30 \times 8 = 240$, and $.3 \times 80 = 24$, we must divide by 10.

14. **(A)** Nine fractions are formed:

$$\frac{1}{2}, \frac{1}{3}, \frac{1}{4}, \frac{2}{2}, \frac{2}{3}, \frac{2}{4}, \frac{3}{2}, \frac{3}{3}, \frac{3}{4}$$

Note that although some of these fractions are equivalent, we do have nine distinct fractions.

When you multiply, the three 2s and the three 3s in the numerators cancel with the three 2s and three 3s in the denominators. So, the numerator is 1 and the denominator is $4 \times 4 \times 4 = 64$.

15. **(C)** Multiplying Ezra's incorrect answer by 1,000 would undo the final division he made. At that point he should have multiplied by 1,000. So, to correct his error, he should multiply again by 1,000. In all, Ezra should multiply his incorrect answer by $1{,}000 \times 1{,}000 = 1{,}000{,}000$.

16. **(C)** Each quantity equals $\frac{5 \times 47}{3}$.

17. **(A)** Quantity A: $-\frac{2}{3} \times \frac{3}{5} = -\frac{2}{5}$.

    Quantity B: $-\frac{2}{3} \div \frac{3}{5} = -\frac{2}{3} \times \frac{5}{3} = -\frac{10}{9}$.

    Finally, $\frac{10}{9} > \frac{2}{5} \Rightarrow -\frac{10}{9} < -\frac{2}{5}$.

18. **(A)** Quantity A: $\frac{15}{\frac{1}{15}} = 15 \times 15 = 225$.

19. **(C)** $8 \div \frac{3}{4} = 8 \times \frac{4}{3} = \frac{32}{3} = 10\frac{2}{3}$. Since 10 packages wouldn't be enough, she had to buy 11. (10 packages would weigh only $7\frac{1}{2}$ pounds.)

20. **(B)** You don't need to multiply on this one: since $\frac{11}{12} < 1$, $\frac{11}{12}$ of $\frac{13}{14}$ is less than $\frac{13}{14}$, which is already less than $\frac{14}{15}$.

21. **(C)** Quantity B is the sum of 2 complex fractions:

    $$\frac{\frac{1}{2}}{\frac{2}{3}} + \frac{\frac{2}{3}}{\frac{1}{2}}$$

    Simplifying each complex fraction, by multiplying numerator and denominator by 6, or treating these as the quotient of 2 fractions, we get $\frac{3}{4} + \frac{4}{3}$, which is exactly the value of Quantity A.

22. **(A)** When two fractions have the same numerator, the one with the smaller denominator is bigger, and $2^{100} < 3^{100}$.

23. **(A)** Since Quantity A is the product of 4 negative numbers, it is positive, and so is greater than Quantity B, which, being the product of 3 negative numbers, is negative.

24. **(A)** Quantity A: $\frac{1}{2} \div \frac{1}{3} = \frac{1}{2} \times \frac{3}{1} = \frac{3}{2}$.

    Since Quantity B is the reciprocal of Quantity A, Quantity B = $\frac{2}{3}$.

25. **(B)** If $0 < x < 1$, then $x^2 < x < \sqrt{x}$. In this question, $x = \frac{3}{11}$.

TIP

A percent is just a fraction whose denominator is 100.

12-C. PERCENTS

- Percents
- Solving Percent Problems
- Percent Increase and Decrease
- Practice Exercises
- Answer Explanations

Percents

The word ***percent*** means hundredth. We use the symbol "%" to express the word "percent." For example, "17 percent" means "17 hundredths," and can be written with a % symbol, as a fraction, or as a decimal:

$$17\% = \frac{17}{100} = 0.17$$

KEY FACT C1

- **To convert a percent to a decimal, drop the % symbol and move the decimal point two places to the left, adding 0s if necessary. (Remember that we assume that there is a decimal point to the right of any whole number.)**
- **To convert a percent to a fraction, drop the % symbol, write the number over 100, and reduce.**

$$25\% = 0.25 = \frac{25}{100} = \frac{1}{4} \qquad 100\% = 1.00 = \frac{100}{100} \qquad 12.5\% = 0.125 = \frac{12.5}{100} = \frac{125}{1{,}000} = \frac{1}{8}$$

$$1\% = 0.01 = \frac{1}{100} \qquad \frac{1}{2}\% = 0.5\% = 0.005 = \frac{.5}{100} = \frac{1}{200} \qquad 250\% = 2.50 = \frac{250}{100} = \frac{5}{2}$$

KEY FACT C2

- **To convert a decimal to a percent, move the decimal point two places to the right, adding 0s if necessary, and add the % symbol.**
- **To convert a fraction to a percent, first convert the fraction to a decimal, then convert the decimal to a percent, as indicated above.**

$$0.375 = 37.5\% \qquad 0.3 = 30\% \qquad 1.25 = 125\% \qquad 10 = 1000\%$$

$$\frac{3}{4} = 0.75 = 75\% \qquad \frac{1}{3} = 0.33333\ldots = 33.333\ldots\% = 33\frac{1}{3}\% \qquad \frac{1}{5} = 0.2 = 20\%$$

You should be familiar with the following basic conversions:

$\frac{1}{2} = 50\%$	$\frac{3}{4} = 75\%$	$\frac{4}{10} = \frac{2}{5} = 40\%$	$\frac{8}{10} = \frac{4}{5} = 80\%$
$\frac{1}{3} = 33\frac{1}{3}\%$	$\frac{1}{10} = 10\%$	$\frac{5}{10} = \frac{1}{2} = 50\%$	$\frac{9}{10} = 90\%$
$\frac{2}{3} = 66\frac{2}{3}\%$	$\frac{2}{10} = \frac{1}{5} = 20\%$	$\frac{6}{10} = \frac{3}{5} = 60\%$	$\frac{10}{10} = 1 = 100\%$
$\frac{1}{4} = 25\%$	$\frac{3}{10} = 30\%$	$\frac{7}{10} = 70\%$	

Knowing these conversions can help solve many problems more quickly. For example, the fastest way to find 25% of 32 is not to multiply 32 by 0.25; rather, it is to know that $25\% = \frac{1}{4}$, and that $\frac{1}{4}$ of 32 is 8.

Many questions involving percents can actually be answered more quickly in your head than by using paper and pencil. Since $10\% = \frac{1}{10}$, to take 10% of a number, just divide by 10 by moving the decimal point one place to the left: 10% of 60 is 6. Also, since 5% is half of 10%, then 5% of 60 is 3 (half of 6); and since 30% is 3 times 10%, then 30% of 60 is 18 (3×6).

Practice doing this, because improving your ability to do mental math will add valuable points to your score on the GRE.

CAUTION

Do not confuse 0.5 and 0.5%.
Just as 5 is 100 times 5%, 0.5 is 100 times 0.5% = 0.005.

CAUTION

Although 35% can be written as $\frac{35}{100}$ or 0.35, x% can *only* be written as $\frac{x}{100}$.

Solving Percent Problems

Consider the following three questions:

(i) What is 45% of 200?
(ii) 90 is 45% of what number?
(iii) 90 is what percent of 200?

The arithmetic needed to answer each of these questions is very easy, but unless you set a question up properly, you won't know whether you should multiply or divide. In each case, there is one unknown, which we will call *x*. Now just translate each sentence, replacing "is" by "=" and the unknown by *x*.

(i) $x = 45\%$ of $200 \Rightarrow x = .45 \times 200 = 90$
(ii) $90 = 45\%$ of $x \Rightarrow 90 = .45x \Rightarrow x = 90 \div .45 = 200$
(iii) $90 = x\%$ of $200 \Rightarrow 90 = \frac{x}{\cancel{100}_1}(\cancel{200}^2) \Rightarrow 90 = 2x \Rightarrow x = 45$

EXAMPLE 1

Charlie gave 20% of his baseball cards to Kenne and 15% to Paulie. If he still had 520 cards, how many did he have originally?

SOLUTION.

Originally, Charlie had 100% of the cards (all of them). Since he gave away 35% of them, he has 100% – 35% = 65% of them left. So, 520 is 65% of what number?

$$520 = .65x \Rightarrow x = 520 \div .65 = \mathbf{800}$$

EXAMPLE 2

After Ruth gave 110 baseball cards to Alison and 75 to Susanna, she still had 315 left. What percent of her cards did Ruth give away?

Ⓐ 25% Ⓑ $33\frac{1}{3}$% Ⓒ 37% Ⓓ 40% Ⓔ 50%

SOLUTION. Ruth gave away a total of 185 cards and had 315 left. Therefore, she started with 185 + 315 = 500 cards. So, 185 is what percent of 500?

$$185 = \frac{x}{\cancel{100}_1}(\cancel{500}^5) \Rightarrow 5x = 185 \Rightarrow x = 185 \div 5 = \mathbf{37}$$

Ruth gave away 37% of her cards, (**C**).

Since percent means hundredth, the easiest number to use in any percent problem is 100:

$$a\% \text{ of } 100 = \frac{a}{\cancel{100}_1} \times \cancel{100}^1 = a$$

KEY FACT C3

For any positive number *a*: *a*% of 100 is *a*.

For example: 91.2% of 100 is 91.2; 300% of 100 is 300; and $\frac{1}{2}$% of 100 is $\frac{1}{2}$.

TACTIC C1

In any problem involving percents, use the number 100. (It doesn't matter whether or not 100 is a realistic number—a country can have a population of 100; an apple can cost $100; a man can run 100 miles per hour.)

EXAMPLE 3

In 1985 the populations of town A and town B were the same. From 1985 to 1995 the population of town A increased by 60% while the population of town B decreased by 60%. In 1995, the population of town B was what percent of the population of town A?

Ⓐ 25% Ⓑ 36% Ⓒ 40% Ⓓ 60% Ⓔ 120%

SOLUTION.

On the GRE, do not waste time with a nice algebraic solution. Simply, assume that in 1985 the population of each town was 100. Then, since 60% of 100 is 60, in 1995, the populations were $100 + 60 = 160$ and $100 - 60 = 40$. So, in 1995, town B's population was $\frac{40}{160} = \frac{1}{4}$ = **25%** of town A's (**A**).

Since $a\%$ of b is $\frac{a}{100} \times b = \frac{ab}{100}$, and $b\%$ of a is $\frac{b}{100} \times a = \frac{ba}{100}$, we have the result shown in KEY FACT C4.

KEY FACT C4

For any positive numbers *a* and *b*: *a*% of *b* = *b*% of *a*.

KEY FACT C4 often comes up on the GRE in quantitative comparison questions: Which is greater, 13% of 87 or 87% of 13? Don't multiply—they're equal.

Percent Increase and Decrease

KEY FACT C5

- **The *percent increase* of a quantity is**

$$\frac{\textbf{actual increase}}{\textbf{original amount}} \times 100\%$$

- **The *percent decrease* of a quantity is**

$$\frac{\textbf{actual decrease}}{\textbf{original amount}} \times 100\%$$

For example:

- If the price of a lamp goes from \$80 to \$100, the actual increase is \$20, and the percent increase is $\frac{20}{80} \times 100\% = \frac{1}{4} \times 100\% = 25\%$.
- If a \$100 lamp is on sale for \$80, the actual decrease in price is \$20, and the percent decrease is $\frac{20}{100} \times 100\% = 20\%$.

Notice that the percent increase in going from 80 to 100 is not the same as the percent decrease in going from 100 to 80.

KEY FACT C6

If $a < b$, the percent increase in going from *a* to *b* is *always* greater than the percent decrease in going from *b* to *a*.

KEY FACT C7

- **To increase a number by $k\%$, multiply it by $(1 + k\%)$.**
- **To decrease a number by $k\%$, multiply it by $(1 - k\%)$.**

For example:

- The value of a $1600 investment after a 25% increase is $1,600(1 + 25%) = $1,600(1.25) = $2,000.
- If the investment then loses 25% of its value, it is worth $2,000(1 – 25%) = $2,000(.75) = $1,500.

Note that, after a 25% increase followed by a 25% decrease, the value is $1,500, $100 *less* than the original amount.

KEY FACT C8

An increase of $k\%$ followed by a decrease of $k\%$ is equal to a decrease of $k\%$ followed by an increase of $k\%$, and is *always* less than the original value. The original value is never regained.

EXAMPLE 4

Store B always sells CDs at 60% off the list price.
Store A sells its CDs at 40% off the list price, but often runs a special sale during which it reduces its prices by 20%.

Quantity A	Quantity B
The price of a CD when it is on sale at store A	The price of the same CD at store B

SOLUTION.
Assume the list price of the CD is $100. Store B always sells the CD for $40 ($60 off the list price). Store A normally sells the CD for $60 ($40 off the list price), but on sale reduces its price by 20%. Since 20% of 60 is 12, the sale price is $48 ($60 – $12). The price is greater at Store A.

Notice that a decrease of 40% followed by a decrease of 20% is not the same as a single decrease of 60%; it is less. In fact, a decrease of 40% followed by a decrease of 30% wouldn't even be as much as a single decrease of 60%.

KEY FACT C9

- **A decrease of $a\%$ followed by a decrease of $b\%$ *always* results in a smaller decrease than a single decrease of $(a + b)\%$.**
- **An increase of $a\%$ followed by an increase of $b\%$ *always* results in a larger increase than a single increase of $(a + b)\%$.**
- **An increase (or decrease) of $a\%$ followed by another increase (or decrease) of $a\%$ is *never* the same as a single increase (or decrease) of $2a\%$.**

EXAMPLE 5

Sally and Heidi were both hired in January at the same salary. Sally got two 40% raises, one in July and another in November. Heidi got one 90% raise in October.

Quantity A	Quantity B
Sally's salary at the end of the year	Heidi's salary at the end of the year

SOLUTION.
Since this is a percent problem, assume their salaries were \$100. Quantity A: Sally's salary rose to $100(1.40) = 140$, and then to $140(1.40) = \$196$. Quantity B: Heidi's salary rose to $100(1.90) = \$190$. Quantity **A** is greater.

EXAMPLE 6

In January, the value of a stock increased by 25%, and in February, it decreased by 20%. How did the value of the stock at the end of February compare with its value at the beginning of January?

Ⓐ It was less.
Ⓑ It was the same.
Ⓒ It was 5% greater.
Ⓓ It was more than 5% greater.
Ⓔ It cannot be determined from the information given.

SOLUTION. Assume that at the beginning of January the stock was worth \$100. Then at the end of January it was worth \$125. Since 20% of 125 is 25, during February its value decreased from \$125 to \$100. The answer is **B**.

KEY FACT C10

- **If a number is the result of increasing another number by k%, to find the original number, divide by (1 + k%).**
- **If a number is the result of decreasing another number by k%, to find the original number, divide it by (1 − k%).**

For example, if the population of a town in 1990 was 3,000, and this represents an increase of 20% since 1980, to find the population in 1980, divide 3,000 by (1 + 20%): $3{,}000 \div 1.20 = 2{,}500$.

EXAMPLE 7

From 1989 to 1990, the number of applicants to a college increased 15% to 5,060. How many applicants were there in 1989?

SOLUTION.

The number of applicants in 1989 was 5,060 ÷ 1.15 = **4,400**.

CAUTION

Percents over 100%, which come up most often on questions involving percent increases, are often confusing for students. First of all, be sure you understand that 100% of a number is that number, 200% of a number is 2 times the number, and 1,000% of a number is 10 times the number. If the value of an investment goes from $1,000 to $5,000, it is now worth 5 times, or 500%, as much as it was originally; but there has only been a *400%* increase in value:

$$\frac{\text{actual increase}}{\text{original amount}} \times 100\% = \frac{4{,}000}{1{,}000} \times 100\% = 4 \times 100\% = 400\%$$

EXAMPLE 8

The population of a country doubled every 10 years from 1960 to 1990. What was the percent increase in population during this time?

Ⓐ 200% Ⓑ 300% Ⓒ 700% Ⓓ 800% Ⓔ 1,000%

SOLUTION.

The population doubled three times (once from 1960 to 1970, again from 1970 to 1980, and a third time from 1980 to 1990). Assume that the population was originally 100. Then it increased from 100 to 200 to 400 to 800. So the population in 1990 was 8 times the population in 1960, but this was an increase of 700 people, or **700% (C)**.

PRACTICE EXERCISES—PERCENTS

Discrete Quantitative Questions

1. If 25 students took an exam and 4 of them failed, what percent of them passed?

Ⓐ 4%
Ⓑ 21%
Ⓒ 42%
Ⓓ 84%
Ⓔ 96%

2. Amanda bought a $60 sweater on sale at 5% off. How much did she pay, including 5% sales tax?

Ⓐ $54.15
Ⓑ $57.00
Ⓒ $57.75
Ⓓ $59.85
Ⓔ $60.00

3. What is 10% of 20% of 30%?

Ⓐ 0.006%
Ⓑ 0.6%
Ⓒ 6%
Ⓓ 60%
Ⓔ 6,000%

4. If c is a positive number, 500% of c is what percent of $500c$?

Ⓐ 0.01
Ⓑ 0.1
Ⓒ 1
Ⓓ 10
Ⓔ 100

5. What percent of 50 is b?

Ⓐ $\frac{b}{50}$
Ⓑ $\frac{b}{2}$
Ⓒ $\frac{50}{b}$
Ⓓ $\frac{2}{b}$
Ⓔ $2b$

6. 8 is $\frac{1}{3}$ % of what number?

[ ]

7. During his second week on the job, Mario earned $110. This represented a 25% increase over his earnings of the previous week. How much did he earn during his first week of work?

Ⓐ $82.50
Ⓑ $85.00
Ⓒ $88.00
Ⓓ $137.50
Ⓔ $146.67

8. At Bernie's Bargain Basement everything is sold for 20% less than the price marked. If Bernie buys radios for $80, what price should he mark them if he wants to make a 20% profit on his cost?

Ⓐ $96
Ⓑ $100
Ⓒ $112
Ⓓ $120
Ⓔ $125

9. Mrs. Fisher usually deposits the same amount of money each month into a vacation fund. This year she decided not to make any contributions during November and December. To make the same annual contribution that she had originally planned, by what percent should she increase her monthly deposits from January through October?

Ⓐ $16\frac{2}{3}\%$

Ⓑ 20%

Ⓒ 25%

Ⓓ $33\frac{1}{3}\%$

Ⓔ It cannot be determined from the information given.

10. The price of a loaf of bread was increased by 20%. How many loaves can be purchased for the amount of money that used to buy 300 loaves?

Ⓐ 240

Ⓑ 250

Ⓒ 280

Ⓓ 320

Ⓔ 360

11. If 1 micron = 10,000 angstroms, then 100 angstroms is what percent of 10 microns?

Ⓐ 0.0001%

Ⓑ 0.001%

Ⓒ 0.01%

Ⓓ 0.1%

Ⓔ 1%

12. There are twice as many girls as boys in an English class. If 30% of the girls and 45% of the boys have already handed in their book reports, what percent of the students have not yet handed in their reports?

[ ] %

13. An art dealer bought a Ming vase for $1,000 and later sold it for $10,000. By what percent did the value of the vase increase?

Ⓐ 10%

Ⓑ 90%

Ⓒ 100%

Ⓓ 900%

Ⓔ 1,000%

14. During a sale a clerk was putting a new price tag on each item. On one jacket, he accidentally raised the price by 15% instead of lowering the price by 15%. As a result the price on the tag was $45 too high. What was the original price of the jacket?

[ ] dollars

15. On a test consisting of 80 questions, Eve answered 75% of the first 60 questions correctly. What percent of the other 20 questions does she need to answer correctly for her grade on the entire exam to be 80%?

Ⓐ 85%

Ⓑ 87.5%

Ⓒ 90%

Ⓓ 95%

Ⓔ 100%

Quantitative Comparison Questions

Ⓐ Quantity A is greater.
Ⓑ Quantity B is greater.
Ⓒ The two quantities are equal.
Ⓓ It is impossible to determine which quantity is greater.

16.

Quantity A	Quantity B
400% of 3	300% of 4

17.

n% of 25 is 50

Quantity A	Quantity B
50% of n	75

18.

Quantity A	Quantity B
The price of a television when it is on sale at 25% off	The price of that television when it's on sale at $25 off

19.

The price of cellular phone 1 is 20% more than the price of cellular phone 2.

Quantity A	Quantity B
The price of cellular phone 1 when it is on sale at 20% off	The price of cellular phone 2

20.

Quantity A	Quantity B
$\frac{2}{3}$% of $\frac{3}{4}$	$\frac{3}{4}$% of $\frac{2}{3}$

21.

Quantity A	Quantity B
a% of $\frac{1}{b}$	b% of $\frac{1}{a}$

22.

Bank A pays 5% interest on its savings accounts. Bank B pays 4% interest on its savings accounts.

Quantity A	Quantity B
Percent by which bank B would have to raise its interest rate to match bank A	20%

23.

A mixture of sugar and cinnamon is 20% sugar by weight. To make it sweeter, the amount of sugar is doubled.

Quantity A	Quantity B
The percent of sugar in the new mixture	40%

24.

b is an integer greater than 1, and b equals n% of b^2

Quantity A	Quantity B
n	50

25.

After Ali gave Lior 50% of her money, she had 20% as much as he did.

Quantity A	Quantity B
75% of the amount Lior had originally	150% of the amount Ali had originally

ANSWER KEY

1. **D**	6. **2,400**	11. **D**	16. **C**	21. **D**
2. **D**	7. **C**	12. **65**	17. **A**	22. **A**
3. **B**	8. **D**	13. **D**	18. **D**	23. **B**
4. **C**	9. **B**	14. **150**	19. **B**	24. **D**
5. **E**	10. **B**	15. **D**	20. **C**	25. **C**

ANSWER EXPLANATIONS

1. **(D)** If 4 students failed, then the other 25 – 4 = 21 students passed, and $\frac{21}{25} = 0.84 = 84\%$.

2. **(D)** Since 5% of 60 is 3, Amanda saved \$3, and thus paid \$57 for the sweater. She then had to pay 5% sales tax on the \$57: $.05 \times 57 = 2.85$, so the total cost was \$57 + \$2.85 = \$59.85.

3. **(B)** 10% of 20% of 30% = $.10 \times .20 \times .30 = .006 = .6\%$.

4. **(C)** 500% of $c = 5c$, which is 1% of $500c$.

5. **(E)** $b = \frac{x}{\cancel{100}_{2}}(\cancel{50}^{1}) \Rightarrow b = \frac{x}{2} \Rightarrow x = 2b$

6. **2,400** $8 = \frac{\frac{1}{3}}{100}x = \frac{1}{300}x \Rightarrow x = 8 \times 300 = 2{,}400$

7. **(C)** To find Mario's earnings during his first week, divide his earnings from the second week by 1.25: $110 \div 1.25 = 88$.

8. **(D)** Since 20% of 80 is 16, Bernie wants to get \$96 for each radio he sells. What price should the radios be marked so that after a 20% discount, the customer will pay \$96? If x represents the marked price, then $.80x = 96 \Rightarrow x = 96 \div .80 = 120$.

9. **(B)** Assume that Mrs. Fisher usually contributed \$100 each month, for an annual total of \$1200. Having decided not to contribute for 2 months, the \$1200 will have to be paid in 10 monthly deposits of \$120 each. This is an increase of \$20, and a percent increase of $\frac{\text{actual increase}}{\text{original amount}} \times 100\% = \frac{20}{100} \times 100\% = 20\%$.

10. **(B)** Assume that a loaf of bread used to cost \$1 and that now it costs \$1.20 (20% more). Then 300 loaves of bread used to cost \$300. How many loaves costing \$1.20 each can be bought for \$300? $300 \div 1.20 = 250$.

11. **(D)** 1 micron = 10,000 angstroms $\Rightarrow$ 10 microns = 100,000 angstroms; dividing both sides by 1,000, we get 100 angstroms = $\frac{1}{1{,}000}$ (10 microns); and $\frac{1}{1{,}000} = .001 = 0.1\%$.

12. **65** Assume that there are 100 boys and 200 girls in the class. Then, 45 boys and 60 girls have handed in their reports. So 105 students have handed them in, and 300 – 105 = 195 have not handed them in. What percent of 300 is 195?

$$\frac{195}{300} = .65 = 65\%$$

13. **(D)** The increase in the value of the vase was \$9,000. So the percent increase is

$$\frac{\text{actual increase}}{\text{original cost}} \times 100\% = \frac{9{,}000}{1{,}000} = 9 = 900\%$$

14. **150** If p represents the original price, the jacket was priced at $1.15p$ instead of $.85p$. Since this was a \$45 difference, $45 = 1.15p - .85p = .30p \Rightarrow p = 45 \div .30 = \$150$.

15. **(D)** To earn a grade of 80% on the entire exam, Eve needs to correctly answer 64 questions (80% of 80). So far, she has answered 45 questions correctly (75% of 60). Therefore, on the last 20 questions she needs 64 – 45 = 19 correct answers; and $\frac{19}{20} = 95\%$.

16. **(C)** Quantity A: 400% of $3 = 4 \times 3 = 12$.
Quantity B: 300% of $4 = 3 \times 4 = 12$.

17. **(A)** Since n% of 25 is 50, then 25% of n is also 50, and 50% of n is twice as much: 100. If you don't see that, just solve for n:

$$\frac{n}{\cancelto{4}{100}} \times \cancelto{1}{25} = 50 \Rightarrow \frac{n}{4} = 50 \Rightarrow n = 200 \text{ and } 50\% \text{ of } n = 100$$

18. **(D)** A 25% discount on a \$10 television is much less than \$25, whereas a 25% discount on a \$1,000 television is much more than \$25. (They would be equal only if the regular price of the television were \$100.)

19. **(B)** Assume that the list price of cellular phone 2 is \$100; then the list price of cellular phone 1 is \$120, and on sale at 20% off it costs \$24 less: \$96.

20. **(C)** For *any* numbers a and b: a% of b is equal to b% of a.

21. **(D)**

Quantity A	Quantity B
$a\%$ of $\frac{1}{b}$	$b\%$ of $\frac{1}{a}$
$\frac{a}{100} \times \frac{1}{b} = \frac{a}{100b}$	$\frac{b}{100} \times \frac{1}{a} = \frac{b}{100a}$

Multiply by 100:

$\frac{a}{b}$	$\frac{b}{a}$

The quantities are equal if a and b are equal, and unequal otherwise.

22. **(A)** Bank B would have to increase its rate from 4% to 5%, an actual increase of 1%.

This represents a percent increase of $\frac{1\%}{4\%} \times 100\% = 25\%$.

23. **(B)** Assume that the original mixture consists of 20 grams of sugar and 80 grams of cinnamon. If the amount of sugar is doubled, there would be 40 grams of sugar and 80 grams of cinnamon.

The sugar will then comprise $\frac{40}{120} = \frac{1}{3} = 33\frac{1}{3}$% of the mixture.

24. **(D)** If $b = 2$, then $b^2 = 4$, and $2 = 50\%$ of 4; in this case, the quantities are equal. If $b = 4$, $b^2 = 16$, and 4 is not 50% of 16; in this case, the quantities are not equal.

25. **(C)** Avoid the algebra and just assume Ali started with \$100. After giving Lior \$50, she had \$50 left, which was 20% or one-fifth of what he had. So, Lior had 5 × \$50 = \$250, which means that originally he had \$200.
Quantity A: 75% of \$200 = \$150.
Quantity B: 150% of \$100 = \$150.
The quantities are equal.

12-D. RATIOS AND PROPORTIONS

Ratios

A ***ratio*** is a fraction that compares two quantities that are measured in the same units. The first quantity is the numerator and the second quantity is the denominator.

For example, if there are 4 boys and 16 girls on the debate team, we say that the ratio of the number of boys to the number of girls on the team is 4 to 16, or $\frac{4}{16}$. This is often written 4:16. Since a ratio is just a fraction, it can be reduced or converted to a decimal or a percent. The following are all different ways to express the same ratio:

4 to 16 4:16 $\frac{4}{16}$ 2 to 8 2:8 $\frac{2}{8}$ 1 to 4 1:4 $\frac{1}{4}$ 0.25 25%

CAUTION

Saying that the ratio of boys to girls on the team is 1:4 does *not* mean that $\frac{1}{4}$ of the team members are boys. It means that for each boy on the team there are 4 girls; so for every 5 members of the team, there are 4 girls and 1 boy. Boys, therefore, make up $\frac{1}{5}$ of the team, and girls $\frac{4}{5}$.

KEY FACT D1

If a set of objects is divided into two groups in the ratio of a:b, then the first group contains $\frac{a}{a+b}$ of the objects and the second group contains $\frac{b}{a+b}$ of the objects.

EXAMPLE 1

Last year, the ratio of the number of tennis matches that Central College's women's team won to the number of matches they lost was 7:3. What percent of their matches did the team win?

[ ] %

SOLUTION.

The team won $\frac{7}{7+3} = \frac{7}{10}$ = **70%** of their matches.

EXAMPLE 2

If 45% of the students at a college are male, what is the ratio of male students to female students?

$\frac{\square}{\square}$

TIP

In problems involving percents the best number to use is 100.

SOLUTION.

Assume that there are 100 students. Then 45 of them are male, and 100 – 45 = 55 of them are female. So, the ratio of males to females is $\frac{45}{55} = \mathbf{\frac{9}{11}}$.

If we know how many boys and girls there are in a club, then, clearly, we know not only the ratio of boys to girls, but several other ratios too. For example, if the club has 7 boys and 3 girls: the ratio of boys to girls is $\frac{7}{3}$, the ratio of girls to boys is $\frac{3}{7}$, the ratio of boys to members is $\frac{7}{10}$, the ratio of members to girls is $\frac{10}{3}$, and so on.

However, if we know a ratio, we *cannot* determine how many objects there are. For example, if a jar contains only red and blue marbles, and if the ratio of red marbles to blue marbles is 3:5, there *may* be 3 red marbles and 5 blue marbles, but *not necessarily.* There may be 300 red marbles and 500 blue ones, since the ratio 300:500 reduces to 3:5. In the same way, all of the following are possibilities for the distribution of marbles.

Red	6	12	33	51	150	3,000	$3x$
Blue	10	20	55	85	250	5,000	$5x$

The important thing to observe is that the number of red marbles can be *any* multiple of 3, as long as the number of blue marbles is the *same* multiple of 5.

KEY FACT D2

If two numbers are in the ratio of $a:b$, then for some number x, the first number is ax and the second number is bx. If the ratio is in lowest terms, and if the quantities must be integers, then x is also an integer.

TACTIC

In any ratio problem, write the letter x after each number and use some given information to solve for x.

EXAMPLE 3

If the ratio of men to women in a particular dormitory is 5:3, which of the following could not be the number of residents in the dormitory?

Ⓐ 24 Ⓑ 40 Ⓒ 96 Ⓓ 150 Ⓔ 224

SOLUTION.

If $5x$ and $3x$ are the number of men and women in the dormitory, respectively, then the number of residents in the dormitory is $5x + 3x = 8x$. So, the number of students must be a multiple of 8. Of the five choices, only **150** (**D**) is not divisible by 8.

NOTE: Assume that the ratio of the number of pounds of cole slaw to the number of pounds of potato salad consumed in the dormitory's cafeteria was 5:3. Then, it is possible that a total of exactly 150 pounds was eaten: 93.75 pounds of cole slaw and 56.25 pounds of potato salad. In Example 3, 150 wasn't possible because there had to be a *whole* number of men and women.

EXAMPLE 4

The measures of the two acute angles in a right triangle are in the ratio of 5:13. What is the measure of the larger angle?

Ⓐ 25° Ⓑ 45° Ⓒ 60° Ⓓ 65° Ⓔ 75°

SOLUTION.

Let the measure of the smaller angle be $5x$ and the measure of the larger angle be $13x$. Since the sum of the measures of the two acute angles of a right triangle is 90° (KEY FACT J1, page 456), $5x + 13x = 90 \Rightarrow 18x = 90 \Rightarrow x = 5$.

Therefore, the measure of the larger angle is $13 \times 5 =$ **65° (D)**.

Ratios can be extended to three or four or more terms. For example, we can say that the ratio of freshmen to sophomores to juniors to seniors in a college marching band is 6:8:5:8, which means that for every 6 freshmen in the band there are 8 sophomores, 5 juniors, and 8 seniors.

TIP

TACTIC D1 applies to extended ratios, as well.

EXAMPLE 5

The concession stand at Cinema City sells popcorn in three sizes: large, super, and jumbo. One day, Cinema City sold 240 bags of popcorn, and the ratio of large to super to jumbo was 8:17:15. How many super bags of popcorn were sold that day?

SOLUTION.

Let $8x$, $17x$, and $15x$ be the number of large, super, and jumbo bags of popcorn sold, respectively. Then $8x + 17x + 15x = 240 \Rightarrow 40x = 240 \Rightarrow x = 6$.

The number of super bags sold was $17 \times 6 =$ **102**.

KEY FACT D3

KEY FACT D1 applies to extended ratios, as well. If a set of objects is divided into 3 groups in the ratio $a{:}b{:}c$, then the first group contains $\frac{a}{a+b+c}$ of the objects, the second $\frac{b}{a+b+c}$, and the third $\frac{c}{a+b+c}$.

EXAMPLE 6

If the ratio of large to super to jumbo bags of popcorn sold at Cinema City was 8:17:15, what percent of the bags sold were super?

Ⓐ 20% Ⓑ 25% Ⓒ $33\frac{1}{3}$% Ⓓ 37.5% Ⓔ 42.5%

SOLUTION.

Super bags made up $\frac{17}{8+17+15} = \frac{17}{40} =$ **42.5%** of the total **(E)**.

A jar contains a number of red (R), white (W), and blue (B) marbles. Suppose that R:W = 2:3 and W:B = 3:5. Then, for every 2 red marbles, there are 3 white ones, and for those 3 white ones, there are 5 blue ones. So, R:B = 2:5, and we can form the extended ratio R:W:B = 2:3:5.

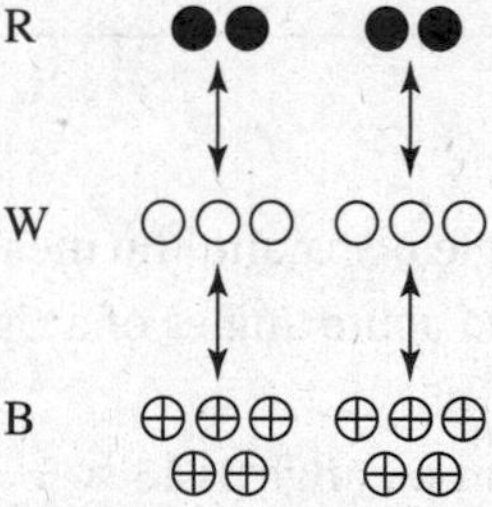

If the ratios were R:W = 2:3 and W:B = 4:5, however, we wouldn't be able to combine them as easily. From the diagram below, you see that for every 8 reds there are 15 blues, so R:B = 8:15.

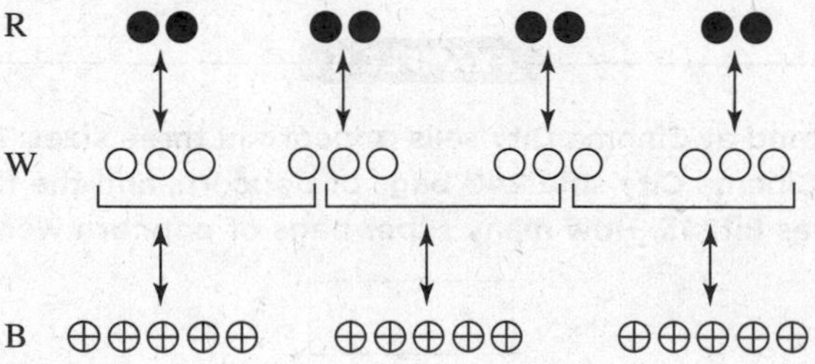

To see this without drawing a picture, we write the ratios as fractions: $\frac{R}{W} = \frac{2}{3}$ and $\frac{W}{B} = \frac{4}{5}$. Then, we multiply the fractions:

$$\frac{R}{\cancel{W}} \times \frac{\cancel{W}}{B} = \frac{2}{3} \times \frac{4}{5} = \frac{8}{15}, \quad \text{so} \quad \frac{R}{B} = \frac{8}{15}$$

Not only does this give us R:B = 8:15, but also, if we multiply both W numbers, $3 \times 4 = 12$, we can write the extended ratio: R:W:B = 8:12:15.

EXAMPLE 7

Jar A and jar B each have 70 marbles, all of which are red, white, or blue.
In jar A, R:W = 2:3 and W:B = 3:5.
In jar B, R:W = 2:3 and W:B = 4:5.

Quantity A	Quantity B
The number of white marbles in jar A	The number of white marbles in jar B

SOLUTION.
From the discussion immediately preceding this example, in jar A the extended ratio R:W:B is 2:3:5, which implies that the white marbles constitute $\frac{3}{2+3+5} = \frac{3}{10}$ of the total: $\frac{3}{10} \times 70 = \mathbf{21}$.

In jar B the extended ratio R:W:B is 8:12:15, so the white marbles are $\frac{12}{8+12+15} = \frac{12}{35}$ of the total: $\frac{12}{35} \times 70 = \mathbf{24}$. The answer is **B**.

Proportions

A ***proportion*** is an equation that states that two ratios are equivalent. Since ratios are just fractions, any equation such as $\frac{4}{6} = \frac{10}{15}$ in which each side is a single fraction is a proportion. Usually the proportions you encounter on the GRE involve one or more variables.

TACTIC
D2

Solve proportions by cross-multiplying: if $\frac{a}{b} = \frac{c}{d}$, then $ad = bc$.

Setting up a proportion is a common way of solving a problem on the GRE.

EXAMPLE 8

If $\frac{3}{7} = \frac{x}{84}$, what is the value of x?

SOLUTION.
Cross-multiply: $3(84) = 7x \Rightarrow 252 = 7x \Rightarrow x = \mathbf{36}$.

EXAMPLE 9

If $\frac{x+2}{17} = \frac{x}{16}$, what is the value of $\frac{x+6}{19}$?

Ⓐ $\frac{1}{2}$ Ⓑ 1 Ⓒ $\frac{3}{2}$ Ⓓ 2 Ⓔ 3

SOLUTION.
Cross-multiply: $16(x + 2) = 17x \Rightarrow 16x + 32 = 17x \Rightarrow x = 32$.

So, $\frac{x+6}{19} = \frac{32+6}{19} = \frac{38}{19} = \mathbf{2}$ **(D)**.

EXAMPLE 10

A state law requires that on any field trip the ratio of the number of chaperones to the number of students must be at least 1:12. If 100 students are going on a field trip, what is the minimum number of chaperones required?

Ⓐ 6 Ⓑ 8 Ⓒ $8\frac{1}{3}$ Ⓓ 9 Ⓔ 12

SOLUTION.
Let x represent the number of chaperones required, and set up a proportion: $\frac{\text{number of chaperones}}{\text{number of students}} = \frac{1}{12} = \frac{x}{100}$. Cross-multiply: $100 = 12x \Rightarrow x = 8\frac{1}{3}$. This, of course, is *not* the answer since, clearly, the number of chaperones must be a whole number. Since x is greater than 8, 8 chaperones would not be enough. The answer is **9 (D)**.

Rates

TIP

A rate can always be written as a fraction.

A ***rate*** is a fraction that compares two quantities measured in different units. The word "per" often appears in rate problems: miles per hour, dollars per week, cents per ounce, students per classroom, and so on.

TACTIC

Set up rate problems just like ratio problems. Solve the proportions by cross-multiplying.

EXAMPLE 11

Brigitte solved 24 math problems in 15 minutes. At this rate, how many problems can she solve in 40 minutes?

Ⓐ 25 Ⓑ 40 Ⓒ 48 Ⓓ 60 Ⓔ 64

SOLUTION.

Handle this rate problem exactly like a ratio problem. Set up a proportion and cross-multiply:

$$\frac{\text{problems}}{\text{minutes}} = \frac{24}{15} = \frac{x}{40} \Rightarrow 15x = 40 \times 24 = 960 \Rightarrow x = \mathbf{64\ (E)}$$

When the denominator in the given rate is 1 unit (1 minute, 1 mile, 1 dollar), the problem can be solved by a single division or multiplication. Consider Examples 12 and 13.

EXAMPLE 12

If Stefano types at the rate of 35 words per minute, how long will it take him to type 987 words?

SOLUTION.

Set up a proportion and cross-multiply:

$$\frac{\text{words typed}}{\text{minutes}} = \frac{35}{1} = \frac{987}{x} \Rightarrow 35x = 987 \Rightarrow x = \frac{987}{35} = \mathbf{28.2}\text{ minutes}$$

EXAMPLE 13

If Mario types at the rate of 35 words per minute, how many words can he type in 85 minutes?

SOLUTION.

Set up a proportion and cross-multiply:

$$\frac{\text{words typed}}{\text{minutes}} = \frac{35}{1} = \frac{x}{85} \Rightarrow x = 35 \times 85 = \mathbf{2{,}975}\text{ words}$$

Notice that in Example 12, all we did was divide 987 by 35, and in Example 13, we multiplied 35 by 85. If you realize that, you don't have to introduce x and set up a proportion. You must know, however, whether to multiply or divide. If you're not absolutely positive which is correct, write the proportion; then you can't go wrong.

CAUTION

In rate problems it is essential that the units in both fractions be the same.

EXAMPLE 14

If 3 apples cost 50¢, how many apples can you buy for $20?

Ⓐ 20 Ⓑ 60 Ⓒ 120 Ⓓ 600 Ⓔ 2,000

SOLUTION.

We have to set up a proportion, but it is *not* $\frac{3}{50} = \frac{x}{20}$. In the first fraction, the denominator represents *cents,* whereas in the second fraction, the denominator represents *dollars.* The units must be the same. We can change 50 cents to 0.5 dollar or we can change 20 dollars to 2000 cents:

$$\frac{3}{50} = \frac{x}{2{,}000} \Rightarrow 50x = 6{,}000 \Rightarrow x = \mathbf{120} \text{ apples (C)}$$

On the GRE, some rate problems involve only variables. They are handled in exactly the same way.

EXAMPLE 15

If *a* apples cost *c* cents, how many apples can be bought for *d* dollars?

Ⓐ $100acd$ Ⓑ $\frac{100d}{ac}$ Ⓒ $\frac{ad}{100c}$ Ⓓ $\frac{c}{100ad}$ Ⓔ $\frac{100ad}{c}$

SOLUTION.

First change *d* dollars to 100*d* cents, and set up a proportion: $\frac{\text{apples}}{\text{cents}} = \frac{a}{c} = \frac{x}{100d}$.

Now cross-multiply: $100ad = cx \Rightarrow x = \frac{\mathbf{100ad}}{c}$ (E).

Most students find problems such as Example 15 very difficult. If you get stuck on such a problem, use TACTIC 2, Chapter 9, page 270, which gives another strategy for handling these problems.

Notice that in rate problems, as one quantity increases or decreases, so does the other. If you are driving at 45 miles per hour, the more hours you drive, the further you go; if you drive fewer miles, it takes less time. If chopped meat costs $3.00 per pound, the less you spend, the fewer pounds you get; the more meat you buy, the more it costs.

In some problems, however, as one quantity increases, the other decreases. These *cannot* be solved by setting up a proportion. Consider the following two examples, which look similar but must be handled differently.

Direct and Indirect Variation

EXAMPLE 16

A hospital needs 150 pills to treat 6 patients for a week. How many pills does it need to treat 10 patients for a week?

SOLUTION.

Example 16 is a standard rate problem. The more patients there are, the more pills are needed.

The *ratio* or *quotient* remains constant: $\frac{150}{6} = \frac{x}{10} \Rightarrow 6x = 1{,}500 \Rightarrow x = \mathbf{250}$.

Rate problems, such as Example 16, are examples of ***direct variation.*** We say that one variable ***varies directly*** with a second variable if their quotient is a constant. In Example 16, the number of pills needed varies directly with the number of patients.

EXAMPLE 17

A hospital has enough pills on hand to treat 10 patients for 14 days. How long will the pills last if there are 35 patients?

SOLUTION.

In Example 17, the situation is different. With more patients, the supply of pills will last for a shorter period of time; if there were fewer patients, the supply would last longer. It is not the ratio that remains constant, it is the *product.*

There are enough pills to last for $10 \times 14 = 140$ patient-days:

$$\frac{140 \text{ patient-days}}{10 \text{ patients}} = 14 \text{ days} \qquad \frac{140 \text{ patient-days}}{35 \text{ patients}} = 4 \text{ days}$$

$$\frac{140 \text{ patient-days}}{70 \text{ patients}} = 2 \text{ days} \qquad \frac{140 \text{ patient-days}}{1 \text{ patient}} = 140 \text{ days}$$

Problems, such as Example 17, are examples of ***indirect variation.*** We say that one variable ***varies indirectly*** with a second variable if their product is a constant. In Example 17, the number of days the pills will last varies indirectly with the number of patients.

TACTIC

If one quantity increases as a second quantity decreases, multiply them; their product will be a constant.

EXAMPLE 18

If 15 workers can pave a certain number of driveways in 24 days, how many days will 40 workers take, working at the same rate, to do the same job?

Ⓐ 6 Ⓑ 9 Ⓒ 15 Ⓓ 24 Ⓔ 40

SOLUTION.

Clearly, the more workers there are, the less time it will take, so use TACTIC D4: multiply. The job takes $15 \times 24 = 360$ worker-days:

$$\frac{360 \text{ worker-days}}{40 \text{ workers}} = \mathbf{9} \text{ days } \mathbf{(B)}$$

Note that it doesn't matter how many driveways have to be paved, as long as the 15 workers and the 40 workers are doing the same job. Even if the question had said, "15 workers can pave 18 driveways in 24 days," the number 18 would not have entered into the solution. This number would be important only if the second group of workers was going to pave a different number of driveways.

EXAMPLE 19

If 15 workers can pave 18 driveways in 24 days, how many days would it take 40 workers to pave 22 driveways?

Ⓐ 6 Ⓑ 9 Ⓒ 11 Ⓓ 15 Ⓔ 18

SOLUTION.

This question is similar to Example 18, except that now the jobs that the two groups of workers are doing are different. The solution, however, starts out exactly the same way. Just as in Example 18, 40 workers can do in 9 days the *same* job that 15 workers can do in 24 days. Since that job is to pave 18 driveways, 40 workers can pave $18 \div 9 = 2$ driveways every day. So, it will take **11** days for them to pave 22 driveways **(C)**.

PRACTICE EXERCISES—RATIOS AND PROPORTIONS

Discrete Quantitative Questions

1. If $\frac{3}{4}$ of the employees in a supermarket are not college graduates, what is the ratio of the number of college graduates to those who are not college graduates?

   Ⓐ 1:3
   Ⓑ 3:7
   Ⓒ 3:4
   Ⓓ 4:3
   Ⓔ 3:1

2. If $\frac{a}{9} = \frac{10}{2a}$, what is the value of a^2?

   Ⓐ $3\sqrt{6}$
   Ⓑ $3\sqrt{5}$
   Ⓒ $9\sqrt{6}$
   Ⓓ 45
   Ⓔ 90

3. If 80% of the applicants to a program were rejected, what is the ratio of the number accepted to the number rejected?

   $\frac{\square}{\square}$

4. Scott can read 50 pages per hour. At this rate, how many pages can he read in 50 minutes?

   Ⓐ 25
   Ⓑ $41\frac{2}{3}$
   Ⓒ $45\frac{1}{2}$
   Ⓓ 48
   Ⓔ 60

5. If all the members of a team are juniors or seniors, and if the ratio of juniors to seniors on the team is 3:5, what percent of the team members are seniors?

   Ⓐ 37.5%
   Ⓑ 40%
   Ⓒ 60%
   Ⓓ 62.5%
   Ⓔ It cannot be determined from the information given.

6. The measures of the three angles in a triangle are in the ratio of 1:1:2. Which of the following statements must be true?

   Indicate *all* such statements.

   [A] The triangle is isosceles.
   [B] The triangle is a right triangle.
   [C] The triangle is equilateral.

7. What is the ratio of the circumference of a circle to its radius?

   Ⓐ 1
   Ⓑ $\frac{\pi}{2}$
   Ⓒ $\sqrt{\pi}$
   Ⓓ π
   Ⓔ 2π

8. The ratio of the number of freshmen to sophomores to juniors to seniors on a college basketball team is 4:7:6:8. What percent of the team are sophomores?

   Ⓐ 16%
   Ⓑ 24%
   Ⓒ 25%
   Ⓓ 28%
   Ⓔ 32%

9. At Central State College the ratio of the number of students taking Spanish to the number taking French is 7:2. If 140 students are taking French, how many are taking Spanish?

[ ] students

10. If $a{:}b = 3{:}5$ and $a{:}c = 5{:}7$, what is the value of $b{:}c$?

Ⓐ 3:7
Ⓑ 21:35
Ⓒ 21:25
Ⓓ 25:21
Ⓔ 7:3

11. If x is a positive number and $\frac{x}{3} = \frac{12}{x}$, then $x =$

Ⓐ 3
Ⓑ 4
Ⓒ 6
Ⓓ 12
Ⓔ 36

12. In the diagram below, $b{:}a = 7{:}2$. What is $b - a$?

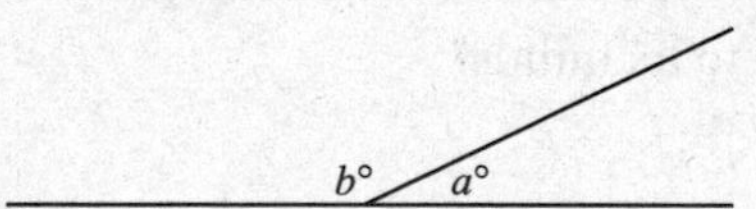

Ⓐ 20
Ⓑ 70
Ⓒ 100
Ⓓ 110
Ⓔ 160

13. A snail can move i inches in m minutes. At this rate, how many feet can it move in h hours?

Ⓐ $\frac{5hi}{m}$
Ⓑ $\frac{60hi}{m}$
Ⓒ $\frac{hi}{12m}$
Ⓓ $\frac{5m}{hi}$
Ⓔ $5him$

14. Gilda can grade t tests in $\frac{1}{x}$ hours. At this rate, how many tests can she grade in x hours?

Ⓐ tx
Ⓑ tx^2
Ⓒ $\frac{1}{t}$
Ⓓ $\frac{x}{t}$
Ⓔ $\frac{1}{tx}$

15. A club had 3 boys and 5 girls. During a membership drive the same number of boys and girls joined the club. How many members does the club have now if the ratio of boys to girls is 3:4?

Ⓐ 12
Ⓑ 14
Ⓒ 16
Ⓓ 21
Ⓔ 28

16. If $\frac{3x-1}{25} = \frac{x+5}{11}$, what is the value of x?

Ⓐ $\frac{3}{4}$
Ⓑ 3
Ⓒ 7
Ⓓ 17
Ⓔ 136

17. If 4 boys can shovel a driveway in 2 hours, how many minutes will it take 5 boys to do the job?

Ⓐ 60
Ⓑ 72
Ⓒ 96
Ⓓ 120
Ⓔ 150

18. If 500 pounds of mush will feed 20 pigs for a week, for how many days will 200 pounds of mush feed 14 pigs?

[ ]

Quantitative Comparison Questions

Ⓐ Quantity A is greater.
Ⓑ Quantity B is greater.
Ⓒ The two quantities are equal.
Ⓓ It is impossible to determine which quantity is greater.

19.

The ratio of red to blue marbles in a jar was 3:5. The same number of red and blue marbles were added to the jar.

Quantity A	Quantity B
The ratio of red to blue marbles now	3:5

20.

Three associates agreed to split the $3,000 profit of an investment in the ratio of 2:5:8.

Quantity A	Quantity B
The difference between the largest and the smallest share	$1,200

21.

The ratio of the number of boys to girls in the chess club is 5:2. The ratio of the number of boys to girls in the glee club is 11:4.

Quantity A	Quantity B
The number of boys in the chess club	The number of boys in the glee club

22.

Sally invited the same number of boys and girls to her party. Everyone who was invited came, but 5 additional boys showed up. This caused the ratio of girls to boys at the party to be 4:5.

Quantity A	Quantity B
The number of people she invited to her party	40

23.

A large jar is full of marbles. When a single marble is drawn at random from the jar, the probability that it is red is $\frac{3}{7}$.

Quantity A	Quantity B
The ratio of the number of red marbles to non-red marbles in the jar	$\frac{1}{2}$

24.

$3a = 2b$ and $3b = 5c$

Quantity A	Quantity B
The ratio of a to c	1

25.

The radius of circle II is 3 times the radius of circle I

Quantity A	Quantity B
$\frac{\text{area of circle II}}{\text{area of circle I}}$	3π

ANSWER KEY

1. **A**	6. **A, B**	12. **C**	18. **4**	24. **A**
2. **D**	7. **E**	13. **A**	19. **A**	25. **B**
3. $\frac{1}{4}$	8. **D**	14. **B**	20. **C**	
	9. **490**	15. **B**	21. **D**	
4. **B**	10. **D**	16. **D**	22. **C**	
5. **D**	11. **C**	17. **C**	23. **A**	

ANSWER EXPLANATIONS

1. **(A)** Of every 4 employees, 3 are not college graduates, and 1 is a college graduate. So the ratio of graduates to nongraduates is 1:3.

2. **(D)** Cross-multiplying, we get: $2a^2 = 90 \Rightarrow a^2 = 45$.

3. $\frac{1}{4}$ If 80% were rejected, 20% were accepted, and the ratio of accepted to rejected is 20:80 = 1:4.

4. **(B)** Set up a proportion: $\frac{50 \text{ pages}}{1 \text{ hour}} = \frac{50 \text{ pages}}{60 \text{ minutes}} = \frac{x \text{ pages}}{50 \text{ minutes}}$,

   and cross-multiply: $50 \times 50 = 60x \Rightarrow 2{,}500 = 60x \Rightarrow x = 41\frac{2}{3}$.

5. **(D)** Out of every 8 team members, 3 are juniors and 5 are seniors. Seniors, therefore, make up $\frac{5}{8} = 62.5\%$ of the team.

6. **(A, B)** It is worth remembering that if the ratio of the measures of the angles of a triangle is 1:1:2, the angles are 45-45-90 (see Section 12-J, page 456). Otherwise, the first step is to write $x + x + 2x = 180 \Rightarrow 4x = 180 \Rightarrow x = 45$.

   Since two of the angles have the same measure, the triangle is isosceles, and since one of the angles measures 90°, it is a right triangle. I and II are true, and, of course, III is false.

7. **(E)** By definition, π is the ratio of the circumference to the diameter of a circle (see Section 12-L, page 488). Therefore, $\pi = \frac{C}{d} = \frac{C}{2r} \Rightarrow 2\pi = \frac{C}{r}$.

8. **(D)** The *fraction* of the team that is sophomores is $\frac{7}{4+7+6+8} = \frac{7}{25}$, and $\frac{7}{25} \times 100\% = 28\%$.

9. **490** Let the number of students taking Spanish be $7x$, and the number taking French be $2x$. Then, $2x = 140 \Rightarrow x = 70 \Rightarrow 7x = 490$.

10. **(D)** Since $\frac{a}{b} = \frac{3}{5}$, $\frac{b}{a} = \frac{5}{3}$. So, $b{:}c = \frac{b}{c} = \frac{b}{\cancel{a}_1} \times \frac{\cancel{a}^1}{c} = \frac{5}{3} \times \frac{5}{7} = \frac{25}{21} = 25{:}21$.

    Alternatively, we could write equivalent ratios with the same value for a:

    $$a{:}b = 3{:}5 = 15{:}25 \text{ and } a{:}c = 5{:}7 = 15{:}21$$

    So, when $a = 15$, $b = 25$, and $c = 21$.

11. **(C)** To solve a proportion, cross-multiply: $\frac{x}{3} = \frac{12}{x} \Rightarrow x^2 = 36 \Rightarrow x = 6$.

12. **(C)** Let $b = 7x$ and $a = 2x$. Then, $7x + 2x = 180 \Rightarrow 9x = 180 \Rightarrow x = 20 \Rightarrow b = 140$ and $a = 40 \Rightarrow b - a = 140 - 40 = 100$.

13. **(A)** Set up the proportion, keeping track of units:

$$\frac{x \text{ feet}}{h \text{ hours}} = \frac{\overset{1}{\cancel{12}}x \text{ inches}}{\underset{5}{\cancel{60}}h \text{ minutes}} = \frac{i \text{ inches}}{m \text{ minutes}} \Rightarrow \frac{x}{5h} = \frac{i}{m} \Rightarrow x = \frac{5hi}{m}$$

14. **(B)** Gilda grades at the rate of $\frac{t \text{ tests}}{\frac{1}{x}\text{hours}} = \frac{tx \text{ tests}}{1 \text{ hour}}$.

Since she can grade tx tests each hour, in x hours she can grade $x(tx) = tx^2$ tests.

15. **(B)** Suppose that x boys and x girls joined the club. Then, the new ratio of boys to girls would be $(3 + x):(5 + x)$, which we are told is 3:4.

So, $\frac{3+x}{5+x} = \frac{3}{4} \Rightarrow 4(3 + x) = 3(5 + x) \Rightarrow 12 + 4x = 15 + 3x \Rightarrow x = 3$.

Therefore, 3 boys and 3 girls joined the other 3 boys and 5 girls: a total of 14.

16. **(D)** Cross-multiplying, we get:

$$11(3x - 1) = 25(x + 5) \Rightarrow 33x - 11 = 25x + 125 \Rightarrow 8x = 136 \Rightarrow x = 17$$

17. **(C)** Since 4 boys can shovel the driveway in 2 hours, or $2 \times 60 = 120$ minutes, the job takes $4 \times 120 = 480$ boy-minutes; and so 5 boys would need

$$\frac{480 \text{ boy-minutes}}{5 \text{ boys}} = 96 \text{ minutes}$$

18. **4** Since 500 pounds will last for 20 pig-weeks = 140 pig-days, 200 pounds will last for $\frac{2}{5} \times 140$ pig-days = 56 pig-days, and $\frac{56 \text{ pig-days}}{14 \text{ pigs}} = 4$ days.

19. **(A)** Assume that to start there were $3x$ red marbles and $5x$ blue ones and that y of each color were added.

	Quantity A	Quantity B
	$\frac{3x+y}{5x+y}$	$\frac{3}{5}$
Cross-multiply:	$5(3x + y)$	$3(5x + y)$
Distribute:	$15x + 5y$	$15x + 3y$
Subtract $15x$:	$5y$	$3y$

Since y is positive, Quantity A is greater.

20. **(C)** The shares are $2x$, $5x$, and $8x$, and their sum is 3,000:

$$2x + 5x + 8x = 3{,}000 \Rightarrow 15x = 3{,}000 \Rightarrow x = 200, \text{ and so } 8x - 2x = 6x = 1{,}200$$

21. **(D)** Ratios alone can't answer the question, "How many?" There could be 5 boys in the chess club or 500. We can't tell.

22. **(C)** Assume that Sally invited x boys and x girls. When she wound up with x girls and $x + 5$ boys, the girl:boy ratio was 4:5. So,

$$\frac{x}{x+5} = \frac{4}{5} \Rightarrow 5x = 4x + 20 \Rightarrow x = 20$$

Sally invited 40 people (20 boys and 20 girls).

23. **(A)** If the probability of drawing a red marble is $\frac{3}{7}$, 3 out of every 7 marbles are red, and 4 out of every 7 are non-red. So the ratio of red:non-red = 3:4, which is greater than $\frac{1}{2}$.

24. **(A)** Multiplying the first equation by 3 and the second by 2 to get the same coefficient of b, we have: $9a = 6b$ and $6b = 10c$. So, $9a = 10c$ and $\frac{a}{c} = \frac{10}{9}$.

25. **(B)** Assume the radius of circle I is 1 and the radius of circle II is 3. Then the areas are π and 9π, respectively. So, the area of circle II is 9 times the area of circle I, and $3\pi > 9$.

12-E. AVERAGES AND STATISTICS

Averages

The ***average*** of a set of n numbers is the sum of those numbers divided by n.

$$\text{average} = \frac{\text{sum of the } n \text{ numbers}}{n} \quad \text{or simply} \quad A = \frac{\text{sum}}{n}$$

If the weights of three children are 80, 90, and 76 pounds, respectively, to calculate the average weight of the children, you would add the three weights and divide by 3:

$$\frac{80+90+76}{3} = \frac{246}{3} = 82$$

The technical name for this type of average is "***arithmetic mean***," and on the GRE those words always appear in parentheses—for example, "What is the average (arithmetic mean) of 80, 90, and 76?"

TIP

On the GRE, you can ignore the words "arithmetic mean." They simply mean "average."

Usually, on the GRE, you are not asked to find an average; rather, you are given the average of a set of numbers and asked for some other information. The key to solving all of these problems is to first find the sum of the numbers. Since $A = \frac{\text{sum}}{n}$, multiplying both sides by n yields the equation: sum = nA.

TACTIC

E1

If you know the average, A, of a set of n numbers, multiply A by n to get their sum.

EXAMPLE 1

One day a supermarket received a delivery of 25 frozen turkeys. If the average (arithmetic mean) weight of a turkey was 14.2 pounds, what was the total weight, in pounds, of all the turkeys?

TIP

Many GRE problems involving averages can be solved using TACTIC E1: sum = *nA*

SOLUTION.

Use TACTIC E1: 25 × 14.2 = **355**.

NOTE: We do not know how much any individual turkey weighed nor how many turkeys weighed more or less than 14.2 pounds. All we know is their total weight.

EXAMPLE 2

Sheila took five chemistry tests during the semester and the average (arithmetic mean) of her test scores was 85. If her average after the first three tests was 83, what was the average of her fourth and fifth tests?

Ⓐ 83 Ⓑ 85 Ⓒ 87 Ⓓ 88 Ⓔ 90

SOLUTION.

- Use TACTIC E1: On her five tests, Sheila earned $5 \times 85 = 425$ points.
- Use TACTIC E1 again: On her first three tests she earned $3 \times 83 = 249$ points.
- Subtract: On her last two tests Sheila earned $425 - 249 = 176$ points.
- Calculate her average on her last two tests: $\frac{176}{2}$ = **88 (D)**.

NOTE: We cannot determine Sheila's grade on even one of the tests.

KEY FACT E1

- **If all the numbers in a set are the same, then that number is the average.**
- **If the numbers in a set are not all the same, then the average must be greater than the smallest number and less than the largest number. Equivalently, at least one of the numbers is less than the average and at least one is greater.**

If Jessica's test grades are 85, 85, 85, and 85, her average is 85. If Gary's test grades are 76, 83, 88, and 88, his average must be greater than 76 and less than 88. What can we conclude if, after taking five tests, Kristen's average is 90? We know that she earned exactly $5 \times 90 = 450$ points, and that either she got a 90 on every test or at least one grade was less than 90 and at least one was over 90. Here are a few of the thousands of possibilities for Kristen's grades:

(a) 90, 90, 90, 90, 90
(b) 80, 90, 90, 90, 100
(c) 83, 84, 87, 97, 99
(d) 77, 88, 93, 95, 97
(e) 50, 100, 100, 100, 100

In (b), 80, the one grade below 90, is *10 points below,* and 100, the one grade above 90, is *10 points above.* In (c), 83 is 7 points below 90, 84 is 6 points below 90, and 87 is 3 points below 90, for a total of $7 + 6 + 3 =$ *16 points below 90*; 97 is 7 points above 90, and 99 is 9 points above 90, for a total of $7 + 9 =$ *16 points above 90.*

These differences from the average are called ***deviations***, and the situation in these examples is not a coincidence.

KEY FACT E2

The total deviation below the average is equal to the total deviation above the average.

EXAMPLE 3

If the average (arithmetic mean) of 25, 31, and x is 37, what is the value of x?

SOLUTION 1.
Use KEY FACT E2. Since 25 is 12 less than 37 and 31 is 6 less than 37, the total deviation below the average is 12 + 6 = 18. Therefore, the total deviation above must also be 18. So, $x = 37 + 18 = \mathbf{55}$.

SOLUTION 2.
Use TACTIC E1. Since the average of the three numbers is 37, the sum of the 3 numbers is $3 \times 37 = 111$. Then,

$$25 + 31 + x = 111 \Rightarrow 56 + x = 111 \Rightarrow x = \mathbf{55}$$

KEY FACT E3

Assume that the average of a set of numbers is *A*. If a number x is added to the set and a new average is calculated, then the new average will be less than, equal to, or greater than *A*, depending on whether x is less than, equal to, or greater than *A*, respectively.

EXAMPLE 4

Quantity A	Quantity B
The average (arithmetic mean) of the integers from 0 to 12	The average (arithmetic mean) of the integers from 1 to 12

TIP

Remember TACTIC 5 from Chapter 10 (page 296). We don't have to *calculate* the averages, we just have to *compare* them.

SOLUTION 1.
Quantity B is the average of the integers from 1 to 12, which is surely greater than 1. Quantity A is the average of those same 12 numbers and 0. Since the extra number, 0, is less than Quantity B, Quantity A must be *less* [KEY FACT E3]. The answer is **B**.

SOLUTION 2.
Clearly the sum of the 13 integers from 0 to 12 is the same as the sum of the 12 integers from 1 to 12. Since that sum is positive, dividing by 13 yields a smaller quotient than dividing by 12 [KEY FACT B4, page 352].

Although in solving Example 4 we didn't calculate the averages, we could have:

$$0 + 1 + 2 + 3 + 4 + 5 + \mathbf{6} + 7 + 8 + 9 + 10 + 11 + 12 = 78 \text{ and } \frac{78}{13} = 6.$$

$$1 + 2 + 3 + 4 + 5 + \mathbf{6} + \mathbf{7} + 8 + 9 + 10 + 11 + 12 = 78 \text{ and } \frac{78}{12} = 6.5.$$

Notice that the average of the 13 *consecutive* integers 0, 1, ... ,12 is the *middle integer*, **6**, and the average of the 12 *consecutive* integers 1, 2, ... ,12 is the *average of the two middle integers*, **6** and **7**. This is a special case of KEY FACT E4.

KEY FACT E4

Whenever *n* numbers form an arithmetic sequence (one in which the difference between any two consecutive terms is the same): (i) if *n* is odd, the average of the numbers is the middle term in the sequence and (ii) if *n* is even, the average of the numbers is the average of the two middle terms, which is the same as the average of the first and last terms.

For example, in the arithmetic sequence 6, 9, 12, 15, 18, the average is the middle number, **12**; in the sequence 10, 20, 30, 40, 50, 60, the average is **35**, the average of the two middle numbers—30 and 40. Note that 35 is also the average of the first and last terms—10 and 60.

EXAMPLE 5

On Thursday, 20 of the 25 students in a chemistry class took a test and their average was 80. On Friday, the other 5 students took the test, and their average was 90. What was the average (arithmetic mean) for the entire class?

SOLUTION.

The class average is calculated by dividing the sum of all 25 test grades by 25.

- The first 20 students earned a total of: $20 \times 80 = 1{,}600$ points
- The other 5 students earned a total of: $5 \times 90 = 450$ points
- Add: altogether the class earned: $1{,}600 + 450 = 2{,}050$ points
- Calculate the class average: $\frac{2{,}050}{25} = \mathbf{82.}$

Weighted Averages

TIP

Without doing any calculations, you should immediately realize that since the grade of 80 is being given more weight than the grade of 90, the average will be closer to 80 than to 90—certainly less than 85.

Notice that the answer to Example 5 is *not* 85, which is the average of 80 and 90. This is because the averages of 80 and 90 were earned by different numbers of students, and so the two averages had to be given different weights in the calculation. For this reason, this is called a ***weighted average***.

KEY FACT E5

To calculate the weighted average of a set of numbers, multiply each number in the set by the number of times it appears, add all the products, and divide by the total number of numbers in the set.

So, the solution to Example 5 should look like this:

$$\frac{20(80)+5(90)}{25} = \frac{1{,}600+450}{25} = \frac{2{,}050}{25} = 82$$

Problems involving *average speed* will be discussed in Section 11-H, but we mention them briefly here because they are closely related to problems on weighted averages.

EXAMPLE 6

For the first 3 hours of his trip, Justin drove at 50 miles per hour. Then, due to construction delays, he drove at only 40 miles per hour for the next 2 hours. What was his average speed, in miles per hour, for the entire trip?

Ⓐ 40 Ⓑ 43 Ⓒ 46 Ⓓ 48 Ⓔ 50

SOLUTION.

This is just a weighted average:

$$\frac{3(50)+2(40)}{5} = \frac{150+80}{5} = \frac{230}{5} = \mathbf{46}$$

Note that in the fractions above, the numerator is the total distance traveled and the denominator the total time the trip took. This is *always* the way to find an average speed. Consider the following slight variation on Example 6.

EXAMPLE 6A

For the first 100 miles of his trip, Justin drove at 50 miles per hour, and then due to construction delays, he drove at only 40 miles per hour for the next 120 miles. What was his average speed, in miles per hour, for the entire trip?

[ ] miles per hour

SOLUTION.

This is not a *weighted* average. Here we immediately know the total distance traveled, 220 miles. To get the total time the trip took, we find the time for each portion and add: the first 100 miles took 100 ÷ 50 = 2 hours, and the next 120 miles took 120 ÷ 40 = 3 hours. So the average speed was $\frac{220}{5}$ = **44** miles per hour.

Notice that in Example 6, since Justin spent more time traveling at 50 miles per hour than at 40 miles per hour, his average speed was closer to 50; in Example 6a, he spent more time driving at 40 miles per hour than at 50 miles per hour, so his average speed was closer to 40.

Median, Mode, and Range

Three other terms that are associated with averages are ***median, mode,*** and ***range.*** In a set of *n* numbers that are arranged in increasing order, the ***median*** is the middle number (if *n* is odd), or the average of the two middle numbers (if *n* is even). The ***mode*** is the number in the set that occurs most often. The ***range*** is the difference between the greatest number and the least number.

EXAMPLE 7

During a 10-day period, Jorge received the following number of phone calls each day: 2, 3, 9, 3, 5, 7, 7, 11, 7, 6. What is the average (arithmetic mean) of the median, mode, and range of this set of data?

Ⓐ 6.5 Ⓑ 6.75 Ⓒ 7 Ⓓ 7.25 Ⓔ 7.5

SOLUTION.
The first step is to write the data in increasing order:

2, 3, 3, 5, 6, 7, 7, 7, 9, 11

- The median is 6.5, the average of the middle two numbers.
- The mode is 7, the number that appears more times than any other.
- The range is 11 – 2 = 9.
- The average of the median, mode, and range is $\frac{6.5+7+9}{3} = \frac{22.5}{3}$ = **7.5 (E).**

Percentiles

The median is actually a special case of a measure called a ***percentile***. In the same way that the median divides a set of data into two roughly equal groups, percentiles divide a set of data into 100 roughly equal groups. P_{63}, the 63rd percentile, for example, is a number with the property that 63% of the data in the group is less than or equal to that number and the rest of the data is greater than that number. Clearly, percentiles are mainly used for large groups of data—it doesn't make much sense to talk about the 63rd percentile of a set of data with 5 or 10 or 20 numbers in it. When you receive your GRE scores in the mail, you will receive a percentile ranking for each of your scores. If you are told that your Verbal score is at the 63rd percentile, that means that your score was higher than the scores of approximately 63% of all GRE test takers (and, therefore, that your score was lower than those of approximately 37% of GRE test takers).

From the definition of percentile, it follows that the median is exactly the same as the 50th percentile. Another term that is often used in analyzing data is ***quartile***. There are three quartiles, Q_1, Q_2, and Q_3, which divide a set of data into four roughly equal groups. Q_1, Q_2, and Q_3 are called the first, second, and third quartiles and are equal to P_{25}, P_{50}, and P_{75}, respectively. So, if M represents the median, then $M = Q_2 = P_{50}$. A measure that is sometimes used to show how spread out the numbers in a set of data are is the ***interquartile range***, which is defined as the difference between the first and third quartiles: $Q_3 - Q_1$.

Boxplots

The interquartile range shows where the middle half of all the data lies. The interquartile range can be graphically illustrated in a diagram called a ***boxplot***. A boxplot extends from the smallest number in the set of data (S) to the largest number in the set of data (L) and has a box representing the interquartile range. The box, which begins and ends at the first and third quartiles, also shows the location of the median (Q_2). The box may be symmetric about the median, but does not need to be, as is illustrated in the two boxplots, below. The upper boxplot shows the distribution of math SAT scores for all students who took the SAT in 2010, while the lower boxplot shows the distribution of math scores for the students at a very selective college.

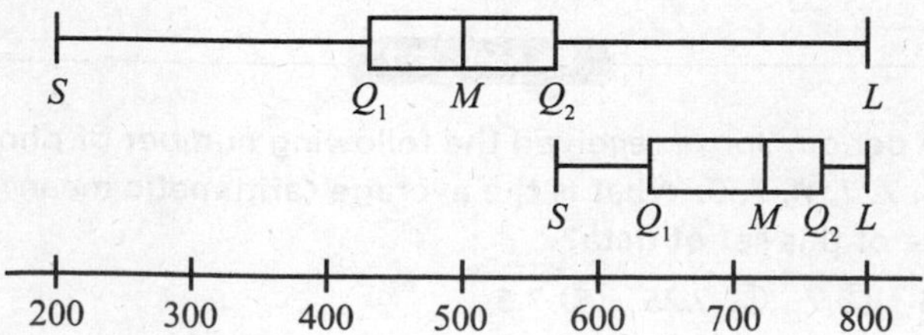

EXAMPLE 8

Twelve hundred 18-year-old boys were weighed, and their weights, in pounds, are summarized in the following boxplot.

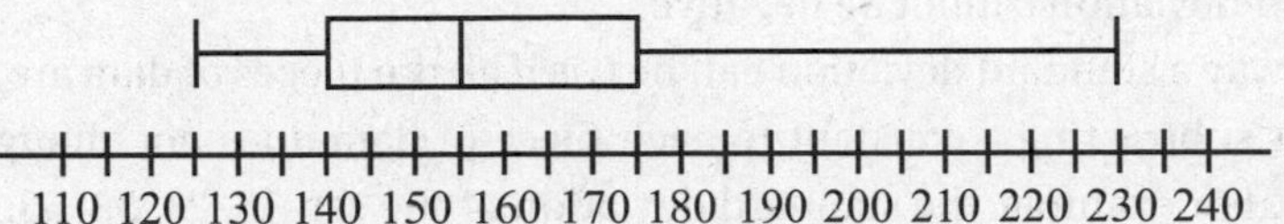

If the 91st percentile of the weights is 200 pounds, approximately how many of the students weigh less than 140 pounds or more than 200 pounds?

Ⓐ 220 Ⓑ 280 Ⓒ 350 Ⓓ 410 Ⓔ 470

SOLUTION.

From the boxplot, we see that the first quartile is 140. So, approximately 25% of the boys weigh less than 140. And since the 91st percentile is 200, approximately 9% of the boys weigh more than 200. So 25% + 9% = 34% of the 1,200 boys fall within the range we are considering.

Finally, 34% of 1,200 = 0.34 × 1,200 = 408, or approximately **410 (D)**.

Standard Deviation

In statistics the ***standard deviation*** is a useful measure that takes a kind of average of how far each piece of data is from the mean. In a distribution in which much of the data is near the mean, the standard deviation tends to be smaller; when the data is more spread out, the standard deviation tends to be larger. It is highly unlikely that you would ever have to calculate a standard deviation on the GRE, but here is how to do it.

Assume a group consists of *n* numerical pieces of data.

STEP 1 Find the mean of the *n* numbers.

STEP 2 Calculate the difference between each of the *n* pieces of data and the mean.

STEP 3 Square each of the *n* differences.

STEP 4 Take the average of the *n* squared differences.

STEP 5 Take the square root of the average just calculated.

EXAMPLE 9

Find the standard deviation of the following five pieces of data:

10, 20, 30, 50, 65

SOLUTION.

- The sum of the five numbers is 175, so the mean is 175 ÷ 5 = 35.
- Calculate the squares of the differences of each number from the mean:

$$(10-35)^2 = (-25)^2 = 625;\ (20-35)^2 = (-15)^2 = 225;\ (30-35)^2 = (-5)^2 = 25;$$
$$(50-35)^2 = (15)^2 = 225;\ (65-35)^2 = (30)^2 = 900$$

- The sum of the five squared differences is 2000, so their average is 2000 ÷ 5 = 400.
- Finally, the standard deviation is 20, the square root of 400.

Here are a few facts about standard deviations you should know:

- A standard deviation cannot be negative.
- The only way a standard deviation can be 0 is if all the pieces of data are the same.
- Adding or subtracting a constant to each piece of data does not change the standard deviation. For example, the standard deviation of the set {13, 23, 33, 53, 68} is 20, since each number in the set is 3 more than each number in the set of data in Example 9.
- Multiplying or dividing each piece of data in a set by a factor greater than 1, multiplies or divides, respectively, the value of the standard deviation by the same factor. For example, the standard deviation of the set {20, 40, 60, 100, 130} is 40, since each number in the set is two times each number in the set of data in Example 9.

Normal Distribution

Sometimes GRE questions about standard deviation concern a ***normal distribution***. The graph of a normal distribution is bell-shaped, symmetrical about the mean (which is approximately equal to both the median and mode). In normal distributions, a little more than two-thirds of the data lie within onc standard deviation of the mean, almost all of it (approximately 95%) lies within two standard deviations of the mean, and essentially all of it lies within three standard deviations of the mean. An example of a normal distribution would be the math SAT scores of all the students who took the SAT on a given date. The mean score is about 500, and the standard deviation is about 100. In the diagram below of a normal distribution, m represents the mean and d represents the standard deviation. The numbers below the letters are the values for the distribution of math SAT scores. The numbers in each region are the percentages of the data that lie in that region. For example, 34% of all students taking the SAT earn between 400 and 500 on the math portion, and only 2.5% of the students earn a score above 700.

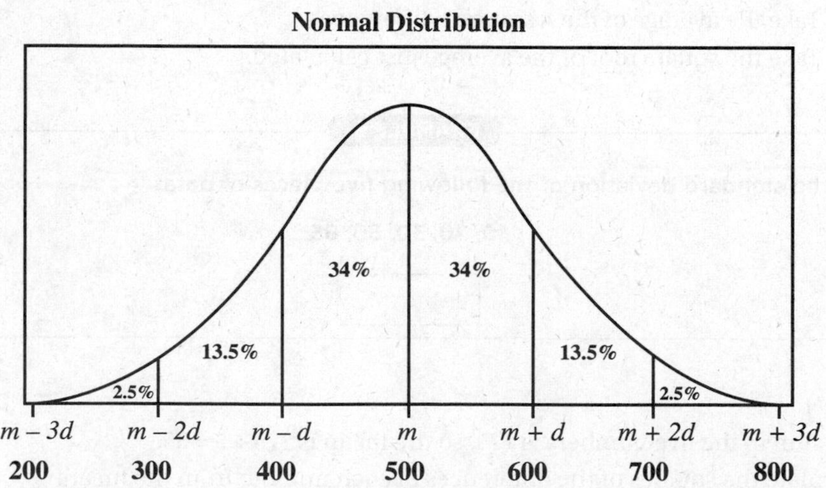

PRACTICE EXERCISES—AVERAGES

Discrete Quantitative Questions

1. Michael's average (arithmetic mean) on 4 tests is 80. What does he need on his fifth test to raise his average to 84?

Ⓐ 82
Ⓑ 84
Ⓒ 92
Ⓓ 96
Ⓔ 100

2. Maryline's average (arithmetic mean) on 4 tests is 80. Assuming she can earn no more than 100 on any test, what is the least she can earn on her fifth test and still have a chance for an 85 average after seven tests?

Ⓐ 60
Ⓑ 70
Ⓒ 75
Ⓓ 80
Ⓔ 85

3. Sandrine's average (arithmetic mean) on 4 tests is 80. Which of the following cannot be the number of tests on which she earned exactly 80 points?

Ⓐ 0
Ⓑ 1
Ⓒ 2
Ⓓ 3
Ⓔ 4

4. What is the average (arithmetic mean) of the positive integers from 1 to 100, inclusive?

Ⓐ 49
Ⓑ 49.5
Ⓒ 50
Ⓓ 50.5
Ⓔ 51

5. If $10a + 10b = 35$, what is the average (arithmetic mean) of a and b?

[ ]

6. If $x + y = 6$, $y + z = 7$, and $z + x = 9$, what is the average (arithmetic mean) of x, y, and z?

Ⓐ $\frac{11}{3}$
Ⓑ $\frac{11}{2}$
Ⓒ $\frac{22}{3}$
Ⓓ 11
Ⓔ 22

7. If the average (arithmetic mean) of 5, 6, 7, and w is 8, what is the value of w?

Ⓐ 8
Ⓑ 12
Ⓒ 14
Ⓓ 16
Ⓔ 24

8. What is the average (arithmetic mean) in degrees of the measures of the five angles in a pentagon?

[ ] degrees

9. If $a + b = 3(c + d)$, which of the following is the average (arithmetic mean) of a, b, c, and d?

Ⓐ $\frac{c+d}{4}$
Ⓑ $\frac{3(c+d)}{8}$
Ⓒ $\frac{c+d}{2}$
Ⓓ $\frac{3(c+d)}{4}$
Ⓔ $c + d$

10. In the diagram below, lines ℓ and m are *not* parallel.

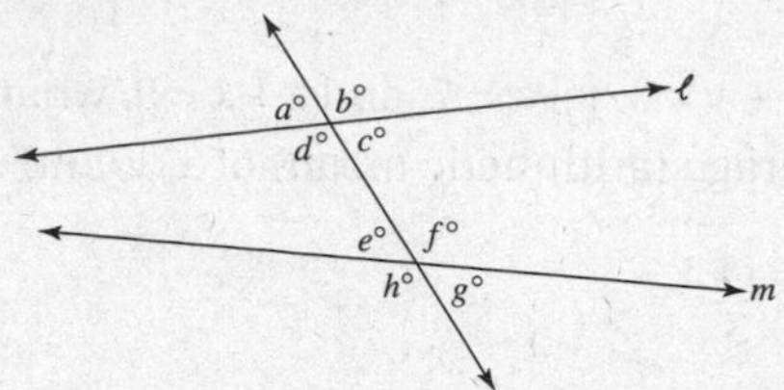

If A represents the average (arithmetic mean) of the degree measures of all eight angles, which of the following is true?

Ⓐ $A = 45$
Ⓑ $45 < A < 90$
Ⓒ $A = 90$
Ⓓ $90 < A < 180$
Ⓔ $A = 180$

11. What is the average (arithmetic mean) of 2^{10} and 2^{20}?

Ⓐ 2^{15}
Ⓑ $2^5 + 2^{10}$
Ⓒ $2^9 + 2^{19}$
Ⓓ 2^{29}
Ⓔ 30

12. Let M be the median and m the mode of the following set of numbers: 10, 70, 20, 40, 70, 90. What is the average (arithmetic mean) of M and m?

Ⓐ 50
Ⓑ 55
Ⓒ 60
Ⓓ 62.5
Ⓔ 65

Quantitative Comparison Questions

Ⓐ Quantity A is greater.
Ⓑ Quantity B is greater.
Ⓒ The two quantities are equal.
Ⓓ It is impossible to determine which quantity is greater.

13.

Quantity A	Quantity B
The average (arithmetic mean) of the measures of the three angles of an equilateral triangle	The average (arithmetic mean) of the measures of the three angles of a right triangle

14.

10 students took a test and the average grade was 80. No one scored exactly 80.

Quantity A	Quantity B
The number of grades over 80	5

15.

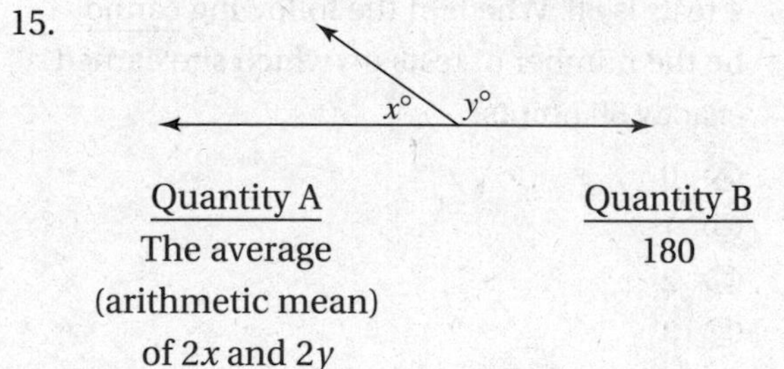

Quantity A	Quantity B
The average (arithmetic mean) of $2x$ and $2y$	180

16.

There are the same number of boys and girls in a club.
The average weight of the boys is 150 pounds.
The average weight of the girls is 110 pounds.

Quantity A	Quantity B
The number of boys weighing over 150	The number of girls weighing over 110

17.

The average (arithmetic mean) of 22, 38, x, and y is 15.

$x > 0$

Quantity A	Quantity B
y	0

18.

List 1: 1, 3, 5, 7, 9

List 2: 11, 13, 15, 17, 19

Quantity A	Quantity B
The standard deviation of the numbers in List 1	The standard deviation of the numbers in List 2

19.

Quantity A	Quantity B
The average (arithmetic mean) of 117, 217, 317	The average (arithmetic mean) of 17, 117, 217, 317

20.

$y > 0$

Quantity A	Quantity B
The average (arithmetic mean) of x and y	The average (arithmetic mean) of x, y, and $2y$

ANSWER KEY

1. **E**	5. **1.75**	9. **E**	13. **C**	17. **B**
2. **C**	6. **A**	10. **C**	14. **D**	18. **C**
3. **D**	7. **C**	11. **C**	15. **C**	19. **A**
4. **D**	8. **108**	12. **D**	16. **D**	20. **D**

ANSWER EXPLANATIONS

1. **(E)** Use TACTIC E1 (page 397). For Michael's average on five tests to be an 84, he needs a total of $5 \times 84 = 420$ points. So far, he has earned $4 \times 80 = 320$ points. Therefore, he needs 100 points more.

2. **(C)** Use TACTIC E1 (page 397). So far, Maryline has earned 320 points. She can survive a low grade on test five if she gets the maximum possible on both the sixth and seventh tests. So, assume she gets two 100s. Then her total for tests 1, 2, 3, 4, 6, and 7 would be 520. For her seven-test average to be 85, she needs a total of $7 \times 85 = 595$ points. Therefore, she needs at least $595 - 520 = 75$ points.

3. **(D)** Since Sandrine's 4-test average is 80, she earned a total of $4 \times 80 = 320$ points. Could Sandrine have earned a total of 320 points with:

0 grades of 80?	Easily; for example, 20, 100, 100, 100 or 60, 70, 90, 100.
1 grade of 80?	Lots of ways; 80, 40, 100, 100, for instance.
2 grades of 80?	Yes; 80, 80, 60, 100.
4 grades of 80?	Sure: 80, 80, 80, 80.
3 grades of 80?	NO! $80 + 80 + 80 + x = 320 \Rightarrow x = 80$, as well.

4. **(D)** Clearly, the sequence of integers from 1 to 100 has 100 terms, and so by KEY FACT E4 (page 400), we know that the average of all the numbers is the average of the two middle ones: 50 and 51. The average, therefore, is 50.5.

5. **1.75** Since $10a + 10b = 35$, dividing both sides of the equation by 10, we get that $a + b = 3.5$. Therefore, the average of a and b is $3.5 \div 2 = 1.75$.

6. **(A)** Whenever a question involves three equations, add them:

$$\begin{array}{r} x + y = 6 \\ y + z = 7 \\ + \quad z + x = 9 \\ \hline 2x + 2y + 2z = 22 \end{array}$$

Divide by 2: $x + y + z = 11$

The average of x, y, and z is $\frac{x+y+z}{3} = \frac{11}{3}$.

7. **(C)** Use TACTIC E1 (page 397): the sum of the 4 numbers is 4 times their average:

$$5 + 6 + 7 + w = 4 \times 8 = 32 \Rightarrow 18 + w = 32 \Rightarrow w = 14$$

8. **108** The average of the measures of the five angles is the sum of their measures divided by 5. The sum is $(5 - 2) \times 180 = 3 \times 180 = 540$ (see Section 12-K, page 473). So, the average is $540 \div 5 = 108$.

9. **(E)** Calculate the average:

$$\frac{a+b+c+d}{4} = \frac{3(c+d)+c+d}{4} = \frac{3c+3d+c+d}{4} = \frac{4c+4d}{4} = c+d$$

10. **(C)** Since $a + b + c + d = 360$, and $e + f + g + h = 360$ (see Section 12-I, page 445), the sum of the measures of all 8 angles is $360 + 360 = 720$, and their average is $720 \div 8 = 90$.

11. **(C)** The average of 2^{10} and 2^{20} is $\frac{2^{10}+2^{20}}{2} = \frac{2^{10}}{2} + \frac{2^{20}}{2} = 2^9 + 2^{19}$.

12. **(D)** Arrange the numbers in increasing order: 10, 20, 40, 70, 70, 90. *M*, the median, is the average of the middle two numbers: $\frac{40+70}{2} = 55$; the mode, *m*, is 70, the number that appears most frequently. The average of *M* and *m*, therefore, is the average of 55 and 70, which is 62.5.

13. **(C)** In *any* triangle, the sum of the measures of the three angles is 180°, and the average of their measures is $180 \div 3 = 60$.

14. **(D)** From KEY FACT E1 (page 398), we know only that *at least one grade was above 80.* In fact, there may have been only one (9 grades of 79 and 1 grade of 89, for example). But there could have been five or even nine (for example, 9 grades of 85 and 1 grade of 35).
Alternative solution. The ten students scored exactly 800 points. Ask, "Could they be equal?" Could there be exactly five grades above 80? Sure, five grades of 100 for 500 points and five grades of 60 for 300 points. Must they be equal? No, eight grades of 100 and two grades of 0 also total 800.

15. **(C)** The average of $2x$ and $2y$ is $\frac{2x+2y}{2} = x + y$, which equals 180.

16. **(D)** It is possible that no boy weighs over 150 (if every single boy weighs exactly 150); on the other hand, it is possible that almost every boy weighs over 150. The same is true for the girls.

17. **(B)** Use TACTIC E1 (page 397): $22 + 38 + x + y = 4(15) = 60 \Rightarrow 60 + x + y = 60 \Rightarrow x + y = 0$. Since it is given that x is positive, y must be negative.

18. **(C)** Do not calculate either standard deviation. Clearly, the mean of List 1 is 5, and the differences between each number and the mean are –4, –2, 0, 2, 4. In List 2, the mean is 15, and again the differences between each number and the mean are –4, –2, 0, 2, 4. Since the differences are the same, the average of the squares of the differences will be the same. The two standard deviations are equal.

19. **(A)** You don't have to calculate the averages. Quantity A is clearly greater than 17, so by KEY FACT E3 (page 399), adding 17 to the set of numbers being averaged must lower the average.

20. **(D)** Use KEY FACT E3 (page 399): If $x < y$, then the average of x and y is less than y, and surely less than $2y$. So, $2y$ has to raise the average. On the other hand, if x is much larger than y, then $2y$ would lower the average.

ALGEBRA

For the GRE you need to know only a small portion of the algebra normally taught in a high school elementary algebra course and none of the material taught in an intermediate or advanced algebra course. Sections 12-F, 12-G, and 12-H review only those topics that you absolutely need for the GRE.

12-F. POLYNOMIALS

- Polynomials
- Arithmetic Operations on Polynomials
- Algebraic Fractions
- Practice Exercises
- Answer Explanations

Polynomials

Even though the terms *monomial, binomial, trinomial,* and *polynomial* are not used on the GRE, you must be able to work with simple polynomials, and the use of these terms will make it easier for us to discuss the important concepts.

A ***monomial*** is any number or variable or product of numbers and variables. Each of the following is a monomial:

$$3 \quad -4 \quad x \quad y \quad 3x \quad -4xyz \quad 5x^3 \quad 1.5xy^2 \quad a^3b^4$$

The number that appears in front of the variables in a monomial is called the *coefficient.* The coefficient of $5x^3$ is 5. If there is no number, the coefficient is 1 or –1, because x means $1x$ and $-ab^2$ means $-1ab^2$.

On the GRE, you could be asked to evaluate a monomial for specific values of the variables.

EXAMPLE 1

What is the value of $-3a^2b$ when $a = -4$ and $b = 0.5$?

Ⓐ -72 Ⓑ -24 Ⓒ 24 Ⓓ 48 Ⓔ 72

SOLUTION.

Rewrite the expression, replacing the letters a and b with the numbers –4 and 0.5, respectively. Make sure to write each number in parentheses. Then evaluate:

$$-3(-4)^2(0.5) = -3(16)(0.5) = \mathbf{-24\ (B)}.$$

CAUTION

Be sure you follow PEMDAS (see Section 12-A): handle exponents before the other operations. In Example 1, you *cannot* multiply -4 by -3, get 12, and then square the 12; you must first square -4.

A ***polynomial*** is a monomial or the sum of two or more monomials. Each monomial that makes up the polynomial is called a ***term*** of the polynomial. Each of the following is a polynomial:

$$2x^2 \quad 2x^2+3 \quad 3x^2-7 \quad x^2+5x-1 \quad a^2b+b^2a \quad x^2-y^2 \quad w^2-2w+1$$

The first polynomial in the above list is a monomial; the second, third, fifth, and sixth polynomials are called ***binomials***, because each has two terms; the fourth and seventh polynomials are called ***trinomials***, because each has three terms. Two terms are called ***like terms*** if they have exactly the same variables and exponents; they can differ only in their coefficients: $5a^2b$ and $-3a^2b$ are like terms, whereas a^2b and b^2a are not.

The polynomial $3x^2 + 4x + 5x + 2x^2 + x - 7$ has 6 terms, but some of them are like terms and can be combined:

$$3x^2 + 2x^2 = 5x^2 \quad \text{and} \quad 4x + 5x + x = 10x.$$

So, the original polynomial is equivalent to the trinomial $5x^2 + 10x - 7$.

TIP

To add, subtract, multiply, and divide polynomials, use the usual laws of arithmetic. To avoid careless errors, before performing any arithmetic operations, write each polynomial in parentheses.

KEY FACT F1

The only terms of a polynomial that can be combined are like terms.

Arithmetic Operations on Polynomials

KEY FACT F2

To add two polynomials, put a plus sign between them, erase the parentheses, and combine like terms.

EXAMPLE 2

What is the sum of $5x^2 + 10x - 7$ and $3x^2 - 4x + 2$?

SOLUTION.

$(5x^2 + 10x - 7) + (3x^2 - 4x + 2)$
$= 5x^2 + 10x - 7 + 3x^2 - 4x + 2$
$= (5x^2 + 3x^2) + (10x - 4x) + (-7 + 2)$
$= \mathbf{8x^2 + 6x - 5}$

KEY FACT F3

To subtract two polynomials, change the minus sign between them to a plus sign and change the sign of every term in the second parentheses. Then just use KEY FACT F2 to add them: erase the parentheses and then combine like terms.

CAUTION

Make sure you get the order right in a subtraction problem.

EXAMPLE 3

Subtract $3x^2 - 4x + 2$ from $5x^2 + 10x - 7$.

SOLUTION.

Be careful. Start with the second polynomial and subtract the first:

$$(5x^2 + 10x - 7) - (3x^2 - 4x + 2) = (5x^2 + 10x - 7) + (-3x^2 + 4x - 2) = \mathbf{2x^2 + 14x - 9}$$

EXAMPLE 4

What is the average (arithmetic mean) of $5x^2 + 10x - 7$, $3x^2 - 4x + 2$, and $4x^2 + 2$?

SOLUTION.

As in any average problem, add and divide:

$$(5x^2 + 10x - 7) + (3x^2 - 4x + 2) + (4x^2 + 2) = 12x^2 + 6x - 3$$

and by the distributive law (KEY FACT A21, page 341),

$$\frac{12x^2 + 6x - 3}{3} = \mathbf{4x^2 + 2x - 1}$$

KEY FACT F4

To multiply monomials, first multiply their coefficients, and then multiply their variables (letter by letter), by adding the exponents (see Section 12-A, page 328).

EXAMPLE 5

What is the product of $3xy^2z^3$ and $-2x^2y^2$?

SOLUTION.

$(3xy^2z^3)(-2x^2y^2) = 3(-2)(x)(x^2)(y^2)(y^2)(z^3) = \mathbf{-6x^3y^4z^3}$.

All other polynomials are multiplied by using the distributive law.

KEY FACT F5

To multiply a monomial by a polynomial, just multiply each term of the polynomial by the monomial.

EXAMPLE 6

What is the product of $2a$ and $3a^2 - 6ab + b^2$?

SOLUTION.

$2a(3a^2 - 6ab + b^2) = \mathbf{6a^3 - 12a^2b + 2ab^2}$.

On the GRE, the only other polynomials that you could be asked to multiply are two binomials.

KEY FACT F6

To multiply two binomials, use the so-called FOIL method, which is really nothing more than the distributive law: Multiply each term in the first parentheses by each term in the second parentheses and simplify by combining terms, if possible.

$$(2x-7)(3x+2) = \underbrace{(2x)(3x)}_{\text{First terms}} + \underbrace{(2x)(2)}_{\text{Outer terms}} + \underbrace{(-7)(3x)}_{\text{Inner terms}} + \underbrace{(-7)(2)}_{\text{Last terms}} =$$

$$6x^2 + 4x - 21x - 14 = 6x^2 - 17x - 14$$

EXAMPLE 7

What is the value of $(x - 2)(x + 3) - (x - 4)(x + 5)$?

SOLUTION.
First, multiply both pairs of binomials:

$$(x-2)(x+3) = x^2 + 3x - 2x - 6 = x^2 + x - 6$$
$$(x-4)(x+5) = x^2 + 5x - 4x - 20 = x^2 + x - 20$$

Now, subtract:

$$(x^2 + x - 6) - (x^2 + x - 20) = x^2 + x - 6 - x^2 - x + 20 = \mathbf{14}$$

KEY FACT F7

The three most important binomial products on the GRE are these:

- $(x-y)(x+y) = x^2 + xy - yx - y^2 = x^2 - y^2$
- $(x-y)^2 = (x-y)(x-y) = x^2 - xy - yx + y^2 = x^2 - 2xy + y^2$
- $(x+y)^2 = (x+y)(x+y) = x^2 + xy + yx + y^2 = x^2 + 2xy + y^2$

TIP

If you memorize these, you won't have to multiply them out each time you need them.

EXAMPLE 8

If $a - b = 7$ and $a + b = 13$, what is the value of $a^2 - b^2$?

SOLUTION.
In Section 12-G, we will review how to solve such a pair of equations; but even if you know how, *you should not do it here.* You do not need to know the values of a and b to answer this question. The moment you see $a^2 - b^2$, you should think $(a - b)(a + b)$. Then:

$$a^2 - b^2 = (a-b)(a+b) = (7)(13) = \mathbf{91}$$

EXAMPLE 9

If $x^2 + y^2 = 36$ and $(x + y)^2 = 64$, what is the value of xy?

SOLUTION.

$$64 = (x + y)^2 = x^2 + 2xy + y^2 = x^2 + y^2 + 2xy = 36 + 2xy$$

Therefore, $2xy = 64 - 36 = 28 \Rightarrow xy =$ **14**.

On the GRE, the only division of polynomials you might have to do is to divide a polynomial by a monomial. You will *not* have to do long division of polynomials.

KEY FACT F8

To divide a polynomial by a monomial, use the distributive law. Then simplify each term by reducing the fraction formed by the coefficients to lowest terms and applying the laws of exponents.

EXAMPLE 10

What is the quotient when $32a^2b + 12ab^3c$ is divided by $8ab$?

SOLUTION.

By the distributive law, $\frac{32a^2b+12ab^3c}{8ab} = \frac{32a^2b}{8ab} + \frac{12ab^3c}{8ab}$.

Now reduce each fraction: $\mathbf{4a + \frac{3}{2}b^2c}$.

On the GRE, the most important way to use the three formulas in KEY FACT F7 is to recognize them in reverse. In other words, whenever you see $x^2 - y^2$, you should realize that it can be rewritten as $(x - y)(x + y)$. This process, which is the reverse of multiplication, is called ***factoring***.

EXAMPLE 11

Quantity A	Quantity B
The value of $x^2 + 4x + 4$ when $x = 95.9$	The value of $x^2 - 4x + 4$ when $x = 99.5$

SOLUTION.

Obviously, you don't want to plug in 95.9 and 99.5 (remember that the GRE *never* requires you to do tedious arithmetic). Recognize that $x^2 + 4x + 4$ is equal to $(x + 2)^2$ and that $x^2 - 4x + 4$ is equal to $(x - 2)^2$. So, Quantity A is just $(95.9 + 2)^2 = 97.9^2$, whereas Quantity B is $(99.5 - 2)^2 = 97.5^2$. Quantity **A** is greater.

EXAMPLE 12

What is the value of $(1{,}000{,}001)^2 - (999{,}999)^2$?

SOLUTION.

Do not even consider squaring 999,999. You know that there has to be an easier way to do this. In fact, if you stop to think, you can get the right answer in a few seconds. This is just $a^2 - b^2$ where $a = 1{,}000{,}001$ and $b = 999{,}999$, so change it to $(a - b)(a + b)$:

$$(1{,}000{,}001)^2 - (999{,}999)^2 = (1{,}000{,}001 - 999{,}999)(1{,}000{,}001 + 999{,}999) = (2)(2{,}000{,}000) = \mathbf{4{,}000{,}000}$$

Algebraic Fractions

Although the coefficients of any of the terms in a polynomial can be fractions, as in $\frac{2}{3}x^2 - \frac{1}{2}x$, the variable itself cannot be in the denominator. An expression such as $\frac{3+x}{x^2}$, which does have a variable in the denominator, is called an ***algebraic fraction.***

Fortunately, you should have no trouble with algebraic fractions, since they are handled just like regular fractions. The rules that you reviewed in Section 12-B (page 350) for adding, subtracting, multiplying, and dividing fractions apply to algebraic fractions, as well.

EXAMPLE 13

What is the sum of the reciprocals of x^2 and y^2?

SOLUTION.

To add $\frac{1}{x^2} + \frac{1}{y^2}$, you need a common denominator, which is x^2y^2.

Multiply the numerator and denominator of $\frac{1}{x^2}$ by y^2 and the numerator and denominator of $\frac{1}{y^2}$ by x^2, and then add:

$$\frac{1}{x^2} + \frac{1}{y^2} = \frac{y^2}{x^2y^2} + \frac{x^2}{x^2y^2} = \mathbf{\frac{x^2 + y^2}{x^2y^2}}$$

Often, the way to simplify algebraic fractions is to factor the numerator or the denominator or both. Consider the following example, which is harder than anything you will see on the GRE, but still quite manageable.

EXAMPLE 14

What is the value of $\frac{4x^3 - x}{(2x+1)(6x-3)}$ when $x = 9{,}999$?

SOLUTION.

Don't use FOIL to multiply the denominator. That's going the wrong way. We want to simplify this fraction by factoring everything we can. First factor an x out of the numerator and notice that what's left is the difference of two squares, which can be factored. Then factor out the 3 in the second factor in the denominator:

$$\frac{4x^3 - x}{(2x+1)(6x-3)} = \frac{x(4x^2-1)}{(2x+1)3(2x-1)} = \frac{x\cancel{(2x-1)}\cancel{(2x+1)}}{3\cancel{(2x+1)}\cancel{(2x-1)}} = \frac{x}{3}$$

So, instead of plugging 9,999 into the original expression, plug it into $\frac{x}{3}$: $9{,}999 \div 3 =$ **3,333.**

PRACTICE EXERCISES—POLYNOMIALS

Discrete Quantitative Questions

1. What is the value of $\frac{a^2 - b^2}{a - b}$ when $a = 117$ and $b = 118$?

2. If $a^2 - b^2 = 21$ and $a^2 + b^2 = 29$, which of the following could be the value of ab?
Indicate *all* possible values.

[A] -10
[B] $5\sqrt{2}$
[C] 10

3. What is the average (arithmetic mean) of $x^2 + 2x - 3$, $3x^2 - 2x - 3$, and $30 - 4x^2$?

(A) $\frac{8x^2 + 4x + 24}{3}$
(B) $\frac{8x^2 + 24}{3}$
(C) $\frac{24 - 4x}{3}$
(D) -12
(E) 8

4. What is the value of $x^2 + 12x + 36$ when $x = 994$?

(A) 11,928
(B) 98,836
(C) 100,000
(D) 988,036
(E) 1,000,000

5. If $c^2 + d^2 = 4$ and $(c - d)^2 = 2$, what is the value of cd?

(A) 1
(B) $\sqrt{2}$
(C) 2
(D) 3
(E) 4

6. What is the value of $(2x + 3)(x + 6) - (2x - 5)(x + 10)$?

(A) 32
(B) 16
(C) 68
(D) $4x^2 + 30x + 68$
(E) $4x^2 + 30x - 32$

7. If $\frac{1}{a} + \frac{1}{b} = \frac{1}{c}$ and $ab = c$, what is the average of a and b?

(A) 0
(B) $\frac{1}{2}$
(C) 1
(D) $\frac{c}{2}$
(E) $\frac{a+b}{2c}$

8. If $x^2 - y^2 = 28$ and $x - y = 8$, what is the average of x and y?

(A) 1.75
(B) 3.5
(C) 7
(D) 8
(E) 10

9. Which of the following is equal to

$\left(\frac{1}{a}+a\right)^2-\left(\frac{1}{a}-a\right)^2$?

Ⓐ 0

Ⓑ 4

Ⓒ $\frac{1}{a^2}-a^2$

Ⓓ $\frac{2}{a^2}-2a^2$

Ⓔ $\frac{1}{a^2}-4-a^2$

10. If $\left(\frac{1}{a}+a\right)^2=100$, what is the value of $\frac{1}{a^2}+a^2$?

Ⓐ 10

Ⓑ 64

Ⓒ 98

Ⓓ 100

Ⓔ 102

Quantitative Comparison Questions

Ⓐ Quantity A is greater.

Ⓑ Quantity B is greater.

Ⓒ The two quantities are equal.

Ⓓ It is impossible to determine which quantity is greater.

11.

$n<0$

Quantity A	Quantity B
$-2n^2$	$(-2n)^2$

12.

$d<c$

Quantity A	Quantity B
$(c-d)(c+d)$	$(c-d)(c-d)$

13.

$x=-3$ and $y=2$

Quantity A	Quantity B
$-x^2y^3$	0

14.

Quantity A	Quantity B
$(r+s)(r-s)$	$r(s+r)-s(r+s)$

15.

Quantity A	Quantity B
$\frac{5x^2-20}{x-2}$	$4x+8$

ANSWER KEY

1. **235**	4. **E**	7. **B**	10. **C**	13. **B**
2. **A, C**	5. **A**	8. **A**	11. **B**	14. **C**
3. **E**	6. **C**	9. **B**	12. **D**	15. **D**

ANSWER EXPLANATIONS

1. **235** $\frac{a^2-b^2}{a-b} = \frac{(a-b)(a+b)}{a-b} = a + b = 117 + 118 = 235$

2. **(A, C)** Adding the two equations, we get that $2a^2 = 50 \Rightarrow a^2 = 25 \Rightarrow b^2 = 4$. So, $a = 5$ or -5 and $b = 2$ or -2. The only possibilities for their product are 10 and -10. (Only A and C are true.)

3. **(E)** To find the average, take the sum of the three polynomials and then divide by 3. Their sum is $(x^2 + 2x - 3) + (3x^2 - 2x - 3) + (30 - 4x^2) = 24$, and $24 \div 3 = 8$.

4. **(E)** You can avoid messy, time-consuming arithmetic if you recognize that $x^2 + 12x + 36 = (x + 6)^2$. The value is $(994 + 6)^2 = 1{,}000^2 = 1{,}000{,}000$.

5. **(A)** Start by squaring $c - d$: $2 = (c - d)^2 = c^2 - 2cd + d^2 = c^2 + d^2 - 2cd = 4 - 2cd$. So, $2 = 4 - 2cd \Rightarrow 2cd = 2 \Rightarrow cd = 1$.

6. **(C)** First multiply out both pairs of binomials: $(2x + 3)(x + 6) = 2x^2 + 15x + 18$ and $(2x - 5)(x + 10) = 2x^2 + 15x - 50$.
Now subtract: $(2x^2 + 15x + 18) - (2x^2 + 15x - 50) = 18 - (-50) = 68$.

7. **(B)** $\frac{1}{c} = \frac{1}{a} + \frac{1}{b} = \frac{a+b}{ab} = \frac{a+b}{c} \Rightarrow 1 = a + b \Rightarrow \frac{a+b}{2} = \frac{1}{2}$

8. **(A)** $x^2 - y^2 = (x - y)(x + y) \Rightarrow 28 = 8(x + y) \Rightarrow x + y = 28 \div 8 = 3.5$

   Finally, the average of x and y is $\frac{x+y}{2} = \frac{3.5}{2} = 1.75$.

9. **(B)** Expand each square: $\left(\frac{1}{a}+a\right)^2 = \frac{1}{a^2} + 2\left(\frac{1}{a}\right)(a) + a^2 = \frac{1}{a^2} + 2 + a^2$.

   Similarly, $\left(\frac{1}{a}-a\right)^2 = \frac{1}{a^2} - 2 + a^2$.

   Subtract: $\left(\frac{1}{a^2}+2+a^2\right)-\left(\frac{1}{a^2}-2+a^2\right) = 4$.

10. **(C)** $100 = \left(\frac{1}{a}+a\right)^2 = \frac{1}{a^2} + 2 + a^2 \Rightarrow \frac{1}{a^2} + a^2 = 98$

11. **(B)** Since n is negative, n^2 is positive, and so $-2n^2$ is negative. Therefore, Quantity A is negative, whereas Quantity B is positive.

12. **(D)** $c > d \Rightarrow c - d$ is positive,

	Quantity A	Quantity B
so divide each side by $c - d$:	$c + d$	$c - d$
Subtract c from each quantity:	d	$-d$

If $d = 0$ the quantities are equal; if $d = 1$, they aren't.

13. **(B)** Quantity A: $-(-3)^2 2^3 = -(9)(8) = -72$.

14. **(C)** Quantity B: $r(s+r) - s(r+s) = rs + r^2 - sr - s^2 = r^2 - s^2$
Quantity A: $(r+s)(r-s) = r^2 - s^2$.

15. **(D)** Quantity A: $\frac{5x^2-20}{x-2} = \frac{5(x^2-4)}{x-2} = \frac{5\cancel{(x-2)}(x+2)}{\cancel{x-2}} = 5(x+2)$.

Quantity B: $4x + 8 = 4(x+2)$. If $x = -2$, both quantities are 0; for any other value of x the quantities are unequal.

12-G. SOLVING EQUATIONS AND INEQUALITIES

The basic principle that you must adhere to in solving any *equation* is that you can manipulate it in any way, as long as *you do the same thing to both sides*. For example, you may always add the same number to each side; subtract the same number from each side; multiply or divide each side by the same number (except 0); square each side; take the square root of each side (if the quantities are positive); or take the reciprocal of each side. These comments apply to inequalities, as well, except you must be very careful, because some procedures (such as multiplying or dividing by a negative number and taking reciprocals) reverse inequalities (see Section 12-A, page 328).

First-Degree Equations and Inequalities

Most of the equations and inequalities that you will have to solve on the GRE have only one variable and no exponents. The following simple six-step method can be used on all of them.

EXAMPLE 1

If $\frac{1}{2}x + 3(x - 2) = 2(x + 1) + 1$, what is the value of x?

SOLUTION.

Follow the steps outlined in the following table.

Step	What to Do	Example 1
1	Get rid of fractions and decimals by multiplying both sides by the Lowest Common Denominator (LCD).	Multiply each term by 2: $x + 6(x - 2) = 4(x + 1) + 2$
2	Get rid of all parentheses by using the distributive law.	$x + 6x - 12 = 4x + 4 + 2$
3	Combine like terms on each side.	$7x - 12 = 4x + 6$
4	By adding or subtracting, get all the variables on one side.	Subtract $4x$ from each side: $3x - 12 = 6$
5	By adding or subtracting, get all the plain numbers on the other side.	Add 12 to each side: $3x = 18$
6	Divide both sides by the coefficient of the variable.*	Divide both sides by 3: $x = 6$

*Note: If you start with an inequality and in Step 6 you divide by a negative number, remember to reverse the inequality (see KEY FACT A24, page 342).

Example 1 is actually harder than any equation on the GRE, because it required all six steps. On the GRE that never happens. Think of the six steps as a list of questions that must be answered. Ask if each step is necessary. If it isn't, move on to the next one; if it is, do it.

Let's look at Example 2, which does not require all six steps.

EXAMPLE 2

For what real number n is it true that $3(n - 20) = n$?

SOLUTION. Do whichever of the six steps are necessary.

Step	Question	Yes/No	What to Do
1	Are there any fractions or decimals?	No	
2	Are there any parentheses?	Yes	Get rid of them: $3n - 60 = n$
3	Are there any like terms to combine?	No	
4	Are there variables on both sides?	Yes	Subtract n from each side: $2n - 60 = 0$
5	Is there a plain number on the same side as the variable?	Yes	Add 60 to each side: $2n = 60$
6	Does the variable have a coefficient?	Yes	Divide both sides by 2: $n = 30$

TACTIC

Memorize the six steps *in order* and use this method whenever you have to solve this type of equation or inequality.

EXAMPLE 3

Three brothers divided a prize as follows. The oldest received $\frac{2}{5}$ of it, the middle brother received $\frac{1}{3}$ of it, and the youngest received the remaining \$120. What was the value of the prize?

SOLUTION.

If x represents the value of the prize, then $\frac{2}{5}x + \frac{1}{3}x + 120 = x$.

Solve this equation using the six-step method.

Step	Question	Yes/No	What to Do
1	Are there any fractions or decimals?	Yes	To get rid of them, multiply by 15. $15\left(\frac{2}{5}x\right) + 15\left(\frac{1}{3}x\right) +$ $15(120) = 15(x)$ $6x + 5x + 1{,}800 = 15x$
2	Are there any parentheses?	No	
3	Are there any like terms to combine?	Yes	Combine them: $11x + 1{,}800 = 15x$
4	Are there variables on both sides?	Yes	Subtract $11x$ from each side: $1{,}800 = 4x$
5	Is there a plain number on the same side as the variable?	No	
6	Does the variable have a coefficient?	Yes	Divide both sides by 4: $x = 450$

Sometimes on the GRE, you are given an equation with several variables and asked to solve for one of them in terms of the others.

TIP

In applying the six-step method, you shouldn't actually write out the table, as we did in Examples 1–4, since it would be too time consuming. Instead, use the method as a guideline and mentally go through each step, doing whichever ones are required.

TACTIC G2

When you have to solve for one variable in terms of the others, treat all of the others as if they were numbers, and apply the six-step method.

EXAMPLE 4

If $a = 3b - c$, what is the value of b in terms of a and c?

SOLUTION.

To solve for *b*, treat *a* and *c* as numbers and use the six-step method with *b* as the variable.

Step	Question	Yes/No	What to Do
1	Are there any fractions or decimals?	No	
2	Are there any parentheses?	No	
3	Are there any like terms to combine?	No	
4	Are there variables on both sides?	No	Remember: the only variable is *b*.
5	Is there a plain number on the same side as the variable?	Yes	Remember: we're considering *c* as a number, and it is on the same side as *b*, the variable. Add *c* to both sides: $a + c = 3b$.
6	Does the variable have a coefficient?	Yes	Divide both sides by 3: $b = \frac{a+c}{3}$

Sometimes when solving equations, you may see a shortcut. For example, to solve $7(w-3) = 42$, it saves time to start by dividing both sides by 7, getting $w-3 = 6$, rather than by using the distributive law to eliminate the parentheses. Similarly, if you have to solve a proportion such as $\frac{x}{7} = \frac{3}{5}$, it is easier to cross-multiply, getting $5x = 21$, than to multiply both sides by 35 to get rid of the fractions (although that's exactly what cross-multiplying accomplishes). Other shortcuts will be illustrated in the problems at the end of the section. If you spot such a shortcut, use it; but if you don't, be assured that the six-step method *always* works.

EXAMPLE 5

If $x - 4 = 11$, what is the value of $x - 8$?

Ⓐ −15 Ⓑ −7 Ⓒ −1 Ⓓ 7 Ⓔ 15

SOLUTION.

Going immediately to Step 5, add 4 to each side: $x = 15$. But this is *not* the answer. You need the value not of x, but of $x - 8$: $15 - 8 =$ **7 (D)**.

As in Example 5, on the GRE you are often asked to solve for something other than the simple variable. In Example 5, you could have been asked for the value of x^2 or $x + 4$ or $(x-4)^2$, and so on.

TACTIC

TIP

Very often, solving the equation is not the quickest way to answer the question. Consider Example 6.

As you read each question on the GRE, on your scrap paper write down whatever you are looking for, and circle it. This way you will always be sure that you are answering the question that is asked.

EXAMPLE 6

If $2x - 5 = 98$, what is the value of $2x + 5$?

SOLUTION.

The first thing you should do is write $2x + 5$ on your paper and circle it. The fact that you are asked for the value of something other than x should alert you to look at the question carefully to see if there is a shortcut.

- The best approach here is to observe that $2x + 5$ is 10 more than $2x - 5$, so the answer is **108** (10 more than 98).
- Next best would be to do only one step of the six-step method, add 5 to both sides: $2x = 103$. Now, add 5 to both sides: $2x + 5 = 103 + 5 = 108$.
- The *worst* method would be to divide $2x = 103$ by 2, get $x = 51.5$, and then use that to calculate $2x + 5$.

EXAMPLE 7

If w is an integer, and the average (arithmetic mean) of 3, 4, and w is less than 10, what is the greatest possible value of w?

Ⓐ 9 Ⓑ 10 Ⓒ 17 Ⓓ 22 Ⓔ 23

SOLUTION.

Set up the inequality: $\frac{3+4+w}{3} < 10$. Do Step 1 (get rid of fractions by multiplying by 3): $3 + 4 + w < 30$. Do Step 3 (combine like terms): $7 + w < 30$. Finally, do Step 5 (subtract 7 from each side): $w < 23$. Since w is an integer, the most it can be is **22 (D)**.

The six-step method also works when there are variables in denominators.

EXAMPLE 8

For what value of x is $\frac{4}{x} + \frac{3}{5} = \frac{10}{x}$?

Ⓐ 5 Ⓑ 10 Ⓒ 20 Ⓓ 30 Ⓔ 50

SOLUTION. Multiply each side by the LCD, $5x$:

$$5\cancel{x}\left(\frac{4}{\cancel{x}}\right) + \cancel{5}x\left(\frac{3}{\cancel{5}}\right) = 5\cancel{x}\left(\frac{10}{\cancel{x}}\right) \Rightarrow 20 + 3x = 50$$

Now solve normally: $20 + 3x = 50 \Rightarrow 3x = 30$ and so $x =$ **10 (B)**.

EXAMPLE 9

If x is positive, and $y = 5x^2 + 3$, which of the following is an expression for x in terms of y?

Ⓐ $\sqrt{\frac{y}{5} - 3}$ Ⓑ $\sqrt{\frac{y-3}{5}}$ Ⓒ $\frac{\sqrt{y-3}}{5}$ Ⓓ $\frac{\sqrt{y}-3}{5}$ Ⓔ $\frac{\sqrt{y}-\sqrt{3}}{5}$

SOLUTION.

The six-step method works when there are no exponents. However, we can treat x^2 as a single variable, and use the method as far as possible:

$$y = 5x^2 + 3 \Rightarrow y - 3 = 5x^2 \Rightarrow \frac{y-3}{5} = x^2$$

Now take the square root of each side; since x is positive, the only solution is $x = \sqrt{\frac{y-3}{5}}$ **(B)**.

CAUTION

Doing the same thing to each *side* of an equation does *not* mean doing the same thing to each *term* of the equation. Study Examples 10 and 11 carefully.

NOTE

You cannot just take the reciprocal of each term; the answer is not $a = b + c$. Here are two solutions.

EXAMPLE 10

If $\frac{1}{a} = \frac{1}{b} + \frac{1}{c}$, what is a in terms of b and c?

SOLUTION 1.
First add the fractions on the right hand side:

$$\frac{1}{a} = \frac{1}{b} + \frac{1}{c} = \frac{b+c}{bc}$$

Now, take the reciprocal of each *side*: $a = \frac{bc}{b+c}$.

SOLUTION 2.
Use the six-step method. Multiply each term by abc, the LCD:

$$\cancel{a}bc\left(\frac{1}{\cancel{a}}\right) = a\cancel{b}c\left(\frac{1}{\cancel{b}}\right) + ab\cancel{c}\left(\frac{1}{\cancel{c}}\right) \Rightarrow bc = ac + ab = a(c+b) \Rightarrow a = \mathbf{\frac{bc}{c+b}}$$

EXAMPLE 11

If $a > 0$ and $a^2 + b^2 = c^2$, what is a in terms of b and c?

SOLUTION. $a^2 + b^2 = c^2 \Rightarrow a^2 = c^2 - b^2$. Be careful: you *cannot* now take the square root of each *term* and write, $a = c - b$. Rather, you must take the square root of each *side*:

$$a = \sqrt{a^2} = \sqrt{c^2 - b^2}$$

Quadratic Equations

There are a few other types of equations that you could have to solve on the GRE. Fortunately, they are quite easy. You probably will not have to solve a quadratic equation. However, if you do, you will *not* need the quadratic formula, and you will not have to factor a trinomial. Here are two examples.

EXAMPLE 12

If x is a positive number and $x^2 + 64 = 100$, what is the value of x?

Ⓐ 6 Ⓑ 12 Ⓒ 13 Ⓓ 14 Ⓔ 36

SOLUTION. When there is an x^2-term, but no x-term, we just have to take a square root:

$$x^2 + 64 = 100 \Rightarrow x^2 = 36 \Rightarrow x = \sqrt{36} = \mathbf{6\ (A)}$$

EXAMPLE 13

What is the largest value of x that satisfies the equation $2x^2 - 3x = 0$?

Ⓐ 0 Ⓑ 1.5 Ⓒ 2 Ⓓ 2.5 Ⓔ 3

SOLUTION.
When an equation has an x^2-term and an x-term but no constant term, the way to solve it is to factor out the x and to use the fact that if the product of two numbers is 0, one of them must be 0 (KEY FACT A3, page 329):

$$2x^2 - 3x = 0 \Rightarrow x(2x - 3) = 0$$
$$x = 0 \text{ or } 2x - 3 = 0$$
$$x = 0 \text{ or } 2x = 3$$
$$x = 0 \text{ or } x = 1.5$$

The largest value is **1.5 (B)**.

Exponential Equations

In another type of equation that occasionally appears on the GRE, the variable is in the exponent. These equations are particularly easy and are basically solved by inspection.

EXAMPLE 14

If $2^{x+3} = 32$, what is the value of 3^{x+2}?

Ⓐ 5 Ⓑ 9 Ⓒ 27 Ⓓ 81 Ⓔ 125

SOLUTION.
How many 2s do you have to multiply together to get 32? If you don't know that it's 5, just multiply and keep track. Count the 2s on your fingers as you say to yourself, "2 times 2 is 4, times 2 is 8, times 2 is 16, times 2 is 32." Then

$$2^{x+3} = 32 = 2^5 \Rightarrow x + 3 = 5 \Rightarrow x = 2$$

Therefore, $x + 2 = 4$, and $3^{x+2} = 3^4 = 3 \times 3 \times 3 \times 3 =$ **81 (D)**.

Occasionally, both sides of an equation have variables in the exponents. In that case, it is necessary to write both exponentials with the same base.

EXAMPLE 15

If $4^{w+3} = 8^{w-1}$, what is the value of w?

Ⓐ 0 Ⓑ 1 Ⓒ 2 Ⓓ 3 Ⓔ 9

SOLUTION.
Since it is necessary to have the same base on each side of the equation, write $4 = 2^2$ and $8 = 2^3$. Then

$$4^{w+3} = (2^2)^{w+3} = 2^{2(w+3)} = 2^{2w+6} \quad \text{and} \quad 8^{w-1} = (2^3)^{w-1} = 2^{3(w-1)} = 2^{3w-3}$$

So, $2^{2w+6} = 2^{3w-3} \Rightarrow 2w + 6 = 3w - 3 \Rightarrow w =$ **9 (E)**.

Systems of Linear Equations

The equations $x + y = 10$ and $x - y = 2$ each have lots of solutions (infinitely many, in fact). Some of them are given in the tables below.

$x + y = 10$

x	5	6	4	1	1.2	10	20
y	5	4	6	9	8.8	0	-10
$x + y$	10	10	10	10	10	10	10

$x - y = 2$

x	5	6	2	0	2.5	19	40
y	3	4	0	-2	.5	17	38
$x - y$	2	2	2	2	2	2	2

However, only one pair of numbers, $x = 6$ and $y = 4$, satisfy both equations simultaneously: $6 + 4 = 10$ and $6 - 4 = 2$. This then is the only solution of the ***system of equations***: $\begin{Bmatrix} x+y=10 \\ x-y=2 \end{Bmatrix}$.

Addition Method

A system of equations is a set of two or more equations involving two or more variables. To solve such a system, you must find values for each of the variables that will make each equation true. In an algebra course you learn several ways to solve systems of equations. On the GRE, the most useful way to solve them is to add or subtract (usually add) the equations. After demonstrating this method, we will show in Example 19 one other way to handle some systems of equations.

TACTIC

To solve a system of equations, add or subtract them. If there are more than two equations, add them.

EXAMPLE 16

$x + y = 10$

$x - y = 2$

Quantity A	Quantity B
x	y

SOLUTION.

Add the two equations:

$$\begin{aligned} x + y &= 10 \\ + \; x - y &= 2 \\ \hline 2x \quad &= 12 \\ x &= 6 \end{aligned}$$

Replacing x with 6 in $x + y = 10$ yields $y = 4$. So, Quantity **A** is greater.

EXAMPLE 17

If $3a + 5b = 10$ and $5a + 3b = 30$, what is the average (arithmetic mean) of a and b?

[ ]

SOLUTION.

Add the two equations:

$$\begin{array}{r} 3a+5b=10 \\ +\,5a+3b=30 \\ \hline 8a+8b=40 \end{array}$$

Divide both sides by 8: $a + b = 5$

The average of a and b is: $\frac{a+b}{2} = \frac{5}{2} = \mathbf{2.5}$

NOTE: It is not only unnecessary to first solve for a and b ($a = 7.5$ and $b = -2.5$), but, because that procedure is so much more time-consuming, it would be foolish to do so.

TIP

On the GRE, most problems involving systems of equations do not require you to solve the system. They usually ask for something other than the values of each variable. Read the questions very carefully, circle what you need, and do no more than is required.

EXAMPLE 18

$$7a - 3b = 200$$
$$7a + 3b = 100$$

Quantity A	Quantity B
a	b

SOLUTION.

Don't actually solve the system. Add the equations:

$$14a = 300 \Rightarrow 7a = 150$$

So, replacing $7a$ with 150 in the second equation, we get $150 + 3b = 100$; so $3b$, and hence b, must be negative, whereas a is positive. Therefore, $a > b$, and Quantity **A** is greater.

TIP

Remember TACTIC 5, Chapter 10 (page 296). On quantitative comparison questions, you don't need to know the value of the quantity in each column; you only need to know which one is greater.

Substitution Method

Occasionally on the GRE, it is as easy, or easier, to solve the system by substitution.

TACTIC G5

If one of the equations in a system of equations consists of a single variable equal to some expression, substitute that expression for the variable in the other equation.

EXAMPLE 19

$x + y = 10$

$y = x - 2$

Quantity A	Quantity B
x	y

SOLUTION.

Since the second equation states that a single variable (y), is equal to some expression ($x - 2$), substitute that expression for y in the first equation: $x + y = 10$ becomes $x + (x - 2) = 10$. Then, $2x - 2 = 10$, $2x = 12$, and $x = 6$. As always, to find the value of the other variable (y), plug the value of x into one of the two original equations: $y = 6 - 2 = 4$. Quantity **A** is greater.

PRACTICE EXERCISES—EQUATIONS/INEQUALITIES

Discrete Quantitative Questions

1. If $4x + 12 = 36$, what is the value of $x + 3$?

Ⓐ 3
Ⓑ 6
Ⓒ 9
Ⓓ 12
Ⓔ 18

2. If $7x + 10 = 44$, what is the value of $7x - 10$?

Ⓐ $-6\frac{6}{7}$
Ⓑ $4\frac{6}{7}$
Ⓒ $14\frac{6}{7}$
Ⓓ 24
Ⓔ 34

3. If $4x + 13 = 7 - 2x$, what is the value of x?

Ⓐ $-\frac{10}{3}$
Ⓑ -3
Ⓒ -1
Ⓓ 1
Ⓔ $\frac{10}{3}$

4. If $x - 4 = 9$, what is the value of $x^2 - 4$?

5. If $ax - b = c - dx$, what is the value of x in terms of a, b, c, and d?

Ⓐ $\frac{b+c}{a+d}$
Ⓑ $\frac{c-b}{a-d}$
Ⓒ $\frac{b+c-d}{a}$
Ⓓ $\frac{c-b}{a+d}$
Ⓔ $\frac{c}{b}-\frac{d}{a}$

6. If $\frac{1}{3}x+\frac{1}{6}x+\frac{1}{9}x = 33$, what is the value of x?

Ⓐ 3
Ⓑ 18
Ⓒ 27
Ⓓ 54
Ⓔ 72

7. If $3x - 4 = 11$, what is the value of $(3x - 4)^2$?

Ⓐ 22
Ⓑ 36
Ⓒ 116
Ⓓ 121
Ⓔ 256

8. If $64^{12} = 2^{a-3}$, what is the value of a?

Ⓐ 9
Ⓑ 15
Ⓒ 69
Ⓓ 72
Ⓔ 75

9. If the average (arithmetic mean) of $3a$ and $4b$ is less than 50, and a is twice b, what is the largest possible integer value of a?

Ⓐ 9
Ⓑ 10
Ⓒ 11
Ⓓ 19
Ⓔ 20

10. If $\frac{1}{a-b} = 5$, then $a =$

Ⓐ $b + 5$
Ⓑ $b - 5$
Ⓒ $b + \frac{1}{5}$
Ⓓ $b - \frac{1}{5}$
Ⓔ $\frac{1-5b}{5}$

11. If $x = 3a + 7$ and $y = 9a^2$, what is y in terms of x?

Ⓐ $(x-7)^2$

Ⓑ $3(x-7)^2$

Ⓒ $\frac{(x-7)^2}{3}$

Ⓓ $\frac{(x+7)^2}{3}$

Ⓔ $(x+7)^2$

12. If $4y - 3x = 5$, what is the smallest integer value of x for which $y > 100$?

Quantitative Comparison Questions

Ⓐ Quantity A is greater.
Ⓑ Quantity B is greater.
Ⓒ The two quantities are equal.
Ⓓ It is impossible to determine which quantity is greater.

13.

$$a + b = 13$$
$$a - b = 13$$

Quantity A	Quantity B
b	13

14.

$$\frac{2^{a-1}}{2^{b+1}} = 8$$

Quantity A	Quantity B
a	b

15.

$$4x^2 = 3x$$

Quantity A	Quantity B
x	1

16.

$$a + b = 1$$
$$b + c = 2$$
$$c + a = 3$$

Quantity A	Quantity B
The average (arithmetic mean) of a, b, and c	1

17.

$$3x - 4y = 5$$
$$y = 2x$$

Quantity A	Quantity B
x	y

18.

$$\frac{x}{2} - 2 > \frac{x}{3}$$

Quantity A	Quantity B
x	12

19.

$$3r - 5s = 17$$
$$2r - 6s = 7$$

Quantity A	Quantity B
The average (arithmetic mean) of r and s	10

20.

$$\frac{1}{c} = 1 + \frac{1}{d}$$

c and d are positive

Quantity A	Quantity B
c	d

ANSWER KEY

1. **C**	5. **A**	9. **D**	13. **B**	17. **A**
2. **D**	6. **D**	10. **C**	14. **A**	18. **A**
3. **C**	7. **D**	11. **A**	15. **B**	19. **B**
4. **165**	8. **E**	12. **132**	16. **C**	20. **B**

ANSWER EXPLANATIONS

1. **(C)** The easiest method is to recognize that $x + 3$ is $\frac{1}{4}$ of $4x + 12$ and, therefore, equals $\frac{1}{4}$ of 36, which is 9. If you don't see that, solve normally:

$$4x + 12 = 36 \Rightarrow 4x = 24 \Rightarrow x = 6 \text{ and so } x + 3 = 9$$

2. **(D)** Subtracting 20 from each side of $7x + 10 = 44$ gives $7x - 10 = 24$. If you don't see that, subtract 10 from each side, getting $7x = 34$. Then subtract 10 to get $7x - 10 = 24$. The worst alternative is to divide both sides of $7x = 34$ by 7 to get $x = \frac{34}{7}$; then you have to multiply by 7 to get back to 34, and then subtract 10.

3. **(C)** Add $2x$ to each side: $6x + 13 = 7$. Subtract 13 from each side: $6x = -6$. Divide by 6: $x = -1$.

4. **165** $x - 4 = 9 \Rightarrow x = 13 \Rightarrow x^2 = 169$ and so $x^2 - 4 = 165$

5. **(A)** Treat a, b, c, and d as constants, and use the six-step method to solve for x:

$$ax - b = c - dx \Rightarrow ax - b + dx = c \Rightarrow ax + dx = c + b \Rightarrow x(a + d) = b + c \Rightarrow x = \frac{b+c}{a+d}$$

6. **(D)** Multiply both sides by 18, the LCD:

$$18\left(\frac{1}{3}x + \frac{1}{6}x + \frac{1}{9}x\right) = 18(33) \Rightarrow 6x + 3x + 2x = 594 \Rightarrow 11x = 594 \Rightarrow x = 54$$

It's actually easier not to multiply out 18×33; leave it in that form, and then divide by 11: $\frac{18 \times \cancel{33}^{3}}{\cancel{11}_{1}} = 3 \times 18 = 54$.

7. **(D)** Be alert. Since you are given the value of $3x - 4$, and want the value of $(3x - 4)^2$, just square both sides: $11^2 = 121$. If you don't see that, you'll waste time solving the equation $3x - 4 = 11$(getting that $x = 5$), only to use that value to calculate that $3x - 4$ is equal to 11, which you aready knew.

8. **(E)** $2^{a-3} = 64^{12} = (2^6)^{12} = 2^{72} \Rightarrow a - 3 = 72$, and so $a = 75$.

9. **(D)** Since $a = 2b$, $2a = 4b$. Therefore, the average of $3a$ and $4b$ is the average of $3a$ and $2a$, which is $2.5a$. Therefore, $2.5a < 50 \Rightarrow a < 20$. So the largest *integer* value of a is 19.

10. **(C)** Taking the reciprocal of each side, we get $a - b = \frac{1}{5}$. So $a = b + \frac{1}{5}$.

11. **(A)** $x = 3a + 7 \Rightarrow x - 7 = 3a \Rightarrow a = \dfrac{x-7}{3}$.

Therefore, $y = 9a^2 = 9\left(\dfrac{x-7}{3}\right)^2 = 9\dfrac{(x-7)^2}{3^2} = (x-7)^2$.

12. **132** Solving for y yields $y = \dfrac{5+3x}{4}$.

Then, since $y > 100$: $\dfrac{5+3x}{4} > 100 \Rightarrow 5 + 3x > 400 \Rightarrow 3x > 395 \Rightarrow x > 131.666$.

The smallest integer value of x is 132.

13. **(B)** Adding the two equations, we get that $2a = 26$. Therefore, $a = 13$ and $b = 0$.

14. **(A)** Express each side of $\dfrac{2^{a-1}}{2^{b+1}} = 8$ as a power of 2:

$8 = 2^3$ and $\dfrac{2^{a-1}}{2^{b+1}} = 2^{(a-1)-(b+1)} = 2^{a-b-2}$.

Therefore, $a - b - 2 = 3 \Rightarrow a = b + 5$, and so a is greater.

15. **(B)** $4x^2 = 3x \Rightarrow 4x^2 - 3x = 0 \Rightarrow x(4x - 3) = 0$.

So,

$$x = 0 \text{ or } 4x - 3 = 0 \Rightarrow$$
$$x = 0 \text{ or } 4x = 3 \Rightarrow$$
$$x = 0 \text{ or } x = \frac{3}{4}$$

There are two possible values of x, both of which are less than 1.

16. **(C)** When we add all three equations, we get

$$2a + 2b + 2c = 6 \Rightarrow a + b + c = 3, \text{ and so } \frac{a+b+c}{3} = 1$$

17. **(A)** Use substitution. Replace y in the first equation with $2x$:

$$3x - 4(2x) = 5 \Rightarrow 3x - 8x = 5 \Rightarrow -5x = 5 \Rightarrow x = -1 \Rightarrow y = -2$$

18. **(A)** Multiply both sides by 6, the LCD:

$$6\left(\frac{x}{2} - 2\right) > 6\left(\frac{x}{3}\right) \Rightarrow 3x - 12 > 2x \Rightarrow -12 > -x \Rightarrow x > 12$$

19. **(B)** The first thing to try is to add the equations. That yields $5r - 11s = 24$, which does not appear to be useful. So now try to subtract the equations. That yields $r + s = 10$. So the average of r and s is $\dfrac{r+s}{2} = \dfrac{10}{2} = 5$.

20. **(B)** Multiply both sides of the given equation by cd, the LCD of the fractions:

$$cd\left(\frac{1}{c}\right) = cd\left(1 + \frac{1}{d}\right) \Rightarrow d = cd + c = c(d+1) \Rightarrow c = \frac{d}{d+1}$$

Since d is positive, $d + 1 > 1$, and so $\dfrac{d}{d+1} < d$. So $c < d$.

12-H. WORD PROBLEMS

On a typical GRE you will see several word problems, covering almost every math topic for which you are responsible. In this chapter you have already seen word problems on consecutive integers in Section A; fractions and percents in Sections B and C; ratios and rates in Section D; and averages in Section E. Later in this chapter you will see word problems involving probability, circles, triangles, and other geometric figures. A few of these problems can be solved with just arithmetic, but most of them require basic algebra.

To solve word problems algebraically, you must treat algebra as a foreign language and learn to translate "word for word" from English into algebra, just as you would from English into French or Spanish or any other language. When translating into algebra, we use some letter (often *x*) to represent the unknown quantity we are trying to determine. It is this translation process that causes difficulty for some students. Once translated, solving is easy using the techniques we have already reviewed. Consider the following pairs of typical GRE questions. The first ones in each pair (1A and 2A) would be considered easy, whereas the second ones (1B and 2B) would be considered harder.

EXAMPLE 1A

What is 4% of 4% of 40,000?

EXAMPLE 1B

In a lottery, 4% of the tickets printed can be redeemed for prizes, and 4% of those tickets have values in excess of $100. If the state prints 40,000 tickets, how many of them can be redeemed for more than $100?

EXAMPLE 2A

If $x + 7 = 2(x - 8)$, what is the value of x?

EXAMPLE 2B

In 7 years Erin will be twice as old as she was 8 years ago. How old is Erin now?

Once you translate the words into arithmetic expressions or algebraic equations, Examples 1A and 1B and 2A and 2B are identical. The problem that many students have is doing the translation. It really isn't very difficult, and we'll show you how. First, though, look over the following English to algebra "dictionary."

English Words	Mathematical Meaning	Symbol
Is, was, will be, had, has, will have, is equal to, is the same as	Equals	=
Plus, more than, sum, increased by, added to, exceeds, received, got, older than, farther than, greater than	Addition	+
Minus, fewer, less than, difference, decreased by, subtracted from, younger than, gave, lost	Subtraction	−
Times, of, product, multiplied by	Multiplication	×
Divided by, quotient, per, for	Division	÷, $\frac{a}{b}$
More than, greater than	Inequality	>
At least	Inequality	≥
Fewer than, less than	Inequality	<
At most	Inequality	≤
What, how many, etc.	Unknown quantity	x (or some quantity

Let's use our dictionary to translate some phrases and sentences.

1. The sum of 5 and some number is 13. $5 + x = 13$
2. John was 2 years younger than Sam. $J = S - 2$
3. Bill has at most $100. $B \leq 100$
4. The product of 2 and a number exceeds that number by 5 (is 5 more than). $2N = N + 5$

In translating statements, you first must decide what quantity the variable will represent. Often it's obvious. Other times there is more than one possibility.

Let's translate and solve the two questions from the beginning of this section, and then we'll look at a few new ones.

TIP

In all word problems on the GRE, remember to write down and circle what you are looking for. Don't answer the wrong question!

EXAMPLE 1B

In a lottery, 4% of the tickets printed can be redeemed for prizes, and 4% of those tickets have values in excess of $100. If the state prints 40,000 tickets, how many of them can be redeemed for more than $100?

SOLUTION.

Let x = the number of tickets worth more than \$100. Then

$$x = 4\% \text{ of } 4\% \text{ of } 40{,}000 = .04 \times .04 \times 40{,}000 = \mathbf{64}$$

which is also the solution to Example 1a.

EXAMPLE 2B

In 7 years Erin will be twice as old as she was 8 years ago. How old is Erin now?

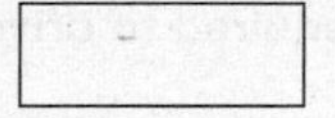

SOLUTION.

Let x = Erin's age now. Then 8 years ago she was $x - 8$, and 7 years from now she will be $x + 7$. So,

$$x + 7 = 2(x - 8) \Rightarrow x + 7 = 2x - 16 \Rightarrow 7 = x - 16 \Rightarrow x = \mathbf{23}$$

which is also the solution to Example 2a.

Most algebraic word problems on the GRE are not too difficult, and if you can do the algebra, that's usually the best way. But if, after studying this section, you still get stuck on a question during the test, don't despair. Use the tactics that you learned in Chapter 9, especially TACTIC 1 (page 268)—backsolving.

TIP

In problems involving ages, remember that "years ago" means you need to subtract, and "years from now" means you need to add.

Age Problems

EXAMPLE 3

In 1980, Judy was 3 times as old as Adam, but in 1984 she was only twice as old as he was. How old was Adam in 1990?

Ⓐ 4 Ⓑ 8 Ⓒ 12 Ⓓ 14 Ⓔ 16

SOLUTION.

Let x be Adam's age in 1980 and fill in the table below.

Year	Judy	Adam
1980	$3x$	x
1984	$3x + 4$	$x + 4$

Now translate: Judy's age in 1984 was twice Adam's age in 1984:

$$3x + 4 = 2(x + 4) = 2x + 8$$

$$3x + 4 = 2x + 8 \Rightarrow x + 4 = 8, \text{ and so } x = 4.$$

So, Adam was 4 in 1980. However, 4 is *not* the answer to this question. Did you remember to circle what you're looking for? The question *could have* asked for Adam's age in 1980 (Choice A) or 1984 (Choice B) or Judy's age in any year whatsoever (Choice C is 1980 and Choice E is 1984); but it didn't. It asked for *Adam's age in 1990.* Since he was 4 in 1980, then 10 years later, in 1990, he was **14** (**D**).

TIP

It is often very useful to organize the data from a word problem in a table.

Distance and Rate Problems

Distance problems all depend on three variations of the same formula:

$$\text{distance} = \text{rate} \times \text{time} \qquad \text{rate} = \frac{\text{distance}}{\text{time}} \qquad \text{time} = \frac{\text{distance}}{\text{rate}}$$

These are usually abbreviated, $d = rt$, $r = \frac{d}{t}$, and $t = \frac{d}{r}$.

EXAMPLE 4

How much longer, in *seconds*, is required to drive 1 mile at 40 miles per hour than at 60 miles per hour?

 **seconds**

SOLUTION.

The time to drive 1 mile at 40 miles per hour is given by

$$t = \frac{1}{40}\text{ hour} = \frac{1}{\cancel{40}_{2}} \times \cancel{60}^{3}\text{ minutes} = 1\frac{1}{2}\text{ minutes}$$

The time to drive 1 mile at 60 miles per hour is given by $t = \frac{1}{60}$ hour = 1 minute.

The difference is $\frac{1}{2}$ minute = **30** seconds.

Note that this solution used the time formula given, but required only arithmetic, not algebra. Example 5 requires an algebraic solution.

EXAMPLE 5

Avi drove from his home to college at 60 miles per hour. Returning over the same route, there was a lot of traffic, and he was only able to drive at 40 miles per hour. If the return trip took 1 hour longer, how many miles did he drive each way?

SOLUTION.

Let x = the number of hours Avi took going to college and make a table.

	rate	time	distance
Going	60	x	$60x$
Returning	40	$x + 1$	$40(x + 1)$

Since he drove the same distance going and returning,

$$60x = 40(x + 1) \Rightarrow 60x = 40x + 40 \Rightarrow 20x = 40, \text{ and so } x = 2.$$

Now be sure to answer the correct question. When $x = 2$, Choices A, B, and C are the time in hours that it took going, returning, and round-trip; Choices D and E are the distances each way and round-trip. You could have been asked for any of the five. If you circled what you're looking for, you won't make a careless mistake. Avi drove **120** miles each way, and so the correct answer is **D**.

The d in $d = rt$ stands for "distance," but it could really be any type of work that is performed at a certain ***rate***, r, for a certain amount of time, t. Example 5 need not be about distance. Instead of driving 120 miles at 60 miles per hour for 2 hours, Avi could have read 120 pages at a rate of 60 pages per hour for 2 hours; or planted 120 flowers at the rate of 60 flowers per hour for 2 hours; or typed 120 words at a rate of 60 words per minute for 2 minutes.

Miscellaneous Problems

Examples 6 and 7 illustrate two additional word problems of the type that you might find on the GRE.

EXAMPLE 6

Lindsay is trying to collect all the cards in a special commemorative set of baseball cards. She currently has exactly $\frac{1}{4}$ of the cards in that set.

When she gets 10 more cards, she will then have $\frac{1}{3}$ of the cards. How many cards are in the set?

Ⓐ 30 Ⓑ 60 Ⓒ 120 Ⓓ 180 Ⓔ 240

SOLUTION.

Let x be the number cards in the set. First, translate this problem from English into algebra: $\frac{1}{4}x + 10 = \frac{1}{3}x$. Now, use the six-step method of Section 12-G (page 421) to solve the equation. Multiply by 12 to get, $3x + 120 = 4x$, and then subtract $3x$ from each side: $x =$ **120 (C)**.

EXAMPLE 7

Jen, Ken, and Len have a total of \$390. Jen has 5 times as much as Len, and Ken has $\frac{3}{4}$ as much as Jen. How much money does Ken have?

Ⓐ \$40 Ⓑ \$78 Ⓒ \$150 Ⓓ \$195 Ⓔ \$200

Suppose, for example, that in this problem you let x represent the amount of money that Ken has. Then since Ken has $\frac{3}{4}$ as much as Jen, Jen has $\frac{4}{3}$ as much as Ken: $\frac{4}{3}x$; and Jen would have $\frac{1}{5}$ of that: $\left(\frac{1}{5}\right)\left(\frac{4}{3}x\right)$. It is much easier here to let x represent the amount of money Len has.

TIP

You often have a choice as to what to let the variable represent. Don't necessarily let it represent what you're looking for; rather, choose what will make the problem easiest to solve.

SOLUTION.

Let x represent the amount of money Len has. Then $5x$ is the amount that Jen has, and $\frac{3}{4}(5x)$ is the amount that Ken has. Since the total amount of money is \$390,

$$x + 5x + \frac{15}{4}x = 390$$

Multiply by 4 to get rid of the fraction: $4x + 20x + 15x = 1{,}560$.
Combine like terms and then divide: $39x = 1{,}560 \Rightarrow x = 40$.

So Len has \$40, Jen has $5 \times 40 =$ \$200, and Ken has $\frac{3}{4}(200) =$ **\$150 (C)**.

PRACTICE EXERCISES—WORD PROBLEMS

Discrete Quantitative Questions

1. Howard has three times as much money as Ronald. If Howard gives Ronald \$50, Ronald will then have three times as much money as Howard. How much money, in dollars, do the two of them have together?

   [ ] dollars

2. In the afternoon, Beth read 100 pages at the rate of 60 pages per hour; in the evening, when she was tired, she read another 100 pages at the rate of 40 pages per hour. What was her average rate of reading for the day?

   Ⓐ 45
   Ⓑ 48
   Ⓒ 50
   Ⓓ 52
   Ⓔ 55

3. If the sum of five consecutive integers is S, what is the largest of those integers in terms of S?

   Ⓐ $\frac{S-10}{5}$
   Ⓑ $\frac{S+4}{4}$
   Ⓒ $\frac{S+5}{4}$
   Ⓓ $\frac{S-5}{2}$
   Ⓔ $\frac{S+10}{5}$

4. As a fund-raiser, the school band was selling two types of candy: lollipops for 40 cents each and chocolate bars for 75 cents each. On Monday, they sold 150 candies and raised 74 dollars. How many lollipops did they sell?

   Ⓐ 75
   Ⓑ 90
   Ⓒ 96
   Ⓓ 110
   Ⓔ 120

5. A jar contains only red, white, and blue marbles. The number of red marbles is $\frac{4}{5}$ the number of white ones, and the number of white ones is $\frac{3}{4}$ the number of blue ones. If there are 470 marbles in all, how many of them are blue?

   Ⓐ 120
   Ⓑ 135
   Ⓒ 150
   Ⓓ 184
   Ⓔ 200

6. The number of shells in Judy's collection is 80% of the number in Justin's collection. If Justin has 80 more shells than Judy, how many shells do they have altogether?

   [ ] shells

7. What is the greater of two numbers whose product is 900, if the sum of the two numbers exceeds their difference by 30?

   Ⓐ 15
   Ⓑ 60
   Ⓒ 75
   Ⓓ 90
   Ⓔ 100

8. On a certain project the only grades awarded were 80 and 100. If 10 students completed the project and the average of their grades was 94, how many earned 100?

   Ⓐ 2
   Ⓑ 3
   Ⓒ 5
   Ⓓ 7
   Ⓔ 8

9. If $\frac{1}{2}x$ years ago Adam was 12, and $\frac{1}{2}x$ years from now he will be $2x$ years old, how old will he be $3x$ years from now?

Ⓐ 18
Ⓑ 24
Ⓒ 30
Ⓓ 54
Ⓔ It cannot be determined from the information given.

10. Since 1950, when Barry was discharged from the army, he has gained 2 pounds every year. In 1980 he was 40% heavier than in 1950. What percent of his 1995 weight was his 1980 weight?

Ⓐ 80
Ⓑ 85
Ⓒ 87.5
Ⓓ 90
Ⓔ 95

Quantitative Comparison Questions

Ⓐ **Quantity A is greater.**
Ⓑ **Quantity B is greater.**
Ⓒ **The two quantities are equal.**
Ⓓ **It is impossible to determine which quantity is greater.**

11.

Lindsay is twice as old as she was 10 years ago.
Kimberly is half as old as she will be in 10 years.

Quantity A	Quantity B
Lindsay's age now	Kimberly's age now

12.

Boris spent $\frac{1}{4}$ of his take-home pay on Saturday and $\frac{1}{3}$ of what was left on Sunday. The rest he put in his savings account.

Quantity A	Quantity B
The amount of his take-home pay that he spent	The amount of his take-home pay that he saved

13.

In 8 years, Tiffany will be 3 times as old as she is now.

Quantity A	Quantity B
The number of years until Tiffany will be 6 times as old as she is now	16

14.

Rachel put exactly 50 cents worth of postage on an envelope using only 4-cent stamps and 7-cent stamps.

Quantity A	Quantity B
The number of 4-cent stamps she used	The number of 7-cent stamps she used

15.

Car A and Car B leave from the same spot at the same time.
Car A travels due north at 40 mph.
Car B travels due east at 30 mph.

Quantity A	Quantity B
Distance from Car A to Car B 9 hours after they left	450 miles

ANSWER KEY

1. **100**	4. **D**	7. **B**	10. **C**	13. **A**
2. **B**	5. **E**	8. **D**	11. **A**	14. **D**
3. **E**	6. **720**	9. **D**	12. **C**	15. **C**

ANSWER EXPLANATIONS

1. **100**

	Ronald	Howard
At the beginning	x	$3x$
After the gift	$x + 50$	$3x - 50$

After the gift, Ronald will have 3 times as much money as Howard:
$x + 50 = 3(3x - 50) \Rightarrow x + 50 = 9x - 150 \Rightarrow 8x = 200$, and so $x = 25$.

So Ronald has \$25 and Howard has \$75, for a total of \$100.

2. **(B)** Beth's average rate of reading is determined by dividing the total number of pages she read (200) by the total amount of time she spent reading. In the afternoon she read for $\frac{100}{60} = \frac{5}{3}$ hours, and in the evening for $\frac{100}{40} = \frac{5}{2}$ hours, for a total time of $\frac{5}{3} + \frac{5}{2} = \frac{10}{6} + \frac{15}{6} = \frac{25}{6}$ hours. So, her average rate was $200 \div \frac{25}{6} = 200 \times \frac{6}{25} = 48$ pages per hour.

3. **(E)** Let the 5 consecutive integers be n, $n + 1$, $n + 2$, $n + 3$, $n + 4$. Then,
$S = n + n + 1 + n + 2 + n + 3 + n + 4 = 5n + 10 \Rightarrow 5n = S - 10 \Rightarrow n = \frac{S-10}{5}$.

Choice A, therefore, is the *smallest* of the integers; the *largest* is

$$n + 4 = \frac{S-10}{5} + 4 = \frac{S-10}{5} + \frac{20}{5} = \frac{S+10}{5}$$

4. **(D)** Let x represent the number of chocolate bars sold; then $150 - x$ is the number of lollipops sold. We must use the same units, so we could write 75 cents as .75 dollars or 74 dollars as 7400 cents. Let's avoid the decimals: x chocolates sold for $75x$ cents and $(150 - x)$ lollipops sold for $40(150 - x)$ cents. So,

$$7{,}400 = 75x + 40(150 - x) = 75x + 6{,}000 - 40x = 6{,}000 + 35x \Rightarrow$$
$$1{,}400 = 35x \Rightarrow x = 40 \text{ and } 150 - 40 = 110$$

5. **(E)** If b is the number of blue marbles, then there are $\frac{3}{4}b$ white ones, and $\frac{4}{5}\left(\frac{3}{4}b\right) = \frac{3}{5}b$ red ones.

Therefore, $470 = b + \frac{3}{4}b + \frac{3}{5}b = b\left(1 + \frac{3}{4} + \frac{3}{5}\right) = \frac{47}{20}b$.

So, $b = 470 \div \frac{47}{20} = \overset{10}{\cancel{470}} \times \frac{20}{\underset{1}{\cancel{47}}} = 200$.

6. **720** If x is the number of shells in Justin's collection, then Judy has $.80x$. Since Justin has 80 more shells than Judy,

$$x = .80x + 80 \Rightarrow .20x = 80 \Rightarrow x = 80 \div .20 = 400$$

So Justin has 400 and Judy has 320: a total of 720.

7. **(B)** If x represents the greater and y the smaller of the two numbers, then $(x + y) = 30 + (x - y) \Rightarrow y = 30 - y \Rightarrow 2y = 30$, and so $y = 15$. Since $xy = 900$, $x = 900 \div 15 = 60$.

8. **(D)** If x represents the number of students earning 100, then $10 - x$ is the number of students earning 80. So

$$94 = \frac{100x+80(10-x)}{10} \Rightarrow 94 = \frac{100x+800-80x}{10} = \frac{20x+800}{10} \Rightarrow$$

$$94 \times 10 = 940 = 20x + 800 \Rightarrow 140 = 20x, \text{ and } x = 7$$

9. **(D)** Since $\frac{1}{2}x$ years ago, Adam was 12, he is now $12 + \frac{1}{2}x$. So $\frac{1}{2}x$ years from now, he will be $12 + \frac{1}{2}x + \frac{1}{2}x = 12 + x$. But, we are told that at that time he will be $2x$ years old. So, $12 + x = 2x \Rightarrow x = 12$.

Thus, he is now $12 + 6 = 18$, and $3x$ or 36 years from now he will be $18 + 36 = 54$.

10. **(C)** Let x be Barry's weight in 1950. By 1980, he had gained 60 pounds (2 pounds per year for 30 years) and was 40% heavier: $60 = .40x \Rightarrow x = 60 \div .4 = 150$. So in 1980, he weighed 210. Fifteen years later, in 1995, he weighed 240: $\frac{210}{240} = \frac{7}{8} = 87.5\%$.

11. **(A)** You can do the simple algebra, but you might realize that if in the past 10 years Lindsay's age doubled, she was 10 and is now 20. Similarly, Kimberly is now 10 and in 10 years will be 20.
Here is the algebra: if x represents Lindsay's age now,

$$x = 2(x - 10) \Rightarrow x = 2x - 20 \Rightarrow x = 20$$

Similarly, Kimberly is now 10 and will be 20 in 10 years.

12. **(C)** Let x represent the amount of Boris's take-home pay. On Saturday, he spent $\frac{1}{4}x$ and still had $\frac{3}{4}x$; but on Sunday, he spent $\frac{1}{3}$ of that: $\frac{1}{\cancel{3}}\left(\frac{\cancel{3}}{4}x\right) = \frac{1}{4}x$.

Therefore, he spent $\frac{1}{4}$ of his take-home pay each day.

So, he spent $\frac{1}{2}$ of his pay and saved $\frac{1}{2}$ of his pay.

13. **(A)** If x represents Tiffany's age now, then in 8 years she will be $x + 8$, and so $x + 8 = 3x \Rightarrow 8 = 2x \Rightarrow x = 4$.

Tiffany will be 6 times as old 20 years from now, when she will be 24.

14. **(D)** If x and y represent the number of 4-cent stamps and 7-cent stamps that Rachel used, respectively, then $4x + 7y = 50$. This equation has infinitely many solutions but only 2 in which x and y are both positive integers: $y = 2$ and $x = 9$ or $y = 6$ and $x = 2$.

15. **(C)** Draw a diagram. In 9 hours Car A drove 360 miles north and Car B drove 270 miles east. These are the legs of a right triangle, whose hypotenuse is the distance between them. Use the Pythagorean theorem if you don't recognize that this is just a $3x$–$4x$–$5x$ right triangle: the legs are 90×3 and 90×4, and the hypotenuse is $90 \times 5 = 450$.

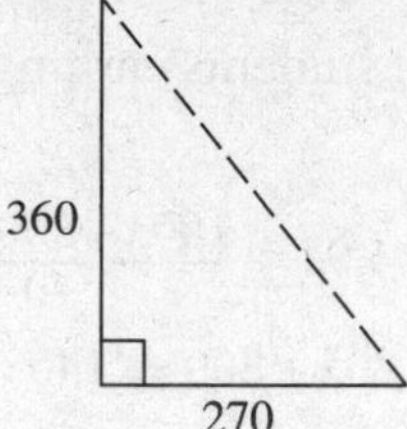

GEOMETRY

Although about 30% of the math questions on the GRE have to do with geometry, there are only a relatively small number of facts you need to know—far less than you would learn in a geometry course—and, of course, there are no proofs. In the next six sections we will review all of the geometry that you need to know to do well on the GRE. We will present the material exactly as it appears on the GRE, using the same vocabulary and notation, which might be slightly different from the terminology you learned in your high school math classes. The numerous examples in the next six sections will show you exactly how these topics are treated on the GRE.

12-I. LINES AND ANGLES

Angles

An ***angle*** is formed by the intersection of two line segments, rays, or lines. The point of intersection is called the ***vertex***. On the GRE, angles are always measured in degrees.

KEY FACT I1

Angles are classified according to their degree measures.

- **An acute angle measures less than 90°.**
- **A right angle measures 90°.**
- **An obtuse angle measures more than 90° but less than 180°.**
- **A straight angle measures 180°.**

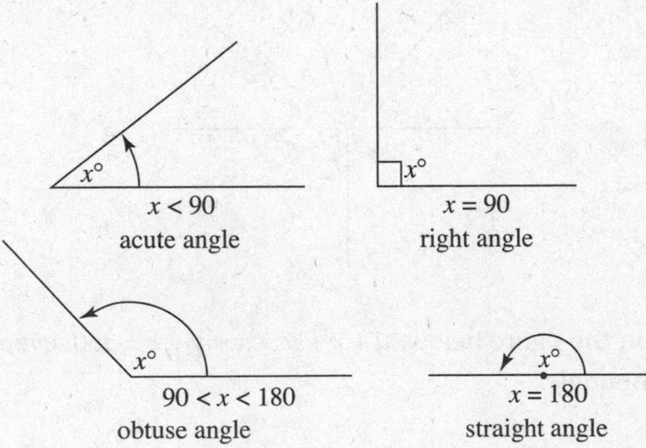

NOTE: The small square in the second angle in the figure above is *always* used to mean that the angle is a right angle. On the GRE, if an angle has a square in it, it must measure exactly 90°, *whether or not you think that the figure has been drawn to scale.*

KEY FACT I2

If two or more angles form a straight angle, the sum of their measures is 180°.

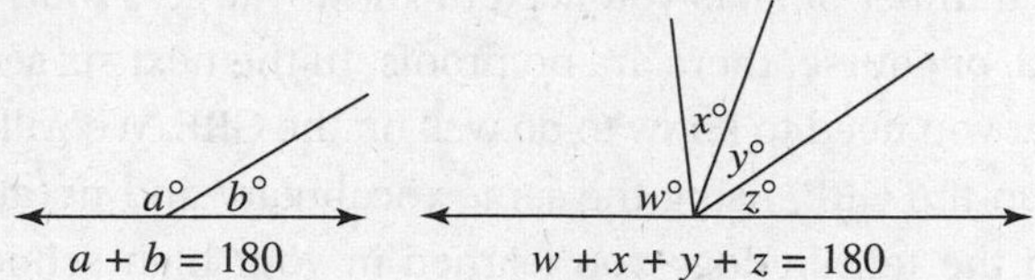

EXAMPLE 1

In the figure below, *R*, *S*, and *T* are all on line ℓ. What is the average of *a*, *b*, *c*, *d*, and *e*?

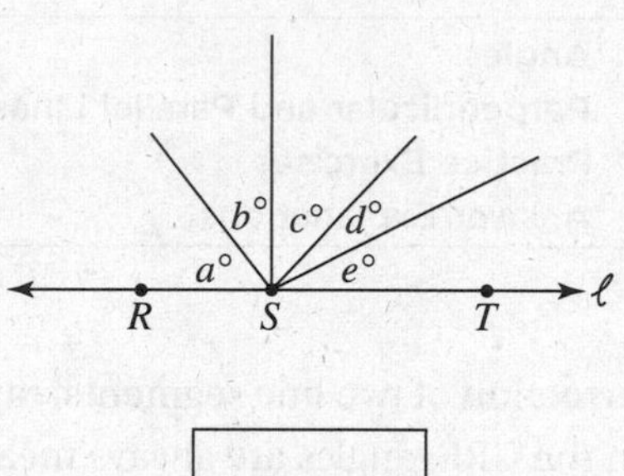

SOLUTION.

Since $\angle RST$ is a straight angle, by KEY FACT I2, the sum of *a, b, c, d,* and *e* is 180, and so their average is $\frac{180}{5}$ = **36.**

In the figure below, since $a + b + c + d = 180$ and $e + f + g = 180$, $a + b + c + d + e + f + g = 180 + 180 = 360$.

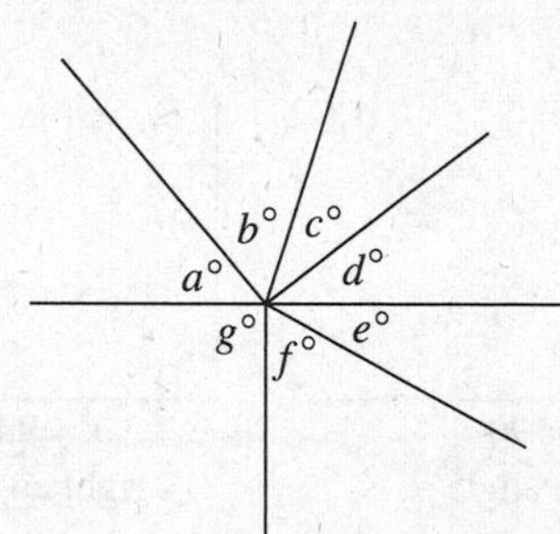

It is also true that in the figure below, $u + v + w + x + y + z = 360$, even though none of the angles forms a straight angle.

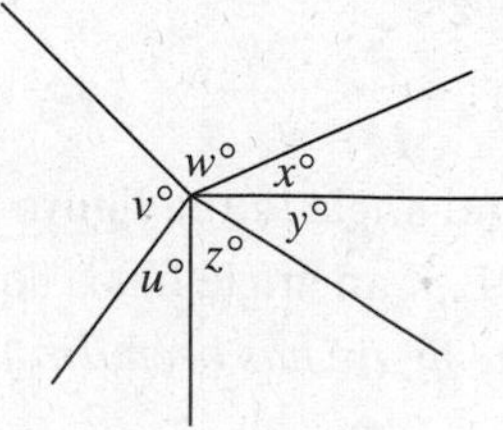

KEY FACT I3

The sum of all the measures of all the angles around a point is 360°.

NOTE: This fact is particularly important when the point is the center of a circle, as we shall see in Section 12-L (page 488).

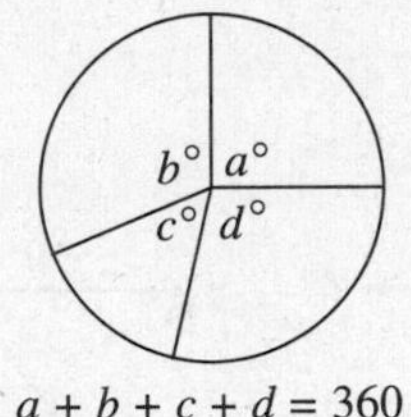

$a + b + c + d = 360$

When two lines intersect, four angles are formed. The two angles in each pair of opposite angles are called ***vertical angles***.

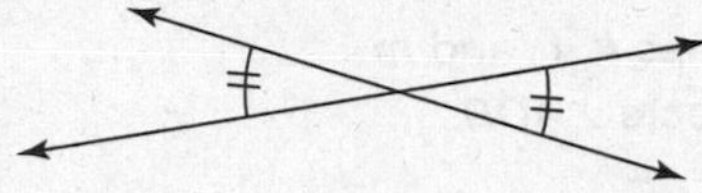

KEY FACT I4

Vertical angles have equal measures.

EXAMPLE 2

In the figure at the right, what is the value of x?

Ⓐ 6 Ⓑ 8 Ⓒ 10 Ⓓ 20 Ⓔ 40

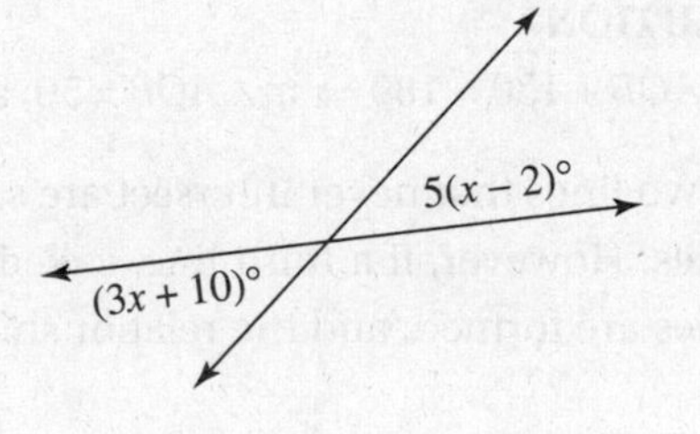

SOLUTION.

Since the measures of vertical angles are equal, $3x + 10 = 5(x - 2) \Rightarrow 3x + 10 = 5x - 10 \Rightarrow 3x + 20 = 5x \Rightarrow 20 = 2x \Rightarrow x = \mathbf{10}$ **(C)**.

KEY FACT I5

If one of the angles formed by the intersection of two lines (or line segments) is a right angle, then all four angles are right angles.

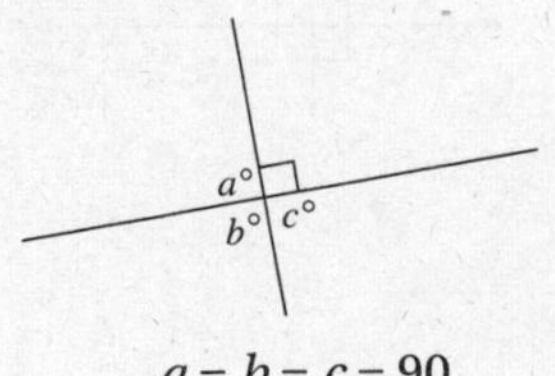

$a = b = c = 90$

Perpendicular and Parallel Lines

Two lines that intersect to form right angles are called ***perpendicular***.

In the figures below, line ℓ divides $\angle ABC$ into two equal parts, and line k divides line segment DE into two equal parts. Line ℓ is said to ***bisect*** the angle, and line k ***bisects*** the line segment. Point M is called the ***midpoint*** of segment DE.

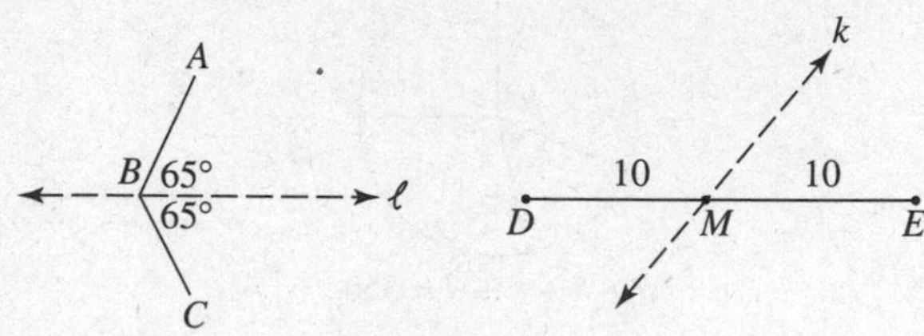

EXAMPLE 3

In the figure at the right, lines k, ℓ, and m intersect at O. If line m bisects $\angle AOB$, what is the value of x?

Ⓐ 25 Ⓑ 35 Ⓒ 45 Ⓓ 50 Ⓔ 60

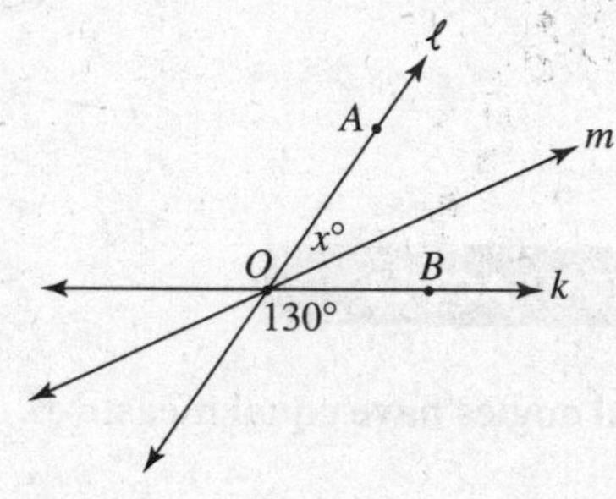

SOLUTION.

$m\angle AOB + 130 = 180 \Rightarrow m\angle AOB = 50$; and since m bisects $\angle AOB$, $x =$ **25 (A)**.

Two lines that never intersect are said to be parallel. Consequently, parallel lines form no angles. However, if a third line, called a ***transversal***, intersects a pair of parallel lines, eight angles are formed, and the relationships among these angles are very important.

KEY FACT I6

If a pair of parallel lines is cut by a transversal that is perpendicular to the parallel lines, all eight angles are right angles.

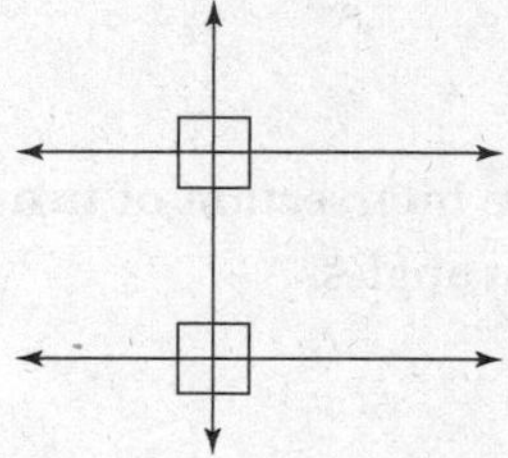

KEY FACT I7

If a pair of parallel lines is cut by a transversal that is not perpendicular to the parallel lines,

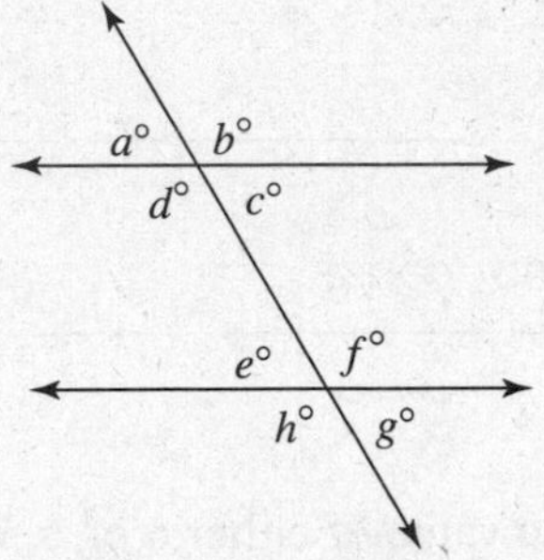

- **Four of the angles are acute and four are obtuse;**
- **The four acute angles are equal: $a = c = e = g$;**
- **The four obtuse angles are equal: $b = d = f = h$;**
- **The sum of any acute angle and any obtuse angle is 180°: for example, $d + e = 180$, $c + f = 180$, $b + g = 180$, ...**

KEY FACT I8

If a pair of lines that are not parallel is cut by a transversal, *none* of the properties listed in KEY FACT I7 is true.

You must know KEY FACT I7—virtually every GRE has at least one question based on it. However, you do *not* need to know the special terms you learned in high school for these pairs of angles; those terms are not used on the GRE.

EXAMPLE 4

In the figure below, *AB* is parallel to *CD*. What is the value of *x*?

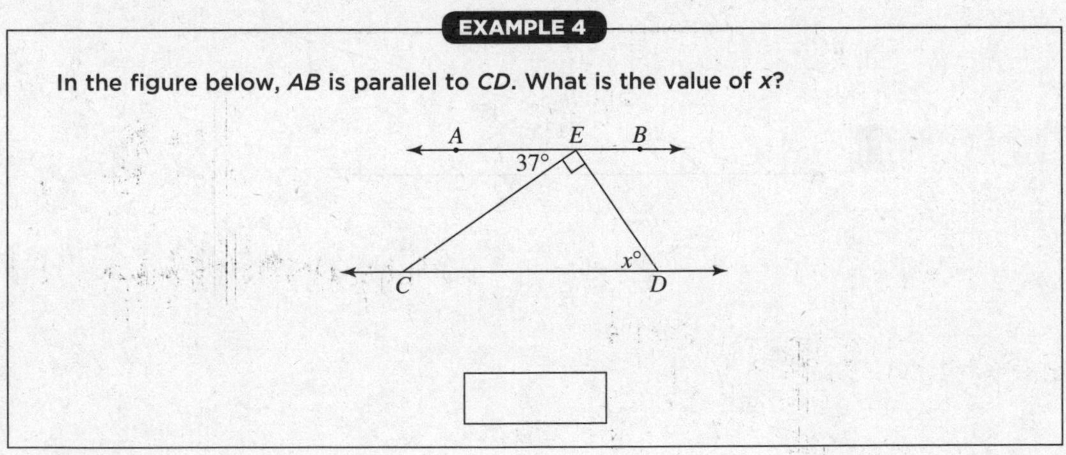

SOLUTION.

Let y be the measure of $\angle BED$. Then by KEY FACT I2:

$$37 + 90 + y = 180 \Rightarrow 127 + y = 180 \Rightarrow y = 53$$

Since *AB* is parallel to *CD*, by KEY FACT I7, $x = y \Rightarrow x = \mathbf{53}$.

EXAMPLE 5

In the figure below, lines ℓ and k are parallel. What is the value of $a + b$?

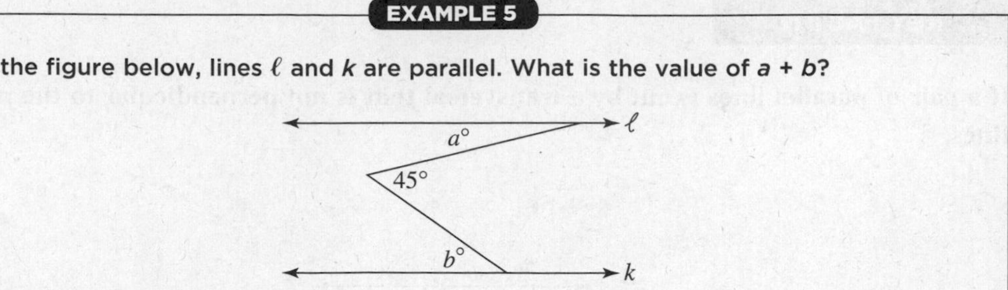

Ⓐ 45 Ⓑ 60 Ⓒ 75 Ⓓ 90 Ⓔ 135

SOLUTION.

It is impossible to determine the value of either a or b. We can, however, find the value of $a + b$. We draw a line through the vertex of the angle parallel to ℓ and k. Then, looking at the top two lines, we see that $a = x$, and looking at the bottom two lines, we see that $b = y$. So, $a + b = x + y =$ **45 (A)**.

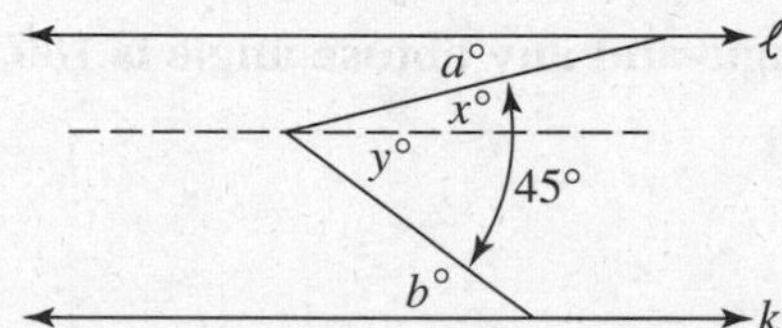

Alternative solution. Draw a different line and use a Key Fact from Section 12-J (page 456) on triangles. Extend one of the line segments to form a triangle. Since ℓ and k are parallel, the measure of the third angle in the triangle equals a. Now, use the fact that the sum of the measures of the three angles in a triangle is 180° or, even easier, that the given 45° angle is an external angle of the triangle, and so is equal to the sum of a and b.

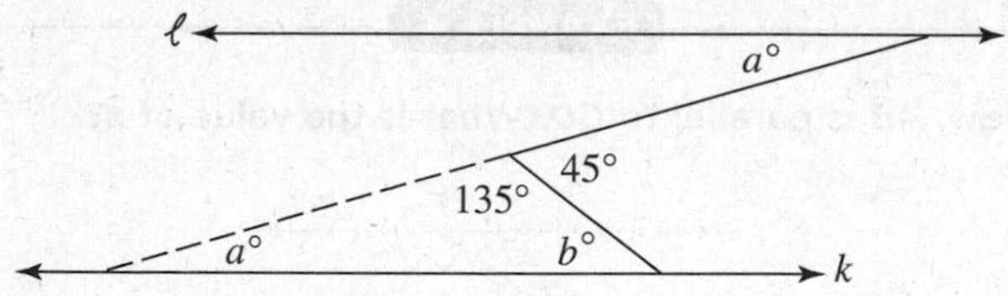

PRACTICE EXERCISES—LINES AND ANGLES

Discrete Quantitative Questions

1. In the figure below, what is the average (arithmetic mean) of the measures of the five angles?

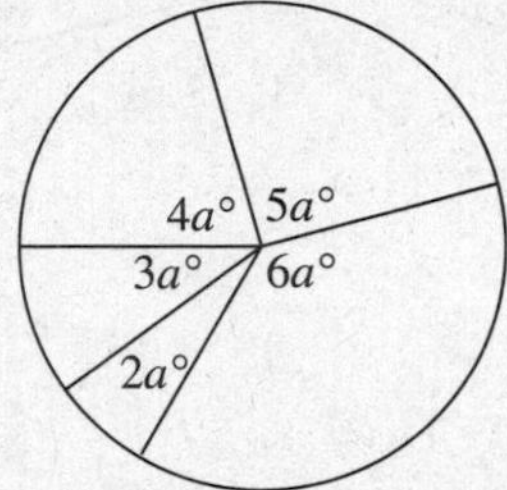

Ⓐ 36
Ⓑ 45
Ⓒ 60
Ⓓ 72
Ⓔ 90

2. In the figure below, what is the value of $\frac{b+a}{b-a}$?

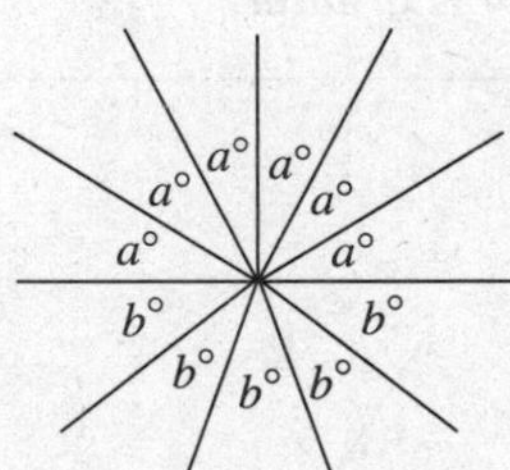

Ⓐ 1
Ⓑ 10
Ⓒ 11
Ⓓ 30
Ⓔ 36

3. In the figure below, what is the value of b?

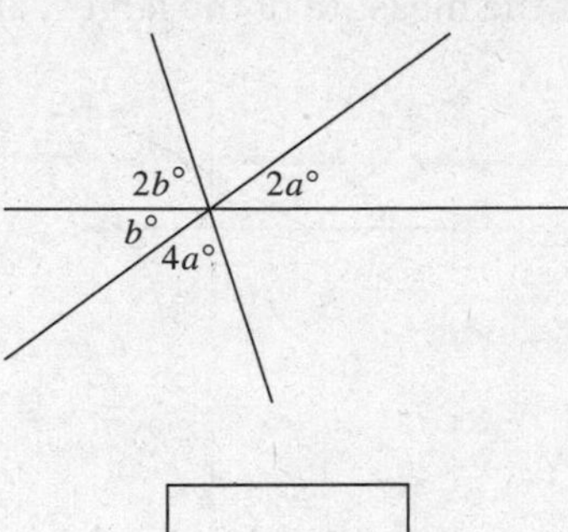

4. In the figure below, what is the value of x if $y:x = 3:2$?

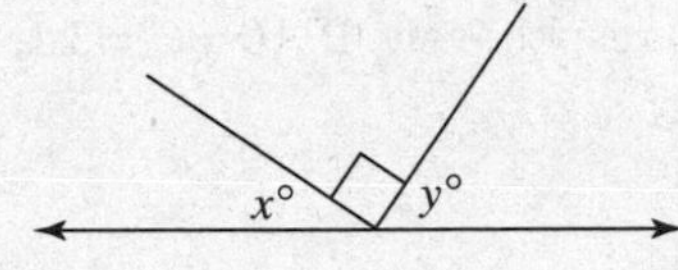

Ⓐ 18
Ⓑ 27
Ⓒ 36
Ⓓ 45
Ⓔ 54

5. What is the measure, in degrees, of the angle formed by the minute and hour hands of a clock at 1:50?

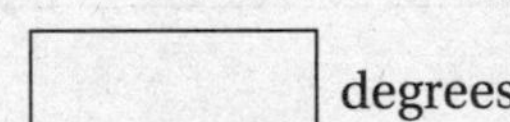 degrees

6. Concerning the figure below, if $a = b$, which of the following statements must be true?

Indicate *all* such statements.

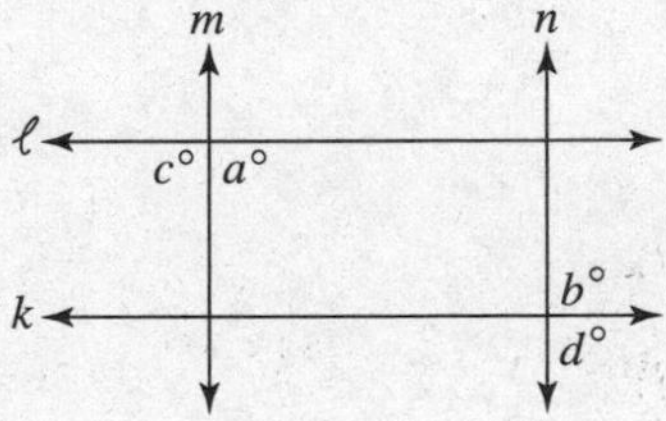

Ⓐ $c = d$
Ⓑ ℓ and k are parallel
Ⓒ m and ℓ are perpendicular

7. In the figure below, $a:b = 3:5$ and $c:b = 2:1$. What is the measure of the largest angle?

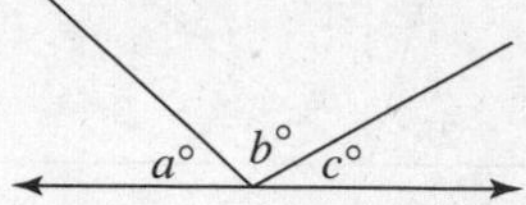

Ⓐ 30
Ⓑ 45
Ⓒ 50
Ⓓ 90
Ⓔ 100

8. A, B, and C are points on a line with B between A and C. Let M and N be the midpoints of AB and BC, respectively. If $AB:BC = 3:1$, what is $MN:BC$?

Ⓐ 1:2
Ⓑ 2:3
Ⓒ 1:1
Ⓓ 3:2
Ⓔ 2:1

9. In the figure below, lines k and ℓ are parallel. What is the value of $y - x$?

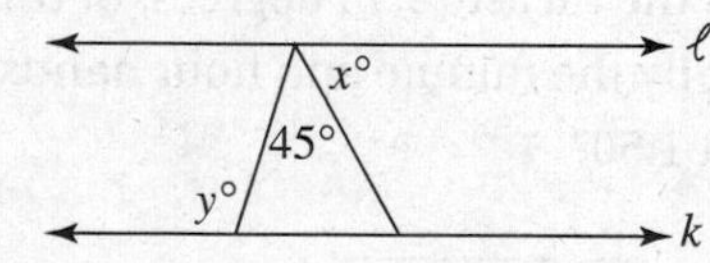

Ⓐ 15
Ⓑ 30
Ⓒ 45
Ⓓ 60
Ⓔ 75

10. In the figure below, line m bisects $\angle AOC$ and line ℓ bisects $\angle AOB$. What is the measure of $\angle DOE$?

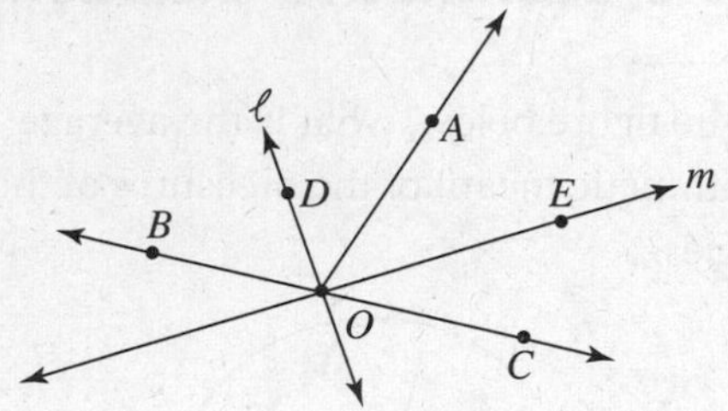

Ⓐ 75
Ⓑ 90
Ⓒ 100
Ⓓ 105
Ⓔ 120

Quantitative Comparison Questions

Ⓐ Quantity A is greater.
Ⓑ Quantity B is greater.
Ⓒ The two quantities are equal.
Ⓓ It is impossible to determine which quantity is greater.

11.

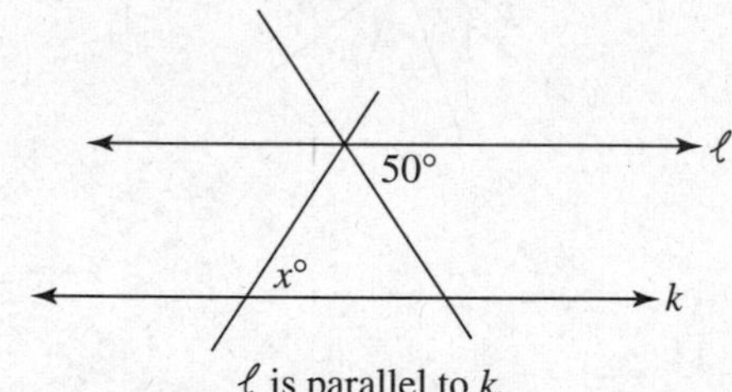

ℓ is parallel to k.

Quantity A	Quantity B
x	50

12.

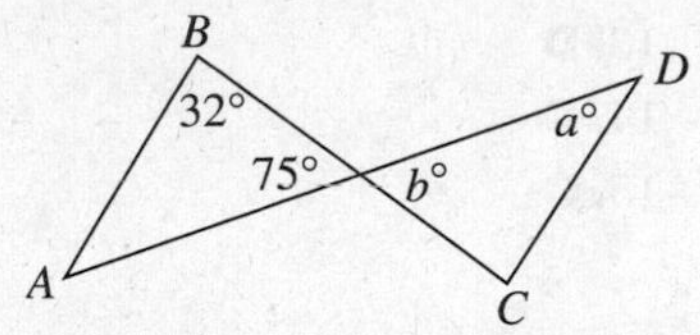

AB is parallel to *CD*.

Quantity A	Quantity B
a	b

13.

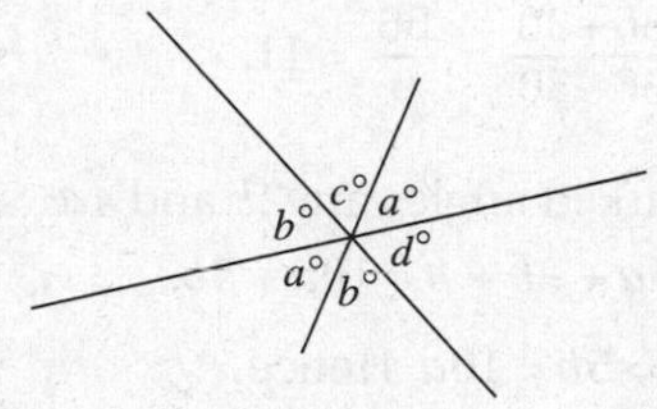

Quantity A	Quantity B
$a + b + c + d$	$2a + 2b$

14.

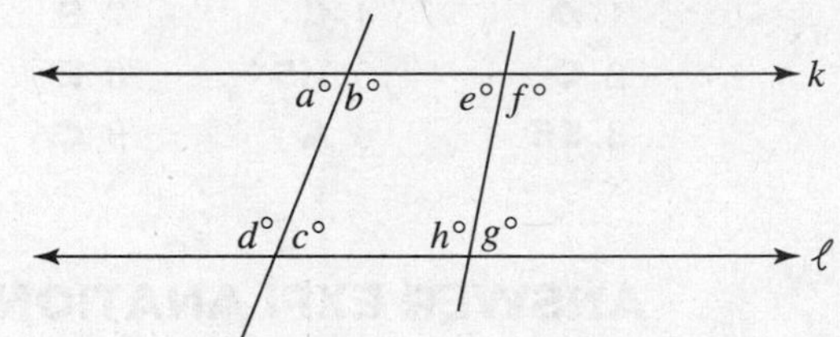

Quantity A	Quantity B
$a + b + c + d$	$e + f + g + h$

15.

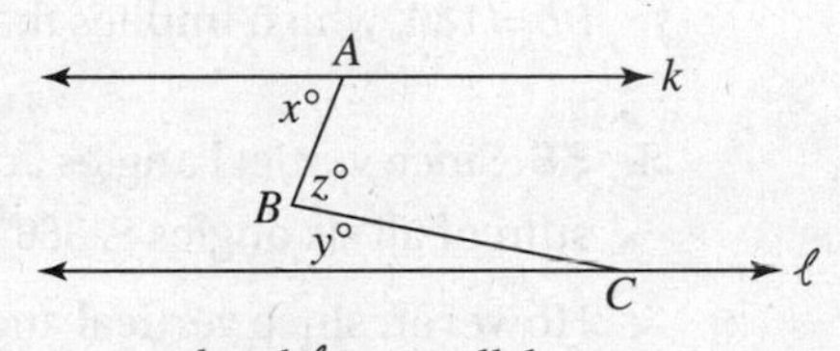

k and *ℓ* are parallel.

Quantity A	Quantity B
z	$x + y$

ANSWER KEY

1. **D**	4. **C**	7. **E**	10. **B**	13. **D**
2. **C**	5. **115**	8. **E**	11. **D**	14. **C**
3. **36**	6. **A**	9. **C**	12. **B**	15. **C**

ANSWER EXPLANATIONS

1. **(D)** The markings in the five angles are irrelevant. The sum of the measures of the five angles is 360°, and $360 \div 5 = 72$. If you calculated the measure of each angle you should have gotten 36, 54, 72, 90, and 108; but you would have wasted time.

2. **(C)** From the diagram, we see that $6a = 180$, which implies that $a = 30$, and that $5b = 180$, which implies that $b = 36$. So, $\frac{b+a}{b-a} = \frac{36+30}{36-30} = \frac{66}{6} = 11$.

3. **36** Since vertical angles are equal, the two unmarked angles are $2b$ and $4a$. Since the sum of all six angles is 360°, $360 = 4a + 2b + 2a + 4a + 2b + b = 10a + 5b$.

   However, since vertical angles are equal, $b = 2a \Rightarrow 5b = 10a$. Hence,

   $$360 = 10a + 5b = 10a + 10a = 20a, \text{ so } a = 18 \text{ and } b = 36.$$

4. **(C)** Since $x + y + 90 = 180$, $x + y = 90$. Also, since $y{:}x = 3{:}2$, $y = 3t$ and $x = 2t$. Therefore, $3t + 2t = 90 \Rightarrow 5t = 90$. So $t = 18$, and $x = 2(18) = 36$.

5. **115** For problems such as this, always draw a diagram. The measure of each of the 12 central angles from one number to the next on the clock is 30°. At 1:50 the minute hand is pointing at 10, and the hour hand has gone $\frac{50}{60} = \frac{5}{6}$ the way from 1 to 2. So from 10 to 1 on the clock is 90°, and from 1 to the hour hand is $\frac{5}{6}(30°) = 25°$, for a total of $90° + 25° = 115°$.

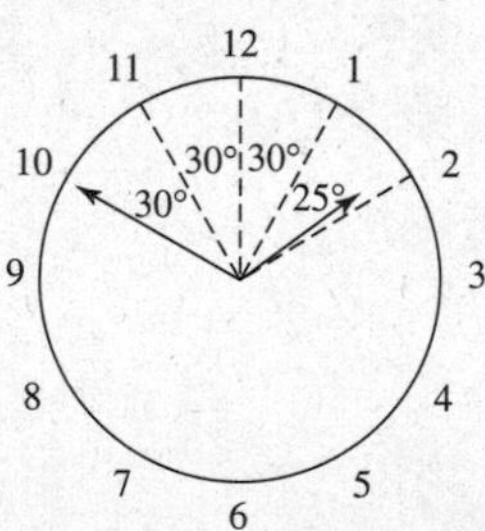

6. **(A)** No conclusions can be made about the lines; they could form any angles whatsoever. (B and C are both false.) Since $a = b$,

   $$c = 180 - a = 180 - b = d$$

   (A is true.)

7. **(E)** Since $a{:}b = 3{:}5$, then $a = 3x$ and $b = 5x$. $c{:}b = c{:}5x = 2{:}1 \Rightarrow c = 10x$. Then, $3x + 5x + 10x = 180 \Rightarrow 18x = 180$. So, $x = 10$ and $c = 10x = 100$.

8. **(E)** If a diagram is not provided on a geometry question, draw one on your scrap paper. From the figure below, you can see that $MN{:}BC = 2{:}1$.

9. **(C)** Since the lines are parallel, the angle marked y and the sum of the angles marked x and 45 are equal: $y = x + 45 \Rightarrow y - x = 45$.

10. **(B)** Let $x = \frac{1}{2}\text{m}\angle AOC$, and $y = \frac{1}{2}\text{m}\angle AOB$.

    Then, $x + y = \frac{1}{2}\text{m}\angle AOC + \frac{1}{2}\text{m}\angle AOB = \frac{1}{2}(180) = 90$.

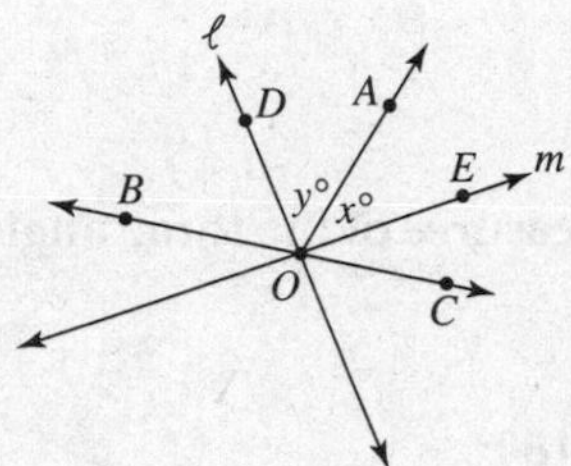

11. **(D)** No conclusion can be made: x could equal 50 or be more or less.

12. **(B)** Since $\text{m}\angle A + 32 + 75 = 180$, $\text{m}\angle A = 73$; and since AB is parallel to CD, $a = 73$, whereas, because vertical angles are equal, $b = 75$.

13. **(D)**

	Quantity A	Quantity B
	$a + b + c + d$	$2a + 2b$
Subtract a and b from each quantity:	$c + d$	$a + b$
Since $b = d$, subtract them:	c	a

There is no way to determine whether a is less than, greater than, or equal to c.

14. **(C)** Whether the lines are parallel or not, $a + b = c + d = e + f = g + h = 180$.

    Each quantity is equal to 360.

15. **(C)** Extend line segment AB to form a transversal. Since $w + z = 180$ and $w + (x + y) = 180$, it follows that $z = x + y$.

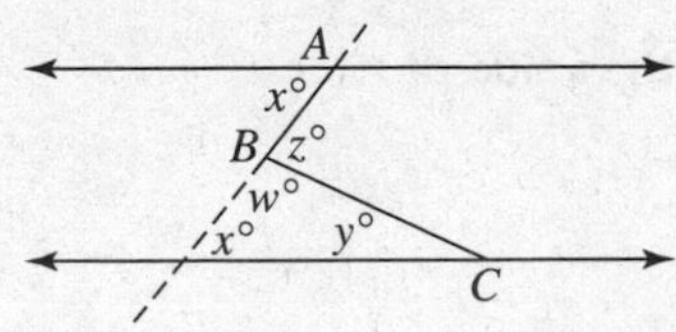

12-J. TRIANGLES

- Sides and Angles of a Triangle
- Classification of Triangles
- Right Triangles
- Pythagorean Theorem
- Special Right Triangles
- Triangle Inequality
- Perimeter and Area
- Practice Exercises
- Answer Explanations

Sides and Angles of a Triangle

More geometry questions on the GRE pertain to triangles than to any other topic. To answer them, there are several important facts that you need to know about the angles and sides of triangles. The KEY FACTS in this section are extremely useful. Read them carefully, a few times if necessary, and *make sure you learn them all.*

KEY FACT J1

In any triangle, the sum of the measures of the three angles is 180°:

$$x + y + z = 180°$$

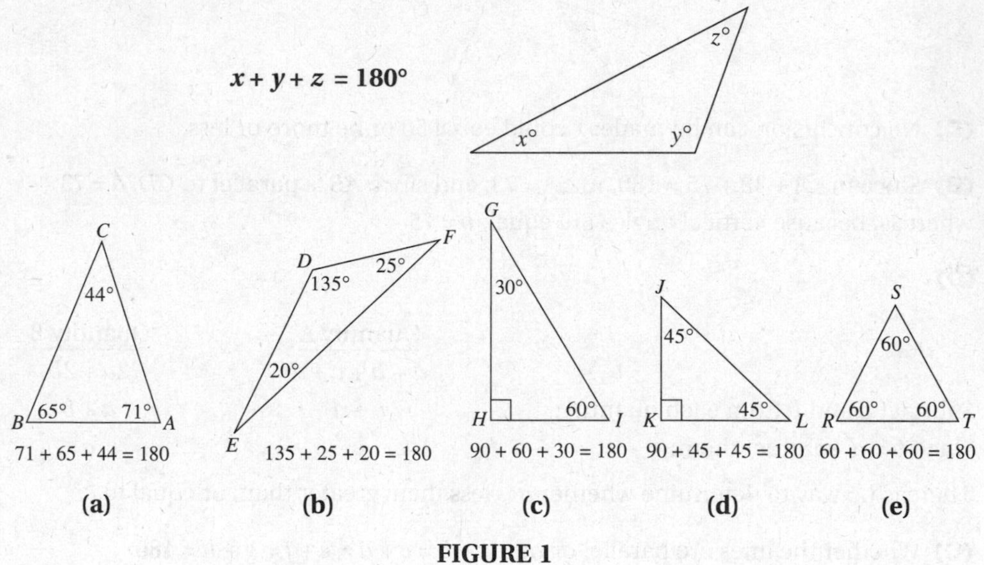

FIGURE 1

Figure 1 (a–e) illustrates KEY FACT J1 for five different triangles, which will be discussed below.

EXAMPLE 1

In the figure below, what is the value of *x*?

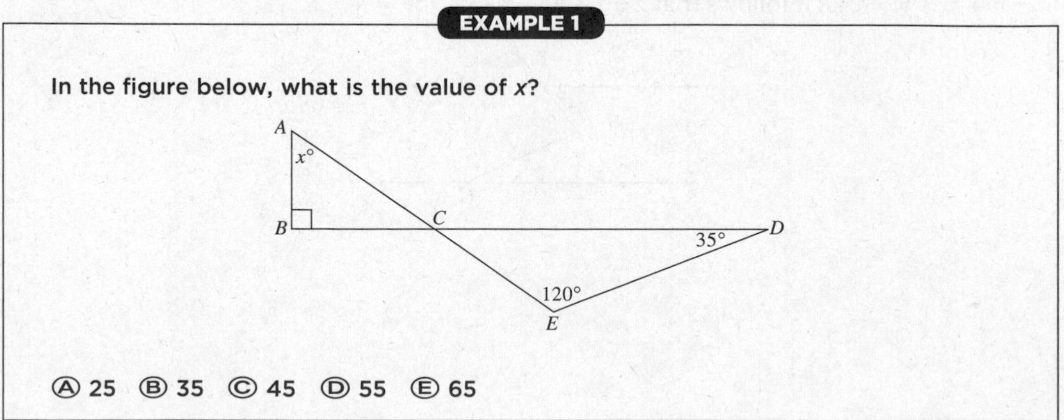

Ⓐ 25 Ⓑ 35 Ⓒ 45 Ⓓ 55 Ⓔ 65

SOLUTION.

Use KEY FACT J1 twice: first, for $\triangle CDE$ and then for $\triangle ABC$.

- $m\angle DCE + 120 + 35 = 180 \Rightarrow m\angle DCE + 155 = 180 \Rightarrow m\angle DCE = 25$.
- Since vertical angles are equal, $m\angle ACB = 25$ (see KEY FACT I6, page 448).
- $x + 90 + 25 = 180 \Rightarrow x + 115 = 180$, and so $x =$ **65 (E)**.

EXAMPLE 2

In the figure at the right, what is the value of *a*?

Ⓐ 45 Ⓑ 60 Ⓒ 75 Ⓓ 120 Ⓔ 135

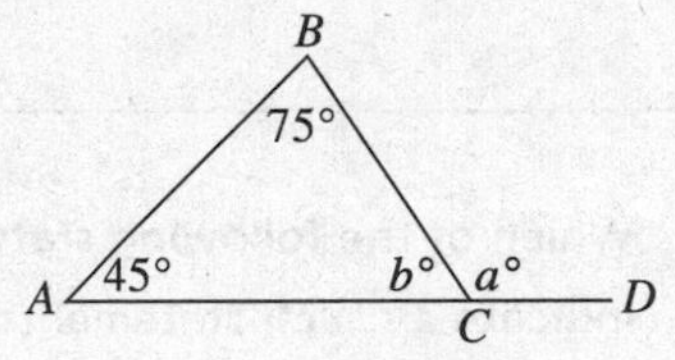

SOLUTION.

First find the value of b: $180 = 45 + 75 + b = 120 + b \Rightarrow b = 60$.

Then, $a + b = 180 \Rightarrow a = 180 - b = 180 - 60 =$ **120 (D)**.

In Example 2, $\angle BCD$, which is formed by one side of $\triangle ABC$ and the extension of another side, is called an ***exterior angle***. Note that to find a we did not have to first find b; we could have just added the other two angles: $a = 75 + 45 = 120$. This is a useful fact to remember.

KEY FACT J2

The measure of an exterior angle of a triangle is equal to the sum of the measures of the two opposite interior angles.

KEY FACT J3

In any triangle:

- **the longest side is opposite the largest angle;**
- **the shortest side is opposite the smallest angle;**
- **sides with the same length are opposite angles with the same measure.**

CAUTION

In KEY FACT J3 the condition "in any triangle" is crucial. If the angles are not in the same triangle, none of the conclusions hold. For example, in the figures below, *AB* and *DE* are *not* equal even though they are each opposite a 90° angle, and *QS* is not the longest side in the figure, even though it is opposite the largest angle in the figure.

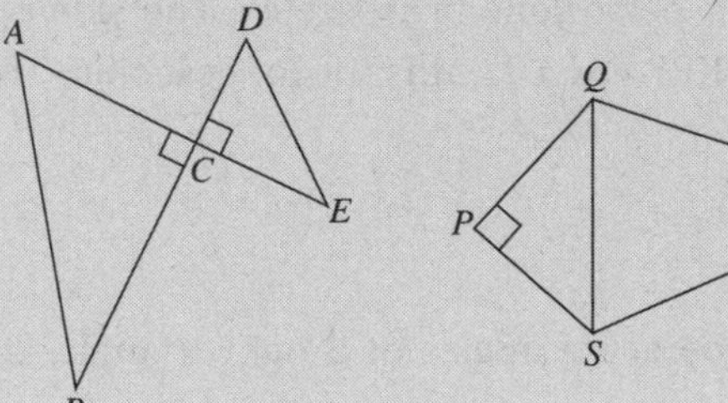

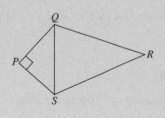

Consider triangles *ABC*, *JKL*, and *RST* in Figure 1 on page 457.

- In $\triangle ABC$: *BC* is the longest side since it is opposite angle *A*, the largest angle (71°). Similarly, *AB* is the shortest side since it is opposite angle *C*, the smallest angle (44°). So $AB < AC < BC$.
- In $\triangle JKL$: angles *J* and *L* have the same measure (45°), so $JK = KL$.
- In $\triangle RST$: since all three angles have the same measure (60°), all three sides have the same length: $RS = ST = TR$.

EXAMPLE 3

Which of the following statements concerning the length of side *YZ* is true? Indicate *all* such statements.

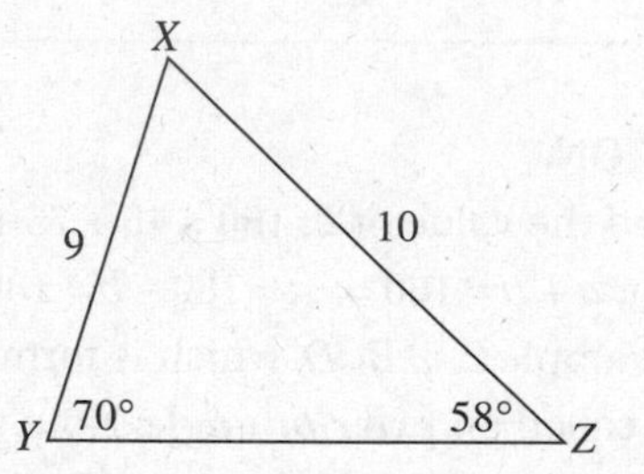

[A] $YZ < 9$

[B] $YZ = 9$

[C] $9 < YZ < 10$

[D] $YZ = 10$

[E] $YZ < 10$

SOLUTION.

Since the five answer choices are mutually exclusive, only one of them can be true.

- By KEY FACT J1, $m\angle X + 70 + 58 = 180 \Rightarrow m\angle X = 52$.
- So, *X* is the smallest angle.
- Therefore, by KEY FACT J3, *YZ* is the shortest side. So $\boldsymbol{YZ < 9}$ **(A)**.

Classification of Triangles

Name	Lengths of the Sides	Measures of the Angles	Examples from Figure 1
scalene	all 3 different	all 3 different	*ABC, DEF, GHI*
isosceles	2 the same	2 the same	*JKL*
equilateral	all 3 the same	all 3 the same	*RST*

Acute triangles are triangles such as *ABC* and *RST*, in which all three angles are acute. An acute triangle could be scalene, isosceles, or equilateral.

Obtuse triangles are triangles such as *DEF*, in which one angle is obtuse and two are acute. An obtuse triangle could be scalene or isosceles.

Right triangles are triangles such as *GHI* and *JKL*, which have one right angle and two acute ones. A right triangle could be scalene or isosceles. The side opposite the 90° angle is called the ***hypotenuse***, and by KEY FACT J3, it is the longest side. The other two sides are called the ***legs***.

Right Triangles

If x and y are the measures of the acute angles of a right triangle, then by KEY FACT J1, $90 + x + y = 180 \Rightarrow x + y = 90$.

KEY FACT J4

In any right triangle, the sum of the measures of the two acute angles is 90°.

EXAMPLE 4

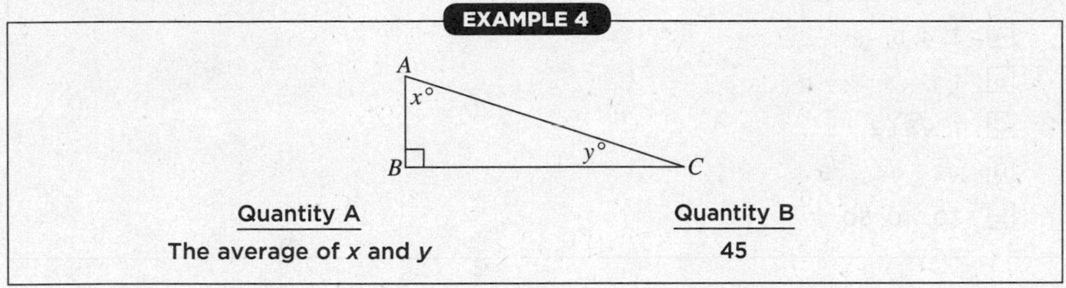

Quantity A	Quantity B
The average of x and y	45

SOLUTION.

Since the diagram indicates that $\triangle ABC$ is a right triangle, then, by KEY FACT J1, $x + y = 90$. So the average of x and $y = \frac{x+y}{2} = \frac{90}{2} = 45$.

The quantities are equal **(C)**.

Pythagorean Theorem

The most important facts concerning right triangles are the **Pythagorean theorem** and its converse, which are given in KEY FACT J5 and repeated as the first line of KEY FACT J6.

TIP

The Pythagorean theorem is probably the most important theorem you need to know. Be sure to review all of its uses.

KEY FACT J5

Let a, b, and c be the sides of $\triangle ABC$, with $a \le b \le c$.
If $\triangle ABC$ is a right triangle, $a^2 + b^2 = c^2$.
If $a^2 + b^2 = c^2$, then $\triangle ABC$ is a right triangle.

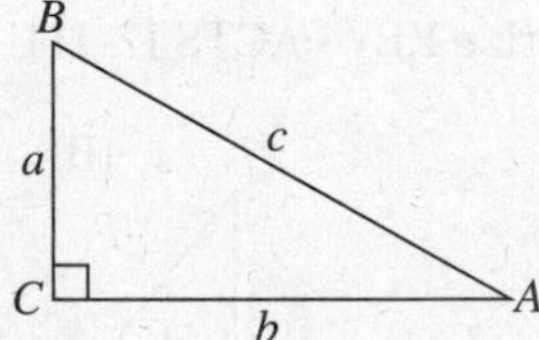

KEY FACT J6

Let a, b, and c be the sides of $\triangle ABC$, with $a \le b \le c$.

- **$a^2 + b^2 = c^2$ if and only if angle C is a right angle. ($\triangle ABC$ is a right triangle.)**
- **$a^2 + b^2 < c^2$ if and only if angle C is obtuse. ($\triangle ABC$ is an obtuse triangle.)**
- **$a^2 + b^2 > c^2$ if and only if angle C is acute. ($\triangle ABC$ is an acute triangle.)**

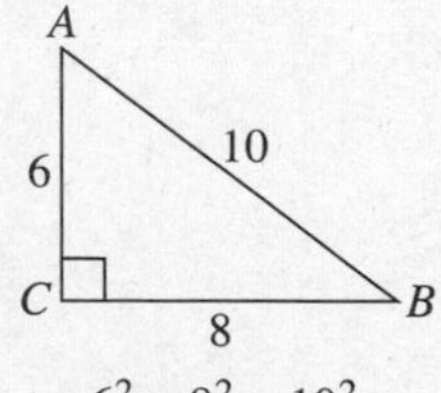

$6^2 + 8^2 = 10^2$

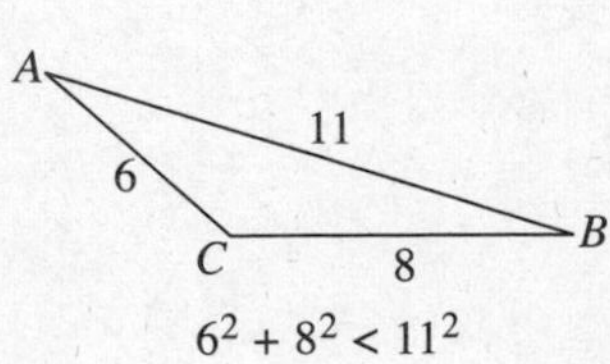

$6^2 + 8^2 < 11^2$

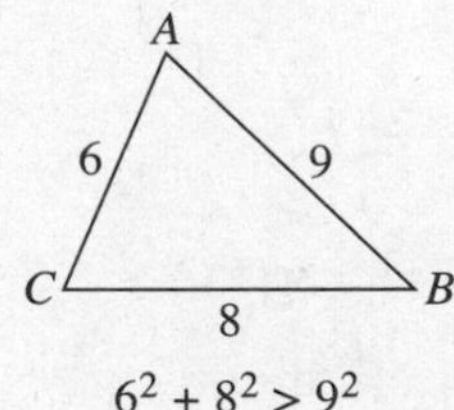

$6^2 + 8^2 > 9^2$

EXAMPLE 5

Which of the following triples are *not* the sides of a right triangle? Indicate *all* such triples.

[A] 3, 4, 5

[B] 1, 1, $\sqrt{3}$

[C] 1, $\sqrt{3}$, 2

[D] $\sqrt{3}$, $\sqrt{4}$, $\sqrt{5}$

[E] 30, 40, 50

SOLUTION.

Just check each choice.

(A) $3^2 + 4^2 = 9 + 16 = 25 = 5^2$ These *are* the sides of a right triangle.

(B) $1^2 + 1^2 = 1 + 1 = 2 \neq (\sqrt{3})^2$ These *are not* the sides of a right triangle.

(C) $1^2 + (\sqrt{3})^2 = 1 + 3 = 4 = 2^2$ These *are* the sides of a right triangle.

(D) $(\sqrt{3})^2 + (\sqrt{4})^2 = 3 + 4 = 7 \neq (\sqrt{5})^2$ These *are not* the sides of a right triangle.

(E) $30^2 + 40^2 = 900 + 1{,}600 = 2{,}500 = 50^2$ These *are* the sides of a right triangle.

The answer is **B** and **D.**

Below are the right triangles that appear most often on the GRE. You should recognize them immediately whenever they come up in questions. Carefully study each one, and memorize KEY FACTS J7–J11.

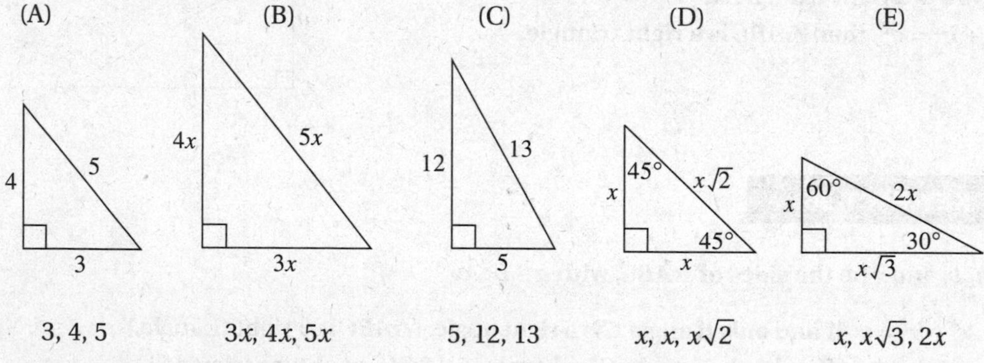

On the GRE, the most common right triangles whose sides are integers are the 3-4-5 triangle (A) and its multiples (B).

KEY FACT J7

For any positive number *x*, there is a right triangle whose sides are 3*x*, 4*x*, 5*x*.

For example:

$x = 1$	3, 4, 5	$x = 5$	15, 20, 25
$x = 2$	6, 8, 10	$x = 10$	30, 40, 50
$x = 3$	9, 12, 15	$x = 50$	150, 200, 250
$x = 4$	12, 16, 20	$x = 100$	300, 400, 500

NOTE: The only other right triangle with integer sides that you should recognize immediately is the one whose sides are 5, 12, 13 (C).

TIP

KEY FACT J7 applies even if *x* is not an integer. For example:
$x = .5$ 1.5, 2, 2.5
$x = \pi$ 3π, 4π, 5π

Special Right Triangles

Let x = length of each leg, and h = length of the hypotenuse, of an isosceles right triangle (D). By the Pythagorean theorem (KEY FACT J5), $x^2 + x^2 = h^2$.

So, $2x^2 = h^2$, and $h = \sqrt{2x^2} = x\sqrt{2}$.

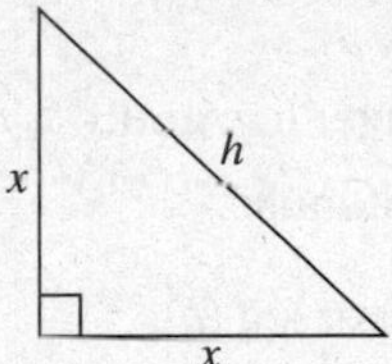

KEY FACT J8

In a 45-45-90 right triangle, the sides are *x*, *x*, and $x\sqrt{2}$. So,

- **by multiplying the length of a leg by $\sqrt{2}$, you get the hypotenuse.**
- **by dividing the hypotenuse by $\sqrt{2}$, you get the length of each leg.**

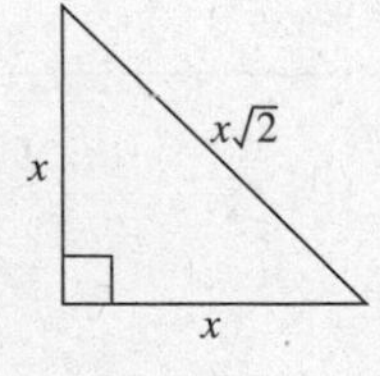

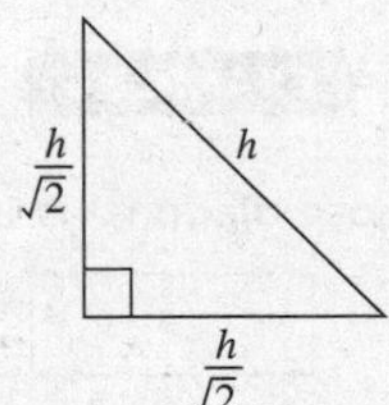

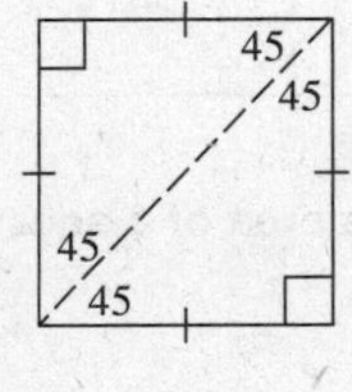

KEY FACT J9

The diagonal of a square divides the square into two isosceles right triangles.

The last important right triangle is the one whose angles measure 30°, 60°, and 90° **(E)**.

KEY FACT J10

An altitude divides an equilateral triangle into two 30-60-90 right triangles.

Let $2x$ be the length of each side of equilateral $\triangle ABC$ in which altitude AD is drawn. Then $\triangle ABD$ is a 30-60-90 right triangle, and its sides are x, $2x$, and h.

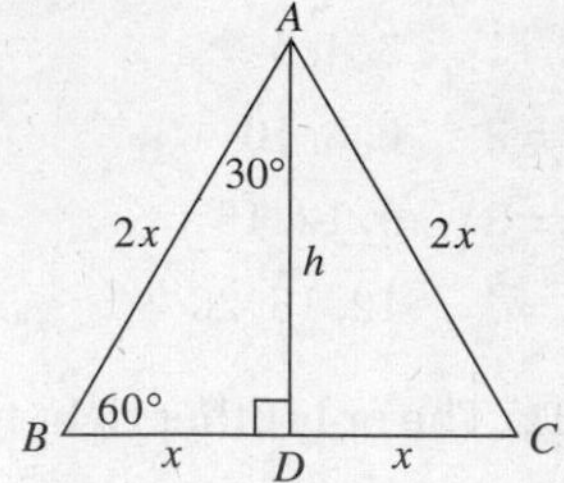

By the Pythagorean theorem,

$$x^2 + h^2 = (2x)^2 = 4x^2$$

So $h^2 = 3x^2$, and $h = \sqrt{3x^2} = x\sqrt{3}$.

KEY FACT J11

In a 30-60-90 right triangle the sides are x, $x\sqrt{3}$, and $2x$.

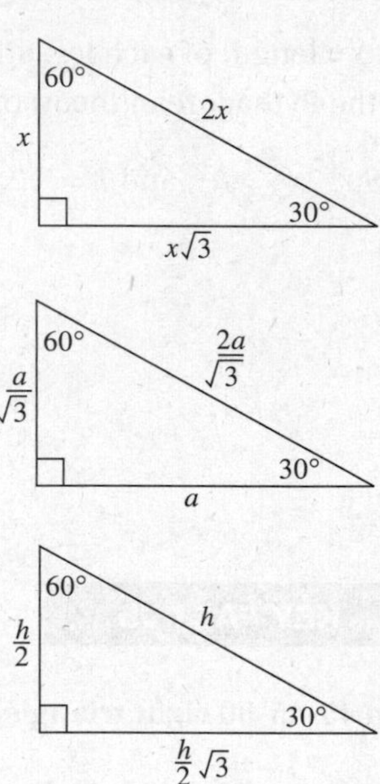

If you know the length of the shorter leg (x),

- multiply it by $\sqrt{3}$ to get the longer leg, and
- multiply it by 2 to get the hypotenuse.

If you know the length of the longer leg (a),

- divide it by $\sqrt{3}$ to get the shorter leg, and
- multiply the shorter leg by 2 to get the hypotenuse.

If you know the length of the hypotenuse (h),

- divide it by 2 to get the shorter leg, and
- multiply the shorter leg by $\sqrt{3}$ to get the longer leg.

EXAMPLE 6

What is the area of a square whose diagonal is 10?

SOLUTION.

Draw a diagonal in a square of side s, creating a 45-45-90 right triangle. By KEY FACT J8:

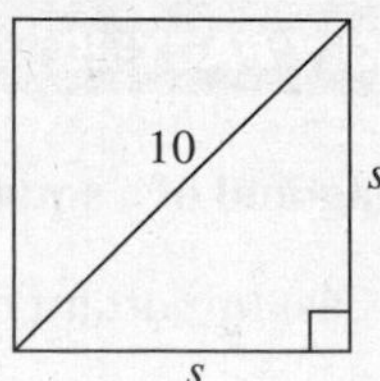

$$s = \frac{10}{\sqrt{2}} \text{ and } A = s^2 = \left(\frac{10}{\sqrt{2}}\right)^2 = \frac{100}{2} = \mathbf{50}$$

EXAMPLE 7

In the diagram at the right, if $BC = \sqrt{6}$, what is the value of CD?

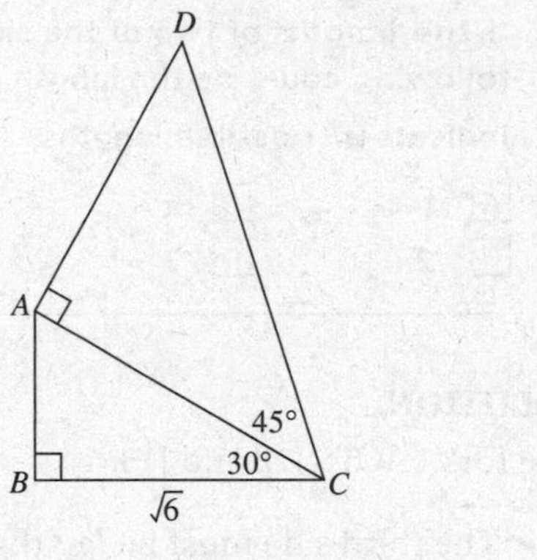

Ⓐ $2\sqrt{2}$

Ⓑ $4\sqrt{2}$

Ⓒ $2\sqrt{3}$

Ⓓ $2\sqrt{6}$

Ⓔ 4

SOLUTION.
Since $\triangle ABC$ and $\triangle DAC$ are 30-60-90 and 45-45-90 right triangles, respectively, use KEY FACTS J11 and J8.

- Divide the longer leg, BC, by $\sqrt{3}$ to get the shorter leg, AB: $\frac{\sqrt{6}}{\sqrt{3}} = \sqrt{2}$.
- Multiply AB by 2 to get the hypotenuse: $AC = 2\sqrt{2}$.
- Since AC is also a leg of isosceles right $\triangle DAC$, to get hypotenuse CD, multiply AC by $\sqrt{2}$: $CD = 2\sqrt{2} \times \sqrt{2} = 2 \times 2 =$ **4 (E)**.

Triangle Inequality

The important results in KEY FACTS J12 and J13 are known as the triangle inequality.

KEY FACT J12

The sum of the lengths of any two sides of a triangle is greater than the length of the third side.

The best way to remember this is to see that $x + y$, the length of the path from A to C through B, is greater than z, the length of the direct path from A to C.

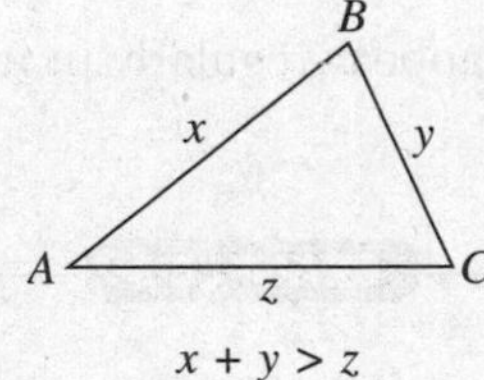

$x + y > z$

NOTE: If you subtract x from each side of $x + y > z$, you see that $z - x < y$.

KEY FACT J13

The difference of the lengths of any two sides of a triangle is less than the length of the third side.

EXAMPLE 8

If the lengths of two of the sides of a triangle are 6 and 7, which of the following could be the length of the third side?

Indicate *all* possible lengths.

Ⓐ 1
Ⓑ 2
Ⓒ π
Ⓓ 7
Ⓔ 12
Ⓕ 13
Ⓖ 15

SOLUTION.

Use KEY FACTS J12 and J13.

- The third side must be *less* than $6 + 7 = 13$. (Eliminate F and G.)
- The third side must be *greater* than $7 - 6 = 1$. (Eliminate A.)
- *Any* number between 1 and 13 could be the length of the third side.

The answer is **B**, **C**, **D**, **E**.

The following diagram illustrates several triangles, two of whose sides have lengths of 6 and 7.

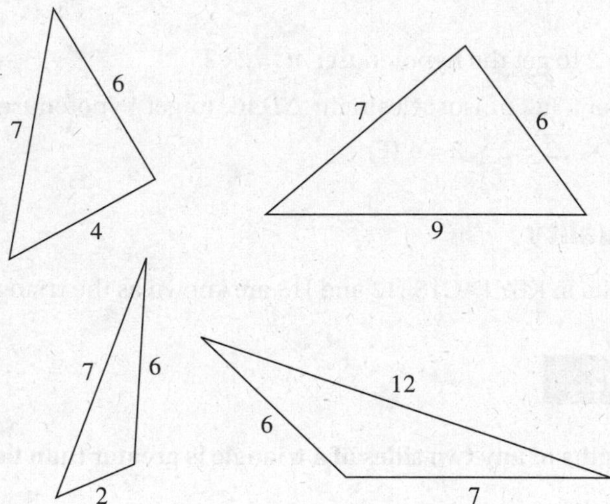

Perimeter and Area

On the GRE, two other terms that appear regularly in triangle problems are ***perimeter*** and ***area*** (see Section 12-K, page 473).

EXAMPLE 9

In the figure at the right, what is the perimeter of $\triangle ABC$?

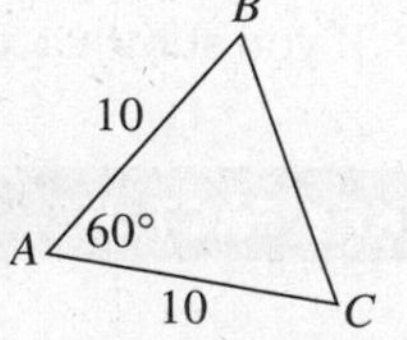

Ⓐ $20 + 10\sqrt{2}$
Ⓑ $20 + 10\sqrt{3}$
Ⓒ 25
Ⓓ 30
Ⓔ 40

SOLUTION.

First use KEY FACTS J3 and J1 to find the measures of the angles.

- Since $AB = AC$, $m\angle B = m\angle C$. Represent each of them by x.
- Then, $x + x + 60 = 180 \Rightarrow 2x = 120 \Rightarrow x = 60$.
- Since the measure of each angle of $\triangle ABC$ is 60, the triangle is equilateral.
- So $BC = 10$, and the perimeter is $10 + 10 + 10 =$ **30 (D)**.

KEY FACT J14

The area of a triangle is given by $A = \frac{1}{2}bh$, where b is the base and h is the height.

NOTE:

1. *Any* side of the triangle can be taken as the ***base***.
2. The ***height*** or ***altitude*** is a line segment drawn to the base or, if necessary, to an extension of the base from the opposite vertex.
3. In a right triangle, either leg can be the base and the other the height.
4. The height may be outside the triangle. [See the figure below.]

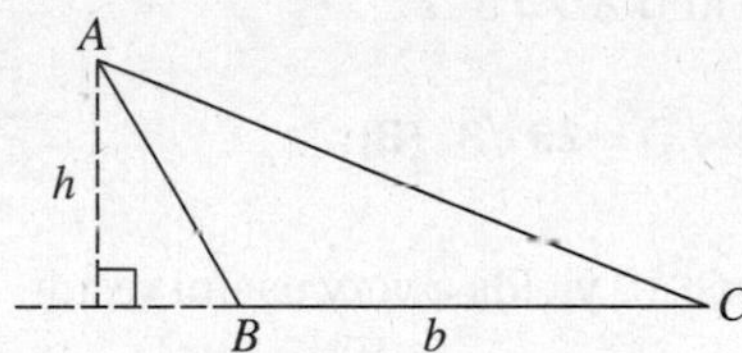

Note: $\triangle ABC$ is obtuse.

TIP

If one endpoint of the base of a triangle is the vertex of an obtuse angle, then the height drawn to that base will be outside the triangle.

In the figure below:

- If AC is the base, BD is the height.
- If AB is the base, CE is the height.
- If BC is the base, AF is the height.

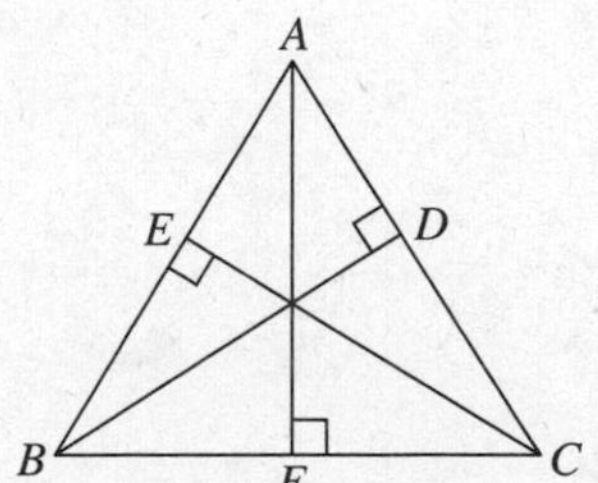

EXAMPLE 10

What is the area of an equilateral triangle whose sides are 10?

Ⓐ 30 Ⓑ $25\sqrt{3}$ Ⓒ 50 Ⓓ $50\sqrt{3}$ Ⓔ 100

SOLUTION.

Draw an equilateral triangle and one of its altitudes.

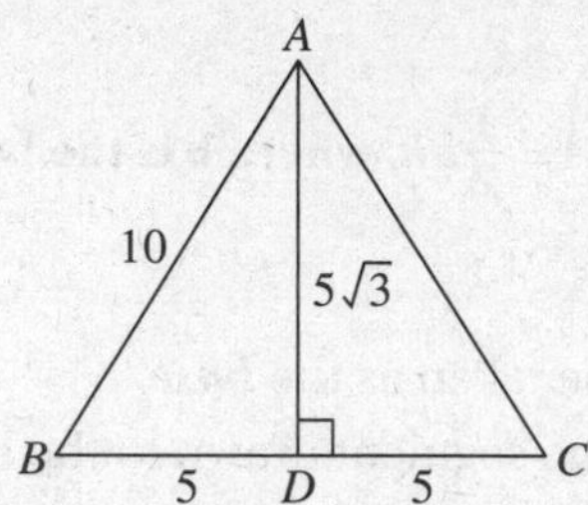

- By KEY FACT J10, $\triangle ABD$ is a 30-60-90 right triangle.
- By KEY FACT J11, $BD = 5$ and $AD = 5\sqrt{3}$.
- The area $\triangle ABC = \frac{1}{2}(10)(5\sqrt{3}) = \mathbf{25\sqrt{3}}$ **(B)**.

Replacing 10 by s in Example 10 yields a very useful result.

TIP

Learn this formula for the area of an equilateral triangle. It can save you time.

KEY FACT J15

If A represents the area of an equilateral triangle with side s, then $A = \frac{s^2\sqrt{3}}{4}$.

PRACTICE EXERCISES—TRIANGLES

Discrete Quantitative Questions

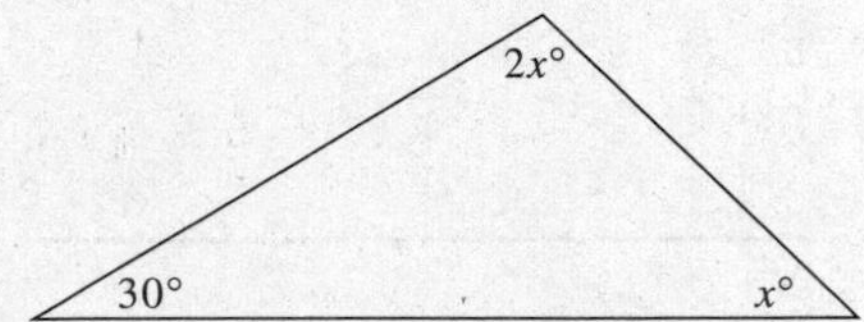

1. In the triangle above, what is the value of x?

   Ⓐ 20
   Ⓑ 30
   Ⓒ 40
   Ⓓ 50
   Ⓔ 60

2. If the difference between the measures of the two smaller angles of a right triangle is 8°, what is the measure, in degrees, of the smallest angle?

   Ⓐ 37
   Ⓑ 41
   Ⓒ 42
   Ⓓ 49
   Ⓔ 53

3. What is the area of an equilateral triangle whose altitude is 6?

   Ⓐ 18
   Ⓑ $12\sqrt{3}$
   Ⓒ $18\sqrt{3}$
   Ⓓ 36
   Ⓔ $24\sqrt{3}$

4. Two sides of a right triangle are 12 and 13. Which of the following *could be* the length of the third side?

   Indicate *all* possible lengths.

   [A] 2
   [B] 5
   [C] $\sqrt{31}$
   [D] 11
   [E] $\sqrt{313}$

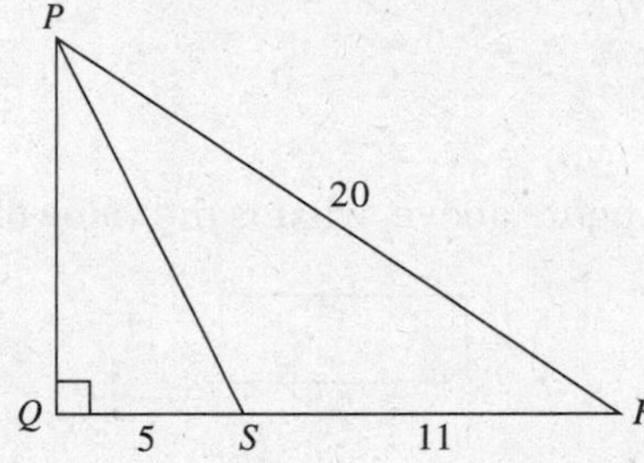

5. What is the value of PS in the triangle above?

   Ⓐ $5\sqrt{2}$
   Ⓑ 10
   Ⓒ 11
   Ⓓ 13
   Ⓔ $12\sqrt{2}$

6. If the measures of the angles of a triangle are in the ratio of 1:2:3, and if the length of the smallest side of the triangle is 10, what is the length of the longest side?

   Ⓐ $10\sqrt{2}$
   Ⓑ $10\sqrt{3}$
   Ⓒ 15
   Ⓓ 20
   Ⓔ 30

7. What is the value of x in the figure below?

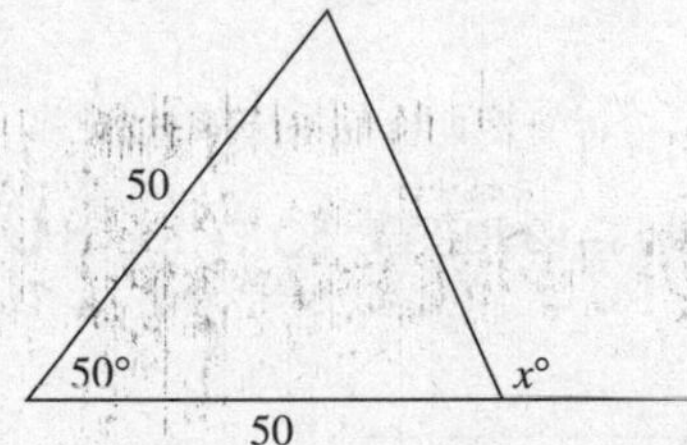

[ ]

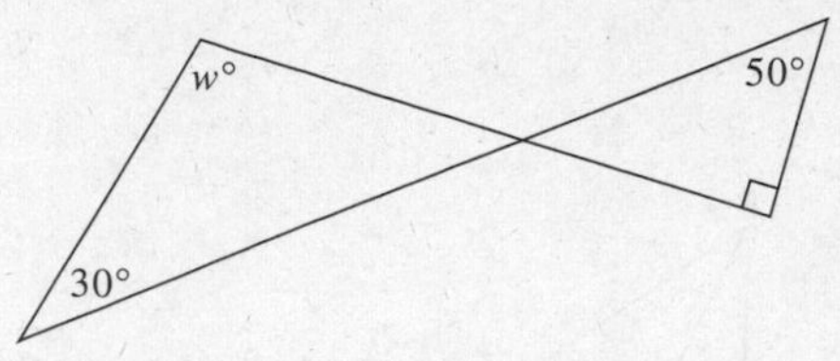

8. In the figure above, what is the value of w?

QUESTIONS 9–10 REFER TO THE FOLLOWING FIGURE.

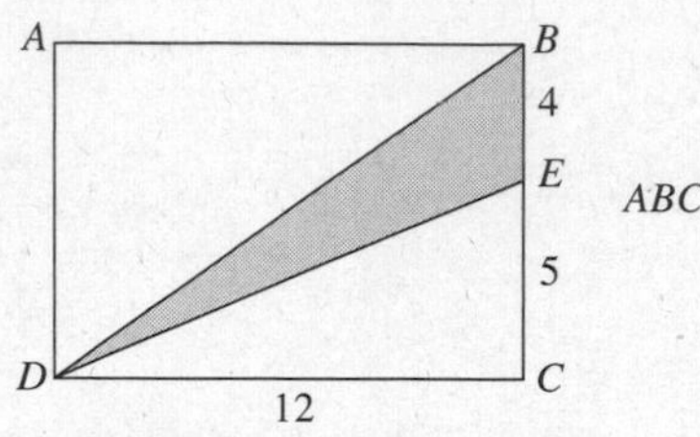

9. What is the area of $\triangle BED$?

Ⓐ 12
Ⓑ 24
Ⓒ 36
Ⓓ 48
Ⓔ 60

10. What is the perimeter of $\triangle BED$?

Ⓐ $19 + 5\sqrt{2}$
Ⓑ 28
Ⓒ $17 + \sqrt{185}$
Ⓓ 32
Ⓔ 36

QUESTIONS 11–12 REFER TO THE FOLLOWING FIGURE.

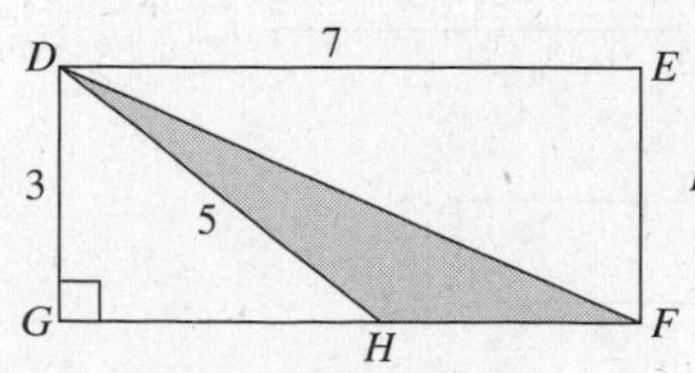

11. What is the area of $\triangle DFH$?

Ⓐ 3
Ⓑ 4.5
Ⓒ 6
Ⓓ 7.5
Ⓔ 10

12. What is the perimeter of $\triangle DFH$?

Ⓐ $8 + \sqrt{41}$
Ⓑ $8 + \sqrt{58}$
Ⓒ 16
Ⓓ 17
Ⓔ 18

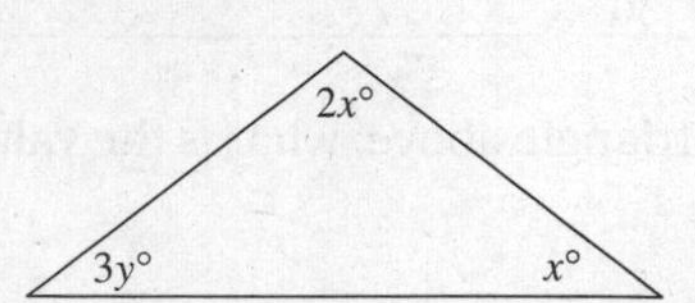

13. Which of the following expresses a true relationship between x and y in the figure above?

Ⓐ $y = 60 - x$
Ⓑ $y = x$
Ⓒ $x + y = 90$
Ⓓ $y = 180 - 3x$
Ⓔ $x = 90 - 3y$

QUESTIONS 14–15 REFER TO THE FOLLOWING FIGURE.

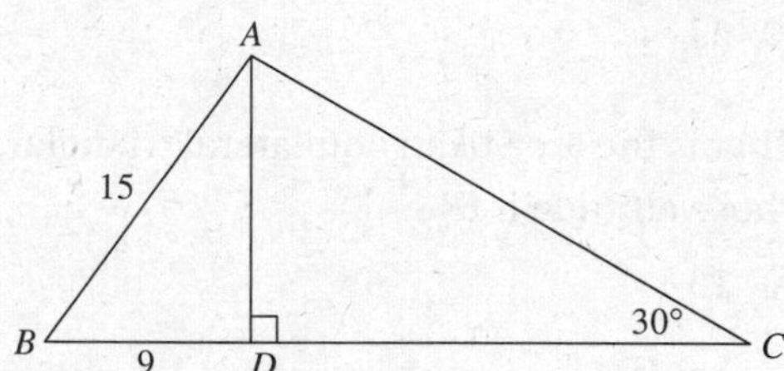

14. What is the perimeter of $\triangle ABC$?

Ⓐ 48
Ⓑ $48 + 12\sqrt{2}$
Ⓒ $48 + 12\sqrt{3}$
Ⓓ 60
Ⓔ $60 + 6\sqrt{3}$

15. What is the area of $\triangle ABC$?

Ⓐ 108
Ⓑ $54 + 72\sqrt{2}$
Ⓒ $54 + 72\sqrt{3}$
Ⓓ 198
Ⓔ 216

Quantitative Comparison Questions

Ⓐ Quantity A is greater.
Ⓑ Quantity B is greater.
Ⓒ The two quantities are equal.
Ⓓ It is impossible to determine which quantity is greater.

16.

The lengths of two sides of a triangle are 7 and 11.

Quantity A	Quantity B
The length of the third side	4

17.

Quantity A	Quantity B
The ratio of the length of a diagonal to the length of a side of a square	$\sqrt{2}$

18.

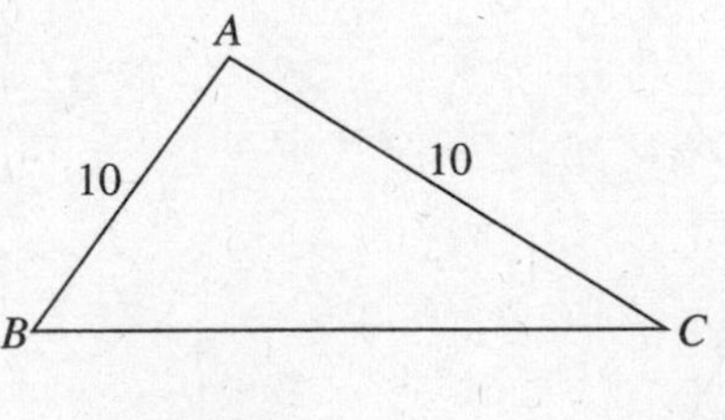

Quantity A	Quantity B
The perimeter of $\triangle ABC$	30

QUESTIONS 19–20 REFER TO THE FOLLOWING FIGURE.

19.

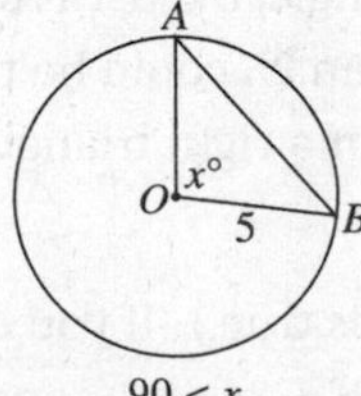

$90 < x$

Quantity A	Quantity B
The length of AB	7

20.

Quantity A	Quantity B
The perimeter of $\triangle AOB$	20

21.

Quantity A	Quantity B
The area of an equilateral triangle whose sides are 10	The area of an equilateral triangle whose altitude is 10

QUESTIONS 22–23 REFER TO THE FOLLOWING FIGURE IN WHICH THE HORIZONTAL AND VERTICAL LINES DIVIDE SQUARE *ABCD* INTO 16 SMALLER SQUARES.

22.

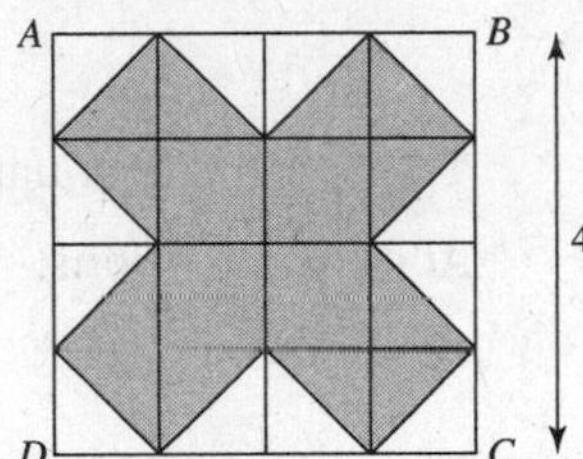

Quantity A	Quantity B
The perimeter of the shaded region	The perimeter of the square

23.

Quantity A	Quantity B
The area of the shaded region	The area of the white region

24.

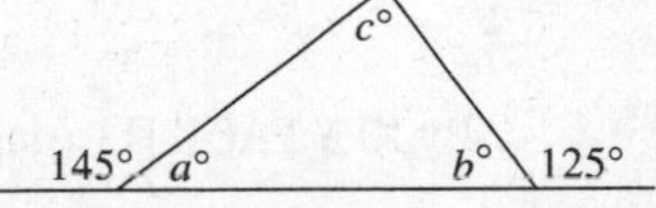

Quantity A	Quantity B
$a + b$	c

25.

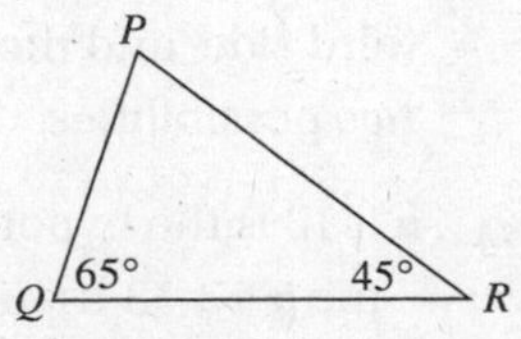

Quantity A	Quantity B
PR	QR

ANSWER KEY

1. **D**	6. **D**	11. **B**	16. **A**	21. **B**
2. **B**	7. **115**	12. **B**	17. **C**	22. **A**
3. **B**	8. **110**	13. **A**	18. **D**	23. **A**
4. **B, E**	9. **B**	14. **C**	19. **A**	24. **C**
5. **D**	10. **D**	15. **C**	20. **B**	25. **B**

ANSWER EXPLANATIONS

1. **(D)** $x + 2x + 30 = 180 \Rightarrow 3x + 30 = 180 \Rightarrow 3x = 150 \Rightarrow x = 50$

2. **(B)** Draw a diagram and label it.

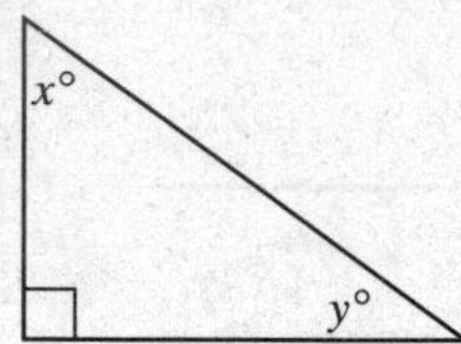

Then write the equations: $x + y = 90$ and $x - y = 8$.

Add the equations:

$$\begin{array}{r} x + y = 90 \\ + x - y = \ \ 8 \\ \hline 2x = 98 \end{array}$$

So $x = 49$ and $y = 90 - 49 = 41$.

3. **(B)** Draw altitude AD in equilateral $\triangle ABC$.

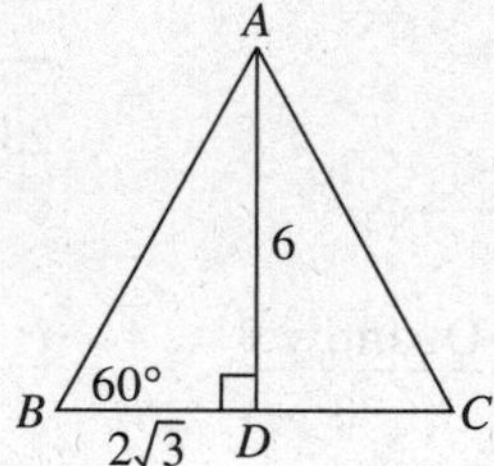

By KEY FACT J11 (page 462), $BD = \dfrac{6}{\sqrt{3}} = \dfrac{6\sqrt{3}}{3} = 2\sqrt{3}$, and BD is one half the base. So, the area is $2\sqrt{3} \times 6 = 12\sqrt{3}$.

4. **(B, E)** If the triangle were not required to be a right triangle, by KEY FACTS J11 and J12 (pages 462–463) *any* number greater than 1 and less than 25 could be the length of the third side, and the answer would be A, B, C, D, E. But for a right triangle, there are only *two* possibilities:

- If 13 is the hypotenuse, then the legs are 12 and 5. (B is true.) (If you didn't recognize the 5-12-13 triangle, use the Pythagorean theorem: $12^2 + x^2 = 13^2$, and solve.)
- If 12 and 13 are the two legs, then use the Pythagorean theorem to find the hypotenuse: $12^2 + 13^2 = c^2 \Rightarrow c^2 = 144 + 169 = 313 \Rightarrow c = \sqrt{313}$. (E is true.)

5. **(D)** Use the Pythagorean theorem twice, unless you recognize the common right triangles in this figure (*which you should*). Since $PR = 20$ and $QR = 16$, $\triangle PQR$ is a $3x$-$4x$-$5x$ right triangle with $x = 4$. So $PQ = 12$, and $\triangle PQS$ is a right triangle whose legs are 5 and 12. The hypotenuse, PS, therefore, is 13.

6. **(D)** If the measures of the angles are in the ratio of 1:2:3,

$$x + 2x + 3x = 180 \Rightarrow 6x = 180 \Rightarrow x = 30$$

So the triangle is a 30-60-90 right triangle, and the sides are a, $2a$, and $a\sqrt{3}$. Since $a = 10$, then $2a$, the length of the longest side, is 20.

7. **115** Label the other angles in the triangle.

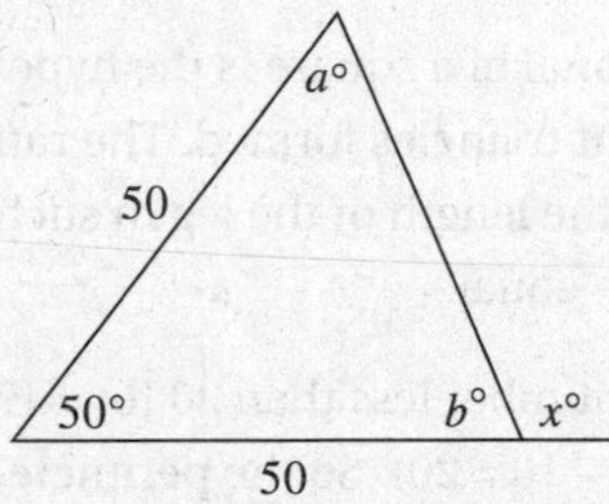

$50 + a + b = 180 \Rightarrow a + b = 130$, and since the triangle is isosceles, $a = b$. Therefore, a and b are each 65, and $x = 180 - 65 = 115$.

8. **110** Here, $50 + 90 + a = 180 \Rightarrow a = 40$, and since vertical angles are equal, $b = 40$. Then, $40 + 30 + w = 180 \Rightarrow w = 110$.

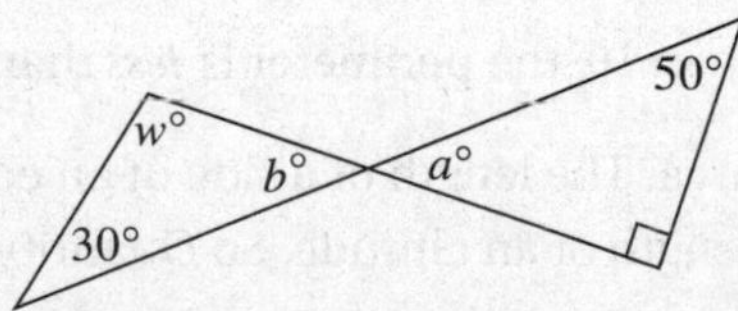

9. **(B)** You could calculate the area of the rectangle and subtract the area of the two white right triangles, but you shouldn't. It is easier to solve this problem if you realize that the shaded area is a triangle whose base is 4 and whose height is 12. The area is $\frac{1}{2}(4)(12) = 24$.

10. **(D)** Since both BD and ED are the hypotenuses of right triangles, their lengths can be calculated by the Pythagorean theorem, but these are triangles you should recognize: the sides of $\triangle DCE$ are 5-12-13, and those of $\triangle BAD$ are 9-12-15 ($3x$-$4x$-$5x$, with $x = 3$). So the perimeter of $\triangle BED$ is $4 + 13 + 15 = 32$.

11. **(B)** Since $\triangle DGH$ is a right triangle whose hypotenuse is 5 and one of whose legs is 3, the other leg, GH, is 4. Since $GF = DE$ is 7, HF is 3. Now, $\triangle DFH$ has a base of 3 (HF) and a height of 3 (DG), and its area is $\frac{1}{2}(3)(3) = 4.5$.

12. **(B)** In $\triangle DFH$, we already have that $DH = 5$ and $HF = 3$; we need only find DF, which is the hypotenuse of $\triangle DEF$. By the Pythagorean theorem, $(DF)^2 = 3^2 + 7^2 = 9 + 49 = 58 \Rightarrow DF = \sqrt{58}$.

So the perimeter is $3 + 5 + \sqrt{58} = 8 + \sqrt{58}$.

13. **(A)** $x + 2x + 3y = 180 \Rightarrow 3x + 3y = 180$. So $x + y = 60$, and $y = 60 - x$.

14. **(C)** $\triangle ABD$ is a right triangle whose hypotenuse is 15 and one of whose legs is 9, so this is a $3x$-$4x$-$5x$ triangle with $x = 3$; so $AD = 12$. Now $\triangle ADC$ is a 30-60-90 triangle, whose shorter leg is 12. Hypotenuse AC is 24, and leg CD is $12\sqrt{3}$. So the perimeter is $24 + 15 + 9 + 12\sqrt{3} = 48 + 12\sqrt{3}$.

15. **(C)** From the solution to 14, we have the base $(9 + 12\sqrt{3})$ the height (12) of $\triangle ABC$. Then, the area is $\frac{1}{2}(12)(9 + 12\sqrt{3}) = 54 + 72\sqrt{3}$.

16. **(A)** Any side of a triangle must be greater than the difference of the other two sides (KEY FACT J13, page 463), so the third side is greater than $11 - 7 = 4$.

17. **(C)** Draw a diagram. A diagonal of a square is the hypotenuse of each of the two 45-45-90 right triangles formed. The ratio of the length of the hypotenuse to the length of the leg in such a triangle is $\sqrt{2}:1$, so the quantities are equal.

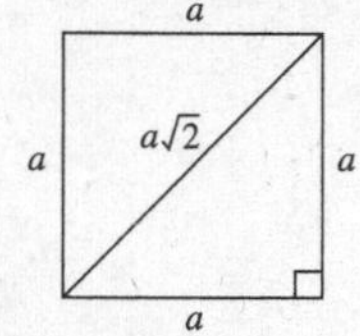

18. **(D)** BC can be any positive number less than 20 (by KEY FACTS J12 and J13, page 463, $BC > 10 - 10 = 0$ and $BC < 10 + 10 = 20$). So the perimeter can be any number greater than 20 and less than 40.

19. **(A)** Since OA and OB are radii, they are each equal to 5. With no restrictions on x, AB could be any positive number less than 10, and the bigger x is, the bigger AB is. If x were 90, AB would be $5\sqrt{2}$, but we are told that $x > 90$, so $AB > 5\sqrt{2} > 7$.

20. **(B)** Since AB must be less than 10, the perimeter is *less* than 20.

21. **(B)** Don't calculate either area. The length of a side of an equilateral triangle is *greater* than the length of an altitude. So Quantity B is larger since it is the area of a triangle whose sides are greater.

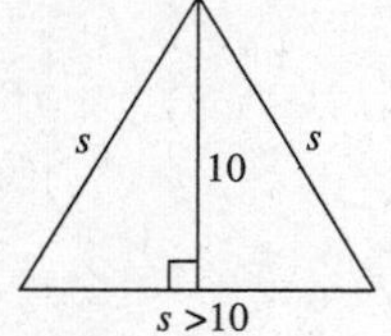

22. **(A)** Quantity A: The perimeter of the shaded region consists of 12 line segments, each of which is the hypotenuse of a 45-45-90 right triangle whose legs are 1. So each line segment is $\sqrt{2}$, and the perimeter is $12\sqrt{2}$. Quantity B: The perimeter of the square is 16.
To compare $12\sqrt{2}$ and 16, square them: $(12\sqrt{2})^2 = 144 \times 2 = 288$; $16^2 = 256$.

23. **(A)** The white region consists of 12 right triangles, each of which has an area of $\frac{1}{2}$, for a total area of 6. Since the area of the large square is 16, the area of the shaded region is $16 - 6 = 10$.

24. **(C)** Since $a = 180 - 145 = 35$ and $b = 180 - 125 = 55$, $a + b = 35 + 55 = 90$. Therefore, $180 = a + b + c = 90 + c \Rightarrow c = 90$.

25. **(B)** Since $65 + 45 = 110$, $m\angle P = 70$. Since $\angle P$ is the largest angle, QR, the side opposite it, is the largest side.

12-K. QUADRILATERALS AND OTHER POLYGONS

- The Angles of a Polygon
- Special Quadrilaterals
- Perimeter and Area of Quadrilaterals
- Practice Exercises
- Answer Explanations

A ***polygon*** is a closed geometric figure made up of line segments. The line segments are called ***sides*** and the endpoints of the line segments are called ***vertices*** (each one is called a ***vertex***). Line segments inside the polygon drawn from one vertex to another are called ***diagonals***. The simplest polygons, which have three sides, are the triangles which you just studied in Section J. A polygon with four sides is called a ***quadrilateral***. The only other terms you should be familiar with are ***pentagon***, ***hexagon***, ***octagon***, and ***decagon***, which are the names for polygons with five, six, eight, and ten sides, respectively.

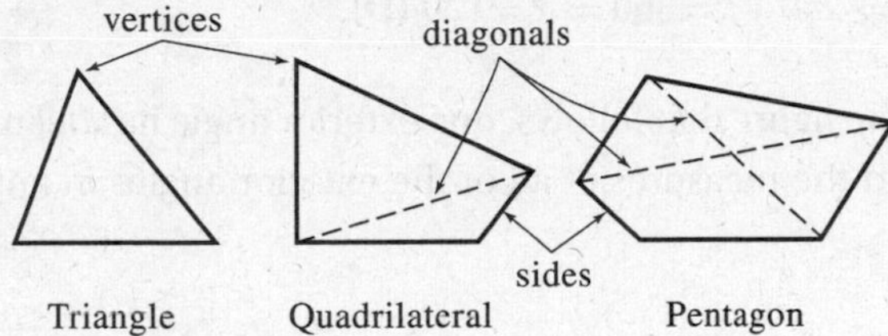

In this section we will present a few facts about polygons and quadrilaterals in general, but the emphasis will be on reviewing the key facts you need to know about four special quadrilaterals.

The Angles of a Polygon

Every quadrilateral has two diagonals. If you draw in either one, you will divide the quadrilateral into two triangles. Since the sum of the measures of the three angles in each of the triangles is 180°, the sum of the measures of the angles in the quadrilateral is 360°.

KEY FACT K1

In any quadrilateral, the sum of the measures of the four angles is 360°.

In exactly the same way, any polygon can be divided into triangles by drawing in all of the diagonals emanating from one vertex.

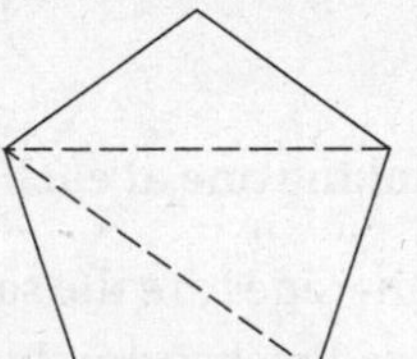

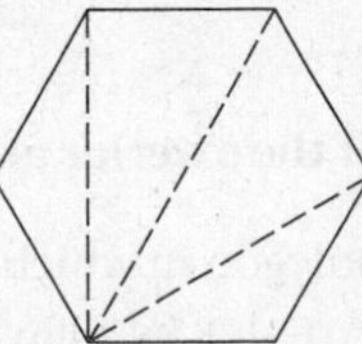

Notice that the pentagon is divided into three triangles, and the hexagon is divided into four triangles. In general, an n-sided polygon is divided into $(n - 2)$ triangles, which leads to KEY FACT K2.

KEY FACT K2

The sum of the measures of the n angles in a polygon with n sides is $(n-2) \times 180°$.

EXAMPLE 1

In the figure at the right, what is the value of x?

Ⓐ 60 Ⓑ 90 Ⓒ 100 Ⓓ 120 Ⓔ 150

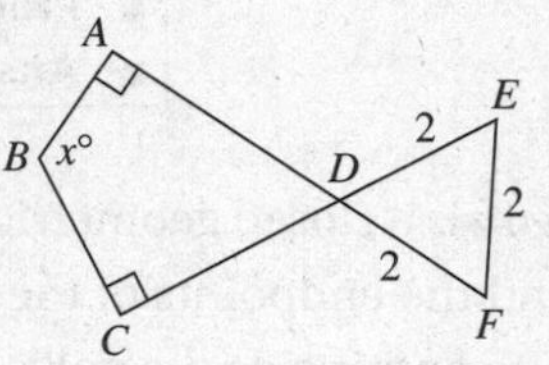

SOLUTION.
Since $\triangle DEF$ is equilateral, all of its angles measure 60°; also, since the two angles at vertex D are vertical angles, their measures are equal. Therefore, the measure of $\angle D$ in quadrilateral $ABCD$ is 60°. Finally, since the sum of the measures of all four angles of $ABCD$ is 360°, $60 + 90 + 90 + x = 360 \Rightarrow 240 + x = 360 \Rightarrow x =$ **120 (D)**.

In the polygons in the figure that follows, one exterior angle has been drawn at each vertex. Surprisingly, if you add the measures of all of the exterior angles in any of the polygons, the sums are equal.

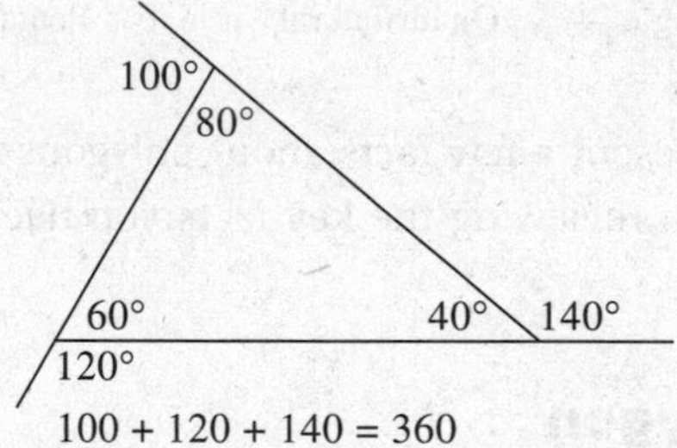

100 + 120 + 140 = 360

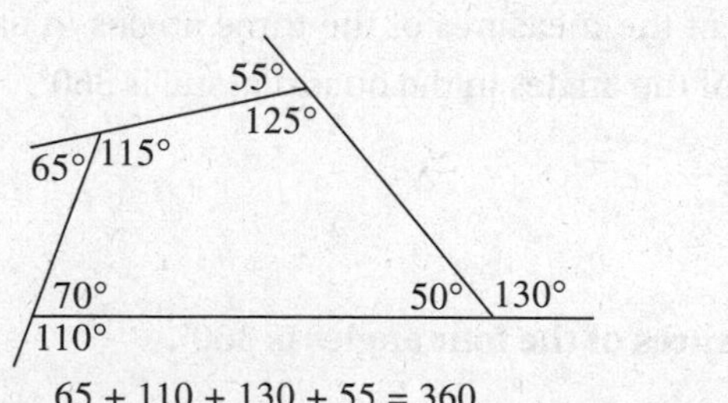

65 + 110 + 130 + 55 = 360

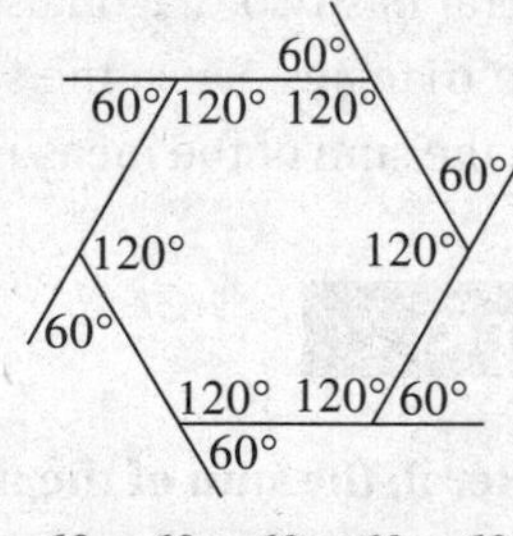

60 + 60 + 60 + 60 + 60 + 60 = 360

KEY FACT K3

In any polygon, the sum of the exterior angles, taking one at each vertex, is 360°.

A ***regular polygon*** is a polygon in which all of the sides are the same length and each angle has the same measure. KEY FACT K4 follows immediately from this definition and from KEY FACTS K2 and K3.

KEY FACT K4

In any regular polygon the measure of each interior angle is $\frac{(n-2)\times 180°}{n}$ and the measure of each exterior angle is $\frac{360°}{n}$.

EXAMPLE 2

What is the measure, in degrees, of each interior angle in a regular decagon?

[ ] degrees

SOLUTION 1.

The measure of each of the 10 interior angles is

$$\frac{(10-2)\times 180°}{10} = \frac{8\times 180°}{10} = \frac{1{,}440°}{10} = \mathbf{144°}$$

SOLUTION 2.

The measure of each of the 10 exterior angles is 36° (360° ÷ 10). Therefore, the measure of each interior angle is 180° – 36° = **144°**.

Special Quadrilaterals

A ***parallelogram*** is a quadrilateral in which both pairs of opposite sides are parallel.

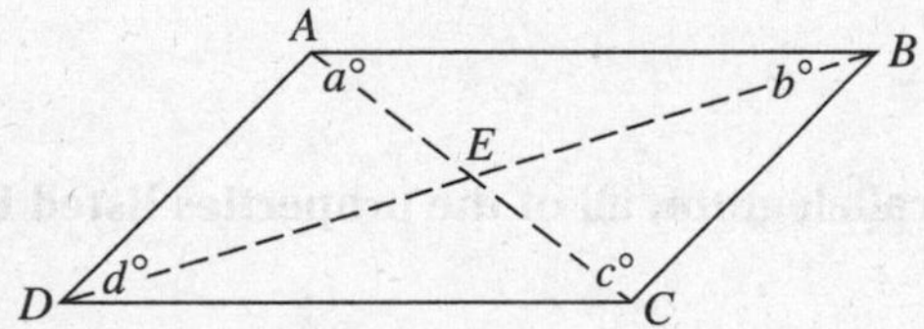

KEY FACT K5

Parallelograms have the following properties:

- **Opposite sides are equal: *AB* = *CD* and *AD* = *BC*.**
- **Opposite angles are equal: $a = c$ and $b = d$.**
- **Consecutive angles add up to 180°: $a + b = 180$, $b + c = 180$, $c + d = 180$, and $a + d = 180$.**
- **The two diagonals bisect each other: *AE* = *EC* and *BE* = *ED*.**
- **A diagonal divides the parallelogram into two triangles that have the exact same size and shape. (The triangles are congruent.)**

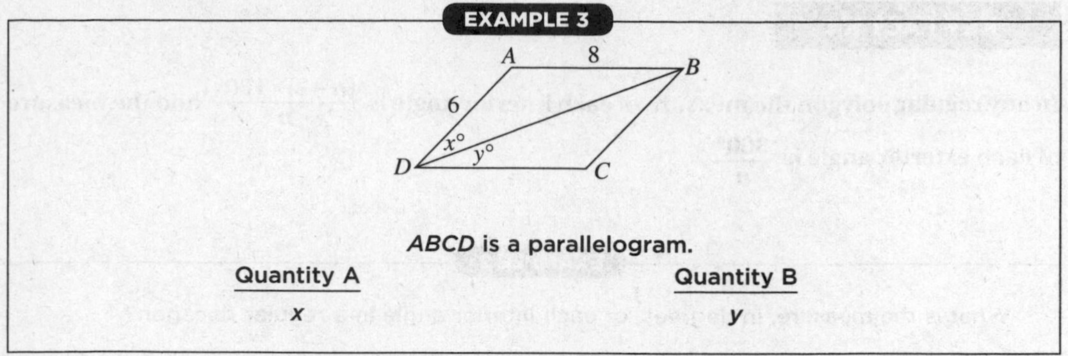

SOLUTION.
In $\triangle ABD$ the larger angle is opposite the larger side (KEY FACT J2, page 457); so $x > m\angle ABD$. However, since AB and CD are parallel sides cut by transversal BD, $y = m\angle ABD$. Therefore, $x > y$. Quantity **A** is greater.

A ***rectangle*** is a parallelogram in which all four angles are right angles. Two adjacent sides of a rectangle are usually called the ***length*** (ℓ) and the ***width*** (w). Note in the right-hand figure that the length is not necessarily greater than the width.

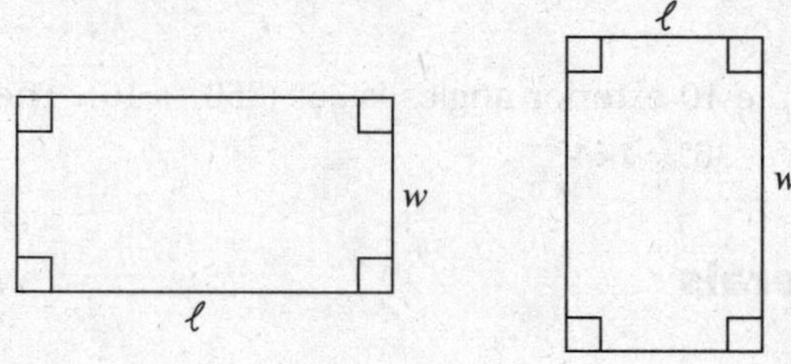

KEY FACT K6

TIP

A rectangle is a parallelogram.

Since a rectangle is a parallelogram, all of the properties listed in KEY FACT K5 hold for rectangles. In addition:

- **The measure of each angle in a rectangle is 90°.**
- **The diagonals of a rectangle have the same length: $AC = BD$.**

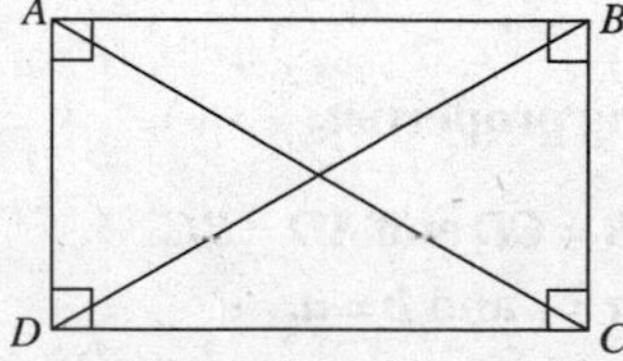

A ***square*** is a rectangle in which all four sides have the same length.

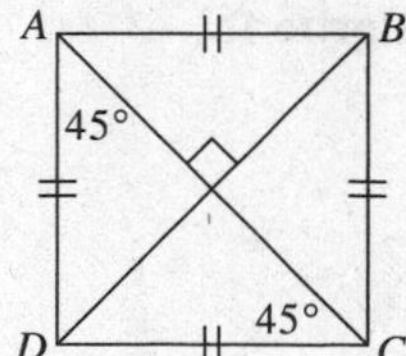

KEY FACT K7

Since a square is a rectangle, all of the properties listed in KEY FACTS K5 and K6 hold for squares. In addition:

- **All four sides have the same length.**
- **Each diagonal divides the square into two 45-45-90 right triangles.**
- **The diagonals are perpendicular to each other: $AC \perp BD$.**

TIP

A square is a rectangle and, hence, a parallelogram.

EXAMPLE 4

What is the length of each side of a square if its diagonals are 10?

Ⓐ 5 Ⓑ 7 Ⓒ $5\sqrt{2}$ Ⓓ $10\sqrt{2}$ Ⓔ $10\sqrt{3}$

SOLUTION.

Draw a diagram.

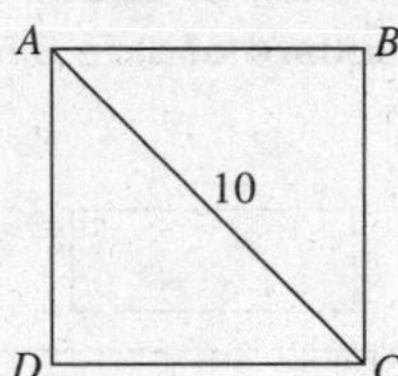

In square *ABCD*, diagonal *AC* is the hypotenuse of $\triangle ABC$ a 45-45-90 right triangle, and side *AB* is a leg of that triangle. By KEY FACT J7 (page 461),

$$AB = \frac{AC}{\sqrt{2}} = \frac{10}{\sqrt{2}} \times \frac{\sqrt{2}}{\sqrt{2}} = \frac{10\sqrt{2}}{2} = \mathbf{5\sqrt{2}\ (C)}$$

A ***trapezoid*** is a quadrilateral in which one pair of sides is parallel and the other pair of sides is not parallel. The parallel sides are called the ***bases*** of the trapezoid. The two bases are never equal. In general, the two nonparallel sides are not equal; if they are, the trapezoid is called an ***isosceles trapezoid***.

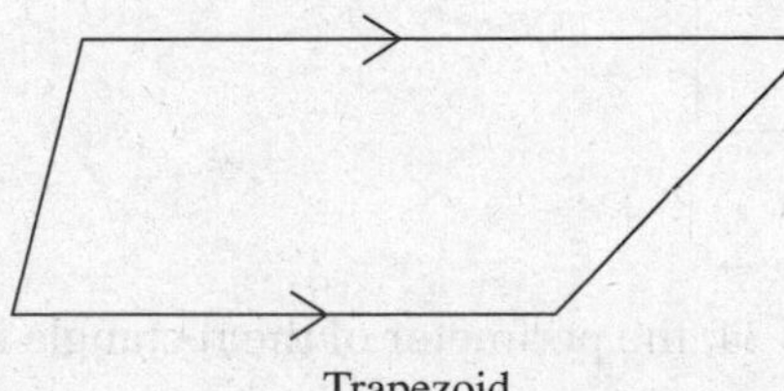

Trapezoid

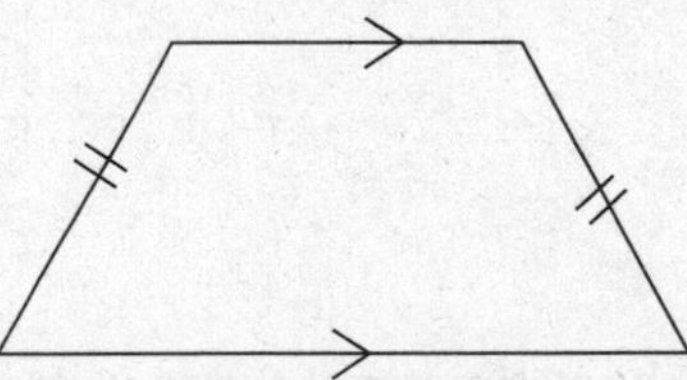

Isoceles trapezoid

The ***perimeter*** (P) of any polygon is the sum of the lengths of all of its sides.

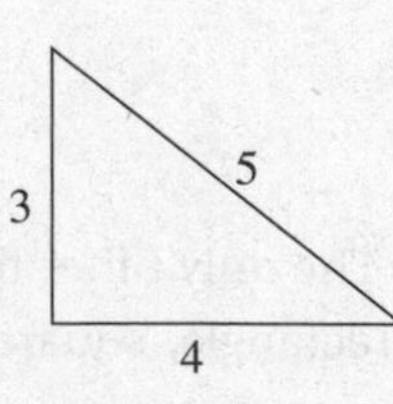

$P = 3 + 4 + 5 = 12$

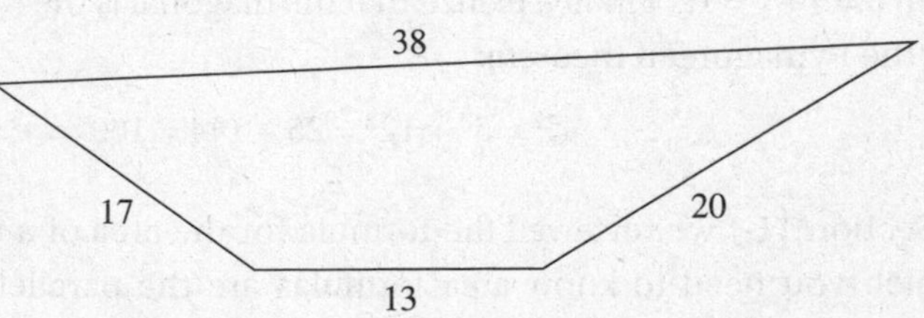

$P = 13 + 17 + 20 + 38 = 88$

Perimeter and Area of Quadrilaterals

KEY FACT K8

In a rectangle, $P = 2(\ell + w)$; in a square, $P = 4s$.

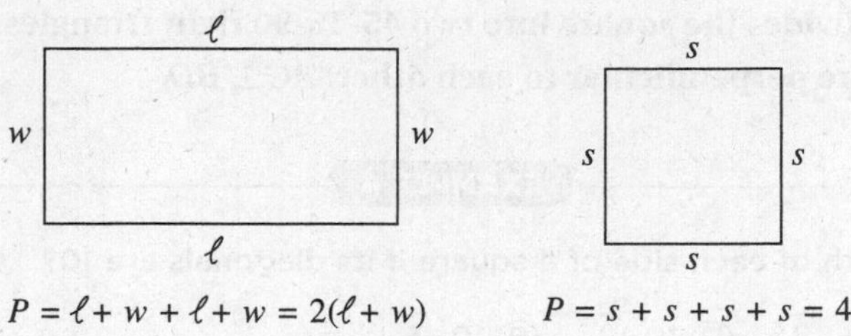

EXAMPLE 5

The length of a rectangle is 7 more than its width. If the perimeter of the rectangle is the same as the perimeter of a square of side 8.5, what is the length of a diagonal of the rectangle?

SOLUTION.

Don't do anything until you have drawn a diagram.

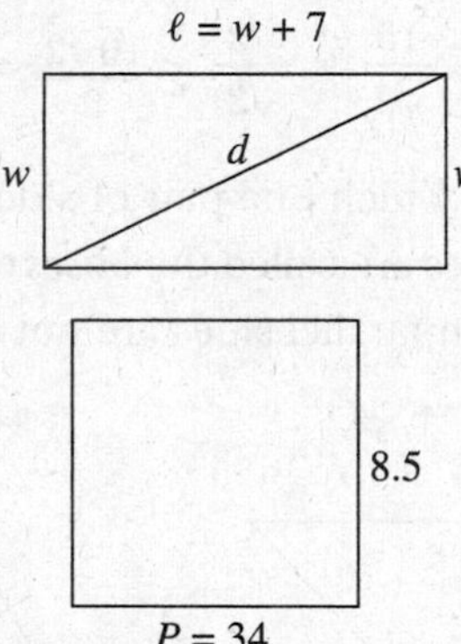

Since the perimeter of the square $= 4 \times 8.5 = 34$, the perimeter of the rectangle is also 34: $2(\ell + w) = 34 \Rightarrow \ell + w = 17$. Replacing ℓ by $w + 7$, we get:

$$w + 7 + w = 17 \Rightarrow 2w + 7 = 17 \Rightarrow 2w = 10 \Rightarrow w = 5$$

Then $\ell = 5 + 7 = 12$. Finally, realize that the diagonal is the hypotenuse of a 5-12-13 triangle, or use the Pythagorean theorem:

$$d^2 = 5^2 + 12^2 = 25 + 144 = 169 \Rightarrow d = \mathbf{13}$$

In Section 11-J we reviewed the formula for the area of a triangle. The only other figures for which you need to know area formulas are the parallelogram, rectangle, square, and trapezoid.

KEY FACT K9

Here are the area formulas you need to know:

- **For a parallelogram: $A = bh$.**
- **For a rectangle: $A = \ell w$.**
- **For a square: $A = s^2$ or $A = \frac{1}{2}d^2$.**
- **For a trapezoid: $A = \frac{1}{2}(b_1 + b_2)h$.**

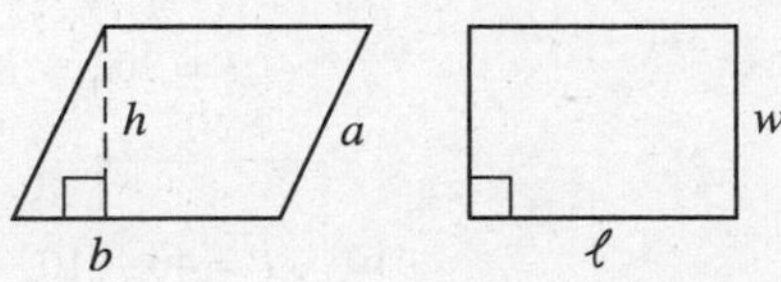

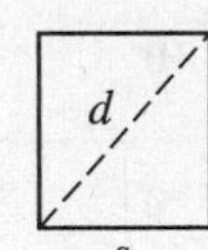

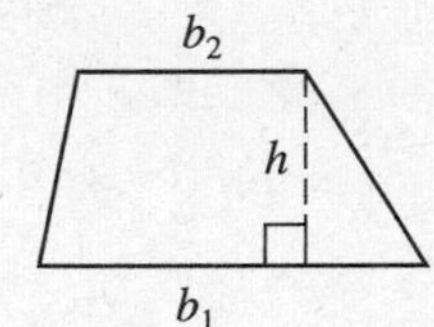

TIP

Be sure to learn the alternative formula for the area of a square: $A = \frac{1}{2}d^2$, where d is the length of a diagonal.

EXAMPLE 6

In the figure below, the area of parallelogram *ABCD* is 40. What is the area of rectangle *AFCE*?

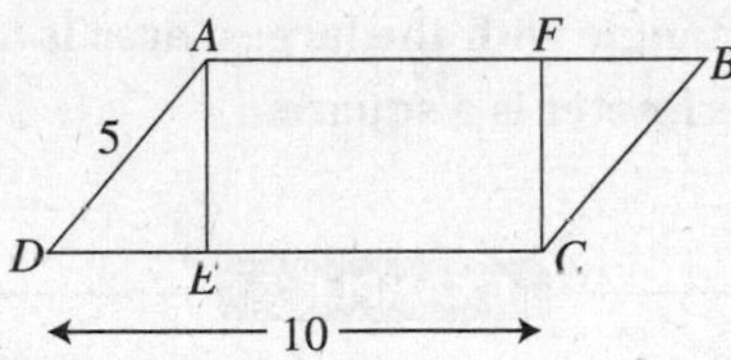

Ⓐ 20 Ⓑ 24 Ⓒ 28 Ⓓ 32 Ⓔ 36

SOLUTION.

Since the base, *CD*, is 10 and the area is 40, the height, *AE*, must be 4. Then $\triangle AED$ must be a 3-4-5 right triangle with $DE = 3$, which implies that $EC = 7$. So the area of the rectangle is $7 \times 4 =$ **28 (C)**.

Two rectangles with the same perimeter can have different areas, and two rectangles with the same area can have different perimeters. These facts are a common source of questions on the GRE.

RECTANGLES WHOSE PERIMETERS ARE 100

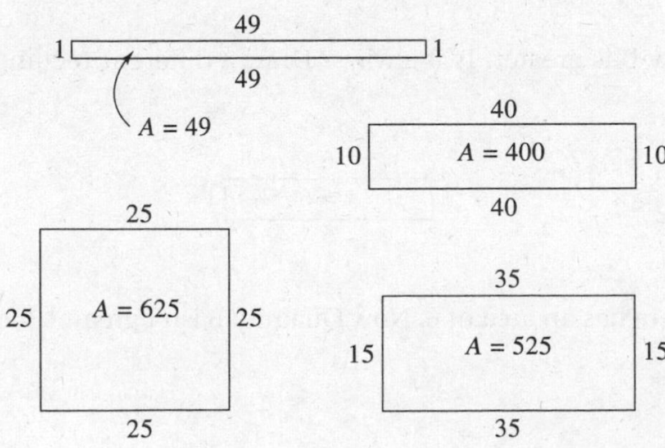

RECTANGLES WHOSE AREAS ARE 100

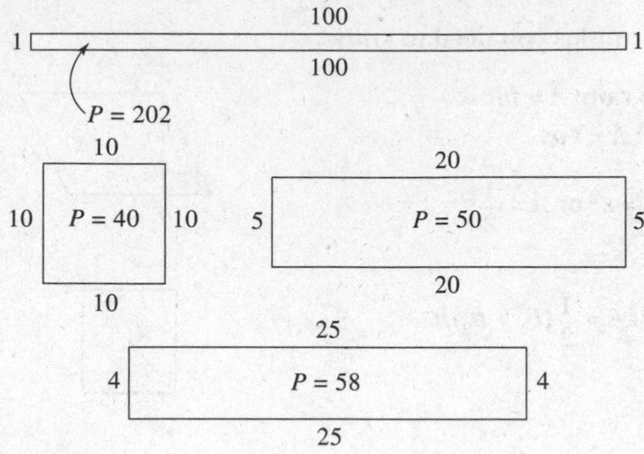

KEY FACT K10

For a given perimeter, the rectangle with the largest area is a square. For a given area, the rectangle with the smallest perimeter is a square.

EXAMPLE 7

Quantity A	Quantity B
The area of a rectangle whose perimeter is 12	The area of a rectangle whose perimeter is 14

SOLUTION.

Draw any rectangles whose perimeters are 12 and 14 and compute their areas. As drawn below, Quantity A = 8 and Quantity B = 12.

4
2 $A = 8$ 2
4

4
3 $A = 12$ 3
4

This time Quantity B is greater. Is it always? Draw a different rectangle whose perimeter is 14.

6
1 $A = 6$ 1
6

The one drawn here has an area of 6. Now Quantity B isn't greater. The answer is **D**.

EXAMPLE 8

Quantity A	Quantity B
The area of a rectangle whose perimeter is 12	10

SOLUTION.

There are many rectangles of different areas whose perimeters are 12. But the largest area is 9, when the rectangle is a 3×3 square. Quantity **B** is greater.

PRACTICE EXERCISES—QUADRILATERALS AND OTHER POLYGONS

Discrete Quantitative Questions

1. If the length of a rectangle is 4 times its width, and if its area is 144, what is its perimeter?

QUESTIONS 2–3 REFER TO THE DIAGRAM BELOW IN WHICH THE DIAGONALS OF SQUARE *ABCD* INTERSECT AT *E*.

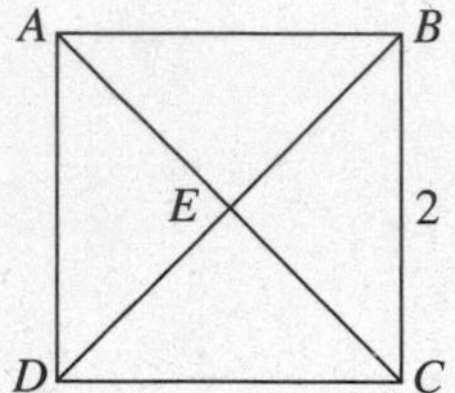

2. What is the area of $\triangle DEC$?

Ⓐ $\frac{1}{2}$
Ⓑ 1
Ⓒ $\sqrt{2}$
Ⓓ 2
Ⓔ $2\sqrt{2}$

3. What is the perimeter of $\triangle DEC$?

Ⓐ $1+\sqrt{2}$
Ⓑ $2+\sqrt{2}$
Ⓒ 4
Ⓓ $2+2\sqrt{2}$
Ⓔ 6

---

4. If the angles of a five-sided polygon are in the ratio of 2:3:3:5:5, what is the measure of the smallest angle?

Ⓐ 20
Ⓑ 40
Ⓒ 60
Ⓓ 80
Ⓔ 90

5. If in the figures below, the area of rectangle *ABCD* is 100, what is the area of rectangle *EFGH*?

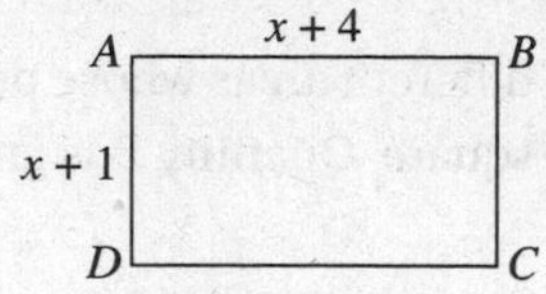

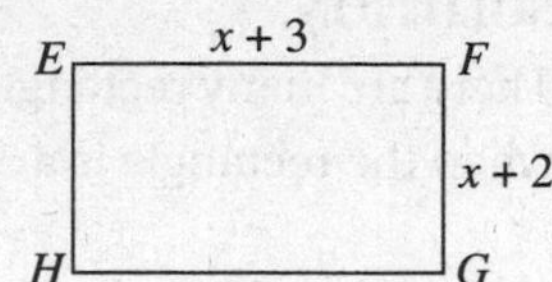

Ⓐ 98
Ⓑ 100
Ⓒ 102
Ⓓ 104
Ⓔ 106

QUESTIONS 6–7 REFER TO A RECTANGLE IN WHICH THE LENGTH OF EACH DIAGONAL IS 12, AND ONE OF THE ANGLES FORMED BY THE DIAGONAL AND A SIDE MEASURES 30°.

6. What is the area of the rectangle?

Ⓐ 18
Ⓑ 72
Ⓒ $18\sqrt{3}$
Ⓓ $36\sqrt{3}$
Ⓔ $36\sqrt{2}$

7. What is the perimeter of the rectangle?

Ⓐ 18
Ⓑ 24
Ⓒ $12+12\sqrt{3}$
Ⓓ $18+6\sqrt{3}$
Ⓔ $24\sqrt{2}$

8. How many sides does a polygon have if the measure of each interior angle is 8 times the measure of each exterior angle?

Ⓐ 8
Ⓑ 9
Ⓒ 10
Ⓓ 12
Ⓔ 18

9. The length of a rectangle is 5 more than the side of a square, and the width of the rectangle is 5 less than the side of the square. If the area of the square is 45, what is the area of the rectangle?

Ⓐ 20
Ⓑ 25
Ⓒ 45
Ⓓ 50
Ⓔ 70

QUESTIONS 10–11 REFER TO THE FOLLOWING FIGURE, IN WHICH *M*, *N*, *O*, AND *P* ARE THE MIDPOINTS OF THE SIDES OF RECTANGLE *ABCD*.

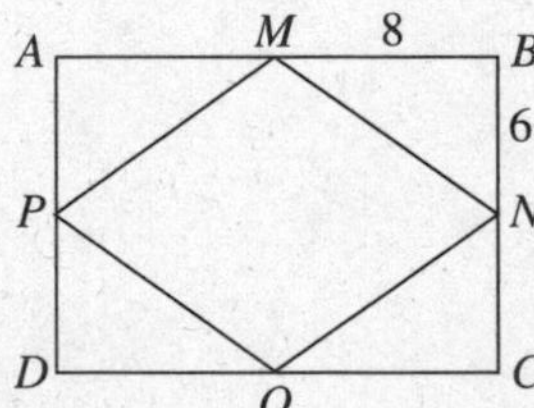

10. What is the perimeter of quadrilateral *MNOP*?

Ⓐ 24
Ⓑ 32
Ⓒ 40
Ⓓ 48
Ⓔ 60

11. What is the area of quadrilateral *MNOP*?

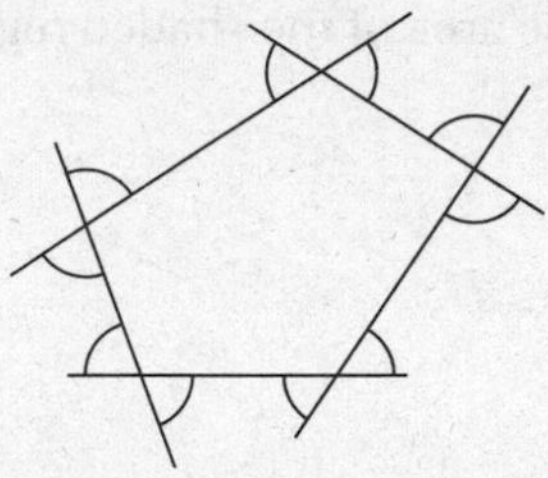

12. In the figure above, what is the sum of the measures of all of the marked angles?

Ⓐ 360
Ⓑ 540
Ⓒ 720
Ⓓ 900
Ⓔ 1,080

13. In quadrilateral *WXYZ*, the measure of angle *Z* is 10 more than twice the average of the measures of the other three angles. What is the measure of angle *Z*?

Ⓐ 100
Ⓑ 105
Ⓒ 120
Ⓓ 135
Ⓔ 150

QUESTIONS 14–15 REFER TO THE FOLLOWING FIGURE, IN WHICH *M* AND *N* ARE THE MIDPOINTS OF TWO OF THE SIDES OF SQUARE *ABCD*.

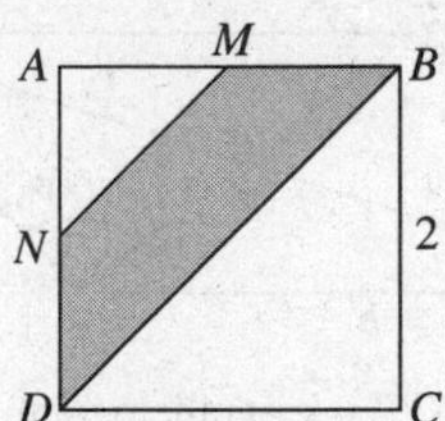

14. What is the perimeter of the shaded region?

Ⓐ 3
Ⓑ $2 + 3\sqrt{2}$
Ⓒ $3 + 2\sqrt{2}$
Ⓓ 5
Ⓔ 8

15. What is the area of the shaded region?

Ⓐ 1.5
Ⓑ 1.75
Ⓒ 3
Ⓓ $2\sqrt{2}$
Ⓔ $3\sqrt{2}$

Quantitative Comparison Questions

Ⓐ Quantity A is greater.
Ⓑ Quantity B is greater.
Ⓒ The two quantities are equal.
Ⓓ It is impossible to determine which quantity is greater.

16.

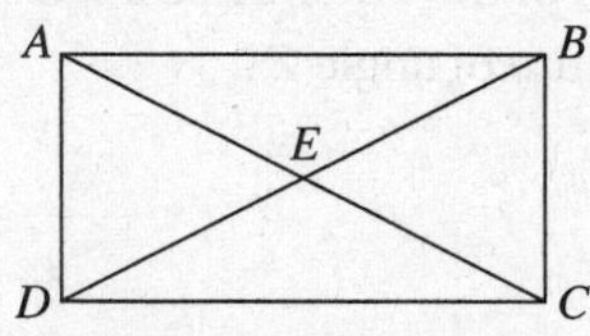

ABCD is a rectangle.

Quantity A	Quantity B
The area of $\triangle AED$	The area of $\triangle EDC$

17.

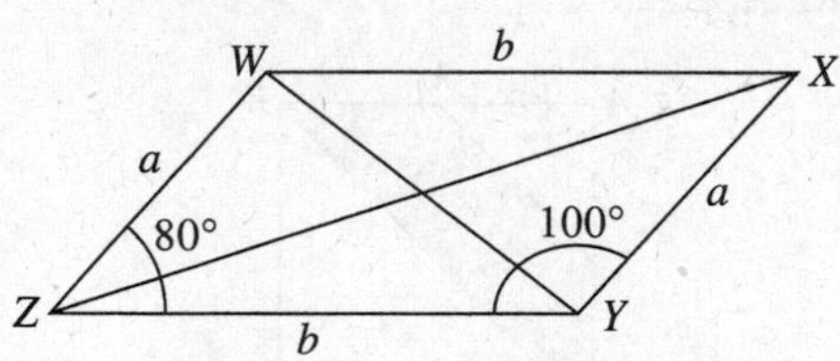

WXYZ is a parallelogram.

Quantity A	Quantity B
Diagonal *WY*	Diagonal *XZ*

18.

Quantity A	Quantity B
The perimeter of a 30-60-90 right triangle whose shorter leg is $2x$	The perimeter of an octagon, each of whose sides is x

19.

Quantity A	Quantity B
The perimeter of a rectangle whose area is 50	28

20.

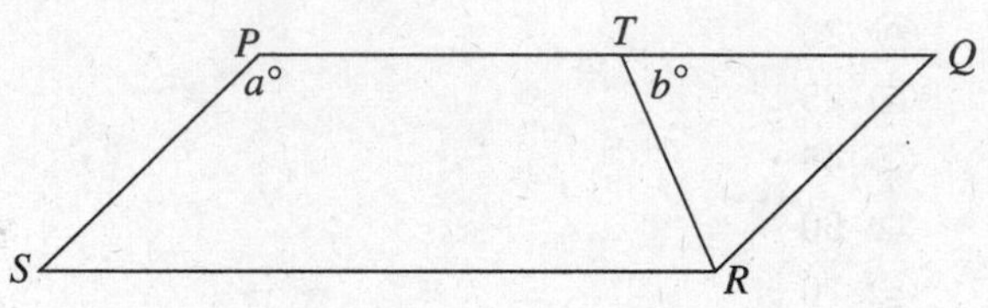

In parallelogram *PQRS*, *TR* bisects $\angle QRS$.

Quantity A	Quantity B
a	$2b$

ANSWER KEY

1. **60**	5. **C**	9. **A**	13. **150**	17. **B**
2. **B**	6. **D**	10. **C**	14. **B**	18. **A**
3. **D**	7. **C**	11. **96**	15. **A**	19. **A**
4. **C**	8. **E**	12. **C**	16. **C**	20. **C**

ANSWER EXPLANATIONS

1. **60** Draw a diagram and label it.

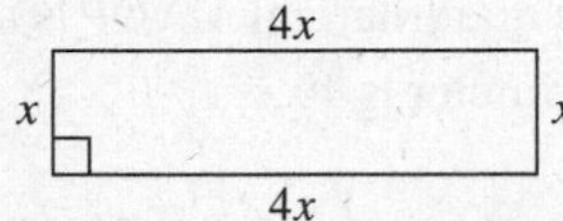

Since the area is 144, then $144 = (4x)(x) = 4x^2 \Rightarrow x^2 = 36 \Rightarrow x = 6$.
So the width is 6, the length is 24, and the perimeter is 60.

2. **(B)** The area of the square is $2^2 = 4$, and each triangle is one-fourth of the square. So the area of $\triangle DEC$ is 1.

3. **(D)** $\triangle DEC$ is a 45-45-90 right triangle whose hypotenuse, DC, is 2.
Therefore, each of the legs is $\frac{2}{\sqrt{2}} = \sqrt{2}$. So the perimeter is $2 + 2\sqrt{2}$.

4. **(C)** The sum of the angles of a five-sided polygon is $(5 - 2) \times 180 = 3 \times 180 = 540$.
Therefore, $540 = 2x + 3x + 3x + 5x + 5x = 18x$.
So, $x = 540 \div 18 = 30$.
The measure of the smallest angle is $2x = 2 \times 30 = 60$.

5. **(C)** The area of rectangle $ABCD$ is $(x + 1)(x + 4) = x^2 + 5x + 4$.
The area of rectangle $EFGH$ is $(x + 2)(x + 3) = x^2 + 5x + 6$, which is exactly 2 more than the area of rectangle $ABCD$: $100 + 2 = 102$.

6. **(D)** Draw a picture and label it.

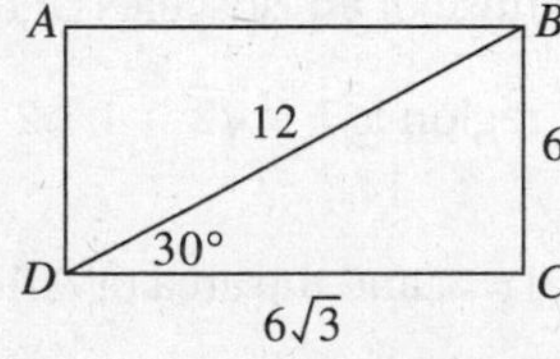

Since $\triangle BCD$ is a 30-60-90 right triangle, BC is 6 (half the hypotenuse) and CD is $6\sqrt{3}$.
So the area is $\ell w = 6(6\sqrt{3}) = 36\sqrt{3}$.

7. **(C)** The perimeter of the rectangle is $2(\ell + w) = 2(6 + 6\sqrt{3}) = 12 + 12\sqrt{3}$.

8. **(E)** The sum of the degree measures of an interior and exterior angle is 180, so $180 = 8x + x = 9x \Rightarrow x = 20$.

Since the sum of the measures of all the exterior angles is 360, there are $360 \div 20 = 18$ angles and 18 sides.

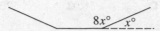

9. **(A)** Let x represent the side of the square. Then the dimensions of the rectangle are $(x + 5)$ and $(x - 5)$, and its area is $(x + 5)(x - 5) = x^2 - 25$.
Since the area of the square is 45, $x^2 = 45 \Rightarrow x^2 - 25 = 45 - 25 = 20$.

10. **(C)** Each triangle surrounding quadrilateral *MNOP* is a 6-8-10 right triangle. So each side of *MNOP* is 10, and its perimeter is 40.

11. **96** The area of each of the triangles is $\frac{1}{2}(6)(8) = 24$, so together the four triangles have an area of 96. The area of the rectangle is $16 \times 12 = 192$. Therefore, the area of quadrilateral *MNOP* is $192 - 96 = 96$.
Note: Joining the midpoints of the four sides of *any* quadrilateral creates a parallelogram whose area is one-half the area of the original quadrilateral.

12. **(C)** Each of the 10 marked angles is an exterior angle of the pentagon. If we take one angle at each vertex, the sum of those five angles is 360; the sum of the other five is also 360: $360 + 360 = 720$.

13. **150** Let W, X, Y, and Z represent the measures of the four angles. Since $W + X + Y + Z = 360$, $W + X + Y = 360 - Z$. Also,

$$Z = 10 + 2\left(\frac{W+X+Y}{3}\right) = 10 + 2\left(\frac{360-Z}{3}\right).$$

So $Z = 10 + \frac{2}{3}(360) - \frac{2}{3}Z = 10 + 240 - \frac{2}{3}Z \Rightarrow \frac{5}{3}Z = 250 \Rightarrow Z = 150$.

14. **(B)** Since M and N are midpoints of sides of length 2, AM, MB, AN, and ND are all 1.

$MN = \sqrt{2}$, since it's the hypotenuse of an isosceles right triangle whose legs are 1; and

$BD = 2\sqrt{2}$, since it's the hypotenuse of an isosceles right triangle whose legs are 2.

So the perimeter of the shaded region is $1 + \sqrt{2} + 1 + 2\sqrt{2} = 2 + 3\sqrt{2}$.

15. **(A)** The area of $\triangle ABD = \frac{1}{2}(2)(2) = 2$, and the area of $\triangle AMN$ is $\frac{1}{2}(1)(1) = 0.5$.

So the area of the shaded region is $2 - 0.5 = 1.5$.

16. **(C)** The area of $\triangle AED$ is $\frac{1}{2}w\left(\frac{\ell}{2}\right) = \frac{\ell w}{4}$.

The area of $\triangle EDC$ is $\frac{1}{2}\ell\left(\frac{w}{2}\right) = \frac{\ell w}{4}$.

Note: Each of the four small triangles has the same area.

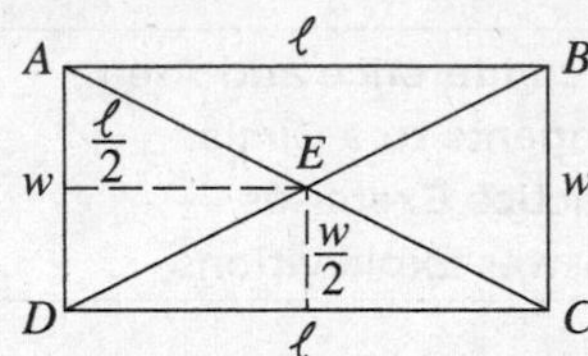

17. **(B)** By KEY FACT J5, since $\angle Z$ is acute and $\angle Y$ is obtuse, $(WY)^2 < a^2 + b^2$, whereas $(XZ)^2 > a^2 + b^2$.

18. **(A)** Since an octagon has eight sides, Quantity B is $8x$.
Quantity A: By KEY FACT J10, page 462, the hypotenuse of the triangle is $4x$, and the longer leg is $2x\sqrt{3}$. So the perimeter is $2x + 4x + 2x\sqrt{3}$. Since $\sqrt{3} > 1$, then

$2x + 4x + 2x\sqrt{3} > 2x + 4x + 2x = 8x.$

19. **(A)** The perimeter of a rectangle of area 50 can be as large as we like, but the least it can be is when the rectangle is a square. In that case, each side is $\sqrt{50}$, which is greater than 7, and so the perimeter is greater than 28.

20. **(C)** *TR* is a transversal cutting the parallel sides *PQ* and *RS*. So $b = x$ and $2b = 2x$.
But since the opposite angles of a parallelogram are equal, $a = 2x$.
So $a = 2b$.

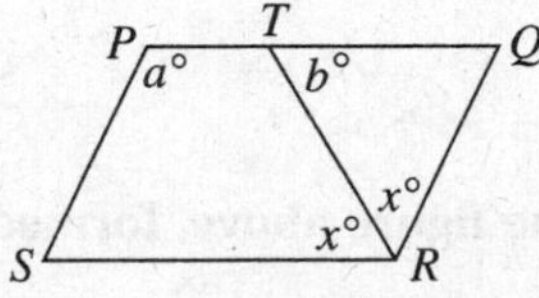

12-L. CIRCLES

- Circumference and Area
- Tangents to a Circle
- Practice Exercises
- Answer Explanations

A ***circle*** consists of all the points that are the same distance from one fixed point called the ***center***. That distance is called the ***radius*** of the circle. The figure below is a circle of radius 1 unit whose center is at the point *O*. *A*, *B*, *C*, *D*, and *E*, which are each 1 unit from *O*, are all points on the circle. It is customary to name a circle by referring to its center. Hence, the circle below is called circle *O*. The word *radius* is also used to represent any of the line segments joining the center and a point on the circle. The plural of ***radius*** is ***radii***. In circle *O*, below, *OA*, *OB*, *OC*, *OD*, and *OE* are all radii. If a circle has radius *r*, each of the radii is *r* units long.

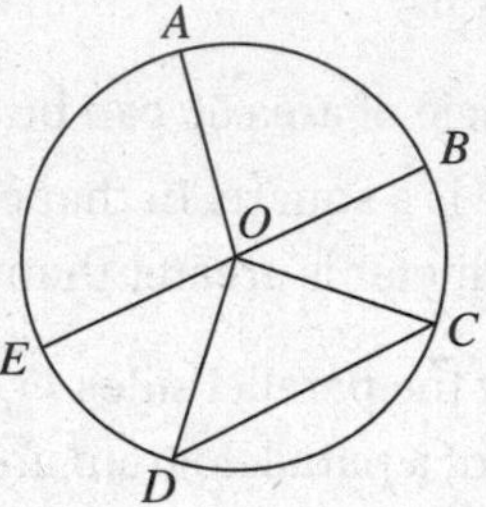

KEY FACT L1

Any triangle, such as △*COD* in the figure above, formed by connecting the endpoints of two radii, is isosceles.

EXAMPLE 1

If *P* and *Q* are points on circle *O*, what is the value of *x*?

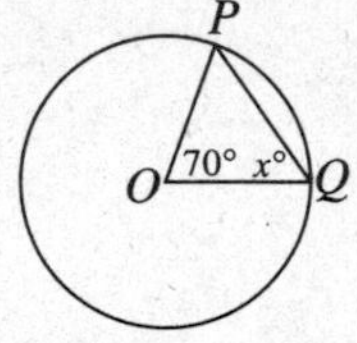

SOLUTION.

Since △*POQ* is isosceles, angles *P* and *Q* have the same measure. Then, $70 + x + x = 180 \Rightarrow 2x = 110 \Rightarrow x = $ **55**.

A line segment, such as *CD* in circle *O* at the beginning of this section, both of whose endpoints are on a circle, is called a ***chord***. A chord such as *BE*, which passes through the center of the circle, is called a ***diameter***. Since *BE* is the sum of two radii, *OB* and *OE*, it is twice as long as a radius.

KEY FACT L2

If *d* is the diameter and *r* the radius of a circle, $d = 2r$.

KEY FACT L3

A diameter is the longest chord that can be drawn in a circle.

EXAMPLE 2

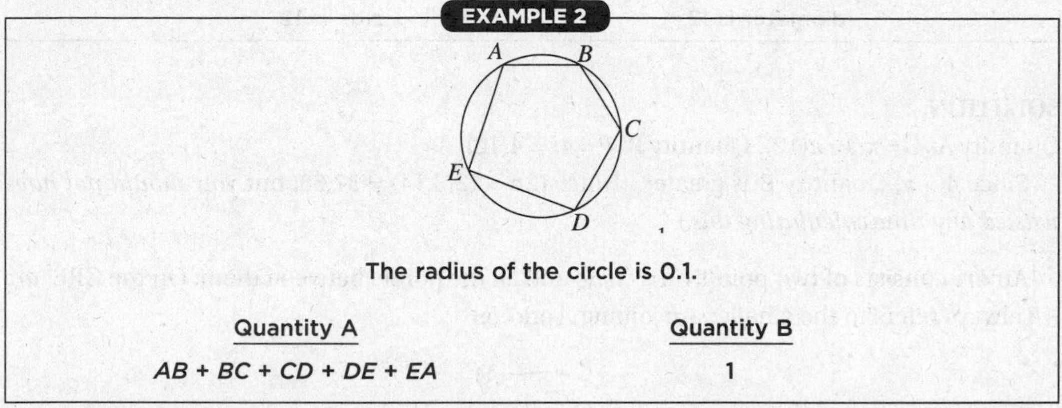

The radius of the circle is 0.1.

Quantity A	Quantity B
$AB + BC + CD + DE + EA$	1

SOLUTION.

Since the radius of the circle is 0.1, the diameter is 0.2. Therefore, the length of each of the five sides of pentagon *ABCDE* is less than 0.2, and the sum of their lengths is less than $5 \times 0.2 = 1$. The answer is **B**.

Circumference and Area

The total length around a circle, from *A* to *B* to *C* to *D* to *E* and back to *A*, is called the ***circumference*** of the circle. In every circle the ratio of the circumference to the diameter is exactly the same and is denoted by the symbol π (the Greek letter "pi").

KEY FACT L4

- $\pi = \dfrac{\textbf{circumference}}{\textbf{diameter}} = \dfrac{C}{d}$
- $C = \pi d$
- $C = 2\pi r$

KEY FACT L5

The value of π is approximately 3.14.

On GRE questions that involve circles, you are almost always expected to leave your answer in terms of π. So *don't* multiply by 3.14 until the final step, and then only if you have to. If you are ever stuck on a problem whose answers involve π, use your calculator to evaluate the answer or to test the answers. For example, assume that you think that an answer is about 50, and the answer choices are 4π, 6π, 12π, 16π, and 24π. Since π is slightly greater than 3, these choices are a little greater than 12, 18, 36, 48, and 72. The answer must be 16π. (To the nearest hundredth, 16π is actually 50.27, but approximating it by 48 was close enough.)

TIP

The answer choices to GRE multiple-choice questions involving circles always involve π. So you *never have to* multiply by 3.14.

EXAMPLE 3

Quantity A	Quantity B
The circumference of a circle whose diameter is 12	The perimeter of a square whose side is 12

SOLUTION.

Quantity A: $C = \pi d = \pi(12)$. Quantity B: $P = 4s = \mathbf{4}(12)$.

Since $4 > \pi$, Quantity **B** is greater. (Note: $12\pi = 12(3.14) = 37.68$, but *you should not have wasted any time calculating this.*)

An ***arc*** consists of two points on a circle and all the points between them. On the GRE, *arc AB* always refers to the smaller arc joining *A* and *B*.

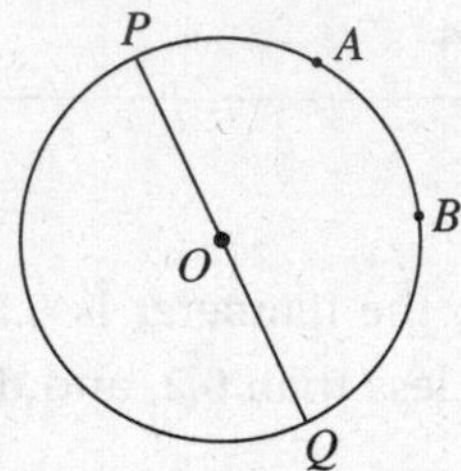

If we wanted to refer to the large arc going from *A* to *B* through *P* and *Q*, we would refer to it as arc *APB* or arc *AQB*. If two points, such as *P* and *Q* in circle *O*, are the endpoints of a diameter, they divide the circle into two arcs called ***semicircles***.

An angle whose vertex is at the center of a circle is called a ***central angle***.

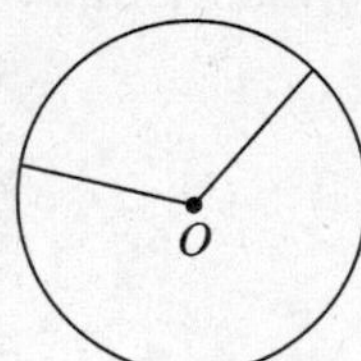

KEY FACT L6

The degree measure of a complete circle is 360°.

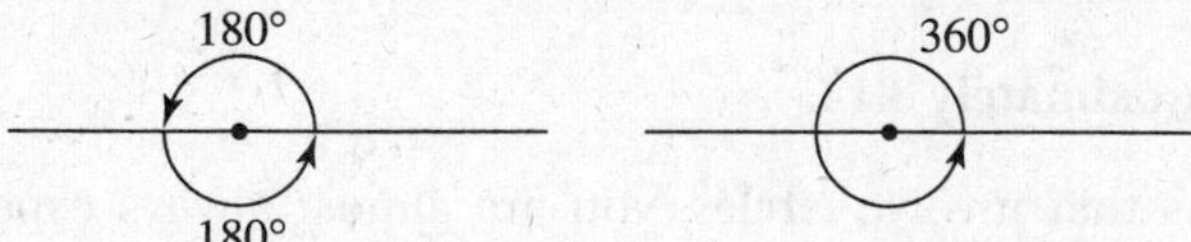

KEY FACT L7

The degree measure of an arc equals the degree measure of the central angle that intercepts it.

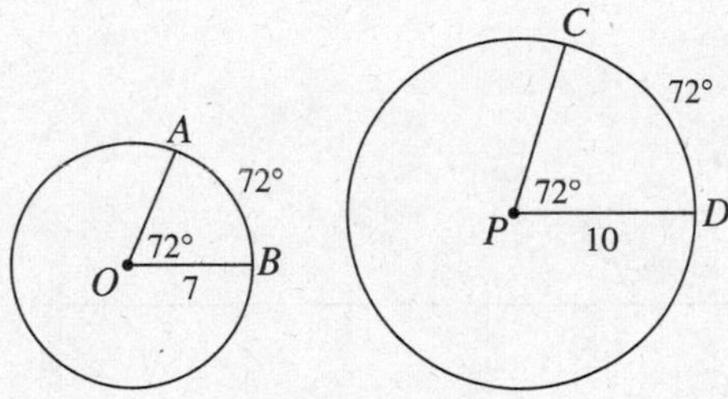

CAUTION

Degree measure is *not* a measure of length. In the circles above, arc *AB* and arc *CD* each measure 72°, even though arc *CD* is much longer.

How long *is* arc *CD*? Since the radius of Circle *P* is 10, its diameter is 20, and its circumference is 20π. Since there are 360° in a circle, arc *CD* is $\frac{72}{360}$, or $\frac{1}{5}$, of the circumference: $\frac{1}{5}(20\pi) = 4\pi$.

KEY FACT L8

The formula for the area of a circle of radius r is $A = \pi r^2$.

The area of Circle *P*, below KEY FACT L7, is $\pi(10)^2 = 100\pi$ square units. The area of sector *CPD* is $\frac{1}{5}$ of the area of the circle: $\frac{1}{5}(100\pi) = 20\pi$.

KEY FACT L9

If an arc measures $x°$, the length of the arc is $\frac{x}{360}(2\pi r)$, and the area of the sector formed by the arc and 2 radii is $\frac{x}{360}(\pi r^2)$.

Examples 4 and 5 refer to the circle below.

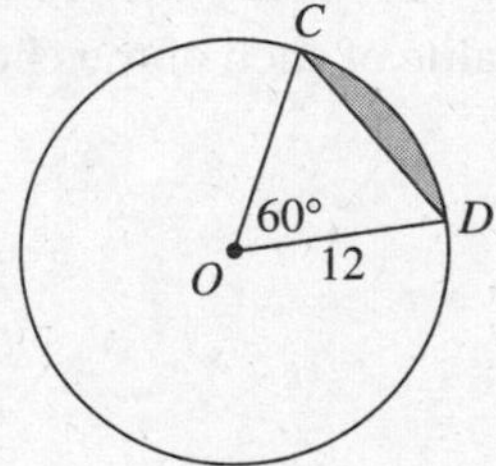

EXAMPLE 4

What is the area of the shaded region?

Ⓐ $144\pi - 144\sqrt{3}$

Ⓑ $144\pi - 36\sqrt{3}$

Ⓒ $144 - 72\sqrt{3}$

Ⓓ $24\pi - 36\sqrt{3}$

Ⓔ $24\pi - 72\sqrt{3}$

SOLUTION.

The area of the shaded region is equal to the area of sector *COD* minus the area of $\triangle COD$. The area of the circle is $\pi(12)^2 = 144\pi$.

- Since $\frac{60}{360} = \frac{1}{6}$, the area of sector *COD* is $\frac{1}{6}(144\pi) = 24\pi$.
- Since $m\angle O = 60°$, $m\angle C + \angle D = 120°$ and since $\triangle COD$ is isosceles, $m\angle C = m\angle D$. So, they each measure 60°, and the triangle is equilateral.
- By KEY FACT J15 (page 466), area of $\triangle COD = \frac{12^2\sqrt{3}}{4} = \frac{144\sqrt{3}}{4} = 36\sqrt{3}$. So the area of the shaded region is $\mathbf{24\pi - 36\sqrt{3}}$ **(D)**.

EXAMPLE 5

What is the perimeter of the shaded region?

Ⓐ $12 + 4\pi$

Ⓑ $12 + 12\pi$

Ⓒ $12 + 24\pi$

Ⓓ $12\sqrt{2} + 4\pi$

Ⓔ $12\sqrt{2} + 24\pi$

SOLUTION.

Since $\triangle COD$ is equilateral, $CD = 12$. Since the circumference of the circle is $2\pi(12) = 24\pi$, arc $CD = \frac{1}{6}(24\pi) = 4\pi$. So the perimeter is $\mathbf{12 + 4\pi}$ **(A)**.

Suppose that in Example 5 you see that $CD = 12$, but you don't remember how to find the length of arc *CD*. From the diagram, it is clear that it is slightly longer than *CD*, say 13. So you know that the perimeter is *about* 25. Now, mentally, using 3 for π, or with your calculator, using 3.14 for π, approximate the value of each of the choices and see which one is closest to 25. Only Choice A is even close.

Tangents to a Circle

A line and a circle or two circles are ***tangent*** if they have only one point of intersection. A circle is ***inscribed*** in a triangle or square if it is tangent to each side. A polygon is ***inscribed*** in a circle if each vertex is on the circle.

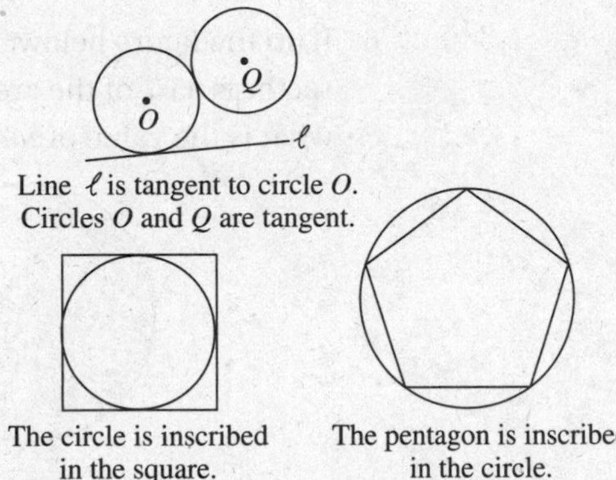

Line ℓ is tangent to circle O.
Circles O and Q are tangent.

The circle is inscribed in the square.

The pentagon is inscribed in the circle.

KEY FACT L10

If a line is tangent to a circle, a radius (or diameter) drawn to the point where the tangent touches the circle is perpendicular to the tangent line.

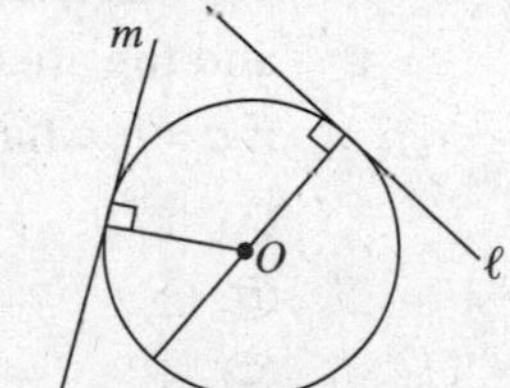

Lines ℓ and m are tangent to circle O.

EXAMPLE 6

A is the center of a circle whose radius is 8, and B is the center of a circle whose diameter is 8. If these two circles are tangent to one another, what is the area of the circle whose diameter is AB?

Ⓐ 12π Ⓑ 36π Ⓒ 64π Ⓓ 144π Ⓔ 256π

SOLUTION.
Draw a diagram.

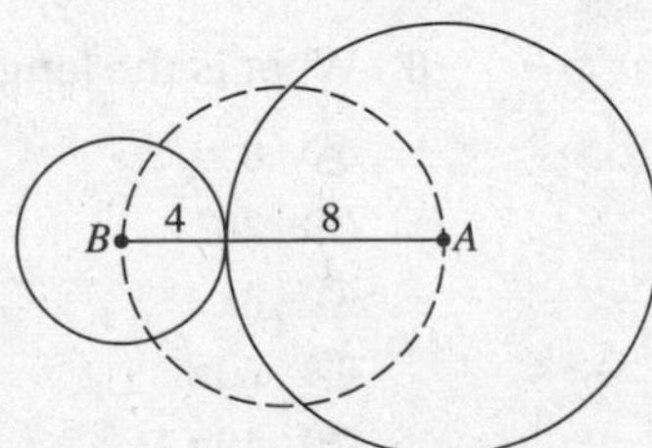

Since the diameter, AB, of the dotted circle is 12, its radius is 6, and its area is $\pi(6)^2 = \mathbf{36\pi}$ **(B)**.

PRACTICE EXERCISES—CIRCLES

Discrete Quantitative Questions

1. What is the circumference of a circle whose area is 100π?

Ⓐ 10
Ⓑ 20
Ⓒ 10π
Ⓓ 20π
Ⓔ 25π

2. What is the area of a circle whose circumference is π?

Ⓐ $\frac{\pi}{4}$
Ⓑ $\frac{\pi}{2}$
Ⓒ π
Ⓓ 2π
Ⓔ 4π

3. What is the area of a circle that is inscribed in a square of area 2?

Ⓐ $\frac{\pi}{4}$
Ⓑ $\frac{\pi}{2}$
Ⓒ π
Ⓓ $\pi\sqrt{2}$
Ⓔ 2π

4. A square of area 2 is inscribed in a circle. What is the area of the circle?

Ⓐ $\frac{\pi}{4}$
Ⓑ $\frac{\pi}{2}$
Ⓒ π
Ⓓ $\pi\sqrt{2}$
Ⓔ 2π

5. A 5×12 rectangle is inscribed in a circle. What is the radius of the circle?

6. If, in the figure below, the area of the shaded sector is 85% of the area of the entire circle, what is the value of w?

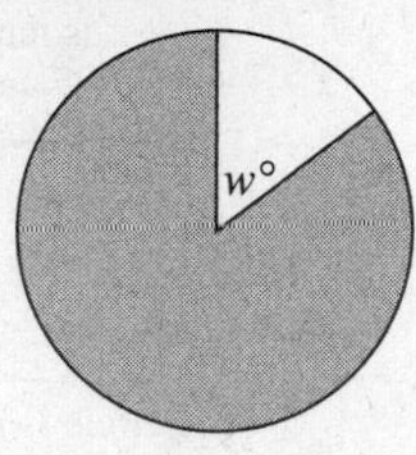

Ⓐ 15
Ⓑ 30
Ⓒ 45
Ⓓ 54
Ⓔ 60

7. The circumference of a circle is $a\pi$ units, and the area of the circle is $b\pi$ square units. If $a = b$, what is the radius of the circle?

Ⓐ 1
Ⓑ 2
Ⓒ 3
Ⓓ π
Ⓔ 2π

QUESTIONS 8–9 REFER TO THE FOLLOWING FIGURE.

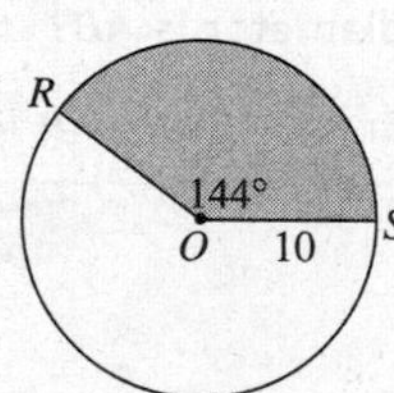

8. What is the length of arc RS?

Ⓐ 8
Ⓑ 20
Ⓒ 8π
Ⓓ 20π
Ⓔ 40π

9. What is the area of the shaded sector?

Ⓐ 8
Ⓑ 20
Ⓒ 8π
Ⓓ 20π
Ⓔ 40π

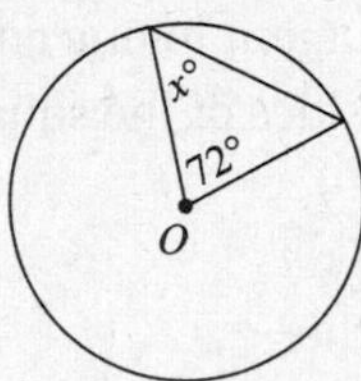

10. In the figure above, what is the value of x?

11. If A is the area and C the circumference of a circle, which of the following is an expression for A in terms of C?

Ⓐ $\frac{C^2}{4\pi}$

Ⓑ $\frac{C^2}{4\pi^2}$

Ⓒ $2C\sqrt{\pi}$

Ⓓ $2C^2$

Ⓔ $\frac{C^2\sqrt{\pi}}{4}$

12. What is the area of a circle whose radius is the diagonal of a square whose area is 4?

Ⓐ 2π
Ⓑ $2\pi\sqrt{2}$
Ⓒ 4π
Ⓓ 8π
Ⓔ 16π

Quantitative Comparison Questions

Ⓐ Quantity A is greater.
Ⓑ Quantity B is greater.
Ⓒ The two quantities are equal.
Ⓓ It is impossible to determine which quantity is greater.

13.

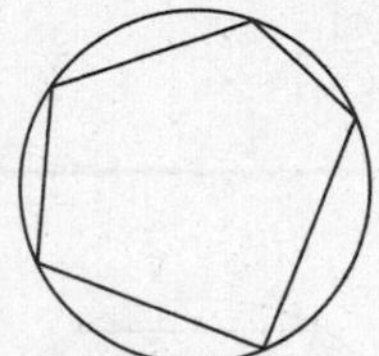

Quantity A	Quantity B
The perimeter of the pentagon	The circumference of the circle

14.

The circumference of a circle is C inches.
The area of the same circle is A square inches.

Quantity A	Quantity B
$\frac{C}{A}$	$\frac{A}{C}$

15.

Quantity A	Quantity B
The area of a circle of radius 2	The area of a semicircle of radius 3

16.

C is the circumference of a circle of radius r

Quantity A	Quantity B
$\frac{C}{r}$	6

17.

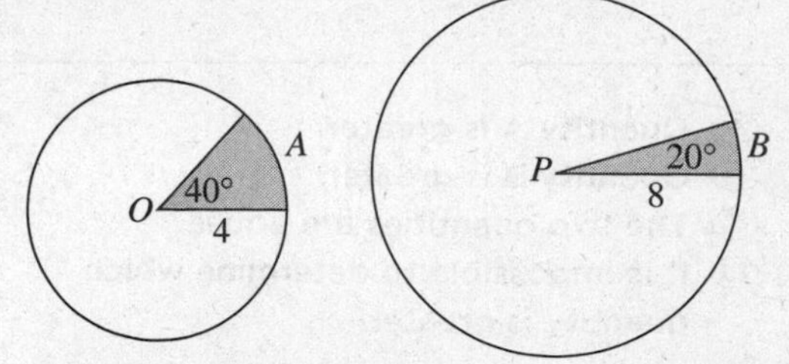

Quantity A	Quantity B
The area of sector A	The area of sector B

18.

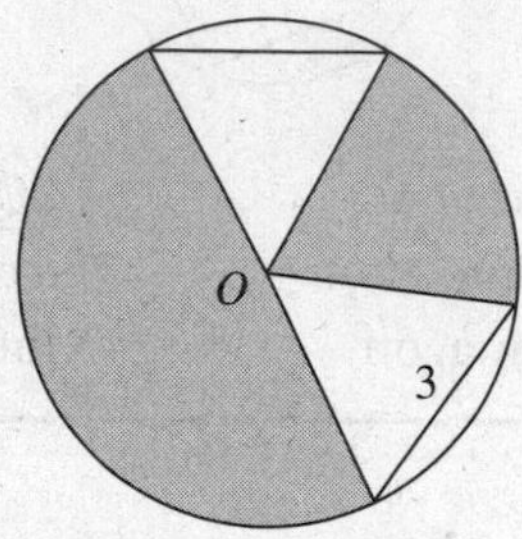

Each of the triangles is equilateral.

Quantity A	Quantity B
The area of the shaded region	6π

19.

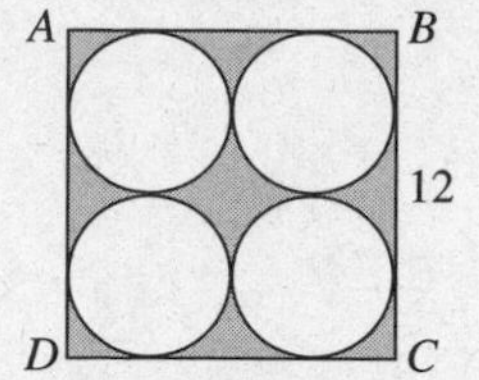

Figure 1

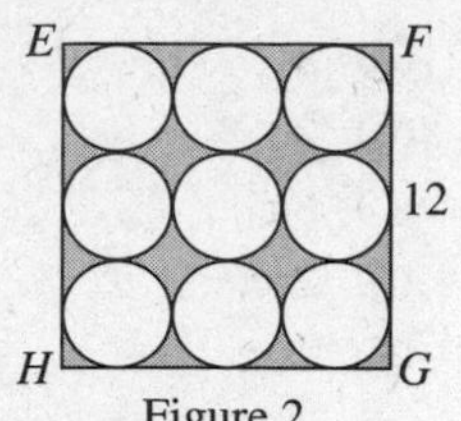

Figure 2

ABCD and *EFGH* are squares, and all circles are tangent to one another and to the sides of the squares.

Quantity A	Quantity B
The area of the shaded region in Figure 1	The area of the shaded region in Figure 2

20.

A square and a circle have equal areas.

Quantity A	Quantity B
The perimeter of the square	The circumference of the circle

ANSWER KEY

1. **D**	5. **6.5**	9. **E**	13. **B**	17. **B**
2. **A**	6. **D**	10. **54**	14. **D**	18. **C**
3. **B**	7. **B**	11. **A**	15. **B**	19. **C**
4. **C**	8. **C**	12. **D**	16. **A**	20. **A**

ANSWER EXPLANATIONS

1. **(D)** $A = \pi r^2 = 100\pi \Rightarrow r^2 = 100 \Rightarrow r = 10 \Rightarrow C = 2\pi r = 2\pi(10) = 20\pi$

2. **(A)** $C = 2\pi r = \pi \Rightarrow 2r = 1 \Rightarrow r = \frac{1}{2} \Rightarrow A = \pi r^2 = \pi\left(\frac{1}{2}\right)^2 = \frac{1}{4}\pi = \frac{\pi}{4}$

3. **(B)** Draw a diagram.

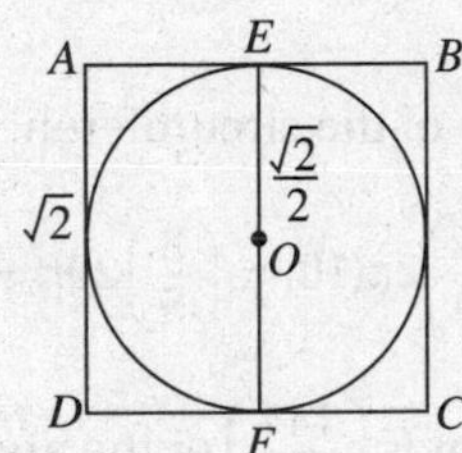

Since the area of square $ABCD$ is 2, $AD = \sqrt{2}$.

Then diameter $EF = \sqrt{2}$ and radius $OE = \frac{\sqrt{2}}{2}$. Then the area of the circle is

$\pi\left(\frac{\sqrt{2}}{2}\right)^2 = \frac{2}{4}\pi = \frac{\pi}{2}$.

4. **(C)** Draw a diagram.

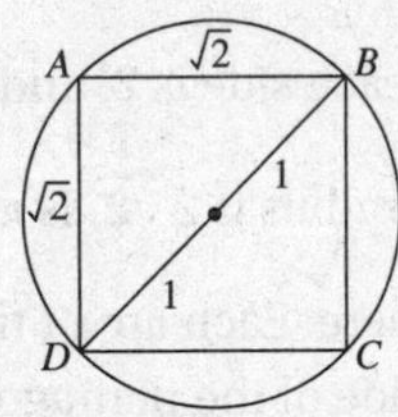

Since the area of square $ABCD$ is 2, $AD = \sqrt{2}$. Then, since $\triangle ABD$ is an isosceles right triangle, diagonal $BD = \sqrt{2} \times \sqrt{2} = 2$.

But BD is also a diameter of the circle. So the diameter is 2 and the radius is 1. Therefore, the area is $\pi(1)^2 = \pi$.

5. **6.5** Draw a diagram.

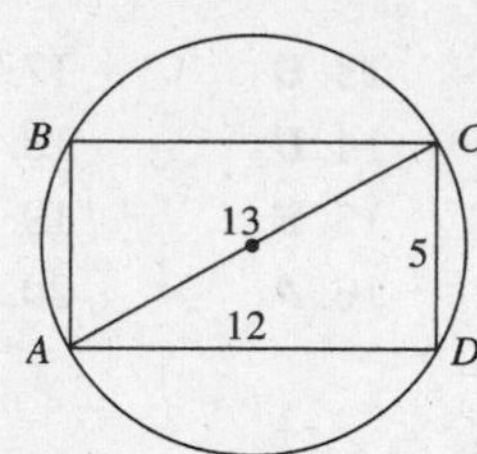

By the Pythagorean theorem (or by recognizing a 5-12-13 triangle), we see that diagonal AC is 13. But AC is also a diameter of the circle, so the diameter is 13 and the radius is 6.5.

6. **(D)** Since the shaded area is 85% of the circle, the white area is 15% of the circle. So, w is 15% of 360°: $0.15 \times 360 = 54$.

7. **(B)** Since $C = a\pi = b\pi = A$, we have $2\pi r = \pi r^2 \Rightarrow 2r = r^2 \Rightarrow r = 2$.

8. **(C)** The length of arc RS is $\frac{144}{360}$ of the circumference:

$$\left(\frac{144}{360}\right)2\pi(10) = \left(\frac{2}{5}\right)20\pi = 8\pi$$

9. **(E)** The area of the shaded sector is $\left(\frac{144}{360}\right)$ of the area of the circle:

$$\left(\frac{144}{360}\right)\pi(10)^2 = \left(\frac{2}{5}\right)100\pi = 40\pi$$

10. **54** Since two of the sides are radii of the circles, the triangle is isosceles. So the unmarked angle is also x:

$$180 = 72 + 2x \Rightarrow 2x = 108 \Rightarrow x = 54$$

11. **(A)** $C = 2\pi r \Rightarrow r = \frac{C}{2\pi} \Rightarrow A = \pi\left(\frac{C}{2\pi}\right)^2 = \pi\left(\frac{C^2}{4\pi^2}\right) = \frac{C^2}{4\pi}$

12. **(D)** If the area of the square is 4, each side is 2, and the length of a diagonal is $2\sqrt{2}$. The area of a circle whose radius is $2\sqrt{2}$ is $\pi(2\sqrt{2})^2 = 8\pi$.

13. **(B)** There's nothing to calculate here. Each arc of the circle is clearly longer than the corresponding chord, which is a side of the pentagon. So the circumference, which is the sum of all the arcs, is greater than the perimeter, which is the sum of all the chords.

14. **(D)** Quantity A: $\frac{C}{A} = \frac{2\pi r}{\pi r^2} = \frac{2}{r}$.

Quantity B: $\frac{A}{C} = \frac{r}{2}$.

If $r = 2$, the quantities are equal; otherwise, they're not.

15. **(B)** Quantity A: $A = \pi(2)^2 = 4\pi$.

Quantity B: The area of a semicircle of radius 3 is $\frac{1}{2}\pi(3)^2 = \frac{1}{2}(9\pi) = 4.5\pi$.

16. **(A)** By KEY FACT L4 (page 489), $\pi = \frac{C}{d} = \frac{C}{2r} \Rightarrow \frac{C}{r} = 2\pi$, which is greater than 6.

17. **(B)** The area of sector A is $\frac{40}{360}(16\pi) = \frac{16\pi}{9}$.

    The area of sector B is $\frac{20}{360}(64\pi) = \frac{64\pi}{18} = \frac{32\pi}{9}$.

    So sector B is twice as big as sector A.

18. **(C)** Since the triangles are equilateral, the two white central angles each measure 60°, and their sum is 120°. So the white area is $\frac{120}{360} = \frac{1}{3}$ of the circle, and the shaded area is $\frac{2}{3}$ of the circle. The area of the circle is $\pi(3)^2 = 9\pi$, so the shaded area is $\frac{2}{3}(9\pi) = 6\pi$.

19. **(C)** Since $BC = 12$, the diameter of each circle in Figure 1 is 6, and so the radius of each circle is 3. So the area of each circle is 9π, and the total area of the 4 circles is 36π. Since $FG = 12$, the diameter of each circle in Figure 2 is 4, and so the radius of each circle is 2. So the area of each circle is 4π, and the total area of the 9 circles is 36π. Since both squares have sides of 12, their areas are equal, and since their white areas are equal, so are their shaded areas.

20. **(A)** Let A represent the area of the square and the circle.

    Quantity A: $A = s^2 \Rightarrow s = \sqrt{A} \Rightarrow P = 4\sqrt{A}$.

    Quantity B: $A = \pi r^2 \Rightarrow r = \sqrt{\frac{A}{\pi}} = \frac{\sqrt{A}}{\sqrt{\pi}}$.

    So $C = 2\pi\left(\frac{\sqrt{A}}{\sqrt{\pi}}\right) = 2\sqrt{\pi}\sqrt{A}$.

    Since $\pi \approx 3.14$, $\sqrt{\pi} \approx 1.77 \Rightarrow 2\sqrt{\pi} \approx 3.54$. Quantity A is $4\sqrt{A}$; Quantity B is $3.54\sqrt{A}$. Quantity A is greater.

12-M. SOLID GEOMETRY

- Rectangular Solids
- Cylinders
- Practice Exercises
- Answer Explanations

There are very few solid geometry questions on the GRE, and they cover only a few elementary topics. Basically, all you need to know are the formulas for the volume and surface areas of rectangular solids (including cubes) and cylinders.

Rectangular Solids

A ***rectangular solid*** or ***box*** is a solid formed by six rectangles, called ***faces***. The sides of the rectangles are called ***edges***. As shown in the diagram below (left), the edges are called the ***length, width***, and ***height***. A ***cube*** is a rectangular solid in which the length, width, and height are equal; so all the edges are the same length.

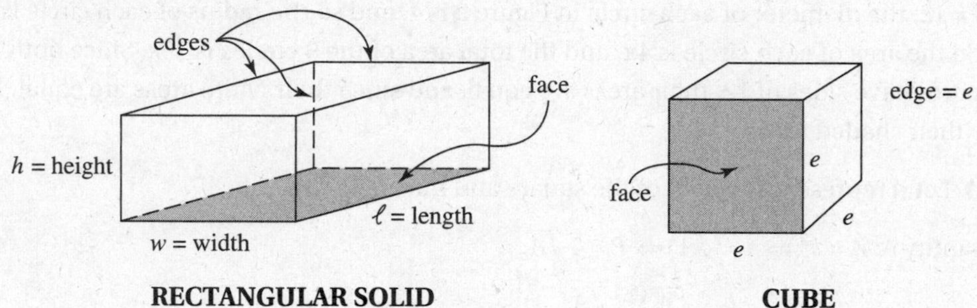

The ***volume*** of a solid is the amount of space it takes up and is measured in ***cubic units***. One cubic unit is the amount of space occupied by a cube all of whose edges are one unit long. In the figure above (right), if each edge of the cube is 1 inch long, then the area of each face is 1 square inch, and the volume of the cube is 1 cubic inch.

KEY FACT M1

Let ℓ, w, and h represent the length, width, and height, respectively, of a rectangular solid. If the rectangular solid is a cube, then $\ell = w = h$, and so each edge has the same length, which is represented by e.

The formulas for the volume (V) of a rectangular solid and a cube are:

$$V = \ell wh \quad \text{and} \quad V = e \cdot e \cdot e = e^3$$

EXAMPLE 1

The base of a rectangular tank is 12 feet long and 8 feet wide; the height of the tank is 30 inches. If water is pouring into the tank at the rate of 2 cubic feet per second, how many minutes will be required to fill the tank?

Ⓐ 1 Ⓑ 2 Ⓒ 10 Ⓓ 120 Ⓔ 240

SOLUTION.

Draw a diagram. In order to express all of the dimensions of the tank in the same units, convert 30 inches to 2.5 feet. Then the volume of the tank is $12 \times 8 \times 2.5 = 240$ cubic feet. At 2 cubic feet per second, it will take $240 \div 2 = 120$ seconds = **2** minutes to fill the tank (**B**).

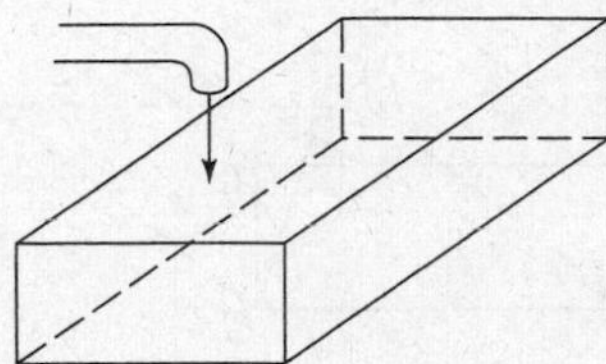

The ***surface area*** of a rectangular solid is the sum of the areas of the six faces. Since the top and bottom faces are equal, the front and back faces are equal, and the left and right faces are equal, we can calculate the area of one from each pair and then double the sum. In a cube, each of the six faces has the same area.

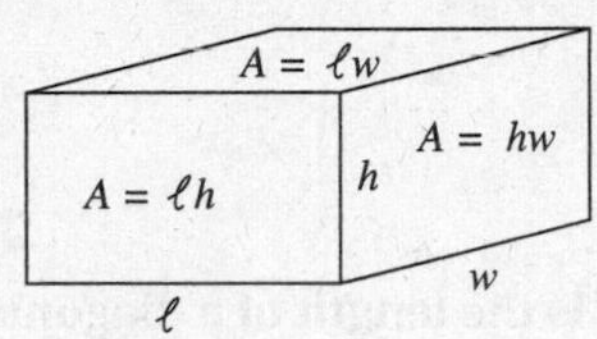

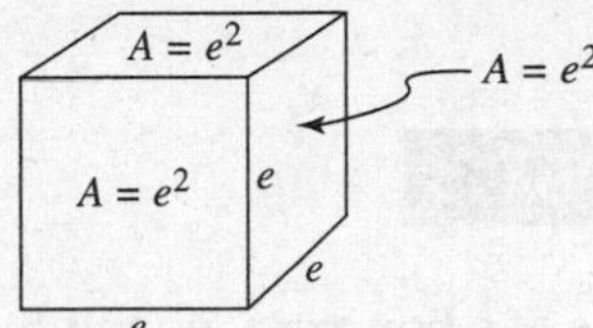

KEY FACT M2

The formulas for the surface area (*A*) of a rectangular solid and a cube are:

$$A = 2(\ell + w + h) \qquad \text{and} \qquad A = 6e^2$$

EXAMPLE 2

The volume of a cube is v cubic *yards*, and its surface area is a square *feet*. If $v = a$, what is the length in *inches* of each edge?

 inches

SOLUTION.

Draw a diagram.

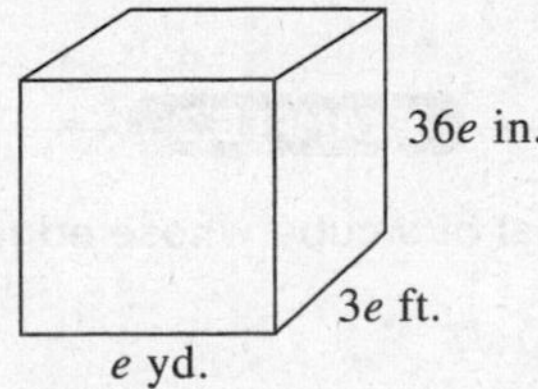

If e is the length of the edge in yards, $3e$ is the length in feet, and $36e$ the length in inches. Therefore, $v = e^3$ and $a = 6(3e)^2 = 6(9e^2) = 54e^2$. Since $v = a$, $e^3 = 54e^2$, and $e = 54$. So the length of each edge is $36(54) =$ **1,944** inches.

A ***diagonal*** of a box is a line segment joining a vertex on the top of the box to the opposite vertex on the bottom. A box has 4 diagonals, all the same length. In the box below they are line segments *AG, BH, CE,* and *DF.*

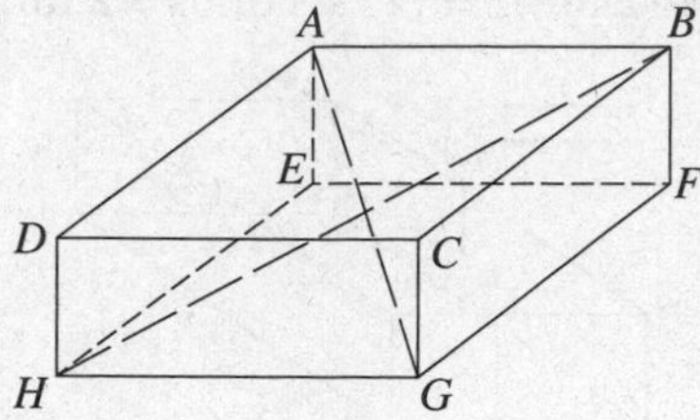

KEY FACT M3

A diagonal of a box is the longest line segment that can be drawn between two points on the box.

KEY FACT M4

If the dimensions of a box are ℓ, w, and h, and if d is the length of a diagonal, then $d^2 = \ell^2 + w^2 + h^2$ and $d = \sqrt{\ell^2 + w^2 + h^2}$.

For example, in the box below: $d^2 = 3^2 + 4^2 + 12^2 = 9 + 16 + 144 = 169 \Rightarrow d = 13$.

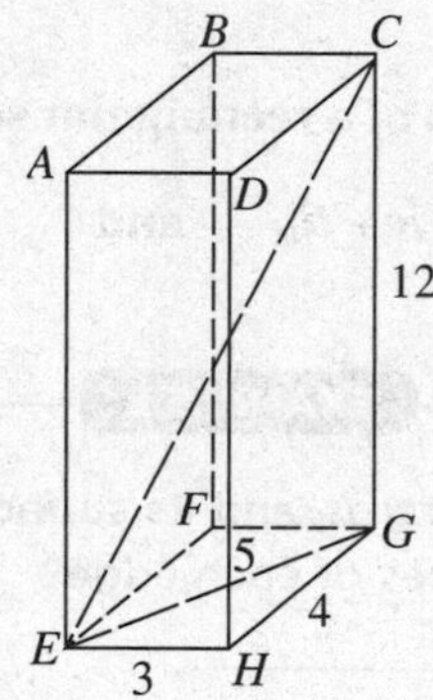

This formula is really just an extended Pythagorean theorem. *EG* is the diagonal of rectangular base *EFGH.* Since the sides of the base are 3 and 4, *EG* is 5. Now, $\triangle CGE$ is a right triangle whose legs are 12 and 5, so diagonal *CE* is 13.

EXAMPLE 3

What is the length of a diagonal of a cube whose edges are 1?

Ⓐ 1 Ⓑ 2 Ⓒ 3 Ⓓ $\sqrt{2}$ Ⓔ $\sqrt{3}$

SOLUTION.
Use the formula:

$$d^2 = 1^2 + 1^2 + 1^2 = 3 \Rightarrow d = \sqrt{3} \text{ (E)}$$

Without the formula you would draw a diagram and label it. Since the base is a 1×1 square, its diagonal is $\sqrt{2}$. Then the diagonal of the cube is the hypotenuse of a right triangle whose legs are 1 and $\sqrt{2}$, so

$$d^2 = 1^2 + (\sqrt{2})^2 = 1 + 2 = 3, \text{ and } d = \sqrt{3}$$

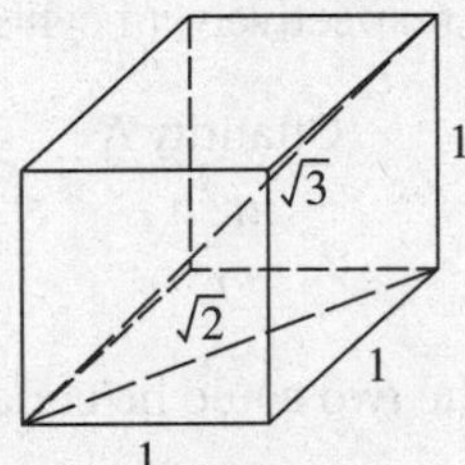

Cylinders

A ***cylinder*** is similar to a rectangular solid except that the base is a circle instead of a rectangle. The volume of a cylinder is the area of its circular base (πr^2) times its height (h). The surface area of a cylinder depends on whether you are envisioning a tube, such as a straw, without a top or bottom, or a can, which has both a top and a bottom.

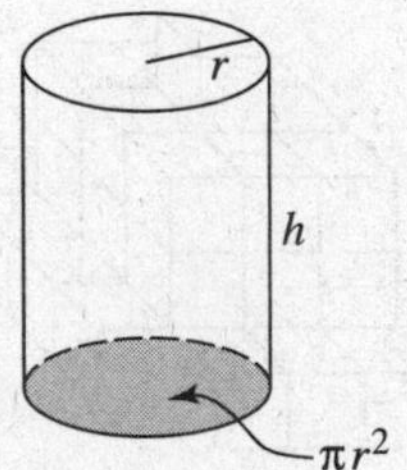

KEY FACT M5

If h and r represent the height and the radius of the circular base of a cylinder, then the formulas for the volume (V), surface area (A), and total area (T) of the cylinder are:

- $V = \pi r^2 h$
  [Note: This is the area of the circular base multiplied by the height.]
- $A = 2\pi rh$
  [Note: This is the circumference of the circular base multiplied by the height.]
- $T = 2\pi rh + 2\pi r^2$
  [Note: this is the surface area, plus the area of the two circular bases.]

EXAMPLE 4

The radius of cylinder II equals the height of cylinder I.
The height of cylinder II equals the radius of cylinder I.

Quantity A	Quantity B
The volume of cylinder I	The volume of cylinder II

SOLUTION.
Let r and h be the radius and height, respectively, of cylinder I. Then

	Quantity A	Quantity B
	πr^2h	πh^2r
Divide each quantity by πrh:	r	h

Either r or h could be greater, or the two could be equal. The answer is **D**.

These are the only formulas you need to know. Any other solid geometry questions that might appear on the GRE would require you to visualize a situation and reason it out, rather than to apply a formula.

EXAMPLE 5

How many small cubes are needed to construct the tower in the figure below?

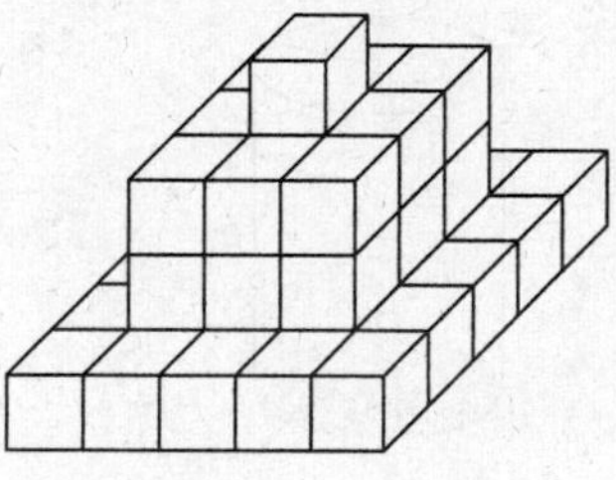

SOLUTION.
You need to "see" the answer. The top level consists of 1 cube, the second and third levels consist of 9 cubes each, and the bottom layer consists of 25 cubes. The total is $1 + 9 + 9 + 25 =$ **44**.

PRACTICE EXERCISES—SOLID GEOMETRY

Discrete Quantitative Questions

1. The sum of the lengths of all the edges of a cube is 6 centimeters. What is the volume, in cubic centimeters, of the cube?

Ⓐ $\frac{1}{8}$
Ⓑ $\frac{1}{4}$
Ⓒ $\frac{1}{2}$
Ⓓ 1
Ⓔ 8

2. What is the volume of a cube whose surface area is 150?

3. What is the surface area of a cube whose volume is 64?

Ⓐ 16
Ⓑ 64
Ⓒ 96
Ⓓ 128
Ⓔ 384

4. What is the number of cubic inches in one cubic foot?

Ⓐ 12
Ⓑ 24
Ⓒ 144
Ⓓ 684
Ⓔ 1728

5. A solid metal cube of edge 3 feet is placed in a rectangular tank whose length, width, and height are 3, 4, and 5 feet, respectively. What is the volume, in cubic feet, of water that the tank can now hold?

Ⓐ 20
Ⓑ 27
Ⓒ 33
Ⓓ 48
Ⓔ 60

6. A 5-foot-long cylindrical pipe has an inner diameter of 6 feet and an outer diameter of 8 feet. If the total surface area (inside and out, including the ends) is $k\pi$, what is the value of k?

Ⓐ 7
Ⓑ 40
Ⓒ 48
Ⓓ 70
Ⓔ 84

7. The height, h, of a cylinder is equal to the edge of a cube. If the cylinder and cube have the same volume, what is the radius of the cylinder?

Ⓐ $\frac{h}{\sqrt{\pi}}$
Ⓑ $h\sqrt{\pi}$
Ⓒ $\frac{\sqrt{\pi}}{h}$
Ⓓ $\frac{h^2}{\pi}$
Ⓔ πh^2

8. A rectangular tank has a base that is 10 centimeters by 5 centimeters and a height of 20 centimeters. If the tank is half full of water, by how many centimeters will the water level rise if 325 cubic centimeters of water are poured into the tank?

Ⓐ 3.25
Ⓑ 6.5
Ⓒ 16.25
Ⓓ 32.5
Ⓔ 65

9. If the height of a cylinder is 4 times its circumference, what is the volume of the cylinder in terms of its circumference, C?

Ⓐ $\frac{C^3}{\pi}$

Ⓑ $\frac{2C^3}{\pi}$

Ⓒ $\frac{2C^2}{\pi^2}$

Ⓓ $\frac{\pi C^2}{4}$

Ⓔ $4\pi C^3$

10. Three identical balls fit snugly into a cylindrical can: the radius of the spheres equals the radius of the can, and the balls just touch the bottom and the top of the can. If the formula for the volume of a sphere is $V = \frac{4}{3}\pi r^3$, what fraction of the volume of the can is taken up by the balls?

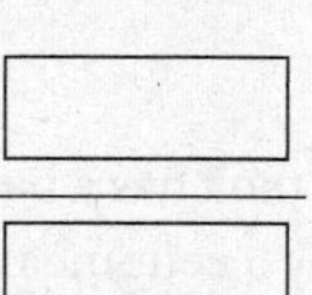

Quantitative Comparison Questions

Ⓐ Quantity A is greater.
Ⓑ Quantity B is greater.
Ⓒ The two quantities are equal.
Ⓓ It is impossible to determine which quantity is greater.

11.

Jack and Jill each roll a sheet of 9×12 paper to form a cylinder.
Jack tapes the two 9-inch edges together.
Jill tapes the two 12-inch edges together.

Quantity A	Quantity B
The volume of Jack's cylinder	The volume of Jill's cylinder

12.

Quantity A	Quantity B
The volume of a cube whose edges are 6	The volume of a box whose dimensions are 5, 6, and 7

13.

A is the surface area of a rectangular box in square units.
V is the volume of the same box in cubic units.

Quantity A	Quantity B
A	V

14.

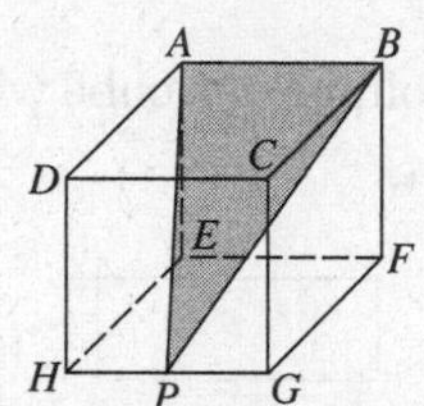

P is a point on edge GH of cube $ABCDEFGH$.
Each edge of the cube is 1.

Quantity A	Quantity B
The area of $\triangle ABP$	1

15.

Quantity A	Quantity B
The volume of a sphere whose radius is 1	The volume of a cube whose edge is 1

ANSWER KEY

1. **A**	4. **E**	7. **A**	10. $\frac{2}{3}$	12. **A**	14. **B**
2. **125**	5. **C**	8. **B**	11. **A**	13. **D**	15. **A**
3. **C**	6. **E**	9. **A**			

ANSWER EXPLANATIONS

1. **(A)** Since a cube has 12 edges, we have $12e = 6 \Rightarrow e = \frac{1}{2}$. Therefore, $V = e^3 = \left(\frac{1}{2}\right)^3 = \frac{1}{8}$.

2. **125** Since the surface area is 150, each of the 6 faces is a square whose area is $150 \div 6 = 25$. So the edges are all 5, and the volume is $5^3 = 125$.

3. **(C)** Since the volume of the cube is 64, we have $e^3 = 64 \Rightarrow e = 4$. The surface area is $6e^2 = 6 \times 16 = 96$.

4. **(E)** The volume of a cube whose edges are 1 foot can be expressed in either of two ways:

$$(1 \text{ foot})^3 = 1 \text{ cubic foot or}$$
$$(12 \text{ inches})^3 = 1728 \text{ cubic inches.}$$

5. **(C)** The volume of the tank is $3 \times 4 \times 5 = 60$ cubic units, but the solid cube is taking up $3^3 = 27$ cubic units. Therefore, the tank can hold $60 - 27 = 33$ cubic units of water.

6. **(E)** Draw a diagram and label it.

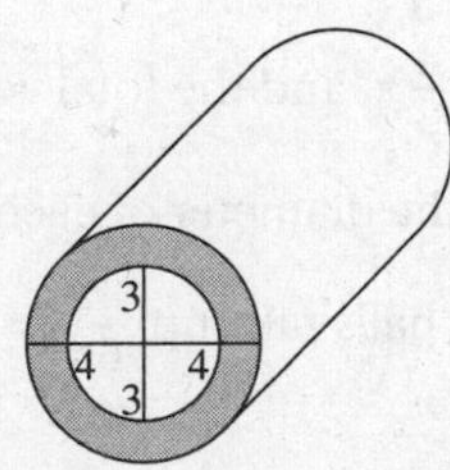

Since the surface of a cylinder is given by $A = 2\pi rh$, the area of the exterior is $2\pi(4)(5) = 40\pi$, and the area of the interior is $2\pi(3)(5) = 30\pi$. The area of *each* shaded end is the area of the outer circle minus the area of the inner circle: $16\pi - 9\pi = 7\pi$, so the total surface area is

$$40\pi + 30\pi + 7\pi + 7\pi = 84\pi \Rightarrow k = 84$$

7. **(A)** Since the volumes are equal, $\pi r^2 h = e^3 = h^3$.

Therefore, $\pi r^2 = h^2 \Rightarrow r^2 = \frac{h^2}{\pi} \Rightarrow r = \frac{h}{\sqrt{\pi}}$.

8. **(B)** Draw a diagram.

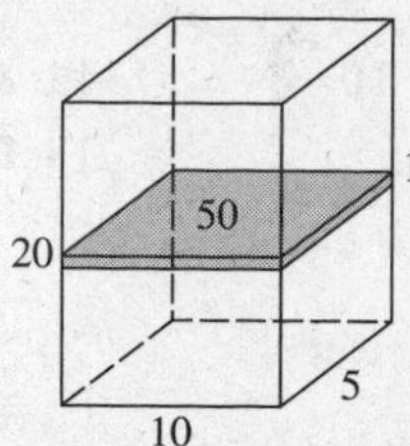

Since the area of the base is $5 \times 10 = 50$ square centimeters, each 1 centimeter of depth has a volume of 50 cubic centimeters. Therefore, 325 cubic centimeters will raise the water level $325 \div 50 = 6.5$ centimeters.

(Note that we didn't use the fact that the tank was half full, except to be sure that the tank didn't overflow. Since the tank was half full, the water was 10 centimeters deep, and the water level could rise by 6.5 centimeters. Had the tank been three-fourths full, the water would have been 15 centimeters deep and the extra water would have caused the level to rise 5 centimeters, filling the tank; the rest of the water would have spilled out.)

9. **(A)** Since $V = \pi r^2 h$, we need to express r and h in terms of C. It is given that $h = 4C$ and since $C = 2\pi r$, then $r = \frac{C}{2\pi}$. Therefore, $V = \pi\left(\frac{C}{2\pi}\right)^2(4C) = \pi\left(\frac{C^2}{4\pi^2}\right)(4C) = \frac{C^3}{\pi}$.

10. $\frac{2}{3}$ To avoid using r, assume that the radii of the spheres and the can are 1. Then the volume of each ball is $\frac{4}{3}\pi(1)^3 = \frac{4}{3}\pi$, and the total volume of the 3 balls is $3\left(\frac{4}{3}\pi\right) = 4\pi$. Since the height of the can is 6 (the diameter of each sphere is 2), the volume of the can is $\pi(1)^2(6) = 6\pi$. So the balls take up $\frac{4\pi}{6\pi} = \frac{2}{3}$ of the can.

11. **(A)** Drawing a diagram makes it easier to visualize the problem. The volume of a cylinder is $\pi r^2 h$. In each case, we know the height but have to determine the radius in order to calculate the volume.

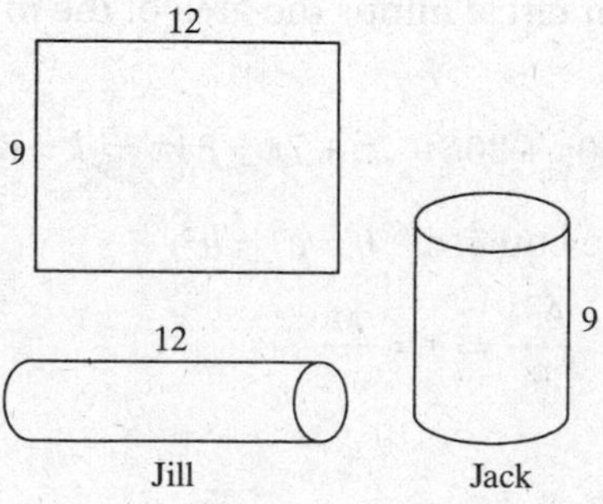

Jack's cylinder has a circumference of 12:

$$2\pi r = 12 \Rightarrow r = \frac{12}{2\pi} = \frac{6}{\pi} \Rightarrow V = \pi\left(\frac{6}{\pi}\right)^2(9) = \pi\left(\frac{36}{\pi^2}\right)(9) = \frac{324}{\pi}$$

Jill's cylinder has a circumference of 9:

$$2\pi r = 9 \Rightarrow r = \frac{9}{2\pi} \Rightarrow V = \pi\left(\frac{9}{2\pi}\right)^2 (12) = \pi\left(\frac{81}{4\pi^2}\right)(12) = \frac{243}{\pi}$$

12. **(A)** Quantity A: $V = 6^3 = 216$. Quantity B: $V = 5 \times 6 \times 7 = 210$.

13. **(D)** There is no relationship between the two quantities. If the box is a cube of edge 1, $A = 6$ and $V = 1$. If the box is a cube of edge 10, $A = 600$ and $V = 1{,}000$.

14. **(B)** The base, *AB*, of $\triangle ABP$ is 1. Since the diagonal is the longest line segment in the cube, the height, *h*, of the triangle is definitely less than the diagonal, which is

    $\sqrt{1^2+1^2+1^2} = \sqrt{3}$.

    So the area of the triangle is less than $\frac{1}{2}(1)\sqrt{3} \approx .87$, which is less than 1.

    (You could also have just calculated the area: $h = BG = \sqrt{2}$, so the area is $\frac{1}{2}\sqrt{2} \approx .71$.)

15. **(A)** You probably don't know how to find the volume of a sphere; fortunately, you don't need to. You should be able to visualize that the sphere is *much* bigger than the cube. (In fact, it is more than 4 times the size.)

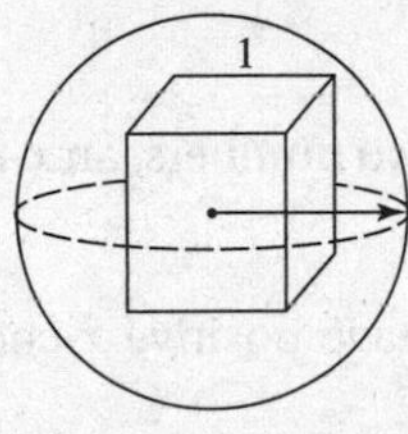

12-N. COORDINATE GEOMETRY

- The Coordinate Plane
- Distance Between Two Points
- Slope
- Equation of Lines
- Practice Exercises
- Answer Explanations

The GRE has very few questions on coordinate geometry. Most often they deal with the coordinates of points and occasionally with the slope of a line. You will *never* have to draw a graph.

The Coordinate Plane

The coordinate plane is formed by two perpendicular number lines called the ***x-axis*** and ***y-axis***, which intersect at the ***origin***. The axes divide the plane into four ***quadrants***, labeled I, II, III, and IV.

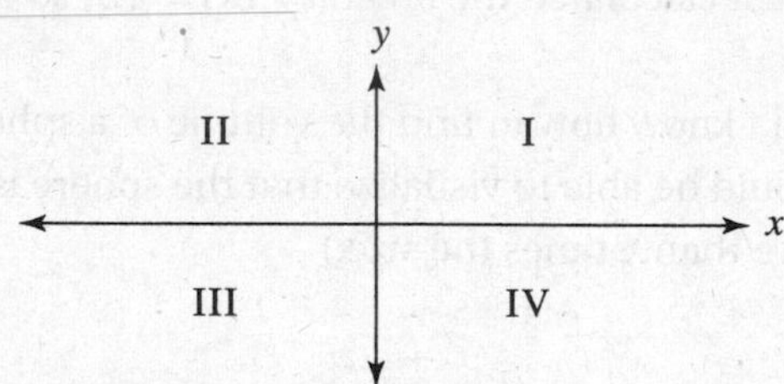

Each point in the plane is assigned two numbers, an ***x-coordinate*** and a ***y-coordinate***, which are written as an ordered pair, **(*x*, *y*)**.

- Points to the right of the *y*-axis have positive *x*-coordinates, and those to the left have negative *x*-coordinates.
- Points above the *x*-axis have positive *y*-coordinates, and those below it have negative *y*-coordinates.
- If a point is on the *x*-axis, its *y*-coordinate is 0.
- If a point is on the *y*-axis, its *x*-coordinate is 0.

For example, point *A* in the following figure is labeled (2, 3), since it is 2 units to the right of the *y*-axis and 3 units above the *x*-axis. Similarly, *B*(–3, –5) is in Quadrant III, 3 units to the left of the *y*-axis and 5 units below the *x*-axis. The origin, which is the point of intersection of the *x*-axis and *y*-axis, has coordinates (0, 0).

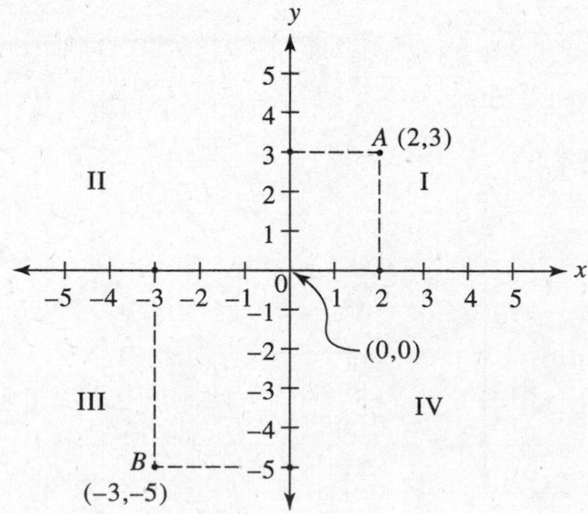

EXAMPLE 1

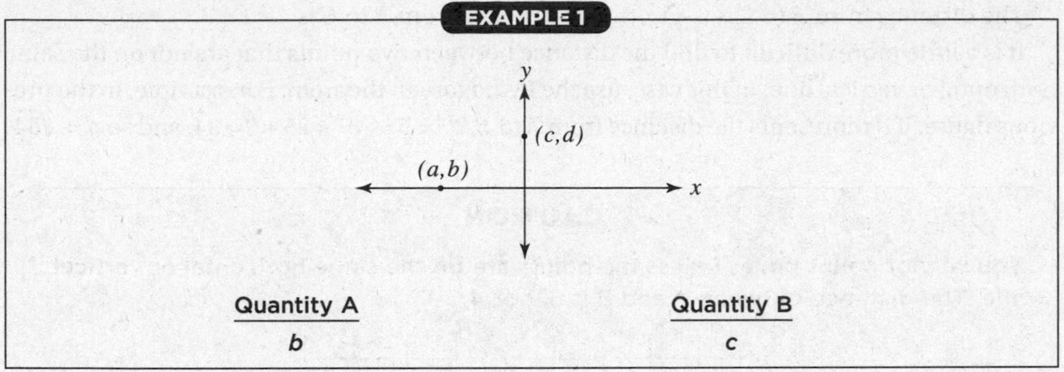

SOLUTION.
Since (a, b) lies on the x-axis, $b = 0$. Since (c, d) lies on the y-axis, $c = 0$. The answer is **C**.

EXAMPLE 2

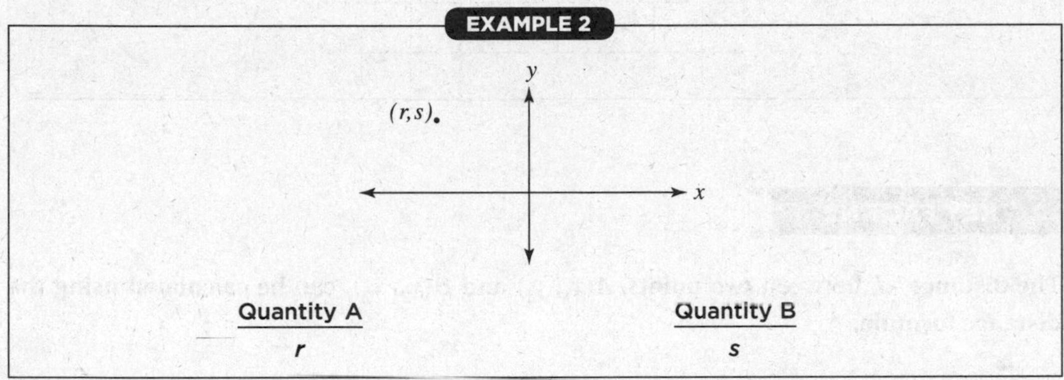

SOLUTION.
Since (r, s) is in Quadrant II, r is negative and s is positive. The answer is **B**.

Distance Between Two Points

Often a question requires you to calculate the distance between two points. This is easiest when the points lie on the same horizontal or vertical line.

KEY FACT N1

- **All the points on a horizontal line have the same y-coordinate. To find the distance between them, subtract their x-coordinates.**
- **All the points on a vertical line have the same x-coordinate. To find the distance between them, subtract their y-coordinates.**

If the points have been plotted on a graph, you can find the distance between them by counting boxes.

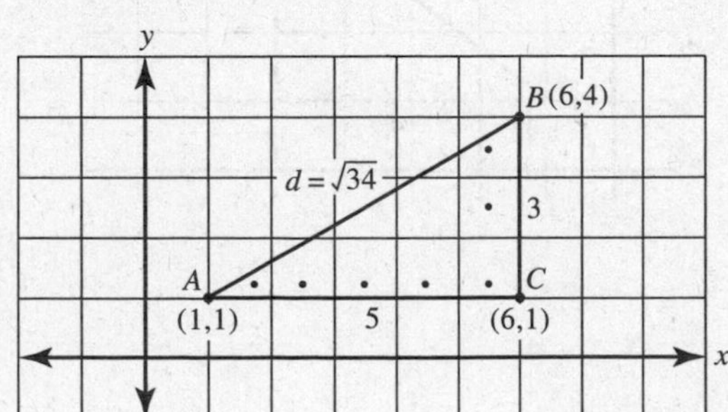

The distance from A to C is $6 - 1 = 5$. The distance from B to C is $4 - 1 = 3$.

It is a little more difficult to find the distance between two points that are not on the same horizontal or vertical line. In this case, use the Pythagorean theorem. For example, in the previous figure, if d represents the distance from A to B, $d^2 = 5^2 + 3^2 = 25 + 9 = 34$, and so $d = \sqrt{34}$.

CAUTION

You *cannot* count boxes unless the points are on the same horizontal or vertical line. The distance between *A* and *B* is 5, not 4.

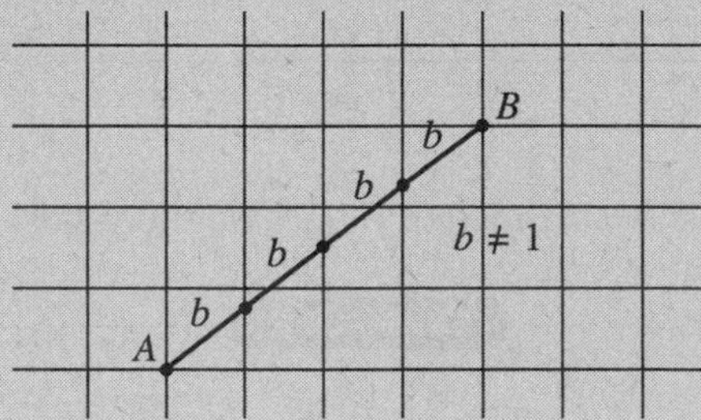

KEY FACT N2

The distance, *d*, between two points, $A(x_1, y_1)$ and $B(x_2, y_2)$, can be calculated using the distance formula:

$$d = \sqrt{(x_2 - x_1)^2 + (y_2 - y_1)^2}$$

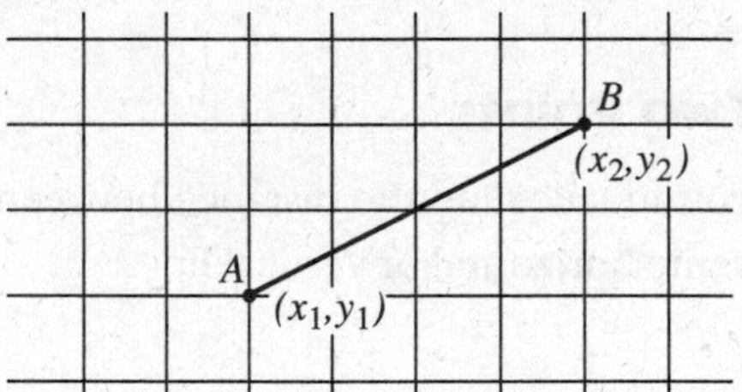

TIP

The "distance formula" is nothing more than the Pythagorean theorem. If you ever forget the formula, and you need the distance between two points that do not lie on the same horizontal or vertical line, do as follows: create a right triangle by drawing a horizontal line through one of the points and a vertical line through the other, and then use the Pythagorean theorem.

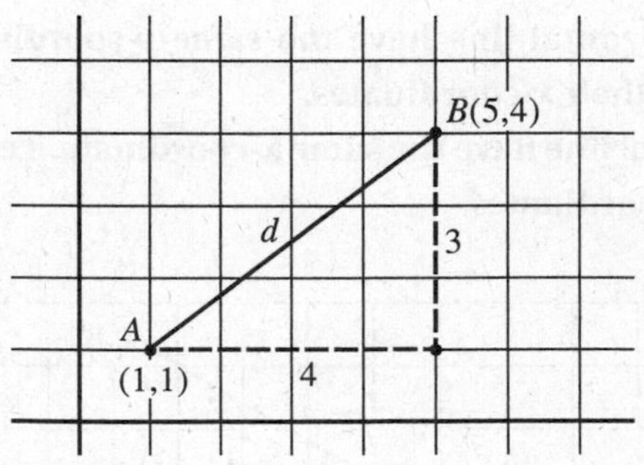

Examples 3–4 refer to the triangle in the following figure.

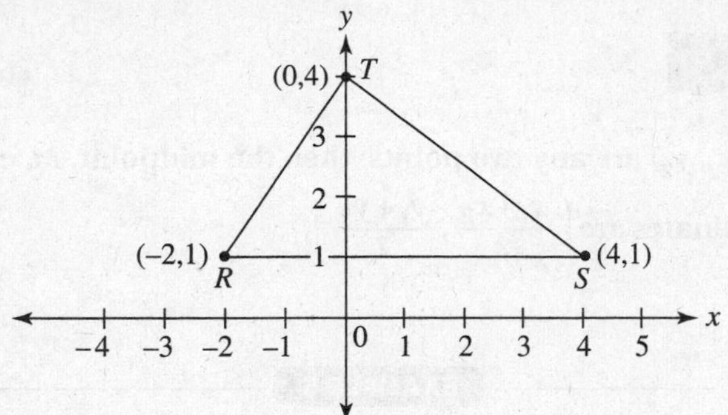

EXAMPLE 3

What is the area of $\triangle RST$?

SOLUTION.
$R(-2, 1)$ and $S(4, 1)$ lie on the same horizontal line, so $RS = 4 - (-2) = 6$. Let that be the base of the triangle. Then the height is the distance along the vertical line from T to RS: $4 - 1 = 3$. The area is $\frac{1}{2}(6)(3) = \mathbf{9}$.

EXAMPLE 4

What is the perimeter of $\triangle RST$?

Ⓐ 13 Ⓑ 14 Ⓒ 16 Ⓓ $11 + \sqrt{13}$ Ⓔ $11 + \sqrt{61}$

SOLUTION.
The perimeter is $RS + ST + RT$. From the solution to Example 3, you know that $RS = 6$. Also, $ST = 5$, since it is the hypotenuse of a 3-4-5 right triangle. To calculate RT, either use the distance formula:

$$RT = \sqrt{(-2-0)^2 + (1-4)^2} = \sqrt{(-2)^2 + (-3)^2} = \sqrt{4+9} = \sqrt{13}$$

or the Pythagorean theorem: $RT^2 = 2^2 + 3^2 = 4 + 9 = 13 \Rightarrow RT = \sqrt{13}$.

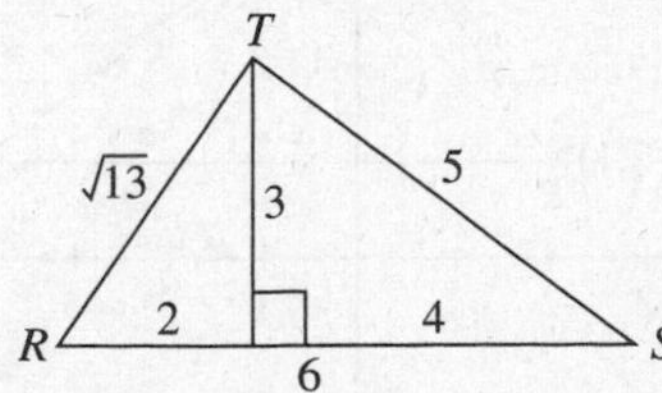

So the perimeter is: $6 + 5 + \sqrt{13} = \mathbf{11 + \sqrt{13}}$ **(D)**.

The Midpoint of a Segment

KEY FACT N3

- **If $P(x_1, y_1)$ and $Q(x_2, y_2)$ are any two points, then the midpoint, M, of segment $\overline{PQ}$ is the point whose coordinates are $\left(\frac{x_1+x_2}{2}, \frac{y_1+y_2}{2}\right)$.**

EXAMPLE 5

$A(2, -3)$ and $B(8, 5)$ are the endpoints of a diameter of a circle. What are the coordinates of the center of the circle?

Ⓐ (3, 1) Ⓑ (3, 4) Ⓒ (5, 1) Ⓓ (5, 4) Ⓔ (10, 2)

SOLUTION.
The center of a circle is the midpoint of any diameter. Therefore, the coordinates are $\left(\frac{2+8}{2}, \frac{-3+5}{2}\right) = \left(\frac{10}{2}, \frac{2}{2}\right) =$ **(5, 1) (C).**

Slope

The ***slope*** of a line is a number that indicates how steep the line is.

KEY FACT N4

- **Vertical lines *do not have slopes.***
- **To find the slope of any other line proceed as follows:**

  1. Choose any two points $A(x_1, y_1)$ and $B(x_2, y_2)$ on the line.
  2. Take the differences of the y-coordinates, $y_2 - y_1$, and the x-coordinates, $x_2 - x_1$.
  3. Divide: slope $= \frac{y_2 - y_1}{x_2 - x_1}$.

We will illustrate the next KEY FACT by using this formula to calculate the slopes of sides RS, RT, and ST of $\triangle RST$ from Example 3: $R(-2, 1)$, $S(4, 1)$, $T(0, 4)$.

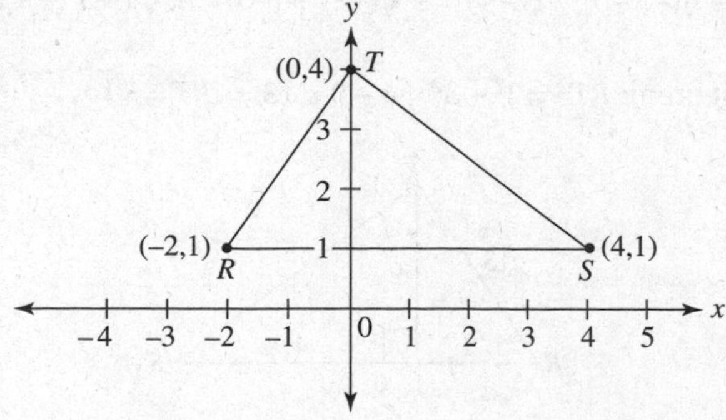

KEY FACT N5

- **The slope of any horizontal line is 0:**

$$\text{slope of } RS = \frac{1-1}{4-(-2)} = \frac{0}{6} = 0$$

- **The slope of any line that goes up as you move from left to right is positive:**

$$\text{slope of } RT = \frac{4-1}{0-(-2)} = \frac{3}{2}$$

- **The slope of any line that goes down as you move from left to right is negative:**

$$\text{slope of } ST = \frac{1-4}{4-0} = \frac{-3}{4} = -\frac{3}{4}$$

EXAMPLE 6

Line ℓ passes through (1, 2) and (3, 5)
Line m is perpendicular to ℓ

Quantity A	Quantity B
The slope of ℓ	The slope of m

SOLUTION.
First, make a quick sketch.

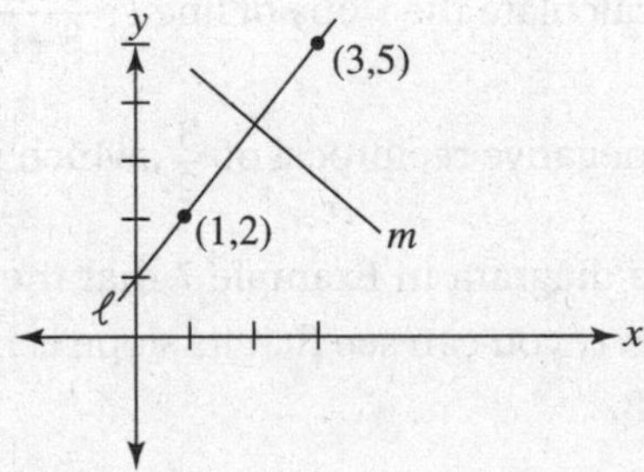

Do not use the formula to calculate the slope of ℓ. Simply notice that ℓ slopes upward, so its slope is positive, whereas m slopes downward, so its slope is negative. Quantity A is greater.

The next key fact concerns the relationship between the slopes of parallel and perpendicular lines.

KEY FACT N6

- **If two nonvertical lines are parallel, their slopes are equal.**
- **If two nonvertical lines are perpendicular, the product of their slopes is –1.**

If the product of two numbers, r and s, is -1, then

$$rs = -1 \Rightarrow r = \frac{1}{s}$$

Therefore, another way to express the second part of KEY FACT N6 is to say that, **if two nonvertical lines are perpendicular, the slope of one is the negative reciprocal of the slope of the other.**

EXAMPLE 7

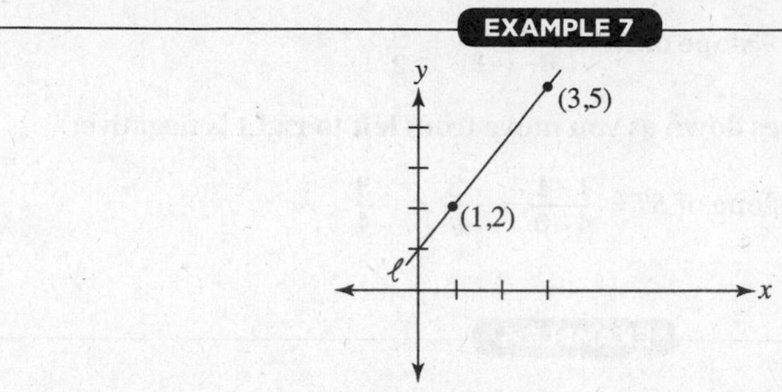

In the figure above, line ℓ passes through points (1, 2) and (3, 5). Line *m* (not shown) is perpendicular to ℓ. What is the slope of line *m*?

Ⓐ $-\frac{3}{2}$ Ⓑ $-\frac{2}{3}$ Ⓒ 0 Ⓓ $\frac{2}{3}$ Ⓔ $\frac{3}{2}$

SOLUTION.

First, use the slope formula to calculate the slope of line ℓ: $\frac{5-2}{3-1} = \frac{3}{2}$.

Then the slope of line m is the negative reciprocal of $\frac{3}{2}$, which is $-\frac{2}{3}$ **(B).**

Note that you can see from the diagram in Example 7 that the slope of ℓ is positive. If you sketch any line perpendicular to ℓ, you can see that its slope is negative. So immediately you know the answer must be A or B.

Equations of Lines

Every line that is drawn in the coordinate plane has an equation. All the points on a horizontal line have the same y-coordinate. For example, in the following figure, horizontal line ℓ passes through (–3, 3), (0, 3), (2, 3), (5, 3), and (10, 3).

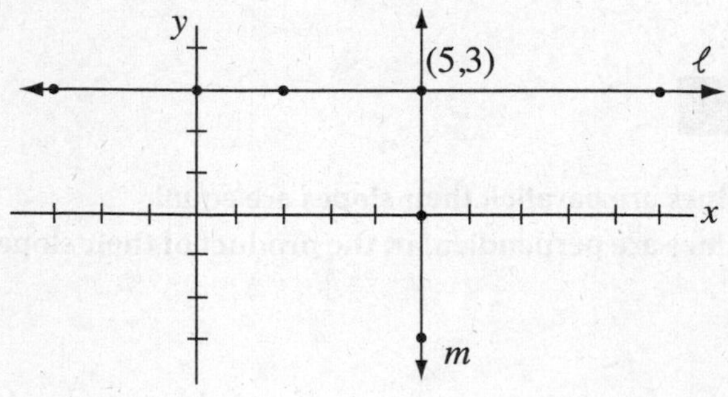

The equation of line ℓ is $y = 3$.

Similarly, every point on vertical line m has an x-coordinate equal to 5, and the equation of m is $x = 5$.

Every other line in the coordinate plane has an equation that can be written in the form $y = mx + b$, where m is the slope of the line and b is the y-intercept—the y-coordinate of the point where the line crosses the y-axis. These facts are summarized in KEY FACT N7.

KEY FACT N7

- **For any real number a: $x = a$ is the equation of the vertical line that crosses the x-axis at $(a, 0)$.**
- **For any real number b: $y = b$ is the equation of the horizontal line that crosses the y-axis at $(0, b)$.**
- **For any real numbers b and m: $y = mx + b$ is the equation of the line that crosses the y-axis at $(0, b)$ and whose slope is m.**

On the GRE, you won't have to graph a line, but you may have to recognize the graph of a line. In a multiple-choice question, you may be given the graph of a line and asked which of the five choices is the equation of that line; or you may be given the equation of a line and asked which of the five choices is the correct graph.

EXAMPLE 8

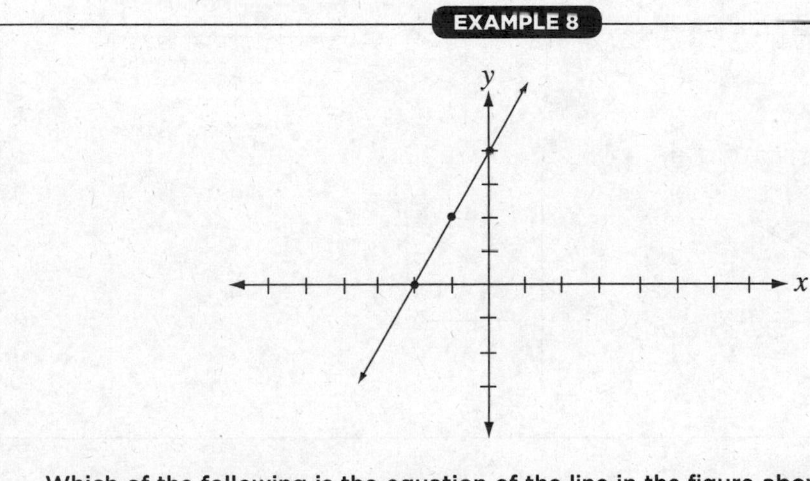

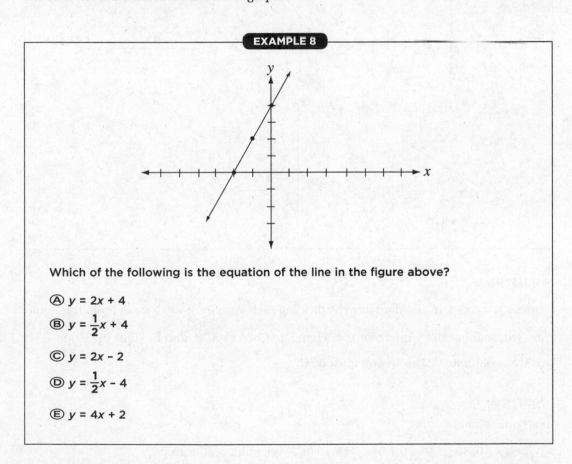

Which of the following is the equation of the line in the figure above?

Ⓐ $y = 2x + 4$

Ⓑ $y = \frac{1}{2}x + 4$

Ⓒ $y = 2x - 2$

Ⓓ $y = \frac{1}{2}x - 4$

Ⓔ $y = 4x + 2$

There are two different ways to handle this question.

SOLUTION 1.

Since the line is neither horizontal nor vertical, its equation has the form $y = mx + b$. Since the line crosses the y-axis at 4, $b = 4$. Also, since the line passes through (–2, 0) and (0, 4), its slope is $\frac{4-0}{0-(-2)} = \frac{4}{2} = 2$.

So $m = 2$, and the equation is $\mathbf{y = 2x + 4}$ **(A)**.

SOLUTION 2.

Test some points. Since the line passes through (0, 4), $y = 4$ when $x = 0$. Plug in 0 for x in the five choices; only in A and B does y equal 4. The line also passes through (–2, 0), so when $x = -2$, $y = 0$.

- $2(-2) + 4 = -4 + 4 = 0$, so A works.
- $\frac{1}{2}(-2) + 4 = -1 + 4 = 3$, so B does not work.

EXAMPLE 9

Which of the following is the graph of the line whose equation is $3y = 2x + 6$?

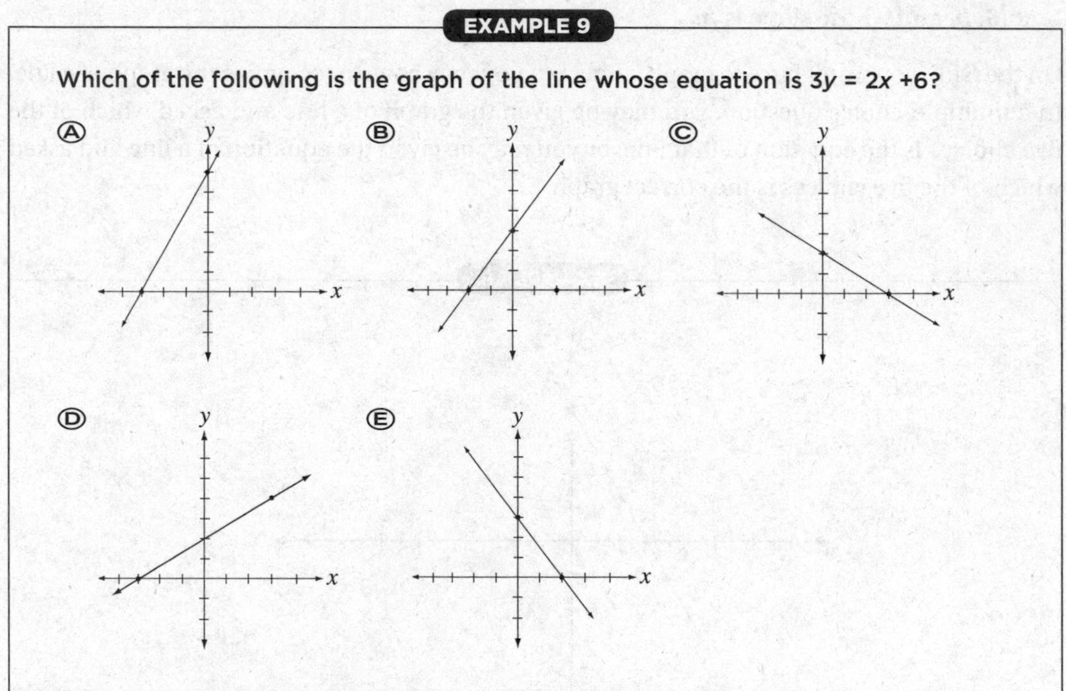

SOLUTION 1.

Express $3y = 2x + 6$ in standard form by dividing each term by 3: $y = \frac{2}{3}x + 2$. From this equation, you see that the y-intercept is 2. Eliminate Choices A, B, and E. Since the slope $\frac{2}{3}$ is positive, eliminate C. The answer must be **D**.

SOLUTION 2.

Test some points.

- When $x = 0$, $3y = 2(0) + 6 = 6 \Rightarrow y = 2$, so (0, 2) is a point on the graph.
- When $x = 3$, $3y = 2(3) + 6 = 12 \Rightarrow y = 4$, so (3, 4) is on the graph.

Only Choice **D** passes through both (0, 2) and (3, 4).

PRACTICE EXERCISES—COORDINATE GEOMETRY

Discrete Quantitative Questions

1. What is the slope of the line that passes through points (0, –2) and (3, 0)?

$$\frac{\boxed{}}{\boxed{}}$$

2. If the coordinates of $\triangle RST$ are $R(0, 0)$, $S(7, 0)$, and $T(2, 5)$, what is the sum of the slopes of the three sides of the triangle?

Ⓐ –1.5
Ⓑ 0
Ⓒ 1.5
Ⓓ 2.5
Ⓔ 3.5

3. If $A(-1, 1)$ and $B(3, -1)$ are the endpoints of one side of square *ABCD*, what is the area of the square?

Ⓐ 12
Ⓑ 16
Ⓒ 20
Ⓓ 25
Ⓔ 36

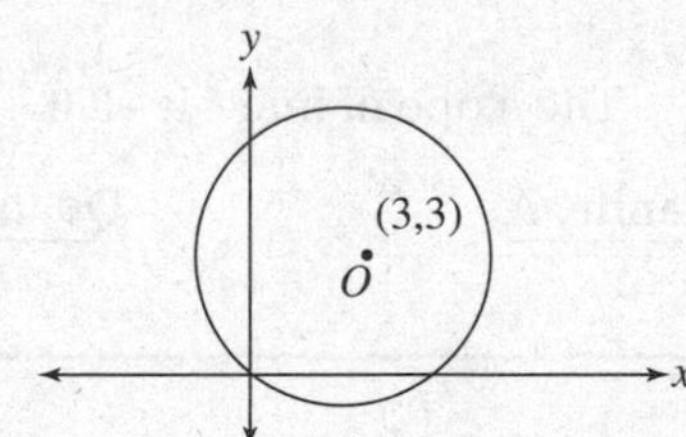

4. If the area of circle *O* above is $k\pi$, what is the value of k?

Ⓐ 3
Ⓑ 6
Ⓒ 9
Ⓓ 18
Ⓔ 27

5. If $P(2, 1)$ and $Q(8, 1)$ are two of the vertices of a rectangle, which of the following could *not* be another of the vertices?

Ⓐ (2, 8)
Ⓑ (8, 2)
Ⓒ (2, –8)
Ⓓ (–2, 8)
Ⓔ (8, 8)

6. A circle whose center is at (6, 8) passes through the origin. Which of the following points is *not* on the circle?

Ⓐ (12, 0)
Ⓑ (6, –2)
Ⓒ (16, 8)
Ⓓ (–2, 12)
Ⓔ (–4, 8)

QUESTIONS 7–8 CONCERN PARALLELOGRAM *JKLM*, WHOSE COORDINATES ARE $J(-5, 2)$, $K(-2, 6)$, $L(5, 6)$, $M(2, 2)$.

7. What is the area of parallelogram *JKLM*?

Ⓐ 35
Ⓑ 28
Ⓒ 24
Ⓓ 20
Ⓔ 12

8. What is the perimeter of parallelogram *JKLM*?

$\boxed{}$

9. If (a, b) and $\left(\frac{1}{a}, b\right)$ are two distinct points, what is the slope of the line that passes through them?

Ⓐ 0
Ⓑ $\frac{1}{b}$
Ⓒ $\frac{1-a^2}{a}$
Ⓓ $\frac{a^2-1}{a}$
Ⓔ undefined

10. If $c \neq 0$ and the slope of the line passing through $(-c, c)$ and $(3c, a)$ is 1, which of the following is an expression for a in terms of c?

Ⓐ $-3c$
Ⓑ $-\frac{c}{3}$
Ⓒ $2c$
Ⓓ $3c$
Ⓔ $5c$

Quantitative Comparison Questions

Ⓐ Quantity A is greater.
Ⓑ Quantity B is greater.
Ⓒ The two quantities are equal.
Ⓓ It is impossible to determine which quantity is greater.

11.

m is the slope of one of the diagonals of a square.

Quantity A	Quantity B
m^2	1

12.

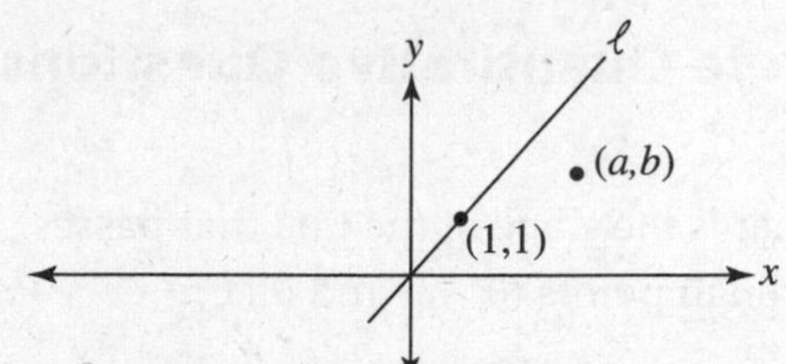

Quantity A	Quantity B
$a - b$	0

13.

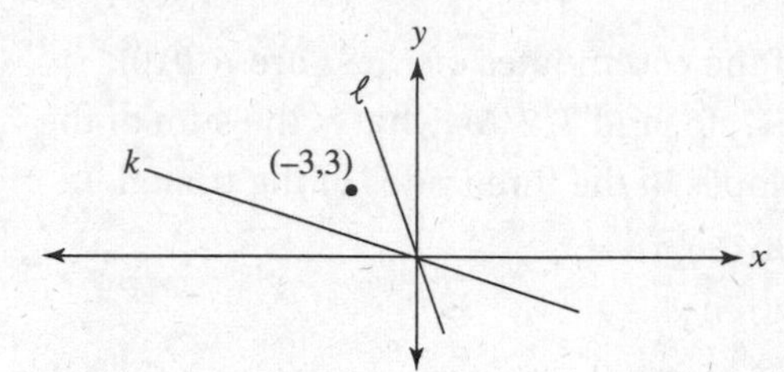

Quantity A	Quantity B
The slope of line k	The slope of line ℓ

14.

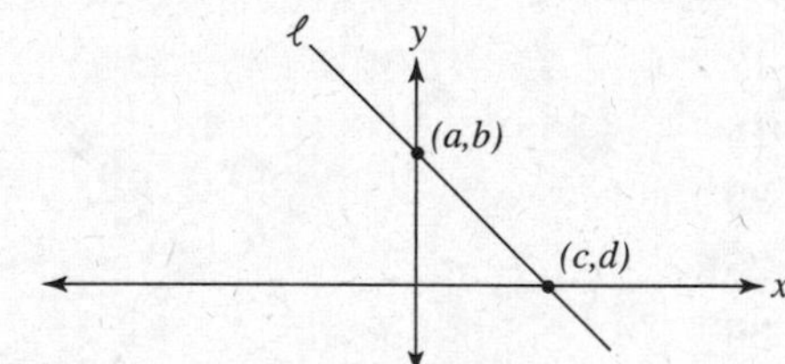

The slope of line ℓ is –0.8.

Quantity A	Quantity B
c	b

15.

The distance from $(b, 5)$ to $(c, -3)$ is 10.

$b < c$

Quantity A	Quantity B
$c - b$	6

ANSWER KEY

1. $\frac{2}{3}$	4. **D**	7. **B**	10. **E**	13. **A**
2. **C**	5. **D**	8. **24**	11. **D**	14. **A**
3. **C**	6. **D**	9. **A**	12. **A**	15. **C**

ANSWER EXPLANATIONS

1. $\frac{2}{3}$ If you sketch the line, you see immediately that the slope of the line is positive.

   Without even knowing the slope formula, therefore, you can eliminate Choices A, B, and C. To determine the actual slope, use the formula: $\frac{y_2 - y_1}{x_2 - x_1} = \frac{0-(-2)}{3-0} = \frac{2}{3}$.

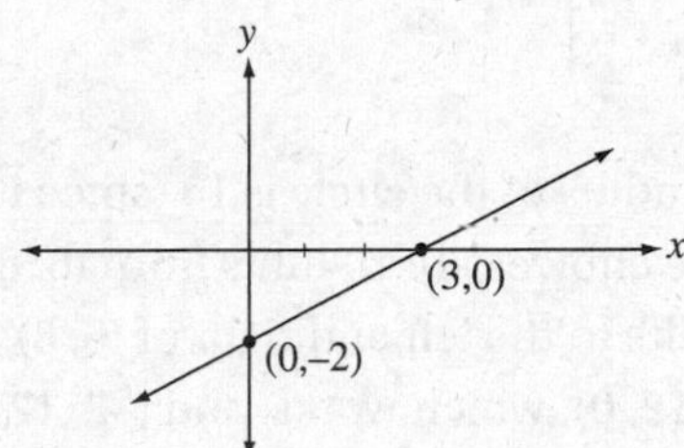

2. **(C)** Sketch the triangle, and then calculate the slopes.

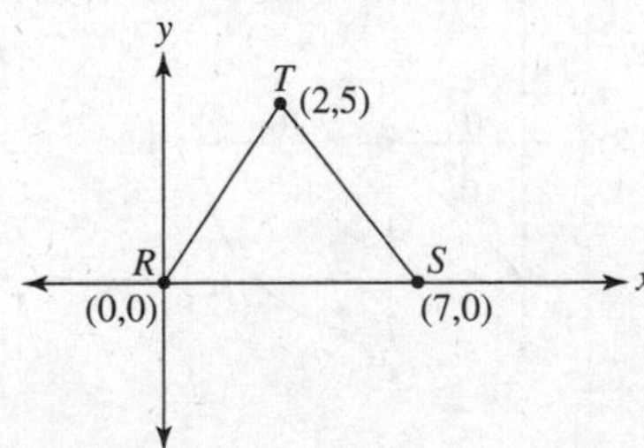

   Since *RS* is horizontal, its slope is 0.

   The slope of $RT = \frac{5-0}{2-0} = 2.5$. The slope of $ST = \frac{5-0}{2-7} = \frac{5}{-5} = -1$.

   Now add: $0 + 2.5 + (-1) = 1.5$

3. **(C)** Draw a diagram and label it. The area of square *ABCD* is s^2, where $s = AB$, the length of a side. By the Pythagorean theorem:

$$s^2 = 2^2 + 4^2 = 4 + 16 = 20$$

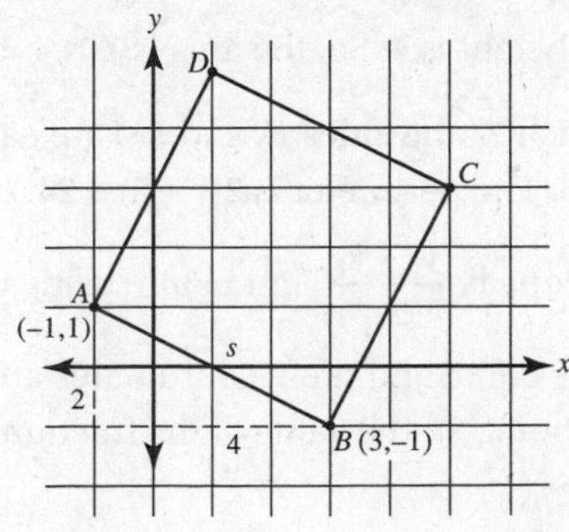

4. **(D)** Since the line segment joining (3, 3) and (0, 0) is a radius of the circle, $r^2 = 3^2 + 3^2 = 18$. Therefore, area $= \pi r^2 = 18\pi \Rightarrow k = 18$. Note that you do not actually have to find that the value of r is $3\sqrt{2}$.

5. **(D)** Draw a diagram. Any point whose x-coordinate is 2 or 8 could be another vertex. Of the choices, only (–2, 8) is *not* possible.

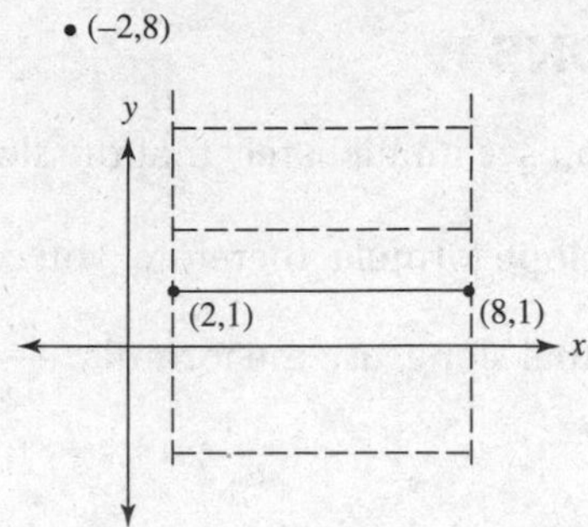

6. **(D)** Draw a diagram. The radius of the circle is 10 (since it's the hypotenuse of a 6-8-10 right triangle). Which of the choices are 10 units from (6, 8)? First, check the easy ones: (–4, 8) and (16, 8) are 10 units to the left and right of (6, 8), and (6, –2) is 10 units below. What remains is to check (12, 0), which works, and (–2, 12), which doesn't.

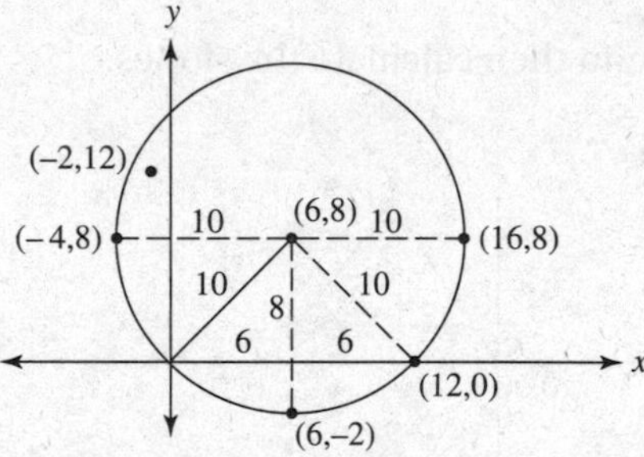

Here is the diagram for solutions 7 and 8.

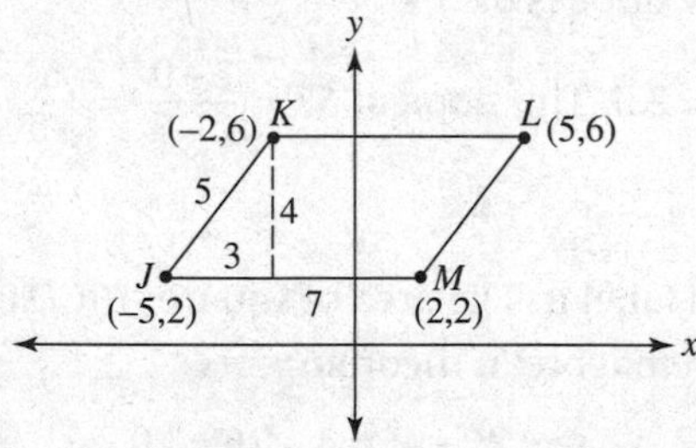

7. **(B)** The base is 7 and the height is 4. So, the area is $7 \times 4 = 28$.

8. **24** Sides *JM* and *KL* are each 7, and sides *JK* and *LM* are each the hypotenuse of a 3-4-5 right triangle, so they are 5. The perimeter is $2(7 + 5) = 24$.

9. **(A)** The formula for the slope is $\frac{y_2 - y_1}{x_2 - x_1}$, but before using it, look.

Since the y-coordinates are equal and the x-coordinates are not equal, the numerator is 0 and the denominator is not 0. So the value of the fraction is 0.

10. **(E)** The slope is equal to $\frac{y_2-y_1}{x_2-x_1} = \frac{a-c}{3c-(-c)} = \frac{a-c}{4c} = 1.$

So $a - c = 4c$ and $a = 5c$.

11. **(D)** If the sides of the square are horizontal and vertical, then m is 1 or –1, and m^2 is 1. But the square could be positioned any place, and the slope of a diagonal could be any number.

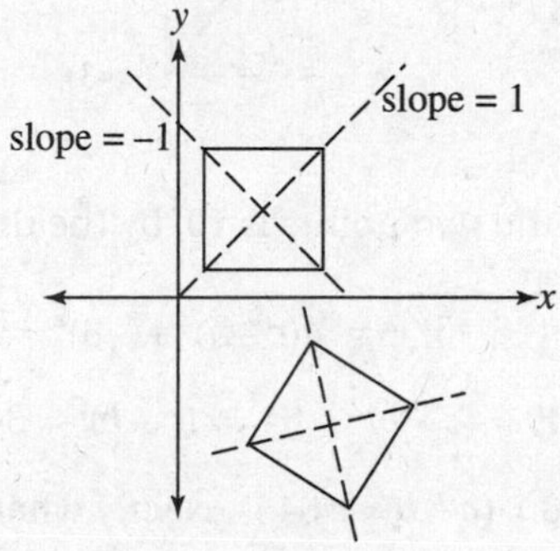

12. **(A)** Line ℓ, which goes through (0, 0) and (1, 1), also goes through (a, a), and since (a, b) is below (a, a), $b < a$. Therefore, $a - b$ is positive. Quantity A is greater.

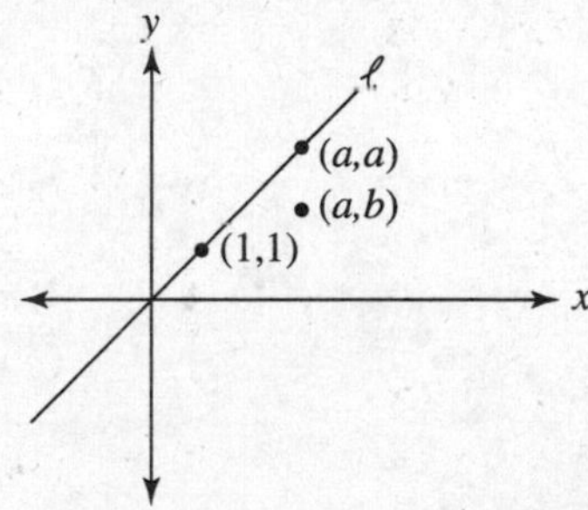

13. **(A)** The line going through (–3, 3) and (0, 0) has slope –1. Since ℓ is steeper, its slope is a number such as –2 or –3; since k is less steep, its slope is a number such as –0.5 or –0.3. Therefore, the slope of k is greater.

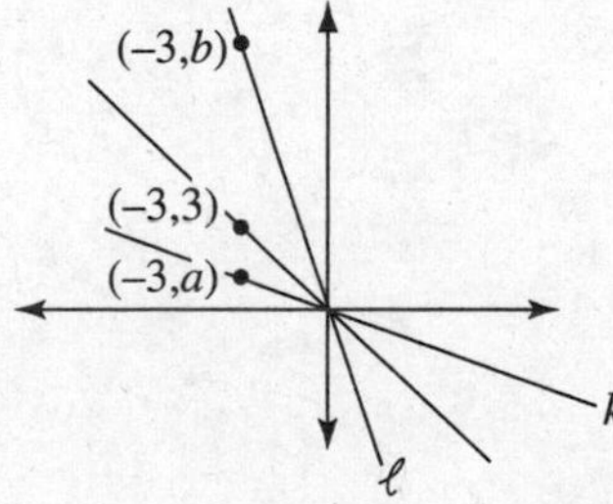

14. **(A)** Since (a, b) is on the y-axis, $a = 0$; and since (c, d) is on the x-axis, $d = 0$.

Then by the slope formula, $-0.8 = \frac{0-b}{c-0} = -\frac{b}{c} \Rightarrow b = 0.8c$.

Since b and c are both positive, $b < c$.

15. **(C)** Draw a diagram.

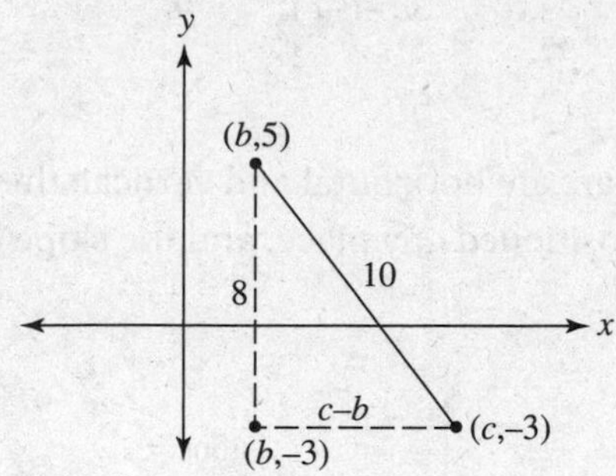

Since the distance between the two points is 10, by the distance formula:

$$10 = \sqrt{(c-b)^2+(-3-5)^2} = \sqrt{(c-b)^2+(-8)^2} = \sqrt{(c-b)^2+64}$$

Squaring both sides gives $100 = (c-b)^2 + 64 \Rightarrow (c-b)^2 = 36$. So $c - b = 6$.

Notice that the equation $100 = (c-b)^2 + 64$ is exactly what you could have gotten immediately by using the Pythagorean theorem: $10^2 = (c-b)^2 + 8^2$.

MISCELLANEOUS TOPICS

12-O. COUNTING AND PROBABILITY

Some questions on the GRE begin, "How many ... ." In these problems you are being asked to count something: how many apples can she buy, how many dollars did he spend, how many pages did she read, how many numbers satisfy a certain property, or how many ways are there to complete a particular task. Sometimes these problems can be handled by simple arithmetic. Other times it helps to use TACTIC 8 from Chapter 8 (page 259) and systematically make a list. Occasionally it helps to know the counting principle and other strategies that we will review in this section.

Counting

USING ARITHMETIC TO COUNT

The following three examples require only arithmetic. But be careful; they are not the same.

EXAMPLE 1

Brian bought some apples. If he entered the store with $113 and left with $109, how much, in dollars, did the apples cost?

EXAMPLE 2

Scott was selling tickets for the school play. One day he sold tickets numbered 109 through 113. How many tickets did he sell that day?

EXAMPLE 3

Brian is the 109th person in a line and Scott is the 113th person. How many people are there between Brian and Scott?

SOLUTIONS 1–3.

- It may seem that each of these examples requires a simple subtraction: 113 – 109 = 4. In Example 1, Brian did spend **$4** on apples; in Example 2, however, Scott sold **5** tickets; and in Example 3, only **3** people are on line between Brian and Scott!
- Assume that Brian went into the store with 113 one-dollar bills, numbered 1 through 113; he spent the 4 dollars numbered 113, 112, 111, and 110, and still had the dollars numbered 1 through 109; Scott sold the 5 tickets numbered 109, 110, 111, 112, and 113; and between Brian and Scott the 110th, 111th, and 112th persons—3 people—were on line.

In Example 1, you just needed to subtract: 113 – 109 = 4. In Example 2, you need to subtract *and then add 1*: 113 – 109 + 1 = 4 + 1 = 5. And in Example 3, you need to subtract and then *subtract 1 more*: 113 – 109 – 1 = 3. Although Example 1 is too easy for the GRE, questions such as Examples 2 and 3 do appear, because they're not as obvious and they require that little extra thought. *When do you have to add or subtract 1*?

The issue is whether or not the first and last numbers are included. In Example 1, Brian spent dollar number 113, but he still had dollar number 109 when he left the store. In Example 2, Scott sold both ticket number 109 and ticket 113. In Example 3, neither Scott (the 113th person) nor Brian (the 109th person) was to be counted.

KEY FACT O1

To count how many integers there are between two integers, follow these rules:

- **If exactly one of the endpoints is included, subtract.**
- **If both endpoints are included, subtract and add 1.**
- **If neither endpoint is included, subtract and subtract 1 more.**

EXAMPLE 4

From 1:09 to 1:13, Adam read pages 109 through 113 in his English book. What was his rate of reading, in pages per minute?

SOLUTION.

Since Adam read both pages 109 and 113, he read 113 – 109 + 1 = 5 pages. He started reading during the minute that started at 1:09 (and ended at 1:10). Since he stopped reading at 1:13, he did not read during the minute that began at 1:13 (and ended at 1:14). So he read for 1:13 – 1:09 = 4 minutes. He read at the rate of $\frac{5}{4}$ pages per minute.

TACTIC O1 Systematically Making a List

When a question asks "How many ... ?" and the numbers in the problem are small, just systematically list all of the possibilities.

Proper use of TACTIC O1 eliminates the risk of making an error in arithmetic. In Example 4, rather than even thinking about whether or not to add 1 or subtract 1 after subtracting the number of pages, you could have just quickly jotted down the numbers of the pages Adam read (109, 110, 111, 112, 113), and then counted them.

EXAMPLE 5

Ariel has 4 paintings in the basement. She is going to bring up 2 of them and hang 1 in her den and 1 in her bedroom. In how many ways can she choose which paintings go in each room?

SOLUTION.
Label the paintings 1, 2, 3, and 4, write B for bedroom and D for den, and make a list.

B-D	B-D	B-D	B-D
1-2	2-1	3-1	4-1
1-3	2-3	3-2	4-2
1-4	2-4	3-4	4-3

There are **12** ways to choose which paintings go in each room.

In Example 5, making a list was feasible, but if Ariel had 10 paintings and needed to hang 4 of them, it would be impossible to list all the different ways of hanging them. In such cases, we need the ***counting principle***.

The Counting Principle

KEY FACT O2

If two jobs need to be completed and there are *m* ways to do the first job and *n* ways to do the second job, then there are $m \times n$ ways to do one job followed by the other. This principle can be extended to any number of jobs.

In Example 5, the first job was to pick 1 of the 4 paintings and hang it in the bedroom. That could be done in 4 ways. The second job was to pick a second painting to hang in the den. That job could be accomplished by choosing any of the remaining 3 paintings. So there are $4 \times 3 =$ **12** ways to hang 2 of the paintings.

Now, assume that there are 10 paintings to be hung in 4 rooms. The first job is to choose one of the 10 paintings for the bedroom. The second job is to choose one of the 9 remaining paintings to hang in the den. The third job is to choose one of the 8 remaining paintings for the living room. Finally, the fourth job is to pick one of the 7 remaining paintings for the dining room. These 4 jobs can be completed in $10 \times 9 \times 8 \times 7 =$ **5,040** ways.

EXAMPLE 6

How many integers are there between 100 and 1,000 all of whose digits are odd?

[ ]

SOLUTION.

We're looking for three-digit numbers, such as 135, 711, 353, and 999, in which all three digits are odd. Note that we are *not* required to use three different digits. Although you certainly wouldn't want to list all of them, you could count them by listing some of them and seeing if a pattern develops.

- In the 100s there are 5 numbers that begin with 11: 111, 113, 115, 117, 119.
- Similarly, there are 5 numbers that begin with 13: 131, 133, 135, 137, 139.
- There are 5 that begin with 15; 5 that begin with 17; and 5 that begin with 19.
- A total of $5 \times 5 = 25$ in the 100s.
- In the same way there are 25 in the 300s, 25 in the 500s, 25 in the 700s, and 25 in the 900s, for a grand total of $5 \times 25 =$ **125**.

You can actually do this in less time than it takes to read this paragraph.

The best way to solve Example 6, however, is to use the counting principle. Think of writing a three-digit number as three jobs that need to be done. The first job is to select one of the five odd digits and use it as the digit in the hundreds place. The second job is to select one of the five odd digits to be the digit that goes in the tens place. Finally, the third job is to select one of the five odd digits to be the digit in the units place. Each of these jobs can be done in 5 ways. So the total number of ways is $5 \times 5 \times 5 =$ **125**.

EXAMPLE 7

How many different arrangements are there of the letters *A*, *B*, *C*, and *D*?

(A) 4 (B) 6 (C) 8 (D) 12 (E) 24

Since from the choices given, we know that the answer is a relatively small number, we could just use TACTIC O1 and systematically list them: *ABCD, ABDC, ACBD*, ... However, this method would not be suitable if you had to arrange as few as 5 or 6 letters and would be essentially impossible if you had to arrange 10 or 20 letters.

SOLUTION.

Think of the act of arranging the four letters as four jobs that need to be done, and use the counting principle. The first job is to choose one of the four letters to write in the first position; there are 4 ways to complete that job. The second job is to choose one of the remaining three letters to write in the second position; there are 3 ways to complete that job. The third job is to choose one of the two remaining letters to write in the third position; there are 2 ways to complete that job. Finally, the fourth job is to choose the one remaining letter and to write it; that can be done in 1 way. So, the total number of arrangements of the letters *A*, *B*, *C*, and *D* is: $4 \times 3 \times 2 \times 1 =$ **24**.

Permutations and Combinations

PERMUTATIONS

Example 7 is a special case of a more general situation. Any order or arrangement of a set of objects is called a ***permutation*** of those objects. So what Example 7 asks is, "How many permutations are there of the letters *A*, *B*, *C*, and *D*?" The answer is (4)(3)(2)(1) = 24. More generally, the number of permutations of a set of *n* objects is:

$$n(n-1)(n-2)\cdots(3)(2)(1)$$

This product occurs so frequently in mathematics that it has been given a special name and symbol. It is called ***n factorial*** and is written ***n*!**.

By special convention 0! = 1, 1! = 1; and for all positive integers greater than 1:

$$n! = n(n-1)(n-2)\cdots(3)(2)(1)$$

For example:

$2! = (2)(1) = 2$
$3! = (3)(2)(1) = 6$
$4! = (4)(3)(2)(1) = 24$
$5! = (5)(4)(3)(2)(1) = 120$
$10! = (10)(9)(8)(7)(6)(5)(4)(3)(2)(1) = 3{,}628{,}800$

As you can see, factorials get big very quickly. When written out, 20! is a 19-digit number, and 50! is 65 digits long. Sometimes we want to know how many ways there are to order only some of the objects of a given set.

EXAMPLE 8

How many different 4-letter arrangements are there of the letters *A*, *B*, *C*, *D*, *E*, *F*, and *G*?

SOLUTION.

Proceed exactly as we did in Example 7. There are 7 choices for the first letter, 6 for the second letter, 5 for the third letter, and 4 for the fourth letter. So, there are $7 \times 6 \times 5 \times 4 =$ **840** ways to arrange 4 of the 7 letters.

Example 8 is also a special case of a more general situation. What Example 8 asks is, "How many permutations of 7 letters are there, if we take only 4 of them?" In general, ${}_nP_k$ represents the number of ***permutations of n objects taken k at a time***. Note that in Example 8,

$${}_7P_4 = 7 \times 6 \times 5 \times 4 = \frac{7\times6\times5\times4\times(3\times2\times1)}{(3\times2\times1)} = \frac{7!}{3!}$$

In general,

$$_nP_k = \frac{n!}{(n-k)!}$$

Note that

$$_nP_n = \frac{n!}{(n-n)!} = \frac{n!}{0!} = \frac{n!}{1} = n!$$

COMBINATIONS

Sometimes the order of the objects doesn't matter. If there are 10 students in a club and one is chosen to be president, a second to be secretary, and a third to be treasurer, *the order matters.* President Amy, secretary Bob, and treasurer Chris is a different scenario from president Bob, secretary Chris, and treasurer Amy. But if the club needs to choose three members to serve on a committee, *the order in which they are chosen doesn't matter.* The committee consisting of Amy, Bob, and Chris is exactly the same as the committee consisting of Bob, Chris, and Amy. When order doesn't matter, we talk about the number of ***combinations of n objects taken k at a time***, for which the symbol is $_nC_k$. The number of ways of choosing a president, secretary, and treasurer from a 10-person club is $_{10}P_3 = \frac{10!}{7!} = 10 \times 9 \times 8 = 720$. The number of 3-person committees that can be chosen from a 10-person club is much smaller. The 3! permutations of *A*, *B*, and *C* (representing Amy, Bob, and Chris):

ABC, ACB, BAC, BCA, CAB, CBA

all represent the same committee. So to get the value of $_{10}C_3$, we have to divide $_{10}P_3$ by 3!. In general,

$$_nC_k = \frac{_nP_k}{k!} = \frac{\frac{n!}{(n-k)!}}{k!} = \frac{n!}{k!(n-k)!}$$

Note: Choosing a committee of 3 people from a group of 10 people could be accomplished by choosing the other 7 people *not* to be on the committee. So, $_{10}C_3 = {}_{10}C_7$, and more generally, $_nC_k = {}_nC_{n-k}$.

Venn Diagrams

A ***Venn diagram*** is a figure with two or three overlapping circles, usually enclosed in a rectangle, which is used to solve certain counting problems. To illustrate this, assume that a school has 100 seniors. The following Venn diagram, which divides the rectangle into four regions, shows the distribution of those students in the band and the orchestra.

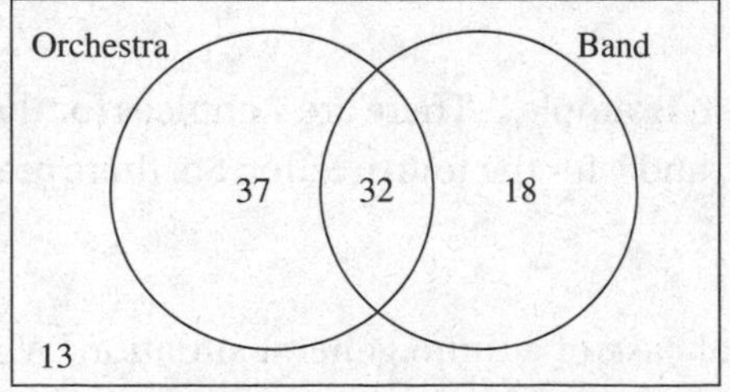

The 32 written in the part of the diagram where the two circles overlap represents the 32 seniors who are in both band and orchestra. The 18 written in the circle on the right represents the 18 seniors who are in band but not in orchestra, while the 37 written in the left circle represents the 37 seniors who are in orchestra but not in band. Finally, the 13 written in the rectangle outside of the circles represents the 13 seniors who are in neither band nor orchestra. The numbers in all four regions must add up to the total number of seniors: $32 + 18 + 37 + 13 = 100$. Note that there are 50 seniors in the band—32 who are also in the orchestra and 18 who are not in the orchestra. Similarly, there are $32 + 37 = 69$ seniors in the orchestra. Be careful: the 50 names on the band roster and the 69 names on the orchestra roster add up to 119 names—more than the number of seniors. That's because 32 names are on both lists and so have been counted twice. The number of seniors who are in band or orchestra is only $119 - 32 = 87$. Those 87 together with the 13 seniors who are in neither make up the total of 100.

On the GRE, Venn diagrams are used in two ways. It is possible to be given a Venn diagram and asked a question about it, as in Example 8. More often, you will come across a problem, such as Example 9, that you will be able to solve more easily if you think to draw a Venn diagram.

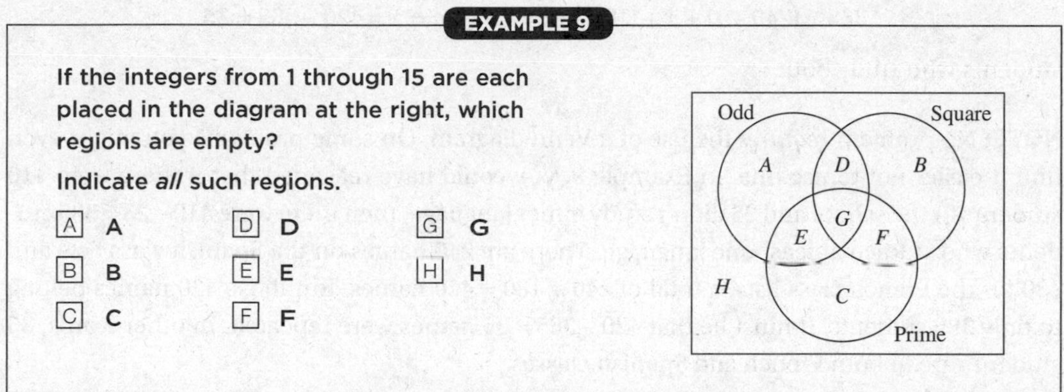

If the integers from 1 through 15 are each placed in the diagram at the right, which regions are empty?

Indicate *all* such regions.

- [A] A
- [B] B
- [C] C
- [D] D
- [E] E
- [F] F
- [G] G
- [H] H

SOLUTION.

The easiest way is just to put each of the numbers from 1 through 15 in the appropriate region.

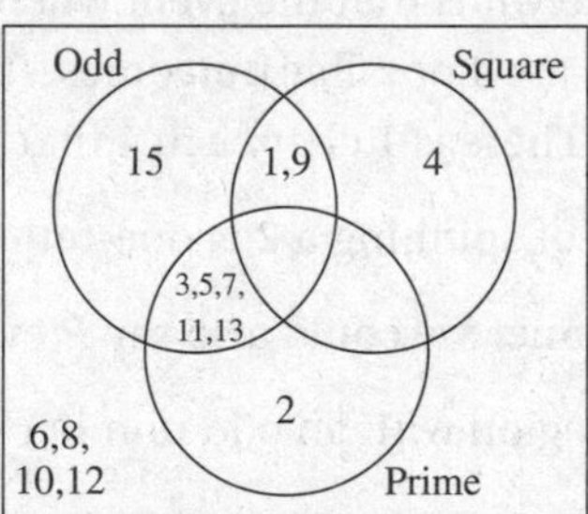

The empty regions are **F** and **G**.

EXAMPLE 10

Of the 410 students at H. S Truman High School, 240 study Spanish and 180 study French. If 25 students study neither language, how many study both?

SOLUTION.
Draw a Venn diagram.

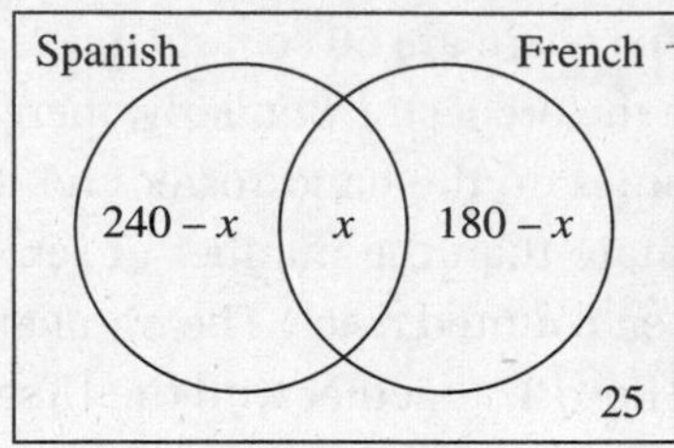

Let x represent the number of students who study both languages, and write x in the part of the diagram where the two circles overlap. Then the number who study only Spanish is $240 - x$, and the number who study only French is $180 - x$. The number who study at least one of the languages is $410 - 25 = 385$, so we have

$$385 = (240 - x) + x + (180 - x) = 420 - x \Rightarrow x = 420 - 385 = \mathbf{35}$$

students who study both.

NOTE: No problem *requires* the use of a Venn diagram. On some problems you might even find it easier not to use one. In Example 9, you could have reasoned that if there were 410 students in the school and 25 didn't study either language, then there were 410 – 25 = 385 students who studied at least one language. There are 240 names on the Spanish class lists and 180 on the French class lists, a total of 240 + 180 = 420 names. But those 420 names belong to only 385 students. It must be that 420 – 385 = 35 names were repeated. In other words, 35 students are in both French and Spanish classes.

Probability

The ***probability*** that an ***event*** will occur is a number between 0 and 1, usually written as a fraction, which indicates how likely it is that the event will happen. For example, if you spin the spinner in the diagram, there are 4 possible outcomes. It is equally likely that the spinner will stop in any of the 4 regions. There is 1 chance in 4 that it will stop in the region marked 2. So we say that the probability of spinning a 2 is one-fourth and write $P(2) = \frac{1}{4}$. Since 2 is the only even number on the spinner we could also say $P(\text{even}) = \frac{1}{4}$. There are 3 chances in 4 that the spinner will land in a region with an odd number in it, so $P(\text{odd}) = \frac{3}{4}$.

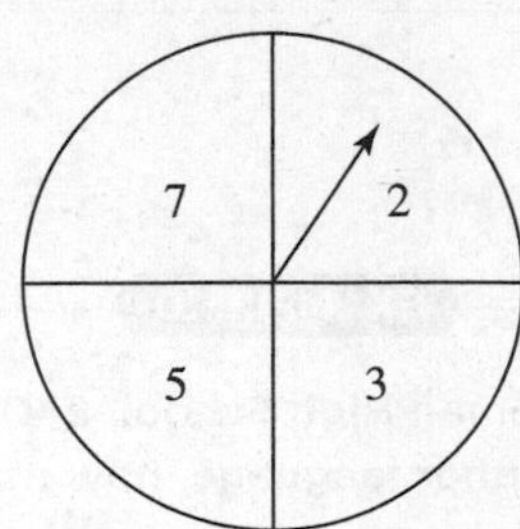

KEY FACT O3

If *E* is any event, the probability that *E* will occur is given by

$$P(E) = \frac{\textbf{number of favorable outcomes}}{\textbf{total number of possible outcomes}}$$

assuming that the possible outcomes are all equally likely.

In the preceding example, each of the 4 regions is the same size, so it is equally likely that the spinner will land on the 2, 3, 5, or 7. Therefore,

$$P(\text{odd}) = \frac{\text{number of ways of getting an odd number}}{\text{total number of possible outcomes}} = \frac{3}{4}$$

Note that the probability of *not* getting an odd number is 1 minus the probability of getting an odd number: $1 - \frac{3}{4} = \frac{1}{4}$. Let's look at some other probabilities associated with spinning this spinner once.

$$P(\text{number} > 10) = \frac{\text{number of ways of getting a number} > 10}{\text{total number of possible outcomes}} = \frac{0}{4} = 0$$

$$P(\text{prime number}) = \frac{\text{number of ways of getting a prime number}}{\text{total number of possible outcomes}} = \frac{4}{4} = 1$$

$$P(\text{number} < 4) = \frac{\text{number of ways of getting a number} < 4}{\text{total number of possible outcomes}} = \frac{2}{4} = \frac{1}{2}$$

KEY FACT O4

Let *E* be an event, and *P*(*E*) the probability it will occur.

- If E is ***impossible*** (such as getting a number greater than 10), ***P*(*E*) = 0.**
- If it is ***certain*** that *E* will occur (such as getting a prime number), ***P*(*E*) = 1.**
- In all cases $\mathbf{0 \le P(E) \le 1}$.
- The probability that event *E* will not occur is **1 – *P*(*E*).**
- If 2 or more events are mutually exclusive and constitute all the outcomes, the sum of their probabilities is 1.

  [For example, $P(\text{even}) + P(\text{odd}) = \frac{1}{4} + \frac{3}{4} = 1$.]
- The more likely it is that an event will occur, the higher its probability (the closer to 1 it is); the less likely it is that an event will occur, the lower its probability (the closer to 0 it is).

Even though probability is defined as a fraction, we can write probabilities as decimals or percents, as well.

Instead of writing $P(E) = \frac{1}{2}$, we write $P(E) = .50$ or $P(E) = 50\%$.

EXAMPLE 11

An integer between 100 and 999, inclusive, is chosen at random. What is the probability that all the digits of the number are odd?

$$\frac{\boxed{}}{\boxed{}}$$

SOLUTION.

By KEY FACT O1, since both endpoints are included, there are 999 – 100 + 1 = 900 integers between 100 and 999. In Example 6, we saw that there are 125 three-digit numbers all of whose digits are odd. So the probability is

$$\frac{\text{number of favorable outcomes}}{\text{total number of possible outcomes}} = \frac{125}{900} = \frac{\mathbf{5}}{\mathbf{36}}$$

NOTE: On a numeric entry question it is not necessary to reduce fractions, so $\frac{125}{900}$ is perfectly acceptable.

KEY FACT O5

If an experiment is done two (or more) times, the probability that first one event will occur and then a second event will occur is the product of the probabilities.

EXAMPLE 12

A fair coin is flipped three times. What is the probability that the coin lands heads each time?

$$\frac{\boxed{}}{\boxed{}}$$

SOLUTION.

When a fair coin is flipped:

$$P(\text{head}) = \frac{1}{2} \text{ and } P(\text{tail}) = \frac{1}{2}$$

By KEY FACT O5, $P(3 \text{ heads}) =$

$$P(\text{head 1st time}) \times P(\text{head 2nd time}) \times P(\text{head 3rd time}) = \frac{1}{2} \times \frac{1}{2} \times \frac{1}{2} = \frac{\mathbf{1}}{\mathbf{8}}$$

Another way to handle problems such as Example 12 is to make a list of all the possible outcomes. For example, if a coin is tossed three times, the possible outcomes are

head, head, head	head, head, tail
head, tail, head	head, tail, tail
tail, head, head	tail, head, tail
tail, tail, head	tail, tail, tail

On the GRE, of course, if you choose to list the outcomes on your scrap paper, you should abbreviate and just write HHH, HHT, and so on. In any event, there are eight possible outcomes, and only one of them (HHH) is favorable. So the probability is $\frac{1}{8}$.

EXAMPLE 13

Three fair coins are flipped.

Quantity A	Quantity B
The probability of getting more heads than tails	The probability of getting more tails than heads

SOLUTION.

From the list of the 8 possible outcomes mentioned, you can see that in 4 of them (HHH, HHT, HTH, THH) there are more heads than tails, and that in 4 of them (TTT, TTH, THT, HTT) there are more tails than heads. Each probability is $\frac{4}{8}$. The answer is **C**.

In Example 12, it wasn't even necessary to calculate the two probabilities. Since heads and tails are equally likely, when several coins are flipped, it is just as likely to have more heads as it is to have more tails. This is typical of quantitative comparison questions on probability; you usually can tell which of the two probabilities is greater without having to calculate either one. This is another instance where you can use TACTIC 5 from Chapter 10 (page 296): don't calculate, compare.

EXAMPLE 14

The numbers from 1 to 1,000 are each written on a slip of paper and placed in a box. Then 1 slip is removed.

Quantity A	Quantity B
The probability that the number drawn is a multiple of 5	The probability that the number drawn is a multiple of 7

SOLUTION.

Since there are many more multiples of 5 than there are of 7, it is more likely that a multiple of 5 will be drawn. Quantity **A** is greater.

PRACTICE EXERCISES—COUNTING AND PROBABILITY

Discrete Quantitative Questions

1. Alyssa completed exercises 6–20 on her math review sheet in 30 minutes. At this rate, how long, in minutes, will it take her to complete exercises 29–57?

Ⓐ 56
Ⓑ 57
Ⓒ 58
Ⓓ 60
Ⓔ 65

2. A diner serves a lunch special, consisting of soup or salad, a sandwich, coffee or tea, and a dessert. If the menu lists 3 soups, 2 salads, 7 sandwiches, and 8 desserts, how many different lunches can you choose? (*Note*: Two lunches are different if they differ in any aspect.)

Ⓐ 22
Ⓑ 280
Ⓒ 336
Ⓓ 560
Ⓔ 672

3. Dwight Eisenhower was born on October 14, 1890 and died on March 28, 1969. What was his age, in years, at the time of his death?

Ⓐ 77
Ⓑ 78
Ⓒ 79
Ⓓ 80
Ⓔ 81

4. How many four-digit numbers have only even digits?

[ ]

5. There are 27 students on the college debate team. What is the probability that at least 3 of them have their birthdays in the same month?

Ⓐ 0
Ⓑ $\frac{3}{27}$
Ⓒ $\frac{3}{12}$
Ⓓ $\frac{1}{2}$
Ⓔ 1

6. Let A be the set of primes less than 6, and B be the set of positive odd numbers less than 6. How many different sums of the form $a + b$ are possible, if a is in A and b is in B?

Ⓐ 6
Ⓑ 7
Ⓒ 8
Ⓓ 9
Ⓔ 10

7. There are 100 people on a line. Aviva is the 37th person and Naomi is the 67th person. If a person on line is chosen at random, what is the probability that the person is standing between Aviva and Naomi?

$\frac{[\ ]}{[\ ]}$

8. A jar has 5 marbles, 1 of each of the colors red, white, blue, green, and yellow. If 4 marbles are removed from the jar, what is the probability that the yellow one was removed?

Ⓐ $\frac{1}{20}$
Ⓑ $\frac{1}{5}$
Ⓒ $\frac{1}{4}$
Ⓓ $\frac{4}{5}$
Ⓔ $\frac{5}{4}$

9. Josh works on the second floor of a building. There are 10 doors to the building and 8 staircases from the first to the second floor. Josh decided that each day he would enter by one door and leave by a different one, and go up one staircase and down another. How many days could Josh do this before he had to repeat a path he had previously taken?

Ⓐ 80
Ⓑ 640
Ⓒ 800
Ⓓ 5040
Ⓔ 6400

10. A jar contains 20 marbles: 4 red, 6 white, and 10 blue. If you remove marbles one at a time, randomly, what is the minimum number that must be removed to be certain that you have at least 2 marbles of each color?

Ⓐ 6
Ⓑ 10
Ⓒ 12
Ⓓ 16
Ⓔ 18

11. At the audition for the school play, n people tried out. If k people went before Judy, who went before Liz, and m people went after Liz, how many people tried out between Judy and Liz?

Ⓐ $n - m - k - 2$
Ⓑ $n - m - k - 1$
Ⓒ $n - m - k$
Ⓓ $n - m - k + 1$
Ⓔ $n - m - k + 2$

12. In a group of 100 students, more students are on the fencing team than are members of the French club. If 70 are in the club and 20 are neither on the team nor in the club, what is the minimum number of students who could be both on the team and in the club?

Ⓐ 10
Ⓑ 49
Ⓒ 50
Ⓓ 60
Ⓔ 61

13. From a group of four boys and six girls, how many ways are there to choose five of the children, if you must choose at least two boys and two girls?

[ ]

QUESTIONS 14–15 REFER TO THE FOLLOWING DIAGRAM.

A is the set of positive integers less than 20; B is the set of positive integers that contain the digit 7; and C is the set of primes.

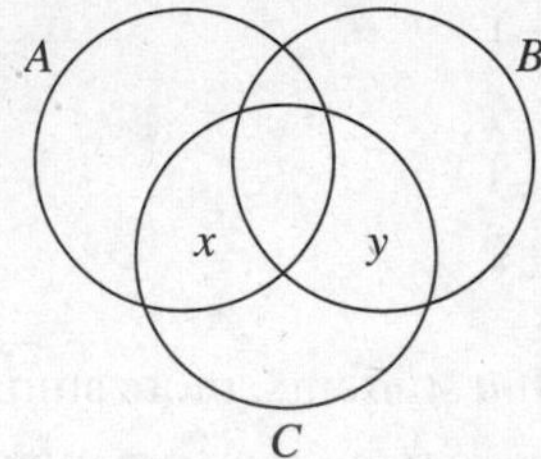

14. How many numbers are in the region labeled x?

Ⓐ 4
Ⓑ 5
Ⓒ 6
Ⓓ 7
Ⓔ 8

15. What is the sum of all the numbers less than 50 that are in the region labeled y?

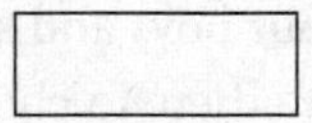

Quantitative Comparison Questions

Ⓐ Quantity A is greater.
Ⓑ Quantity B is greater.
Ⓒ The two quantities are equal.
Ⓓ It is impossible to determine which quantity is greater.

16.

Quantity A	Quantity B
The probability of getting no heads when a fair coin is flipped 7 times	The probability of getting 7 heads when a fair coin is flipped 7 times

17.

A jar contains 4 marbles: 2 red and 2 white. 2 marbles are chosen at random.

Quantity A	Quantity B
The probability that the marbles chosen are the same color	The probability that the marbles chosen are different colors

18.

Quantity A	Quantity B
The number of ways to assign a number from 1 to 5 to each of 4 people	The number of ways to assign a number from 1 to 5 to each of 5 people

19.

A congressional committee consisting of 10 Democrats and 10 Republicans is to choose a subcommittee consisting of 4 Democrats and 6 Republicans.

Quantity A	Quantity B
The number of ways the 4 Democrats can be chosen	The number of ways the 6 Republicans can be chosen

20.

Quantity A	Quantity B
The probability a number chosen at random from the primes between 100 and 199 is odd.	.99

ANSWER KEY

1. **C**	5. **E**	9. **D**	13. **180**	17. **B**
2. **D**	6. **B**	10. **E**	14. **C**	18. **C**
3. **B**	7. $\frac{29}{100}$	11. **A**	15. **84**	19. **C**
4. **500**	8. **D**	12. **E**	16. **C**	20. **A**

ANSWER EXPLANATIONS

1. **(C)** Alyssa completed 20 – 6 + 1 = 15 exercises in 30 minutes, which is a rate of 1 exercise every 2 minutes. Therefore, to complete 57 – 29 + 1 = 29 exercises would take her 58 minutes.

2. **(D)** You can choose your soup or salad in any of 5 ways, your beverage in any of 2 ways, your sandwich in 7 ways, and your dessert in 8 ways. The counting principle says to multiply: $5 \times 2 \times 7 \times 8 = 560$. (Note that if you got soup *and* a salad, then instead of 5 choices for the first course there would have been $2 \times 3 = 6$ choices for the first two courses.)

3. **(B)** His last birthday was in October 1968, when he turned 78: 1968 – 1890 = 78.

4. **500** The easiest way to solve this problem is to use the counting principle. The first digit can be chosen in any of 4 ways (2, 4, 6, 8), whereas the second, third, and fourth digits can be chosen in any of 5 ways (0, 2, 4, 6, 8). Therefore, the total number of four-digit numbers all of whose digits are even is $4 \times 5 \times 5 \times 5 = 500$.

5. **(E)** If there were no month in which at least 3 students had a birthday, then each month would have the birthdays of at most 2 students. But that's not possible. Even if there were 2 birthdays in January, 2 in February, ... , and 2 in December, that would account for only 24 students. It is guaranteed that with more than 24 students, at least one month will have 3 or more birthdays. The probability is 1.

6. **(B)** $A = \{2, 3, 5\}$ and $B = \{1, 3, 5\}$. Any of the 3 numbers in A could be added to any of the 3 numbers in B, so there are 9 sums that could be formed. However, there could be some duplication. List the sums systematically; first add 1 to each number in A, then 3, and then 5: 3, 4, 6; 5, 6, 10; 7, 8, 10. There are 7 different sums.

7. $\mathbf{\frac{29}{100}}$ There are 67 – 37 – 1 = 29 people between Aviva and Naomi, so, the probability that one of them is chosen is $\frac{29}{100}$.

8. **(D)** It is equally likely that any one of the 5 marbles will be the one that is not removed. So, the probability that the yellow one is left is $\frac{1}{5}$ and the probability that it is removed is $\frac{4}{5}$.

9. **(D)** This is the counting principle at work. Each day Josh has four jobs to do: choose 1 of the 10 doors to enter and 1 of the 9 other doors to exit; choose 1 of the 8 staircases to go up and 1 of the other 7 to come down. This can be done in $10 \times 9 \times 8 \times 7 = 5{,}040$ ways. So on each of 5,040 days Josh could choose a different path.

10. **(E)** In a problem like this the easiest thing to do is to see what could go wrong in your attempt to get 2 marbles of each color. If you were really unlucky, you might remove 10 blue ones in a row, followed by all 6 white ones. At that point you would have 16 marbles, and you still wouldn't have even 1 red one. The next 2 marbles, however, must both be red. The answer is 18.

11. **(A)** It may help to draw a line and label it:

$$(\underline{\quad k \quad})\overset{J}{\bullet}(\underline{\qquad\quad})\overset{L}{\bullet}(\underline{\quad m \quad})$$

From the n people who tried out, subtract the k people who went before Judy and the m people who went after Liz, and then subtract 2 more (for Judy and Liz). The number of people to try out between Judy and Liz was $n - k - m - 2 = n - m - k - 2$.

12. **(E)** Draw a Venn diagram, letting x be the number of students who are on the team and in the club.

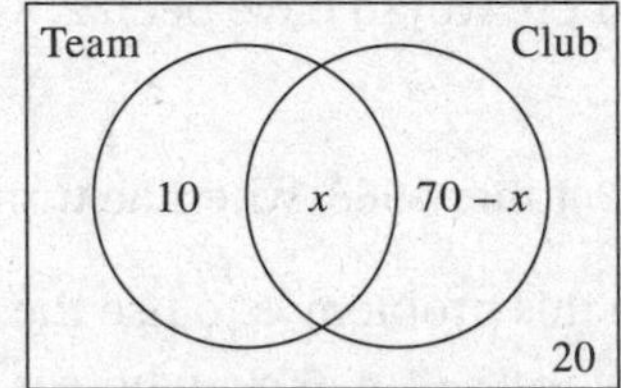

Of the 100 students, 70 are in the club, so 30 are not in the club. Of these 30, 20 are also not on the team, so 10 are on the team but not in the club.
Since more students are on the team than in the club, $10 + x > 70 \Rightarrow x > 60$. Since x must be an integer, the least it can be is 61.

13. **180** There are two possibilities: we can choose two boys and three girls or three boys and two girls.

By the counting principle, the number of ways of choosing two boys and three girls is

(the number of ways of choosing 2 of the 4 boys) times
(the number of ways of choosing 3 of the 6 girls):

$$_4C_2 \times {}_6C_3 = \frac{4!}{2!2!} \times \frac{6!}{3!3!} = 6 \times 20 = 120$$

Similarly, the number of ways of choosing three boys and two girls is

$$_4C_3 \times {}_6C_2 = \frac{4!}{3!1!} \times \frac{6!}{2!4!} = 4 \times 15 = 60$$

The total number of ways to choose the five children is 120 + 60 = 180.

14. **(C)** The region labeled x contains all of the primes less than 20 that do *not* contain the digit 7. They are 2, 3, 5, 11, 13, 19.

15. **84** Region y consists of primes that contain the digit 7 and are greater than 20. There are two of them that are less than 50: 37 and 47. Their sum is 84.

16. **(C)** Don't calculate the probabilities. The probability of no heads is equal to the probability of no tails; but no tails means all heads.

17. **(B)** The simplest solution is to notice that whatever color the first marble is, there is only 1 more marble of that color, but there are 2 of the other color, so it is twice as likely that the marbles will be of different colors.

18. **(C)** By the counting principle, Quantity A is 5·4·3·2 and Quantity B is 5·4·3·2·1. Clearly, the quantities are equal.

19. **(C)** Quantity A is ${}_{10}C_4$ and Quantity B is ${}_{10}C_6$. Since ${}_{10}C_4 = {}_{10}C_6$, the quantities are equal.

20. **(A)** Every prime between 100 and 199 is odd (the only even prime is 2). So Quantity A is 1, which is greater than .99.

12-P. SEQUENCES

- Repeating Sequences
- Arithmetic Sequences
- Geometric Sequences
- Practice Exercises
- Answer Explanations

On a typical GRE math test, there are often one or two questions about sequences. In this section, you will read about the different types of sequences that could be the source of a GRE question.

A ***sequence*** is a list of objects separated by commas. Most often, the objects are numbers, but they don't have to be. A sequence can be finite, such as 2, 5, 10, 17, 26, or can be infinite, such as 2, 4, 6, 8, 10, ... The numbers in the list are called the ***terms*** of the sequence.

The terms of a sequence don't have to follow any regular pattern or rule. Suppose John tossed a die 100 times and recorded the outcomes. If you saw the first 10 terms of that sequence—4, 6, 6, 2, 5, 3, 5, 4, 4, 2—you would have no way of knowing what the 11th term is.

On the GRE, however, there is always a definite rule that determines the terms of a sequence. If Mary creates a sequence of 100 terms by writing down the number 5 and then continually adding 3 to each term, the first 10 terms would be 5, 8, 11, 14, 17, 20, 23, 26, 29, 32. Not only do you know what the eleventh term of her sequence is, as you will see, you can easily calculate the 88th, or any other, term.

On the GRE, the most common type of question concerning sequences gives you a rule and asks you to find a particular term. The three types of sequences that occur most often are repeating sequences, arithmetic sequences, and geometric sequences.

Repeating Sequences

A sequence whose terms repeat in a cyclical pattern is called a ***repeating sequence***. For example, the following three sequences are repeating sequences:

a, b, c, a, b, c, a, b, c, a, b, c, ...
0, 1, 0, 1, 0, 1, 0, 1, 0, 1, 0, 1, ...
7, 1, 4, 2, 8, 5, 7, 1, 4, 2, 8, 5, ...

Sometimes we use the notation $\{a_n\}$ for a squence. Here a_n represents the n-th term of the sequence: a_1 is the first term, a_2 is the second term, and so on.

KEY FACT P1

When a sequence consists of a group of *k* terms that repeat in the same order indefinitely, to find the *n*th term, find the remainder, *r*, when *n* is divided by *k*. The *r*th term and the *n*th term are equal.

The fraction $\frac{5}{7}$ is equivalent to the repeating decimal 0.714285714285... in which the six digits, 7, 1, 4, 2, 8, 5, repeat indefinitely. Examples 1 and 2 refer to this sequence of digits.

EXAMPLE 1

What is the 1,000th digit to the right of the decimal point in the expansion of $\frac{5}{7}$?

Ⓐ 1 Ⓑ 2 Ⓒ 4 Ⓓ 7 Ⓔ 8

SOLUTION.

Use KEY FACT P1. Since the repeating portion consists of 6 digits, divide 1,000 by 6.

$$1{,}000 \div 6 = 166.666... \Rightarrow \text{the quotient is } 166$$

$$166 \times 6 = 996 \Rightarrow \text{the remainder is } 1{,}000 - 996 = 4$$

Therefore, the 1,000th term is the same as the 4th term, namely **2 (B)**.

EXAMPLE 2

What is the sum of the 101st through the 106th digits in the decimal expression of $\frac{5}{7}$?

SOLUTION.

You could repeat what was done in Example 1 six times, but, of course, you shouldn't. Any six consecutive terms of this sequence consist, in some order, of the same six digits—7, 1, 4, 2, 8, 5—whose sum is **27**. In this case, the order is 8, 5, 7, 1, 4, 2, but you do not need to know that.

Consider the following sequence, called the Fibonacci sequence, after the 13th century Italian mathematician: $a_1 = 1$, $a_2 = 1$, and for all $n > 2$, $a_n = a_{n-1} + a_{n-2}$. Then $a_3 = a_2 + a_1 = 1 + 1 = 2$; $a_4 = 2 + 1 = 3$; $a_5 = 3 + 2 = 5$; $a_6 = 5 + 3 = 8$, and so on. Clearly this is *not* a repeating sequence, and it would be totally unreasonable to ask you to find the 100th term. However, there are some questions, such as the one in Example 3, that you could be asked.

EXAMPLE 3

Of the first 100 terms of the Fibonacci sequence, how many are odd?

SOLUTION.

The sequence itself does not form a repeating sequence, but its pattern of odd (O) and even (E) terms does:

1	1	2	3	5	8	13	21	34
O	O	E	O	O	E	O	O	E

Note that the Os and Es form a repeating sequence:

$$\boxed{\text{O O E}}, \ \boxed{\text{O O E}}, \ \boxed{\text{O O E}}, \ \ldots$$

The first 99 terms consist of 33 sets of $\boxed{\text{O O E}}$. Since each set contains two Os and one E, of the first 99 terms, 66 are odd and 33 are even. The 100th term is the first term in the next set and so is O. In all, there are **67** odd terms.

Arithmetic Sequences

An ***arithmetic sequence*** is a sequence such as 5, 8, 11, 14, 17, ... in which the difference between any two consecutive terms is the same. In this sequence, the difference is 3 ($8 - 5 = 3$; $11 - 8 = 3$; $14 - 11 = 3$, ...). An easy way to find the *n*th term of such a sequence is to start with the first term and add the common difference $n - 1$ times. Here, the 5th term is 17, which can be obtained by taking the first term, 5, and adding the common difference, 3, four times: $5 + 4(3) = 17$. In the same way, the 100th term is $5 + 99(3) = 5 + 297 = 302$.

KEY FACT P2

If $a_1, a_2, a_3, \ldots$ is an arithmetic sequence whose common difference is d, then $a_n = a_1 + (n - 1)d$.

EXAMPLE 4

If the 8th term of an arithmetic sequence is 10 and the 20th term is 58, what is the first term?

$\boxed{}$

SOLUTION.
Use KEY FACT P2 twice and subtract:

$$\begin{aligned} a_{20} &= a_1 + 19d = 58 \\ a_8 &= a_1 + 7d = 10 \\ \hline & \quad 12d = 48 \Rightarrow d = 4 \end{aligned}$$

Then

$$10 = a_1 + 7d = a_1 + 7(4) = a_1 + 28 \Rightarrow a_1 = \mathbf{-18}$$

Geometric Sequences

A ***geometric sequence*** is a sequence such as 3, 6, 12, 24, 48, ... in which the ratio between any two consecutive terms is the same. In this sequence, the ratio is

$$\frac{6}{3} = 2; \ \frac{12}{6} = 2; \ \frac{24}{12} = 2; \ldots$$

An easy way to find the *n*th term of a geometric sequence is to start with the first term and multiply it by the common ratio $n - 1$ times. Here the 5th term is 48, which can be obtained by taking the first term, 3, and multiplying it by the common ratio, 2, four times: $3 \times 2 \times 2 \times 2 \times 2 = 3 \times 2^4 = 3 \times 16 = 48$. In the same way, the 100th term is 3×2^{99}.

KEY FACT P3

If $a_1, a_2, a_3, \ldots$ is a geometric sequence whose common ratio is r, then $a_n = a_1r^{n-1}$.

EXAMPLE 5

What is the 12th term of the sequence 3, –6, 12, –24, 48, –96, . . . ?

SOLUTION.

This is a geometric sequence whose common ratio is –2. By KEY FACT P3,

$$a_{12} = a_1(-2)^{11} = 3(-2)^{11} = 3(-2{,}048) = \mathbf{-6{,}144}$$

PRACTICE EXERCISES—SEQUENCES

1. $\{a_n\}$ and $\{b_n\}$ are two sequences defined as follows: $a_1 = 10$ and for $n > 1$, $a_n = a_{n-1} + 3$; $b_1 = 100$ and for all $n > 1$, $b_n = b_{n-1} - 3$. What is $a_{16} + b_{16}$?

   Ⓐ 45
   Ⓑ 55
   Ⓒ 90
   Ⓓ 110
   Ⓔ 200

2. What is the 500th digit to the right of the decimal point when $\frac{15}{37}$ is expressed as a decimal?

   Ⓐ 0
   Ⓑ 3
   Ⓒ 4
   Ⓓ 5
   Ⓔ 7

3. July 4, 2009 was a Saturday. What day of the week was July 4, 2011? (Note: 2009, 2010, and 2011 were all regular years with 365 days.)

   Ⓐ Sunday
   Ⓑ Monday
   Ⓒ Tuesday
   Ⓓ Friday
   Ⓔ Saturday

4. The number of bacteria in a culture increases by 20% every 20 minutes. If there are 1,000 bacteria present at noon on a given day, to the nearest thousand, how many will be present at midnight of the same day?

   Ⓐ 9,000
   Ⓑ 43,000
   Ⓒ 174,000
   Ⓓ 591,000
   Ⓔ 709,000

5. A gum ball dispenser is filled with exactly 1,000 pieces of gum. The gum balls always come out in the following order: 1 red, 2 blue, 3 green, 4 yellow, and 5 white. After the fifth white, the pattern repeats, starting with 1 red, and so on. What is the color of the last gum ball to come out of the machine?

   Ⓐ red
   Ⓑ blue
   Ⓒ green
   Ⓓ yellow
   Ⓔ white

6. $\{a_n\}$ is an arithmetic sequence. If $a_{21} = 57$ and $a_{89} = 227$, what is a_{333}?

   Ⓐ 367
   Ⓑ 417
   Ⓒ 587
   Ⓓ 793
   Ⓔ 837

ANSWER KEY

1. **(D)**
2. **(A)**
3. **(B)**
4. **(E)**
5. **(D)**
6. **(E)**

ANSWER EXPLANATIONS

1. **(D)** $\{a_n\}$ and $\{b_n\}$ are arithmetic sequences whose common differences are 3 and –3, respectively. Sequence II is an arithmetic sequence whose common difference is –3.

$$a_{16} = 10 + 15(3) = 10 + 45 = 55$$
$$b_{16} = 100 + 15(-3) = 100 - 45 = 55$$

$a_{16} + b_{16} = 55 + 55 = 110.$

2. **(A)** Use your calculator to divide: $15 \div 37 = 0.405405405$. So the question is equivalent to asking, "What is the 500th term in the repeating sequence 4, 0, 5, 4, 0, 5, 4, 0, 5, ... ?" Since there are 3 terms in the repeating portion, divide 500 by 3:

$$500 \div 3 = 166.66 \Rightarrow \text{the quotient is } 166$$
$$166 \times 3 = 498 \Rightarrow \text{the remainder is } 500 - 498 = 2$$

So the 500th term was the same as the second term: 0.

3. **(B)** July 4, 2011 was exactly 2 years $= 2 \times 365 = 730$ days after July 4, 2009. The days of the week form a repeating sequence in which 7 terms repeat.

$$730 \div 7 = 104.2857... \Rightarrow \text{the quotient is } 104$$
$$104 \times 7 = 728 \Rightarrow \text{the remainder is } 730 - 728 = 2$$

So 730 days after a Saturday will always be the same day as 2 days after a Saturday, namely Monday.

4. **(E)** Every 20 minutes, the number of bacteria present is muliplied by a factor of 1.2. This creates a geometric sequence whose first term is 1,000 and whose common ratio is 1.2:

$$1{,}000,\ 1{,}200,\ 1{,}440,\ 1{,}728,\ ...$$

The 12 hours from noon to midnight consist of 36 20-minute intervals. So the number of bacteria at midnight is

$$1{,}000 \times (1.2)^{36} = 1{,}000(708.8) = 708{,}800 \approx 709{,}000$$

5. **(D)** Since the pattern repeats itself after every 15 gum balls, divide 1,000 by 15. The quotient is 66, and the remainder is 10. Therefore, the 1,000th gum ball is the same color as the 10th gum ball, which is yellow.

6. **(E)** Since $a_n = a_1 + (n-1)d$, we have

$$57 = a_{21} = a_1 + 20d$$
$$227 = a_{89} = a_1 + 88d$$

Subtracting the first equation from the second yields

$$170 = 68d \Rightarrow d = 2.5$$

So $57 = a_1 + 20(2.5) = a_1 + 50 \Rightarrow a_1 = 7$.
Finally, a_{333}, the 333rd term, is

$$7 + 332(2.5) = 7 + 830 = \mathbf{837}$$

Math Reference 13

All of the math that you need to know to excel on the GRE has been covered in the discussion of data interpretation questions in Chapter 11 and the 16 sections of math review in Chapter 12. If while taking the GRE you get stuck on a question, you may still be able to answer it correctly by using one of the tactics that are covered in Chapters 8, 9, and 10. To minimize the chance of getting stuck in the first place, we recommend that you take a little time to review the most important definitions, facts, and formulas you need to know. They are all listed below with page references so, if you have forgotten any of them, you may quickly go to the appropriate page to find the information you need as well as worked-out questions based on those facts.

IMPORTANT DEFINITIONS, FACTS, AND FORMULAS

1. **Sum:** the result of an addition: 8 is the sum of 6 and 2 (page 329)
2. **Difference:** the result of a subtraction: 4 is the difference of 6 and 2 (page 329)
3. **Product:** the result of a multiplication: 12 is the product of 6 and 2 (page 329)
4. **Quotient:** the result of a division: 3 is the quotient of 6 and 2 (page 329)
5. **Integers:** {... , –3, –2, –1, 0, 1, 2, 3, ...} (page 332)
6. **Remainder:** when 15 is divided by 6, the quotient is 2 and the remainder is 3: $15 = 6 \times 2 + 3$ (page 333)
7. **Factor or Divisor:** any integer that leaves no remainder (i.e., a remainder of 0) when it is divided into another integer: 1, 2, 5, 10 are the factors (or divisors) of 10 (page 334)
8. **Multiple:** the product of one integer by a second integer: 7, 14, 21, 28, ... are multiples of 7 ($7 = 1 \times 7$, $14 = 2 \times 7$, and so on) (page 334)
9. **Even integers:** the multiples of 2: {... , –4, –2, 0, 2, 4, ...} (page 336)
10. **Odd integers:** the non-multiples of 2: {... , –3, –1, 1, 3, 5, ...} (page 336)
11. **Consecutive integers:** two or more integers, written in sequence, each of which is 1 more than the preceding one. For example: (page 332)

    $7, 8, 9 \qquad -2, -1, 0, 1, 2 \qquad n, n+1, n+2$

12. **Prime number:** a positive integer that has exactly two divisors. The first few primes are 2, 3, 5, 7, 11, 13, 17 (*not* 1). (page 334)

13. Exponent: a number written as a superscript: the 3 in 7^3. On the GRE, exponents are almost always positive integers:

$$2^n = 2 \times 2 \times 2 \times \cdots \times 2, \text{ where 2 appears as a factor } n \text{ times.}$$

(page 336)

14. Laws of Exponents:

For any numbers b, c, m, and n:

(i) $b^m b^n = b^{m+n}$ (ii) $\dfrac{b^m}{b^n} = b^{m-n}$ (iii) $(b^m)^n = b^{mn}$

(iv) $b^m c^m = (bc)^m$

(page 337)

15. Square root of a positive number: if a is positive, $\sqrt{a}$ is the only positive number whose square is a: $\left(\sqrt{a}\right)^2 = \sqrt{a} \times \sqrt{a} = a$.

(page 338)

16. The product and the quotient of signed numbers: The product and the quotient of two positive numbers or two negative numbers are positive; the product and the quotient of a positive number and a negative number are negative. (page 330)

- The product of an *even* number of negative factors is positive.
- The product of an *odd* number of negative factors is negative.

17. For any positive numbers a and b:

$\sqrt{ab} = \sqrt{a} \times \sqrt{b}$ and $\sqrt{\dfrac{a}{b}} = \dfrac{\sqrt{a}}{\sqrt{b}}$

(page 339)

18. The **Distributive Law**: for any real numbers a, b, and c:

- $a(b + c) = ab + ac$
- $a(b - c) = ab - ac$

and, if $a \neq 0$,

- $\dfrac{b+c}{a} = \dfrac{b}{a} + \dfrac{c}{a}$
- $\dfrac{b-c}{a} = \dfrac{b}{a} - \dfrac{c}{a}$

(page 341)

19. Inequalities: for any numbers a and b:

- $a > b$ means that $a - b$ is positive.
- $a < b$ means that $a - b$ is negative.

(page 342)

20. To compare two fractions, convert them to decimals by dividing the numerator by the denominator. (page 351)

21. To multiply two fractions, multiply their numerators and multiply their denominators:

$$\frac{3}{5}\times\frac{4}{7}=\frac{3\times4}{5\times7}=\frac{12}{35}$$

(page 356)

22. To divide any number by a fraction, multiply that number by the reciprocal of the fraction.

$$\frac{3}{5}\div\frac{2}{3}=\frac{3}{5}\times\frac{3}{2}=\frac{9}{10}$$

(page 358)

23. To add or subtract fractions with the same denominator, add or subtract the numerators and keep the denominator:

$$\frac{4}{9}+\frac{1}{9}=\frac{5}{9} \quad \text{and} \quad \frac{4}{9}-\frac{1}{9}=\frac{3}{9}=\frac{1}{3}$$

(page 358)

24. To add or subtract fractions with different denominators, first rewrite the fractions as equivalent fractions with the same denominator:

$$\frac{1}{6}+\frac{3}{4}=\frac{2}{12}+\frac{9}{12}=\frac{11}{12}$$

(page 358)

25. Percent: a fraction whose denominator is 100:

$$15\% = \frac{15}{100} = 0.15$$

(page 368)

26. The **percent increase** of a quantity is

$$\frac{\text{actual increase}}{\text{original amount}} \times 100\%$$

The **percent decrease** of a quantity is

$$\frac{\text{actual decrease}}{\text{original amount}} \times 100\%$$

(page 371)

27. Ratio: a fraction that compares two quantities that are measured in the same units.

The ratio *2 to 3* can be written $\frac{2}{3}$ or 2:3. (page 381)

28. In any ratio problem, write the letter x after each number and use some given information to solve for x. (page 383)

29. Proportion: an equation that states that two ratios (fractions) are equal.

Solve proportions by cross-multiplying: if $\frac{a}{b}=\frac{c}{d}$, then $ad = bc$. (page 385)

30. Average (arithmetic mean) of a set of n numbers: the sum of those numbers divided by n:

$$\text{average} = \frac{\text{sum of the numbers}}{n} \quad \text{or simply } A = \frac{\text{sum}}{n}$$

(page 397)

31. Tactic for average problems: If you know the average, A, of a set of n numbers, multiply A by n to get their sum: sum = nA. (page 397)

32. To multiply two binomials, use the FOIL method: multiply each term in the first parentheses by each term in the second parentheses and simplify by combining terms, if possible.

$$(2x-7)(3x+2) = \underset{\text{First terms}}{(2x)(3x)} + \underset{\text{Outer terms}}{(2x)(2)} + \underset{\text{Inner terms}}{(-7)(3x)} + \underset{\text{Last terms}}{(-7)(2)} =$$

$$6x^2 + 4x - 21x - 14 = 6x^2 - 17x - 14$$

(page 413)

33. The three most **important binomial products** on the GRE are these:

- $(x-y)(x+y) = x^2 - y^2$
- $(x-y)^2 = (x-y)(x-y) = x^2 - 2xy + y^2$
- $(x+y)^2 = (x+y)(x+y) = x^2 + 2xy + y^2$

(page 413)

34. All **distance problems** involve one of three variations of the same formula:

$$\text{distance} = \text{rate} \times \text{time} \qquad \text{rate} = \frac{\text{distance}}{\text{time}}$$

$$\text{time} = \frac{\text{distance}}{\text{rate}}$$

(page 438)

35. Linear equations and inequalities: use the 6-step method to solve linear equations and inequalities. (page 421)

36.

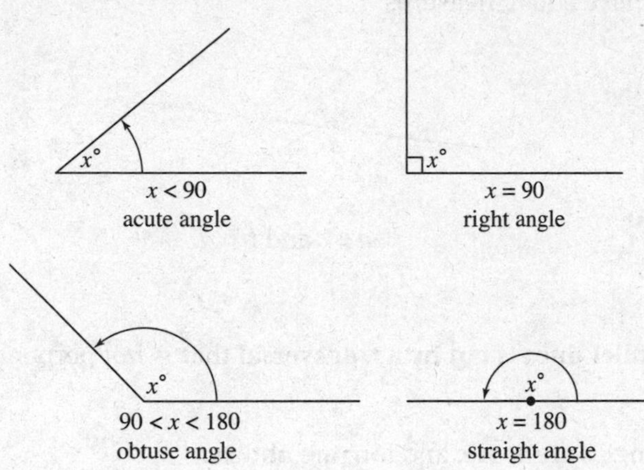

(page 445)

37. If two or more angles form a **straight angle**, the sum of their measures is 180°.

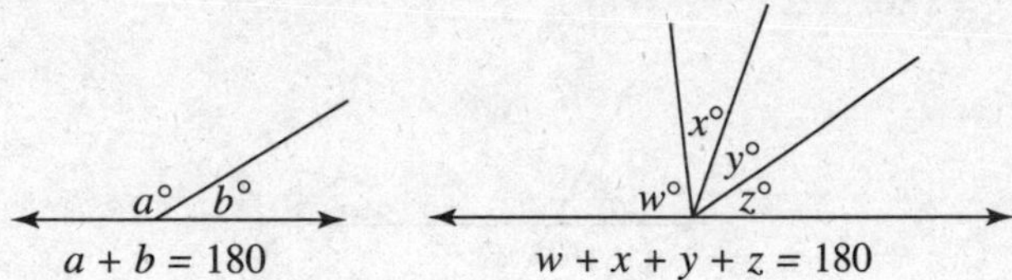

(page 445)

38. The sum of all the measures of all the angles around a point is 360°.

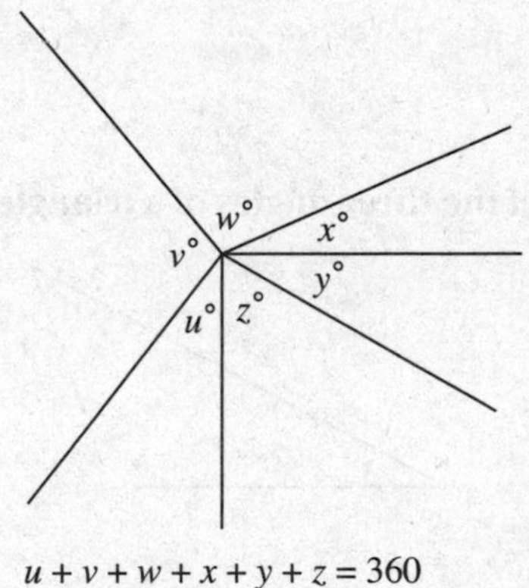

(page 447)

39. Vertical angles are the opposite angles formed by the intersecting lines.

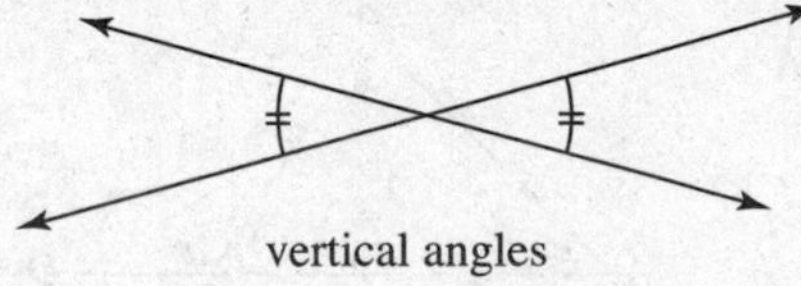

(page 447)

Vertical angles have equal measures.

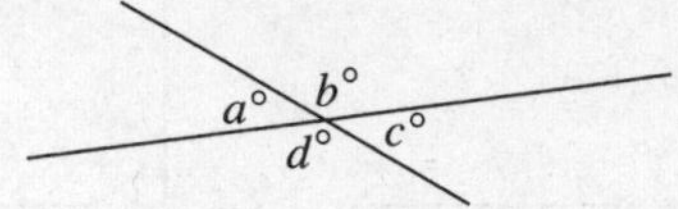

$a = c$ and $b = d$.

(page 447)

40. If a pair of **parallel lines** is **cut by a transversal** that is *not* perpendicular to the parallel lines:

- Four of the angles are acute, and four are obtuse.
- All four acute angles are equal: $a = c = e = g$.
- All four obtuse angles are equal: $b = d = f = h$.
- The sum of any acute angle and any obtuse angle is 180°: for example, $d + e = 180$, $c + f = 180$, $b + g = 180$, … .

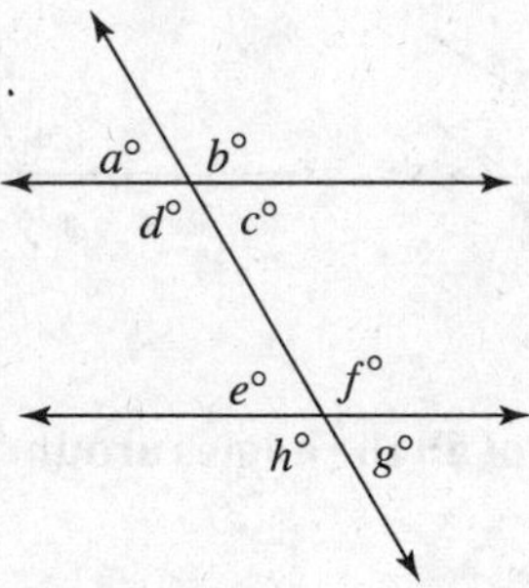

(page 449)

41. The sum of the measures of the three angles of a triangle is 180°:

$x + y + z = 180$.

(page 456)

42. The measure of an exterior angle of a triangle is equal to the sum of the measures of the two opposite interior angles.

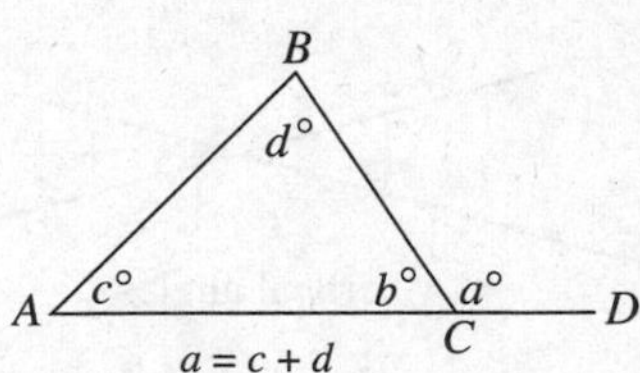

(page 457)

43. The lengths of the sides of a triangle

In any triangle:

- the longest side is opposite the largest angle;
- the shortest side is opposite the smallest angle;
- sides with the same length are opposite angles with the same measure.

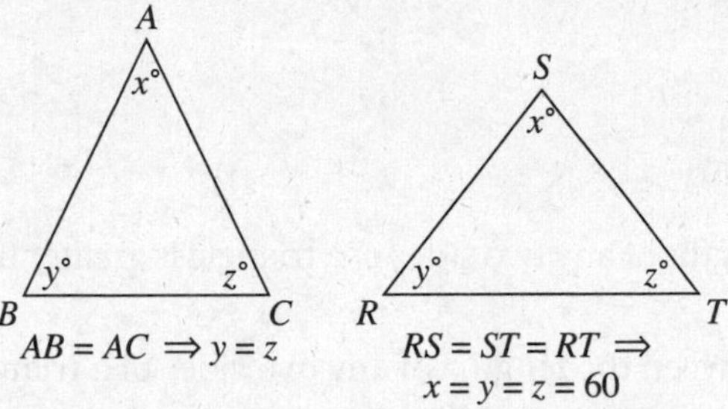

(page 457)

44. In any **right triangle**, the sum of the measures of the two acute angles is 90°.

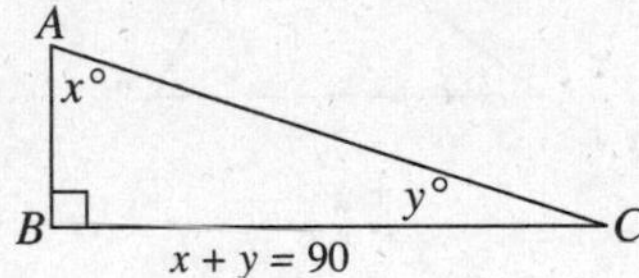

(page 459)

45. Pythagorean theorem

In a right triangle with legs a, b, and hypotenuse c: $a^2 + b^2 = c^2$.

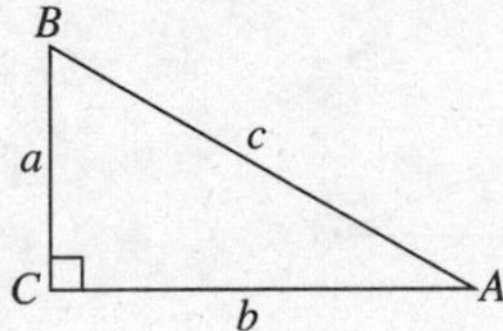

(page 459)

46. In a **45-45-90 right triangle**, the sides are x, x, and $x\sqrt{2}$.

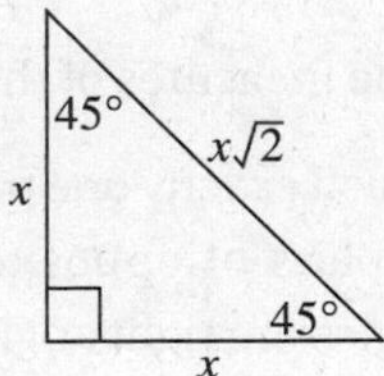

(page 461)

47. In a **30-60-90 right triangle**, the sides are x, $x\sqrt{3}$, and $2x$.

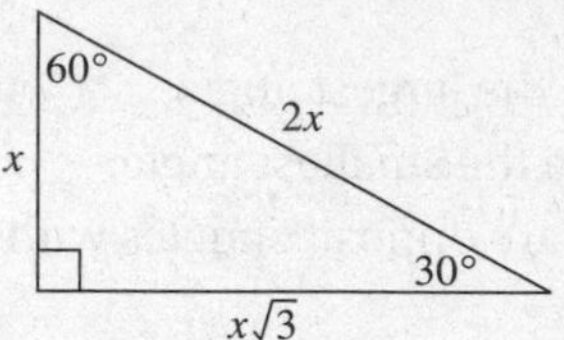

(page 462)

48. The triangle inequality

- The sum of the lengths of any two sides of a triangle is greater than the length of the third side.
- The difference between the lengths of any two sides of a triangle is less than the length of the third side.

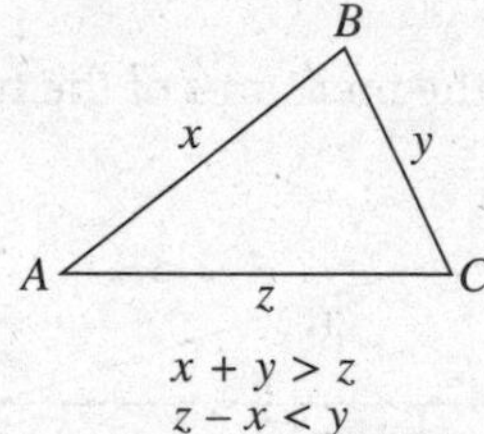

$$x + y > z$$
$$z - x < y$$

(page 463)

49. The **area of a triangle** is given by $A = \frac{1}{2}bh$, where b = base and h = height.

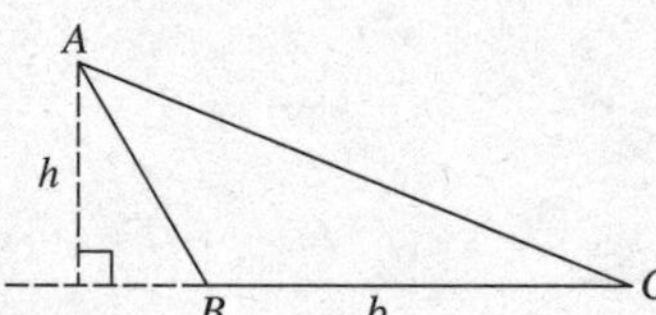

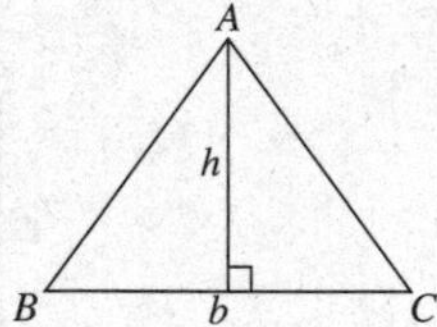

(page 465)

50. If A represents the **area of an equilateral triangle** with side s, then $A = \frac{s^2\sqrt{3}}{4}$. (page 466)

51. In any **quadrilateral**, the sum of the measures of the four angles is 360°. (page 473)

52. A **trapazoid** is a quadrilateral in which exactly one pair of sides is parallel. A **parallelogram** is a quadrilateral in which both pairs of opposite sides are parallel. A **rectangle** is a parallelogram in which all four angles are right angles. A **square** is a rectangle in which all four sides have the same length. (page 475)

53. Properties of a parallelogram

In parallelogram *ABCD*:

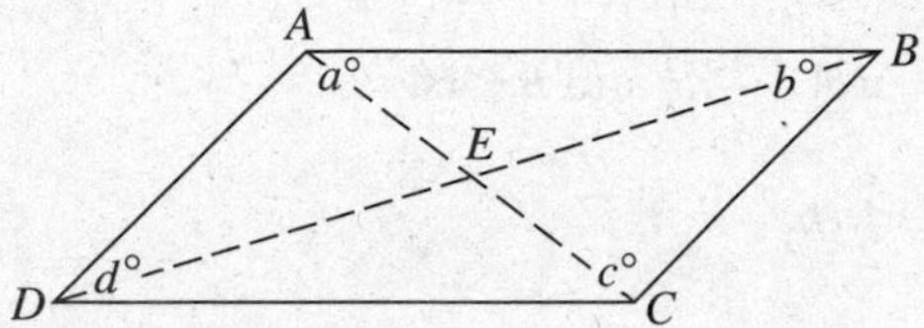

- Opposite sides are equal: $AB = CD$ and $AD = BC$.
- Opposite angles are equal: $a = c$ and $b = d$.
- Consecutive angles add up to 180°: $a + b = 180$, $b + c = 180$, and so on.
- The two diagonals bisect each other: $AE = EC$ and $BE = ED$.

(page 475)

54. Properties of a rectangle

In any rectangle:

- The measure of each angle in a rectangle is 90°.
- The diagonals of a rectangle have the same length: $AC = BD$.

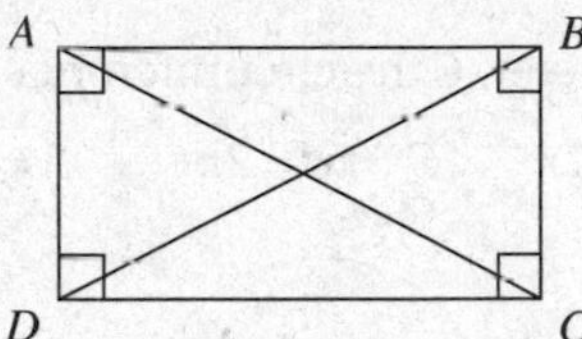

(page 476)

55. Properties of a square

In any square:

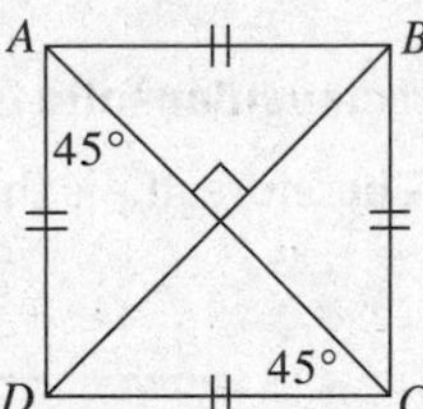

- All four sides have the same length.
- Each diagonal divides the square into two 45-45-90 right triangles.
- The diagonals are perpendicular to each other: $AC \perp BD$.

(page 477)

56. Formulas for perimeter and area:

- For a parallelogram: $A = bh$ and $P = 2(a + b)$.
- For a rectangle: $A = \ell w$ and $P = 2(\ell + w)$.
- For a square: $A = s^2$ or $A = \frac{1}{2}d^2$ and $P = 4s$.
- For a trapezoid: $A = \frac{1}{2}(b_1 + b_2)h$.

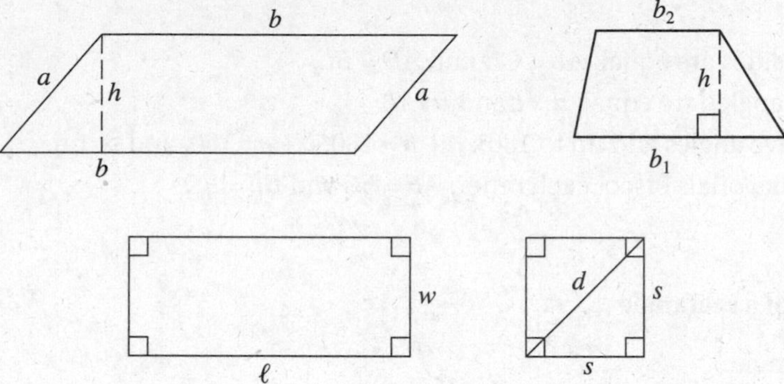

(page 478)

57. Circle formulas

Let r be the radius, d the diameter, C the circumference, and A the area of a circle. Then

$$d = 2r \qquad C = \pi d = 2\pi r \qquad A = \pi r^2$$

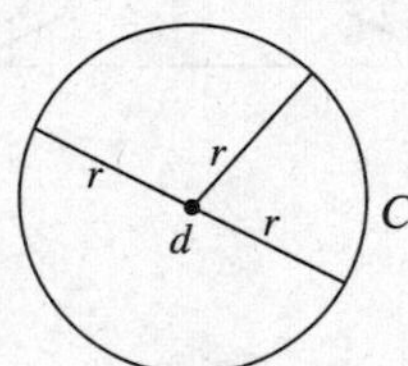

(page 489)

58. The formula for the volume of a rectangular solid is $V = \ell wh$.

In a cube, all the edges are equal. Therefore, if e is the edge, the formula for the volume is $V = e^3$.

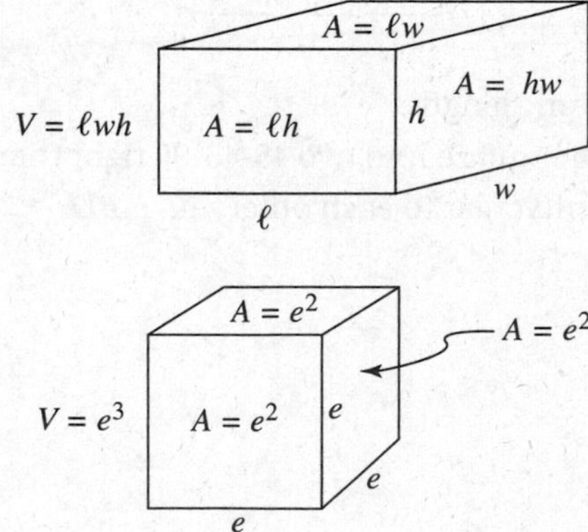

(page 500)

59. The formula for the surface area of a rectangular solid is $A = 2(\ell w + \ell h + wh)$.

The formula for the surface area of a cube is $A = 6e^2$. (page 501)

60. The formula for the volume, *V*, of a cylinder is $V = \pi r^2 h$.

The surface area, *A*, of the side of the cylinder is $A = 2\pi rh$. The area of the top and bottom are each πr^2.

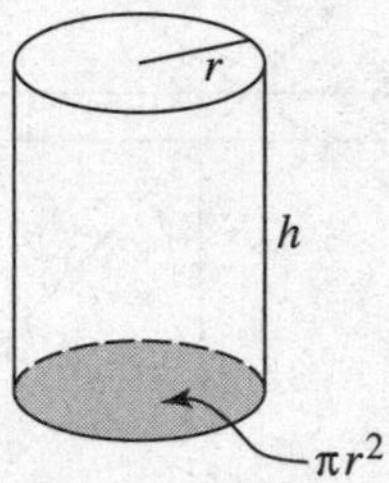

(page 503)

61. The distance, *d*, between two points, $A(x_1, y_1)$ and $B(x_2, y_2)$, can be calculated using the distance formula:

$$d = \sqrt{(x_2 - x_1)^2 + (y_2 - y_1)^2}$$

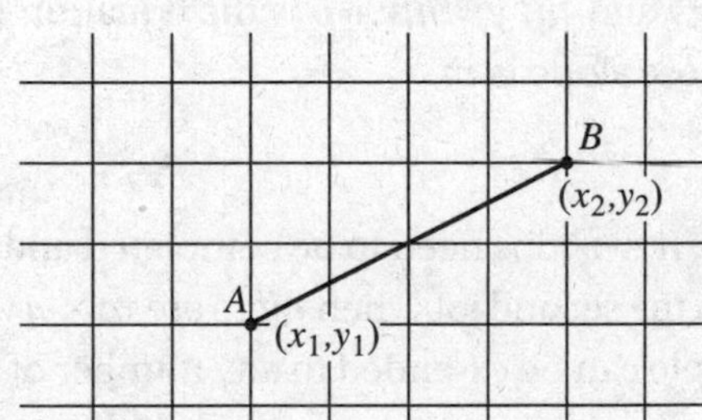

(page 512)

62. Slope formula

The slope of line *AB* is given by slope $= \dfrac{y_2 - y_1}{x_2 - x_1}$

(page 514)

63. Slope facts:

- The slope of any horizontal line is 0.
- The slope of any line that goes up as you move from left to right is positive.
- The slope of any line that goes down as you move from left to right is negative.

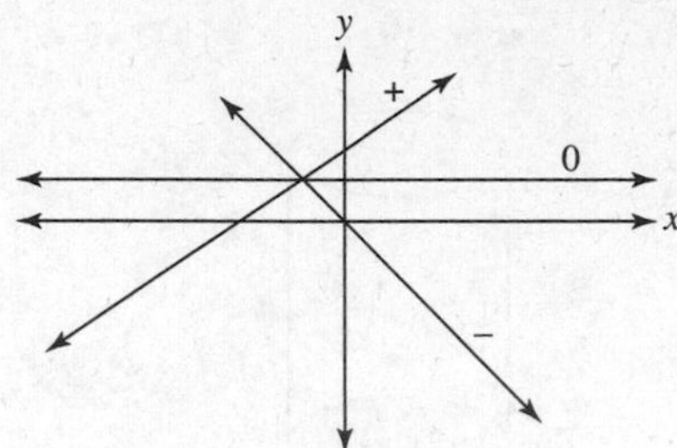

(page 515)

64. Formula for the equation of a line:

- For any real number *a*: $x = a$ is the equation of the vertical line that crosses the *x*-axis at $(a, 0)$.
- For any real number *b*: $y = b$ is the equation of the horizontal line that crosses the *y*-axis at $(0, b)$.
- For any real numbers *b* and *m*: $y = mx + b$ is the equation of the line that crosses the *y*-axis at $(0, b)$ and whose slope is *m*.

(page 517)

65. The Counting Principle: If two jobs need to be completed and there are *m* ways to do the first job and *n* ways to do the second job, then there are $m \times n$ ways to do one job followed by the other. This principle can be extended to any number of jobs. (page 527)

66. If *E* is any event, the **probability** that *E* will occur is given by

$$P(E) = \frac{\text{number of favorable outcomes}}{\text{total number of possible outcomes}}$$

assuming that all of the possible outcomes are equally likely. (page 533)

67. Probability facts:

Let *E* be an event, and let $P(E)$ be the probability that it will occur.

- If *E* is **impossible**, then $\mathbf{P(E) = 0}$.
- If it is **certain** that *E* will occur, then $\mathbf{P(E) = 1}$.
- In all other cases, $\mathbf{0 < P(E) < 1}$.
- The probability that event *E* will *not* occur is $\mathbf{1 - P(E)}$.
- If an experiment is done 2 (or more) times, the probability that first one event will occur, and then a second event will occur, is the product of the probabilities.

To review facts about **data interpretation** and **statistics**, including **line graphs**, **bar graphs**, **circle graphs**, **scatter plots**, **box plots**, **mean**, **median**, **mode**, **range**, **percentile**, **standard deviation**, and **normal distributions**, see Chapter 11 (pages 307–326) and Section E of Chapter 12 (pages 397–409).

PART 5
Model Tests

Model Tests

14

This chapter is designed to give you further experience in what to expect on the verbal, quantitative, and analytical writing sections of the Graduate Record Examination General Test. These tests should serve as a basis for analysis, which for some may signal the need for further drill before taking the actual test, and for others, may indicate that preparation for this part of the test is adequate. For the best results, take these tests only after reviewing your weak areas, found as a result of completing our Diagnostic Test.

Remember that the actual GRE Test you take will be done on a computer. Therefore, we strongly recommend that, in addition to completing these model tests, you take the computer-delivered model test online at *barronsbooks.com/TP/GRE/*. Note that the model tests in this book follow the exact same format as the test you will be taking. In each of the model tests in this book, the order of the five sections is analytical writing, verbal, quantitative, verbal, quantitative. On the actual computerized GRE that you take, the sections can appear in any order, except that Section 1 will definitely be the writing section.

To best simulate actual test conditions, find a quiet place to work. Have a stopwatch or a clock handy so that you can keep perfect track of the time. Go through each section by answering the questions in the order in which they appear. If you don't know the answer to a question, guess, making an educated guess, if possible, and move on. Practice pacing yourself so that you use all your time and just finish each section in the time allowed. Do not spend too much time on any one question. If you get stuck, just guess and go on to the next question.

After you have devoted the specified time allowed for each section of a model examination, refer to the correct answers furnished, determine your raw score, judge your progress, and plan further study. You should then carefully study the explanations for the correct answers of those questions that gave you difficulty. If you find that a particular topic needs further review, refer to the earlier part of the book where this topic is treated before attempting to take the next model test. If you follow this procedure, by the time you complete the second test in this chapter you will feel confident about your success.

ANSWER SHEET
Model Test 1

Section 2

1. Ⓐ Ⓑ Ⓒ Ⓓ Ⓔ Ⓕ
2. Ⓐ Ⓑ Ⓒ Ⓓ Ⓔ Ⓕ
3. Ⓐ Ⓑ Ⓒ Ⓓ Ⓔ Ⓕ
4. Ⓐ Ⓑ Ⓒ Ⓓ Ⓔ Ⓕ
5. Ⓐ Ⓑ Ⓒ Ⓓ Ⓔ Ⓕ
6. Ⓐ Ⓑ Ⓒ Ⓓ Ⓔ
7. Ⓐ Ⓑ Ⓒ Ⓓ Ⓔ
8. Ⓐ Ⓑ Ⓒ Ⓓ Ⓔ
9. Ⓐ Ⓑ Ⓒ Ⓓ Ⓔ
10. Ⓐ Ⓑ Ⓒ Ⓓ Ⓔ
11. Ⓐ Ⓑ Ⓒ Ⓓ Ⓔ Ⓕ
12. Ⓐ Ⓑ Ⓒ Ⓓ Ⓔ Ⓕ
13. Ⓐ Ⓑ Ⓒ Ⓓ Ⓔ Ⓕ Ⓖ Ⓗ Ⓘ
14. Ⓐ Ⓑ Ⓒ Ⓓ Ⓔ Ⓕ
15. Ⓐ Ⓑ Ⓒ Ⓓ Ⓔ Ⓕ Ⓖ Ⓗ Ⓘ
16. Ⓐ Ⓑ Ⓒ Ⓓ Ⓔ
17. Ⓐ Ⓑ Ⓒ Ⓓ Ⓔ
18. Ⓐ Ⓑ Ⓒ Ⓓ Ⓔ
19. Ⓐ Ⓑ Ⓒ Ⓓ Ⓔ
20. Ⓐ Ⓑ Ⓒ Ⓓ

Section 3

1. Ⓐ Ⓑ Ⓒ Ⓓ
2. Ⓐ Ⓑ Ⓒ Ⓓ
3. Ⓐ Ⓑ Ⓒ Ⓓ
4. Ⓐ Ⓑ Ⓒ Ⓓ
5. Ⓐ Ⓑ Ⓒ Ⓓ
6. Ⓐ Ⓑ Ⓒ Ⓓ
7. Ⓐ Ⓑ Ⓒ Ⓓ
8. Ⓐ Ⓑ Ⓒ Ⓓ
9. Ⓐ Ⓑ Ⓒ Ⓓ Ⓔ
10. 
11. [ ]
12. Ⓐ Ⓑ Ⓒ Ⓓ Ⓔ
13. Ⓐ Ⓑ Ⓒ Ⓓ
14. Ⓐ Ⓑ Ⓒ Ⓓ Ⓔ
15. Ⓐ Ⓑ Ⓒ Ⓓ Ⓔ
16. Ⓐ Ⓑ Ⓒ
17. Ⓐ Ⓑ Ⓒ Ⓓ Ⓔ
18. Ⓐ Ⓑ Ⓒ
19. Ⓐ Ⓑ Ⓒ Ⓓ Ⓔ
20. Ⓐ Ⓑ Ⓒ Ⓓ Ⓔ

ANSWER SHEET
Model Test 1

Section 4

1. Ⓐ Ⓑ Ⓒ Ⓓ Ⓔ Ⓕ
2. Ⓐ Ⓑ Ⓒ Ⓓ Ⓔ Ⓕ
3. Ⓐ Ⓑ Ⓒ Ⓓ Ⓔ Ⓕ
4. Ⓐ Ⓑ Ⓒ Ⓓ Ⓔ Ⓕ
5. Ⓐ Ⓑ Ⓒ Ⓓ Ⓔ Ⓕ
6. Ⓐ Ⓑ Ⓒ Ⓓ Ⓔ
7. Ⓐ Ⓑ Ⓒ Ⓓ Ⓔ
8. Ⓐ Ⓑ Ⓒ Ⓓ Ⓔ
9. Ⓐ Ⓑ Ⓒ Ⓓ Ⓔ
10. Ⓐ Ⓑ Ⓒ Ⓓ Ⓔ
11. Ⓐ Ⓑ Ⓒ Ⓓ Ⓔ
12. Ⓐ Ⓑ Ⓒ Ⓓ Ⓔ Ⓕ
13. Ⓐ Ⓑ Ⓒ Ⓓ Ⓔ Ⓕ
14. Ⓐ Ⓑ Ⓒ Ⓓ Ⓔ Ⓕ
15. Ⓐ Ⓑ Ⓒ Ⓓ Ⓔ Ⓕ
16. Ⓐ Ⓑ Ⓒ Ⓓ Ⓔ Ⓕ
17. Ⓐ Ⓑ Ⓒ Ⓓ Ⓔ
18. Ⓐ Ⓑ Ⓒ Ⓓ Ⓔ
19. Ⓐ Ⓑ Ⓒ Ⓓ Ⓔ
20. Ⓐ Ⓑ Ⓒ Ⓓ Ⓔ

Section 5

1. Ⓐ Ⓑ Ⓒ Ⓓ
2. Ⓐ Ⓑ Ⓒ Ⓓ
3. Ⓐ Ⓑ Ⓒ Ⓓ
4. Ⓐ Ⓑ Ⓒ Ⓓ
5. Ⓐ Ⓑ Ⓒ Ⓓ
6. Ⓐ Ⓑ Ⓒ Ⓓ
7. Ⓐ Ⓑ Ⓒ Ⓓ
8. Ⓐ Ⓑ Ⓒ Ⓓ Ⓔ
9. Ⓐ Ⓑ Ⓒ Ⓓ Ⓔ
10. Ⓐ Ⓑ Ⓒ Ⓓ Ⓔ Ⓕ
11. Ⓐ Ⓑ Ⓒ Ⓓ Ⓔ
12. Ⓐ Ⓑ Ⓒ Ⓓ Ⓔ
13. 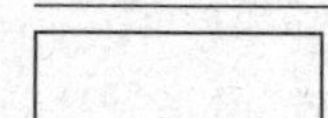
14. Ⓐ Ⓑ Ⓒ Ⓓ Ⓔ
15. Ⓐ Ⓑ Ⓒ Ⓓ Ⓔ
16. Ⓐ Ⓑ Ⓒ Ⓓ Ⓔ
17.
18. Ⓐ Ⓑ Ⓒ Ⓓ Ⓔ
19.
20. Ⓐ Ⓑ Ⓒ Ⓓ Ⓔ

SECTION 1 ANALYTICAL WRITING

TIME: 60 MINUTES—2 WRITING TASKS

Task 1: Analyze an Issue

30 MINUTES

Directions: In 30 minutes, compose an essay on the topic below. You may not write on any other topic.

The topic is presented in a one- to two-sentence quotation commenting on an issue of general concern. Your essay may support, refute, or qualify the views expressed in the quotation. Whatever you write, however, must be relevant to the issue under discussion, and you must support your viewpoint with reasons and examples derived from your studies and/or experience.

If you will be taking the computer-delivered test, write your essay using a word-processing program with its spelling and grammar checker turned off. If you will be taking the paper-delivered test, write your essay on lined paper using a #2 pencil.

Faculty members from various institutions will evaluate your essay, judging it on the basis of your skill in the following areas:

- ✔ Coverage of each of the elements in the task instructions
- ✔ Analysis of the statement's implications
- ✔ Organization and articulation of your ideas
- ✔ Use of relevant examples and arguments to support your case
- ✔ Handling of the mechanics, grammar, and usage of standard written English

ISSUE TASK

"We venerate loyalty—to our schools, employers, institutions, friends—as a virtue. Loyalty, however, can be at least as detrimental an influence as it can be a beneficial one."

Compose an essay that identifies how greatly you concur (or differ) with the statement provided, describing in detail the rationale for your argument. As you build and provide evidence for your argument, include examples that demonstrate circumstances in which the statement could (or could not) be valid. Be sure to explain the impact these examples have on your argument.

Task 2: Analyze an Argument

30 MINUTES

Directions: In 30 minutes, prepare a critical analysis of an argument expressed in a short paragraph, following the specific task instructions provided. You may not offer an analysis of any other argument.

Be sure to support your analysis with evidence (reasons and/or examples) but **do not present your personal views on the topic.** Your job is to analyze the elements of an argument, not to support or contradict that argument.

If you will be taking the computer-delivered test, write your essay using a word-processing program with its spelling and grammar checker turned off. If you will be taking the paper-delivered test, write your essay on lined paper using a #2 pencil.

Faculty members from various institutions will evaluate your essay, judging it on the basis of your skill in the following areas:

- ✔ Coverage of each of the elements in the task instructions
- ✔ Identification and assessment of the argument's main elements
- ✔ Organization and articulation of your thoughts
- ✔ Use of relevant examples and arguments to support your case
- ✔ Handling of the mechanics, grammar, and usage of standard written English

ARGUMENT TASK

The following appeared in a petition presented by Classen University students to the school's administration.

"The purpose of higher education is to prepare students for the future, but Classen students ar at a serious disadvantage in the competition for post-college employment due to the University's burdensome breadth requirements. Classen's job placement rate is substantially lower than placement rates of many top-ranked schools. Classen students would be more attractive to employers if they had more time to take advanced courses in their specialty, rather than being required to spend fifteen percent of their time at Classen taking courses outside of their subject area. We demand, therefore, that the University abandon or drastically cut back on its breadth requirements."

Compose an essay that identifies the questions that must be answered before reaching a conclusion about whether the prediction and the argument supporting it make sense. In writing your essay you should describe the impact that the answers to these questions would have on your assessment of the prediction.

SECTION 2 VERBAL REASONING

TIME: 30 MINUTES—20 QUESTIONS

Directions: For each of the following sentences, select the two answers of the six choices given that, when substituted in the sentence, both logically complete the sentence as a whole and create sentences that are equivalent to one another in meaning.

QUESTIONS 1–5

1. It seems ironic that the preacher's sermon, intended to reconcile the feuding brothers, served only to ________ them further.

   A intimidate
   B estrange
   C avenge
   D arbitrate
   E commiserate
   F disaffect

2. In recent years, the British seem to have become ________ Americanisms: even members of Parliament fall into baseball metaphors, although very few Britons understand the rules of the game.

   A critical of
   B indifferent to
   C enamored of
   D aggrieved by
   E tired of
   F hooked on

3. The general was such a contrarian that, at times when it appeared that the only sane action would be to ________, he became all the more determined to fight to the bitter end.

   A capitulate
   B remonstrate
   C exonerate
   D submit
   E repeat
   F resist

4. Some critics of the administration maintained that it was ________ of the White House to describe its proposal to reduce welfare payments to single parents as "tough love": the plan, in their opinion, while decidedly tough, was not loving at all.

   A witty
   B accurate
   C disingenuous
   D diplomatic
   E mendacious
   F salient

5. A perfectionist is someone who feels ________ when he makes even the most minuscule of errors.

   A vexation
   B hostility
   C indifference
   D chagrin
   E condemnation
   F bafflement

Directions: The next questions are based on the content of the following passage. Read the passage and then determine the best answer choice for each question. Base your choice on what this passage *states directly* or *implies*, not on any information you may have gained elsewhere.

For each of Questions 6–10, select one answer choice unless otherwise instructed.

QUESTIONS 6–10 ARE BASED ON THE FOLLOWING PASSAGE.

There can be no doubt that the emergence of the Negro writer in the post-war period stemmed, in part, from the fact that he was inclined to exploit the opportunity to write about himself. It was more than that, however. The movement that has variously been called the "Harlem Renaissance," the "Black Renaissance," and the "New Negro Movement" was essentially a part of the growing interest of American literary circles in the immediate and pressing social and economic problems. This growing interest coincided with two developments in Negro life that fostered the growth of the New Negro Movement. These two factors, the keener realization of injustice and the improvement of the capacity for expression, produced a crop of Negro writers who constituted the "Harlem Renaissance."

The literature of the Harlem Renaissance was, for the most part, the work of a race-conscious group. Through poetry, prose, and song, the writers cried out against social and economic wrongs. They protested against segregation and lynching. They demanded higher wages, shorter hours, and better conditions of work. They stood for full social equality and first-class citizenship. The new vision of social and economic freedom that they had did not force them to embrace the several foreign ideologies that sought to sink their roots in some American groups during the period.

The writers of the Harlem Renaissance, bitter and cynical as some of them were, gave little attention to the propaganda of the socialists and communists. The editors of the *Messenger* ventured the opinion that the New Negro was the "product of the same world-wide forces that have brought into being the great liberal and radical movements that are now seizing the reins of power in all the civilized countries of the world." Such forces may have produced the New Negro, but the more articulate of the group did not resort to advocating the type of political action that would have subverted American constitutional government. Indeed, the writers of the Harlem Renaissance were not so much revolting against the system as they were protesting its inefficient operation. In this approach they proved as characteristically American as any writers of the period.

6. Which of the following is implied by the statement that the writers of the Harlem Renaissance "were not so much revolting against the system as they were protesting its inefficient operation" (lines 49–52)?

Ⓐ Black writers played only a minor part in protesting the injustices of the period.
Ⓑ Left to itself, the system was certain to function efficiently.
Ⓒ Black writers in general were not opposed to the system as such.
Ⓓ In order for the system to operate efficiently, blacks must seize the reins of power in America.
Ⓔ Black writers were too caught up in aesthetic questions to identify the true nature of the conflict.

7. With which of the following statements regarding the writers of the Harlem Renaissance would the author most likely agree?

Ⓐ They needed to increase their commitment to international solidarity.
Ⓑ Their awareness of oppression caused them to reject American society.
Ⓒ They transformed their increasing social and political consciousness into art.
Ⓓ Their art suffered from their overinvolvement in political crusades.
Ⓔ Their detachment from their subject matter lessened the impact of their work.

8. The information in the passage suggests that the author is most likely

Ⓐ a historian concerned with presenting socially conscious black writers of the period as loyal Americans
Ⓑ a literary critic who questions the conclusions of historians about the Harlem Renaissance
Ⓒ an educator involved in fostering creating writing programs for minority youths
Ⓓ a black writer of fiction bent on discovering new facts about his literary roots
Ⓔ a researcher with questions about the validity of his sources

9. Which of the following statements best describes the organization of lines 34–48 of the passage ("The writers . . . constitutional government")?

Ⓐ The author cites an authority supporting a previous statement and then qualifies the original statement to clarify its implications.
Ⓑ The author makes a point, quotes an observation apparently contradicting that point, and then resolves the inconsistency by limiting the application of his original statement.
Ⓒ The author makes a negative comment and then modifies it by rephrasing his original comment to eliminate its negative connotations.
Ⓓ The author summarizes an argument, quotes an observation in support of that argument, and then advances an alternative hypothesis to explain potential contradictions in that argument.
Ⓔ The author states a thesis, quotes a statement relevant to that thesis, and then presents two cases, both of which corroborate the point of the original statement.

10. The passage supplies information for answering which of the following questions?

Ⓐ What factors led to the stylistic improvement in the literary work of black writers in the post-war period?
Ⓑ Who were the leading exponents of protest literature during the Harlem Renaissance?
Ⓒ Why were the writers of the Harlem Renaissance in rebellion against foreign ideological systems?
Ⓓ How did black writers in the post-war period define the literary tradition to which they belonged?
Ⓔ With what specific socioeconomic causes did the black writers of the post-war period associate themselves?

Directions: Each of the following sentences or groups of sentences contains one, two, or three blanks. These blanks signify that a word or set of words has been left out. Below each sentence are columns of words or sets of words. For each blank, pick the *one* word or set of words from the corresponding column that *best* completes the text.

11. Like the theory of evolution, the big-bang model of the universe's formation has undergone modification and (i) ________, but it has (ii) ________ all serious challenges.

Blank (i)
Ⓐ refinement
Ⓑ evaluation
Ⓒ refutation

Blank (ii)
Ⓓ resisted
Ⓔ acknowledged
Ⓕ misdirected

12. A rigid and conventional thinker, he lacked both the (i) ________ to adapt to changing conditions and the (ii) ________ to be innovative.

Blank (i)
Ⓐ volatility
Ⓑ refinement
Ⓒ flexibility

Blank (ii)
Ⓓ creativity
Ⓔ discipline
Ⓕ impertinence

13. Perugino's initial fame brought him considerable wealth and prestige, if not (i) ________ glory: some years after having been lauded as the most famous artist in Italy, his reputation having suffered a decline, Perugino was (ii) ________ by the acerbic Michelangelo as an artistic (iii) ________.

Blank (i)
Ⓐ mundane
Ⓑ enduring
Ⓒ ephemeral

Blank (ii)
Ⓓ derided
Ⓔ claimed
Ⓕ emulated

Blank (iii)
Ⓖ virtuoso
Ⓗ bumpkin
Ⓘ precursor

14. Rather than portraying Joseph II as a radical reformer whose reign was strikingly (i) ________, the play *Amadeus* depicts him as (ii) ________ thinker, too wedded to orthodox theories of musical composition to appreciate an artist of Mozart's genius.

Blank (i)
Ⓐ dissipated
Ⓑ enlightened
Ⓒ placid

Blank (ii)
Ⓓ a revolutionary
Ⓔ an iconoclastic
Ⓕ a doctrinaire

15. Some critics maintain that fixed poetic forms, which require a specific number of lines and syllables, invite and may even (i) ________ wordiness; when no such (ii) ________ exists, the poet can easily spot and (iii) ________ superfluities.

Blank (i)
Ⓐ curtail
Ⓑ encourage
Ⓒ juxtapose

Blank (ii)
Ⓓ constraint
Ⓔ lyricism
Ⓕ subterfuge

Blank (ii)
Ⓖ foster
Ⓗ brandish
Ⓘ eliminate

16. University training enables a graduate to see things as they are, to go right to the point, to disentangle a twisted ________ of thought.

Ⓐ line
Ⓑ lack
Ⓒ mass
Ⓓ plethora
Ⓔ skein

Directions: Questions 17 through 20 are based on the content of the following passages. Read the passage and then determine the best answer choice for each question. Base your choice on what the passage *states directly* or *implies*, not on any information you may have gained elsewhere.

For each of Questions 17–20, select one answer choice unless otherwise instructed.

QUESTIONS 17–19 ARE BASED ON THE FOLLOWING PASSAGE.

As the works of dozens of women writers have been rescued from what E. P. Thompson calls "the enormous condescension of posterity," and considered in relation to each other, the lost continent of the female tradition has risen like Atlantis from the sea of English literature. It is now becoming clear that, contrary to Mill's theory, women have had a literature of their own all along. The woman novelist, according to Vineta Colby, was "really neither single nor anomalous," but she was also more than a "register and spokesman for her age." She was part of a tradition that had its origins before her age, and has carried on through our own.

Many literary historians have begun to reinterpret and revise the study of women writers. Ellen Moers sees women's literature as an international movement, "apart from, but hardly subordinate to the mainstream: an undercurrent, rapid and powerful. This 'movement' began in the late eighteenth century, was multinational, and produced some of the greatest literary works of two centuries, as well as most of the lucrative pot-boilers." Patricia Meyer Spacks, in *The Female Imagination*, finds that "for readily discernible historical reasons women have characteristically concerned themselves with matters more or less peripheral to male concerns, or at least slightly skewed from them. The differences between traditional female preoccupations and roles and male ones make a difference in female writing." Many other critics are beginning to agree that when we look at women writers collectively we can see an imaginative continuum, the recurrence of certain patterns, themes, problems, and images from generation to generation.

17. In the second paragraph of the passage the author's attitude toward the literary historians cited can best be described as one of

Ⓐ irony
Ⓑ ambivalence
Ⓒ disparagement
Ⓓ receptiveness
Ⓔ awe

Directions: For the following question, consider each of the choices separately and select *all* that apply.

18. The passage supplies information for answering which of the following questions?

[A] Does the author believe the female literary tradition to be richer in depth than its masculine counterpart?
[B] Which literary historian maintains that the female literary tradition transcends national boundaries?
[C] Does Moers share Mill's concern over the ephemeral nature of female literary renown?
[D] What patterns, themes, images, and problems recur sufficiently in the work of women writers to belong to the female imaginative continuum?
[E] Did Mill acknowledge the existence of a separate female literary tradition?

19. In the first paragraph, the author fails to make use of the technique of

Ⓐ extended metaphor
Ⓑ numeration and classification
Ⓒ classical allusion
Ⓓ direct quotation
Ⓔ comparison and contrast

Directions: For the following question, consider each of the choices separately and select *all* that apply.

QUESTION 20 IS BASED ON THE FOLLOWING PASSAGE.

In 1798 Thomas Malthus wrote "An Essay on the Principle of Population," in which he postulates that food supply never can keep pace with the rate of increase in human population. Increase the supply of food, Malthus argues, and population will rise to meet this increase. This, he asserts, means that the race between population and resources can never be truly won by any sociocultural system. Therefore, some measure of social inequality is inevitable in all human societies.

20. Which of the following statements, if true, would tend to undermine Malthus's argument?

[A] The rate of population increase has begun to decline in Northern Europe, but the food supply has not diminished.
[B] In many nations, the increase in human population has far outstripped the food-producing capacity.
[C] Human population growth may be limited by the use of contraception.
[D] For many ethnic and religious groups, artificial control of conception is morally unacceptable.

SECTION 3 QUANTITATIVE ABILITY

TIME: 35 MINUTES—20 QUESTIONS

Directions: In each of Questions 1-8, there are two quantities—Quantity A and Quantity B. You are to compare those quantities, taking into consideration any additional information given. The correct answer to such a question is

Ⓐ if Quantity A is greater;

Ⓑ if Quantity B is greater;

Ⓒ if the two quantities are equal;

Ⓓ if it is impossible to determine which quantity is greater.

Note: The given information, if any, is always centered above the two quantities. In any question, if a symbol or letter appears more than once, it represents the same thing each time.

1.

Quantity A	Quantity B
The sum of the positive divisors of 19	The product of the positive divisors of 19

2.

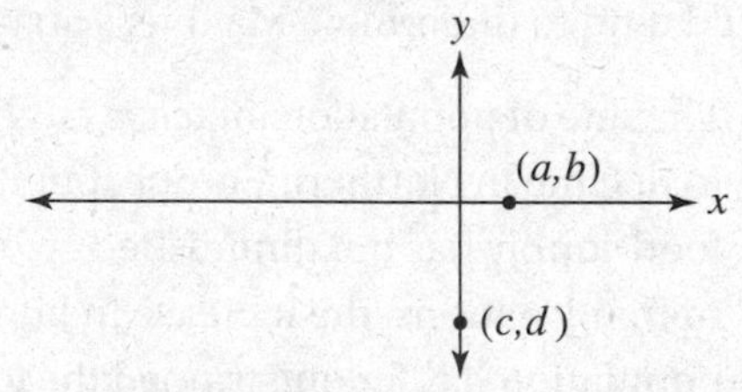

Quantity A	Quantity B
$a + b$	$c + d$

3.

Quantity A	Quantity B
$5(r + t)$	$5r + t$

4.

Quantity A	Quantity B
The average (arithmetic mean) of all the positive multiples of 5 less than 26	The average (arithmetic mean) of all the positive multiples of 7 less than 26

5.

c and *d* are positive

$$\frac{1}{c} = 1 + \frac{1}{d}$$

Quantity A	Quantity B
c	d

6.

A number is a *palindrome* if it reads exactly the same from right to left as it does from left to right. For example, 959 and 24742 are palindromes.

Quantity A	Quantity B
The probability that a three-digit number chosen at random is a palindrome	$\frac{1}{10}$

7.

Jack and Jill each bought the same TV set using a 10% off coupon. Jack's cashier took 10% off the price and then added 8.5% sales tax. Jill's cashier first added the tax and then took 10% off the total price.

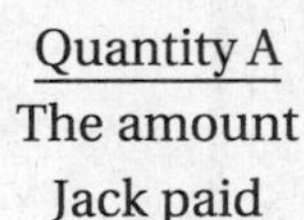

Quantity A	Quantity B
The amount Jack paid	The amount Jill paid

8.

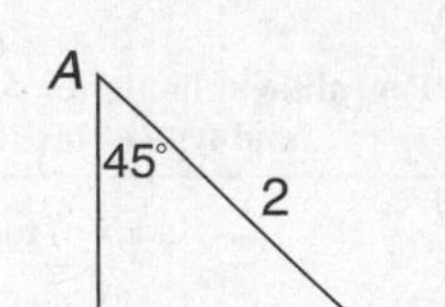

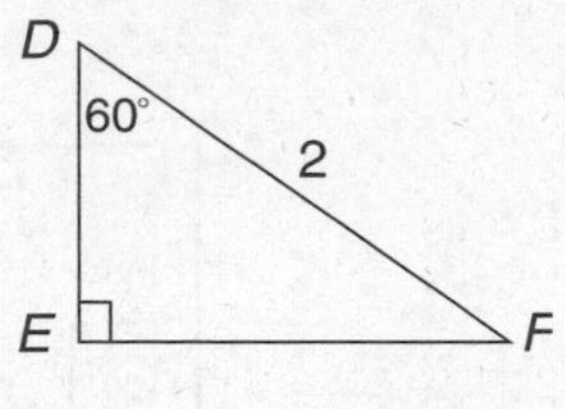

Quantity A	Quantity B
The area of $\triangle ABC$	The area of $\triangle DEF$

Directions: Questions 9–20 have three different formats. Unless a question has its own directions that specifically state otherwise, each question has five answer choices, exactly one of which is correct.

9. If it is now June, what month will it be 400 months from now?

Ⓐ January
Ⓑ April
Ⓒ June
Ⓓ October
Ⓔ December

Directions: The answer to the following question is a fraction. Enter the numerator in the upper box and the denominator in the lower box.

10. If $\frac{5}{9}$ of the members of the school chorus are boys, what is the ratio of girls to boys in the chorus?

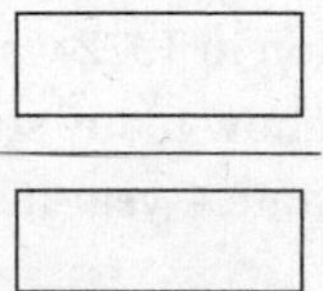

Directions: For the following question, enter your answer in the box.

11. What is the volume of a cube whose total surface area is 54?

12. If A is 25 kilometers east of B, which is 12 kilometers south of C, which is 9 kilometers west of D, how far is it, in kilometers, from A to D?

Ⓐ 20
Ⓑ $5\sqrt{34}$
Ⓒ $5\sqrt{41}$
Ⓓ $10\sqrt{13}$
Ⓔ 71

Directions: For the following question, consider each of the choices separately and select *all* that apply.

13. The math scores of all the students who took the SAT in January 2015 formed a normal distribution with a mean of 500 and a standard deviation of 100. Which of the following statements must be true?

Indicate *all* such statements.

[A] Fewer than 4% of the students scored above 700.
[B] More students scored between 500 and 550 than between 600 and 700.
[C] More than 80% of the students scored above 400.
[D] If a student is chosen at random, the probability that his or her math score is less than 600 is greater than $\frac{4}{5}$.

QUESTIONS 14–16 REFER TO THE FOLLOWING GRAPHS.

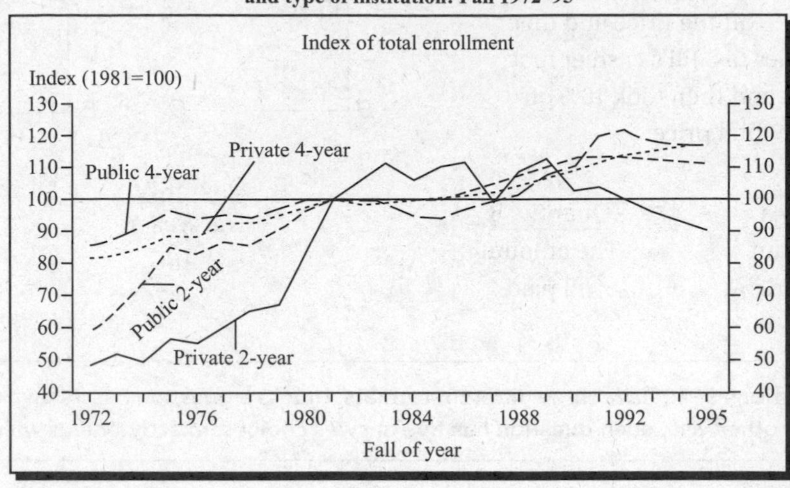

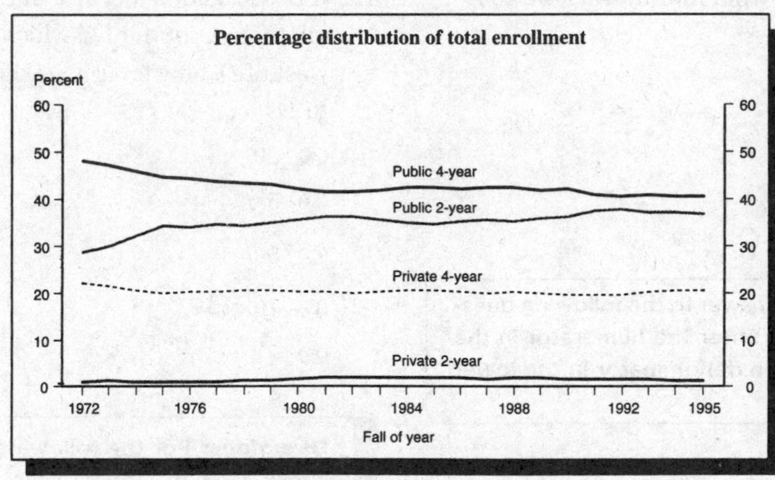

SOURCE: U.S. Department of Education.

14. In 1995 the number of students enrolled in public institutions of higher education was approximately how many times the number of students enrolled in private institutions of higher education?

Ⓐ 2
Ⓑ 2.5
Ⓒ 3
Ⓓ 3.5
Ⓔ 4

15. If the total enrollment in institutions of higher education in 1972 was 5,000,000, approximately how many students were enrolled in private 4-year institutions in 1995?

Ⓐ 1,000,000
Ⓑ 1,100,000
Ⓒ 1,250,000
Ⓓ 1,500,000
Ⓔ 1,650,000

Directions: For the following question, consider each of the choices separately and select *all* that apply.

16. Based on the information in the two graphs, which of the following statements are true?

Indicate *all* such statements.

[A] The number of students enrolled in private 2-year institutions was approximately the same in 1981 and 1987.

[B] The percentage of students enrolled in private 2-year institutions was approximately the same in 1981 and 1987.

[C] From 1972 to 1995, the percentage of college students who were enrolled in 2-year institutions rose by more than 25%.

---

17. Which of the following expresses the area of a circle in terms of *C*, its circumference?

Ⓐ $\frac{C^2}{4\pi}$

Ⓑ $\frac{C^2}{2\pi}$

Ⓒ $\frac{\sqrt{C}}{2\pi}$

Ⓓ $\frac{C\pi}{4}$

Ⓔ $\frac{C}{4\pi}$

Directions: For the following question, consider each of the choices separately and select *all* that apply.

18. If the lengths of two of the sides of a triangle are 9 and 10, which of the following could be the length of the third side?

Indicate *all* such lengths.

[A] 1
[B] 11
[C] 21

19. If *p* pencils cost *c* cents at the same rate, how many pencils can be bought for *d* dollars?

Ⓐ cdp

Ⓑ $100\,cdp$

Ⓒ $\frac{dp}{100c}$

Ⓓ $\frac{100cd}{p}$

Ⓔ $\frac{100dp}{c}$

20. If 3 children are chosen at random from a group of 5 boys and 5 girls, what is the probability that the 3 children chosen are all boys?

Ⓐ $\frac{1}{15}$

Ⓑ $\frac{1}{12}$

Ⓒ $\frac{1}{5}$

Ⓓ $\frac{1}{3}$

Ⓔ $\frac{1}{2}$

SECTION 4 VERBAL REASONING

TIME: 30 MINUTES—20 QUESTIONS

Directions: For each of the following sentences, select the **two** answers of the six choices given that, when substituted in the sentence, both logically complete the sentence as a whole **and** create sentences that are equivalent to one another in meaning.

1. From papayas in Hawaii to canola in Canada, the spread of pollen or seeds from genetically engineered plants is evolving from ________ scientific worry into a significant practical problem.

   A a toxic
   B a theoretical
   C a radical
   D an abstract
   E an overblown
   F an analogous

2. When facts are ________ and data hard to come by, even scientists occasionally throw aside the professional pretense of objectivity and tear into each other with shameless appeals to authority and arguments that are unabashedly ad hominem.

   A elusive
   B established
   C demonstrable
   D ineluctable
   E uncertain
   F relevant

3. You may wonder how the expert on fossil remains is able to trace descent through teeth, which seem ________ pegs upon which to hang whole ancestries.

   A novel
   B reliable
   C flimsy
   D specious
   E inadequate
   F academic

4. During the military takeover, the constitution was not abolished, but some of its clauses temporarily were ________ as the armed forces took over the administration.

   A suspended
   B notarized
   C under construction
   D put in abeyance
   E left undefined
   F widely promulgated

5. Woolf ________ conventional notions of truth: in her words, one cannot receive from any lecture "a nugget of pure truth" to wrap up between the pages of one's notebook and keep on the mantelpiece forever.

   A anticipates
   B articulates
   C makes light of
   D mocks
   E pays heed to
   F puts up with

Directions: The next questions are based on the content of the following passage. Read the passage and then determine the best answer choice for each question. Base your choice on what this passage *states directly* or *implies*, not on any information you may have gained elsewhere.

For each of Questions 6–10, select one answer choice unless otherwise instructed.

QUESTION 6 IS BASED ON THE FOLLOWING PASSAGE.

Contemporary literary scholars have come to discard the once-conventional image of English theater in the time of Elizabeth I as an anomalous literary wonder, a sudden flowering of creativity rooted not in the dramatic traditions of England but the theater of ancient Greece and Rome. While acknowledging the debt of the Elizabethan playwrights to the dramas of Terence, Plautus, and Seneca, and to the *Poetics* of Aristotle, the majority of theater scholars today regard Elizabethan drama as being organically related to traditional English drama, above all to the medieval cycles of mystery and morality plays.

Directions: For the following question, consider each of the choices separately and select *all* that apply.

6. Which of the following is NOT consistent with the passage above?

   [A] Theater historians have significantly altered their views of the origins of Elizabethan drama.

   [B] England had a native dramatic tradition antedating the Elizabethan era.

   [C] Although Elizabethan drama deals with English subject matter, it derives its form and method solely from classical Greek and Roman theater.

   [D] Once envisioned as a historical and literary anomaly, Elizabethan drama now is interpreted as part of a historical continuum.

   [E] Modern theater scholars view Elizabethan drama as a direct offshoot of Greek and Roman dramatic traditions.

QUESTION 7 IS BASED ON THE FOLLOWING PASSAGE.

The current trend toward specialization in nearly all occupational groups is exactly the opposite of what the educational system needs. World problems today are so diverse, complex, and interrelated that only the generalist stands a chance of understanding the broad picture. Unless our schools stress a truly broad, liberal education, the world will crumble around us as we each expertly perform our own narrow function.

7. Which of the following statements, if true, would not weaken the conclusion drawn above?

   (A) Many of the world's problems can be solved only by highly specialized experts working on specific problems.

   (B) Relatively few generalists are needed to coordinate the work of the many specialists.

   (C) Specialization does not necessarily entail losing the ability to see the broad picture.

   (D) Increasingly complex problems require a growing level of technical expertise that can be acquired only through specialization.

   (E) Even the traditional liberal education is becoming more highly specialized today.

QUESTIONS 8–10 ARE BASED ON THE FOLLOWING PASSAGE.

Given the persistent and intransigent nature of the American race system, which proved quite impervious to black attacks, Du Bois in his speeches and writings moved from one proposed solution to another, and the salience of various parts of his philosophy changed as his perceptions of the needs and strategies of black America shifted over time. Aloof and autonomous in his personality, Du Bois did not hesitate to depart markedly from whatever was the current mainstream of black thinking when he perceived that the conventional wisdom being enunciated by black spokesmen was proving inadequate to the task of advancing the race. His willingness to seek different solutions often placed him well in advance of his contemporaries, and this, combined with a strong-willed, even arrogant personality made his career as a black leader essentially a series of stormy conflicts.

Thus Du Bois first achieved his role as a major black leader in the controversy that arose over the program of Booker T. Washington, the most prominent and influential black leader at the opening of the twentieth century. Amidst the wave of lynchings, disfranchisement, and segregation laws, Washington, seeking the good will of powerful whites, taught blacks not to protest against discrimination, but to elevate themselves through industrial education, hard work, and property accumulation; then, they would ultimately obtain recognition of their citizenship rights. At first Du Bois agreed with this gradualist strategy, but in 1903 with the publication of his most influential book, *Souls of Black Folk,* he became the chief leader of the onslaught against Washington that polarized the black community into two wings—the "conservative" supporters of Washington and his "radical" critics.

8. Which of the following statements about W. E. B. Du Bois does the passage best support?
   - Ⓐ He sacrificed the proven strategies of earlier black leaders to his craving for political novelty.
   - Ⓑ Preferring conflict to harmony, he followed a disruptive course that alienated him from the bulk of his followers.
   - Ⓒ He proved unable to change with the times in mounting fresh attacks against white racism.
   - Ⓓ He relied on the fundamental benevolence of the white population for the eventual success of his movement.
   - Ⓔ Once an adherent of Washington's policies, he ultimately lost patience with them for their inefficacy.

9. It can be inferred that Booker T. Washington in comparison with W. E. B. Du Bois could not be described as
   - Ⓐ submissive to the majority
   - Ⓑ concerned with financial success
   - Ⓒ versatile in adopting strategies
   - Ⓓ traditional in preaching industry
   - Ⓔ respectful of authority

10. The author's attitude toward Du Bois's departure from conventional black policies can best be described as
    - Ⓐ skeptical
    - Ⓑ derisive
    - Ⓒ shocked
    - Ⓓ approving
    - Ⓔ resigned

Directions: Each of the following sentences or groups of sentences contains one, two, or three blanks. These blanks signify that a word or set of words has been left out. Below each sentence are columns of words or sets of words. For each blank, pick the *one* word or set of words from the corresponding column that *best* completes the text.

11. As any visitor to Claude Monet's final home at Giverny can ________, Japanese prints were the artist's passion: his home overflows with works by Hiroshige, Utamaro, and other Japanese masters.

Ⓐ portray
Ⓑ attest
Ⓒ contest
Ⓓ rectify
Ⓔ invalidate

12. Breaking with established musical traditions, Stravinsky was (i) ________ composer whose (ii) ________ works infuriated the traditionalists of his day.

Blank (i)
Ⓐ a derivative
Ⓑ an uncontroversial
Ⓒ an iconoclastic

Blank (ii)
Ⓓ hackneyed
Ⓔ heterodox
Ⓕ euphonious

13. While the disease is in (i)________ state it is almost impossible to determine its existence by (ii) ________.

Blank (i)
Ⓐ a critical
Ⓑ a latent
Ⓒ an overt

Blank (ii)
Ⓓ postulate
Ⓔ methodology
Ⓕ observation

14. The paleontologist's (i) ________ orthodoxy meant that the evidence he had so painstakingly gathered would inevitably be (ii) ________ by his more conventional colleagues.

Blank (i)
Ⓐ break with
Ⓑ dependence on
Ⓒ reputation for

Blank (ii)
Ⓓ considered
Ⓔ contested
Ⓕ classified

MODEL TEST 1

15. An essential purpose of the criminal justice system is to enable purgation to take place; that is, to provide a (i) __________ by which a community expresses its collective (ii) __________ the transgression of the criminal.

Blank (i)
Ⓐ catharsis
Ⓑ disclaimer
Ⓒ prototype

Blank (ii)
Ⓓ empathy with
Ⓔ indifference to
Ⓕ outrage at

16. In a classic example of scholarly (i) ________, the poet and scholar A. E. Housman once assailed a German rival for relying on manuscripts "as a drunkard relies on lampposts, for support rather than (ii) ________."

Blank (i)
Ⓐ productivity
Ⓑ invective
Ⓒ detachment

Blank (ii)
Ⓓ stability
Ⓔ illumination
Ⓕ credibility

Directions: The next questions are based on the content of the following passage. Read the passage and then determine the best answer choice for each question. Base your choice on what this passage *states directly* or *implies*, not on any information you may have gained elsewhere.

For each of Questions 17–20, select *one* answer choice unless otherwise instructed.

QUESTION 17 IS BASED ON THE FOLLOWING PASSAGE.

Exquisitely adapted for life in one of Earth's harshest environments, polar bears can survive for 20 years or more on the Arctic Circle's glacial ice. At home in a waste where temperatures reach minus 50 degrees Fahrenheit, these largest members of the bear family are a striking example of natural selection at work. With two layers of fur over a subcutaneous layer of blubber, polar bears are well adapted to resist heat loss. Their broad, snowshoe-like paws and sharp, curved claws enable them to traverse the ice with ease. Formidable hunters, these monarchs of the icy waste even possess the capacity to scent prey from a distance of 20 miles.

17. In the context of the passage's final sentence, "capacity" most nearly means

Ⓐ faculty
Ⓑ stature
Ⓒ dimensions
Ⓓ spaciousness
Ⓔ intelligence

QUESTIONS 18–20 ARE BASED ON THE FOLLOWING PASSAGE.

At night, schools of prey and predators are almost always spectacularly illuminated by the bioluminescence produced by the microscopic and larger plankton. The reason for the ubiquitous production of light by the microorganisms of the sea remains obscure, and suggested explanations are controversial. It has been suggested that light is a kind of inadvertent by-product of life in transparent organisms. It has also been hypothesized that the emission of light on disturbance is advantageous to the plankton in making the predators of the plankton conspicuous to *their* predators! Unquestionably, it does act this way. Indeed, some fisheries base the detection of their prey on the bioluminescence that the fish excite. It is difficult, however, to defend the thesis that this effect was the direct factor in the original development of bioluminescence, since the effect was of no advantage to the individual microorganism that first developed it. Perhaps the luminescence of a microorganism also discourages attack by light-avoiding predators and is of initial survival benefit to the individual. As it then becomes general in the population, the effect of revealing plankton predators to their predators would also become important.

18. The primary topic of the passage is which of the following?

Ⓐ The origin of bioluminescence in plankton predators
Ⓑ The disadvantages of bioluminescence in microorganisms
Ⓒ The varieties of marine bioluminescent life forms
Ⓓ Symbiotic relationships between predators and their prey
Ⓔ Hypotheses on the causes of bioluminescence in plankton

19. The author mentions the activities of fisheries in order to provide an example of

Ⓐ how ubiquitous the phenomenon of bioluminescence is coastally
Ⓑ how predators do make use of bioluminescence in locating their prey
Ⓒ how human intervention imperils bioluminescent microorganisms
Ⓓ how nocturnal fishing expeditions are becoming more and more widespread
Ⓔ how limited bioluminescence is as a source of light for human use

20. The passage provides an answer to which of the following questions?

Ⓐ What is the explanation for the phenomenon of bioluminescence in marine life?
Ⓑ Does the phenomenon of plankton bioluminescence have any practical applications?
Ⓒ Why do only certain specimens of marine life exhibit the phenomenon of bioluminescence?
Ⓓ How does underwater bioluminescence differ from atmospheric bioluminescence?
Ⓔ What are the steps that take place as an individual microorganism becomes bioluminescent?

SECTION 5 QUANTITATIVE ABILITY

TIME: 35 MINUTES—20 QUESTIONS

Directions: In each of Questions 1–7, there are two quantities—Quantity A and Quantity B. You are to compare those quantities, taking into consideration any additional information given. The correct answer to such a question is

Ⓐ if Quantity A is greater;
Ⓑ if Quantity B is greater;
Ⓒ if the two quantities are equal;
Ⓓ if it is impossible to determine which quantity is greater.

Note: The given information, if any, is always centered above the two quantities. In any question, if a symbol or letter appears more than once, it represents the same thing each time.

1.

Quantity A	Quantity B
$\frac{1}{\pi}$	$\frac{1}{\sqrt{10}}$

2.

n is an odd positive integer

$700 < n < 800$

Quantity A	Quantity B
The number of the prime factors of n	The number of prime factors of $2n$

3.

$x < y$

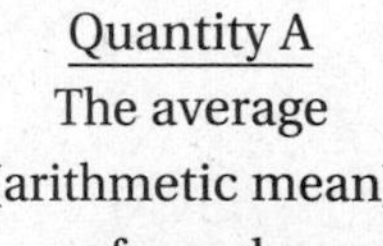

Quantity A	Quantity B
The average (arithmetic mean) of x and y	The average (arithmetic mean) of x, y, and y

4.

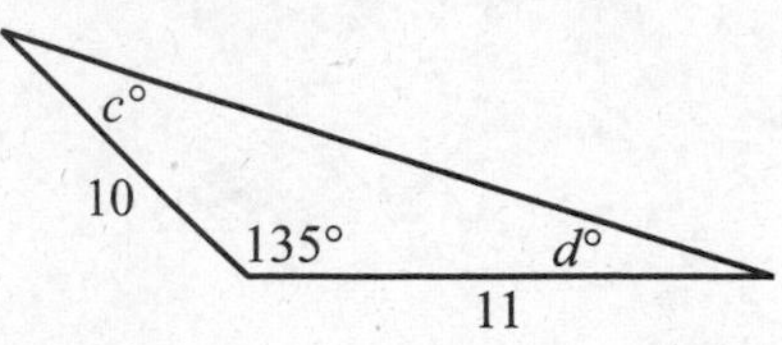

Quantity A	Quantity B
c	d

5.

$0 < a < b$

Quantity A	Quantity B
$a\%$ of $\frac{1}{b}$	$b\%$ of $\frac{1}{a}$

6.

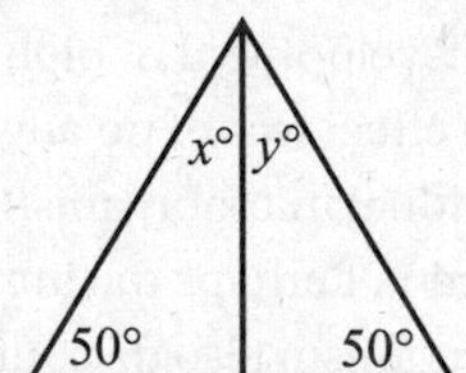

Quantity A	Quantity B
x	y

7.

Line l passes through

$(-\sqrt{2}, \sqrt{3})$ and $(\sqrt{2}, -\sqrt{3})$.

Line m is perpendicular to line l.

Quantity A	Quantity B
The slope of l	The slope of m

Directions: Questions 8–20 have three different formats. Unless a question has its own directions that specifically state otherwise, each question has five answer choices, exactly one of which is correct.

8. In the figure below, what is the average (arithmetic mean) of the measures of the five angles?

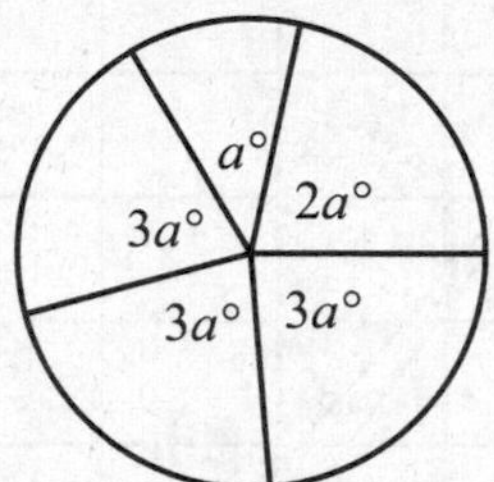

Ⓐ 36
Ⓑ 45
Ⓒ 60
Ⓓ 72
Ⓔ 90

9. Camille's average on her 6 math tests this marking period is 75. Fortunately for Camille, her teacher drops each student's lowest grade, and this raises her average to 85. What was her lowest grade?

Ⓐ 20
Ⓑ 25
Ⓒ 30
Ⓓ 40
Ⓔ 50

Directions: For Questions 10 and 11, consider each of the choices separately and select *all* that apply.

10. If the area of a rectangle is 40, which of the following could be the perimeter of the rectangle?

Indicate *all* such areas.

A 20
B 40
C 200
D 400
E 2,000
F 4,000

11. Which of the following is an equation of a line that is perpendicular to the line whose equation is $2x + 3y = 4$?
Indicate *all* such equations.

A $3x + 2y = 4$
B $3x - 2y = 4$
C $2x - 3y = 4$
D $4 - 3x = -2y$
E $4 + 2x = 3y$

MODEL TEST 1

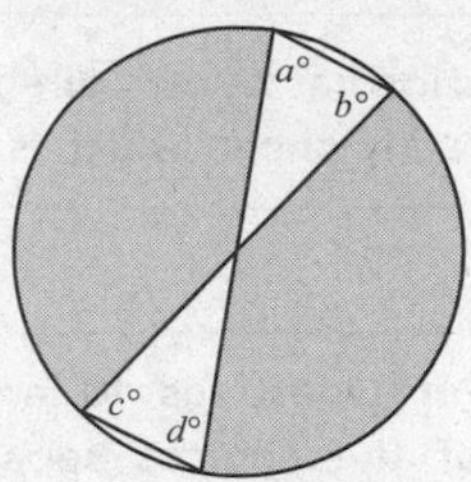

12. In the figure above, the diameter of the circle is 20 and the area of the shaded region is 80π. What is the value of $a + b + c + d$?

Ⓐ 144
Ⓑ 216
Ⓒ 240
Ⓓ 270
Ⓔ 288

Directions: The answer to the following question is a fraction. Enter the numerator in the upper box and the denominator in the lower box.

13. Each integer from 1 to 50 whose units digit is a 3 is written on a slip of paper and placed in a box. If two slips of paper are drawn at random, what is the probability that both the numbers picked are prime?

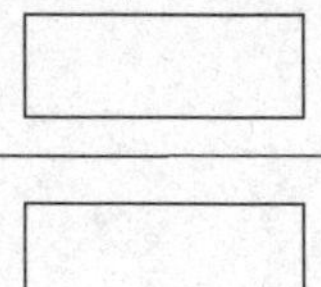

QUESTIONS 14–16 REFER TO THE FOLLOWING GRAPH.

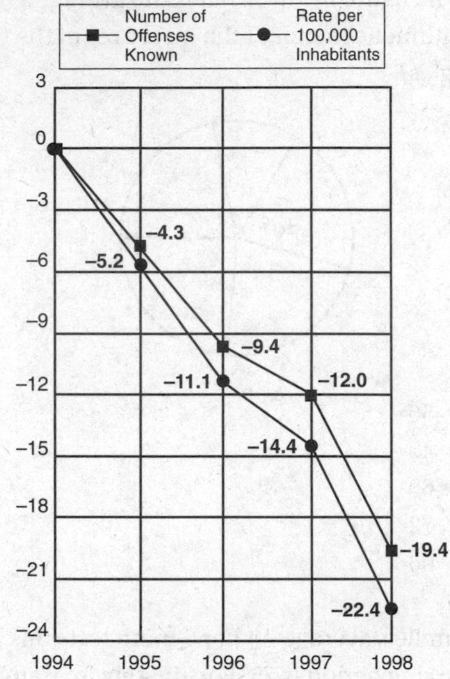

Source: U.S. Department of Justice, Federal Bureau of Investigation.

14. If 1,000,000 vehicles were stolen in 1994, how many were stolen in 1996?

Ⓐ 889,000
Ⓑ 906,000
Ⓒ 940,000
Ⓓ 1,094,000
Ⓔ 1,100,000

15. By what percent did the number of vehicles stolen decrease from 1997 to 1998?

Ⓐ 7.4%
Ⓑ 8.0%
Ⓒ 8.4%
Ⓓ 12.0%
Ⓔ 19.4%

16. To the nearest percent, by what percent did the population of the United States increase from 1994 to 1998?

Ⓐ 1%
Ⓑ 2%
Ⓒ 3%
Ⓓ 4%
Ⓔ 5%

Directions: For the following question enter your answer in the box.

17. If the average (arithmetic mean) of v, w, x, y, and z is 12.3, and the average of v and w is 45.6, what is the average of x, y, and z?

[ ]

18. At Tyler High School, there are twice as many girls than boys on the yearbook staff. At one staff meeting, the percentage of girls attending was twice the percentage of boys. What percent of those attending were boys?

Ⓐ 20
Ⓑ 25
Ⓒ 30
Ⓓ 33
Ⓔ 50

Directions: For the following question enter your answer in the box.

19. If four boys can shovel a driveway in two hours, how many minutes would it take five boys to shovel that driveway? (Assume that each boy works at the same rate.)

[ ] minutes

20. In 1950 Roberto was four times as old as Juan. In 1955, Roberto was three times as old as Juan. How old was Roberto when Juan was born?

Ⓐ 5
Ⓑ 10
Ⓒ 20
Ⓓ 30
Ⓔ 40

MODEL TEST 1

ANSWER KEY

Section 1—Analytical Writing

The Analytical Writing sections are scored holistically, in accordance with the following guidelines.

First, estimate your score on the Issue Essay by using the following rubric.

	Argument	Support	Structure	Fluency	Conventions
6	Presents a clear and perceptive argument that responds to the specific task instructions	Provides strong reasoning and/or examples to fully support its thesis	Is focused and very well organized and has logical and skillful transitions between ideas	Expresses ideas clearly and fluently, with sophisticated word choice and varied sentence structure	Displays impressive command of the grammar, usage, and mechanics of standard written English
5	Presents a clear and thoughtful argument that responds to the specific task instructions	Provides logical reasoning and/or appropriate examples to support its thesis	Is focused and well organized and has logical transitions between ideas	Expresses ideas effectively, with appropriate word choice and varied sentence structure	Displays solid command of the grammar, usage, and mechanics of standard written English
4	Presents a clear argument that adequately responds to the specific task instructions	Provides adequate reasoning and/or examples to support its thesis	Is reasonably well focused and organized	Expresses ideas effectively, with appropriate word choice	Displays command of the grammar, usage, and mechanics of standard written English
3	Presents an argument that is somewhat unclear or that does not clearly respond to the specific task instructions	Makes unsupported claims or has limited relevant examples to support its thesis	Is minimally focused and/or organized	Is somewhat unclear due to incorrect word choice or sentence structure	Includes infrequent major or frequent minor errors in grammar, usage, and/or mechanics
2	Presents an argument that is unclear or fails to address the specific task instructions	Provides nearly no relevant examples or reasons to support its thesis	Is unfocused and/or disorganized	Is unclear due to frequent incorrect word choice or sentence structure	Includes significant errors in grammar, usage, and/or mechanics that render its meaning unclear
1	Presents an argument that demonstrates severely limited understanding of the topic	Provides little to no examples or reasoning that are related to the assigned topic	Is extremely disorganized or excessively short	Is very unclear due to pervasive incorrect word choice or sentence structure	Includes pervasive errors in grammar, usage, and/or mechanics that render it indecipherable
0	Addresses a topic other than the one assigned, is written in a language other than English, is nothing more than the words in the topic and/or task instructions, is nothing more than random characters, is not legible.				

As you examine the rubric you will notice that all of the scores below four are shaded gray. The reason for this is that ETS, the maker of the GRE, states that essays scoring below four display **one or more** of the characteristics listed in the shaded area. In other words, if your essay displays even one characteristic listed in the shaded area, that low score will determine your overall score. If all of your essay's characteristics are found in the boxes above the shaded area, your score should be the average of the five scores (for argument, support, structure, fluency, and writing conventions).

SCORING THE ISSUE ESSAY

Using the Issue Essay rubric, check the box in each column that best describes your work. If each of the boxes you have checked is above the shaded area, add those five scores together and calculate their average.

Example:

Argument	4
Support	4
Structure	5
Fluency	4
Conventions	4
Total	21

The average is 4.2, rounded down to a likely score of 4.

If, however, **any** of your scores fall into the shaded area of the rubric, the lowest score marked will be your final score.

Next, estimate your score on the Argument Essay by using the following rubric.

	Argument	Support	Structure	Fluency	Conventions
6	Pinpoints the elements of the argument at issue and evaluates them with great insight	Provides detailed and persuasive support for its main points	Expresses ideas clearly and is very well organized, with logical and clear transitions between ideas	Expresses ideas clearly and fluently, with sophisticated word choice and varied sentence structure	Displays impressive command of the grammar, usage, and mechanics of standard written English
5	Pinpoints the elements of the argument at issue and evaluates them thoughtfully	Provides thoughtful and persuasive support for its main points	Expresses ideas clearly and is well organized, with suitable transitions between ideas	Expresses ideas effectively, with appropriate word choice and varied sentence structure	Displays solid command of the grammar, usage, and mechanics of standard written English
4	Identifies the elements of the argument at issue and evaluates them, but may include less relevant points	Provides sufficient, though possibly uneven, support for its main points	Expresses ideas reasonably clearly and is organized, but transitions between ideas are inadequate or absent	Expresses ideas effectively, with appropriate word choice	Displays command of the grammar, usage, and mechanics of standard written English
3	Fails to distinguish or evaluate the most relevant elements of the argument, though some relevant aspects may be discussed	Provides support that is sometimes irrelevant to its main points	Expresses ideas with little depth and/or organizes them illogically	Is somewhat unclear due to incorrect word choice or sentence structure	Includes infrequent major or frequent minor errors in grammar, usage, and/or mechanics
2	Fails to evaluate the argument using logic, but may provide the writer's personal views on the topic	Provides support that is generally irrelevant to its main points	Expresses ideas inadequately and organizes them illogically	Is unclear due to frequent incorrect word choice or sentence structure	Includes significant errors in grammar, usage, and/or mechanics that render its meaning unclear
1	Fails to demonstrate any grasp of the argument at issue	Provides no support for its main points	Is extremely disorganized or excessively short	Is very unclear due to pervasive incorrect word choice or sentence structure	Includes pervasive errors in grammar, usage, and/or mechanics that render it indecipherable
0	Addresses a topic other than the one assigned, is written in a language other than English, is nothing more than the words in the topic and/or task instructions, is nothing more than random characters, is not legible.				

SCORING THE ARGUMENT ESSAY

Using the Argument Essay rubric, check the box in each column that best describes your work. If each of the boxes you have checked is above the shaded area, add those five scores together and calculate their average.

CALCULATING YOUR OVERALL SCORE

To determine your overall Analytical Writing score, add the scores for both essays (Issue and Argument) together and divide by 2. The overall score is given in half-point increments, so you should round up to the nearest half point when calculating this score. As an example, if you earn a score of 5 on the Issue Essay and a score of 4.5 on the Argument Essay, your overall Analytical Writing score will be 4.75, rounded up to 5.

Section 2—Verbal Reasoning

1. **B, F**	6. **C**	11. **A, D**	16. **E**
2. **C, F**	7. **C**	12. **C, D**	17. **D**
3. **A, D**	8. **A**	13. **B, D, H**	18. **B, E**
4. **C, E**	9. **B**	14. **B, F**	19. **B**
5. **A, D**	10. **E**	15. **B, D, I**	20. **A, C**

Note: The letters in brackets following the Quantitative Ability answers in Sections 3 and 5 refer to the sections of Chapter 12 in which you can find the information you need to answer the questions. For example, 12. A [J] means that the answer to question 12 is A, and that the solution requires information found in Section 12-J: Triangles. Also, 14. D [11] means that the answer to question 14 is D and is based on information in Chapter 11: Data Interpretation.

Section 3—Quantitative Ability

1. **A** [A]	6. **C** [O]	11. **27** [M]	16. **A, B, C** [11]
2. **A** [N]	7. **C** [C]	12. **A** [J]	17. **A** [L]
3. **D** [A]	8. **A** [J]	13. **A, B, C, D** [E]	18. **B** [J]
4. **A** [A, E]	9. **D** [A]	14. **D** [11]	19. **E** [D]
5. **B** [B]	10. **4/5** [B, D]	15. **E** [11]	20. **B** [0]

Section 4—Verbal Reasoning

1. **B, D**	6. **C, E**	11. **B**	16. **B, E**
2. **A, E**	7. **E**	12. **C, E**	17. **A**
3. **C, E**	8. **E**	13. **B, F**	18. **E**
4. **A, D**	9. **C**	14. **A, E**	19. **B**
5. **C, D**	10. **D**	15. **A, F**	20. **B**

Section 5—Quantitative Ability

1. **A** [A]	6. **D** [J]	11. **B, D** [N]	16. **D** [11]
2. **B** [A]	7. **B** [N]	12. **E** [L]	17. **-9.9** [E]
3. **B** [E]	8. **D** [E, L]	13. **3/5** [O]	18. **A** [C]
4. **A** [J]	9. **B** [E]	14. **B** [11]	19. **96** [D]
5. **B** [C]	10. **B, C, D, E, F** [L]	15. **C** [11]	20. **D** [H]

ANSWER EXPLANATIONS

Section 1—Analytical Writing

PROMPT #1

"We venerate loyalty—to our schools, employers, institutions, friends—as a virtue. Loyalty, however, can be at least as detrimental an influence as it can be a beneficial one."

Compose an essay that identifies how greatly you concur (or differ) with the statement provided, describing in detail the rationale for your argument. As you build and provide evidence for your argument, include examples that demonstrate circumstances in which the statement could (or could not) be valid. Be sure to explain the impact these examples have on your argument.

SCORE 6 ISSUE ESSAY

In press coverage of the epidemic of violence in some urban area like Chicago, there is frequent reference to a "Code of the Streets" that counsels residents, "don't be a snitch." Law enforcement officials decry this loyalty as misguided and ultimately harmful, agreeing with those who argue that loyalty "can be as detrimental an influence as it can be a beneficial one." They are, of course, correct. Loyalty can be detrimental. Their error comes in failing to recognize that this observation applies to themselves as much as it does to the members of the community whose silence they criticize.

The "Code of the Streets" has an analog in the "Blue Code of Silence" that places loyalty to fellow police officers, right or wrong, above the interests and safety of the community. News stories abound with examples of incidents in which police officers describe events one way, only to have their stories contradicted by video evidence. It is not surprising that police officers who have behaved improperly might stretch the truth, or even concoct stories out of whole cloth, in order to avoid being held responsible for their actions. The actions of lawless police officers are a serious problem, but the loyalty of their brothers and sisters in blue is even more detrimental. The inability of the majority of law-abiding police officers to speak out against the misconduct of so-called bad apples undermines the legitimacy of law enforcement as a whole in many of the communities that need its help the most.

Though the "Code of the Streets" and the "Blue Code of Silence" demonstrate that loyalty can be detrimental, the solution is not to embrace disloyalty. It is, after all, difficult to imagine how valuing betrayal could lead to better consequences. The problem in these instances is not really loyalty per se, but a mistaken understanding of community. So long as police officers and members of the public feel that they are not members of one community, their loyalty will be misguided, focused on protecting their own (be they police officers or civilians) from threatening and lawless others (be they police officers or civilians). If we could break down this divide and accept that we are all members of the same community, our loyalty to that greater community would shatter both the "Code of the Streets" and the "Blue Code of Silence." When we learn to embrace our historic enemies as members of a single human community, rather than combatants from warring factions, loyalty will be a venerable virtue. Until that distant day, it will remain, as often as not, an abhorrent vice.

APPLYING THE RUBRIC	
Argument	6
Support	6
Structure	5
Fluency	6
Conventions	6
Total	29

The average is 5.8, rounded up to a likely score of 6.

ARGUMENT The essay presents a clear and perceptive argument that loyalty can be as detrimental as it is beneficial. The writer does an especially good job of presenting instances in which loyalty can have consequences that fracture communities and threaten public safety. The argument is also quite sophisticated, proposing an additional factor that may cause loyalty to be harmful and suggesting that, absent that reason, loyalty might be a virtue.

SUPPORT The essay includes two strong examples of groups whose loyalty to their members does great harm to the larger community, though it focuses more deeply on a single group—police officers.

STRUCTURE The essay is well focused and does not stray from the task of proving its thesis. Its organization is clear, and transitions between paragraphs are logical.

FLUENCY The essay displays sophisticated and powerful vocabulary. Its sentence structure is varied throughout.

CONVENTIONS Outstanding. The essay includes no noticeable errors in grammar, usage, or mechanics.

SCORE 5 ISSUE ESSAY

Loyalty is considered a virtue in our culture, but where is the breaking point at which one decides that loyalty does more damage than good? Can loyalty be more detrimental than beneficial?

Recently, professional football player Colin Kaepernick came under fire from patriotic Americans for his decision to "take a knee" when the national anthem is played at NFL football games. Kaepernick cited the number of African-Americans killed by police as one of many examples that the United States does not value the lives of its African-American citizens. He questioned why he should demonstrate loyalty or patriotism to a country that treats some people as second-class citizens. Across America—especially on the internet—pundits, both professional and amateur, weighed in on the subject. Even among those who claimed to agree with his motivation, many took the stance that he was somehow still protesting in the "wrong" way. "He can be upset," they said, "but he's being unpatriotic, disrespectful, disloyal." Loyalty to country was seen as a virtue, and criticism, as un-American.

Interestingly enough, loyalty as a fan also became part of the debate around Kaepernick's protest. If Kaep's team, the 49ers, is "your" team, are you allowed to break ranks with them in protest of his disloyalty? Does that make you a fair-weather fan? Is it fair to the other players on the team if you, as a fan, jump ship because one player is doing something you don't like? Of course, if loyalty is hierarchical, loyalty to country must outweigh loyalty to team. The order of importance is God, country, family, and football (though some fans disagree with the order of the last two). This is the American way.

Or is it?

If a hallmark of American citizenship is freedom, is loyalty in the form of patriotism a virtue? Loyalty to our country, especially post-September 11, can be seen as a form of collective strength. But does blind allegiance to an ideal vision of what America could and should be require that we turn a blind eye to what America is? In other areas of life, we know that pretending that toxic behavior and attitudes are acceptable simply because we are loyal to those who engage in such behaviors cannot only be harmful to ourselves, but also to the perpetrator. Why isn't the same true of loyalty to country? If your child's school was harming children, would you allow it to continue out of loyalty to the institution? Or would your loyalty to the school end the second someone's child was in danger? Why, then, do we not have the same standard for the ill treatment of adults? If an institution is abusive, must we remain loyal despite the abuse because it could be worse elsewhere? Is "America—love it or leave it" the only acceptable response when our country fails to live up to its lofty goals? Is this a standard of loyalty we would live by when it came to any subject other than patriotism?

The answer to this question is clearly no. Loyalty can clearly be detrimental in so many circumstances. We would never stand by and let a teacher abuse students because of loyalty to the school. When Penn State was found guilty of covering up an employee's sexual abuse of children, the public was rightly horrified at the behavior of the individuals who knew about the abuse but remained silent as a result of their loyalty to the institution. Similarly, we do not expect victims of spousal abuse to remain with their abusers. We counsel them that their abusers do not deserve their loyalty, and that they must inform the authorities of their situation. We encourage them to testify against their abusers in court so that justice can be done. It is high time that we recognize that our country too can do wrong, and that it must be corrected and held accountable when it does so. Turning a blind eye to our nation's failures out of loyalty is harmful and wrong. When we see our nation behave unjustly, we should "take a knee" with Colin Kaepernick.

APPLYING THE RUBRIC

Argument	5
Support	6
Structure	5
Fluency	5
Conventions	5
Total	26

The average is 5.2, rounded down to a likely score of 5.

ARGUMENT The essay presents a clear and thoughtful argument that loyalty, even loyalty to country, can be detrimental.

SUPPORT The essay includes compelling examples that provide strong support for its thesis. The Penn State example is especially persuasive, demonstrating terrible consequences of remaining silent out of loyalty to an institution. The Colin Kaepernick example is engaging, while also demonstrating the complexity of choosing to criticize one's country.

STRUCTURE The essay is generally well focused, though the Kaepernick/49ers story at the start runs a bit long, slightly obscuring the essay's thesis. Transitions between paragraphs are logical, and the thesis becomes crystal clear in the final paragraph.

FLUENCY The ideas in the essay are clear, and its vocabulary use is appropriate and effective, if a bit colloquial at times. Sentence structure is varied.

CONVENTIONS The essay demonstrates solid command of the grammar, usage, and mechanics of standard written English. There are few, if any, obvious errors.

SCORE 4 ISSUE ESSAY

I agree that loyalty is detrimental, especially blind loyalty. Loyalty should be conditional upon the other institution or person meeting certain standards. Loyalty is a virtue in that it is indicative of the faith that one person holds in the other. However, this faith should not be given without inhibition, but should be given on a merit basis.

I think blindly pledging loyalty to a political party can be detrimental. In pre-World War II Germany, Adolf Hitler's militant Nazism and charisma gained him a large following—large enough to place him at the head of Germany at the time and allowed him to lead the country to commit atrocious horrors upon Jews, homosexuals, the disabled, and other minorities not fitting into his vision for what Germany should look like. If people weren't so ready to blindly pledge loyalty but were more autonomous, perhaps concentration camps wouldn't have occurred, or perhaps not on the scale that they did.

Blindly giving loyalty to an employer can also have a dangerous outcome. Say, for example, there is a factory and the company running the factory knows of safety hazards, but doesn't report them to avoid the cost of fixing the safety hazards. The employees see the safety hazards too, but don't report them because of company loyalty. Worst-case scenario is that there could be a serious injury or worse if the danger goes unreported. This would all be because people were too loyal to go over the company's head and do something about the concern.

There are nevertheless benefits of loyalty. It can be good to feel as if you can rely on someone, and likewise for them be able to rely on you. It makes things predictable in that you know how things will run, assuming conditions run their course. However, that is not how it always is—sometimes events blindside us. For these unplanned and uncharacteristic events, loyalty not only can be, but should be, questioned. If a large enough and horrendous enough crime were committed by my friend, I definitely would question my loyalty to him or her. If I, however, decided instead to protect my guilty friend and hide this person, not only would I be obstructing justice (a crime unto itself) but I would also be hurting society by allowing a crime like this to go unpunished.

Loyalty is detrimental when it is blind and its continual questioning is beneficial to society.

APPLYING THE RUBRIC

Argument	5
Support	5
Structure	4
Fluency	4
Conventions	4
Total	22

The average is 4.4, rounded down to a likely score of 4.

ARGUMENT The essay presents a clear argument that misplaced loyalty can lead to devastating consequences. Though the analysis could be more sophisticated, it admits some complexity to the issue, granting that loyalty can provide comfort and reliability.

SUPPORT The essay includes two strong examples that provide strong support for its thesis. The third, contrasting example (the friend who commits a crime) is a bit muddled and underdeveloped.

STRUCTURE The essay is reasonably well focused, though the transitions between paragraphs are abrupt. The conclusion is too short, and fails to adequately summarize the essay's arguments.

FLUENCY The ideas in the essay are clear, and its vocabulary use is generally appropriate, with a few distracting errors. The essay sounds awkward in places, but it is generally effective despite this.

CONVENTIONS The essay demonstrates adequate command of the grammar, usage, and mechanics of standard written English. There are several minor errors, but not enough to obscure meaning.

PROMPT #2

The following appeared in a petition presented by Classen University students to the school's administration.

"The purpose of higher education is to prepare students for the future, but Classen students are at a serious disadvantage in the competition for post-college employment due to the University's burdensome breadth requirements. Classen's job placement rate is substantially lower than placement rates of many top-ranked schools. Classen students would be more attractive to employers if they had more time to take advanced courses in their specialty, rather than being required to spend fifteen percent of their time at Classen taking courses outside of their subject area. We demand, therefore, that the University abandon or drastically cut back on its breadth requirements."

Compose an essay that identifies the questions that must be answered before reaching a conclusion about whether the prediction and the argument supporting it make sense. In writing your essay you should describe the impact that the answers to these questions would have on your assessment of the prediction.

SCORE 6 ARGUMENT ESSAY

As the technology sector of the US economy has burgeoned, the argument for increasing education in STEM subjects (Science, Technology, Engineering, and Math) and consequently decreasing time spent on the Humanities has grown popular. The students at Classen University echo this argument (that education should focus on preparing workers to meet the needs of the economy) in their petition demanding a decrease in the University's breadth requirements. Though their argument is a popular one, it is grounded on a number of questionable premises that bear further examination.

The Classen students start off on the wrong foot by making the unsubstantiated claim that "the purpose of higher education is to prepare students for the future." But is preparing students for the future truly higher education's sole purpose? If Classen's petitioning students are wrong about the answer to this question, their claim is flawed from the outset. While it is unarguable that preparing students for the future is *a* purpose of higher education, there is no consensus on a single, overriding purpose. Additionally, even if the students are correct that preparation for the future is the primary purpose of higher education, their focus on career preparation and employment is based on a very narrow view of that future. During the course of their lives these students will be citizens, community members, parents, and friends, not just workers. Perhaps a university education could and should prepare students for these roles as well.

Granting, for the sake of argument, that the purpose of higher education is to prepare students for employment, the students' case for decreasing breadth requirements is still weak because it fails to answer several additional important questions. The first among these is whether the top-ranked schools to which they compare Classen actually have fewer breadth requirements than Classen. If they do not, there is little reason to believe that decreasing Classen's breadth requirements will, in fact, improve the job placement rate of its graduates.

Another crucial question that remains unanswered by the students' petition is whether the demographics of the student body at Classen are similar to those of the student population of the top-ranked schools to which Classen is being compared. Are Classen's students as academically strong as those at these unnamed schools? Does Classen have a greater number of students for whom English is not their first language? Does Classen serve a student population with an unusually high percentage of students who are the first in their families to attend college? Do the students at the top-ranked schools come from wealthier families than do those at Classen? Because these factors all influence student success both in school and after graduation, answering the aforementioned questions is essential to evaluating whether Classen is indeed doing a poor job of preparing its graduates for employment.

Finally, even if the students are correct that Classen is doing a poor job of preparing its graduates for employment, it is not clear that decreasing breadth requirements is the solution to this problem. The students assert that graduates "would be more attractive to employers if they had more time to take advanced courses in their specialty," but they offer no evidence for this claim. What are employers looking for in potential employees? This question must be answered before an effective solution to the low job placement rate of Classen graduates can be crafted. If employers want to hire graduates with work experience, the solution may lie in a summer internship program. If they want employees with substantial advanced coursework in their specialty, the students' proposal may be sound. But if they require employees with a broad range of knowledge and the ability to attack problems flexibly and take different perspectives into account, more, rather than fewer, breadth requirements may be in order.

APPLYING THE RUBRIC

Argument	6
Support	6
Structure	6
Fluency	6
Conventions	6
Total	30

The average is 6.

ARGUMENT The essay successfully pinpoints a number of problematic elements in the provided argument, explaining how its strength depends on the answers to several unanswered questions. The essay explicitly and thoughtfully describes the impact that these answers would have on the reliability of the students' argument.

SUPPORT The essay provides detailed and persuasive support for its main points, introducing a number of rival factors that might explain the poor job placement rate of Classen University students.

STRUCTURE The essay is well organized, expressing its position clearly and in a logicalprogression. Transitions between ideas are well executed, and the essay builds to a strong conclusion, suggesting that the best solution to Classen students' poor employment results may be the inverse of the plan advocated by the students.

FLUENCY The essay reads smoothly and uses sophisticated vocabulary. Sentence structure is varied.

CONVENTIONS Outstanding. The essay includes no noticeable errors in grammar, usage, or mechanics.

SCORE 5 ARGUMENT ESSAY

Classen students have presented a demand to their administration that breadth requirements be either drastically reduced or eliminated. In considering this demand, the University must evaluate two main points. First, do the students demonstrate an understanding of the purpose of a University education and know where breadth requirements fit into this purpose? Second, do the students make a clear case that the disadvantages that they attribute to the breadth requirements are in fact the sole reason for their lower job placement rates, and upon what do they base this case? Only with this information can the administration make a reasoned decision about whether to reduce or remove breadth requirements.

The students' assertion that "higher education is to prepare students for the future" is arguably a given. However, their definition of preparation for the future seems to be limited solely to job placement. However, while the university has a role to play in preparing for the work force, career preparation is not the sole purpose of higher education, and I suspect that nowhere in the mission statement of the school does the University state that its main focus is job training. Scholarship is important, both to individuals and to the greater culture. If it were not so, we could simply send students to various trade schools. While undergraduates should have opportunities to take advanced coursework in their fields, as the students assert, graduate school is the place to focus more intently on a particular field. While it may be frustrating for students to wade through other requirements before getting to that point, their frustration does not warrant scrapping the entire system.

Furthermore, the students have not considered or addressed the reality that breadth requirements are often instituted by schools because of feedback from employers—directly and culturally—that students are not socially or intellectually prepared for adult life. In other words, just as colleges admit students not solely on the basis of one skill or talent, so too do employers want employees with life skills, critical thinking skills, and other analytical skills in addition to the practical skills in their fields. Breadth requirements actually prepare students to do advanced work in their fields, by helping them learn how to learn, learn how to negotiate subjects with which they may be less familiar, and learn how to work with others whose strengths and interests lie in different areas than their own.

Even assuming that it's true that job placement is the sole goal of a college education (it isn't), the students have shown no evidence that Classen's lower job placement rate is the fault of breadth requirements. They are vague about "many top-ranked schools," without citing those schools, their course requirements, or their job placement rates. Perhaps the schools are top-ranked for other reasons, and those reasons are part of employers' motivation for hiring the students. In fact, what if some of the schools with higher job placement rates actually have more broad requirements? What if the very reason their graduates do better in the workforce is precisely because they experienced varied subject matter, teaching styles, and skills practice than do students who focus more exclusively within their own fields?

The simplicity of the Classen students' demands is actually exemplary of precisely why they need breadth requirements in the first place. Correlation is not causation (science classes teach that); their thesis is flawed (English classes teach that); the market needs varied skills (economics classes teach that); and their lack of understanding of greater socio-cultural influences on education means they are not considering the full extent of their demands (sociology classes teach that). Their demand statement is Freshman 101 level; they cannot use it to argue against the existence of Freshman 101 when they haven't passed the course yet.

APPLYING THE RUBRIC

Argument	5
Support	6
Structure	5
Fluency	5
Conventions	5
Total	26

The average is 5.2, rounded down to a likely score of 5.

ARGUMENT The essay successfully pinpoints two questions that must be answered in order to assess the argument in the Classen students' petition, and it evaluates their impact thoughtfully. If there is any weakness here it is only that the essay focuses somewhat more on the views of its author than it does on how different answers to the questions posed might lead to different conclusions about the strength of the students' argument.

SUPPORT The essay provides detailed support for its main points, especially in its exploration of other factors that might be driving Classen students' low job placement rate.

STRUCTURE The essay is well organized, with effective transitions between ideas. It could, however, be a bit clearer about which of the two questions it is addressing in each paragraph.

FLUENCY The essay expresses its ideas clearly, using appropriate vocabulary and varied sentence structure.

CONVENTIONS The essay displays solid command of the conventions of standard written English.

SCORE 4 ARGUMENT ESSAY

I disagree with this petition. I think that a well-rounded education is a beneficial one. When young, it is difficult to know what you want to do and having a requirement to take different classes in different disciplines can be good to allow students the opportunity to explore different disciplines. Furthermore, there are many factors at play for job placement and classes don't necessarily play that large of a part in that measurement. In addition, job placement isn't necessarily the only reason that people go to college.

First of all, taking different classes allows students to explore different topics of interest, all while fulfilling degree requirements. This is very beneficial to ensure that they truly do like what they plan to study for four years in the process of obtaining a bachelor's degree. Also, it is only fifteen percent of the classes, and that is less than a fifth so it is a very small percentage of classes that this petition is referring to.

Moreover, there are plenty of factors at play for getting jobs—classes just being one. We need to ask what factors are important in getting jobs to understand whether decreasing breadth requirements can help. There is a saying that "life isn't *what* you know but *who* you know," and there is definitely some truth to that. Networking is a very important skill that can't be learned in a class but is more taught through life. Furthermore, the petition is comparing job placements to other, larger and more prestigious universities where there are presumably larger budgets, more resources, and a more competitive student pool. All of these factors can change job placement rates. For example, larger and more prestigious companies might tend to prefer to higher from more prestigious universities. Though it's obviously not impossible to get positions at these firms, attending certain universities can arguably provide "leg up" to some individual students applying for certain positions at certain firms, thus affecting the job placement rates.

In addition, the petition begins with, "[the] purpose of higher education is to prepare students for the future," and I completely agree with this statement, but I measure future preparation in a different way. Preparedness for the future can't be quantitately measured through percentage of students landing jobs, or even how long these students last at these companies. Instead, being prepared for the future has more of a qualitative essence—it can't be measured through numerical evidence but is demonstrated by happiness and ability for students to meet any problems and struggles that life throws at them.

APPLYING THE RUBRIC

Argument	4
Support	5
Structure	4
Fluency	4
Conventions	4
Total	21

The average is 4.2, rounded down to a likely score of 4.

ARGUMENT The essay identifies and evaluates many elements of the argument provided, but its examination of questions that would need to be answered in order to evaluate the argument could be better. Only one of the essay's four paragraphs examines these questions, which are the main requirement of the task instructions.

SUPPORT The essay provides thoughtful and persuasive support for its main points.

STRUCTURE The essay expresses its ideas clearly and has adequate transitions (using words like "first of all" and "in addition." Despite this, the order in which the essay presents its points appears somewhat random, and the conclusion is abrupt.

FLUENCY The essay generally uses vocabulary effectively to express its ideas.

CONVENTIONS The essay generally displays command of the conventions of standard written English, despite the presence of a few minor errors that do not interfere with meaning.

Section 2—Verbal Reasoning

1. **(B, F)** The verbs *estrange* and *disaffect* are synonyms; both mean to make unfriendly or to distance. The two words can be used interchangeably here. Think of "estranged couples" getting a divorce and "disaffected voters" leaving a political party.

2. **(C, F)** Baseball metaphors are examples of Americanisms, American idioms enthusiastically embraced by Britons despite the British lack of understanding of the original context of these terms. The Britons are *hooked on* or *enamored of* them.

3. **(A, D)** A contrarian is someone who takes a contrary view or action, one who makes decisions that contradict prevailing wisdom. Because he is a contrarian, the general is resolved to fight to the bitter end; clearly, the wise or sane course would be to *capitulate* or *submit.* Note that *submit* here is a synonym for yielding or giving in, not for asserting or proposing something.

4. **(C, E)** If the plan, though tough, is not loving, then it certainly would not be *accurate* for the White House to describe it as tough love. It would not be particularly *witty* or *salient* (strikingly conspicuous) for the White House to do so. It might indeed have been *diplomatic* (tactful) for the White House to describe the plan as tough love. However, critics of the administration would be unlikely to put such a positive spin on the administration's description. Also, none of the other choices are synonyms for *diplomatic.* Only two choices remain: *disingenuous* and *mendacious.* To be disingenuous is to be insincere or untruthful. Likewise, to be mendacious is to be untruthful.

5. **(A, D)** Perfectionists expect perfection of themselves. Therefore, when they make even tiny errors, they feel *vexation* (annoyance with themselves) and *chagrin* (annoyance mixed with humiliation).

6. **(C)** The fact that the writers were more involved with fighting problems in the system than with attacking the system itself suggests that fundamentally they *were not opposed to the* democratic system of government.

   Choice A is incorrect. The fact that the writers did not revolt against the system does not necessarily imply that they played a minor role in fighting abuses of the system.

   Choice B is incorrect. There is nothing in the statement that would imply that, *left to itself, the system was certain to function efficiently.*

   Choice D is incorrect. There is nothing in the statement that would imply that *in order for the system to operate efficiently, blacks must seize the reins of power in America.*

   Choice E is incorrect. There is nothing in the statement that would imply that *Black writers were too caught up in aesthetic questions to identify the true nature of the conflict.*

7. **(C)** In lines 6–12, the author mentions the growing interest in social and economic problems among the writers of the Harlem Renaissance. They used poetry, prose, and song to cry out against social and economic wrongs. Thus, they *transformed their increasing social and political consciousness into art.*

   Choice A is incorrect. The author distrusts the foreign ideologies (lines 28–34) with their commitment to international solidarity.

   Choice B is incorrect. The author states that the writers wished to contribute to American culture; they did not totally reject American society, but wished to improve it.

   Choices D and E are incorrect. Neither is implied by the author.

8. **(A)** The author's evident concern to distinguish Negro writers from those who "embraced" socialist and communist propaganda (lines 28–34) suggest that he is a historian concerned with presenting these writers as loyal Americans.

   Choice B is incorrect. The author touches on literature only in relationship to historical events.

   Choices C, D, and E are incorrect. There is nothing in the passage to suggest any of these interpretations.

9. **(B)** The author makes the point that the writers essentially ignored socialist and communist propaganda. This point is apparently contradicted by the *Messenger* quote asserting that the same forces that produced socialism and communism *produced* the New Negro (and thus the new black writer). The author then *limits the application of his original* assertion by giving only qualified assent to that assertion. ("Such forces *may* have produced the New Negro.")

10. **(E)** Choice E is answerable on the basis of this passage.

    The passage cites the battles for better working conditions, desegregation, and social and political equality in which the black writers of the period were engaged. These were *specific socioeconomic causes* with which the writers associated themselves.

    Choice A is unanswerable on the basis of this passage. The passage mentions an "improvement in the capacity for expression" in the period, but cites no factors leading to this stylistic improvement.

    Choice B is unanswerable on the basis of this passage. The passage mentions no specific names.

    Choice C is unanswerable on the basis of this passage. The passage states the writers did not "embrace the several foreign ideologies that sought to sink their roots" in America. However, it nowhere suggests that the writers were *in rebellion* against these foreign ideologies.

    Choice D is unanswerable on the basis of this passage. No such information is supplied by the passage.

11. **(A, D)** The author concedes that the big-bang theory has been changed somewhat: it has undergone *refinement* or polishing. However, he denies that its validity has been threatened seriously by any rival theories: it has *resisted* or defied all challenges.

    The use of the support signal *and* indicates that the first missing word is similar in meaning to "modification." The use of the contrast signal *but* indicates that the second missing word is contrary in meaning to "undergone modification."

12. **(C, D)** Someone described as "rigid and conventional" would lack both the *flexibility* (adaptability) to adjust to changes and the *creativity* (inventiveness; imagination) to come up with new, innovative ideas.

13. **(B, D, H)** The phrases "some years after having been lauded" and "his reputation having suffered a decline" provide the key to unlocking this sentence. The subject here is the change in Perugino's reputation. In the beginning, he received wealth and status, but his fame did not last: he did not win *enduring* glory. Instead, Michaelangelo *derided* (ridiculed; mocked) him as an artistic *bumpkin* (clod; oaf).

14. **(B, F)** The play *Amadeus* portrays Joseph II as "wedded to orthodox theories of musical composition." Thus, it depicts him as a *doctrinaire* thinker, dogmatic about which theories or doctrines he accepts. This view of Emperor Joseph is in contrast with his image as a reformer whose reign was impressively *enlightened* (liberal; civilized) for the period.

The best way to attack this sentence is to complete the second blank first. Note that the second blank immediately precedes a long descriptive phrase that clarifies what kind of thinker Joseph II was.

15. **(B, D, I)** The adverb *even* (indeed) is used here as an intensive to stress something. Not only do fixed poetic forms *invite* wordiness, they may even *encourage* it. Because these fixed forms require the poet to write a specific number of lines or syllables, they place a *constraint* (limitation; restriction) on the poet. Without that constraint, the poet might have an easier time spotting and *eliminating* unnecessary syllables and words.

16. **(E)** One would have to disentangle a *skein* or coiled and twisted bundle of yarn. Note how the presence of the verb *disentangle,* which may be used both figuratively and literally, influences the writer's choice of words. In this case, while *line* is a possible choice, the word does not possess the connotations of twistings and tangled contortions that make *skein* a more suitable choice.

17. **(D)** The author opens the paragraph by stating that many literary critics have begun reinterpreting the study of women's literature. She then goes on to cite individual comments that support her assertion. Clearly, she is *receptive* or open to the ideas of these writers, for they and she share a common sense of the need to reinterpret their common field.

    Choices A and B are incorrect. The author cites the literary critics straightforwardly, presenting their statements as evidence supporting her thesis.

    Choice C is incorrect. The author does not *disparage* or belittle these critics. By quoting them respectfully she implicitly acknowledges their competence.

    Choice E is incorrect. The author quotes the critics as acknowledged experts in the field. However, she does not look on these critics with *awe* (an overwhelming feeling of reverence, admiration, or fear).

18. **(B, E)** Question B is answerable on the basis of the passage. According to lines 19–20, Ellen Moers "sees women's literature as an international movement," in other words, as a movement that *transcends national boundaries.*

    Likewise, Question E is answerable on the basis of the passage. According to lines 9–10, Mill disbelieved in the idea that women "have had a literature of their own all along."

19. **(B)** The writer neither lists (*enumerates*) nor sorts (*classifies*) anything in the opening paragraph.

    Choice A is incorrect. The writer likens the female tradition to a lost continent and develops the metaphor by describing the continent "rising . . . from the sea of English literature."

    Choice C is incorrect. The author refers or *alludes* to the classical legend of Atlantis.

    Choice D is incorrect. The author quotes Colby and Thompson.

    Choice E is incorrect. The author contrasts the revised view of women's literature with Mill's view.

20. **(A, C)** The statement that "The rate of population increase has begun to decline in Northern Europe, but the food supply has not diminished" weakens Malthus's postulate that food supply cannot keep pace with the rate of increase of human population. Likewise, if "[h]uman population growth may be limited by the use of contraception," then it is possible that increasing the supply of food might not necessarily be followed by an increase in human population.

Section 3—Quantitative Ability

Two asterisks (**) indicate an alternative method of solving.

1. **(A)** The only positive divisors of 19 are 1 and 19. So, Quantity A equals $1 + 19 = 20$, and Quantity B equals $1 \times 19 = 19$. Quantity A is greater.

2. **(A)** Since (a, b) is on the positive portion of the x-axis, a is positive and $b = 0$; so $a + b$ is positive. Also, since (c, d) is on the negative portion of the y-axis, $c = 0$ and d is negative; so $c + d$ is negative. Quantity A is greater.

3. **(D)** By the distributive law (KEY FACT A21, page 341), Quantity A is $5r + 5t$. Subtracting $5r$ from each of Quantity A and Quantity B, we are left with $5t$ and t, respectively. So quantities A and B are equal if $t = 0$ and unequal otherwise. Neither quantity is always greater, and the two quantities are not always equal (D).

4. **(A)** Quantity A: there are 5 positive multiples of 5 less than 26: 5, 10, 15, 20, 25; their average is 15, the middle one [KEY FACT E5, page 400].

   Quantity B: there are 3 positive multiples of 7 less than 26: 7, 14, 21; their average is 14.

   Quantity A is greater.

5. **(B)** Since $\frac{1}{c} = 1 + \frac{1}{d}$, then $1 = \frac{1}{c} - \frac{1}{d} = \frac{d-c}{cd}$.

   Therefore, $d - c = cd$, which is positive, since both c and d are. Then, $d - c$ is positive, and so $d > c$.

   Quantity B is greater.

6. **(C)** The simplest solution is to realize that there is one palindrome between 100 and 109 (101), one between 390 and 399 (393), one between 880 and 889 (888), and in general, one out of every 10 numbers. So the probability is $\frac{1}{10}$. The answer is (C).

   **The more direct solution is to count the number of 3-digit palindromes. Either systematically make a list and notice that there are 10 of them between 100 and 199, and 10 in each of the hundreds from the 100s to the 900s, for a total of 90; or use the counting principle (KEY FACT O2, page 527): the hundreds digit can be chosen in any of 9 ways (any of the digits from 1 through 9), the tens digit in any of 10 ways (any of the digits from 0 through 9), and the units digit, since it must match the hundreds digit, can be chosen in only 1 way ($9 \times 10 \times 1 = 90$). Since there are 900 three-digit numbers, the probability is $\frac{90}{900} = \frac{1}{10}$.

7. **(C)** Let P = the price of the TV set. Then Jack paid $1.085(.90P)$, whereas Jill paid $.90(1.085P)$. The quantities are equal (C).

   **Use TACTIC 2 in Chapter 10 (page 290), and choose a convenient number: assume the TV cost \$100. Jack paid \$90 plus \$7.65 tax (8.5% of \$90) for a total of \$97.65. Jill's cashier rang up \$100 plus \$8.50 tax and then deducted \$10.85 (10% of \$108.50) for a final cost of \$97.65.

8. **(A)** Quantity A: Since $\triangle ABC$ is a 45-45-90 right triangle whose hypotenuse is 2, by KEY FACT J8 (page 461), the length of each leg is $\frac{2}{\sqrt{2}} = \sqrt{2}$, and the area is $\frac{1}{2}(\sqrt{2})(\sqrt{2}) = \frac{1}{2}(2) = 1$.

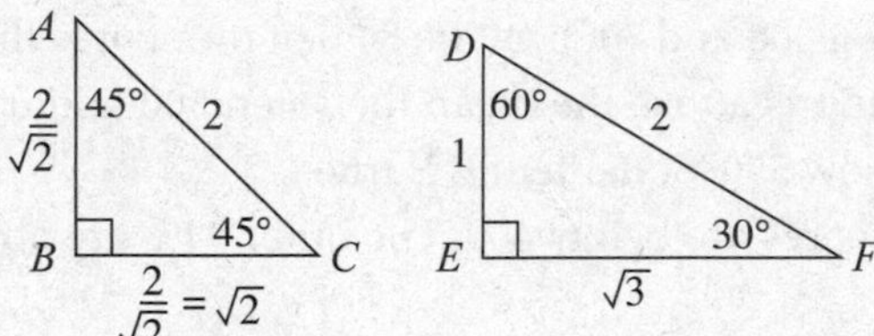

Quantity B: Since $\triangle DEF$ is a 30-60-90 right triangle whose hypotenuse is 2, by KEY FACT J11 (page 462) the shorter leg is 1, the longer leg is $\sqrt{3}$, and the area is $\frac{1}{2}(\sqrt{3})(1) = \frac{\sqrt{3}}{2}$, which is less than 1 because $\sqrt{3}$ is less than 2.

Quantity A is greater.

9. **(D)** Since $400 = 12 \times 33 + 4$, 100 months is 4 months more than 33 years. 33 years from June it will again be June, and 4 months later it will be October.

**Look for a pattern. Since there are 12 months in a year, after every 12 months it will again be June; i.e., it will be June after 12, 24, 36, 48, ... , 120, ... , 360 months. So, 396 (33×12) months from now, it will again be June. Count 4 more months to October.

10. $\frac{\mathbf{4}}{\mathbf{5}}$ Use TACTIC 3 in Chapter 9, page 273: pick an easy-to-use number for the number of members of the chorus. Since $\frac{5}{9}$ of the members are boys, assume there are 9 members, 5 of whom are boys. Then the other 4 are girls, and the ratio of girls to boys is 4 to 5, or $\frac{4}{5}$.

11. **27** Since the surface area of the cube is 54, the area of each of the six square faces is: $54 \div 6 = 9$. Therefore, each edge is 3, and by KEY FACT M1, page 500, the volume is $3^3 = 27$.

12. **(A)** Use TACTIC 1 in Chapter 8, page 248: draw a diagram. See the figure below on the left. Then form rectangle $BCDE$ by drawing $DE \perp AB$, yielding the figure on the right

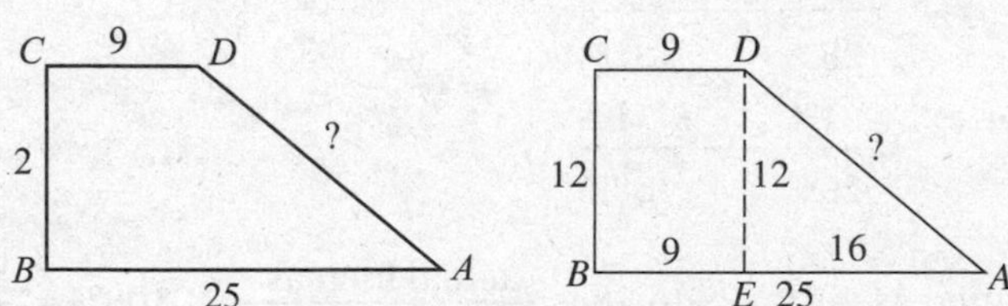

Then, $BE = 9$, $AE = 16$, and $DE = 12$. Finally, $DA = 20$, because right triangle AED is a 3-4-5 triangle in which each side is multiplied by 4. If you don't realize that, use the Pythagorean theorem to get DA:

$$(DA)^2 = (AE)^2 + (DE)^2 = 256 + 144 = 400 \Rightarrow DA = 20$$

13. **(A, B, C, D)**
   - In a normal distribution, 5% of the data lie outside of two standard deviations from the mean, in this case less than 300 and greater than 700. That 5% is equally divided: 2.5% below 300 and 2.5% above 700. Statement A is true.
   - About 13.5% of the scores lie between one and two standard deviations above the mean (here, between 600 and 700). Of the 34% of the scores that are between one and two standard deviations above the mean (between 500 and 600), well more than half (about 19%) are below 550. Statement B is true.
   - About 16% of the scores are below 400. The other 84% are above 400. Statement C is true.
   - This is essentially the same as Statement C. About 84% of the scores are below 600. Since 84% is greater than $\frac{4}{5}$, Statement D is true.

14. **(D)** From the bottom graph, we can estimate the percentage distribution of total enrollment to be:

Public 4-year	41%	Private 4-year	21%
Public 2-year	37%	Private 2-year	1%
Total public	78%	Total private	22%

$78 \div 22 \approx 3.5$, so there were 3.5 times as many students enrolled in public institutions as private ones.

15. **(E)** In 1972, enrollment in private 4-year institutions was approximately 1,100,000 (22% of the total enrollment of 5,000,000). By 1995, the index for private 4-year institutions had increased from 80 to 120, a 50% increase. Therefore, the number of private 4-year students enrolled in 1995 was approximately 1,650,000 (50% more than the 1,100,000 students enrolled in 1972).

16. **(A, B, C)**
   - From the top graph, we see that for every 100 students enrolled in private 2-year institutions in 1981, the number increased to about 110 in 1983, stayed between 105 and 110 until 1986, and then dropped back to 100 in 1987. Statement A is true.
   - From the bottom graph, we see that the percentage of students enrolled in 2-year private institutions remained constant at about 2% from 1981 to 1987. Statement B is true.
   -

	1972	1995
Public 2-year	28%	37%
Private 2-year	1%	1%
Total	29%	38%

The percent increase from 29 to 38 is $\frac{\text{actual increase}}{\text{original amount}} \times 100\% = \frac{9}{29} \times 100\% = 31\%$, well more than 25%. Statement C is true.

17. **(A)** Since by KEY FACT L4 (page 489), $C = 2\pi r$, then $r = \frac{C}{2\pi}$, and by KEY FACT L8 (page 491), the area of the circle is $\pi r^2 = \pi\left(\frac{C}{2\pi}\right)^2 = \pi\left(\frac{C^2}{4\pi}\right) = \frac{C^2}{4\pi}$.

18. **(B)** By the triangle inequality (KEY FACTS J12 and J13, page 463),
   - The third side must be *less* than 9 + 10 = 19. (C is false.)
   - The third side must be *greater* than 10 – 9 = 1. (A is false.)
   - *Any* number between 1 and 19 could be the length of the third side. (B is true.)

19. **(E)** Since p pencils cost c cents, each pencil costs $\frac{c}{p}$ cents. By dividing the number of cents we have by $\frac{c}{p}$, we find out how many pencils we can buy. Since d dollars equals $100d$ cents, we divide $100d$ by $\frac{c}{p}$, which is equivalent to multiplying $100d$ by $\frac{p}{c}$:

$$100d\left(\frac{p}{c}\right) = \frac{100dp}{c}$$

   You will probably prefer the alternative solution below.

   **Use TACTIC 2 in Chapter 10, page 290: replace variables with numbers. Assume 2 pencils cost 10 cents. So, pencils cost 5 cents each or 20 for one dollar. So, for 3 dollars, we can buy 60 pencils. Which of the choices equals 60 when $p = 2$, $c = 10$, and $d = 3$? Only $\frac{100dp}{c}$.

20. **(B)** The probability that an event will occur is

$$\frac{\text{number of favorable outcomes}}{\text{total number of possible outcomes}}$$

   Here, the number of favorable outcomes is the number of ways of choosing 3 of the 5 boys:

$${}_5C_3 = \frac{5!}{3!2!} = \frac{5\times4\times\cancel{(3\times2\times1)}}{\cancel{(3\times2\times1)}(2\times1)} = 10$$

   The total number of outcomes is the number of ways of choosing 3 of the 10 children:

$${}_5C_3 = \frac{10!}{3!7!} = \frac{10\times9\times8\times\cancel{(7\times6\times5\times4\times3\times2\times1)}}{3\times2\times1\cancel{(7\times6\times5\times4\times3\times2\times1)}} = 120$$

   The probability that the 3 children chosen are all boys is $\frac{10}{120} = \frac{1}{12}$.

Section 4—Verbal Reasoning

1. **(B, D)** The spread of genetically engineered matter has become "a significant practical problem." Thus, it is no longer merely a *theoretical* (hypothetical; lacking practical application) or *abstract* worry.
2. **(A, E)** Under certain circumstances scientists attack each other with *ad hominem* arguments (personal attacks) and shameless appeals to authority. When is this likely to occur? When facts are *established* or *demonstrable* or *ineluctable* (unavoidable) or *relevant*? Hardly. Under such circumstances they would rely on the facts to establish their case. It is when facts prove *elusive* (hard to pin down) or *uncertain* that they lose control and, in doing so, abandon their pretense of objectivity.
3. **(C, E)** If "you may wonder" how the expert reaches his conclusions, it appears that it is questionable to rely on teeth for guidance in interpreting fossils. Choices C and E, *flimsy* and *inadequate*, create the element of doubt that the clause tries to develop. Choice D,

specious, also creates an element of doubt; however, nothing in the context justifies the idea that the reasoning is specious or false.

Note that here you are dealing with an extended metaphor. Picture yourself hanging a heavy winter coat on a slim wooden peg. Wouldn't you worry that the peg might prove inadequate or flimsy?

4. **(A, D)** If armed forces take over a country's administration, then that country is under military law rather than constitutional law. However, in this military takeover, the constitution has *not* been abolished or stamped out. Instead, some of its provisions merely have been *suspended* (rendered inoperative for a time) or *put in abeyance* (temporarily set aside).
5. **(C, D)** The second clause presents an example of literary mockery or sarcastic jesting. The abstract idea of preserving a nugget of pure truth is appealing; the concrete example of setting it up on the mantelpiece *makes light of* or *mocks* the whole idea.
6. **(C, E)** The passage asserts that literary scholars now *reject* the idea that Elizabethan drama has it roots in classical Greek and Roman drama. Therefore, it would be inconsistent with the passage to assert Statement C ("Although Elizabethan drama deals with English subject matter, it derives its form and method solely from classical Greek and Roman theater"). Likewise, it would be inconsistent with the passage to assert Statement E ("Modern theater scholars view Elizabethan drama as a direct offshoot of Greek and Roman dramatic traditions").
7. **(E)** Choice E does not weaken the argument, because the argument specifically calls for "a truly broad, liberal education." Choice E, however, merely refers to "the traditional liberal education," which is not necessarily the truly broad and liberal education the author has in mind.

   Choice A weakens the argument: it exposes the argument's failure to acknowledge that many specific problems may be solved by persons who don't understand the broad picture.

   Choice B weakens the argument: it exposes the assumption that because generalists are needed, *all* persons should be educated as generalists.

   Choice C weakens the argument: it exposes the false dichotomy between specialization and seeing the broad picture.

   Choice D weakens the argument: it attacks the implicit assumption that fewer specialists are needed.
8. **(E)** The last sentence points out that Du Bois originally agreed with Washington's program.

   Choice A is incorrect. Nothing in the passage suggests that Du Bois sacrificed effective strategies out of a desire to try something new.

   Choice B is incorrect. Du Bois gained in influence, effectively winning away large numbers of blacks from Washington's policies.

   Choice C is incorrect. Du Bois's quickness to depart from conventional black wisdom when it proved inadequate to the task of advancing the race shows him to be well able to change with the times.

   Choice D is incorrect. Washington, not Du Bois, is described as seeking the good will of powerful whites.

9. **(C)** The author does *not* portray Washington as versatile. Instead, he portrays Du Bois as versatile.

Choice A is incorrect. The author portrays Washington as submissive to the majority; he shows him teaching blacks not to protest.

Choice B is incorrect. The author portrays Washington as concerned with financial success; he shows him advocating property accumulation.

Choice D is incorrect. The author portrays Washington as traditional in preaching industry; he shows him advocating hard work.

Choice E is incorrect. The author portrays Washington as respectful of authority; he shows him deferring to powerful whites.

10. **(D)** Although the author points out that Du Bois's methods led him into conflicts, he describes Du Bois as "often . . . well in advance of his contemporaries" and stresses that his motives for departing from the mainstream were admirable. Thus, his attitude can best be described as *approving*.

11. **(B)** The fact that Monet's home was filled to overflowing with works by Japanese artists would be sufficient reason for someone to *attest* (declare; bear witness) that Japanese prints were Monet's passion.

12. **(C, E)** The key phrase here is "Breaking with established musical traditions." Someone who breaks with traditions is by definition *iconoclastic* (unorthodox; radical; irreverent of tradition). The musical creations of an iconoclastic composer would most likely be *heterodox* or unorthodox as well.

13. **(B, F)** A disease in a *latent* state has yet to manifest itself and emerge into view. Therefore it is almost impossible to determine its existence by *observation.*

The key phrase here is "almost impossible to determine its existence." By its very nature, it would *not* be almost impossible to determine the existence of a disease in its *critical* (acute) or *overt* (apparent; unconcealed) state.

14. **(A, E)** The key phrase here is "his more conventional colleagues." The paleontologist described here is less conventional than his colleagues. What then is his relationship to orthodoxy (conventionality)? He has departed from conventional ways, has made a *break with* orthodoxy. Therefore, his more conventional colleagues would *contest* (challenge) the evidence he has gathered.

15. **(A, F)** Here the task is to determine the communal reaction to crime. The writer maintains that the criminal justice system of punishments allows the community to purge itself of its anger, its sense of *outrage* at the criminal's acts. Thus, it provides a *catharsis* or purgation for the community.

It is unlikely that an essential purpose of the criminal justice system would be the provision of either a *disclaimer* (denial or disavowal, as in disavowing responsibility for a legal claim) or a *prototype* (model; exemplar).

16. **(B, E)** The key word here is *assailed.* Housman is attacking his rival. Thus he is in the tradition of scholarly *invective* (vehement verbal attack), criticizing his foe for turning to manuscripts merely for confirmation or support of old theories and not for enlightenment or *illumination.* Again, note the use of figurative language, in this case the simile of the drunkard.

17. **(A)** The capacity of polar bears to scent prey at a great distance is their *faculty* or ability to do so. Note that *faculty* here is being used with a secondary meaning.

18. **(E)** The author first states that the reason for bioluminescence in underwater microorganisms is obscure and then proceeds to enumerate various hypotheses.

19. **(B)** The author does not deny that predators make use of bioluminescence in locating their prey. Instead, he gives an example of human predators (fishers) who are drawn to their prey (the fish that prey on plankton) by the luminescence of the plankton.

20. **(B)** As the previous answer makes clear, the phenomenon of plankton bioluminescence does have practical applications. It is a valuable tool for fisheries interested in increasing their catch of fish that prey on plankton.

Section 5—Quantitative Ability

Two asterisks (**) indicate an alternative method of solving.

1. **(A)** $\pi \approx 3.14$ and $\sqrt{10} \approx 3.16$. So $\pi < \sqrt{10}$.

   By KEY FACT A24 (page 342), for any positive numbers a and b, if $a < b$,

   then $\frac{1}{a} > \frac{1}{b}$. So $\frac{1}{\pi} > \frac{1}{\sqrt{10}}$.

2. **(B)** It is irrelevant that $700 < n < 800$. Every factor of n is a factor of $2n$, but 2 is a prime factor of $2n$, which is not a factor of n (since n is odd). $2n$ has one more prime factor than n. Quantity B is greater.

3. **(B)** Since $x < y$, the average of x and y is less than y, so having another y raises the average. Quantity B is greater.

   ** Plug in the numbers: say $x = 2$ and $y = 4$.

   Quantity A: the average of 2 and 4 is 3.

   Quantity B: the average of 2, 4, and 4 is $10 \div 3 = 3.333$, which is more than 3; the second 4 raised the average.

4. **(A)** By KEY FACT J3 (page 457), in any triangle, if one side is longer than a second side, the angle opposite the longer side is greater than the angle opposite the shorter side, so $c > d$. Quantity A is greater. (It is irrelevant that the third angle is 135°.)

5. **(B)**

   Quantity A: $a\%$ of $\frac{1}{b} = \frac{a}{100} \times \frac{1}{b} = \frac{a}{100b} = \frac{1}{100} \times \frac{a}{b}$

   Quantity B: $a\%$ of $\frac{1}{a} = \frac{b}{100} \times \frac{1}{a} = \frac{b}{100a} = \frac{1}{100} \times \frac{b}{a}$

   Since a and b are positive and $b > a$, $\frac{b}{a} > 1$, and $\frac{a}{b} < 1$.

   So Quantity B is greater.

6. **(D)** Could x and y be equal? Yes, the two small triangles could be right triangles, and x and y could each be 40. Must they be equal? No. On the GRE, diagrams are not necessarily drawn to scale. See the figure below, in which clearly $x < y$. Neither quantity is *always* greater, and the quantities are not *always* equal.

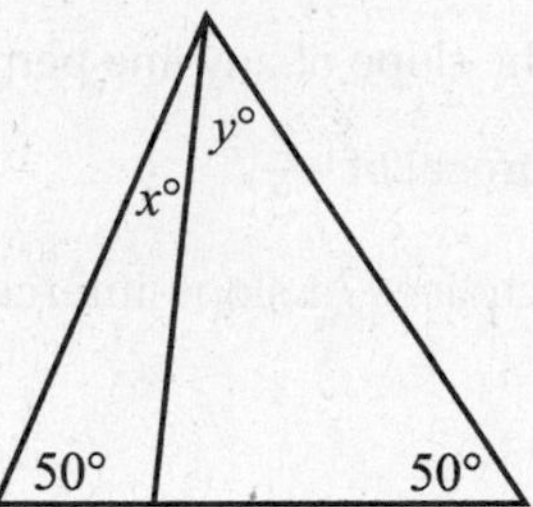

7. **(B)** Don't waste time using the slope formula; just make a quick sketch.

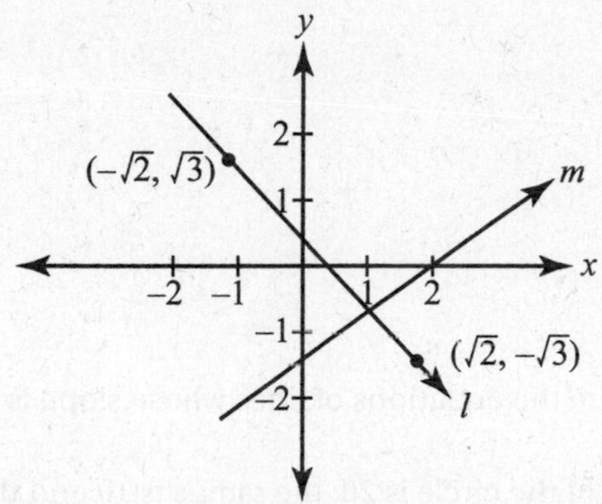

Note that l slopes downward, so its slope is negative, whereas m slopes upward, so its slope is positive. (See KEY FACT N4 on page 514.) Quantity B is greater.

8. **(D)** The markings in the five angles are irrelevant. The sum of the five angles is 360°, and $360 \div 5 = 72$.

   **If you solve the equation $a + 2a + 3a + 3a + 3a = 360$, you get that $12a = 360 \Rightarrow a = 30$, and so the degree measures of the five angles are 30, 60, 90, 90, and 90. You would then find that the average of those five numbers is 72; but all of that is a waste of time.

9. **(B)** By Tactic E1 (page 397), on her six tests combined, Camille earned a total of $6 \times 75 = 450$ points. The total of her five best grades is $5 \times 85 = 425$ points, so her lowest grade was $450 - 425 = 25$.

   **Since Camille's average on her 5 best tests is 85, assume that those grades were each 85. Then each one has a deviation of 10 points above the average of 75, and the total deviation above 75 is $5 \times 10 = 50$ points. Therefore, by KEY FACT E2 (page 398), her one bad grade must have been 50 points below 75.

10. **(B, C, D, E, F)** The perimeter of a rectangle whose area is 40 can be as large as we like (for example, if the length is 4,000 and the width is 0.01, the perimeter is 8,000.02). However, the perimeter is the smallest when the rectangle is a square, in which case each side is $\sqrt{40}$ and the perimeter is $4\sqrt{40}$. Since $\sqrt{40} > 6$, the perimeter is greater than $4 \times 6 = 24$.

    So Choice A, 20, is not possible. All of the other choices are possible.

11. **(B, D)** Rewriting the equation of the given line, $2x + 3y = 4$, in slope-intercept form, we get that $y = -\frac{2}{3}x + \frac{4}{3}$. So by KEY FACT N7 (page 517), the slope of the given line is $-\frac{2}{3}$.

By KEY FACT N6 (page 515), the slope of any line perpendicular to that line must have a slope of $\frac{3}{2}$, the negative reciprocal of $-\frac{2}{3}$.

Rewrite each of the answer choices in slope-intercept form, and see which ones also have a slope of $\frac{3}{2}$.

A: $y = -\frac{3}{2}x + 2$

B: $y = \frac{3}{2}x - 2$

C: $y = \frac{2}{3}x - \frac{4}{3}$

D: $y = \frac{3}{2}x - 2$

E: $y = \frac{2}{3}x + \frac{4}{3}$

Only Choices B and D are the equations of lines whose slope is $\frac{3}{2}$.

12. **(E)** Since the diameter of the circle is 20, the radius is 10 and the area is 100π. Since the area of the shaded region is 80π, it is $\frac{80}{100} = \frac{4}{5}$ of the circle, and the white area is $\frac{1}{5}$ of the circle. So the sum of the measures of the two white central angles is $\frac{1}{5}$ of 360°, or 72°. The sum of the measures of all six angles in the two triangles is 360°, so $a + b + c + d + 72 = 360 \Rightarrow a + b + c + d = 288$.

13. $\frac{3}{5}$ The five numbers are 3, 13, 23, 33, and 43, four of which are prime (all except 33). So the probability that the first number drawn is prime is $\frac{4}{5}$.

If the first number is prime, then three of the remaining four numbers are prime, and the probability is $\frac{3}{4}$ that the second number will be prime.

P(both numbers are prime) =

P(1st number is prime) $\times$ P(2nd number is prime) = $\frac{4}{5} \times \frac{3}{4} = \frac{3}{5}$.

14. **(B)** From 1994 to 1996 there was a 9.4% decrease in the number of vehicles stolen. Since 9.4% of 1,000,000 = 94,000, the number of vehicles stolen in 1996 was 1,000,000 – 94,000 = 906,000. If you can't solve problems such as this, you have to guess.

But since the number of stolen vehicles is clearly decreasing, be sure to eliminate Choices D and E first.

15. **(C)** For simplicity, assume that 1,000 vehicles were stolen in 1994. By 1997, the number had decreased by 12.0% to 880 (12% of 1,000 = 120, and 1,000 – 120 = 880); by 1998, the number had decreased 19.4% to 806 (19.4% of 1,000 = 194 and 1,000 – 194 = 806). So from 1997 to 1998, the number of vehicles stolen decreased by 74 from 880 to 806.

    This represents a decrease of $\frac{74}{880} = .084 = 8.4\%$.

16. **(D)** Simplify the situation by assuming that in 1994 the population was 100,000 and there were 1,000 vehicles stolen. As in the solution to question 15, in 1998 the number of stolen vehicles was 806. At the same time, the number of thefts per 100,000 inhabitants decreased 22.4% from 1,000 to 776. So if there were 776 vehicles stolen for every 100,000 inhabitants, and 806 cars were stolen, the number of inhabitants must have increased.

    To know by how much, solve the proportion: $\frac{776}{100{,}000} = \frac{806}{x}$. Cross-multiplying, we get $776x = 80{,}600{,}000$.

    So, $x = 103{,}800$. Then for every 100,000 inhabitants in 1994, there were 103,800 in 1998, an increase of 3.8%.

17. **–9.9**

    - Since the average of the 5 numbers v, w, x, y, and z is 12.3, their sum is $5 \times 12.3 = 61.5$.
    - Since the average of v and w is 45.6, their sum is $2 \times 45.6 = 91.2$.
    - Then $x + y + z = 61.5 - 91.2 = -29.7$, and $\frac{x+y+z}{3} = \frac{-29.7}{3} = -9.9$.

18. **(A)** Even if you can do the algebra, this type of problem is easier if you use TACTIC 3 in Chapter 9 (page 273): plug in some easy-to-use numbers; assume that there are 100 girls and 50 boys on staff and that 20% of the girls and 10% of the boys attended the meeting. Then, 20 girls and 5 boys were there, and 5 is 20% of 25, the total number attending.

    Of course, you *can* do this algebraically. If x represents the number of boys on staff, then $2x$ is the number of girls. If y% of the boys attended the meeting, then $2y$% of the girls did. So, the number of boys attending was $x\left(\frac{y}{100}\right) = \frac{xy}{100}$, whereas the number of girls attending was $2x\left(\frac{2y}{100}\right) = \frac{4xy}{100}$.

    Therefore, there were 4 times as many girls in attendance as boys: $\frac{4}{5}$ of those at the meeting were girls and $\frac{1}{5}$ or 20% were boys.

19. **96** Since 4 boys can shovel the driveway in 2 hours or $2 \times 60 = 120$ minutes, the job takes $4 \times 120 = 480$ boy-minutes to complete. Therefore, 5 boys will need

    $\frac{\text{480 boy-minutes}}{\text{5 boys}} = 96$ minutes.

MODEL TEST 1

20. **(D)** Make a table to determine Roberto's and Juan's ages. Let x represent Juan's age in 1950, and fill in the table as shown.

	1950	1955
Roberto	$4x$	$4x+5$
Juan	x	$x+5$

In 1955, Roberto was 3 times as old as Juan, so $4x + 5 = 3(x + 5) = 3x + 15$, and so $x = 10$. Therefore, in 1950, Juan was 10 and Roberto was 40. Because Roberto is 30 years older than Juan, Roberto was 30 when Juan was born.

ANSWER SHEET
Model Test 2

Section 2

1. Ⓐ Ⓑ Ⓒ Ⓓ Ⓔ Ⓕ
2. Ⓐ Ⓑ Ⓒ Ⓓ Ⓔ Ⓕ
3. Ⓐ Ⓑ Ⓒ Ⓓ Ⓔ Ⓕ
4. Ⓐ Ⓑ Ⓒ Ⓓ Ⓔ Ⓕ
5. Ⓐ Ⓑ Ⓒ Ⓓ Ⓔ Ⓕ
6. Ⓐ Ⓑ Ⓒ Ⓓ Ⓔ Ⓕ
7. Ⓐ Ⓑ Ⓒ Ⓓ Ⓔ
8. Ⓐ Ⓑ Ⓒ Ⓓ Ⓔ
9. Ⓐ Ⓑ Ⓒ Ⓓ Ⓔ
10. Ⓐ Ⓑ Ⓒ Ⓓ Ⓔ
11. Ⓐ Ⓑ Ⓒ Ⓓ Ⓔ Ⓕ
12. Ⓐ Ⓑ Ⓒ Ⓓ Ⓔ Ⓕ
13. Ⓐ Ⓑ Ⓒ Ⓓ Ⓔ Ⓕ
14. Ⓐ Ⓑ Ⓒ Ⓓ Ⓔ Ⓕ
15. Ⓐ Ⓑ Ⓒ Ⓓ Ⓔ Ⓕ Ⓖ Ⓗ Ⓘ
16. Ⓐ Ⓑ Ⓒ Ⓓ Ⓔ
17. Ⓐ Ⓑ Ⓒ
18. Ⓐ Ⓑ Ⓒ Ⓓ Ⓔ
19. Ⓐ Ⓑ Ⓒ Ⓓ Ⓔ
20. Ⓐ Ⓑ Ⓒ Ⓓ Ⓔ

Section 3

1. Ⓐ Ⓑ Ⓒ Ⓓ
2. Ⓐ Ⓑ Ⓒ Ⓓ
3. Ⓐ Ⓑ Ⓒ Ⓓ
4. Ⓐ Ⓑ Ⓒ Ⓓ
5. Ⓐ Ⓑ Ⓒ Ⓓ
6. Ⓐ Ⓑ Ⓒ Ⓓ
7. Ⓐ Ⓑ Ⓒ Ⓓ
8. Ⓐ Ⓑ Ⓒ Ⓓ
9. Ⓐ Ⓑ Ⓒ Ⓓ Ⓔ
10. Ⓐ Ⓑ Ⓒ Ⓓ Ⓔ
11.
12. Ⓐ Ⓑ Ⓒ Ⓓ Ⓔ
13.
14. Ⓐ Ⓑ Ⓒ Ⓓ Ⓔ
15. Ⓐ Ⓑ Ⓒ Ⓓ Ⓔ
16.
17. Ⓐ Ⓑ Ⓒ Ⓓ Ⓔ
18. Ⓐ Ⓑ Ⓒ Ⓓ Ⓔ
19. Ⓐ Ⓑ Ⓒ Ⓓ Ⓔ
20.

ANSWER SHEET
Model Test 2

Section 4

1. Ⓐ Ⓑ Ⓒ Ⓓ Ⓔ Ⓕ
2. Ⓐ Ⓑ Ⓒ Ⓓ Ⓔ Ⓕ
3. Ⓐ Ⓑ Ⓒ Ⓓ Ⓔ Ⓕ
4. Ⓐ Ⓑ Ⓒ Ⓓ Ⓔ Ⓕ
5. Ⓐ Ⓑ Ⓒ Ⓓ Ⓔ Ⓕ
6. Ⓐ Ⓑ Ⓒ Ⓓ Ⓔ Ⓕ
7. Ⓐ Ⓑ Ⓒ Ⓓ Ⓔ
8. Ⓐ Ⓑ Ⓒ Ⓓ Ⓔ
9. Ⓐ Ⓑ Ⓒ Ⓓ Ⓔ
10. Ⓐ Ⓑ Ⓒ Ⓓ Ⓔ
11. Ⓐ Ⓑ Ⓒ Ⓓ Ⓔ Ⓕ
12. Ⓐ Ⓑ Ⓒ Ⓓ Ⓔ Ⓕ
13. Ⓐ Ⓑ Ⓒ Ⓓ Ⓔ Ⓕ
14. Ⓐ Ⓑ Ⓒ Ⓓ Ⓔ Ⓕ
15. Ⓐ Ⓑ Ⓒ Ⓓ Ⓔ
16. Ⓐ Ⓑ Ⓒ Ⓓ Ⓔ
17. Ⓐ Ⓑ Ⓒ Ⓓ Ⓔ
18. Ⓐ Ⓑ Ⓒ Ⓓ Ⓔ
19. Ⓐ Ⓑ Ⓒ Ⓓ Ⓔ
20. Ⓐ Ⓑ Ⓒ Ⓓ Ⓔ

Section 5

1. Ⓐ Ⓑ Ⓒ Ⓓ
2. Ⓐ Ⓑ Ⓒ Ⓓ
3. Ⓐ Ⓑ Ⓒ Ⓓ
4. Ⓐ Ⓑ Ⓒ Ⓓ
5. Ⓐ Ⓑ Ⓒ Ⓓ
6. Ⓐ Ⓑ Ⓒ Ⓓ
7. Ⓐ Ⓑ Ⓒ Ⓓ
8. Ⓐ Ⓑ Ⓒ Ⓓ Ⓔ
9. Ⓐ Ⓑ Ⓒ Ⓓ Ⓔ
10. ☐
11. Ⓐ Ⓑ Ⓒ Ⓓ Ⓔ
12. Ⓐ Ⓑ Ⓒ Ⓓ Ⓔ
13. Ⓐ Ⓑ Ⓒ Ⓓ Ⓔ
14. ☐
15. Ⓐ Ⓑ Ⓒ Ⓓ Ⓔ
16. Ⓐ Ⓑ Ⓒ Ⓓ Ⓔ
17. ☐
18. Ⓐ Ⓑ Ⓒ Ⓓ Ⓔ Ⓕ
19. Ⓐ Ⓑ Ⓒ Ⓓ Ⓔ
20. Ⓐ Ⓑ Ⓒ Ⓓ Ⓔ

SECTION 1 ANALYTICAL WRITING

TIME: 60 MINUTES—2 WRITING TASKS

Task 1: Analyze an Issue

30 MINUTES

Directions: In 30 minutes, compose an essay on the topic below. You may not write on any other topic.

The topic is presented in a one- to two-sentence quotation commenting on an issue of general concern. Your essay may support, refute, or qualify the views expressed in the quotation. Whatever you write, however, must be relevant to the issue under discussion, and you must support your viewpoint with reasons and examples derived from your studies and/or experience.

If you will be taking the computer-delivered test, write your essay using a word-processing program with its spelling and grammar checker turned off. If you will be taking the paper-delivered test, write your essay on lined paper using a #2 pencil.

Faculty members from various institutions will evaluate your essay, judging it on the basis of your skill in the following areas:

- ☑ Coverage of each of the elements in the task instructions
- ☑ Analysis of the statement's implications
- ☑ Organization and articulation of your ideas
- ☑ Use of relevant examples and arguments to support your case
- ☑ Handling of the mechanics, grammar, and usage of standard written English

ISSUE TASK

"Public secondary school students should be required to pass a standardized national exit exam in order to receive a high school diploma."

Compose an essay that presents your opinion on the policy presented, explicating your rationale for this opinion. As you build and provide evidence for your argument, you must take into account the likely effects of applying the policy and describe the impact these potential effects have on your argument.

Task 2: Analyze an Argument

30 MINUTES

Directions: In 30 minutes, prepare a critical analysis of an argument expressed in a short paragraph, following the specific task instructions provided. You may not offer an analysis of any other argument.

Be sure to support your analysis with evidence (reasons and/or examples) but **do not present your personal views on the topic.** Your job is to analyze the elements of an argument, not to support or contradict that argument.

If you will be taking the computer-delivered test, write your essay using a word-processing program with its spelling and grammar checker turned off. If you will be taking the paper-delivered test, write your essay on lined paper using a #2 pencil.

Faculty members from various institutions will evaluate your essay, judging it on the basis of your skill in the following areas:

- ✔ Coverage of each of the elements in the task instructions
- ✔ Identification and assessment of the argument's main elements
- ✔ Organization and articulation of your thoughts
- ✔ Use of relevant examples and arguments to support your case
- ✔ Handling of the mechanics, grammar, and usage of standard written English

ARGUMENT TASK

The following appeared in a letter to the editor in the journal *Health Matters.*

"Statistics gathered over the past three decades show that the death rate is higher among those who do not have jobs than among those with regular employment. Unemployment, just like heart disease and cancer, is a significant health issue. While many health care advocates promote increased government funding for medical research and public health care, it would be folly to increase government spending if doing so were to affect the nation's economy adversely and ultimately cause a rise in unemployment. A healthy economy means healthy citizens. Reining in government spending is, therefore, the best medicine."

Compose an essay that identifies the questions that must be answered before deciding whether the conclusion and the argument supporting it make sense. In writing your essay you should describe the impact that the answers to these questions would have on your assessment of the conclusion.

SECTION 2 VERBAL REASONING

TIME: 30 MINUTES—20 QUESTIONS

Directions: For each of the following sentences, select the two answers of the six choices given that, when substituted in the sentence, both logically complete the sentence as a whole and create sentences that are equivalent to one another in meaning.

QUESTIONS 1–6

1. Given the human tendency to suspect and disbelieve in processes that take place below the level of consciousness, it is unsurprising that many students of organizational development ________ the impact of the unconscious on business and political behavior and social dynamics.

   A intimate
   B acclaim
   C applaud
   D deny
   E gainsay
   F acknowledge

2. Although the young author had the reputation of being excessively taciturn, he seemed not at all ________ conversation.

   A inclined to
   B averse from
   C capable of
   D skilled at
   E opposed to
   F enamored of

3. To Mrs. Trollope, writing in the 1830s, nothing more clearly illustrated the ________ pervading "the land of the free" than the institution of slavery.

   A sanctimoniousness
   B conservatism
   C hypocrisy
   D rationality
   E liberality
   F orthodoxy

4. To someone as phlegmatic as Paul, it was a shock to find himself attracted to a woman so clearly his opposite in every way: a passionate activist, as ________ in her enthusiasms as in her dislikes.

   A dogmatic
   B ardent
   C haphazard
   D wholehearted
   E abstracted
   F mistaken

5. Soap operas and situation comedies, though given to distortion, are so derivative of contemporary culture that they are inestimable ________ the attitudes and values of our society in any particular decade.

   A contraventions of
   B antidotes to
   C indices of
   D prerequisites for
   E evidence of
   F determinants of

6. Slander is like counterfeit money: many people who would not coin it ________ without qualms.

   A hoard it
   B invest it
   C withdraw it
   D circulate it
   E spread it around
   F complain about it

> **Directions:** The next questions are based on the content of the following passage. Read the passage and then determine the best answer choice for each question. Base your choice on what this passage *states directly* or *implies*, not on any information you may have gained elsewhere.
>
> For each of Questions 6–10, select one answer choice unless otherwise instructed.

QUESTIONS 7–10 ARE BASED ON THE FOLLOWING PASSAGE.

With Meredith's *The Egoist* we enter into a critical problem that we have not yet before faced in these studies. That is the problem offered by a writer of recognizably impressive stature, whose work is informed by a muscular intelligence, whose language has splendor, whose "view of life" wins our respect, and yet for whom we are at best able to feel only a passive appreciation which amounts, practically, to indifference. We should be unjust to Meredith and to criticism if we should, giving in to the inertia of indifference, simply avoid dealing with him and thus avoid the problem along with him. He does not "speak to us," we might say; his meaning is not a "meaning for us"; he "leaves us cold." But do not the challenge and the excitement of the critical problem as such lie in that ambivalence of attitude which allows us to recognize the intelligence and even the splendor of Meredith's work, while, at the same time, we experience a lack of sympathy, a failure of any enthusiasm of response?

7. According to the passage, the work of Meredith is noteworthy for its elements of

   Ⓐ sensibility and artistic fervor
   Ⓑ ambivalence and moral ambiguity
   Ⓒ tension and sense of vitality
   Ⓓ brilliance and linguistic grandeur
   Ⓔ wit and whimsical frivolity

8. The author's discussion of Meredith fails to provide

   Ⓐ an indication of Meredith's customary effect on readers
   Ⓑ an enumeration of the admirable qualities in his work
   Ⓒ a selection of hypothetical comments at Meredith's expense
   Ⓓ an analysis of the critical ramifications of Meredith's effect on readers
   Ⓔ a refutation of the claim that Meredith evokes no sympathy

9. It can be inferred from the passage that the author finds the prospect of appraising Meredith's work critically to be

   Ⓐ counterproductive
   Ⓑ overly formidable
   Ⓒ somewhat tolerable
   Ⓓ markedly unpalatable
   Ⓔ clearly invigorating

10. It can be inferred from the passage that the author would be most likely to agree with which of the following statements about the role of criticism?

    Ⓐ Its prime office should be to make our enjoyment of the things that feed the mind as conscious as possible.
    Ⓑ It should be a disinterested endeavor to learn and propagate the best that is known and thought in the world.
    Ⓒ It should enable us to go beyond personal prejudice to appreciate the virtues of works antipathetic to our own tastes.
    Ⓓ It should dwell upon excellencies rather than imperfections, ignoring such deficiencies as irrelevant.
    Ⓔ It should strive both to purify literature and to elevate the literary standards of the reading public.

Directions: Each of the following sentences or groups of sentences contains one, two, or three blanks. These blanks signify that a word or set of words has been left out. Below each sentence are columns of words or sets of words. For each blank, pick the *one* word or set of words from the corresponding column that *best* completes the text.

11. Whereas off-Broadway theatre over the past several seasons has clearly (i) __________ a talent for experimentation and improvisation, one deficiency in the commercial stage of late has been its marked incapacity for (ii) __________.

Blank (i)
Ⓐ manifested
Ⓑ lampooned
Ⓒ disavowed

Blank (ii)
Ⓓ orthodoxy
Ⓔ spontaneity
Ⓕ burlesque

12. Although she had received many compliments for her (i) __________ in debate, at her inauguration as president of the student body she was surprisingly (ii) __________.

Blank (i)
Ⓐ candor
Ⓑ analysis
Ⓒ fluency

Blank (ii)
Ⓓ inarticulate
Ⓔ inattentive
Ⓕ inconsiderate

13. Even though their subjects and approaches are quite different, each of these filmmakers takes great care to (i) __________ a strong sense of place. In this way, they make their films intimate portraits of not only the characters but also the (ii) __________.

Blank (i)
Ⓐ reject
Ⓑ impart
Ⓒ vitiate

Blank (ii)
Ⓓ settings they emulate
Ⓔ families they abandon
Ⓕ spaces they inhabit

14. In England after 1600, small bass viols called division viols began to (i) __________ larger consort basses. They remained the dominant viol size until they (ii) __________ during the eighteenth century.

Blank (i)
Ⓐ impede
Ⓑ displace
Ⓒ circumvent

Blank (ii)
Ⓓ went out of fashion
Ⓔ gained prominence
Ⓕ achieved closure

15. The perpetual spinning of particles is much like that of a top, with one significant (i) ________: unlike the top, the particles have no need to be wound up, for (ii) ________ is one of their (iii) ________ properties.

Blank (i)
(A) difference
(B) correlation
(C) result

Blank (ii)
(D) circuitousness
(E) rotation
(F) collision

Blank (iii)
(G) intrinsic
(H) hypothetical
(I) intangible

Directions: The passage below is followed by questions based on its content. Once you have read the passage, select the best answer choice that *best* answers each question. Answer all questions on the basis of what is *stated* or implied in the passage.

For each of Questions 16–20, select one answer choice unless otherwise instructed.

QUESTIONS 16–17 ARE BASED ON THE FOLLOWING PASSAGE.

How is a newborn star formed? For the answer to this question, we must look to the familiar physical concept of gravitational instability. It is a simple concept, long known to scientists, having been first recognized by Isaac Newton in the late 1600s.

Let us envision a cloud of interstellar atoms and molecules, slightly admixed with dust. This cloud of interstellar gas is static and uniform. Suddenly, something occurs to disturb the gas, causing one small area within it to condense. As this small area increases in density, becoming slightly denser than the gas around it, its gravitational field likewise increases somewhat in strength. More matter now is attracted to the area, and its gravity becomes even stronger; as a result, it starts to contract, in process increasing in density even more. This in turn further increases its gravity, so that it accumulates still more matter and contracts further still. And so the process continues, until finally the small area of gas gives birth to a gravitationally bound object, a newborn star.

16. It can be inferred from the passage that the author views the information contained within it as

(A) controversial but irrefutable
(B) speculative and unprofitable
(C) uncomplicated and traditional
(D) original but obscure
(E) sadly lacking in elaboration

Directions: For the following question, consider each of the choices separately and select *all that apply*.

17. The author provides information that answers which of the following questions?

    [A] How does the small area's increasing density affect its gravitational field?

    [B] What causes the disturbance that changes the cloud from its original static state?

    [C] What is the end result of the gradually increasing concentration of the small area of gas?

QUESTIONS 18–20 ARE BASED ON THE FOLLOWING PASSAGE.

The Quechua world is submerged, so to speak, in a cosmic magma that weighs heavily upon it. It possesses the rare quality of being as it were interjected into the midst of antagonistic forces, which in turn implies a whole body of social and aesthetic structures whose innermost meaning must be the administration of energy. This gives rise to the social organism known as the *ayllu*, the agrarian community that regulates the procurement of food. The *ayllu* formed the basic structure of the whole Inca empire.

The central idea of this organization was a kind of closed economy, just the opposite of our economic practices, which can be described as open. The closed economy rested on the fact that the Inca controlled both the production and consumption of food. When one adds to this fact the religious ideas noted in the Quechua texts cited by the chronicler Santa Cruz Pachacuti, one comes to the conclusion that in the Andean zone the margin of life was minimal and was made possible only by the system of magic the Quechua constructed through his religion.

Adversities, moreover, were numerous, for the harvest might fail at any time and bring starvation to millions. Hence the whole purpose of the Quechua administrative and ideological system was to carry on the arduous task of achieving *abundance* and staving off shortages. This kind of structure presupposes a state of unremitting anxiety, which could not be resolved by action. The Quechua could not do so because his primordial response to problems was the use of magic, that is, recourse to the unconscious for the solution of external problems. Thus the struggle against the world was a struggle against the dark depths of the Quechua's own psyche, where the solution was found. By overcoming the unconscious, the outer world was also vanquished.

These considerations permit us to classify Quechua culture as absolutely static or, more accurately, as the expression of a mere state of being. Only in this way can we understand the refuge that it took in the germinative center of the cosmic *mandala* as revealed by Quechua art. The Quechua empire was nothing more than a *mandala*, for it was divided into four zones, with Cuzco in the center. Here the Quechua ensconced himself to contemplate the decline of the world as though it were caused by an alien and autonomous force.

18. The term "mandala" as used in the last paragraph most likely means

    (A) an agrarian community
    (B) a kind of superstition
    (C) a closed economic pattern
    (D) a philosophy or way of regarding the world
    (E) a figure composed of four divisions

MODEL TEST 2

19. The author implies that the Quechua world was

Ⓐ uncivilized
Ⓑ highly introspective
Ⓒ vitally energetic
Ⓓ free of major worries
Ⓔ well organized

20. With which of the following statements would the author most likely agree?

Ⓐ Only psychological solutions can remedy economic ills.
Ⓑ The Quechua were renowned for equanimity and unconcern.
Ⓒ The Quechua limited themselves to realizable goals.
Ⓓ Much of Quechua existence was harsh and frustrating.
Ⓔ Modern Western society should adopt some Quechua economic ideas.

SECTION 3 QUANTITATIVE ABILITY

TIME: 35 MINUTES—20 QUESTIONS

Directions: In each of Questions 1-8, there are two quantities—Quantity A and Quantity B. You are to compare those quantities, taking into consideration any additional information given. The correct answer to such a question is

Ⓐ if Quantity A is greater;
Ⓑ if Quantity B is greater;
Ⓒ if the two quantities are equal;
Ⓓ if it is impossible to determine which quantity is greater.

Note: The given information, if any, is always centered above the two quantities. In any question, if a symbol or letter appears more than once, it represents the same thing each time.

1.

m and n are positive integers

$mn = 25$

Quantity A	Quantity B
m	n

2.

Quantity A	Quantity B
65% of a	$\frac{2}{3}$ of a

3.

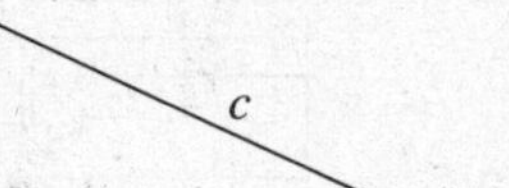

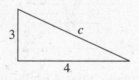

Quantity A	Quantity B
c	5

4.

$a + b = 24$

$a - b = 25$

Quantity A	Quantity B
b	0

5.

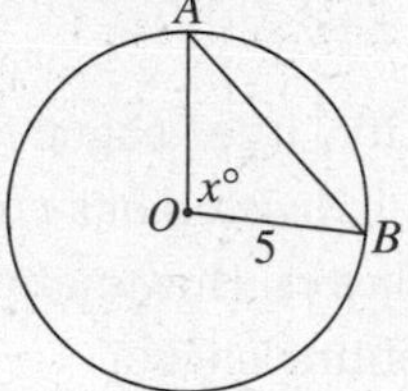

$90 < x$

Quantity A	Quantity B
The length of AB	7

6.

n	Frequency
1	4
2	5
3	2
4	3
5	6

The table above shows the frequency distribution of the values of a variable, n.

Quantity A	Quantity B
The average (arithmetic mean) of the median and mode of the distribution	The range of the distribution

MODEL TEST 2

7.

List 1: 25, 50, 75, 100, 125

List 2: 50, 100, 150, 200, 250

Quantity A	Quantity B
The standard deviation of the data in List 1	The standard deviation of the data in List 2

8.

A school group charters three identical buses and occupies $\frac{4}{5}$ of the seats. After $\frac{1}{4}$ of the passengers leave, the remaining passengers use only two of the buses.

Quantity A	Quantity B
The fraction of the seats on the two buses that are now occupied	$\frac{9}{10}$

Directions: Questions 9–20 have three different formats. Unless a question has its own directions that specifically state otherwise, each question has five answer choices, exactly one of which is correct.

9. The Center City Little League is divided into d divisions. Each division has t teams, and each team has p players. How many players are there in the entire league?

Ⓐ $d + t + p$
Ⓑ dtp
Ⓒ $\frac{pt}{d}$
Ⓓ $\frac{dt}{p}$
Ⓔ $\frac{d}{pt}$

10. In 1980, the cost of p pounds of potatoes was d dollars. In 1990, the cost of $2p$ pounds of potatoes was $\frac{1}{2}d$ dollars. By what percent did the price of potatoes decrease from 1980 to 1990?

Ⓐ 25%
Ⓑ 50%
Ⓒ 75%
Ⓓ 100%
Ⓔ 400%

Directions: The answer to the following question is a fraction. Enter the numerator in the upper box and the denominator in the lower box.

11. A number x is chosen at random from the set of positive integers less than 10. What is the probability that $\frac{9}{x} > x$?

12. A bag contains 3 red, 4 white, and 5 blue marbles. Jason begins removing marbles from the bag at random, one at a time. What is the least number of marbles he must remove to be sure that he has at least one of each color?

Ⓐ 3
Ⓑ 6
Ⓒ 8
Ⓓ 10
Ⓔ 12

Directions: For the following question, enter your answer in the box.

13. Jordan has taken 5 math tests so far this semester. If he gets a 70 on his next test, it will lower the average (arithmetic mean) of his test scores by 4 points. What is his average now?

QUESTIONS 14–16 REFER TO THE FOLLOWING GRAPHS.

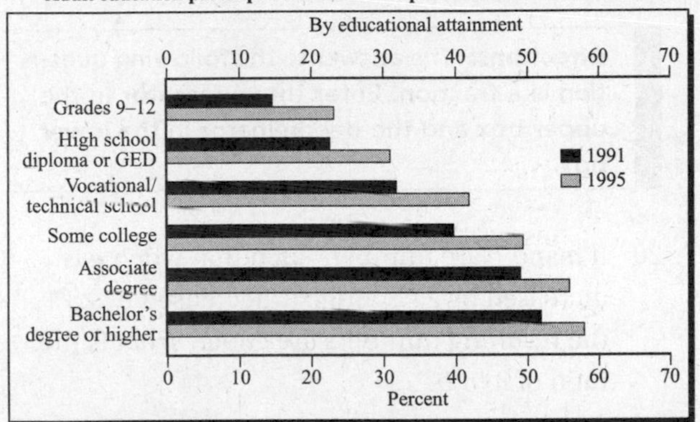

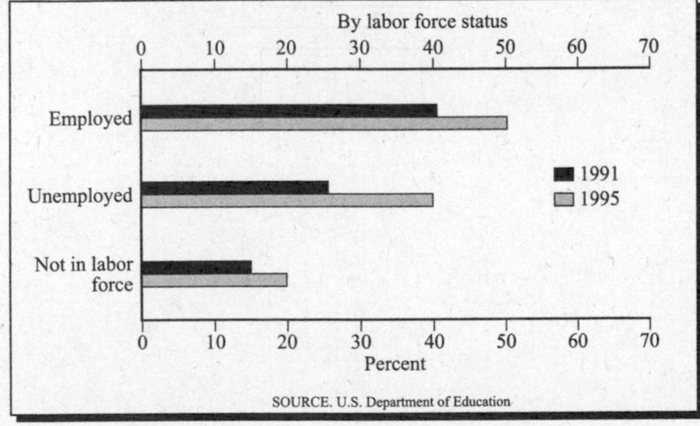

Directions: For the following question, consider each of the choices separately and select *all* that apply.

14. Which of the following is a valid conclusion from the graphs and the fact that the population of the United States was greater in 1995 than in 1991?

Indicate *all* such conclusions.

- [A] In 1991, adults whose highest degree was at least a bachelor's were more than twice as likely to participate in adult education than those whose highest educational attainment was a high school diploma or GED (high school equivalency diploma).
- [B] On a percentage basis, from 1991 to 1995, the greatest increase in the adult education participation rate was among those adults whose highest educational attainment was grades 9–12, without earning a high school diploma.
- [C] In 1995, more people participated in adult education programs than in 1991.
- [D] From 1991 to 1995 the rate of participation in adult education among the groups represented in the graphs increased the least for those who attained at least a bachelor's degree.
- [E] In 1995, more adults with at least a bachelor's degree participated in adult education than did adults who attended some college but did not earn a college degree.

15. If, in the United States in 1995, there were 100 million employed adults and 40 million adults not in the labor force, then approximately what was the ratio of the number of employed adults participating in adult education to the number of people not in the labor force participating in adult education?

Ⓐ 5:4
Ⓑ 5:2
Ⓒ 10:3
Ⓓ 5:1
Ⓔ 6:1

MODEL TEST 2

Directions: For the following question, enter your answer in the box.

16. Assume that in 1996 the unemployment rate was 8%, meaning that 8 out of every 100 adults in the workforce were unemployed. What percentage of adults in the labor force participated in adult education? Round your answer to the nearest whole percent.

 %

---

17. If a and b are the lengths of the legs of a right triangle whose hypotenuse is 10 and whose area is 20, what is the value of $(a + b)^2$?

Ⓐ 100
Ⓑ 120
Ⓒ 140
Ⓓ 180
Ⓔ 200

18. What is the average (arithmetic mean) of 3^{30}, 3^{60}, 3^{90}?

Ⓐ 3^{60}
Ⓑ 3^{177}
Ⓒ $3^{10} + 3^{20} + 3^{30}$
Ⓓ $3^{27} + 3^{57} + 3^{87}$
Ⓔ $3^{29} + 3^{59} + 3^{89}$

19. The figure below consists of four semicircles in a large semicircle. If the small semicircles have radii of 1, 2, 3, and 4, what is the perimeter of the shaded region?

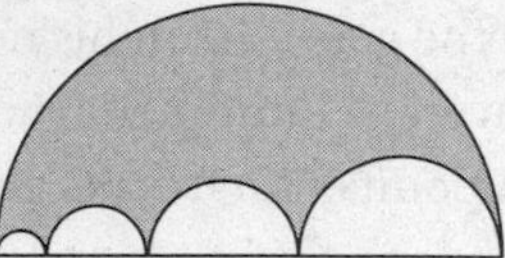

Ⓐ 10π
Ⓑ 20π
Ⓒ 40π
Ⓓ 60π
Ⓔ 100π

Directions: The answer to the following question is a fraction. Enter the numerator in the upper box and the denominator in the lower box.

20. If a and b are numbers such that when a is increased by 25% and b is decreased by 25%, the resulting numbers are equal. What is the ratio of a to b?

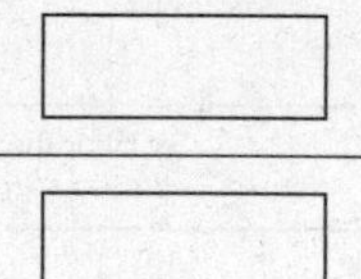

SECTION 4 VERBAL REASONING

TIME: 30 MINUTES—20 QUESTIONS

Directions: For each of the following sentences, select the two answers of the six choices given that, when substituted in the sentence, both logically complete the sentence as a whole and create sentences that are equivalent to one another in meaning.

QUESTIONS 1–6

1. Ironically, the same mayor who preached ______ to his constituents was noted for his extravagance and his free-spending lifestyle.

A righteousness
B radicalism
C economy
D austerity
E repentance
F honesty

2. The portrait painter was disinclined to accept a commission unless she was assured of adequate ______ for the task.

A recompense
B illumination
C personnel
D remuneration
E equipment
F expertise

3. Beginning with the music and dance of the antebellum plantation, jazz, born from a slave culture, would eventually ______ a musical industry that African musicians would dominate for years to come.

A preclude
B spawn
C withstand
D advocate
E disenfranchise
F generate

4. To a sophisticated audience conversant with the wide range of contemporary literary criticism, this brief essay would have been seen as a ______ version of arguments rehearsed in much more detail elsewhere.

A synoptic
B perceptive
C condensed
D generic
E censored
F forensic

5. Among contemporary writers of fiction, Mrs. Woolf is ______ figure, in some ways as radical as James Joyce, in others no more modern than Jane Austen.

A a curious
B an introspective
C a peripheral
D a disinterested
E an anomalous
F a doctrinaire

6. Book publishing has long been ______ profession, partly because for younger editors the best way to win a raise or a promotion was to move on to another publishing house.

A an innovative
B a prestigious
C an itinerant
D a mobile
E a rewarding
F an insular

MODEL TEST 2

Directions: The next questions are based on the content of the following passage. Read the passage and then determine the best answer choice for each question. Base your choice on what this passage *states directly* or *implies*, not on any information you may have gained elsewhere.

For each of Questions 7–9, select one answer choice unless otherwise instructed.

QUESTIONS 7–9 ARE BASED ON THE FOLLOWING PASSAGE.

Mary Shelley herself was the first to point to her fortuitous immersion in the literary and scientific revolutions of her day as the source of her novel *Frankenstein.* Her extreme youth, as well as her sex, have contributed to the generally held opinion that she was not so much an author in her own right as a transparent medium through which passed the ideas of those around her. "All Mrs. Shelley did," writes Mario Praz, "was to provide a passive reflection of some of the wild fantasies which were living in the air about her."

Passive reflections, however, do not produce original works of literature, and *Frankenstein,* if not a great novel, was unquestionably an original one. The major Romantic and minor Gothic tradition to which it *should* have belonged was to the literature of the overreacher: the superman who breaks through normal human limitations to defy the rules of society and infringe upon the realm of God. In the Faust story, hypertrophy of the individual will is symbolized by a pact with the devil. Byron's and Balzac's heroes; the Wandering Jew; the chained and unchained Prometheus: all are overreachers, all are punished by their own excesses—by a surfeit of sensation, of experience, of knowledge and, most typically, by the doom of eternal life. But Mary Shelley's overreacher is different. Frankenstein's exploration of the forbidden boundaries of human science does not cause the prolongation and extension of his own life, but the creation of a new one. He defies mortality not by living forever, but by giving birth.

7. The author quotes Mario Praz primarily in order to

Ⓐ support her own perception of Mary Shelley's uniqueness
Ⓑ illustrate recent changes in scholarly opinions of Shelley
Ⓒ demonstrate Praz's unfamiliarity with Shelley's *Frankenstein*
Ⓓ provide an example of the predominant critical view of Shelley
Ⓔ contrast Praz's statement about Shelley with Shelley's own self-appraisal

8. The author of the passage concedes which of the following about Mary Shelley as an author?

Ⓐ She was unaware of the literary and mythological traditions of the overreacher.
Ⓑ She intentionally parodied the scientific and literary discoveries of her time.
Ⓒ he was exposed to radical artistic and scientific concepts that influenced her work.
Ⓓ She lacked the maturity to create a literary work of absolute originality.
Ⓔ She was not so much an author in her own right as an imitator of the literary works of others.

9. According to the author, Frankenstein parts from the traditional figure of the overreacher in

Ⓐ his exaggerated will
Ⓑ his atypical purpose
Ⓒ the excesses of his method
Ⓓ the inevitability of his failure
Ⓔ his defiance of the deity

Directions: Each of the following sentences or groups of sentences contains one, two, or three blanks. These blanks signify that a word or set of words has been left out. Below each sentence are columns of words or sets of words. For each blank, pick the *one* word or set of words from the corresponding column that *best* completes the text.

QUESTIONS 10–14

10. With units covering such topics as euthanasia, organ transplantation, and patient rights, the course *Religion, Ethics, and Medicine* explores the ways in which religious ideas and concepts ________ the practice of medicine and delivery of health care.

Ⓐ inform
Ⓑ obviate
Ⓒ reiterate
Ⓓ preclude
Ⓔ deny

11. To the embittered ex-philanthropist, all the former recipients of his charity were (i) ________, as stingy with their thanks as they were wasteful of his (ii) ________.

Blank (i)
Ⓐ misers
Ⓑ ingrates
Ⓒ prigs

Blank (ii)
Ⓓ gratitude
Ⓔ largesse
Ⓕ equanimity

12. For centuries, physicists have had good reason to believe in the principle of equivalence propounded by Galileo: it has (i) ________ many rigorous tests that (ii) ________ its accuracy to extraordinary precision.

Blank (i)
Ⓐ predicted
Ⓑ survived
Ⓒ postulated

Blank (ii)
Ⓓ established
Ⓔ compromised
Ⓕ equated

13. The actress had (i) ________ getting people to do things for her, and, to her delight, her new friends proved quite (ii) ________ in finding new ways to meet her needs.

Blank (i)
Ⓐ a knack for
Ⓑ a disinclination for
Ⓒ an indifference to

Blank (ii)
Ⓓ assiduous
Ⓔ dilatory
Ⓕ stoical

14. Although he did not consider himself (i) ________, he felt that the inconsistencies in her story (ii) ________ a certain degree of incredulity on his part.

Blank (i)
Ⓐ an apostate
Ⓑ a skeptic
Ⓒ a hypocrite

Blank (ii)
Ⓓ intimated
Ⓔ dignified
Ⓕ warranted

Directions: The passage below is followed by questions based on its content. Once you have read the passage, select the answer choice that *best* answers each question. Answer all questions on the basis of what is *stated* or *implied* in the passage.

For each of Questions 15–20, select one answer choice unless otherwise instructed.

QUESTIONS 15–17 ARE BASED ON THE FOLLOWING PASSAGE.

(The passage was written in the latter half of the 20th century.)

The coastlines on the two sides of the Atlantic Ocean present a notable parallelism: the easternmost region of Brazil, in Pernambuco, has a convexity that corresponds almost perfectly with the concavity of the African Gulf of Guinea, while the contours of the African coastline between Rio de Oro and Liberia would, by the same approximation, match those of the Caribbean Sea.

Similar correspondences are also observed in many other regions of the Earth. This observation began to awaken scientific interest about sixty years ago, when Alfred Wegener, a professor at the University of Hamburg, used it as a basis for formulating a revolutionary theory in geological science.

According to Wegener, there was originally only one continent or land mass, which he called Pangaea. Inasmuch as continental masses are lighter than the base on which they rest, he reasoned, they must float on the substratum of igneous rock, known as sima, as ice floes float on the sea. Then why, he asked, might continents not be subject to drifting? The rotation of the globe and other forces, he thought, had caused the cracking and, finally, the breaking apart of the original Pangaea, along an extensive line represented today by the longitudinal submerged mountain range in the center of the Atlantic. While Africa seems to have remained static, the Americas apparently drifted toward the west until they reached their present position after more than 100 million years. Although the phenomenon seems fantastic, accustomed as we are to the concept of the rigidity and immobility of the continents, on the basis of the distance that separates them it is possible to calculate that the continental drift would have been no greater than two inches per year.

15. The primary purpose of the passage is to

Ⓐ describe the relative speed of continental movement
Ⓑ predict the future configuration of the continents
Ⓒ refute a radical theory postulating continental movement
Ⓓ describe the reasoning behind a geological theory
Ⓔ explain how to calculate the continental drift per year

16. It can be inferred from the passage that evidence for continental drift has been provided by the

Ⓐ correspondences between coastal contours
Ⓑ proof of an original solitary land mass
Ⓒ level of sima underlying the continents
Ⓓ immobility of the African continent
Ⓔ relative heaviness of the continental masses

17. The passage presents information that would answer which of the following questions?

Ⓐ In what ways do the coastlines of Africa and South America differ from one another?
Ⓑ How much lighter than the substratum of igneous rock below them are the continental masses?
Ⓒ Is the rotation of the globe affecting the stability of the present day continental masses?
Ⓓ According to Wegener's theory, in what direction have the Americas tended to move?
Ⓔ How does Wegener's theory account for the apparent immobility of the African continent?

QUESTIONS 18–20 ARE BASED ON THE FOLLOWING PASSAGE.

During the 1930s, National Association for the Advancement of Colored People (NAACP) attorneys Charles H. Houston, William Hastie, James M. Nabrit, Leon Ransom, and Thurgood Marshall charted a legal strategy designed to end segregation in education. They developed a series of legal cases challenging segregation in graduate and professional schools. Houston believed that the battle against segregation had to begin at the highest academic level in order to mitigate fear of race mixing that could create even greater hostility and reluctance on the part of white judges. After establishing a series of favorable legal precedents in higher education, NAACP attorneys planned to launch an all-out attack on the separate-but-equal doctrine in primary and secondary schools. The strategy proved successful. In four major United States Supreme Court decisions precedents were established that would enable the NAACP to construct a solid legal foundation upon which the *Brown* case could rest: *Missouri ex rel. Gaines* v. *Canada, Registrar of the University of Missouri* (1938); *Sipuel* v. *Board of Regents of the University of Oklahoma* (1948); *McLaurin* v. *Oklahoma State Regents for Higher Education* (1950); and *Sweatt* v. *Painter* (1950).

In the Oklahoma case, the Supreme Court held that the plaintiff was entitled to enroll in the University. The Oklahoma Regents responded by separating black and white students in cafeterias and classrooms. The 1950 McLaurin decision ruled that such internal separation was unconstitutional. In the *Sweatt* ruling, delivered on the same day, the Supreme Court held that the maintenance of separate law schools for whites and blacks was unconstitutional. A year after Herman Sweatt entered the University of Texas law school, desegregation cases were filed in the states of Kansas, South Carolina, Virginia, and

Delaware and in the District of Columbia asking the courts to apply the qualitative test of the *Sweatt* case to the elementary and secondary schools and to declare the separate-but-equal doctrine invalid in the area of public education.

The 1954 *Brown* v. *Board of Education* decision declared that a classification based solely on race violated the 14th Amendment to the United States Constitution. The decision reversed the 1896 *Plessy* v. *Ferguson* ruling, which had established the separate-but-equal doctrine. The *Brown* decision more than any other case launched the "equalitarian revolution" in American jurisprudence and signalled the emerging primacy of equality as a guide to constitutional decisions; nevertheless, the decision did not end state sanctioned segregation. Indeed, the second *Brown* decision, known as *Brown II* and delivered a year later, played a decisive role in limiting the effectiveness and impact of the 1954 case by providing southern states with the opportunity to delay the implementation of desegregation.

18. According to the passage, Houston aimed his legislative challenge at the graduate and professional school level on the basis of the assumption that

Ⓐ the greatest inequities existed at the highest academic and professional levels
Ⓑ the separate-but-equal doctrine applied solely to the highest academic levels
Ⓒ there were clear precedents for reform in existence at the graduate school level
Ⓓ the judiciary would feel less apprehension at desegregation on the graduate level
Ⓔ the consequences of desegregation would become immediately apparent at the graduate school level

19. Which of the following statements is most compatible with the principles embodied in *Plessy* v. *Ferguson* as described in the passage?

Ⓐ Internal separation of whites and blacks within a given school is unconstitutional.
Ⓑ Whites and blacks may be educated in separate schools so long as they offer comparable facilities.
Ⓒ The maintenance of separate professional schools for blacks and whites is unconstitutional.
Ⓓ The separate-but-equal doctrine is inapplicable to the realm of private education.
Ⓔ Blacks may be educated in schools with whites whenever the blacks and whites have equal institutions.

20. The aspect of Houston's work most extensively discussed in the passage is its

Ⓐ psychological canniness
Ⓑ judicial complexity
Ⓒ fundamental efficiency
Ⓓ radical intellectualism
Ⓔ exaggerated idealism

SECTION 5 QUANTITATIVE ABILITY

TIME: 35 MINUTES—20 QUESTIONS

Directions: In each of Questions 1–7, there are two quantities—Quantity A and Quantity B. You are to compare those quantities, taking into consideration any additional information given. The correct answer to such a question is

Ⓐ if Quantity A is greater;

Ⓑ if Quantity B is greater;

Ⓒ if the two quantities are equal;

Ⓓ if it is impossible to determine which quantity is greater.

Note: The given information, if any, is always centered above the two quantities. In any question, if a symbol or letter appears more than once, it represents the same thing each time.

1.

Quantity A	Quantity B
$(-8)^8$	$(-9)^9$

2.

$a > 0$

Quantity A	Quantity B
$\sqrt{a^{18}}$	$(a^2)(a^3)(a^4)$

3.

The price of a large pizza is 30% more than the price of a small pizza.

Quantity A	Quantity B
The price of a large pizza when it is on sale for 30% off.	The price of a small pizza.

4.

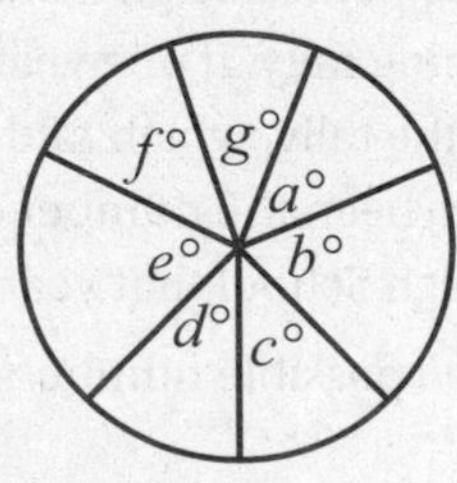

Quantity A	Quantity B
The average (arithmetic mean) of *a*, *b*, *c*, *d*, *e*, *f*, and *g*.	50

5.

A palindrome is an integer that reads the same from left to right as from right to left (ignoring commas). For example, 22; 171; 3,003; and 18,481 are all palindromes.

Quantity A	Quantity B
The number of 5-digit palindromes	The number of 6-digit palindromes

6.

Quantity A	Quantity B
The area of an equilateral triangle whose sides are 6	The area of an isosceles right triangle whose legs are 6

7.

A bag contains four slips of paper, two of which have the number 1 written on them and two of which have the number −1 on them. Two of the slips are chosen at random.

Quantity A	Quantity B
The probability that the product of the two numbers chosen is −1	The probability that the product of the two numbers chosen is 1

Directions: Questions 8–20 have three different formats. Unless a question has its own directions that specifically state otherwise, each question has five answer choices, exactly one of which is correct.

8. John bought a $100 DVD player on sale at 8% off. How much did he pay including 8% sales tax?

Ⓐ $84.64
Ⓑ $92.00
Ⓒ $96.48
Ⓓ $99.36
Ⓔ $100.00

9. The sum of the lengths of all the edges of a cube is 3 feet. What is the volume, in cubic feet, of the cube?

Ⓐ $\frac{1}{64}$
Ⓑ $\frac{1}{8}$
Ⓒ $\frac{1}{4}$
Ⓓ 8
Ⓔ 27

Directions: For the following question enter your answer in the box.

10. Mary read from the top of page 10 to the bottom of page 24 in 30 minutes, At this rate, how long, in minutes, will it take her to read from the top of page 25 to the bottom of page 50?

[ ] minutes

11. For how many positive integers $m \leq 100$ is $(m-5)(m-45)$ positive?

Ⓐ 45
Ⓑ 50
Ⓒ 58
Ⓓ 59
Ⓔ 60

12. The magazine *Modern Crafts* published the instructions for making a circular mosaic whose diameter is 20 centimeters. Geraldine wants to use tiles of the same size as those listed in the magazine article to make a larger mosaic—one that is 30 centimeters in diameter. To have the correct number of tiles for her mosaic, by what factor must she multiply the number of tiles that were listed in the magazine's directions?

Ⓐ 2.25
Ⓑ 2.00
Ⓒ 1.50
Ⓓ 1.44
Ⓔ 0.67

Directions: For the following question, consider each of the choices separately and select *all* that apply.

13. Every year between 70% and 85% of the students at Central High School attend the homecoming rally. If one year 1435 students attended the rally, which of the following could have been the number of students at Central High School that year?

Indicate *all* possible numbers of students.

[A] 1675
[B] 1775
[C] 1875
[D] 1975
[E] 2075

QUESTIONS 14–16 REFER TO THE FOLLOWING GRAPHS.

College Enrollment, by Age and Gender: 1975 and 1995

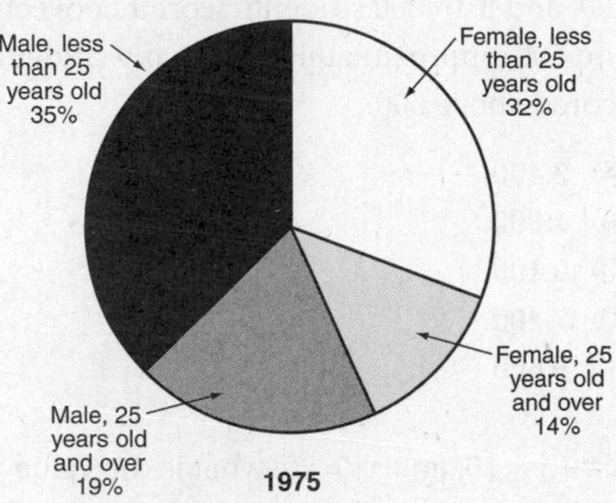

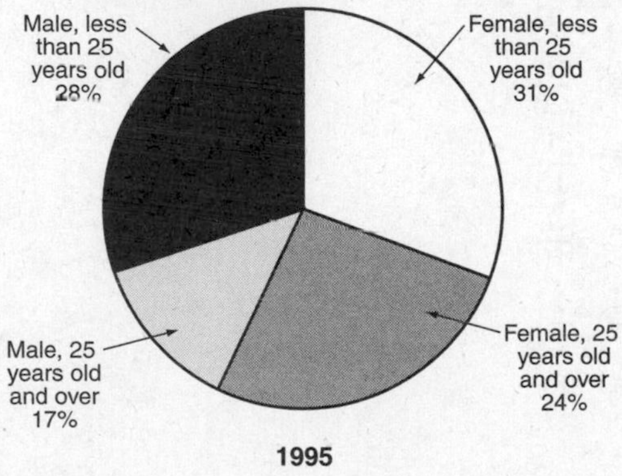

Source: U.S. Bureau of the Census, Current Population Survey.

Directions: For the following question enter your answer in the box.

14. If there were 10,000,000 college students in 1975, how many more male students were there than female students?

[ ]

15. In 1975, approximately what percent of female college students were at least 25 years old?

Ⓐ 14%
Ⓑ 30%
Ⓒ 45%
Ⓓ 69%
Ⓔ 76%

16. If the total number of students enrolled in college was 40% higher in 1995 than in 1975, what is the ratio of the number of male students in 1995 to the number of male students in 1975?

Ⓐ 5:6
Ⓑ 6:7
Ⓒ 7:6
Ⓓ 6:5
Ⓔ 7:5

Directions: For the following question enter your answer in the box.

17. Eric can address 40 envelopes per hour. At this rate, how many envelopes can he address in 99 minutes?

[ ]

MODEL TEST 2

Directions: For the following question, consider each of the choices separately and select *all* that apply.

18. At Florence Pizza, the only slices of pizza available are plain and pepperoni, which cost \$1.50 and \$2.00, respectively. Small, medium, and large cups of soda cost \$1.00, \$1.50, and \$1.75, respectively. Which of the following could be the total cost of two slices of pizza and two sodas?

Indicate *all* such costs.

- [A] \$5.00
- [B] \$5.25
- [C] \$6.00
- [D] \$6.25
- [E] \$7.00
- [F] \$7.25

19. In a normal distribution, 68% of the scores lie within one standard deviation of the mean. If the SAT scores of all the high school juniors in Center City followed a normal distribution with a mean of 500 and a standard deviation of 100, and if 10,200 students scored between 400 and 500, approximately how many students scored above 600?

- (A) 2,400
- (B) 4,800
- (C) 5,100
- (D) 7,200
- (E) 9,600

20. If $x + y = 10$, and $xy = 20$, what is the value of $\frac{1}{x} + \frac{1}{y}$?

- (A) $\frac{1}{20}$
- (B) $\frac{1}{15}$
- (C) $\frac{1}{10}$
- (D) $\frac{1}{2}$
- (E) 2

ANSWER KEY

Section 1—Analytical Writing

The Analytical Writing sections are scored holistically, in accordance with the following guidelines.

First, estimate your score on the Issue Essay by using the following rubric.

	Argument	Support	Structure	Fluency	Conventions
6	Presents a clear and perceptive argument that responds to the specific task instructions	Provides strong reasoning and/or examples to fully support its thesis	Is focused and very well organized and has logical and skillful transitions between ideas	Expresses ideas clearly and fluently, with sophisticated word choice and varied sentence structure	Displays impressive command of the grammar, usage, and mechanics of standard written English
5	Presents a clear and thoughtful argument that responds to the specific task instructions	Provides logical reasoning and/or appropriate examples to support its thesis	Is focused and well organized and has logical transitions between ideas	Expresses ideas effectively, with appropriate word choice and varied sentence structure	Displays solid command of the grammar, usage, and mechanics of standard written English
4	Presents a clear argument that adequately responds to the specific task instructions	Provides adequate reasoning and/or examples to support its thesis	Is reasonably well focused and organized	Expresses ideas effectively, with appropriate word choice	Displays command of the grammar, usage, and mechanics of standard written English
3	Presents an argument that is somewhat unclear or that does not clearly respond to the specific task instructions	Makes unsupported claims or has limited relevant examples to support its thesis	Is minimally focused and/or organized	Is somewhat unclear due to incorrect word choice or sentence structure	Includes infrequent major or frequent minor errors in grammar, usage, and/or mechanics
2	Presents an argument that is unclear or fails to address the specific task instructions	Provides nearly no relevant examples or reasons to support its thesis	Is unfocused and/or disorganized	Is unclear due to frequent incorrect word choice or sentence structure	Includes significant errors in grammar, usage, and/or mechanics that render its meaning unclear
1	Presents an argument that demonstrates severely limited understanding of the topic	Provides little to no examples or reasoning that are related to the assigned topic	Is extremely disorganized or excessively short	Is very unclear due to pervasive incorrect word choice or sentence structure	Includes pervasive errors in grammar, usage, and/or mechanics that render it indecipherable
0	Addresses a topic other than the one assigned, is written in a language other than English, is nothing more than the words in the topic and/or task instructions, is nothing more than random characters, is not legible.				

As you examine the rubric you will notice that all of the scores below four are shaded gray. The reason for this is that ETS, the maker of the GRE, states that essays scoring below four display **one or more** of the characteristics listed in the shaded area. In other words, if your essay displays even one characteristic listed in the shaded area, that low score will determine your overall score. If all of your essay's characteristics are found in the boxes above the shaded area, your score should be the average of the five scores (for argument, support, structure, fluency, and writing conventions).

SCORING THE ISSUE ESSAY

Using the Issue Essay rubric, check the box in each column that best describes your work. If each of the boxes you have checked is above the shaded area, add those five scores together and calculate their average.

Example:

Argument	4
Support	4
Structure	5
Fluency	4
Conventions	4
Total	**21**

The average is 4.2, rounded down to a likely score of 4.

If, however, **any** of your scores fall into the shaded area of the rubric, the lowest score marked will be your final score.

Next, estimate your score on the Argument Essay by using the following rubric.

	Argument	Support	Structure	Fluency	Conventions
6	Pinpoints the elements of the argument at issue and evaluates them with great insight	Provides detailed and persuasive support for its main points	Expresses ideas clearly and is very well organized, with logical and clear transitions between ideas	Expresses ideas clearly and fluently, with sophisticated word choice and varied sentence structure	Displays impressive command of the grammar, usage, and mechanics of standard written English
5	Pinpoints the elements of the argument at issue and evaluates them thoughtfully	Provides thoughtful and persuasive support for its main points	Expresses ideas clearly and is well organized, with suitable transitions between ideas	Expresses ideas effectively, with appropriate word choice and varied sentence structure	Displays solid command of the grammar, usage, and mechanics of standard written English
4	Identifies the elements of the argument at issue and evaluates them, but may include less relevant points	Provides sufficient, though possibly uneven, support for its main points	Expresses ideas reasonably clearly and is organized, but transitions between ideas are inadequate or absent	Expresses ideas effectively, with appropriate word choice	Displays command of the grammar, usage, and mechanics of standard written English
3	Fails to distinguish or evaluate the most relevant elements of the argument, though some relevant aspects may be discussed	Provides support that is sometimes irrelevant to its main points	Expresses ideas with little depth and/or organizes them illogically	Is somewhat unclear due to incorrect word choice or sentence structure	Includes infrequent major or frequent minor errors in grammar, usage, and/or mechanics
2	Fails to evaluate the argument using logic, but may provide the writer's personal views on the topic	Provides support that is generally irrelevant to its main points	Expresses ideas inadequately and organizes them illogically	Is unclear due to frequent incorrect word choice or sentence structure	Includes significant errors in grammar, usage, and/or mechanics that render its meaning unclear
1	Fails to demonstrate any grasp of the argument at issue	Provides no support for its main points	Is extremely disorganized or excessively short	Is very unclear due to pervasive incorrect word choice or sentence structure	Includes pervasive errors in grammar, usage, and/or mechanics that render it indecipherable
0	Addresses a topic other than the one assigned, is written in a language other than English, is nothing more than the words in the topic and/or task instructions, is nothing more than random characters, is not legible.				

SCORING THE ARGUMENT ESSAY

Using the Argument Essay rubric, check the box in each column that best describes your work. If each of the boxes you have checked is above the shaded area, add those five scores together and calculate their average.

CALCULATING YOUR OVERALL SCORE

To determine your overall Analytical Writing score, add the scores for both essays (Issue and Argument) together and divide by 2. The overall score is given in half-point increments, so you should round up to the nearest half point when calculating this score. As an example, if you earn a score of 5 on the Issue Essay and a score of 4.5 on the Argument Essay, your overall Analytical Writing score will be 4.75, rounded up to 5.

Section 2—Verbal Reasoning

1. **D, E**	6. **D, E**	11. **A, E**	16. **C**
2. **B, E**	7. **D**	12. **C, D**	17. **A, C**
3. **A, C**	8. **E**	13. **B, F**	18. **E**
4. **B, D**	9. **E**	14. **B, D**	19. **B**
5. **C, E**	10. **C**	15. **A, E, G**	20. **D**

Note: The letters in brackets following the Quantitative Ability answers in Sections 3 and 5 refer to the sections of Chapter 12 in which you can find the information you need to answer the questions. For example, 3. D [J] means that the answer to question 3 is D, and that the solution requires information found in Section 12-J: Triangles. Also, 15. B [11] means that the answer to question 15 is B and is based on information in Chapter 11: Data Interpretation.

Section 3—Quantitative Ability

1. **D** [A]	6. **C** [E]	11. **2/9** [O]	16. **49** [11]
2. **D** [B, C]	7. **B** [E]	12. **D** [O]	17. **D** [G, J]
3. **D** [J]	8. **C** [B]	13. **94** [E]	18. **E** [A]
4. **B** [G]	9. **B** [D]	14. **A, B, C, D** [11]	19. **B** [L]
5. **A** [J, L]	10. **C** [C, D]	15. **E** [11]	20. **3/5** [C]

Section 4—Verbal Reasoning

1. **C, D**	6. **C, D**	11. **B, E**	16. **A**
2. **A, D**	7. **D**	12. **B, D**	17. **D**
3. **B, F**	8. **C**	13. **A, D**	18. **D**
4. **A, C**	9. **B**	14. **B, F**	19. **B**
5. **A, E**	10. **A**	15. **D**	20. **A**

Section 5—Quantitative Ability

1. **A** [A]	6. **B** [J]	11. **D** [A, G]	16. **C** [11]
2. **C** [A]	7. **A** [O]	12. **A** [L]	17. **66** [H]
3. **B** [C]	8. **D** [C]	13. **B, C, D** [C, H]	18. **A, C, D, E, F** [A]
4. **A** [E, L]	9. **A** [M]	14. **800,000** [11]	19. **B** [D]
5. **C** [O]	10. **52** [O]	15. **B** [11]	20. **D** [G]

ANSWER EXPLANATIONS

Section 1—Analytical Writing

PROMPT #1

"Public secondary school students should be required to pass a standardized national exit exam in order to receive a high school diploma."

Compose an essay that presents your opinion on the policy presented, explicating your rationale for this opinion. As you build and provide evidence for your argument, you must take into account the likely effects of applying the policy and describe the impact these potential effects have on your argument.

SCORE 6 ISSUE ESSAY

Since the publication of the report, "A Nation at Risk," in the early 1980s, policy makers and pundits have decried the poor quality of American education. They argue that our public schools, once the envy of the world, have lost their way. Business leaders complain that many high school graduates lack basic skills, creating a shortage of qualified workers. Critics also lament the significant achievement gap between students in wealthy suburban communities and their peers in many of the nation's largest urban school systems. This frustration has led many to support the implementation of a standardized national high school exit exam in order to set high standards for all students. Unfortunately, there is no simple answer to the challenges facing the American system of public education, and the consequences of implementing a standardized national high school exit exam are likely to be both counterproductive and discriminatory.

A standardized national high school exit exam is more likely to harm the quality of American education than it is to improve it. Standardized tests are ideal for measuring subject matter knowledge, but they are inadequate instruments for measuring skills like writing and problem solving. If a standardized national high school exit exam is implemented, schools will be evaluated and ranked based on the scores their students achieve. This ranking will create pressure on administrators and teachers to improve student test scores, and "teaching to the test" will be an inevitable consequence. Tragically, because these tests privilege recall of facts over demonstration of skills, school districts will alter their curricula in order to maximize their students' performance on the national test. Class time that was once dedicated to writing and hands-on problem solving will be given over to rote memorization and drill, creating students who are less skilled and prepared than their predecessors.

Not only will a national standardized high school exit exam fail to improve the quality of education in the United States, but it will also exacerbate the inequality for which some propose it as a remedy. Standardized testing cannot shrink the achievement gap between wealthy suburban students and their less fortunate urban counterparts. Without improved resources to address the systemic causes of the achievement gap, students in failing districts will continue to struggle. Only now, with a standardized national test, all students will be held to the same standards, regardless of the advantages or disadvantages they face. The upshot of this is that high school graduation will become a more distant goal for the very students who struggle the most. The dropout rate in large urban districts will rise, and the unfortunate products of these schools will find themselves less employable. As businesses abandon these communities due to a shortage of qualified workers, unemployment will increase. As local economies decline, so too will property values, which are the basis of the taxes that support public education in most areas of the country. Finally, with even fewer resources available, the students in these struggling school districts will fall ever further behind their more fortunate peers.

Adopting a standardized national high school exit exam is a simplistic response to a complicated problem. If we want to improve the quality of education for all students in the United States, we need to recognize that one size does not fit all. We need to develop instruments and methods that better evaluate student skills, and we need to provide resources to address the wealth and opportunity gap that drives the achievement gap. We cannot improve the quality of education if we focus on measuring outputs without doing anything to change inputs.

APPLYING THE RUBRIC

Argument	6
Support	6
Structure	5
Fluency	6
Conventions	6
Total	29

The average is 5.8, rounded up to a likely score of 6.

ARGUMENT The essay presents a clear and perceptive argument that a standardized national high school exit exam will be harmful. The essay is especially good at meeting the requirement to examine the consequences of implementing this policy, doing so by describing the chain of events that could be expected to follow its implementation.

SUPPORT The likely consequences of implementing the policy are well supported by strong reasoning. One excellent example of this is the description of how decreases in the number of high school graduates will harm the economy, affecting tax revenues, ultimately resulting in reduced resources for schools and even poorer educational results.

STRUCTURE The essay is well focused and organized, with logical transitions between ideas.

FLUENCY The essay displays sophisticated and powerful vocabulary. Its sentence structure is varied throughout.

CONVENTIONS Outstanding. The essay includes no noticeable errors in grammar, usage, or mechanics.

SCORE 5 ISSUE ESSAY

High school graduation is a rite of passage, a ritual through which young people show that they have completed one stage of their development and are ready for their next. But what does it actually represent about the education of those young people? What does it certify that they are skilled enough to do, that they are learned enough to understand? In theory, a high school diploma indicates that certain basic skills have been attained. In reality, however, the only thing we know for sure about a person who graduated from high school is that they that completed four years of high school. Even a student who has met state requirements for graduation may have met very different requirements from a student with the same amount of schooling from another state.

Assessment of student success varies dramatically from state to state, district to district, school to school, and even teacher to teacher. Some schools do not even have a common standard for what a passing grade is. Teacher A might consider 55% a D. Teacher B might consider 55% an F. One student with a 55% passes the class, even if just barely. Another does not. Standardization is necessary in that school. But it's easier to manage at a school level than on a national level. We are not willing to put the kind of time and money into standardization that it would take for schools to even educate their faculty about common grading rubrics (even schools that have such rubrics often have no "grade norming" in which teachers undergo professional development training to ensure that they are applying the rubric in similar ways). If we are not willing to fund more professional development for teachers to do something on as small of a scale as their own school, what on earth would demonstrate that we are willing to fund the development of a national standardized test?

While a national standardized test might seem like an obvious solution to ensure that students across the country demonstrate the same knowledge, the actual implementation of such testing would further shift the focus of education toward quantifiable outcomes. The consequence of this is turning students into information regurgitators rather than scholars. The purpose of public education is not just to prepare students for the workforce, but also to prepare them to become responsible citizens.

Completion of high school as a rite of passage is so culturally ingrained that students, and their families, expect that any student who put in their time should be prepared for the world. If a student puts four years into high school and still cannot pass a standardized test, has the student failed or has the system failed? I'm not suggesting we just ignore any possibility of standards in favor of allowing students to bide their time until graduation. I am, however, suggesting that smaller educational communities struggle enough with figuring out how to help students learn; adding to the burdens of overburdened, underfunded schools would mean even fewer graduations for those schools. This would affect already-disadvantaged communities more than it would affect privileged communities. The de facto national exams that exist—the SAT and ACT—are already more accessible to students from better resourced schools, both logistically and in terms of test content. Implementing a standardized national high school exit exam would duplicate this unfairness.

Without standardization, assessment is something of a wildcard. With it, schools become beuracracies in which teachers must focus on delivering measurable results rather than helping young people learn.

APPLYING THE RUBRIC

Argument	5
Support	6
Structure	5
Fluency	5
Conventions	5
Total	26

The average is 5.2, rounded down to a likely score of 5.

ARGUMENT The essay presents a clear and thoughtful argument that the implementation of the proposed policy will negatively change the focus of teaching and present an unfair burden to some schools.

SUPPORT The essay includes concrete examples of how implementing a standardized national high school exit exam will change what schools teach and present a special burden to some schools.

STRUCTURE The essay is generally well focused and organized, though the discussion of the lack of will to fund the teacher training needed to implement standardization at a national level is less clearly a description of the writer's views on the policy than it is an indictment of the likelihood of its being adopted. Transitions between ideas are logical.

FLUENCY The ideas in the essay are clear, and its vocabulary use is appropriate and effective. Sentence structure is varied.

CONVENTIONS The essay demonstrates solid command of the grammar, usage, and mechanics of standard written English, despite the presence of a few minor errors that do not obscure meaning.

SCORE 4 ISSUE ESSAY

It is no secret in America that we have an education crisis. Our students no longer rank at the top of the charts in terms of meeting standardized educational goals. Other countries have surpassed us and now boast better education systems than the one here in the United States. While there are many solutions to this problem, including an increase in funding and a national standard of higher compensation for teachers, this essay will focus on one possible solution. By requiring public secondary school students to pass a standardized national exit exam in order to receive a high school diploma, schools can set an achievable standard that can help return America to the top of the educational charts.

Though they are controversial, there is great need to create a national standard that will strengthen our national education system. Limiting the curriculum a teacher can present may be a good thing. Too often teachers complain about the heavy amount of preparation time that is needed for them to do their jobs. Moving to a strict and standardized testing system could help alleviate this stress. Though the tests do teach a narrow set of skills, they do not have to focus on rote memorization. Many exams also require a critical thinking or analytical section that is not about memorization of facts. A standardized testing still allows students to take elective courses which supplement their test preparation. While these exams can create anxiety, it can also open the door to a conversation about how to manage the this stress and prepare them for the real world. This creates a learning experience that would not otherwise happen. Setting achievable goals is an important part of passage from being a high school student into adult life.

It is clear that the debate about standardized tests will continue. They can be used to determine a standard of education that must be achieved in order to continue with education or enter the workplace. The set of skills taught can be wide and varied, and do not have to exclude other forms of creative education. Finally, since standardized tests are often the metric of entrance into higher education, this type of testing creates an opportunity for learning good test taking skills early on in one's educational career, which is a skill that cannot be underestimated.

APPLYING THE RUBRIC	
Argument	4
Support	4
Structure	4
Fluency	4
Conventions	4
Total	20

The average is 4.

ARGUMENT The essay presents a clear argument that adequately responds to the task instructions. In answering common fears about standardized testing, it describes ways in which these concerns could be worked around. The argument would be stronger, however, if it examined the likelihood of these scenarios.

SUPPORT The essay includes adequate reasoning and some specific descriptions of how a number of the feared consequences of a standardized national exit exam could be avoided.

STRUCTURE The essay is reasonably well focused and organized, though the introduction is a bit misleading. It focuses more on the need for improved education than it does on the ultimate subject of the essay, the possibility of avoiding some of the negative consequences of standardized testing.

FLUENCY The ideas in the essay are clear, and its vocabulary use is generally appropriate.

CONVENTIONS The essay demonstrates adequate command of the grammar, usage, and mechanics of standard written English. There are a few minor errors, but not enough to obscure meaning.

PROMPT #2

The following appeared in a letter to the editor in the journal *Health Matters*.

"Statistics gathered over the past three decades show that the death rate is higher among those who do not have jobs than among those with regular employment. Unemployment, just like heart disease and cancer, is a significant health issue. While many health care advocates promote increased government funding for medical research and public health care, it would be folly to increase government spending if doing so were to affect the nation's economy adversely and ultimately cause a rise in unemployment. A healthy economy means healthy citizens. Reining in government spending is, therefore, the best medicine."

Compose an essay that identifies the questions that must be answered before deciding whether the conclusion and the argument supporting it make sense. In writing your essay you should describe the impact that the answers to these questions would have on your assessment of the conclusion.

SCORE 6 ARGUMENT ESSAY

According to a letter to the editor of *Health Matters*, three decades of research shows that people without jobs have a higher death rate than those who work. Thus, argues the writer, any public policy that increases spending on healthcare and medical research is misguided if that spending would destabilize the economy and thereby increase unemployment. The writer concludes, therefore, that decreased government spending will create a healthier population. This conclusion seems, on its face, both simplistic and unlikely. To test it, there are two questions that must be answered.

The first and most fundamental question raised by the letter's conclusion is whether unemployment does, in fact, cause death. Correlation is not causation. In other words, the fact that two conditions exist in proximity to one another does not mean one is the cause of the other. Higher mortality among people without jobs does not necessarily mean that unemployment causes higher mortality. For one thing, the writer does not specify whether people without regular employment are the same as "unemployed" people. Elderly people do not have regular employment because they are retired, and they have a high mortality rate because they are elderly. Their lack of employment does not cause their high mortality rate. The same is true of people who suffer from serious illnesses like cancer and heart disease. They lack regular employment because they are sick, and they suffer from high mortality for the same reason. The correlation between lack of regular employment and high mortality does not prove that the former causes the latter.

The second question that must be answered in order to evaluate the claim that reducing government spending saves lives is whether that spending would be great enough to cause harm to the economy. The writer makes this broad claim about government spending in the context of spending on healthcare and medical research, thus the question is properly whether this spending in particular would harm the economy. There are several reasons to think that it would not. First, government spending on healthcare keeps people in good health so that they can work. Without that spending more people will be too ill to work, and they, as a result, depend on government programs for their support. In this way, government spending on healthcare may strengthen the economy and, in the long run, reduce or stabilize government spending overall.

An additional way in which government spending on healthcare and medical research may strengthen the economy is by providing jobs. When the government funds healthcare and research, it doesn't just pour money into a hole to nowhere. Those monies enter the economy as wages for doctors, nurses, and researchers. They pay construction workers who build hospitals, custodians, and cafeteria workers. This in turn increases overall employment, raising revenue from income taxes and decreasing spending on social welfare programs. There are logical reasons to conclude that government spending on healthcare and medical research would strengthen the economy, while the claim that it would harm the economy is an unwarranted assertion.

"Reining in government spending" sounds like an admirable goal. Curtailing financial crisis through fiscal responsibility is, by definition, a good idea. But the claim that increased government spending on healthcare and medical research will have the paradoxical effect of increasing the death rate is supported by neither evidence nor reasoning.

APPLYING THE RUBRIC

Argument	6
Support	6
Structure	6
Fluency	5
Conventions	6
Total	29

The average is 5.8, rounded up to a likely score of 6.

ARGUMENT The essay successfully identifies two questions that must be answered in order to evaluate the argument presented. The essay explicitly and thoroughly answers these questions, providing well-reasoned explanations that support the essay's thesis on the relationship between government health spending and mortality rates.

SUPPORT The essay provides detailed and persuasive support for its main points, in one case describing how the argument's author has likely confused correlation for causation, and in the other case outlining theories for how government health spending might logically strengthen, rather than weaken, the economy.

STRUCTURE The essay is well organized, expressing its position clearly and in a logical progression. Transitions between the main ideas in the essay are clear, and the concluding paragraph summarizes the essay's argument well.

FLUENCY The essay expresses ideas effectively, with appropriate word choice and varied sentence structure.

CONVENTIONS The essay displays impressive command of the conventions of standard written English, with no noticeable errors in grammar, usage, or mechanics.

SCORE 5 ISSUE ESSAY

In this letter to the editor of *Health Matters*, there are many questions that stand to be answered and little to no proof to hold up its conclusion. There are three main assumptions underlying its conclusion that the government should not spend more money on healthcare: 1. unemployment causes death in citizens, 2. government spending is a problem that outweighs the benefits of government-funded medical research, and 3. government spending creates unemployment. No evidence exists to substantiate any of the claims made.

First and foremost is the question of whether unemployment causes death. It is important to remember correlation does not mean causation. In other words, just because two things might happen at the same time doesn't mean that one causes the other. In this instance, the author clearly thinks that unemployment causes an earlier death, but doesn't think that they are merely correlated. But there are many other reasons for the correlation between unemployment and death. If an individual is unemployed, chances are their stress levels are higher. Furthermore, there might be a reason they don't have a job. For example, they could be sick and that sickness might be the reason they both don't have a job and they die earlier. In another instance, they could have a substance use disorder that would prevent them from being a productive worker without receiving help first.

The second assumption is that government spending is a problem that outweighs the government funding medical research. But does it? I think not. For example, the US government funds over 90% of the world's research on substance use disorders through NIDA (National Institute on Drug Abuse). Without the government, a lot of major medical breakthroughs wouldn't happen because there is no way at this point in time that the private sector would pitch in enough to fund as many innovations as the government helps create.

The final question is whether government spending on medical research causes unemployment. Once again, no data is provided for this. No economic theory is stated or quantitative data is presented to solidify this claim. Based on history, I would think that government spending actually creates jobs. During World War II, the American economy was booming and the government was spending lots of money on the war effort.

In sum, there are many assumptions made in this letter to the editor, with very limited evidence offered in support. A little data would go a long way toward supporting the author's case. Without it, the argument has no merit.

APPLYING THE RUBRIC

Argument	5
Support	5
Structure	5
Fluency	4
Conventions	5
Total	24

The average is 4.8, rounded up to a likely score of 5.

ARGUMENT The essay successfully pinpoints and responds thoughtfully to three questions that must be answered in order to assess the conclusion that government health spending is counterproductive.

SUPPORT The essay provides thoughtful and reasonably persuasive support for its main points. It is strong in its discussion of alternate causality, but weaker in its use of World War II as proof that government spending strengthens the economy (the scale of spending in these two instances does not seem comparable).

STRUCTURE The essay is well organized, with suitable (though not always smooth) transitions between ideas.

FLUENCY The essay generally uses vocabulary effectively to express its ideas, though it reads awkwardly in places.

CONVENTIONS The essay displays solid command of the conventions of standard written English.

SCORE 4 ARGUMENT ESSAY

There is no way to accept at face value the letter to the editor in *Health Matters*. The author of the letter makes several logical leaps that require further examination. While the analogy of the healthy economy draws up images of prosperity for everyone, the conclusions this author makes are fundamentally flawed.

There are any number of reasons for the correlation between death rate and employment; this author examines none of them. To accept this premise I would need to know if "regular employment" included retired people, older people, veterans or others on permanent disability, and children. Unless the statistical data of death rate was limited to eligible workers of working age, then the statistics presented are skewed in favor of the author's ultimate point. They use this shocking claim to draw in the reader and the analogy of health to appeal to the broadest set of people. Health is not a politicized issue; everyone, conceivably, wants to be healthy. However, this analogy is still just an assertion used to support an argument for reducing government spending.

To create a healthy society and cure diseases like cancer, heart disease, and, per the author, unemployment, government spending will likely have to increase. Another question I would need to answer to evaluate the conclusion is where the author thinks money to combat unemployment is going to come from. Other than a thinly veiled jab at healthcare professionals for seeking increased funding, the author has no identifiable solution. I would also need to know whether healthcare spending was going to "affect the nation's economy adversely" and lead to the spike in unemployment promised by the author. It would seem likely that more funding for "medical research and public health care" would create more jobs rather than less of them.

Ultimately, this author uses their health metaphor to assert that "Reining in government spending is . . . the best medicine." This health metaphor has come full circle; earlier in the letter, the author argues that increased spending for medical research would lead to a rise in unemployment, but has no problem touting his solution as the best medicine.

APPLYING THE RUBRIC

Argument	4
Support	4
Structure	4
Fluency	4
Conventions	4
Total	20

The average is 4.

ARGUMENT The essay identifies and responds to questions that must be answered in order to evaluate the argument presented. The essay's discussion of the argument's use of health as a metaphor is, however, somewhat tangential to the task at hand.

SUPPORT The essay provides sufficient support for its main points, though it does a better job of identifying where the argument provided lacks support than it does in offering counterexamples or reasoning.

STRUCTURE The essay expresses its ideas reasonably clearly, and but could benefit from more graceful transitions. The internal organization of the second and third paragraph, could be stronger.

FLUENCY The essay generally uses vocabulary appropriately to express its ideas.

CONVENTIONS The essay generally displays command of the conventions of standard written English, despite the presence of a few minor errors that do not interfere with meaning.

Section 2—Verbal Reasoning

1. **(D, E)** Note the two key phrases "Given the human tendency to suspect and disbelieve in" and "it is unsurprising that." People who view the unconscious with suspicion or disbelieve in it are as a consequence likely to *deny* or *gainsay* (contradict) its effect on human interactions.
2. **(B, E)** In contrast to his reputation, the author is not markedly taciturn (uncommunicative; disinclined to talk). In fact, he seems inclined to talk. In other words, he is not at all *averse from* or *opposed to* conversation.
3. **(A, C)** To call a country "the land of the free" while allowing the institution of slavery to exist struck Mrs. Trollope as evidence of *hypocrisy* or *sanctimoniousness* (the act of making a false display of righteousness or piety).
4. **(B, D)** The key word here is "passionate." Paul finds himself attracted to a woman who is *ardent* (fervent; keen) and *wholehearted* (fully enthusiastic) about her likes and dislikes.

5. **(C, E)** Soap operas and situation comedies are derivative of contemporary culture: they take their elements from that culture. Therefore, they serve as *evidence* or *indices* (signs, indications) of what is going on in that culture; they both point to and point up the social attitudes and values they portray.

   Note that the soap operas and comedies here cannot be *determinants* of our society's attitudes and values: they derive from these attitudes and values; they do not determine them.

6. **(D, E)** Whatever word or phrase you choose here must apply equally well both to slander and to counterfeit money. People who would not make up a slanderous statement *circulate* or *spread* slander by passing it on. So too people who would not coin or make counterfeit money *circulate* or *spread around* counterfeit money by passing it on.

   Note how the extended metaphor here influences the writer's choice of words.

7. **(D)** The author cites Meredith's intelligence (*brilliance*) and his splendor of language (*linguistic grandeur*).

8. **(E)** Rather than refuting the claim, the author clearly acknowledges Meredith's inability to evoke the reader's sympathy.

   Choice A is incorrect. From the start the author points out how Meredith leaves readers cold.

   Choice B is incorrect. The author reiterates Meredith's virtues, citing muscular intelligence and literary merit.

   Choice C is incorrect. The author quotes several such imagined criticisms.

   Choice D is incorrect. The author indicates that if readers choose to avoid dealing with Meredith they shall be doing a disservice to the cause of criticism.

   Only Choice E remains. It is the correct answer.

9. **(E)** Speaking of the "challenge and excitement of the critical problem as such," the author clearly finds the prospect of appraising Meredith critically to be stirring and *invigorating*.

10. **(C)** The author wishes us to be able to recognize the good qualities of Meredith's work while at the same time we continue to find it personally unsympathetic. Thus, she would agree that criticism should enable us to appreciate the virtues of works we dislike.

    Choices A, B, and E are unsupported by the passage.

    Choice D is incorrect. While the author wishes the reader to be aware of Meredith's excellences, she does not suggest that the reader should ignore those qualities in Meredith that make his work unsympathetic. Rather, she wishes the reader to come to appreciate the very ambivalence of his critical response.

11. **(A, E)** The off-Broadway and Broadway theatres are contrasted here. The former has *manifested* or shown a talent for improvisation, extemporaneous or spontaneous performance. The latter has manifested no such talent for *spontaneity*.

    Note the use of *whereas* to establish the contrast.

12. **(C, D)** People had complimented her for her *fluency* or eloquence; it was therefore surprising that she proved *inarticulate* or tongue-tied at her inauguration.

    Note the use of *although* and *surprisingly* to signal the contrast.

13. **(B, F)** The filmmakers wish neither to *reject* nor to *vitiate* (impair; weaken) a strong sense of place. Instead, they take pains to *impart* (communicate; convey) a strong sense of the places they film as well as of the characters they film. Thus, their films become portraits of the *spaces* their characters *inhabit*.

14. **(B, D)** The key phrase here is "they remained the dominant viol size." The text is discussing changes over time in the popularity of different sizes of bass viols. Before 1600, larger consort bass viols were in fashion. After 1600, the larger consort bass viols were *displaced* by the smaller division viols. The division viols continued to be popular until some time in the 1700s, when they *went out of fashion.*

15. **(A, E, G)** Particles have no need to be wound up because the property of spinning (*rotation*) is built into their makeup: it is *intrinsic.* That is the significant *difference* between the spinning of particles and the spinning of tops.

16. **(C)** To the author the concept is both simple and traditional, dating as it does from Newton's time.

17. **(A, C)** Question A is answerable on the basis of the passage. As the area's density increases, its gravitational field increases in strength. Likewise, Question C is answerable on the basis of the passage. The end result of the process is the formation of a gravitationally bound object, a newborn star. Remember, you must have selected *both* A and C to receive credit for this question.

    Question B is not answerable on the basis of the passage. The passage nowhere states what disturbs the gas.

18. **(E)** The passage compares the Quechua empire to a *mandala* because "it was divided into four parts." Thus, a *mandala* is most likely a "figure composed of four divisions."

19. **(B)** The author refers to the Quechua as existing in "a state of unremitting anxiety, which could not be resolved by action" and which the Quechua could only deal with by looking into himself and struggling with the depths of his own psyche. This suggests that the Quechua world was *highly introspective.*

20. **(D)** Both the unremitting anxiety of Quechua life and the recurring harvest failures that brought starvation to millions illustrate the *harshness and frustration* of Quechua existence.

Section 3—Quantitative Ability

Two asterisks (**) indicate an alternative method of solving.

1. **(D)** Use TACTIC 4, Chapter 10 (page 294). Could m and n be equal? Sure, if each is 5. Eliminate Choices A and B. Must they be equal? No, not if $m = 1$ and $n = 25$. Eliminate Choice C, as well. Neither quantity is always greater, and the two quantities are not always equal (D).

2. **(D)** Since $\frac{2}{3} = 66\frac{2}{3}\%$, which is clearly more than 65%, it *appears* that Quantity B is greater. *Be careful!* That would be true if a were positive, but no restrictions are placed on a. If $a = 0$, the columns are equal; if a is negative, Quantity A is greater. Neither quantity is always greater, and the two quantities are not always equal (D).

    **Use TACTIC 1, Chapter 10 (page 285). Just let $a = 0$, and then let $a = 1$.

3. **(D)** Use TACTIC 4, Chapter 10 (page 294). Could the quantities be equal? Could $c = 5$? Sure, if this is a 3-4-5 right triangle. Must $c = 5$? No; if the triangle is not a right triangle, c could be less than or more than 5.

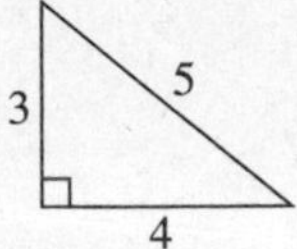

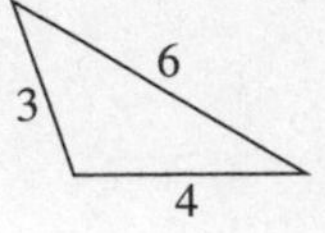

Neither quantity is *always* greater, and the quantities are not *always* equal (D). (*Note*: Since the figure may not be drawn to scale, do *not* assume that the triangle has a right angle.)

4. **(B)** You don't *have* to solve for a and b. If $a - b > a + b$, then $-b > b$, and so b is negative and Quantity B is greater.
   **You *could* solve. Adding the two equations yields $2a = 49 \Rightarrow a = 24.5 \Rightarrow b = -0.5$.

5. **(A)** Since in the given figure OA and OB are radii, each is equal to 5. With no restrictions on x, AB could be any positive number less than 10; and the larger x is, the larger AB is. If x were 90, AB would be $5\sqrt{2}$, but we are told that $x > 90$, so $AB > 5\sqrt{2} > 7$.

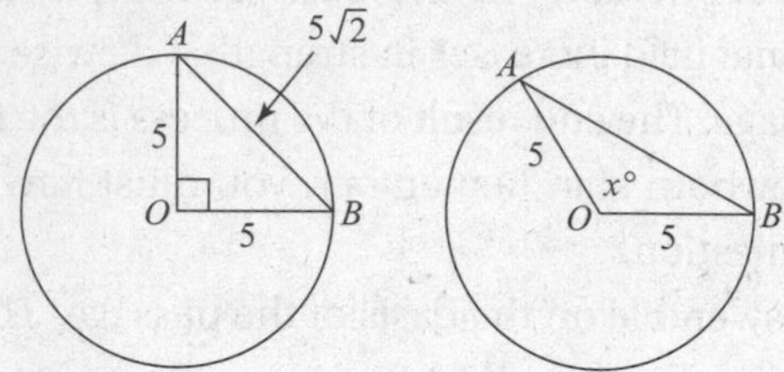

6. **(C)** The distribution consists of 20 numbers: four 1's, five 2's, two 3's, three 4's, and six 5's:

   1, 1, 1, 1, 2, 2, 2, 2, 2, 3, 3, 4, 4, 4, 5, 5, 5, 5, 5, 5

   - The median is the average of the two middle numbers, which are both 3, so the median is 3.
   - The mode is 5, since there are more 5's than any other number.
   - So the quantity in Column A is 4, the average of 3 and 5.
   - Since the range of a set of data is the difference between the largest and smallest values, the range is $5 - 1 = 4$.
   - So, the quantity in Column B is also 4.
   - The quantities are equal.

7. **(B)** Do not waste any time evaluating the two standard deviations. We don't need the values of the two quantities, we only need to know which quantity is greater. The standard deviation is a measure of how far, on average, the pieces of data are from the mean. The closer the data are to the mean, the smaller the standard deviation; the farther the data are from the mean, the greater the standard deviation. In List 1, the mean is 75, and the five data points are 50, 25, 0, 25, and 50, respectively, away from the mean. In List 2, the mean is 150, and the five data points are 100, 50, 0, 50, and 100, respectively, away from the mean. The data in List 2 are farther from its mean than the data in List 1 are from its mean, so the standard deviation of List 2 is greater.

8. **(C)** If there are x seats on each bus, then the group is using $\frac{4}{5}(3x) = \frac{12}{5}x$ seats. After $\frac{1}{4}$ of them get off, $\frac{3}{4}$ of them, or $\frac{3}{4}\left(\frac{12}{5}x\right) = \frac{9}{5}x$ remain.

What fraction of the $2x$ seats on the two buses are now being used?

$$\frac{\frac{9}{5}x}{2x} = \frac{\frac{9}{5}}{2} = \frac{9}{10}.$$

**To avoid the algebra, use TACTIC 2 in Chapter 10 (page 290): choose appropriate numbers. Assume there are 20 seats on each bus. At the beginning, the group is using 48 of the 60 seats on the three buses. When 12 people left, the 36 remaining people used $\frac{36}{40} = \frac{9}{10}$ of the 40 seats on two buses.

9. **(B)** Since d divisions each have t teams, multiply to get dt teams; and since each team has p players, multiply the number of teams (dt) by p to get the total number of players: dtp.

**Use TACTIC 2, Chapter 9 (page 270). Pick three easy-to-use numbers for t, d, and p. Assume that there are 2 divisions, each consisting of 4 teams, so, there are $2 \times 4 = 8$ teams. Then assume that each team has 10 players, for a total of $8 \times 10 = 80$ players. Now check the choices. Which one is equal to 80 when $d = 2$, $t = 4$, and $p = 10$? Only dtp.

10. **(C)** Since, in 1990, $2p$ pounds of potatoes cost $\frac{1}{2}d$ dollars, p pounds cost half as much: $\frac{1}{2}\left(\frac{1}{2}d\right) = \frac{1}{4}d$. This is $\frac{1}{4}$, or 25%, as much as the cost in 1980, which represents a decrease of 75%.

**In this type of problem it is *often* easier to use TACTIC 2, Chapter 9 (page 270): replace the variables with numbers. Assume that 1 pound of potatoes cost \$100 in 1980. Then in 1990, 2 pounds cost \$50, so 1 pound cost \$25. This is a decrease of \$75 in the cost of 1 pound of potatoes, and

$$\% \text{ decrease} = \frac{\text{actual decrease}}{\text{original amount}} \times 100\% = \frac{75}{100} \times 100\% = 75\%$$

11. $\mathbf{\frac{2}{9}}$ There are nine positive integers less than 10: 1, 2, ... , 9. For which of them is $\frac{9}{x} > x$?

Only 1 and 2: $\frac{9}{1} > 1$ and $\frac{9}{2} > 2$. When $x = 3$, $\frac{9}{x} = x$, and for all the others $\frac{9}{x} < x$.

The probability is $\frac{2}{9}$.

12. **(D)** If Jason were really unlucky, what could go wrong in his attempt to get one marble of each color? Well, his first nine picks *might* yield five blue marbles and four white ones. But then the tenth marble would be red, and now he would have at least one of each color. The answer is 10.

13. **94** If a represents Jordan's average after 5 tests, then he has earned a total of $5a$ points (see TACTIC E1, page 397). A grade of 70 on the sixth test will lower his average 4 points to $a - 4$. Therefore,

$$a - 4 = \frac{5a + 70}{6} \Rightarrow 6(a - 4) = 5a + 70 \Rightarrow 6a - 24 = 5a + 70 \Rightarrow 6a = 5a + 94 \Rightarrow a = 94$$

**Assume Jordan's average is *a* because he earned *a* on each of his first 5 tests. Since after getting a 70 on his sixth test his average will be $a - 4$, the deviation on each of the first 5 tests is 4, for a total deviation above the average of 20 points. So, the total deviation below must also be 20 [KEY FACT E3, page 399]. Therefore, 70 is 20 less than the new average of $a - 4$:

$$70 = (a - 4) - 20 \Rightarrow a = 94$$

**Use TACTIC 1, Chapter 9 (page 268): backsolve. Start with Choice C, 86. If his 5-test average was 90, he had 450 points and a 70 on the sixth test would give him a total of 520 points, and an average of $520 \div 6 = 86.666$. So, the 70 lowered his average 3.333 points. That's not enough. Eliminate Choices A, B, and C. Try Choices D or E. Choice E, 94, works.

14. **(A, B, C, D)**

(A) In 1991, more than 50% of the adults whose highest degree was at least a bachelor's degree participated in adult education, whereas those whose highest educational attainment was a high school diploma or GED (high school equivalency diploma) fewer than 25% participated. (A is true.)

(B) From 1991 to 1995, among those adults whose highest educational attainment was grades 9–12, without earning a high school diploma, the rate of participation in adult education increased from about 15% to 23%, an increase of about 50%. None of the other groups had nearly that great an increase. (B is true.)

(C) Since the population of the country grew between 1991 and 1995, and the rate of participation in adult education programs increased in every category, the total number of people participating had to increase. (C is true.)

(D) From 1991 to 1995 the rate of participation in adult education for those who had attained at least a bachelor's degree increased from about 52% to 58%, the least increase of any group on both an absolute and percent basis. (D is true.)

(E) Without knowing how many adults have earned a college degree and how many have attended some college without earning a college degree, it is impossible to make this conclusion. For example, 50% of 100,000,000 is much more than 58% of 50,000,000. (E is false.)

15. **(E)** 50% of 100,000,000 = 50,000,000; 20% of 40,000,000 = 8,000,000. 50,000,000:8,000,000 = 50:8 = 6.25:1, which is closest to choice E, 6:1.

16. **(49)** Assume that there were 1,000 adults in the workforce. Then 80 were unemployed and 920 were employed. Since 50% of the employed adults and 40% of the unemployed adults participated in adult education, the number of participants was 50% of 920 + 40% of 80 = 460 + 32 = 492.

So, the rate of participation was $\frac{492}{1{,}000} = \frac{49.2}{100} = 49.2\%$.

Rounded to the nearest whole percent, the answer is 49.

MODEL TEST 2

17. **(D)**

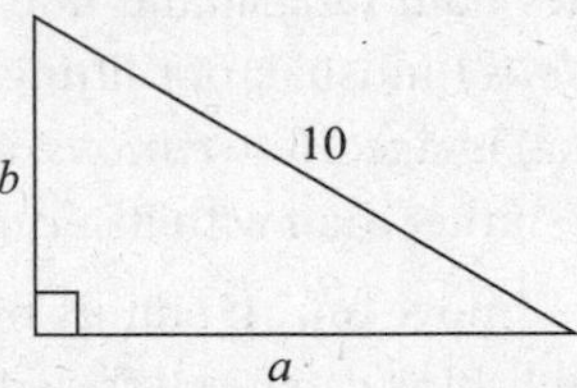

By the Pythagorean theorem,

$$a^2 + b^2 = 10^2 = 100$$

and since the area is 20, $\frac{1}{2}ab = 20 \Rightarrow ab = 40.$

Expand:

$$(a + b)^2 = a^2 + 2ab + b^2 = (a^2 + b^2) + 2ab$$

Then

$$(a^2 + b^2) + 2ab = 100 + 2(40) = 180$$

18. **(E)** To find the average of three numbers, divide their sum by 3: $\frac{3^{30} + 3^{60} + 3^{90}}{3}$.

Now use the distributive law (see KEY FACT A21, page 341) and divide each term in the numerator by 3: $\frac{3^{30}}{3} + \frac{3^{60}}{3} + \frac{3^{90}}{3} = 3^{29} + 3^{59} + 3^{89}$.

19. **(B)** Since the radii of the four small semicircles in the figure are 1, 2, 3, and 4, their diameters are 2, 4, 6, and 8; so the diameter of the large semicircle is $2 + 4 + 6 + 8 = 20$, and its radius is 10. The perimeter of the shaded region is the sum of the circumferences of all five semicircles. Since the circumference of a circle is πd or $2\pi r$, the circumference of a semicircle is πr, so the perimeter is $\pi + 2\pi + 3\pi + 4\pi + 10\pi = 20\pi$.

20. $\mathbf{\frac{3}{5}}$ $a + 25\%(a) = 1.25a$, and $b - 25\%(b) = 0.75b$.

So, $1.25a = .75b$, and $\frac{a}{b} = \frac{.75}{1.25} = \frac{3}{5}$

Section 4—Verbal Reasoning

1. **(C, D)** The key phrase here is "his extravagance and his free-spending lifestyle." *Ironically* is an implicit contrast signal: it indicates that you are looking for an antonym or near-antonym to *extravagance.* The mayor practices extravagance but preaches thrift, that is, *economy* (financial prudence) or *austerity* (strict economy; restraint).
2. **(A, D)** Working on commission, the portrait painter seeks proper *recompense* or *remuneration* (payment or reward for services) for undertaking the job.
3. **(B, F)** Stripped of descriptive phrases, the sentence simply states that jazz would *spawn* or *generate* (give rise to) an industry. Note that the verb *spawn* occurs here with a secondary meaning.
4. **(A, C)** Several clues suggest that this *brief* essay is an abridgment or synopsis of more extensive critiques ("arguments rehearsed in much more detail elsewhere"). Thus, it can be described as a *condensed* (shortened) or *synoptic* (concise; summary) version.

5. **(A, E)** If Mrs. Woolf combines both radical and non-radical elements in her fictions, then she presents *an anomalous* (unusual; not fitting into a common or familiar pattern) or *curious* (highly unusual) image. Here *curious* occurs with its secondary meaning (arousing interest or curiosity) rather than with its primary meaning (inquisitive).
6. **(C, D)** The key phrase here is "move on." If editors have to travel from firm to firm to succeed in their field, then publishing can be classified as an *itinerant* or *mobile* profession, a profession marked by traveling.
7. **(D)** Immediately before quoting Praz, the author states that the general view of Shelley depicts her as "a transparent medium through which passed the ideas of those around her." The quotation from Praz provides an excellent example of this particular point of view.

   To answer this question correctly, you do not need to read the passage in its entirety. Quickly scroll through the passage, scanning for the name Praz; read only the context in which it appears.
8. **(C)** The opening sentence points out that Shelley herself acknowledged the influence of her unplanned immersion in the scientific and literary revolutions of her time. Clearly, the author of the passage concedes this as true of Shelley.
9. **(B)** The concluding paragraph distinguishes Frankenstein from the other overreachers in his desire not to extend his own life but to impart life to another (by creating his monster). Thus, his purpose is *atypical* of the traditional overreacher.

   To say that someone *parts from* the traditional figure of the overreacher is to say that he *differs* from it. Thus, to answer this question quickly, scan the passage looking for *overreacher* and *different* (or their synonyms).
10. **(A)** Clearly religious ideas and concepts do not *obviate* (hinder), *preclude* (rule out), or *deny* the practice of medicine and delivery of health care. Neither do they *reiterate* (repeat) the practice of medicine. However, religious ideas and concepts do *inform* (pervade; permeate, with obvious effect) medical practices.
11. **(B, E)** The embittered benefactor thinks of them as *ingrates* (ungrateful persons) because they do not thank him sufficiently for his generosity. He does not think of them as *misers* (hoarders of wealth): although they are stingy in expressing thanks, they are extravagant in spending money, that is, being "wasteful of his largesse." He certainly does not think of them as *prigs* (self-righteous fuss-budgets): the specific attribute he resents in them is ingratitude, not self-righteousness, or exaggerated propriety.
12. **(B, D)** The physicists have had good reason to believe in the principle because it has *survived* rigorous or strict tests. These tests have *established* (proved) that the principle is accurate.

    Note how the second clause supports the first, explaining why the physicists have had reason to be confident in the principle.
13. **(A, D)** The actress had *a knack* or talent for getting people to do things for her and was delighted that her new friends were *assiduous* (diligent) in finding new ways to meet her needs.

    Note that it is useful to focus first on the second blank as you answer this question. The key phrase here is "to her delight." The actress would have no particular cause for delight if her new friends proved *dilatory* (tardy; slow) or *stoical* (impassive; unemotional) in finding new ways to meet her needs.

14. **(B, F)** The presence of inconsistencies (discrepancies; contradictions) in someone's story would *warrant* (justify) some incredulity (disbelief) on anyone's part. Even someone who was not a *skeptic* (person who maintains a doubting attitude) would be justified in doubting such a tale.

15. **(D)** The author takes the reader through Wegener's reasoning step by step, describing what led Wegener to reach his conclusions.

16. **(A)** Since the existence of the correspondences between the various coastal contours was used by Wegener as a basis for formulating his theory of continental drift, it can be inferred that the correspondences provide evidence for the theory.

    Choice B is incorrect. The passage does not indicate that Pangaea's existence has been proved.

    Choice C is incorrect. It is the relative heaviness of sima, not the level or depth of sima, that suggested the possibility of the lighter continents drifting.

    Choice D is incorrect. Mobility rather than immobility would provide evidence for continental drift.

    Choice E is incorrect. The continents are lighter than the underlying sima.

17. **(D)** Choice D is answerable on the basis of the passage. The next-to-the-last sentence of the second paragraph states that the Americas "apparently drifted toward the west."

18. **(D)** Houston believed that the battle had to begin at the graduate level "to mitigate fear" (relieve *apprehension*) of race-mixing and miscegenation that might otherwise have caused the judges to rule against the NAACP-sponsored complaints.

19. **(B)** The separate-but-equal doctrine established by *Plessy* v. *Ferguson* allows the existence of racially segregated schools.

20. **(A)** In assessing the possible effects on judges of race-mixing in the lower grades, Houston was *psychologically canny,* shrewd in seeing potential dangers and in figuring strategies to avoid these dangers.

Section 5—Quantitative Ability

Two asterisks (**) indicate an alternative method of solving.

1. **(A)** By KEY FACT A5 (page 330), the product of 8 negative numbers is positive and the product of 9 negative numbers is negative. Therefore, Quantity A is positive and Quantity B is negative. So, Quantity A is greater.

2. **(C)**

   Quantity A: Since $(a^9)(a^9) = (a^{18})$, and since $a > 0$, $\sqrt{a^{18}} = a^9$.

   Quantity B: $(a^2)(a^3)(a^4) = a^{2+3+4} = a^9$.

   The quantities are equal.

3. **(B)** Assume that the price of a small pizza is \$10; then the price of a large pizza is \$10 + 0.30(\$10) = \$10 + \$3 = \$13.

   On sale at 30% off, a large pizza costs 30% less than \$13.

   $$\$13 - 0.30(\$13) = \$13 - \$3.90 = \$9.10$$

   So, Quantity B is \$10 and Quantity A is \$9.10.

4. **(A)** There is not enough information provided to determine the values of *a, b, c, d, e, f,* and *g,* but they are irrelevant. By the note following KEY FACT L7 (page 491), the sum of

MODEL TEST 2

the measures of the seven angles is 360°, and so their average is $360° \div 7 \approx 51.4°$. Quantity A is greater.

5. **(C)** There are 9 ways to choose the first digit of a 5-digit palindrome (any of the digits from 1 to 9); there are 10 ways to choose the second digit and 10 ways to choose the third digit (any of the digits from 0 to 9). Since the fourth digit must be the same as the second digit, there is only 1 way to choose it. Finally, the fifth digit must be the same as the first digit, so again, there is only 1 choice.

   Therefore, the number of 5-digit palindromes is $9 \times 10 \times 10 \times 1 \times 1 = 900$. In exactly the same way, the number of 6-digit palindromes is $9 \times 10 \times 10 \times 1 \times 1 \times 1 = 900$.

   The quantities are equal.

   **There is a 1-1 correspondence between the set of 5-digit palindromes and the set of 6-digit palindromes: *abcba* corresponds to *abccba*. So the two sets have the same number of members.

6. **(B)**

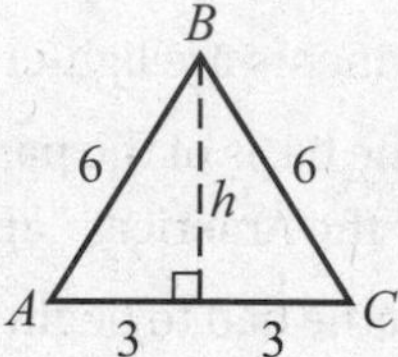

Quantity A: If h is the height of equilateral triangle ABC, then by the Pythagorean theorem $3^2 + h^2 = 6^2 \Rightarrow h^2 = 27 \Rightarrow h = 3\sqrt{3}$. So the area of triangle ABC is

$$A = \frac{1}{2}bh = \frac{1}{2}(6)(3\sqrt{3}) = 9\sqrt{3} \approx 15.59$$

Alternatively, if you know the special formula for the area of an equilateral triangle (KEY FACT J15, page 466), you don't have to find h:

$$A = \frac{6^2\sqrt{3}}{4} = \frac{36\sqrt{3}}{4} = 9\sqrt{3} \approx 15.59$$

Quantity B:

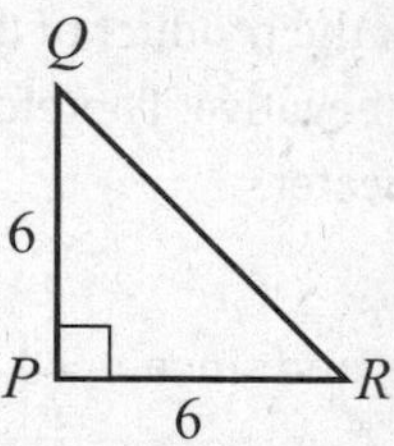

The area of isosceles triangle PQR is $\frac{1}{2}(6)(6) = 18$.

7. **(A)** The simplest solution is to notice that if a 1 is chosen first, of the remaining three slips, two of them have –1 on them and one of them has 1 on it. So there are 2 chances in 3 that the second number will be –1 and the product will be –1. Similarly, if a –1 is chosen first, there are 2 chances in 3 that the second number will be 1 and, again, the product will be –1.

   Quantity A is $\frac{2}{3}$ and Quantity B is $\frac{1}{3}$.

**Given 4 numbers a, b, c, and d, there are 6 possible products: ab, ac, ad, bc, bd, and cd. If $a = b = 1$ and $c = d = -1$, then 4 of these products equal -1 and two of them equal 1.

So Quantity A is $\frac{4}{6} = \frac{2}{3}$ and Quantity B is $\frac{2}{6} = \frac{1}{3}$.

8. **(D)** Since 8% of 100 is 8, John saved \$8, and thus paid \$92 for the DVD player. He then had to pay 8% sales tax on the \$92: $0.08 \times 92 = 7.36$, so the total cost was \$92 + \$7.36 = \$99.36.

9. **(A)**

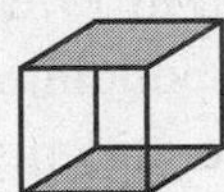

A cube has 12 edges. (In the diagram, each shaded square base has 4 edges, and there are 4 edges connecting the two bases.) So if e represents the length of each edge, we have that $12e = 3 \Rightarrow e = \frac{1}{4}$. Since by KEY FACT M1 (page 500) $V = e^3$, we have

$$V = \left(\frac{1}{4}\right)^3 = \frac{1}{64} \text{ cubic feet}$$

10. **52** How many pages did Mary read in 30 minutes? Since Mary started on page 10, she read the first 24 pages, except pages 1–9: She read $24 - 9 = 15$ pages. So she read at the rate of 15 pages every 30 minutes, or 1 page every 2 minutes. Similarly, if Mary reads pages 25 through 50, she will read $50 - 24 = 26$ pages. At the rate of 1 page every 2 minutes it will take her 52 minutes to read 26 pages.

11. **(D)**
   - If $(m-5)(m-45)$ is positive, either both factors are positive or both factors are negative.
   - If both factors are negative, m must be less than 5, so m could be 1, 2, 3, or 4 (4 values).
   - If both factors are positive, m must be greater than 45, so m could be 46, 47, ..., 100 (55 values).
   - The answer is $4 + 55 = 59$.

12. **(A)** Since the diameters of the two mosaics are 30 and 20, the radii are 15 and 10, respectively. So the area of the larger mosaic is $\pi(15)^2 = 225\pi$, whereas the area of the smaller mosaic is $\pi(10)^2 = 100\pi$. So the area of the larger mosaic is 2.25 times the area of the smaller mosaic, and hence will require 2.25 times as many tiles.
**The ratio of the diameters is $\frac{30}{20} = \frac{3}{2}$. So the ratio of the area is $\left(\frac{3}{2}\right)^2 = \frac{9}{4} = 2.25$.

13. **(B, C, D)** Let S = the number of students at Central High School that year.
If 70% of the students attended the rally, then $0.70S = 1{,}435$, and so $S = 1{,}435 \div 0.70 = 2{,}050$.
If 85% of the students attended the rally, then $0.85S = 1{,}435$, and so $S = 1{,}435 \div 0.85 = 1{,}688$.
So, S must satisfy the inequality $1{,}688 < S < 2{,}050$.
Only Choices B, C, and D are in this range.

14. **800,000** From the top graph, we see that in 1975, 54% (35% + 19%) of all college students were male, and the other 46% were female. So there were 5,400,000 males and 4,600,000 females—a difference of 800,000.

15. **(B)** In 1975, of every 100 college students, 46 were female—32 of whom were less than 25 years old, and 14 of whom were 25 years old and over. So, 14 of every 46 female students were at least 25 years old. Finally, $\frac{14}{46} = .30 = 30\%$.

16. **(C)** From the two graphs, we see that in 1975 54% (35% + 19%) of all college students were male, whereas in 1995 the corresponding figure was 45% (28% + 17%). For simplicity, assume that there were 100 college students in 1975, 54 of whom were male. Then in 1995, there were 140 college students, 63 of whom were male (45% of 140 = 63). So the ratio of the number of male students in 1995 to the number of male students in 1975 is 63:54 = 7:6.

17. **66** Let x represent the number of envelopes Eric can address in 99 minutes and set up a proportion:

$$\frac{40 \text{ envelopes}}{1 \text{ hour}} = \frac{40 \text{ envelopes}}{60 \text{ minutes}} = \frac{2 \text{ envelopes}}{3 \text{ minutes}} = \frac{x \text{ envelopes}}{99 \text{ minutes}} \Rightarrow$$

$$2 \times 99 = 3x \Rightarrow 198 = 3x \Rightarrow x = 66$$

18. **(A, C, D, E, F)** Start with the least expensive option: 2 regular slices and 2 small sodas.
    - This option costs $5.00. (A is true.)
    - Changing anything would add at least 50 cents to the cost so $5.25 is *not* possible. (B is false.)
    - Increasing two items by 50 cents each—say, buying 2 medium sodas instead of 2 small sodas—brings the cost to $6.00. (C is true.)
    - Now replacing a medium soda with a large soda adds 25 cents, so $6.25 is also possible. (D is true.)
    - 2 pepperoni slices and 2 medium sodas cost $7.00. (E is true.)
    - Replacing one of those medium sodas with a large soda adds 25 cents, so $7.25 is possible, too. (F is true.)

19. **(B)** Since a normal distribution is symmetric about the mean, and since in a normal distribution 68% of the scores are within one standard deviation of the mean, 34% are within one standard deviation below the mean, and 34% are within one standard deviation above the mean. The other 32% are more than one standard deviation from the mean, 16% are more than one standard deviation below the mean, and 16% are more than one standard deviation above the mean.

    So 16% score below 400, 34% between 400 and 500, 34% between 500 and 600, and 16% above 600. Set up a proportion.

$$\frac{\text{number of students}}{\text{percent of total}} = \frac{10{,}200}{34} = \frac{x}{16} \Rightarrow \frac{16 \times 10{,}200}{34} = x \Rightarrow x = 4{,}800$$

20. **(D)** $\frac{1}{x}+\frac{1}{y}=\frac{y}{xy}+\frac{x}{xy}=\frac{x+y}{xy}=\frac{10}{20}=\frac{1}{2}$.

    **Estimate. If $x = 7$ and $y = 3$, then $x + y = 10$ and $xy = 21$. That's not exactly right; we are told that $xy = 20$. But it's close. Then $\frac{1}{x}+\frac{1}{y}=\frac{1}{7}+\frac{1}{3} \approx .476$. So guess $\frac{1}{2}$.

MODEL TEST 2

Index

E

F

G

H

Q

NOTES

MAXIMIZE YOUR MATH SKILLS!

BARRON'S E-Z SERIES

Specially structured to maximize learning with a minimum of time and effort, these books promote fast skill building through lively cartoons and other fun features.

E-Z ALGEBRA
(978-0-7641-4257-4)
$16.99, *Can$19.99*

E-Z CALCULUS
(978-0-7641-4461-5)
$16.99, *Can$19.99*

E-Z GEOMETRY
(978-0-7641-3918-5)
$16.99, *Can$19.99*

E-Z TRIGONOMETRY
(978-0-7641-4251-2)
$16.99, *Can$19.99*

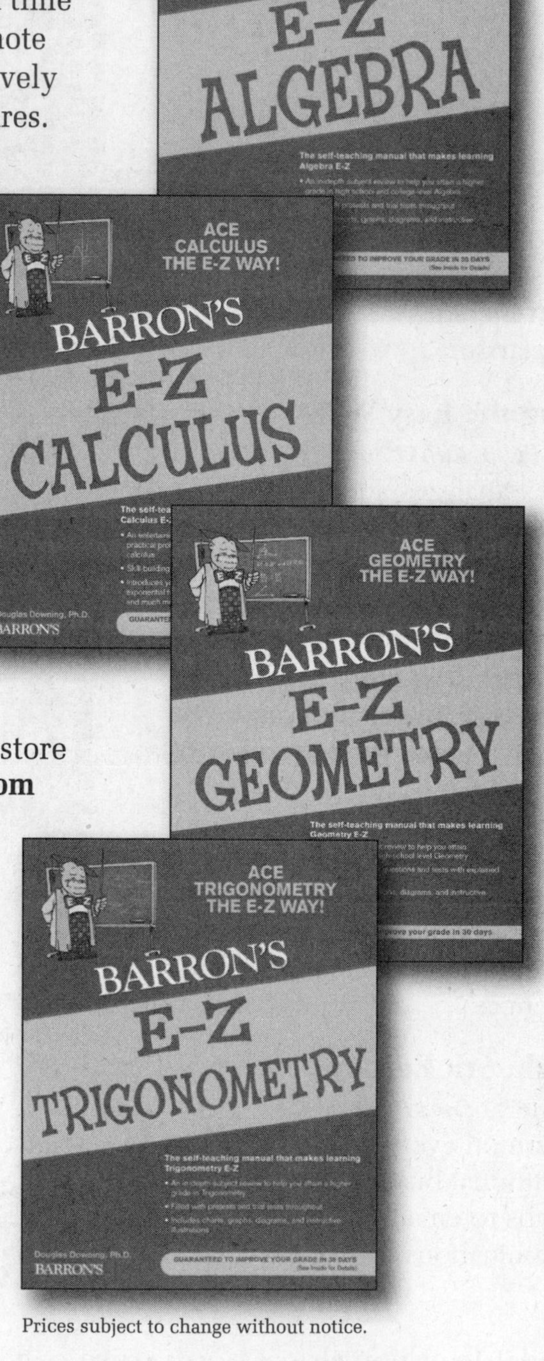

Available at your local book store or visit **www.barronseduc.com**

Barron's Educational Series, Inc.
250 Wireless Blvd.
Hauppauge, N.Y. 11788
Call toll-free: 1-800-645-3476

In Canada:
Georgetown Book Warehouse
34 Armstrong Ave.
Georgetown, Ontario L7G 4R9
Call toll-free: 1-800-247-7160

Prices subject to change without notice.

(#44a) R5/16